AF685796

NEW PERSPECTIVES ON

Microsoft® Access® 2013

COMPREHENSIVE

Joseph J. Adamski
Grand Valley State University

Kathleen T. Finnegan

Sharon Scollard
Mohawk College

CENGAGE Learning®

Australia • Brazil • Japan • Korea • Mexico • Singapore • Spain • United Kingdom • United States

CENGAGE Learning®

New Perspectives on Microsoft Access 2013, Comprehensive

Product Director: Kathleen McMahon

Senior Director of Development: Marah Bellegarde

Senior Product Team Manager: Donna Gridley

Associate Product Manager: Amanda Lyons

Product Development Manager: Leigh Hefferon

Senior Content Developer: Kathy Finnegan

Content Developer: Julia Leroux-Lindsey

Developmental Editor: Sasha Vodnik

Product Assistant: Melissa Stehler

Marketing Director: Elinor Gregory

Senior Market Development Manager: Eric LaScola

Market Development Manager: Kristie Clark

Marketing Manager: Gretchen Swann

Marketing Coordinator: Elizabeth Murphy

Senior Content Project Manager: Jennifer Goguen McGrail

Composition: GEX Publishing Services

Art Director: GEX Publishing Services

Text Designer: Althea Chen

Cover Art: © Janaka Dharmasena/Shutterstock

Copyeditor: Michael Beckett

Proofreader: Lisa Weidenfeld

Indexer: Alexandra Nickerson

For product information and technology assistance, contact us at
Cengage Learning Customer & Sales Support, 1-800-354-9706

For permission to use material from this text or product, submit all requests online at **www.cengage.com/permissions**
Further permissions questions can be emailed to
permissionrequest@cengage.com

Library of Congress Control Number: 2013947743

ISBN-13: 978-1-285-09920-0

ISBN-10: 1-285-09920-6

Cengage Learning
200 First Stamford Place, 4th Floor
Stamford, CT 06902
USA

Cengage Learning is a leading provider of customized learning solutions with office locations around the globe, including Singapore, the United Kingdom, Australia, Mexico, Brazil, and Japan. Locate your local office at:
international.cengage.com/global

Cengage Learning products are represented in Canada by Nelson Education, Ltd.

To learn more about Cengage Learning, visit **www.cengage.com.**

Purchase any of our products at your local college store or at our preferred online store **www.cengagebrain.com**

Printed in the United States of America
2 3 4 5 6 7 19 18 17 16 15 14

Preface

The New Perspectives Series' critical-thinking, problem-solving approach is the ideal way to prepare students to transcend point-and-click skills and take advantage of all that Microsoft Office 2013 has to offer.

In developing the New Perspectives Series, our goal was to create books that give students the software concepts and practical skills they need to succeed beyond the classroom. We've updated our proven case-based pedagogy with more practical content to make learning skills more meaningful to students.

With the New Perspectives Series, students understand *why* they are learning *what* they are learning, and are fully prepared to apply their skills to real-life situations.

"This text provides real-world examples that guide learners through the material with clear explanations and rich graphics. The progression of lessons allows students to incorporate new concepts into their existing knowledge and continuously build to a high level of achievement and understanding."

—Christine Yero
Madison Area Technical College

About This Book

This book provides complete coverage of Microsoft Access 2013, and includes the following:

- Detailed, hands-on instruction of Microsoft Access 2013, including creating and maintaining a database, querying a database, creating forms and reports, integrating Access with other programs, creating macros, and securing a database
- Coverage of important database concepts, including guidelines for designing databases and setting field properties, defining table relationships, object dependencies, normalization, and Access naming conventions

New for this edition!

- Each tutorial has been updated with new case scenarios throughout, which provide a rich and realistic context for students to apply the concepts and skills presented.
- A new Troubleshoot type of Case Problem, in which certain steps of the exercise require students to identify and correct errors—which are intentionally placed in the files students work with—promotes problem solving and critical thinking.
- The content has been developed so that students and instructors can work seamlessly on either the Windows 7 or Windows 8 operating system.

System Requirements

This book assumes a typical installation of Microsoft Access 2013 and Microsoft Windows 8 Professional. (You can also complete the material in this text using another version of Windows 8 or using Windows 7. You may see only minor differences in how some windows look.) The browser used for any steps that require a browser is Internet Explorer 10.

www.cengage.com/series/newperspectives

"The clear step-by-step instructions, real-world data files, and helpful figures make New Perspectives texts excellent for courses taught in the classroom, the hybrid/blended format, or entirely online."
—Sylvia Amito'elau
Coastline Community College

The New Perspectives Approach

Context
Each tutorial begins with a problem presented in a "real-world" case that is meaningful to students. The case sets the scene to help students understand what they will do in the tutorial.

Hands-on Approach
Each tutorial is divided into manageable sessions that combine reading and hands-on, step-by-step work. Colorful screenshots help guide students through the steps. **Trouble?** tips anticipate common mistakes or problems to help students stay on track and continue with the tutorial.

VISUAL OVERVIEW

Visual Overviews
Each session begins with a Visual Overview, a two-page spread that includes colorful, enlarged screenshots with numerous callouts and key term definitions, giving students a comprehensive preview of the topics covered in the session, as well as a handy study guide.

PROSKILLS

ProSkills Boxes and Exercises
ProSkills boxes provide guidance for how to use the software in real-world, professional situations, and related ProSkills exercises integrate the technology skills students learn with one or more of the following soft skills: decision making, problem solving, teamwork, verbal communication, and written communication.

KEY STEP

Key Steps
Important steps are highlighted in yellow with attached margin notes to help students pay close attention to completing the steps correctly and avoid time-consuming rework.

INSIGHT

InSight Boxes
InSight boxes offer expert advice and best practices to help students achieve a deeper understanding of the concepts behind the software features and skills.

TIP

Margin Tips
Margin Tips provide helpful hints and shortcuts for more efficient use of the software. The Tips appear in the margin at key points throughout each tutorial, giving students extra information when and where they need it.

REVIEW

APPLY

Assessment
Retention is a key component to learning. At the end of each session, a series of Quick Check questions helps students test their understanding of the material before moving on. Engaging end-of-tutorial Review Assignments and Case Problems have always been a hallmark feature of the New Perspectives Series. Colorful bars and headings identify the type of exercise, making it easy to understand both the goal and level of challenge a particular assignment holds.

REFERENCE

TASK REFERENCE

GLOSSARY/INDEX

Reference
Within each tutorial, Reference boxes appear before a set of steps to provide a succinct summary and preview of how to perform a task. In addition, a complete Task Reference at the back of the book provides quick access to information on how to carry out common tasks. Finally, each book includes a combination Glossary/Index to promote easy reference of material.

www.cengage.com/series/newperspectives

Our Complete System of Instruction

Coverage To Meet Your Needs

Whether you're looking for just a small amount of coverage or enough to fill a semester-long class, we can provide you with a textbook that meets your needs.

- Brief books typically cover the essential skills in just 2 to 4 tutorials.
- Introductory books build on those skills and contain an average of 5 to 8 tutorials.
- Comprehensive books are great for a full-semester class, and contain 9 to 12+ tutorials.

So if the book you're holding does not provide the right amount of coverage for you, there's probably another offering available. Go to our Web site or contact your Cengage Learning sales representative to find out what else we offer.

CourseCasts – Learning on the Go. Always available…always relevant.

Want to keep up with the latest technology trends relevant to you? Visit http://coursecasts.course.com to find a library of weekly updated podcasts, CourseCasts, and download them to your mp3 player. Ken Baldauf, host of CourseCasts, is a faculty member of the Florida State University Computer Science Department where he is responsible for teaching technology classes to thousands of FSU students each year. Ken is an expert in the latest technology trends; he gathers and sorts through the most pertinent news and information for CourseCasts so your students can spend their time enjoying technology, rather than trying to figure it out. Open or close your lecture with a discussion based on the latest CourseCast. Visit us at http://coursecasts.course.com to learn on the go!

Instructor Resources

We offer more than just a book. We have all the tools you need to enhance your lectures, check students' work, and generate exams in a new, easier-to-use and completely revised package. This book's Instructor's Manual, ExamView testbank, PowerPoint presentations, data files, solution files, figure files, and a sample syllabus are all available on a single CD-ROM or for downloading at http://www.cengage.com.

SAM: Skills Assessment Manager

Get your students workplace-ready with SAM, the premier proficiency-based assessment and training solution for Microsoft Office! SAM's active, hands-on environment helps students master computer skills and concepts that are essential to academic and career success. Skill-based assessments, interactive trainings, business-centric projects, and comprehensive remediation engage students in mastering the latest Microsoft Office programs on their own, allowing instructors to spend class time teaching. SAM's efficient course setup and robust grading features provide faculty with consistency across sections. Fully interactive MindTap Readers integrate market-leading Cengage Learning content with SAM, creating a comprehensive online student learning environment.

Certification Prep Tool

This textbook was developed to instruct on the Microsoft® Office® 2013 certification objectives. Microsoft Corporation has developed a set of standardized, performance-based examinations that you can take to demonstrate your overall expertise with Microsoft Office 2013 programs. Microsoft Office 2013 certification provides a number of benefits for you:

- Differentiate yourself in the employment marketplace from those who are not Microsoft Office Specialist or Expert certified.

- Prove skills and expertise when using Microsoft Office 2013.
- Perform at a higher skill level in your job.
- Work at a higher professional level than those who are not certified.
- Broaden your employment opportunities and advance your career more rapidly.

For more information about Microsoft Office 2013 certification, including a complete list of certification objectives, visit the Microsoft web site, http://www.microsoft.com/learning. To see which Microsoft Office 2013 certification objectives are addressed by the contents of this text and where each is included in the text, visit the Certification resource on the Student Companion Site located on www.cengagebrain.com. For detailed instructions about accessing available resources, visit www.cengage.com/ct/student download or contact your instructor for information about accessing the required files.

Acknowledgments

The authors wish to thank the following reviewers for their helpful feedback, valuable insights, and dedication to this project: Cliff Brozo, Monroe College; Deborah Franklin, Bryant & Stratton College; Debi Griggs, Bellevue College; Karen Miller, Hohokus of Hackensack School; and Christine Yero, Madison Area Technical College. Many thanks to everyone on the New Perspectives team, especially Donna Gridley for her leadership and inspiration; Amanda Lyons and Melissa Stehler for their contributions and support; Julia Leroux-Lindsey for her outstanding management of this project, keeping us all on task and focused through many hoops and hurdles; and Jennifer Goguen McGrail for her tireless efforts and expertise in guiding us through the production process. Thanks as well to the following Manuscript Quality Assurance (MQA) staff members for their diligent efforts in ensuring the quality and accuracy of this text: Chris Scriver, MQA Project Leader; and John Freitas, Serge Palladino, Susan Pedicini, and Danielle Shaw, MQA Testers.

Special thanks go to Sasha Vodnik, Developmental Editor, for his incredible attention to detail, his willingness to go the extra mile, and, above all, his positive attitude and friendship, which helped to turn a challenging project into a fun endeavor. To my co-author, Sharon Scollard, more thanks than I can express for her expertise and guidance, but most especially for her true spirit of collaboration and teamwork, which made it a pleasure to complete this book. Many thanks to Cindi DelFavero for her special contributions to this text. Finally, I am extremely grateful for the love and support of my wonderful parents, Ed and Mary Curran, and for being lucky enough to have the two best sons in the world, Connor and Devon, who make this all worthwhile.
–Kathleen T. Finnegan

I would like to express my gratitude and appreciation to the people whose dedication was invaluable in producing this book. Sasha Vodnik, Developmental Editor, made countless positive contributions and always had words of encouragement right when I needed them. Kathy Finnegan, co-author and Senior Product Manager, regardless of the hat she wore, always had words of wisdom, and I don't think we've had a single conversation without sharing a good laugh. Many thanks also to Joe Adamski, whose love for teaching and technology shines through this material, which forms such a strong foundation. Finally, with all my heart, I'd like to thank my children, Angela, Robyn and Andrew. They keep me grounded, they keep me laughing, and they're the top three records in my database.
–Sharon Scollard

BRIEF CONTENTS

TABLE OF CONTENTS

Managing Your Files

Organizing Files and Folders with Windows 8

OBJECTIVES

- Explore the differences between Windows 7 and Windows 8
- Plan the organization of files and folders
- Use File Explorer to view and manage libraries, folders, and files
- Open and save files
- Create folders
- Copy and move files and folders
- Compress and extract files

Case | *Savvy Traveler*

After spending a summer traveling in Italy, Matt Marino started Savvy Traveler, a travel company that organizes small tours in Europe. To market his company, Matt created flyers, brochures, webpages, and other materials that describe the tours he offers. Matt uses the Savvy Traveler office computer to locate and store photos, illustrations, and text documents he can include in his marketing materials. He recently hired you to help manage the office. To keep Matt connected to the office while traveling, he just purchased a new laptop computer running Windows 8. He is familiar with Windows 7, so he needs an overview explaining how Windows 8 is different. Matt asks you to train him on using Windows 8 to organize his files and folders. Although he has only a few files, he knows it's a good idea to set up a logical organization now so he can find his work later as he stores more files and folders on the computer.

In this tutorial, you'll explore the differences between Windows 7 and Windows 8, especially those related to file management tools. You'll also work with Matt to devise a plan for managing his files. You'll learn how Windows 8 organizes files and folders, and then create files and folders yourself and organize them on Matt's computer. You'll also use techniques to display the information you need in folder windows, and explore options for working with compressed files.

STARTING DATA FILES

FM →

Tutorial	Review	Case1	Case2
Artists.rtf	Banner.png	Fall Classes.rtf	Budget1.xlsx
Chianti.jpg	Colosseum.jpg	Instructors.txt	Budget2.xlsx
Florence.jpg	Lectures.xlsx	Kings Canyon.jpg	Report1.xlsx
List.rtf	Rome.jpg	Mojave.jpg	Report2.xlsx
Logo.png	Rome.rtf	Redwoods.jpg	Report3.xlsx
Market.jpg	Schedule.rtf	Spring Classes.rtf	Report4.xlsx
Marketing.txt	Tours.rtf	Summer Classes.rtf	Tips1.rtf
Tour Rates.rtf		Winter Classes.rtf	Tips1 – Copy.rtf
Tuscany.rtf		Workshops.rtf	Tips2.rtf
		Yosemite.jpg	Tips2 – Copy.rtf

Visual Overview:

You use the Change your view button to change the size of the icons in the window.

In Windows 7, you use **Windows Explorer** to navigate the contents of your computer.

Use the arrow buttons in the Address bar to navigate to other locations on your computer.

The **file path** is a notation that indicates a file's location on your computer.

Use the Search box to search for files in the current folder.

The Windows Explorer **toolbar** provides buttons for completing tasks.

Windows Explorer includes a **navigation pane**, which displays icons and links to resources and locations on your computer.

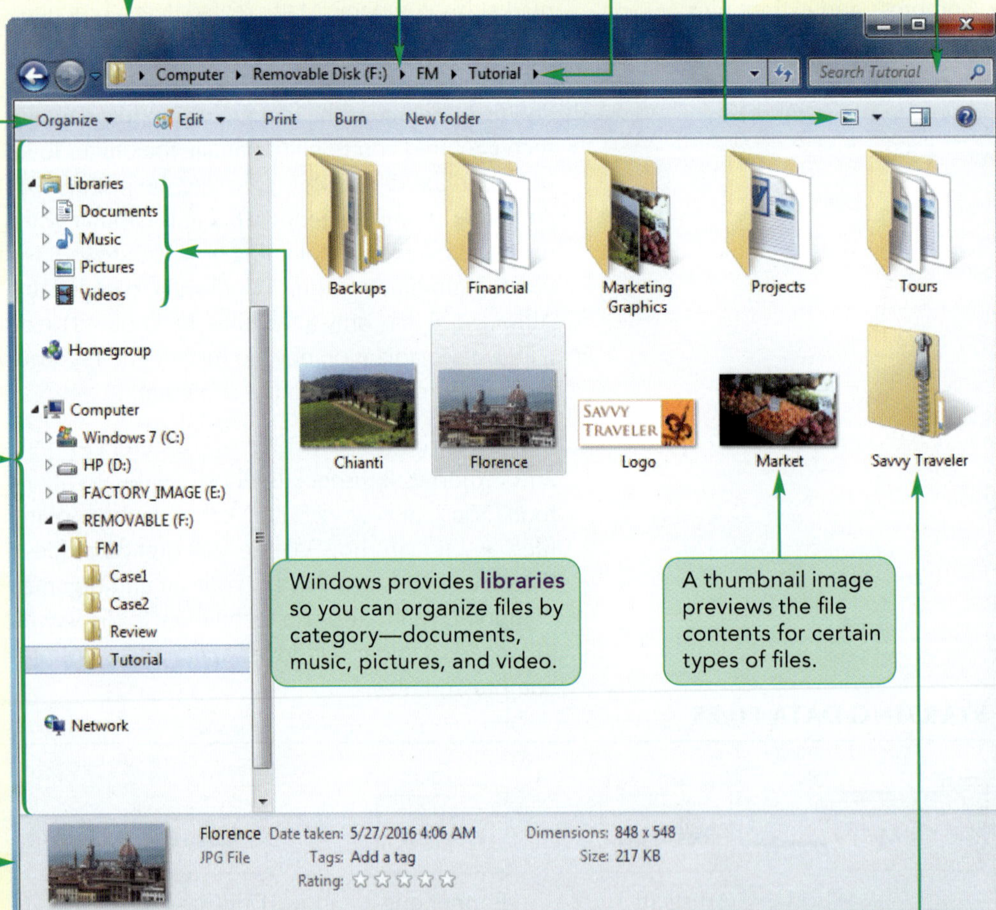

Windows provides **libraries** so you can organize files by category—documents, music, pictures, and video.

A thumbnail image previews the file contents for certain types of files.

By default, Windows Explorer includes the **Details pane** at the bottom of the window, which displays the properties of the selected object.

The zipped folder icon indicates a **compressed folder**, which stores files so they take up less disk space.

Windows 7

Photos courtesy of Lisa Ruffolo

Comparing Windows 7 & Windows 8

The **View tab** on the ribbon contains options for specifying how the information displays in File Explorer.

Windows provides **libraries** so you can organize files by category—documents, music, pictures, and videos.

The **Quick Access toolbar** contains buttons for viewing properties and creating a folder.

Use the arrow buttons in the Address bar to navigate to other locations on your computer.

The **file path** in the Address bar shows a file's location on your computer.

In Windows 8, you use **File Explorer** to navigate the contents of your computer.

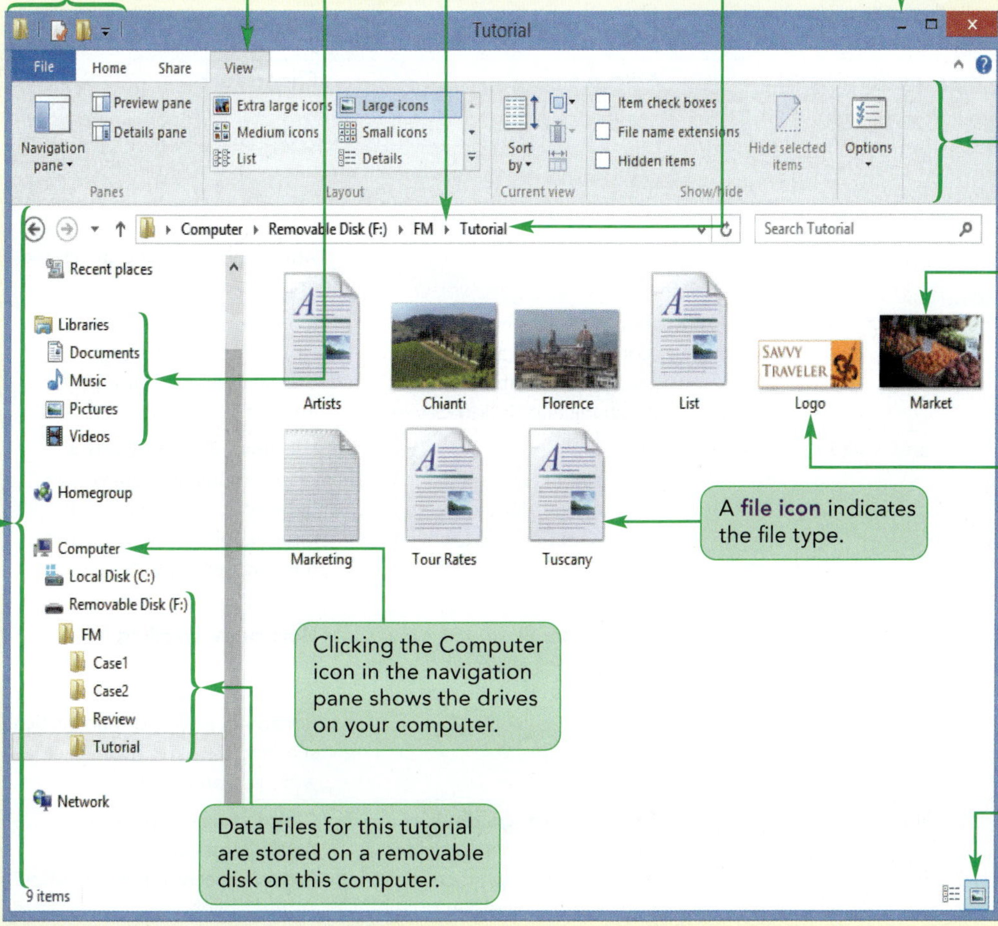

File Explorer includes a ribbon with tools organized on tabs for working with files and folders.

A thumbnail image previews the file contents for certain types of files.

A **filename** is the name you give to a file when you save it to identify the file's contents.

A **file icon** indicates the file type.

Clicking the Computer icon in the navigation pane shows the drives on your computer.

You can use the Large icons view button on the status bar or in the Layout group on the View tab to switch to Large icons view.

Data Files for this tutorial are stored on a removable disk on this computer.

File Explorer includes a **navigation pane**, which displays icons and links to resources and locations on your computer.

Windows 8

Exploring the Differences Between Windows 7 and Windows 8

Windows 8, the most recent version of the Microsoft operating system, is significantly different from Windows 7, the previous version. The major difference is that Windows 8 is designed for touchscreen computers such as tablets and laptops with touch-activated displays, though it runs on computers with more traditional pointing devices such as a mouse or a trackpad. This design change affects many of the fundamental Windows features you use to work on a computer. Figure 1 compares how to perform typical tasks in Windows 7 and Windows 8.

Figure 1 Comparing Windows 7 and Windows 8

Task	Windows 7 Method	Windows 8 Method
Start applications (sometimes called apps)	**Start menu** Open the Start menu by clicking the Start button.	**Start screen** The Start screen appears when you start Windows.
Access applications, documents, settings, and other resources	**Start menu** Use the Start menu, All Programs list, and Search box.	**Charms bar** The Charms bar appears when you point to the upper-right or lower-right corner of the screen, and displays buttons, called charms, for interacting with Windows 8 and accessing applications.
Select objects and commands	**Icons** Icons are small and detailed, designed for interaction with mechanical pointing devices.	**Icons and tiles** Icons and tiles are large and simplified, designed for interaction with your fingertips.
Open and work in applications	**Desktop** Applications all use a single desktop interface featuring windows and dialog boxes.	**Windows 8 and desktop** Applications use one of two interfaces: the Windows 8 interface (featuring tiles and a full-screen layout) or the desktop.
Display content out of view	**Vertical scrolling** Applications allow more vertical scrolling than horizontal scrolling.	**Horizontal scrolling** The Start screen and applications allow more horizontal scrolling than vertical scrolling to take advantage of wide-screen monitors.
Store files	**Physical storage devices** Windows primarily provides access to disks physically connected to the computer.	**Cloud storage locations** A Microsoft user account provides access to information stored online.
Enter text	**Physical keyboard** Type on the keyboard attached to the computer.	**On-screen keyboard** If your computer does not have a physical keyboard, type using the on-screen keyboard.

Although Windows 7 introduced a few gestures for touchscreen users, Windows 8 expands the use of gestures and interactions. In Windows 8, you can use touch gestures to do nearly everything you can do with a pointing device. Figure 2 lists common Windows 8 interactions and their touch and mouse equivalents.

Figure 2 Windows 8 touch and mouse interactions

Interaction	Touch Gesture	Mouse Action
Display a ScreenTip, text that identifies the name or purpose of the button	Touch and hold (or press) an object such as a button.	Point to an object such as a button.
Display an Apps bar, which displays options related to the current task and access to the Apps screen	Swipe from the top or bottom of the screen toward the center.	Right-click the bottom edge of the screen.
Display the Charms bar	Swipe from the right edge of the screen toward the center.	Point to the upper-right or lower-right corner of the screen.
Display thumbnails of open apps (the Switch List)	Swipe from the left edge of the screen toward the center.	Point to the upper-left corner of the screen, and then drag the pointer down.
Drag an object	Press and then drag.	Click, hold, and then drag.
Scroll the Start screen	Swipe from the right edge of the screen to the left.	Click the scroll arrows, or drag the scroll bar.
Select an object or perform an action such as starting an app	Tap the object.	Click the object.
Zoom	Pinch two fingers to zoom out or move the fingers apart to zoom in.	Click the Zoom button.

Despite the substantial differences between how you interact with Windows 7 and Windows 8, the steps you follow to perform work in either operating system are the same. In a typical computer session, you start an application and open a **file**, often referred to as a document, which is a collection of data that has a name and is stored on a computer. You view, add, or change the file contents, and then save and close the file. You can complete all of these steps using Windows 7 or Windows 8. Because most of your work involves files, you need to understand how to save and organize files so you can easily find and open them when necessary.

Organizing Files and Folders

Knowing how to save, locate, and organize computer files makes you more productive when you are working with a computer. After you create a file, you can open it, edit its contents, print the file, and save it again—usually using the same application you used to create the file. You organize files by storing them in folders. A **folder** is a container for files. You need to organize files and folders so that you can find them easily and work efficiently.

A file cabinet is a common metaphor for computer file organization. As shown in Figure 3, a computer is like a file cabinet that has two or more drawers—each drawer is a storage device, or **disk**. Each disk contains folders that hold files. To make it easy to retrieve files, you arrange them logically into folders. For example, one folder might contain financial data, another might contain your creative work, and another could contain information you're gathering for an upcoming vacation.

Figure 3 **Computer as a file cabinet**

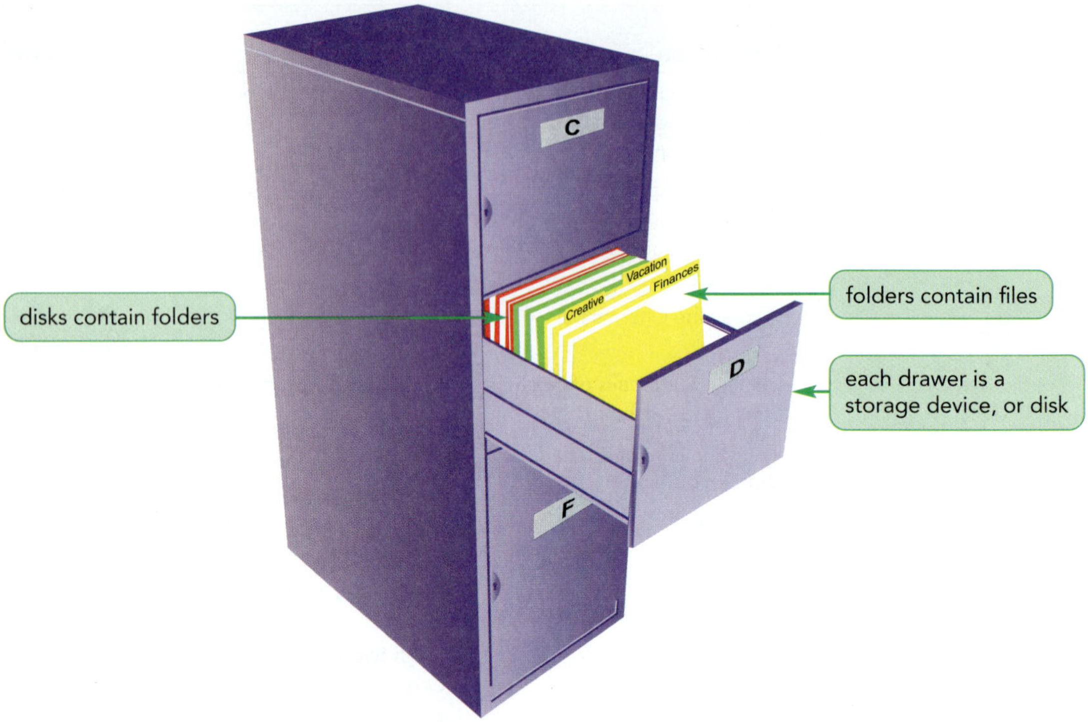

A computer can store folders and files on different types of disks, ranging from removable media—such as **USB drives** (also called USB flash drives) and digital video discs (DVDs)—to **hard disks**, or fixed disks, which are permanently housed in a computer. Hard disks are the most popular type of computer storage because they provide an economical way to store many gigabytes of data. (A **gigabyte**, or **GB**, is about 1 billion bytes, with each byte roughly equivalent to a character of data.)

To have your computer access a removable disk, you must insert the disk into a **drive**, which is a device that can retrieve and sometimes record data on a disk. A computer's hard disk is already contained in a drive inside the computer, so you don't need to insert it each time you use the computer.

A computer distinguishes one drive from another by assigning each a drive letter. The hard disk is assigned to drive C. The remaining drives can have any other letters, but are usually assigned in the order that the drives were installed on the computer—so your USB drive might be drive D or drive F.

Understanding How to Organize Files and Folders

Windows stores thousands of files in many folders on the hard disk of your computer. These are system files that Windows needs to display the Start screen and desktop, use drives, and perform other operating system tasks. To keep the system stable and to find files quickly, Windows organizes the folders and files in a hierarchy, or **file system**. At the top of the hierarchy, Windows stores folders and important files that it needs when you turn on the computer. This location is called the **root directory** and is usually drive C (the hard disk). As Figure 4 shows, the root directory contains all the other folders and files on the computer. The figure also shows that folders can contain other folders. An effectively organized computer contains a few folders in the root directory, and those folders contain other folders, also called **subfolders**.

Figure 4 Organizing folders and files on a hard disk

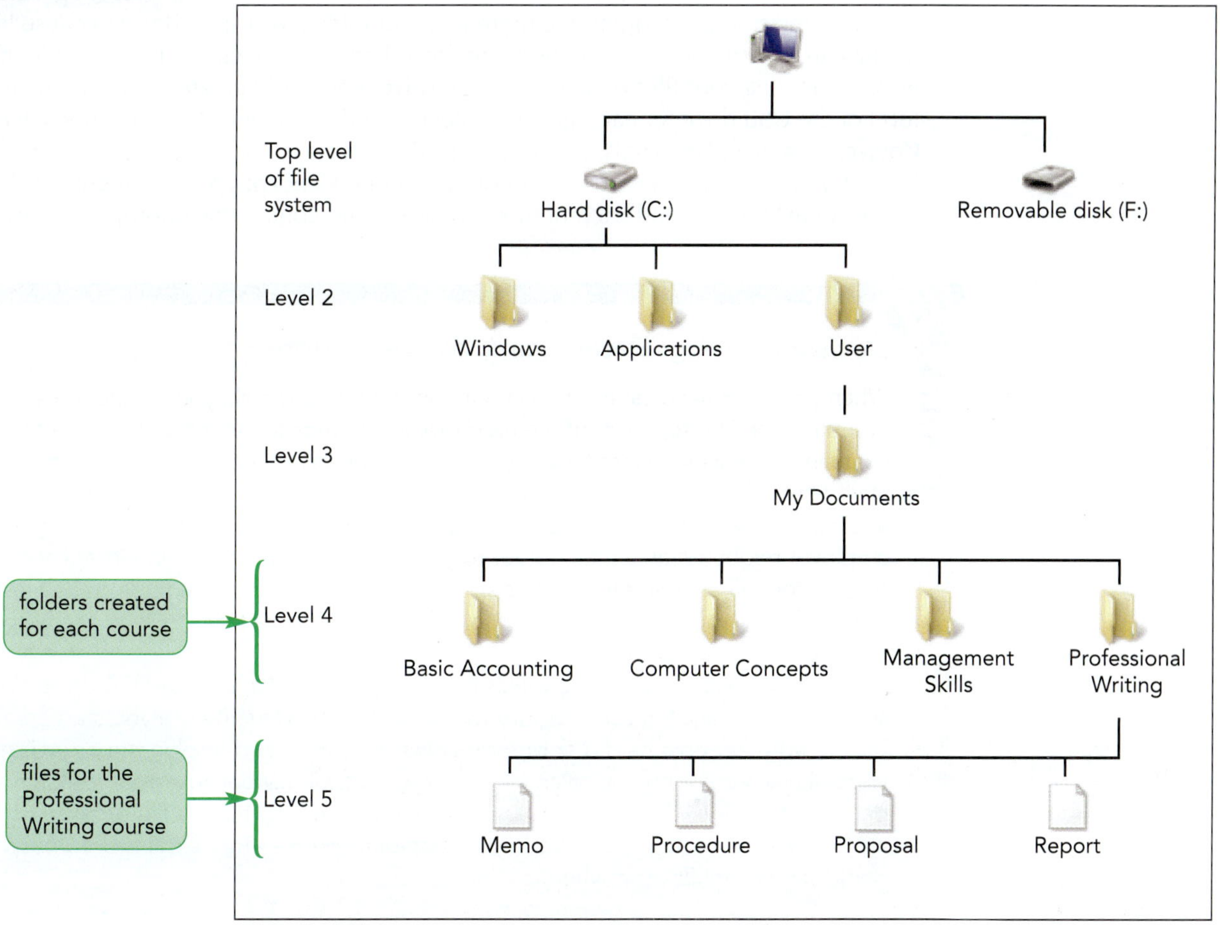

The root directory is the top level of the hard disk and is for system files and folders only. You should not store your own work in the root directory because your files could interfere with Windows or an application. (If you are working in a computer lab, you might not be allowed to access the root directory.)

Do not delete or move any files or folders from the root directory of the hard disk; doing so could disrupt the system so that you can't start or run the computer. In fact, you should not reorganize or change any folder that contains installed software because Windows 8 expects to find the files for specific applications within certain folders. In Figure 4, folders containing software are stored at Level 2 of the file system. If you reorganize or change these folders, Windows 8 can't locate and start the applications stored in those folders. Likewise, you should not make changes to the folder (usually named Windows) that contains the Windows 8 operating system.

Level 2 of the file system also includes a folder for your user account, such as the User folder. This folder contains all of your system settings, preferences, and other user account information. It also contains subfolders, such as the My Documents folder, for your personal files. The folders in Level 3 of the file system are designed to contain subfolders for your personal files. You can create as many subfolders at Level 4 of the file system as you need to store other folders and files and keep them organized.

Figure 4 shows how you could organize your files on a hard disk if you were taking a full semester of business classes. To duplicate this organization, you would open the main folder for your documents, such as My Documents, create four folders—one each for the Basic Accounting, Computer Concepts, Management Skills, and Professional Writing courses—and then store the writing assignments you complete in the Professional Writing folder.

If you store your files on removable media, such as a USB drive, you can use a simpler organization because you do not have to account for system files. In general, the larger the storage medium, the more levels of folders you should use because large media can store more files and, therefore, need better organization. For example, if you were organizing your files on a 12 GB USB drive, you could create folders in the top level of the USB drive for each general category of documents you store—one each for Courses, Creative, Financials, and Vacation. The Courses folder could then include one folder for each course (Basic Accounting, Computer Concepts, Management Skills, and Professional Writing), and each of those folders could contain the appropriate files.

PROSKILLS

Decision Making: Determining Where to Store Files

When you create and save files on your computer's hard disk, you should store them in subfolders. The top level of the hard disk is off-limits for your files because they could interfere with system files. If you are working on your own computer, store your files within the My Documents folder in the Documents library, which is where many applications save your files by default. When you use a computer on the job, your employer might assign a main folder to you for storing your work. In either case, if you simply store all your files in one folder, you will soon have trouble finding the files you want. Instead, you should create subfolders within a main folder to separate files in a way that makes sense for you.

Even if you store most of your files on removable media, such as USB drives, you still need to organize those files into folders and subfolders. Before you start creating folders, whether on a hard disk or removable disk, you need to plan the organization you will use. Following your plan increases your efficiency because you don't have to pause and decide which folder to use when you save your files. A file organization plan also makes you more productive in your computer work—the next time you need a particular file, you'll know where to find it.

Exploring Files and Folders

As shown in the Visual Overview, you use File Explorer in Windows 8 to explore the files and folders on your computer. File Explorer displays the contents of your computer by using icons to represent drives, folders, and files. When you open File Explorer, it shows the contents of the Windows built-in libraries by default. Windows provides these libraries so you can organize files by category—documents, music, pictures, and video. A library can display these categories of files together, no matter where the files are actually stored. For example, you might keep some music files in a folder named Albums on your hard disk. You might also keep music files in a Songs folder on a USB drive. Although the Albums and Songs folders are physically stored in different locations, you can set up the Music library to display both folders in the same File Explorer window. You can then search and arrange the files as a single collection to quickly find the music you want to open and play. In this way, you use libraries to organize your files into categories so you can easily locate and work with files.

The File Explorer window is divided into two sections, called panes. The left pane is the navigation pane, which contains icons and links to locations on your computer. The right pane displays the contents of the location selected in the navigation pane. If the navigation pane showed all the contents on your computer at once, it could be a very long list. Instead, you open drives and folders only when you want to see what they contain. For example, to display the hierarchy of the folders and other locations on your computer, you select the Computer icon in the navigation pane, and then select the icon for a drive, such as Local Disk (C:) or Removable Disk (F:). You can then open and explore folders on that drive.

If a folder contains undisplayed subfolders, an expand icon appears to the left of the folder icon. (The same is true for drives.) To view the folders contained in an object, you click the expand icon. A collapse icon then appears next to the folder icon; click the collapse icon to hide the folder's subfolders. To view the files contained in a folder, you click the folder icon, and the files appear in the right pane. See Figure 5.

Figure 5 **Viewing files in File Explorer**

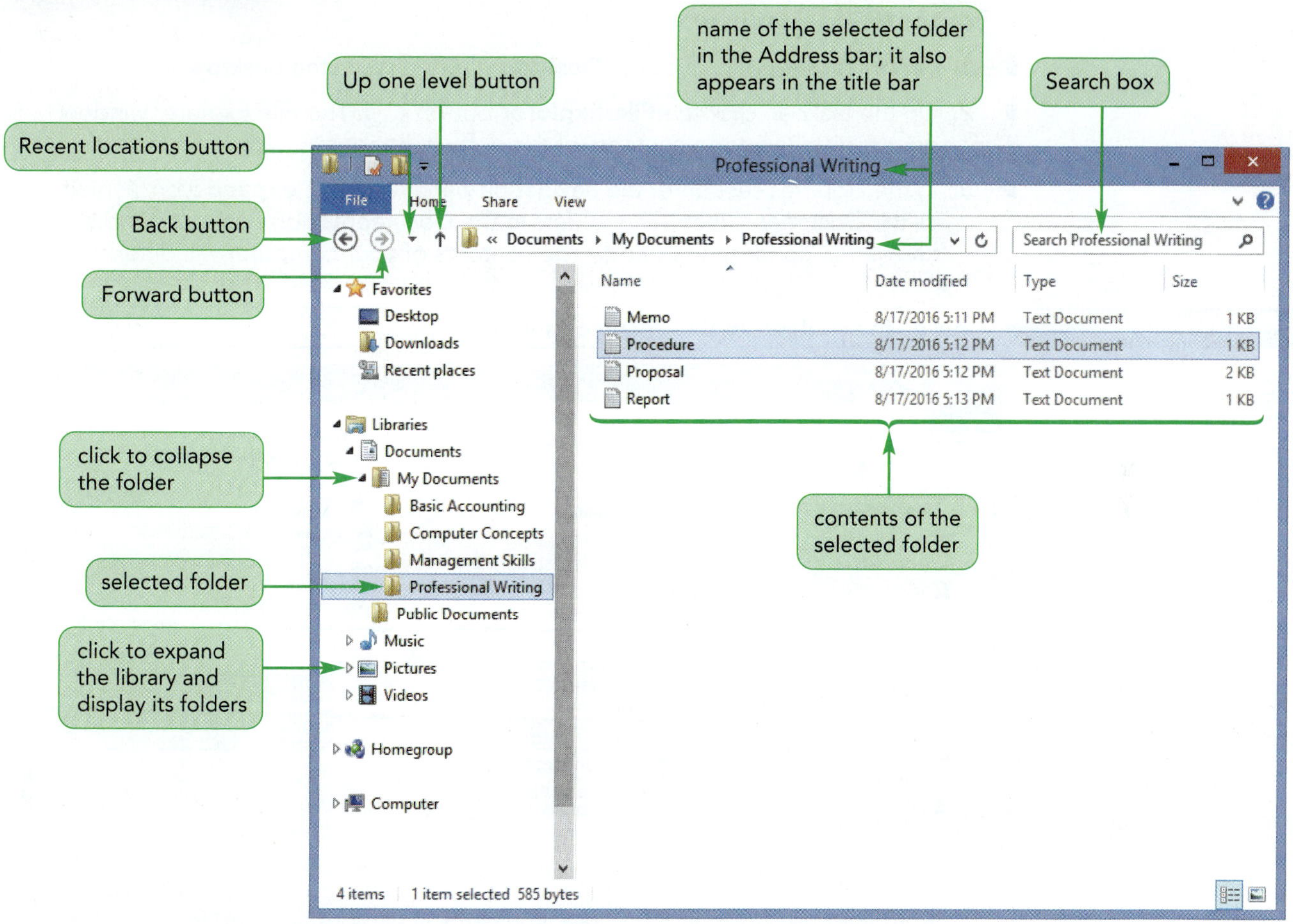

Using the navigation pane helps you explore your computer and orients you to your current location. As you move, copy, delete, and perform other tasks with the files and folders in the right pane of File Explorer, you can refer to the navigation pane to see how your changes affect the overall organization of the selected location.

In addition to using the navigation pane, you can explore your computer in File Explorer using the following navigation techniques:

- Opening drives and folders in the right pane—To view the contents of a drive or folder, double-click the drive or folder icon in the right pane of File Explorer.
- Using the Address bar—You can use the Address bar to navigate to a different folder. The Address bar displays the file path for your current folder. (Recall that a file path shows the location of a folder or file.) Click a folder name such as My Documents in the Address bar to navigate to that folder, or click an arrow button to navigate to a different location in the folder's hierarchy.
- Clicking the Back, Forward, Recent locations, and Up to buttons—Use the Back, Forward, and Recent locations buttons to navigate to other folders you have already opened. Use the Up to button to navigate up to the folder containing the current folder.
- Using the Search box—To find a file or folder stored in the current folder or its subfolders, type a word or phrase in the Search box. The search begins as soon as you

start typing. Windows finds files based on text in the filename, text within the file, and other properties of the file.

You'll practice using some of these navigation techniques later in the tutorial. Right now, you'll show Matt how to open File Explorer. Your computer should be turned on and displaying the Start screen.

To open File Explorer:

1. On the Start screen, click the **Desktop** tile to display the desktop.
2. On the taskbar, click the **File Explorer** button. The File Explorer window opens, displaying the contents of the default libraries.
3. In the Libraries section of the navigation pane, click the **expand** icon next to the Documents icon. The folders in the Documents library appear in the navigation pane; see Figure 6. The contents of your computer will differ.

Figure 6 Viewing the contents of the Documents library

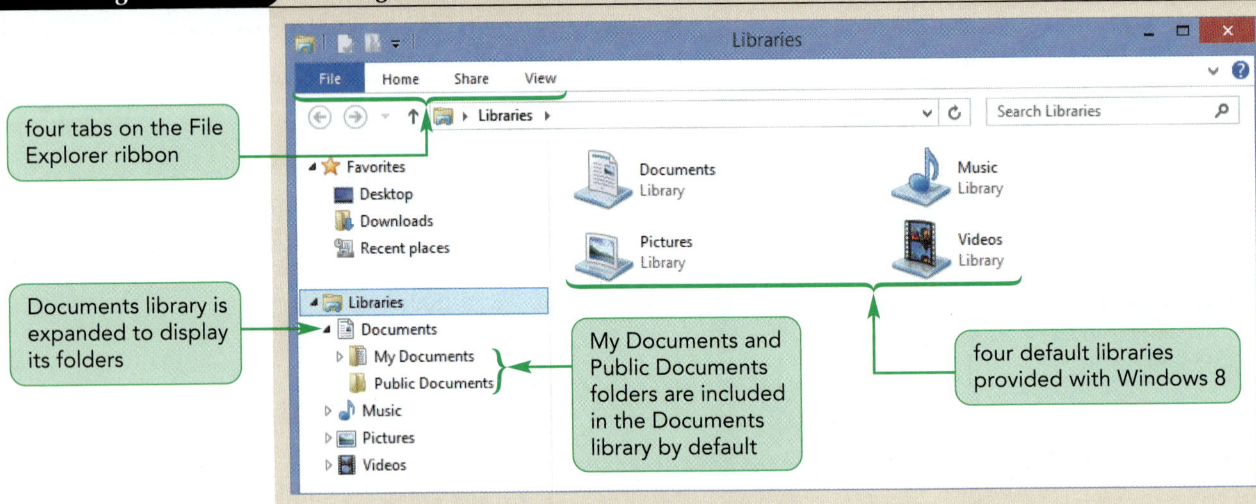

Trouble? If your window displays icons in a size or arrangement different from the one shown in the figure, you can still explore files and folders. The same is true for all the figures in this tutorial.

4. In the navigation pane, click the **My Documents** folder to display its contents in the right pane.

TIP

When you are working in the navigation pane, you only need to click a folder to open it; you do not need to double-click it.

As Figure 6 shows, the File Explorer window includes a ribbon, which is collapsed by default so it displays only tab names, such as File, Home, Share, and View. The Visual Overview shows the expanded ribbon, which displays the options for the selected tab. You'll work with the ribbon and learn how to expand it later in the tutorial.

Navigating to Your Data Files

To navigate to the files you want, it helps to know the file path because the file path tells you exactly where the file is stored in the hierarchy of drives and folders on your computer. For example, Matt has a file named "Logo," which contains an image of the company's logo. If Matt stored the Logo file in a folder named "Marketing" and saved that folder in a folder named "Savvy Traveler" on drive F (a USB drive) on his computer, the Address bar would show the following file path for the Logo file:

Computer ▸ Removable Disk (F:) ▸ Savvy Traveler ▸ Marketing ▸ Logo.png

This path has five parts, with each part separated by an arrow button:

- Computer—The main container for the file, such as "Computer" or "Network"
- Removable Disk (F:)—The drive name, including the drive letter followed by a colon, which indicates a drive rather than a folder
- Savvy Traveler—The top-level folder on drive F
- Marketing—A subfolder in the Savvy Traveler folder
- Logo.png—The name of the file

Although File Explorer uses arrow buttons to separate locations in a file path, printed documents use backslashes (\ ). For example, if you read an instruction to open the Logo file in the Savvy Traveler\Marketing folder on your USB drive, you know you must navigate to the USB drive attached to your computer, open the Savvy Traveler folder, and then open the Marketing folder to find the Logo file.

File Explorer displays the file path in the Address bar so you can keep track of your current location as you navigate between drives and folders. You can use File Explorer to navigate to the Data Files you need for this tutorial. Before you perform the following steps, you should know where you stored your Data Files, such as on a USB drive. The following steps assume that drive is Removable Disk (F:), a USB drive. If necessary, substitute the appropriate drive on your system when you perform the steps.

To navigate to your Data Files:

1. Make sure your computer can access your Data Files for this tutorial. For example, if you are using a USB drive, insert the drive into the USB port.

   Trouble? If you don't have the starting Data Files, you need to get them before you can proceed. Your instructor will either give you the Data Files or ask you to obtain them from a specified location (such as a network drive). If you have any questions about the Data Files, see your instructor or technical support person for assistance.

2. In the navigation pane of File Explorer, click the **expand** icon ▷ next to the Computer icon to display the drives on your computer, if necessary.
3. Click the **expand** icon ▷ next to the drive containing your Data Files, such as Removable Disk (F:). A list of the folders on that drive appears below the drive name.
4. If the list of folders does not include the FM folder, continue clicking the **expand** icon ▷ to navigate to the folder that contains the FM folder.
5. Click the **expand** icon ▷ next to the FM folder to expand the folder, and then click the **FM** folder so that its contents appear in the navigation pane and in the right pane of the folder window. The FM folder contains the Case1, Case2, Review, and Tutorial folders, as shown in Figure 7. The other folders on your computer might vary.

Figure 7 Navigating to the FM folder

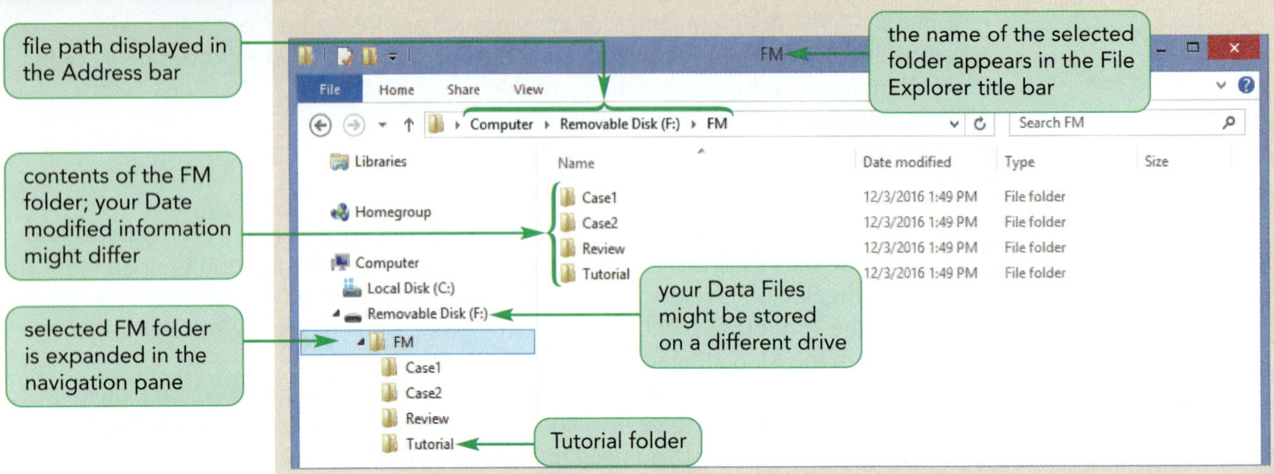

6. In the navigation pane, click the **Tutorial** folder. The files it contains appear in the right pane.

You can change the appearance of the File Explorer window to suit your preferences. You'll do so next so you can see more details about folders and files.

Changing the View

TIP

The default view for any folder in the Pictures library is Large icons view, which provides a thumbnail image of the file contents.

File Explorer provides eight ways to view the contents of a folder: Extra large icons, Large icons, Medium icons, Small icons, List, Details, Tiles, and Content. For example, the files in the Tutorial folder are currently displayed in Details view, which is the default view for all folders except those stored in the Pictures library. Details view displays a small icon to identify each file's type and lists file details in columns, such as the date the file was last modified, the file type, and the size of the file. Although only Details view lists the file details, you can see these details in any other view by pointing to a file to display a ScreenTip.

To change the view of File Explorer to any of the eight views, you use the View tab on the ribbon. To switch to Details view or Large icons view, you can use the view buttons on the status bar.

REFERENCE

Changing the View in File Explorer

- Click a view button on the status bar.

or

- Click the View tab on the ribbon.
- In the Layout group, click the view option; or click the More button, if necessary, and then click a view option.

You'll show Matt how to change the view of the Tutorial folder in the File Explorer window.

To change the view of the Tutorial folder in File Explorer:

1. On the ribbon, click the **View** tab.
2. In the Layout group, click **Medium icons**. The files appear in Medium icons view in File Explorer. See Figure 8.

Figure 8 Files in the Tutorial folder in Medium icons view

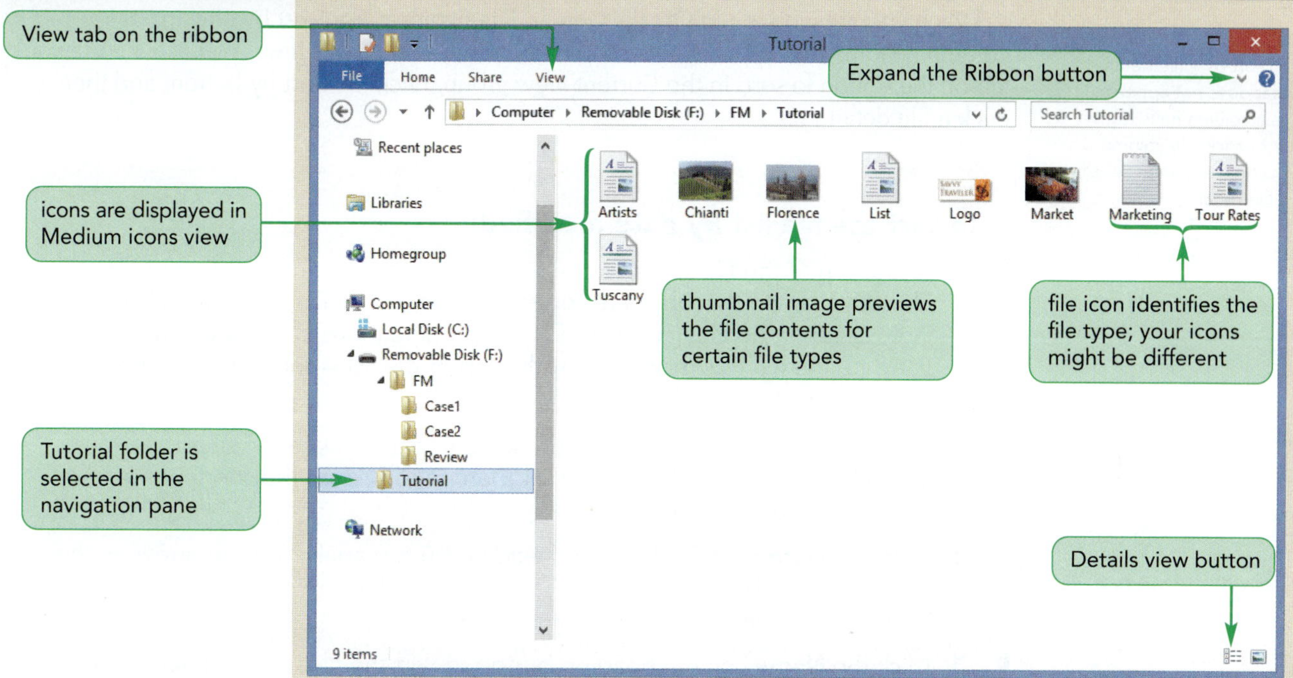

Photos courtesy of Lisa Ruffolo

Because the icons used to identify types of files depend on the applications installed on your computer, the file icons that appear in your window might be different.

3. On the status bar, click the **Large icons view** button. The window shows the files with large icons and no file details.

TIP

When you change the view, it only changes the view for the currently selected folder.

When you clicked the View tab in the previous steps, the ribbon expanded so you could select an option and then collapsed after you clicked the Medium icons option. You can keep the ribbon expanded in the File Explorer window so you can easily access all of its options. You'll show Matt how to expand the ribbon and then use the View tab to switch to Details view.

To expand the ribbon in File Explorer:

1. Click the **Expand the Ribbon** button to expand the ribbon. The Expand the Ribbon button changes to the Minimize the Ribbon button, which you could click if you wanted to collapse the ribbon.
2. On the View tab, in the Layout group, click **Details**. The window shows the files with small icons and lists the file details.

No matter which view you use, you can sort the file list by the name of the files or another detail, such as size, type, or date. When you **sort** files, you list them in ascending order (A to Z, 0 to 9, or earliest to latest date) or descending order (Z to A, 9 to 0, or latest to earliest date) by a file detail. If you're viewing music files, you can sort by details such as contributing artists or album title; and if you're viewing picture files, you can sort by details such as date taken or size. Sorting can help you find a particular file in a long file listing. For example, suppose you want to work on a document that you know you edited on June 4, 2016, but you can't remember the name of the file. You can sort the file list by date modified to find the file you want.

When you are working in Details view in File Explorer, you sort by clicking a column heading that appears at the top of the file list. In other views, you use the View tab on the ribbon to sort. In the Current view group, click the Sort by button, and then click a file detail.

TIP

To sort by a file detail that does not appear as a column heading, right-click any column heading and then select a file detail.

To sort the file list by date modified:

1. At the top of the file list, click the **Date modified** column heading button. The down arrow that appears above the label of the Date modified button indicates that the files are sorted in descending (newest to oldest) order by the date the file was modified. At the top of the list is the List file, which was modified on June 18, 2016.

   Trouble? If your folder window does not contain a Date modified column, right-click any column heading, click Date modified on the shortcut menu, and then repeat Step 1.

2. Click the **Date modified** column heading button again. The up arrow on the Date modified button indicates that the sort order is reversed, with the files listed in ascending (oldest to newest) order.

3. Click the **Name** column heading button to sort the files in alphabetical order by name. The Artists file is now listed first.

Now that Matt is comfortable working in File Explorer, you're ready to show him how to manage his files and folders.

Managing Files and Folders

As discussed earlier, you manage your personal files and folders by storing them according to a logical organization so that they are easy to find later. You can organize files as you create, edit, and save them, or you can do so later by creating folders, if necessary, and then moving and copying files into the folders.

To create a file-organization plan for Matt's files, you can review Figure 8 and look for files that logically belong together. In the Tutorial folder, Chianti, Florence, Logo, and Market are all graphics files that Matt uses for marketing and sales. He created the Artists and Tuscany files to describe Italian tours. The Marketing and Tour Rates files relate to business finances. Matt thinks the List file contains a task list for completing a project, but he isn't sure of its contents. He does recall creating the file using WordPad.

If the List file does contain a project task list, you can organize the files by creating four folders—one for graphics, one for tours, another for the financial files, and a fourth folder for projects. When you create a folder, you give it a name, preferably one that describes its contents. A folder name can have up to 255 characters, and any character is allowed, except / \ : * ? " < > and |. Considering these conventions, you could create four folders to contain Matt's files, as follows:

- Marketing Graphics folder—Chianti, Florence, Logo, and Market files
- Tours folder—Artists and Tuscany files
- Financial folder—Marketing and Tour Rates files
- Projects folder—List file

Before you start creating folders according to this plan, you need to verify the contents of the List file. You can do so by opening the file.

Opening a File

TIP

To select the default application for opening a file, right-click the file in File Explorer, point to Open with, and then click Choose default application. Click an application in the list that opens, and then click OK.

You can open a file from a running application or from File Explorer. To open a file in a running application, you select the application's Open command to access the Open dialog box, which you use to navigate to the file you want, select the file, and then open it. In the Open dialog box, you use the same tools that are available in File Explorer to navigate to the file you want to open. If the application you want to use is not running, you can open a file by double-clicking it in the right pane of File Explorer. The file usually opens in the application that you used to create or edit it.

Occasionally, File Explorer will open the file in an application other than the one you want to use to work with the file. For example, double-clicking a digital picture file usually opens the picture in a picture viewer application. If you want to edit the picture, you must open the file in a graphics editing application. When you need to specify an application to open a file, you can right-click the file, point to Open with on the shortcut menu, and then click the name of the application that you want to use.

Matt says that he might want to edit the List file to add another task. You'll show him how to use File Explorer to open the file in WordPad, which he used to create the file, and then edit it.

To open and edit the List file:

1. In the right pane of File Explorer, right-click the **List** file, and then point to **Open with** on the shortcut menu to display a list of applications that can open the file. See Figure 9.

   Trouble? If a list does not appear when you point to Open with on the shortcut menu, click Open with to display a window asking how you want to open this file.

Figure 9 Shortcut menu for opening a file

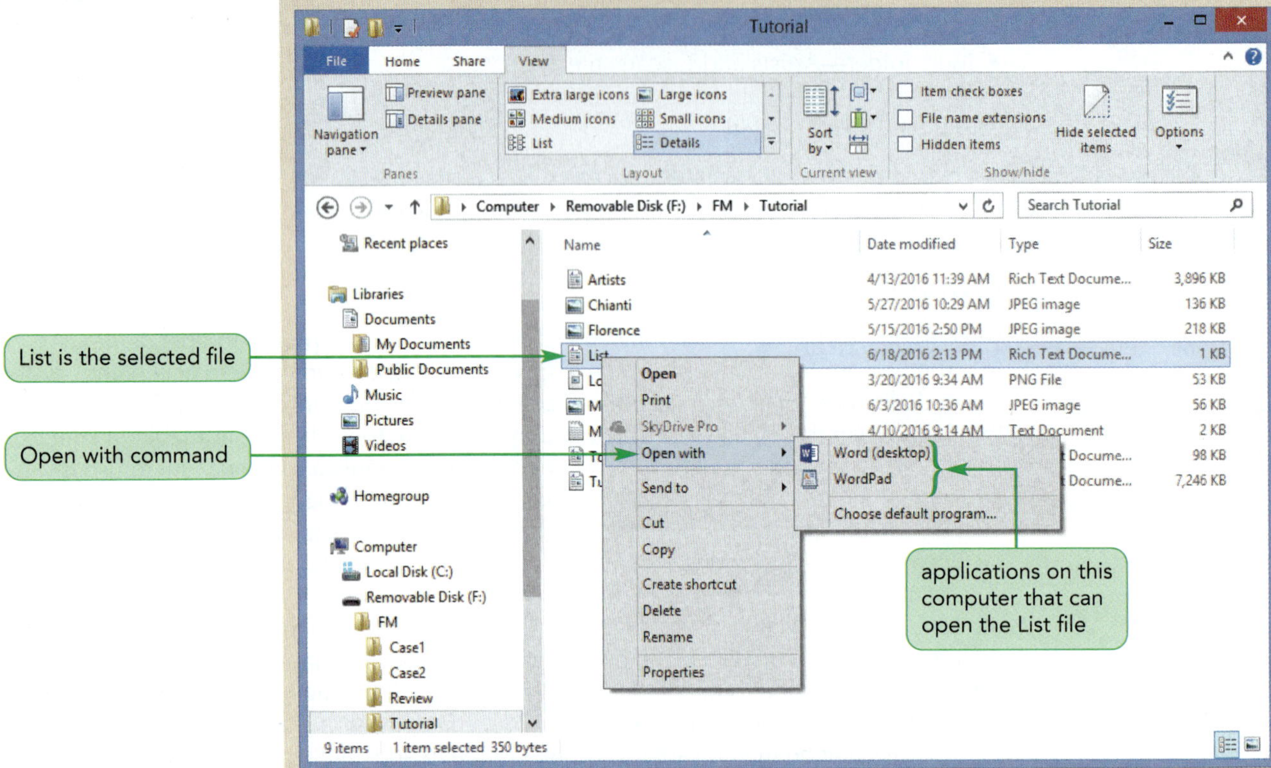

2. Click **WordPad** to open the List file in WordPad. The file contains a task list for the marketing project, which includes three items.

   Trouble? If you had to click Open with instead of pointing to it, in the window that asks how you want to open this file, click Keep using WordPad.

3. Press the **Ctrl+End** keys to move the insertion point to the end of the document, press the **Enter** key if necessary to start a new line, and then type **4. Review the Tours in Italy webpage.**

TIP

In File Explorer, you can also double-click a file to open it in the default application for that file type.

Now that you've added text to the List file, you need to save it to preserve the changes you made.

Saving a File

As you are creating or editing a file, you should save it frequently so you don't lose your work. When you save a file, you need to decide what name to use for the file and where to store it. Most applications provide a default location for saving a file, which makes it easy to find the file again later. However, you can select a different location depending on where you want to store the file.

Besides a storage location, every file must have a filename, which provides important information about the file, including its contents and purpose. A filename such as Italian Tours.docx has the following three parts:

- Main part of the filename—When you save a file, you need to provide only the main part of the filename, such as "Italian Tours."
- Dot—The dot (.) separates the main part of the filename from the extension.
- Extension—The **extension** includes the three or four characters that follow the dot in the filename and identify the file's type.

Similar to folder names, the main part of a filename can have up to 255 characters. This gives you plenty of room to name your file accurately enough so that you'll recognize the contents of the file just by looking at the filename. You can use spaces and certain punctuation symbols in your filenames. However, filenames cannot contain the symbols / \ : * ? " < > or | because these characters have special meanings in Windows 8.

Windows and other software add the dot and the extension to a filename, though File Explorer does not display them by default. Instead, File Explorer shows the file icon associated with the extension or a thumbnail for some types of files, such as graphics. For example, in a file named Italian Tours.docx, the docx extension identifies the file as one created in Microsoft Word, a word-processing application. File Explorer displays this file using a Microsoft Word icon and the main part of its filename. For a file named Italian Tours.png, the png extension identifies the file as one created in a graphics application such as Paint. In Details view or List view, File Explorer displays this file using a Paint icon and the main part of its filename. In other views, File Explorer does not use an icon, but displays the file contents in a thumbnail. File Explorer treats the Italian Tours.docx and Italian Tours.png files differently because their extensions distinguish them as different types of files, even though the main parts of their filenames are identical.

When you save a new file, you use the Save As dialog box to provide a filename and select a location for the file. You can create a folder for the new file at the same time you save the file. When you edit a file you saved previously, you can use the application's Save command to save your changes to the file, keeping the same name and location. If you want to save the edited file with a different name or in a different location, however, you need to use the Save As dialog box to specify the new name or location.

As with the Open dialog box, you specify the file location in the Save As dialog box using the same navigation techniques and tools that are available in File Explorer. You might need to click the Browse Folders button to expand the Save As dialog box so it displays these tools. In addition, the Save As dialog box always includes a File name box where you specify a filename.

INSIGHT

Saving Files on SkyDrive

Some Windows 8 applications, such as Microsoft Office, include SkyDrive as a location for saving and opening files. **SkyDrive** is a Microsoft service that provides up to 7 GB of online storage space for your files at no charge. You can purchase additional space if you need it. For example, if you create a document in Microsoft Word, your SkyDrive appears as a location for saving the document. (Your SkyDrive appears with your username, such as Matt's SkyDrive.) If you have a Microsoft account, you can select a folder on your SkyDrive to save the document online. (If you don't have a Microsoft account, you can sign up for one by visiting the SkyDrive website.) Because the file is stored online, it takes up no storage space on your computer and is available from any computer with an Internet connection. You access the document by opening it in Word or by visiting the SkyDrive website, and then signing in to your Microsoft account. To share the document with other people, you can send them a link to the document via email. They can use the link to access the document even if they do not have a Microsoft account.

One reason that Matt had trouble remembering the contents of the List file is that "List" is not a descriptive name. A better name for this file is Task List. You will save this document in the Tutorial subfolder of the FM folder provided with your Data Files. You will also use the Save As dialog box to specify a new name for the file as you save it.

To save the List file with a new name:

1. On the ribbon in the WordPad window, click the **File** tab to display commands for working with files.
2. Click **Save as** to open the Save As dialog box, as shown in Figure 10. The Tutorial folder is selected as the storage location for this file because you opened the file from this folder.

Figure 10 Saving a file using the Save As dialog box

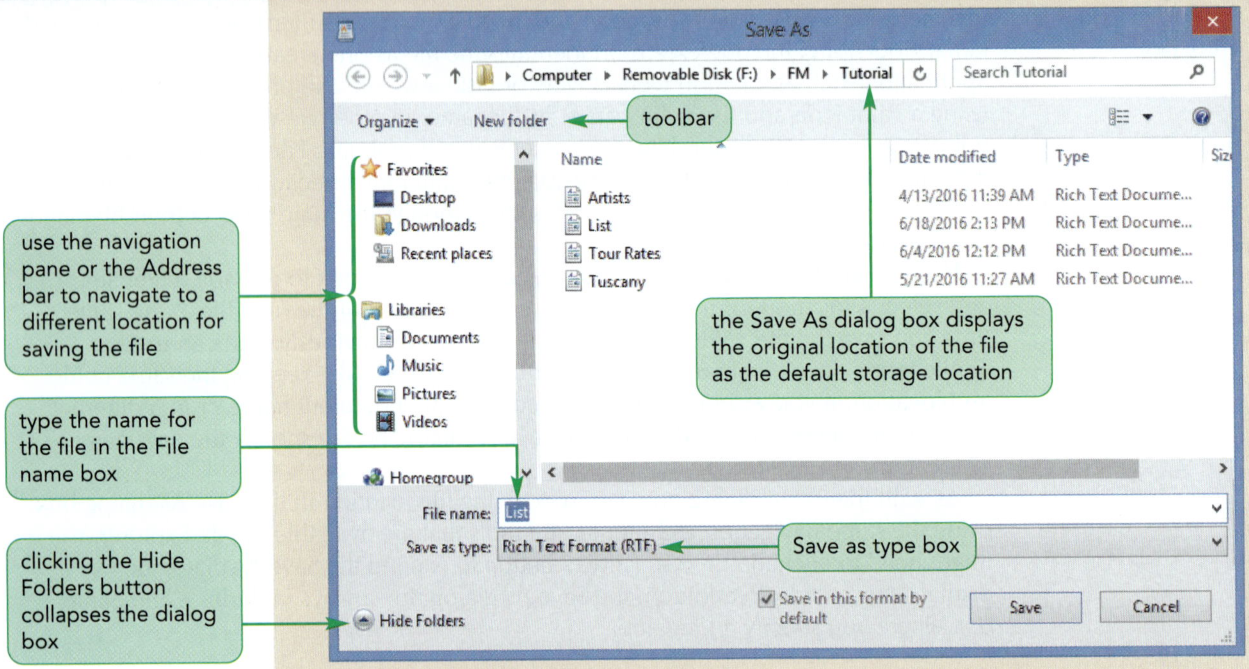

Trouble? If the navigation pane does not appear in the Save As dialog box, click the Browse Folders button. The Browse Folders button toggles to become the Hide Folders button.

3. With the current filename selected in the File name box, type **Task List**. The Save as type box shows that WordPad will save this file as a Rich Text Format (RTF) file, which is the default file type for WordPad files.

   Trouble? If the current filename is not selected in the File name box, drag to select the text in the File name box and then type Task List.

4. Click the **Save** button. The Save As dialog box closes, WordPad saves the Task List file in the Tutorial folder, and the new filename appears in the WordPad title bar.
5. On the title bar, click the **Close** button × to close WordPad.

TIP

To change the file type, click the Save as type box, and then click a file type such as Text Document.

Now you're ready to start creating the folders you need to organize Matt's files.

Creating Folders

You originally proposed creating four new folders for Matt's files: Marketing Graphics, Tours, Financial, and Projects. Matt asks you to create these folders now. After that, you'll move his files to the appropriate folders. You create folders in File Explorer using one of three methods: using the New folder button in the New group on the Home tab; using the New folder button on the Quick Access Toolbar; or right-clicking to display a shortcut menu that includes the New command.

INSIGHT

Guidelines for Creating Folders

Consider the following guidelines as you create folders:

- Keep folder names short yet descriptive of the folder's contents. Long folder names can be more difficult to display in their entirety in folder windows, so use names that are short but clear. Choose names that will be meaningful later, such as project names or course numbers.
- Create subfolders to organize files. If a file list in File Explorer is so long that you must scroll the window, you should probably organize those files into subfolders.
- Develop standards for naming folders. Use a consistent naming scheme that is clear to you, such as one that uses a project name as the name of the main folder, and includes step numbers in each subfolder name (for example, 1-Outline, 2-First Draft, 3-Final Draft, and so on).

In the following steps, you will create the four folders for Matt in your Tutorial folder. Because it is easier to work with files using large file icons, you'll switch to Large icons view first.

To create the folders:

1. On the status bar in the File Explorer window, click the **Large icons view** button to switch to Large icons view.
2. Click the **Home** tab to display the Home tab on the ribbon.
3. In the New group, click the **New folder** button. A folder icon with the label "New folder" appears in the right pane of the File Explorer window. See Figure 11.

Figure 11 Creating a new folder in the Tutorial folder

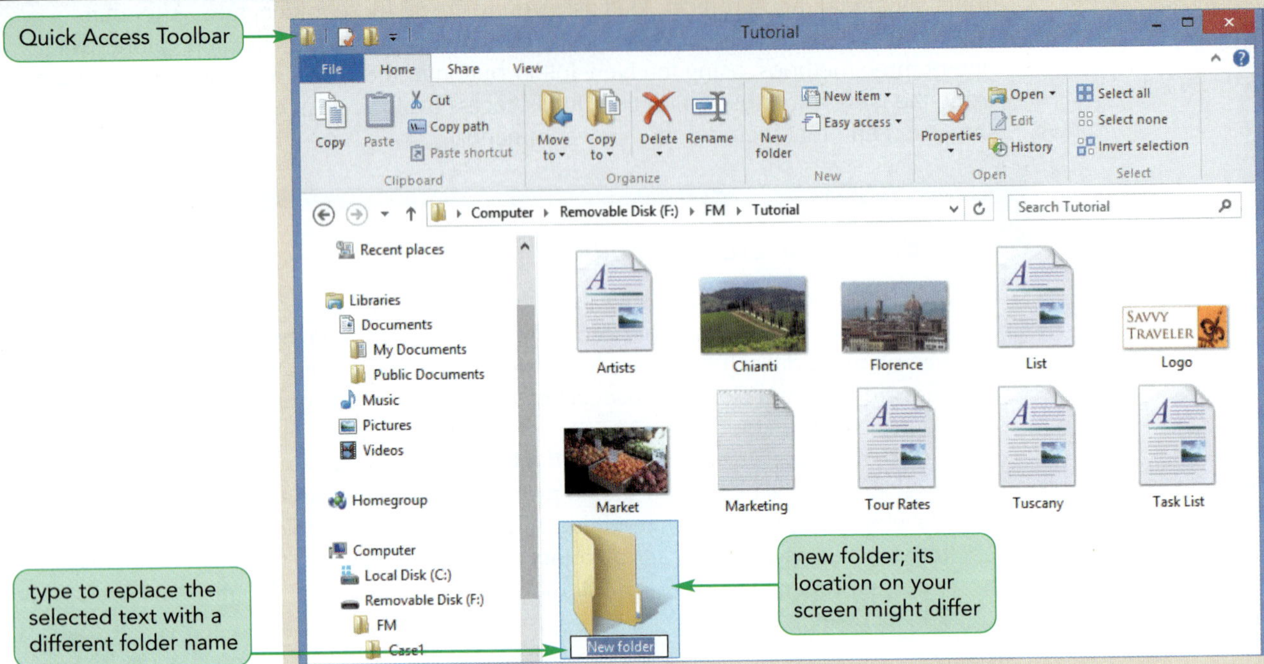

Photos courtesy of Lisa Ruffolo

Trouble? If the "New folder" name is not selected, right-click the new folder, click Rename on the shortcut menu, and then continue with Step 4.

Windows uses "New folder" as a placeholder, and selects the text so that you can replace it immediately by typing a new name. You do not need to press the Backspace or Delete key to delete the text.

4. Type **Marketing Graphics** as the folder name, and then press the **Enter** key. The new folder is named Marketing Graphics and is the selected item in the right pane. To create a second folder, you can use a shortcut menu.
5. In the right pane, right-click a blank area, point to **New** on the shortcut menu, and then click **Folder**. A folder icon appears in the right pane with the "New folder" text selected.
6. Type **Tours** as the name of the new folder, and then press the **Enter** key. To create the third folder, you can use the Quick Access Toolbar.
7. On the Quick Access Toolbar, click the **New folder** button, type **Financial**, and then press the **Enter** key to create and name the folder.
8. Create a new folder in the Tutorial folder named **Projects**.

After creating four folders, you're ready to organize Matt's files by moving them into the appropriate folders.

Moving and Copying Files and Folders

You can either move or copy a file from its current location to a new location. **Moving** a file removes it from its current location and places it in a new location that you specify. **Copying** a file places a duplicate version of the file in a new location that you specify, while leaving the original file intact in its current location. You can also move and copy folders. When you do, you move or copy all the files contained in the folder. (You'll practice copying folders in a Case Problem at the end of this tutorial.)

In File Explorer, you can move and copy files by using the Move to or Copy to buttons in the Organize group on the Home tab; using the Copy and Cut commands on a file's shortcut menu; or using keyboard shortcuts. When you copy or move files using these methods, you are using the **Clipboard**, a temporary storage area for files and information that you copy or move from one location to place in another.

You can also move files by dragging the files in the File Explorer window. You will now organize Matt's files by moving them to the appropriate folders you have created. You'll start by moving the Marketing file to the Financial folder by dragging the file.

To move the Marketing file by dragging it:

1. In File Explorer, point to the **Marketing** file in the right pane, and then press and hold the mouse button.
2. While still pressing the mouse button, drag the **Marketing** file to the **Financial** folder. See Figure 12.

Figure 12 Dragging a file to move it to a folder

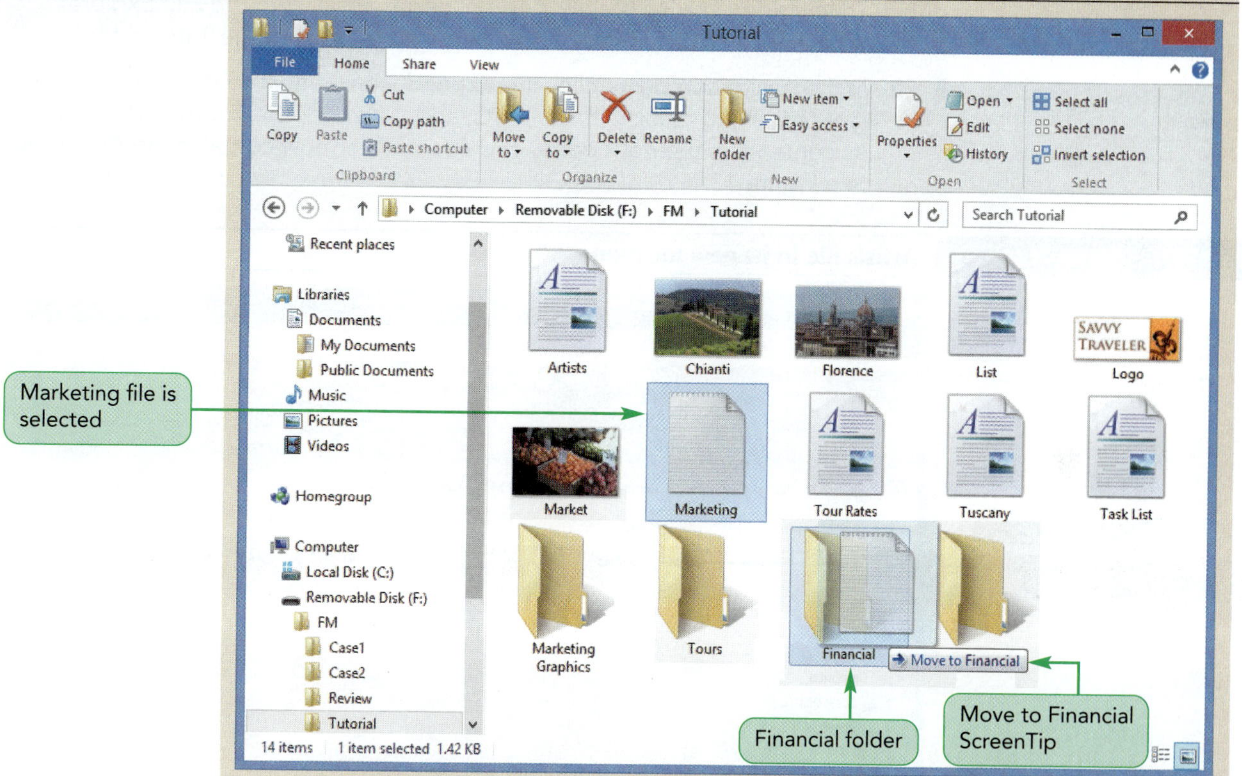

TIP

If you drag a file or folder to a location on a different drive, the file is copied, not moved, to preserve the file in its original location.

3. When the Move to Financial ScreenTip appears, release the mouse button. The Marketing file is removed from the main Tutorial folder and stored in the Financial subfolder.

   Trouble? If you released the mouse button before the Move to Financial ScreenTip appeared, press the Ctrl+Z keys to undo the move, and then repeat Steps 1–3.

   Trouble? If you moved the Market file instead of the Marketing file, press the Ctrl+Z keys to undo the move, and then repeat Steps 1–3.

4. In the right pane, double-click the **Financial** folder to verify that it contains the Marketing file.

Trouble? If the Marketing file does not appear in the Financial folder, you probably moved it to a different folder. Press the Ctrl+Z keys to undo the move, and then repeat Steps 1–3.

5. Click the **Back** button on the Address bar to return to the Tutorial folder.

You'll move the remaining files into the folders using the Clipboard.

To move files using the Clipboard:

1. Right-click the **Artists** file, and then click **Cut** on the shortcut menu. Although the file icon still appears selected in the right pane of File Explorer, Windows removes the Artists file from the Tutorial folder and stores it on the Clipboard.
2. In the right pane, right-click the **Tours** folder, and then click **Paste** on the shortcut menu. Windows pastes the Artists file from the Clipboard to the Tours folder. The Artists file icon no longer appears in the File Explorer window, which is currently displaying the contents of the Tutorial folder.
3. In the navigation pane, click the **expand** icon next to the Tutorial folder, if necessary, to display its contents, and then click the **Tours** folder to view its contents in the right pane. The Tours folder now contains the Artists file. See Figure 13.

Figure 13 Artists file in its new location

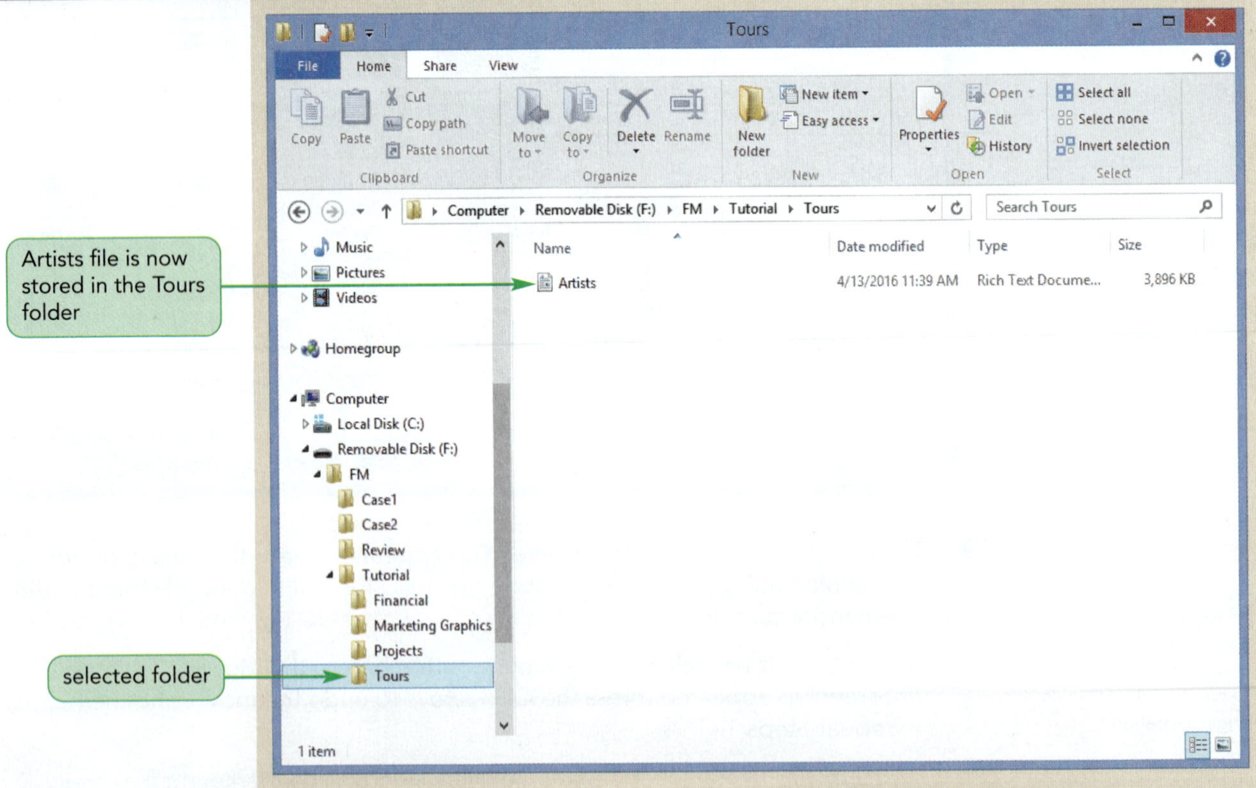

Next, you'll use the Clipboard again to move the Tuscany file from the Tutorial folder to the Tours folder. But this time, you'll access the Clipboard using the ribbon.

4. On the Address bar, point to the **Up to** button [↑] to display its ScreenTip (Up to "Tutorial"), click the **Up to** button [↑] to return to the Tutorial folder, and then click the **Tuscany** file to select it.
5. On the Home tab, in the Clipboard group, click the **Cut** button to remove the Tuscany file from the Tutorial folder and temporarily store it on the Clipboard.
6. In the Address bar, click the **arrow** button [▶] to the right of "Tutorial" to display a list of subfolders in the Tutorial folder, and then click **Tours** to display the contents of the Tours folder in File Explorer.
7. In the Clipboard group, click the **Paste** button to paste the Tuscany file in the Tours folder. The Tours folder now contains the Artists and Tuscany files.

Finally, you'll move the Task List file from the Tutorial folder to the Projects folder using the Move to button in the Organize group on the Home tab. This button and the Copy to button are ideal when you want to move or copy files without leaving the current folder. When you select a file and then click the Move to or Copy to button, a list of locations appears, including all of the Windows libraries and one or more folders you open frequently. You can click a location in the list to move the selected file to that library or folder. You can also select the Choose location option to open the Move Items or Copy Items dialog box, and then select a location for the file, which you'll do in the following steps.

To move the Task List file using the Move to button:

1. In the Address bar, click **Tutorial** to return to the Tutorial folder, and then click the **Task List** file to select it.
2. On the Home tab, in the Organize group, click the **Move to** button to display a list of locations to which you can move the selected file. The Projects folder is not included on this list because you haven't opened it yet.
3. Click **Choose location** to open the Move Items dialog box. See Figure 14.

Figure 14 Move Items dialog box

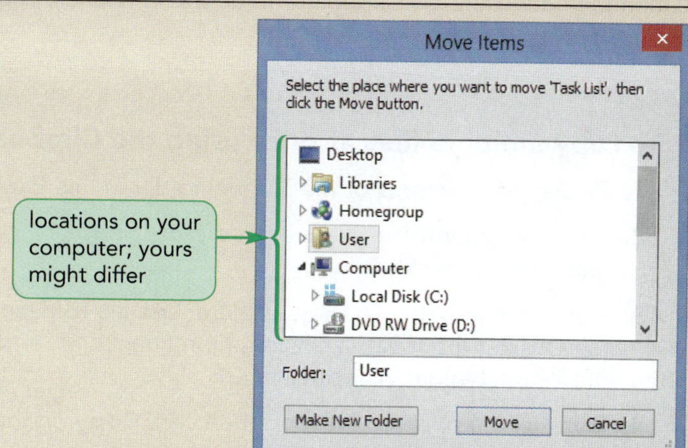

4. If necessary, scroll the list of locations, and then click the **expand** icon [▷] next to the drive containing your Data Files, such as Removable Disk (F:).

5. Navigate to the FM ▸ Tutorial folder, and then click the **Projects** folder to select it.
6. Click the **Move** button to close the dialog box and move the Task List file to the Projects folder.
7. Open the Projects folder to confirm that it contains the Task List file.

One way to save steps when moving or copying multiple files or folders is to select all the files and folders you want to move or copy, and then work with them as a group. You can use several techniques to select multiple files or folders at the same time, which are described in Figure 15.

Figure 15 **Selecting multiple files or folders**

Items to Select in the Right Pane of File Explorer	Method
Files or folders listed together	Click the first item, press and hold the Shift key, click the last item, and then release the Shift key. *or* Drag the pointer to create a selection box around all the items you want to include.
Files or folders not listed together	Press and hold the Ctrl key, click each item you want to select, and then release the Ctrl key.
All files and folders	On the Home tab, in the Select group, click the Select all button.
Items to Deselect in the Right Pane of File Explorer	**Method**
Single file or folder in a selected group	Press and hold the Ctrl key, click each item you want to remove from the selection, and then release the Ctrl key.
All selected files and folders	Click a blank area of the File Explorer window.

Next, you'll copy the four graphics files from the Tutorial folder to the Marketing Graphics folder using the Clipboard. To do this efficiently, you will select multiple files at once.

To copy multiple files at once using the Clipboard:

1. Display the contents of the Tutorial folder in File Explorer.
2. Click the **Chianti** file, press and hold the **Shift** key, click the **Market** file, and then release the **Shift** key.
3. Press and hold the **Ctrl** key, click the **List** file to deselect it, and then release the **Ctrl** key. Four files—Chianti, Florence, Logo, and Market—are selected in the Tutorial folder window.
4. Right-click a selected file, and then click **Copy** on the shortcut menu. Windows copies the selected files to the Clipboard.
5. Right-click the **Marketing Graphics** folder, and then click **Paste** on the shortcut menu.
6. Open the **Marketing Graphics** folder to verify it contains the four files you copied, and then return to the Tutorial folder.

7. Right-click the **Tour Rates** file, and then click **Copy** on the shortcut menu.
8. In the right pane, double-click the **Financial** folder to open it, right-click a blank area of the right pane, and then click **Paste** on the shortcut menu.

INSIGHT

Duplicating Your Folder Organization

If you work on two computers, such as one computer at an office or school and another computer at home, you can duplicate the folders you use on both computers to simplify the process of transferring files from one computer to another. For example, if you have four folders in your My Documents folder on your work computer, create these same four folders on a USB drive and in the My Documents folder of your home computer. If you change a file on the hard disk of your home computer, you can copy the most recent version of the file to the corresponding folder on your USB drive so the file is available when you are at work. You also then have a **backup**, or duplicate copy, of important files. Having a backup of your files is invaluable if your computer has a fatal error.

All the files that originally appeared in the Tutorial folder are now stored in appropriate subfolders. You can streamline the organization of the Tutorial folder by deleting the duplicate files you no longer need.

Deleting Files and Folders

TIP

In most cases, a file deleted from a USB drive does not go into the Recycle Bin. Instead, it is deleted when Windows 8 removes its icon, and the file cannot be recovered.

You should periodically delete files and folders you no longer need so that your main folders and disks don't get cluttered. In File Explorer, you delete a file or folder by deleting its icon. When you delete a file from a hard disk, Windows 8 removes the file from the folder but stores the file contents in the Recycle Bin. The Recycle Bin is an area on your hard disk that holds deleted files until you remove them permanently. When you delete a folder from the hard disk, the folder and all of its files are stored in the Recycle Bin. If you change your mind and want to retrieve a deleted file or folder, you can double-click the Recycle Bin on the desktop, right-click the file or folder you want to retrieve, and then click Restore. However, after you empty the Recycle Bin, you can no longer recover the files it contained.

Because you copied the Chianti, Florence, Logo, Market, and Tour Rates files to the subfolders in the Tutorial folder, you can safely delete the original files. You can also delete the List file because you no longer need it. You can delete a file or folder using various methods, including using a shortcut menu or selecting one or more files and then pressing the Delete key.

To delete files in the Tutorial folder:

1. Display the Tutorial folder in the File Explorer window.
2. In the right pane, click **Chianti**, press and hold the **Shift** key, click **Tour Rates**, and then release the **Shift** key. All files in the Tutorial folder are now selected. None of the subfolders should be selected.
3. Right-click the selected files, and then click **Delete** on the shortcut menu. A message box appears, asking if you're sure you want to permanently delete these files.

Make sure you have copied the selected files to the Marketing Graphics and Financial folders before completing this step.

4. Click the **Yes** button to confirm that you want to delete the files.

Renaming Files

After creating and naming a file or folder, you might realize that a different name would be more meaningful or descriptive. You can easily rename a file or folder by using the Rename command on the file's shortcut menu.

Now that you've organized Matt's files into folders, he reviews your work and notes that the Artists file was originally created to store text specifically about Florentine painters and sculptors. You can rename that file to give it a more descriptive filename.

To rename the Artists file:

1. In the right pane of the File Explorer window, double-click the **Tours** folder to display its contents.
2. Right-click the **Artists** file, and then click **Rename** on the shortcut menu. The filename is highlighted and a box appears around it.
3. Type **Florentine Artists**, and then press the **Enter** key. The file now appears with the new name.

   Trouble? If you make a mistake while typing and you haven't pressed the Enter key yet, press the Backspace key until you delete the mistake and then complete Step 3. If you've already pressed the Enter key, repeat Steps 2 and 3 to rename the file again.

   Trouble? If your computer is set to display filename extensions, a message might appear asking if you are sure you want to change the filename extension. Click the No button, and then repeat Steps 2 and 3.

TIP

To rename a file, you can also click the file, pause, click it again to select the filename, and then type to enter a new filename.

Working with Compressed Files

You compress a file or a folder of files so it occupies less space on the disk. It can be useful to compress files before transferring them from one location to another, such as from your hard disk to a removable disk or vice versa, or from one computer to another via email. You can then transfer the files more quickly. Also, if you or your email contacts can send and receive files only up to a certain size, compressing large files might make them small enough to send and receive. Compare two folders—a folder named Photos that contains files totaling about 8.6 MB, and a compressed folder containing the same files but requiring only 6.5 MB of disk space. In this case, the compressed files use about 25 percent less disk space than the uncompressed files.

You can compress one or more files in File Explorer using the Zip button, which is located in the Send group on the Share tab of the ribbon. Windows stores the compressed files in a special type of folder called an **archive**, or a compressed folder. File Explorer uses an icon of a folder with a zipper to represent a compressed folder. To compress additional files or folders, you drag them into the compressed folder. You can open a file directly from a compressed folder, although you cannot modify the file. To edit and save a compressed file, you must extract it first. When you **extract** a file, you create an uncompressed copy of the file in a folder you specify. The original file remains in the compressed folder.

Matt suggests that you compress the files and folders in the Tutorial folder so that you can more quickly transfer them to another location.

To compress the folders and files in the Tutorial folder:

1. In File Explorer, navigate to the Tutorial folder, and then select all the folders in the Tutorial folder.
2. Click the **Share** tab on the ribbon.
3. In the Send group, click the **Zip** button. After a few moments, a new compressed folder appears in the Tutorial window with the filename selected. By default, File Explorer uses the name of the first selected item as the name of the compressed folder. You'll replace the name with a more descriptive one.
4. Type **Savvy Traveler**, and then press the **Enter** key to rename the compressed folder. See Figure 16.

TIP

Another way to compress files is to select the files, right-click the selection, point to Send to on the shortcut menu, and then click Compressed (zipped) folder.

Figure 16 Compressing files and folders

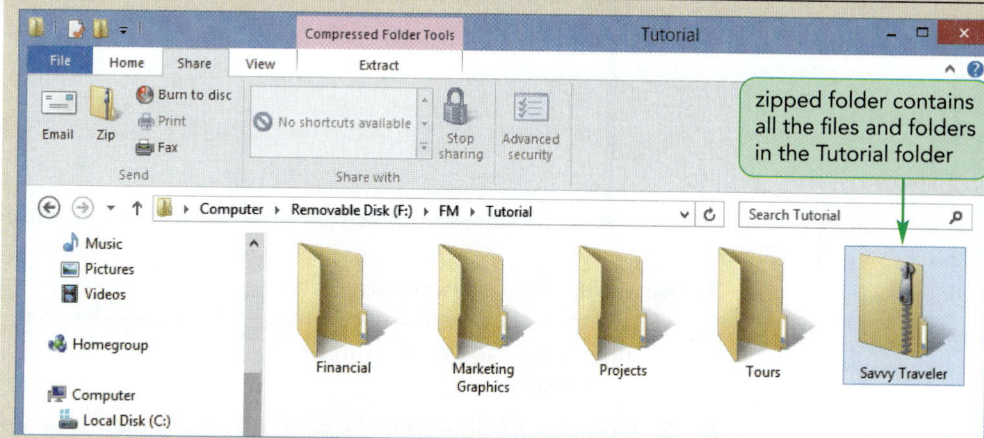

5. Double-click the **Savvy Traveler** compressed folder to open it, open the **Tours** folder, and then note the size of the compressed Tuscany file, which is 1,815 KB.
6. Navigate back to the Tutorial folder.

You can move and copy the files and folders from an opened compressed folder to other locations, although you cannot rename the files. More often, you extract all of the files from the compressed folder to a new location that you specify, preserving the files in their original folders as appropriate.

To extract the compressed files:

1. Click the **Savvy Traveler** compressed folder to select it, and then click the **Compressed Folder Tools Extract** tab on the ribbon.
2. In the Extract all group, click the **Extract all** button. The Extract Compressed (Zipped) Folders Wizard starts and opens the Select a Destination and Extract Files dialog box.
3. Press the **End** key to deselect the path in the box and move the insertion point to the end of the path, press the **Backspace** key as many times as necessary to delete the Savvy Traveler text, and then type **Backups**. The final three parts of the path in the box should be \FM\Tutorial\Backups. See Figure 17.

Figure 17 Extracting files from a compressed folder

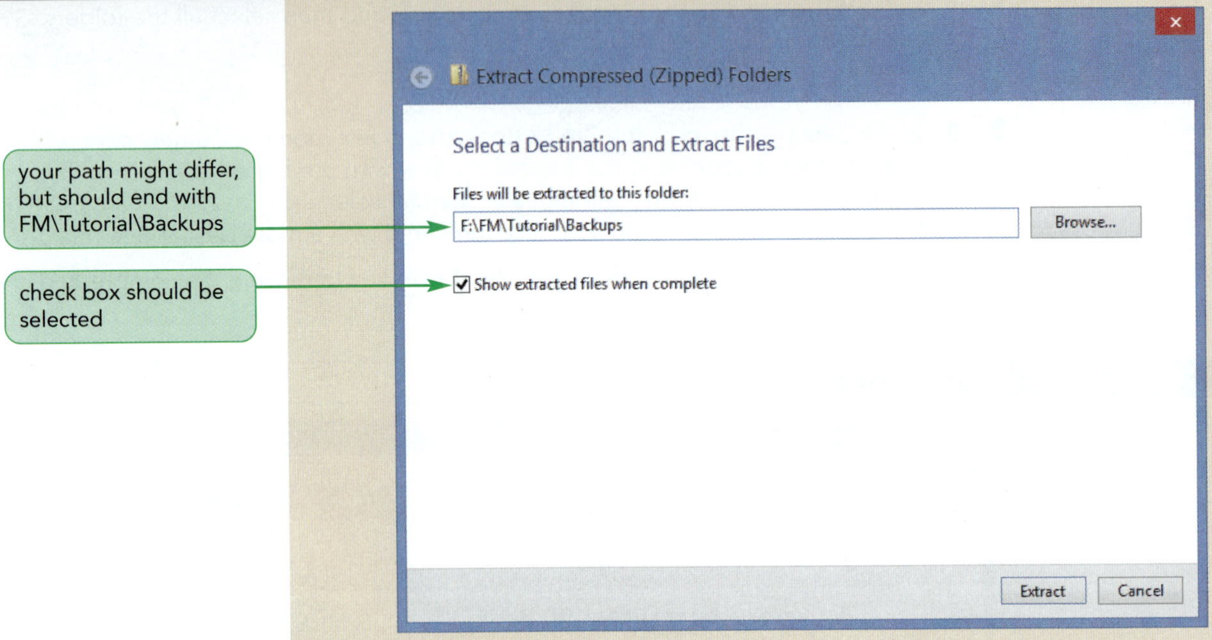

4. Make sure the Show extracted files when complete check box is checked, and then click the **Extract** button. Windows extracts the files and then opens the Backups folder, showing the Financial, Marketing Graphics, Projects, and Tours folders.
5. Open each folder to make sure it contains the files you worked with in this tutorial. When you open the Tours folder, note the uncompressed size of the Tuscany file, which is about four times as large as its compressed version.
6. Close all open windows.

In this tutorial, you examined the purpose of organizing files and folders, and you planned and created an organization for a set of related files and folders. You also explored your computer using File Explorer and learned how to navigate to your Data Files using the navigation pane. You used File Explorer to manage files and folders by opening and saving files; creating folders; and selecting, moving, and copying files. You also renamed and deleted files according to your organization plan. Finally, you compressed and extracted files.

REVIEW

Quick Check

1. You organize files by storing them in ____________.
2. What is the purpose of the Address bar in File Explorer?
3. A filename ____________ identifies the file's type and indicates the application that created the file.
4. Explain how to use File Explorer to navigate to a file in the following location: E: ▸ Courses ▸ Computer Basics ▸ Operating Systems.txt.
5. One way to move files and folders is to use the ____________, a temporary storage area for files and information that you copied or moved from one place and plan to use somewhere else.
6. What happens if you click the first file in a folder window, press the Shift key, click the last file, and then release the Shift key?
7. When you delete a file from a hard disk, Windows removes the file from the folder but stores the file contents in the ____________.
8. Describe how to compress a file or folder.
9. What are the benefits of compressing files and folders?

PRACTICE

Review Assignments

Data Files needed for the Review Assignments: Banner.png, Colosseum.jpg, Lectures.xlsx, Rome.jpg, Rome.rtf, Schedule.rtf, Tours.rtf

Matt has saved a few files from his old computer to a removable disk. He gives you these files in a single, unorganized folder, and asks you to organize them logically into subfolders. To do this, you will need to devise a plan for managing the files, and then create the subfolders you need. Next, you will rename, copy, move, and delete files, and then perform other management tasks to make it easy for Matt to work with these files and folders. Complete the following steps:

1. Use File Explorer to navigate to and open the FM ▸ Review folder provided with your Data Files. Examine the seven files in this folder and consider the best way to organize the files.
2. Open the **Rome** text file in WordPad, and then add the following tip to the end of the document: **Dine on the Italian schedule, with the main meal in the middle of the day.**
3. Save the document as **Rome Dining Tips** in the Review folder. Close the WordPad window.
4. In the Review folder, create three folders: **Business**, **Destinations**, and **Supplements**.
5. To organize the files into the correct folders, complete the following steps:
   - Move the Banner and Schedule files from the Review folder to the Business folder.
   - Move the Colosseum and Rome JPEG image files and the Rome Dining Tips and Tours text files to the Destinations folder.
   - Copy the Lectures file to the Supplements folder.
6. Copy the Tours file in the Destinations folder to the Business folder.
7. Rename the Schedule file in the Business folder as **2016 Schedule**. Rename the Lectures file in the Supplements folder as **On-site Lectures**.
8. Delete the Lectures file and the Rome text file from the Review folder.
9. Create a compressed (zipped) folder in the Review folder named **Rome** that contains all the files and folders in the Review folder.
10. Extract the contents of the Rome compressed folder to a new folder named **Rome Backups** in the Review folder. (*Hint:* The file path will end with \FM\Review\Rome Backups.)
11. Close the File Explorer window.

APPLY

Case Problem 1

See the Starting Data Files section at the beginning of this tutorial for the list of Data Files needed for this Case Problem.

Bay Shore Arts Center Casey Sullivan started the Bay Shore Arts Center in Monterey, California, to provide workshops and courses on art and photography. Attracting students from the San Francisco and San José areas, Casey's business has grown and she now holds classes five days a week. She recently started a course on fine art landscape photography, which has quickly become her most popular offering. Casey hired you to help her design new classes and manage other parts of her growing business, including maintaining electronic business files and communications. Your first task is to organize the files on her new Windows 8 computer. Complete the following steps:

1. Open File Explorer. In the FM ▸ Case1 folder provided with your Data Files, create three folders: **Classes**, **Landscapes**, and **Management**.
2. Move the Fall Classes, Spring Classes, Summer Classes, and Winter Classes files from the Case1 folder to the Classes folder.
3. Rename the four files in the Classes folder by deleting the word "Classes" from each filename.
4. Move the four JPEG image files from the Case1 folder to the Landscapes folder.
5. Copy the remaining two files to the Management folder.
6. Copy the Workshops file to the Classes folder.
7. Delete the Instructors and Workshops files from the Case1 folder.
8. Make a copy of the Landscapes folder in the Case1 folder. The name of the duplicate folder appears as Landscapes – Copy. Rename the Landscapes – Copy folder as **California Photos**.
9. Copy the Workshops file from the Classes folder to the California Photos folder. Rename this file **California Workshops**.
10. Compress the graphics files in the California Photos folder in a new compressed folder named **Photos**.
11. Move the compressed Photos folder to the Case1 folder.
12. Close File Explorer.

TROUBLESHOOT

Case Problem 2

See the Starting Data Files section at the beginning of this tutorial for the list of Data Files needed for this Case Problem.

Charlotte Area Business Incubator Antoine Jackson is the director of the Charlotte Area Business Incubator, a service run by the University of North Carolina in Charlotte to consult with new and struggling small businesses. You work as an intern at the business incubator and spend part of your time organizing client files. Since Antoine started using Windows 8, he has been having trouble finding files on his computer. He sometimes creates duplicates of files and then doesn't know which copy is the most current. Complete the following steps:

1. Navigate to the FM ▸ Case2 folder provided with your Data Files, and then examine the files in this folder. Based on the filenames and file types, begin to create an organization plan for the files.
2. **Troubleshoot** Open the Tips1 and the Tips1 – Copy files and consider the problem these files could cause. Close the files and then fix the problem, renaming one or more files as necessary to reflect the contents.
3. **Troubleshoot** Open the Tips2 and the Tips2 – Copy files and compare their contents. Change the filenames to clarify the purpose and contents of the files.
4. Complete the organization plan for Antoine's files. In the FM ▸ Case2 folder, create the subfolders you need according to your plan.
5. Move the files in the Case2 folder to the subfolders you created. When you finish, the Case2 folder should contain at least two subfolders containing files.
6. Rename the spreadsheet files in each subfolder according to the following descriptions.
   - Budget1: **Website budget**
   - Budget2: **Marketing budget**
   - Report1: **Travel expense report**
   - Report2: **Project expense report**
   - Report3: **Balance sheet**
   - Report4: **Event budget**
7. **Troubleshoot** Make sure all files have descriptive names that accurately reflect their contents.
8. **Troubleshoot** Based on the work you did in Steps 6 and 7, move files as necessary to improve the file organization.
9. Close File Explorer.

TUTORIAL 1

Creating a Database

Tracking Patient, Visit, and Billing Data

OBJECTIVES

Session 1.1

- Learn basic database concepts and terms
- Start and exit Access
- Explore the Microsoft Access window and Backstage view
- Create a blank database
- Create and save a table in Datasheet view
- Enter field names and records in a table datasheet
- Open a table using the Navigation Pane

Session 1.2

- Open an Access database
- Copy and paste records from another Access database
- Navigate a table datasheet
- Create and navigate a simple query
- Create and navigate a simple form
- Create, preview, navigate, and print a simple report
- Use Help in Access
- Learn how to compact, back up, and restore a database

Case | *Chatham Community Health Services*

Chatham Community Health Services, a nonprofit health clinic located in Hartford, Connecticut, provides a range of medical services to patients of all ages. The clinic specializes in the areas of pulmonology, cardiac care, and chronic disease management. Cindi Rodriguez, the office manager for Chatham Community Health Services, oversees a small staff and is responsible for maintaining the medical records of the clinic's patients.

In order to best manage the clinic, Cindi and her staff rely on electronic medical records for patient information, billing, inventory control, purchasing, and accounts payable. Several months ago, the clinic upgraded to **Microsoft Access 2013** (or simply **Access**), a computer program used to enter, maintain, and retrieve related data in a format known as a database. Cindi and her staff want to use Access to store information about patients, billing, vendors, and products. She asks for your help in creating the necessary Access database.

STARTING DATA FILES

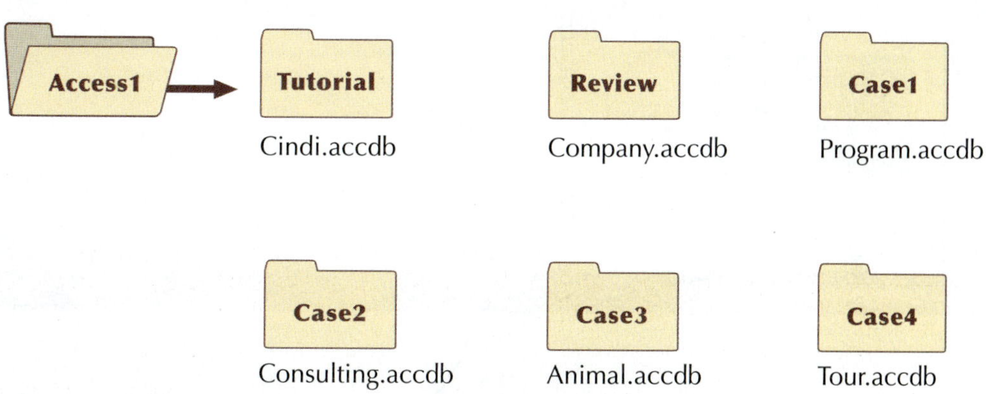

Session 1.1 Visual Overview:

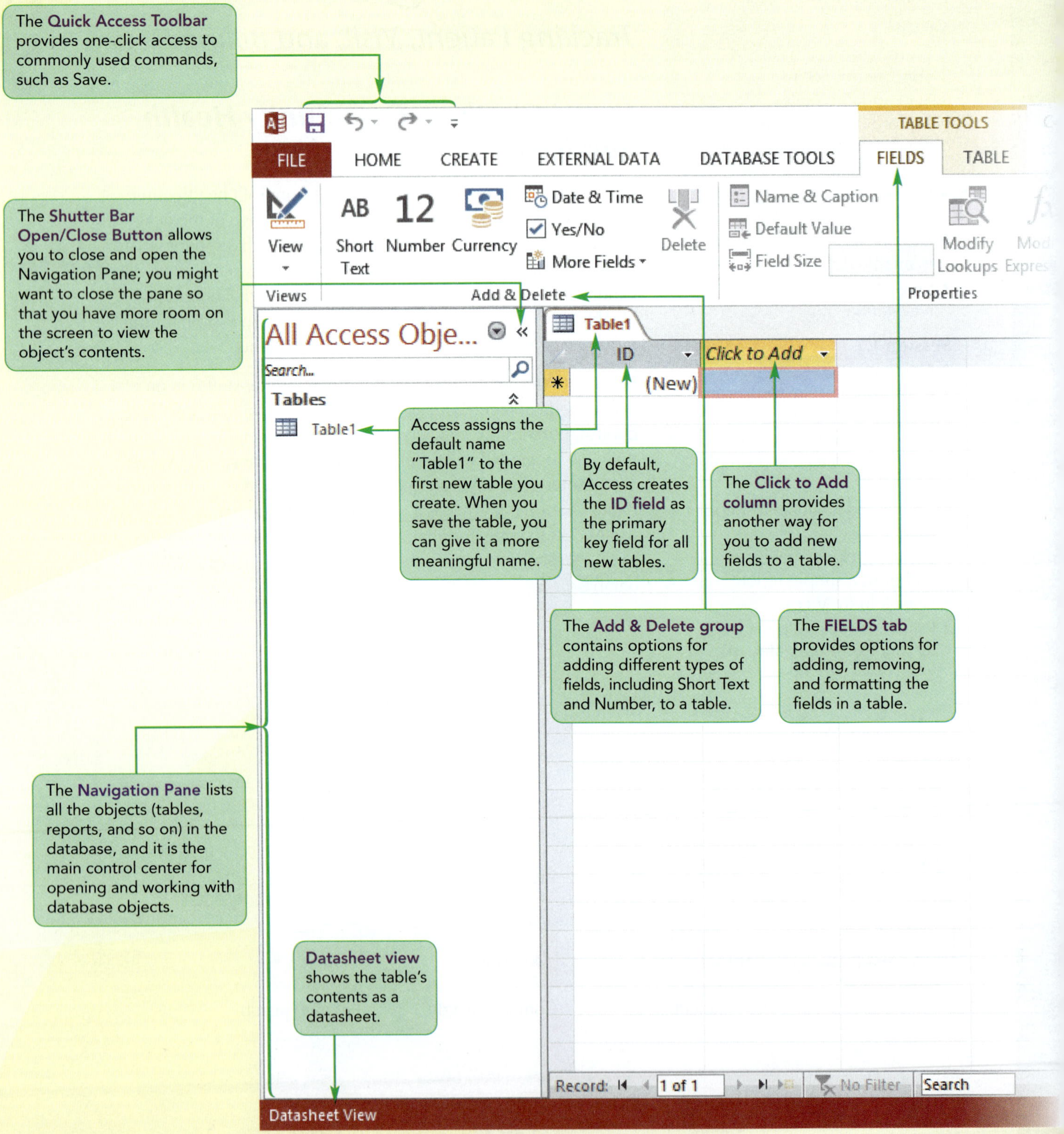

The Access Window

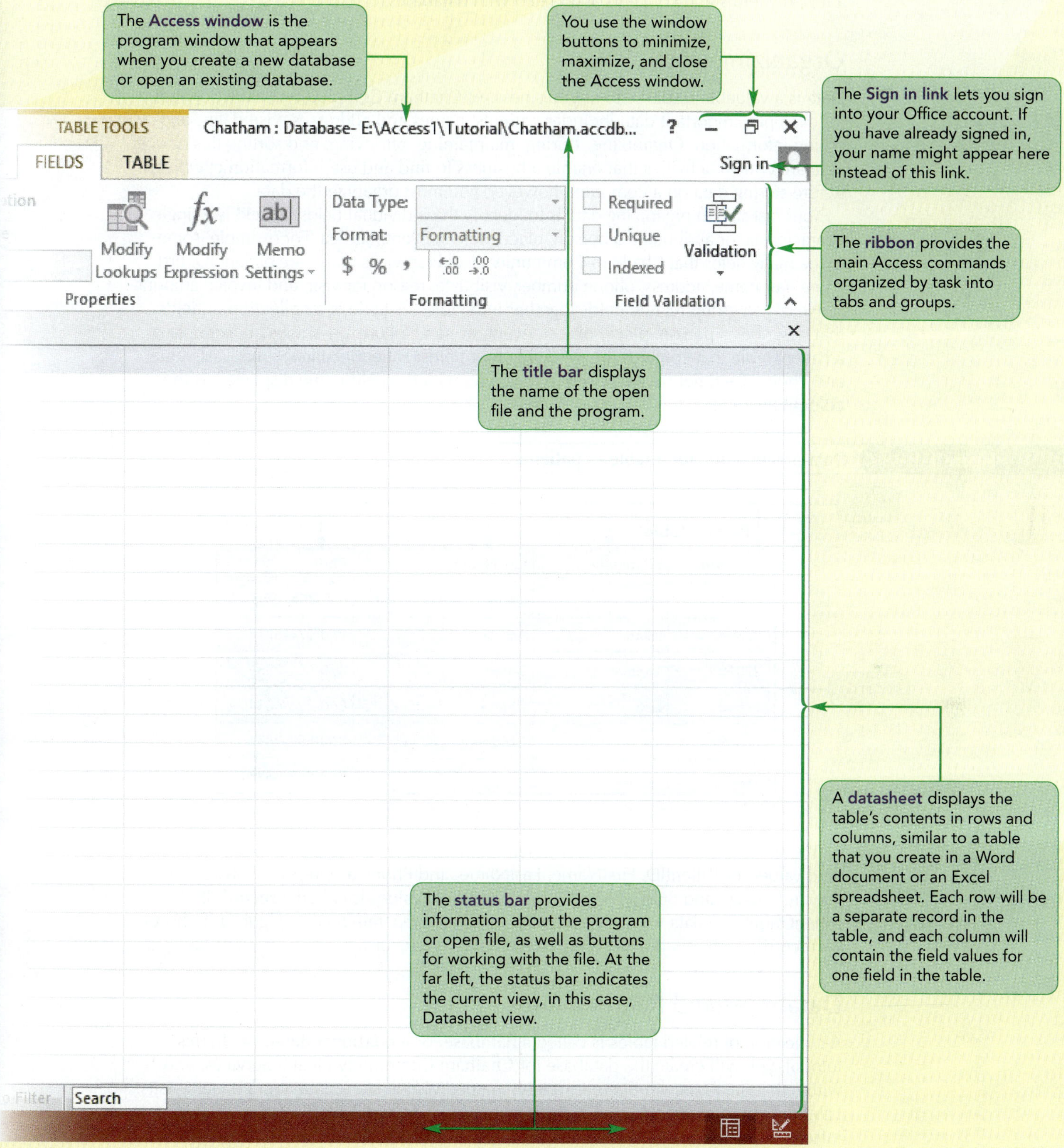

Introduction to Database Concepts

Before you begin using Access to create the database for Cindi, you need to understand a few key terms and concepts associated with databases.

Organizing Data

Data is a valuable resource to any business. At Chatham Community Health Services, for example, important data includes patients' names and addresses, visit dates, and billing information. Organizing, storing, maintaining, retrieving, and sorting this type of data are critical activities that enable a business to find and use information effectively. Before storing data on a computer, however, you must organize the data.

Your first step in organizing data is to identify the individual fields. A **field** is a single characteristic or attribute of a person, place, object, event, or idea. For example, some of the many fields that Chatham Community Health Services tracks are patient ID, first name, last name, address, phone number, visit date, reason for visit, and invoice amount.

Next, you group related fields together into tables. A **table** is a collection of fields that describes a person, place, object, event, or idea. Figure 1-1 shows an example of a Patient table that contains the following four fields: PatientID, FirstName, LastName, and Phone. Each field is a column in the table, with the field name displayed as the column heading.

Figure 1-1 **Data organization for a table of patients**

fields

records

Patient table

PatientID	FirstName	LastName	Phone
22501	Edward	Darcy	860-305-3985
22504	Lilian	Aguilar	860-374-5724
22510	Thomas	Booker	860-661-2539
22512	Lisa	Chang	860-226-6034
22529	Robert	Goldberg	860-552-2873
22537	Amrita	Mehta	860-552-0375

The specific content of a field is called the **field value**. In Figure 1-1, the first set of field values for PatientID, FirstName, LastName, and Phone are, respectively: 22501; Edward; Darcy; and 860-305-3985. This set of field values is called a **record**. In the Patient table, the data for each patient is stored as a separate record. Figure 1-1 shows six records; each row of field values in the table is a record.

Databases and Relationships

A collection of related tables is called a **database**, or a **relational database**. In this tutorial, you will create the database for Chatham Community Health Services, and within that database, you'll create a table named Visit to store data about patient visits. Later on, you'll create two more tables, named Patient and Billing, to store related information about patients and their invoices.

As Cindi and her staff use the database that you will create, they will need to access information about patients and their visits. To obtain this information, you must have a way to connect records in the Patient table to records in the Visit table. You connect the records in the separate tables through a **common field** that appears in both tables.

In the sample database shown in Figure 1-2, each record in the Patient table has a field named PatientID, which is also a field in the Visit table. For example, Robert Goldberg is the fifth patient in the Patient table and has a PatientID field value of 22529. This same PatientID field value, 22529, appears in two records in the Visit table. Therefore, Robert Goldberg is the patient who made these two visits.

Figure 1-2 Database relationship between tables for patients and visits

Patient table

PatientID	FirstName	LastName	Phone
22501	Edward	Darcy	860-305-3985
22504	Lilian	Aguilar	860-374-5724
22510	Thomas	Booker	860-661-2539
22512	Lisa	Chang	860-226-6034
22529	Robert	Goldberg	860-552-2873
22537	Amrita	Mehta	860-552-0375

primary keys

common field

foreign key

two visits for Robert Goldberg

Visit table

VisitID	PatientID	VisitDate	Reason
1539	22504	11/18/2015	Annual wellness visit
1549	22501	11/30/2015	Influenza
1564	22512	1/5/2016	Annual wellness visit
1610	22529	2/9/2016	Sinusitis
1613	22510	2/11/2016	Hypertension
1688	22529	4/12/2016	Annual wellness visit
1690	22537	4/13/2016	Varicella

Each PatientID value in the Patient table must be unique so that you can distinguish one patient from another. These unique PatientID values also identify each patient's specific visits in the Visit table. The PatientID field is referred to as the primary key of the Patient table. A **primary key** is a field, or a collection of fields, whose values uniquely identify each record in a table. No two records can contain the same value for the primary key field. In the Visit table, the VisitID field is the primary key because Chatham Community Health Services assigns each visit a unique identification number.

When you include the primary key from one table as a field in a second table to form a relationship between the two tables, it is called a **foreign key** in the second table, as shown in Figure 1-2. For example, PatientID is the primary key in the Patient table and a foreign key in the Visit table. The PatientID field must have the same characteristics in both tables. Although the primary key PatientID contains unique values in the Patient table, the same field as a foreign key in the Visit table does not necessarily contain unique values. The PatientID value 22529, for example, appears two times in the Visit table because Robert Goldberg made two visits to the clinic. Each foreign key value, however, must match one of the field values for the primary key in the other table. In the example shown in Figure 1-2, each PatientID value in the Visit table must match a PatientID value in the Patient table. The two tables are related, enabling users to connect the facts about patients with the facts about their visits to the clinic.

INSIGHT

Storing Data in Separate Tables

When you create a database, you must create separate tables that contain only fields that are directly related to each other. For example, in the Chatham database, the patient and visit data should not be stored in the same table because doing so would make the data difficult to update and prone to errors. Consider the patient Robert Goldberg and his visits to the clinic, and assume that he has many more than just two visits. If all the patient and visit data were stored in the same table, so that each record (row) contained all the information about each visit and the patient, the patient data would appear multiple times in the table. This causes problems when the data changes. For example, if Robert Goldberg's phone number changed, you would have to update the multiple occurrences of the phone number throughout the table. Not only would this be time-consuming, it would increase the likelihood of errors or inconsistent data.

Relational Database Management Systems

To manage its databases, a company uses a database management system. A **database management system (DBMS)** is a software program that lets you create databases and then manipulate the data they contain. Most of today's database management systems, including Access, are called relational database management systems. In a **relational database management system**, data is organized as a collection of tables. As stated earlier, a relationship between two tables in a relational DBMS is formed through a common field.

A relational DBMS controls the storage of databases and facilitates the creation, manipulation, and reporting of data, as illustrated in Figure 1-3.

Figure 1-3 Relational database management system

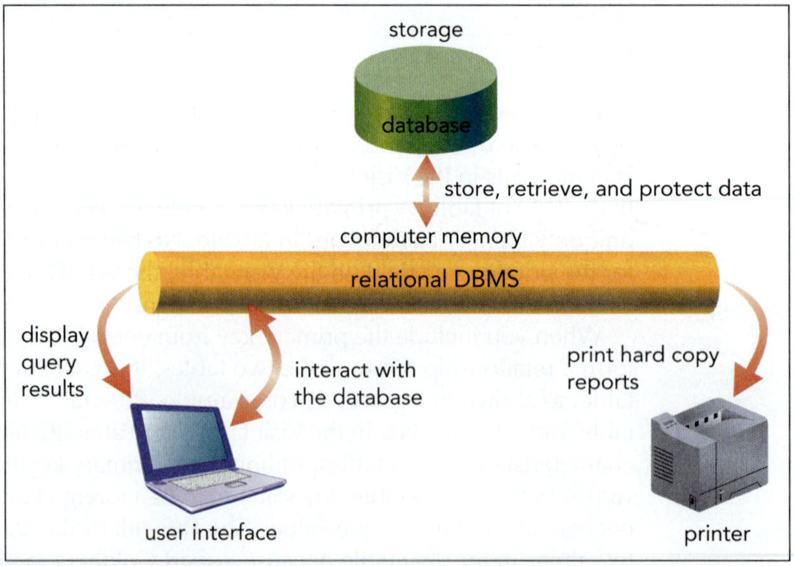

relational DBMS provides the following functions:

create database structures containing fields, tables, and table

/ add new records, change field values in existing records, and delete

ilt-in query language, which lets you obtain immediate answers to the
ıeries) you ask about your data.

ilt-in report generator, which lets you produce professional-looking,
ts from your data.

›ases through security, control, and recovery facilities.

n such as Chatham Community Health Services benefits from a
›ecause it allows users working in different groups to share the same
ne user can enter data into a database, and more than one user can retrieve and analyze data that other users have entered. For example, the database for Chatham Community Health Services will contain only one copy of the Visit table, and all employees will use it to access visit information.

Finally, unlike other software programs, such as spreadsheet programs, a DBMS can handle massive amounts of data and can be used to create relationships among multiple tables. Each Access database, for example, can be up to two gigabytes in size, can contain up to 32,768 objects (tables, reports, and so on), and can have up to 255 people using the database at the same time. For instructional purposes, the databases you will create and work with throughout this text contain a relatively small number of records compared to databases you would encounter outside the classroom, which would likely contain tables with very large numbers of records.

Starting Access and Creating a Database

Now that you've learned some database terms and concepts, you're ready to start Access and create the Chatham database for Cindi.

To start Access:

1. Display the Windows Start screen, if necessary.

   Using Windows 7? To complete Step 1, click the Start button on the taskbar.

2. Click the **Access 2013** tile. Access starts and displays the Recent screen in Backstage view. See Figure 1-4.

Figure 1-4 **Recent screen in Backstage view**

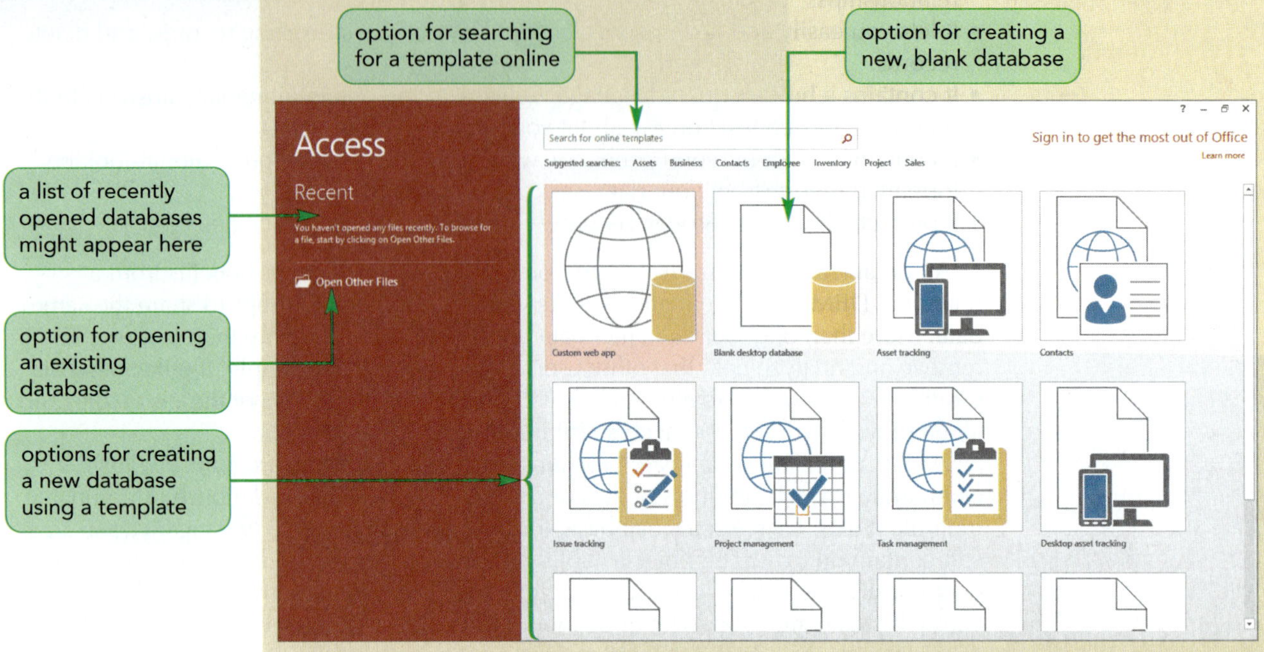

Trouble? If you don't see the Access 2013 tile on your Start screen, type Access to display the Apps screen with the Access 2013 tile highlighted, and then click the tile.

Using Windows 7? To complete Step 2, point to All Programs on the Start menu, click Microsoft Office 2013, and then click Access 2013.

When you start Access, the first screen that appears is Backstage view, which is the starting place for your work in Access. **Backstage view** contains commands that allow you to manage Access files and options. The Recent screen in Backstage view provides options for you to create a new database or open an existing database. To create a new database that does not contain any data or objects, you use the Blank desktop database option. If the database you need to create contains objects that match those found in common databases, such as databases that store data about contacts or tasks, you can use one of the templates provided with Access. A **template** is a predesigned database that includes professionally designed tables, reports, and other database objects that can make it quick and easy for you to create a database. You can also search for a template online using the Search box.

In this case, the templates provided do not match Cindi's needs for the clinic's database, so you need to create a new, blank database from scratch.

To create the new Chatham database:

1. Make sure you have the Access starting Data Files on your computer.

   Trouble? If you don't have the starting Data Files, you need to get them before you can proceed. Your instructor will either give you the Data Files or ask you to obtain them from a specified location (such as a network drive). If you have any questions about the Data Files, see your instructor or technical support person for assistance.

2. Click the **Blank desktop database** option (see Figure1-4). The Blank desktop database screen opens.

Be sure to type **Chatham** or you'll create a database named Database1.

3. In the File Name box, type **Chatham** to replace the selected database name provided by Access, Database1. Next you need to specify the location for the file.
4. Click the **Browse** button to the right of the File Name box. The File New Database dialog box opens.
5. Navigate to the drive and folder where you are storing your files, as specified by your instructor.
6. Make sure the "Save as type" box displays "Microsoft Access 2007 – 2013 Databases."

   Trouble? If your computer is set up to show filename extensions, you will see the Access filename extension ".accdb" in the File name box.

TIP

If you don't type the filename extension, Access adds it automatically.

7. Click the **OK** button. You return to the Blank desktop database screen, and the File Name box now shows the name Chatham.accdb. The filename extension ".accdb" identifies the file as an Access 2007 - 2013 database.
8. Click the **Create** button. Access creates the new database, saves it to the specified location, and then opens an empty table named Table1.

   Trouble? If you see only ribbon tab names and no buttons, click the HOME tab to expand the ribbon, and then in the bottom-right corner of the ribbon, click the Pin the ribbon button.

Refer back to the Session 1.1 Visual Overview and spend some time becoming familiar with the components of the Access window.

INSIGHT

Understanding the Database File Type

Access 2013 uses the .accdb file extension, which is the same file extension used for databases created with Microsoft Access 2007 and 2010. To ensure compatibility between these earlier versions and the Access 2013 software, new databases created using Access 2013 have the same file extension and file format as Access 2007 and Access 2010 databases. This is why the File New Database dialog box provides the Microsoft Access 2007 - 2013 Databases option in the "Save as type" box. In addition, the notation "(Access 2007 - 2013 file format)" appears in the title bar next to the name of an open database in Access 2013, confirming that database files with the .accdb extension can be used in Access 2007, Access 2010, and Access 2013.

Working in Touch Mode

TIP

On a touch device, you *tap* instead of *click*.

If you are working on a touch device, such as a tablet, you can switch to Touch Mode in Access to make it easier for you to tap buttons on the ribbon and perform other touch actions. Your screens will not match those shown in the book exactly, but this will not cause any problems.

Note: The following steps assume that you are using a mouse. If you are instead using a touch device, please read these steps but don't complete them, so that you remain working in Touch Mode.

To switch to Touch Mode:

1. On the Quick Access Toolbar, click the **Customize Quick Access Toolbar** button. A menu opens listing buttons you can add to the Quick Access Toolbar as well as other options for customizing the toolbar.

   Trouble? If the Touch/Mouse Mode command on the menu has a checkmark next to it, press the Esc key to close the menu, and then skip to Step 3.

2. Click **Touch/Mouse Mode**. The Quick Access Toolbar now contains the Touch/Mouse Mode button, which you can use to switch between Mouse Mode, the default display, and Touch Mode.

3. On the Quick Access Toolbar, click the **Touch/Mouse Mode** button. A menu opens with two commands: Mouse, which shows the ribbon in the standard display and is optimized for use with the mouse; and Touch, which provides more space between the buttons and commands on the ribbon and is optimized for use with touch devices. The icon next to Mouse is shaded red to indicate that it is selected.

   Trouble? If the icon next to Touch is shaded red, press the Esc key to close the menu and skip to Step 5.

4. Click **Touch**. The display switches to Touch Mode with more space between the commands and buttons on the ribbon. See Figure 1-5.

Figure 1-5 Ribbon displayed in Touch Mode

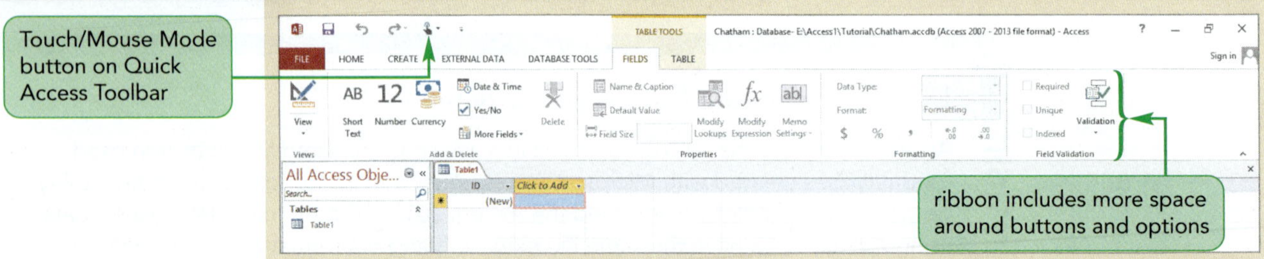

The figures in this text show the standard Mouse Mode display, and the instructions assume you are using a mouse to click and select options, so you'll switch back to Mouse Mode.

Trouble? If you are using a touch device and want to remain in Touch Mode, skip Steps 5 and 6.

5. On the Quick Access Toolbar, click the **Touch/Mouse Mode** button, and then click **Mouse**. The ribbon returns to the standard display, as shown in the Session 1.1 Visual Overview.

6. On the Quick Access Toolbar, click the **Customize Quick Access Toolbar** button, and then click **Touch/Mouse Mode** to deselect it. The Touch/Mouse Mode button is removed from the Quick Access Toolbar.

Creating a Table in Datasheet View

Tables contain all the data in a database and are the fundamental objects for your work in Access. There are different ways to create a table in Access, including entering the fields and records for the table directly in Datasheet view.

REFERENCE

Creating a Table in Datasheet View

- On the ribbon, click the CREATE tab.
- In the Tables group, click the Table button.
- Rename the default ID primary key field and change its data type, if necessary; or accept the default ID field with the AutoNumber data type.
- In the Add & Delete group on the FIELDS tab, click the button for the type of field you want to add to the table (for example, click the Short Text button), and then type the field name; or, in the table datasheet, click the Click to Add column heading, click the type of field you want to add from the list that opens, and then press the Tab or Enter key to move to the next column in the datasheet. Repeat this step to add all the necessary fields to the table.
- In the first row below the field names, enter the value for each field in the first record, pressing the Tab or Enter key to move from one field to the next.
- After entering the value for the last field in the first record, press the Tab or Enter key to move to the next row, and then enter the values for the next record. Continue this process until you have entered all the records for the table.
- On the Quick Access Toolbar, click the Save button, enter a name for the table, and then click the OK button.

For Chatham Community Health Services, Cindi needs to track information about each patient visit at the clinic. She asks you to create the Visit table according to the plan shown in Figure 1-6.

Figure 1-6 **Plan for the Visit table**

Field	Purpose
VisitID	Unique number assigned to each visit; will serve as the table's primary key
PatientID	Unique number assigned to each patient; common field that will be a foreign key to connect to the Patient table
VisitDate	Date on which the patient visited the clinic
Reason	Reason/diagnosis for the patient visit
WalkIn	Whether the patient visit was a walk-in or a scheduled appointment

As shown in Cindi's plan, she wants to store data about visits in five fields, including fields to contain the date of each visit, the reason for the visit, and if the visit was a walk-in or scheduled appointment. These are the most important aspects of a visit and, therefore, must be tracked. Also, notice that the VisitID field will be the primary key for the table; each visit at Chatham Community Health Services has a unique number assigned to it, so this field is the logical choice for the primary key. Finally, the PatientID field is needed in the Visit table as a foreign key to connect the information about visits to patients. The data about patients and their bills will be stored in separate tables, which you will create later.

Notice the name of each field in Figure 1-6. You need to name each field, table, and other object in an Access database.

PROSKILLS

Decision Making: Naming Fields in Access Tables

One of the most important tasks in creating a table is deciding what names to specify for the table's fields. Keep the following guidelines in mind when you assign field names:

- A field name can consist of up to 64 characters, including letters, numbers, spaces, and special characters, except for the period (.), exclamation mark (!), grave accent (`), and square brackets ([ ]).
- A field name cannot begin with a space.
- Capitalize the first letter of each word in a field name that combines multiple words, for example VisitDate.
- Use concise field names that are easy to remember and reference, and that won't take up a lot of space in the table datasheet.
- Use standard abbreviations, such as Num for Number, Amt for Amount, and Qty for Quantity, and use them consistently throughout the database. For example, if you use Num for Number in one field name, do not use the number sign (#) for Number in another.
- Give fields descriptive names so that you can easily identify them when you view or edit records.
- Although Access supports the use of spaces in field names (and in other object names), experienced database developers avoid using spaces because they can cause errors when the objects are involved in programming tasks.

By spending time obtaining and analyzing information about the fields in a table, and understanding the rules for naming Access fields, you can create a well-designed table that will be easy for others to use.

Renaming the Default Primary Key Field

As noted earlier, Access provides the ID field as the default primary key for a new table you create in Datasheet view. Recall that a primary key is a field, or a collection of fields, whose values uniquely identify each record in a table. However, according to Cindi's plan, the VisitID field should be the primary key for the Visit table. You'll begin by renaming the default ID field to create the VisitID field.

TIP

A **shortcut menu** opens when you right-click an object and provides options for working with that object.

To rename the ID field to the VisitID field:

1. Right-click the **ID** column heading to open the shortcut menu, and then click **Rename Field**. The column heading ID is selected, so that whatever text you type next will replace it.
2. Type **VisitID** and then click the row below the heading. The column heading changes to VisitID, and the insertion point moves to the row below the heading. See Figure 1-7.

   Trouble? If you make a mistake while typing the field name, use the Backspace key to delete characters to the left of the insertion point or the Delete key to delete characters to the right of the insertion point. Then type the correct text. To correct a field name by replacing it entirely, press the Esc key, and then type the correct text.

Figure 1-7 **ID field renamed to VisitID**

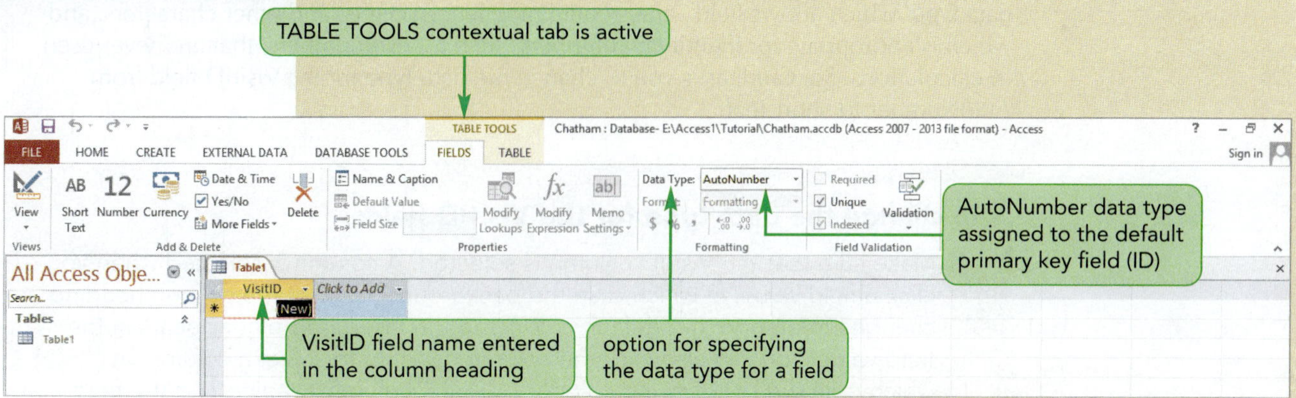

The **insertion point** is a flashing cursor that shows where text you type will be inserted. In this case, it is hidden within the selected field value (New).

Notice that the TABLE TOOLS tab is active on the ribbon. This is an example of a **contextual tab**, which is a tab that appears and provides options for working with a specific object that is selected—in this case, the table you are creating. As you work with other objects in the database, other contextual tabs will appear with commands and options related to each selected object.

INSIGHT

Buttons and Labels on the Ribbon

Depending on the size of the monitor you are using and your screen resolution settings, you might see more or fewer buttons on the ribbon, and you might not see labels next to certain buttons. The screenshots in these tutorials were created using a screen resolution setting of 1366 x 768 with the program window maximized. If you are using a smaller monitor or a lower screen resolution, some buttons will appear only as icons, with no labels next to them, because there is not enough room on the ribbon to display the labels.

You have renamed the default primary key field, ID, to VisitID. However, the VisitID field still retains the characteristics of the ID field, including its data type. Your next task is to change the data type of this field.

Changing the Data Type of the Default Primary Key Field

Notice the Formatting group on the FIELDS tab. One of the options available in this group is the Data Type option (see Figure 1-7). Each field in an Access table must be assigned a data type. The **data type** determines what field values you can enter for the field. In this case, the AutoNumber data type is displayed. Access assigns the AutoNumber data type to the default ID primary key field because the **AutoNumber** data type automatically inserts a unique number in this field for every record, beginning with the number 1 for the first record, the number 2 for the second record, and so on. Therefore, a field using the AutoNumber data type can serve as the primary key for any table you create.

Visit numbers at Chatham Community Health Services are specific, four-digit numbers, so the AutoNumber data type is not appropriate for the VisitID field, which is the primary key field in the table you are creating. A better choice is the **Short Text** data type, which allows field values containing letters, digits, and other characters, and which is appropriate for identifying numbers, such as visit numbers, that are never used in calculations. So, Cindi asks you to change the data type for the VisitID field from AutoNumber to Short Text.

To change the data type for the VisitID field:

1. Make sure that the VisitID column is selected. A column is selected when you click a field value, in which case the background color of the column heading changes to orange (the default color) and the insertion point appears in the field value. You can also click the column heading to select a column, in which case the background color of both the column heading and the field value changes (the default colors are gray and blue, respectively).
2. In the Formatting group on the FIELDS tab, click the **Data Type arrow**, and then click **Short Text**. The VisitID field is now a Short Text field. See Figure 1-8.

Figure 1-8 Short Text data type assigned to the VisitID field

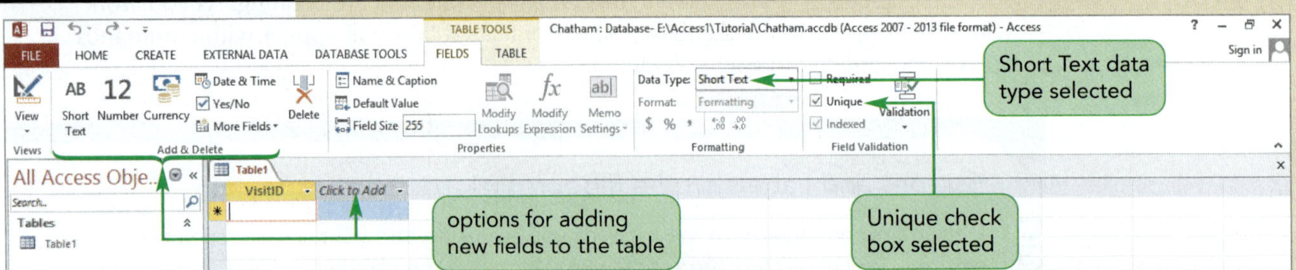

Note the Unique check box in the Field Validation group. This check box is selected because the VisitID field assumed the characteristics of the default primary key field, ID, including the fact that each value in the field must be unique. Because this check box is selected, no two records in the Visit table will be allowed to have the same value in the VisitID field.

With the VisitID field created and established as the primary key, you can now enter the rest of the fields in the Visit table.

Adding New Fields

When you create a table in Datasheet view, you can use the options in the Add & Delete group on the FIELDS tab to add fields to your table. You can also use the Click to Add column in the table datasheet to add new fields. (See Figure 1-8.) You'll use both methods to add the four remaining fields to the Visit table. The next field you need to add is the PatientID field. Similar to the VisitID field, the PatientID field will contain numbers that will not be used in calculations, so it should be a Short Text field.

To add the rest of the fields to the Visit table:

1. In the Add & Delete group on the FIELDS tab, click the **Short Text** button. Access adds a new field named "Field1" to the right of the VisitID field. See Figure 1-9.

Figure 1-9 **New Short Text field added to the table**

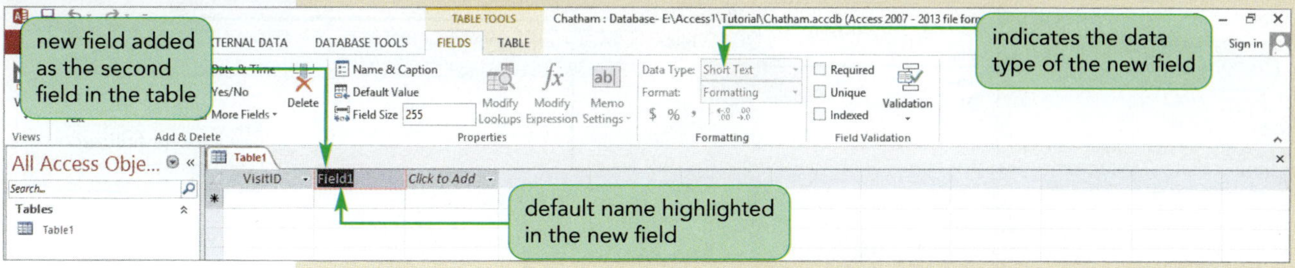

The text "Field1" is selected, so you can simply type the new field name to replace it.

2. Type **PatientID**. The second field is added to the table. Next, you'll add the VisitDate field. Because this field will contain date values, you'll add a field with the **Date/Time** data type, which allows field values in a variety of date and time formats.
3. In the Add & Delete group, click the **Date & Time** button. Access adds a third field to the table, this time with the Date/Time data type.
4. Type **VisitDate** to replace the highlighted name "Field1." The fourth field in the Visit table is the Reason field, which will contain brief descriptions of the reason for the visit to the clinic. You'll add another Short Text field—this time using the Click to Add column.
5. Click the **Click to Add** column heading. Access displays a list of available data types from which you can choose the data type for the new field you're adding.
6. Click **Short Text** in the list. Access adds a fourth field to the table.
7. Type **Reason** to replace the highlighted name "Field1," and then press the **Enter** key. The Click to Add column becomes active and displays the list of field data types.

   The fifth and final field in the Visit table is the WalkIn field, which will indicate whether or not the visit was a walk-in (that is, the patient did not have a scheduled appointment). The **Yes/No** data type is suitable for this field because it is used to define fields that store values representing one of two options—true/false, yes/no, or on/off.

TIP

You can also type the first letter of a data type to select it and close the Click to Add list.

8. Click **Yes/No** in the list, and then type **WalkIn** to replace the highlighted name "Field1."

   Trouble? If you pressed the Tab or Enter key after typing the WalkIn field name, press the Esc key to close the Click to Add list.

9. Click in the row below the VisitID column heading. All five fields are now entered for the Visit table. See Figure 1-10.

Figure 1-10 **Table with all fields entered**

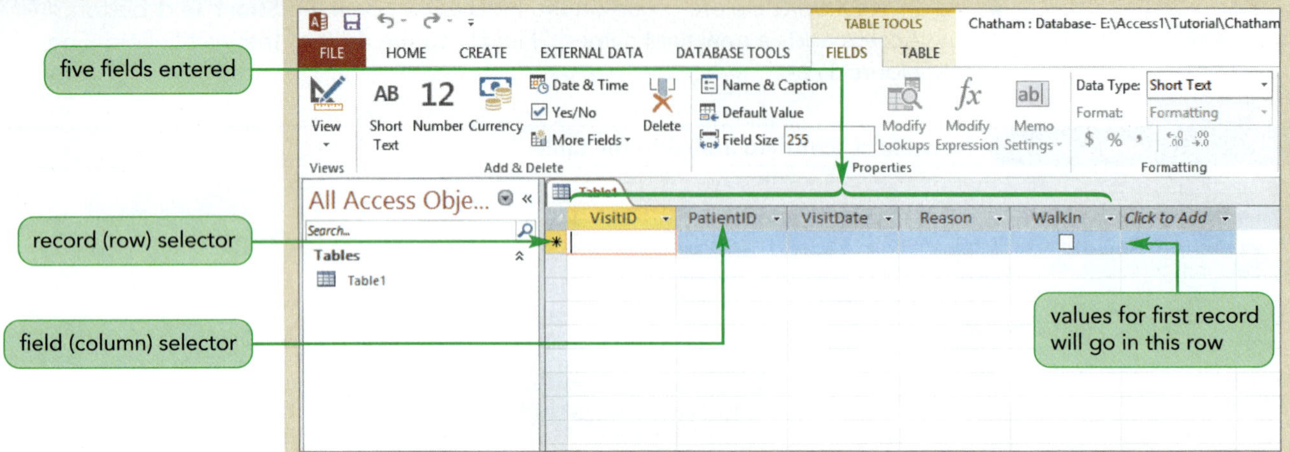

The table contains three Short Text fields (VisitID, PatientID, and Reason), one Date/Time field (VisitDate), and one Yes/No field (WalkIn). You'll learn more about field data types in the next tutorial.

As noted earlier, Datasheet view shows a table's contents in rows (records) and columns (fields). Each column is headed by a field name inside a field selector, and each row has a record selector to its left (see Figure 1-10). Clicking a **field selector** or a **record selector** selects that entire column or row (respectively), which you then can manipulate. A field selector is also called a **column selector**, and a record selector is also called a **row selector**.

Entering Records

With the fields in place for the table, you can now enter the field values for each record. Cindi requests that you enter eight records in the Visit table, as shown in Figure 1-11.

Figure 1-11 **Visit table records**

VisitID	PatientID	VisitDate	Reason	WalkIn
1550	22549	12/1/2015	Influenza	Yes
1527	22522	11/9/2015	Allergies - environmental	Yes
1555	22520	12/7/2015	Annual wellness visit	No
1542	22537	11/24/2015	Influenza	Yes
1530	22510	11/10/2015	Seborrheic dermatitis	No
1564	22512	1/5/2016	Annual wellness visit	No
1575	22513	1/13/2016	Broken leg	Yes
1538	22500	11/17/2015	Migraine	Yes

To enter records in a table datasheet, you type the field values below the column headings for the fields. The first record you enter will go in the first row (see Figure 1-10).

Be sure to type the numbers "0" and "1" and not the letters "O" and "I" in the field value.

To enter the first record for the Visit table:

1. In the first row for the VisitID field, type **1550** (the VisitID field value for the first record), and then press the **Tab** key. Access adds the field value and moves the insertion point to the right, into the PatientID column. See Figure 1-12.

Figure 1-12 First field value entered

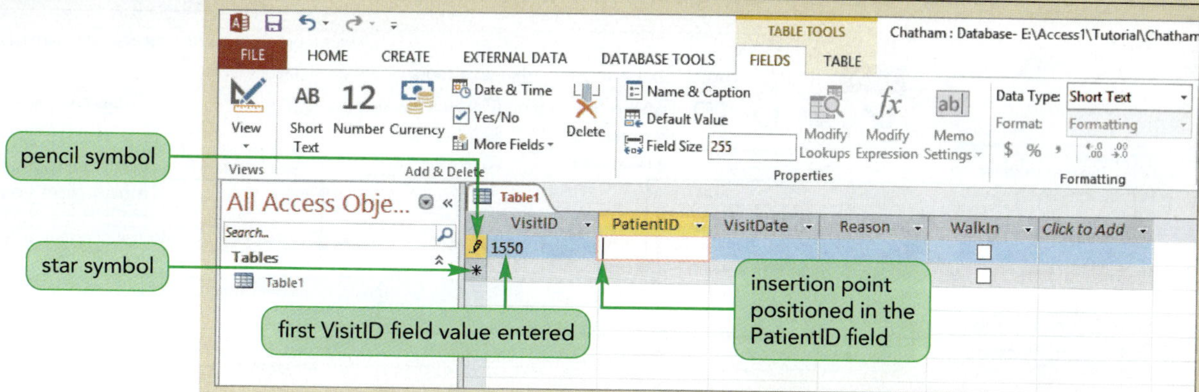

Trouble? If you make a mistake when typing a value, use the Backspace key to delete characters to the left of the insertion point or the Delete key to delete characters to the right of the insertion point. Then type the correct value. To correct a value by replacing it entirely, press the Esc key, and then type the correct value.

Notice the pencil symbol that appears in the row selector for the new record. The **pencil symbol** indicates that the record is being edited. Also notice the star symbol that appears in the row selector for the second row. The **star symbol** identifies the second row as the next row available for a new record.

2. Type **22549** (the PatientID field value for the first record), and then press the **Tab** key. Access enters the field value and moves the insertion point to the VisitDate column.

3. Type **12/1/15** (the VisitDate field value for the first record), and then press the **Tab** key. Access displays the year as "2015" even though you entered only the final two digits of the year. This is because the VisitDate field has the Date/Time data type, which automatically formats dates with four-digit years.

   Trouble? Depending on your Windows date setting, your VisitDate field values might be displayed in a different format. This difference will not cause any problems.

4. Type **Influenza** (the Reason field value for the first record), and then press the **Tab** key to move to the WalkIn column.

   Recall that the WalkIn field is a Yes/No field. Notice the check box displayed in the WalkIn column. By default, the value for any Yes/No field is "No"; therefore, the check box is initially empty. For Yes/No fields with check boxes, you press the Tab key to leave the check box unchecked, or you press the spacebar to insert a checkmark in the check box. The record you are entering in the table is for a walk-in visit, so you need to insert a checkmark in the check box to indicate "Yes."

TIP

You can also click a check box in a Yes/No field to insert or remove a checkmark.

5. Press the **spacebar** to insert a checkmark, and then press the **Tab** key. The first record is entered into the table, and the insertion point is positioned in the VisitID field for the second record. The pencil symbol is removed from the first row because the record in that row is no longer being edited. The table is now ready for you to enter the second record. See Figure 1-13.

Figure 1-13 **Datasheet with first record entered**

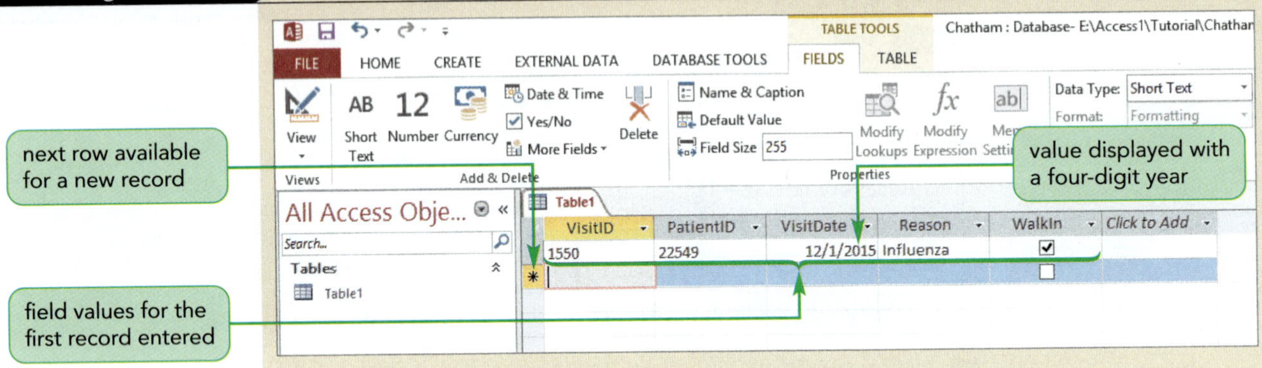

Now you can enter the remaining seven records in the Visit table.

To enter the remaining records in the Visit table:

TIP

You can also press the Enter key instead of the Tab key to move from one field to another, and to the next row.

1. Referring to Figure 1-11, enter the values for records 2 through 8, pressing the **Tab** key to move from field to field and to the next row for a new record. Keep in mind that you do not have to type all four digits of the year in the VisitDate field values; you can enter only the final two digits and Access will display all four. Also, for any WalkIn field values of "No," be sure to press the Tab key to leave the check box empty.

   Trouble? If you enter a value in the wrong field by mistake, such as entering a Reason field value in the VisitDate field, a menu might open with options for addressing the problem. If this happens, click the "Enter new value" option in the menu. You'll return to the field with the incorrect value highlighted, which you can then replace by typing the correct value.

   Notice that not all of the Reason field values are fully displayed. To see more of the table datasheet and the full field values, you'll close the Navigation Pane and resize the Reason column.

2. At the top of the Navigation Pane, click the **Shutter Bar Open/Close Button** «. The Navigation Pane closes, and only the complete table datasheet is displayed.

3. Place the pointer on the vertical line to the right of the Reason field name until the pointer changes to a ↔ shape, and then double-click the vertical line. All the Reason field values are now fully displayed. See Figure 1-14.

Figure 1-14 Datasheet with eight records entered

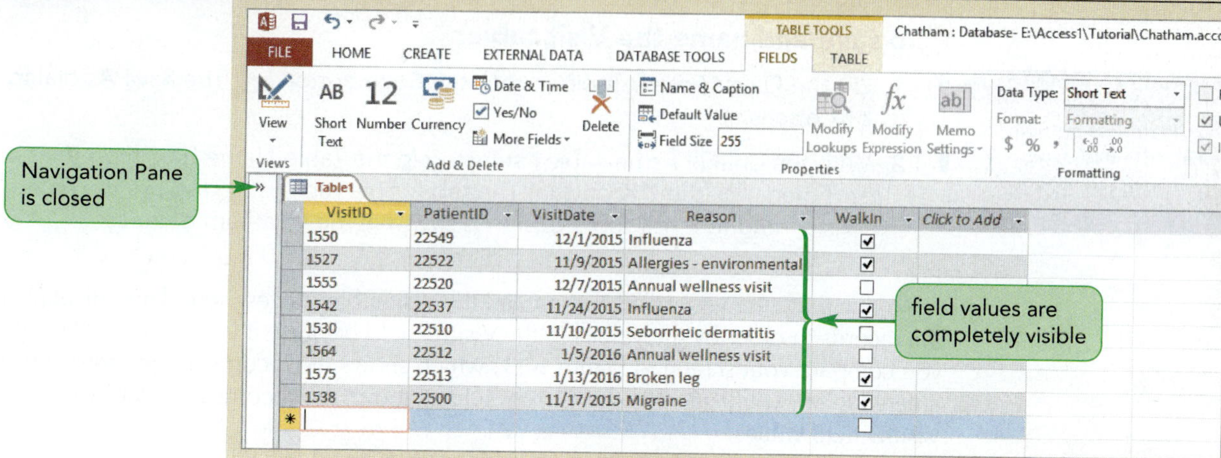

When you resize a datasheet column by double-clicking the column dividing line, you are sizing the column to its **best fit**—that is, so the column is just wide enough to display the longest visible value in the column, including the field name.

Carefully compare your VisitID and PatientID values with those in the figure, and correct any errors before continuing.

4. Compare your table to the one in Figure 1-14. If any of the field values in your table do not match those shown in the figure, you can correct a field value by clicking to position the insertion point in the value, and then using the Backspace key or Delete key to delete incorrect text. Then type the correct text and press the Enter key. To correct a value in the WalkIn field, simply click the check box to add or remove the checkmark as appropriate. Also, be sure the spelling and capitalization of field names in your table match those shown in the figure exactly, and that there are no spaces between words. To correct a field name, double-click it to select it, and then type the correct name; or use the Rename Field option on the shortcut menu to rename a field with the correct name.

Saving a Table

The records you enter are immediately stored in the database as soon as you enter them; however, the table's design—the field names and characteristics of the fields themselves, plus any layout changes to the datasheet—are not saved until you save the table. When you save a new table for the first time, you should give it a name that best identifies the information it contains. Like a field name, a table name can contain up to 64 characters, including spaces.

REFERENCE

Saving a Table

- Make sure the table you want to save is open.
- On the Quick Access Toolbar, click the Save button. The Save As dialog box opens.
- In the Table Name box, type the name for the table.
- Click the OK button.

According to Cindi's plan, you need to save the table with the name "Visit."

To save and name the Visit table:

TIP

You can also use the Save command in Backstage view to save and name a new table.

1. On the Quick Access Toolbar, click the **Save** button. The Save As dialog box opens.
2. With the default name Table1 selected in the Table Name box, type **Visit**, and then click the **OK** button. The tab for the table now displays the name "Visit," and the Visit table design is saved in the Chatham database.

Notice that after you saved and named the Visit table, Access sorted and displayed the records in order by the values in the VisitID field because it is the primary key. If you compare your screen to Figure 1-11, which shows the records in the order you entered them, you'll see that the current screen shows the records in order by the VisitID field values.

Cindi asks you to add two more records to the Visit table. When you add a record to an existing table, you must enter the new record in the next row available for a new record; you cannot insert a row between existing records for the new record. In a table with just a few records, such as the Visit table, the next available row is visible on the screen. However, in a table with hundreds of records, you would need to scroll the datasheet to see the next row available. The easiest way to add a new record to a table is to use the New button, which scrolls the datasheet to the next row available so you can enter the new record.

To enter additional records in the Visit table:

1. If necessary, click the first record's VisitID field value (**1527**) to make it the current record.
2. On the ribbon, click the **HOME** tab.
3. In the Records group, click the **New** button. The insertion point is positioned in the next row available for a new record, which in this case is row 9. See Figure 1-15.

Figure 1-15 **Entering a new record**

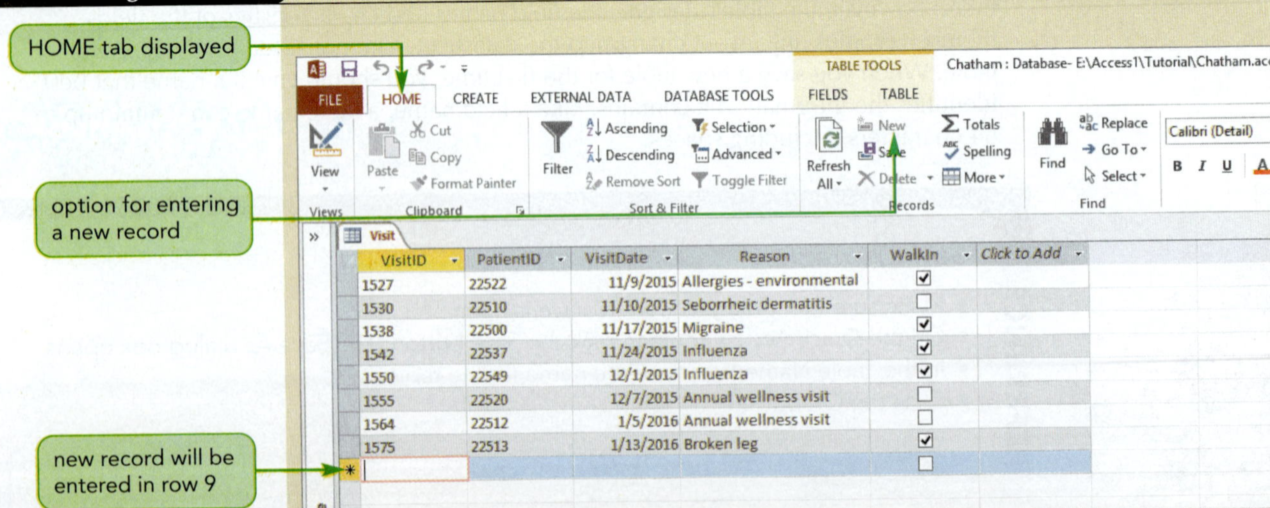

4. With the insertion point in the VisitID field for the new record, type **1548** and then press the **Tab** key.

5. Complete the entry of this record by entering each value shown below, pressing the **Tab** key to move from field to field:

   PatientID = **22519**

   VisitDate = **11/30/2015**

   Reason = **Hypertension**

   WalkIn = **No (unchecked)**

6. Enter the values for the next new record, as follows, and then press the **Tab** key after entering the WalkIn field value:

   VisitID = **1560**

   PatientID = **22514**

   VisitDate = **12/15/2015**

   Reason = **Influenza**

   WalkIn = **Yes (checked)**

   Your datasheet should now look like the one shown in Figure 1-16.

Figure 1-16 Datasheet with additional records entered

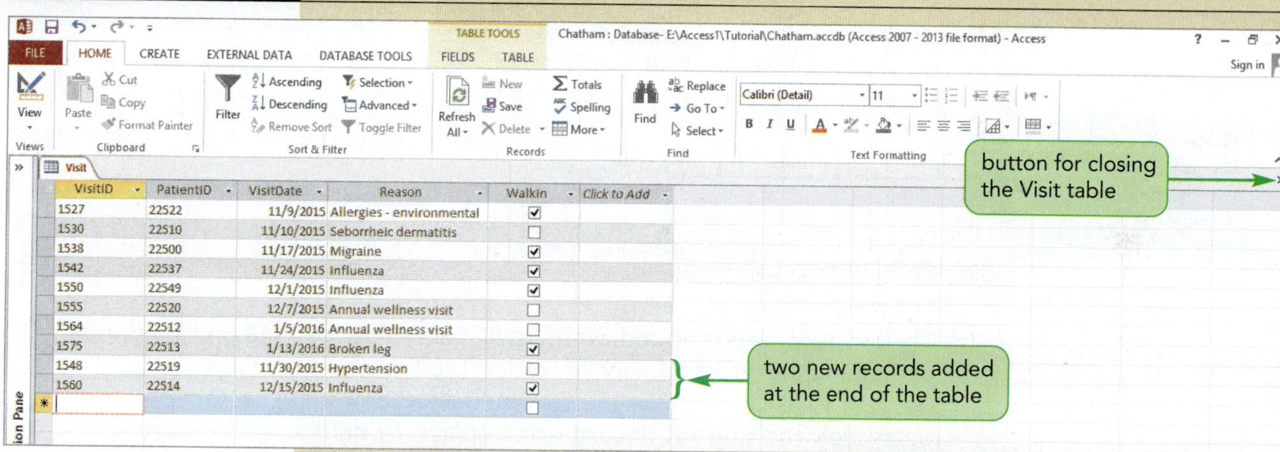

The new records you added appear at the end of the table, and are not sorted in order by the primary key field values. For example, VisitID 1548 should be the fifth record in the table, placed between VisitID 1542 and VisitID 1550. When you add records to a table datasheet, they appear at the end of the table. The records are not displayed in primary key order until you either close and reopen the table or switch between views.

7. Click the **Close** button on the object tab (see Figure 1-16 for the location of this button). The Visit table closes, and the main portion of the Access window is now blank because no database object is currently open. The Chatham database file is still open, as indicated by the filename in the Access window title bar.

Opening a Table

The tables in a database are listed in the Navigation Pane. You open a table, or any Access object, by double-clicking the object name in the Navigation Pane. Next, you'll open the Visit table so you can see the order of all the records you've entered.

To open the Visit table:

1. On the Navigation Pane, click the **Shutter Bar Open/Close Button** » to open the pane. Note that the Visit table is listed.
2. Double-click **Visit** to open the table in Datasheet view. See Figure 1-17.

Figure 1-17 Table with 10 records entered and displayed in primary key order

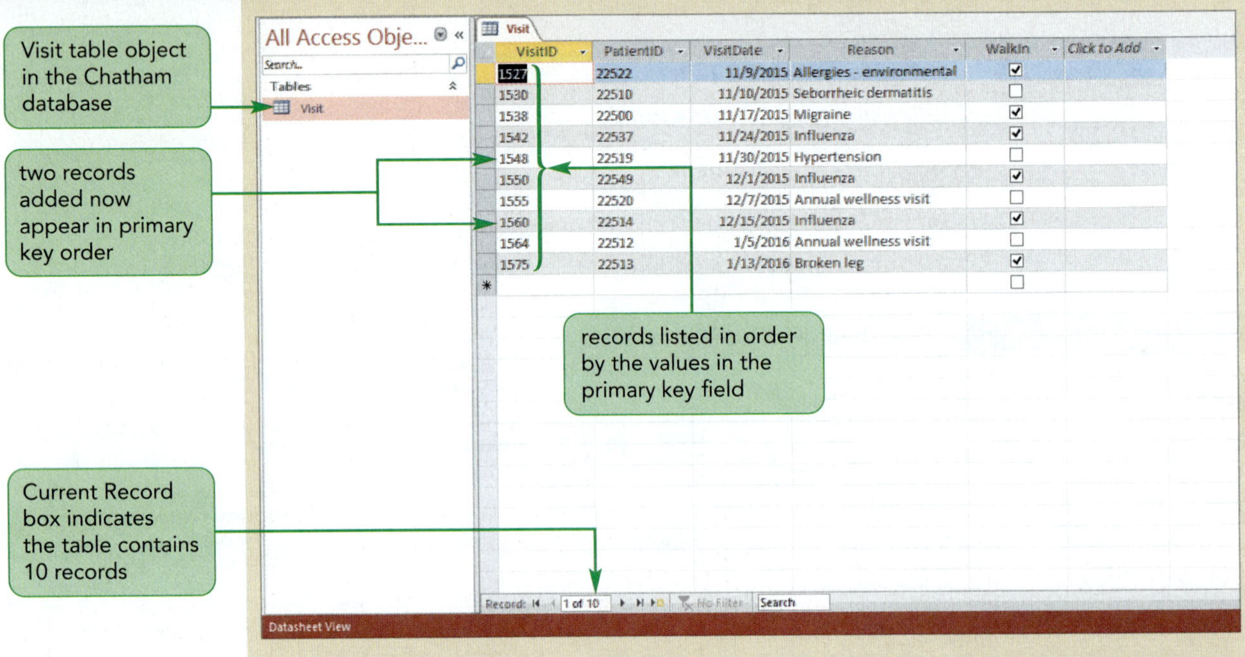

The two records you added, with VisitID field values of 1548 and 1560, now appear in the correct primary key order. The table now contains a total of 10 records, as indicated by the Current Record box at the bottom of the datasheet. The **Current Record box** displays the number of the current record as well as the total number of records in the table.

Each record contains a unique VisitID value because this field is the primary key. Other fields, however, can contain the same value in multiple records; for example, note the three values of "Influenza" in the Reason field.

Closing a Table and Exiting Access

When you are finished working in an Access table, it's a good idea to close the table so that you do not make unintended changes to the table data. You can close a table by clicking its Close button on the object tab, as you did earlier. Or, if you want to close the Access program as well, you can click the program's Close button. When you do, any open tables are closed, the active database is closed, and you exit the Access program.

To close the Visit table and exit Access:

TIP

To close a database without exiting Access, click the FILE tab to display Backstage view, and then click Close.

1. Click the **Close** button ✕ on the program window title bar. Access closes the Visit table and the Chatham database, and then the Access program closes.

INSIGHT

Saving a Database

Unlike the Save buttons in other Office programs, the Save button on the Quick Access Toolbar in Access does not save the active document (database). Instead, you use the Save button to save the design of an Access object, such as a table (as you saw earlier), or to save datasheet format changes, such as resizing columns. Access does not have a button or option you can use to save the active database.

Access saves changes to the active database automatically when you change or add a record or close the database. If your database is stored on a removable medium, such as a USB drive, you should never remove the drive while the database file is open. If you do, Access will encounter problems when it tries to save the database, which might damage the database. Make sure you close the database first before removing the drive.

Now that you've become familiar with database concepts and Access, and created the Chatham database and the Visit table, Cindi wants you to add more records to the table and work with the data stored in it to create database objects including a query, form, and report. You'll complete these tasks in the next session.

REVIEW

Session 1.1 Quick Check

1. A(n) ______________ is a single characteristic of a person, place, object, event, or idea.
2. You connect the records in two separate tables through a(n) ______________ that appears in both tables.
3. The ______________, whose values uniquely identify each record in a table, is called a(n) ______________ when it is placed in a second table to form a relationship between the two tables.
4. The ______________ is the area of the Access window that lists all the objects in a database, and it is the main control center for opening and working with database objects.
5. What is the name of the field that Access creates, by default, as the primary key field for a new table in Datasheet view?
6. Which group on the FIELDS tab contains the options you use to add new fields to a table?
7. What does a pencil symbol at the beginning of a record represent? What does a star symbol represent?
8. Explain how the saving process in Access is different from saving in other Office programs.

Session 1.2 Visual Overview:

The **CREATE tab** provides options for creating various database objects, including tables, forms, and reports. The options appear on the tab grouped by object type.

The Forms group contains options for creating a **form**, which is a database object you use to enter, edit, and view records in a database.

The **Query Wizard button** opens a dialog box with different types of wizards that guide you through the steps to create a query. One of these, the **Simple Query Wizard**, allows you to select records and fields quickly to display in the query results.

You use the options in the Tables group to create a table in Datasheet view or in Design view.

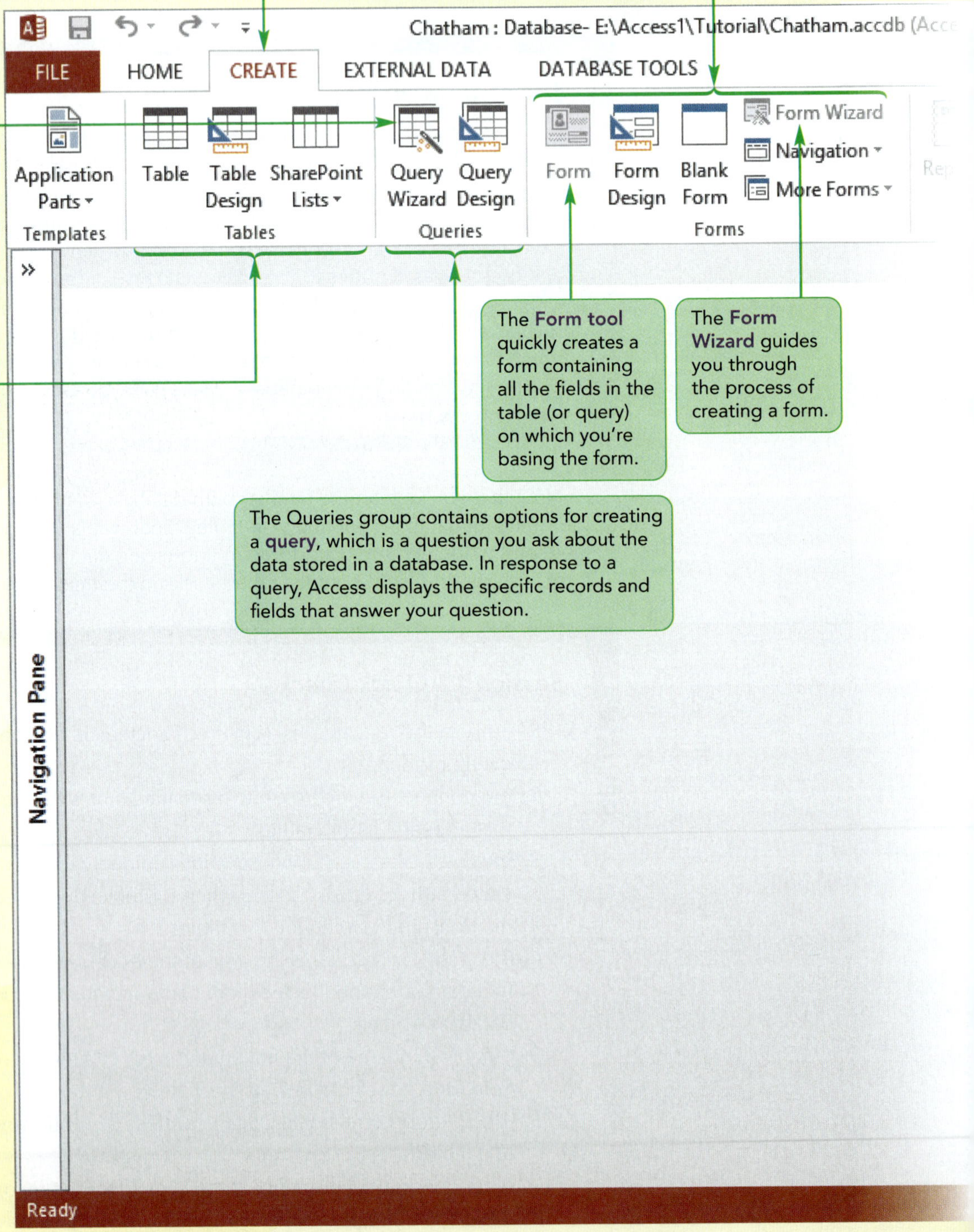

The **Form tool** quickly creates a form containing all the fields in the table (or query) on which you're basing the form.

The **Form Wizard** guides you through the process of creating a form.

The Queries group contains options for creating a **query**, which is a question you ask about the data stored in a database. In response to a query, Access displays the specific records and fields that answer your question.

The CREATE Tab Options

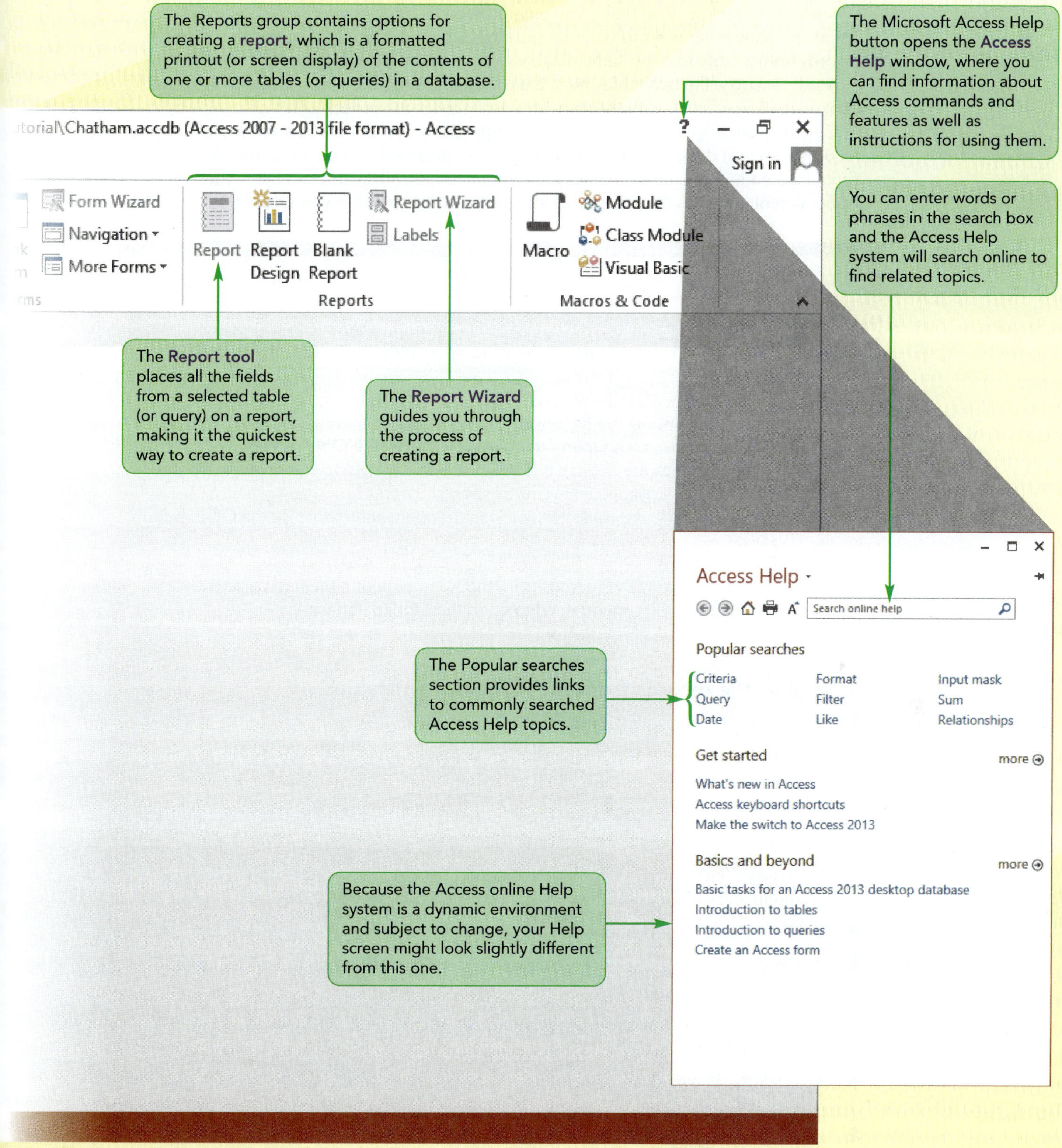

Copying Records from Another Access Database

When you created the Visit table, you entered records directly into the table datasheet. There are many other ways to enter records in a table, including copying and pasting records from a table into the same database or into a different database. To use this method, however, the two tables must have the same structure—that is, the tables must contain the same fields, with the same design, in the same order.

Cindi has already created a table named Appointment that contains additional records with visit data. The Appointment table is contained in a database named Cindi located in the Access1 ▸ Tutorial folder included with your Data Files. The Appointment table has the same table structure as the Visit table you created.

REFERENCE

Opening a Database

- Start Access and display the Recent screen in Backstage view.
- Click the name of the database you want to open in the list of recently opened databases.

or

- Start Access and display the Recent screen in Backstage view.
- In the navigation bar, click Open Other Files to display the Open screen.
- Click Computer, click the Browse button, and then navigate to the drive and folder containing the database file you want to open.
- Click the name of the database file you want to open, and then click the Open button.

Your next task is to copy the records from the Appointment table and paste them into your Visit table. To do so, you need to open the Cindi database.

To copy the records from the Appointment table:

1. Display the Windows Start screen, if necessary.

   Using Windows 7? To complete Step 1, click the Start button on the taskbar.

2. Click the **Access 2013** tile. Access starts and displays the Recent screen in Backstage view.

   Using Windows 7? To complete Step 2, click All Programs on the Start menu, click Microsoft Office 2013, and then click Access 2013.

3. Click **Open Other Files** to display the Open screen in Backstage view.
4. On the Open screen, click **Computer**. The right side of the screen now shows folder information for your computer.

   Trouble? If you are storing your files on SkyDrive, click SkyDrive, and then log in if necessary.

5. Click the **Browse** button, and then navigate to the drive that contains your Data Files.
6. Navigate to the **Access1 ▸ Tutorial** folder, click the database file named **Cindi**, and then click the **Open** button. The Cindi database opens in the Access program window. Note that the database contains only one object, the Appointment table.

Trouble? If a security warning appears below the ribbon indicating that some active content has been disabled, click the Enable Content button next to the warning. Access provides this warning because some databases might contain content that could harm your computer. Because the Cindi database does not contain objects that could be harmful, you can open it safely. If you are accessing the file over a network, you might also see a dialog box asking if you want to make the file a trusted document; click Yes.

7. In the Navigation Pane, double-click **Appointment** to open the Appointment table in Datasheet view. The table contains 76 records and the same five fields, with the same characteristics, as the fields in the Visit table. See Figure 1-18.

Figure 1-18 **Appointment table in the Cindi database**

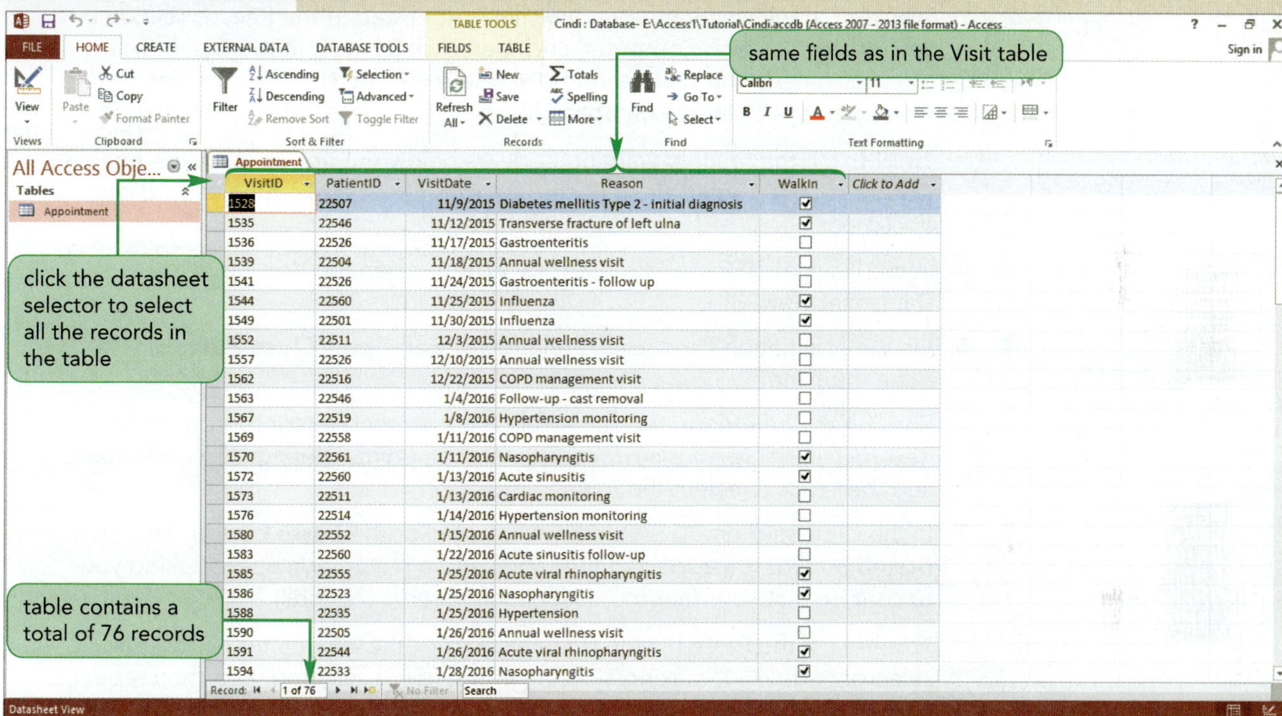

Cindi wants you to copy all the records in the Appointment table. You can select all the records by clicking the **datasheet selector**, which is the box to the left of the first field name in the table datasheet (see Figure 1-18).

8. Click the **datasheet selector** to the left of the VisitID field, as shown in Figure 1-18. Access selects all the records in the table.
9. In the Clipboard group on the HOME tab, click the **Copy** button. All the records are copied to the Clipboard.
10. Click the **Close 'Appointment'** button ✕ on the object tab. A dialog box opens asking if you want to save the data you copied to the Clipboard. This dialog box opens only when you copy a large amount of data to the Clipboard.
11. Click the **Yes** button. The dialog box closes, and then the Appointment table closes.

With the records copied to the Clipboard, you can now paste them into the Visit table. First you need to close the Cindi database while still keeping the Access program open, and then open the Chatham database.

To close the Cindi database and then paste the records into the Visit table:

1. Click the **FILE** tab to display Backstage view, and then click **Close** in the navigation bar to close the Cindi database. You return to the HOME tab in the Access program window.
2. Click the **FILE** tab to return to Backstage view, and then click **Open** in the navigation bar. The Recent section of the Open screen shows a list of the recently opened database files. This list should include the Chatham database.
3. In the Recent section of the screen, click **Chatham** to open the Chatham database file.

   Trouble? If the Chatham database file is not listed in the Recent section on your computer, click Computer, and then click Browse. In the Open dialog box, navigate to the drive and folder where you are storing your files, and then open the Chatham database file.

   Trouble? If the security warning appears below the ribbon, click the Enable Content button, and then, if necessary, click Yes to make the file a trusted document.
4. In the Navigation Pane, double-click **Visit** to open the Visit table in Datasheet view.
5. On the Navigation Pane, click the **Shutter Bar Open/Close Button** « to close the pane.
6. Position the pointer on the star symbol in the row selector for row 11 (the next row available for a new record) until the pointer changes to a ➡ shape, and then click to select the row.
7. In the Clipboard group on the HOME tab, click the **Paste** button. The pasted records are added to the table, and a dialog box opens asking you to confirm that you want to paste all the records (76 total).

   Trouble? If the Paste button isn't active, click the ➡ pointer on the row selector for row 11, making sure the entire row is selected, and then repeat Step 7.
8. Click the **Yes** button. The dialog box closes, and the pasted records are highlighted. See Figure 1-19. Notice that the table now contains a total of 86 records—10 records that you entered and 76 records that you copied and pasted.

Figure 1-19 Visit table after copying and pasting records

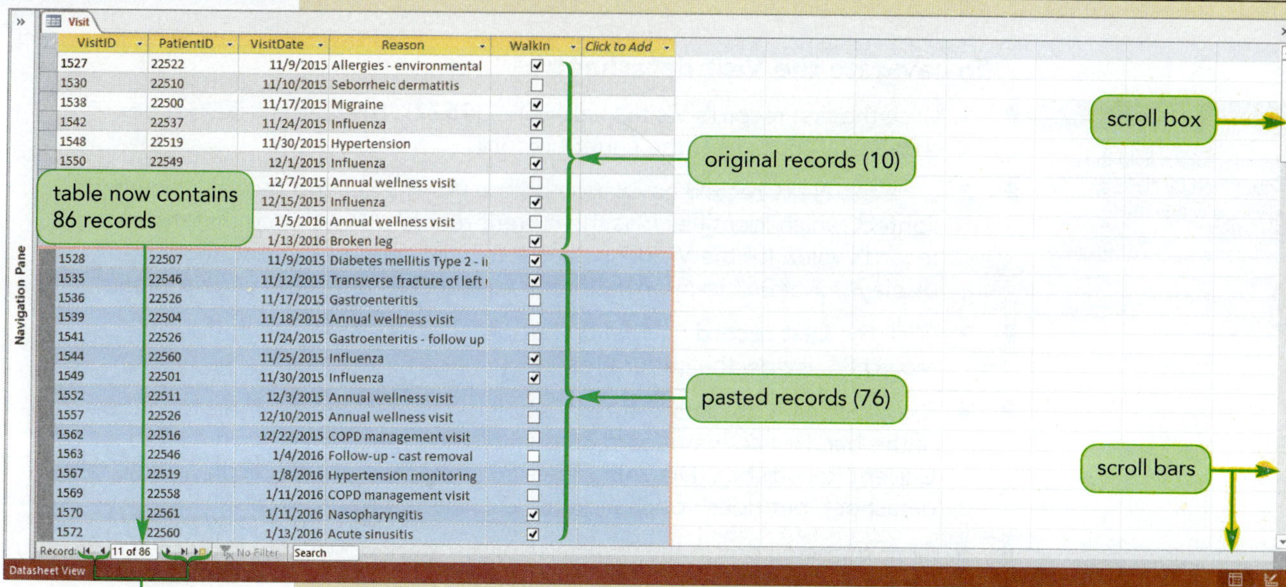

Not all the Reason field values are completely visible, so you need to resize this column to its best fit.

9. Place the pointer on the vertical line to the right of the Reason field name until the pointer changes to a ✛ shape, and then double-click the vertical line. The Reason field values are now fully displayed.

Navigating a Datasheet

The Visit table now contains 86 records, but only some of the records are visible on the screen. To view fields or records not currently visible on the screen, you can use the horizontal and vertical scroll bars shown in Figure 1-19 to navigate the data. The **navigation buttons**, shown in Figure 1-19 and also described in Figure 1-20, provide another way to move vertically through the records. The Current Record box appears between the two sets of navigation buttons and displays the number of the current record as well as the total number of records in the table. Figure 1-20 shows which record becomes the current record when you click each navigation button. Note the New (blank) record button, which works in the same way as the New button on the HOME tab you used earlier to enter a new record in the table.

Figure 1-20 Navigation buttons

Navigation Button	Record Selected	Navigation Button	Record Selected
	First record		Last record
	Previous record		New (blank) record
	Next record		

Cindi suggests that you use the various navigation techniques to move through the Visit table and become familiar with its contents.

TIP

You can make a field the current field by clicking anywhere within the column for that field.

To navigate the Visit datasheet:

1. Click the first record's VisitID field value (**1527**). The Current Record box shows that record 1 is the current record.
2. Click the **Next record** navigation button ▶. The second record is now highlighted, which identifies it as the current record. Also, notice that the second record's value for the VisitID field is selected, and the Current Record box displays "2 of 86" to indicate that the second record is the current record.
3. Click the **Last record** navigation button ▶|. The last record in the table, record 86, is now the current record.
4. Drag the scroll box in the vertical scroll bar (see Figure 1-19) up to the top of the bar. Notice that record 86 is still the current record, as indicated in the Current Record box. Dragging the scroll box changes the display of the table datasheet, but does not change the current record.
5. Drag the scroll box in the vertical scroll bar back down until you can see the end of the table and the current record (record 86).
6. Click the **Previous record** navigation button ◀. Record 85 is now the current record.
7. Click the **First record** navigation button |◀. The first record is now the current record and is visible on the screen.

   As you moved through the datasheet, you might have noticed that not all the Reason field values are fully displayed. When you resize a column to its best fit, the column expands to fully display only the field values that are visible on the screen at that time. To make sure all field values are displayed for the entire table, you need to scroll through the datasheet and repeat the resizing process.
8. Drag the scroll box down to display more of the table, until you see other Reason field values that are not fully displayed. Then use the ✛ pointer to resize the field.
9. Repeat Step 8, as necessary, until you reach the bottom of the table and have resized all the Reason field values, and then drag the scroll box back up to display the beginning of the table.

The Visit table now contains all the data about patient visits for Chatham Community Health Services. To better understand how to work with this data, Cindi asks you to create simple objects for the other main types of database objects—queries, forms, and reports.

Creating a Simple Query

As noted earlier, a query is a question you ask about the data stored in a database. When you create a query, you tell Access which fields you need and what criteria it should use to select the records that will answer your question. Then Access displays only the information you want, so you don't have to navigate through the entire database for the information. In the Visit table, for example, Cindi might create a query to display only those records for visits that occurred in a specific month. Even though a query can display table information in a different way, the information still exists in the table as it was originally entered.

Cindi wants to see a list of all the visit dates and reasons for visits in the Visit table. She doesn't want the list to include all the fields in the table, such as PatientID and WalkIn. To produce this list for Cindi, you'll use the Simple Query Wizard to create a query based on the Visit table.

To start the Simple Query Wizard:

1. On the ribbon, click the **CREATE** tab.
2. In the Queries group on the CREATE tab, click the **Query Wizard** button. The New Query dialog box opens.
3. Make sure **Simple Query Wizard** is selected, and then click the **OK** button. The first Simple Query Wizard dialog box opens. See Figure 1-21.

Figure 1-21 First Simple Query Wizard dialog box

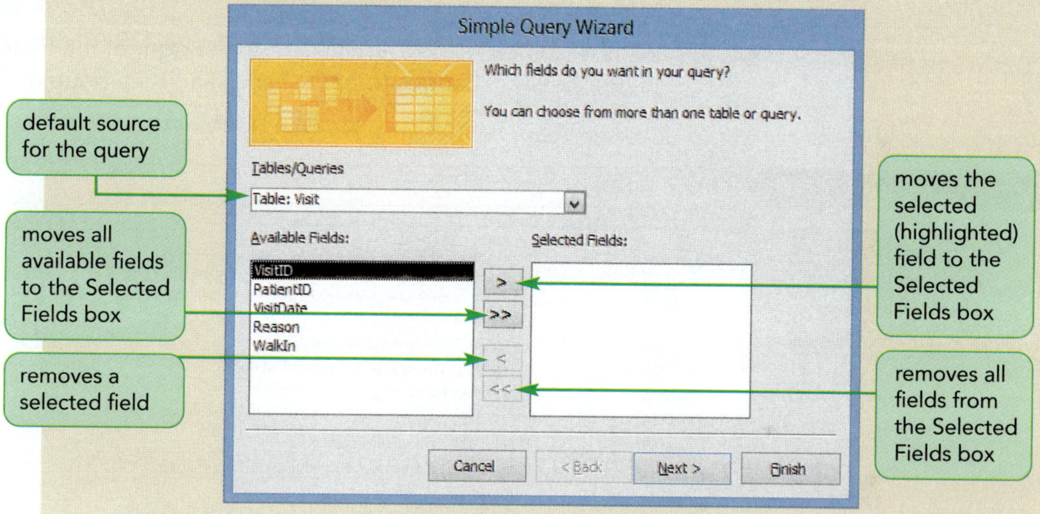

Because the Visit table is the only object in the Chatham database, it is listed in the Tables/Queries box by default. If the database contained more objects, you could click the Tables/Queries arrow and choose another table or a query as the basis for the new query you are creating. The Available Fields box lists all the fields in the Visit table.

You need to select fields from the Available Fields box to include them in the query. To select fields one at a time, click a field and then click the > button. The selected (highlighted) field moves from the Available Fields box on the left to the Selected Fields box on the right. To select all the fields, click the >> button. If you change your mind or make a mistake, you can remove a field by clicking it in the Selected Fields box and then clicking the < button. To remove all fields from the Selected Fields box, click the << button.

Each Simple Query Wizard dialog box contains buttons on the bottom that allow you to move to the previous dialog box (Back button), move to the next dialog box (Next button), or cancel the creation process (Cancel button). You can also finish creating the object (Finish button) and accept the wizard's defaults for the remaining options.

Cindi wants her list to include data from only the following fields: VisitID, VisitDate, and Reason. You need to select these fields to include them in the query.

TIP

You can also double-click a field to move it from the Available Fields box to the Selected Fields box.

To create the query using the Simple Query Wizard:

1. Click **VisitID** in the Available Fields box to select the field (if necessary), and then click the > button. The VisitID field moves to the Selected Fields box.
2. Repeat Step 1 for the fields **VisitDate** and **Reason**, and then click the **Next** button. The second, and final, Simple Query Wizard dialog box opens and asks you to choose a name (title) for your query. Access suggests the name "Visit Query" because the query you are creating is based on the Visit table. You'll change the suggested name to "VisitList."
3. Click at the end of the suggested name, use the **Backspace** key to delete the word "Query" and the space, and then type **List**. Now you can view the query results.
4. Click the **Finish** button to complete the query. Access displays the query results in Datasheet view, on a new tab named "VisitList." A query datasheet is similar to a table datasheet, showing fields in columns and records in rows—but only for those fields and records you want to see, as determined by the query specifications you select.
5. Place the pointer on the vertical line to the right of the Reason field name until the pointer changes to a ✛ shape, and then double-click the vertical line to resize the Reason field. See Figure 1-22.

Figure 1-22 **Query results**

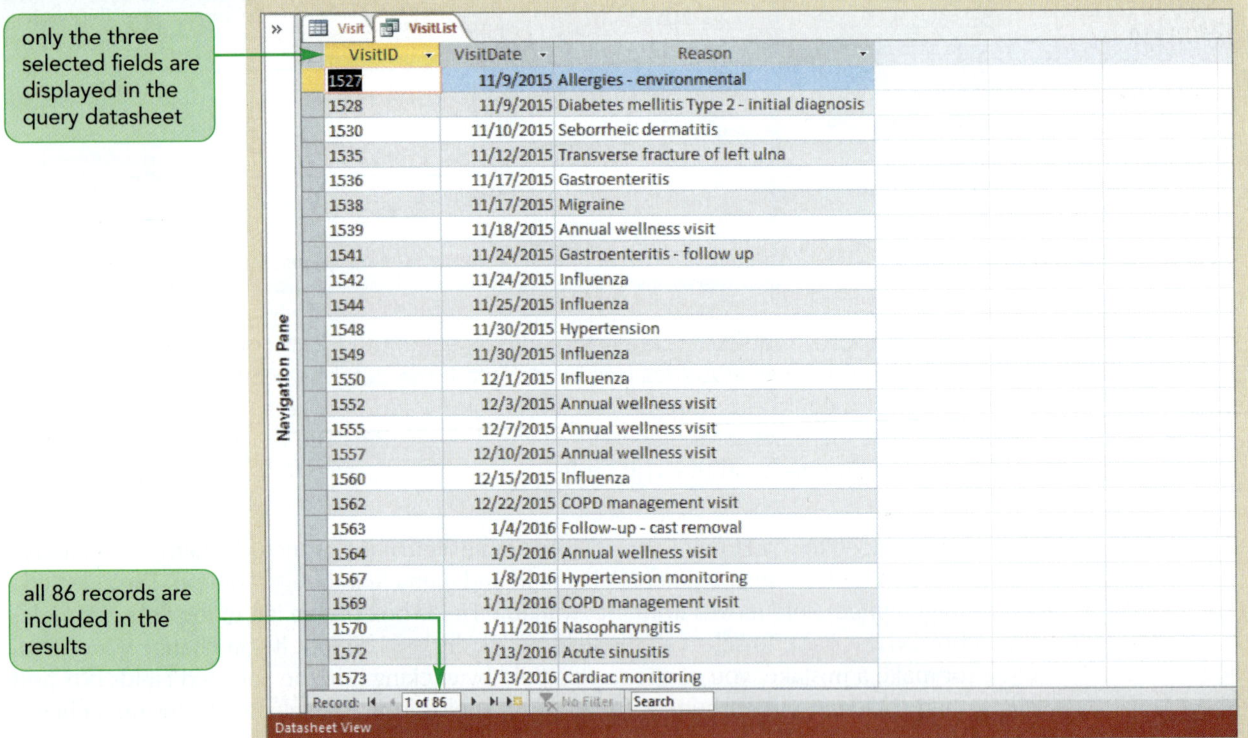

The VisitList query datasheet displays the three selected fields for each record in the Visit table. The fields are shown in the order you selected them in the Simple Query Wizard, from left to right. The records are listed in order by the primary key field, VisitID. Even though the query datasheet displays only the three fields you chose for the query, the Visit table still includes all the fields for all records.

Notice that the navigation buttons are located at the bottom of the window. You navigate a query datasheet in the same way that you navigate a table datasheet.

6. Click the **Last record** navigation button ▶|. The last record in the query datasheet is now the current record.
7. Click the **Previous record** navigation button ◀. Record 85 in the query datasheet is now the current record.
8. Click the **First record** navigation button |◀. The first record is now the current record.
9. Click the **Close 'VisitList'** button ✕ on the object tab. A dialog box opens asking if you want to save the changes to the layout of the query. This dialog box opens because you resized the Reason column.
10. Click the **Yes** button to save the query layout changes and close the query.

The query results are not stored in the database; however, the query design is stored as part of the database with the name you specified. You can re-create the query results at any time by opening the query again. When you open the query at a later date, the results displayed will reflect up-to-date information to include any new records entered in the Visit table.

Next, Cindi asks you to create a form for the Visit table so that Chatham Community Health Services employees can use the form to enter and work with data in the table easily.

Creating a Simple Form

As noted earlier, you use a form to enter, edit, and view records in a database. Although you can perform these same functions with tables and queries, forms can present data in many customized and useful ways.

Cindi wants a form for the Visit table that shows all the fields for one record at a time, with fields listed one below another in a column. This type of form will make it easier for her staff to focus on all the data for a particular visit. You'll use the Form tool to create this form quickly and easily.

To create the form using the Form tool:

1. Make sure the Visit table is still open in Datasheet view. The table or other database object you're using as the basis for the form must either be open or selected in the Navigation Pane when you use the Form tool.

   Trouble? If the Visit table is not open, click the Shutter Bar Open/Close Button » to open the Navigation Pane. Then double-click Visit to open the Visit table in Datasheet view. Click the Shutter Bar Open/Close Button « to close the pane.

2. Make sure the CREATE tab is displayed.
3. In the Forms group, click the **Form** button. The Form tool creates a simple form showing every field in the Visit table and places it on a tab named "Visit." Access assigns this name because the form is based on the Visit table. See Figure 1-23.

Figure 1-23 **Form created by the Form tool**

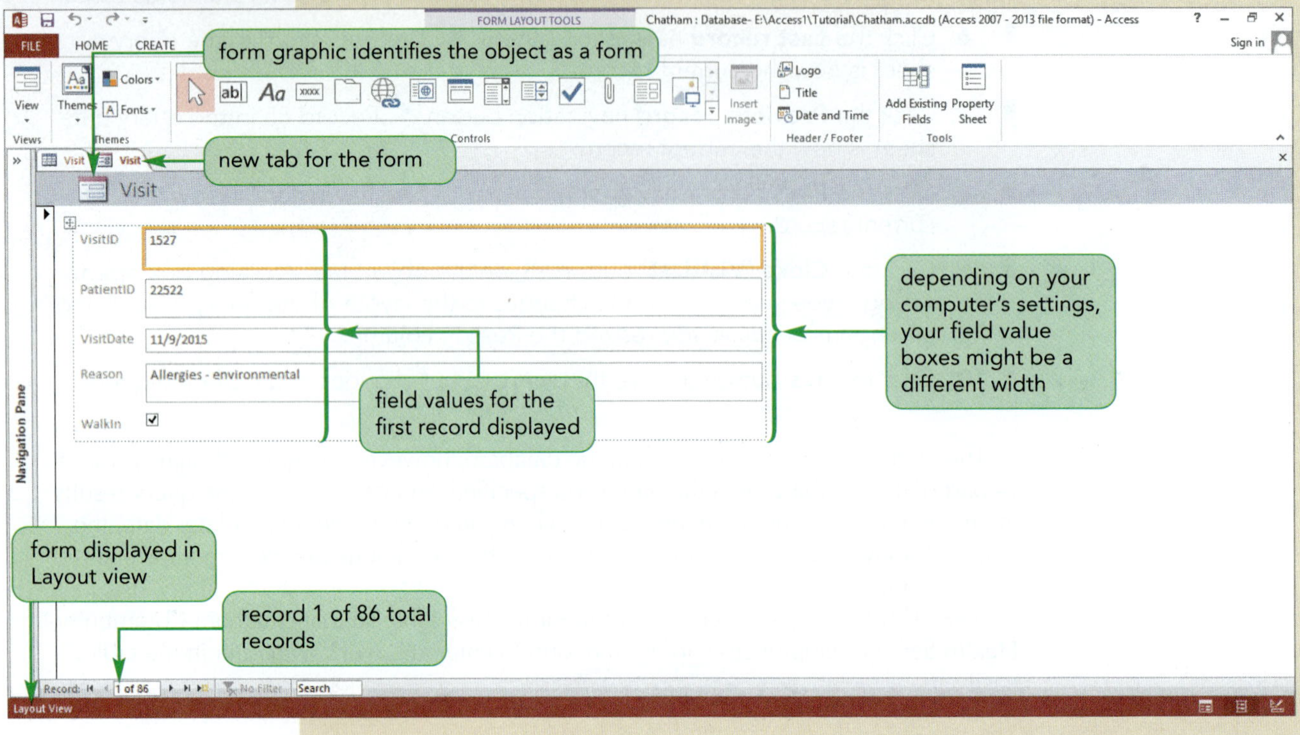

Trouble? Depending on the size of your monitor and your screen resolution settings, the fields in your form might appear in multiple columns instead of a single column. This difference will not present any problems.

The form displays one record at a time in the Visit table, providing another view of the data that is stored in the table and allowing you to focus on the values for one record. Access displays the field values for the first record in the table and selects the first field value (VisitID) by placing a border around the value. Each field name appears on a separate line and on the same line as its field value, which appears in a box to the right. Depending on your computer's settings, the field value boxes in your form might be wider or narrower than those shown in the figure. As indicated in the status bar, the form is displayed in Layout view. In **Layout view**, you can make design changes to the form while it is displaying data, so that you can see the effects of the changes you make immediately.

To view, enter, and maintain data using a form, you must know how to move from field to field and from record to record. Notice that the form contains navigation buttons, similar to those available in Datasheet view, which you can use to display different records in the form. You'll use these now to navigate the form; then you'll save and close the form.

To navigate, save, and close the form:

1. Click the **Next record** navigation button ▶. The form now displays the values for the second record in the Visit table.
2. Click the **Last record** navigation button ▶| to move to the last record in the table. The form displays the information for VisitID 1700.
3. Click the **Previous record** navigation button ◀ to move to record 85.

4. Click the **First record** navigation button [I◀] to return to the first record in the Visit table.

   Next, you'll save the form with the name "VisitData" in the Chatham database. Then the form will be available for later use.

5. On the Quick Access Toolbar, click the **Save** button. The Save As dialog box opens.

6. In the Form Name box, click at the end of the highlighted word "Visit," type **Data**, and then press the **Enter** key. Access saves the form as VisitData in the Chatham database and closes the dialog box. The tab containing the form now displays the name VisitData.

7. Click the **Close 'VisitData'** button [X] on the object tab to close the form.

INSIGHT

Saving Database Objects

In general, it is best to save a database object—query, form, or report—only if you anticipate using the object frequently or if it is time consuming to create, because all objects use storage space and increase the size of the database file. For example, you most likely would not save a form you created with the Form tool because you can re-create it easily with one mouse click. (However, for the purposes of this text, you usually need to save the objects you create.)

After attending a staff meeting, Cindi returns with another request. She would like to see the information in the Visit table presented in a more readable and professional format. You'll help Cindi by creating a report.

Creating a Simple Report

As noted earlier, a report is a formatted printout (or screen display) of the contents of one or more tables or queries. You'll use the Report tool to quickly produce a report based on the Visit table for Cindi. The Report tool creates a report based on the selected table or query.

To create the report using the Report tool:

1. With the Visit table open in Datasheet view, click the **CREATE** tab on the ribbon.

2. In the Reports group, click the **Report** button. The Report tool creates a simple report showing every field in the Visit table and places it on a tab named "Visit." Again, Access assigns this name because the object you created (the report) is based on the Visit table. See Figure 1-24.

Figure 1-24 Report created by the Report tool

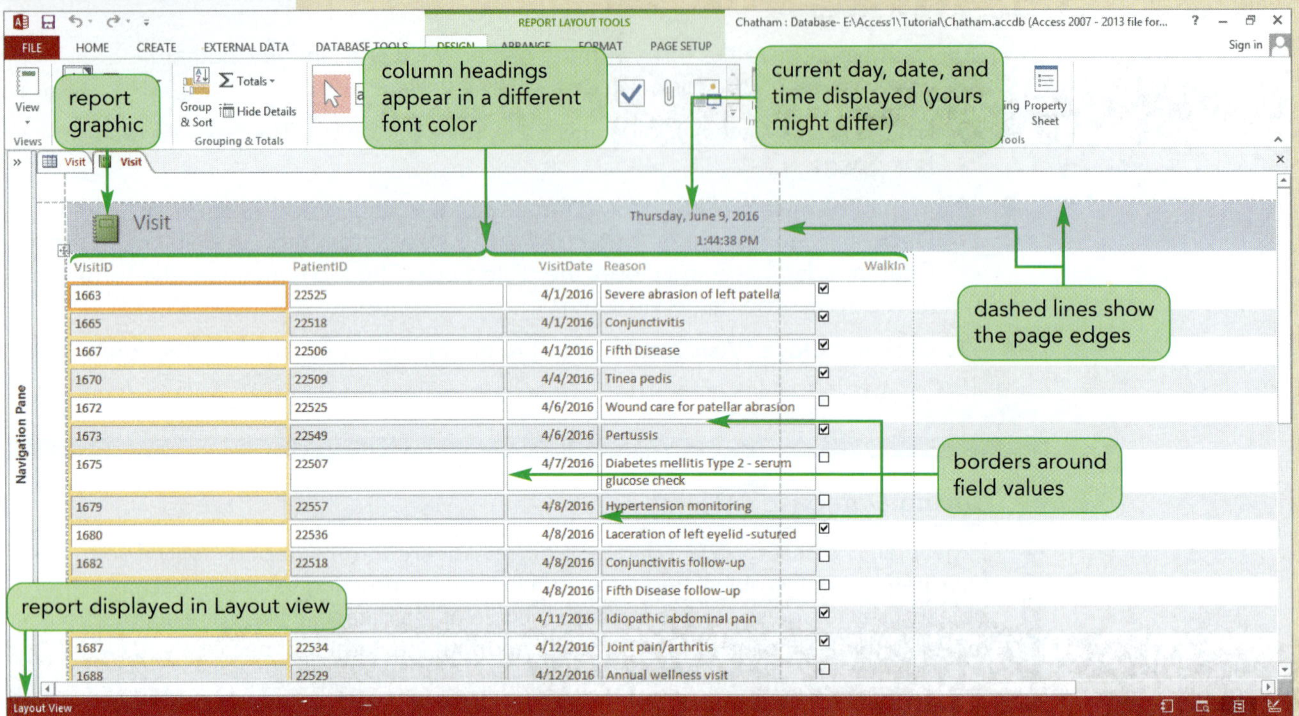

Trouble? The records in your report might appear in a different order from the records shown in Figure 1-24. This difference will not cause any problems.

The report shows each field in a column, with the field values for each record in a row, similar to a table or query datasheet. However, the report offers a more visually appealing format for the data, with the column headings in a different color, borders around each field value, a graphic of a report at the top left, and the current day, date, and time at the top right. Also notice the dashed horizontal and vertical lines on the top and right, respectively; these lines mark the edges of the page and show where text will print on the page.

The report needs some design changes to better display the data. The columns are much wider than necessary for the VisitID and PatientID fields, and the Reason and WalkIn field values and borders are not completely displayed within the page area defined by the dashed lines, which means they would not appear on the same page as the rest of the fields in the printed report. You can resize the columns easily in Layout view.

To resize the VisitID and PatientID columns:

1. Position the pointer on the right border of any field value in the VisitID column until the pointer changes to a ↔ shape.
2. Click and drag the mouse to the left; dark outlines surround the field name and each field value to show the column width as you change it. Drag to the left until the column is slightly wider than the VisitID field name.
3. Release the mouse button. The VisitID column is now narrower, and the other four columns have shifted to the left. The Reason and WalkIn fields, values, and borders are now completely within the page area. See Figure 1-25.

Figure 1-25 Report after resizing the VisitID column

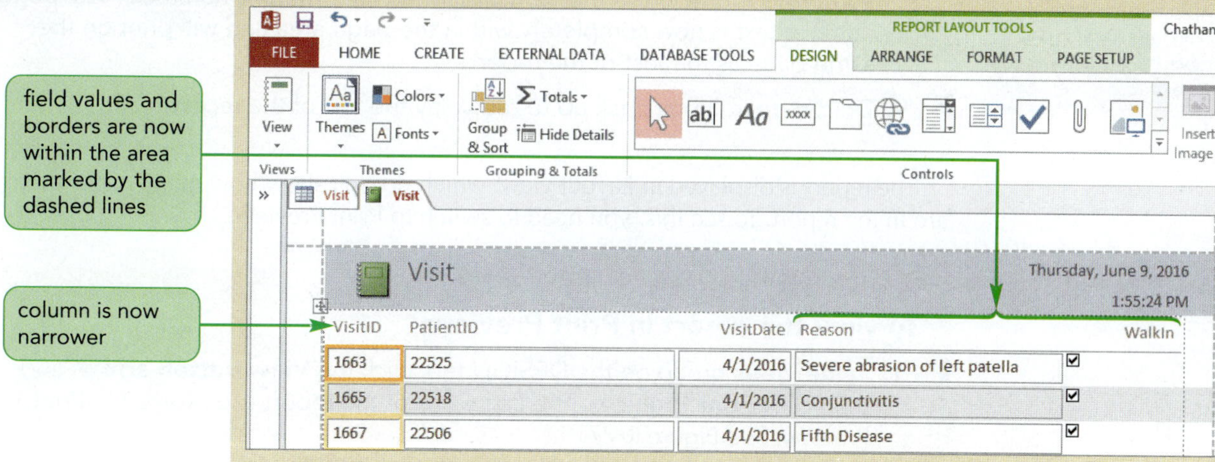

4. Click the first field value for PatientID to establish the field as the current field.
5. Position the pointer on the right border of the first value in the PatientID column until the pointer changes to ↔, click and drag to the left until the column is slightly wider than its field name, and then release the mouse button.
6. Drag the scroll box on the vertical scroll bar all the way down to the bottom of the report to check its entire layout.

   The Report tool displays the number "86" at the bottom left of the report, showing the total number of records in the report and the table on which it is based—the Visit table. The Report tool also displays the page number at the bottom right, but the text "Page 1 of 1" appears cut off through the vertical dashed line. This will cause a problem when you print the report, so you need to move this text to the left.
7. Click anywhere on the words **Page 1 of 1**. An orange outline appears around the text, indicating it is selected. See Figure 1-26.

Figure 1-26 Report page number selected

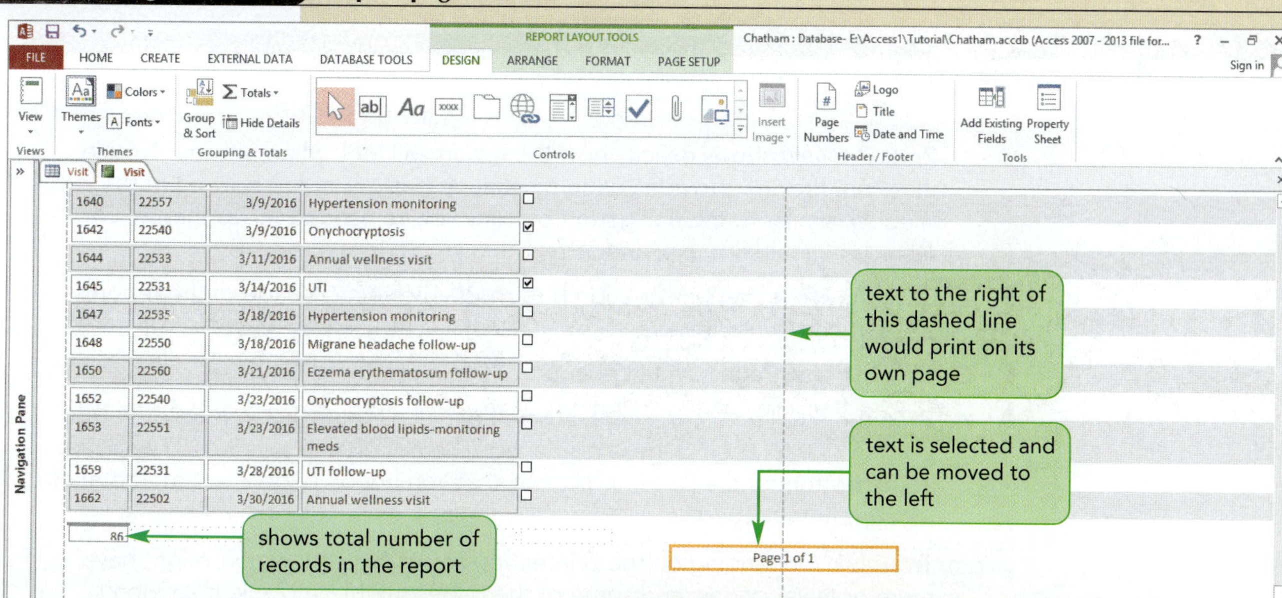

With the text selected, you can use the keyboard arrow keys to move it.

TIP

You can also use the mouse to drag the selected page number, but the arrow key is more precise.

8. Press the ← key repeatedly until the selected box containing the page number is to the left of the vertical dashed line (roughly 35 times). The page number text is now completely within the page area and will print on the same page as the rest of the report.
9. Drag the scroll box back up to redisplay the top of the report.

The report is displayed in Layout view, which doesn't show how many pages there are in the report. To see this, you need to switch to Print Preview.

To view the report in Print Preview:

1. In the Views group on the DESIGN tab, click the **View button arrow**, and then click **Print Preview**. The first page of the report is displayed in Print Preview. See Figure 1-27.

Figure 1-27 First page of the report in Print Preview

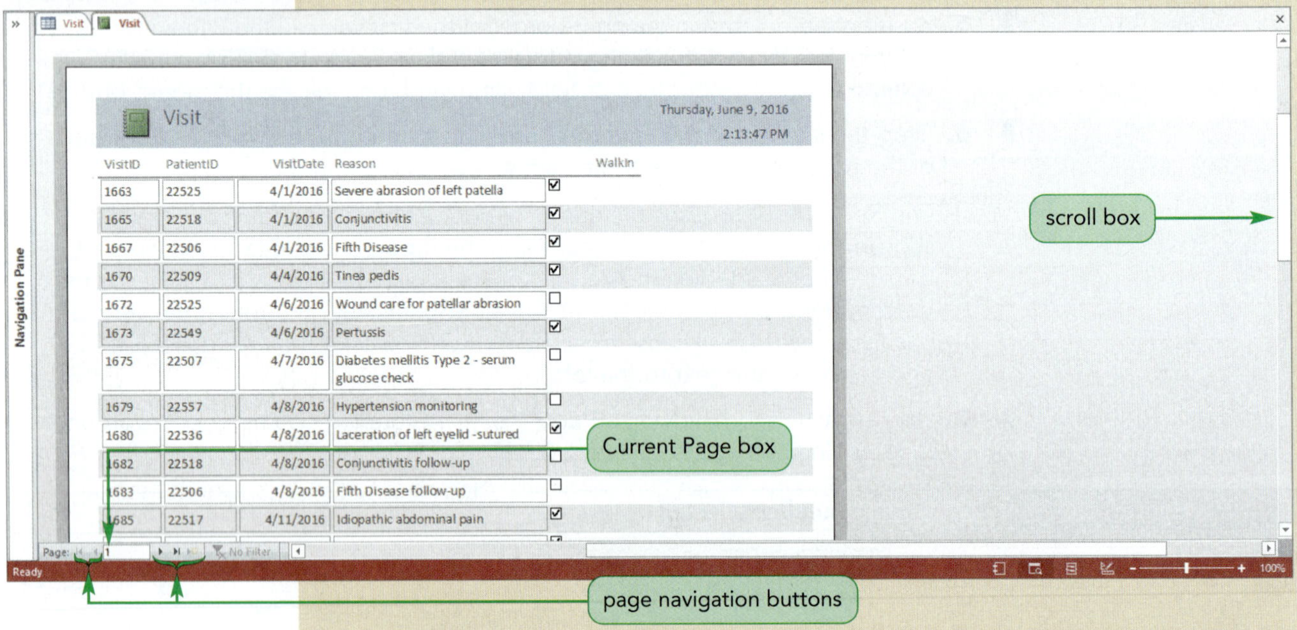

Print Preview shows exactly how the report will look when printed. Notice that Print Preview provides page navigation buttons at the bottom of the window, similar to the navigation buttons you've used to move through records in a table, query, and form.

2. Click the **Next Page** navigation button ▶. The second page of the report is displayed in Print Preview.
3. Click the **Last Page** navigation button ▶| to move to the last page of the report.
4. Drag the scroll box in the vertical scroll bar (see Figure 1-27) down until the bottom of the report page is displayed. The notation "Page 3 of 3" appears at the bottom of the page, indicating that you are on page 3 out of a total of 3 pages in the report.

   Trouble? Depending on the printer you are using, your report might have more or fewer pages, and some of the pages might be blank. If so, don't worry. Different printers format reports in different ways, sometimes affecting the total number of pages and the number of records printed per page.

5. Click the **First Page** navigation button [First Page] to return to the first page of the report, and then drag the scroll box in the vertical scroll bar back up so that the top of the report is displayed.

   Next you'll save the report as VisitDetails, and then print it.

6. On the Quick Access Toolbar, click the **Save** button [Save]. The Save As dialog box opens.

7. In the Report Name box, click at the end of the highlighted word "Visit," type **Details,** and then press the **Enter** key. Access saves the report as VisitDetails in the Chatham database and closes the dialog box. The tab containing the report now displays the name "VisitDetails."

Printing a Report

After creating a report, you might need to print it to distribute it to others who need to view the report's contents. You can print a report without changing any print settings, or display the Print dialog box and select options for printing.

REFERENCE

Printing a Report

- Open the report in any view, or select the report in the Navigation Pane.
- Click the FILE tab to display Backstage view, click Print, and then click Quick Print to print the report with the default print settings.

or

- Open the report in any view, or select the report in the Navigation Pane.
- Click the FILE tab, click Print, and then click Print (or, if the report is displayed in Print Preview, click the Print button in the Print group on the PRINT PREVIEW tab). The Print dialog box opens, in which you can select the options you want for printing the report.

Cindi asks you to print the entire report with the default settings, so you'll use the Quick Print option in Backstage view.

Note: To complete the following steps, your computer must be connected to a printer. Check with your instructor first to see if you should print the report.

To print the report and then close it:

1. On the ribbon, click the **FILE** tab to display Backstage view.

2. In the navigation bar, click **Print**, and then click **Quick Print**. The report prints with the default print settings, and you return to the report in Print Preview.

   Trouble? If your report did not print, make sure that your computer is connected to a printer, and that the printer is turned on and ready to print. Then repeat Steps 1 and 2.

3. Click the **Close 'VisitDetails'** button [X] on the object tab to close the report.

4. Click the **Close 'Visit'** button [X] on the object tab to close the Visit table.

   Trouble? If you are asked to save changes to the layout of the table, click Yes.

You can also use the Print dialog box to print other database objects, such as table and query datasheets. Most often, these objects are used for viewing and entering data, and reports are used for printing the data in a database.

Viewing Objects in the Navigation Pane

The Chatham database now contains four objects—the Visit table, the VisitList query, the VisitData form, and the VisitDetails report. When you work with the database file—such as closing it, opening it, or distributing it to others—the file includes all the objects you created and saved in the database. You can view and work with these objects in the Navigation Pane.

To view the objects in the Chatham database:

1. On the Navigation Pane, click the **Shutter Bar Open/Close Button** » to open the pane. See Figure 1-28.

Figure 1-28 Chatham database objects displayed in the Navigation Pane

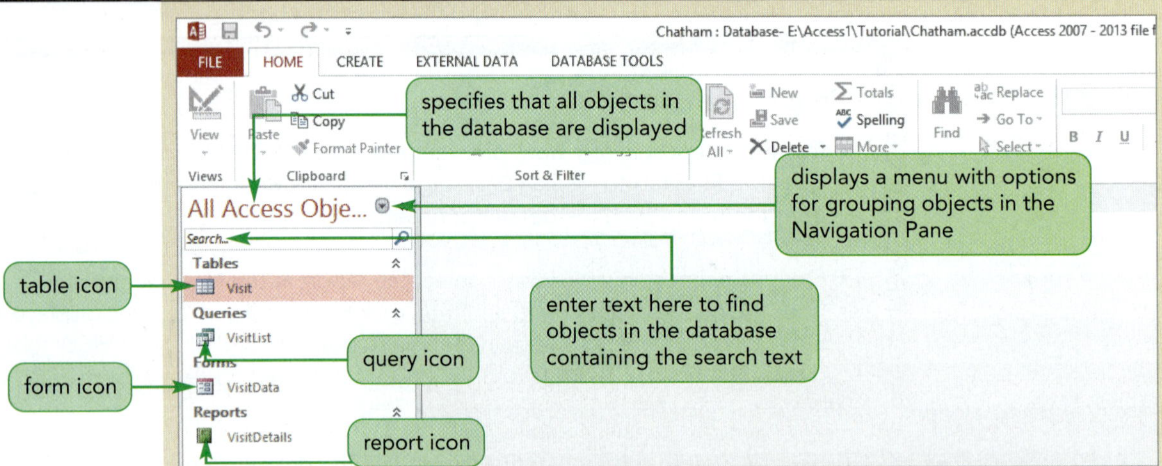

The Navigation Pane currently displays the default category, **All Access Objects**, which lists all the database objects in the pane. Each object type (Tables, Queries, Forms, and Reports) appears in its own group. Each database object (the Visit table, the VisitList query, the VisitData form, and the VisitDetails report) has a unique icon to its left to indicate the type of object. This makes it easy for you to identify the objects and choose which one you want to open and work with.

The arrow on the All Access Objects bar displays a menu with options for various ways to group and display objects in the Navigation Pane. The Search box enables you to enter text for Access to find; for example, you could search for all objects that contain the word "Visit" in their names. Note that Access searches for objects only in the categories and groups currently displayed in the Navigation Pane.

As you continue to build the Chatham database and add more objects to it in later tutorials, you'll use the options in the Navigation Pane to manage those objects.

Using Microsoft Access Help

The Access program provides a Help system you can use to search for information about specific Access features. You start Help by clicking the Microsoft Access Help button in the top right of the Access window, or by pressing the F1 key. You'll use Help now to learn more about the Navigation Pane.

To search for information about the Navigation Pane in Help:

1. Click the **Microsoft Access Help** button ? on the title bar. The Access Help window opens, as shown earlier in the Session 1.2 Visual Overview.
2. Click in the search box, type **Navigation Pane**, and then press the **Enter** key. The Access Help window displays a list of topics related to the Navigation Pane.
3. Click the topic **Manage database objects in the Navigation Pane**. The Access Help window displays the article you selected. See Figure 1-29.

Figure 1-29 Article displayed in the Access Help window

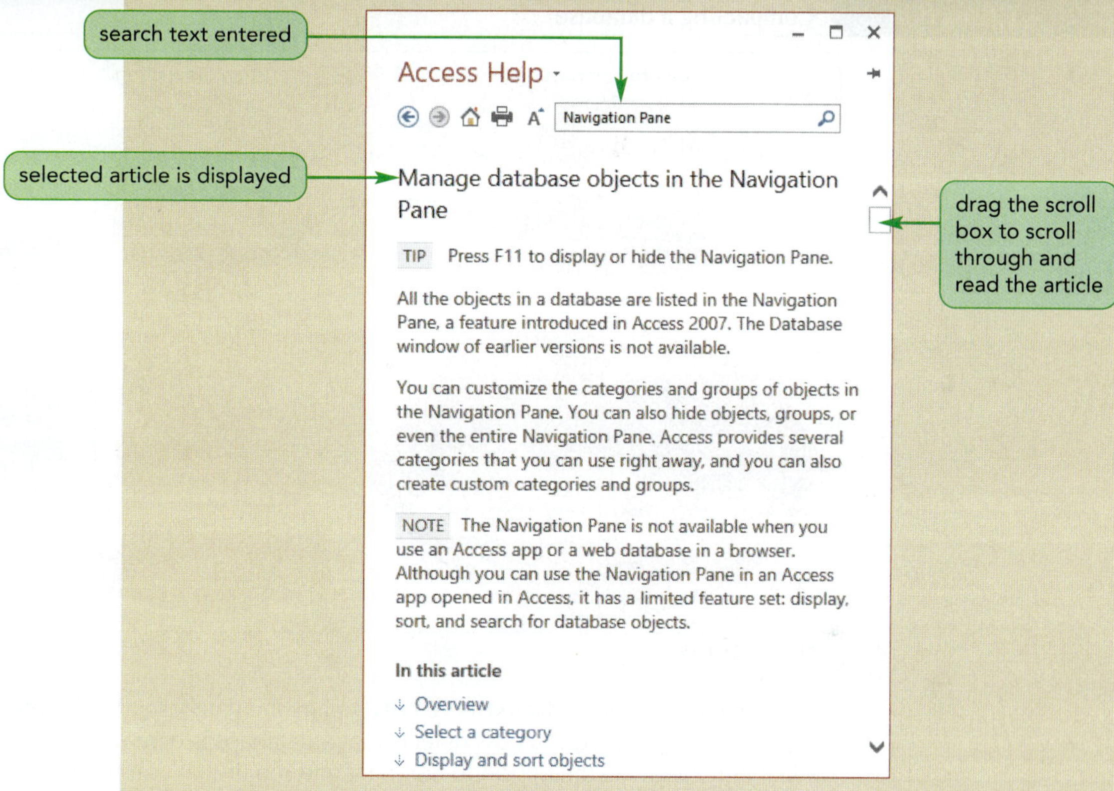

Trouble? If the article on managing database objects is not listed in your Help window, choose another article related to the Navigation Pane to read.

4. Scroll through the article to read detailed information about working with the Navigation Pane.
5. When finished, click the **Close** button ✕ on the Access Help window to close it.

The Access Help system is an important reference tool for you to use if you need additional information about databases in general, details about specific Access features, or support with problems you might encounter.

Managing a Database

One of the main tasks involved in working with database software is managing your databases and the data they contain. Some of the activities involved in database management include compacting and repairing a database and backing up and restoring a database. By managing your databases, you can ensure that they operate in the most efficient way, that the data they contain is secure, and that you can work with the data effectively.

Compacting and Repairing a Database

Whenever you open an Access database and work in it, the size of the database increases. Further, when you delete records or when you delete or replace database objects—such as queries, forms, and reports—the storage space that had been occupied by the deleted or replaced records or objects does not automatically become available for other records or objects. To make the space available, and also to increase the speed of data retrieval, you must compact the database. **Compacting** a database rearranges the data and objects in a database to decrease its file size, thereby making more storage space available and enhancing the performance of the database. Figure 1-30 illustrates the compacting process.

Figure 1-30 Compacting a database

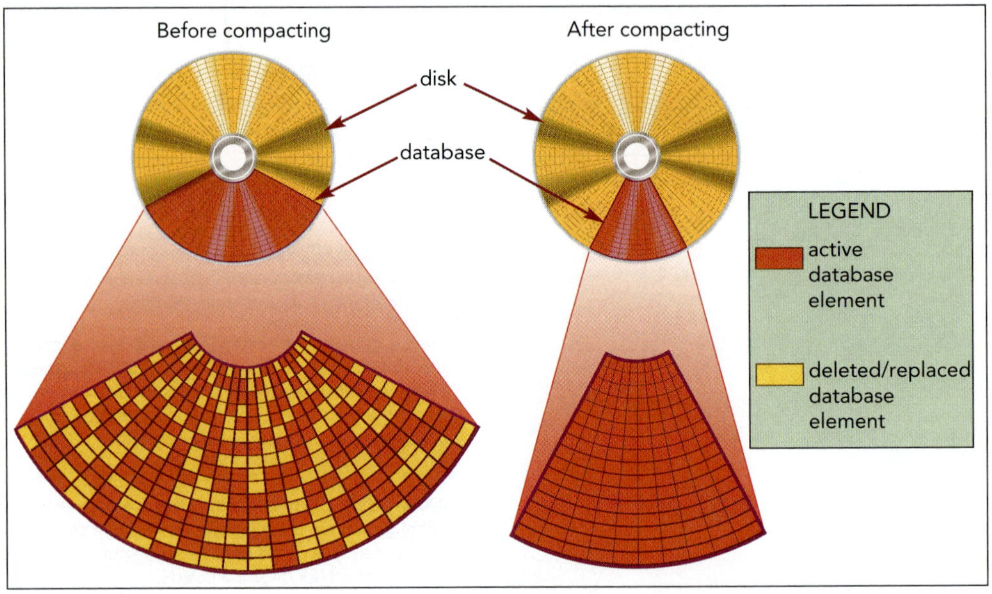

When you compact a database, Access repairs the database at the same time, if necessary. In some cases, Access detects that a database is damaged when you try to open it and gives you the option to compact and repair it at that time. For example, the data in your database might become damaged, or corrupted, if you exit the Access program suddenly by turning off your computer. If you think your database might be damaged because it is behaving unpredictably, you can use the Compact & Repair Database option to fix it.

REFERENCE

Compacting and Repairing a Database

- Make sure the database file you want to compact and repair is open.
- Click the FILE tab to display the Info screen in Backstage view.
- Click the Compact & Repair Database button.

Access also allows you to set an option to compact and repair a database file automatically every time you close it. The Compact on Close option is available in the Current Database section of the Access Options dialog box, which you open from

Backstage view by clicking the Options command in the navigation bar. By default, the Compact on Close option is turned off.

Next, you'll compact the Chatham database manually using the Compact & Repair Database option. This will make the database smaller and allow you to work with it more efficiently. After compacting the database, you'll close it.

To compact and repair the Chatham database:

1. On the ribbon, click the **FILE** tab to display the Info screen in Backstage view.
2. Click the **Compact & Repair Database** button. Access closes Backstage view and returns to the HOME tab. Although nothing visible happens on the screen, Access compacts the Chatham database, making it smaller, and repairs it at the same time.
3. Click the **FILE** tab to return to the Info screen, and then click **Close** in the navigation bar. Access closes the Chatham database.

Backing Up and Restoring a Database

Backing up a database is the process of making a copy of the database file to protect your database against loss or damage. The Back Up Database command enables you to back up your database file from within the Access program, while you are working on your database. To use this option, click the FILE tab to display the Info screen in Backstage view, click Save As in the navigation bar, click Back Up Database in the Advanced section of the Save Database As pane, and then click the Save As button. In the Save As dialog box that opens, Access provides a default filename for the backup copy that consists of the same filename as the database you are backing up (for example, "Chatham"), and an underscore character, plus the current date. This filenaming system makes it easy for you to keep track of your database backups and when they were created. To restore a backup database file, you simply copy the backup from the location where it is stored to your hard drive, or whatever device you use to work in Access, and start working with the restored database file. (You will not actually back up the Chatham database in this tutorial unless directed by your instructor to do so.)

INSIGHT

Planning and Performing Database Backups

Experienced database users make it a habit to back up a database before they work with it for the first time, keeping the original data intact. They also make frequent backups while continuing to work with a database; these backups are generally on flash drives, recordable CDs or DVDs, external or network hard drives, or cloud-based storage (such as SkyDrive). Also, it is recommended to store the backup copy in a different location from the original. For example, if the original database is stored on a flash drive, you should not store the backup copy on the same flash drive. If you lose the drive or the drive is damaged, you would lose both the original database and its backup copy.

If the original database file and the backup copy have the same name, restoring the backup copy might replace the original. If you want to save the original file, rename it before you restore the backup copy. To ensure that the restored database has the most current data, you should update the restored database with any changes made to the original between the time you created the backup copy and the time the original database became damaged or lost.

By properly planning for and performing backups, you can avoid losing data and prevent the time-consuming effort required to rebuild a lost or damaged database.

In the following tutorials, you'll help Cindi complete and maintain the Chatham database, and you'll use it to meet the specific information needs of the clinic's employees.

PROSKILLS

Decision Making: When to Use Access vs. Excel

Using a spreadsheet application like Microsoft Excel to manage lists or tables of information works well when the data is simple, such as a list of contacts or tasks. As soon as the data becomes complex enough to separate into tables that need to be related, you start to see the limitations of using a spreadsheet application. The strength of a database application such as Access is in its ability to easily relate one table of information to another. Consider a table of contacts that includes home addresses, with a separate row for each person living at the same address. When an address changes, it's too easy to make a mistake and not update the home address for each person who lives there. To ensure you have the most accurate data at all times, it's important to have only one instance of each piece of data. By creating separate tables that are related, and keeping only one instance of each piece of data, you'll ensure the integrity of the data. Trying to accomplish this in Excel is a complex process, whereas Access is specifically designed for this functionality.

Another limitation of using Excel instead of Access to manage data has to do with the volume of data. Although a spreadsheet can hold thousands of records, a database can hold millions. A spreadsheet containing thousands of pieces of information is cumbersome to use. Think of large-scale commercial applications such as enrollment at a college or tracking customers for a large company. It's hard to imagine managing such information in an Excel spreadsheet. Instead, you'd use a database. Finally, with an Access database, multiple users can access the information it contains at the same time. Although an Excel spreadsheet can be shared, there can be problems when users try to open and edit the same spreadsheet at the same time.

When you're trying to decide whether to use Excel or Access, ask yourself the following questions.

1. Do you need to store data in separate tables that are related to each other?
2. Do you have a very large amount of data to store?
3. Will more than one person need to access the data at the same time?

If you answer "yes" to any of these questions, an Access database is most likely the appropriate application to use.

REVIEW

Session 1.2 Quick Check

1. To copy the records from a table in one database to another table in a different database, the two tables must have the same ______________.
2. A(n) ______________ is a question you ask about the data stored in a database.
3. The quickest way to create a form is to use the ______________.
4. Which view enables you to see the total number of pages in a report and navigate through the report pages?
5. In the Navigation Pane, each database object has a unique ______________ to its left that identifies the object's type.
6. ______________ a database rearranges the data and objects in a database to decrease its file size and enhance the speed and performance of the database.
7. ________________ a database is the process of making a copy of the database file to protect the database against loss or damage.

ASSESS

SAM Projects

Put your skills into practice with SAM Projects! SAM Projects for this tutorial can be found online. If you have a SAM account, go to www.cengage.com/sam2013 to download the most recent Project Instructions and Start Files.

PRACTICE

Review Assignments

Data File needed for the Review Assignments: Company.accdb

For Chatham Community Health Services, Cindi asks you to create a new database to contain information about the vendors that the clinic works with to obtain medical supplies and equipment for the clinic, and the vendors who service and maintain the equipment. Complete the following steps:

1. Create a new, blank database named **Vendor** and save it in the folder where you are storing your files, as specified by your instructor.
2. In Datasheet view for the Table1 table, rename the default ID primary key field to **SupplierID**. Change the data type of the SupplierID field to Short Text.
3. Add the following 10 fields to the new table in the order shown; all of them are Short Text fields *except* InitialContact, which is a Date/Time field: **Company**, **Category**, **Address**, **City**, **State**, **Zip**, **Phone**, **ContactFirst**, **ContactLast**, and **InitialContact**. Resize the columns as necessary so that the complete field names are displayed. Save the table as **Supplier**.
4. Enter the records shown in Figure 1-31 in the Supplier table. For the first record, be sure to enter your first name in the ContactFirst field and your last name in the ContactLast field.

   Note: When entering field values that are shown on multiple lines in the figure, do not try to enter the values on multiple lines. The values are shown on multiple lines in the figure for page spacing purposes only.

Figure 1-31 **Supplier table records**

SupplierID	Company	Category	Address	City	State	Zip	Phone	ContactFirst	ContactLast	InitialContact
ARE318	Aresco Surgical, Inc.	Supplies	48 Vienna St	Bridgeport	CT	06601	203-774-3048	*Student First*	*Student Last*	9/2/2015
GRE364	Greinke Labs, Inc.	Supplies	451 Summit Dr	Tiverton	RI	02878	401-208-9843	Evan	Brighton	1/12/2016
DUR368	Durasurg Equipment, Inc.	Equipment	74 Jessie St	Roanoke	VA	24036	540-340-3829	Kristin	Taylor	12/1/2015
STE472	Sterile Labs of CT, Inc.	Service	938 Gormley Ave	North Branford	CT	06517	203-537-5940	Carmine	San Marcos	11/3/2015
GSE420	GSE Medical, Inc.	Equipment	583 Renovo Dr	Claremont	NH	03743	603-202-4951	John	Vereen	9/10/2015

5. Cindi created a database named Company that contains a Business table with supplier data. The Supplier table you created has the same design as the Business table. Copy all the records from the **Business** table in the **Company** database (located in the Access1 ▸ Review folder provided with your Data Files) and then paste them at the end of the Supplier table in the Vendor database.

6. Resize all datasheet columns to their best fit, and then save the Supplier table.
7. Close the Supplier table, and then use the Navigation Pane to reopen it. Note that the records are displayed in primary key order by the values in the SupplierID field.
8. Use the Simple Query Wizard to create a query that includes the Company, Category, ContactFirst, ContactLast, and Phone fields (in that order) from the Supplier table. Name the query **SupplierList**, and then close the query.
9. Use the Form tool to create a form for the Supplier table. Save the form as **SupplierInfo**, and then close it.
10. Use the Report tool to create a report based on the Supplier table. In Layout view, resize all fields except the Company field, so that each field is slightly wider than the longest entry (either the field name itself or an entry in the field). Display the report in Print Preview and verify that all the fields fit across two pages in the report. Save the report as **SupplierDetails**, and then close it.
11. Close the Supplier table, and then compact and repair the Vendor database.
12. Close the Vendor database.

APPLY

Case Problem 1

Data File needed for this Case Problem: Program.accdb

GoGopher! Amol Mehta, a recent college graduate living in Boulder, Colorado, spent months earning money by running errands and completing basic chores for family members and acquaintances, while looking for full-time employment. As his list of customers needing such services continued to grow, Amol decided to start his own business called GoGopher! The business, which Amol operates completely online from his home, offers customers a variety of services—from grocery shopping and household chores to yard work and pet care—on a subscription basis. Clients become members of GoGopher! by choosing the plan that best suits their needs. Each plan provides a certain number of tasks per month to members, for a specified period of time. Amol wants to use Access to maintain information about the members who have joined GoGopher! and the types of plans offered. He needs your help in creating this database. Complete the following:

1. Create a new, blank database named **Gopher** and save it in the folder where you are storing your files, as specified by your instructor.
2. In Datasheet view for the Table1 table, rename the default primary key ID field to **PlanID**. Change the data type of the PlanID field to Short Text.
3. Add the following three fields to the new table in the order shown: **PlanDescription** (a Short Text field), **PlanCost** (a Currency field), and **FeeWaived** (a Yes/No field). Save the table as **Plan**.
4. Enter the records shown in Figure 1-32 in the Plan table. Note: When entering the PlanCost field values, you do not have to type the dollar signs, commas, or decimal places; Access will enter them automatically.

Figure 1-32 **Plan table records**

PlanID	PlanDescription	PlanCost	FeeWaived
301	20 tasks per month for 12 months	$6,000.00	Yes
311	10 tasks per month for 3 months	$750.00	No
304	10 tasks per month for 12 months	$3,000.00	Yes
303	15 tasks per month for 12 months	$4,500.00	Yes
312	8 tasks per month for 3 months	$600.00	No

when entering currency values, you do not have to type the dollar signs, commas, or decimal places

5. Amol created a database named Program that contains a Service table with plan data. The Plan table you created has the same design as the Service table. Copy all the records from the **Service** table in the **Program** database (located in the Access1 ▸ Case1 folder provided with your Data Files) and then paste them at the end of the Plan table in the Gopher database.

6. Resize all datasheet columns to their best fit, and then save the Plan table.
7. Close the Plan table, and then use the Navigation Pane to reopen it. Note that the records are displayed in primary key order by the values in the PlanID field.
8. Use the Simple Query Wizard to create a query that includes the PlanID, PlanDescription, and PlanCost fields from the Plan table. In the second Simple Query Wizard dialog box, select the Detail option. (This option appears because the query includes a Currency field.) Save the query as **PlanData**, and then close the query.
9. Use the Form tool to create a form for the Plan table. Save the form as **PlanInfo**, and then close it.
10. Use the Report tool to create a report based on the Plan table. In Layout view, resize the PlanID field so it is slightly wider than the longest entry, which is the field name in this case. Also, resize the box containing the total amount that appears below the PlanCost column by clicking the box and then dragging its bottom border down so that the amount is fully displayed. (The Report Tool calculated this total automatically.) Display the report in Print Preview; then verify that all the fields are within the page area and all field values are fully displayed. Save the report as **PlanList**, print the report (only if asked by your instructor to do so), and then close it.
11. Close the Plan table, and then compact and repair the Gopher database.
12. Close the Gopher database.

APPLY

Case Problem 2

Data File needed for this Case Problem: Consulting.accdb

O'Brien Educational Services After teaching English in a public high school for 15 years, Karen O'Brien decided to channel her experience in education in a new direction and founded O'Brien Educational Services, a small educational consulting company located in South Bend, Indiana. The company offers tutoring services to high school students to help prepare them for standardized tests, such as the SAT and the ACT. The company provides group, private, and semi-private tutoring sessions to best meet the needs of its students. As her business continues to expand, Karen wants to use Access to maintain information about the tutors who work for her, the students who sign up for tutoring, and the contracts they sign. She needs your help in creating this database. Complete the following steps:

1. Create a new, blank database named **OBrien** and save it in the folder where you are storing your files, as specified by your instructor.
2. In Datasheet view for the Table1 table, rename the default primary key ID field to **TutorID**. Change the data type of the TutorID field to Short Text.
3. Add the following five fields to the new table in the order shown; all of them are Short Text fields *except* HireDate, which is a Date/Time field: **FirstName**, **LastName**, **Degree**, **School**, and **HireDate**. Resize the columns, if necessary, so that the complete field names are displayed. Save the table as **Tutor**.
4. Enter the records shown in Figure 1-33 in the Tutor table. For the first record, be sure to enter your first name in the FirstName field and your last name in the LastName field.

Figure 1-33 **Tutor table records**

TutorID	FirstName	LastName	Degree	School	HireDate
31-1200	*Student First*	*Student Last*	BA	Pierre University	8/2/2015
68-8234	Caitlin	Shea	MS	Towns University	1/5/2016
55-1234	Samuel	Glick	BA	Manoog College	7/23/2016
69-2254	Sachi	Hatanaka	MA	Wyman College	3/23/2015
71-1698	Richard	Keating	Ph.D	Hobert University	5/3/2015

5. Karen created a database named Consulting that contains an Instructor table with tutor data. The Tutor table you created has the same design as the Instructor table. Copy all the records from the **Instructor** table in the **Consulting** database (located in the Access1 ► Case2 folder provided with your Data Files) and then paste them at the end of the Tutor table in the OBrien database.
6. Resize all datasheet columns to their best fit, and then save the Tutor table.
7. Close the Tutor table, and then use the Navigation Pane to reopen it. Note that the records are displayed in primary key order by the values in the TutorID field.
8. Use the Simple Query Wizard to create a query that includes the FirstName, LastName, and HireDate fields from the Tutor table. Save the query as **StartDate**, and then close the query.
9. Use the Form tool to create a form for the Tutor table. Save the form as **TutorInfo**, and then close it.
10. Use the Report tool to create a report based on the Tutor table. In Layout view, resize the TutorID, FirstName, LastName, and Degree fields so they are slightly wider than the longest entry (either the field name itself or an entry in the field). All six fields should fit within the page area after you resize the specified fields. At the bottom of the report, move the text "Page 1 of 1" to the left so it is within the page area. Display the report in Print Preview; then verify that the fields and page number fit within the page area, and that all field values are fully displayed. Save the report as **TutorList**, print the report (only if asked by your instructor to do so), and then close it.
11. Close the Tutor table, and then compact and repair the OBrien database.
12. Close the OBrien database.

CHALLENGE

Case Problem 3

Data File needed for this Case Problem: Animal.accdb

Rosemary Animal Shelter Ryan Lang is the director of the Rosemary Animal Shelter in Cobb County, Georgia. The main goals of the shelter, which has several locations in the county, are to rescue dogs and cats and to find people who will adopt them. The shelter was established by Rosemary Hanson, who dedicated her life to rescuing pets and finding good homes for them. Residents of Cobb County generously donate money, food, and equipment in support of the shelter. Some of these patrons also adopt animals from the shelter. Ryan has asked you to create an Access database to manage information about the animals, patrons, and donations. Complete the following steps:

1. Create a new, blank database named **Shelter** and save it in the folder where you are storing your files, as specified by your instructor.
2. In Datasheet view for the Table1 table, rename the default primary key ID field to **PatronID**. Change the data type of the PatronID field to Short Text.
3. Add the following four Short Text fields to the new table in the order shown: **Title**, **FirstName**, **LastName**, and **Phone**. Save the table as **Patron**.
4. Enter the records shown in Figure 1-34 in the Patron table. For the first record, be sure to enter your title in the Title field, your first name in the FirstName field, and your last name in the LastName field.

Figure 1-34 Patron table records

PatronID	Title	FirstName	LastName	Phone
30405	*Student Title*	*Student First*	*Student Last*	770-427-9300
33287	Dr.	Ali	Haddad	770-528-8973
32189	Mrs.	Gini	Smith	770-499-2775
36028	Mr.	Michael	Carlucci	678-283-6334
30753	Ms.	Cynthia	Crosby	678-444-2676

5. Ryan created a database named Animal that contains a Donor table with data about patrons. The Patron table you created has the same design as the Donor table. Copy all the records from the **Donor** table in the **Animal** database (located in the Access1 ▸ Case3 folder provided with your Data Files) and then paste them at the end of the Patron table in the Shelter database.
6. Resize all datasheet columns to their best fit, and then save the Patron table.
7. Close the Patron table, and then use the Navigation Pane to reopen it. Note that the records are displayed in primary key order by the values in the PatronID field.

Explore 8. Use the Simple Query Wizard to create a query that includes all the fields in the Patron table *except* the Title field. (*Hint*: Use the >> and < buttons to select the necessary fields.) Save the query using the name **PatronPhoneList**.

Explore 9. The query results are displayed in order by the PatronID field values. You can specify a different order by sorting the query. Display the HOME tab. Then, click the insertion point anywhere in the LastName column to make it the current field. In the Sort & Filter group on the HOME tab, click the Ascending button. The records are now listed in order by the values in the LastName field. Save and close the query.

Explore 10. Use the Form tool to create a form for the Patron table. In the new form, navigate to record 15 (the record with PatronID 33765), and then print the form *for the current record only*. (*Hint*: You must use the Print dialog box in order to print only the current record. Go to Backstage view, click Print in the navigation bar, and then click Print to open the Print dialog box. Click the Selected Record(s) option button and then click the OK button to print the current record.) Save the form as **PatronInfo**, and then close it.

11. Use the Report tool to create a report based on the Patron table. In Layout view, resize each field so it is slightly wider than the longest entry (either the field name itself or an entry in the field). All five fields should fit within the page area after resizing. At the bottom of the report, move the text "Page 1 of 1" to the left so it is within the page area. Display the report in Print Preview, then verify that the fields and page number fit within the page area and that all field values are fully displayed. Save the report as **PatronList**. Print the report (only if asked by your instructor to do so), and then close it.
12. Close the Patron table, and then compact and repair the Shelter database.
13. Close the Shelter database.

CHALLENGE

Case Problem 4

Data File needed for this Case Problem: Tour.accdb

Stanley EcoTours Janice and Bill Stanley live in Pocatello, Idaho, and are the proud owners and operators of Stanley EcoTours. Their passion is to encourage people to visit natural areas around the world in a responsible manner that does not harm the environment. Their advertising has drawn clients from Idaho, Wyoming, Montana, and Canada. As the interest in ecotourism grows, Janice and Bill's business is also expanding to include more tours in Africa and South America. Because of the growth in business that they anticipate, Janice and Bill realize their current recordkeeping system is inadequate. They would like you to build an Access database to manage information about guests, tours, and reservations. Complete the following:

1. Create a new, blank database named **Stanley** and save it in the folder where you are storing your files, as specified by your instructor.
2. In Datasheet view for the Table1 table, rename the default primary key ID field to **GuestID**. Change the data type of the GuestID field to Short Text.
3. Add the following eight Short Text fields to the new table in the order shown: **GuestFirst**, **GuestLast**, **Address**, **City**, **State/Prov**, **PostalCode**, **Country**, and **Phone**. Save the table as **Guest**.

4. Enter the records shown in Figure 1-35 in the Guest table. For the first record, be sure to enter your first name in the GuestFirst field and your last name in the GuestLast field.

Figure 1-35 **Guest table records**

GuestID	GuestFirst	GuestLast	Address	City	State/Prov	PostalCode	Country	Phone
401	*Student First*	*Student Last*	10 Winter Ave	Boise	ID	83702	USA	208-344-0975
417	Isabelle	Rouy	227 Front Ln	Calgary	AB	T1Y 2N7	Canada	403-226-0065
403	Brian	Anderson	5003 Grant Blvd	Great Falls	MT	59401	USA	406-761-4515
425	Kelly	Skolnik	15 Tobin Dr	Red Deer	AB	T4N 3D5	Canada	403-755-1597
420	Alberto	Lopez	991 Crestview Dr	Butte	MT	59701	USA	406-782-1183

5. Bill created a database named Tour that contains a Customer table with data about guests. The Guest table you created has the same design as the Customer table. Copy all the records from the **Customer** table in the **Tour** database (located in the Access1 ▸ Case4 folder provided with your Data Files) and then paste them at the end of the Guest table in the Stanley database.
6. Resize all datasheet columns to their best fit, and then save the Guest table.
7. Close the Guest table, and then use the Navigation Pane to reopen it. Note that the records are displayed in primary key order.
8. Use the Simple Query Wizard to create a query that includes the following fields from the Guest table, in the order shown: GuestID, GuestLast, GuestFirst, State/Prov, and Phone. Name the query **GuestData**.

Explore 9. The query results are displayed in order by the GuestID field values. You can specify a different order by sorting the query. Display the HOME tab. Then, click the insertion point anywhere in the State/Prov column to make it the current field. In the Sort & Filter group on the HOME tab, click the Ascending button. The records are now listed in order by the values in the State/Prov field. Save and close the query.

Explore 10. Use the Form tool to create a form for the Guest table. In the new form, navigate to record 10 (the record with GuestID 412), and then print the form *for the current record only*. (*Hint*: You must use the Print dialog box in order to print only the current record. Go to Backstage view, click Print in the navigation bar, and then click Print to open the Print dialog box. Click the Selected Record(s) option button and then click the OK button to print the current record.) Save the form as **GuestInfo**, and then close it.

11. Use the Report tool to create a report based on the Guest table. In Layout view, resize each field so it is slightly wider than the longest entry (either the field name itself or an entry in the field). At the bottom of the report, move the text "Page 1 of 1" to the left so it is within the page area on the report's first page. Display the report in Print Preview and notice that the columns of the report are still spread across two pages, even after resizing the fields. Save the report as **GuestList**.

Explore 12. In the Close Preview group, click the Close Print Preview button to return to the report in Layout view. To make more room on the first page, you'll delete the Address, PostalCode, and Country columns from the report. Click anywhere in the Address column to make it active. Click the ARRANGE tab (one of the REPORT LAYOUT TOOLS contextual tabs), and then click the Select Column button in the Rows & Columns group. Click the HOME tab, and then click the Delete button in the Records group to delete the selected column from the report. Repeat this process to delete the PostalCode and Country columns. The remaining six fields should now all fit on the report's first page.

13. Display the report in Print Preview again, then verify that the fields and page number fit within the page area and that all field values are fully displayed.
14. Save the report, print it (only if asked by your instructor to do so), and then close it.
15. Close the Guest table, and then compact and repair the Stanley database.
16. Close the Stanley database.

TUTORIAL 2

Building a Database and Defining Table Relationships

Creating the Billing and Patient Tables

OBJECTIVES

Session 2.1

- Learn the guidelines for designing databases and setting field properties
- Create a table in Design view
- Define fields, set field properties, and specify a table's primary key
- Modify the structure of a table
- Change the order of fields in Design view
- Add new fields in Design view
- Change the Format property for a field in Datasheet view
- Modify field properties in Design view

Session 2.2

- Import data from an Excel worksheet
- Create a table by importing an existing table structure
- Add fields to a table with the Data Type gallery
- Delete and rename fields
- Change the data type for a field in Design view
- Set the Default Value property for a field
- Add data to a table by importing a text file
- Define a relationship between two tables

Case | ***Chatham Community Health Services***

The Chatham database currently contains one table, the Visit table. Cindi Rodriguez also wants to track information about the clinic's patients and the invoices sent to them for services provided by Chatham Community Health Services. This information includes such items as each patient's name and address, and the amount and billing date for each invoice.

In this tutorial, you'll create two new tables in the Chatham database—named Billing and Patient—to contain the additional data Cindi wants to track. You will use two different methods for creating the tables, and learn how to modify the fields. After adding records to the tables, you will define the necessary relationships between the tables in the Chatham database to relate the tables, enabling Cindi and her staff to work with the data more efficiently.

STARTING DATA FILES

Access1 →

Tutorial
Chatham.accdb *(cont.)*
Invoices.xlsx
Kelly.accdb
Patient.txt

Review
Supplies.xlsx
Vendor.accdb *(cont.)*

Case1
Customers.txt
Gopher.accdb *(cont.)*

Case2
Agreements.xlsx
Client.accdb
OBrien.accdb *(cont.)*
Students.txt

Case3
Animals.txt
Donations.xlsx
Shelter.accdb *(cont.)*

Case4
Bookings.txt
Stanley.accdb *(cont.)*
Travel.accdb

Session 2.1 Visual Overview:

Design view allows you to define or modify a table structure or the properties of the fields in a table.

The default name for a new table you create in Design view is Table1. This name appears on the tab for the new table.

The top portion of the Table window in Design view is called the **Table Design grid**. Here, you enter values for the Field Name, Data Type, and Description field properties.

After you assign a data type to a field, the General tab displays additional field properties for that data type. Initially, most field properties are assigned default values.

When defining the fields in a table, you can move from the Table Design grid to the Field Properties pane by pressing the **F6 key**.

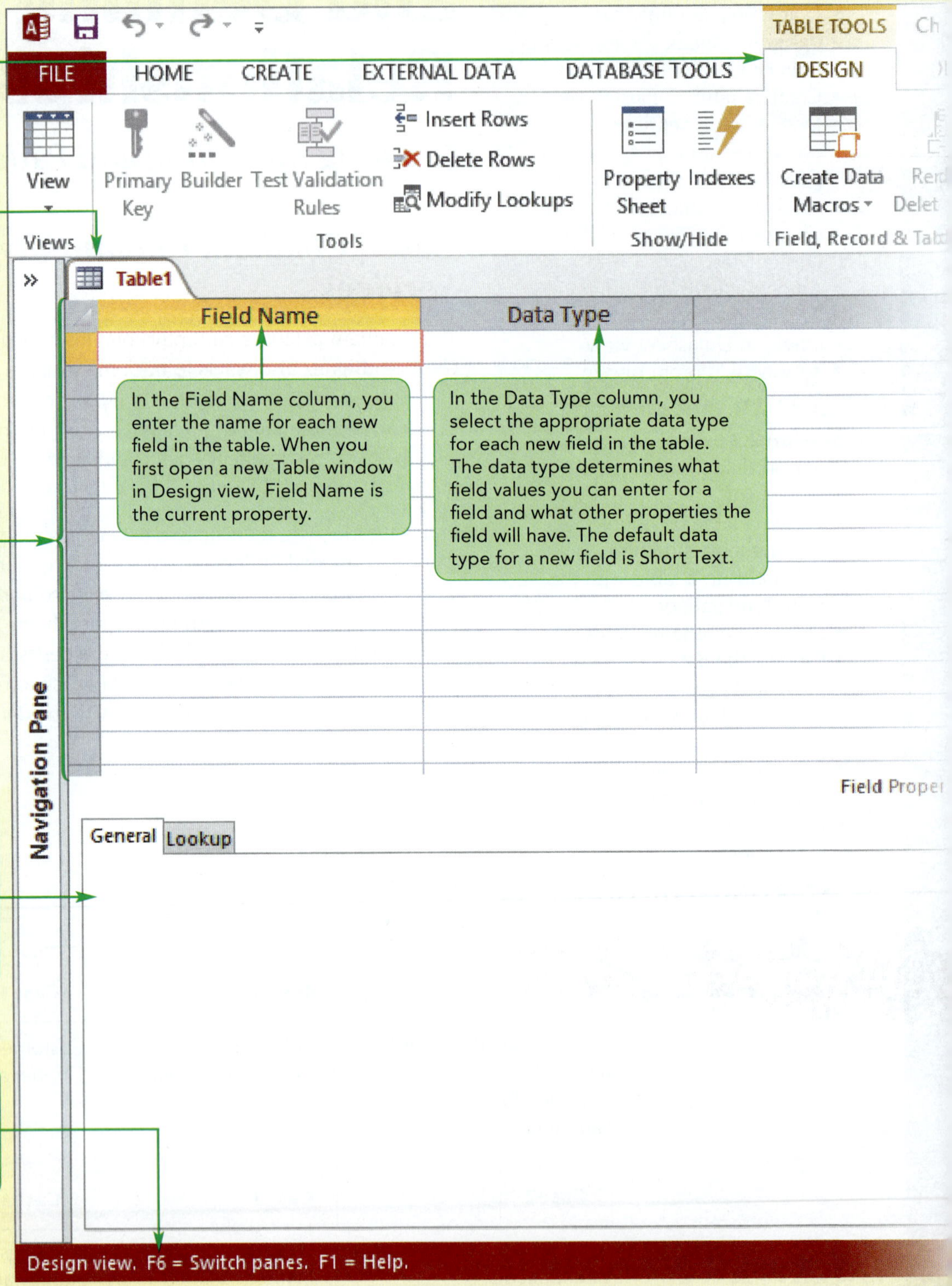

In the Field Name column, you enter the name for each new field in the table. When you first open a new Table window in Design view, Field Name is the current property.

In the Data Type column, you select the appropriate data type for each new field in the table. The data type determines what field values you can enter for a field and what other properties the field will have. The default data type for a new field is Short Text.

Table Window in Design View

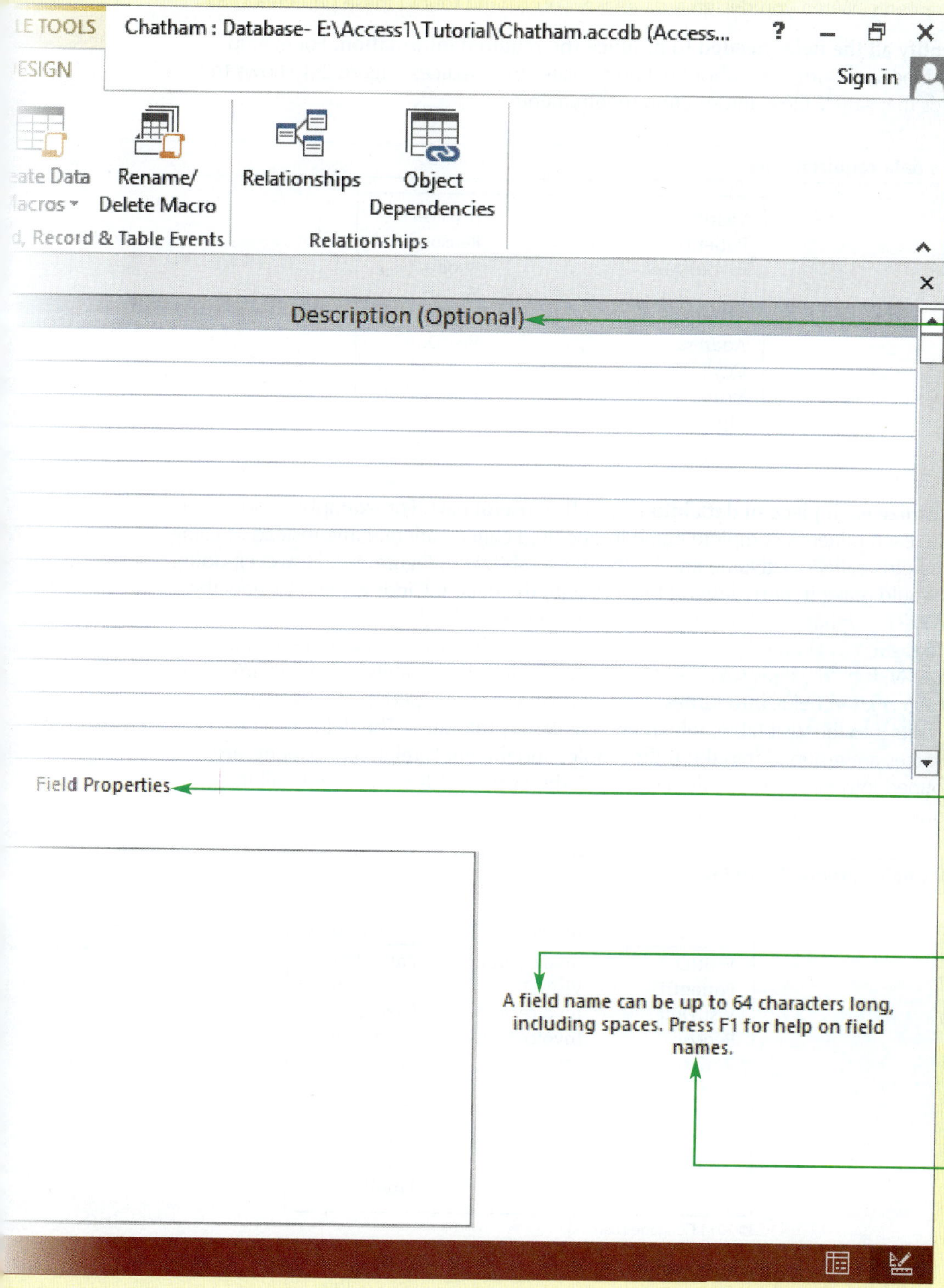

You can use the **Description property** to enter an optional description for a field to explain its purpose or usage. A field's Description property can be up to 255 characters long, and its value appears on the status bar when you view the table datasheet.

The bottom portion of the Table window in Design view is called the **Field Properties pane**. Here, you select values for all other field properties, most of which are optional.

The purpose or characteristics of the current property (Field Name, in this case) appear in this section of the Field Properties pane.

You can display more complete Help information about the current property by pressing the **F1 key**.

Guidelines for Designing Databases

A database management system can be a useful tool, but only if you first carefully design the database so that it meets the needs of its users. In database design, you determine the fields, tables, and relationships needed to satisfy the data and processing requirements. When you design a database, you should follow these guidelines:

- **Identify all the fields needed to produce the required information.** For example, Cindi needs information about patients, visits, and invoices. Figure 2-1 shows the fields that satisfy these information requirements.

Figure 2-1 Cindi's data requirements

VisitID	InvoiceDate
PatientID	Reason
InvoiceAmt	Phone
FirstName	WalkIn
LastName	Email
Address	VisitDate
City	InvoiceNum
State	InvoicePaid
Zip	BirthDate

- **Organize each piece of data into its smallest useful part.** For example, Cindi could store each patient's complete name in one field called PatientName instead of using two fields called FirstName and LastName, as shown in Figure 2-1. However, doing so would make it more difficult to work with the data. If Cindi wanted to view the records in alphabetical order by last name, she wouldn't be able to do so with field values such as "Ben Li" and "Amanda Fox" stored in a PatientName field. She could do so with field values such as "Li" and "Fox" stored separately in a LastName field.
- **Group related fields into tables.** For example, Cindi grouped the fields related to visits into the Visit table, which you created in Tutorial 1. The fields related to invoices are grouped into the Billing table, and the fields related to patients are grouped into the Patient table. Figure 2-2 shows the fields grouped into all three tables for the Chatham database.

Figure 2-2 Cindi's fields grouped into tables

Visit table	Billing table	Patient table
VisitID	InvoiceNum	PatientID
PatientID	VisitID	LastName
VisitDate	InvoiceDate	FirstName
Reason	InvoiceAmt	BirthDate
WalkIn	InvoicePaid	Phone
		Address
		City
		State
		Zip
		Email

- **Determine each table's primary key.** Recall that a primary key uniquely identifies each record in a table. For some tables, one of the fields, such as a credit card number, naturally serves the function of a primary key. For other tables, two or more fields might be needed to function as the primary key. In these cases, the primary key is called a **composite key**. For example, a school grade table would use a combination of student number, term, and course code to serve as the primary key. For a third category of tables, no single field or combination of fields can uniquely identify a record in a table. In these cases, you need to add a field whose sole purpose is to serve as the table's primary key. For Cindi's tables, VisitID is the primary key for the Visit table, InvoiceNum is the primary key for the Billing table, and PatientID is the primary key for the Patient table.
- **Include a common field in related tables.** You use the common field to connect one table logically with another table. For example, Cindi's Visit and Patient tables include the PatientID field as a common field. Recall that when you include the primary key from one table as a field in a second table to form a relationship, the field in the second table is called a foreign key; therefore, the PatientID field is a foreign key in the Visit table. With this common field, Cindi can find all visits to the clinic made by a particular patient; she can use the PatientID value for a patient and search the Visit table for all records with that PatientID value. Likewise, she can determine which patient made a particular visit by searching the Patient table to find the one record with the same PatientID value as the corresponding value in the Visit table. Similarly, the VisitID field is a common field, serving as the primary key in the Visit table and a foreign key in the Billing table.
- **Avoid data redundancy.** When you store the same data in more than one place, **data redundancy** occurs. With the exception of common fields to connect tables, you should avoid data redundancy because it wastes storage space and can cause inconsistencies. An inconsistency would exist, for example, if you type a field value one way in one table and a different way in the same table or in a second table. Figure 2-3, which contains portions of potential data stored in the Patient and Visit tables, shows an example of incorrect database design that has data redundancy in the Visit table. In Figure 2-3, the LastName field in the Visit table is redundant, and one value for this field was entered incorrectly, in three different ways.

Figure 2-3 **Incorrect database design with data redundancy**

Patient table

PatientID	Last Name	FirstName	Address
22542	Diaz	Anna	93 Gates Ln
22544	Sutherland	Max	48 Vine St
22546	Ingram	Julia	834 Kiefer Rd
22560	Lewis	Patrice	15 Prince Rd
22561	Shaw	Daniel	33 Agnes Ct

data redundancy

Visit table

VisitID	PatientID	Last Name	VisitDate	WalkIn
1535	22546	Ingraham	11/12/2015	Yes
1570	22561	Shaw	1/11/2016	Yes
1571	22546	Ingrams	1/15/2016	No
1591	22544	Sutherland	1/26/2016	Yes
1601	22542	Diaz	2/2/2016	No
1620	22546	Engram	3/7/2016	No
1638	22560	Lewis	3/11/2016	Yes

inconsistent data

- **Determine the properties of each field.** You need to identify the **properties**, or characteristics, of each field so that the DBMS knows how to store, display, and process the field values. These properties include the field's name, data type, maximum number of characters or digits, description, valid values, and other field characteristics. You will learn more about field properties later in this tutorial.

The Billing and Patient tables you need to create will contain the fields shown in Figure 2-2. Before creating these new tables in the Chatham database, you first need to learn some guidelines for setting field properties.

Guidelines for Setting Field Properties

As just noted, the last step of database design is to determine which values to assign to the properties, such as the name and data type, of each field. When you select or enter a value for a property, you **set** the property. Access has rules for naming fields and objects, assigning data types, and setting other field properties.

Naming Fields and Objects

You must name each field, table, and other object in an Access database. Access stores these items in the database, using the names you supply. It's best to choose a field or object name that describes the purpose or contents of the field or object so that later you can easily remember what the name represents. For example, the three tables in the Chatham database are named Visit, Billing, and Patient because these names suggest their contents. Note that a table or query name must be unique within a database. A field name must be unique within a table, but it can be used again in another table.

Assigning Field Data Types

Each field must have a data type, which is either assigned automatically by Access or specifically by the table designer. The data type determines what field values you can enter for the field and what other properties the field will have. For example, the Billing table will include an InvoiceDate field, which will store date values, so you will assign the Date/Time data type to this field. Then Access will allow you to enter and manipulate only dates or times as values in the InvoiceDate field.

Figure 2-4 lists the most commonly used data types in Access, describes the field values allowed for each data type, explains when you should use each data type, and indicates the field size of each data type. You can find more complete information about all available data types in Access Help.

Figure 2-4 Common data types

Data Type	Description	Field Size
Short Text	Allows field values containing letters, digits, spaces, and special characters. Use for names, addresses, descriptions, and fields containing digits that are *not used in calculations*.	0 to 255 characters; default is 255
Long Text	Allows field values containing letters, digits, spaces, and special characters. Use for long comments and explanations.	1 to 65,535 characters; exact size is determined by entry
Number	Allows positive and negative numbers as field values. A number can contain digits, a decimal point, commas, a plus sign, and a minus sign. Use for fields that will be used in calculations, except those involving money.	1 to 15 digits
Date/Time	Allows field values containing valid dates and times from January 1, 100 to December 31, 9999. Dates can be entered in month/day/year format, several other date formats, or a variety of time formats, such as 10:35 PM. You can perform calculations on dates and times, and you can sort them. For example, you can determine the number of days between two dates.	8 bytes
Currency	Allows field values similar to those for the Number data type, but is used for storing monetary values. Unlike calculations with Number data type decimal values, calculations performed with the Currency data type are not subject to round-off error.	Accurate to 15 digits on the left side of the decimal point and to 4 digits on the right side
AutoNumber	Consists of integer values created automatically by Access each time you create a new record. You can specify sequential numbering or random numbering, which guarantees a unique field value, so that such a field can serve as a table's primary key.	9 digits
Yes/No	Limits field values to yes and no, on and off, or true and false. Use for fields that indicate the presence or absence of a condition, such as whether an order has been filled or whether an invoice has been paid.	1 character
Hyperlink	Consists of text used as a hyperlink address, which can have up to four parts: the text that appears in a field or control; the path to a file or page; a location within the file or page; and text displayed as a ScreenTip.	Up to 65,535 characters total for the four parts of the hyperlink

Setting Field Sizes

The **Field Size property** defines a field value's maximum storage size for Short Text, Number, and AutoNumber fields only. The other data types have no Field Size property because their storage size is either a fixed, predetermined amount or is determined automatically by the field value itself, as shown in Figure 2-4. A Short Text field has a default field size of 255 characters; you can also set its field size by entering a number from 0 to 255. For example, the FirstName and LastName fields in the Patient table will be Short Text fields with sizes of 20 characters and 25 characters, respectively. These field sizes will accommodate the values that will be entered in each of these fields.

PROSKILLS

Decision Making: Specifying the Field Size Property for Number Fields

When you use the Number data type to define a field, you need to decide what the Field Size setting should be for the field. You should set the Field Size property based on the largest value that you expect to store in that field. Access processes smaller data sizes faster, using less memory, so you can optimize your database's performance and its storage space by selecting the correct field size for each field. Field Size property settings for Number fields are as follows:

- **Byte**: Stores whole numbers (numbers with no fractions) from 0 to 255 in one byte
- **Integer**: Stores whole numbers from –32,768 to 32,767 in two bytes
- **Long Integer** (default): Stores whole numbers from –2,147,483,648 to 2,147,483,647 in four bytes
- **Single**: Stores positive and negative numbers to precisely seven decimal places in four bytes
- **Double**: Stores positive and negative numbers to precisely 15 decimal places in eight bytes
- **Replication ID**: Establishes a unique identifier for replication of tables, records, and other objects in databases created using Access 2003 and earlier versions in 16 bytes
- **Decimal**: Stores positive and negative numbers to precisely 28 decimal places in 12 bytes

Choosing an appropriate field size is important to optimize efficiency. For example, it would be wasteful to use the Long Integer field size for a Number field that will store only whole numbers ranging from 0 to 255 because the Long Integer field size uses four bytes of storage space. A better choice would be the Byte field size, which uses one byte of storage space to store the same values. By first gathering and analyzing information about the number values that will be stored in a Number field, you can make the best decision for the field's Field Size property and ensure the most efficient user experience for the database.

Setting the Caption Property for Fields

The **Caption property** for a field specifies how the field name is displayed in database objects, including table and query datasheets, forms, and reports. If you don't set the Caption property, Access displays the field name as the column heading or label for a field. For example, field names such as InvoiceAmt and InvoiceDate in the Billing table can be difficult to read. Setting the Caption property for these fields to "Invoice Amt" and "Invoice Date" would make it easier for users to read the field names and work with the database.

INSIGHT

Setting the Caption Property vs. Naming Fields

Although Access allows you to include spaces in field names, this practice is not recommended because the spaces cause problems when you try to perform more complex tasks with the data in your database. Setting the Caption property allows you to follow best practices for naming fields, such as not including spaces in field names, while still providing users with more readable field names in datasheets, forms, and reports.

In Tutorial 1, you created the Chatham database file and, within that file, you created the Visit table working in Datasheet view. According to her plan for the Chatham database, Cindi also wants to track information about the invoices the clinic sends to its patients. Next, you'll create the Billing table for Cindi—this time, working in Design view.

Creating a Table in Design View

Creating a table in Design view involves entering the field names and defining the properties for the fields, specifying a primary key for the table, and then saving the table structure. Cindi documented the design for the new Billing table by listing each field's name and data type; each field's size and description (if applicable); and any other properties to be set for each field. See Figure 2-5.

Figure 2-5 **Design for the Billing table**

Field Name	Data Type	Field Size	Description	Other
InvoiceNum	Short Text	5	Primary key	Caption = Invoice Num
VisitID	Short Text	4	Foreign key	Caption = Visit ID
InvoiceAmt	Currency			Format = Currency Decimal Places = 2 Caption = Invoice Amt
InvoiceDate	Date/Time			Format = mm/dd/yyyy Caption = Invoice Date
InvoicePaid	Yes/No			Caption = Invoice Paid

You'll use Cindi's design as a guide for creating the Billing table in the Chatham database.

To begin creating the Billing table:

1. Start Access and open the **Chatham** database you created in Tutorial 1.

   Trouble? If the security warning is displayed below the ribbon, click the Enable Content button.

2. If the Navigation Pane is open, click the **Shutter Bar Open/Close Button** « to close it.
3. On the ribbon, click the **CREATE** tab.
4. In the Tables group, click the **Table Design** button. A new table named Table1 opens in Design view. Refer to the Session 2.1 Visual Overview for a complete description of the Table window in Design view.

Defining Fields

When you first create a table in Design view, the insertion point is located in the first row's Field Name box, ready for you to begin defining the first field in the table. You enter values for the Field Name, Data Type, and Description field properties, and then select values for all other field properties in the Field Properties pane. These other properties will appear when you move to the first row's Data Type box.

REFERENCE

Defining a Field in Design View

- In the Field Name box, type the name for the field, and then press the Tab key.
- Accept the default Short Text data type, or click the arrow and select a different data type for the field. Press the Tab key.
- Enter an optional description for the field, if necessary.
- Use the Field Properties pane to type or select other field properties, as appropriate.

The first field you need to define is the InvoiceNum field. This field will be the primary key for the Billing table. Each invoice at Chatham Community Health Services is assigned a specific five-digit number. Although the InvoiceNum field will contain these number values, the numbers will never be used in calculations; therefore, you'll assign the Short Text data type to this field. Any time a field contains number values that will not be used in calculations—such as phone numbers, zip codes, and so on—you should use the Short Text data type instead of the Number data type.

To define the InvoiceNum field:

TIP

You can also press the Enter key to move from one property to the next in the Table Design grid.

1. Type **InvoiceNum** in the first row's Field Name box, and then press the **Tab** key to advance to the Data Type box. The default data type, Short Text, appears highlighted in the Data Type box, which now also contains an arrow, and the field properties for a Short Text field appear in the Field Properties pane. See Figure 2-6.

Figure 2-6 Table window after entering the first field name

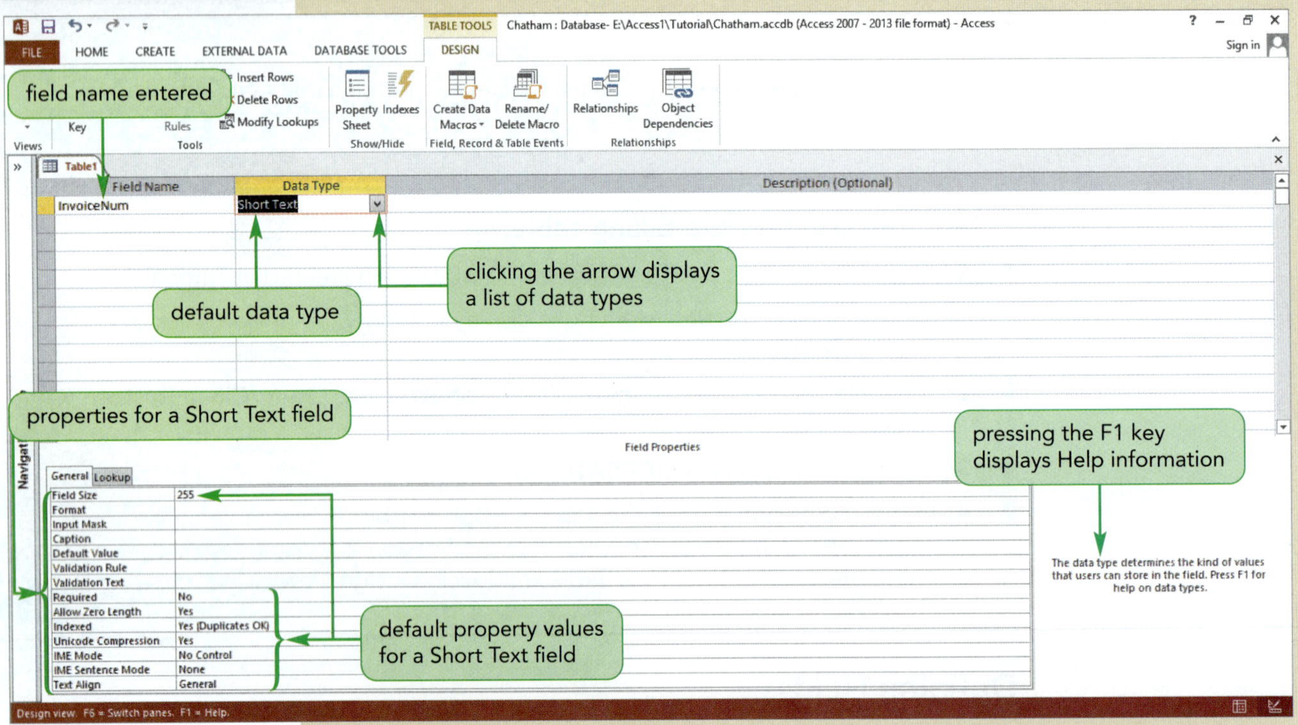

Notice that the right side of the Field Properties pane now provides an explanation for the current property, Data Type.

Trouble? If you make a typing error, you can correct it by clicking to position the insertion point, and then using either the Backspace key to delete characters to the left of the insertion point or the Delete key to delete characters to the right of the insertion point. Then type the correct text.

Because the InvoiceNum field values will not be used in calculations, you will accept the default Short Text data type for the field.

2. Press the **Tab** key to accept Short Text as the data type and to advance to the Description (Optional) box.

Next you'll enter the Description property value as "Primary key." The value you enter for the Description property will appear on the status bar when you view the table datasheet. Note that specifying "Primary key" for the Description property does *not* establish the current field as the primary key; you use a button on the ribbon to specify the primary key in Design view, which you will do later in this session.

3. Type **Primary key** in the Description (Optional) box.

   Notice the Field Size property for the field. The default setting of 255 for Short Text fields is displayed. You need to change this number to 5 because all invoice numbers at Chatham Community Health Services contain only five digits.

4. Double-click the number **255** in the Field Size property box to select it, and then type **5**.

   Finally, you need to set the Caption property for the field so that its name appears with a space, as "Invoice Num."

5. Click the **Caption** property box, and then type **Invoice Num**. The definition of the first field is complete. See Figure 2-7.

Figure 2-7 **InvoiceNum field defined**

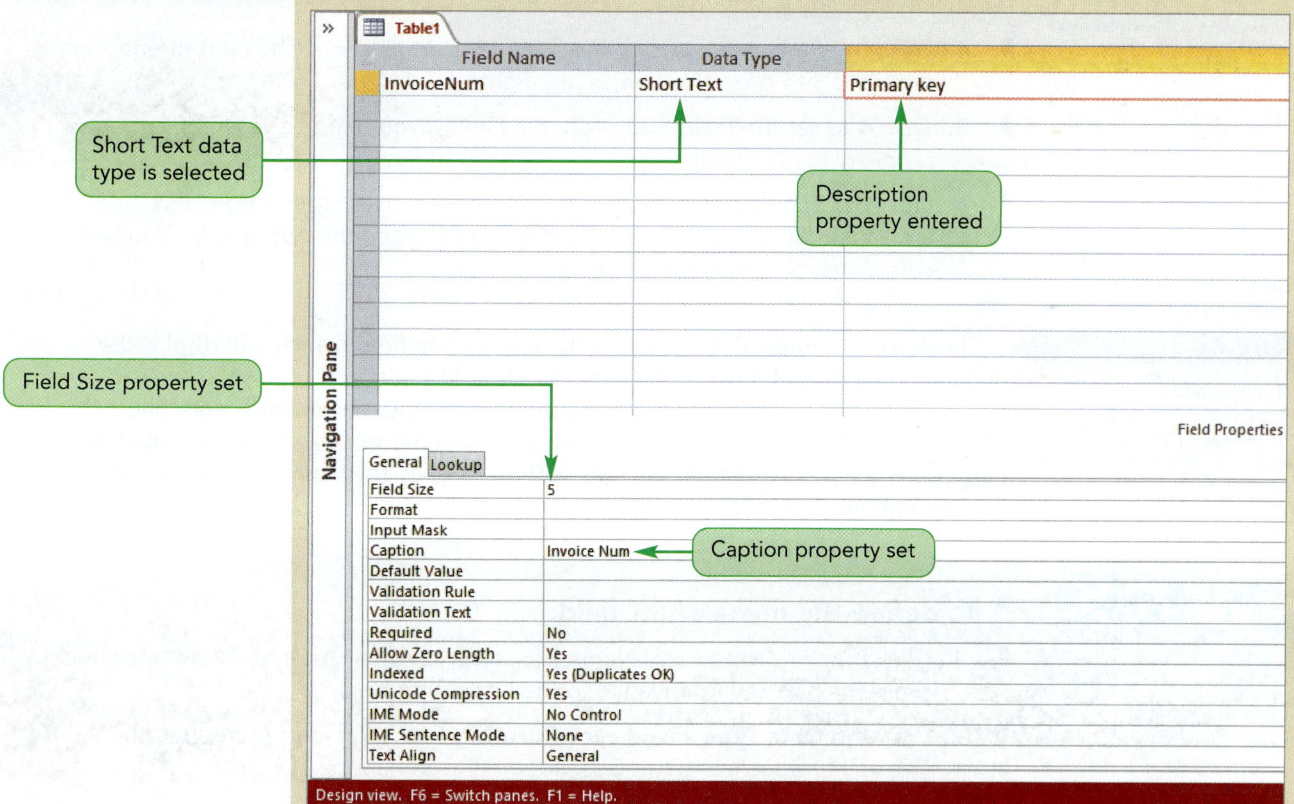

Cindi's Billing table design (Figure 2-5) shows VisitID as the second field. Because Cindi and other staff members need to relate information about invoices to the visit data in the Visit table, the Billing table must include the VisitID field, which is the Visit table's primary key. Recall that when you include the primary key from one table as a field in a second table to connect the two tables, the field is a foreign key in the second table. The field must be defined in the same way in both tables—that is, the field properties, including field size and data type, must match exactly.

Next, you will define VisitID as a Short Text field with a field size of 4. Later in this session, you'll change the Field Size property for the VisitID field in the Visit table to 4 so that the field definition is the same in both tables.

To define the VisitID field:

1. In the Table Design grid, click the second row's Field Name box, type **VisitID** in the box, and then press the **Tab** key to advance to the Data Type box.
2. Press the **Tab** key to accept Short Text as the field's data type. Because the VisitID field is a foreign key to the Visit table, you'll enter "Foreign key" in the Description (Optional) box to help users of the database understand the purpose of this field.
3. Type **Foreign key** in the Description (Optional) box. Next, you'll change the Field Size property to 4.
4. Press the **F6** key to move to the Field Properties pane. The current entry for the Field Size property, 255, is highlighted.
5. Type **4** to set the Field Size property. Finally, you need to set the Caption property for this field.
6. Press the **Tab** key until the insertion point is in the Caption box, and then type **Visit ID** (be sure to include a space between the two words). You have completed the definition of the second field.

TIP

The quickest way to move back to the Table Design grid is to use the mouse.

The third field in the Billing table is the InvoiceAmt field, which will display the dollar amount of each invoice the clinic sends to its patients. Cindi wants the values to appear with two decimal places because invoice amounts include cents. She also wants the values to include dollar signs, so that the values will be formatted as currency when they are printed in bills sent to patients. The Currency data type is the appropriate choice for this field.

To define the InvoiceAmt field:

1. Click the third row's Field Name box, type **InvoiceAmt** in the box, and then press the **Tab** key to advance to the Data Type box.
2. Click the **Data Type** arrow, click **Currency** in the list, and then press the **Tab** key to advance to the Description (Optional) box.

   According to Cindi's design (Figure 2-5), you do not need to enter a description for this field. If you've assigned a descriptive field name and the field does not fulfill a special function (such as primary key), you usually do not enter a value for the optional Description property. InvoiceAmt is a field that does not require a value for its Description property.

   Cindi wants the InvoiceAmt field values to be displayed with two decimal places. The **Decimal Places property** specifies the number of decimal places that are displayed to the right of the decimal point.

TIP

You can display the arrow and the list simultaneously by clicking the right side of a box.

3. In the Field Properties pane, click the **Decimal Places** box to position the insertion point there. An arrow appears on the right side of the Decimal Places box. When you position the insertion point or select text in many boxes, Access displays an arrow, which you can click to display a list with options.
4. Click the **Decimal Places** arrow, and then click **2** in the list to specify two decimal places for the InvoiceAmt field values.
5. Press the **Tab** key until the insertion point is in the Caption box, and then type **Invoice Amt**. The definition of the third field is now complete. See Figure 2-8.

Figure 2-8 **Table window after defining the first three fields**

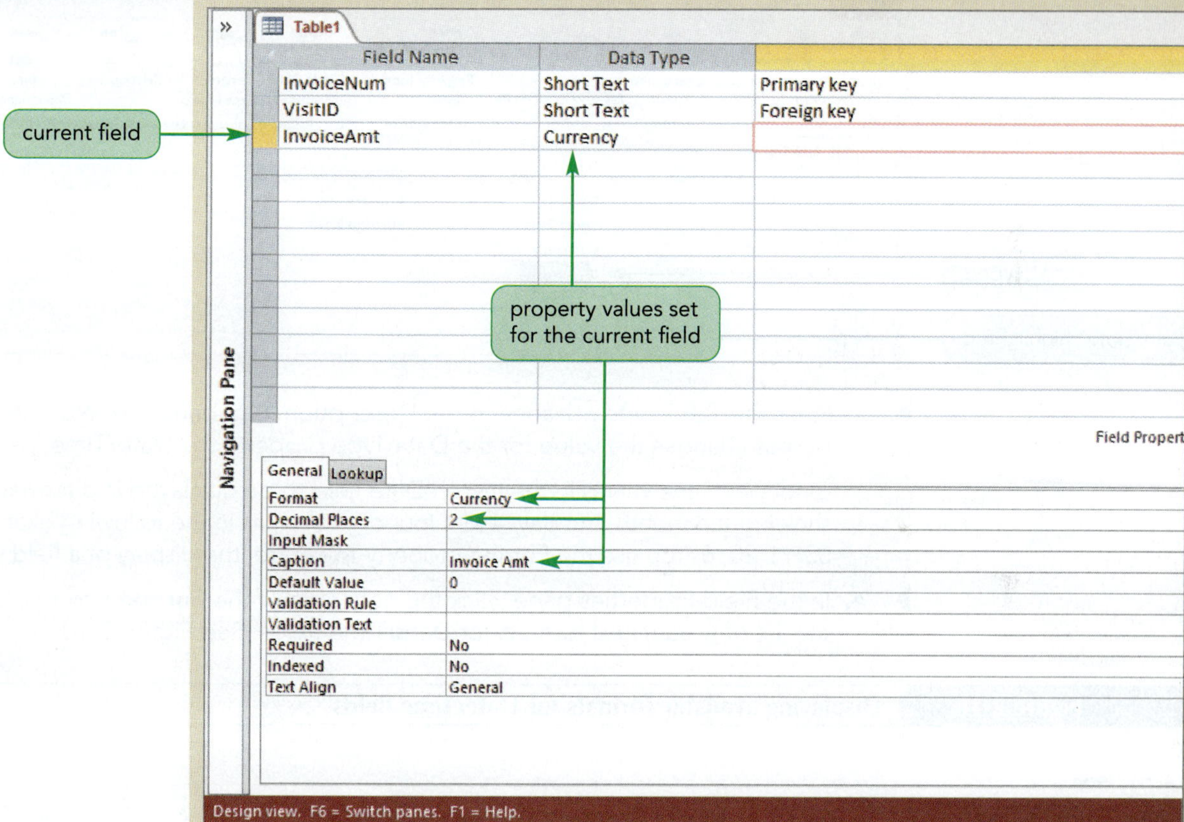

Notice that the Format property is set to "Currency," which formats the values with dollar signs.

The fourth field in the Billing table is the InvoiceDate field. This field will contain the dates on which invoices are generated for the clinic's patients. You'll define the InvoiceDate field using the Date/Time data type. Also, according to Cindi's design (Figure 2-5), the date values should be displayed in the format mm/dd/yyyy, which is a two-digit month, a two-digit day, and a four-digit year.

To define the InvoiceDate field:

1. Click the fourth row's Field Name box, type **InvoiceDate**, and then press the **Tab** key to advance to the Data Type box.

   You can select a value from the Data Type list as you did for the InvoiceAmt field. Alternately, you can type the property value in the box or type just the first character of the property value.

2. Type **d**. The value in the fourth row's Data Type box changes to "date/Time," with the letters "ate/Time" highlighted. See Figure 2-9.

Figure 2-9 Selecting a value for the Data Type property

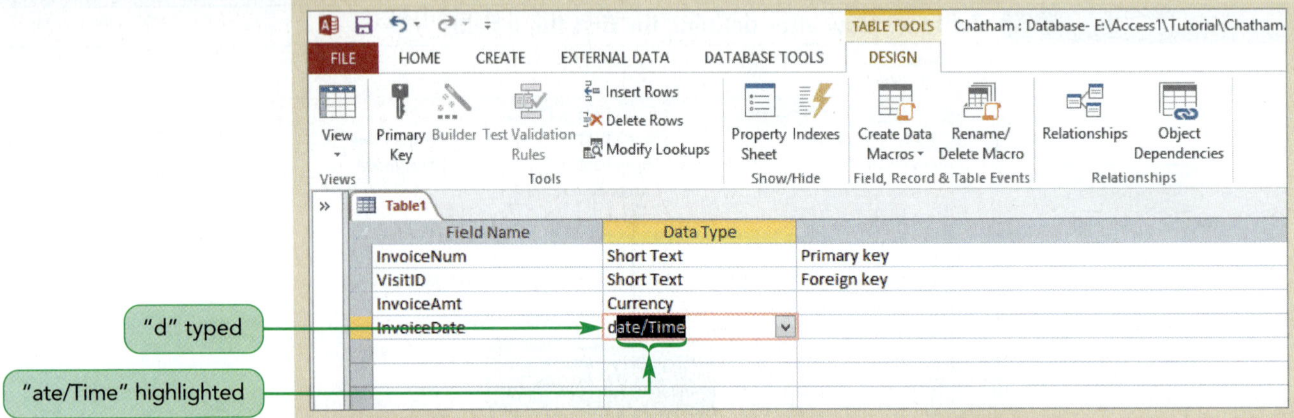

3. Press the **Tab** key to advance to the Description (Optional) box. Note that Access changes the value for the Data Type property to "Date/Time."

   Cindi wants the values in the InvoiceDate field to be displayed in a format showing the month, the day, and a four-digit year, as in the following example: 03/11/2016. You use the Format property to control the display of a field value.

4. In the Field Properties pane, click the right side of the **Format** box to display the list of predefined formats for Date/Time fields. See Figure 2-10.

Figure 2-10 Displaying available formats for Date/Time fields

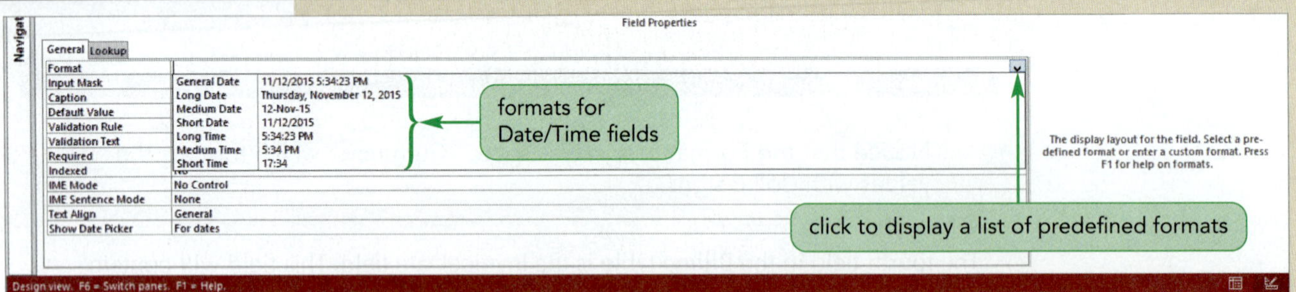

Trouble? If you see an arrow instead of a list of predefined formats, click the arrow to display the list.

As noted in the right side of the Field Properties pane, you can either choose a predefined format or enter a custom format. Even though the Short Date format seems to match the format Cindi wants, it displays only one digit for months that contain only one digit. For example, it would display the month of March with only the digit "3"—as in 3/11/2016—instead of displaying the month with two digits, as in 03/11/2016.

Because none of the predefined formats matches the exact layout Cindi wants for the InvoiceDate values, you need to create a custom date format. Figure 2-11 shows some of the symbols available for custom date and time formats.

Figure 2-11 Symbols for some custom date formats

Symbol	Description
/	date separator
d	day of the month in one or two numeric digits, as needed (1 to 31)
dd	day of the month in two numeric digits (01 to 31)
ddd	first three letters of the weekday (Sun to Sat)
dddd	full name of the weekday (Sunday to Saturday)
w	day of the week (1 to 7)
ww	week of the year (1 to 53)
m	month of the year in one or two numeric digits, as needed (1 to 12)
mm	month of the year in two numeric digits (01 to 12)
mmm	first three letters of the month (Jan to Dec)
mmmm	full name of the month (January to December)
yy	last two digits of the year (01 to 99)
yyyy	full year (0100 to 9999)

Cindi wants the dates to be displayed with a two-digit month (mm), a two-digit day (dd), and a four-digit year (yyyy). You'll enter this custom format now.

5. Click the **Format** arrow to close the list of predefined formats, and then type **mm/dd/yyyy** in the Format box.
6. Press the **Tab** key until the insertion point is in the Caption box, and then type **Invoice Date**. See Figure 2-12.

Figure 2-12 Specifying the custom date format

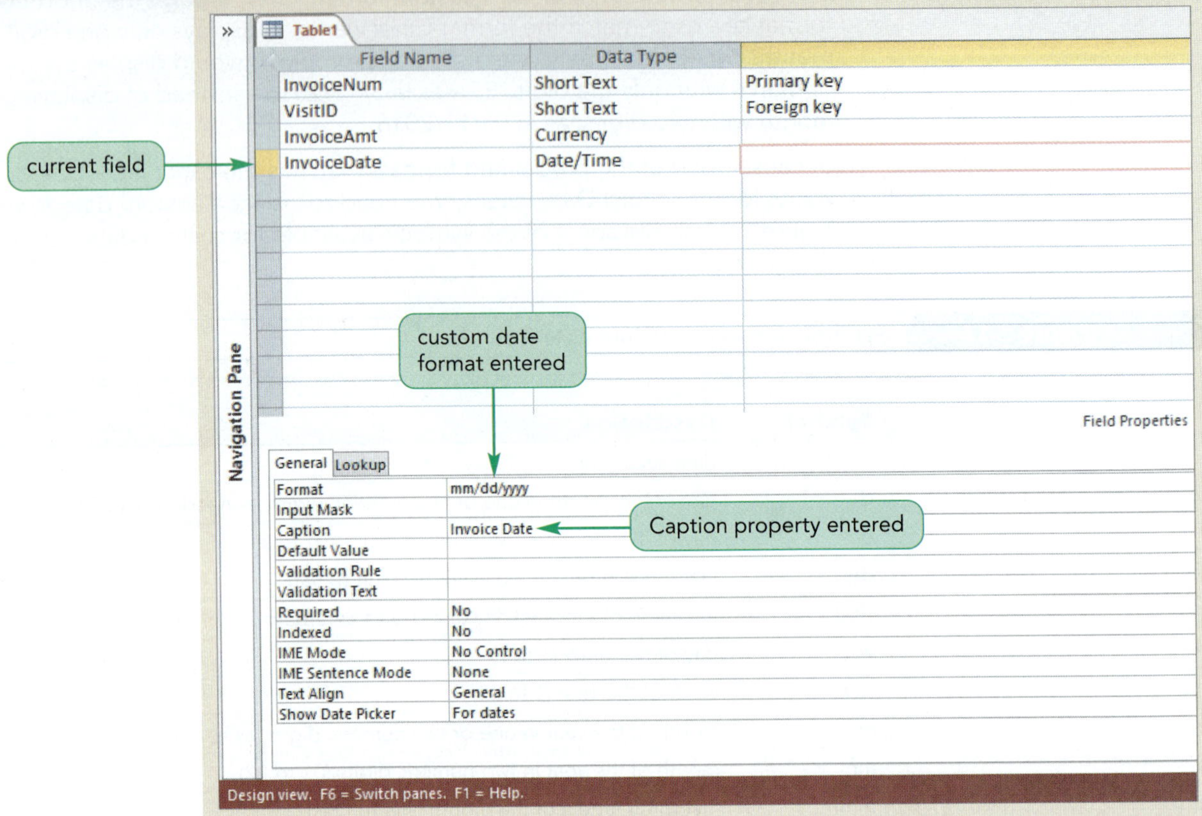

The fifth, and final, field to be defined in the Billing table is InvoicePaid. This field will be a Yes/No field to indicate the payment status of each invoice record stored in the Billing table. Recall that the Yes/No data type is used to define fields that store true/false, yes/no, and on/off field values. When you create a Yes/No field in a table, the default Format property is set to Yes/No.

To define the InvoicePaid field:

1. Click the fifth row's Field Name box, type **InvoicePaid**, and then press the **Tab** key to advance to the Data Type box.
2. Type **y**. Access completes the data type as "yes/No."
3. Press the **Tab** key to select the Yes/No data type and move to the Description (Optional) box. In the Field Properties pane, note that the default format of "Yes/No" is selected, so you do not have to change this property.
4. In the Field Properties pane, click the Caption box, and then type **Invoice Paid**.

You've finished defining the fields for the Billing table. Next, you need to specify the primary key for the table.

Specifying the Primary Key

As you learned earlier, the primary key for a table uniquely identifies each record in the table.

REFERENCE

Specifying a Primary Key in Design View

- Display the table in Design view.
- Click in the row for the field you've chosen to be the primary key to make it the active field. If the primary key will consist of two or more fields, click the row selector for the first field, press and hold down the Ctrl key, and then click the row selector for each additional primary key field.
- In the Tools group on the DESIGN tab, click the Primary Key button.

According to Cindi's design, you need to specify InvoiceNum as the primary key for the Billing table. You can do so while the table is in Design view.

To specify InvoiceNum as the primary key:

1. Click in the row for the InvoiceNum field to make it the current field.
2. In the Tools group on the DESIGN tab, click the **Primary Key** button. The Primary Key button in the Tools group is now highlighted, and a key symbol appears in the row selector for the first row, indicating that the InvoiceNum field is the table's primary key. See Figure 2-13.

TIP

This button is a toggle; you can click it to remove the key symbol.

Figure 2-13 InvoiceNum field selected as the primary key

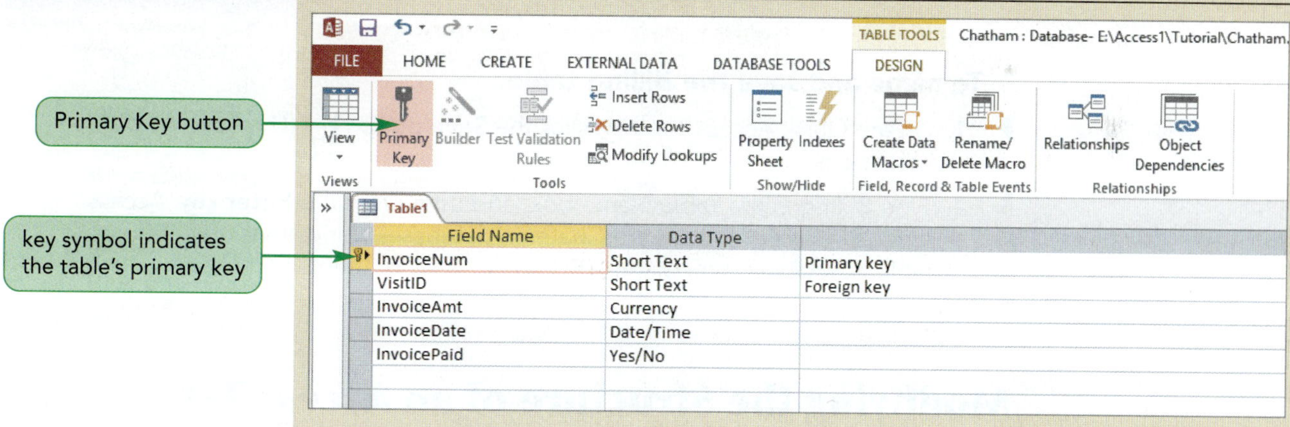

INSIGHT

Understanding the Importance of the Primary Key

Although Access does not require a table to have a primary key, including a primary key offers several advantages:

- A primary key uniquely identifies each record in a table.
- Access does not allow duplicate values in the primary key field. For example, if a record already exists in the Visit table with a VisitID value of 1550, Access prevents you from adding another record with this same value in the VisitID field. Preventing duplicate values ensures the uniqueness of the primary key field.
- When a primary key has been specified, Access forces you to enter a value for the primary key field in every record in the table. This is known as **entity integrity**. If you do not enter a value for a field, you have actually given the field a **null value**. You cannot give a null value to the primary key field because entity integrity prevents Access from accepting and processing that record.
- You can enter records in any order, but Access displays them by default in order of the primary key's field values. If you enter records in no specific order, you are ensured that you will later be able to work with them in a more meaningful, primary key sequence.
- Access responds faster to your requests for specific records based on the primary key.

Saving the Table Structure

The last step in creating a table is to name the table and save the table's structure. When you save a table structure, the table is stored in the database file (in this case, the Chatham database file). Once the table is saved, you can enter data into it. According to Cindi's plan, you need to save the table you've defined as "Billing."

To name and save the Billing table:

1. On the Quick Access Toolbar, click the **Save** button. The Save As dialog box opens.
2. Type **Billing** in the Table Name box, and then press the **Enter** key. Access saves the Billing table in the Chatham database. Notice that the tab for the table now displays the name "Billing" instead of "Table1."

Modifying the Structure of an Access Table

Even a well-designed table might need to be modified. Some changes that you can make to a table's structure in Design view include changing the order of fields and adding new fields.

After meeting with her assistant, Kelly Schwarz, and reviewing the structure of the Billing table, Cindi has changes she wants you to make to the table. First, she wants the InvoiceAmt field to be moved so that it appears right before the InvoicePaid field. Then, she wants you to add a new Short Text field named InvoiceItem to the table to include information about what the invoice is for, such as office visits, lab work, and so on. Cindi would like the InvoiceItem field to be inserted between the InvoiceDate and InvoiceAmt fields.

Moving a Field in Design View

To move a field, you use the mouse to drag it to a new location in the Table Design grid. Although you can move a field in Datasheet view by dragging its column heading to a new location, doing so rearranges only the *display* of the table's fields; the table structure is not changed. To move a field permanently, you must move the field in Design view.

Next, you'll move the InvoiceAmt field so that it is before the InvoicePaid field in the Billing table.

To move the InvoiceAmt field:

1. Position the pointer on the row selector for the InvoiceAmt field until the pointer changes to a ➡ shape.
2. Click the **row selector** to select the entire InvoiceAmt row.
3. Place the pointer on the row selector for the InvoiceAmt field until the pointer changes to ⇖, and then click and drag to the row selector for the InvoicePaid field. Notice that as you drag, the pointer changes to ⇖. See Figure 2-14.

Figure 2-14 Moving the InvoiceAmt field in the table structure

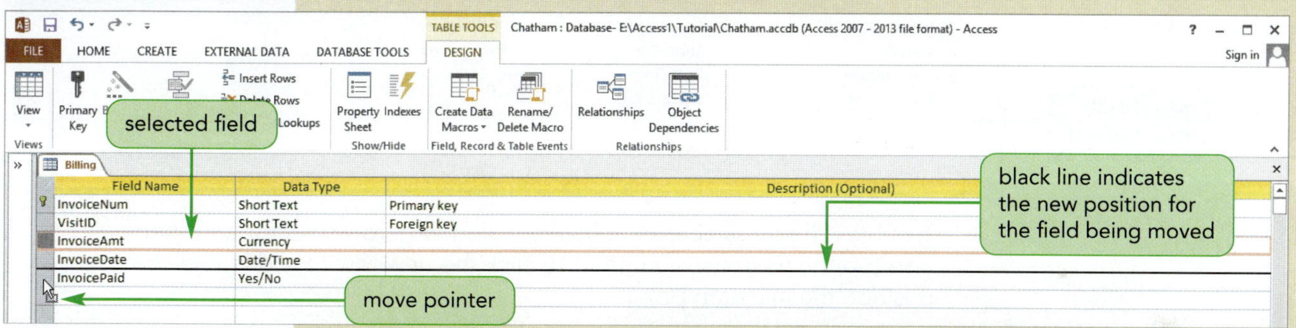

4. Release the mouse button. The InvoiceAmt field now appears between the InvoiceDate and InvoicePaid fields in the table structure.

   Trouble? If the InvoiceAmt field did not move, repeat Steps 1 through 4, making sure you hold down the mouse button during the drag operation.

Adding a Field in Design View

To add a new field between existing fields, you must insert a row. You begin by selecting the row below where you want the new field to be inserted.

REFERENCE

Adding a Field Between Two Existing Fields

- In the Table window in Design view, select the row below where you want the new field to be inserted.
- In the Tools group on the DESIGN tab, click the Insert Rows button.
- Define the new field by entering the field name, data type, optional description, and any property specifications.

Next, you need to add the InvoiceItem field to the Billing table structure between the InvoiceAmt and InvoicePaid fields.

To add the InvoiceItem field to the Billing table:

1. Click the **InvoicePaid** Field Name box. You need to establish this field as the current field so that the row for the new record will be inserted above this field.
2. In the Tools group on the DESIGN tab, click the **Insert Rows** button. Access adds a new, blank row between the InvoiceAmt and InvoicePaid fields. The insertion point is positioned in the Field Name box for the new row, ready for you to type the name for the new field. See Figure 2-15.

Figure 2-15 Table structure after inserting a row

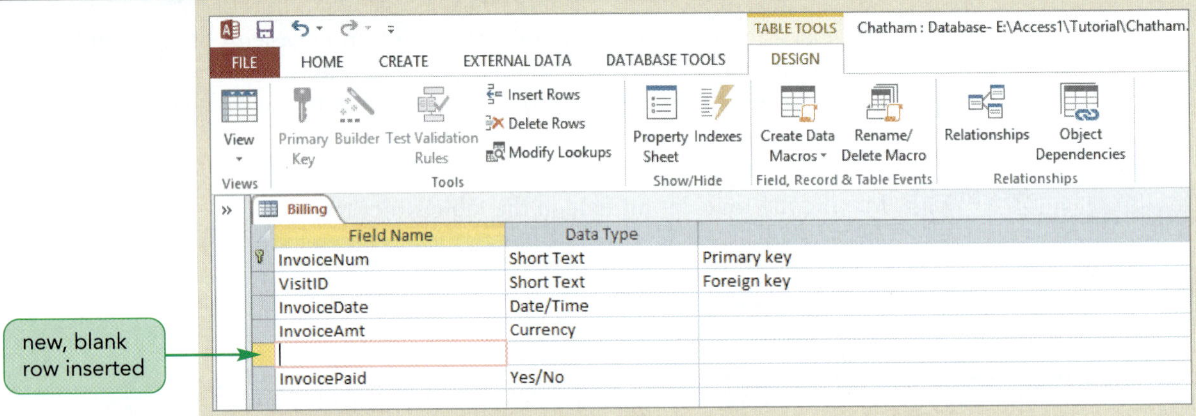

Trouble? If you selected the InvoicePaid field's row selector and then inserted the new row, you need to click the new row's Field Name box to position the insertion point in it.

You'll define the InvoiceItem field in the new row of the Billing table. This field will be a Short Text field with a field size of 40, and you need to set the Caption property to include a space between the words in the field name.

3. Type **InvoiceItem**, press the **Tab** key to move to the Data Type property, and then press the **Tab** key again to accept the default Short Text data type.
4. Press the **F6** key to move to the Field Size box and to select the default field size, and then type **40**.
5. Press the **Tab** key until the insertion point is in the Caption box, and then type **Invoice Item**. The definition of the new field is complete. See Figure 2-16.

Figure 2-16 **InvoiceItem field added to the Billing table**

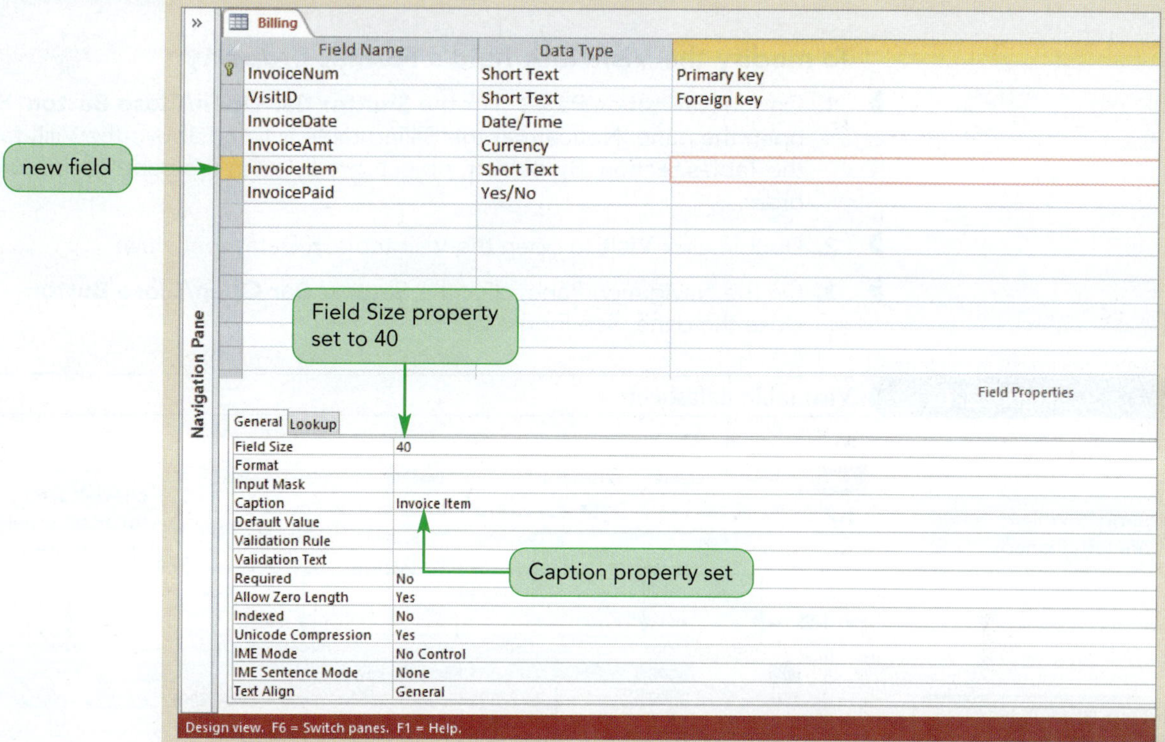

6. On the Quick Access Toolbar, click the **Save** button to save the changes to the Billing table structure.
7. Click the **Close 'Billing'** button on the object tab to close the Billing table.

Modifying Field Properties

With the Billing table design complete, you can now go back and modify the properties of the fields in the Visit table you created in Tutorial 1, as necessary. You can make some changes to properties in Datasheet view; for others, you'll work in Design view.

Changing the Format Property in Datasheet View

The Formatting group on the FIELDS tab in Datasheet view allows you to modify some formatting for certain field types. When you format a field, you change the way data is displayed, but not the actual values stored in the table.

Next, you'll check the properties of the VisitDate field in the Visit table to see if any changes are needed to improve the display of the date values.

To modify the VisitDate field's Format property:

1. On the Navigation Pane, click the **Shutter Bar Open/Close Button** » to open the pane. Notice that the Billing table is listed above the Visit table in the Tables section. By default, objects are listed in the pane in alphabetical order.
2. Double-click **Visit** to open the Visit table in Datasheet view.
3. On the Navigation Pane, click the **Shutter Bar Open/Close Button** « to close the pane. See Figure 2-17.

Figure 2-17 Visit table datasheet

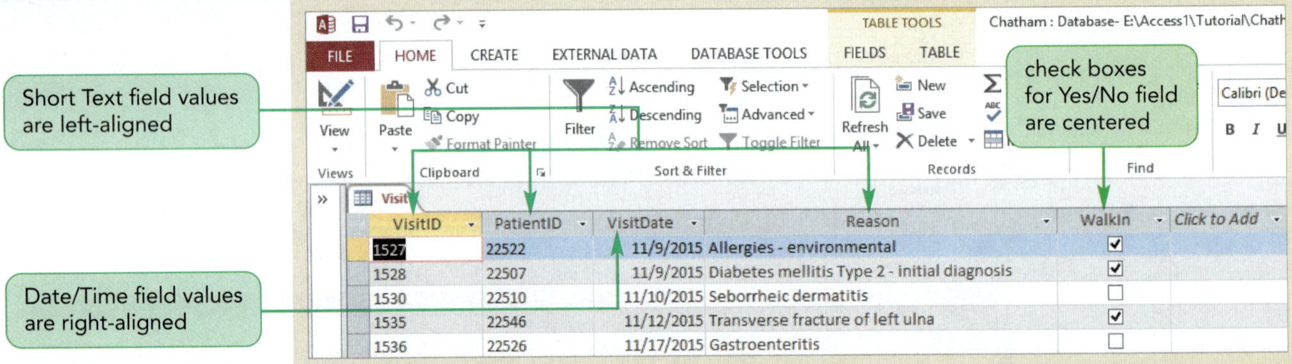

Notice that the values in the three Short Text fields—VisitID, PatientID, and Reason—appear left-aligned within their boxes, and the values in the Date/Time field (VisitDate) appear right-aligned. In Access, values for Short Text fields are left-aligned, and values for Number, Date/Time, and Currency fields are right-aligned. The WalkIn field is a Yes/No field, so its values appear in check boxes that are centered within the column.

4. On the ribbon, click the **FIELDS** tab.
5. Click the first field value in the VisitDate column. The Data Type option shows that this field is a Date/Time field.

   By default, Access assigns the General Date format to Date/Time fields. Note the Format option in the Formatting group; this is the same as the Format property in the Field Properties pane in Design view. Even though the Format box is empty, the VisitDate field has the General Date format applied to it. The General Date format includes settings for date or time values, or a combination of date and time values. However, Cindi wants *only date values* to be displayed in the VisitDate field, so she asks you to specify the Short Date format for the field.
6. In the Formatting group, click the **Format arrow**, and then click **Short Date**. See Figure 2-18.

Figure 2-18 VisitDate field after modifying the format

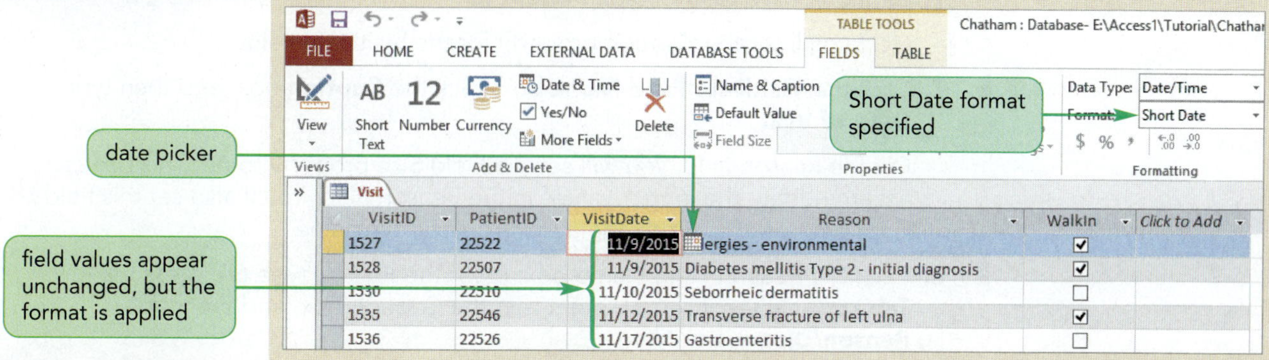

> **TIP**
>
> When working with date values, you can type dates directly or click the date picker shown in Figure 2-18 to select a date from an interactive calendar.

Although no change is apparent in the worksheet—the VisitDate field values already appear with the Short Date setting (for example, 11/9/2015), as part of the default General Date format—the field now has the Short Date format applied to it. This ensures that only date field values, and not time or date/time values, are allowed in the field.

Changing Properties in Design View

Recall that each of the Short Text fields in the Visit table—VisitID, PatientID, and Reason—still has the default field size of 255, which is too large for the data contained in these fields. Also, the VisitID and PatientID fields need descriptions to identify them as the primary and foreign keys, respectively, in the table. Finally, each of these fields needs a caption either to include a space between the words in the field name or to make the name more descriptive. You can make all of these property changes more easily in Design view.

> **TIP**
>
> You can also click the Design View button in the far right of the status bar to switch to Design view.

To modify the Field Size, Description, and Caption field properties:

1. In the Views group on the FIELDS tab, click the **View** button. The table is displayed in Design view with the VisitID field selected. You need to enter a Description property value for this field, the primary key in the table, and change its Field Size property to 4 because each visit number at Chatham Community Health Services consists of four digits.
2. Press the **Tab** key until the insertion point is in the Description (Optional) box, and then type **Primary key**.
3. Press the **F6** key to move to and select the default setting of 255 for the Field Size property, and then type **4**. Next you need to set the Caption property for this field.
4. Press the **Tab** key until the insertion point is in the Caption box, and then type **Visit ID**.

   Next you need to enter a Description property value for the PatientID field, a foreign key in the table, and set its Field Size property to 5 because each PatientID number at Chatham Community Health Services consists of five digits. You also need to set this field's Caption property.
5. Click the **Description (Optional)** box for the PatientID field, and then type **Foreign key**.

6. Press the **F6** key, type **5**, press the **Tab** key until the insertion point is in the Caption box, and then type **Patient ID**.

   Next you'll set the Caption property for the VisitDate field.

7. Click the **VisitDate** Field Name box, click the **Caption** box, and then type **Date of Visit**.

   For the Reason field, you will set the Field Size property to 60. This size can accommodate the longer values in the Reason field. You'll also set this field's Caption property to provide a more descriptive name.

8. Click the **Reason** Field Name box, press the **F6** key, type **60**, press the **Tab** key until the insertion point is in the Caption box, and then type **Reason/Diagnosis**.

   Finally, you'll set the Caption property for the WalkIn field.

9. Click the **WalkIn** Field Name box, click the **Caption** box, and then type **Walk-in?** See Figure 2-19.

Figure 2-19 Visit table after modifying field properties

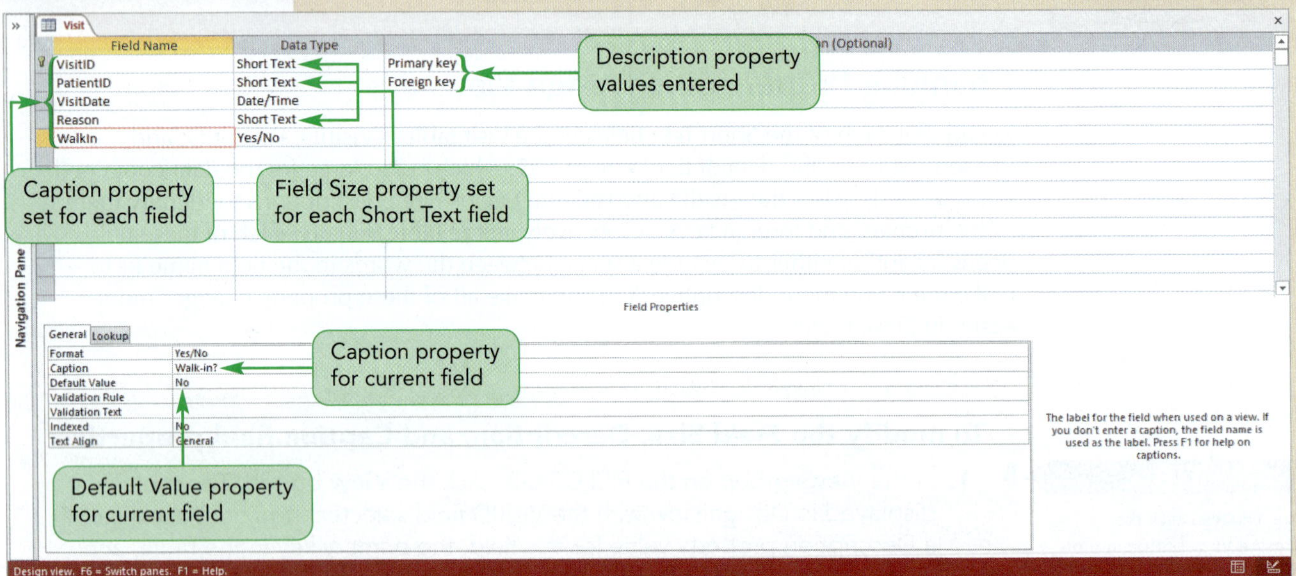

Notice that the WalkIn field's Default Value property is automatically set to "No," which means the check box for this field will be empty for each new record. This is the default for this property for any Yes/No field. You can set the Default Value property for other types of fields to make data entry easier. You'll learn more about setting this property in the next session.

The changes to the Visit table's properties are now complete, so you can save the table and view the results of your changes in Datasheet view.

To save and view the modified Visit table:

1. On the Quick Access Toolbar, click the **Save** button to save the modified table. A dialog box opens informing you that some data may be lost because you decreased the field sizes. Because all of the values in the VisitID, PatientID, and Reason fields contain the same number of or fewer characters than the new Field Size properties you set for each field, you can ignore this message.
2. Click the **Yes** button.
3. In the Views group on the DESIGN tab, click the **View** button to display the Visit table in Datasheet view. Notice that each column (field) heading now displays the text you specified in the Caption property for that field. See Figure 2-20.

Figure 2-20 Modified Visit table in Datasheet view

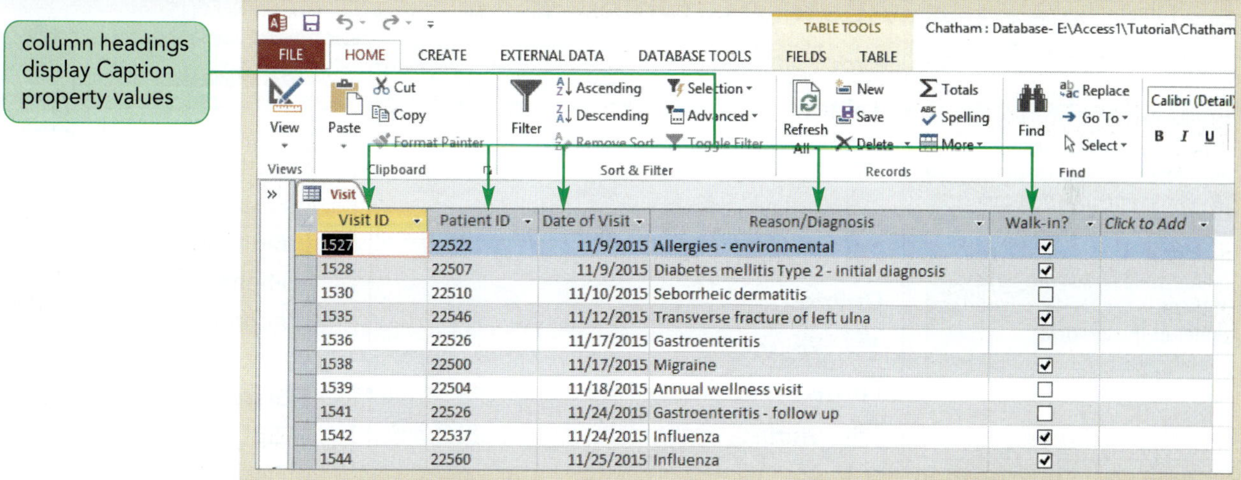

4. Click the **Close 'Visit'** button on the object tab to close the Visit table.
5. If you are not continuing to Session 2.2, click the **FILE** tab, and then click **Close** in the navigation bar to close the Chatham database.

You have created the Billing table and made modifications to its design. In the next session, you'll add records to the Billing table and create the Patient table in the Chatham database.

REVIEW

Session 2.1 Quick Check

1. What guidelines should you follow when designing a database?
2. What is the purpose of the Data Type property for a field?
3. The ____________ property specifies how a field's name is displayed in database objects, including table and query datasheets, forms, and reports.
4. For which three types of fields can you assign a field size?
5. The default Field Size property setting for a Short Text field is ____________.
6. In Design view, which key do you press to move from the Table Design grid to the Field Properties pane?
7. List three reasons why you should specify a primary key for an Access table.

Session 2.2 Visual Overview:

Click the Close button to close the Relationships window.

You click the Show Table button to open the Show Table dialog box. From there, you can choose a table to add to the Relationships window.

The Relationships window illustrates the relationships among a database's tables. Using this window, you can view or change existing relationships, define new relationships between tables, and rearrange the layout of the tables in the window.

The key symbol next to a field name indicates that the field is the table's primary key. For example, PatientID is the primary key for the Patient table.

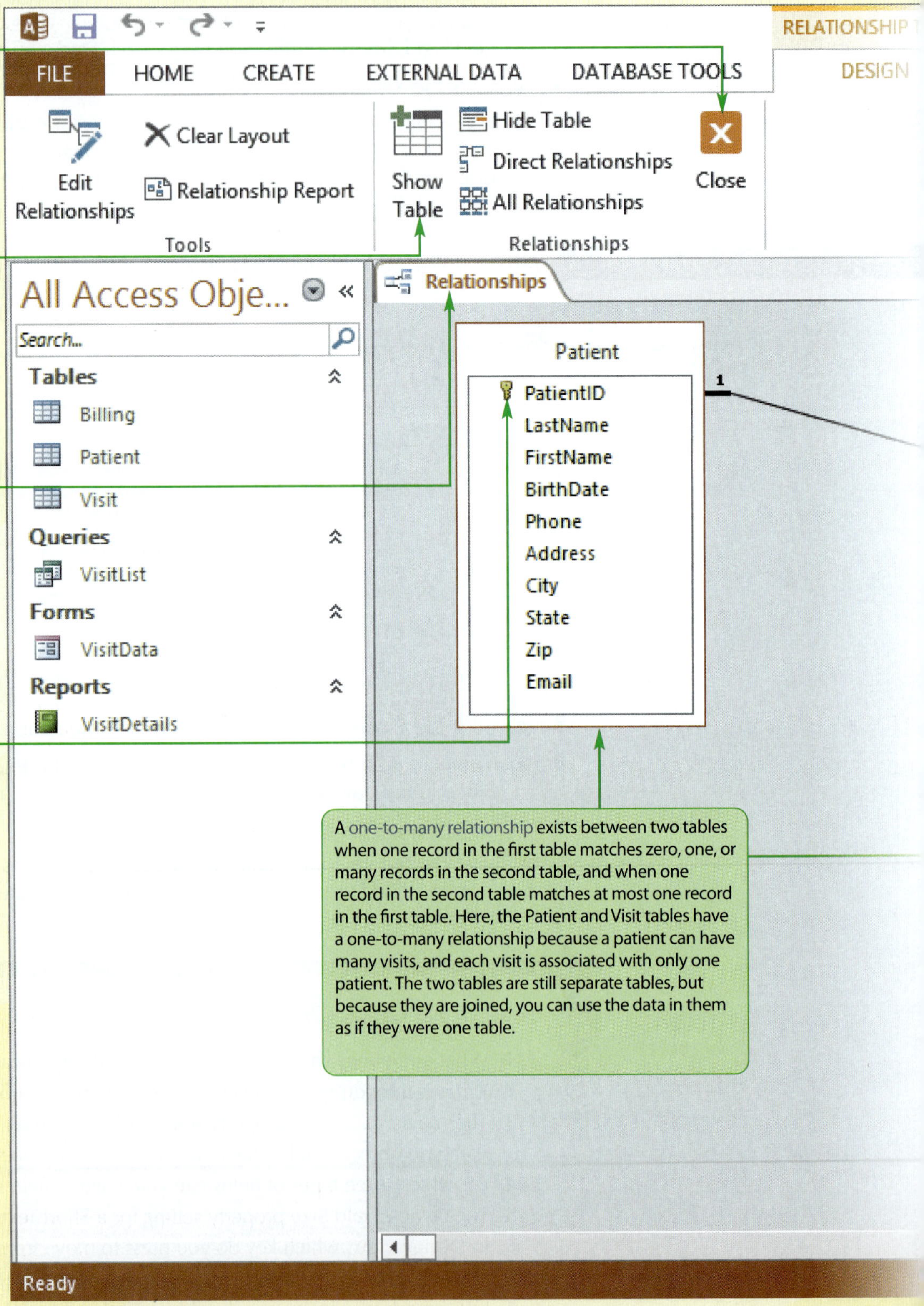

A one-to-many relationship exists between two tables when one record in the first table matches zero, one, or many records in the second table, and when one record in the second table matches at most one record in the first table. Here, the Patient and Visit tables have a one-to-many relationship because a patient can have many visits, and each visit is associated with only one patient. The two tables are still separate tables, but because they are joined, you can use the data in them as if they were one table.

Understanding Table Relationships

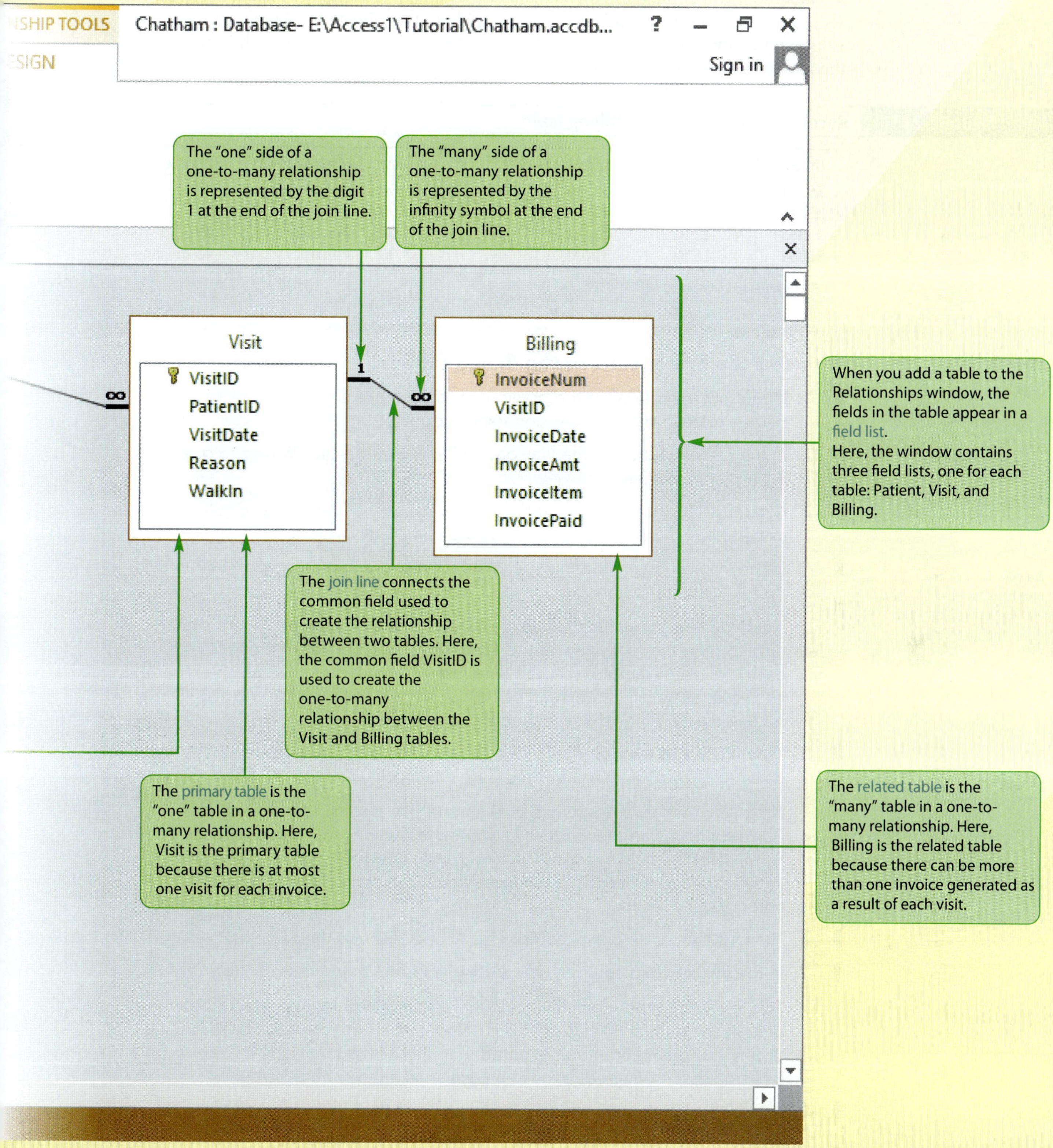

Adding Records to a New Table

Before you can begin to define the table relationships illustrated in the Session 2.2 Visual Overview, you need to finish creating the tables in the Chatham database.

The Billing table design is complete. Now, Cindi would like you to add records to the table so it will contain the invoice data for Chatham Community Health Services. As you learned earlier, you add records to a table in Datasheet view by typing the field values in the rows below the column headings for the fields. You'll begin by entering the records shown in Figure 2-21.

Figure 2-21 Records to be added to the Billing table

Invoice Num	Visit ID	Invoice Date	Invoice Amt	Invoice Item	Invoice Paid
35801	1527	11/10/2015	$100.00	Office visit	Yes
35818	1536	11/18/2015	$100.00	Office visit	Yes
35885	1570	01/12/2016	$85.00	Pharmacy	No
35851	1550	12/02/2015	$85.00	Pharmacy	No

To add the first record to the Billing table:

1. If you took a break after the previous session, make sure the Chatham database is open and the Navigation Pane is open.
2. In the Tables section of the Navigation Pane, double-click **Billing** to open the Billing table in Datasheet view.
3. Close the Navigation Pane, and then use the ✛ pointer to resize columns, as necessary, so that the field names are completely visible.
4. In the Invoice Num column, type **35801**, press the **Tab** key, type **1527** in the Visit ID column, and then press the **Tab** key.

Be sure to type the numbers "0" and "1" and *not* the letters "O" and "I" in the field values.

   Next you need to enter the invoice date. Recall that you specified a custom date format, mm/dd/yyyy, for the InvoiceDate field. You do not need to type each digit; for example, you can type just "3" instead of "03" for the month, and you can type "16" instead of "2016" for the year. Access will display the full value according to the custom date format.

5. Type **11/10/15** and then press the **Tab** key. Notice that Access displays the date "11/10/2015" in the Invoice Date column.

   Next you need to enter the invoice amount for the first record. This is a Currency field with the Currency format and two decimal places specified. Because of the field's properties, you do not need to type the dollar sign, comma, or zeroes for the decimal places; Access will display these items automatically for you.

6. Type **100** and then press the **Tab** key. Access displays the value as "$100.00."
7. In the Invoice Item column, type **Office visit** and then press the **Tab** key.

   The last field in the table, InvoicePaid, is a Yes/No field. Recall that the default value for any Yes/No field is "No"; therefore, the check box is initially empty. For the record you are entering in the Billing table, the invoice has been paid, so you need to insert a checkmark in the check box.

8. Press the **spacebar** to insert a checkmark, and then press the **Tab** key. The values for the first record are entered. See Figure 2-22.

Figure 2-22 First record entered in the Billing table

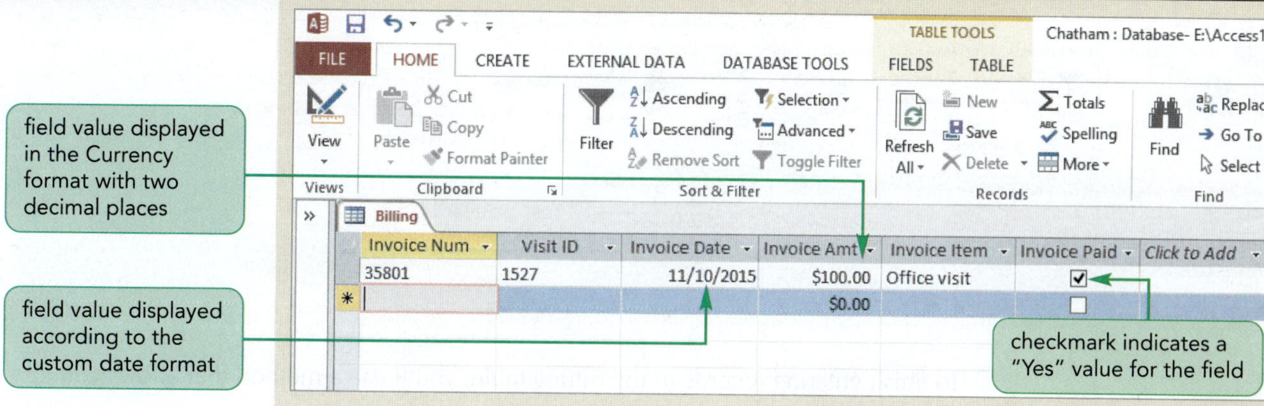

Now you can add the remaining three records. As you do, you'll learn a keyboard shortcut for inserting the value from the same field in the previous record. A **keyboard shortcut** is a key or combination of keys you press to complete an action more efficiently.

To add the next three records to the Billing table:

1. Refer to Figure 2-21 and enter the values in the second record's Invoice Num, Visit ID, and Invoice Date columns.

   Notice that the value in the second record's Invoice Amt column is $100.00. This value is the exact same value as in the first record. You can quickly insert the value from the same column in the previous record using the **Ctrl + '** (apostrophe) keyboard shortcut. To use this shortcut, you press and hold down the Ctrl key, press the ' key once, and then release both keys. (The plus sign in the keyboard shortcut indicates you're pressing two keys at once; you do not press the + key.)

2. With the insertion point in the Invoice Amt column, press the **Ctrl + '** keys. Access inserts the value "$100.00" in the Invoice Amt column for the second record.

3. Press the **Tab** key to move to the Invoice Item column. Again, the value you need to enter in this column—Office visit—is the same as the value for this column in the previous record. So, you can use the keyboard shortcut again.

4. With the insertion point in the Invoice Item column, press the **Ctrl + '** keys. Access inserts the value "Office visit" in the Invoice Item column for the second record.

5. Press the **Tab** key to move to the Invoice Paid column, press the **spacebar** to insert a checkmark in the check box, and then press the **Tab** key. The second record is entered in the Billing table.

6. Refer to Figure 2-21 to enter the values for the third and fourth records, using the Ctrl + ' keys to enter the values in the fourth record's Invoice Amt and Invoice Item columns. Also, for both records, the invoices have not been paid. Therefore, be sure to press the Tab key to leave the Invoice Paid column values unchecked (signifying "No"). Your table should look like the one in Figure 2-23.

Figure 2-23 **Billing table with four records added**

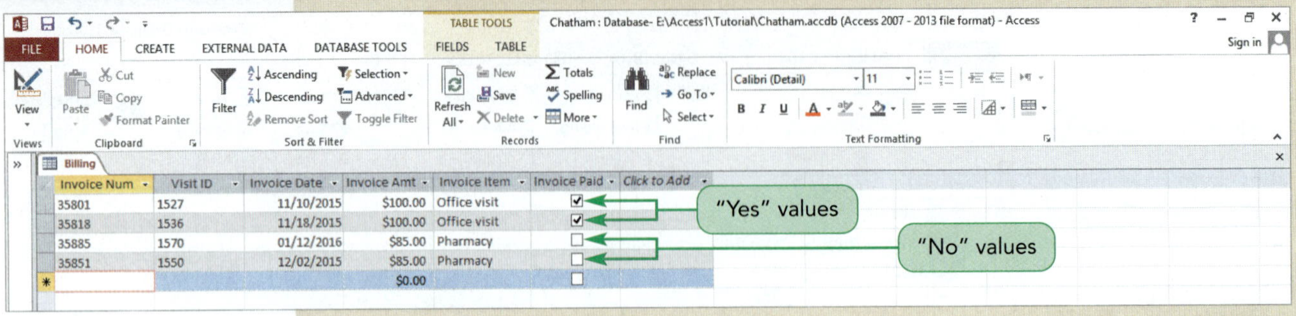

To finish entering records in the Billing table, you'll use a method that allows you to import the data.

Importing Data from an Excel Worksheet

Often, the data you want to add to an Access table exists in another file, such as a Word document or an Excel workbook. You can bring the data from other files into Access in different ways. For example, you can copy and paste the data from an open file, or you can **import** the data, which is a process that allows you to copy the data from a source without having to open the source file.

Cindi had been using Excel to track invoice data for Chatham Community Health Services and already created a worksheet, named "Invoices," containing this data. You'll import this Excel worksheet into your Billing table to complete the entry of data in the table. To use the import method, the columns in the Excel worksheet must match the names and data types of the fields in the Access table.

INSIGHT

Caption Property Values and the Import Process

When you import data from an Excel worksheet into an Access table, any Caption property values set for the fields in the table are not considered in the import process. For example, your Access table could have fields such as InvoiceDate and InvoiceAmt with Caption property values of Invoice Date and Invoice Amt, respectively. If the Excel worksheet you are importing has the column headings Invoice Date and Invoice Amt, you might think that the data matches and you can proceed with the import. However, if the underlying field names in the Access table do not match the Excel worksheet column headings exactly, the import process will fail. It's a good idea to double-check to make sure that the actual Access field names—and not just the column headings displayed in a table datasheet (as specified by the Caption property)—match the Excel worksheet column headings. If there are differences, you can change the column headings in the Excel worksheet to match the Access table field names before you import the data, ensuring that the process will work correctly.

The Invoices worksheet contains the following columns: InvoiceNum, VisitID, InvoiceDate, InvoiceAmt, InvoiceItem, and InvoicePaid. These column headings match the field names in the Billing table exactly, so you can import the data. Before you import data into a table, you need to close the table.

To import the Invoices worksheet into the Billing table:

1. Click the **Close 'Billing'** button on the object tab to close the Billing table. A dialog box opens asking if you want to save the changes to the table layout. This dialog box opens because you resized the table columns.
2. Click the **Yes** button in the dialog box.
3. On the ribbon, click the **EXTERNAL DATA** tab.
4. In the Import & Link group on the EXTERNAL DATA tab, click the **Excel** button. The Get External Data - Excel Spreadsheet dialog box opens. See Figure 2-24.

Figure 2-24 Get External Data - Excel Spreadsheet dialog box

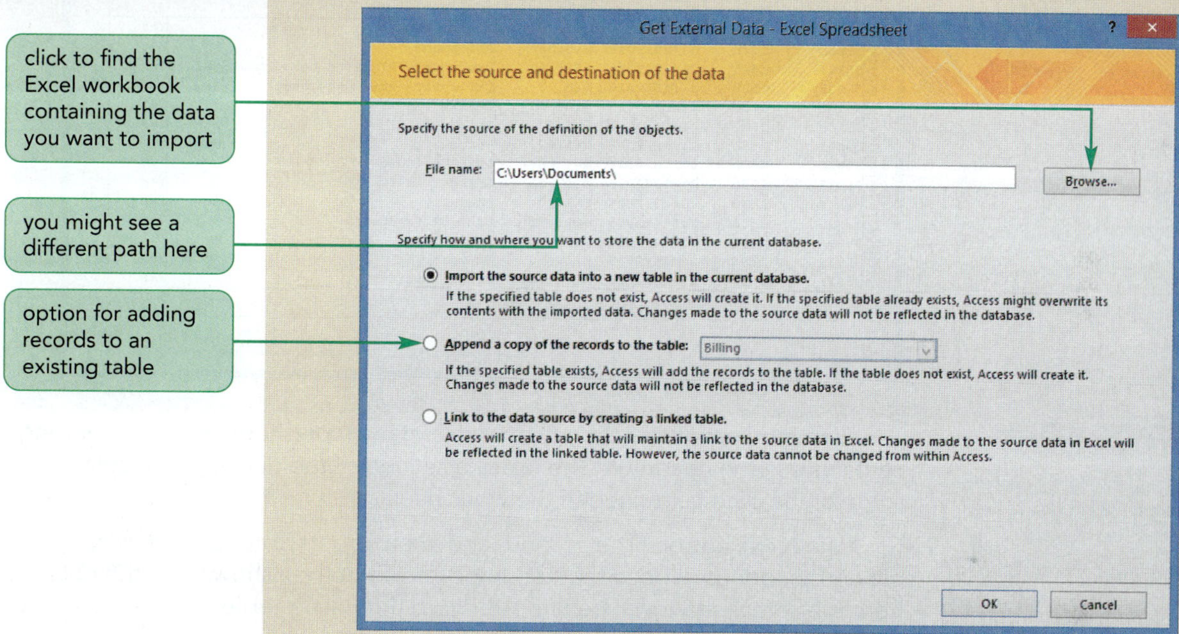

Trouble? If the Export - Excel Spreadsheet dialog box opens instead of the dialog box shown in Figure 2-24, you probably clicked the Excel button in the Export group. If so, click the Cancel button in the dialog box, and then repeat Step 4, being sure to click the Excel button in the Import & Link group.

The dialog box provides options for importing the entire worksheet as a new table in the current database, adding the data from the worksheet to an existing table, or linking the data in the worksheet to the table. You need to add, or append, the worksheet data to the Billing table.

5. Click the **Browse** button. The File Open dialog box opens. The Excel workbook file is named "Invoices" and is located in the Access1 ▸ Tutorial folder provided with your Data Files.
6. Navigate to the **Access1 ▸ Tutorial** folder, where your starting Data Files are stored, and then double-click the **Invoices** Excel file. You return to the dialog box.
7. Click the **Append a copy of the records to the table** option button. The box to the right of this option becomes active and displays the Billing table name, because it is the first table listed in the Navigation Pane.

   Trouble? If another table name appears in this box, click the arrow on the box, and then click Billing.

8. Click the **OK** button. The first Import Spreadsheet Wizard dialog box opens. See Figure 2-25.

Figure 2-25 **First Import Spreadsheet Wizard dialog box**

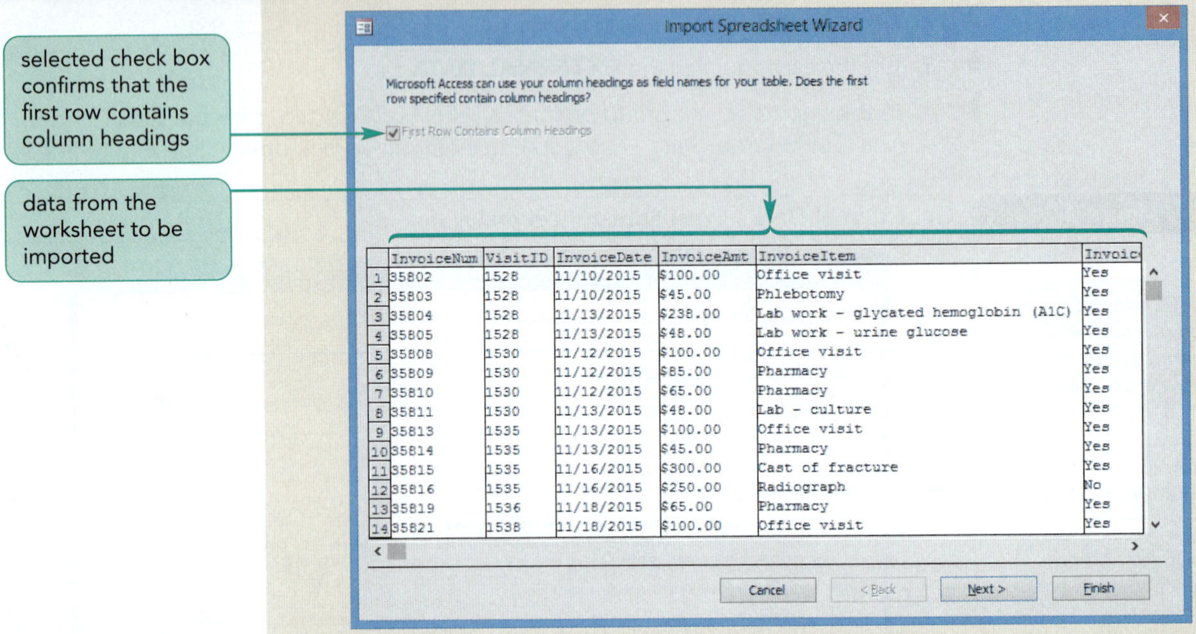

TIP

Carefully check the data to make sure it should be imported into the selected table.

The dialog box confirms that the first row of the worksheet you are importing contains column headings. The bottom section of the dialog box displays some of the data contained in the worksheet.

9. Click the **Next** button. The second, and final, Import Spreadsheet Wizard dialog box opens. Notice that the Import to Table box shows that the data from the spreadsheet will be imported into the Billing table.

10. Click the **Finish** button. A dialog box opens asking if you want to save the import steps. If you needed to repeat this same import procedure many times, it would be a good idea to save the steps for the procedure. However, you don't need to save these steps because you'll be importing the data only one time. Once the data is in the Billing table, Cindi will no longer use Excel to track invoice data.

11. Click the **Close** button in the dialog box to close it without saving the steps.

The data from the Invoices worksheet has been added to the Billing table. Next, you'll open the table to view the new records.

To open the Billing table and view the imported data:

1. Open the Navigation Pane, and then double-click **Billing** in the Tables section to open the table in Datasheet view.

2. Resize the Invoice Item column to its best fit, scrolling the worksheet and resizing, as necessary.

3. Press the **Ctrl + Home** keys to scroll to the top of the datasheet. Notice that the table now contains a total of 204 records—four records you entered plus 200 records imported from the Invoices worksheet. The records are displayed in primary key order by the values in the Invoice Num column. See Figure 2-26.

Figure 2-26 **Billing table after importing data from Excel**

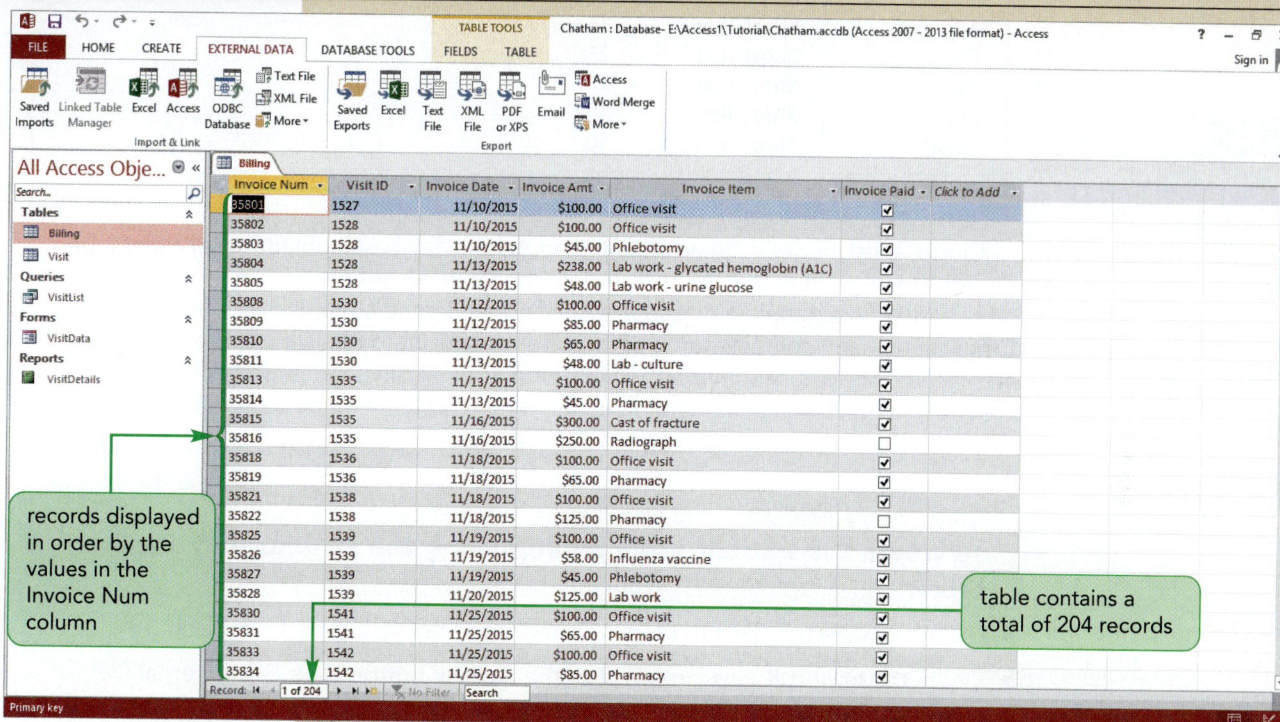

4. Save and close the Billing table, and then close the Navigation Pane.

Two of the tables—Visit and Billing—are now complete. According to Cindi's plan for the Chatham database, you need to create a third table, named "Patient," to track data about the clinic's patients. You'll use a different method to create this table.

Creating a Table by Importing an Existing Table Structure

If another Access database contains a table—or even just the design, or structure, of a table—that you want to include in your database, you can import the table and any records it contains or import only the table structure into your database.

Cindi documented the design for the new Patient table by listing each field's name and data type, as well as any applicable field size, description, and caption property values, as shown in Figure 2-27. Note that each field in the Patient table, except BirthDate, will be a Short Text field, and the PatientID field will be the table's primary key.

Figure 2-27 **Design for the Patient table**

Field Name	Data Type	Field Size	Description	Caption
PatientID	Short Text	5	Primary key	Patient ID
LastName	Short Text	25		Last Name
FirstName	Short Text	20		First Name
BirthDate	Date/Time			Date of Birth
Phone	Short Text	14		
Address	Short Text	35		
City	Short Text	25		
State	Short Text	2		
Zip	Short Text	10		
Email	Short Text	50		

Cindi's assistant Kelly already created an Access database containing a Patient table design. She never entered any records into the table because she wasn't sure if the table design was complete or correct. After reviewing the table design, both Kelly and Cindi agree that it contains some of the fields they want to track, but that some changes are needed. So, you can import the table structure in Kelly's database to create the Patient table in the Chatham database, and then modify the imported table to produce the final table structure according to Cindi's design.

To create the Patient table by importing the structure of another table:

1. Make sure the EXTERNAL DATA tab is the active tab on the ribbon.
2. In the Import & Link group, click the **Access** button. The Get External Data - Access Database dialog box opens. This dialog box is similar to the one you used earlier when importing the Excel spreadsheet.
3. Click the **Browse** button. The File Open dialog box opens. The Access database file from which you need to import the table structure is named "Kelly" and is located in the Access1 ▸ Tutorial folder provided with your Data Files.
4. Navigate to the **Access1 ▸ Tutorial** folder, where your starting Data Files are stored, and then double-click the **Kelly** database file. You return to the dialog box.
5. Make sure the **Import tables, queries, forms, reports, macros, and modules into the current database** option button is selected, and then click the **OK** button. The Import Objects dialog box opens. The dialog box contains tabs for importing all the different types of Access database objects—tables, queries, forms, and so on. The Tables tab is the current tab.
6. Click the **Options** button in the dialog box to see all the options for importing tables. See Figure 2-28.

Figure 2-28 **Import Objects dialog box**

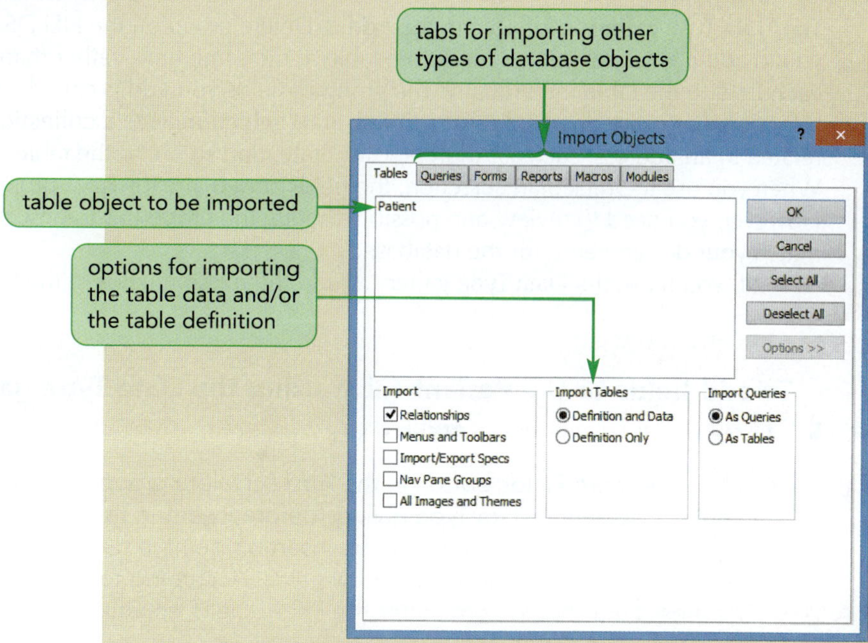

Note the Import Tables section of the dialog box, which contains options for importing the definition and data—that is, the structure of the table and any records contained in the table—or the definition (structure) only. You need to import only the structure of the Patient table Kelly created.

7. On the Tables tab, click **Patient** to select this table.
8. In the Import Tables section of the dialog box, click the **Definition Only** option button, and then click the **OK** button. Access creates the Patient table in the Chatham database using the structure of the Patient table in the Kelly database, and opens a dialog box asking if you want to save the import steps.
9. Click the **Close** button to close the dialog box without saving the import steps.
10. Open the Navigation Pane and note that the Patient table is listed in the Tables section.
11. Double-click **Patient** to open the table, and then close the Navigation Pane. The Patient table opens in Datasheet view. The table contains no records. See Figure 2-29.

Figure 2-29 **Imported Patient table in Datasheet view**

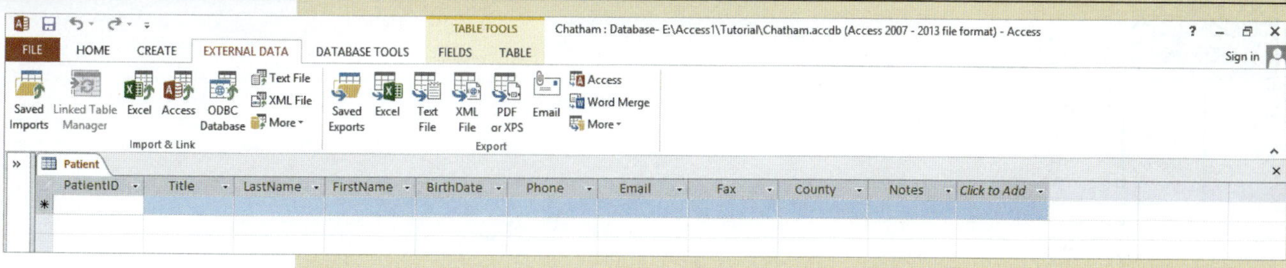

The table structure you imported contains some of the fields Cindi wants, but not all (see Figure 2-27); it also contains some fields Cindi does not want in the Patient table. You can add the missing fields using the Data Type gallery.

Adding Fields to a Table Using the Data Type Gallery

The **Data Type gallery**, available in the Add & Delete group on the FIELDS tab, allows you to add a group of related fields to a table at the same time, rather than adding each field to the table individually. The group of fields you add is called a **Quick Start selection**. For example, the **Address Quick Start selection** adds a collection of fields related to an address, such as Address, City, State, and so on, to the table at one time. When you use a Quick Start selection, the fields added already have properties set. However, you need to review and possibly modify the properties to ensure the fields match your design needs for the database.

Next, you'll use the Data Type gallery to add the missing fields to the Patient table.

To add fields to the Patient table using the Data Type gallery:

1. On the ribbon, click the **FIELDS** tab.

   Note the More Fields button in the Add & Delete group; this button allows you to display the Data Type gallery. Before inserting fields from the Data Type gallery, you need to place the insertion point in the field to the right of where you want to insert the new fields. According to Cindi's design, the Address field should come after the Phone field, so you need to make the next field, Email, the active field.

Make sure the correct field is active before adding new fields.

2. Click the first row in the **Email** field to make it the active field.
3. In the Add & Delete group, click the **More Fields** button. The Data Type gallery opens and displays options for different types of fields you can add to your table.
4. Scroll the gallery down so the Quick Start section is visible. See Figure 2-30.

Figure 2-30 Patient table with the Data Type gallery displayed

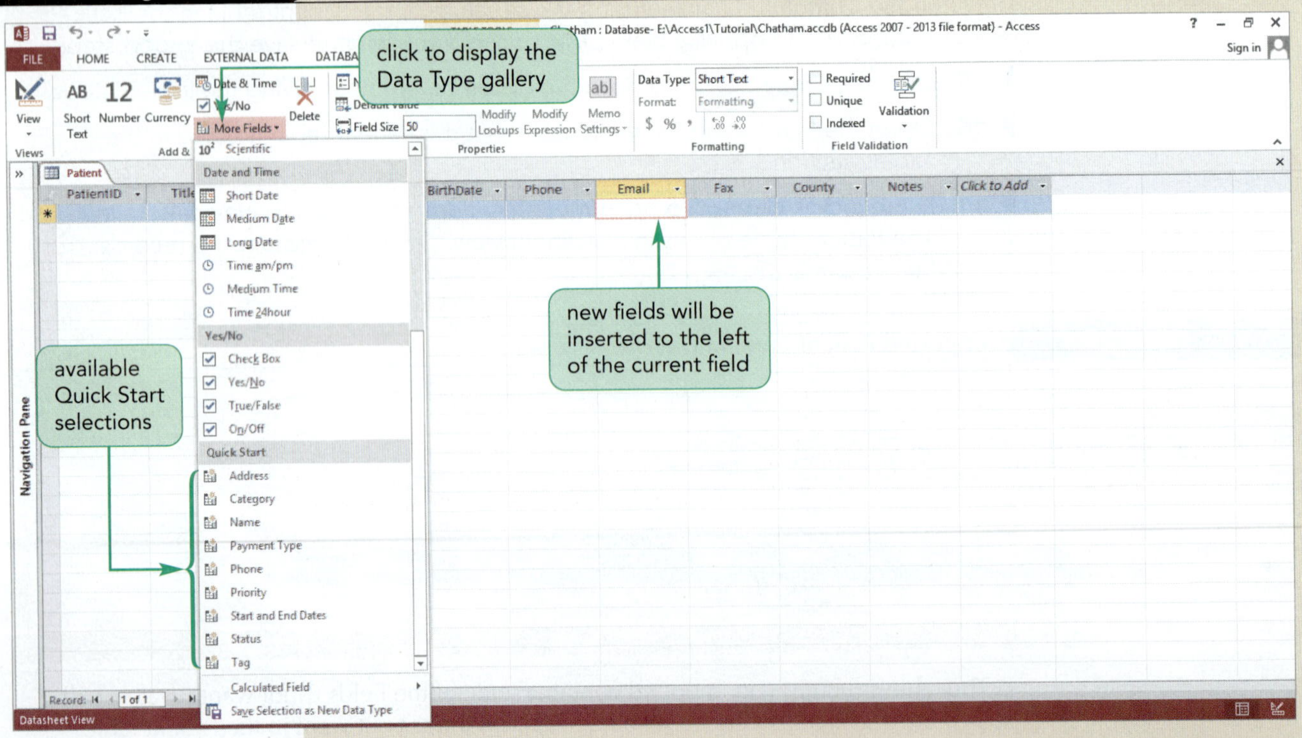

The Quick Start section provides options that will add multiple, related fields to the table at one time. The new fields will be inserted to the left of the current field.

5. In the Quick Start section, click **Address**. Access adds five fields to the table: Address, City, State Province, ZIP Postal, and Country Region. See Figure 2-31.

Figure 2-31 **Patient table after adding fields from the Data Type gallery**

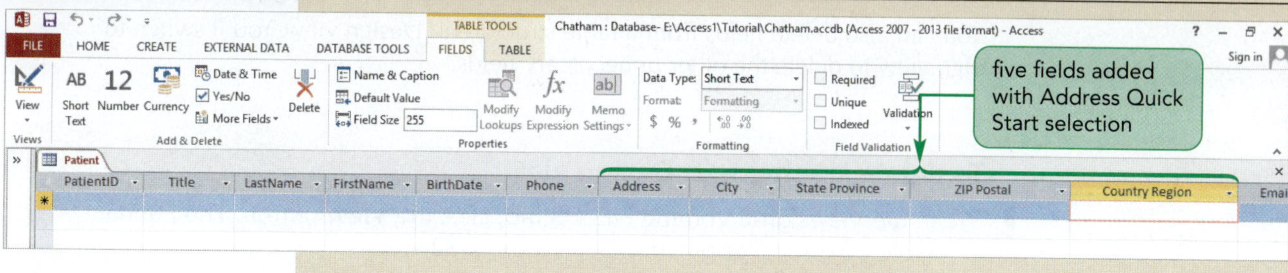

Modifying the Imported Table

Refer back to Cindi's design for the Patient table (Figure 2-27). To finalize the table design, you need to modify the imported table by deleting fields, renaming fields, and changing field data types. You'll begin by deleting fields.

Deleting Fields from a Table Structure

After you've created a table, you might need to delete one or more fields. When you delete a field, you also delete all the values for that field from the table. So, before you delete a field, you should make sure that you want to do so and that you choose the correct field to delete. You can delete fields in either Datasheet view or Design view.

REFERENCE

Deleting a Field from a Table Structure

- In Datasheet view, click anywhere in the column for the field you want to delete.
- In the Add & Delete group on the FIELDS tab, click the Delete button.

or

- In Design view, click the Field Name box for the field you want to delete.
- In the Tools group on the DESIGN tab, click the Delete Rows button.

The Address Quick Start selection added a field named "Country Region" to the Patient table. Cindi doesn't need a field to store country data because all Chatham Community Health Services patients are located in the United States. You'll begin to modify the Patient table structure by deleting the Country Region field.

To delete the Country Region field from the table in Datasheet view:

1. Click the first row in the **Country Region** field (if necessary).
2. In the Add & Delete group on the FIELDS tab, click the **Delete** button. The Country Region field is removed and the first field, PatientID, is now the active field.

You can also delete fields from a table structure in Design view. You'll switch to Design view to delete the other unnecessary fields.

To delete the fields in Design view:

1. In the Views group on the FIELDS tab, click the **View** button. The Patient table opens in Design view. See Figure 2-32.

Figure 2-32 Patient table in Design view

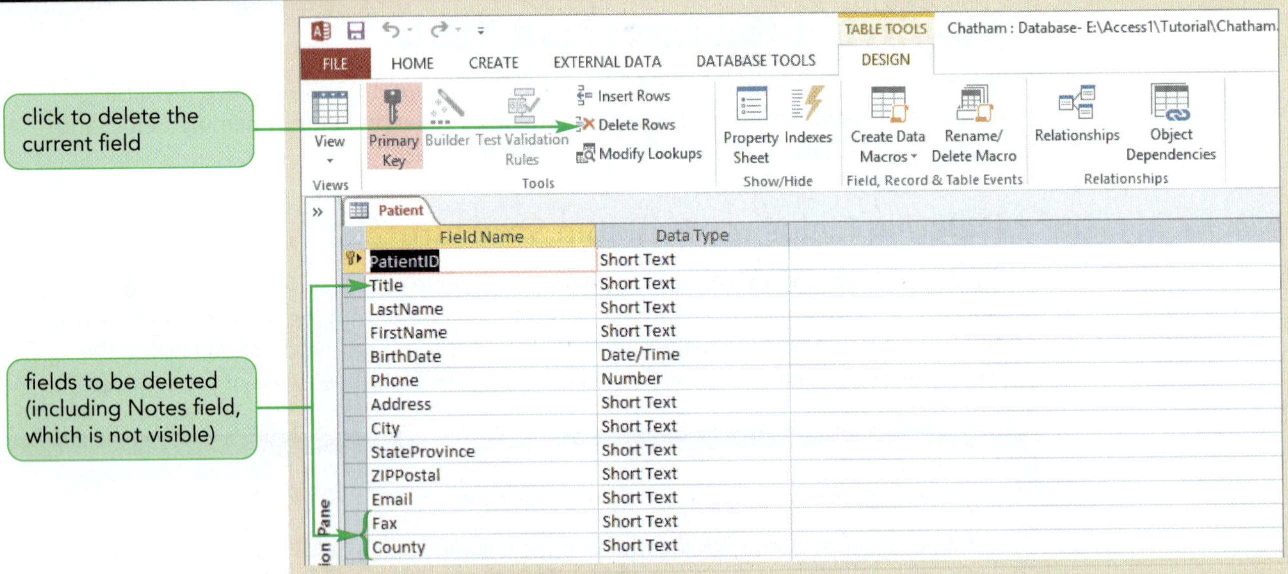

2. Click the **Title** Field Name box to make it the current field.
3. In the Tools group on the DESIGN tab, click the **Delete Rows** button. The Title field is removed from the Patient table structure.

   You'll delete the Fax, County, and Notes fields next. Instead of deleting these fields individually, you'll select and delete them at the same time.
4. Click and hold down the mouse button on the row selector for the **Fax** field, and then drag the mouse to select the **County** and **Notes** fields.
5. Release the mouse button. The rows for the three fields are outlined in a red box, meaning all three fields are selected.

6. In the Tools group, click the **Delete Rows** button. See Figure 2-33.

Figure 2-33 Patient table after deleting fields

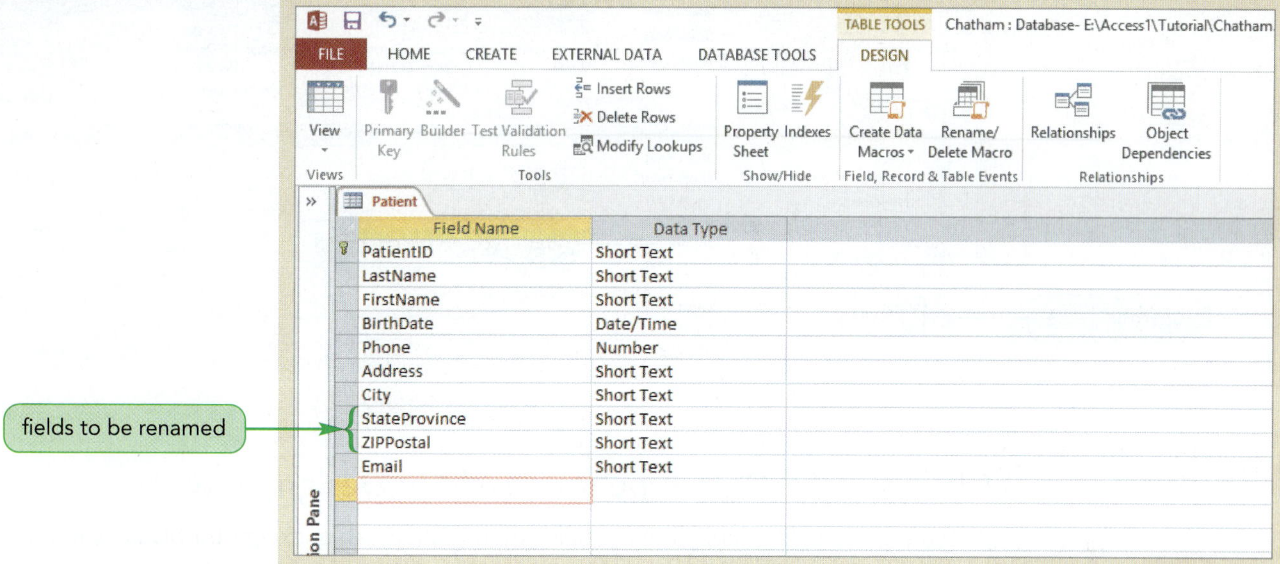

Renaming Fields in Design View

To match Cindi's design for the Patient table, you need to rename the StateProvince and ZIPPostal fields. In Tutorial 1, you renamed the default primary key field (ID) in Datasheet view. You can also rename fields in Design view by simply editing the names in the Table Design grid.

To rename the fields in Design view:

1. Click to position the insertion point to the right of the word **StateProvince** in the eighth row's Field Name box, and then press the **Backspace** key eight times to delete the word "Province." The name of the eighth field is now State.

   You can also select an entire field name and then type new text to replace it.

2. In the ninth row's Field Name box, drag to select the text **ZIPPostal**, and then type **Zip**. The text you type replaces the original text. See Figure 2-34.

Figure 2-34 Patient table after renaming fields

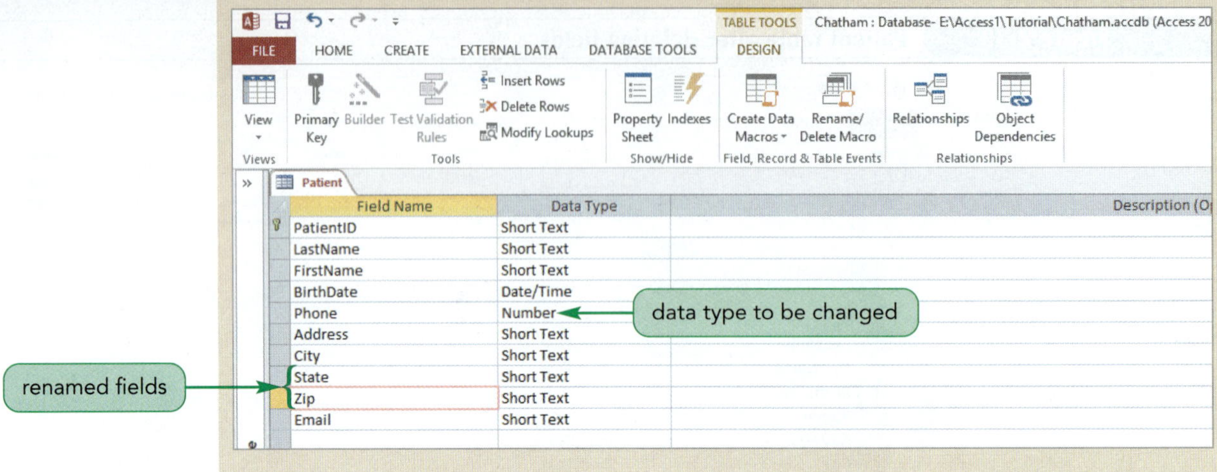

Changing the Data Type for a Field in Design View

According to Cindi's plan, all of the fields in the Patient table, except BirthDate, should be Short Text fields. The table structure you imported specifies the Number data type for the Phone field; you need to change this to Short Text. In Tutorial 1, you used an option in Datasheet view to change a field's data type. You can also change the data type for a field in Design view.

To change the data type of the Phone field in Design view:

1. Click the right side of the **Data Type** box for the Phone field to display the list of data types.
2. Click **Short Text** in the list. The Phone field is now a Short Text field. Note that, by default, the Field Size property is set to 255. According to Cindi's plan, the Phone field should have a Field Size property of 14. You'll make this change next.
3. Press the **F6** key to move to and select the default Field Size property, and then type **14**.

Each of the remaining fields you added using the Address Quick Start selection—Address, City, State, and Zip—also has the default field size of 255. You need to change the Field Size property for these fields to match Cindi's design. You'll also delete any Caption property values for these fields because the field names match how Cindi wants them displayed, so captions are unnecessary.

To change the Field Size and Caption properties for the fields:

1. Click the **Address** Field Name box to make it the current field.
2. Press the **F6** key to move to and select the default Field Size property, and then type **35**.

   Note that the Caption property setting for this field is the same as the field name. This field doesn't need a caption, so you can delete this value.
3. Press the **Tab** key until the the word Address is selected in the Caption box, and then press the **Delete** key. The Caption property value is removed.
4. Repeat Steps 1 through 3 to change the Field Size property for the City field to **25** and to delete its Caption property value.
5. Change the Field Size property for the State field to **2**, and then delete its Caption property value.
6. Change the Field Size property for the Zip field to **10**, and then delete its Caption property value.
7. On the Quick Access Toolbar, click the **Save** button to save your changes to the Patient table.

Finally, Cindi would like you to set the Description property for the Patient ID field and the Caption property for the PatientID, LastName, FirstName, and BirthDate fields. You'll make these changes now.

To enter the Description and Caption property values:

1. Click the **Description (Optional)** box for the PatientID field, and then type **Primary key**.
2. In the Field Properties pane, click the **Caption** box.

   After you leave the Description (Optional) box, the Property Update Options button appears below this box for the PatientID field. When you change a field's property in Design view, you can use this button to update the corresponding property on forms and reports that include the modified field. For example, if the Chatham database included a form that contained the PatientID field, you could choose to **propagate**, or update, the modified Description property in the form by clicking the Property Update Options button, and then choosing the option to make the update everywhere the field is used. The text on the Property Update Options button varies depending on the task; in this case, if you click the button, the option is "Update Status Bar Text everywhere PatientID is used."

   Because the Chatham database does not include any forms or reports that are based on the Patient table, you do not need to update the properties, so you can ignore the button for now. In most cases, however, it is a good idea to perform the update.
3. In the Caption box for the PatientID field, type **Patient ID**.
4. Click the **LastName** Field Name box to make it the current field.
5. Click the **Caption** box, and then type **Last Name**.
6. Click the **FirstName** Field Name box to make it the current field, click the **Caption** box, and then type **First Name**.

7. Click the **BirthDate** Field Name box to make it the current field, click the **Caption** box, and then type **Date of Birth**. See Figure 2-35.

Figure 2-35 Patient table after entering description and captions

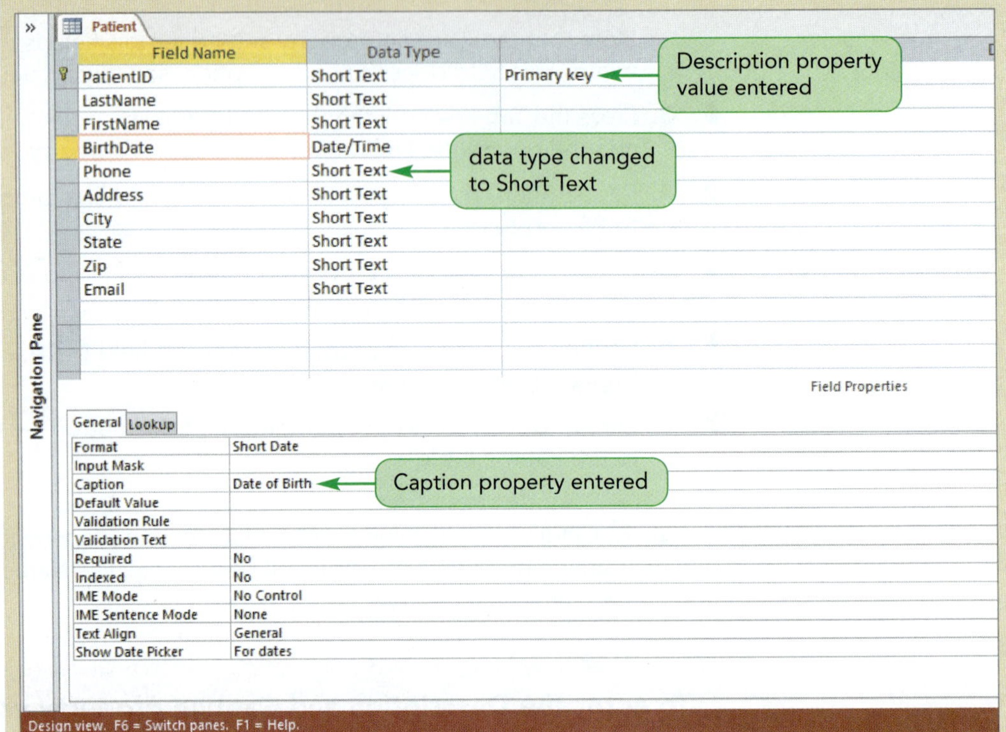

8. On the Quick Access Toolbar, click the **Save** button to save your changes to the Patient table.

9. In the Views group on the DESIGN tab, click the **View** button to display the table in Datasheet view.

10. Resize each column to its best fit, and then click in the first row for the **Patient ID** column. See Figure 2-36.

Figure 2-36 **Modified Patient table in Datasheet view**

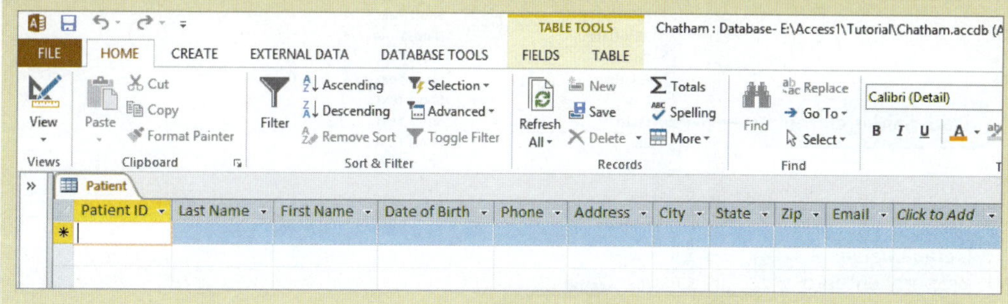

After viewing the Patient table datasheet, both Cindi and Kelly agree that data entry would be made easier if the State field value of "CT" was automatically filled in for each new record added to the table, because all of the clinic's patients live in Connecticut. You can accomplish this by setting the Default Value property for the field.

Setting the Default Value Property for a Field

The **Default Value property** for a field specifies what value will appear, by default, for the field in each new record you add to a table. Recall the InvoicePaid field in the Billing table; this is a Yes/No field, which automatically includes a Default Value property setting of "No." That's why the check box for the InvoicePaid field is initially empty for a new record in the Billing table.

Because all the patients at Chatham Community Health Services live in Connecticut, you'll specify a default value of "CT" for the State field in the Patient table. With this setting, each new record in the Patient table will have the correct State field value entered automatically.

To set the Default Value property for the State field:

1. In the Views group on the HOME tab, click the **View** button to display the Patient table in Design view.
2. Click the **State** Field Name box to make it the current field.
3. In the Field Properties pane, click the **Default Value** box, type **CT** and then press the Tab key. See Figure 2-37.

Figure 2-37 Specifying the Default Value property for the State field

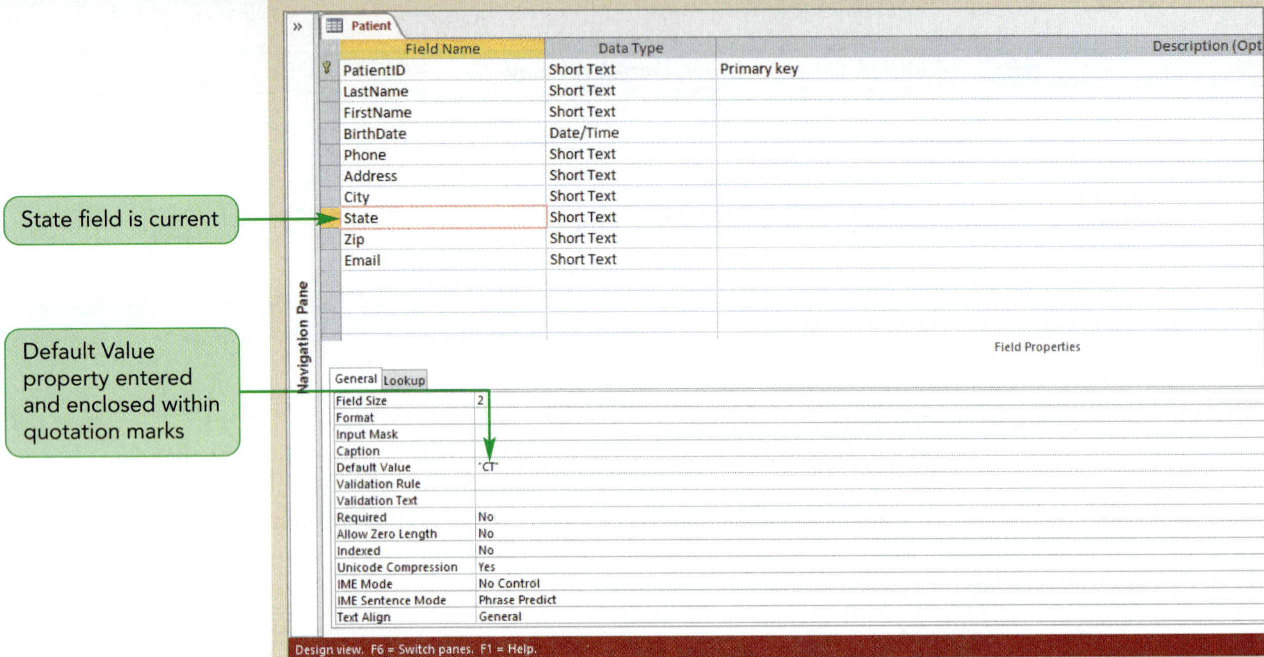

Note that a text entry in the Default Value property must be enclosed within quotation marks. If you do not type the quotation marks, Access adds them for you. However, for some entries, you would receive an error message indicating invalid syntax if you omitted the quotation marks. In such cases, you have to enter the quotation marks yourself.

4. On the Quick Access Toolbar, click the **Save** button to save your changes to the Patient table.

TIP

You can change the value in a record from the default value to another value, if necessary.

5. In the Views group on the DESIGN tab, click the **View** button to display the table in Datasheet view. Note that the State field for the first row now displays the default value "CT" as specified by the Default Value property. Each new record entered in the table will automatically have this State field value entered.

With the Patient table design set, you can now enter records in it. You'll begin by entering two records, and then you'll use a different method to add the remaining records.

Note: *Be sure to enter your last name and first name where indicated.*

To add two records to the Patient table:

1. Enter the following values in the columns in the first record; note that you can press Tab to move past the default State field value:

   Patient ID = **22500**

   Last Name = ***[student's last name]***

   First Name = ***[student's first name]***

   Date of Birth = **2/28/1994**

   Phone = **860-938-2822**

   Address = **501 Perkins Dr**

   City = **Hartford**

   State = **CT**

   Zip = **06120**

   Email = **student1@example.edu**

2. Enter the following values in the columns in the second record:

   Patient ID = **22533**

   Last Name = **Rowe**

   First Name = **Christina**

   Date of Birth = **12/5/1941**

   Phone = **860-552-5920**

   Address = **27 Tracey Ct**

   City = **Windsor**

   State = **CT**

   Zip = **06095**

   Email = **c.rowe@example.com**

3. Resize columns to their best fit, as necessary, and then save and close the Patient table.

Before Cindi decided to store data using Access, Kelly managed the clinic's patient data in a different system. She exported that data into a text file and now asks you to import it into the new Patient table. You can import the data contained in this text file to add the remaining records to the Patient table.

Adding Data to a Table by Importing a Text File

There are many ways to import data into an Access database. So far, you've learned how to add data to an Access table by importing an Excel spreadsheet, and you've created a new table by importing the structure of an existing table. You can also import data contained in text files.

To complete the entry of records in the Patient table, you'll import the data contained in Kelly's text file. The file is named "Patient" and is located in the Access1 ▸ Tutorial folder provided with your Data Files.

To import the data contained in the Patient text file:

1. On the ribbon, click the **EXTERNAL DATA** tab.
2. In the Import & Link group, click the **Text File** button. The Get External Data - Text File dialog box opens. This dialog box is similar to the one you used earlier when importing the Excel spreadsheet and the Access table structure.
3. Click the **Browse** button. The File Open dialog box opens.
4. Navigate to the Access1 ▸ Tutorial folder, where your starting Data Files are stored, and then double-click the **Patient** file. You return to the dialog box.
5. Click the **Append a copy of the records to the table** option button. The box to the right of this option becomes active. Next, you need to select the table to which you want to add the data.
6. Click the arrow on the box, and then click **Patient**.
7. Click the **OK** button. The first Import Text Wizard dialog box opens. The dialog box indicates that the data to be imported is in a delimited format. A **delimited text file** is one in which fields of data are separated by a character such as a comma or a tab. In this case, the dialog box shows that data is separated by the comma character in the text file.
8. Make sure the **Delimited** option button is selected in the dialog box, and then click the **Next** button. The second Import Text Wizard dialog box opens. See Figure 2-38.

Figure 2-38 Second Import Text Wizard dialog box

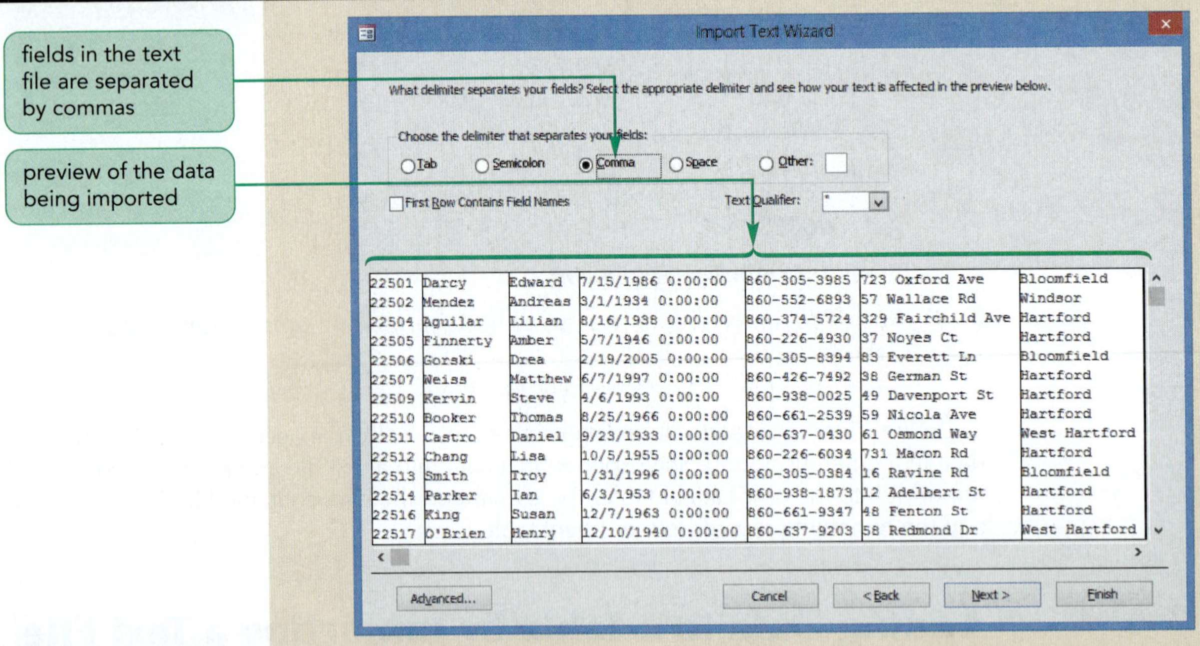

TIP
Carefully check the data to make sure it should be imported into the selected table.

This dialog box asks you to confirm the delimiter character that separates the fields in the text file you're importing. Access detects that the comma character is used in the Patient text file and selects this option. The bottom area of the dialog box provides a preview of the data you're importing.

9. Make sure the **Comma** option button is selected, and then click the **Next** button. The third, and final, Import Text Wizard dialog box opens. Notice that the Import to Table box shows that the data will be imported into the Patient table.

10. Click the **Finish** button. A dialog box opens asking if you want to save the import steps. You'll only import the patient data once, so you can close the dialog box without saving the import steps.
11. Click the **Close** button in the dialog box to close it without saving the import steps.

Cindi asks you to open the Patient table in Datasheet view so she can see the results of importing the text file.

To view the Patient table datasheet:

1. Open the Navigation Pane, and then double-click **Patient** to open the Patient table in Datasheet view. The Patient table contains a total of 51 records.
2. Close the Navigation Pane.
3. Resize columns to their best fit, scrolling the table datasheet as necessary, so that all field values are displayed. When finished, scroll back to display the first fields in the table, and then click the first row's Patient ID field. See Figure 2-39.

Figure 2-39 Patient table after importing data from the text file

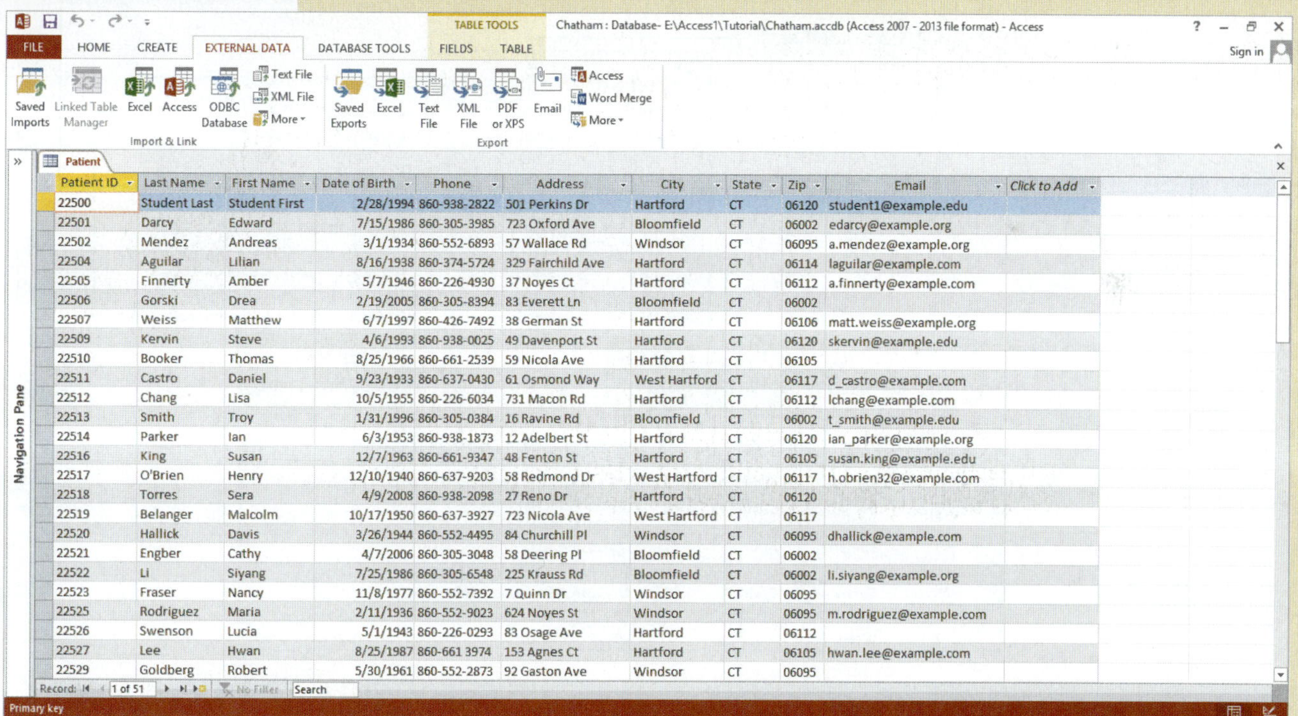

Patient ID	Last Name	First Name	Date of Birth	Phone	Address	City	State	Zip	Email	Click to Add
22500	Student Last	Student First	2/28/1994	860-938-2822	501 Perkins Dr	Hartford	CT	06120	student1@example.edu	
22501	Darcy	Edward	7/15/1986	860-305-3985	723 Oxford Ave	Bloomfield	CT	06002	edarcy@example.org	
22502	Mendez	Andreas	3/1/1934	860-552-6893	57 Wallace Rd	Windsor	CT	06095	a.mendez@example.org	
22504	Aguilar	Lilian	8/16/1938	860-374-5724	329 Fairchild Ave	Hartford	CT	06114	laguilar@example.com	
22505	Finnerty	Amber	5/7/1946	860-226-4930	37 Noyes Ct	Hartford	CT	06112	a.finnerty@example.com	
22506	Gorski	Drea	2/19/2005	860-305-8394	83 Everett Ln	Bloomfield	CT	06002		
22507	Weiss	Matthew	6/7/1997	860-426-7492	38 German St	Hartford	CT	06106	matt.weiss@example.org	
22509	Kervin	Steve	4/6/1993	860-938-0025	49 Davenport St	Hartford	CT	06120	skervin@example.edu	
22510	Booker	Thomas	8/25/1966	860-661-2539	59 Nicola Ave	Hartford	CT	06105		
22511	Castro	Daniel	9/23/1933	860-637-0430	61 Osmond Way	West Hartford	CT	06117	d_castro@example.com	
22512	Chang	Lisa	10/5/1955	860-226-6034	731 Macon Rd	Hartford	CT	06112	lchang@example.com	
22513	Smith	Troy	1/31/1996	860-305-0384	16 Ravine Rd	Bloomfield	CT	06002	t_smith@example.edu	
22514	Parker	Ian	6/3/1953	860-938-1873	12 Adelbert St	Hartford	CT	06120	ian_parker@example.org	
22516	King	Susan	12/7/1963	860-661-9347	48 Fenton St	Hartford	CT	06105	susan.king@example.edu	
22517	O'Brien	Henry	12/10/1940	860-637-9203	58 Redmond Dr	West Hartford	CT	06117	h.obrien32@example.com	
22518	Torres	Sera	4/9/2008	860-938-2098	27 Reno Dr	Hartford	CT	06120		
22519	Belanger	Malcolm	10/17/1950	860-637-3927	723 Nicola Ave	West Hartford	CT	06117		
22520	Hallick	Davis	3/26/1944	860-552-4495	84 Churchill Pl	Windsor	CT	06095	dhallick@example.com	
22521	Engber	Cathy	4/7/2006	860-305-3048	58 Deering Pl	Bloomfield	CT	06002		
22522	Li	Siyang	7/25/1986	860-305-6548	225 Krauss Rd	Bloomfield	CT	06002	li.siyang@example.org	
22523	Fraser	Nancy	11/8/1977	860-552-7392	7 Quinn Dr	Windsor	CT	06095		
22525	Rodriguez	Maria	2/11/1936	860-552-9023	624 Noyes St	Windsor	CT	06095	m.rodriguez@example.com	
22526	Swenson	Lucia	5/1/1943	860-226-0293	83 Osage Ave	Hartford	CT	06112		
22527	Lee	Hwan	8/25/1987	860-661 3974	153 Agnes Ct	Hartford	CT	06105	hwan.lee@example.com	
22529	Goldberg	Robert	5/30/1961	860-552-2873	92 Gaston Ave	Windsor	CT	06095		

4. Save and close the Patient table, and then open the Navigation Pane.

The Chatham database now contains three tables—Patient, Visit, and Billing—and the tables contain all the necessary records. Your final task is to complete the database design by defining the necessary relationships between its tables.

Defining Table Relationships

One of the most powerful features of a relational database management system is its ability to define relationships between tables. You use a common field to relate one table to another. The process of relating tables is often called performing a **join**. When you join tables that have a common field, you can extract data from them as if they were one larger table. For example, you can join the Patient and Visit tables by using the PatientID field in both tables as the common field. Then you can use a query, form, or report to extract selected data from each table, even though the data is contained in two separate tables, as shown in Figure 2-40. The PatientVisits query shown in Figure 2-40 includes the PatientID, LastName, and FirstName fields from the Patient table, and the VisitDate and Reason fields from the Visit table. The joining of records is based on the common field of PatientID. The Patient and Visit tables have a type of relationship called a one-to-many relationship.

Figure 2-40 One-to-many relationship and sample query

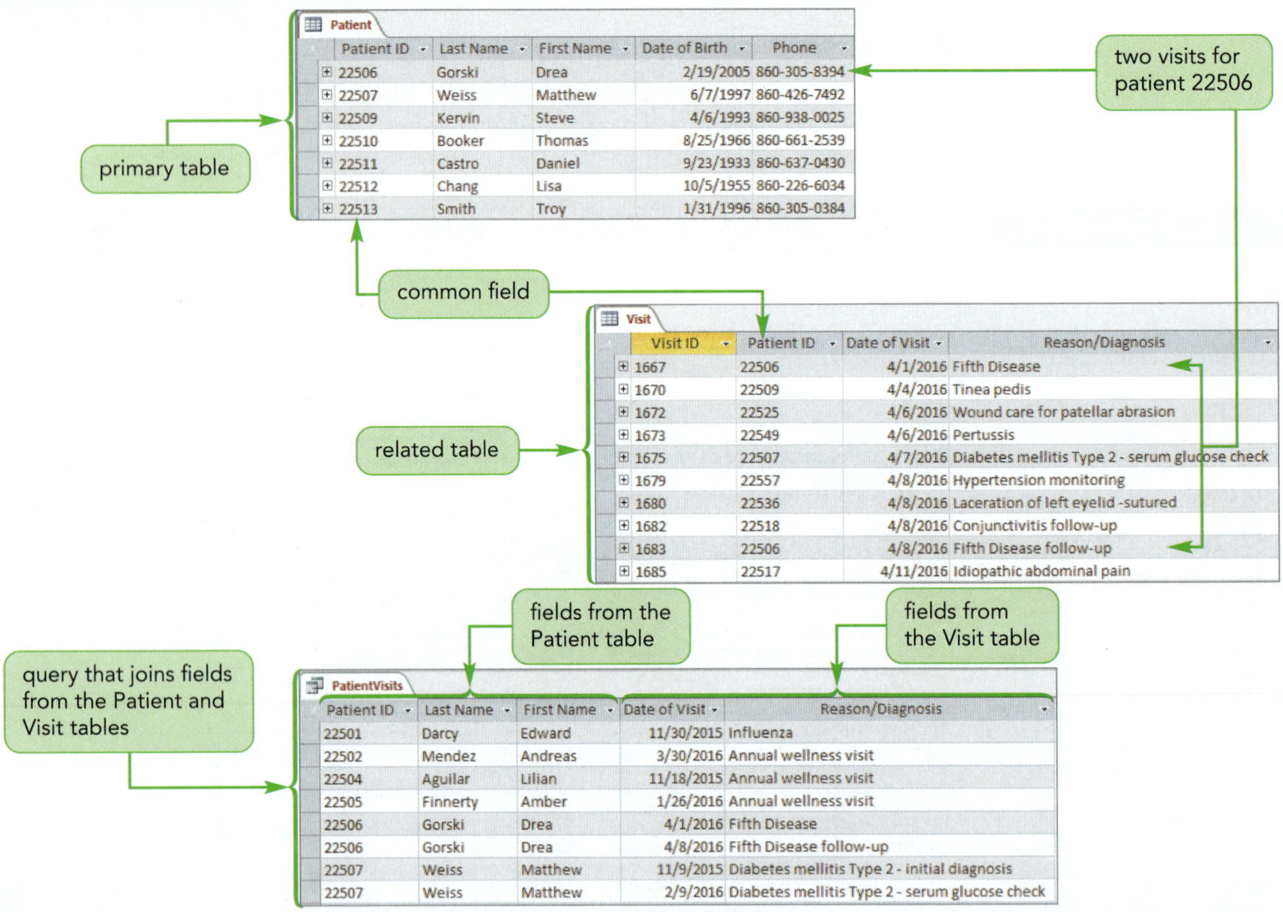

One-to-Many Relationships

As shown earlier in the Session 2.2 Visual Overview, a one-to-many relationship exists between two tables when one record in the first table matches zero, one, or many records in the second table, and when one record in the second table matches at most one record in the first table. For example, as shown in Figure 2-40, patient 22506 has two visits in the Visit table. Other patients have one or more visits. Every visit has a single matching patient.

Access refers to the two tables that form a relationship as the primary table and the related table. The primary table is the "one" table in a one-to-many relationship; in Figure 2-40, the Patient table is the primary table because there is only one patient for each visit. The related table is the "many" table; in Figure 2-40, the Visit table is the related table because a patient can have zero, one, or many visits.

Because related data is stored in two tables, inconsistencies between the tables can occur. Referring to Figure 2-40, consider the following three scenarios:

- Cindi adds a record to the Visit table for a new patient, Jack Perry, using PatientID 22570. She did not first add the new patient's information to the Patient table, so this visit does not have a matching record in the Patient table. The data is inconsistent, and the visit record is considered to be an **orphaned record**.
- In another situation, Cindi changes the PatientID in the Patient table for Drea Gorski from 22506 to 22601. Because there is no longer a patient with the PatientID 22506 in the Patient table, this change creates two orphaned records in the Visit table, and the database is inconsistent.
- In a third scenario, Cindi deletes the record for Drea Gorski, patient 22506, from the Patient table because this patient moved and no longer receives medical services from Chatham Community Health Services. The database is again inconsistent; two records for patient 22506 in the Visit table have no matching record in the Patient table.

You can avoid these types of problems and avoid having inconsistent data in your database by specifying referential integrity between tables when you define their relationships.

Referential Integrity

Referential integrity is a set of rules that Access enforces to maintain consistency between related tables when you update data in a database. Specifically, the referential integrity rules are as follows:

- When you add a record to a related table, a matching record must already exist in the primary table, thereby preventing the possibility of orphaned records.
- If you attempt to change the value of the primary key in the primary table, Access prevents this change if matching records exist in a related table. However, if you choose the **Cascade Update Related Fields option**, Access permits the change in value to the primary key and changes the appropriate foreign key values in the related table, thereby eliminating the possibility of inconsistent data.
- When you attempt to delete a record in the primary table, Access prevents the deletion if matching records exist in a related table. However, if you choose the **Cascade Delete Related Records option**, Access deletes the record in the primary table and also deletes all records in related tables that have matching foreign key values.

INSIGHT

Understanding the Cascade Delete Related Records Option

Although there are advantages to using the Cascade Delete Related Records option for enforcing referential integrity, its use does present risks as well. You should rarely select the Cascade Delete Related Records option because doing so might cause you to inadvertently delete records you did not intend to delete. It is best to use other methods for deleting records that give you more control over the deletion process.

Defining a Relationship Between Two Tables

When two tables have a common field, you can define a relationship between them in the Relationships window (see the Session 2.2 Visual Overview). Next, you need to define a one-to-many relationship between the Patient and Visit tables, with Patient as the primary table and Visit as the related table, and with PatientID as the common field (the primary key in the Patient table and a foreign key in the Visit table). You'll also define a one-to-many relationship between the Visit and Billing tables, with Visit as the primary table and Billing as the related table, and with VisitID as the common field (the primary key in the Visit table and a foreign key in the Billing table).

To define the one-to-many relationship between the Patient and Visit tables:

1. On the ribbon, click the **DATABASE TOOLS** tab.
2. In the Relationships group, click the **Relationships** button. The Show Table dialog box opens. See Figure 2-41.

Figure 2-41 Show Table dialog box

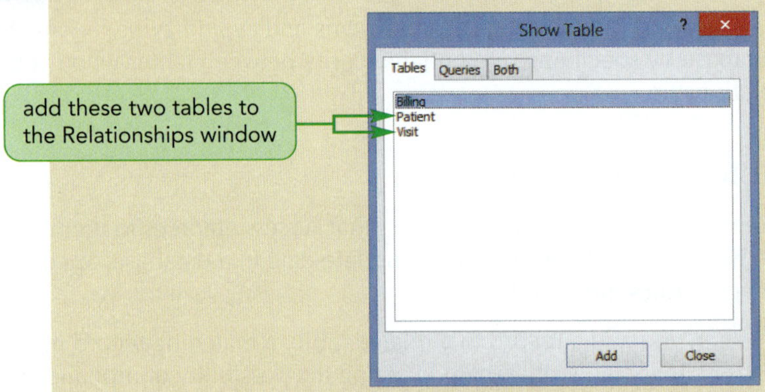

You must add each table participating in a relationship to the Relationships window. Because the Patient table is the primary table in the relationship, you'll add it first.

TIP

You can also double-click a table in the Show Table dialog box to add it to the Relationships window.

3. Click **Patient**, and then click the **Add** button. The Patient table's field list is added to the Relationships window.

   Trouble? If you add the same table more than once to the Relationships window, click the Close button in the Show Table box, right-click the field list for the duplicate table, and then click Hide Table. Then in the Relationships group on the DESIGN tab, click the Show Table button to reopen the Show Table dialog box.

4. Click **Visit**, and then click the **Add** button. The Visit table's field list is added to the Relationships window.
5. Click the **Close** button in the Show Table dialog box to close it.

So that you can view all the fields and complete field names, you'll resize the Patient table field list.

6. Use the ↕ pointer to drag the bottom of the Patient table field list to lengthen it until the vertical scroll bar disappears and all the fields are visible.

To form the relationship between the two tables, you drag the common field of PatientID from the primary table to the related table. Then Access opens the Edit Relationships dialog box, in which you select the relationship options for the two tables.

7. Click **PatientID** in the Patient field list, and then drag it to **PatientID** in the Visit field list. When you release the mouse button, the Edit Relationships dialog box opens. See Figure 2-42.

Figure 2-42 **Edit Relationships dialog box**

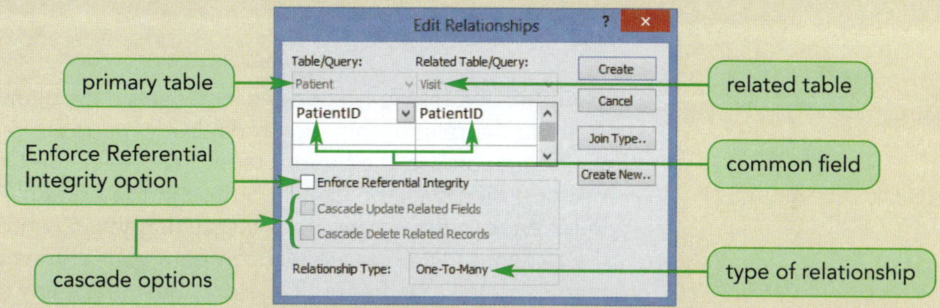

The primary table, related table, common field, and relationship type (One-To-Many) appear in the dialog box. Note that Access correctly identifies the "One" side of the relationship and places the primary table Patient in the Table/Query section of the dialog box; similarly, Access correctly identifies the "Many" side of the relationship and places the related table Visit in the Related Table/Query section of the dialog box.

8. Click the **Enforce Referential Integrity** check box.

After you click the Enforce Referential Integrity check box, the two cascade options become available. If you select the Cascade Update Related Fields option, Access will update the appropriate foreign key values in the related table when you change a primary key value in the primary table. You will *not* select the Cascade Delete Related Records option because doing so could cause you to delete records that you do not want to delete; this option is rarely selected.

9. Click the **Cascade Update Related Fields** check box.

10. Click the **Create** button to define the one-to-many relationship between the two tables and to close the dialog box. The completed relationship appears in the Relationships window, with the join line connecting the common field of PatientID in each table. See Figure 2-43.

Figure 2-43 **Defined relationship in the Relationships window**

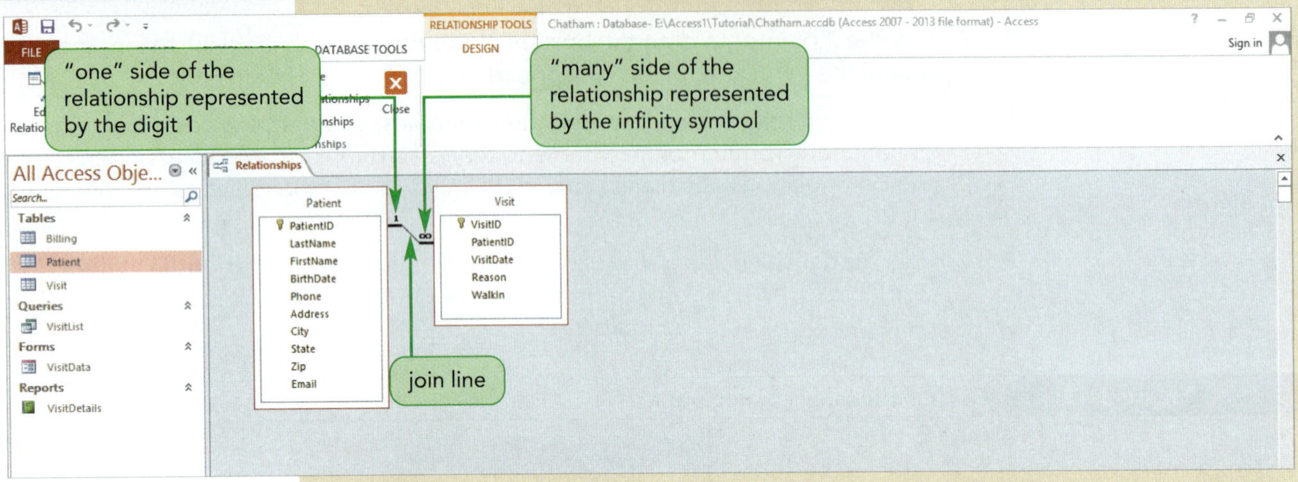

Trouble? If a dialog box opens indicating a problem that prevents you from creating the relationship, you most likely made a typing error when entering the two records in the Patient table. If so, click the OK button in the dialog box and then click the Cancel button in the Edit Relationships dialog box. Refer back to the earlier steps instructing you to enter the two records in the Patient table and carefully compare your entries with those shown in the text, especially the PatientID field values. Make any necessary corrections to the data in the Patient table, and then repeat Steps 7 through 10. If you still receive an error message, ask your instructor for assistance.

Now you need to define the one-to-many relationship between the Visit and Billing tables. In this relationship, Visit is the primary ("one") table because there is at most one visit for each invoice. Billing is the related ("many") table because there are zero, one, or many invoices that are generated for each patient visit. For example, some visits require lab work or pharmacy charges, which are invoiced separately.

To define the relationship between the Visit and Billing tables:

1. In the Relationships group on the DESIGN tab, click the **Show Table** button. The Show Table dialog box opens.
2. Make sure the **Billing** table is selected on the Tables tab, click the **Add** button, and then click the **Close** button to close the Show Table dialog box. The Billing table's field list appears in the Relationships window to the right of the Visit table's field list.
3. Use the pointer to drag the bottom of the Billing table field list to lengthen it until the vertical scroll bar disappears.

   Because the Visit table is the primary table in this relationship, you need to drag the VisitID field from the Visit field list to the Billing field list.
4. Click and drag the **VisitID** field in the Visit field list to the **VisitID** field in the Billing field list. When you release the mouse button, the Edit Relationships dialog box opens.
5. Click the **Enforce Referential Integrity** check box, and then click the **Cascade Update Related Fields** check box.

TIP

You can also use the mouse to drag a table from the Navigation Pane to add it to the Relationships window.

6. Click the **Create** button to define the one-to-many relationship between the two tables and to close the dialog box. The completed relationship appears in the Relationships window. See Figure 2-44.

Figure 2-44 **Both relationships defined**

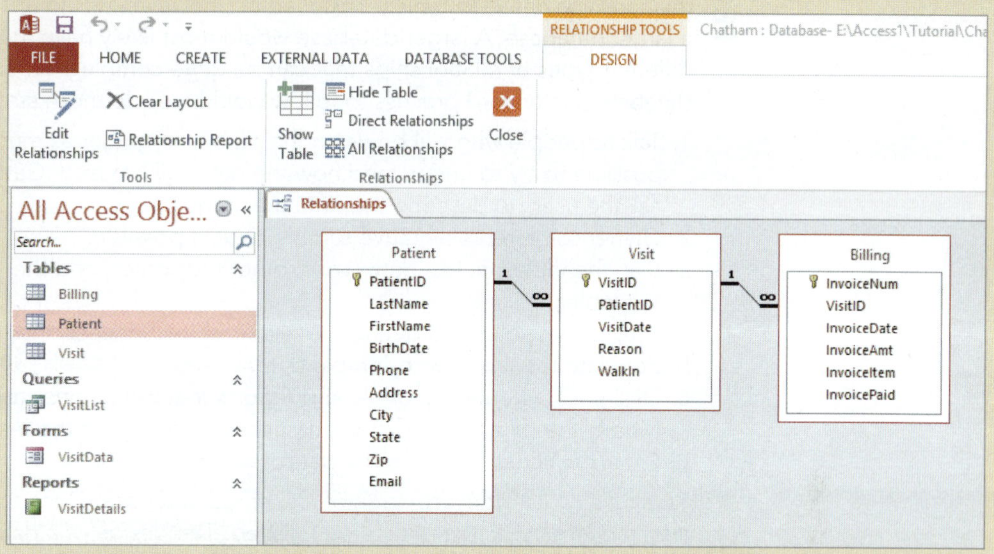

Trouble? If a dialog box opens indicating a problem that prevents you from creating the relationship, you most likely made a typing error when entering the two records in the Visit table. If so, click the OK button in the dialog box and then click the Cancel button in the Edit Relationships dialog box. Refer back to the steps in Tutorial 1 instructing you to enter the records in the Visit table and carefully compare your entries with those shown in the text, especially the VisitID field values. Make any necessary corrections to the data in the Visit table, and then repeat Steps 4 through 6. If you still receive an error message, ask your instructor for assistance.

With both relationships defined, you have connected the data among the three tables in the Chatham database.

7. On the Quick Access Toolbar, click the **Save** button to save the layout in the Relationships window.
8. In the Relationships group on the DESIGN tab, click the **Close** button to close the Relationships window.
9. Click the **FILE** tab on the ribbon to display Backstage view.
10. Click the **Compact & Repair Database** button. Access compacts and repairs the Chatham database.
11. Click the **FILE** tab, and then click **Close** to close the Chatham database.

PROSKILLS

Problem Solving: Creating a Larger Database

When you create a small database that contains only a few tables, and the data and the reports you want to generate from it are fairly simple, you could follow the process outlined in this text: create the tables, populate them, and then define the necessary relationships between tables. This method, however, would not be suitable for creating a larger database. A larger database would most likely have many more tables and different types of relationships that can be quite complex. When creating a large database, a standard process to follow would include these steps:

1. Talk to people who will be using the data, and gather as much documentation as possible to try to understand how the data will be used. Gather sample reports, and ask the users to describe the data they require.
2. Gather some representative sample data, if possible.
3. Plan the tables, fields, data types, other properties, and the relationships between the tables.
4. Create the tables and define the relationships between them.
5. Populate the tables with sample data.
6. Design some queries, forms, and reports that will be needed, and then test them.
7. Modify the database structure, if necessary, based on the results of your tests.
8. Enter the actual data into the database tables.

Testing is critical at every stage of creating a database. Once the database is finalized and implemented, it's not actually finished. The design of a database evolves as new functionality is required and as the data that is gathered changes.

REVIEW

Session 2.2 Quick Check

1. What is the keyboard shortcut for inserting the value from the same field in the previous record into the current record?
2. ______________ data is a process that allows you to copy the data from a source without having to open the source file.
3. The ______________ gallery allows you to add a group of related fields to a table at the same time, rather than adding each field to the table individually.
4. What is the effect of deleting a field from a table structure?
5. A(n) ______________ text file is one in which fields of data are separated by a character such as a comma or a tab.
6. The ______________ is the "one" table in a one-to-many relationship, and the ______________ is the "many" table in the relationship.
7. ______________ is a set of rules that Access enforces to maintain consistency between related tables when you update data in a database.

ASSESS

SAM Projects

Put your skills into practice with SAM Projects! SAM Projects for this tutorial can be found online. If you have a SAM account, go to www.cengage.com/sam2013 to download the most recent Project Instructions and Start Files.

PRACTICE

Review Assignments

Data Files needed for the Review Assignments: Vendor.accdb *(cont. from Tutorial 1)* and Supplies.xlsx

In addition to tracking information about the vendors Chatham Community Health Services works with, Cindi also wants to track information about their products and services. First, Cindi asks you to modify the necessary properties in the existing Supplier table in the Vendor database; then she wants you to create a new table in the Vendor database to contain product data. Complete the following:

1. Open the **Vendor** database you created in Tutorial 1.
2. Open the **Supplier** table in Design view, and set the field properties as shown in Figure 2-45.

Figure 2-45 Field properties for the Supplier table

Field Name	Data Type	Description	Field Size	Other
SupplierID	Short Text	Primary key	6	Caption = Supplier ID
Company	Short Text		50	
Category	Short Text		15	
Address	Short Text		35	
City	Short Text		25	
State	Short Text		2	
Zip	Short Text		10	
Phone	Short Text		14	Caption = Contact Phone
ContactFirst	Short Text		20	Caption = Contact First Name
ContactLast	Short Text		25	Caption = Contact Last Name
InitialContact	Date/Time			Format = Short Date Caption = Initial Contact

3. Save the Supplier table. Click the Yes button when a message appears indicating some data might be lost. Switch to Datasheet view and resize columns, as necessary, to their best fit. Then save and close the Supplier table.
4. Create a new table in Design view, using the table design shown in Figure 2-46.

Figure 2-46 **Design for the Product table**

Field Name	Data Type	Description	Field Size	Other
ProductID	Short Text	Primary key	5	Caption = Product ID
SupplierID	Short Text	Foreign key	6	Caption = Supplier ID
ProductName	Short Text		75	Caption = Product Name
Price	Currency			Format = Standard Decimal Places = 2
TempControl	Yes/No			Caption = Temp Controlled?
Sterile	Yes/No			Caption = Sterile?
Units	Number		Integer	Decimal Places = 0 Caption = Units/Case Default Value = [no entry]

5. Specify ProductID as the primary key, and then save the table as **Product**.
6. Modify the table structure by adding a new field named **Weight** (data type: **Number**; field size: **Single**; Decimal Places: **2**; Caption: **Weight in Lbs**; Default Value: [no entry]) between the Price and TempControl fields. Then move the **Units** field so that it is positioned between the Price and Weight fields.
7. Enter the records shown in Figure 2-47 in the Product table. Resize all datasheet columns to their best fit. When finished, save and close the Product table.

Figure 2-47 **Records for the Product table**

Product ID	Supplier ID	Product Name	Price	Units/Case	Weight in Lbs	Temp Controlled?	Sterile?
SS582	DUR368	Stethoscopes	65.00	1	1	No	No
AL487	COU392	Alcohol wipes	15.00	1000	12	Yes	Yes

8. Use the Import Spreadsheet Wizard to add data to the Product table. The data you need to import is contained in the Supplies workbook, which is an Excel file located in the Access1 ▸ Review folder provided with your Data Files.
   a. Specify the Supplies workbook as the source of the data.
   b. Select the option for appending the data.
   c. Select Product as the table.
   d. In the Import Spreadsheet Wizard dialog boxes, make sure Access confirms that the first row contains column headings, and import to the Product table. Do not save the import steps.
9. Open the **Product** table in Datasheet view and resize columns to their best fit, as necessary. Then save and close the Product table.
10. Define a one-to-many relationship between the primary Supplier table and the related Product table. Resize the table field lists so that all field names are visible. Select the referential integrity option and the cascade updates option for the relationship.
11. Save the changes to the Relationships window and close it, compact and repair the Vendor database, and then close the database.

APPLY

Case Problem 1

Data Files needed for this Case Problem: Gopher.accdb *(cont. from Tutorial 1)* and Customers.txt

GoGopher! Amol Mehta wants to use the Gopher database to track information about members who join his online business, which provides a variety of services on a subscription basis, and the plans in which members are enrolled. He asks you to help maintain this database. Complete the following:

1. Open the **Gopher** database you created in Tutorial 1.
2. Open the **Plan** table in Design view, and change the following field properties:
   a. PlanID: Enter **Primary key** for the description, change the field size to **3**, and enter **Plan ID** for the caption.
   b. PlanDescription: Change the field size to **40** and enter **Plan Description** for the caption.
   c. PlanCost: Change the format to **Standard**, specify **0** decimal places, and enter **Plan Cost** for the caption.
   d. FeeWaived: Enter **Fee Waived** for the caption.
3. Save and close the Plan table. Click the Yes button when a message appears indicating some data might be lost.
4. Create a new table in Design view, using the table design shown in Figure 2-48.

Figure 2-48 **Design for the Member table**

Field Name	Data Type	Description	Field Size	Other
MemberID	Short Text	Primary key	4	Caption = Member ID
PlanID	Short Text	Foreign key	3	Caption = Plan ID
FirstName	Short Text		20	Caption = First Name
LastName	Short Text		25	Caption = Last Name
Phone	Short Text		14	
Expiration	Date/Time	Date when membership expires		Format = Short Date Caption = Expiration Date

5. Specify MemberID as the primary key, and then save the table as **Member**.
6. Use the Address Quick Start selection in the Data Type gallery to add five fields between the LastName and Phone fields.
7. Switch to Design view, and then make the following changes to the Member table design:
   a. Address field: Change the name of this field to **Street**, change the field size to **40**, and delete the entry for the caption.
   b. City field: Change the field size to **25** and delete the entry for the caption.
   c. StateProvince field: Change the name of this field to **State**, change the field size to **2**, delete the entry for the caption, and enter **CO** for the default value.
   d. ZIPPostal field: Change the name of this field to **Zip**, change the field size to **10**, and delete the entry for the caption.
   e. Delete the **CountryRegion** field from the Member table structure.
   f. Add a new field named **DateJoined** (data type: **Date/Time**; format: **Short Date**; Caption: **Date Joined**) between the Phone and Expiration fields.
8. Enter the records shown in Figure 2-49 in the Member table. Be sure to enter your first and last names in the appropriate fields for the first new record. Resize all datasheet columns to their best fit. When finished, save and close the Member table.

Figure 2-49 **Records for the Member table**

Member ID	Plan ID	First Name	Last Name	Street	City	State	Zip	Phone	Date Joined	Expiration Date
1200	311	*Student First*	*Student Last*	45 Lakeview Dr	Boulder	CO	80301	303-559-1238	11/1/2015	2/1/2016
1210	312	Todd	Grant	6 Rosebriar Rd	Erie	CO	80516	303-674-2140	1/20/2016	4/20/2016

9. Use the Import Text File Wizard to add data to the Member table. The data you need to import is contained in the Customers text file, which is located in the Access1 ▸ Case1 folder provided with your Data Files.
   a. Specify the Customers text file as the source of the data.
   b. Select the option for appending the data.
   c. Select Member as the table.
   d. In the Import Text File Wizard dialog boxes, choose the options to import delimited data, to use a comma delimiter, and to import the data into the Member table. Do not save the import steps.
10. Open the **Member** table in Datasheet view and resize columns to their best fit, as necessary. Then save and close the Member table.
11. Define a one-to-many relationship between the primary Plan table and the related Member table. Resize the Member table field list so that all field names are visible. Select the referential integrity option and the cascade updates option for this relationship.
12. Save the changes to the Relationships window and close it, compact and repair the Gopher database, and then close the database.

APPLY

Case Problem 2

Data Files needed for this Case Problem: OBrien.accdb *(cont. from Tutorial 1)*, Client.accdb, Students.txt, and Agreements.xlsx

O'Brien Educational Services Karen O'Brien plans to use the OBrien database to maintain information about the students, tutors, and contracts for her educational services company. Karen asks you to help her build the database by updating one table and creating two new tables in the database. Complete the following:

1. Open the **OBrien** database you created in Tutorial 1.
2. Open the **Tutor** table in Design view, and set the field properties as shown in Figure 2-50.

Figure 2-50 **Field properties for the Tutor table**

Field Name	Data Type	Description	Field Size	Other
TutorID	Short Text	Primary key	7	Caption = Tutor ID
FirstName	Short Text		20	Caption = First Name
LastName	Short Text		25	Caption = Last Name
Degree	Short Text		7	
School	Short Text		50	
HireDate	Date/Time			Format = Short Date Caption = Hire Date

3. Add a new field as the last field in the Tutor table with the field name **Groups**, the **Yes/No** data type, and the caption **Groups Only**.
4. Save the Tutor table. Click the Yes button when a message appears indicating some data might be lost.

5. In the table datasheet, specify that the following tutors conduct group tutoring sessions only: Student First/Student Last (i.e., your name), Amy Hawkins, Lori Burns, Samuel Glick, and Caitlin Shea. Close the Tutor table.
6. Karen created a table named Student in the Client database that is located in the Access1 ▸ Case2 folder provided with your Data Files. Import the structure of the Student table in the Client database into a new table named Student in the OBrien database. Do not save the import steps.
7. Open the **Student** table in Datasheet view, and then add the following two fields to the end of the table: **BirthDate** (Date/Time field) and **Gender** (Short Text field).
8. Use the Phone Quick Start selection in the Data Type gallery to add four fields related to phone numbers between the Zip and BirthDate fields. (*Hint:* Be sure to make the BirthDate field the active field before adding the new fields.)
9. Display the Student table in Design view, delete the BusinessPhone and FaxNumber fields, and then save and close the Student table.
10. Reopen the Student table and modify its design so that it matches the design in Figure 2-51, *including the revised field names and data types*.

    Note: You must type the quotation marks around the Default Property value for the State field.

Figure 2-51 **Field properties for the Student table**

Field Name	Data Type	Description	Field Size	Other
StudentID	Short Text	Primary key	7	Caption = Student ID
LastName	Short Text		25	Caption = Last Name
FirstName	Short Text		20	Caption = First Name
Address	Short Text		35	
City	Short Text		25	
State	Short Text		2	Default Value = "IN"
Zip	Short Text		10	
HomePhone	Short Text		14	
CellPhone	Short Text		14	Caption = Cell Phone
BirthDate	Date/Time			Format = Short Date Caption = Date of Birth
Gender	Short Text	F(emale), M(ale)	1	

you must type the quotation marks for this Default Value property

11. Move the LastName field so it follows the FirstName field.
12. Save your changes to the table design, and then add the records shown in Figure 2-52 to the Student table.

Figure 2-52 **Records for the Student table**

Student ID	First Name	Last Name	Address	City	State	Zip	Home Phone	Cell Phone	Date of Birth	Gender
TUR8005	Lynne	Turner	6 Crowell Ct	South Bend	IN	46614	574-245-2125	574-245-8842	7/24/2002	F
CHA8034	Henry	Chang	1401 Lauren Dr	Oscela	IN	46561	574-607-3045	574-674-2410	10/5/1999	M

13. Resize the fields to their best fit, and then save and close the Student table.
14. Use the Import Text File Wizard to add data to the Student table. The data you need to import is contained in the Students text file, which is located in the Access1 ▸ Case2 folder provided with your Data Files.
    a. Specify the Students text file as the source of the data.
    b. Select the option for appending the data.

c. Select Student as the table.

d. In the Import Text File Wizard dialog boxes, choose the options to import delimited data, to use a comma delimiter, and to import the data into the Student table. Do not save the import steps.

15. Open the **Student** table in Datasheet view, resize columns in the datasheet to their best fit (as necessary), and then save and close the table.
16. Create a new table in Design view, using the table design shown in Figure 2-53.

Figure 2-53 Design for the Contract table

Field Name	Data Type	Description	Field Size	Other
ContractID	Short Text	Primary key	4	Caption = Contract ID
StudentID	Short Text	Foreign key	7	Caption = Student ID
TutorID	Short Text	Foreign key	7	Caption = Tutor ID
SessionType	Short Text		15	Caption = Session Type
Length	Number		Integer	Decimal Places = 0 Caption = Length (Hrs) Default Value = [no entry]
NumSessions	Number		Integer	Decimal Places = 0 Caption = Number of Sessions Default Value = [no entry]
Cost	Currency			Format = Currency Decimal Places = 0 Default Value = [no entry]
Assessment	Yes/No	Pre-assessment exam complete		Caption = Assessment Complete

17. Specify ContractID as the primary key, and then save the table using the name **Contract**.
18. Add a new field to the Contract table, between the TutorID and SessionType fields, with the field name **ContractDate**, the **Date/Time** data type, the description **Date contract is signed**, the **Short Date** format, and the caption **Contract Date**. Save and close the Contract table.
19. Use the Import Spreadsheet Wizard to add data to the Contract table. The data you need to import is contained in the Agreements workbook, which is an Excel file located in the Access1 ▸ Case2 folder provided with your Data Files.
    a. Specify the Agreements workbook as the source of the data.
    b. Select the option for appending the data to the table.
    c. Select Contract as the table.
    d. In the Import Spreadsheet Wizard dialog boxes, choose the Agreements worksheet, make sure Access confirms that the first row contains column headings, and import to the Contract table. Do not save the import steps.
20. Open the **Contract** table and add the records shown in Figure 2-54. (*Hint*: Use the New (blank) record button in the navigation buttons to add a new record.)

Figure 2-54 Records for the Contract table

Contract ID	Student ID	Tutor ID	Contract Date	Session Type	Length (Hrs)	Number of Sessions	Cost	Assessment Complete
5168	LUF8037	68-8234	8/30/2016	Group	3	12	$1,440	Yes
5172	GOS8029	71-1698	9/7/2016	Private	2	6	$720	Yes

21. Resize columns in the datasheet to their best fit (as necessary), and then save and close the Contract table.

22. Define the one-to-many relationships between the database tables as follows: between the primary Student table and the related Contract table, and between the primary Tutor table and the related Contract table. Resize the table field lists so that all field names are visible. Select the referential integrity option and the cascade updates option for each relationship.
23. Save the changes to the Relationships window and close it, compact and repair the OBrien database, and then close the database.

CHALLENGE

Case Problem 3

Data Files needed for this Case Problem: Shelter.accdb *(cont. from Tutorial 1)*, Donations.xlsx, and Animals.txt

Rosemary Animal Shelter Ryan Lang wants to use the Shelter database to maintain information about the patrons, animals, and donations for his not-for-profit agency. Ryan asks you to help him maintain the database by updating one table and creating two new ones. Complete the following:

1. Open the **Shelter** database you created in Tutorial 1.
2. Open the **Patron** table in Design view, and then change the following field properties:
   a. PatronID: Enter **Primary key** for the description, change the field size to **5**, and enter **Patron ID** for the caption.
   b. Title: Change the field size to **4**.
   c. FirstName: Change the field size to **20** and enter **First Name** for the caption.
   d. LastName: Change the field size to **25** and enter **Last Name** for the caption.
   e. Phone: Change the field size to **14.**
3. Save and close the Patron table. Click the Yes button when a message appears indicating some data might be lost.

Explore 4. Use the Import Spreadsheet Wizard to create a table in the Shelter database. As the source of the data, specify the Donations workbook, which is located in the Access1 ▸ Case3 folder provided with your Data Files. Select the option to import the source data into a new table in the database.

Explore 5. Complete the Import Spreadsheet Wizard dialog boxes as follows:
   a. Select Donation as the worksheet you want to import.
   b. Specify that the first row contains column headings.
   c. Accept the field options suggested by the wizard, and do not skip any fields.
   d. Choose DonationID as your own primary key.
   e. Import the data to a table named **Donation**, and do not save the import steps.

6. Open the Donation table in Datasheet view, and then delete the Requires Pickup field.
7. Open the Donation table in Design view, and then modify the table so it matches the design shown in Figure 2-55, including changes to data types, field name, and field position. For the Short Text fields, delete any formats specified in the Format property boxes.

Figure 2-55 **Design for the Donation table**

Field Name	Data Type	Description	Field Size	Other
DonationID	Short Text	Primary key	4	Caption = Donation ID
PatronID	Short Text	Foreign key	5	Caption = Patron ID
DonationDate	Date/Time			Format = mm/dd/yyyy Caption = Donation Date
Description	Short Text		30	
DonationValue	Currency	Dollar amount or estimated value		Format = Currency Decimal Places = 2 Caption = Donation Value Default Value = [no entry]

8. Save your changes to the table design, click Yes for the message about lost data, and then switch to Datasheet view.
9. Resize the columns in the Donation datasheet to their best fit.

Explore 10. Ryan decides that the values in the Donation Value column would look better without the two decimal places. Make this field the current field in the datasheet. Then, in the Formatting group on the FIELDS tab, use the Decrease Decimals button to remove the two decimal places and the period from these values. Switch back to Design view, and note that the Decimal Places property for the DonationValue field is now set to 0.

11. Save and close the Donation table.
12. Use Design view to create a table using the table design shown in Figure 2-56.

Figure 2-56 Design for the Animal table

Field Name	Data Type	Description	Field Size	Other
AnimalID	Short Text	Primary key	3	Caption = Animal ID
AnimalName	Short Text		15	Caption = Animal Name
Age	Short Text		2	Caption = Age at Arrival
Gender	Short Text		6	
AnimalType	Short Text		5	Caption = Animal Type
Description	Short Text		60	
ArrivalDate	Date/Time			Format = Short Date Caption = Arrival Date
AdoptionDate	Date/Time			Format = Short Date Caption = Adoption Date
Adopted	Yes/No			
PatronID	Short Text		5	Caption = Patron ID

13. Specify AnimalID as the primary key, save the table as **Animal**, and then close the table.
14. Use the Import Text File Wizard to add data to the Animal table. The data you need to import is contained in the Animals text file, which is located in the Access1 ▸ Case3 folder provided with your Data Files.
    a. Specify the Animals text file as the source of the data.
    b. Select the option for appending the data.
    c. Select Animal as the table.
    d. In the Import Text File Wizard dialog boxes, choose the options to import delimited data, to use a comma delimiter, and to import the data into the Animal table. Do not save the import steps.
15. Open the Animal table in Datasheet view, and resize all columns to their best fit.
16. Display the Animal table in Design view. Move the PatronID field to make it the second field in the table, and enter the description **Foreign key** for the PatronID field. Then move the Adopted field so it is positioned between the ArrivalDate and AdoptionDate fields. Save the modified Animal table design.
17. Switch to Datasheet view, and then add the records shown in Figure 2-57 to the Animal table. (*Hint*: Use the New (blank) record button in the navigation buttons to add a new record.) Close the table when finished.

Figure 2-57 Records for the Animal table

Animal ID	Patron ID	Animal Name	Age at Arrival	Gender	Animal Type	Description	Arrival Date	Adopted	Adoption Date
B45		Gizmo	12	Male	Dog	Hound mix	3/6/2016	No	
R39	38398	Simba	3	Female	Cat	Siamese	4/12/2016	Yes	5/14/2016

18. Define the one-to-many relationships between the database tables as follows: between the primary Patron table and the related Animal table, and between the primary Patron table and the related Donation table. (*Hint:* Place the Patron table as the middle table in the Relationships window to make it easier to join the tables.) Resize the Animal field list so that all field names are visible. Select the referential integrity option and the cascade updates option for each relationship.
19. Save the changes to the Relationships window and close it, compact and repair the Shelter database, and then close the database.

CHALLENGE

Case Problem 4

Data Files needed for this Case Problem: Stanley.accdb (*cont. from Tutorial 1*), Travel.accdb, and Bookings.txt

Stanley EcoTours Janice and Bill Stanley use the Stanley database to track the data about the tours they offer to clients of their ecotourism business. They ask you to help them maintain this database. Complete the following:

1. Open the **Stanley** database you created in Tutorial 1.
2. Open the **Guest** table in Design view and change the following field properties:
   a. GuestID: Enter **Primary key** for the description, change the field size to **3**, and enter **Guest ID** for the caption.
   b. GuestFirst: Change the field size to **20** and enter **Guest First Name** for the caption.
   c. GuestLast: Change the field size to **25** and enter **Guest Last Name** for the caption.
   d. Address: Change the field size to **35**.
   e. City: Change the field size to **25**.
   f. State/Prov: Change the field size to **2**.
   g. PostalCode: Change the field size to **10** and enter **Postal Code** for the caption.
   h. Country: Change the field size to **15**.
   i. Phone: Change the field size to **14**.
3. Save the Guest table, click the Yes button when a message appears indicating some data might be lost, resize the Guest First Name and Guest Last Name columns in Datasheet view to their best fit, and then save and close the table.

Explore 4. In addition to importing the structure of an existing Access table, you can also import both the structure *and* the data contained in a table to create a new table. Import the **Trip** table structure and data from the **Travel** database into a new table in the **Stanley** database as follows:
   a. Start the process for importing an Access table structure.
   b. As the source of the data, specify the Travel database, which is located in the Access1 ▸ Case4 folder provided with your Data Files.
   c. Select the option button to import tables, queries, forms, reports, macros, and modules into the current database.
   d. In the Import Objects dialog box, select the Trip table, click the Options button, and then make sure that the correct option is selected to import the table's data and structure (definition).
   e. Do not save your import steps.

Explore 5. Using a shortcut menu in the Navigation Pane, rename the Trip table as **Tour** to give this name to the new table in the Stanley database.

6. Open the **Tour** table in Design view, delete the VIPDiscount field, and then move the PricePerPerson field so that it appears between the Country and SingleSupplement fields.

7. Change the following properties:
   a. TourID: Enter the description **Primary key**, change the field size to **4**, and enter **Tour ID** for the caption.
   b. TourName: Enter **Tour Name** for the caption.
   c. PricePerPerson: Enter **Price Per Person** for the caption.
   d. SingleSupplement: Enter the description **Additional charge for single accommodation**, and enter **Single Supplement** for the caption.
   e. TourType: Change the field size to **15**, and enter **Tour Type** for the caption.
   f. Nights: Enter **Num of Nights** for the caption.
8. Save the modified table, click the Yes button when a message appears indicating some data might be lost, and then display the table in Datasheet view. Resize all datasheet columns to their best fit, and then save and close the table.
9. In Design view, create a table using the table design shown in Figure 2-58.

Figure 2-58 **Design for the Reservation table**

Field Name	Data Type	Description	Field Size	Other
ReservationID	Short Text	Primary key	3	Caption = Reservation ID
GuestID	Short Text	Foreign key	3	Caption = Guest ID
TourID	Short Text	Foreign key	4	Caption = Tour ID
StartDate	Date/Time			Caption = Start Date
People	Number	Number of people in the party	Integer	Decimal Places = 0 Default Value = [no entry]

10. Specify ReservationID as the primary key, and then save the table as **Reservation**.

Explore 11. Refer back to Figure 2-11 to review the custom date formats. Change the Format property of the StartDate field to a custom format that displays dates in a format similar to 05/25/16. Save and close the Reservation table.

12. Use the Import Text File Wizard to add data to the Reservation table. The data you need to import is contained in the Bookings text file, which is located in the Access1 ▸ Case4 folder provided with your Data Files.
    a. Specify the Bookings text file as the source of the data.
    b. Select the option for appending the data.
    c. Select Reservation as the table.
    d. In the Import Text File Wizard dialog boxes, choose the options to import delimited data, to use a comma delimiter, and to import the data into the Reservation table. Do not save the import steps.
13. Resize columns in the **Reservation** table datasheet to their best fit (as necessary), verify that the date values in the StartDate field are displayed correctly according to the custom format, and then save and close the table.
14. Define the one-to-many relationships between the database tables as follows: between the primary Guest table and the related Reservation table, and between the primary Tour table and the related Reservation table. (*Hint:* Place the Reservation table as the middle table in the Relationships window to make it easier to join the tables.) Resize the Guest and Tour field lists so that all field names are visible. Select the referential integrity option and the cascade updates option for each relationship.
15. Save the changes to the Relationships window and close it, compact and repair the Stanley database, and then close the database.

TUTORIAL 3

Maintaining and Querying a Database

Updating and Retrieving Information About Patients, Visits, and Invoices

OBJECTIVES

Session 3.1
- Find, modify, and delete records in a table
- Hide and unhide fields in a datasheet
- Work in the Query window in Design view
- Create, run, and save queries
- Update data using a query datasheet
- Create a query based on multiple tables
- Sort data in a query
- Filter data in a query

Session 3.2
- Specify an exact match condition in a query
- Use a comparison operator in a query to match a range of values
- Use the And and Or logical operators in queries
- Change the font size and alternate row color in a datasheet
- Create and format a calculated field in a query
- Perform calculations in a query using aggregate functions and record group calculations
- Change the display of database objects in the Navigation Pane

Case | *Chatham Community Health Services*

At a recent meeting, Cindi Rodriguez and her staff discussed the importance of maintaining accurate information about the clinic's patients, visits, and invoices, and regularly monitoring the business activities of Chatham Community Health Services. For example, Kelly Schwarz, Cindi's assistant, needs to make sure she has up-to-date contact information, such as phone numbers and email addresses, for all the clinic's patients. The office staff also must monitor billing activity to ensure that invoices are paid on time and in full. Ethan Ward, a staff member who handles marketing and community outreach efforts for the clinic, tracks patient activity to develop new strategies for promoting services provided by the clinic. In addition, Cindi is interested in analyzing other aspects of the business related to patient visits and finances. You can satisfy all these informational needs for Chatham Community Health Services by updating data in the Chatham database and by creating and using queries that retrieve information from the database.

STARTING DATA FILES

Access1 →

Tutorial
Chatham.accdb *(cont.)*

Review
Vendor.accdb *(cont.)*

Case1
Gopher.accdb *(cont.)*

Case2
OBrien.accdb *(cont.)*

Case3
Shelter.accdb *(cont.)*

Case4
Stanley.accdb *(cont.)*
Tour.accdb

Session 3.1 Visual Overview:

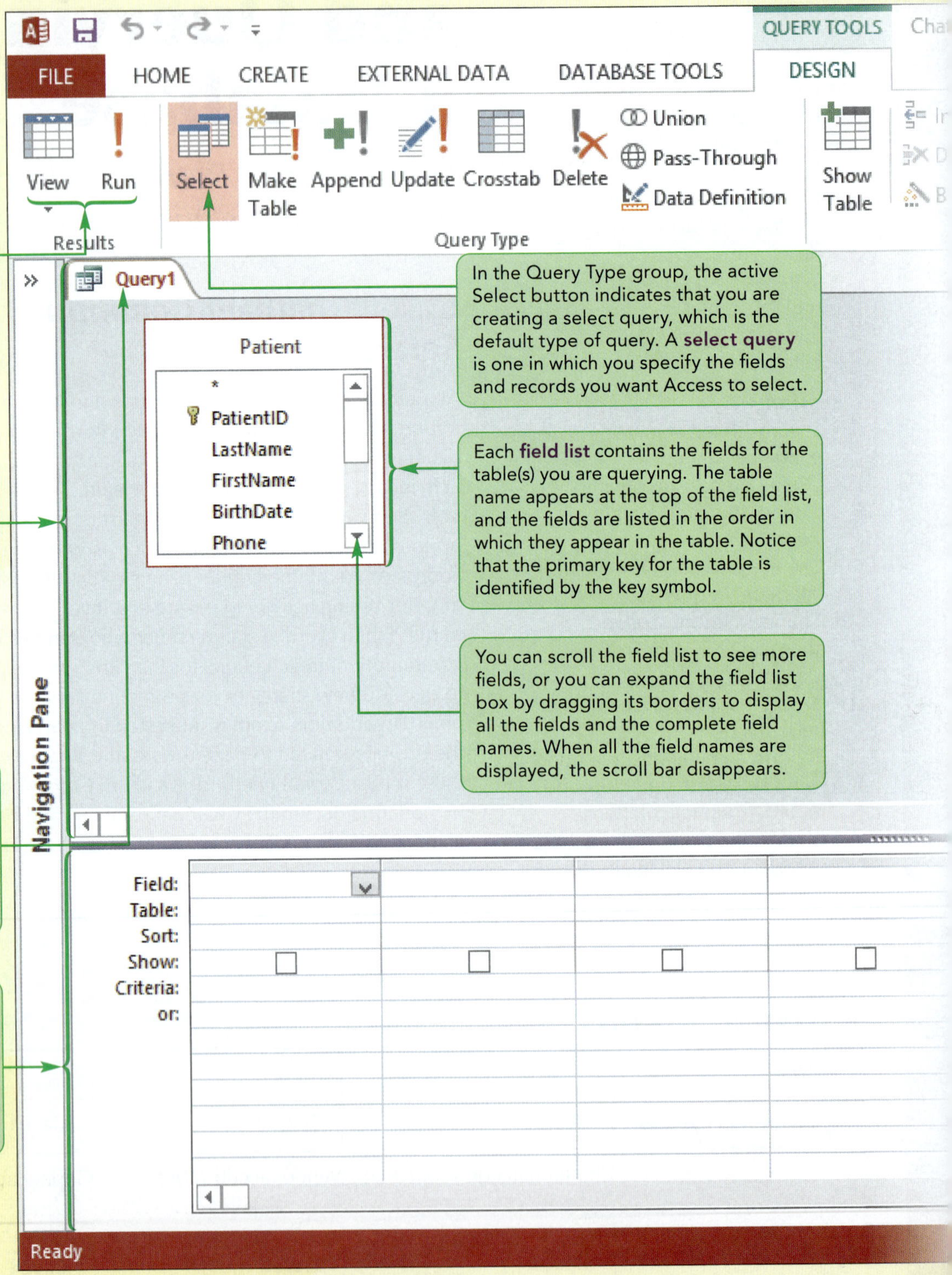

When you are constructing a query, you can see the results at any time by clicking the View button or the Run button. In response, Access displays the query datasheet, which contains the set of fields and records that results from answering, or **running**, the query.

In the Query Type group, the active Select button indicates that you are creating a select query, which is the default type of query. A **select query** is one in which you specify the fields and records you want Access to select.

The top portion of the Query window in Design view contains the field list (or lists) for the table(s) used in the query.

Each **field list** contains the fields for the table(s) you are querying. The table name appears at the top of the field list, and the fields are listed in the order in which they appear in the table. Notice that the primary key for the table is identified by the key symbol.

You can scroll the field list to see more fields, or you can expand the field list box by dragging its borders to display all the fields and the complete field names. When all the field names are displayed, the scroll bar disappears.

The default query name, Query1, is displayed on the tab for the query. You change the default query name to a more meaningful one when you save the query.

The bottom portion of the Query window in Design view contains the design grid. In the **design grid**, you include the fields and record selection criteria for the information you want to see.

Query Window in Design View

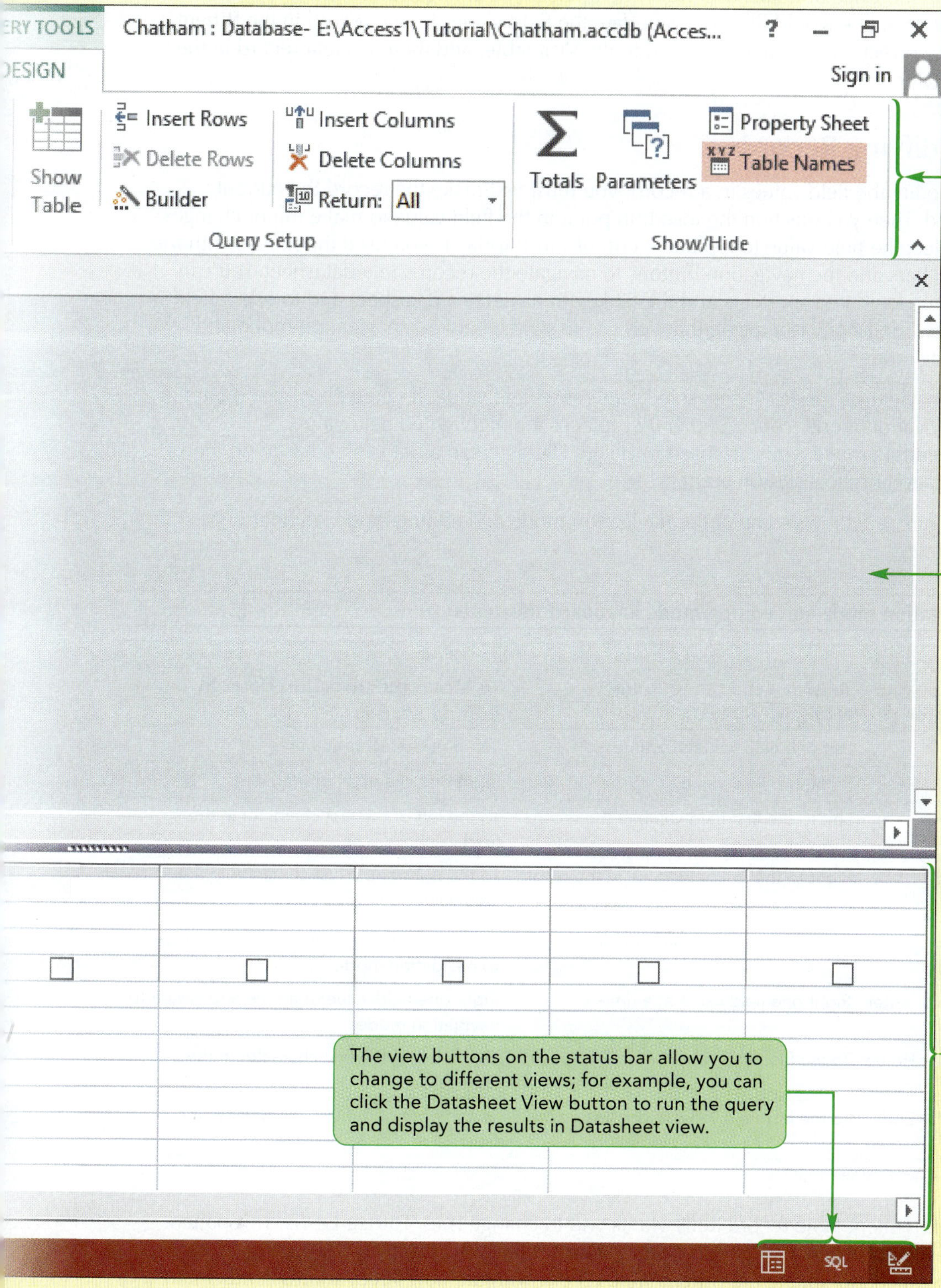

The ribbon displays the QUERY TOOLS DESIGN tab with options for creating and running queries. Note the Query Type group on the DESIGN tab; it provides buttons you can click to create various types of queries.

In Design view, you specify the data you want to view by constructing a query by example. When you use **query by example (QBE)**, you give Access an example of the information you are requesting. Access then retrieves the information that precisely matches your example.

Each column in the design grid contains specifications about a field you will use in the query. You can choose a single field for your query by double-clicking its name in the field list to place the field in the next available design grid column.

The view buttons on the status bar allow you to change to different views; for example, you can click the Datasheet View button to run the query and display the results in Datasheet view.

Updating a Database

Updating, or **maintaining**, a database is the process of adding, modifying, and deleting records in database tables to keep them current and accurate. After reviewing the data in the Chatham database, Kelly identified some changes that need to be made to the data. She would like you to update the field values in one record in the Patient table, correct an error in one record in the Visit table, and then delete a record in the Visit table.

Modifying Records

To modify the field values in a record, you must first make the record the current record. Then you position the insertion point in the field value to make minor changes, or select the field value to replace it entirely. In Tutorial 1, you used the mouse with the scroll bars and the navigation buttons to navigate the records in a datasheet. You can also use keyboard shortcuts and the F2 key to navigate a datasheet and to select field values. The **F2 key** is a toggle that you use to switch between navigation mode and editing mode:

- In **navigation mode**, Access selects an entire field value. If you type while you are in navigation mode, your typed entry replaces the highlighted field value.
- In **editing mode**, you can insert or delete characters in a field value based on the location of the insertion point.

Figure 3-1 shows some of the navigation mode and editing mode keyboard shortcuts.

Figure 3-1 Navigation mode and editing mode keyboard shortcuts

Press	To Move the Selection in Navigation Mode	To Move the Insertion Point in Editing Mode
←	Left one field value at a time	Left one character at a time
→	Right one field value at a time	Right one character at a time
Home	Left to the first field value in the record	To the left of the first character in the field value
End	Right to the last field value in the record	To the right of the last character in the field value
↑ or ↓	Up or down one record at a time	Up or down one record at a time and switch to navigation mode
Tab or Enter	Right one field value at a time	Right one field value at a time and switch to navigation mode
Ctrl + Home	To the first field value in the first record	To the left of the first character in the field value
Ctrl + End	To the last field value in the last record	To the right of the last character in the field value

The Patient table record Kelly wants you to change is for Patrice Lewis. This patient recently moved to another location in Windsor and also changed her email address, so you need to update the Patient table record with the new street address and email address.

To open the Patient table in the Chatham database:

1. Start Access and open the **Chatham** database you created and worked with in Tutorials 1 and 2.

   Trouble? If the security warning is displayed below the ribbon, click the Enable Content button.

2. Open the **Patient** table in Datasheet view.

The Patient table contains many fields. Sometimes, when updating data in a table, it can be helpful to remove the display of some fields on the screen.

Hiding and Unhiding Fields

TIP

Hiding a field removes it from the datasheet display *only*; the field and its contents are still part of the table.

When you are viewing a table or query datasheet in Datasheet view, you might want to temporarily remove certain fields from the displayed datasheet, making it easier to focus on the data you're interested in viewing. The **Hide Fields** command allows you to remove the display of one or more fields, and the **Unhide Fields** command allows you to redisplay any hidden fields. Hiding fields can be especially useful in a table with many fields.

To make it easier to modify the patient record, you'll first hide a couple of fields in the Patient table.

To hide fields in the Patient table and modify the patient record:

1. Right-click the **Date of Birth** field name to display the shortcut menu, and then click **Hide Fields** on the shortcut menu. The Date of Birth column is removed from the datasheet display.
2. Right-click the **Phone** field name, and then click **Hide Fields** on the shortcut menu. The Phone column is removed from the datasheet display.

   With the fields hidden, you can now update the patient record. The record you need to modify is near the end of the table and has a PatientID field value of 22560.
3. Drag the vertical scroll box down until you see the last records in the table.
4. Click the PatientID field value **22560**, for Patrice Lewis. The field value is not selected, indicating you are in editing mode.
5. Press the **Tab** key to move to the Last Name field value, Lewis. The field value is selected, indicating you are in navigation mode.
6. Press the **Tab** key twice to move to the Address field and select its field value, type **83 Highland St**, press the **Tab** key four times to move to the Email field, type **plewis5@example.org**, and then press the **Tab** key. The changes to the record are complete. See Figure 3-2.

Figure 3-2 Table after changing field values in a record

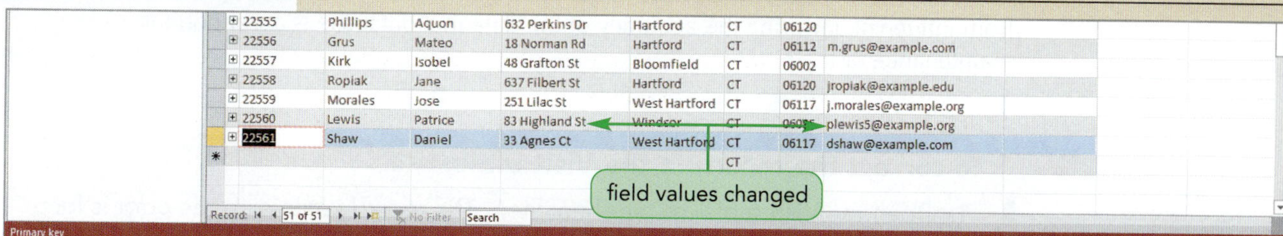

Access saves changes to field values when you move to a new field or another record, or when you close the table. You don't have to click the Save button to save changes to field values or records.

Note that the PatientID field value for the last record in the table is selected, indicating you are in navigation mode.

7. Press the **Ctrl+Home** keys to move to the first field value in the first record.

   With the changes to the record complete, you can unhide the hidden fields.

8. Right-click any field name to display the shortcut menu, and then click **Unhide Fields**. The Unhide Columns dialog box opens. See Figure 3-3.

Figure 3-3 Unhide Columns dialog box

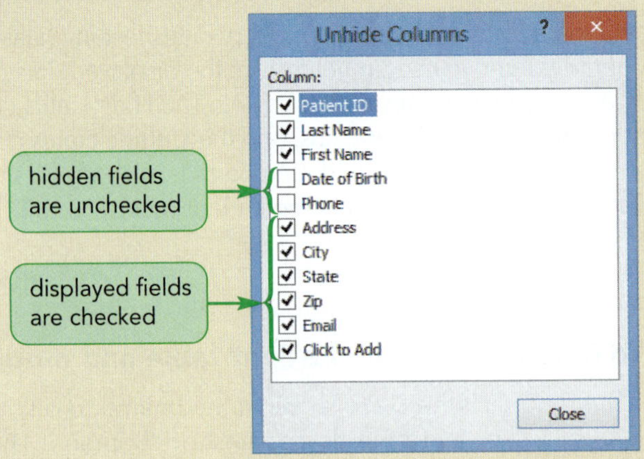

All currently displayed fields are checked in this dialog box, and all hidden fields are unchecked. To redisplay them, you simply click their check boxes to select them.

9. In the Unhide Columns dialog box, click the **Date of Birth** check box to select it, click the **Phone** check box to select it, and then click the **Close** button to close the dialog box. The two hidden fields are now displayed in the datasheet.

10. Close the Patient table. A dialog box opens asking if you want to save changes to the layout of the Patient table. This box appears because you hid fields and redisplayed them.

    In this case, you can click either the Yes button or the No button, because no changes were actually made to the table layout or design.

11. Click the **No** button to close the dialog box.

Next you need to correct an error in the Visit table for a visit made by Jane Ropiak, Patient ID 22558. A staff member incorrectly entered "COPD management visit" as the reason for the visit, when the patient actually came to the clinic that day suffering from influenza. Ensuring the accuracy of the data in a database is an important maintenance task.

To correct the record in the Visit table:

1. Open the **Visit** table in Datasheet view. The record containing the error is for Visit ID 1635.

2. Scroll down the Visit table until you locate Visit ID **1635**, and then click at the end of the **Reason** field value for this record. Because the field value is not selected, you are in editing mode.
3. Press the **Backspace** key until the current entry for the Reason field is deleted, type **Influenza**, and then press the **Enter** key twice. The record now contains the correct value in the Reason field, and Access saves this change automatically in the Visit table.

The next update Kelly asks you to make is to delete a record in the Visit table. One of the clinic's patients, Robert Goldberg, recently notified Kelly that he received an invoice for an annual wellness visit, but that he had cancelled this scheduled appointment to the clinic. Because this patient visit did not take place, the record for this visit needs to be deleted from the Visit table. Rather than scrolling through the table to locate the record to delete, you can have Access find the data for you.

Finding Data in a Table

Access provides options you can use to locate specific field values in a table. Instead of scrolling the Visit table datasheet to find the visit that you need to delete—the record for Visit ID 1688—you can use the Find command to find the record. The **Find command** allows you to search a table or query datasheet, or a form, to locate a specific field value or part of a field value. This feature is particularly useful when searching a table that contains a large number of records.

TIP

You can click any value in the column containing the field you want to search to make the field current.

To search for the record in the Visit table:

1. Make sure the VisitID field value **1638** is still selected. You need to search the VisitID field to find the record containing the value 1688, so the insertion point is already correctly positioned in the field you want to search.
2. Make sure the **HOME** tab is displayed on the ribbon.
3. In the Find group, click the **Find** button. The Find and Replace dialog box opens. See Figure 3-4.

Figure 3-4 Find and Replace dialog box

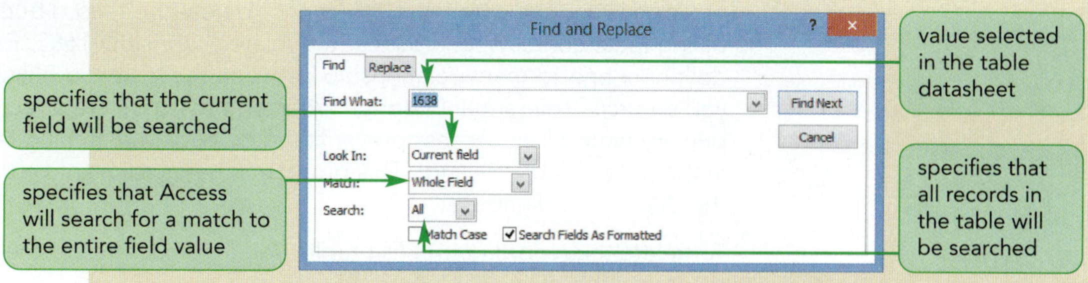

The field value 1638 appears in the Find What box because this value is selected in the table datasheet. The Look In box indicates that the current field will be searched for the value. The Match box indicates that the Find command will match the whole field value, which is correct for your search. You also can choose to search for only part of a field value, such as when you need to find all Visit IDs that start with a certain value. The Search box indicates that all the records in the table will be searched for the value you want to find. You also can choose to search up or down from the currently selected record.

Trouble? Some of the settings in your dialog box might be different from those shown in Figure 3-4 depending on the last search performed on the computer you're using. If so, change the settings so that they match those in the figure.

4. Make sure the value 1638 is selected in the Find What box, type **1688** to replace the selected value, and then click the **Find Next** button. Access scrolls the datasheet to record 81 and selects the field value you specified.
5. Click the **Cancel** button to close the Find and Replace dialog box.

Deleting Records

To delete a record, you need to select the record in Datasheet view, and then delete it using the Delete button in the Records group on the HOME tab or the Delete Record option on the shortcut menu.

REFERENCE

Deleting a Record

- With the table open in Datasheet view, click the row selector for the record you want to delete.
- In the Records group on the HOME tab, click the Delete button (or right-click the row selector for the record, and then click Delete Record on the shortcut menu).
- In the dialog box asking you to confirm the deletion, click the Yes button.

Now that you have found the record with Visit ID 1688, you can delete it. To delete a record, you must first select the entire row for the record.

To delete the record:

1. Click the row selector for the record containing the VisitID field value **1688**, which should still be highlighted. The entire row is selected.
2. In the Records group on the HOME tab, click the **Delete** button. A dialog box opens and indicates that you cannot delete the record because the Billing table contains records that are related to VisitID 1688. Recall that you defined a one-to-many relationship between the Visit and Billing tables and you enforced referential integrity. When you try to delete a record in the primary table (Visit), Access prevents the deletion if matching records exist in the related table (Billing). This protection helps to maintain the integrity of the data in the database.

   To delete the record in the Visit table, you first must delete the related records in the Billing table.
3. Click the **OK** button in the dialog box to close it. Notice the plus sign that appears at the beginning of each record in the Visit table. The **plus sign** indicates that the Visit table is the primary table related to another table—in this case, the Billing table.
4. Scroll the datasheet down until you see the rest of the records in the table, so that you have room to view the related records for the visit record.

5. Click the **plus sign** next to VisitID 1688. Access displays the one related record from the Billing table for this visit. See Figure 3-5.

Figure 3-5 Related record from the Billing table in the subdatasheet

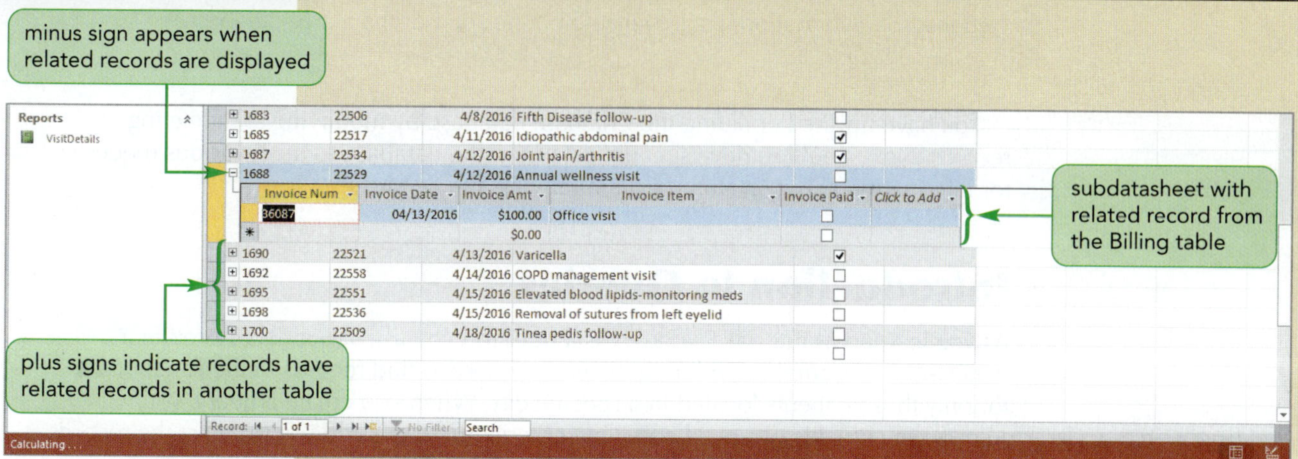

TIP

The plus sign changes to a minus sign for the current record when its related records are displayed.

The related record from the Billing table is displayed in a **subdatasheet**. When you first open a table that is the primary table in a one-to-many relationship, the subdatasheet containing the records from the related table is not displayed. You need to click the plus sign, also called the **expand indicator**, to display the related records in the subdatasheet. When the subdatasheet is open, you can navigate and update it, just as you can using a table datasheet.

You need to delete the record in the Billing table that is related to Visit ID 1688 before you can delete this visit record. The record is for the invoice that was mistakenly sent to the patient, Robert Goldberg, who had cancelled his annual wellness visit at the clinic. You could open the Billing table and find the related record. However, an easier way is to delete the record right in the subdatasheet. The record will be deleted from the Billing table automatically.

6. In the Billing table subdatasheet, click the row selector for invoice number **36087**. The entire row is selected.
7. In the Records group on the HOME tab, click the **Delete** button. Access opens a dialog box asking you to confirm the deletion of one record. Because the deletion of a record is permanent and cannot be undone, Access prompts you to make sure that you want to delete the record.
8. Click the **Yes** button to confirm the deletion and close the dialog box. The record is removed from the Billing table, and the subdatasheet is now empty.
9. Click the **minus sign** next to VisitID 1688 to close the subdatasheet.

Now that you have deleted the related record in the Billing table, you can delete the record for Visit ID 1688. You'll use the shortcut menu to do so.

Be sure to select the correct record before deleting it.

10. Right-click the row selector for the record for Visit ID **1688**. Access selects the record and displays the shortcut menu.
11. Click **Delete Record** on the shortcut menu, and then click the **Yes** button in the dialog box to confirm the deletion. The record is deleted from the Visit table.
12. Close the Visit table.

INSIGHT

Process for Deleting Records

When working with more complex databases that are managed by a database administrator, you typically need special permission to delete records from a table. Many companies also follow the practice of archiving records before deleting them so that the information is still available but not part of the active database.

You have finished updating the Chatham database by modifying and deleting records. Next, you'll retrieve specific data from the database to meet various requests for information about Chatham Community Health Services.

Introduction to Queries

As you learned in Tutorial 1, a query is a question you ask about data stored in a database. For example, Cindi might create a query to find records in the Patient table for only those patients located in a specific city. When you create a query, you tell Access which fields you need and what criteria Access should use to select the records. Access provides powerful query capabilities that allow you to do the following:

- Display selected fields and records from a table
- Sort records
- Perform calculations
- Generate data for forms, reports, and other queries
- Update data in the tables in a database
- Find and display data from two or more tables

Most questions about data are generalized queries in which you specify the fields and records you want Access to select. These common requests for information, such as "Which patients are located in Bloomfield?" or "How many invoices have been paid?" are select queries. The answer to a select query is returned in the form of a datasheet. The result of a query is also referred to as a **recordset** because the query produces a set of records that answers your question.

INSIGHT

Designing Queries vs. Using a Query Wizard

More specialized, technical queries, such as finding duplicate records in a table, are best formulated using a Query Wizard. A **Query Wizard** prompts you for information by asking a series of questions and then creates the appropriate query based on your answers. In Tutorial 1, you used the Simple Query Wizard to display only some of the fields in the Visit table; Access provides other Query Wizards for more complex queries. For common, informational queries, designing your own query is more efficient than using a Query Wizard.

Ethan wants you to create a query to display the patient ID, last name, first name, city, and email address for each record in the Patient table. He needs this information to complete an email campaign advertising a special blood pressure screening being offered to patients of Chatham Community Health Services. You'll open the Query window in Design view to create the query for Ethan.

To open the Query window in Design view:

1. Close the Navigation Pane so that more of the workspace is displayed.
2. On the ribbon, click the **CREATE** tab. Access displays the options for creating different database objects.
3. In the Queries group, click the **Query Design** button. The Show Table dialog box opens on the Query window in Design view. See Figure 3-6.

Figure 3-6 Show Table dialog box

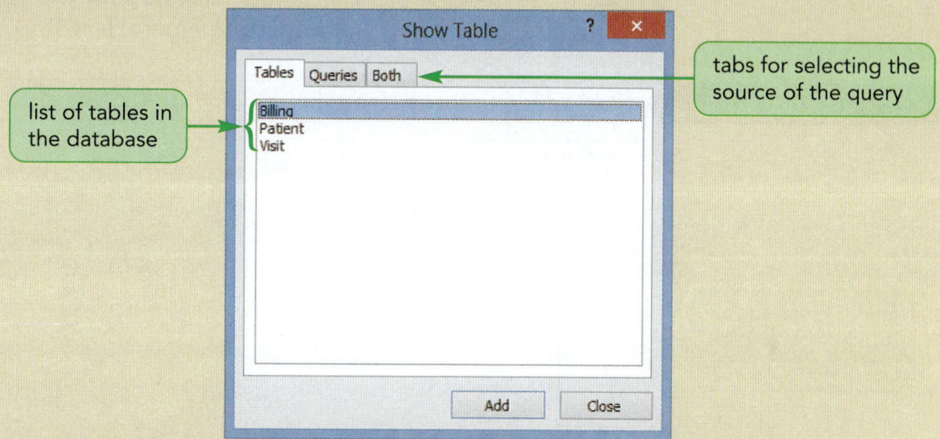

The Show Table dialog box lists all the tables in the Chatham database. You can choose to base a query on one or more tables, on other queries, or on a combination of tables and queries. The query you are creating will retrieve data from the Patient table, so you need to add this table to the Query window.

4. Click **Patient** in the Tables list, click the **Add** button, and then click the **Close** button. Access places the Patient table's field list in the Query window and closes the Show Table dialog box. Refer to the Session 3.1 Visual Overview to familiarize yourself with the Query window in Design view.

   Trouble? If you add the wrong table to the Query window, right-click the bar at the top of the field list containing the table name, and then click Remove Table on the shortcut menu. To add the correct table to the Query window, click the Show Table button in the Query Setup group on the DESIGN tab to redisplay the Show Table dialog box, and then repeat Step 4.

Now you'll create and run Ethan's query to display selected fields from the Patient table.

Creating and Running a Query

The default table datasheet displays all the fields in the table in the same order as they appear in the table. In contrast, a query datasheet can display selected fields from a table, and the order of the fields can be different from that of the table, enabling those viewing the query results to see only the information they need and in the order they want.

Ethan wants the PatientID, LastName, FirstName, City, and Email fields from the Patient table to appear in the query results. You'll add each of these fields to the design grid. First you'll resize the Patient table field list to display all of the fields.

To select the fields for the query, and then run the query:

1. Position the pointer on the bottom border of the Patient field list until the pointer changes to a ↕ shape, and then click and drag the pointer down until the vertical scroll bar in the field list disappears and all fields in the Patient table are displayed in the list.

   Note that it's not necessary to resize the field list in order to create the query, but doing so enables you to see all the fields in the list, making it easier to select fields to include in the query.

2. In the Patient field list, double-click **PatientID** to place the field in the design grid's first column Field box. See Figure 3-7.

Figure 3-7 **Field added to the design grid**

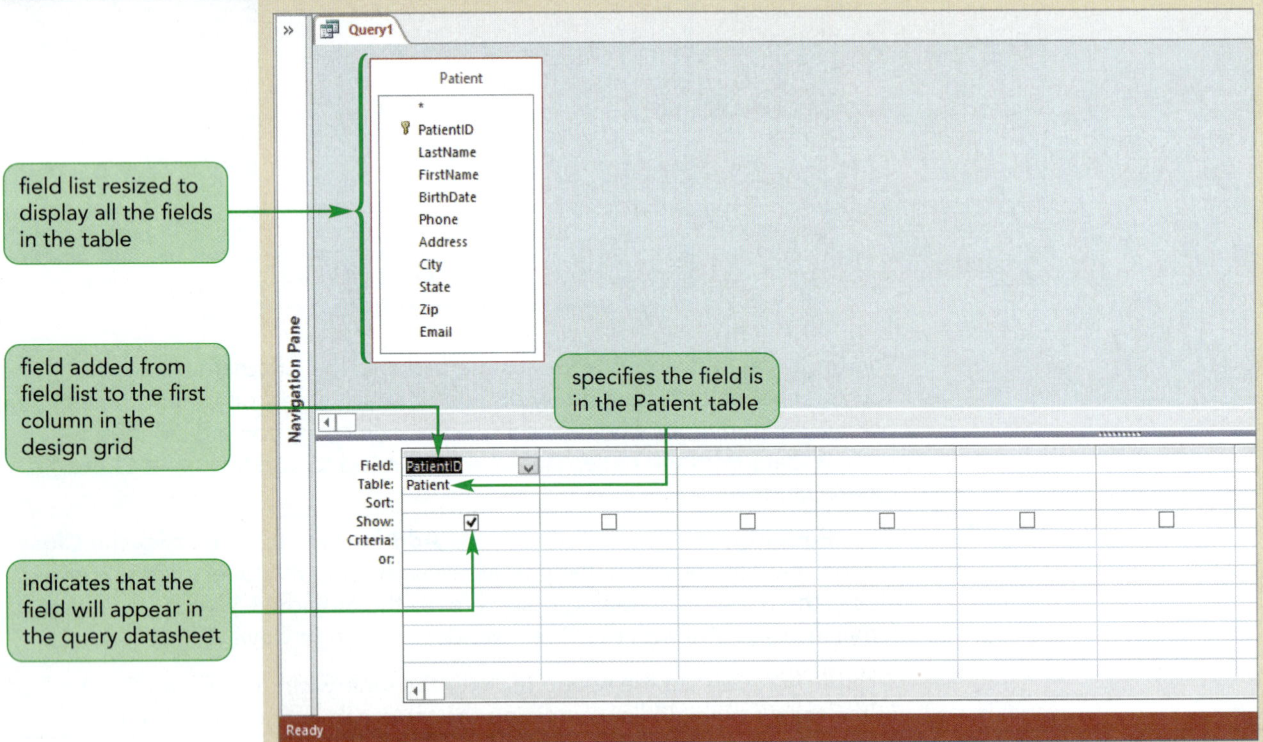

In the design grid's first column, the field name PatientID appears in the Field box, the table name Patient appears in the Table box, and the checkmark in the Show check box indicates that the field will be displayed in the datasheet when you run the query. Sometimes you might not want to display a field and its values in the query results. For example, if you are creating a query to list all patients located in Windsor, and you assign the name "WindsorPatients" to the query, you do not need to include the City field value for each record in the query results—the query design only lists patients with the City field value of "Windsor." Even if you choose not to display a field in the query results, you can still use the field as part of the query to select specific records or to specify a particular sequence for the records in the datasheet.

You can also add a field to the design grid using the arrow on the Field box; this arrow appears when you click the right side of an empty Field box.

TIP

You can also use the mouse to drag a field from the field list to a column in the design grid.

3. In the design grid, click the right side of the second column's Field box to display a menu listing all the fields in the Patient table, and then click **LastName**. Access adds this field to the second column in the design grid.
4. Use the method you prefer to add the **FirstName**, **City**, and **Email** fields to the design grid in that order.

   Trouble? If you accidentally add the wrong field to the design grid, you can remove the field from the grid. Select the field's column by clicking the pointer ⬇ on the field selector, which is the thin bar above the Field box, for the field you want to delete, and then press the Delete key (or in the Query Setup group on the DESIGN tab, click the Delete Columns button).

   Having selected the five fields for Ethan's query, you can now run the query.
5. In the Results group on the DESIGN tab, click the **Run** button. Access runs the query and displays the results in Datasheet view. See Figure 3-8.

Figure 3-8 Datasheet displayed after running the query

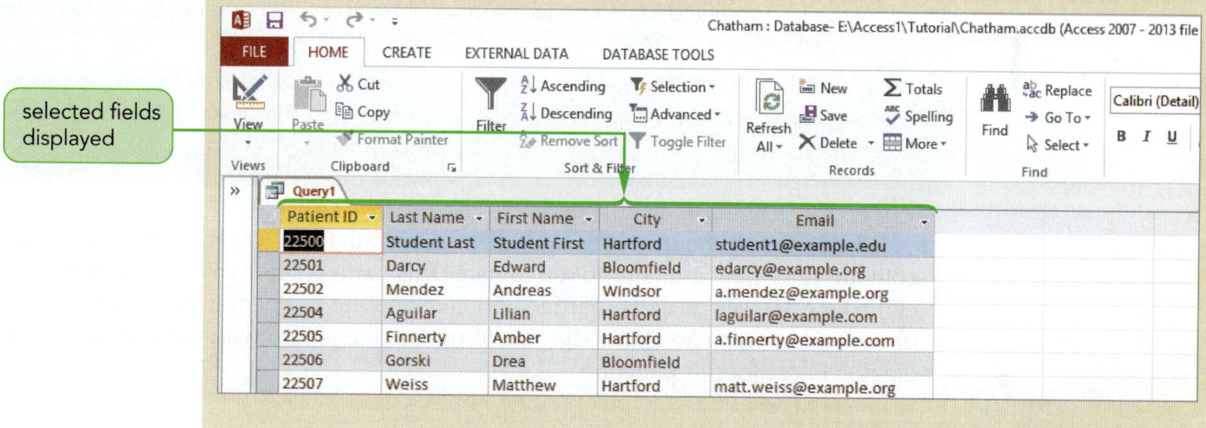

The five fields you added to the design grid appear in the datasheet in the same order as they appear in the design grid. The records are displayed in primary key sequence by PatientID. Access selected all 51 records from the Patient table for display in the query datasheet. Ethan asks you to save the query as "PatientEmail" so that he can easily retrieve the same data again.

6. On the Quick Access Toolbar, click the **Save** button. The Save As dialog box opens.
7. In the Query Name box, type **PatientEmail** and then press the **Enter** key. Access saves the query with the specified name in the Chatham database and displays the name on the tab for the query.

PROSKILLS

Decision Making: Comparing Methods for Adding All Fields to the Design Grid

If the query you are creating includes every field from the specified table, you can use one of the following three methods to transfer all the fields from the field list to the design grid:

- Double-click (or click and drag) each field individually from the field list to the design grid. Use this method if you want the fields in your query to appear in an order that is different from the order in the field list.
- Double-click the asterisk at the top of the field list. Access places the table name followed by a period and an asterisk (as in "Patient.*") in the Field box of the first column in the design grid, which signifies that the order of the fields is the same in the query as it is in the field list. Use this method if you don't need to sort the query or specify conditions based on the fields in the table you added in this way (for example, in a query based on more than one table). The advantage of using this method is that you do not need to change the query if you add or delete fields from the underlying table structure. Such changes are reflected automatically in the query.
- Double-click the field list title bar to highlight all the fields, and then click and drag one of the highlighted fields to the first column in the design grid. Access places each field in a separate column and arranges the fields in the order in which they appear in the field list. Use this method when you need to sort your query or include record selection criteria.

By choosing the most appropriate method to add all the table fields to the query design grid, you can work more efficiently and ensure that the query produces the results you want.

When viewing the query results, Ethan noticed that the record for one of the patients contains information that is not up to date. This patient, Nancy Fraser, had informed the clinic that she was recently married and changed her last name; she also provided a new email address. So Ethan asks you to update the record with the new last name and email address for this patient.

Updating Data Using a Query

A query datasheet is temporary and its contents are based on the criteria in the query design grid; however, you can still update the data in a table using a query datasheet. In this case, Ethan has changes he wants you to make to a record in the Patient table. Instead of making the changes in the table datasheet, you can make them in the PatientEmail query datasheet because the query is based on the Patient table. The underlying Patient table will be updated with the changes you make.

To update data using the PatientEmail query datasheet:

1. Locate the record with PatientID 22523, Nancy Fraser (record 21 in the query datasheet).
2. In the Last Name column for this record, double-click **Fraser** to select the name, and then type **Bennett**.
3. Press the **Tab** key three times to move to the Email column, type **n.bennett@example.com** and then press the **Tab** key.
4. Close the PatientEmail query, and then open the Navigation Pane. Note that the PatientEmail query is listed in the Queries section of the Navigation Pane.

Now you'll check the Patient table to verify that the changes you made in the query datasheet are reflected in the Patient table.

5. Open the **Patient** table in Datasheet view, and then close the Navigation Pane.
6. Locate the record for PatientID 22523 (record 21). Notice that the changes you made in the query datasheet to the Last Name and Email field values were made to the record in the Patient table.
7. Close the Patient table.

INSIGHT

Query Datasheet vs. Table Datasheet

Although a query datasheet looks just like a table datasheet and appears in Datasheet view, the contents of a query datasheet are temporary and are based on the criteria you establish in the design grid. Whenever you run a query, the results displayed reflect the current data in the underlying table. In contrast, a table datasheet shows the permanent data in a table. However, you can update data while viewing a query datasheet, just as you can when working in a table datasheet or form.

Kelly also wants to view specific information in the Chatham database. She would like to review the visit data for patients while also viewing certain contact information for them. So, she needs to see data from both the Patient table and the Visit table at the same time.

Creating a Multitable Query

A multitable query is a query based on more than one table. If you want to create a query that retrieves data from multiple tables, the tables must have a common field. In Tutorial 2, you established a relationship between the Patient (primary) and Visit (related) tables based on the common PatientID field that exists in both tables, so you can now create a query to display data from both tables at the same time. Specifically, Kelly wants to view the values in the City, FirstName, and LastName fields from the Patient table and the VisitDate and Reason fields from the Visit table.

To create the query using the Patient and Visit tables:

1. On the ribbon, click the **CREATE** tab.
2. In the Queries group, click the **Query Design** button. Access opens the Show Table dialog box. You need to add the Patient and Visit tables to the Query window.
3. Click **Patient** in the Tables list, click the **Add** button, click **Visit**, click the **Add** button, and then click the **Close** button. The Patient and Visit field lists appear in the Query window, and the Show Table dialog box closes.
4. Use the ⇕ pointer to resize the Patient and Visit field lists so that all the fields in each list are displayed and the vertical scroll bars disappear.

   The one-to-many relationship between the two tables is shown in the Query window in the same way that Access indicates a relationship between two tables in the Relationships window. Note that the join line is thick at both ends; this signifies that you selected the option to enforce referential integrity. If you had not selected this option, the join line would be thin at both ends and neither the "1" nor the infinity symbol would appear, even though the tables have a one-to-many relationship.

You need to place the City, FirstName, and LastName fields (in that order) from the Patient field list into the design grid, and then place the VisitDate and Reason fields from the Visit field list into the design grid. This is the order in which Kelly wants to view the fields in the query results.

5. In the Patient field list, double-click **City** to place this field in the design grid's first column Field box.
6. Repeat Step 5 to add the **FirstName** and **LastName** fields from the Patient table to the second and third columns of the design grid.
7. Repeat Step 5 to add the **VisitDate** and **Reason** fields (in that order) from the Visit table to the fourth and fifth columns of the design grid. The query specifications are complete, so you can now run the query.
8. In the Results group on the DESIGN tab, click the **Run** button. Access runs the query and displays the results in Datasheet view. See Figure 3-9.

Figure 3-9 **Datasheet for query based on the Patient and Visit tables**

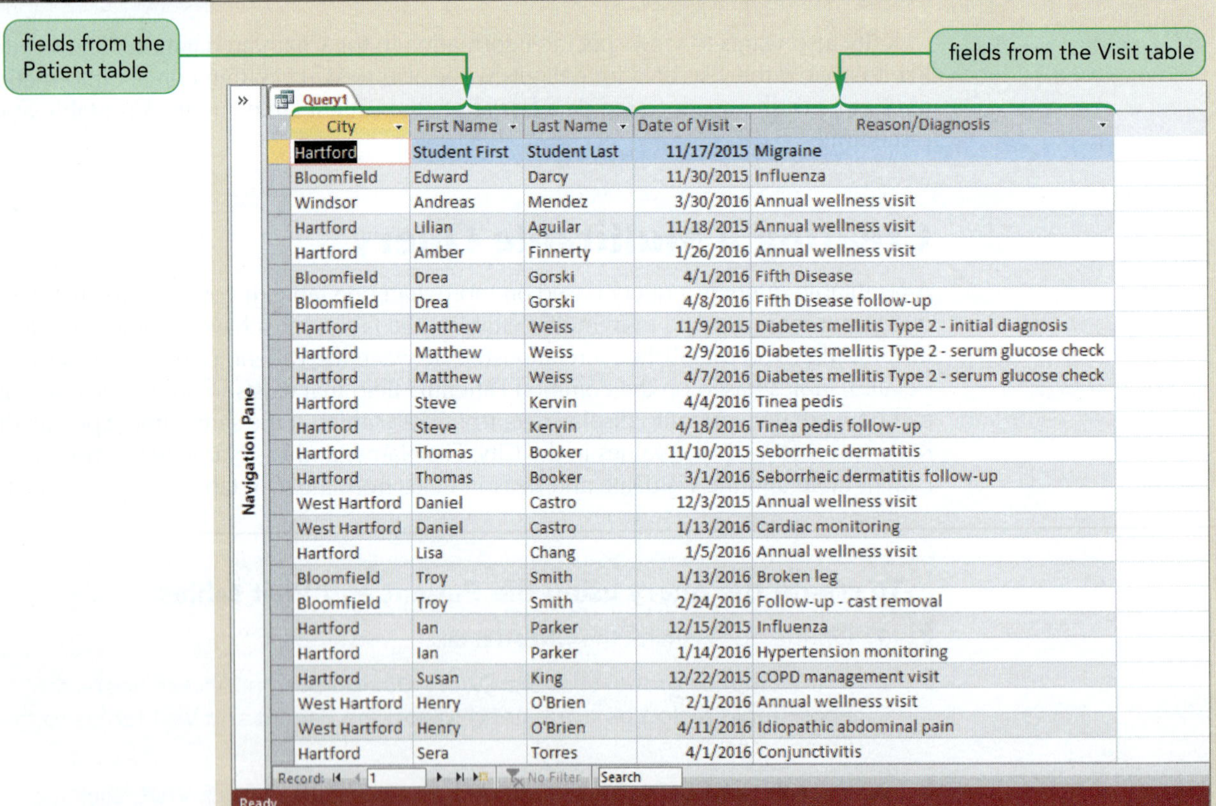

City	First Name	Last Name	Date of Visit	Reason/Diagnosis
Hartford	Student First	Student Last	11/17/2015	Migraine
Bloomfield	Edward	Darcy	11/30/2015	Influenza
Windsor	Andreas	Mendez	3/30/2016	Annual wellness visit
Hartford	Lilian	Aguilar	11/18/2015	Annual wellness visit
Hartford	Amber	Finnerty	1/26/2016	Annual wellness visit
Bloomfield	Drea	Gorski	4/1/2016	Fifth Disease
Bloomfield	Drea	Gorski	4/8/2016	Fifth Disease follow-up
Hartford	Matthew	Weiss	11/9/2015	Diabetes mellitis Type 2 - initial diagnosis
Hartford	Matthew	Weiss	2/9/2016	Diabetes mellitis Type 2 - serum glucose check
Hartford	Matthew	Weiss	4/7/2016	Diabetes mellitis Type 2 - serum glucose check
Hartford	Steve	Kervin	4/4/2016	Tinea pedis
Hartford	Steve	Kervin	4/18/2016	Tinea pedis follow-up
Hartford	Thomas	Booker	11/10/2015	Seborrheic dermatitis
Hartford	Thomas	Booker	3/1/2016	Seborrheic dermatitis follow-up
West Hartford	Daniel	Castro	12/3/2015	Annual wellness visit
West Hartford	Daniel	Castro	1/13/2016	Cardiac monitoring
Hartford	Lisa	Chang	1/5/2016	Annual wellness visit
Bloomfield	Troy	Smith	1/13/2016	Broken leg
Bloomfield	Troy	Smith	2/24/2016	Follow-up - cast removal
Hartford	Ian	Parker	12/15/2015	Influenza
Hartford	Ian	Parker	1/14/2016	Hypertension monitoring
Hartford	Susan	King	12/22/2015	COPD management visit
West Hartford	Henry	O'Brien	2/1/2016	Annual wellness visit
West Hartford	Henry	O'Brien	4/11/2016	Idiopathic abdominal pain
Hartford	Sera	Torres	4/1/2016	Conjunctivitis

Only the five selected fields from the Patient and Visit tables appear in the datasheet. The records are displayed in order according to the values in the PatientID field because it is the primary key field in the primary table, even though this field is not included in the query datasheet.

Kelly plans on frequently tracking the data retrieved by the query, so she asks you to save it as "PatientVisits."

9. On the Quick Access Toolbar, click the **Save** button. The Save As dialog box opens.

10. In the Query Name box, type **PatientVisits** and then press the **Enter** key. Access saves the query and displays its name on the object tab.

Kelly decides she wants the records displayed in alphabetical order by city. Because the query displays data in order by the field values in the PatientID field, which is the primary key for the Patient table, you need to sort the records by the City field to display the data in the order Kelly wants.

Sorting Data in a Query

Sorting is the process of rearranging records in a specified order or sequence. Sometimes you might need to sort data before displaying or printing it to meet a specific request. For example, Kelly might want to review visit information arranged by the VisitDate field because she needs to know which months are the busiest for Chatham Community Health Services in terms of patient visits. Cindi might want to view billing information arranged by the InvoiceAmt field because she monitors the finances of the clinic.

When you sort data in a query, you do not change the sequence of the records in the underlying tables. Only the records in the query datasheet are rearranged according to your specifications.

To sort records, you must select the **sort field**, which is the field used to determine the order of records in the datasheet. In this case, Kelly wants the data sorted alphabetically by city, so you need to specify City as the sort field. Sort fields can be Short Text, Number, Date/Time, Currency, AutoNumber, or Yes/No fields, but not Long Text, Hyperlink, or Attachment fields. You sort records in either ascending (increasing) or descending (decreasing) order. Figure 3-10 shows the results of each type of sort for these data types.

Figure 3-10 **Sorting results for different data types**

Data Type	Ascending Sort Results	Descending Sort Results
Short Text	A to Z (alphabetical)	Z to A (reverse alphabetical)
Number	lowest to highest numeric value	highest to lowest numeric value
Date/Time	oldest to most recent date	most recent to oldest date
Currency	lowest to highest numeric value	highest to lowest numeric value
AutoNumber	lowest to highest numeric value	highest to lowest numeric value
Yes/No	yes (checkmark in check box) then no values	no then yes values

Access provides several methods for sorting data in a table or query datasheet and in a form. One of the easiest ways is to use the AutoFilter feature for a field.

Using an AutoFilter to Sort Data

TIP

You can also use the Ascending and Descending buttons in the Sort & Filter group on the HOME tab to quickly sort records based on the currently selected field in a datasheet.

As you've probably noticed when working in Datasheet view for a table or query, each column heading has an arrow to the right of the field name. This arrow gives you access to the **AutoFilter** feature, which enables you to quickly sort and display field values in various ways. When you click this arrow, a menu opens with options for sorting and displaying field values. The first two options on the menu enable you to sort the values in the current field in ascending or descending order. Unless you save the datasheet or form after you've sorted the records, the rearrangement of records is temporary.

Next, you'll use an AutoFilter to sort the PatientVisits query results by the City field.

To sort the records using an AutoFilter:

1. Click the **arrow** on the City column heading to display the AutoFilter menu. See Figure 3-11.

Figure 3-11 **Using AutoFilter to sort records in the datasheet**

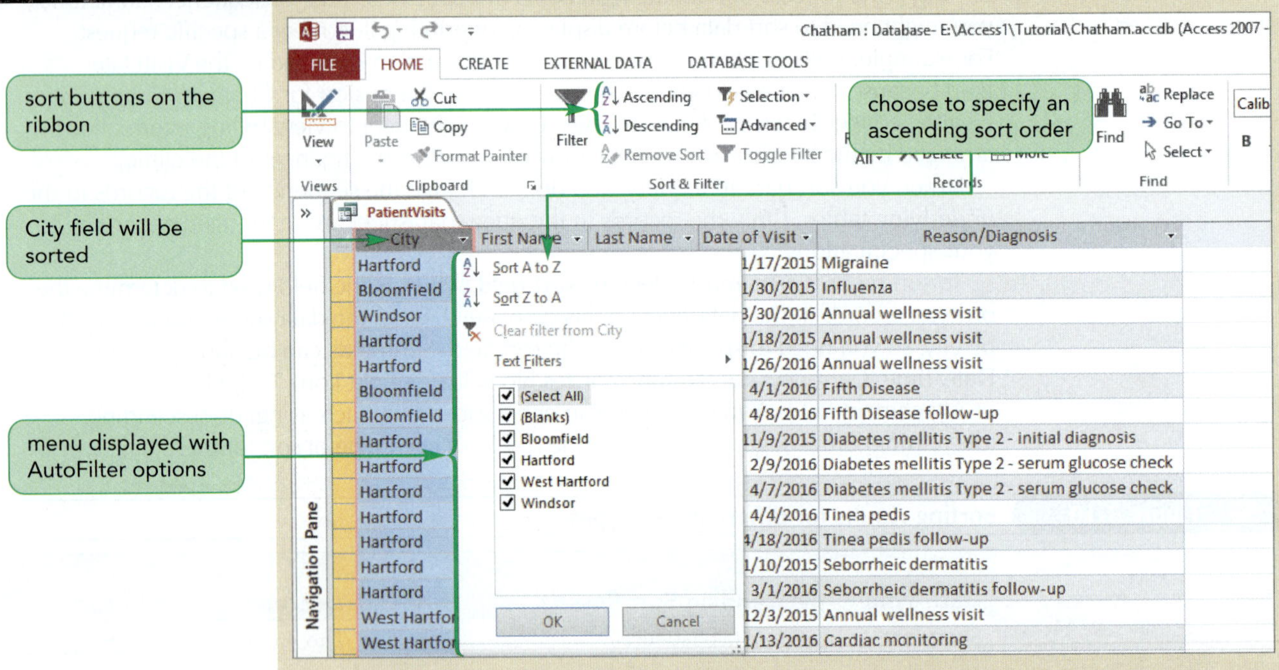

Kelly wants the data sorted in ascending (alphabetical) order by the values in the City field, so you need to select the first option in the menu.

2. Click **Sort A to Z**. The records are rearranged in ascending alphabetical order by city. A small, upward-pointing arrow appears on the right side of the City column heading. This arrow indicates that the values in the field have been sorted in ascending order. If you used the same method to sort the field values in descending order, a small downward-pointing arrow would appear there instead.

After viewing the query results, Kelly decides that she would also like to see the records arranged by the values in the VisitDate field, so that the data is presented in chronological order. She still wants the records to be arranged by the City field values as well. To produce the results Kelly wants, you need to sort using two fields.

Sorting on Multiple Fields in Design View

Sort fields can be unique or nonunique. A sort field is **unique** if the value in the sort field for each record is different. The PatientID field in the Patient table is an example of a unique sort field because each patient record has a different value in this primary key field. A sort field is **nonunique** if more than one record can have the same value for the sort field. For example, the City field in the Patient table is a nonunique sort field because more than one record can have the same City value.

TIP

The primary sort field is *not* the same as a table's primary key. A table has at most one primary key, which must be unique, whereas any field in a table can serve as a primary sort field.

When the sort field is nonunique, records with the same sort field value are grouped together, but they are not sorted in a specific order within the group. To arrange these grouped records in a specific order, you can specify a **secondary sort field**, which is a second field that determines the order of records that are already sorted by the **primary sort field** (the first sort field specified).

Access lets you select up to 10 different sort fields. When you use the buttons on the ribbon to sort by more than one field, the sort fields must be in adjacent columns in the datasheet. (Note that you cannot use an AutoFilter to sort on more than one field. This method works for a single field only.) You can specify only one type of sort—either ascending or descending—for the selected columns in the datasheet. You highlight the adjacent columns, and Access sorts first by the first column and then by each remaining highlighted column in order from left to right.

Kelly wants the records sorted first by the City field values, as they currently are, and then by the VisitDate values. The two fields are in the correct left-to-right order in the query datasheet, but they are not adjacent, so you cannot use the Ascending and Descending buttons on the ribbon to sort them. You could move the City field to the left of the VisitDate field in the query datasheet, but both columns would have to be sorted with the same sort order. This is not what Kelly wants—she wants the City field values sorted in ascending order so that they are in the correct alphabetical order, for ease of reference; and she wants the VisitDate field values to be sorted in descending order, so that she can focus on the most recent patient visits first. To sort the City and VisitDate fields with different sort orders, you must specify the sort fields in Design view.

In the Query window in Design view, Access first uses the sort field that is leftmost in the design grid. Therefore, you must arrange the fields you want to sort from left to right in the design grid, with the primary sort field being the leftmost. In Design view, multiple sort fields do not have to be adjacent to each other, as they do in Datasheet view; however, they must be in the correct left-to-right order.

REFERENCE

Sorting a Query Datasheet

- In the query datasheet, click the arrow on the column heading for the field you want to sort.
- In the menu that opens, click Sort A to Z for an ascending sort, or click Sort Z to A for a descending sort.

or

- In the query datasheet, select the column or adjacent columns on which you want to sort.
- In the Sort & Filter group on the HOME tab, click the Ascending button or the Descending button.

or

- In Design view, position the fields serving as sort fields from left to right.
- Click the right side of the Sort box for each field you want to sort, and then click Ascending or Descending for the sort order.

To achieve the results Kelly wants, you need to modify the query in Design view to specify the sort order for the two fields.

TIP

In Design view, the sort fields do not have to be adjacent, and fields that are not sorted can appear between the sort fields.

To select the two sort fields in Design view:

1. In the Views group on the HOME tab, click the **View** button to open the query in Design view. The fields are currently in the correct left-to-right order in the design grid, so you only need to specify the sort order for the two fields.

   First, you need to specify an ascending sort order for the City field. Even though the records are already sorted by the values in this field, you need to modify the query so that this sort order, and the sort order you will specify for the VisitDate field, are part of the query's design. Any time the query is run, the records will be sorted according to these specifications.

2. Click the right side of the **City Sort** box to display the arrow and the sort options, and then click **Ascending**. You've selected an ascending sort order for the City field, which will be the primary sort field. The City field is a Short Text field, and an ascending sort order will display the field values in alphabetical order.

3. Click the right side of the **VisitDate Sort** box, click **Descending**, and then click in one of the empty text boxes below the VisitDate field to deselect the setting. You've selected a descending sort order for the VisitDate field, which will be the secondary sort field because it appears to the right of the primary sort field (City) in the design grid. The VisitDate field is a Date/Time field, and a descending sort order will display the field values with the most recent dates first. See Figure 3-12.

Figure 3-12 Selecting two sort fields in Design view

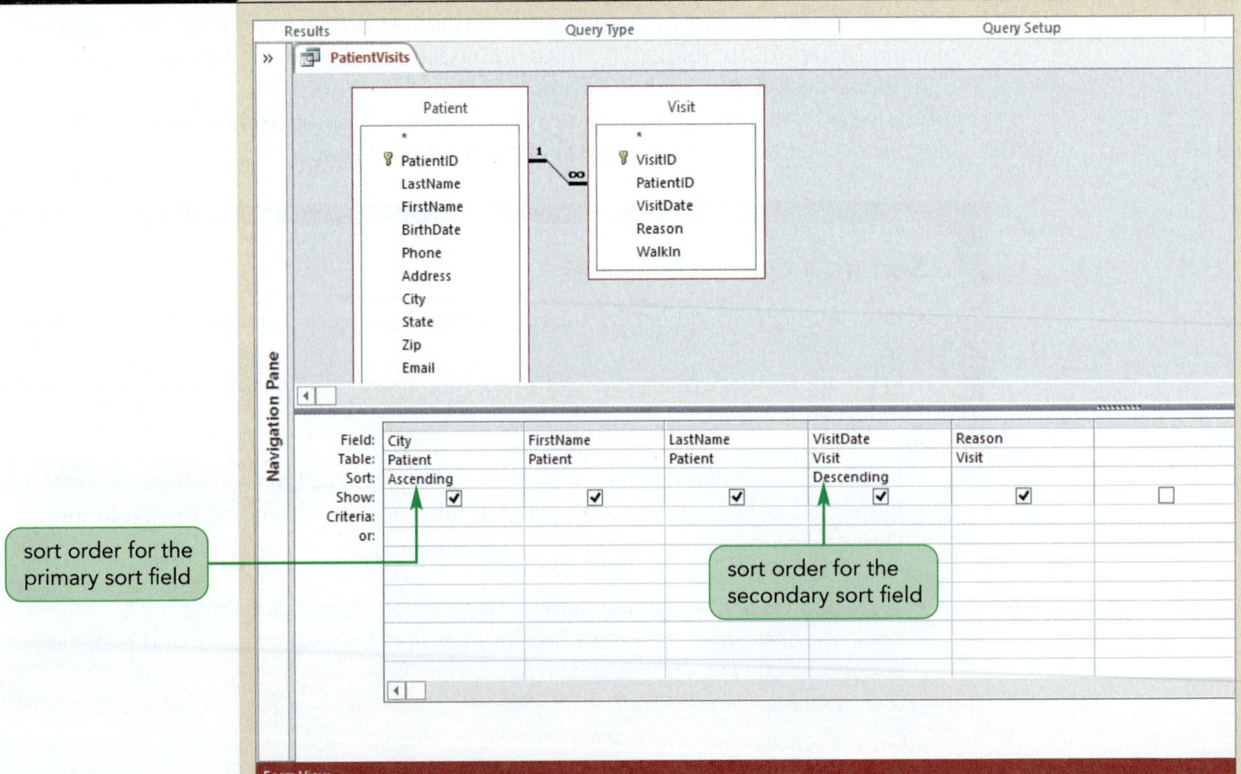

You have finished your query changes, so now you can run the query and then save the modified query with the same name.

4. In the Results group on the DESIGN tab, click the **Run** button. Access runs the query and displays the query datasheet. The records appear in ascending order based on the values in the City field. Within groups of records with the same City field value, the records appear in descending order by the values of the VisitDate field. See Figure 3-13.

Figure 3-13 Datasheet sorted on two fields

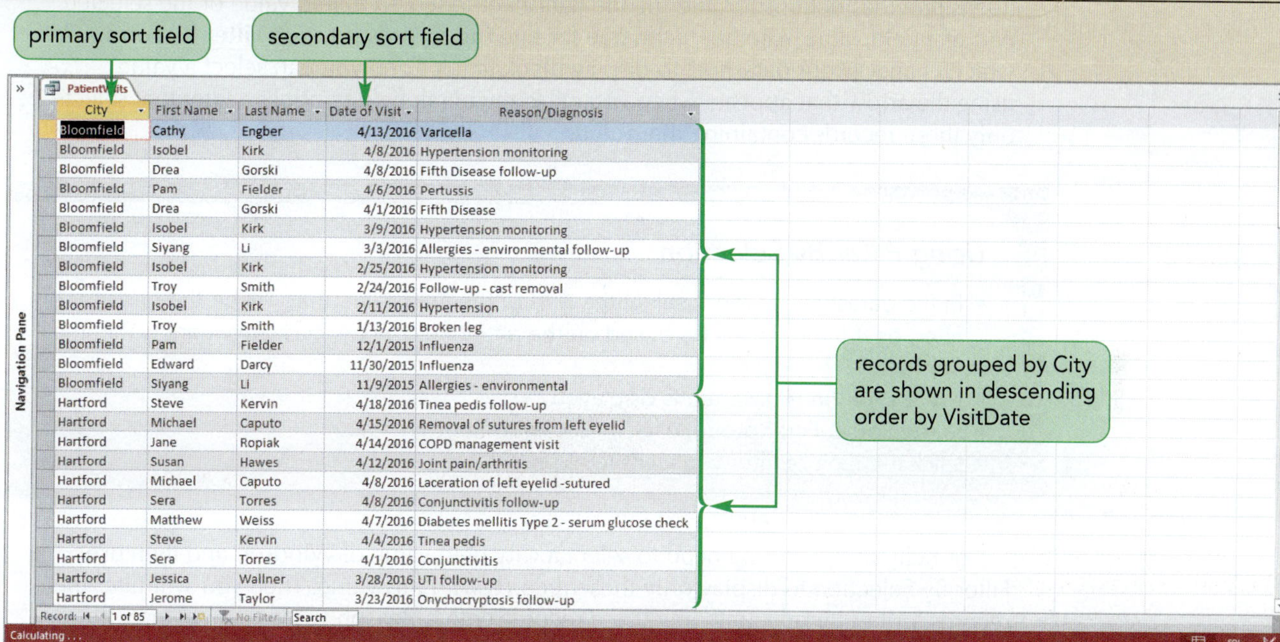

When you save the query, all of your design changes—including the selection of the sort fields—are saved with the query. The next time Kelly runs the query, the records will appear sorted by the primary and secondary sort fields.

5. On the Quick Access Toolbar, click the **Save** button to save the revised PatientVisits query.

Kelly knows that Chatham Community Health Services has seen an increase in the number of patients from Windsor. She would like to focus briefly on the information for patients in that city only. Also, she is interested in knowing how many patients from Windsor have had annual wellness exams. She is concerned that, although more patients are coming to the clinic from this city, not enough of them are scheduling wellness visits. Selecting only the records with a City field value of "Windsor" and a Reason field value beginning with "Annual" is a temporary change that Kelly wants in the datasheet, so you do not need to switch to Design view and change the query. Instead, you can apply a filter.

Filtering Data

A **filter** is a set of restrictions you place on the records in an open datasheet or form to *temporarily* isolate a subset of the records. A filter lets you view different subsets of displayed records so that you can focus on only the data you need. Unless you save a query or form with a filter applied, an applied filter is not available the next time you run the query or open the form.

The simplest technique for filtering records is Filter By Selection. **Filter By Selection** lets you select all or part of a field value in a datasheet or form, and then display only those records that contain the selected value in the field. You can also use the AutoFilter feature to filter records. When you click the arrow on a column heading, the menu that opens provides options for filtering the datasheet based on a field value or the selected part of a field value. Another technique for filtering records is to use **Filter By Form**, which changes your datasheet to display blank fields. Then you can select a value using the arrow that appears when you click any blank field to apply a filter that selects only those records containing that value.

REFERENCE

Using Filter By Selection

- In the datasheet or form, select the part of the field value that will be the basis for the filter; or, if the filter will be based on the entire field value, click anywhere within the field value.
- Make sure the HOME tab is displayed.
- In the Sort & Filter group, click the Selection button.
- Click the type of filter you want to apply.

For Kelly's request, you need to select a City field value of Windsor, and then use Filter By Selection to display only those records with this value. Then you will filter the records further by selecting only those records with a Reason value that begins with "Annual" (for Annual wellness visit).

To display the records using Filter By Selection:

1. In the query datasheet, locate the first occurrence of a City field containing the value **Windsor**, and then click anywhere within that field value.
2. In the Sort & Filter group on the HOME tab, click the **Selection** button. A menu opens with options for the type of filter to apply. See Figure 3-14.

Figure 3-14 **Using Filter By Selection**

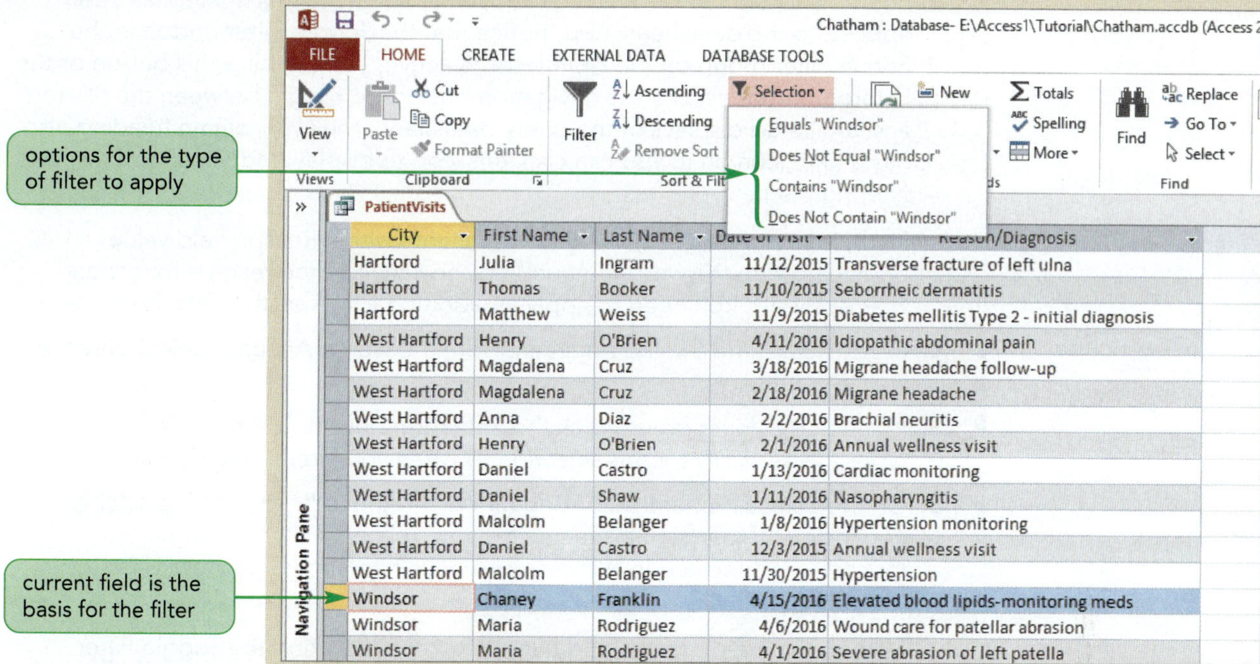

The menu provides options for displaying only those records with a City field value that equals the selected value (in this case, Windsor); does not equal the value; contains the value somewhere within the field; or does not contain the value somewhere within the field. You want to display all the records whose City field value equals Windsor.

3. In the Selection menu, click **Equals "Windsor"**. Access displays the filtered results. Only the 24 records that have a City field value of Windsor appear in the datasheet. See Figure 3-15.

Figure 3-15 **Datasheet after applying the filter**

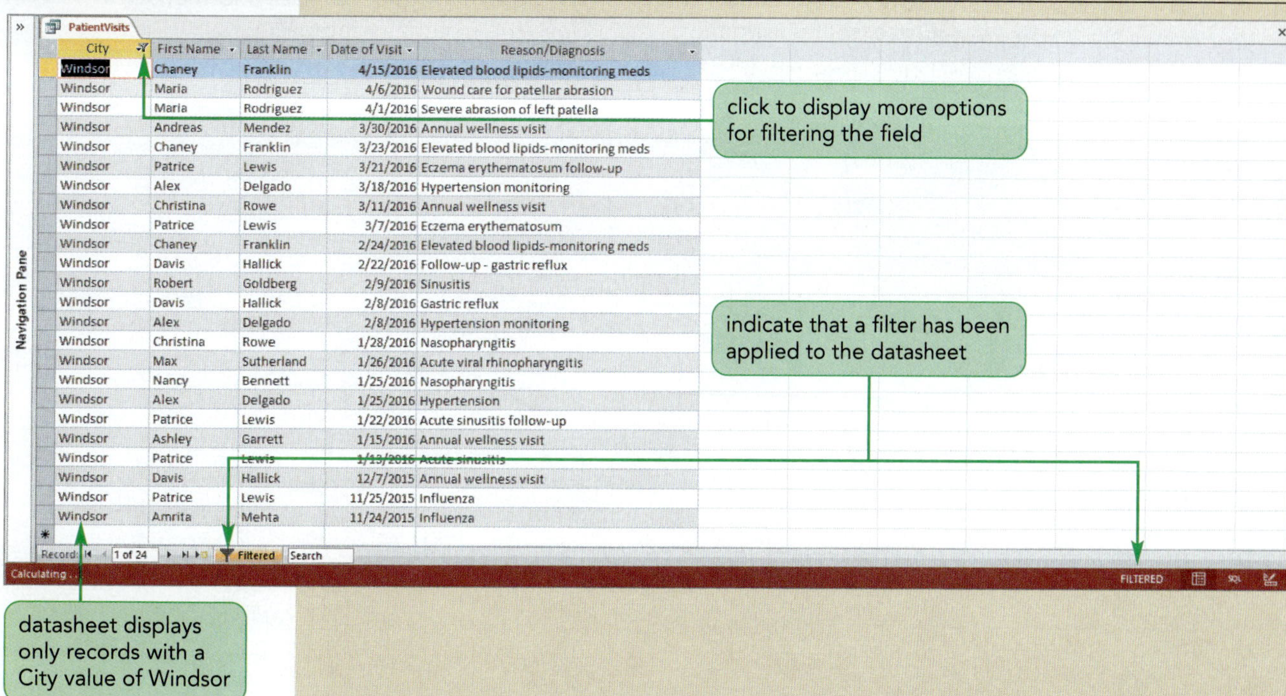

The button labeled "Filtered" to the right of the navigation buttons and the notation "FILTERED" on the status bar both indicate that a filter has been applied to the datasheet. Also, notice that the Toggle Filter button in the Sort & Filter group on the HOME tab is active; you can click this button or the Filtered button next to the navigation buttons to toggle between the filtered and unfiltered displays of the query datasheet. The City column heading also has a filter icon on it; you can click this icon to display additional options for filtering the field.

Next, Kelly wants to view only those records with a Reason field value beginning with the word "Annual" so she can view the records for annual wellness visits. You need to apply an additional filter to the datasheet.

4. In any Reason field value beginning with the word "Annual," select only the word **Annual**.
5. In the Sort & Filter group, click the **Selection** button. The same four filter types are available for this selection as when you filtered the City field.
6. On the Selection menu, click **Begins With "Annual"**. The second filter is applied to the query datasheet, which now shows only the four records for customers located in Windsor who have had annual wellness visits at the clinic.

Now you can redisplay all the query records by clicking the Toggle Filter button, which you use to switch between the filtered and unfiltered displays.

TIP

The ScreenTip for this button is Remove Filter.

7. In the Sort & Filter group, click the **Toggle Filter** button. Access removes the filter and redisplays all 85 records in the query datasheet.
8. Close the PatientVisits query. Access asks if you want to save your changes to the design of the query—in this case, the filtered display, which is still available through the Toggle Filter button. Kelly does not want the query saved with the filter because she doesn't need to view the filtered information on a regular basis.
9. Click the **No** button to close the query without saving the changes.
10. If you are not continuing to Session 3.2, click the **FILE** tab, and then click **Close** in the navigation bar to close the Chatham database.

REVIEW

Session 3.1 Quick Check

1. In Datasheet view, what is the difference between navigation mode and editing mode?
2. What command can you use in Datasheet view to remove the display of one or more fields from the datasheet?
3. What is a select query?
4. Describe the field list and the design grid in the Query window in Design view.
5. How are a table datasheet and a query datasheet similar? How are they different?
6. For a Date/Time field, how do the records appear when sorted in ascending order?
7. When you define multiple sort fields in Design view, describe how the sort fields must be positioned in the design grid.
8. A(n) ______________ is a set of restrictions you place on the records in an open datasheet or form to isolate a subset of records temporarily.

Session 3.2 Visual Overview:

When creating queries in Design view, you can enter criteria so that Access will display only selected records in the query results.

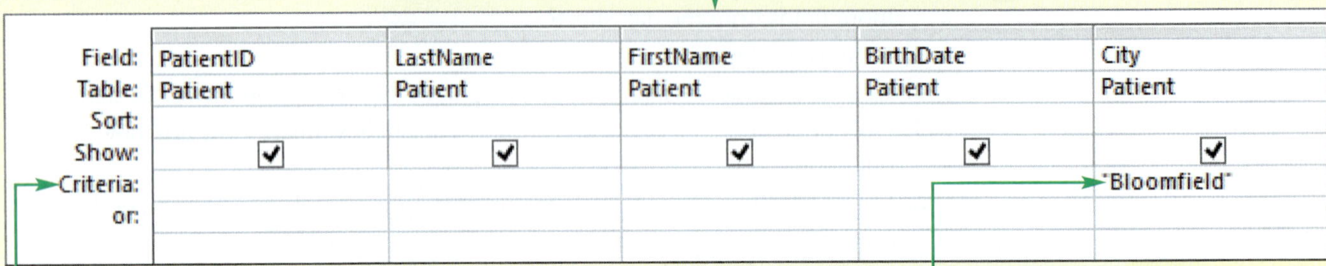

To define a condition for a field, you place the condition in the field's Criteria box in the design grid.

To tell Access which records you want to select, you must specify a condition as part of the query. A **condition** is a criterion, or rule, that determines which records are selected.

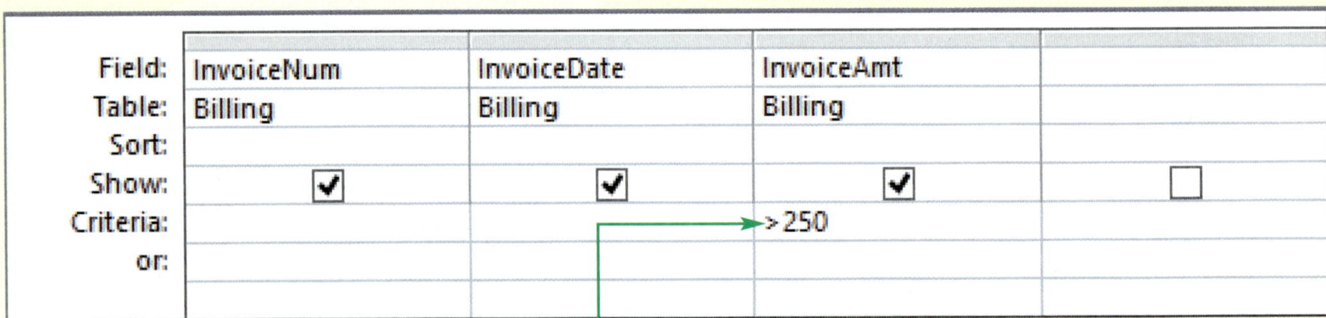

A condition usually consists of an operator, often a comparison operator, and a value. A **comparison operator** asks Access to compare the value in a field to the condition value and to select all the records for which the condition is true.

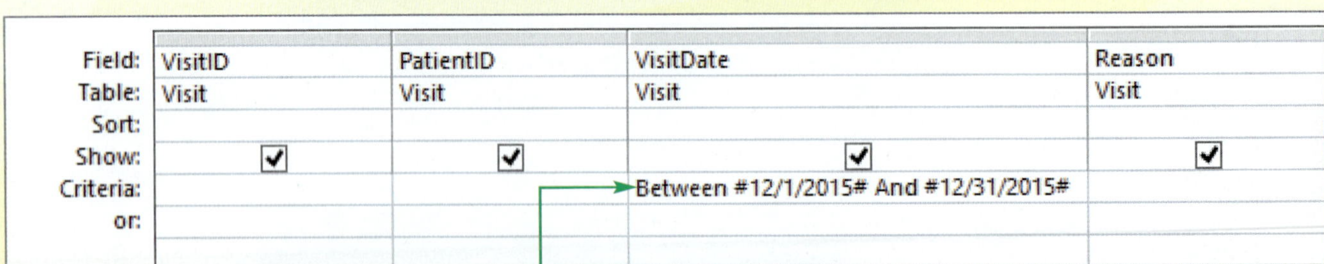

Most comparison operators (such as Between...And...) ask Access to select records that match a range of values for the condition—in this case, all records with dates that fall within the range shown.

Selection Criteria in Queries

The results of a query containing selection criteria include only the records that meet the specified criteria.

BloomfieldPatients

Patient ID	Last Name	First Name	Date of Birth	City
22501	Darcy	Edward	7/15/1986	Bloomfield
22506	Gorski	Drea	2/19/2005	Bloomfield
22513	Smith	Troy	1/31/1996	Bloomfield
22521	Engber	Cathy	4/7/2006	Bloomfield
22522	Li	Siyang	7/25/1986	Bloomfield
22549	Fielder	Pam	12/6/1978	Bloomfield
22557	Kirk	Isobel	11/18/1965	Bloomfield
*				

The results of this query show only patients from Bloomfield because the condition "Bloomfield" in the City field's Criteria box specifies that Access should select records only with City field values of Bloomfield. This type of condition is called an **exact match** because the value in the specified field must match the condition exactly in order for the record to be included in the query results.

LargeInvoiceAmts

Invoice Num	Invoice Date	Invoice Amt
35815	11/16/2015	$300.00
35900	01/20/2016	$300.00
36002	03/15/2016	$450.00
36074	04/12/2016	$450.00
*		$0.00

The results of this query show only those invoices with amounts greater than $250 because the condition >250, which uses the greater than comparison operator, specifies that Access should select records only with InvoiceAmt field values over $250.

DecemberVisits

Visit ID	Patient ID	Date of Visit	Reason/Diagnosis
1550	22549	12/1/2015	Influenza
1552	22511	12/3/2015	Annual wellness visit
1555	22520	12/7/2015	Annual wellness visit
1557	22526	12/10/2015	Annual wellness visit
1560	22514	12/15/2015	Influenza
1562	22516	12/22/2015	COPD management visit
*			

The results of this query show only those patient visits that took place in December 2015 because the condition in the VisitDate's Criteria box specifies that Access should select records only with a visit date between 12/1/2015 and 12/31/2015.

Defining Record Selection Criteria for Queries

Cindi wants to display patient and visit information for all patients who live in Bloomfield. She is considering having the clinic hold a health fair in Bloomfield, with a special emphasis on hypertension, so she is interested in knowing more about the patients from this city. For this request, you could create a query to select the correct fields and all records in the Patient and Visit tables, select a City field value of Bloomfield in the query datasheet, and then click the Selection button and choose the appropriate filter option to display the information for only those patients in Bloomfield. However, a faster way of displaying the data Cindi needs is to create a query that displays the selected fields and only those records in the Patient and Visit tables that satisfy a condition.

Just as you can display selected fields from a database in a query datasheet, you can display selected records. To tell Access which records you want to select, you must specify a condition as part of the query, as illustrated in the Session 3.2 Visual Overview. A condition usually includes one of the comparison operators shown in Figure 3-16.

Figure 3-16 **Access comparison operators**

Operator	Meaning	Example
=	equal to (optional; default operator)	="Hall"
<>	not equal to	<>"Hall"
<	less than	<#1/1/99#
<=	less than or equal to	<=100
>	greater than	>"C400"
>=	greater than or equal to	>=18.75
Between … And …	between two values (inclusive)	Between 50 And 325
In ()	in a list of values	In ("Hall", "Seeger")
Like	matches a pattern that includes wildcards	Like "706*"

Specifying an Exact Match

For Cindi's request, you need to create a query that will display only those records in the Patient table with the value Bloomfield in the City field. This type of condition is an exact match because the value in the specified field must match the condition exactly in order for the record to be included in the query results. You'll create the query in Design view.

To create the query in Design view:

1. If you took a break after the previous session, make sure that the Chatham database is open and the Navigation Pane is closed.
2. On the ribbon, click the **CREATE** tab.
3. In the Queries group, click the **Query Design** button. The Show Table dialog box opens. You need to add the Patient and Visit tables to the Query window.
4. Click **Patient** in the Tables list, click the **Add** button, click **Visit**, click the **Add** button, and then click the **Close** button.

5. Use the pointer to resize both field lists so that all the fields are displayed and the vertical scroll bars disappear.
6. Add the following fields from the Patient table to the design grid in the order shown: **LastName**, **FirstName**, **Phone**, **Address**, **City**, and **Email**.

   Cindi also wants information from the Visit table included in the query results.
7. Add the following fields from the Visit table to the design grid in the order shown: **VisitID**, **VisitDate**, and **Reason**. See Figure 3-17.

Figure 3-17 Design grid after adding fields from both tables

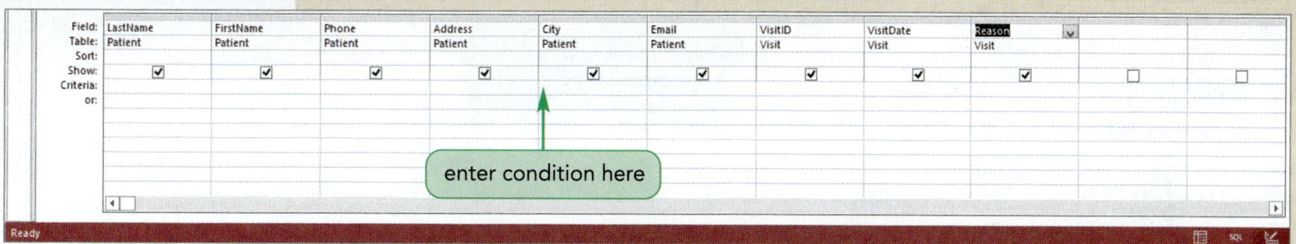

The field lists for the Patient and Visit tables appear in the top portion of the window, and the join line indicating a one-to-many relationship connects the two tables. The fields you selected appear in the design grid.

To display the information Cindi wants, you need to enter the condition for the City field in its Criteria box (see Figure 3-17). Cindi wants to display only those records with a City field value of Bloomfield.

To enter the exact match condition, and then save and run the query:

1. Click the **City Criteria** box, type **Bloomfield**, and then press the **Enter** key. The condition changes to "Bloomfield".

   Access automatically enclosed the condition you typed in quotation marks. You must enclose text values in quotation marks when using them as selection criteria. If you omit the quotation marks, however, Access will include them automatically in most cases. Some words—including "in" and "select"—are special keywords in Access that are reserved for functions and commands. If you want to enter one of these keywords as the condition, you must type the quotation marks around the text or Access will display an error message and will not allow the condition to be entered.
2. On the Quick Access Toolbar, click the **Save** button to open the Save As dialog box.
3. In the Query Name box, type **BloomfieldPatients** and then press the **Enter** key. Access saves the query with the specified name and displays the name on the object tab.
4. In the Results group on the DESIGN tab, click the **Run** button. Access runs the query and displays the selected field values for only those records with a City field value of Bloomfield. A total of 14 records is selected and displayed in the datasheet. See Figure 3-18.

Figure 3-18 **Datasheet displaying selected fields and records**

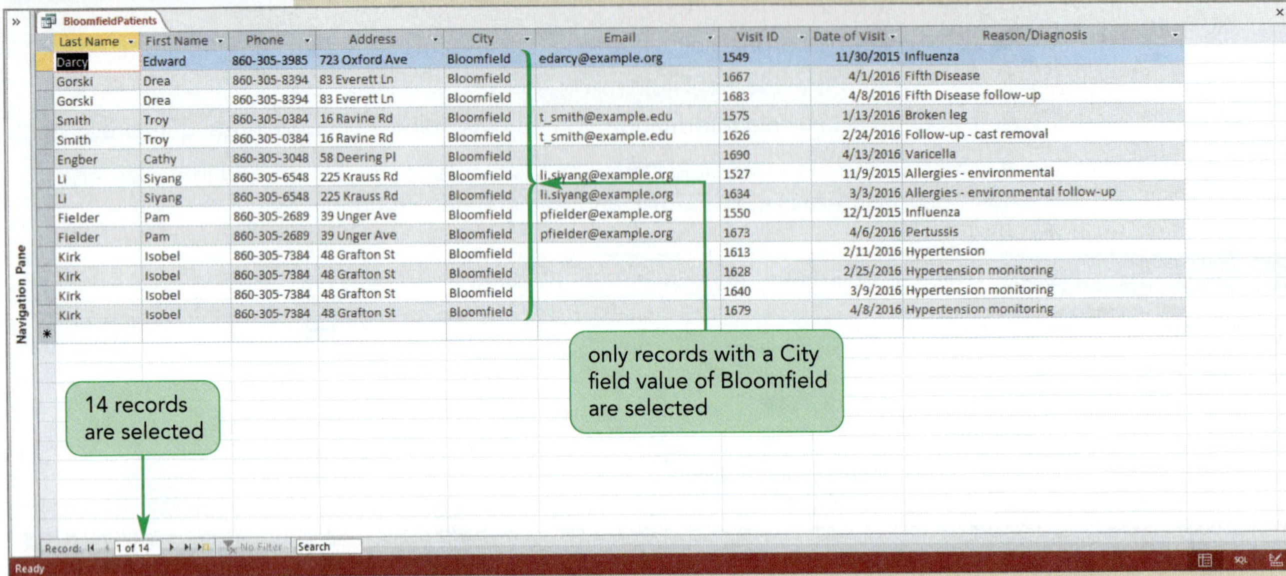

Last Name	First Name	Phone	Address	City	Email	Visit ID	Date of Visit	Reason/Diagnosis
Darcy	Edward	860-305-3985	723 Oxford Ave	Bloomfield	edarcy@example.org	1549	11/30/2015	Influenza
Gorski	Drea	860-305-8394	83 Everett Ln	Bloomfield		1667	4/1/2016	Fifth Disease
Gorski	Drea	860-305-8394	83 Everett Ln	Bloomfield		1683	4/8/2016	Fifth Disease follow-up
Smith	Troy	860-305-0384	16 Ravine Rd	Bloomfield	t_smith@example.edu	1575	1/13/2016	Broken leg
Smith	Troy	860-305-0384	16 Ravine Rd	Bloomfield	t_smith@example.edu	1626	2/24/2016	Follow-up - cast removal
Engber	Cathy	860-305-3048	58 Deering Pl	Bloomfield		1690	4/13/2016	Varicella
Li	Siyang	860-305-6548	225 Krauss Rd	Bloomfield	li.siyang@example.org	1527	11/9/2015	Allergies - environmental
Li	Siyang	860-305-6548	225 Krauss Rd	Bloomfield	li.siyang@example.org	1634	3/3/2016	Allergies - environmental follow-up
Fielder	Pam	860-305-2689	39 Unger Ave	Bloomfield	pfielder@example.org	1550	12/1/2015	Influenza
Fielder	Pam	860-305-2689	39 Unger Ave	Bloomfield	pfielder@example.org	1673	4/6/2016	Pertussis
Kirk	Isobel	860-305-7384	48 Grafton St	Bloomfield		1613	2/11/2016	Hypertension
Kirk	Isobel	860-305-7384	48 Grafton St	Bloomfield		1628	2/25/2016	Hypertension monitoring
Kirk	Isobel	860-305-7384	48 Grafton St	Bloomfield		1640	3/9/2016	Hypertension monitoring
Kirk	Isobel	860-305-7384	48 Grafton St	Bloomfield		1679	4/8/2016	Hypertension monitoring

Cindi realizes that it's not necessary to include the City field values in the query results. The name of the query, BloomfieldPatients, indicates that the query design includes all patients who live in Bloomfield, so the City field values are unnecessary and repetitive. Also, she decides that she would prefer the query datasheet to show the fields from the Visit table first, followed by the Patient table fields. You need to modify the query to produce the results Cindi wants.

Modifying a Query

After you create a query and view the results, you might need to make changes to the query if the results are not what you expected or require. First, Cindi asks you to modify the BloomfieldPatients query so that it does not display the City field values in the query results.

To remove the display of the City field values:

1. In the Views group on the HOME tab, click the **View** button. The BloomfieldPatients query opens in Design view.

   You need to keep the City field as part of the query design because it contains the defined condition for the query. You only need to remove the display of the field's values from the query results.

2. Click the **City Show** check box to remove the checkmark. The query will still find only those records with the value Bloomfield in the City field, but the query results will not display these field values.

Next, you need to change the order of the fields in the query so that the visit information is listed first.

To move the Visit table fields to precede the Patient table fields:

1. Position the pointer on the VisitID field selector until the pointer changes to a ⬇ shape, and then click to select the field. See Figure 3-19.

Figure 3-19 Selected VisitID field

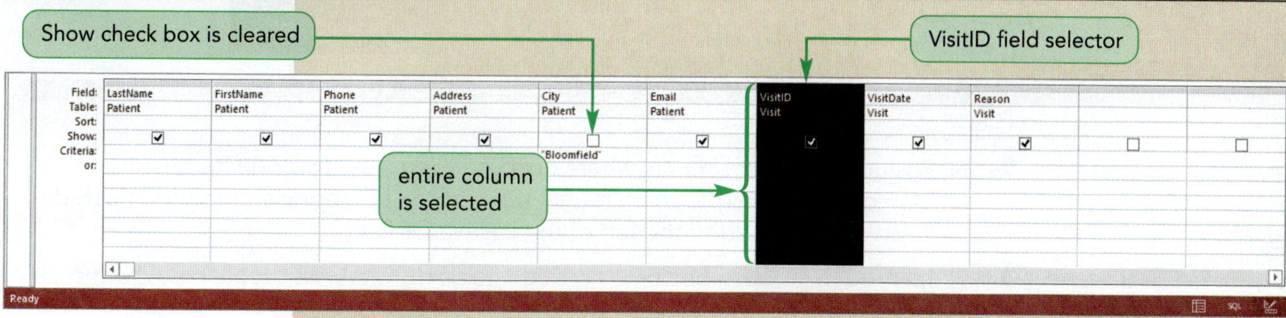

2. Position the pointer on the VisitID field selector, and then click and hold down the mouse button; notice that the pointer changes to the move pointer and a black vertical line appears to the left of the selected field. This line represents the selected field when you drag the mouse to move it.
3. Drag to the left until the vertical line representing the selected field is positioned to the left of the LastName field. See Figure 3-20.

Figure 3-20 Dragging the field in the design grid

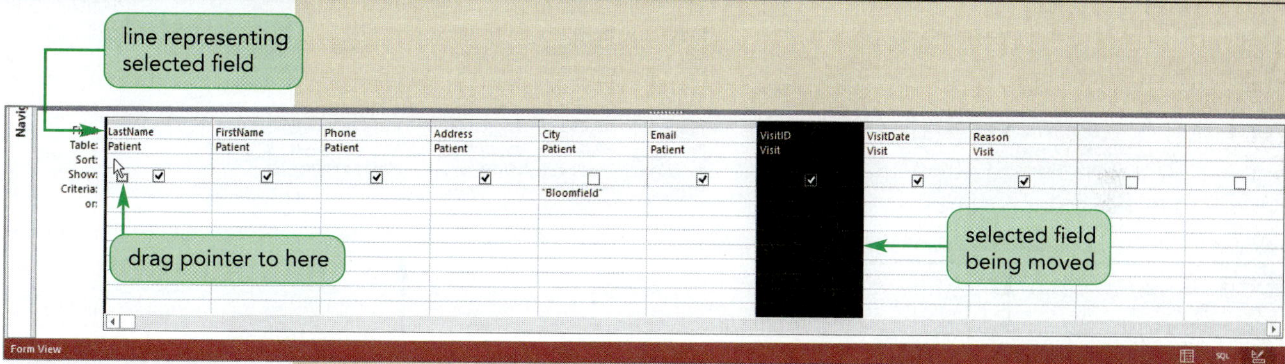

> **TIP**
> Instead of moving a field by dragging, you can also delete the field and then add it back to the design grid in the location you want.

4. Release the mouse button. The VisitID field moves to the left of the LastName field.

   You can also select and move multiple fields at once. You need to select and move the VisitDate and Reason fields so that they follow the VisitID field in the query design. To select multiple fields, you click and drag the mouse over the field selectors for the fields you want.

5. Click and hold the pointer ⬇ on the VisitDate field selector, drag the pointer to the right to select the Reason field, and then release the mouse button. Both fields are now selected. See Figure 3-21.

Figure 3-21 **Multiple fields selected to be moved**

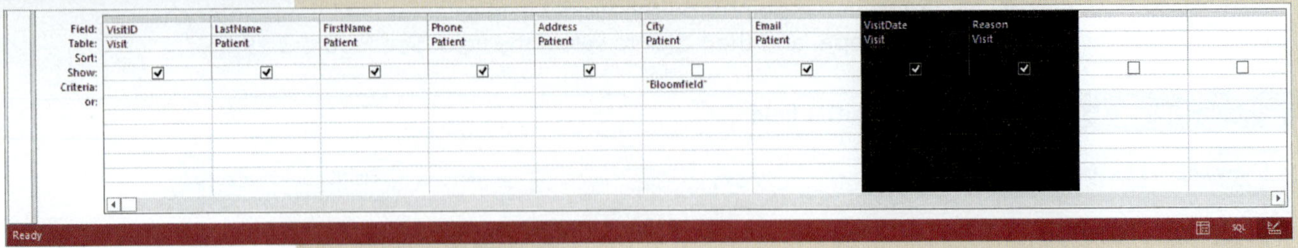

6. Position the pointer anywhere near the top of the two selected fields, and then click and drag to the left until the vertical line representing the selected fields is positioned to the left of the LastName field.
7. Release the mouse button. The three fields from the Visit table are now the first three fields in the query design.

   You have finished making the modifications to the query Cindi requested, so you can now run the query.
8. In the Results group on the DESIGN tab, click the **Run** button. Access displays the results of the modified query. See Figure 3-22.

Figure 3-22 **Results of the modified query**

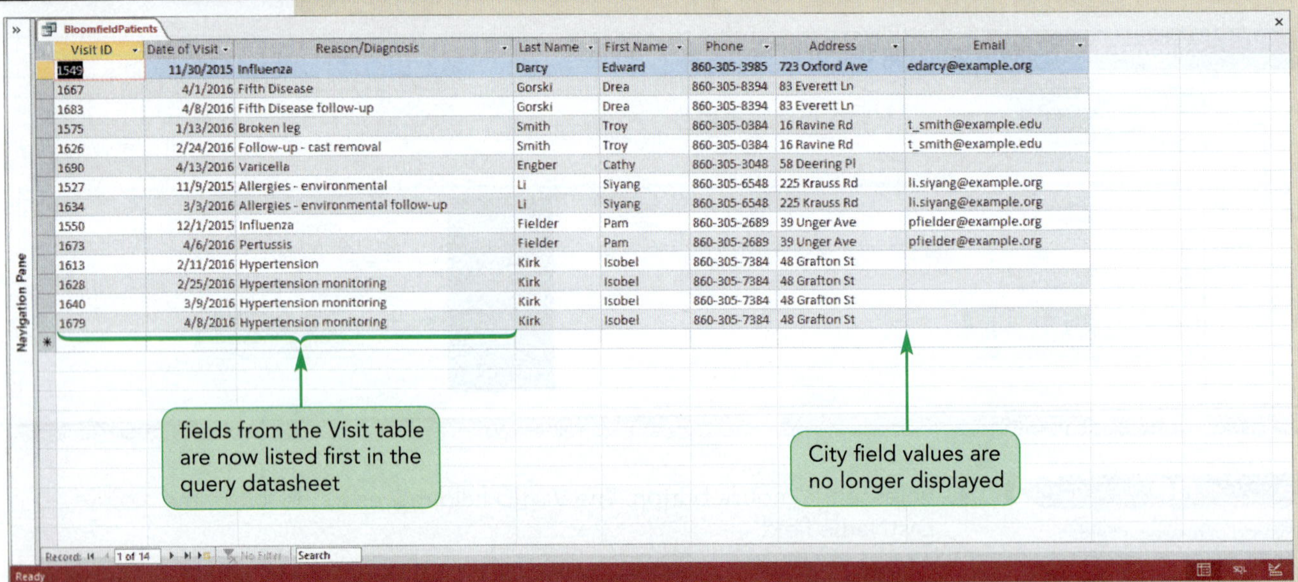

   Note that the City field values are no longer displayed in the query results.
9. Save and close the BloomfieldPatients query.

After viewing the query results, Cindi decides that she would like to see the same fields, but only for those records with a VisitDate field value before 1/1/2016. She is interested to know which patients of Chatham Community Health Services in all cities have not been to the clinic recently, so that her staff can follow up with these patients by sending them reminder notes or emails. To create the query that will produce the results Cindi wants, you need to use a comparison operator to match a range of values—in this case, any VisitDate value less than 1/1/2016.

Using a Comparison Operator to Match a Range of Values

After you create and save a query, you can double-click the query name in the Navigation Pane to run the query again. You can then click the View button to change its design. You can also use an existing query as the basis for creating another query. Because the design of the query you need to create next is similar to the BloomfieldPatients query, you will copy, paste, and rename this query to create the new query. Using this approach keeps the BloomfieldPatients query intact.

To create the new query by copying the BloomfieldPatients query:

1. Open the Navigation Pane. Note that the BloomfieldPatients query is listed in the Queries section.

   You need to use the shortcut menu to copy the BloomfieldPatients query and paste it in the Navigation Pane; then you'll give the copied query a different name.

2. In the Queries section of the Navigation Pane, right-click **BloomfieldPatients** to select it and display the shortcut menu.
3. Click **Copy** on the shortcut menu.
4. Right-click the empty area near the bottom of the Navigation Pane, and then click **Paste** on the shortcut menu. The Paste As dialog box opens with the text "Copy Of BloomfieldPatients" in the Query Name box. Because Cindi wants the new query to show data for patients who have not visited the clinic recently, you'll name the new query "EarlierVisits."
5. In the Query Name box, type **EarlierVisits** and then press the **Enter** key. The new query appears in the Queries section of the Navigation Pane.
6. Double-click the **EarlierVisits** query to open, or run, the query. The design of this query is currently the same as the original BloomfieldPatients query.
7. Close the Navigation Pane.

Next, you need to open the query in Design view and modify its design to produce the results Cindi wants—to display only those records with VisitDate field values that are earlier than, or less than, 1/1/2016.

To modify the design of the new query:

1. In the Views group on the HOME tab, click the **View** button to display the query in Design view.
2. Click the **VisitDate Criteria** box, type **<1/1/2016** and then press the **Tab** key. See Figure 3-23.

Figure 3-23 Criteria entered for the VisitDate field

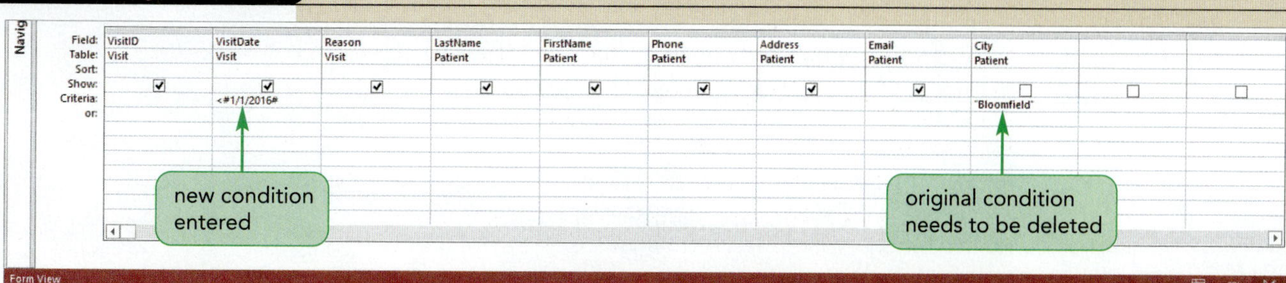

Note that Access automatically encloses the date criteria with number signs. The condition specifies that a record will be selected only if its VisitDate field value is less than (earlier than) 1/1/2016. Before you run the query, you need to delete the condition for the City field. Recall that the City field is part of the query, but its values are not displayed in the query results. When you modified the query to remove the City field values from the query results, Access moved the field to the end of the design grid. You need to delete the City field's condition, specify that the City field values should be included in the query results, and then move the field back to its original position following the Address field.

3. Press the **Tab** key six times until the condition for the City field is highlighted, and then press the **Delete** key. The condition for the City field is removed.
4. Click the **Show** check box for the City field to insert a checkmark so that the field values will be displayed in the query results.
5. Use the pointer to select the City field, drag the selected field to the left of the Email field, and then click in an empty box to deselect the City field. See Figure 3-24.

Figure 3-24 Design grid after moving the City field

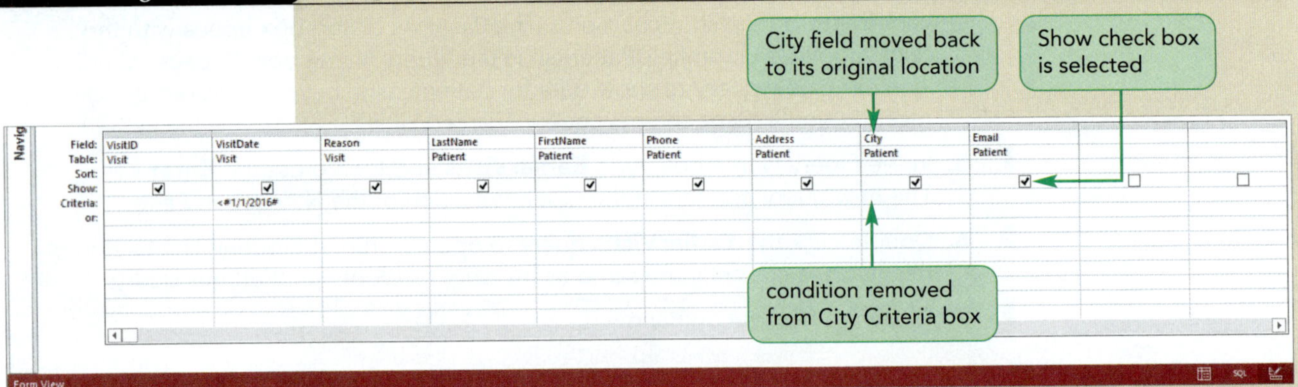

6. In the Results group on the DESIGN tab, click the **Run** button. Access runs the query and displays the selected fields for only those records with a VisitDate field value less than 1/1/2016. The query displays a total of 18 records. See Figure 3-25.

Figure 3-25 **Running the modified query**

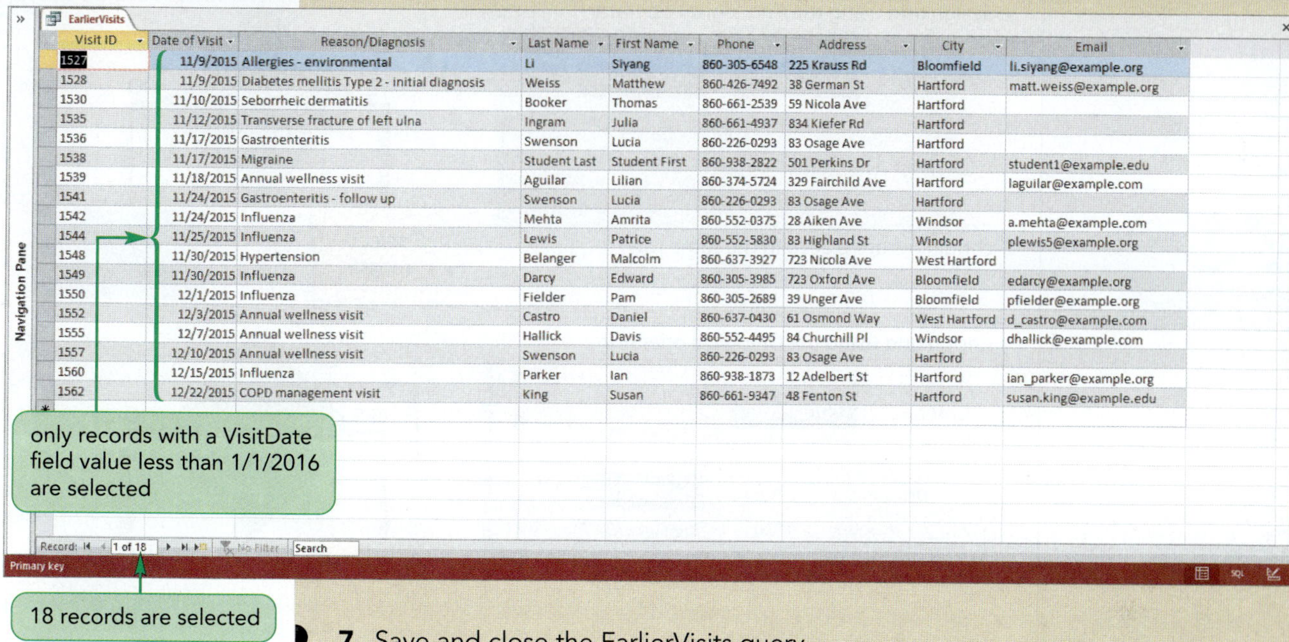

Visit ID	Date of Visit	Reason/Diagnosis	Last Name	First Name	Phone	Address	City	Email
1527	11/9/2015	Allergies - environmental	Li	Siyang	860-305-6548	225 Krauss Rd	Bloomfield	li.siyang@example.org
1528	11/9/2015	Diabetes mellitis Type 2 - initial diagnosis	Weiss	Matthew	860-426-7492	38 German St	Hartford	matt.weiss@example.org
1530	11/10/2015	Seborrheic dermatitis	Booker	Thomas	860-661-2539	59 Nicola Ave	Hartford	
1535	11/12/2015	Transverse fracture of left ulna	Ingram	Julia	860-661-4937	834 Kiefer Rd	Hartford	
1536	11/17/2015	Gastroenteritis	Swenson	Lucia	860-226-0293	83 Osage Ave	Hartford	
1538	11/17/2015	Migraine	Student Last	Student First	860-938-2822	501 Perkins Dr	Hartford	student1@example.edu
1539	11/18/2015	Annual wellness visit	Aguilar	Lilian	860-374-5724	329 Fairchild Ave	Hartford	laguilar@example.com
1541	11/24/2015	Gastroenteritis - follow up	Swenson	Lucia	860-226-0293	83 Osage Ave	Hartford	
1542	11/24/2015	Influenza	Mehta	Amrita	860-552-0375	28 Aiken Ave	Windsor	a.mehta@example.com
1544	11/25/2015	Influenza	Lewis	Patrice	860-552-5830	83 Highland St	Windsor	plewis5@example.org
1548	11/30/2015	Hypertension	Belanger	Malcolm	860-637-3927	723 Nicola Ave	West Hartford	
1549	11/30/2015	Influenza	Darcy	Edward	860-305-3985	723 Oxford Ave	Bloomfield	edarcy@example.org
1550	12/1/2015	Influenza	Fielder	Pam	860-305-2689	39 Unger Ave	Bloomfield	pfielder@example.org
1552	12/3/2015	Annual wellness visit	Castro	Daniel	860-637-0430	61 Osmond Way	West Hartford	d_castro@example.com
1555	12/7/2015	Annual wellness visit	Hallick	Davis	860-552-4495	84 Churchill Pl	Windsor	dhallick@example.com
1557	12/10/2015	Annual wellness visit	Swenson	Lucia	860-226-0293	83 Osage Ave	Hartford	
1560	12/15/2015	Influenza	Parker	Ian	860-938-1873	12 Adelbert St	Hartford	ian_parker@example.org
1562	12/22/2015	COPD management visit	King	Susan	860-661-9347	48 Fenton St	Hartford	susan.king@example.edu

7. Save and close the EarlierVisits query.

Cindi continues to analyze patient visits to Chatham Community Health Services. She is especially concerned about being proactive and reaching out to older patients well in advance of flu season. With this in mind, she would like to see a list of all patients who are age 60 or older and who have visited the clinic suffering from influenza. She wants to track these patients in particular so that her staff can contact them early for flu shots. To produce this list, you need to create a query containing two conditions—one for the patient's date of birth and another for the reason/diagnosis for each patient visit.

Defining Multiple Selection Criteria for Queries

Multiple conditions require you to use **logical operators** to combine two or more conditions. When you want a record selected only if two or more conditions are met, you need to use the **And logical operator**. In this case, Cindi wants to see only those records with a BirthDate field value less than or equal to 12/31/1956 *and* a Reason field value of "Influenza." If you place conditions in separate fields in the *same* Criteria row of the design grid, all conditions in that row must be met in order for a record to be included in the query results. However, if you place conditions in *different* Criteria rows, a record will be selected if at least one of the conditions is met. If none of the conditions are met, Access does not select the record. When you place conditions in different Criteria rows, you are using the **Or logical operator**. Figure 3-26 illustrates the difference between the And and Or logical operators.

Figure 3-26 **Logical operators And and Or for multiple selection criteria**

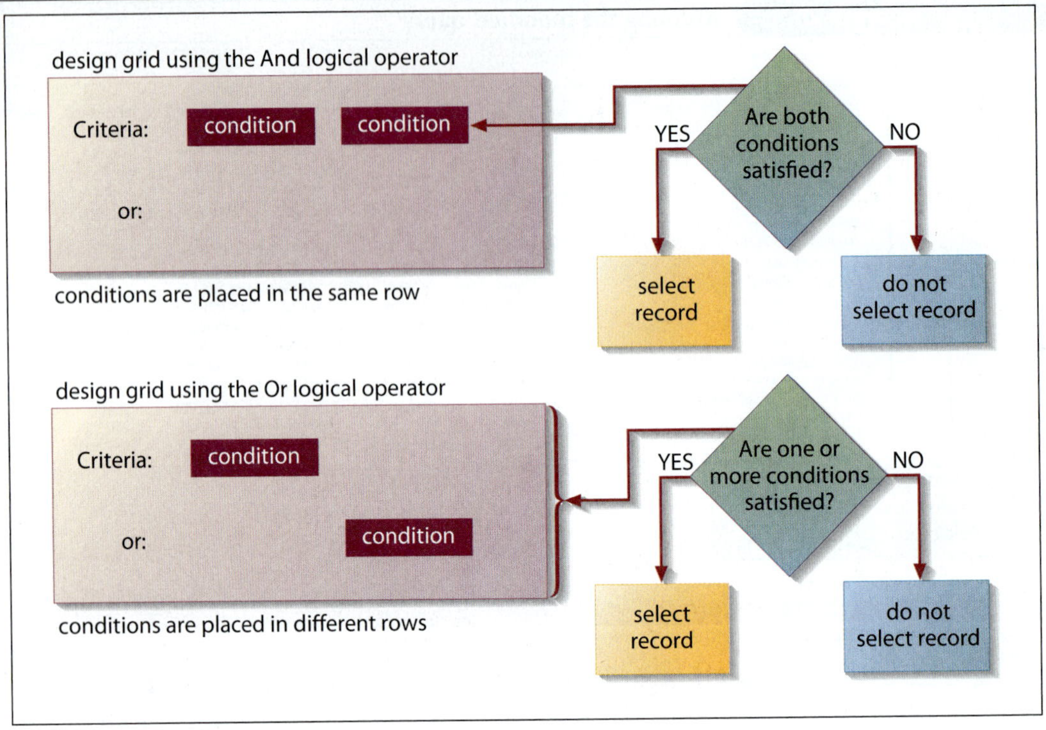

The And Logical Operator

To create the query for Cindi, you need to use the And logical operator to show only the records for patients who were born on or before 12/31/1956 *and* who have visited the clinic because of influenza. You'll create a new query based on both the Patient and Visit tables to produce the necessary results. In the query design, both conditions you specify will appear in the same Criteria row; therefore, the query will select records only if both conditions are met.

To create a new query using the And logical operator:

1. On the ribbon, click the **CREATE** tab.
2. In the Queries group, click the **Query Design** button.
3. Add the **Patient** and **Visit** tables to the Query window, and then close the Show Table dialog box. Resize both field lists to display all the field names.
4. Add the following fields from the Patient field list to the design grid in the order shown: **FirstName**, **LastName**, **BirthDate**, **Phone**, and **City**.
5. Add the **VisitDate** and **Reason** fields from the Visit table to the design grid.

   Now you need to enter the two conditions for the query.
6. Click the **BirthDate Criteria** box, and then type **<=12/31/1956**.
7. Press the **Tab** key four times to move to the **Reason Criteria** box, type **Influenza**, and then press the **Tab** key. See Figure 3-27.

Figure 3-27 Query to find older patients who have had influenza

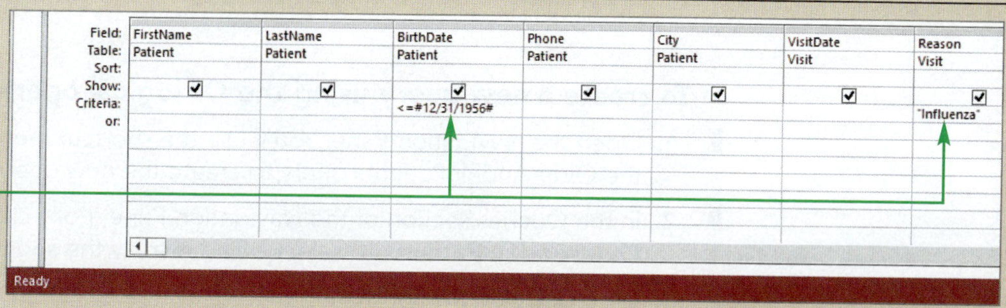

8. Run the query. Access displays only those records that meet both conditions: a BirthDate field value less than or equal to 12/31/1956 *and* a Reason field value of Influenza. Two records are selected for two different patients. See Figure 3-28.

Figure 3-28 Results of query using the And logical operator

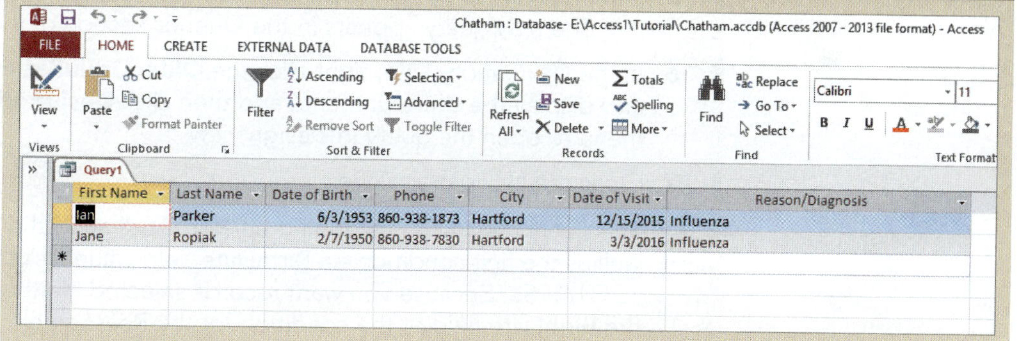

9. On the Quick Access Toolbar, click the **Save** button, and then save the query as **OlderAndFluPatients**.
10. Close the query.

Cindi meets with staff member Ethan to discuss the issue of influenza and keeping patients informed about receiving flu shots at the clinic. After viewing the results of the OlderAndFluPatients query, Ethan suggests that the clinic should reach out to all elderly patients regarding flu shots, because this segment of the population is particularly susceptible to the flu. In addition, he thinks they should contact any patient who has visited the clinic suffering from influenza to keep these patients informed about flu shots well in advance of flu season. To help with their planning, Cindi and Ethan have asked you to produce a list of all patients who were born on or before 12/31/1956 or who visited the clinic because of influenza. To create this query, you need to use the Or logical operator.

The Or Logical Operator

To create the query that Cindi and Ethan requested, your query must select a record when either one of two conditions is satisfied or when both conditions are satisfied. That is, a record is selected if the BirthDate field value is less than or equal to 12/31/1956 *or* if the Reason field value is Influenza *or* if both conditions are met. You will enter the condition for the BirthDate field in the Criteria row and the condition for the Reason field in the "or" criteria row, thereby using the Or logical operator.

To display the information Cindi and Ethan want to view, you'll create a new query based on the existing OlderAndFluPatients query, since it already contains the necessary fields. Then you'll specify the conditions using the Or logical operator.

To create a new query using the Or logical operator:

1. Open the Navigation Pane. You'll use the shortcut menu to copy and paste the OlderAndFluPatients query to create the new query.
2. In the Queries section of the Navigation Pane, right-click **OlderAndFluPatients** to select it and display the shortcut menu.
3. Click **Copy** on the shortcut menu.
4. Right-click the empty area near the bottom of the Navigation Pane, and then click **Paste** on the shortcut menu. The Paste As dialog box opens with the text "Copy Of OlderAndFluPatients" in the Query Name box. Because Cindi wants the new query to show data for all older patients or patients who have visited the clinic due to influenza, you'll name the new query "OlderOrFluPatients."
5. In the Query Name box, type **OlderOrFluPatients** and then press the **Enter** key. The new query appears in the Queries section of the Navigation Pane.
6. In the Navigation Pane, right-click the **OlderOrFluPatients** query to select it and display the shortcut menu, and then click **Design View** on the shortcut menu to open the query in Design view.
7. Close the Navigation Pane.

   The query already contains all the fields Cindi and Ethan want to view, as well as the first condition—a BirthDate field value less than or equal to 12/31/1956. Because you want records selected if either the condition for the BirthDate field or the condition for the Reason field is satisfied, you must delete the existing condition for the Reason field in the Criteria row and then enter this same condition in the "or" row of the design grid for the Reason field.
8. In the design grid, click at the end of the **Reason Criteria** box and then press the **Backspace** key until the condition "Influenza" is deleted.
9. Press the ↓ key to move to the "or" row for the Reason field, type **Influenza**, and then press the **Tab** key. See Figure 3-29.

Figure 3-29 Query window with the Or logical operator

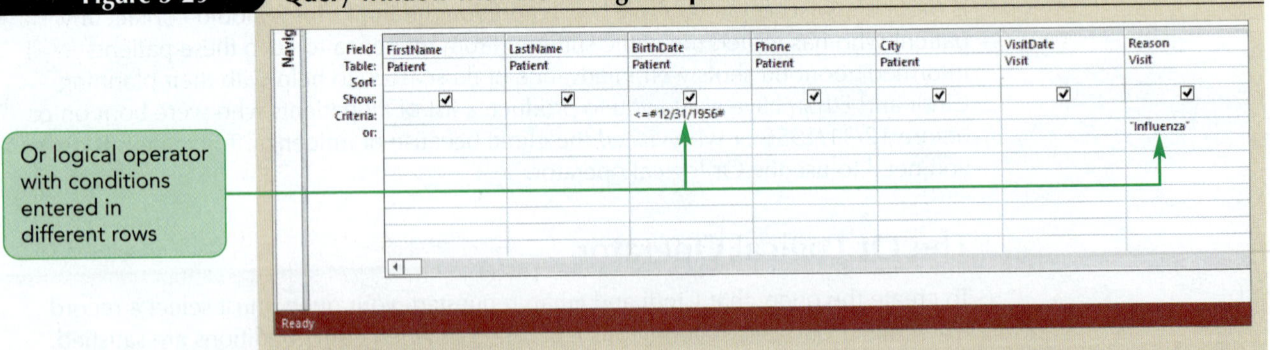

Cindi wants the list displayed in descending order by BirthDate to better analyze the data.

10. Click the right side of the **BirthDate Sort** box, and then click **Descending**.

11. Run the query. Access displays only those records that meet either condition: a BirthDate field value less than or equal to 12/31/1956 *or* a Reason field value of Influenza. Access also selects records that meet both conditions. The query displays a total of 38 records. The records in the query datasheet appear in descending order based on the values in the BirthDate field. See Figure 3-30.

Figure 3-30 Results of query using the Or logical operator

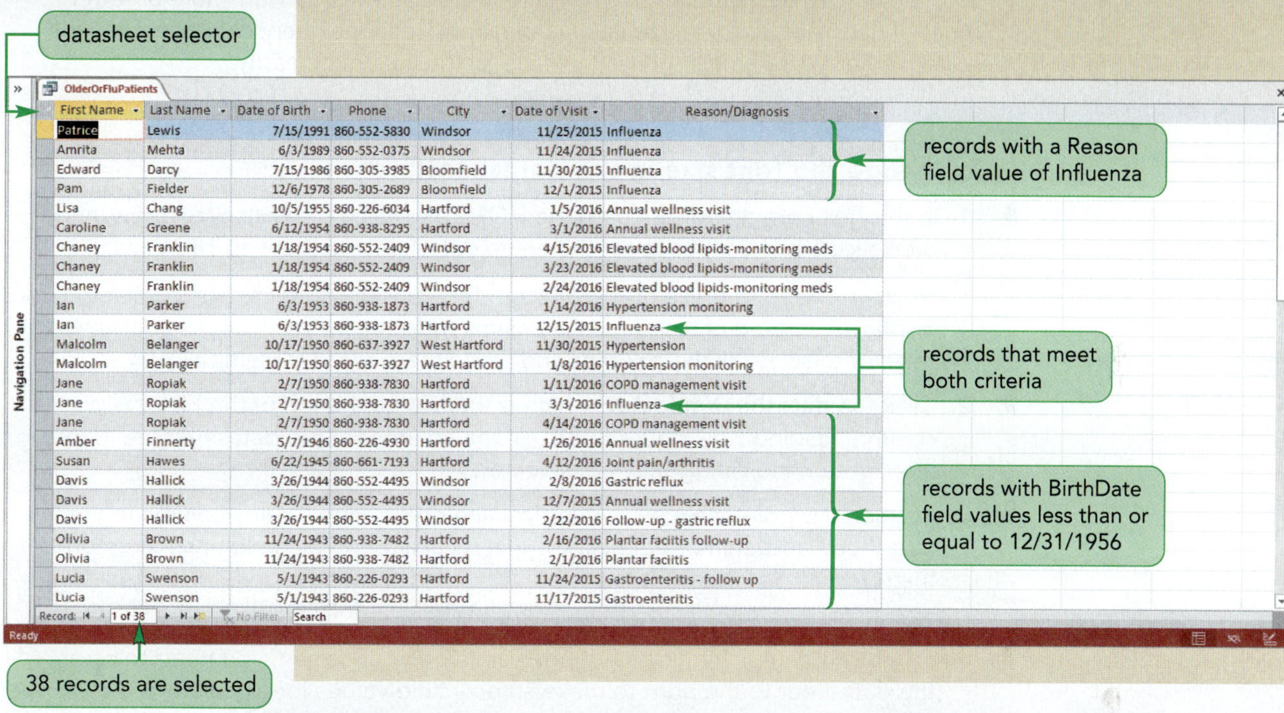

First Name	Last Name	Date of Birth	Phone	City	Date of Visit	Reason/Diagnosis
Patrice	Lewis	7/15/1991	860-552-5830	Windsor	11/25/2015	Influenza
Amrita	Mehta	6/3/1989	860-552-0375	Windsor	11/24/2015	Influenza
Edward	Darcy	7/15/1986	860-305-3985	Bloomfield	11/30/2015	Influenza
Pam	Fielder	12/6/1978	860-305-2689	Bloomfield	12/1/2015	Influenza
Lisa	Chang	10/5/1955	860-226-6034	Hartford	1/5/2016	Annual wellness visit
Caroline	Greene	6/12/1954	860-938-8295	Hartford	3/1/2016	Annual wellness visit
Chaney	Franklin	1/18/1954	860-552-2409	Windsor	4/15/2016	Elevated blood lipids-monitoring meds
Chaney	Franklin	1/18/1954	860-552-2409	Windsor	3/23/2016	Elevated blood lipids-monitoring meds
Chaney	Franklin	1/18/1954	860-552-2409	Windsor	2/24/2016	Elevated blood lipids-monitoring meds
Ian	Parker	6/3/1953	860-938-1873	Hartford	1/14/2016	Hypertension monitoring
Ian	Parker	6/3/1953	860-938-1873	Hartford	12/15/2015	Influenza
Malcolm	Belanger	10/17/1950	860-637-3927	West Hartford	11/30/2015	Hypertension
Malcolm	Belanger	10/17/1950	860-637-3927	West Hartford	1/8/2016	Hypertension monitoring
Jane	Ropiak	2/7/1950	860-938-7830	Hartford	1/11/2016	COPD management visit
Jane	Ropiak	2/7/1950	860-938-7830	Hartford	3/3/2016	Influenza
Jane	Ropiak	2/7/1950	860-938-7830	Hartford	4/14/2016	COPD management visit
Amber	Finnerty	5/7/1946	860-226-4930	Hartford	1/26/2016	Annual wellness visit
Susan	Hawes	6/22/1945	860-661-7193	Hartford	4/12/2016	Joint pain/arthritis
Davis	Hallick	3/26/1944	860-552-4495	Windsor	2/8/2016	Gastric reflux
Davis	Hallick	3/26/1944	860-552-4495	Windsor	12/7/2015	Annual wellness visit
Davis	Hallick	3/26/1944	860-552-4495	Windsor	2/22/2016	Follow-up - gastric reflux
Olivia	Brown	11/24/1943	860-938-7482	Hartford	2/16/2016	Plantar faciitis follow-up
Olivia	Brown	11/24/1943	860-938-7482	Hartford	2/1/2016	Plantar faciitis
Lucia	Swenson	5/1/1943	860-226-0293	Hartford	11/24/2015	Gastroenteritis - follow up
Lucia	Swenson	5/1/1943	860-226-0293	Hartford	11/17/2015	Gastroenteritis

INSIGHT

Understanding the Results of Using And vs. Or

When you use the And logical operator to define multiple selection criteria in a query, you *narrow* the results produced by the query because a record must meet more than one condition to be included in the results. For example, the OlderAndFluPatients query you created resulted in only 2 records. When you use the Or logical operator, you *broaden* the results produced by the query because a record must meet only one of the conditions to be included in the results. For example, the OlderOrFluPatients query you created resulted in 38 records. This is an important distinction to keep in mind when you include multiple selection criteria in queries, so that the queries you create will produce the results you want.

Cindi would like to spend some time reviewing the results of the OlderOrFluPatients query. To make this task easier, she asks you to change how the datasheet is displayed.

Changing a Datasheet's Appearance

You can make many formatting changes to a datasheet to improve its appearance or readability. Many of these modifications are familiar types of changes you can also make in Word documents or Excel spreadsheets, such as modifying the font type, size, color, and the alignment of text. You can also apply different colors to the rows and columns in a datasheet to enhance its appearance.

Modifying the Font Size

Depending on the size of the monitor you are using or the screen resolution, you might need to increase or decrease the size of the font in a datasheet to view more or fewer columns of data. Cindi asks you to change the font size in the query datasheet from the default 11 points to 14 points so that she can read the text more easily.

To change the font size in the datasheet:

1. In the Text Formatting group on the HOME tab, click the **Font Size** arrow, and then click **14**. The font size for the entire datasheet increases to 14 points.

   Next, you need to resize the columns to their best fit, so that all field values are displayed. Instead of resizing each column individually, you'll use the datasheet selector to select all the columns and resize them at the same time.

2. Click the **datasheet selector**, which is the box to the left of the First Name column heading (see Figure 3-30). All the columns in the datasheet are highlighted, indicating they are selected.
3. Position the pointer ↔ on the vertical line on the right of any column in the datasheet, and then double-click the vertical line. All the columns visible on the screen are resized to their best fit. Scroll down and repeat the resizing, as necessary, to make sure that all field values are fully displayed.

   Trouble? If all the columns are not visible on your screen, you need to scroll the datasheet to the right to make sure all field values for all columns are fully displayed. If you need to resize any columns, click a field value first to deselect the columns before resizing an individual column.

4. Click any value in the First Name column to make it the current field and to deselect the columns in the datasheet.

Changing the Alternate Row Color in a Datasheet

TIP

When choosing a row color, be sure not to select a color that is too dark because it might obscure the data rather than enhance it.

Access uses themes to format the objects in a database. A **theme** is a predefined set of formats including colors, fonts, and other effects that enhance an object's appearance and usability. When you create a database, Access applies the Office theme to objects as you create them. By default, the Office theme formats every other row in a datasheet with a gray background color to distinguish one row from another, making it easier to view and read the contents of a datasheet. The gray alternate row color provides a subtle difference compared to the rows that have the default white color. You can change the alternate row color in a datasheet to something more noticeable using the Alternate Row Color button in the Text Formatting group on the HOME tab. Cindi suggests that you change the alternate row color in the datasheet to see the effect of using this feature.

To change the alternate row color in the datasheet:

1. In the Text Formatting group on the HOME tab, click the **Alternate Row Color** button arrow to display the gallery of color choices. See Figure 3-31.

Figure 3-31 Gallery of color choices for alternate row color

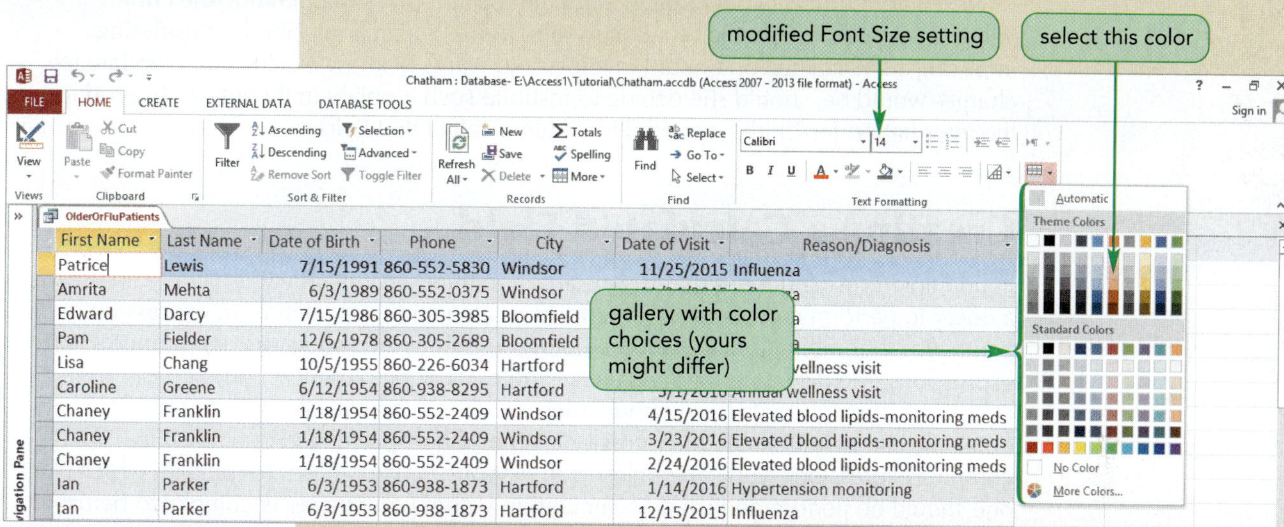

TIP

The name of the color appears in a ScreenTip when you point to a color in the gallery.

The Theme Colors section provides colors from the default Office theme, so that your datasheet's color scheme matches the one in use for the database. The Standard Colors section provides many standard color choices. You might also see a Recent Colors section, with colors that you have recently used in a datasheet. At the bottom of the gallery, you could also choose the No Color option, which sets each row's background color to white; or the More Colors option, which creates a custom color. You'll use one of the theme colors.

2. In the Theme Colors section, click the color box for **Orange, Accent 2, Lighter 60%** (third row, sixth color box). The alternate row color is applied to the query datasheet. See Figure 3-32.

Figure 3-32 Datasheet formatted with alternate row color

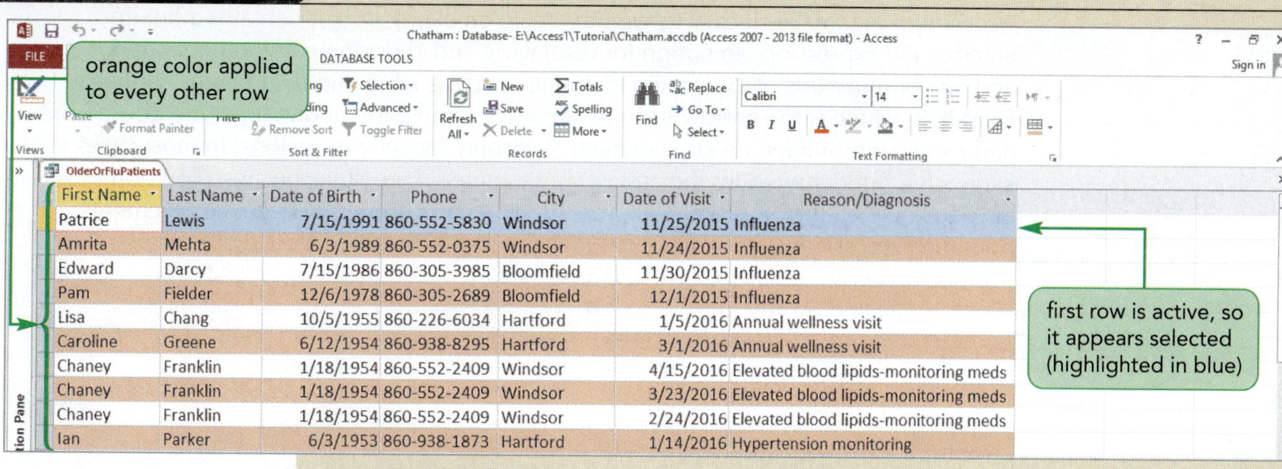

Every other row in the datasheet uses the selected theme color. Cindi likes how the datasheet looks with this color scheme, so she asks you to save the query.

3. Save and close the OlderOrFluPatients query. The query is saved with both the increased font size and the orange alternate row color.

Next, Cindi turns her attention to some financial aspects of operating the clinic. She wants to use the Chatham database to perform calculations. She is considering imposing a 2% late fee on unpaid invoices and wants to know exactly what the late fee charges would be, should she decide to institute such a policy in the future. To produce the information for Cindi, you need to create a calculated field.

Creating a Calculated Field

In addition to using queries to retrieve, sort, and filter data in a database, you can use a query to perform calculations. To perform a calculation, you define an **expression** containing a combination of database fields, constants, and operators. For numeric expressions, the data types of the database fields must be Number, Currency, or Date/Time; the constants are numbers such as .02 (for the 2% late fee); and the operators can be arithmetic operators (+ – * /) or other specialized operators. In complex expressions, you can enclose calculations in parentheses to indicate which one should be performed first; any calculation within parentheses is completed before calculations outside the parentheses. In expressions without parentheses, Access performs basic calculations using the following order of precedence: multiplication and division before addition and subtraction. When operators have equal precedence, Access calculates them in order from left to right.

To perform a calculation in a query, you add a calculated field to the query. A **calculated field** is a field that displays the results of an expression. A calculated field that you create with an expression appears in a query datasheet or in a form or report; however, it does not exist in a database. When you run a query that contains a calculated field, Access evaluates the expression defined by the calculated field and displays the resulting value in the query datasheet, form, or report.

To enter an expression for a calculated field, you can type it directly in a Field box in the design grid. Alternately, you can open the Zoom box or Expression Builder and use either one to enter the expression. The **Zoom box** is a dialog box that you can use to enter text, expressions, or other values. To use the Zoom box, however, you must know all the parts of the expression you want to create. **Expression Builder** is an Access tool that makes it easy for you to create an expression; it contains a box for entering the expression, an option for displaying and choosing common operators, and one or more lists of expression elements, such as table and field names. Unlike a Field box, which is too narrow to show an entire expression at one time, the Zoom box and Expression Builder are large enough to display longer expressions. In most cases, Expression Builder provides the easiest way to enter expressions because you don't have to know all the parts of the expression; you can choose the necessary elements from the Expression Builder dialog box, which also helps to prevent typing errors.

REFERENCE

Using Expression Builder

- Create and save the query in which you want to include a calculated field.
- Open the query in Design view.
- In the design grid, click the Field box in which you want to create an expression.
- In the Query Setup group on the DESIGN tab, click the Builder button.
- Use the expression elements and common operators to build the expression, or type the expression directly in the expression box.
- Click the OK button.

To produce the information Cindi wants, you need to create a new query based on the Billing and Visit tables and, in the query, create a calculated field that will multiply each InvoiceAmt field value by .02 to calculate the proposed 2% late fee.

To create the new query and the calculated field:

1. On the ribbon, click the **CREATE** tab.
2. In the Queries group, click the **Query Design** button. The Show Table dialog box opens.

   Cindi wants to see data from both the Visit and Billing tables, so you need to add these two tables to the Query window.
3. Add the **Visit** and **Billing** tables to the Query window, and then close the Show Table dialog box. The field lists appear in the Query window, and the one-to-many relationship between the Visit (primary) and Billing (related) tables is displayed.
4. Resize the two field lists so that all field names are visible.
5. Add the following fields to the design grid in the order given: **VisitID**, **PatientID**, and **VisitDate** from the Visit table; and **InvoiceItem**, **InvoicePaid**, and **InvoiceAmt** from the Billing table.

   Cindi is interested in viewing data only for unpaid invoices because a late fee would apply only to them, so you need to enter the necessary condition for the InvoicePaid field. Recall that InvoicePaid is a Yes/No field. The condition you need to enter is the word "No" in the Criteria box for this field, so that Access will retrieve the records for unpaid invoices only.
6. In the **InvoicePaid Criteria** box, type **No**. As soon as you type the letter "N," a menu appears with options for entering various functions for the criteria. You don't need to enter a function, so you can close this menu.
7. Press the **Esc** key to close the menu.
8. Press the **Tab** key. The query name you'll use will indicate that the data is for unpaid invoices, so you don't need to include the InvoicePaid values in the query results.
9. Click the **InvoicePaid Show** check box to remove the checkmark.
10. Save the query with the name **UnpaidInvoiceLateFee**.

You must close the menu or you'll enter a function, which will cause an error.

Now you can use Expression Builder to create the calculated field for the InvoiceAmt field.

TIP

You must first save and name a query in order for its fields to be listed in the Expression Categories section.

To create the calculated field:

1. Click the blank Field box to the right of the InvoiceAmt field. This field will contain the expression.
2. In the Query Setup group on the DESIGN tab, click the **Builder** button. The Expression Builder dialog box opens.

   The insertion point is positioned in the large box at the top of the dialog box, ready for you to enter the expression. The Expression Categories section of the dialog box lists the fields from the query so you can include them in the expression. The Expression Elements section contains options for including other elements in the expression, including functions, constants, and operators. If the expression you're entering is a simple one, you can type it in the box; if it's more complex, you can use the options in the Expression Elements section to help you build the expression.

   The expression for the calculated field will multiply the InvoiceAmt field values by the numeric constant .02 (which represents a 2% late fee).
3. In the Expression Categories section of the dialog box, double-click **InvoiceAmt**. The field name is added to the expression box, within brackets and with a space following it. In an expression, all field names must be enclosed in brackets.

   Next you need to enter the multiplication operator, which is the asterisk (*), followed by the constant.
4. Type * (an asterisk) and then type **.02**. You have finished entering the expression. See Figure 3-33.

Figure 3-33 **Completed expression for the calculated field**

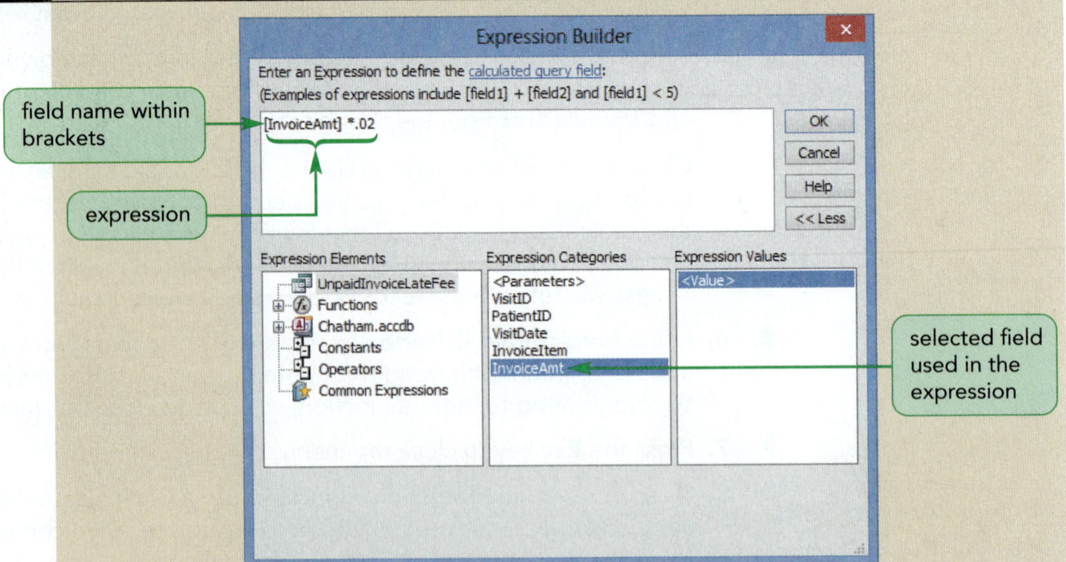

If you're not sure which operator to use, you can click Operators in the Expression Elements section to display a list of available operators in the center section of the dialog box.

5. Click the **OK** button. Access closes the Expression Builder dialog box and adds the expression to the design grid in the Field box for the calculated field.

   When you create a calculated field, Access uses the default column name "Expr1" for the field. You need to specify a more meaningful column name so it will appear in the query results. You'll enter the name "LateFee," which better describes the field's contents.

6. Click to the left of the text "Expr1:" at the beginning of the expression, and then press the **Delete** key five times to delete the text **Expr1**. *Do not delete the colon*; it is needed to separate the calculated field name from the expression.

7. Type **LateFee**. Next, you'll set this field's Caption property so that the field name will appear as "Late Fee" in the query datasheet.

8. In the Show/Hide group on the DESIGN tab, click the **Property Sheet** button. The Property Sheet for the current field, LateFee, opens on the right side of the window. See Figure 3-34.

Figure 3-34 **Property Sheet for the calculated field**

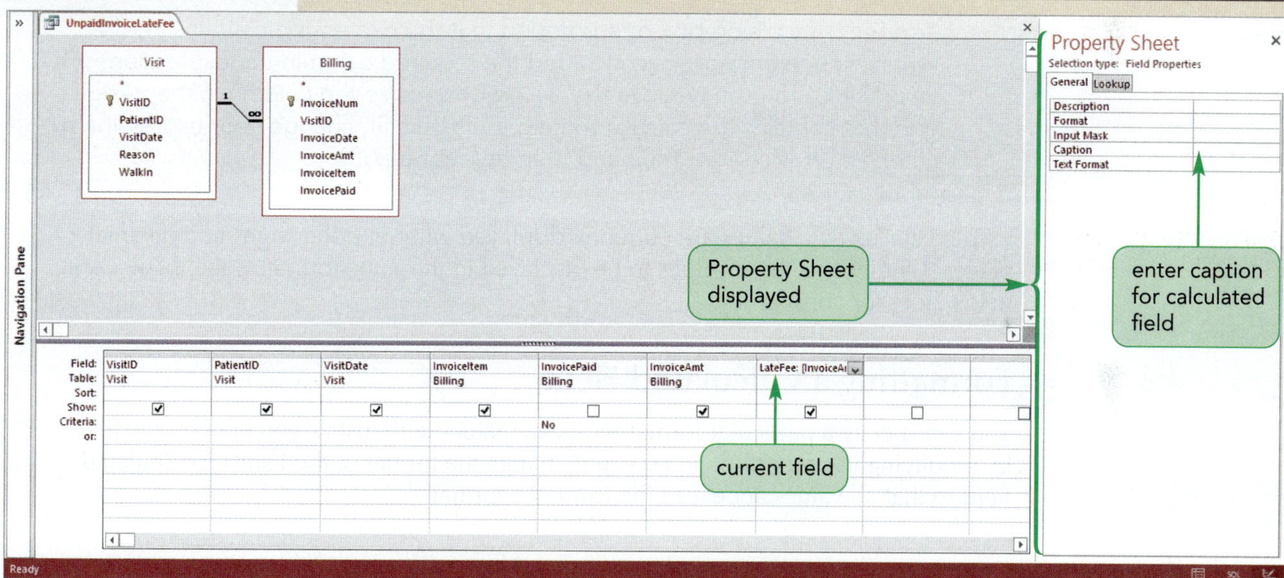

9. Click in the Caption box of the Property Sheet, type **Late Fee** and then close the Property Sheet.

10. Run the query. Access displays the query datasheet, which contains the specified fields and the calculated field with the caption "Late Fee." See Figure 3-35.

Figure 3-35 Datasheet displaying the calculated field

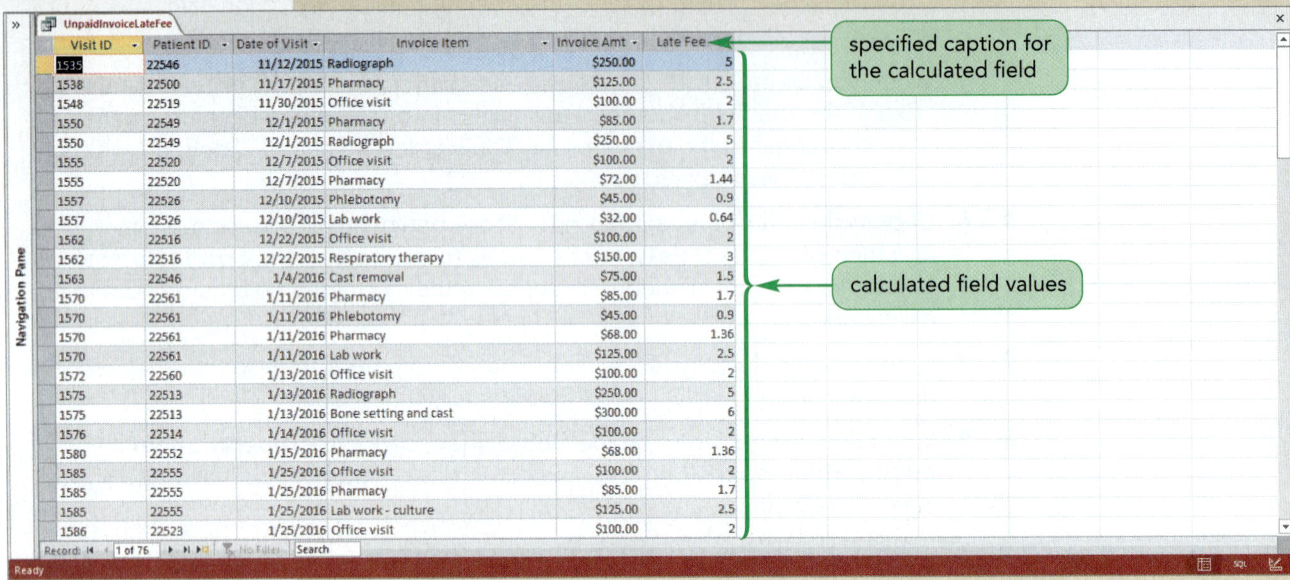

Visit ID	Patient ID	Date of Visit	Invoice Item	Invoice Amt	Late Fee
1535	22546	11/12/2015	Radiograph	$250.00	5
1538	22500	11/17/2015	Pharmacy	$125.00	2.5
1548	22519	11/30/2015	Office visit	$100.00	2
1550	22549	12/1/2015	Pharmacy	$85.00	1.7
1550	22549	12/1/2015	Radiograph	$250.00	5
1555	22520	12/7/2015	Office visit	$100.00	2
1555	22520	12/7/2015	Pharmacy	$72.00	1.44
1557	22526	12/10/2015	Phlebotomy	$45.00	0.9
1557	22526	12/10/2015	Lab work	$32.00	0.64
1562	22516	12/22/2015	Office visit	$100.00	2
1562	22516	12/22/2015	Respiratory therapy	$150.00	3
1563	22546	1/4/2016	Cast removal	$75.00	1.5
1570	22561	1/11/2016	Pharmacy	$85.00	1.7
1570	22561	1/11/2016	Phlebotomy	$45.00	0.9
1570	22561	1/11/2016	Pharmacy	$68.00	1.36
1570	22561	1/11/2016	Lab work	$125.00	2.5
1572	22560	1/13/2016	Office visit	$100.00	2
1575	22513	1/13/2016	Radiograph	$250.00	5
1575	22513	1/13/2016	Bone setting and cast	$300.00	6
1576	22514	1/14/2016	Office visit	$100.00	2
1580	22552	1/15/2016	Pharmacy	$68.00	1.36
1585	22555	1/25/2016	Office visit	$100.00	2
1585	22555	1/25/2016	Pharmacy	$85.00	1.7
1585	22555	1/25/2016	Lab work - culture	$125.00	2.5
1586	22523	1/25/2016	Office visit	$100.00	2

Trouble? If a dialog box opens noting that the expression contains invalid syntax, you might not have included the required colon in the expression. Click the OK button to close the dialog box, resize the column in the design grid that contains the calculated field to its best fit, change your expression to LateFee: [InvoiceAmt]*0.02 and then repeat Step 10.

The LateFee field values are currently displayed without dollar signs and decimal places. Cindi wants these values to be displayed in the same format as the InvoiceAmt field values for consistency.

Formatting a Calculated Field

You can specify a particular format for a calculated field, just as you can for any field, by modifying its properties. Next, you'll change the format of the LateFee calculated field so that all values appear in the Currency format.

To format the calculated field:

1. Switch to Design view.
2. In the design grid, click in the **LateFee** calculated field to make it the current field, if necessary.
3. In the Show/Hide group on the DESIGN tab, click the **Property Sheet** button to open the Property Sheet for the calculated field.

   You need to change the Format property to Currency, which displays values with a dollar sign and two decimal places.
4. In the Property Sheet, click the right side of the **Format** box to display the list of formats, and then click **Currency**.
5. Close the Property Sheet for the calculated field, and then run the query. The amounts in the LateFee calculated field are now displayed with dollar signs and two decimal places.

6. Save and close the UnpaidInvoiceLateFee query.

PROSKILLS

Problem Solving: Creating a Calculated Field vs. Using the Calculated Field Data Type

You can also create a calculated field using the Calculated Field data type, which lets you store the result of an expression as a field in a table. However, database experts caution users against storing calculations in a table for several reasons. First, storing calculated data in a table consumes valuable space and increases the size of the database. The preferred approach is to use a calculated field in a query; with this approach, the result of the calculation is not stored in the database—it is produced only when you run the query—and it is always current. Second, the Calculated Field data type provides limited options for creating a calculation, whereas a calculated field in a query provides more functions and options for creating expressions. Third, including a field in a table using the Calculated Field data type limits your options if you need to upgrade the database at some point to a more robust DBMS, such as Oracle or SQL Server, that doesn't support this data type; you would need to redesign your database to eliminate this data type. Finally, most database experts agree that including a field in a table whose value is dependent on other fields in the table violates database design principles. To avoid such problems, it's best to create a query that includes a calculated field to perform the calculation you want, instead of creating a field in a table that uses the Calculated Field data type.

To better analyze costs at Chatham Community Health Services, Cindi wants to view more detailed information about patient invoices. Specifically, she would like to know the minimum, average, and maximum invoice amounts. She asks you to determine these statistics from data in the Billing table.

Using Aggregate Functions

You can calculate statistical information, such as totals and averages, on the records displayed in a table datasheet or selected by a query. To do this, you use the Access aggregate functions. **Aggregate functions** perform arithmetic operations on selected records in a database. Figure 3-36 lists the most frequently used aggregate functions.

Figure 3-36 **Frequently used aggregate functions**

Aggregate Function	Determines	Data Types Supported
Average	Average of the field values for the selected records	AutoNumber, Currency, Date/Time, Number
Count	Number of records selected	AutoNumber, Currency, Date/Time, Long Text, Number, OLE Object, Short Text, Yes/No
Maximum	Highest field value for the selected records	AutoNumber, Currency, Date/Time, Number, Short Text
Minimum	Lowest field value for the selected records	AutoNumber, Currency, Date/Time, Number, Short Text
Sum	Total of the field values for the selected records	AutoNumber, Currency, Date/Time, Number

Working with Aggregate Functions Using the Total Row

If you want to quickly perform a calculation using an aggregate function in a table or query datasheet, you can use the Totals button in the Records group on the HOME tab. When you click this button, a row labeled "Total" appears at the bottom of the datasheet. You can then choose one of the aggregate functions for a field in the datasheet, and the results of the calculation will be displayed in the Total row for that field.

Cindi wants to know the total amount of all invoices for the clinic. You can quickly display this amount using the Sum function in the Total row in the Billing table datasheet.

To display the total amount of all invoices in the Billing table:

1. Open the Navigation Pane, open the **Billing** table in Datasheet view, and then close the Navigation Pane.
2. Make sure the HOME tab is displayed.
3. In the Records group, click the **Totals** button. Access adds a row with the label "Total" to the bottom of the datasheet.
4. Scroll to the bottom of the datasheet to view the last records in the datasheet and the Total row. You want to display the sum of all the values in the Invoice Amt column.
5. In the Total row, click the **Invoice Amt** column. An arrow appears on the left side of the field.
6. Click the **arrow** to display the menu of aggregate functions. The functions displayed depend on the data type of the current field; in this case, the menu provides functions for a Currency field. See Figure 3-37.

Figure 3-37 Using aggregate functions in the Total row

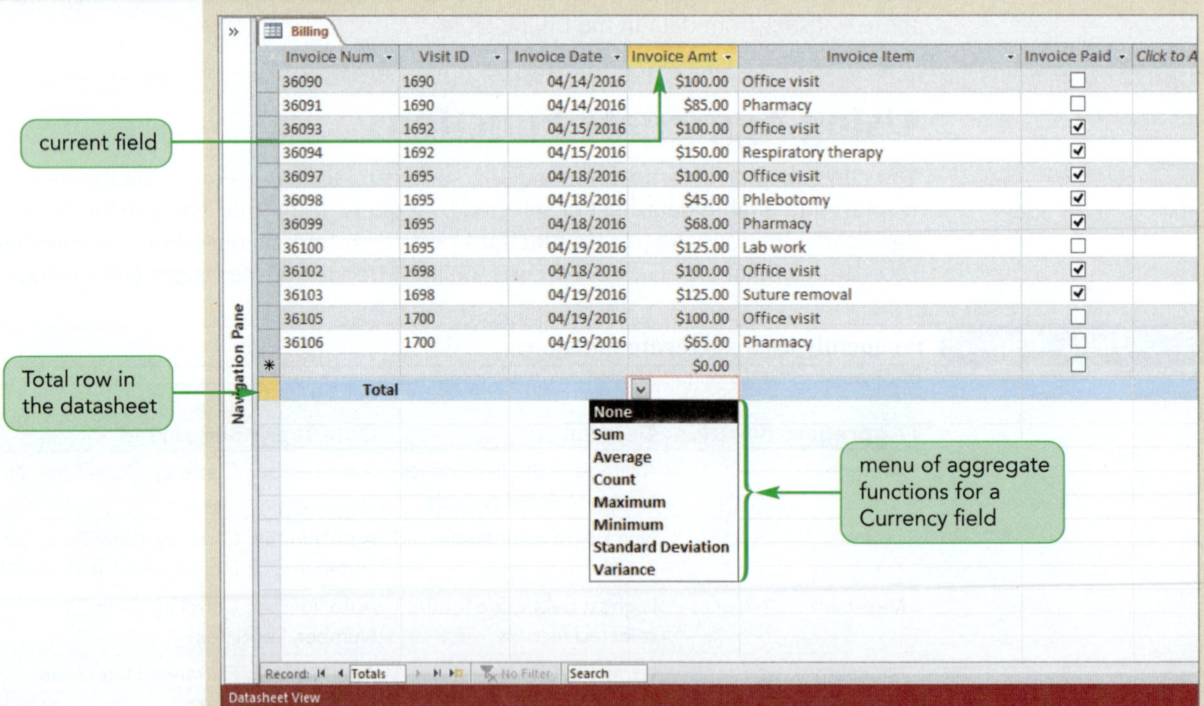

7. Click **Sum** in the menu. Access adds all the values in the Invoice Amt column and displays the total $20,603.00 in the Total row for the column.

   Cindi doesn't want to change the Billing table to always display this total. You can remove the Total row by clicking the Totals button again; this button works as a toggle to switch between the display of the Total row with the results of any calculations in the row, and the display of the datasheet without this row.

8. In the Records group, click the **Totals** button. Access removes the Total row from the datasheet.
9. Close the Billing table without saving the changes.

Cindi wants to know the minimum, average, and maximum invoice amounts for Chatham Community Health Services. To produce this information for Cindi, you need to use aggregate functions in a query.

Creating Queries with Aggregate Functions

Aggregate functions operate on the records that meet a query's selection criteria. You specify an aggregate function for a specific field, and the appropriate operation applies to that field's values for the selected records.

To display the minimum, average, and maximum of all the invoice amounts in the Billing table, you will use the Minimum, Average, and Maximum aggregate functions for the InvoiceAmt field.

To calculate the minimum of all invoice amounts:

1. Create a new query in Design view, add the **Billing** table to the Query window, and then close the Show Table dialog box. Resize the Billing field list to display all fields.

   To perform the three calculations on the InvoiceAmt field, you need to add the field to the design grid three times.

2. In the Billing field list, double-click **InvoiceAmt** three times to add three copies of the field to the design grid.

   You need to select an aggregate function for each InvoiceAmt field. When you click the Totals button in the Show/Hide group on the DESIGN tab, a row labeled "Total" is added to the design grid. The Total row provides a list of the aggregate functions that you can select.

3. In the Show/Hide group on the DESIGN tab, click the **Totals** button. A new row labeled "Total" appears between the Table and Sort rows in the design grid. The default entry for each field in the Total row is the Group By operator, which you will learn about later in this tutorial. See Figure 3-38.

Figure 3-38 Total row inserted in the design grid

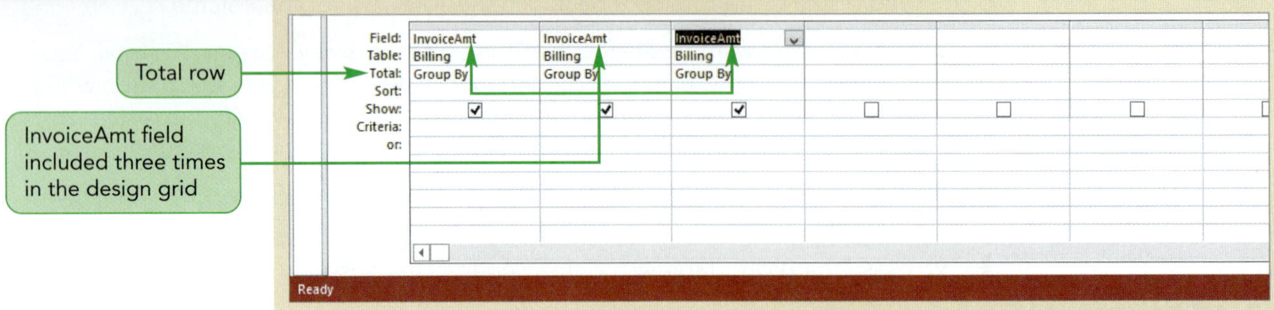

In the Total row, you specify the aggregate function you want to use for a field.

4. Click the right side of the first column's **Total** box, and then click **Min**. This field will calculate the minimum amount of all the InvoiceAmt field values.

   When you run the query, Access automatically will assign a datasheet column name of "MinOfInvoiceAmt" for this field. You can change the datasheet column name to a more descriptive or readable name by entering the name you want in the Field box. However, you must also keep the InvoiceAmt field name in the Field box because it identifies the field to use in the calculation. The Field box will contain the datasheet column name you specify followed by the field name (InvoiceAmt) with a colon separating the two names.

Be sure to type the colon following the name or the query will not work correctly.

5. In the first column's Field box, click to the left of InvoiceAmt, and then type **MinimumInvoiceAmt:** (including the colon).
6. Using the ✥ pointer, double-click the column dividing line between the first two columns so that you can see the complete field name, MinimumInvoiceAmt:InvoiceAmt.

   Next, you need to set the Caption property for this field so that the field name appears with spaces between words in the query datatsheet.

7. In the Show/Hide group on the DESIGN tab, click the **Property Sheet** button to open the Property Sheet for the current field.
8. In the Caption box, type **Minimum Invoice Amt** and then close the Property Sheet.

You'll follow the same process to complete the query by calculating the average and maximum invoice amounts.

To calculate the average and maximum of all invoice amounts:

1. Click the right side of the second column's **Total** box, and then click **Avg**. This field will calculate the average of all the InvoiceAmt field values.
2. In the second column's Field box, click to the left of InvoiceAmt, and then type **AverageInvoiceAmt:**.
3. Resize the second column to fully display the field name, AverageInvoiceAmt:InvoiceAmt.

4. Open the Property Sheet for the current field, and then set its Caption property to **Average Invoice Amt**. Leave the Property Sheet open.
5. Click the right side of the third column's **Total** box, and then click **Max**. This field will calculate the maximum amount of all the InvoiceAmt field values.
6. In the third column's Field box, click to the left of InvoiceAmt, and then type **MaximumInvoiceAmt:**.
7. Resize the third column to fully display the field name, MaximumInvoiceAmt:InvoiceAmt.
8. In the Property Sheet for the current field, set the Caption property to **Maximum Invoice Amt** and then close the Property Sheet. See Figure 3-39.

Figure 3-39 Query with aggregate functions entered

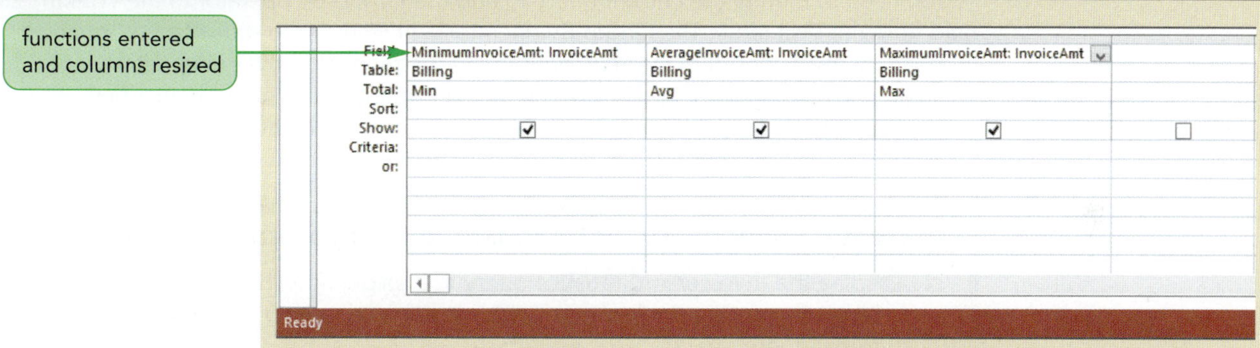

Trouble? Carefully compare your field names to those shown in the figure to make sure they match exactly; otherwise the query will not work correctly.

9. Run the query. Access displays one record containing the three aggregate function results. The single row of summary statistics represents calculations based on all the records selected for the query—in this case, all 203 records in the Billing table.
10. Resize all columns to their best fit so that the column names are fully displayed, and then click the field value in the first column to deselect the value and view the results. See Figure 3-40.

Figure 3-40 Result of the query using aggregate functions

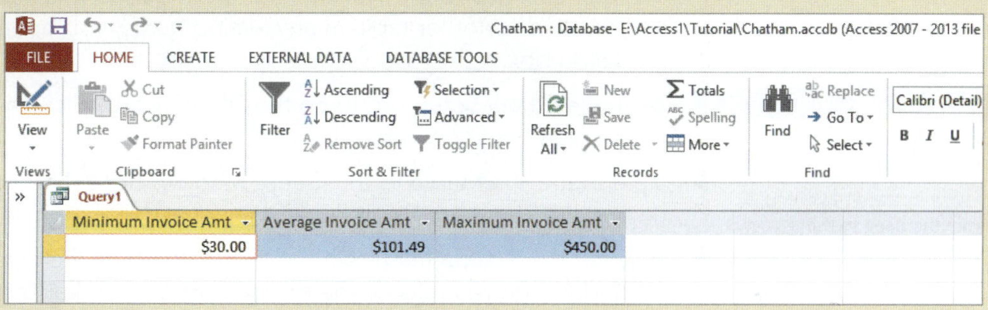

11. Save the query as **InvoiceAmtStatistics**.

Cindi would like to view the same invoice amount statistics (minimum, average, and maximum) as they relate to both scheduled appointments and walk-in visits to the clinic.

Using Record Group Calculations

In addition to calculating statistical information on all or selected records in selected tables, you can calculate statistics for groups of records. For example, you can determine the number of patients in each city or the average invoice amount by city.

To create a query for Cindi's latest request, you can modify the current query by adding the WalkIn field and assigning the Group By operator to it. The **Group By operator** divides the selected records into groups based on the values in the specified field. Those records with the same value for the field are grouped together, and the datasheet displays one record for each group. Aggregate functions, which appear in the other columns of the design grid, provide statistical information for each group.

You need to modify the current query to add the Group By operator to the WalkIn field from the Visit table. The Group By operator will display the statistical information grouped by the values of the WalkIn field for all the records in the query datasheet. To create the new query, you will save the InvoiceAmtStatistics query with a new name, keeping the original query intact, and then modify the new query.

To create a new query with the Group By operator:

1. Display the InvoiceAmtStatistics query in Design view. Because the query is open, you can use Backstage view to save it with a new name, keeping the original query intact.
2. Click the **FILE** tab to display Backstage view, and then click **Save As** in the navigation bar. The Save As screen opens.
3. In the File Types section on the left, click **Save Object As**. The right side of the screen changes to display options for saving the current database object as a new object.
4. Click the **Save As** button. The Save As dialog box opens, indicating that you are saving a copy of the InvoiceAmtStatistics query.
5. Type **InvoiceAmtStatisticsByWalkIn** to replace the highlighted name, and then press the **Enter** key. The new query is saved with the name you specified and displayed in Design view.

   You need to add the WalkIn field to the query. This field is in the Visit table. To include another table in an existing query, you open the Show Table dialog box.

TIP

You could also open the Navigation Pane and drag the Visit table from the pane to the Query window.

6. In the Query Setup group on the DESIGN tab, click the **Show Table** button to open the Show Table dialog box.
7. Add the **Visit** table to the Query window, close the Show Table dialog box, and then resize the Visit field list.
8. Drag the **WalkIn** field from the Visit field list to the first column in the design grid. When you release the mouse button, the WalkIn field appears in the design grid's first column, and the existing fields shift to the right. Group By, the default option in the Total row, appears for the WalkIn field.
9. Run the query. Access displays 2 records—one for each WalkIn group, Yes and No. Each record contains the WalkIn field value for the group and the three aggregate function values. The summary statistics represent calculations based on the 203 records in the Billing table. See Figure 3-41.

Figure 3-41 Aggregate functions grouped by WalkIn

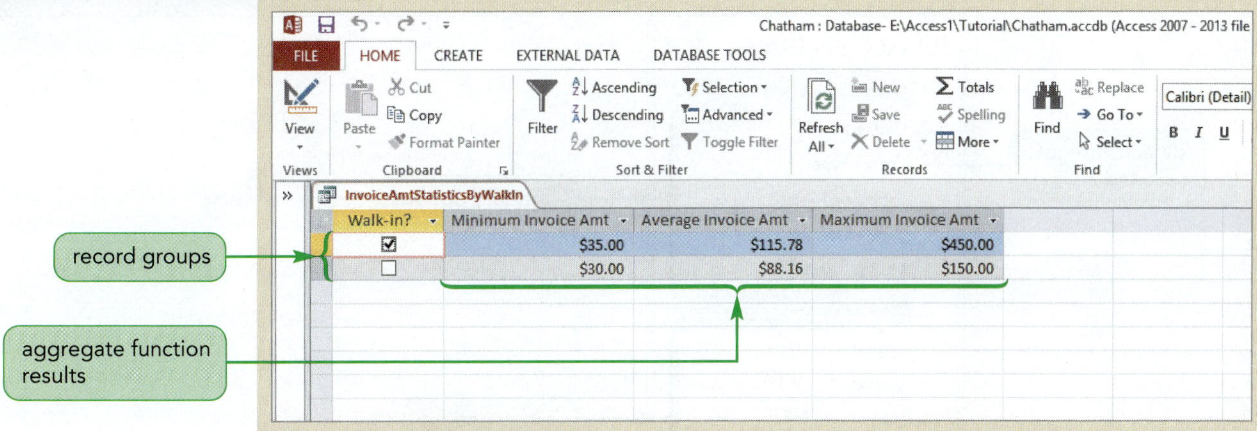

Cindi notes that the invoice amounts for walk-in visits are higher than those for scheduled appointments.

10. Save and close the query.
11. Open the Navigation Pane.

You have created and saved many queries in the Chatham database. The Navigation Pane provides options for opening and managing the queries you've created, as well as the other objects in the database, such as tables, forms, and reports.

Working with the Navigation Pane

As noted earlier, the Navigation Pane is the main area for working with the objects in a database. As you continue to create objects in your database, you might want to display and work with them in different ways. The Navigation Pane provides options for grouping database objects in various ways to suit your needs. For example, you might want to view only the queries created for a certain table or all the query objects in the database.

TIP

You can hide the display of a group's objects by clicking the button to the right of the group name; click the button again to expand the group and display its objects.

The Navigation Pane divides database objects into categories, and each category contains groups. The groups contain one or more objects. The default category is **Object Type**, which arranges objects by type—tables, queries, forms, and reports. The default group is **All Access Objects**, which displays all objects in the database. You can also choose to display only one type of object, such as tables.

The default group name, All Access Objects, appears at the top of the Navigation Pane. Currently, each object type—Tables, Queries, Forms, and Reports—is displayed as a heading, and the objects related to each type are listed below the heading. To group objects differently, you can select another category by using the Navigation Pane menu. You'll try this next.

To group objects differently in the Navigation Pane:

1. At the top of the Navigation Pane, click the **All Access Objects** button. A menu is displayed for choosing different categories and groups. See Figure 3-42.

Figure 3-42 Navigation Pane menu

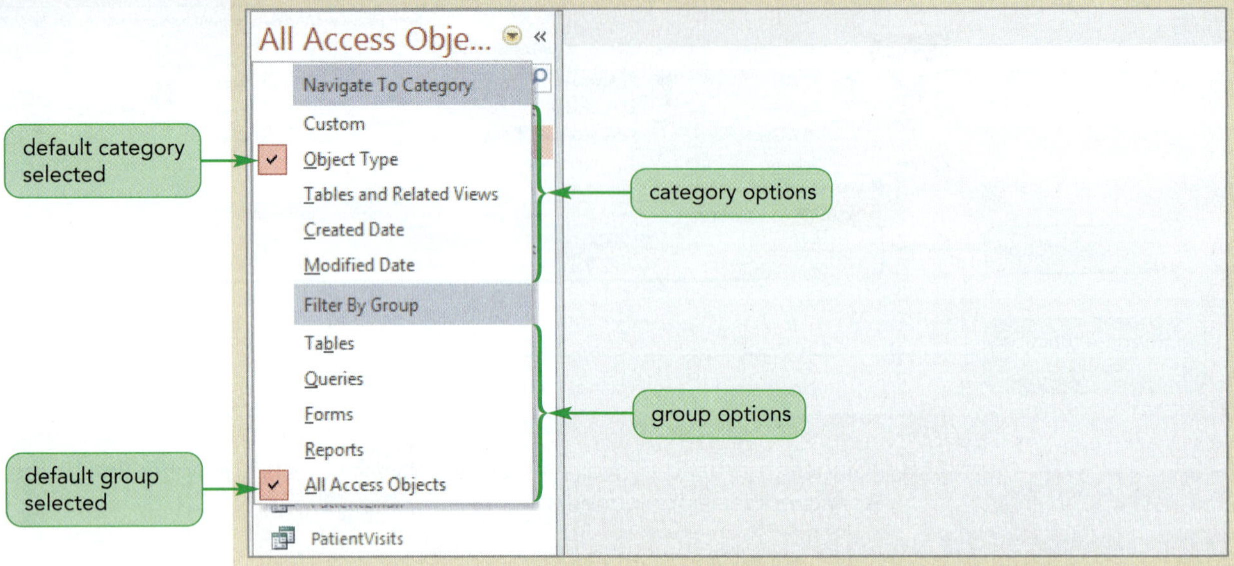

The top section of the menu provides the options for choosing a different category. The Object Type category has a checkmark next to it, signifying that it is the currently selected category. The lower section of the menu provides options for choosing a different group; these options might change depending on the selected category.

2. In the top section of the menu, click **Tables and Related Views**. The Navigation Pane is now grouped into categories of tables, and each table in the database—Visit, Billing, and Patient—is its own group. All database objects related to a table are listed below the table's name. See Figure 3-43.

Figure 3-43 Database objects grouped by table in the Navigation Pane

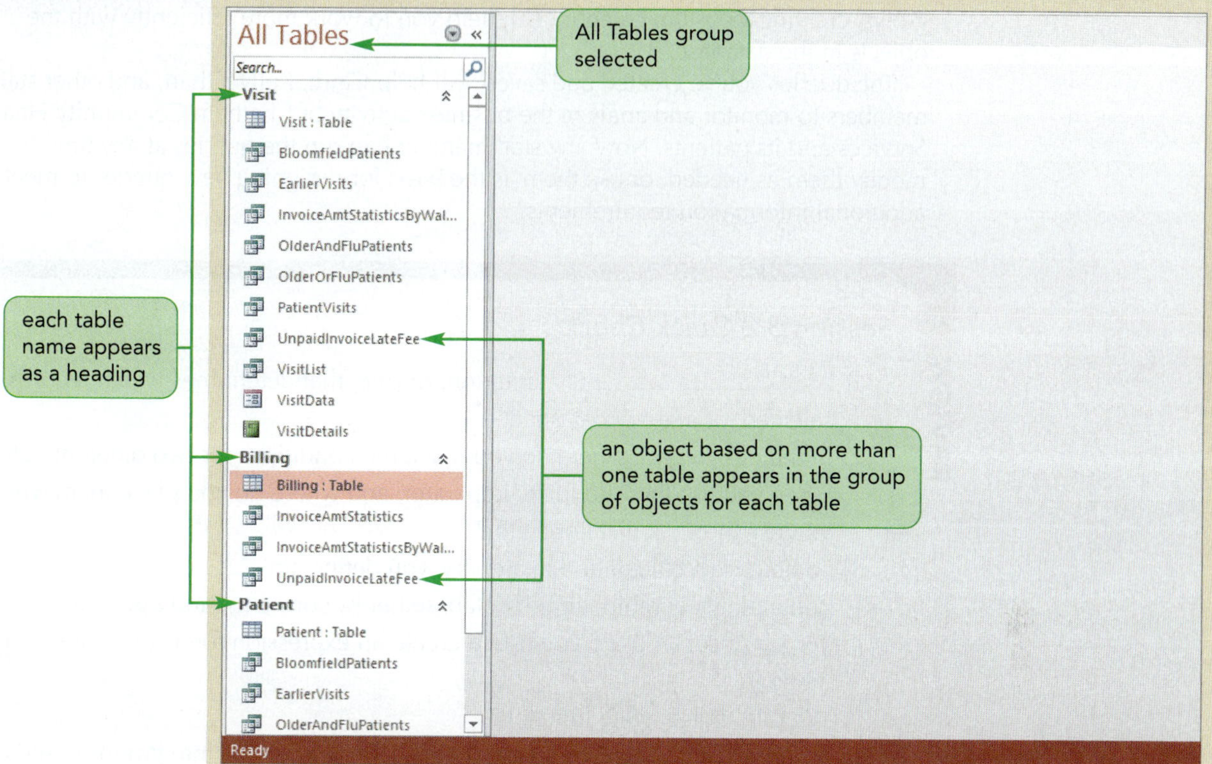

Some objects appear more than once. When an object is based on more than one table, that object appears in the group for each table. For example, the UnpaidInvoiceLateFee query is based on both the Visit and Billing tables, so it is listed in the group for both tables.

You can also choose to display the objects for only one table to better focus on that table.

3. At the top of the Navigation Pane, click the **All Tables** button to display the Navigation Pane menu, and then click **Patient**. The Navigation Pane now shows only the objects related to the Patient table—the table itself plus the six queries you created that include fields from the Patient table.
4. At the top of the Navigation Pane, click the **Patient** button, and then click **Object Type** to return to the default display of the Navigation Pane.
5. Compact and repair the Chatham database, and then close the database.

   Trouble? If a dialog box opens and warns that this action will cause Microsoft Access to empty the Clipboard, click the Yes button to continue.

The default All Access Objects category is a predefined category. You can also create custom categories to group objects in the way that best suits how you want to manage your database objects. As you continue to build a database and the list of objects grows, creating a custom category can help you to work more efficiently with the objects in the database.

The queries you've created and saved will help Cindi, Kelly, Ethan, and other staff members to monitor and analyze the business activity of Chatham Community Health Services and its patients. Now any staff member can run the queries at any time, modify them as needed, or use them as the basis for designing new queries to meet additional information requirements.

REVIEW

Session 3.2 Quick Check

1. A(n) ______________ is a criterion, or rule, that determines which records are selected for a query datasheet.
2. In the design grid, where do you place the conditions for two different fields when you use the And logical operator, and where do you place them when you use the Or logical operator?
3. To perform a calculation in a query, you define a(n) ______________ containing a combination of database fields, constants, and operators.
4. Which Access tool do you use to create an expression for a calculated field in a query?
5. What is an aggregate function?
6. The ______________ operator divides selected records into groups based on the values in a field.
7. What is the default category for the display of objects in the Navigation Pane?

ASSESS

SAM Projects

Put your skills into practice with SAM Projects! SAM Projects for this tutorial can be found online. If you have a SAM account, go to www.cengage.com/sam2013 to download the most recent Project Instructions and Start Files.

PRACTICE

Review Assignments

Data File needed for the Review Assignments: Vendor.accdb *(cont. from Tutorial 2)*

Cindi asks you to update some information in the Vendor database and also to retrieve specific information from the database. Complete the following:

1. Open the **Vendor** database you created and worked with in Tutorials 1 and 2, and then click the Enable Content button next to the security warning, if necessary.
2. Open the **Supplier** table in Datasheet view, and then change the following field values for the record with the Supplier ID GRE364: Address to **1550 W Main St**, Contact Phone to **401-625-2745**, Contact First Name to **Andrew**, and Contact Last Name to **Kline**. Close the table.
3. Create a query based on the Supplier table. Include the following fields in the query, in the order shown: Company, Category, ContactFirst, ContactLast, Phone, and InitialContact. Sort the query in ascending order based on the Category field values. Save the query as **ContactList**, and then run the query.
4. Use the ContactList query datasheet to update the Supplier table by changing the Phone field value for Aresco Surgical, Inc. to **203-335-0054**.
5. Change the size of the font in the ContactList query datasheet to 12 points. Resize columns, as necessary, so that all field values and column headings are visible.
6. Change the alternate row color in the ContactList query datasheet to the Theme Color named Green, Accent 6, Lighter 60%, and then save and close the query.
7. Create a query based on the Supplier and Product tables. Select the Company, Category, and State fields from the Supplier table, and the ProductName, Price, Units, and Weight fields from the Product table. Sort the query results in descending order based on price. Select only those records with a State field value of CT, but do not display the State field values in the query results. Save the query as **CTSuppliers**, run the query, and then close it.
8. Create a query that lists all products that cost more than $200 and are sterile. Display the following fields from the Product table in the query results: ProductID, ProductName, Price, Units, and TempControl. (*Hint:* The Sterile field is a Yes/No field that should not appear in the query results.) Save the query as **HighPriceAndSterile**, run the query, and then close it.
9. Create a query that lists information about suppliers who sell equipment or products that require temperature control. Include the Company, Category, ContactFirst, and ContactLast fields from the Supplier table; and the ProductName, Price, TempControl, and Sterile fields from the Product table. Save the query as **EquipmentOrTempControl**, run the query, and then close it.
10. Create a query that lists only those products that cost $1000 or more, along with a 5% discount amount based on the price of the product. Include the Company field from the Supplier table and the following fields from the Product table in the query: ProductID, ProductName, and Price. Save the query as **HighPriceWithDiscount**. Display the discount in a calculated field named **DiscountAmt** that determines a 5% discount based on the Price field values. Set the Caption property **Discount Amt** for the calculated field. Display the query results in descending order by Price. Save and run the query.

11. Modify the format of the DiscountAmt field in the HighPriceWithDiscount query so that it uses the Standard format and two decimal places. Run the query, resize all columns in the datasheet to their best fit, and then save and close the query.
12. Create a query that calculates the lowest, highest, and average prices for all products using the field names **LowestPrice**, **HighestPrice**, and **AveragePrice**, respectively. Set the Caption property for each field to include a space between the two words in the field name. Run the query, resize all columns in the datasheet to their best fit, save the query as **PriceStatistics**, and then close it.
13. In the Navigation Pane, copy the PriceStatistics query, and then rename the copied query as **PriceStatisticsBySupplier**.
14. Modify the PriceStatisticsBySupplier query so that the records are grouped by the Company field in the Supplier table. The Company field should appear first in the query datasheet. Save and run the query, and then close it.
15. Compact and repair the Vendor database, and then close it.

APPLY

Case Problem 1

Data File needed for this Case Problem: Gopher.accdb *(cont. from Tutorial 2)*

GoGopher! Amol Mehta needs to modify a few records in the Gopher database and analyze the data for members enrolled in his company's various plans. To help Amol, you'll update the Gopher database and create queries to answer his questions. Complete the following:

1. Open the **Gopher** database you created and worked with in Tutorials 1 and 2, and then click the Enable Content button next to the security warning, if necessary.
2. In the **Member** table, find the record for MemberID 1251, and then change the Street value to **75 Hemlock Ln** and the Phone to **303-553-1847**.
3. In the **Member** table, find the record for MemberID 1228, and then delete the record. Close the Member table.
4. Create a query that lists members who did not have to pay a fee when they joined. In the query results, display the FirstName, LastName, and DateJoined fields from the Member table, and the PlanCost field from the Plan table. Sort the records in descending order by the date joined. Select records only for members whose fees were waived. (*Hint:* The FeeWaived field is a Yes/No field that should not appear in the query results.) Save the query as **NoFees**, and then run the query.
5. Use the NoFees query datasheet to update the Member table by changing the Last Name value for Kara Murray to **Seaburg**.
6. Use the NoFees query datasheet to display the total Plan Cost for the selected members. Save and close the query.
7. Create a query that lists the MemberID, FirstName, LastName, DateJoined, PlanDescription, and PlanCost fields for members who joined GoGopher! between April 1, 2016 and April 30, 2016. Save the query as **AprilMembers**, run the query, and then close it.
8. Create a query that lists all members who live in Louisville and whose memberships expire on or after 1/1/2017. Display the following fields from the Member table in the query results: MemberID, FirstName, LastName, Phone, and Expiration. (*Hint:* The City field values should not appear in the query results.) Sort the query results in ascending order by last name. Save the query as **LouisvilleAndExpiration**, run the query, and then close it.
9. Copy and paste the LouisvilleAndExpiration query to create a new query named **LouisvilleOrExpiration**. Modify the new query so that it lists all members who live in Louisville or whose memberships expire on or after 1/1/2017. Display the City field values in the query results following the Phone field values, and sort the query results in ascending order by city (this should be the only sort in the query). Save and run the query.
10. Change the size of the font in the LouisvilleOrExpiration query datasheet to 14 points. Resize columns, as necessary, so that all field values and column headings are visible.

11. Change the alternate row color in the LouisvilleOrExpiration query datasheet to the Theme Color named Blue, Accent 1, Lighter 80%, and then save and close the query.
12. Create a query that calculates the lowest, highest, and average cost for all plans using the field names **LowestCost**, **HighestCost**, and **AverageCost**, respectively. Set the Caption property for each field to include a space between the two words in the field name. Run the query, resize all columns in the datasheet to their best fit, save the query as **CostStatistics**, and then close it.
13. Copy and paste the CostStatistics query to create a new query named **CostStatisticsByCity**.
14. Modify the CostStatisticsByCity query to display the same statistics grouped by City, with City appearing as the first field. (*Hint:* Add the Member table to the query.) Run the query, and then save and close it.
15. Compact and repair the Gopher database, and then close it.

CREATE

Case Problem 2

Data File needed for this Case Problem: OBrien.accdb *(cont. from Tutorial 2)*

O'Brien Educational Services After reviewing the OBrien database, Karen O'Brien wants to modify some records and then view specific information about the students, tutors, and contracts for her educational services company. She asks you to update and query the OBrien database to perform these tasks. Complete the following:

1. Open the **OBrien** database you created and worked with in Tutorials 1 and 2, and then click the Enable Content button next to the security warning, if necessary.
2. In the **Tutor** table, change the following information for the record with TutorID 79-0678: Degree is **BA** and Hire Date is **9/15/2015**. Close the table.
3. In the **Student** table, find the record with the StudentID MCS8051, and then delete the related record in the subdatasheet for this student. Delete the record for StudentID MCS8051, and then close the Student table.
4. Create a query based on the Student table that includes the LastName, FirstName, and CellPhone fields, in that order. Save the query as **StudentCellList**, and then run the query.
5. In the results of the StudentCellList query, change the cell phone number for Haley Gosnold to **574-252-1973**. Close the query.
6. Create a query based on the Tutor and Contract tables. Display the LastName field from the Tutor table, and the StudentID, ContractDate, SessionType, Length, and Cost fields, in that order, from the Contract table. Sort first in ascending order by the tutor's last name, and then in ascending order by the StudentID. Save the query as **SessionsByTutor**, run the query, and the close it.
7. Copy and paste the SessionsByTutor query to create a new query named **GroupSessions**. Modify the new query so that it displays the same information for records with a Group session type only. Do not display the SessionType field values in the query results. Save and run the query, and then close it.
8. Create and save a query that produces the results shown in Figure 3-44. Close the query when you are finished.

Figure 3-44 SouthBendPrivate query results

9. Create and save a query that produces the results shown in Figure 3-45. Close the query when you are finished.

Figure 3-45 OscelaOrSemi query results

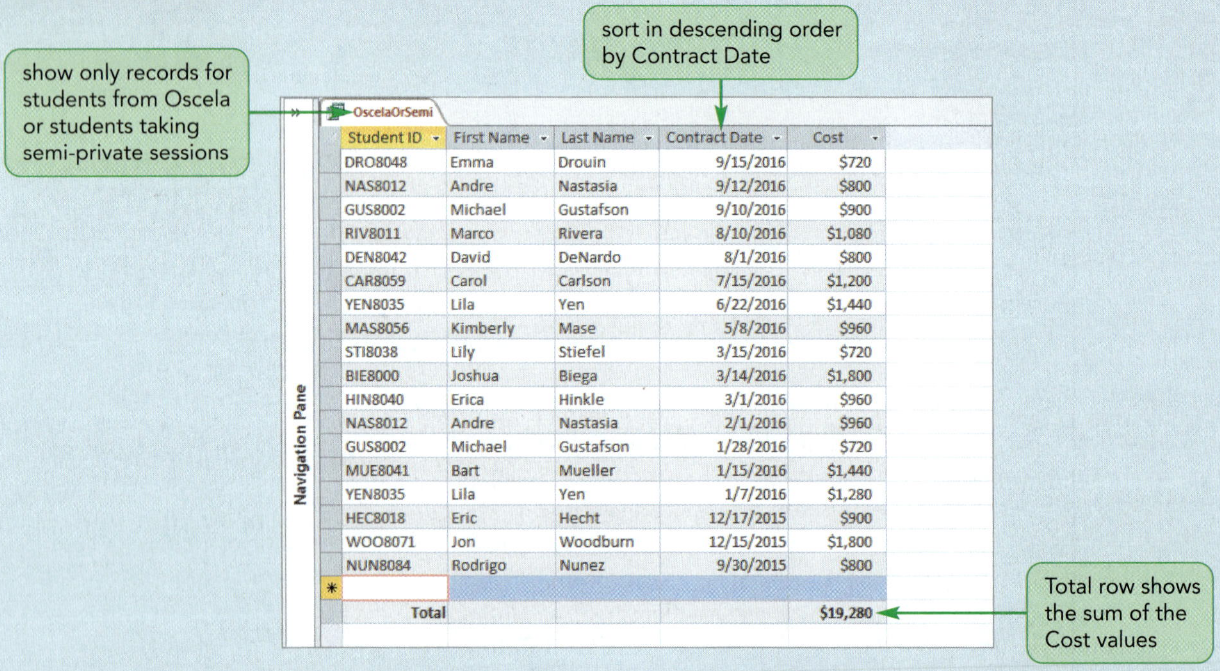

10. Create and save a query to display statistics for the Cost field, as shown in Figure 3-46. Close the query when you are finished.

Figure 3-46 CostStatistics query results

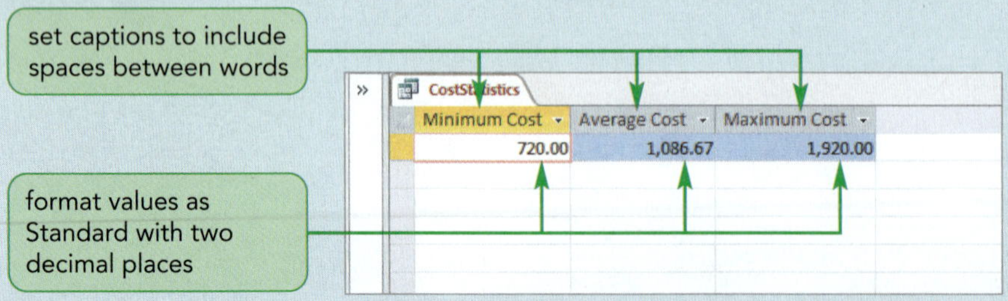

11. Copy and paste the CostStatistics query to create a new query named **CostStatisticsByCity**.
12. Modify the CostStatisticsByCity query to display the same statistics grouped by City, with City appearing as the first field. (*Hint:* Add the Student table to the query.) Run the query, and then save and close it.
13. Compact and repair the OBrien database, and then close it.

CHALLENGE

Case Problem 3

Data File needed for this Case Problem: Shelter.accdb *(cont. from Tutorial 2)*

Rosemary Animal Shelter Ryan Lang needs to modify some records in the Shelter database, and then he wants to find specific information about the animals, patrons, and donations for his not-for-profit agency. Ryan asks you to help him update the database and create queries to find the information he needs. Complete the following:

1. Open the **Shelter** database you created and worked with in Tutorials 1 and 2, and then click the Enable Content button next to the security warning, if necessary.

Explore 2. In the **Patron** table, delete the record with PatronID 36064. (*Hint:* Delete the related record in the Donation subdatasheet first, which you need to display using the Insert Subdatasheet dialog box.) Close the Patron table without saving changes to the table layout.

3. Create a query based on the Animal table that includes the AnimalID, AnimalName, AnimalType, Gender, and ArrivalDate fields, in that order. Save the query as **AnimalsByType**, and then run it.
4. Modify the AnimalsByType query design so that it sorts records in ascending order first by AnimalType and then by Gender. Save and run the query.
5. In the AnimalsByType query datasheet, find the record for the animal with Animal ID D23, and then change the arrival date for this animal to **5/19/2016**. Close the query.
6. Create a query that displays the PatronID, FirstName, and LastName fields from the Patron table, and the Description and DonationValue fields from the Donation table for all donations over $150. Sort the query in ascending order by donation value. Save the query as **LargeDonations**, run the query, and then close it.
7. Copy and paste the LargeDonations query to create a new query named **LargeCashDonations**.

Explore 8. Modify the LargeCashDonations query to display only those records with donations valuing more than $150 in cash. Do not include the Description field values in the query results. Use the query datasheet to calculate the average cash donation. Save and close the query.

9. Create a query that displays the PatronID, FirstName, and LastName fields from the Patron table, and the AnimalName, AnimalType, Age, Gender, and Adopted fields from the Animal table. Specify that the results show records for only those animals that have been adopted. Do not display the Adopted field values in the query results. Save the query as **CatAdoptions**, and then run the query.
10. Filter the results of the CatAdoptions query datasheet to display records for cats only.

Explore 11. Format the datasheet of the CatAdoptions query so that it does not display gridlines, uses an alternate row Standard Color of Purple 2, and displays a font size of 12. (*Hint*: Use the Gridlines button in the Text Formatting group on the HOME tab to select the appropriate gridlines option.) Resize the columns to display the complete field names and values, if necessary. Save and close the query.

Explore 12. Create a query that displays the PatronID, FirstName, and LastName fields from the Patron table, and the Description, DonationDate, and DonationValue fields from the Donation table. Specify that the query include records for noncash donations only or for donations made in the month of June 2016. Sort the records first in ascending order by the patron's last name, and then in descending order by the donation value. Save the query as **NonCashOrJuneDonations**, run the query, and then close it.

13. Copy and paste the NonCashOrJuneDonations query to create a new query named **DonationsAfterStorageCharge**.

Explore 14. Modify the DonationsAfterStorageCharge query so that it displays records for noncash donations made on all dates. Create a calculated field named **NetDonation** that displays the results of subtracting $3.50 from the DonationValue field values to account for the cost of storing each noncash donated item. Set the Caption property **Net Donation** for the calculated field. Display the results in ascending order by donation value. Run the query, and then modify it to format both the DonationValue field and the calculated field as Currency with two decimal places. Run the query again and resize the columns in the datasheet to their best fit, as necessary. Save and close the query.

Explore 15. Create a query based on the **Donation** table that displays the sum, average, and count of the DonationValue field for all donations. Then complete the following:

a. Specify field names of **TotalDonations**, **AverageDonation**, and **NumberofDonations**. Then specify captions to include spaces between words.

b. Save the query as **DonationStatistics**, and then run it. Resize the query datasheet columns to their best fit.

c. Modify the field properties so that the values in the Total Donations and Average Donation columns display two decimal places and the Standard format. Run the query again, and then save and close the query.

d. Copy and paste the DonationStatistics query to create a new query named **DonationStatisticsByDescription**.

e. Modify the DonationStatisticsByDescription query to display the sum, average, and count of the DonationValue field for all donations grouped by Description, with Description appearing as the first field. Sort the records in descending order by Total Donations. Save, run, and then close the query.

16. Compact and repair the Shelter database, and then close it.

TROUBLESHOOT

Case Problem 4

Data File needed for this Case Problem: Stanley.accdb *(cont. from Tutorial 2)* and Tour.accdb

Stanley EcoTours Janice and Bill Stanley need your help to maintain and analyze data about the clients, reservations, and tours for their ecotourism business. Additionally, you'll troubleshoot some problems in another database containing tour information. Complete the following:

1. Open the **Stanley** database you created and worked with in Tutorials 1 and 2, and then click the Enable Content button next to the security warning, if necessary.
2. In the **Guest** table, change the phone number for Paul Barry to **406-497-1068**, and then close the table.
3. Create a query based on the Tour table that includes the TourName, Location, Country, PricePerPerson, and TourType fields, in that order. Sort in ascending order based on the PricePerPerson field values. Save the query as **ToursByPrice**, and then run the query.
4. Use the ToursByPrice query datasheet to display the total Price Per Person for the tours. Save and close the query.

5. Create a query that displays the GuestLast, City, and State/Prov fields from the Guest table, and the ReservationID, StartDate, and People fields from the Reservation table. Save the query as **GuestTourDates**, and then run the query. Change the alternate row color in the query datasheet to the Theme Color Green, Accent 6, Lighter 40%. In Datasheet view, use an AutoFilter to sort the query results from oldest to newest Start Date. Save and close the query.
6. Create a query that displays the GuestFirst, GuestLast, City, ReservationID, TourID, and StartDate fields for all guests from Montana (MT). Do not include the State/Prov field in the query results. Sort the query in ascending order by the guest's last name. Save the query as **MontanaGuests** and then run it. Close the query.
7. Create a query that displays data from all three tables in the database, as follows: the GuestLast, City, State/Prov, and Country fields from the Guest table; the StartDate field from the Reservation table; and the TourName, Location, and TourType fields from the Tour table. Specify that the query select only those records for guests from Canada or guests who are taking Jeep tours. Sort the query in ascending order by Location. Save the query as **CanadaOrJeep**, and then run the query. Resize datasheet columns to their best fit, as necessary, and then save and close the query.
8. Copy and paste the CanadaOrJeep query to create a new query named **IdahoAndJuly**.
9. Modify the IdahoAndJuly query to select all guests from Idaho who are taking a tour starting sometime in the month of July 2016. Do not include the State/Prov field values or the Country field values in the query results. Run the query. Resize datasheet columns to their best fit, as necessary, and then save and close the query.
10. Create a query that displays the ReservationID, StartDate, and People fields from the Reservation table, and the TourName, Location, Country, PricePerPerson, and SingleSupplement fields from the Tour table for all reservations with a People field value of 1. Save the query as **SingleReservations**. Add a field to the query named **TotalCost** that displays the results of adding the SingleSupplement field values to the PricePerPerson field values. Set the Caption property **Total Cost** for the calculated field. Display the results in descending order by TotalCost. Do not include the People field values in the query results. Run the query. Modify the query by formatting the TotalCost field to show 0 decimal places. Run the query, resize datasheet columns to their best fit, as necessary, and then save and close the query.
11. Create a query based on the Tour table that determines the minimum, average, and maximum price per person for all tours. Then complete the following:
    a. Specify field names of **LowestPrice**, **AveragePrice**, and **HighestPrice**.
    b. Set the Caption property for each field to include a space between the two words in the field name.
    c. Save the query as **PriceStatistics**, and then run the query.
    d. In Design view, specify the Standard format and two decimal places for each column.
    e. Run the query, resize all the datasheet columns to their best fit, save your changes, and then close the query.
    f. Create a copy of the PriceStatistics query named **PriceStatisticsByTourType**.
    g. Modify the PriceStatisticsByTourType query to display the price statistics grouped by TourType, with TourType appearing as the first field. Save your changes and then run and close the query.
12. Compact and repair the Stanley database, and then close it.

Troubleshoot 13. Open the **Tour** database located in the Access1 ▸ Case4 folder provided with your Data Files, and then click the Enable Content button next to the security warning, if necessary. Run the BookingByDateAndState query in the Tour database. The query is not producing the desired results. Fix the query so that the data from the Booking table is listed first, the data is sorted only by StartDate in ascending order, and the results do not display country values. Save and close the corrected query.

Troubleshoot 14. Run the WYGuestsFewerPeople query, which displays no records in the results. This query is supposed to show data for guests from Wyoming with fewer than four people in their booking. Find and correct the error in the query design, run the query, and then close it.

Troubleshoot 15. Run the CanadaOrSeptStart query. This query should display the records for all guests who are from Canada or whose booking start date is on or after 9/1/2016. Find and correct the errors in the query design, run the query, and then close it. Compact and repair the Tour database, and then close it.

TUTORIAL 4

ACCESS

Creating Forms and Reports

Using Forms and Reports to Display Patient and Visit Data

OBJECTIVES

Session 4.1

- Create a form using the Form Wizard
- Apply a theme to a form
- Add a picture to a form
- Change the color of text on a form
- Find and maintain data using a form
- Preview and print selected form records
- Create a form with a main form and a subform

Session 4.2

- Create a report using the Report Wizard
- Apply a theme to a report
- Change the alignment of field values on a report
- Move and resize fields in a report
- Insert a picture in a report
- Change the color of text on a report
- Apply conditional formatting in a report
- Preview and print a report

Case | *Chatham Community Health Services*

Cindi Rodriguez wants to continue enhancing the Chatham database to make it easier for her staff to enter, locate, and maintain data. In particular, she wants the database to include a form based on the Patient table to make it easier for staff members to enter and change data about the clinic's patients. She also wants the database to include a form that shows data from both the Patient and Visit tables at the same time. This form will show the visit information for each patient along with the corresponding patient data, providing a complete picture of Chatham Community Health Services patients and their visits to the clinic.

In addition, Ethan Ward would like the database to include a formatted report of patient and visit data so that he and other staff members will have printed output when completing patient analyses and planning strategies for community outreach efforts. He wants the information to be formatted in a professional manner, to make the report appealing and easy to use.

STARTING DATA FILES

Access1 →

Tutorial
Chatham.accdb (*cont.*)
Medical.bmp

Review
Supplies.bmp
Vendor.accdb (*cont.*)

Case1
Gopher.accdb (*cont.*)
Tasks.bmp

Case2
OBrien.accdb (*cont.*)
Tests.bmp

Case3
Animals.bmp
Shelter.accdb (*cont.*)

Case4
Hiking.bmp
Stanley.accdb (*cont.*)
Tour.accdb

Session 4.1 Visual Overview:

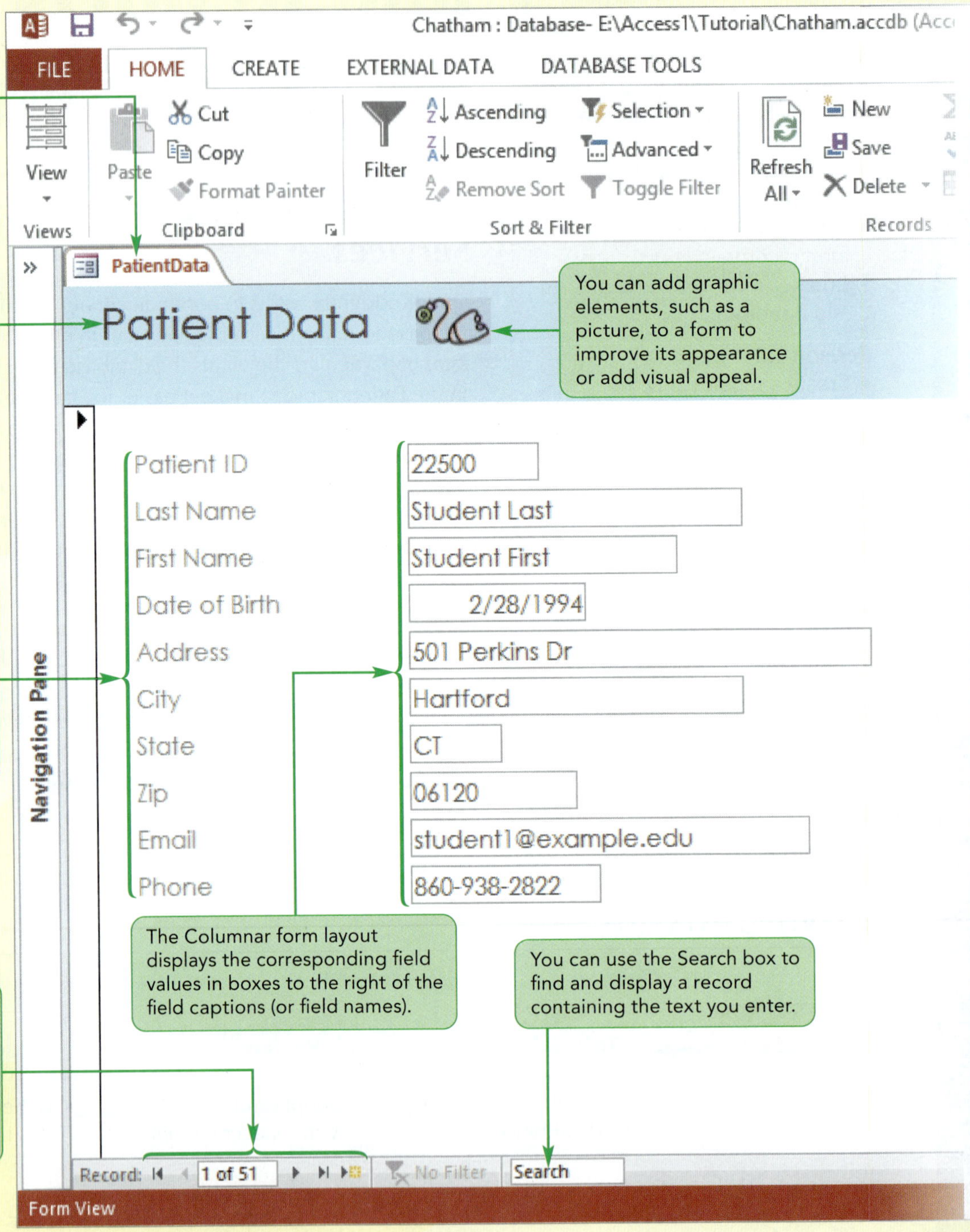

The form object's name is displayed on the tab for the form.

The form title appears at the top of the form. By default, the form object name is used as the form title, but you can edit the title to display the text you want, as done here—a space was added between the two words for readability.

You can add graphic elements, such as a picture, to a form to improve its appearance or add visual appeal.

With the Columnar form layout, the field captions appear in a column on the left side of the form. If captions had not been specified for the fields, the field names would appear here instead.

The Columnar form layout displays the corresponding field values in boxes to the right of the field captions (or field names).

You can use the Search box to find and display a record containing the text you enter.

The navigation buttons allow you to display the first, last, next, or previous record in the form, enter a specific record number and move to that record, and create a new record.

Form Displayed in Form View

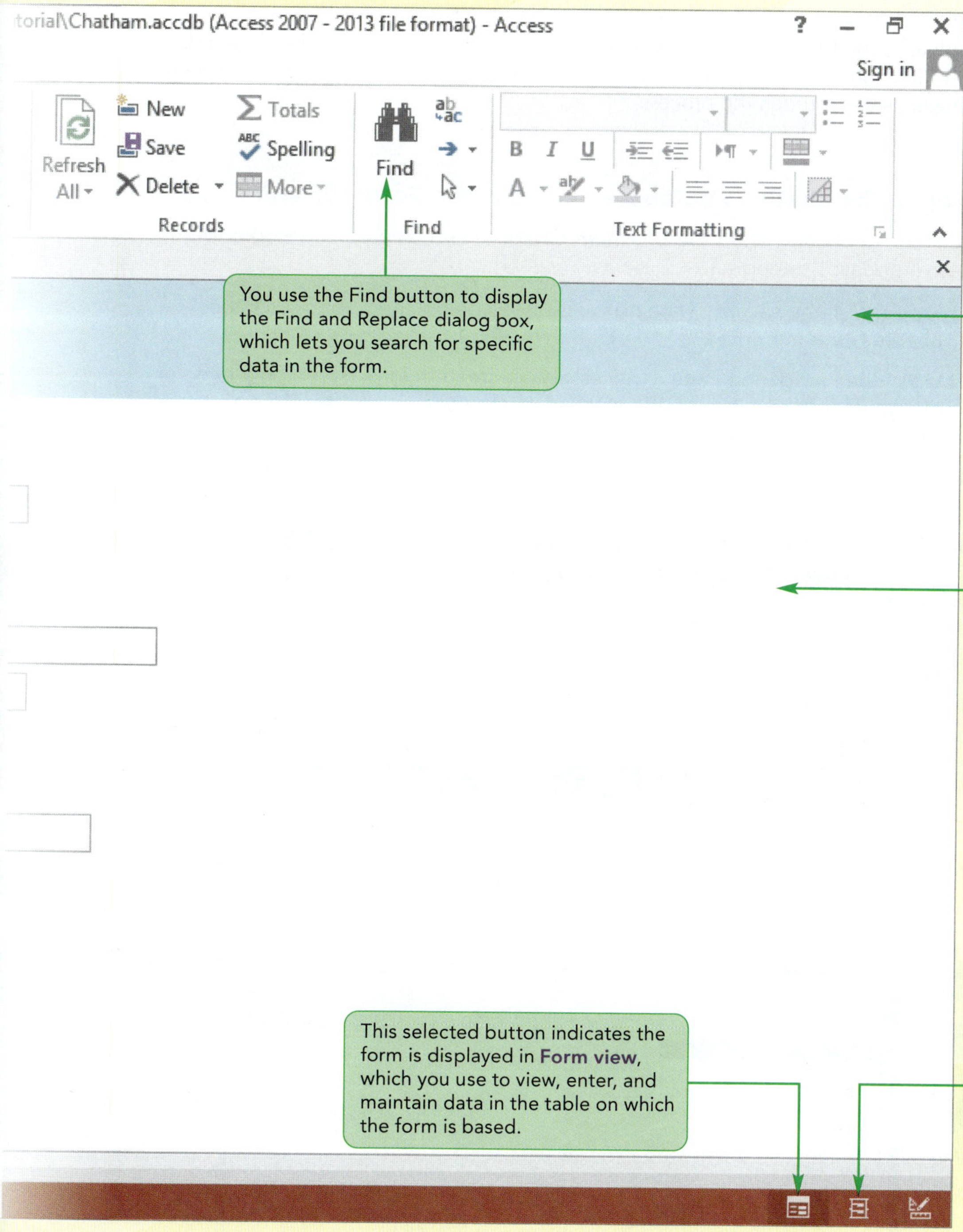

You use the Find button to display the Find and Replace dialog box, which lets you search for specific data in the form.

You can apply a theme to a form, as done here with the PatientData form. A theme is a predefined set of formats including colors, fonts, and other effects that enhance a form's appearance and usability.

The PatientData form was created using the **Form Wizard**, which allows you to choose some or all of the fields in the table or query used as the basis for the form, choose fields from other tables and queries, and display the selected fields in any order on the form.

This selected button indicates the form is displayed in **Form view**, which you use to view, enter, and maintain data in the table on which the form is based.

You can click this button to display the form in **Layout view**, which allows you to modify many aspects of a form's layout and design.

Creating a Form Using the Form Wizard

As you learned in Tutorial 1, a form is an object you use to enter, edit, and view records in a database. You can design your own forms or have Access create them for you automatically. In Tutorial 1, you used the Form tool to create the VisitData form in the Chatham database. Recall that the Form tool creates a form automatically, using all the fields in the selected table or query.

Cindi asks you to create a new form that her staff can use to view and maintain data in the Patient table. To create the form for the Patient table, you'll use the Form Wizard, which guides you through the process.

To open the Chatham database and start the Form Wizard:

1. Start Access and open the **Chatham** database you created and worked with in Tutorials 1 through 3.

   Trouble? If the security warning is displayed below the ribbon, click the Enable Content button.

2. Open the Navigation Pane, if necessary. To create a form based on a table or query, you can select the table or query in the Navigation Pane first, or you can select it using the Form Wizard.
3. In the Tables section of the Navigation Pane, click **Patient** to select the Patient table as the basis for the new form.
4. On the ribbon, click the **CREATE** tab. The Forms group on the CREATE tab provides options for creating various types of forms and designing your own forms.
5. In the Forms group, click the **Form Wizard** button. The first Form Wizard dialog box opens. See Figure 4-1.

Figure 4-1 **First Form Wizard dialog box**

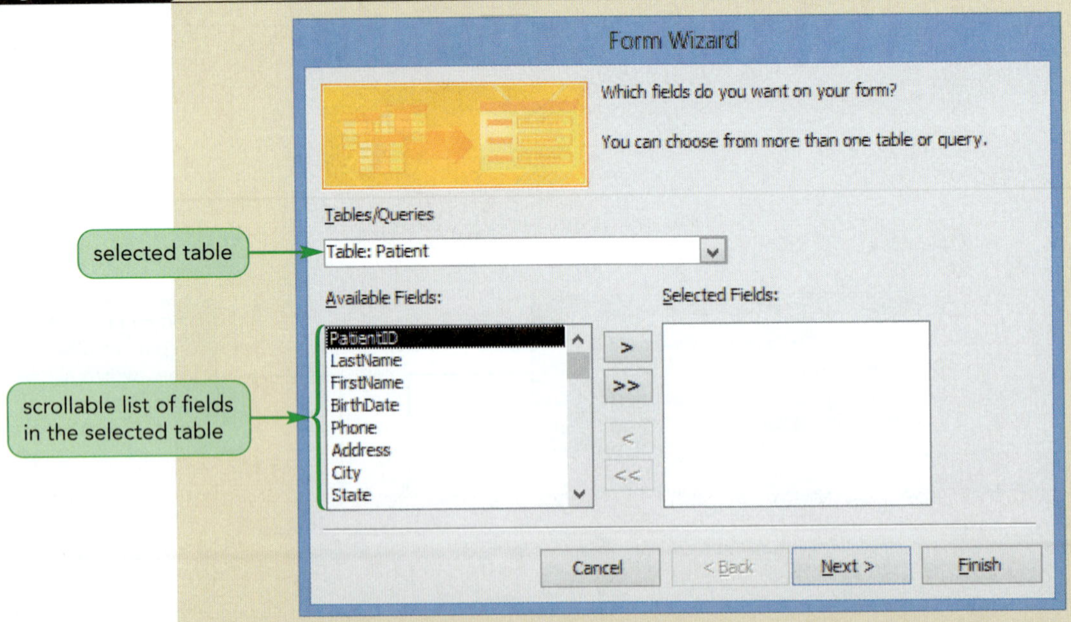

Because you selected the Patient table in the Navigation Pane before starting the Form Wizard, this table is selected in the Tables/Queries box, and the fields for the Patient table are listed in the Available Fields box.

Cindi wants the form to display all the fields in the Patient table, but in a different order. She would like the Phone field to appear at the bottom of the form so that it stands out, making it easier for someone who needs to call patients to use the form and quickly identify the phone number for a patient.

To create the form using the Form Wizard:

1. Click the >> button to move all the fields to the Selected Fields box. Next, you need to remove the Phone field, and then add it back as the last selected field so that it will appear at the bottom of the form.
2. In the Selected Fields box, click the **Phone** field, and then click the < button to move the field back to the Available Fields box.

   To add the Phone field to the end of the form, you need to highlight the last field in the list, and then move the Phone field back to the Selected Fields box. A new field is always added after the selected field in the Selected Fields box.
3. In the Selected Fields box, click the **Email** field.
4. With the Phone field selected in the Available Fields box, click the > button to move the Phone field to the end of the Selected Fields box.
5. Click the **Next** button to display the second Form Wizard dialog box, in which you select a layout for the form. See Figure 4-2.

Figure 4-2 **Choosing a layout for the form**

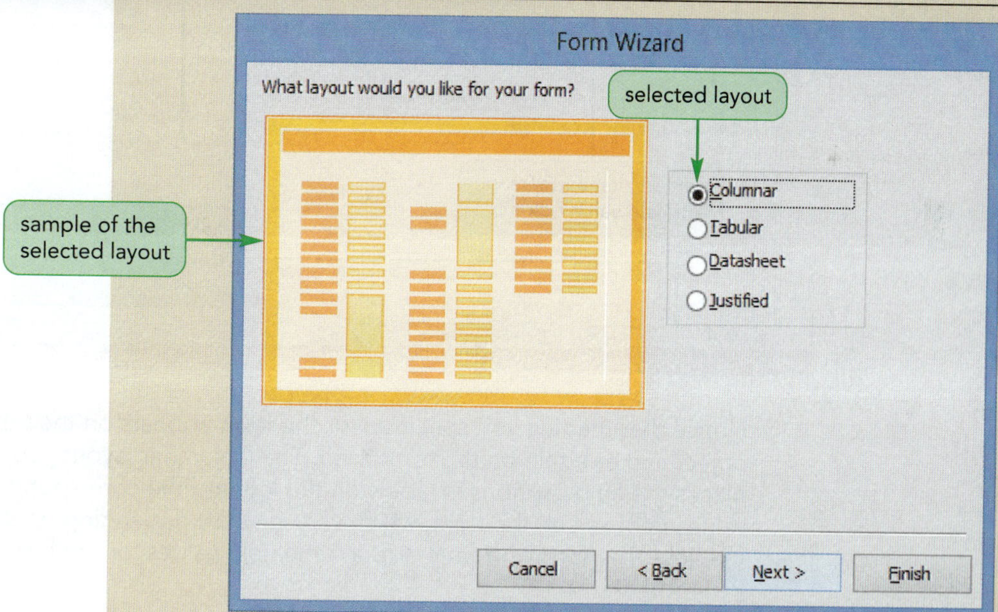

The layout choices are Columnar, Tabular, Datasheet, and Justified. A sample of the selected layout appears on the left side of the dialog box.

6. Click each of the option buttons and review the corresponding sample layout.

   The Tabular and Datasheet layouts display the fields from multiple records at one time, whereas the Columnar and Justified layouts display the fields from one record at a time. Cindi thinks the Columnar layout is the appropriate arrangement for displaying and updating data in the table, so that anyone using the form can focus on just one patient record at a time.

7. Click the **Columnar** option button (if necessary), and then click the **Next** button.

   Access displays the third and final Form Wizard dialog box and shows the Patient table's name as the default form name. "Patient" is also the default title that will appear on the tab for the form.

   You'll use "PatientData" as the form name and, because you don't need to change the form's design at this point, you'll display the form.

8. Click to position the insertion point to the right of Patient in the text box, type **Data**, and then click the **Finish** button.

9. Close the Navigation Pane to display only the Form window. The completed form is displayed in Form view. See Figure 4-3.

Figure 4-3 PatientData form in Form view

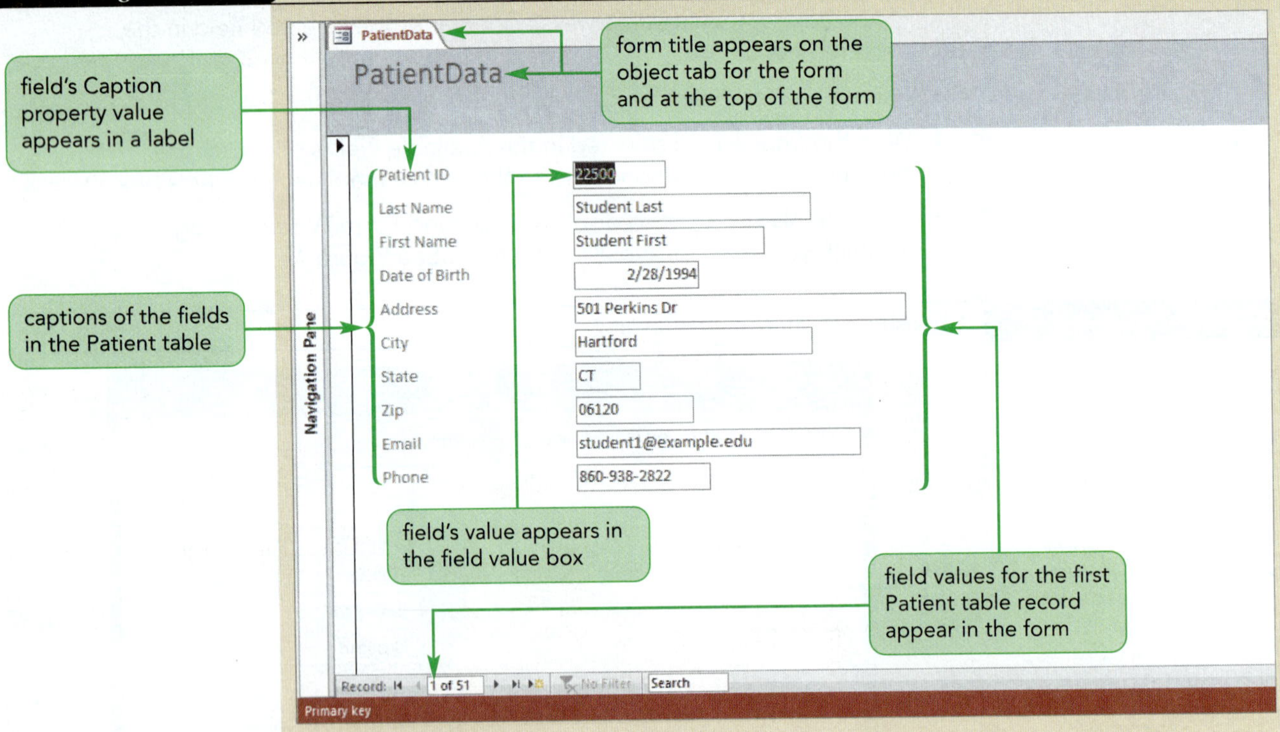

Notice that the title you specified for the form appears on the tab for the object and as a title on the form itself. The Columnar layout you selected places the field captions in labels on the left and the corresponding field values in boxes on the right, which vary in width depending on the size of the field. The form currently displays the field values for the first record in the Patient table.

After viewing the form, Cindi decides that she doesn't like its appearance. The font used in the labels on the left is somewhat light in color and small, making the labels a bit difficult to read. Also, she thinks inserting a graphic on the form would add visual interest, and modifying other form elements—such as the color of the title text—would improve the look of the form. You can make all of these changes working with the form in Layout view.

Modifying a Form's Design in Layout View

TIP

Some form design changes require you to switch to Design view, which gives you a more detailed view of the form's structure.

After you create a form, you might need to modify its design in Layout view to improve its appearance or to make the form easier to use. In Layout view, you see the form as it appears in Form view, but you can still modify the form's design; in Form view, you cannot make any design changes. Because you can see the form and its data while you are modifying the form, Layout view makes it easy for you to see the results of any design changes you make. You can continue to make changes, undo modifications, and rework the design in Layout view to achieve the look you want for the form.

The first modification you'll make to the PatientData form is to change its appearance by applying a theme.

Applying a Theme to a Form

By default, a form you create is formatted with the Office theme, which determines the color and font used on the form. Access, like other Microsoft Office programs, provides many built-in themes, including the Office theme, making it easy for you to create objects with a unified look. You can also create a customized theme if none of the built-in themes suit your needs. To change a form's appearance, you can easily apply a new theme to it.

REFERENCE

Applying a Theme to a Form

- Display the form in Layout view.
- In the Themes group on the DESIGN tab, click the Themes button.
- In the displayed gallery, click the theme you want to apply to all objects; or, right-click the theme to display the shortcut menu, and then choose to apply the theme to the current object only or to all matching objects.

Cindi would like to see if the PatientData form's appearance can be improved with a different theme. To apply a theme, you first need to switch to Layout view.

To apply a theme to the PatientData form:

1. Make sure the HOME tab is displayed.
2. In the Views group, click the **View** button. The form is displayed in Layout view. See Figure 4-4.

Figure 4-4 Form displayed in Layout view

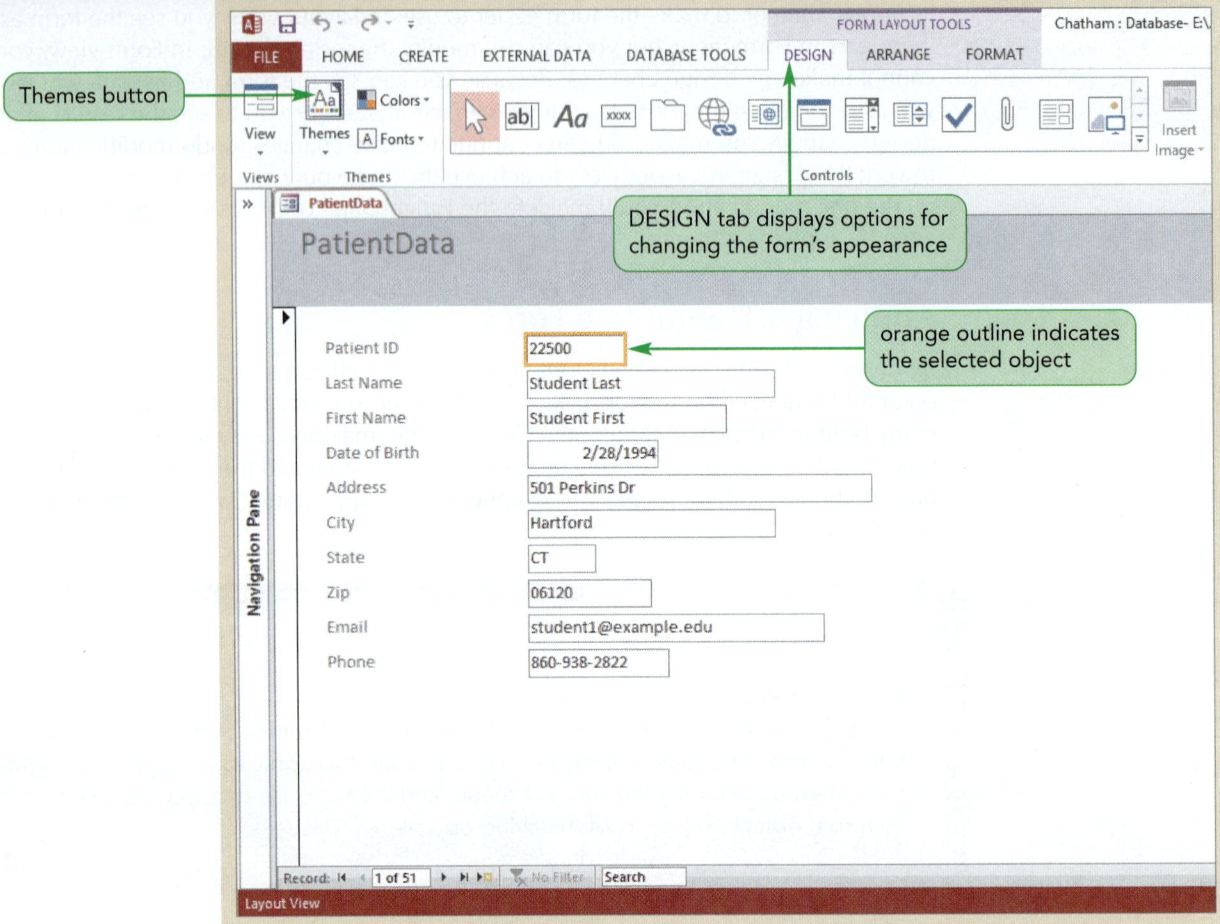

Trouble? If the Field List or Property Sheet opens on the right side of your window, close it before continuing.

You can use Layout view to modify an existing form. In Layout view, an orange outline identifies the currently selected object on the form. In this case, the field value for the PatientID field, 22500, is selected. You need to apply a theme to the PatientData form.

3. In the Themes group on the DESIGN tab, click the **Themes** button. A gallery opens showing the available themes for the form. See Figure 4-5.

Figure 4-5 Themes gallery displayed

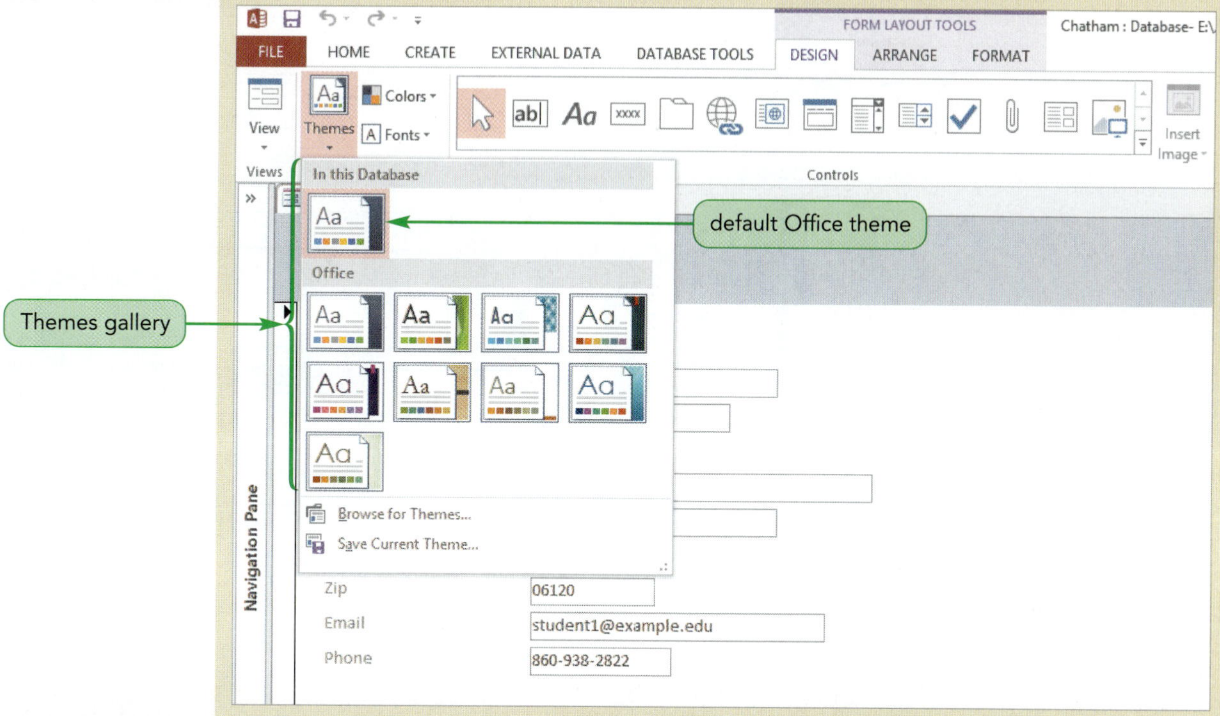

TIP

Themes other than the Office theme are listed in alphabetical order in the gallery.

The Office theme, which is shown in the "In this Database" section and is also the first theme listed in the section containing other themes, is the default theme currently applied in the database. Each theme provides a design scheme for the colors and fonts used in the database objects. You can point to each theme in the gallery to see its name in a ScreenTip. Also, when you point to a theme, the Live Preview feature shows the effect of applying the theme to the open object.

4. In the gallery, point to each of the themes to see how they would format the PatientData form. Notice the changes in color and font type of the text, for example.

   Trouble? If you click a theme by mistake, repeat Step 3 to redisplay the gallery, and then continue to Step 5.

   Cindi likes the Slice theme because of its bright blue color in the title area at the top and its larger font size, which makes the text in the form easier to read. She asks you to apply this theme to the form.

5. Right-click the **Slice** theme. A shortcut menu opens with options for applying the theme. See Figure 4-6.

Figure 4-6 Shortcut menu for applying the theme

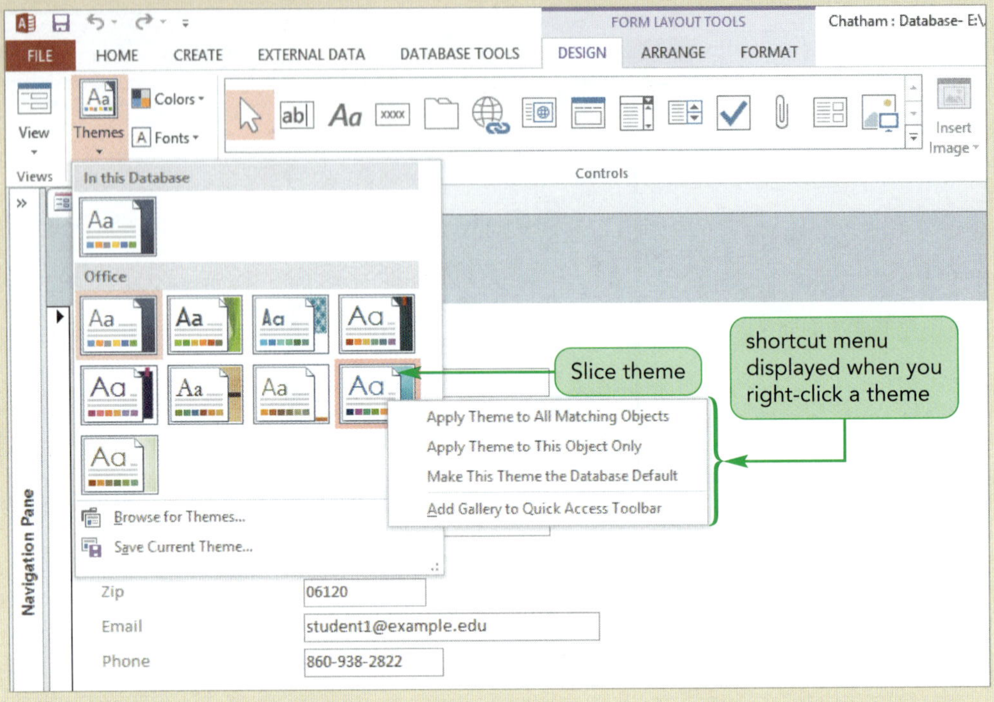

The menu provides options for applying the theme to all matching objects—for example, all the forms in the database—or to the current object only. You can also choose to make the theme the default theme in the database, which means any new objects you create will be formatted with the selected theme. Because Cindi is not sure if all forms in the Chatham database will look better with the Slice theme, she asks you to apply it only to the PatientData form.

Choose this option to avoid applying the theme to other forms in the database.

6. On the shortcut menu, click **Apply Theme to This Object Only**.

The gallery closes, and Access formats the form's colors and fonts with the Slice theme.

Trouble? If you choose the wrong option by mistake, you might have applied the selected theme to other forms and/or reports in the database. Repeat Steps 3 through 6 to apply the Slice theme to the PatientData form. You can also follow the same process to reapply the default Office theme to the other forms and reports in the Chatham database, as directed by your instructor.

INSIGHT

Working with Themes

Themes provide a quick and easy way for you to format the objects in a database with a consistent look, which is a good design principle to follow. In general, all objects of a type in a database—for example, all forms—should have a consistent design. However, keep in mind that when you select a theme in the Themes gallery and choose the option to apply the theme to all matching objects or to make the theme the default for the database, Access might apply it to *all* the existing forms and reports in the database as well as to new forms and reports you create. Although this ensures a consistent design, this approach can cause problems. For example, if you have already created a form or report and its design is suitable, applying a theme that includes a larger font size could cause the text in labels and field value boxes to be cut off or to extend into other objects on the form or report. The colors applied by the theme could also interfere with elements on existing forms and reports. To handle these unintended results, you would have to spend time checking the existing forms and reports and fixing any problems introduced by applying the theme. A better approach is to select the option "Apply Theme to This Object Only," available on the shortcut menu for a theme in the Themes gallery, for each existing form and report. If the newly applied theme causes problems for any individual form or report, you can then reapply the original theme to return the object to its original design.

Next, Cindi asks you to add a picture to the form for visual interest. The picture, which is included on various flyers and other patient correspondence for Chatham Community Health Services, is a small graphic of a stethoscope. You'll add this picture to the form.

Adding a Picture to a Form

A picture is one of many controls you can add and modify on a form. A **control** is an item on a form, report, or other database object that you can manipulate to modify the object's appearance. The controls you can add and modify in Layout view for a form are available in the Controls group and the Header/Footer group on the DESIGN tab. The picture you need to add is contained in a file named Medical.bmp, which is located in the Access1 ▸ Tutorial folder provided with your Data Files.

To add the picture to the form:

1. Make sure the form is still displayed in Layout view and that the DESIGN tab is active.
2. In the Header/Footer group, click the **Logo** button. The Insert Picture dialog box opens.
3. Navigate to the **Access1 ▸ Tutorial** folder provided with your Data Files, click the **Medical** file, and then click the **OK** button. The picture appears as a selected object on top of the form's title. See Figure 4-7.

Figure 4-7 **Form with picture added**

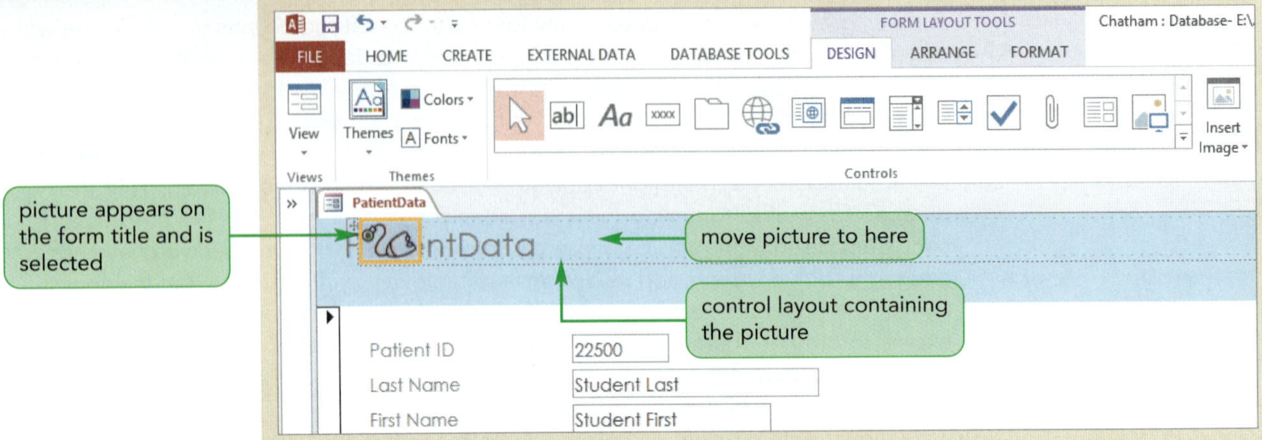

A solid orange outline surrounds the picture, indicating it is selected. The picture is placed in a **control layout**, which is a set of controls grouped together in a form or report so that you can manipulate the set as a single control. The dotted bright blue outline indicates the control layout (see Figure 4-7). The easiest way to move the picture off the form title is to first remove it from the control layout. Doing so allows you to move the picture independently.

4. Right-click the selected picture to display the shortcut menu, point to **Layout**, and then click **Remove Layout**. The picture is removed from the control layout. Now you can move the picture to the right of the form title.
5. Position the pointer on the picture, and then click and drag the picture to the right to move it to the right of the form title.
6. When the pointer is roughly one-half inch to the right of the form's title, release the mouse button. The picture is positioned to the right of the form title.
7. Click in a blank area on the main form (to the right of the field values) to deselect the picture. See Figure 4-8.

   Trouble? Don't be concerned if your picture is not in the exact location as the one shown in Figure 4-8. Just make sure the picture is not blocking any part of the form title and that it appears to the right of the form title and within the blue shaded area at the top of the form. Also, if your picture is too large or too small, you can resize it by first selecting it and then dragging a corner of the orange outline in the appropriate direction to increase or decrease the picture size.

TIP

You can resize a selected image by dragging one of its corners.

Figure 4-8 Form with theme applied and picture repositioned

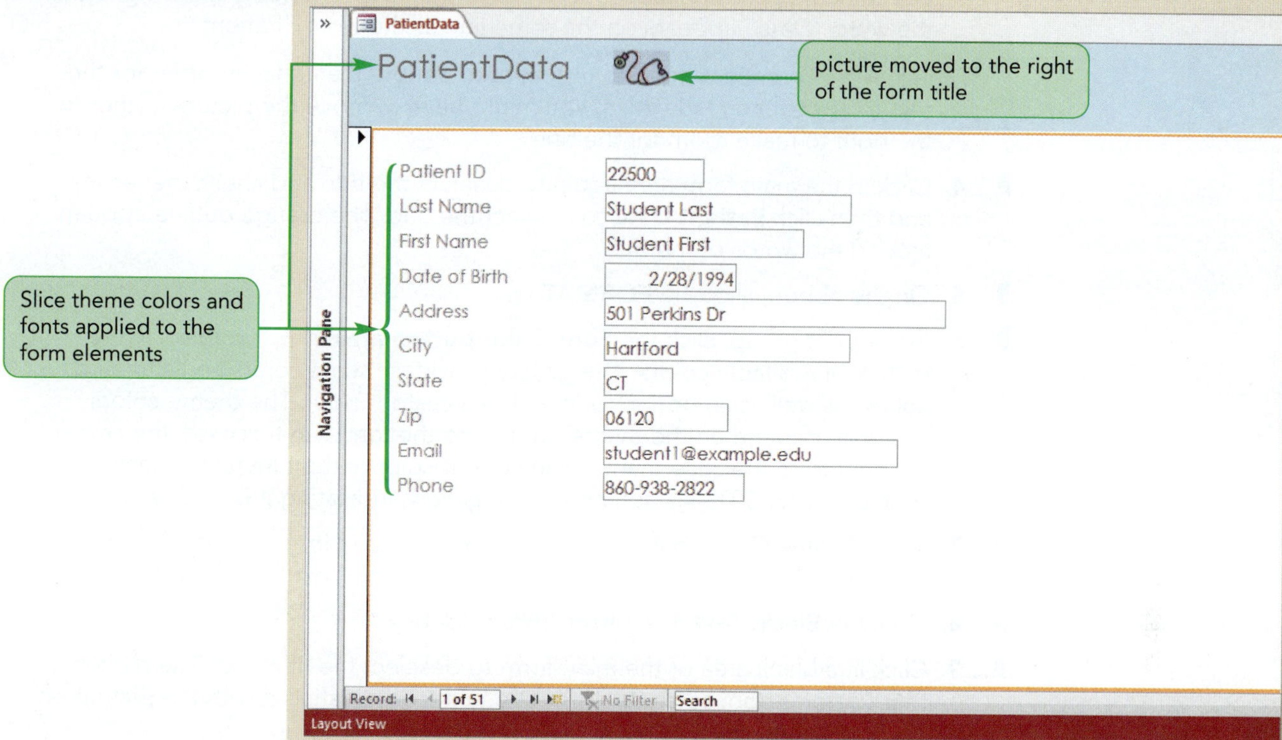

Next, Cindi asks you to change the color of the form title to a darker color so that it will coordinate better with the picture next to the title and stand out more on the form.

Changing the Color of the Form Title

The Font group on the FORMAT tab provides many options you can use to change the appearance of text on a form. For example, you can bold, italicize, and underline text; change the font, font color, and font size; and change the alignment of text. Before you change the color of the "PatientData" title on the form, you'll change the title to two words so it is easier to read.

To change the form title's text and color:

1. Click the **PatientData** form title. An orange box surrounds the title, indicating it is selected.
2. Click between the letters "t" and "D" to position the insertion point, and then press the **spacebar**. The title on the form is now "Patient Data" but the added space caused the words to appear on two lines. You can fix this by resizing the box containing the title.

TIP

Changing the form's title does not affect the form object name; it is still PatientData, as shown on the object tab.

3. Position the pointer on the right vertical line of the box containing the form title until the pointer changes to ↔, and then click and drag to the right until the word "Data" appears on the same line as the word "Patient."

   Trouble? You might need to repeat Step 3 more than once in order for the text to appear correctly. Also, you might have to move the picture further to the right to make room for the title.

4. Click in the main form area again to deselect the title and check the results, and then click **Patient Data** to reselect the title. The orange outline appears around the words of the title.
5. On the ribbon, click the **FORMAT** tab.
6. In the Font group, click the **Font Color button arrow** to display the gallery of available colors. The gallery provides theme colors and standard colors, as well as an option for creating a custom color. The theme colors available depend on the theme applied to the form—in this case, the colors are related to the Slice theme. The current color of the title text—Black, Text 1, Lighter 50%—is outlined in the gallery, indicating it is selected.
7. In the Theme Colors palette, point to the second color box in the fourth row of boxes. The ScreenTip indicates this is the Black, Text 1, Lighter 25% color.
8. Click the **Black, Text 1, Lighter 25%** color box.
9. Click in a blank area of the main form to deselect the title text. The darker black color is applied to the form title text, coordinating it with the picture on the form. See Figure 4-9.

Figure 4-9 **Form title with new color applied**

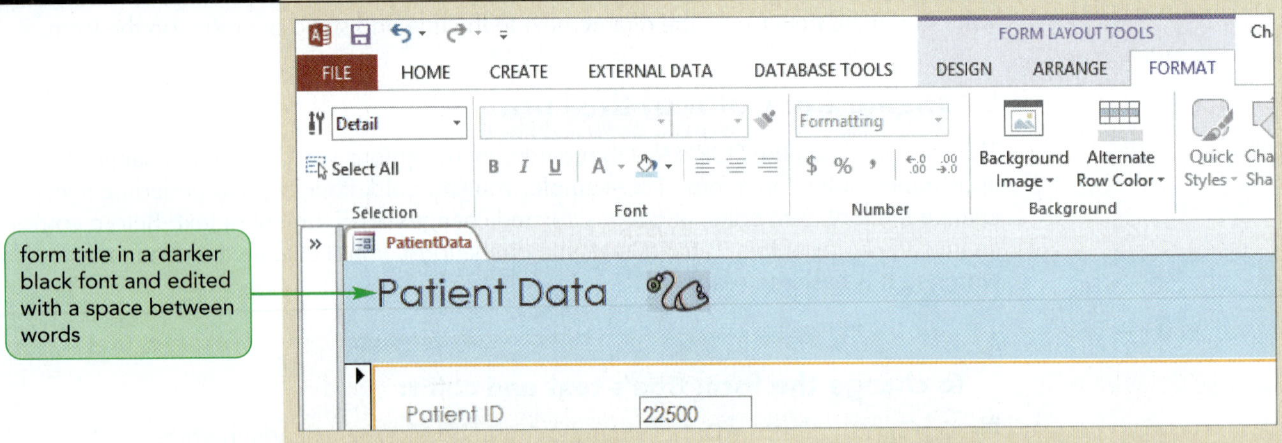

You have made a couple of changes to the form, and should save it now.

10. On the Quick Access Toolbar, click the **Save** button to save the modified form.
11. In the bottom right section of the status bar, click the **Form View** button to display the form in Form view. Refer back to the Session 4.1 Visual Overview; your form should match the PatientData form shown there.

Cindi is pleased with the modified appearance of the form. Later, she plans to revise the existing VisitData form and make the same changes to it, so that it matches the appearance of the PatientData form.

PROSKILLS

Written Communication: Understanding the Importance of Form Design

Similar to any document, a form must convey written information clearly and effectively. When you create a form, it's important to consider how the form will be used, so that its design will accommodate the needs of people using the form to view, enter, and maintain data. For example, if a form in a database mimics a paper form that users will enter data from, the form in the database should have the same fields in the same order as those on the paper form. This will enable users to easily tab from one field to the next in the database form to enter the necessary information from the paper form. Also, it's important to include a meaningful title on the form to identify its purpose and to enhance the appearance of the form. A form that is visually appealing makes working with the database more user-friendly and can improve the readability of the form, thereby helping to prevent errors in data entry. Also, be sure to use a consistent design for the forms in your database whenever possible. Users will expect to see similar elements—titles, pictures, fonts, and so on—in each form contained in a database. A mix of form styles and elements among the forms in a database could lead to problems when working with the forms. Finally, make sure the text on your form does not contain any spelling or grammatical errors. By producing a well-designed and well-written form, you can help to ensure that users will be able to work with the form in a productive and efficient manner.

Navigating a Form

Cindi wants to use the PatientData form to view some data in the Patient table. As you saw earlier, you use Layout view to modify the appearance of a form. To view, navigate, and change data using a form, you need to display the form in Form view. As you learned in Tutorial 1, you navigate a form in the same way that you navigate a table datasheet. Also, the navigation mode and editing mode keyboard shortcuts you used with datasheets in Tutorial 3 are the same when navigating a form.

The PatientData form is already displayed in Form view, so you can use it to navigate through the fields and records of the Patient table.

To navigate the PatientData form:

1. If necessary, click in the Patient ID field value box to make it current.
2. Press the **Tab** key twice to move to the First Name field value box, and then press the **End** key to move to the Phone field value box.
3. Press the **Home** key to move back to the Patient ID field value box. The first record in the Patient table still appears in the form.
4. Press the **Ctrl+End** keys to move to the Phone field value box for record 51, which is the last record in the table. The record number for the current record appears in the Current Record box between the navigation buttons at the bottom of the form.
5. Click the **Previous record** navigation button ◀ to move to the Phone field value box in record 50.
6. Press the ↑ key twice to move to the Zip field value box in record 50.
7. Click to position the insertion point between the numbers "8" and "3" in the Address field value to switch to editing mode, press the **Home** key to move the insertion point to the beginning of the field value, and then press the **End** key to move the insertion point to the end of the field value.

8. Click the **First record** navigation button to move to the Address field value box in the first record. The entire field value is highlighted because you switched from editing mode to navigation mode.
9. Click the **Next record** navigation button to move to the Address field value box in record 2, the next record.

Next, Cindi asks you to find the record for a patient named Sam. The paper form containing all the original contact information for this patient was damaged. Other than the patient's first name, Cindi knows only the street the patient lives on. Now she wants to use the form to view the complete data for this patient so she can contact the patient and make any necessary corrections.

Finding Data Using a Form

As you learned in Tutorial 3, the Find command lets you search for data in a datasheet so you can display only those records you want to view. You can also use the Find command to search for data in a form. You choose a field to serve as the basis for the search by making that field the current field, and then you enter the value you want Access to match in the Find and Replace dialog box.

REFERENCE

Finding Data in a Form or Datasheet

- Open the form or datasheet, and then make the field you want to search the current field.
- In the Find group on the HOME tab, click the Find button to open the Find and Replace dialog box.
- In the Find What box, type the field value you want to find.
- Complete the remaining options, as necessary, to specify the type of search to conduct.
- Click the Find Next button to begin the search.
- Click the Find Next button to continue searching for the next match.
- Click the Cancel button to stop the search operation.

You need to find the record for the patient Cindi wants to contact. In addition to the patient's first name (Sam), Cindi knows the name of the street on which this patient lives—Bunnell Place—so you'll search for the record using the Address field.

To find the record using the PatientData form:

1. Make sure the **Address** field value is still selected for the current record. This is the field you need to search.

   You can search for a record that contains part of the address anywhere in the Address field value. Performing a partial search such as this is often easier than matching the entire field value and is useful when you don't know or can't remember the entire field value.
2. In the Find group on the HOME tab, click the **Find** button. The Find and Replace dialog box opens. The Look In box shows that the current field (in this case, Address) will be searched. You'll search for records that contain the word "bunnell" in the address.

3. In the Find What box, type **bunnell**. Note that you do not have to enter the word as "Bunnell" with a capital letter "B" because the Match Case option is not selected in the Find and Replace dialog box. Access will find any record containing the word "bunnell" with any combination of uppercase and lowercase letters.

4. Click the **Match** arrow to display the list of matching options, and then click **Any Part of Field**. Access will find any record that contains the word "bunnell" in any part of the Address field. See Figure 4-10.

Figure 4-10 Completed Find and Replace dialog box

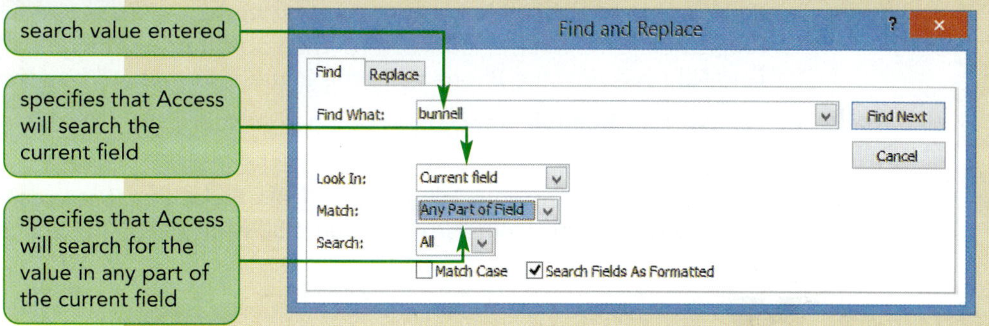

5. Click the **Find Next** button. The PatientData form now displays record 37, which is the record for Sam Boucher (PatientID 22543). The word "Bunnell" is selected in the Address field value box because you searched for this word. Cindi calls the patient and confirms that all the information is correct.

The search value you enter can be an exact value or it can include wildcard characters. A **wildcard character** is a placeholder you use when you know only part of a value or when you want to start or end with a specific character or match a certain pattern. Figure 4-11 shows the wildcard characters you can use when finding data.

Figure 4-11 Wildcard characters

Wildcard Character	Purpose	Example
*	Match any number of characters. It can be used as the first and/or last character in the character string.	th* *finds* the, that, this, therefore, *and so on*
?	Match any single alphabetic character.	a?t *finds* act, aft, ant, apt, *and* art
[]	Match any single character within the brackets.	a[fr]t *finds* aft *and* art *but not* act, ant, *or* apt
!	Match any character not within brackets.	a[!fr]t *finds* act, ant, *and* apt *but not* aft *or* art
-	Match any one of a range of characters. The range must be in ascending order (a to z, not z to a).	a[d-p]t *finds* aft, ant, *and* apt *but not* act *or* art
#	Match any single numeric character.	#72 *finds* 072, 172, 272, 372, *and so on*

Next, to see how a wildcard works, you'll view the records for any patients with phone numbers that contain the exchange 226 as part of the phone number. The exchange consists of the three digits that follow the area code in the phone number. You could search for any record containing the digits 226 in any part of the Phone field, but this search would also find records with the digits 226 in any part of the phone number. To find only those records with the digits 226 as the exchange, you'll use the * wildcard character.

To find the records using the * wildcard character:

1. Make sure the Find and Replace dialog box is still open.
2. Click anywhere in the PatientData form to make it active, and then press the **Tab** key until you reach the Phone field value box. This is the field you want to search.
3. Click the title bar of the Find and Replace dialog box to make it active, and then drag the Find and Replace dialog box to the right so you can see the Phone field on the form, if necessary. The Look In box setting is still Current field, which is now the Phone field; this is the field that will be searched.
4. Double-click **bunnell** in the Find What box to select the entire value, and then type **860-226***.
5. Click the **Match** arrow, and then click **Whole Field**. Because you're using a wildcard character in the search value, you want Access to search the whole field.

   With the settings you've entered, Access will find records in which any field value in the Phone field begins with the area code 860 followed by a hyphen and the exchange 226.
6. Click the **Find Next** button. Access displays record 46, which is the first record found for a customer with the exchange 226. Notice that the search process started from the point of the previously displayed record in the form, which was record 37.
7. Click the **Find Next** button. Access displays record 5, which is the next record found for a customer with the exchange 226. Notice that the search process cycles back through the beginning of the records in the underlying table.
8. Click the **Find Next** button. Access displays record 11, the third record found.
9. Click the **Find Next** button. Access displays record 23, the fourth record found.
10. Click the **Find Next** button. Access displays record 34.
11. Click the **Find Next** button. Access displays record 37 for Sam Boucher; this is the patient record that was active when you started the search process.
12. Click the **Find Next** button. Access displays a dialog box informing you that the search is finished.
13. Click the **OK** button to close the dialog box.
14. Click the **Cancel** button to close the Find and Replace dialog box.

Cindi has identified some patient updates she wants you to make. You'll use the PatientData form to update the data in the Patient table.

Maintaining Table Data Using a Form

Maintaining data using a form is often easier than using a datasheet because you can focus on all the changes for a single record at one time. In Form view, you can edit the field values for a record, delete a record from the underlying table, or add a new record to the table. You already know how to navigate a form and find specific records. Now you'll use the PatientData form to make the changes Cindi wants to the Patient table.

First, you'll update the record for Felipe Ramos. This patient recently moved from Hartford to West Hartford and provided an email address, so you need to update the necessary fields for this patient. In addition to using the Find and Replace dialog box to locate a specific record, you can use the Search box to the right of the navigation buttons. You'll use the Search box to search for the patient's last name, Ramos, and display the patient record in the form.

To change the record using the PatientData form:

1. To the right of the navigation buttons, click the **Search** box and then type **Ramos**. As soon as you start to type, Access begins searching through all fields in the records to match your entry. Record 33 (Felipe Ramos) is now current.

   You need to update this record with the new information for this patient.

2. Select the current entry in the Address field value box, and then type **145 Jackson Dr** to replace it.
3. Click at the beginning of the City field value box, type **West** and then press the **spacebar**. The City field value is now West Hartford.
4. Press the **Tab** key twice to move to and select the Zip field value, and then type **06117**.
5. Press the **Tab** key to move to the Email field value box, and then type **f.ramos@example.org** for the new email address.
6. Click to place the insertion point at the end of the value in the Phone field value box, press the **Backspace** key to delete everything except the area code and first dash, and then type **637-8841**. The Phone field value is now 860-637-8841. The updates to the record are complete. See Figure 4-12.

TIP

Note that the pencil symbol appears in the upper-left corner of the form, indicating that the form is in editing mode.

Figure 4-12 Patient record after changing field values

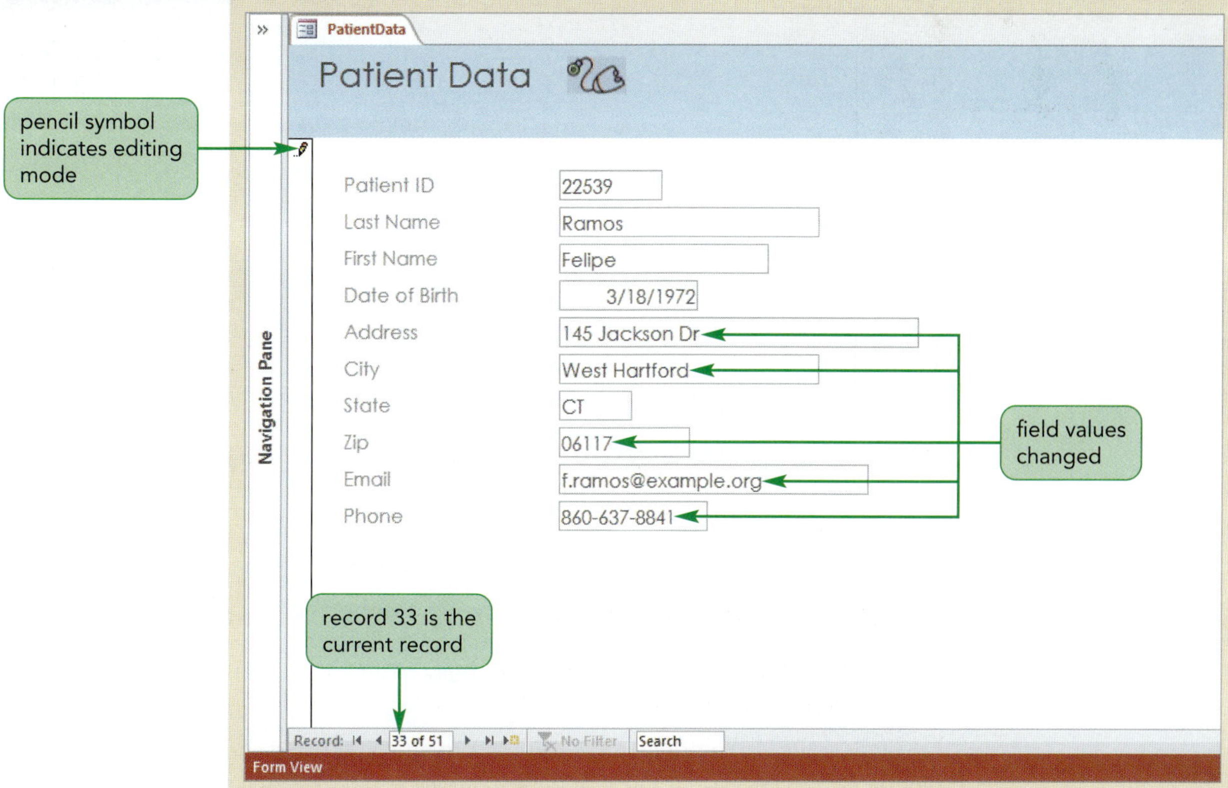

Next, Cindi asks you to add a record for a new patient. This person signed up to be a patient of the clinic at a recent health fair held by Chatham Community Health Services, but has not yet visited the clinic. You'll use the PatientData form to add the new record.

To add the new record using the PatientData form:

1. In the Records group on the HOME tab, click the **New** button. Record 52, the next available new record, becomes the current record. All field value boxes are empty (except the State field, which displays the default value of CT) and the insertion point is positioned in the Patient ID field value box.
2. Refer to Figure 4-13 and enter the value shown for each field. Press the **Tab** key to move from field to field.

Figure 4-13 Completed form for the new record

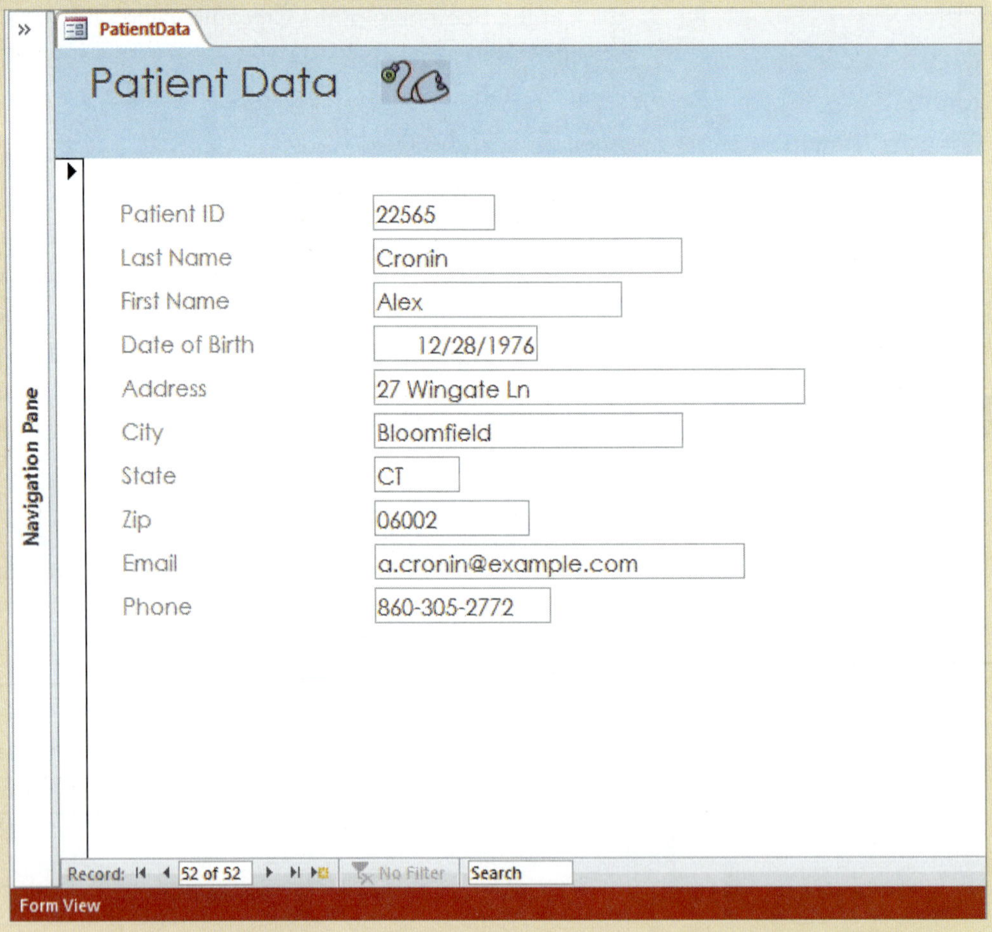

Trouble? Compare your screen with Figure 4-13. If any field value is incorrect, correct it now, using the methods described earlier for editing field values.

3. After entering the Phone field value, press the **Tab** key. Record 53, the next available new record, becomes the current record, and the record for PatientID 22565 is saved in the Patient table.

Cindi would like a printed copy of the PatientData form to show to her staff members. She asks you to print one form record.

Previewing and Printing Selected Form Records

Access prints as many form records as can fit on a printed page. If only part of a form record fits on the bottom of a page, the remainder of the record prints on the next page. Access allows you to print all pages or a range of pages. In addition, you can print the currently selected form record.

Cindi asks you to use the PatientData form to print the first record in the Patient table. Before you do, you'll preview the form record to see how it will look when printed.

To preview the form and print the data for record 1:

1. Click the **First record** navigation button to display record 1 in the form. This is the record in which you have entered your first and last names.
2. Click the **FILE** tab to display Backstage view, click **Print** in the navigation bar, and then click **Print Preview**. The Print Preview window opens, showing the form records for the Patient table. Notice that each record appears in its own form, and that shading is used to distinguish one record from another. See Figure 4-14.

Figure 4-14 Form records displayed in Print Preview

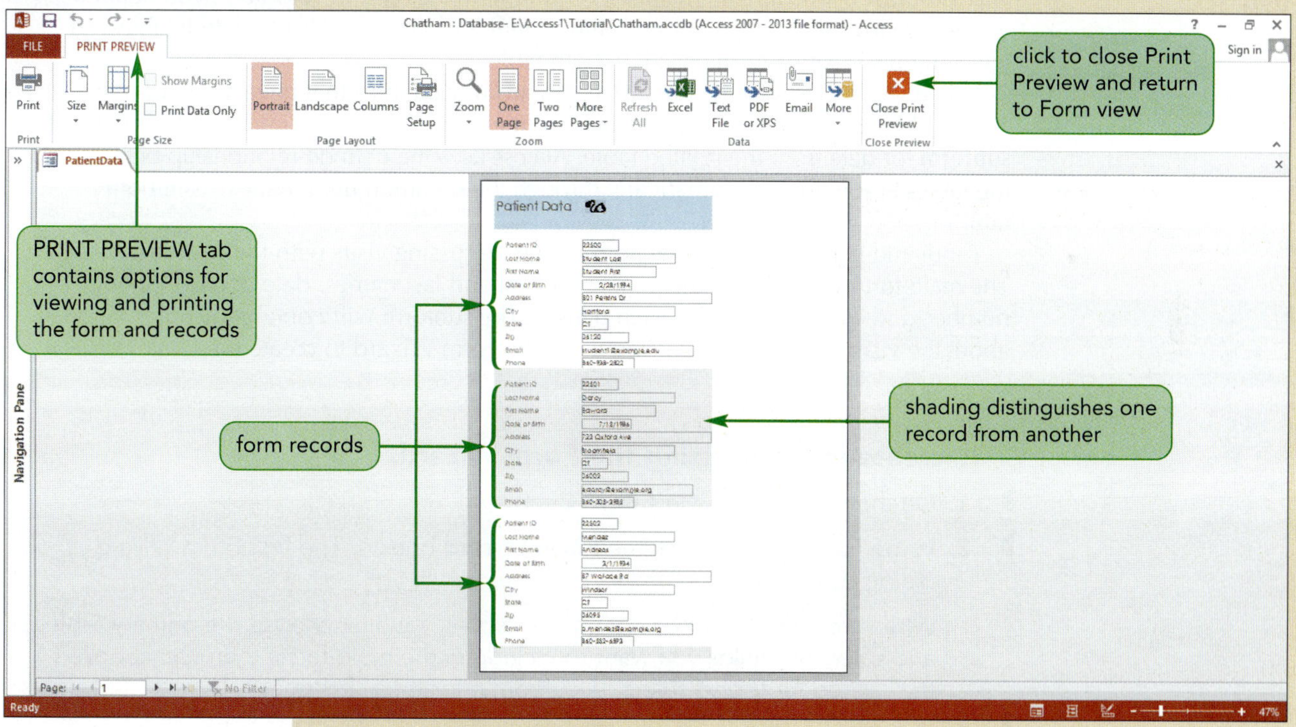

To print one selected record on a page by itself, you need to close Print Preview and then use the Print dialog box.

3. In the Close Preview group on the PRINT PREVIEW tab, click the **Close Print Preview** button. You return to Form view with the first record still displayed.
4. Click the **FILE** tab to display Backstage view again, click **Print** in the navigation bar, and then click **Print**. The Print dialog box opens.

5. Click the **Selected Record(s)** option button to print the current form record (record 1).

   Trouble? Check with your instructor to be sure you should print the form; then continue to the next step. If you should not print the form, click the Cancel button, and then skip to Step 7.

6. Click the **OK** button to close the dialog box and print the selected record.
7. Close the PatientData form.

After reviewing the printed PatientData form with her staff, Cindi realizes that it would be helpful for staff members to also have a form showing information about both patients and their visits.

Creating a Form with a Main Form and a Subform

Cindi would like you to create a form so that she can view the data for each patient and the patient's visits to the clinic at the same time. The type of form you need to create will include a main form and a subform. To create a form based on two tables, you must first define a relationship between the two tables. In Tutorial 2, you defined a one-to-many relationship between the Patient (primary) and Visit (related) tables, so you can now create a form based on both tables.

When you create a form containing data from two tables that have a one-to-many relationship, you actually create a **main form** for data from the primary table and a **subform** for data from the related table. Access uses the defined relationship between the tables to join them automatically through the common field that exists in both tables.

Cindi and her staff will use the form when discussing visits with the clinic's patients. The main form will contain the patient ID, first and last names, date of birth, phone number, and email address for each patient. The subform will contain the information about the visits for each patient. You'll use the Form Wizard to create the form.

To create the form using the Form Wizard:

1. On the ribbon, click the **CREATE** tab.
2. In the Forms group, click the **Form Wizard** button. The first Form Wizard dialog box opens.

   When creating a form based on two tables, you first choose the primary table and select the fields you want to include in the main form; then you choose the related table and select fields from it for the subform.

3. If necessary, click the **Tables/Queries** arrow, and then click **Table: Patient**.

   Cindi wants the form to include only the PatientID, FirstName, LastName, BirthDate, Phone, and Email fields from the Patient table.

4. Click **PatientID** in the Available Fields box (if necessary), and then click the > button to move the field to the Selected Fields box.
5. Repeat Step 4 for the **FirstName**, **LastName**, **BirthDate**, **Phone**, and **Email** fields.

The PatientID field will appear in the main form, so you do not have to include it in the subform. Otherwise, Cindi wants the subform to include all the fields from the Visit table.

6. Click the **Tables/Queries** arrow, and then click **Table: Visit**. The fields from the Visit table appear in the Available Fields box. The quickest way to add the fields you want to include is to move all the fields to the Selected Fields box, and then remove the only field you don't want to include (PatientID).

TIP

The table name (Visit) is included in the PatientID field name to distinguish it from the same field in the Patient table.

7. Click the >> button to move all the fields in the Visit table to the Selected Fields box.

8. Click **Visit.PatientID** in the Selected Fields box, and then click the < button to move the field back to the Available Fields box.

9. Click the **Next** button. The next Form Wizard dialog box opens. See Figure 4-15.

Figure 4-15 Choosing a format for the main form and subform

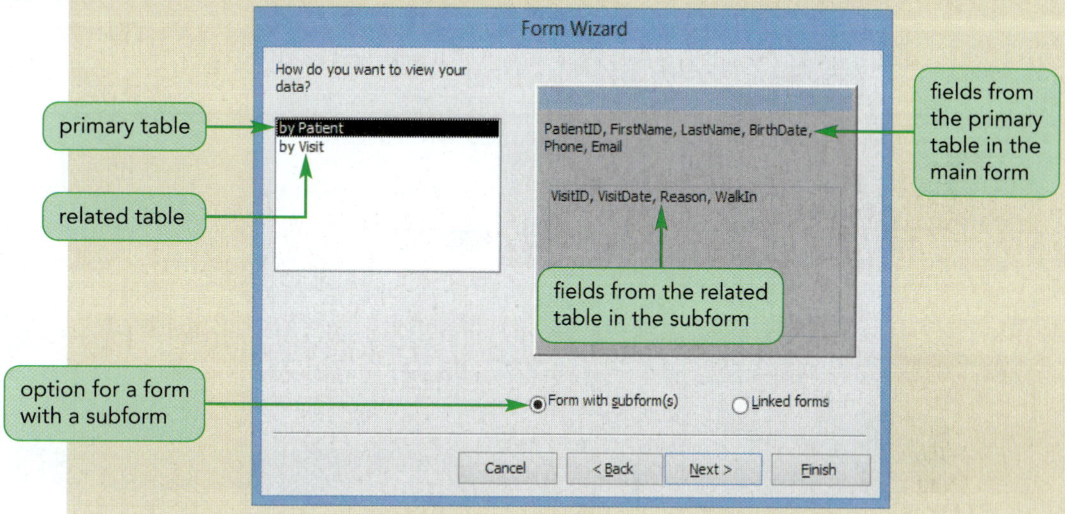

In this dialog box, the section on the left shows the order in which you will view the selected data: first by data from the primary Patient table, and then by data from the related Visit table. The form will be displayed as shown on the right side of the dialog box, with the fields from the Patient table at the top in the main form, and the fields from the Visit table at the bottom in the subform. The selected "Form with subform(s)" option button specifies a main form with a subform. The Linked forms option creates a form structure in which only the main form fields are displayed. A button with the subform's name on it appears on the main form; you can click this button to display the associated subform records.

The default options shown in Figure 4-15 are correct for creating a form with Patient data in the main form and Visit data in the subform.

To finish creating the form:

1. Click the **Next** button. The next Form Wizard dialog box opens, in which you choose the subform layout.

The Tabular layout displays subform fields as a table, whereas the Datasheet layout displays subform fields as a table datasheet. The layout choice is a matter of personal preference. You'll use the Datasheet layout.

2. Click the **Datasheet** option button to select it (if necessary), and then click the **Next** button. The next Form Wizard dialog box opens, in which you choose titles for the main form and the subform.

   You'll use the title "PatientVisits" for the main form and the title "VisitSubform" for the subform. These titles will also be the names for the form objects.

3. In the Form box, click to position the insertion point to the right of the last letter, and then type **Visits**. The main form name is now PatientVisits.
4. In the Subform box, delete the space between the two words so that the subform name appears as **VisitSubform**.
5. Click the **Finish** button. The completed form opens in Form view. See Figure 4-16.

Figure 4-16 **Main form with subform in Form view**

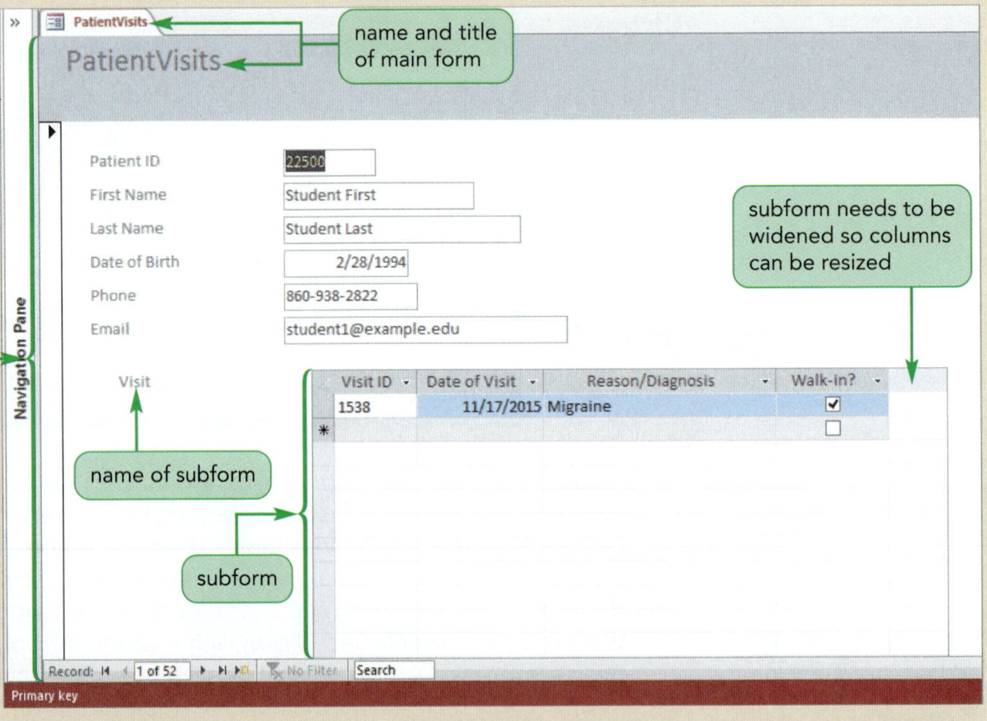

TIP

The PatientVisits form is formatted with the default Office theme because you applied the Slice theme only to the PatientData form.

In the main form, Access displays the fields from the first record in the Patient table in a columnar format. The records in the main form appear in primary key order by PatientID. PatientID 22500 has one related record in the Visit table; this record, for VisitID 1538, is shown in the subform, which uses the datasheet format. The main form name, "PatientVisits," appears on the object tab and as the form title. The name of the subform appears to the left of the subform. Note that only the word "Visit" and not the complete name "VisitSubform" appears on the form. Access displays only the table name for the subform itself, but displays the complete name of the object, "VisitSubform," when you view and work with objects in the Navigation Pane.

The subform designation is necessary in a list of database objects so that you can distinguish the Visit subform from other objects, such as the Visit table, but the subform designation is not needed in the PatientVisits form. Only the table name is required to identify the table containing the records in the subform.

Next, you need to make some changes to the form. First, you'll edit the form title to add a space between the words so that it appears as "Patient Visits." Then, you'll resize the subform. Cindi is concerned that the subform is not wide enough to allow for all the columns to be resized and fully display their field values, especially the Reason/Diagnosis column. To make these changes, you need to switch to Layout view.

To modify the PatientVisits form in Layout view:

1. In the Views group on the HOME tab, click the **View** button to switch to Layout view.
2. Click **PatientVisits** in the blue-gray area at the top of the form. The form title is selected.
3. Click between the letters "t" and "V" to place the insertion point, and then press the **spacebar**. The title on the form is now "Patient Visits."
4. Click in a blank area of the form to the right of the field value boxes to deselect the title. Next, you'll increase the width of the subform.
5. Click the subform. An orange outline surrounds the subform, indicating it is selected.
6. Position the pointer on the right vertical line of the selected subform until the pointer changes to a ↔ shape, and then click and drag to the right approximately two inches. The subform is now wider. See Figure 4-17.

Figure 4-17 Modified form in Layout view

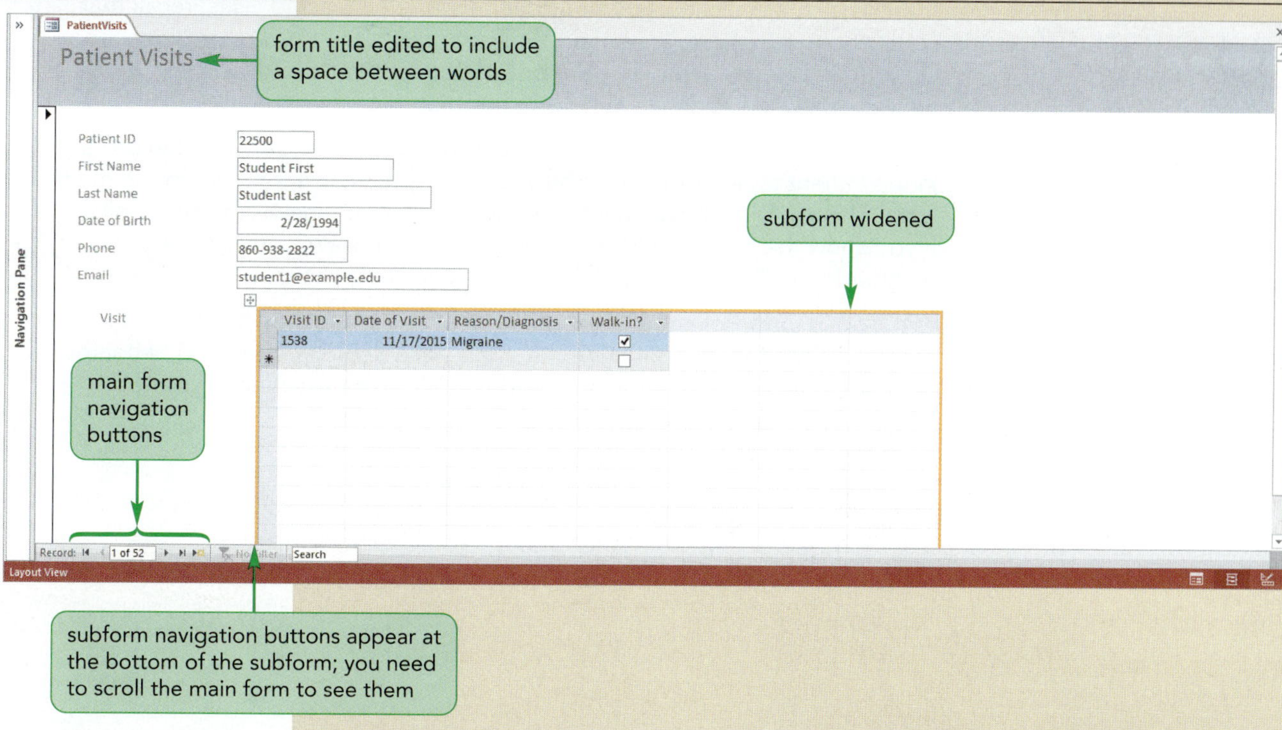

The wider subform will enable you to resize the Reason/Diagnosis column, as necessary, to fully display its field values.

7. On the Quick Access Toolbar, click the **Save** button to save both the main form and the subform.
8. In the Views group on the DESIGN tab, click the **View** button to display the PatientVisits form in Form view.

   Trouble? If the fields in the main form are partially out of view, use the vertical scroll bar to scroll to the top of the form and display the fields.

The form includes two sets of navigation buttons. You use the set of navigation buttons at the bottom of the Form window to select records from the primary table in the main form (see Figure 4-17). The second set of navigation buttons is currently not visible; you need to scroll down the main form to see these buttons, which appear at the bottom of the subform. You use the subform navigation buttons to select records from the related table in the subform.

You'll use the navigation buttons to view different records.

TIP

As you move through the form/subform, notice that some field values in the subform are not completely visible. You can resize any subform field to its best fit to fully display the field values.

To navigate to different main form and subform records:

1. In the main form, click the **Next record** navigation button six times. Record 7 of 52 total records in the Patient table (for Matthew Weiss) becomes the current record in the main form. The subform shows that this patient made three visits to the clinic. Note that the field values in the Reason/Diagnosis column are not fully displayed.
2. Double-click the pointer on the right vertical line of the Reason/Diagnosis column in the subform to resize this field to its best fit and display the complete field values.
3. In the main form, click the **Last record** navigation button. Record 52 in the Patient table (for Alex Cronin) becomes the current record in the main form. The subform shows that this patient currently has no visits; recall that you just entered this record using the PatientData form. Cindi could use the subform to enter the information for this patient's visits to the clinic, and that information will be updated in the Visit table.
4. In the main form, click the **Previous record** navigation button. Record 51 in the Patient table (for Daniel Shaw) becomes the current record in the main form. The subform shows that this patient has made one visit to the clinic.

   If you know the number of the record you want to view, you can enter the number in the Current Record box to move to that record.
5. In the main form, select **51** in the Current Record box, type **47**, and then press the **Enter** key. Record 47 in the Patient table (for Isobel Kirk) becomes the current record in the main form. The subform shows that this patient made four visits to the clinic.

6. In the subform, resize the Reason/Diagnosis column to its best fit to fully display its field values, if necessary.
7. If necessary, use the vertical scroll bar for the main form to scroll down and view the bottom of the subform. Note the navigation buttons for the subform.
8. In the subform, click the **Last record** navigation button ▶|. Record 4 in the Visit table, for Visit ID 1679, becomes the current record in the subform.
9. Save and close the PatientVisits form.
10. If you are not continuing to Session 4.2, click the **FILE** tab, and then click **Close** in the navigation bar to close the Chatham database.

Both the PatientData form and the PatientVisits form you created will enable Cindi and her staff to view, enter, and maintain data easily in the Patient and Visit tables in the Chatham database.

REVIEW

Session 4.1 Quick Check

1. Describe the difference between creating a form using the Form tool and creating a form using the Form Wizard.
2. What is a theme and how do you apply one to an existing form?
3. A(n) ______________ is an item on a form, report, or other database object that you can manipulate to modify the object's appearance.
4. Which table record is displayed in a form when you press the Ctrl+End keys while you are in navigation mode?
5. Which wildcard character matches any single alphabetic character?
6. To print only the current record displayed in a form, you need to select the ______________ option button in the Print dialog box.
7. In a form that contains a main form and a subform, what data is displayed in the main form and what data is displayed in the subform?

Session 4.2 Visual Overview:

The report object's name is displayed on the tab for the report.

The report title appears at the top of the report. By default, the report object name is used as the report title, but you can edit the title to display the text you want, as done here, with spaces added between words for readability.

Fields from the primary Patient table appear first in the report.

Fields from the related Visit table appear below the fields from the primary table.

For a **grouped report**, the data from a record in the primary table (the Patient table in this report) appears as a group, followed on subsequent lines of the report by the joined records from the related table (the Visit table in this report).

The navigation buttons allow you to display the first, last, next, or previous page in the report, or to enter a specific page number and move to that page.

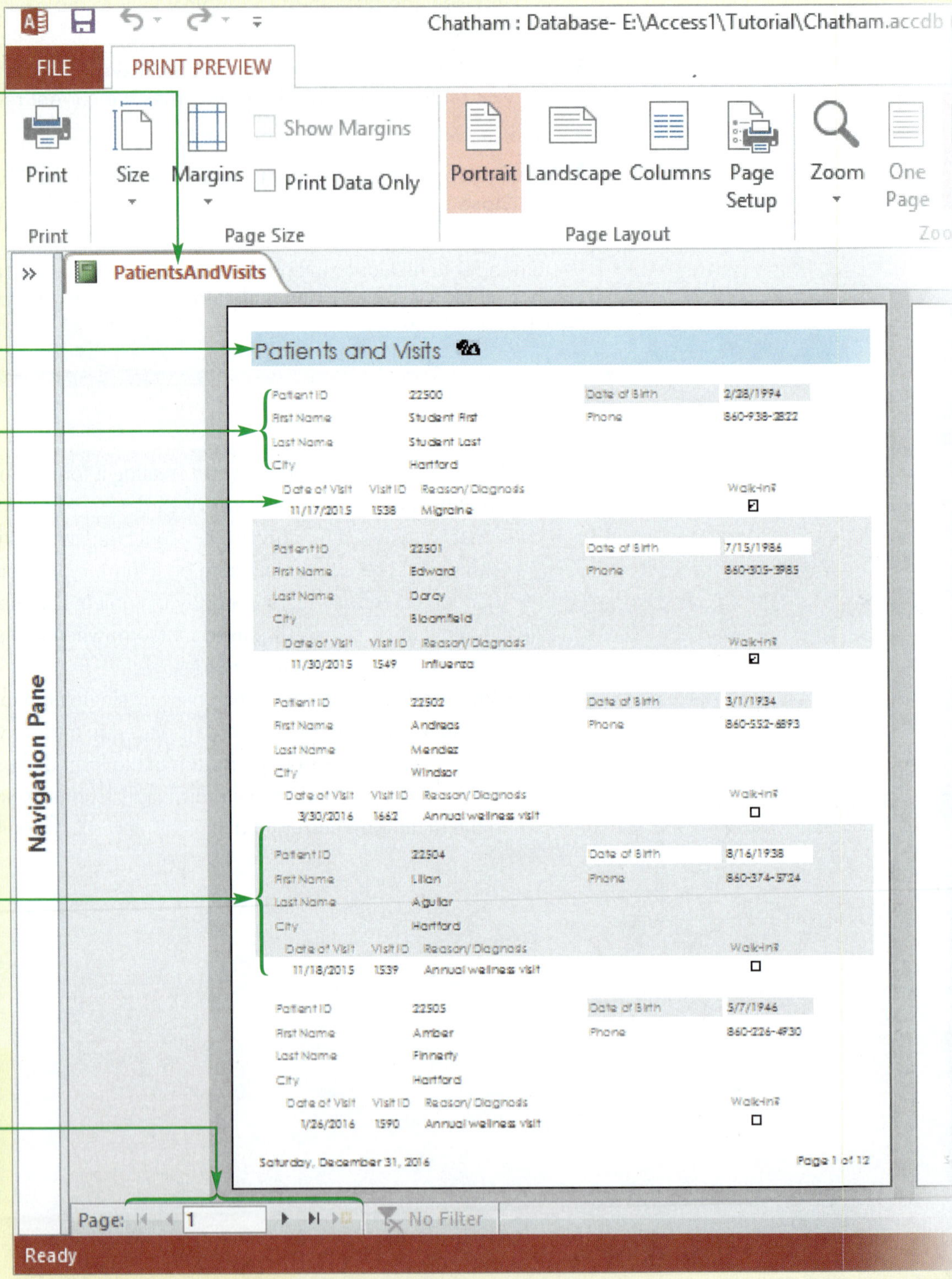

Report Displayed in Print Preview

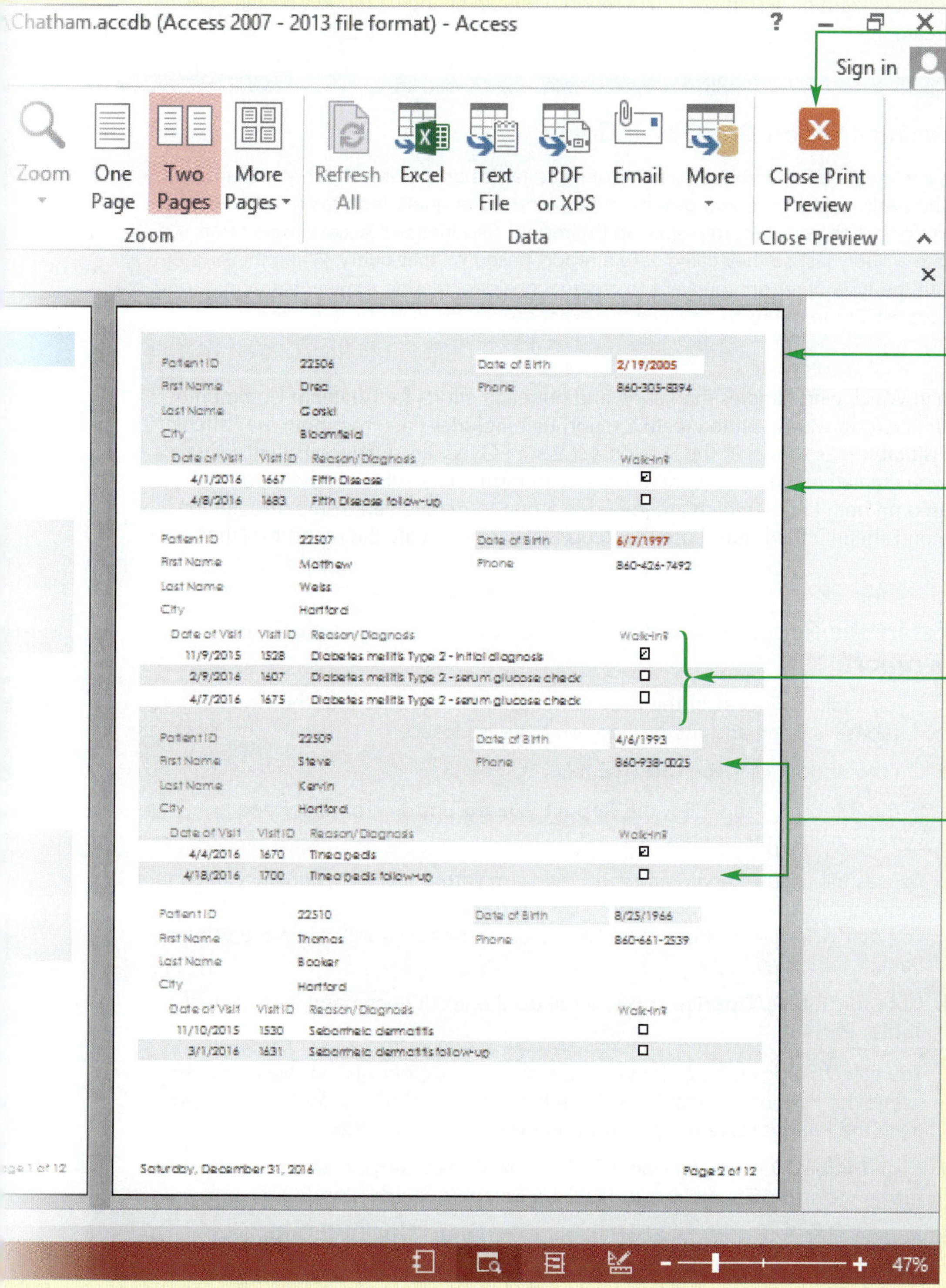

Click this button to close Print Preview and return to the report in the previously displayed view.

The PatientsAndVisits report was created using the **Report Wizard**, which asks you a series of questions and then creates a report based on your answers. This report is based on data in both the Patient and Visit tables, which are joined in a one-to-many relationship through the common PatientID field.

This report uses **portrait orientation**, where the page is taller than it is wide; you can also format a report in **landscape orientation**, where the page is wider than it is tall.

The set of field values for each record in the related table is called a **detail record**. These three detail records are the Visit table records related to the Patient table record for Matthew Weiss.

Shading is used to distinguish one Patient record from another, and one Visit record from another.

Creating a Report Using the Report Wizard

As you learned in Tutorial 1, a report is a formatted printout or screen display of the contents of one or more tables or queries in a database. In Access, you can create your own reports or use the Report Wizard to create them for you. Whether you use the Report Wizard or design your own report, you can change a report's design after you create it.

INSIGHT

Creating a Report Based on a Query

You can create a report based on one or more tables or queries. When you use a query as the basis for a report, you can use criteria and other query features to retrieve only the information you want to display in the report. Experienced Access users often create a query just so they can create a report based on that query. When thinking about the type of report you want to create, consider creating a query first and basing the report on the query, to produce the exact results you want to see in the report.

Ethan Ward, who handles marketing and outreach efforts for Chatham Community Health Services, wants you to create a report that includes data from both the Patient and Visit tables, as shown in the Session 4.2 Visual Overview. Like the PatientVisits form you created earlier, which includes a main form and a subform, the report will be based on both tables, which are joined in a one-to-many relationship through the common PatientID field. You'll use the Report Wizard to create the report for Ethan.

To start the Report Wizard and select the fields to include in the report:

1. If you took a break after the previous session, make sure that the Chatham database is open and the Navigation Pane is closed.
2. On the ribbon, click the **CREATE** tab.
3. In the Reports group, click the **Report Wizard** button. The first Report Wizard dialog box opens.

   As was the case when you created the form with a subform, initially you can choose only one table or query to be the data source for the report. Then you can include data from other tables or queries. You will select the primary Patient table first.
4. Click the **Tables/Queries** arrow, scroll up the list (if necessary), and then click **Table: Patient**.

   You select fields in the order you want them to appear on the report. Ethan wants the PatientID, FirstName, LastName, City, BirthDate, and Phone fields from the Patient table to appear on the report, in that order.
5. Click **PatientID** in the Available Fields box (if necessary), and then click the > button. The field moves to the Selected Fields box.
6. Repeat Step 5 to add the **FirstName**, **LastName**, **City**, **BirthDate**, and **Phone** fields to the report.
7. Click the **Tables/Queries** arrow, and then click **Table: Visit**. The fields from the Visit table appear in the Available Fields box.

The PatientID field will appear on the report with the patient data, so you do not need to include it in the detail records for each visit. Otherwise, Ethan wants all the fields from the Visit table to be included in the report.

8. Click the >> button to move all the fields from the Available Fields box to the Selected Fields box.
9. Click **Visit.PatientID** in the Selected Fields box, click the < button to move the field back to the Available Fields box, and then click the **Next** button. The second Report Wizard dialog box opens. See Figure 4-18.

Figure 4-18 Choosing a grouped or ungrouped report

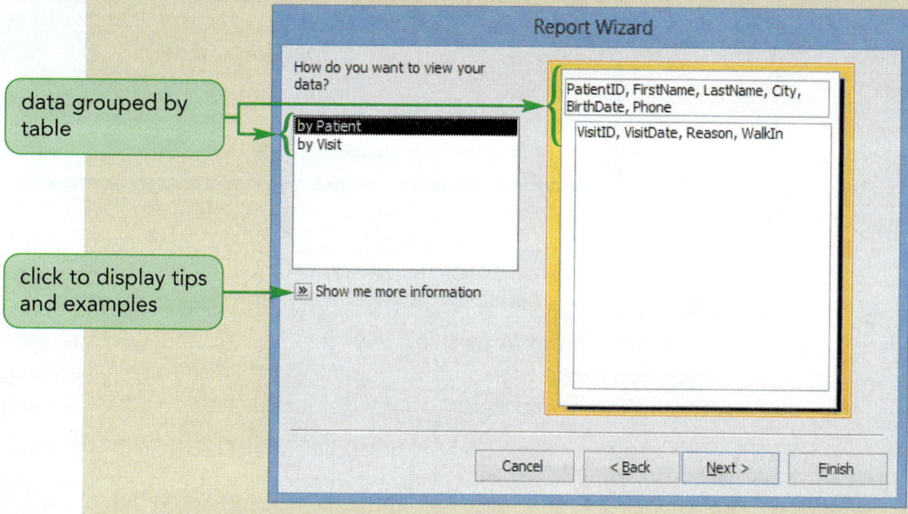

TIP

You can display tips for creating reports and examples of reports by clicking the "Show me more information" button.

You can choose to arrange the selected data grouped by table, which is the default, or ungrouped. You're creating a grouped report; the data from each record in the Patient table will appear in a group, followed by the related records for that patient from the Visit table.

The default options shown on your screen are correct for the report Ethan wants, so you can continue responding to the Report Wizard questions.

To finish creating the report using the Report Wizard:

1. Click the **Next** button. The next Report Wizard dialog box opens, in which you choose additional grouping levels.

   Currently the report contains only one grouping level, which is for the patient's data. Grouping levels are useful for reports with multiple levels, such as those containing monthly, quarterly, and annual totals, or for those containing city and country groups. Ethan's report requires no further grouping levels, so you can accept the default options.
2. Click the **Next** button. The next Report Wizard dialog box opens, in which you choose the sort order for the detail records. See Figure 4-19.

Figure 4-19 Choosing the sort order for detail records

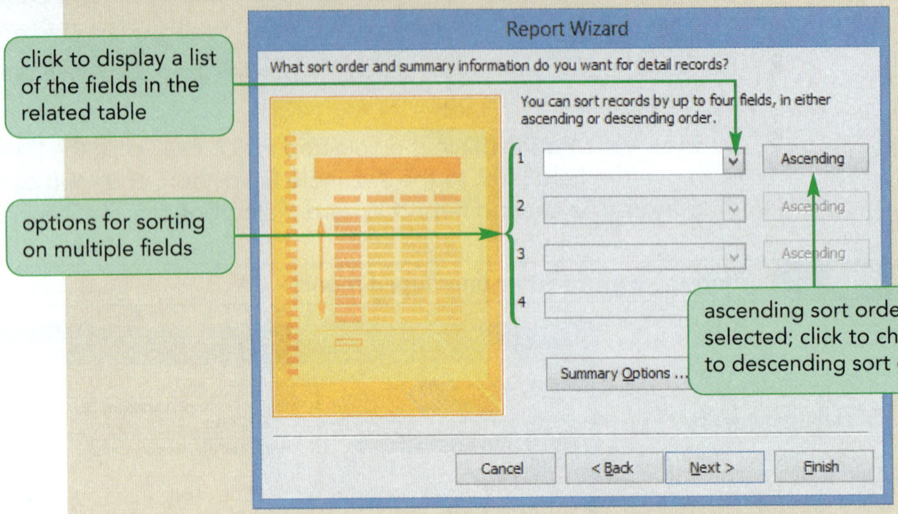

The records from the Visit table for a patient represent the detail records for Ethan's report. He wants these records to appear in ascending order by the value in the VisitDate field, so that the visits will be shown in chronological order. The Ascending option is already selected by default. To change to descending order, you click this same button, which acts as a toggle between the two sort orders. Also, you can sort on multiple fields, as you can with queries.

3. Click the **arrow** on the first box, click **VisitDate**, and then click the **Next** button. The next Report Wizard dialog box opens, in which you choose a layout and page orientation for the report. See Figure 4-20.

Figure 4-20 Choosing the report layout

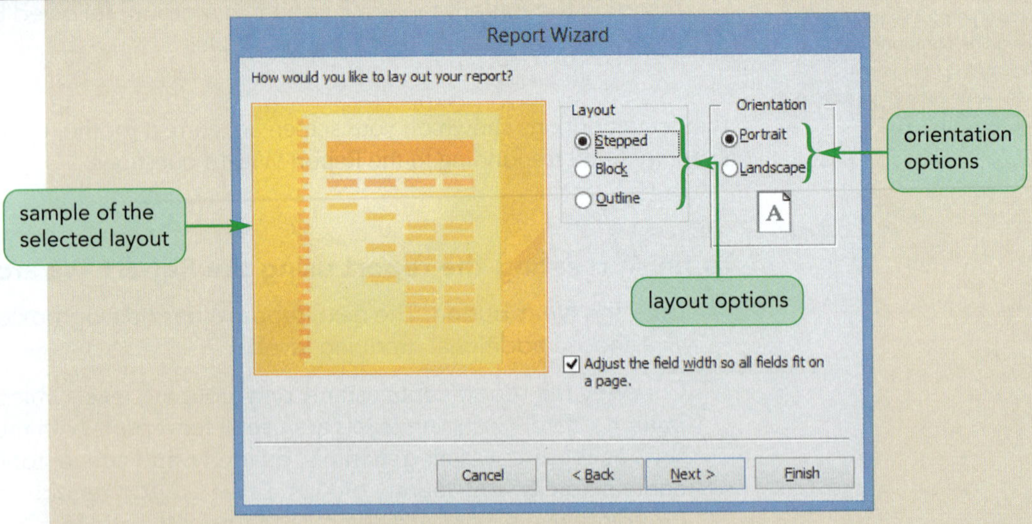

4. Click each layout option and examine each sample that appears.

You'll use the Outline layout for Ethan's report. Also, most of the fields in both the Patient and Visit tables contain relatively short field values, so you'll keep the portrait page orientation. This should provide enough space across the page to display all the field values; you will confirm this when viewing the report created by the wizard.

5. In the Layout section, click the **Outline** option button, and then click the **Next** button. The final Report Wizard dialog box opens, in which you choose a report title, which also serves as the name for the report object in the database.

   Ethan wants the report title "Patients and Visits" at the top of the report. Because the name you enter in this dialog box is also the name of the report object, you'll enter the report name as one word and edit the title on the report later.

6. In the box for the title, enter **PatientsAndVisits** and then click the **Finish** button. The Report Wizard creates the report based on your answers, saves it as an object in the Chatham database, and opens the report in Print Preview.

   To view the entire page, you need to change the Zoom setting.

7. In the Zoom group on the PRINT PREVIEW tab, click the **Zoom button arrow**, and then click **Fit to Window**. The first page of the report is displayed in Print Preview.

8. At the bottom of the window, click the **Next Page** navigation button ▶ to display the second page of the report.

   When a report is displayed in Print Preview, you can use the pointer to toggle between a full-page display and a close-up display of the report.

9. Click the pointer at the center of the report. The display changes to show a close-up view of the report. See Figure 4-21.

Figure 4-21 Close-up view of the report

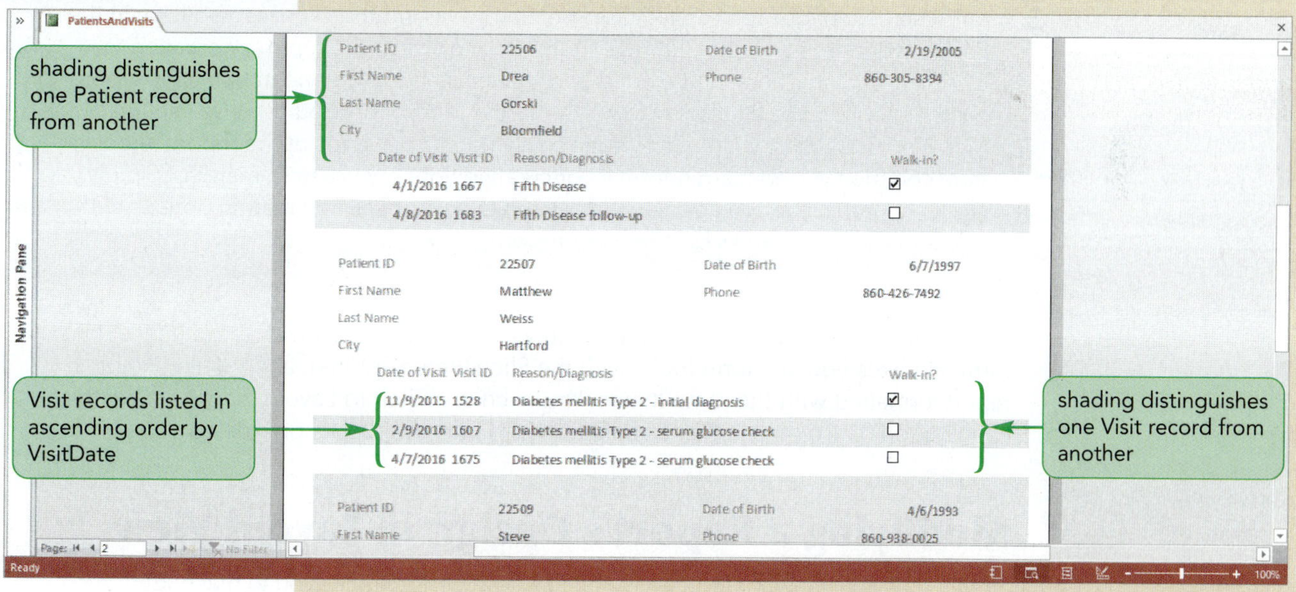

Shading is used to distinguish both one Patient record from another and, within a group of each patient's Visit records, one Visit record from another.

Trouble? Depending on your computer settings, the shading and colors used in your report might look different. This difference should not cause any problems.

The detail records for the Visit table fields appear in ascending order based on the values in the VisitDate field. Because the VisitDate field is used as the basis for sorting records, it appears as the first field in this section, even though you selected the fields in the order in which they appear in the Visit table.

10. Use the vertical scroll bar to scroll to the bottom of the second page, checking the text in the report as you scroll. Notice the current date and page number at the bottom of the page; the Report Wizard included these elements as part of the report's design.

    Trouble? Depending on your computer's settings, the text of the page number might not be completely within the page border. If so, you'll see blank pages every other page as you complete Steps 11 and 12. You'll fix this problem shortly.

11. Click the pointer on the report to zoom back out, and then click the **Next Page** navigation button to move to page 3 of the report.

12. Continue to move through the pages of the report, and then click the **First Page** navigation button to return to the first page.

INSIGHT

Changing a Report's Page Orientation and Margins

When you display a report in Print Preview, you can easily change the report layout using options on the PRINT PREVIEW tab (refer to the Session 4.2 Visual Overview). For example, sometimes fields with longer values cause the report content to overflow onto the next page. You can fix this problem by clicking the Landscape button in the Page Layout group on the PRINT PREVIEW tab to switch the report orientation to landscape, where the page is wider than it is tall. Landscape orientation allows more space for content to fit across the width of the report page. You can also use the Margins button in the Page Size group to change the margins of the report, choosing from commonly used margin formats or creating your own custom margins. Simply click the Margins button arrow to display the menu of available margin options and select the one that works best for your report.

Earlier, when meeting with Cindi, Ethan viewed and worked with the PatientData form. He likes how the form looks with the Slice theme applied, and would like his report formatted with the same theme. You need to switch to Layout view to make this change. You'll also make other modifications to improve the report's design.

Modifying a Report's Design in Layout View

Similar to Layout view for forms, Layout view for reports enables you to make modifications to the report's design. Many of the same options—such as those for applying a theme and changing the color of text—are provided in Layout view for reports.

Applying a Theme to a Report

The same themes available for forms are also available for reports. You can choose to apply a theme to the current report object only, or to all reports in the database. In this case, you'll apply the Slice theme only to the PatientsAndVisits report because Ethan isn't certain if it is the appropriate theme for other reports in the Chatham database.

To apply the Slice theme to the report:

1. On the status bar, click the **Layout View** button. The report is displayed in Layout view.
2. In the Themes group on the DESIGN tab, click the **Themes** button. The "In this Database" section at the top of the gallery shows both the default Office theme and the Slice theme. The Slice theme is included here because you applied it earlier to the PatientData form.
3. At the top of the gallery, right-click the **Slice** theme to display the shortcut menu, and then click **Apply Theme to This Object Only**. The gallery closes and the theme is applied to the report.

   The larger font used by the Slice theme has caused the report title text to be cut off on the right. You'll fix this problem and edit the title text as well.
4. Click the **PatientsAndVisits** title at the top of the report to select it.
5. Place the pointer on the right vertical line of the orange outline surrounding the title, and then click and drag the ↔ pointer to the right until the title is fully displayed.

   Trouble? You might need to repeat Step 5 more than once in order for the text to appear correctly.
6. Click between the letters "s" and "A" in the title, press the **spacebar**, change the capital letter "A" to **a**, place the insertion point between the letters "d" and "V," and then press the **spacebar**. The title is now "Patients and Visits."
7. Click to the right of the report title in the shaded area to deselect the title.

TIP

When you point to the Slice theme, a ScreenTip displays the names of the database objects that use the theme—in this case, the PatientData form.

Ethan views the report and notices some other formatting changes he would like you to make. First, he doesn't like how the BirthDate field values are aligned compared to the Phone field values. You'll fix this next.

Changing the Alignment of Field Values

The FORMAT tab in Layout view, one of the REPORT LAYOUT TOOLS contextual tabs, provides options for you to easily modify the format of various report objects. For example, you can change the alignment of the text in a field value. Recall that Date/Time fields, like BirthDate, automatically right-align their field values, whereas Short Text fields, like Phone, automatically left-align their field values. Ethan asks you to change the alignment of the BirthDate field so its values appear left-aligned, which will improve the format of the report.

To change the alignment of the BirthDate field values:

1. On the ribbon, click the **FORMAT** tab. The ribbon changes to display groups and options for formatting the report. The options for modifying the format of a report are the same as those available for forms.
2. In the report, click the first **BirthDate field value box**, which contains the date 2/28/1994. The field value box is outlined in orange, indicating it is selected. Note that the other BirthDate field value boxes are outlined in a lighter orange, indicating they are selected as well. Any changes you make will be applied to all BirthDate field values throughout the report.

3. In the Font group on the FORMAT tab, click the **Align Left** button. The text in the BirthDate field value boxes is now left-aligned, and the birth dates are aligned with the phone numbers. See Figure 4-22.

Figure 4-22 Report after applying a theme and changing field alignment

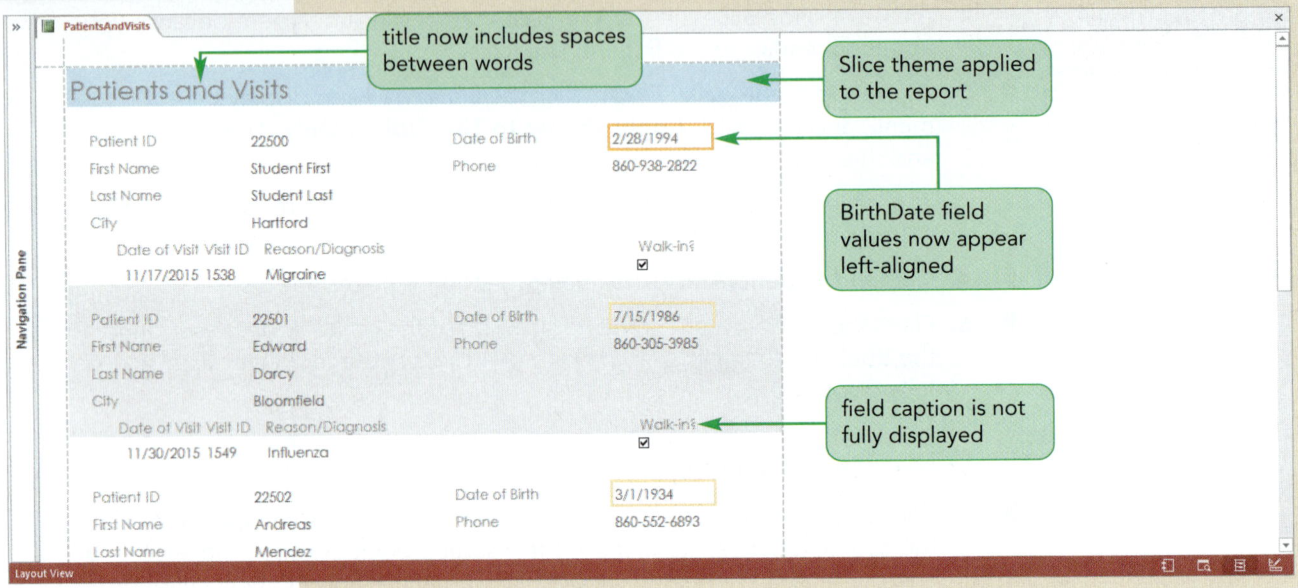

Moving and Resizing Fields on a Report

Working in Layout view, you can resize and reposition fields and field value boxes to improve the appearance of a report or to address the problem of some field values not being completely displayed. In the PatientsAndVisits report, you need to move and resize the WalkIn field label so that the complete caption, Walk-in?, is displayed. Ethan also thinks the report would look better with more room between the VisitDate and VisitID fields, so you'll move the VisitDate field label and associated field value box to the left.

You can select one or more objects on a report and then drag them to a new location; or, for more precise control over the move, you can use the arrow keyboard keys to move selected objects. Ethan asks you to move the WalkIn field's label to the left so it appears centered over its check box, and also to make the label larger.

To move and resize the WalkIn field label:

1. In the report, click the first occurrence of the **Walk-in?** field label. All instances of the label are selected throughout the report.
2. Press the ← key repeatedly until the label is centered (roughly) over its check box.
3. Place the pointer on the right vertical line of the orange outline surrounding the label, and then click and drag the ↔ pointer to the right until the label text is fully displayed.

Next, you need to move the VisitDate field label (Date of Visit) and field value box to the left, to provide more space between the VisitDate field and the VisitID field in the report. You can select both objects and modify them at the same time.

To move the VisitDate field label and field value box:

1. In the report, click the first occurrence of the **Date of Visit** field label, press and hold the **Shift** key, and then click the first occurrence of the field value box, which contains the date 11/17/2015. Both the field label and its associated field value box are selected and can be moved. See Figure 4-23.

Figure 4-23 Report after moving and resizing field label

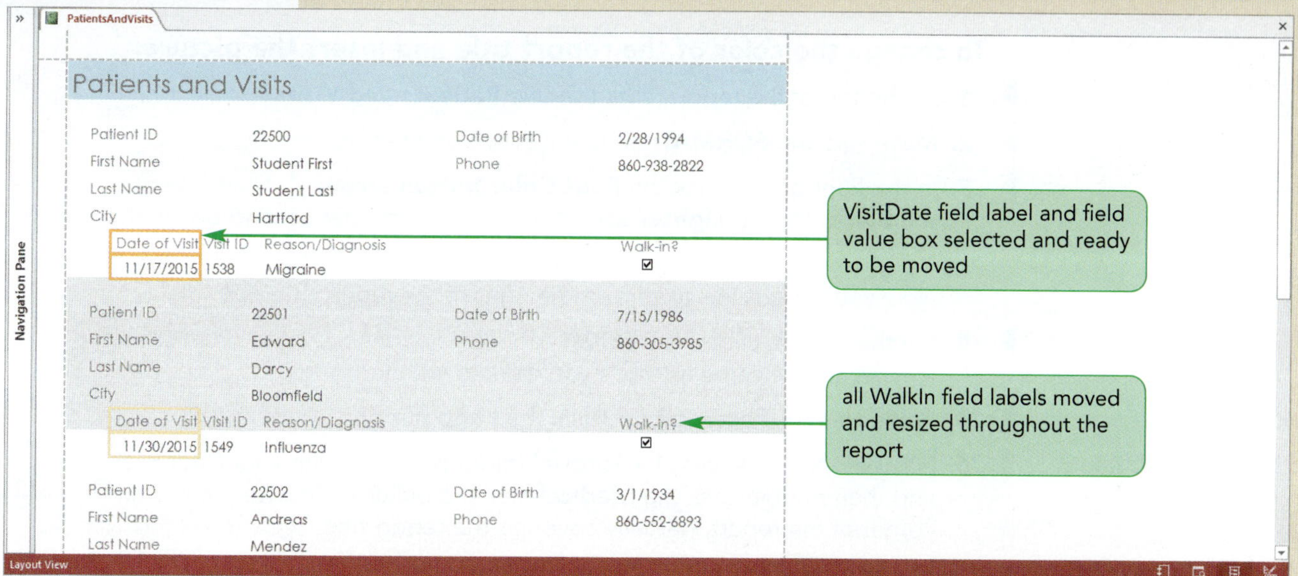

2. Press the ← key four times to move the field label and field value box to the left.

   Trouble? Once you press the left arrow key, the report might jump to display the end of the report. Just continue to press the left arrow key to move the label and value. Then scroll the window back up to display the beginning of the report.

   Ethan is pleased with the changes to the report format, but he is concerned that the larger font size of the theme might have caused other text in the report to be cut off—especially some of the Reason/Diagnosis field values, which are lengthy. You need to check the report for such problems. First, you'll save the design changes you've made.

3. On the Quick Access Toolbar, click the **Save** button to save the modified report.
4. At the top of the report, click to the right of the report title in the shaded area to deselect the VisitDate field label and field value box.
5. Scroll through the report, checking the field labels and field values as you go to make sure all text is fully displayed. When finished, scroll back up to display the top of the report.

Next, Ethan asks you to enhance the report's appearance by inserting the same picture on the PatientsAndVisits report as you included on the PatientData form, and to change the color of the report title to the same darker color used on the form.

Changing the Title Font Color and Inserting a Picture in a Report

You can change the color of text on a report to enhance its appearance. You can also add a picture to a report for visual interest or to identify a particular section of the report. Because Ethan plans to print the report, he asks you to change the report title color to the darker black you applied earlier to the PatientData form and to include the Medical picture to the right of the report title.

To change the color of the report title and insert the picture:

Make sure the title is selected so the picture is inserted in the correct location.

1. At the top of the report, click the title **Patients and Visits** to select it.
2. Make sure the **FORMAT** tab is still active on the ribbon.
3. In the Font group, click the **Font Color button arrow** , and then click the **Black, Text 1, Lighter 25%** color box (fourth row, second box in the Theme Colors palette). The color is applied to the report title.

   Now you'll insert the picture to the right of the report title text.
4. On the ribbon, click the **DESIGN** tab. The options provided on this tab for reports are the same as those you worked with for forms.
5. In the Header/Footer group, click the **Logo** button.
6. Navigate to the **Access1 ▸ Tutorial** folder provided with your Data Files, and then double-click the **Medical** file. The picture is inserted in the top-left corner of the report, partially covering the report title.
7. Position the pointer on the selected picture, and then click and drag it to the right of the report title.
8. Click in a blank area of the shaded bar to deselect the picture. See Figure 4-24.

Figure 4-24 **Report after changing the title font color and inserting the picture**

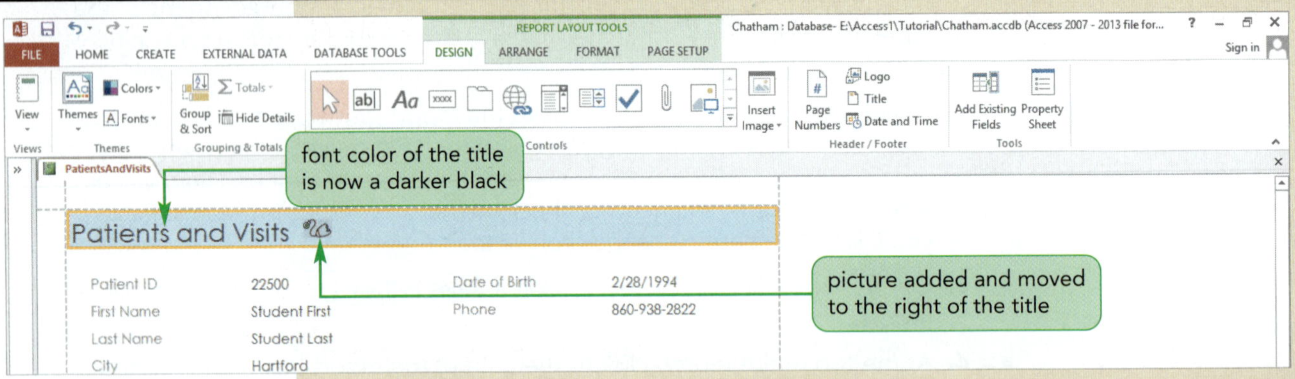

Trouble? Don't be concerned if the picture in your report is not in the exact same location as the one shown in the figure. Just make sure it is to the right of the title text and within the shaded area.

Ethan is pleased with the report's appearance and shows it to Cindi. She also approves of the report's contents and design, but has one final suggestion for the report. She'd like to draw attention to patient records for children and teenagers by formatting their birth dates with a bold, red font. Chatham Community Health Services is planning a special event specifically geared to children and teenagers regarding healthy diets, so this format will make it easier to find these patient records in the report. Because Cindi doesn't want all the birth dates to appear in this font, you need to use conditional formatting.

Using Conditional Formatting in a Report

Conditional formatting in a report (or form) is special formatting applied to certain field values depending on one or more conditions—similar to criteria you establish for queries. If a field value meets the condition or conditions you specify, the formatting is applied to the value.

Cindi would like the PatientsAndVisits report to show any birth date that is greater than 1/1/1997 in a bold, dark red font. This formatting will help to highlight the patient records for children and teenagers. Cindi plans to review this report in a planning meeting for the upcoming special event.

To apply conditional formatting to the BirthDate field in the report:

1. Make sure the report is still displayed in Layout view, and then click the **FORMAT** tab on the ribbon.

   To apply conditional formatting to a field, you must first make it the active field by clicking any field value in the field's column.

TIP

You must select a field *value box*, and not the field *label*, before applying a conditional format.

2. Click the first BirthDate field value, **2/28/1994**, for PatientID 22500. An orange outline appears around the field value box, and a lighter orange outline appears around each BirthDate field value box throughout the entire report. The conditional formatting you specify will affect all the values for the field.
3. In the Control Formatting group on the FORMAT tab, click the **Conditional Formatting** button. The Conditional Formatting Rules Manager dialog box opens. Because you selected a BirthDate field value box, the name of this field is displayed in the "Show formatting rules for" box. Currently, there are no conditional formatting rules set for the selected field. You need to create a new rule.
4. Click the **New Rule** button. The New Formatting Rule dialog box opens. See Figure 4-25.

Figure 4-25 New Formatting Rule dialog box

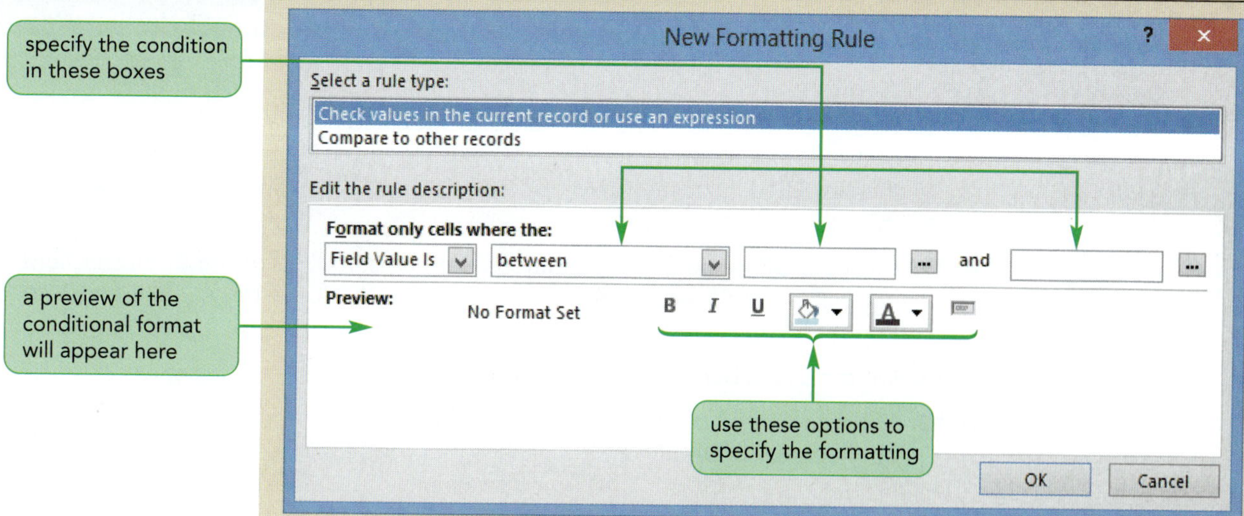

The default setting for "Select a rule type" specifies that Access will check field values and determine if they meet the condition. This is the setting you want. You need to enter the condition in the "Edit the rule description" section of the dialog box. The setting "Field Value Is" means that the conditional format you specify will be applied only when the value for the selected field, BirthDate, meets the condition.

5. Click the **arrow** for the box containing the word "between," and then click **greater than**. Cindi wants only those birth dates greater than 1/1/1997 to be formatted.
6. Click in the next box, and then type **1/1/1997**.
7. In the Preview section, click the **Font color button arrow** and then click the **Dark Red** color box (first color box in the last row of Standard Colors).
8. In the Preview section, click the **Bold** button **B**. The specifications for the conditional formatting are complete. See Figure 4-26.

Figure 4-26 **Conditional formatting set for the BirthDate field**

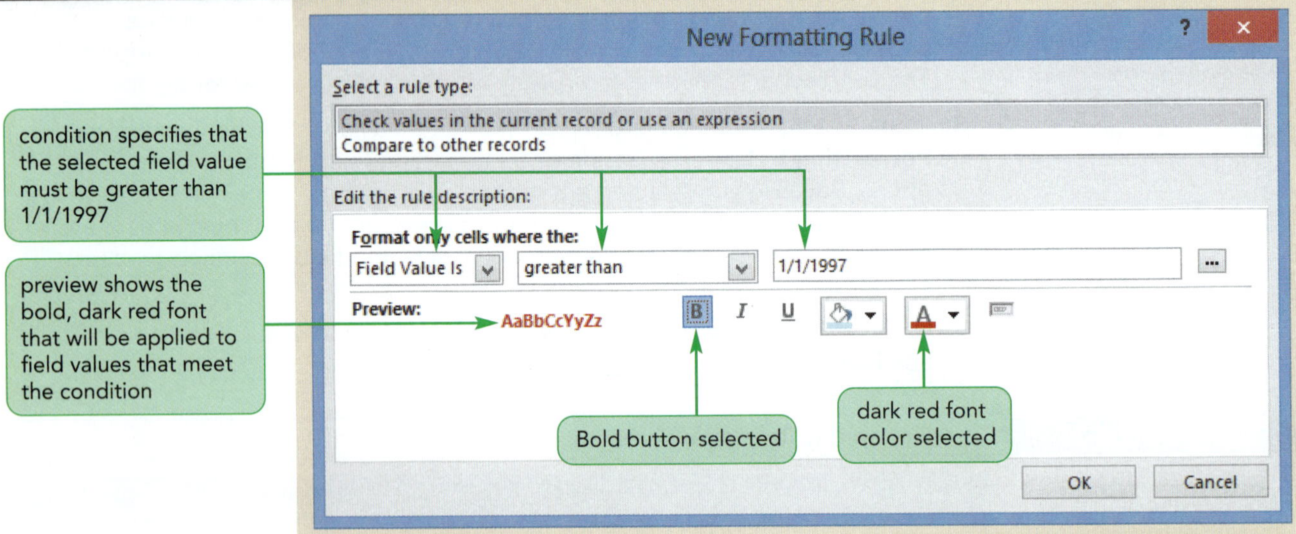

9. Click the **OK** button. The new rule you specified appears in the Rule section of the dialog box as Value > 1/1/1997; the Format section on the right shows the conditional formatting (dark red, bold font) that will be applied based on this rule.
10. Click the **OK** button. The conditional format is applied to the BirthDate field values. To get a better view of the report and the formatting, you'll switch to Print Preview.
11. On the status bar, click the **Print Preview** button.
12. Move to page 2 of the report. Notice that the conditional formatting is applied only to BirthDate field values greater than 1/1/1997. See Figure 4-27.

Figure 4-27 **Viewing the finished report in Print Preview**

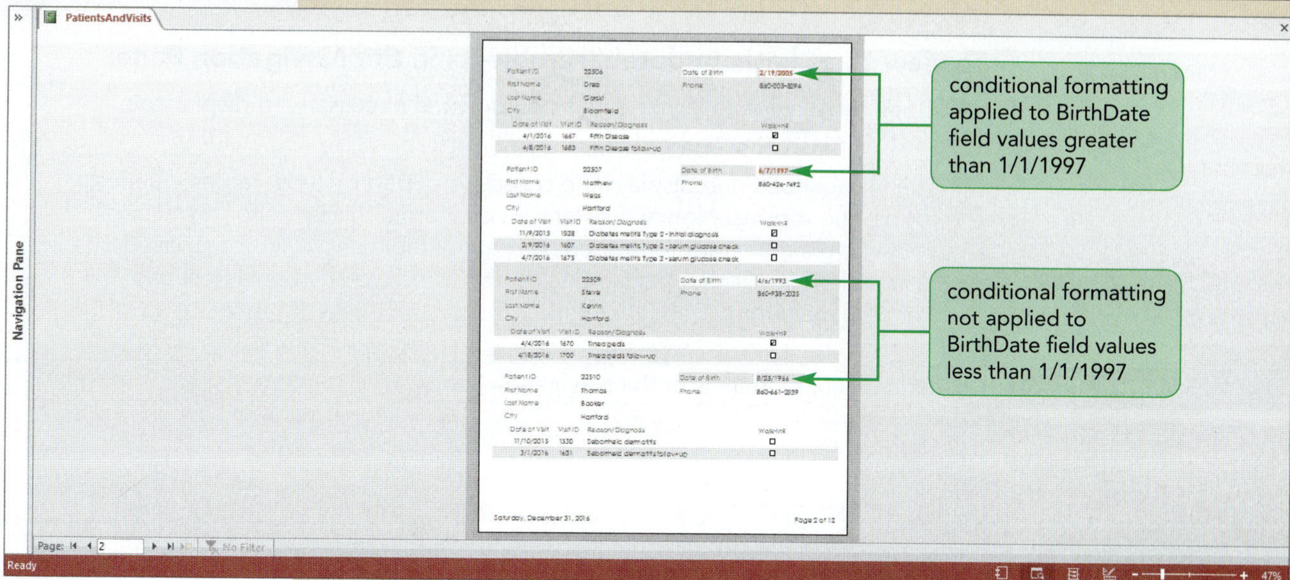

PROSKILLS

Problem Solving: Understanding the Importance of Previewing Reports

When you create a report, it is a good idea to display the report in Print Preview occasionally as you develop it. Doing so will give you a chance to find any formatting problems or other issues so that you can make any necessary corrections before printing the report. It is particularly important to preview a report after you've made changes to its design to ensure that the changes you made have not created new problems with the report's format. Before printing any report, you should preview it so you can determine where the pages will break and make any necessary adjustments. Following this problem-solving approach will not only ensure that the final report looks exactly the way you want it to, but will also save you time and help to avoid wasting paper if you print the report.

The report is now complete. You'll print just the first page of the report so that Cindi and Ethan can view the final results and share the report design with other staff members before printing the entire report. (*Note:* Ask your instructor if you should complete the following printing steps.)

To print page 1 of the report:

1. In the Print group on the PRINT PREVIEW tab, click the **Print** button. The Print dialog box opens.
2. In the Print Range section, click the **Pages** option button. The insertion point now appears in the From box so that you can specify the range of pages to print.
3. Type **1** in the From box, press the **Tab** key to move to the To box, and then type **1**. These settings specify that only page 1 of the report will be printed.
4. Click the **OK** button. The Print dialog box closes, and the first page of the report is printed.
5. Save and close the PatientsAndVisits report.

You've created many different objects in the Chatham database. Before you close it, you'll open the Navigation Pane to view all the objects in the database.

To view the Chatham database objects in the Navigation Pane:

1. Open the Navigation Pane and scroll down, if necessary, to display the bottom of the pane.

   The Navigation Pane displays the objects grouped by type: tables, queries, forms, and reports. Notice the PatientVisits form. This is the form you created containing a main form based on the Patient table and a subform based on the Visit table. The VisitSubform object is also listed; you can open it separately from the main form. See Figure 4-28.

Figure 4-28 Chatham database objects in the Navigation Pane

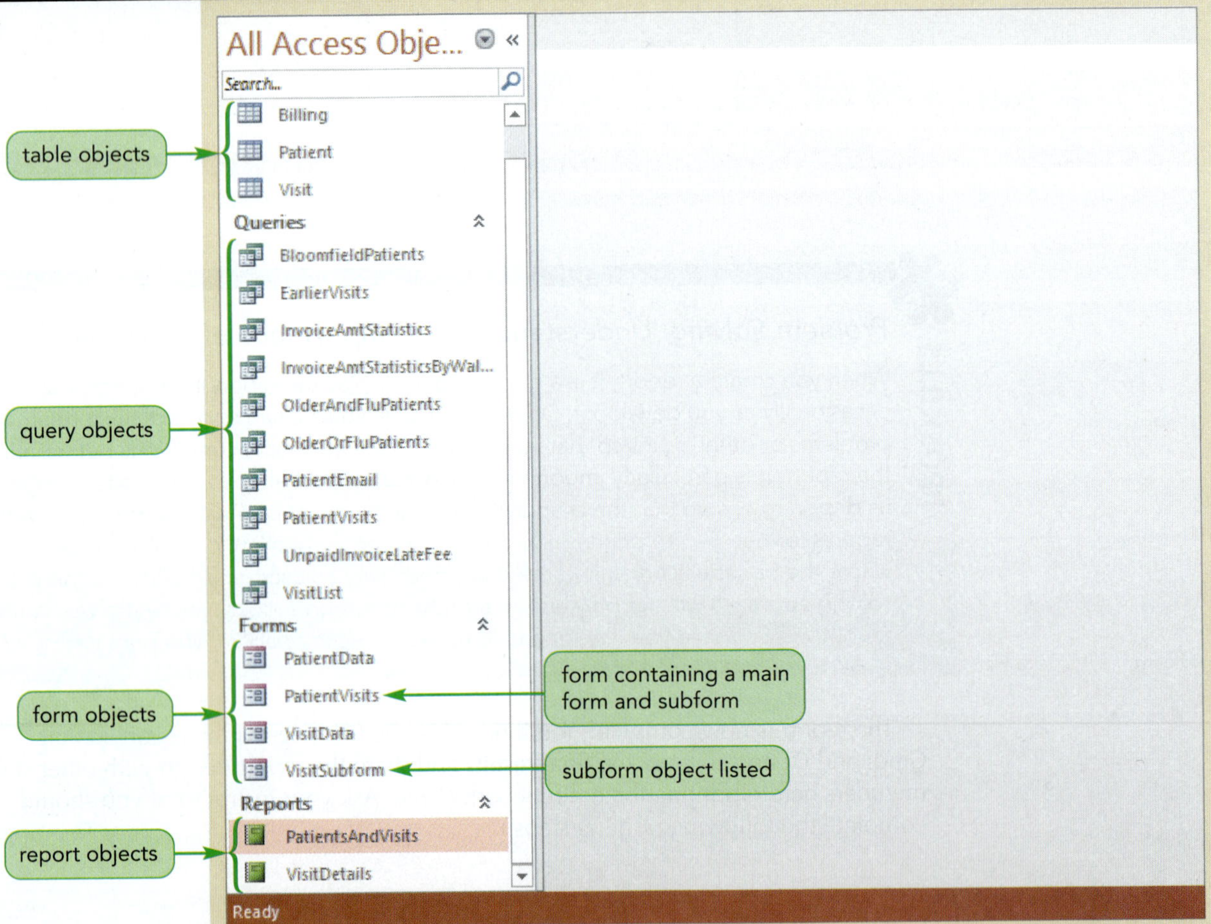

2. Compact and repair the Chatham database, and then close the database.

Cindi is satisfied that the forms you created—the PatientData form and the PatientVisits form—will make it easier to enter, view, and update data in the Chatham database. The PatientsAndVisits report presents important information about the clinic's patients in an attractive and professional format, which will help Ethan and other staff members in their community outreach efforts.

REVIEW

Session 4.2 Quick Check

1. In a(n) ______________ report, the data from a record in the primary table appears together, followed on subsequent lines by the joined records from the related table.
2. When you create a report based on two tables that are joined in a one-to-many relationship, the field values for the records from the related table are called the ______________ records.
3. Identify three types of modifications you can make to a report in Layout view.
4. Describe the process for moving a control to another location on a report in Layout view.
5. When working in Layout view for a report, which key do you press and hold down so that you can click to select multiple controls (field labels, field value boxes, and so on)?
6. ______________ in a report (or form) is special formatting applied to certain field values depending on one or more conditions.

ASSESS

SAM Projects

Put your skills into practice with SAM Projects! SAM Projects for this tutorial can be found online. If you have a SAM account, go to www.cengage.com/sam2013 to download the most recent Project Instructions and Start Files.

PRACTICE

Review Assignments

Data Files needed for the Review Assignments: Vendor.accdb *(cont. from Tutorial 3)* and Supplies.bmp

Cindi asks you to enhance the Vendor database with forms and reports. Complete the following steps:

1. Open the **Vendor** database you created and worked with in Tutorials 1 through 3, and then click the Enable Content button next to the security warning, if necessary.
2. Use the Form Wizard to create a form based on the Product table. Select all fields for the form and the Columnar layout; specify the title **ProductData** for the form.
3. Apply the Facet theme to the ProductData form *only*.
4. Insert the Supplies picture, which is located in the Access1 ▸ Review folder provided with your Data Files, in the ProductData form. Remove the picture from the control layout, and then move the picture to the right of the form title.
5. Drag a bottom corner of the image to increase its size until the items in the picture are all clearly visible. Continue to resize and reposition the image until it is in the location you want, making sure to keep it within the shaded area of the title and to the right of the title.
6. Edit the form title so that it appears as "Product Data" (two words), and change the font color of the form title to the Blue-Gray, Text 2, Darker 25% theme color.
7. Resize the Weight in Lbs field value box so it is the same width (approximately) as the Units/Case field value box above it.
8. Change the alignment of the Price, Units/Case, and Weight in Lbs fields so that their values appear left-aligned in the field value boxes.
9. Save your changes to the form design.
10. Use the ProductData form to update the Product table as follows:
    a. Use the Find command to search for the word "test" anywhere in the ProductName field, and then display the record for the mononucleosis test (ProductID MO269). Change the Price in this record to **49.50**.
    b. Add a new record with the following field values:
       Product ID: **EG400**
       Supplier ID: **SAN481**
       Product Name: **Non-Latex exam gloves**
       Price: **4.75**
       Units/Case: **80**
       Weight in Lbs: **2**
       Temp Controlled?: **no**
       Sterile?: **no**
    c. Save and close the form.
11. Use the Form Wizard to create a form containing a main form and a subform. Select all fields from the Supplier table for the main form, and select ProductID, ProductName, Price, TempControl, and Sterile—in that order—from the Product table for the subform. Use the Datasheet layout. Specify the title **SuppliersAndProducts** for the main form and **ProductSubform** for the subform.

12. Change the form title text to **Suppliers and Products**.
13. Resize the subform to the right, increasing its width by approximately three inches, and then resize all columns in the subform to their best fit, working left to right. Navigate through each record in the main form to make sure all the field values in the subform are completely displayed, resizing subform columns and the subform itself, as necessary. Save and close the SuppliersAndProducts form.
14. Use the Report Wizard to create a report based on the primary Supplier table and the related Product table. Select the SupplierID, Company, City, Category, ContactFirst, ContactLast, and Phone fields—in that order—from the Supplier table, and the ProductID, ProductName, Price, and Units fields from the Product table. Do not specify any additional grouping levels, and sort the detail records in ascending order by ProductID. Choose the Outline layout and Portrait orientation. Specify the title **ProductsBySupplier** for the report.
15. Change the report title text to **Products by Supplier**.
16. Apply the Facet theme to the ProductsBySupplier report *only*.
17. Resize and reposition the following objects in the report in Layout view, and then scroll through the report to make sure all field labels and field values are fully displayed:
    a. Resize the report title so that the text of the title, Products by Supplier, is fully displayed.
    b. Move the ProductName label and field value box to the right a bit (be sure not to move them too far so that the longest product name will still be completely visible).
    c. Resize the Product ID field label on its right side, increasing its width slightly so the label is fully displayed.
    d. Move the Units/Case label and field value box to the right a bit; then resize the label on its left side, increasing its width slightly so the label is fully displayed.
    e. Select the field value boxes *only* (not the field labels) for the following four fields: SupplierID, Company, City, and Category. Then move the four field value boxes to the left until their left edges align (roughly) with the "S" in "Supplier" in the report title.
    f. Resize the Company field value box on its right side, increasing its width slightly so that all company names are fully displayed.
18. Change the color of the report title text to the Blue-Gray, Text 2, Darker 25% theme color.
19. Insert the Supplies picture, which is located in the Access1 ▸ Review folder provided with your Data Files, in the report. Move the picture to the right of the report title. Drag a bottom corner of the image to increase its size until the items in the picture are all clearly visible. Continue to resize and reposition the image until it is in the location you want, making sure to keep it within the shaded area of the title and to the right of the title.
20. Apply conditional formatting so that the Category field values equal to Service appear as dark red and bold.
21. Preview each page of the report, verifying that all the fields fit on the page. If necessary, return to Layout view and make changes so the report prints within the margins of the page and so that all field names and values are completely displayed.
22. Save the report, print its first page (only if asked by your instructor to do so), and then close the report.
23. Compact and repair the Vendor database, and then close it.

APPLY

Case Problem 1

Data Files needed for this Case Problem: Gopher.accdb *(cont. from Tutorial 3)* and Tasks.bmp

GoGopher! Amol Mehta uses the Gopher database to track and view information about the services his company offers. He asks you to create the necessary forms and a report to help him work with this data more efficiently. Complete the following:

1. Open the **Gopher** database you created and worked with in Tutorials 1 through 3, and then click the Enable Content button next to the security warning, if necessary.

2. Use the Form Wizard to create a form based on the Member table. Select all the fields for the form and the Columnar layout. Specify the title **MemberData** for the form.
3. Apply the Wisp theme to the MemberData form *only*.
4. Edit the form title so that it appears as "Member Data" (two words); resize the title so that both words fit on the same line; and then change the font color of the form title to the Dark Red, Accent 1, Darker 25% theme color.
5. Use the Find command to display the record for Marco Krukonis, and then change the Street field value for this record to **75 Woodfield Ave**.
6. Use the MemberData form to add a new record to the Member table with the following field values:

   Member ID: **1261**
   Plan ID: **306**
   First Name: **Taylor**
   Last Name: **Byrne**
   Street: **318 Coolidge Dr**
   City: **Jamestown**
   State: **CO**
   Zip: **80455**
   Phone: **303-751-3152**
   Date Joined: **10/1/2016**
   Expiration Date: **4/1/2017**
7. Save and close the MemberData form.
8. Use the Form Wizard to create a form containing a main form and a subform. Select all the fields from the Plan table for the main form, and select the MemberID, FirstName, LastName, Expiration, and Phone fields from the Member table for the subform. Use the Datasheet layout. Specify the title **MembersByPlan** for the main form and the title **MemberSubform** for the subform.
9. Change the form title text for the main form to **Members by Plan**.
10. Resize all columns in the subform to their best fit, working from left to right; then move through all the records in the main form and check to make sure that all subform field values are fully displayed, resizing the columns as necessary.
11. Save and close the MembersByPlan form.
12. Use the Report Wizard to create a report based on the primary Plan table and the related Member table. Select all the fields from the Plan table, and then select the MemberID, FirstName, LastName, City, Phone, DateJoined, and Expiration fields from the Member table. Do not select any additional grouping levels, and sort the detail records in ascending order by MemberID. Choose the Outline layout and Landscape orientation. Specify the title **MemberPlans** for the report.
13. Apply the Wisp theme to the MemberPlans report *only*.
14. Resize the report title so that the text is fully displayed; edit the report title so that it appears as "Member Plans" (two words); and change the font color of the title to the Dark Red, Accent 1, Darker 25% theme color.
15. Change the alignment of the Plan Cost field so that its values appear left-aligned in the field value boxes.
16. Resize and reposition the following objects in the report in Layout view, and then scroll through the report to make sure all field labels and field values are fully displayed:
    a. Move the FirstName label and field value box to the right a bit (be sure not to move them too far so that the longest first name will still be completely visible).
    b. Resize the MemberID field label on its right side, increasing its width until the label is fully displayed.
    c. Move the Phone label and field value box to the left; then move the DateJoined label and field value box to the left.
    d. Resize the Expiration Date label on its left side, increasing its width until the label is fully displayed.

e. Scroll to the bottom of the report; note that the page number might not be completely within the page border (the dotted vertical line). If necessary, select and move the box containing the text "Page 1 of 1" until the entire text is positioned to the left of the dotted vertical line marking the right page border.

17. Insert the Tasks picture, which is located in the Access1 ▸ Case1 folder provided with your Data Files, in the report. Move the picture to the right of the report title. Drag a bottom corner of the image to increase its size slightly. Continue to resize and reposition the image until it is in the location you want, making sure to keep it within the shaded area of the title and to the right of the title.
18. Apply conditional formatting so that any Expiration field value less than 9/1/2016 appears as bold and with the Red color applied.
19. Preview the entire report to confirm that it is formatted correctly. If necessary, return to Layout view and make changes so that all field labels and field values are completely displayed.
20. Save the report, print its first page (only if asked by your instructor to do so), and then close the report.
21. Compact and repair the Gopher database, and then close it.

CREATE

Case Problem 2

Data Files needed for this Case Problem: OBrien.accdb *(cont. from Tutorial 3)* and Tests.bmp

O'Brien Educational Services Karen O'Brien is using the OBrien database to track and analyze the business activity of her educational consulting company. To make her work easier, you'll create a form and report in the OBrien database. Complete the following:

1. Open the **OBrien** database you created and worked with in Tutorials 1 through 3, and then click the Enable Content button next to the security warning, if necessary.
2. Create the form shown in Figure 4-29.

Figure 4-29 Completed ContractsByTutor form

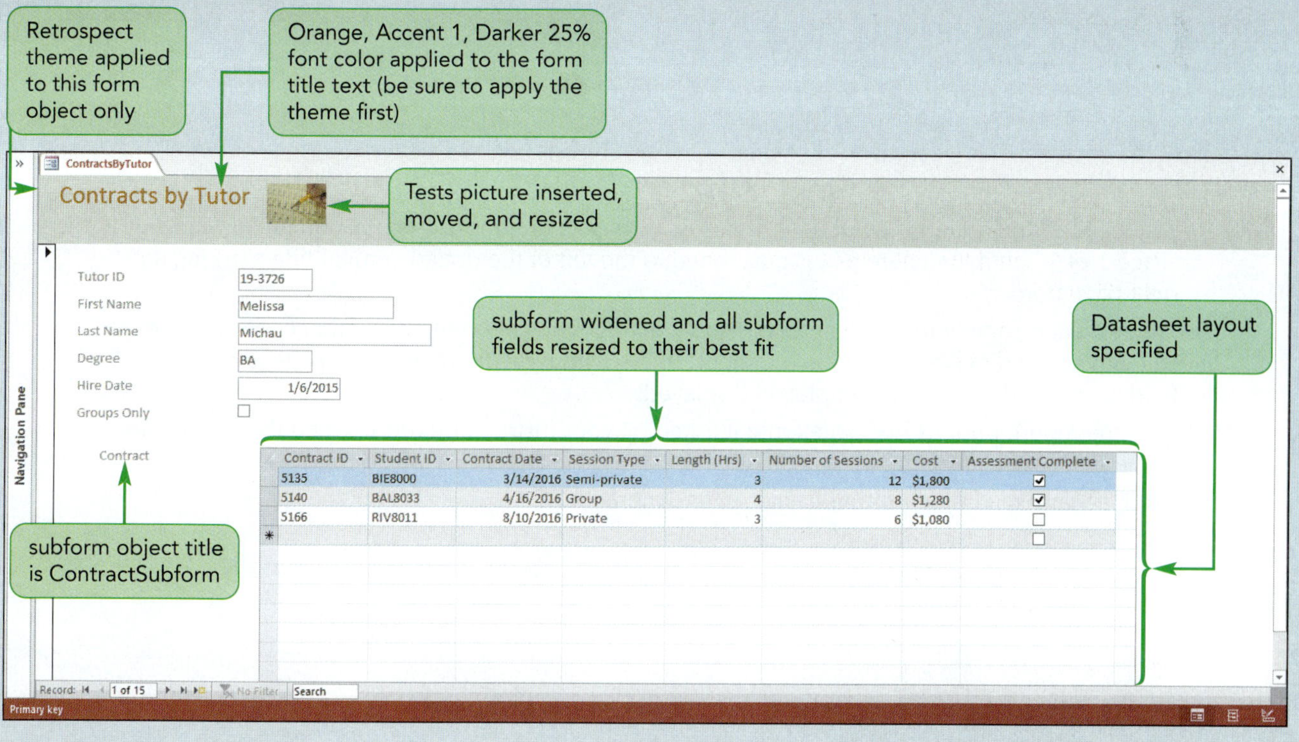

3. Using the form you just created, navigate to the second record in the subform for the third main record, and then change the Assessment Complete field value to **yes**.
4. Use the Find command to move to the record for Samuel Glick, and then change the value in the Groups Only field to **no**.
5. Use the appropriate wildcard character to find all records with a Hire Date field value that begins with the month of March (3). Change the Hire Date field value for Alameda Sarracino (Tutor ID 51-7070) to **3/27/2016**. Save and close the form.
6. Create the report shown in Figure 4-30.

Figure 4-30 Completed TutorsAndContracts report

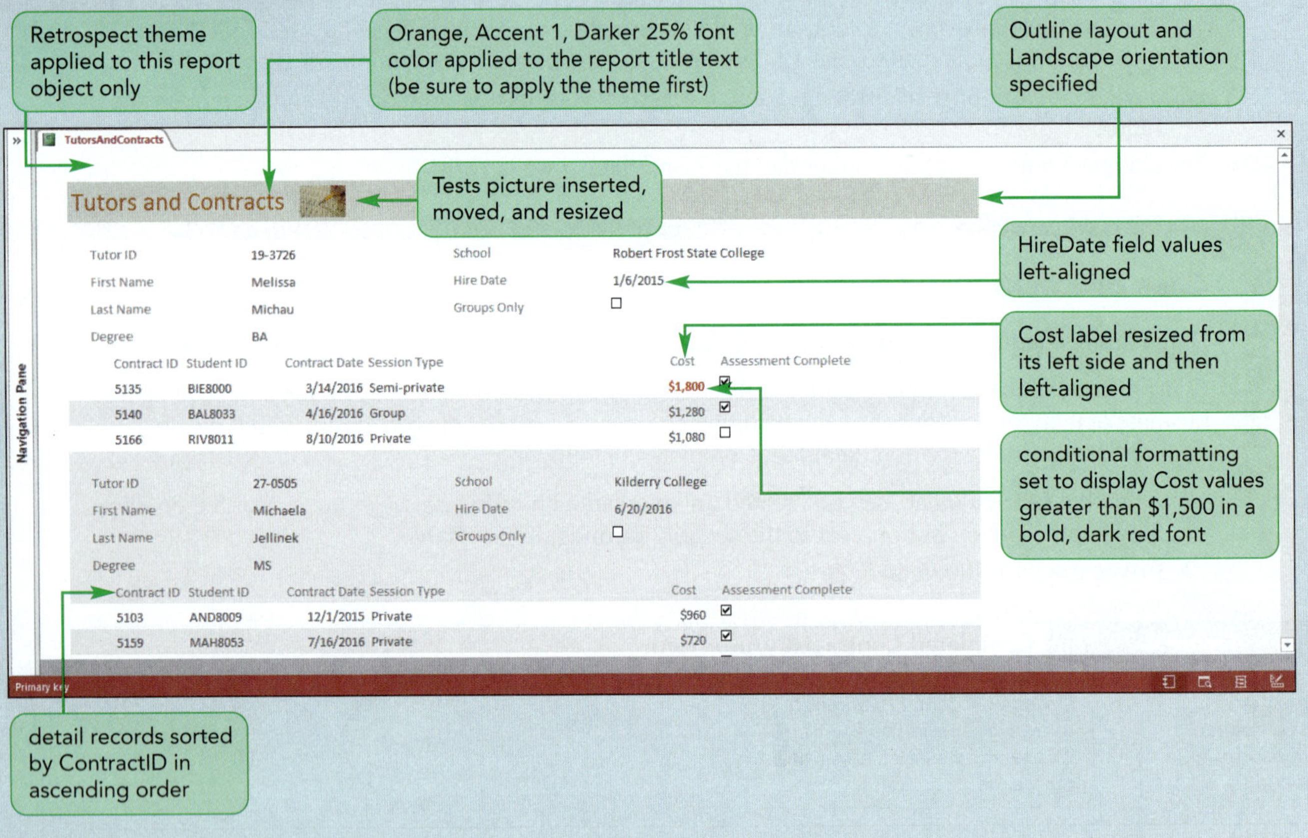

7. Scroll to the bottom of the report; note that the page number might not be completely within the page border (the dotted vertical line). If necessary, select and move the box containing the text "Page 1 of 1" until the entire text is positioned to the left of the dotted vertical line marking the right page border.
8. Preview each page of the report, verifying that all the fields fit on the page. If necessary, return to Layout view and make changes so the report prints within the margins of the page and so that all field names and values are completely displayed.
9. Save the report, print its first page (only if asked by your instructor to do so), and then close the report.
10. Compact and repair the OBrien database, and then close it.

CHALLENGE

Case Problem 3

Data Files needed for this Case Problem: Shelter.accdb *(cont. from Tutorial 3)* and Animals.bmp

Rosemary Animal Shelter Ryan Lang uses the Shelter database to track, maintain, and analyze data about his shelter's patrons, donations, and animals. You'll help Ryan by creating a form and a report based on this data. Complete the following:

1. Open the **Shelter** database you created and worked with in Tutorials 1 through 3, and then click the Enable Content button next to the security warning, if necessary.
2. Use the Form Wizard to create a form based on the Animal table. Select all the fields for the form and the Columnar layout. Specify the title **AnimalInfo** for the form.
3. Apply the Ion theme to the AnimalInfo form *only*.
4. Edit the form title so that it appears as "Animal Info" (two words), and change the font color of the form title to the Green, Accent 4, Darker 25% theme color.

Explore 5. Use the appropriate button in the Font group on the FORMAT tab to underline the form title. Save the form.

6. Use the AnimalInfo form to update the Animal table as follows:
   a. Use the Find command to search for records that contain "beagle" anywhere in the Description field. Display the record for the dog named Gus (AnimalID R98), and then change the Age field value for this record to **3**.
   b. Add a new record with the following values:

      Animal ID: **T80**

      Patron ID: [leave blank]

      Animal Name: **Tessie**

      Age at Arrival: **1**

      Gender: **Female**

      Animal Type: **Dog**

      Description: **Terrier mix**

      Arrival Date: **4/9/16**

      Adopted: **no**

      Adoption Date: [leave blank]

   Explore c. Find the record with AnimalID S35 (for Roggie), and then delete the record. (*Hint:* After displaying the record in the form, you need to select it by clicking the right-pointing triangle in the bar to the left of the field labels. Then use the appropriate button in the Records group on the HOME tab to delete the record. When asked to confirm the deletion, click the Yes button.) Close the form.
7. Use the Form Wizard to create a form containing a main form and a subform. Select all the fields from the Patron table for the main form, and select all fields except PatronID from the Donation table for the subform. Use the Datasheet layout. Specify the name **PatronsAndDonations** for the main form and the title **DonationSubform** for the subform.
8. Apply the Ion theme to the PatronsAndDonations form *only*.
9. Edit the form title so that it appears as "Patrons and Donations." Resize the form title so that the text fits on one line. Change the font color of the title to the Green, Accent 4, Darker 25% theme color.
10. Insert the Animals picture, which is located in the Access1 ▸ Case3 folder provided with your Data Files, in the PatronsAndDonations form. Remove the picture from the control layout, and then move the picture to the right of the form title. Resize the picture so it is approximately double the original size.

Explore 11. Use the appropriate button in the Font group on the FORMAT tab to apply the theme color Green, Accent 4, Lighter 80% as a background color for all the field value boxes in the main form. Then use the appropriate button in the Control Formatting group to change the outline of all the main form field value boxes to have a line thickness of 1 pt. (*Hint:* Select all the field value boxes before making these changes.)

12. Resize the subform to the right, and then resize all columns in the subform to their best fit. Navigate through the records in the main form to make sure all the field values in the subform are completely displayed, resizing subform columns as necessary. Save and close the form.
13. Use the Report Wizard to create a report based on the primary Patron table and the related Donation table. Select all the fields from the Patron table, and select all fields except PatronID from the Donation table. Sort the detail records in *descending* order by DonationValue. Choose the Outline layout and Portrait orientation. Specify the name **PatronsAndDonations** for the report.
14. Apply the Ion theme to the PatronsAndDonations report *only*.
15. Resize the report title so that the text is fully displayed; edit the report title so that it appears as "Patrons and Donations"; and change the font color of the title to the Green, Accent 4, Darker 25% theme color.
16. Move the Donation Value field label and its field value box to the left a bit. Then resize the Donation ID field label on the right to fully display the label. Move the Description field label and its field value box to the right a bit, to provide more space between the Donation Date and Description fields. Finally, resize the Phone field label from its left side to reduce the width of the label box, moving the word "Phone" closer to the phone numbers. Save the report.
17. Insert the Animals picture, which is located in the Access1 ▸ Case3 folder provided with your Data Files, in the PatronsAndDonations report. Move the picture to the right of the report title. Resize the picture so it is approximately double the original size.

Explore 18. Use the appropriate button in the Background group on the FORMAT tab to apply the theme color Green, Accent 4, Lighter 60% as the alternate row color for the fields from the Patron table; then apply the theme color Green, Accent 4, Lighter 80% as the alternate row color for the fields from the Donation table. (*Hint:* You must first select an entire row with no background color for the appropriate fields before applying each alternate row color.) Scroll through the report to find a patron record with multiple donations so you can verify the effect of applying the alternate row color to the Donation fields.

19. Apply conditional formatting so that any DonationValue greater than or equal to 250 is formatted as bold and with the Brown font color.

Explore 20. Preview the report so you can see two pages at once. (*Hint:* Use a button on the PRINT PREVIEW tab.) Check the report to confirm that it is formatted correctly and all field labels and field values are fully displayed. Save the report, print its first page (only if asked by your instructor to do so), and then close the report.

21. Compact and repair the Shelter database, and then close it.

TROUBLESHOOT

Case Problem 4

Data Files needed for this Case Problem: Stanley.accdb *(cont. from Tutorial 3)*, Hiking.bmp, and Tour.accdb

Stanley EcoTours Janice and Bill Stanley use the Stanley database to maintain and analyze data about the clients, reservations, and tours for their ecotourism business. You'll help them by creating a form and a report in the Stanley database. Additionally, you'll troubleshoot some problems in another database containing tour information. Complete the following:

1. Open the **Stanley** database you created and worked with in Tutorials 1 through 3, and then click the Enable Content button next to the security warning, if necessary.
2. Use the Form Wizard to create a form containing a main form and a subform. Select all the fields from the Guest table for the main form, and select all the fields except GuestID from the Reservation table for the subform. Use the Datasheet layout. Specify the title **GuestReservations** for the main form and the title **ReservationSubform** for the subform.
3. Apply the Organic theme to the GuestReservations form *only*.

4. Edit the form title so that it appears with a space between the two words. Change the font color of the title to the Blue-Gray, Accent 3, Darker 25% theme color.
5. Insert the Hiking picture, which is located in the Access1 ▸ Case4 folder provided with your Data Files, in the GuestReservations form. Remove the picture from the control layout, and then move the picture to the right of the form title. Resize the picture so it is approximately double the original size.
6. Resize all columns in the subform to their best fit so that the subform column titles are fully displayed. Save the form.
7. Use the Find command to search for records that contain "AB" in the State/Prov field. Display the record for Isabelle Rouy (GuestID 417), and then change the Address field value for this record to **15 Brookside Dr**. Close the form.
8. Use the Report Wizard to create a report based on the primary Guest table and the related Reservation table. Select all the fields from the Guest table, and then select all the fields except GuestID from the Reservation table. Do not select any additional grouping levels, and sort the detail records in ascending order by ReservationID. Choose the Outline layout and Portrait orientation. Specify the title **GuestsAndReservations** for the report.
9. Apply the Organic theme to the GuestsAndReservations report *only*.
10. Edit the report title so that it appears as "Guests and Reservations"; then change the font color of the title to the Blue-Gray, Accent 3, Darker 25% theme color.
11. Move the Phone field label to the left, and then resize it from its right side to make the label box smaller. Then move the Phone field value box to the left, and then resize it on its right side to make the box bigger and fully display the field value.
12. Insert the Hiking picture, which is located in the Access1 ▸ Case4 folder provided with your Data Files, in the GuestsAndReservations report. Move the picture to the right of the report title. Resize the picture so it is approximately double the original size.
13. Apply conditional formatting so that any People field value greater than or equal to 5 appears as bold and with the Red color applied.
14. Preview the entire report to confirm that it is formatted correctly. If necessary, return to Layout view and make changes so that all field labels and field values are completely displayed.
15. Save the report, print its first page (only if asked by your instructor to do so), and then close the report.
16. Compact and repair the Stanley database, and then close it.

Troubleshoot 17. Open the Tour database located in the Access1 ▸ Case4 folder provided with your Data Files. Open the CustomerData form in the Tour database. The form is not formatted correctly; it should be formatted with the Ion Boardroom theme and the theme color Plum, Accent 1, Darker 25% applied to the title. There are other problems with the form title's format as well. Additionally, some of the field labels are not properly formatted with regard to spacing between words. Identify and fix the problems with the form's format. (*Hint:* To fix the spacing between words in the necessary field labels, use the same procedure you use to fix the spacing between words in the form title text.) Save and close the corrected form.

Troubleshoot 18. Open the CustomerBookings form, which is also not formatted correctly. Modify the form so that it matches the corrected format of the CustomerData form and has a consistent design, including the correctly placed image (Hiking.bmp). Fix the formatting problems with the subform as well, and then save and close the corrected form with subform.

Troubleshoot 19. Open the CustomersAndBookings report. This report should have a consistent format in terms of theme, color, and so on as the two forms. Additionally, some of the field labels are not properly formatted with regard to spacing between words. (*Hint:* To fix the spacing between words in the necessary field labels, use the same procedure you use to fix the spacing between words in the report title text.) Find and fix these formatting errors. The report also has several problems with field labels and field value boxes, where the labels and values are not fully displayed. Locate and correct all of these problems, being sure to scroll through the entire report. Also, the conditional formatting applied to the People field is supposed to use a bold Red font. Edit the rule to correct the conditional formatting. Save the corrected report, and then preview it to identify and correct any remaining formatting problems. Compact and repair the Tour database, and then close it.

ProSkills

Teamwork

Working with a Team to Create a Database

Teamwork is the collaborative effort of individuals working together to achieve a goal. Most organizations rely on teams to complete work tasks, regardless of whether those teams are formal and ongoing or informally organized to achieve a specific goal. Some teams might even be virtual, such as teams that use telecommunications technologies and social networks to complete tasks from different corporate or geographical locations.

When an organization decides to use a database to manage information, the database is rarely planned, created, and maintained by a single individual. In most cases, a team of individuals is assigned to work on different stages of database development. For example, a team might research the needs of the organization, the best database management system to use to meet those needs, and the skills required of the team members to create, update, and maintain the database. Then another team might take over the task of actually creating the database and its objects, inputting the data, and installing the database on the organization's network. Finally, yet another team might conduct training sessions to teach users how to use the database to extract the data they require to perform their jobs.

Regardless of the type of database being created, the roles that individual team members play when working on a team are similar to what you might expect in any situation that requires a collaborative effort.

The Roles of Team Members

If a team is to be successful, individual members must see the value in their respective contributions and what the team as a whole gets out of each member's contribution. This means two important requirements must be met: task performance and social satisfaction. Task performance usually is handled by one or more members who are task specialists. Task specialists spend a lot of time and effort ensuring that the team achieves its goals. They initiate ideas, give opinions, gather information, sort details, and provide motivation to keep the team on track.

Social satisfaction is handled by individuals who strengthen the team's social bonds through encouragement, empathy, conflict resolution, compromise, and tension reduction. Have you ever been on a team where the tension was high, and someone stepped in to tell a joke or tried to soften the blow of criticism? That person held the role of managing social satisfaction.

Both the task specialist and social satisfaction specialist are important roles on teams. These are not the only roles, however. Other roles include team leaders, work coordinators, idea people, and critics. The roles of individual team members are not always mutually exclusive. For example, the task specialist might also be the team leader, and the idea person might also fill the social satisfaction role. As you begin working with your team in this exercise, watch how these roles are filled and how they change as your team completes its work. Perhaps you'll want to discuss upfront which role each member is comfortable filling to see how complementary your collective skill sets turn out to be. What if your team lacks a role? Then you'll need to figure out, as a team, how to move forward so you can complete your work successfully. The following are tips that everyone should respect as work on a team begins:

- Remember that everyone brings something of value to the team.
- Respect and support each other as you work toward the common goal.
- When criticism or questions arise, try to see things from the other person's perspective.
- If someone needs assistance, find ways to encourage or support that person so the team is not affected.
- Deal with negative or unproductive attitudes immediately so they don't damage team energy and attitude.
- Get outside help if the team becomes stuck and can't move forward.
- Provide periodic positive encouragement or rewards for contributions.

The Importance of Technology in Teamwork

Many teams now depend on technology to accomplish work tasks. For example, corporate intranets and networks, email and voice mail, texting and instant messaging, teleconferencing and software collaboration tools, social networks, and cell phones can support teamwork. Each time you work in a group, decide at the outset how the team will use different technologies to communicate and document work activities. Determine how the team will organize and combine deliverable documents or presentation materials. Use whatever technology tools make the most sense for your team, your task, and your skills.

PROSKILLS

Create a Database

Many organizations use Access to manage business data, but Access can also be a valuable tool to track personal data. For example, you might create an Access database to store information about items in a personal collection, such as CDs, DVDs, or books; items related to a hobby, such as coin or stamp collecting, travel, or family history; or items related to sports teams, theater clubs, or other organizations to which you might belong. In this exercise, you'll work with your team members to create a database that will contain information of your choice, using the Access skills and features presented in Tutorials 1 through 4. As a group, you'll choose something the team is interested in tracking, such as members and activities of a college service organization or recruiters and job opportunities at your school.

Using Templates

Access includes templates for creating databases. A **database template** is a database containing predefined tables, queries, forms, and reports. Using a database template can save you time and effort when creating a database. For example, if the database objects available in one of the database templates are suitable for the data you want to store, you can use the template to quickly create a database with the objects already created for you. You can then modify them, as necessary, to suit your needs. Before you begin to create a database with your team members, review the following steps for using a database template.

To create a database using a database template:

1. Make sure the New screen is displayed in Backstage view.
2. Click one of the available Desktop templates, or use the box at the top of the screen to search for templates online. (Note that templates without the word "Desktop" in their names require Sharepoint, so do not choose one of those.)
3. Specify the name for your database and a location in which to save the database file.
4. Click the Create button.
5. Use the resulting database objects to enter, modify, or delete data or database objects.

Work in a Team to Create a Database

Working with your team members, you can decide to use a database template for this exercise if the template fits the data you want to track. Note, however, that you still need to create the additional database objects indicated in the following steps—tables, queries, forms, and reports—to complete the exercise successfully.

Note: Please be sure *not* to include any personal information of a sensitive nature in the database you create to be submitted to your instructor for this exercise. Later on, you can update the data in your database with such information for your own personal use.

1. Meet with your team to determine what data you want to track in your new Access database. Determine how many tables you need and what data will go into each table. Be sure that the data you choose to track lends itself to at least three groupings of related data, that at least twenty items are available to track within each group, and that you'll be able to track multiple types of data. Sketch the layout of the columns (fields) and rows (records) for each table.

Also discuss the field properties for each field, so that team members can document the characteristics needed for each field as they collect data. Consider using a standard form to help each person as he or she collects the necessary data.

Next, assign data gathering and documentation tasks to each team member and set a deadline for finishing this initial task. Consider using Excel workbooks for this task, as you can use them to import the data later when working in Access. When all the data for the fields is collected, meet again as a team to examine the data collected and determine the structure of the database you will create. Finally, assign each team member specific tasks for creating the database objects discussed in the following steps.

2. Create a new Access database to contain the data your team wants to track.
3. Create two or three tables in the database that can be joined through one-to-many relationships.
4. Using the preliminary design work done by team members, define the properties for each field in each table. Make sure to include a mix of data types for the fields (for example, do not include only Short Text fields in each table).
5. As a team, discuss and specify a primary key for each table.
6. Define the necessary one-to-many relationships between the tables in the database with referential integrity enforced.
7. Enter 20 to 30 records in each table. If appropriate, your team can import the data for a table from another source, such as an Excel workbook or a text file.
8. Create 5 to 10 queries based on single tables and multiple tables. Be sure that some of the queries include some or all of the following: exact match conditions, comparison operators, and logical operators.
9. For some of the queries, use various sorting and filtering techniques to display the query results in various ways. Save these queries with the sort and/or filter applied.
10. If possible, and depending on the data your team is tracking, create at least one calculated field in one of the queries.
11. If possible, and depending on the data your team is tracking, use aggregate functions to produce summary statistics based on the data in at least one of the tables.
12. Create at least one form for each table in the database. Enhance each form's appearance with pictures, themes, title colors, and so on.
13. Create at least one form with a main form and subform based on related tables in the database. Enhance the form's appearance as appropriate.
14. Create at least one report based on each table in the database. Enhance each report's appearance with pictures, themes, color, and so on.
15. Apply conditional formatting to the values in at least one of the reports.
16. Submit your team's completed database to your instructor as requested. Include printouts of any database objects, such as reports, if required. Also, provide written documentation that describes the role of each team member and his or her contributions to the team. This documentation should include descriptions of any challenges the team faced while completing this exercise and how the team members worked together to overcome those challenges.

TUTORIAL 5

Creating Advanced Queries and Enhancing Table Design

Making the Clinic Database Easier to Use

OBJECTIVES

Session 5.1
- Review object naming standards
- Use the Like, In, Not, and & operators in queries
- Filter data using an AutoFilter
- Use the IIf function to assign a conditional value to a calculated field in a query
- Create a parameter query

Session 5.2
- Use query wizards to create a crosstab query, a find duplicates query, and a find unmatched query
- Create a top values query

Session 5.3
- Modify table designs using lookup fields, input masks, and data validation rules
- Identify object dependencies
- Review a Long Text field's properties
- Designate a trusted folder

Case | *Chatham Community Health Services*

Chatham Community Health Services is a nonprofit health clinic located in Hartford, Connecticut. It provides a range of medical services to patients of all ages. The clinic specializes in the areas of pulmonology, cardiac care, and chronic disease management. Cindi Rodriguez, the office manager for Chatham Community Health Services, oversees a small staff and is responsible for maintaining the medical records of the clinic's patients.

Cindi and her staff rely on Microsoft Access 2013 to manage electronic medical records for patient information, billing, inventory control, purchasing, and accounts payable. The Chatham staff developed the Clinic database, which contains tables, queries, forms, and reports that Cindi and other staff members use to track patient, visit, and billing information.

Cindi is interested in taking better advantage of the power of Access to make the database easier to use and to create more sophisticated queries. For example, Cindi wants to obtain lists of patients in certain cities. She also needs a summarized list of invoice amounts by city. In this tutorial, you'll modify and customize the Clinic database to satisfy these and other requirements.

STARTING DATA FILES

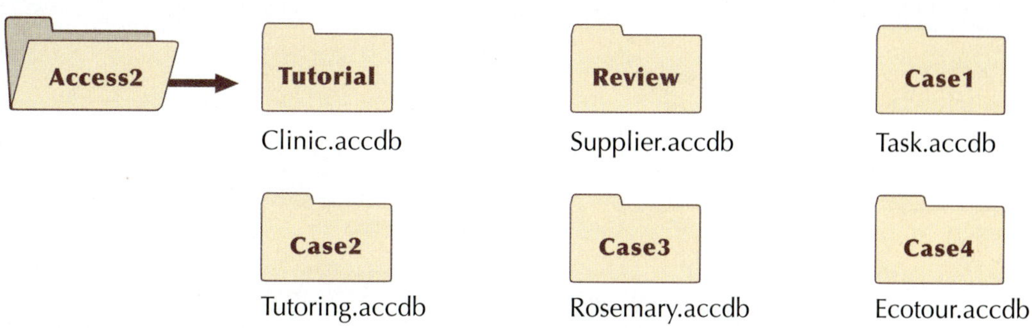

Session 5.1 Visual Overview:

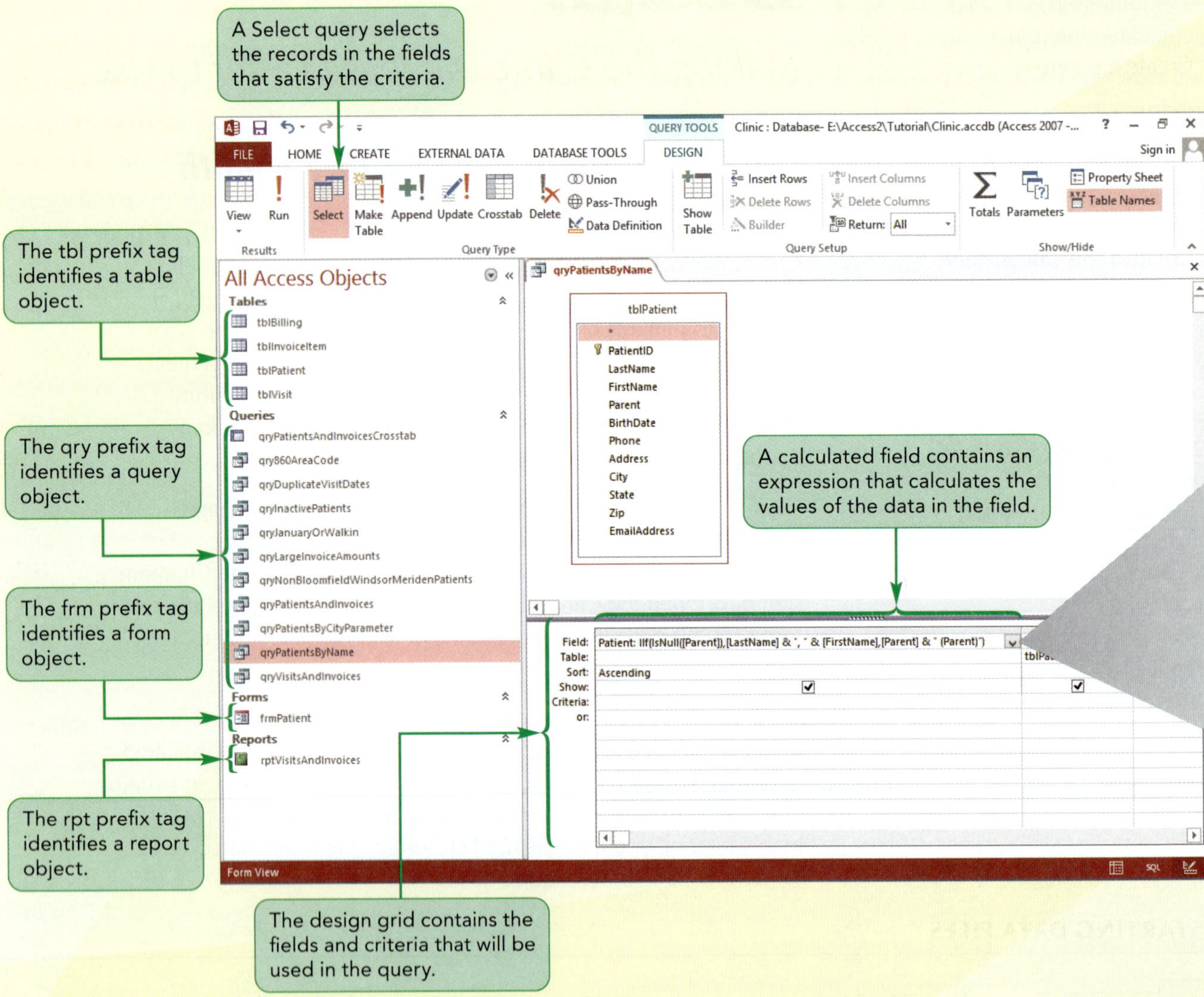

Calculated Field

The name of the new calculated field is placed to the left of the expression, separated with a colon.

The **IIf function** tests a condition and returns one of two values. The function returns the first value if the condition is true, and the second value if the condition is false.

The Expression Builder can be used to create an expression for a calculated field.

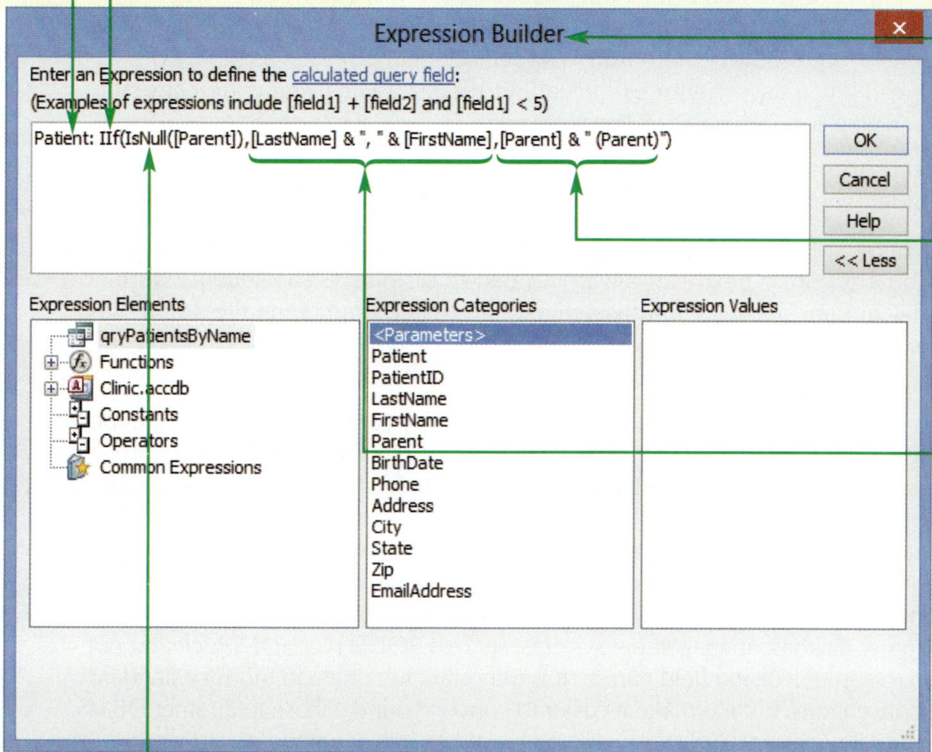

The falsepart of this IIf function will concatenate the data in the Parent field to the string "(Parent)".

The truepart of this IIf function will concatenate the data in the LastName field to a string with a comma and space. It will then concatenate the result to the data in the FirstName field.

The **IsNull function** will return a value of true if the field is empty and will return a value of false if the field is not empty.

Reviewing the Clinic Database

TIP

Read the Microsoft Access Naming Conventions section in the appendix titled "Relational Databases and Database Design" for more information about naming conventions.

Cindi and her staff had no previous database experience when they created the Clinic database; they simply used the wizards and other easy-to-use Access tools. As business continued to grow at Chatham Community Health Services, Cindi realized she needed a database expert to further enhance the Clinic database. She hired Raj Gupta, who has a business information systems degree and nine years of experience developing database systems. Raj spent a few days reviewing the Clinic database, making sure the database adhered to simple naming standards for the objects and field names to make his future work easier.

Before implementing the enhancements for Cindi, you'll review the naming conventions for the object names in the Clinic database.

To review the object naming conventions in the Clinic database:

1. Make sure you have the Access starting Data Files on your computer.

   Trouble? If you don't have the Access Data Files, you need to get them before you can proceed. Your instructor will either give you the Data Files or ask you to obtain them from a specified location (such as a network drive). If you have any questions about the Data Files, see your instructor or technical support person for assistance.

2. Start Access, and then open the **Clinic** database from the Access2 ▸ Tutorial folder where your starting Data Files are stored.

   Trouble? If a security warning is displayed below the ribbon, click the Enable Content button next to the warning text to dismiss it. The security warning may appear because there is active content (a query) in the file and it may not be in a trusted folder.

As shown in Visual Overview 5.1, the Navigation Pane displays the objects grouped by object type. Each object name has a prefix tag—a tbl prefix tag for tables, a qry prefix tag for queries, a frm prefix tag for forms, and a rpt prefix tag for reports. All three characters in each prefix tag are lower case. The word immediately after the three-character prefix begins with an upper case letter. Using object prefix tags, you can readily identify the object type, even when the objects have the same base name—for instance, tblPatient, frmPatient, and rptCustomersAndBilling. In addition, object names have no spaces, because other database management systems, such as SQL Server and Oracle, do not permit spaces in object and field names. It is important to adhere to industry standard naming conventions, both to make it easier to convert your database to another DBMS in the future, if necessary, and to develop personal habits that enable you to work seamlessly with other major DBMSs. If Chatham Community Health Services needs to upscale to one of these other systems in the future, using standard naming conventions means that Raj will have to do less work to make the transition.

PROSKILLS

Teamwork: Following Naming Conventions

Most Access databases have hundreds of fields, objects, and controls. You'll find it easier to identify the type and purpose of these database items when you use a naming convention or standard. Most companies adopt a standard naming convention, such as the one used for the Clinic database, so that multiple people can develop a database, troubleshoot database problems, and enhance and improve existing databases. When working on a database, a team's tasks are difficult, if not impossible, to perform if a standard naming convention isn't used. In addition, most databases and database samples on Web sites and in training books use standard naming conventions that are similar to the ones used for the Clinic database. By following the standard naming convention established by your company or organization, you'll help to ensure smooth collaboration among all team members.

Now you'll create the queries that Cindi needs.

Using a Pattern Match in a Query

You are already familiar with queries that use an exact match or a range of values (for example, queries that use the > or < comparison operators) to select records. Access provides many other operators for creating select queries. These operators let you build more complicated queries that are difficult or impossible to create with exact-match or range-of-values selection criteria.

Cindi created a list of questions she wants to answer using the Clinic database:

- Which patients have the 860 area code?
- What is the patient information for patients located in Bloomfield, Windsor, or Meriden?
- What is the patient information for all patients except those located in Bloomfield, Windsor, or Meriden?
- What is the patient and visit information for patients in Hartford or West Hartford who have invoice amounts for less than $100 or who visited during the winter?
- What are the first and last names of Chatham Community Health Services' patients, or the parent name if it is listed? Children should not be contacted directly.
- What is the patient information for patients in a particular city? This query needs to be flexible to allow the user to specify the city.

Next, you will create the queries necessary to answer these questions. Cindi wants to view the records for all patients located in the 860 area code. These patients are located nearby and Cindi would like to start planning to arrange transportation for any of these patients who have difficulty travelling to the clinic. To answer Cindi's question, you can create a query that uses a pattern match. A **pattern match** selects records with a value for the designated field that matches the pattern of a simple condition value—in this case, patients with the 860 area code. You do this using the Like comparison operator.

The **Like comparison operator** selects records by matching field values to a specific pattern that includes one or more of these wildcard characters: asterisk (*), question mark (?), and number symbol (#). The asterisk represents any string of characters, the question mark represents any single character, and the number symbol represents any single digit. Using a pattern match is similar to using an exact match, except that a pattern match includes wildcard characters.

To create the new query, you must first place the tblPatient table field list in the Query window in Design view.

To create the new query in Design view:

1. If necessary, click the **Shutter Bar Open/Close Button** « at the top of the Navigation Pane to close it.
2. On the ribbon, click the **CREATE** tab.
3. In the Queries group, click the **Query Design** button. Access opens the Show Table dialog box in front of the Query window in Design view.
4. Click **tblPatient** in the Tables box, click the **Add** button, and then click the **Close** button. Access places the tblPatient table field list in the Query window and closes the Show Table dialog box.
5. Drag the bottom border of the tblPatient window down until you can see the full list of fields.
6. Double-click the **title bar** of the tblPatient field list to highlight all the fields, and then drag the highlighted fields to the first column's Field box in the design grid. Access places each field in a separate column in the design grid, in the same order that the fields appear in the table. See Figure 5-1.

TIP

You can also double-click a table name to add the table's field list to the Query window.

Figure 5-1 Adding the fields for the pattern match query

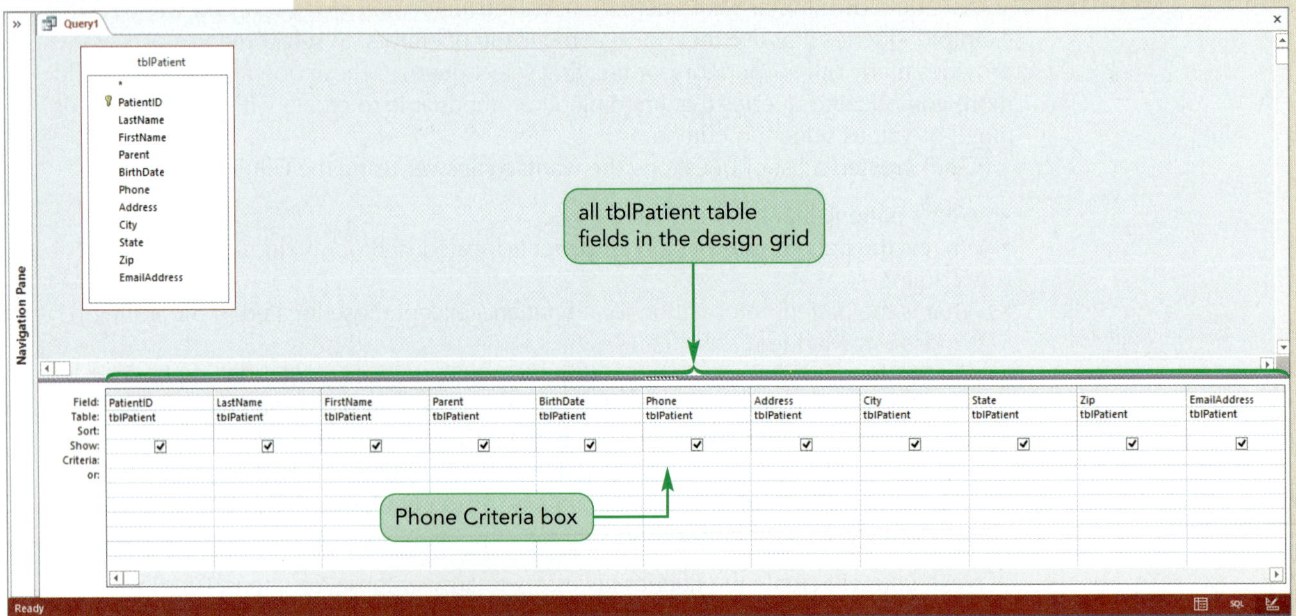

Trouble? If tblPatient.* appears in the first column's Field box, you dragged the * from the field list instead of the highlighted fields. Press the Delete key, and then repeat Step 6.

Now you will enter the pattern match condition Like "860*" for the Phone field. Access will select records with a Phone field value of 860 in positions one through three. The asterisk wildcard character specifies that any characters can appear in the remaining positions of the field value.

TIP

If you omit the Like operator, Access automatically adds it when you run the query.

To specify records that match the indicated pattern:

1. Click the **Phone Criteria** box, and then type **L**. The Formula AutoComplete menu displays a list of functions beginning with the letter L, but the Like operator is not one of the choices in the list. You'll finish typing the condition.
2. Type **ike "860*"**. See Figure 5-2.

Figure 5-2 Record selection based on matching a specific pattern

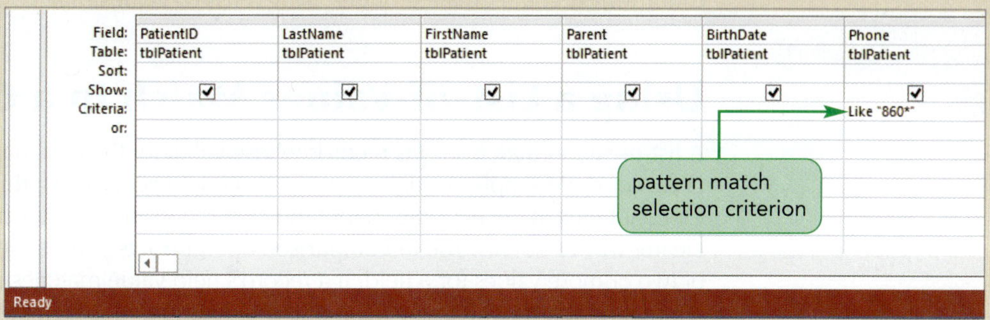

3. Click the **Save** button on the Quick Access Toolbar to open the Save As dialog box.
4. Type **qry860AreaCode** in the Query Name box, and then press the **Enter** key. Access saves the query and displays the name on the object tab.
5. On the DESIGN tab, in the Results group, click the **Run** button. The query results are displayed in the query window. Access finds 46 records with the area code 860 in the Phone field. Not all records fit in the window, and you can scroll down to see more records. See Figure 5-3.

Figure 5-3 tblPatient table records for area code 860

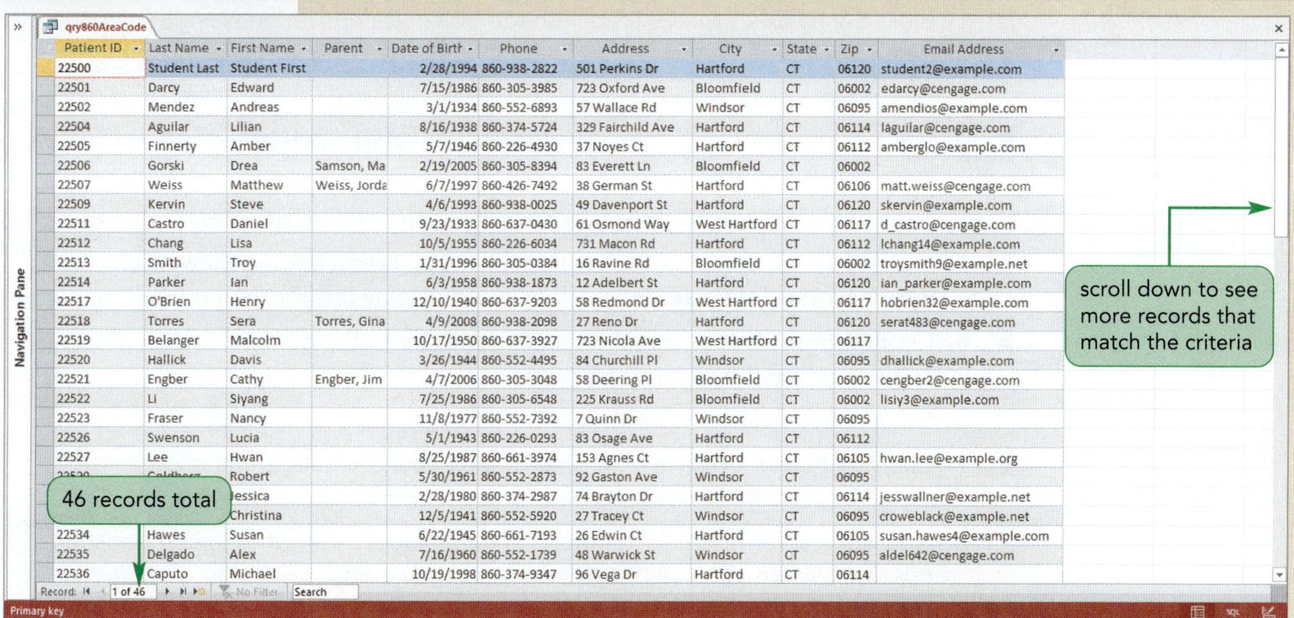

Note that Raj removed the hyphens from the Phone field values; for example, 8609382822 in the first record used to be 860-938-2822. You'll modify the Phone field later in this tutorial to format its values with hyphens.

6. Change the first record in the table, with Patient ID 22500, so the Last Name and First Name columns contain your last and first names, respectively.
7. Close the qry860AreaCode query.

Next, Cindi asks you to create a query that displays information about patients who live in Bloomfield, Windsor, or Meriden. She wants a printout of the patient data for her administrative assistant, who will contact these patients. To produce the results Cindi wants, you'll create a query using a list-of-values match.

Using a List-of-Values Match in a Query

A **list-of-values match** selects records whose value for the designated field matches one of two or more simple condition values. You could accomplish this by including several Or conditions in the design grid, but the In comparison operator provides an easier and clearer way to do this. The **In comparison operator** lets you define a condition with a list of two or more values for a field. If a record's field value matches one value from the list of defined values, then Access selects and includes that record in the query results.

To display the information Cindi requested, you want to select records if their City field value equals Bloomfield, Windsor, or Meriden. These are the values you will use with the In comparison operator. Cindi wants the query to contain the same fields as the qry860AreaCode query, so you'll make a copy of that query and modify it.

To create the query using a list-of-values match:

1. Open the Navigation Pane.
2. In the Queries group on the Navigation Pane, right-click **qry860AreaCode** and then click **Copy** on the shortcut menu.

   Trouble? If you don't see the qry860AreaCode query in the Queries group, press the F5 function key to refresh the object listings in the Navigation pane.
3. Right-click in the empty area in the Navigation Pane below the report and click **Paste**.
4. In the Query Name box, type **qryBloomfieldWindsorMeridenPatients** and then press the **Enter** key.

   To modify the copied query, you need to open it in Design view.
5. In the Queries group on the Navigation Pane, right-click **qryBloomfield WindsorMeridenPatients** to select it and display the shortcut menu.
6. Click **Design View** on the shortcut menu to open the query in Design view, and then close the Navigation Pane.

   You need to delete the existing condition from the Phone field.
7. Click the **Phone Criteria** box, press the **F2** key to highlight the entire condition, and then press the **Delete** key to remove the condition.

   Now you can enter the criterion for the new query using the In comparison operator. When you use this operator, you must enclose the list of values you want to match within parentheses and separate the values with commas. In addition, for fields defined using the Text data type, you enclose each value in quotation marks, although Access adds the quotation marks if you omit them. For fields defined using the Number or Currency data type, you don't enclose the values in quotation marks.

8. Right-click the **City Criteria** box to open the shortcut menu, click **Zoom** to open the Zoom dialog box, and then type **In ("Bloomfield","Windsor", "Meriden")**, as shown in Figure 5-4.

Figure 5-4 Record selection based on matching field values to a list of values

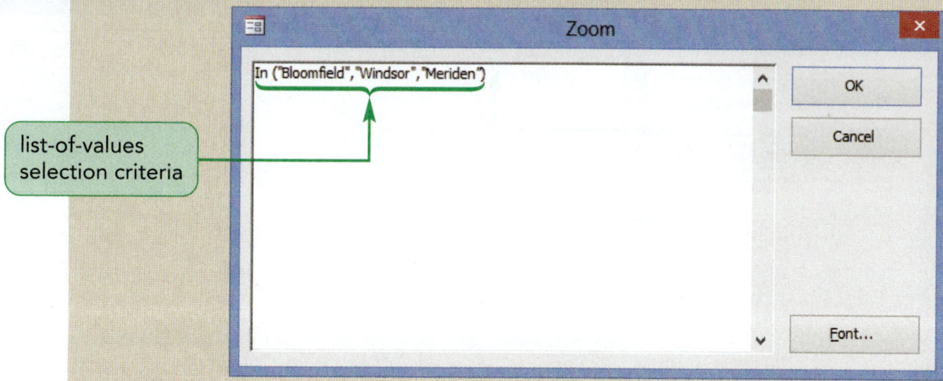

TIP

After clicking in a box, you can also open its Zoom dialog box by holding down the Shift key and pressing the F2 key.

9. Click the **OK** button to close the Zoom dialog box, and then save and run the query. Access displays the recordset, which shows the 20 records with Bloomfield, Windsor, or Meriden in the City field.
10. Close the query.

Cindi also asks her assistant to contact Chatham Community Health Services patients who don't live in Bloomfield, Windsor, or Meriden. You can provide Cindi with this information by creating a query with the Not logical operator.

Using the Not Logical Operator in a Query

The **Not logical operator** negates a criterion or selects records for which the designated field does not match the criterion. For example, if you enter *Not "Windsor"* in the Criteria box for the City field, the query results show records that do not have the City field value Windsor—that is, records of all patients not located in Windsor.

To create Cindi's query, you will combine the Not logical operator with the In comparison operator to select patients whose City field value is not in the list *("Bloomfield", "Windsor","Meriden")*. The qryBloomfieldWindsorMeridenPatients query has the fields that Cindi needs to see in the query results. Cindi doesn't need to keep the qryBloomfieldWindsorMeridenPatients query, so you'll rename and then modify the query.

TIP

You can rename any type of object, including a table, in the Navigation Pane using the Rename command on the shortcut menu.

To create the query using the Not logical operator:

1. Open the Navigation Pane.
2. In the Queries group, right-click **qryBloomfieldWindsorMeridenPatients**, and then on the shortcut menu click **Rename**.
3. Position the insertion point after "qry," type **Non**, and then press the **Enter** key. The query name is now qryNonBloomfieldWindsorMeridenPatients.
4. Open the **qryNonBloomfieldWindsorMeridenPatients** query in Design view, and then close the Navigation Pane.

   You need to change the existing condition in the City field to add the Not logical operator.

5. Click the **City Criteria** box, open the Zoom dialog box, click at the beginning of the expression, type **Not**, and then press the **spacebar**. See Figure 5-5.

Figure 5-5 **Record selection based on not matching a list of values**

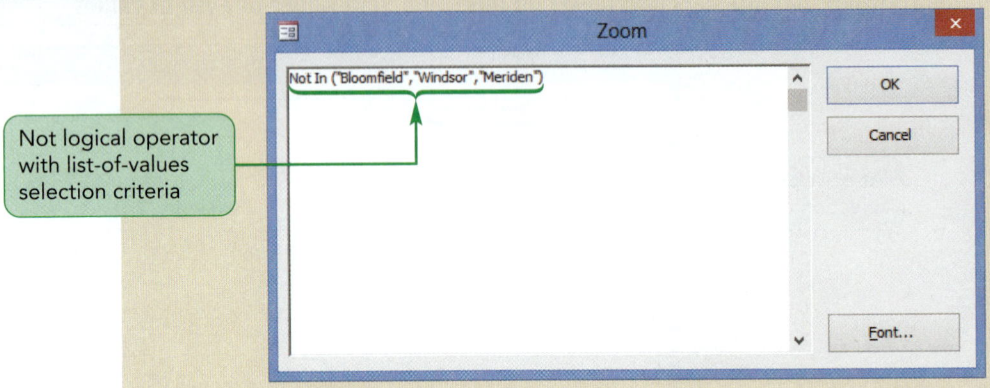

6. Click the **OK** button, and then save and run the query. The recordset displays only those records with a City field value that is not Bloomfield, Windsor, or Meriden. The recordset includes a total of 31 patient records.
7. Scroll down the datasheet to make sure that no Bloomfield or Windsor or Meriden patients appear in your results.

   Now you can close and delete the query, because Cindi does not need to run this query again.

TIP

You can delete any type of object, including a table, in the Navigation Pane using the Delete command on the shortcut menu.

8. Close the query, and then open the Navigation Pane.
9. Right-click **qryNonBloomfieldWindsorMeridenPatients**, click **Delete** on the shortcut menu, and then click **Yes** in the dialog box warning that deleting this object will remove it from all groups.

You now are ready to answer Cindi's question about patients in Hartford or West Hartford that have invoice amounts for less than $100 or that visited during the winter.

Using an AutoFilter to Filter Data

Cindi wants to view the patient last and first names, cities, visit dates, walk-in statuses, and visit reasons for patients in Hartford or West Hartford who either walked in without an appointment or visited during the first week in January. The qryJanuaryOrWalkin query contains the same fields Cindi wants to view. This query also uses the Or logical operator to select records if the Walkin field has a value of true or if the VisitDate field value is between 1/1/2016 and 1/7/2016. These are two of the conditions needed to answer Cindi's question. You could modify the qryJanuaryOrWalkin query in Design view to further restrict the records selected to patients located only in Hartford or West Hartford. However, you can use the AutoFilter feature to choose the city restrictions faster and with more flexibility. You previously used the AutoFilter feature to sort records, and you previously used Filter By Selection to filter records. Now you'll use the AutoFilter feature to filter records.

To filter the records using an AutoFilter:

1. Open the **qryJanuaryOrWalkin** query in Design view, and then close the Navigation Pane.

The true condition for the Walkin field selects records for patients who walked in without an appointment, and the Between #1/1/2016# And #1/7/2016# condition for the VisitDate field selects records for patients whose visit date was in the first week of January 2016. Although the Walkin field is a yes/no field, these values are represented by true (yes) and false (no). Because the conditions are in two different rows, the query uses the Or logical operator. If you wanted to answer Cindi's question in Design view, you would add a condition for the City field, using either the Or logical operator—"Hartford" Or "West Hartford"—or the In comparison operator—In ("Hartford","West Hartford"). If you were to use Like *Hartford instead of the In function, the asterisk wildcard (*) would include East Hartford as well as Hartford and West Hartford. You'd place the condition for the City field in both the Criteria row and in the Or row. The query recordset would include a record only if both conditions in either row are satisfied. Instead of changing the conditions in Design view, though, you'll choose the information Cindi wants using an AutoFilter.

2. Run the query, and then click the **arrow** on the City column heading to display the AutoFilter menu. See Figure 5-6.

Figure 5-6 **Using an AutoFilter to filter records in the query recordset**

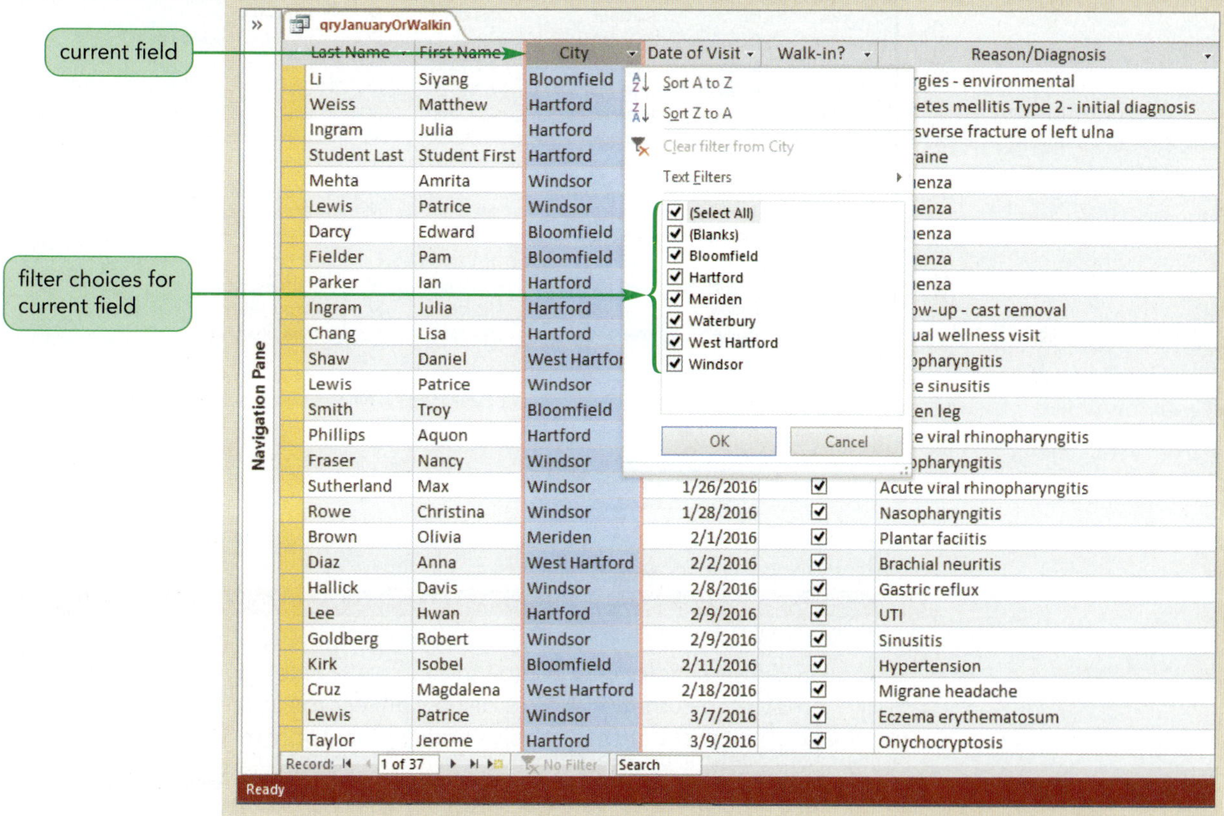

The AutoFilter menu lists all City field values that appear in the recordset. A check mark next to an entry indicates that records with that City field value appear in the recordset. To filter for selected City field values, you uncheck the cities you don't want selected and leave checked the cities you do want selected. You can click the "(Select All)" check box to select or deselect all field values. The "(Blanks)" option includes null values when checked and excludes null values when unchecked. (Recall that a null field value is the absence of a value for the field.)

3. Click the **(Select All)** check box to deselect all check boxes, click the **Hartford** check box, and then click the **West Hartford** check box.

   The two check boxes indicate that the AutoFilter will include only Hartford and West Hartford City field values.

4. Click the **OK** button. Access displays the 18 records for patients in Hartford and West Hartford who walked in without an appointment, or who had a visit in the first week in January. See Figure 5-7.

Figure 5-7 Using an AutoFilter to filter records in the query recordset

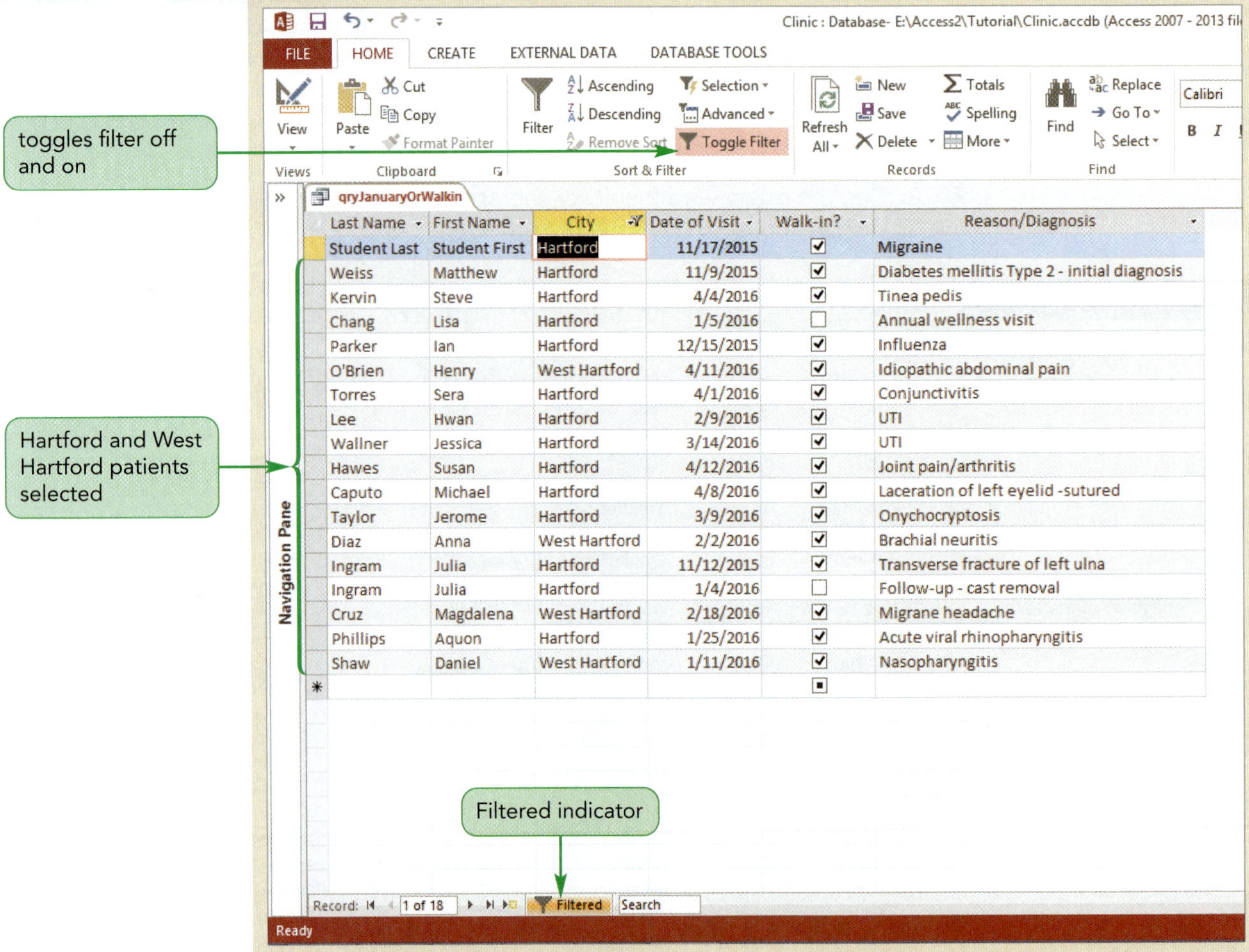

You click the Toggle Filter button in the Sort & Filter group on the HOME tab to remove the current filter and display all records in the query. If you click the Toggle Filter button a second time, you reapply the filter.

5. On the HOME tab, in the Sort & Filter group, click the **Toggle Filter** button. Access removes the filter, and all 37 records appear in the recordset.

6. Click the **Toggle Filter** button. Access applies the City filter, displaying the 18 records for patients in Hartford and West Hartford.

7. Save the query and close it.

Next, Cindi wants to view all fields from the tblPatient table, along with the patient name or the parent name if the patient is a child.

Assigning a Conditional Value to a Calculated Field

If a field in a record does not contain any information at all, it has a null value. Such a field is also referred to as a null field. A field in a record that contains any data at all—even a single space—is nonnull. Records for patients who are adults have nonnull FirstName and LastName field values and null Parent field values in the tblPatient table, while records for children have nonnull values for all three fields. Cindi wants to view records from the tblPatient table in order by the Parent value, if it's nonnull, and at the same time in order by the LastName and then FirstName field values, if the Parent field value is null. To produce this information for Cindi, you need to create a query that includes all fields from the tblPatient table and then add a calculated field that will display the patient name—either the Parent field value, which is input using the form LastName, FirstName, or the LastName and FirstName field values, separated by a comma and a space.

To combine the LastName and FirstName fields, you'll use the expression *LastName & ", " & FirstName*. The **& (ampersand) operator** is a concatenation operator that joins text expressions. **Concatenation** refers to joining two or more text fields or characters encapsulated in quotes. When you join the LastName field value to the string that contains the comma and space, you are concatenating these two strings. If the LastName field value is Fernandez and the FirstName field value is Sabrina, for example, the result of the expression *LastName & ", " & FirstName* is *Fernandez & ", " & Sabrina* which results in *Fernandez, Sabrina*.

INSIGHT

Using Concatenation

IT professionals generally refer to a piece of text data as a string. Most programming languages include the ability to join two or more strings using concatenation.

Imagine you're working with a database table that contains Title, FirstName, and LastName values for people who have made donations, and you've been asked to add their names to a report. You could add each individual field separately, but the data would look awkward, with each field in a separate column. Alternatively, you could create a calculated field with an expression that combines the fields with spaces into a more readable format, such as "Mr. Jim Sullivan". To do this, you would concatenate the fields with a space separator. The expression to perform this task might look like *=Title & " " & FirstName & " " & LastName.*

To display the correct patient value, you'll use the IIf function. The IIf (Immediate If) function assigns one value to a calculated field or control if a condition is true, and a second value if the condition is false. The IIf function has three parts: a condition that is true or false, the result when the condition is true, and the result when the condition is false. Each part of the IIf function is separated by a comma. The condition you'll use is *IsNull(Parent)*. The IsNull function tests a field value or an expression for a null value; if the field value or expression is null, the result is true; otherwise, the result is false. The expression *IsNull(Parent)* is true when the Parent field value is null, and is false when the Parent field value is not null.

For the calculated field, you'll enter *IIf(IsNull(Parent),LastName & ", " & FirstName, Parent & " (Parent)")*. You interpret this expression as follows: If the Parent field value is null, then set the calculated field value to the concatenation of the LastName field value and the text string ", " and the FirstName field value. If the Parent field value is not null, then set the calculated field value to the Parent field value and the text string "(Parent)" to indicate the patient name is the parent of a child patient.

Now you're ready to create Cindi's query to display the patient name.

To create the query to display the patient name:

1. Click the **CREATE** tab, and then in the Queries group, click the **Query Design** button. The Show Table dialog box opens on top of the Query window in Design View.
2. Click **tblPatient** in the Tables box, click the **Add** button, and then click the **Close** button. The tblPatient table field list is placed in the Query window and the Show Table dialog box closes.

   Cindi wants all fields from the tblPatient table to appear in the query recordset, with the new calculated field in the first column.
3. Drag the bottom border of the tblPatient field list down until all fields are visible, double-click the **title bar** of the tblPatient field list to highlight all the fields, and then drag the highlighted fields to the second column's Field box in the design grid. Access places each field in a separate column in the design grid starting with the second column, in the same order that the fields appear in the table.

   Trouble? If you accidentally drag the highlighted fields to the first column in the design grid, click the PatientID Field box, and then in the Query Setup group, click the Insert Columns button. Continue with Step 4.

TIP

After clicking in a box, you can also open its Expression Builder dialog box by holding down the Ctrl key and pressing the F2 key.

4. Right-click the blank Field box to the left of the PatientID field, and then click **Build** on the shortcut menu. The Expression Builder dialog box opens.

   Cindi wants to use "Patient" as the name of the calculated field, so you'll type that name, followed by a colon, and then you'll choose the IIf function.
5. Type **Patient:** and then press the **spacebar**.
6. Double-click **Functions** in the Expression Elements (left) column, and then click **Built-In Functions**.

Make sure you double-click instead of single-click the IIf function.

7. Scroll down the Expression Categories (middle) column, click **Program Flow**, and then in the Expression Values (right) column, double-click **IIf**. Access adds the IIf function with four placeholders to the right of the calculated field name in the expression box. See Figure 5-8.

Figure 5-8 IIf function inserted for the calculated field

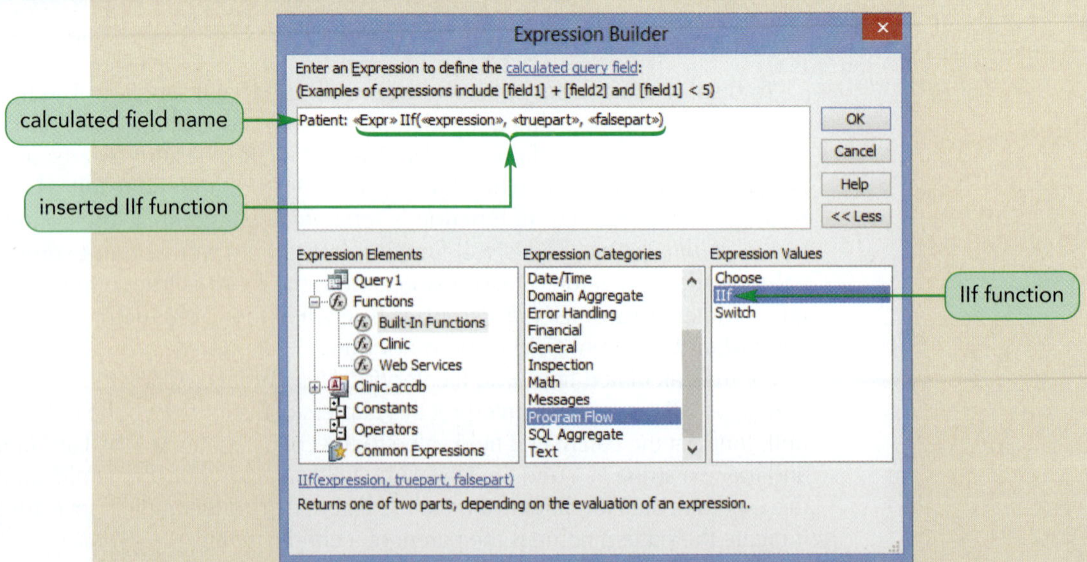

The expression you will create does not need the leftmost placeholder (<<Expr>>), so you'll delete it. You'll replace the second placeholder (<<expression>>) with the condition using the IsNull function, the third placeholder (<<truepart>>) with the expression using the & operator, and the fourth placeholder (<<falsepart>>) with the Parent field name and expression to include the " (Parent)" text.

8. Click **<<Expr>>** in the expression box, and then press the **Delete** key. The first placeholder is deleted.
9. Click **<<expression>>** in the expression box, and then click **Inspection** in the Expression Categories (middle) column.
10. Double-click **IsNull** in the Expression Values (right) column, click **<<expression>>** in the expression box, and then type **Parent**. You've completed the entry of the condition in the IIf function. See Figure 5-9.

Figure 5-9 **After entering the condition for the calculated field's IIf function**

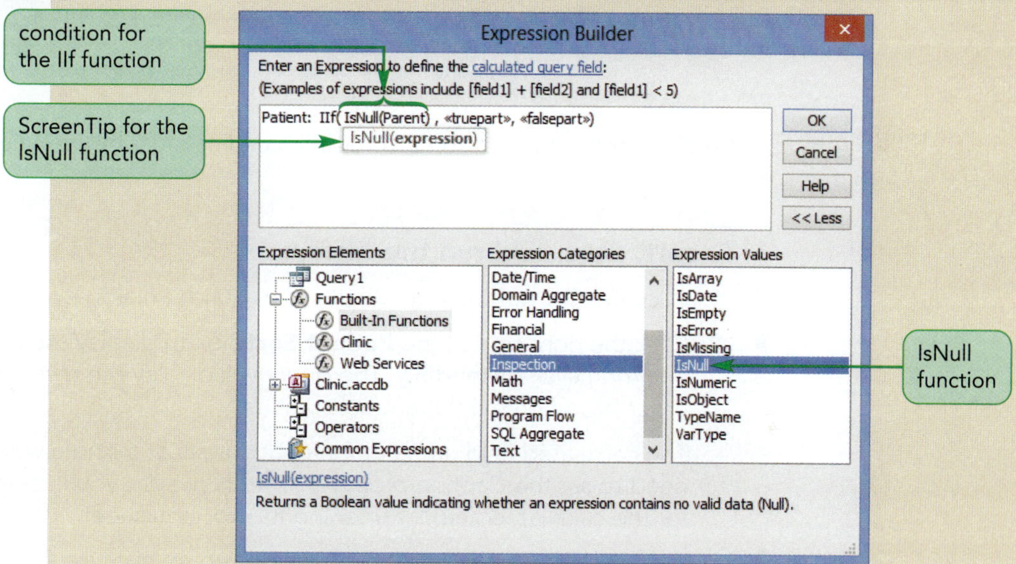

After you typed the first letter of "Parent," the Formula AutoComplete box displayed a list of functions beginning with the letter P, and a ScreenTip for the IsNull function was displayed above the box. The box closed after you typed the third letter, but the ScreenTip remains on the screen.

> **TIP**
> The expression "[tblPatient]![Parent]", meaning the Parent field in the tblPatient table, is the same as "Parent".

Instead of typing the field name of Parent in the previous step, you could have double-clicked Clinic.accdb in the Expression Elements column, double-clicked Tables in the Expression Elements column, clicked tblPatient in the Expression Elements column, and then double-clicked Parent in the Expression Categories column.

Now you'll replace the third placeholder and then the fourth placeholder.

11. Click **<<truepart>>**, and then type **LastName & ", " & FirstName** to finish creating the calculated field. Be sure you type a space after the comma within the quotation marks.
12. Click **<<falsepart>>**, and then type **Parent & " (Parent)"**. Be sure you type a space after the first quotation mark. See Figure 5-10.

Figure 5-10 Completed calculated field

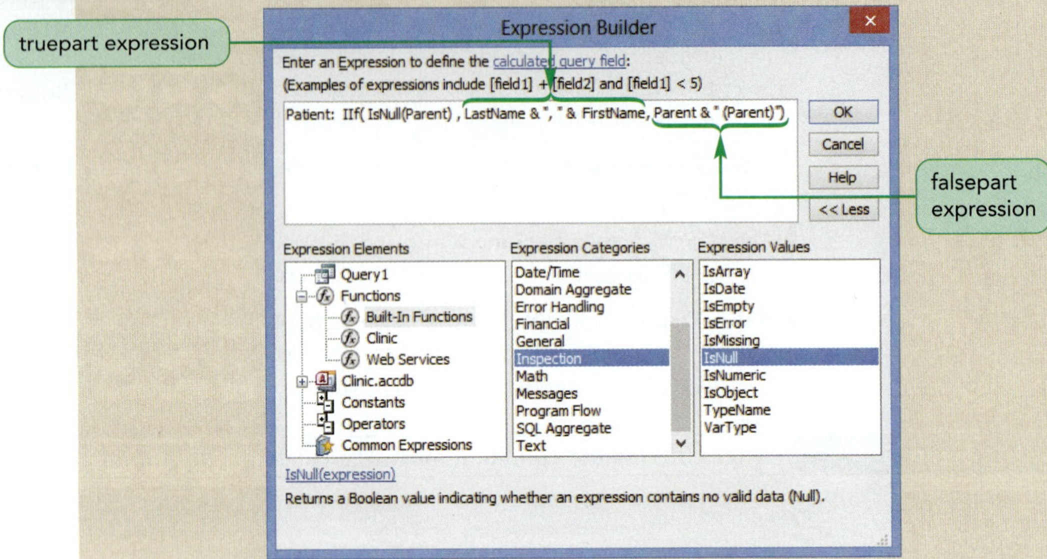

Cindi wants the query to sort records in ascending order by the Patient calculated field.

To sort, save, and run the query:

1. Click the **OK** button in the Expression Builder dialog box to close it.
2. Click the right side of the **Patient Sort** box to display the sort order options, and then click **Ascending**. The query will display the records in alphabetical order based on the Patient field values.

   The calculated field name of Patient consists of a single word, so you do not need to set the Caption property for it. However, you'll review the properties for the calculated field by opening its property sheet.
3. On the DESIGN tab, in the Show/Hide group, click the **Property Sheet** button. The property sheet opens and displays the properties for the Patient calculated field. See Figure 5-11.

Figure 5-11 Property sheet for the Patient calculated field

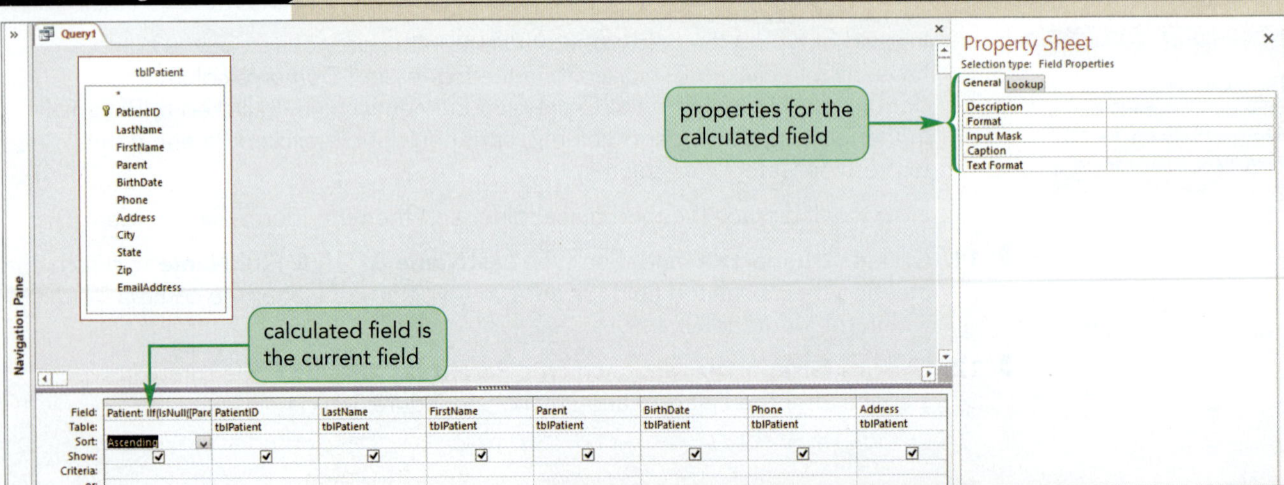

Among the properties for the calculated field, which is the current field, is the Caption property. Leaving the Caption property set to null means that the column name for the calculated field in the query recordset will be Patient, which is the calculated field name. The Property Sheet button is a toggle, so you'll click it again to close the property sheet.

4. Click the **Property Sheet** button again to close the property sheet.
5. Save the query as **qryPatientsByName**, run the query, and then resize the Patient column to its best fit. Access displays all records from the tblPatient table in alphabetical order by the Patient field. See Figure 5-12.

Figure 5-12 Completed query displaying the Patient calculated field

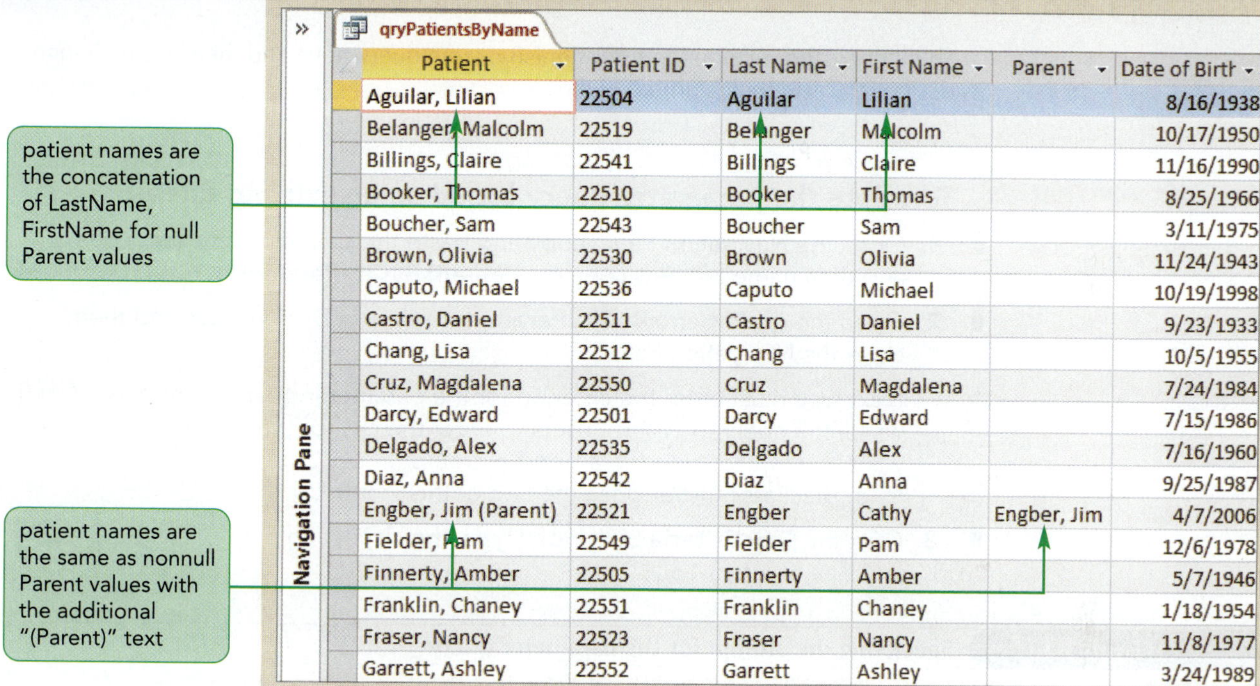

Patient	Patient ID	Last Name	First Name	Parent	Date of Birth
Aguilar, Lilian	22504	Aguilar	Lilian		8/16/1938
Belanger, Malcolm	22519	Belanger	Malcolm		10/17/1950
Billings, Claire	22541	Billings	Claire		11/16/1990
Booker, Thomas	22510	Booker	Thomas		8/25/1966
Boucher, Sam	22543	Boucher	Sam		3/11/1975
Brown, Olivia	22530	Brown	Olivia		11/24/1943
Caputo, Michael	22536	Caputo	Michael		10/19/1998
Castro, Daniel	22511	Castro	Daniel		9/23/1933
Chang, Lisa	22512	Chang	Lisa		10/5/1955
Cruz, Magdalena	22550	Cruz	Magdalena		7/24/1984
Darcy, Edward	22501	Darcy	Edward		7/15/1986
Delgado, Alex	22535	Delgado	Alex		7/16/1960
Diaz, Anna	22542	Diaz	Anna		9/25/1987
Engber, Jim (Parent)	22521	Engber	Cathy	Engber, Jim	4/7/2006
Fielder, Pam	22549	Fielder	Pam		12/6/1978
Finnerty, Amber	22505	Finnerty	Amber		5/7/1946
Franklin, Chaney	22551	Franklin	Chaney		1/18/1954
Fraser, Nancy	22523	Fraser	Nancy		11/8/1977
Garrett, Ashley	22552	Garrett	Ashley		3/24/1989

6. Save and close the query.

You're now ready to create the query to satisfy Cindi's request for information about patients in a particular city.

Creating a Parameter Query

Cindi's next request is for records in the qryPatientsByName query for patients in a particular city. For this query, she wants to specify a city, such as Windsor or Hartford, each time she runs the query.

To create this query, you will copy, rename, and modify the qryPatientsByName query. You could create a simple condition using an exact match for the City field, but you would need to change it in Design view every time you run the query. Alternatively, Cindi or a member of her staff could filter the qryPatientsByName query for the city records they want to view. Instead, you will create a parameter query. A **parameter query** displays a dialog box that prompts the user to enter one or more criteria values when the query is run. In this case, you want to create a query that prompts for the city and selects only those patient records with that City field value from the table. You will enter the prompt in the Criteria box for the City field. When Access runs the query, it will open a dialog box and prompt you to enter the city. Access will then create the query results, just as if you had changed the criteria in Design view.

REFERENCE

Creating a Parameter Query

- Create a select query that includes all fields to appear in the query results.
- Choose the sort fields and set the criteria that do not change when you run the query.
- Decide which fields to use as prompts when the query runs. In the Criteria box for each of these fields, type the prompt you want to appear in a dialog box when you run the query, and enclose the prompt in brackets.

You'll copy and rename the qryPatientsByName query now, and then you'll change its design to create the parameter query.

To create the parameter query based on an existing query:

1. Open the Navigation Pane, copy and paste the qryPatientsByName query, and then name the new copy **qryPatientsByCityParameter**.
2. Open the **qryPatientsByCityParameter** query in Design view, and then close the Navigation Pane.

   Next, you must enter the criterion for the parameter query. In this case, Cindi wants the query to prompt users to enter the city for the patient records they want to view. You need to enter the prompt in the Criteria box for the City field. Brackets must enclose the text of the prompt.
3. Click the **City Criteria** box, type **[Type the city:]**, and then press the **Enter** key. See Figure 5-13.

Figure 5-13 Specifying the prompt for the parameter query

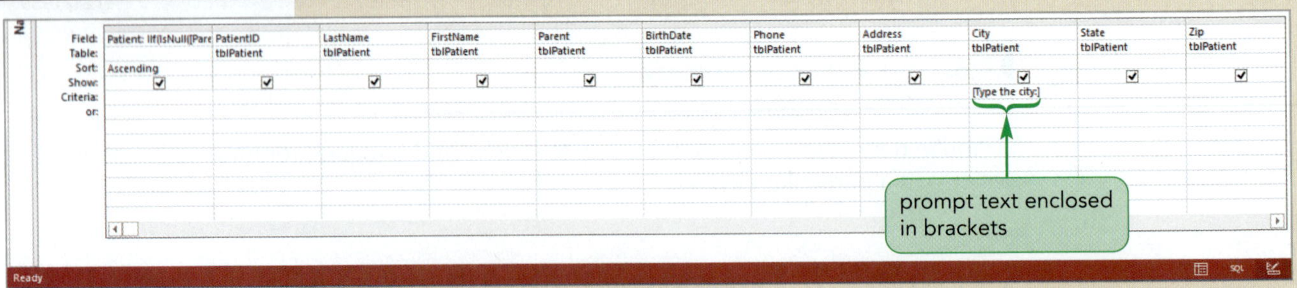

4. Save and run the query. Access displays a dialog box prompting you for the name of the city. See Figure 5-14

Figure 5-14 **Enter Parameter Value dialog box**

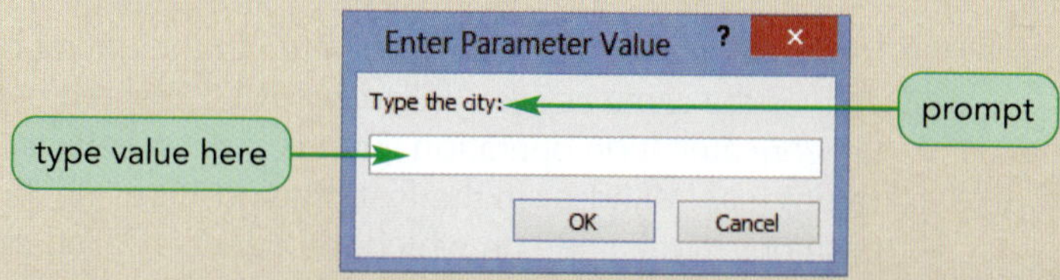

TIP

You must enter a value that matches the spelling of a City field value, but you can use either lowercase or uppercase letters.

The bracketed text you specified in the Criteria box of the City field appears above a box, in which you must type a City field value. Cindi wants to see all patients in Waterbury.

5. Type **Waterbury**, press the **Enter** key, and then scroll the datasheet to the right, if necessary, to display the City field values. The recordset displays the data for the two patients in Waterbury. See Figure 5-15.

Figure 5-15 **Results of the parameter query**

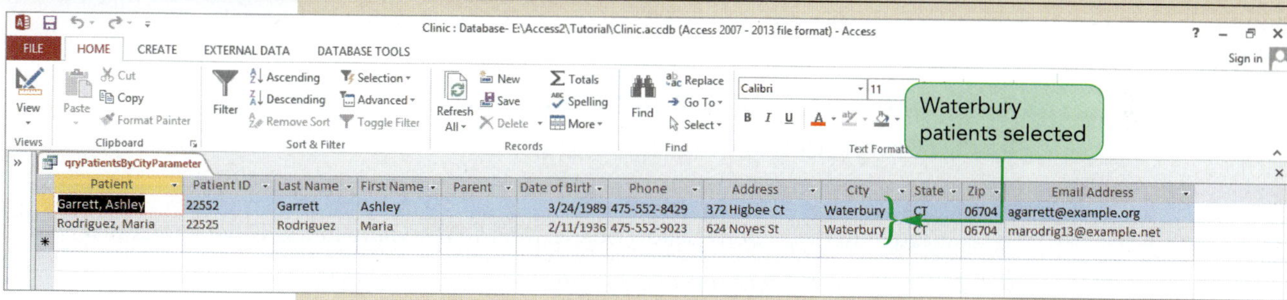

Cindi asks what happens if she doesn't enter a value in the dialog box when she runs the qryPatientsByCityParameter query. You can run the query again to show Cindi the answer to her question.

6. Switch to Design view, and then run the query. The Enter Parameter Value dialog box opens.

   If you click the OK button or press the Enter key, you'll run the parameter query without entering a value for the City field criterion.

7. Click the **OK** button. Access displays no records in the query results.

When you run the parameter query and enter "Waterbury" in the dialog box, Access runs the query just as if you had entered "Waterbury" in the City Criteria box in the design grid, and displays all Waterbury patient records. When you do not enter a value in the dialog box, Access runs the query as if you had entered "null" in the City Criteria box. Because none of the records has a null City field value, Access displays no records. Cindi asks if there's a way to display records for a selected City field value when she enters its value in the dialog box and to display all records when she doesn't enter a value.

Creating a More Flexible Parameter Query

Most users want a parameter query to display the records that match the parameter value the user enters or to display all records when the user doesn't enter a parameter value. To provide this functionality, you can change the value in the Criteria box in the design grid for the specified column. For example, you could change an entry for a City field from *[Type the city:]* to *Like [Type the city:] & "*"*. That is, you can prefix the Like operator to the original criterion and concatenate the criterion to a wildcard character. When you run the parameter query with this new entry, Access will display one of the following recordsets:

- If you enter a specific City field value in the dialog box, such as *Windsor*, the entry is the same as *Like "Windsor" & "*"*, which becomes *Like "Windsor*"* after the concatenation operation. That is, Access selects all records whose City field values have Windsor in the first nine positions and any characters in the remaining positions. If the table on which the query is based contains records with City field values of Windsor, Access displays only those records. However, if the table on which the query is based also contains records with City field values of Windsor City, then Access would display both the Windsor and the Windsor City records.
- If you enter a letter in the dialog box, such as *W*, the entry is the same as *Like "W*"*, and the recordset displays all records with City field values that begin with the letter W, which would include Waterbury, West Hartford, Windsor, and Windsor City.
- If you enter no value in the dialog box, the entry is the same as *Like Null & "*"*, which becomes *Like "*"* after the concatenation operation, and the recordset displays all records.

Now you'll modify the parameter query to satisfy Cindi's request and you'll test the new version of the query.

To modify and test the parameter query:

1. Switch to Design view.
2. Click the **City Criteria** box, and then open the Zoom dialog box.

   You'll use the Zoom dialog box to modify the value in the City Criteria box.
3. Click to the left of the expression in the Zoom dialog box, type **Like**, press the **spacebar**, and then press the **End** key.
4. Press the **spacebar**, type **&**, press the **spacebar**, and then type **"*"** as shown in Figure 5-16.

Be sure you type "*" at the end of the expression.

Figure 5-16 Modified City Criteria value in the Zoom dialog box

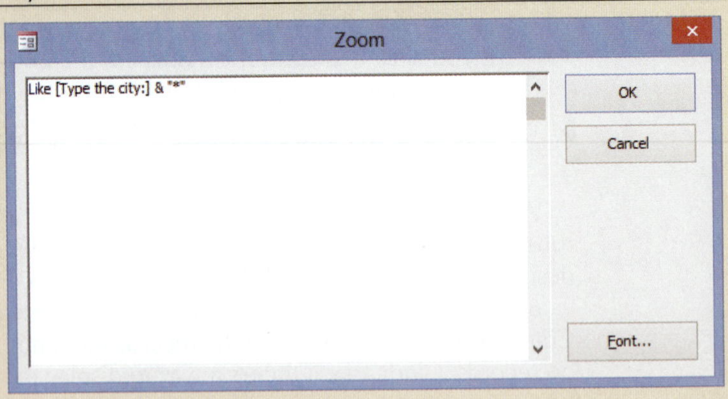

Now you can test the modified parameter query.

5. Click the **OK** button to close the Zoom dialog box, save your query design changes, and then run the query.

   First, you'll test the query to display patients in Windsor.
6. Type **Windsor**, and then press the **Enter** key. The recordset displays the data for the 10 patients in Windsor.

   Now you'll test the query without entering a value when prompted.

7. Switch to Design view, run the query, and then click the **OK** button. The recordset displays all 51 original records from the tblPatient table.

   Finally, you'll test how the query performs when you enter W in the dialog box.

8. On the HOME tab, in the Records group, click the **Refresh All** button to open the Enter Parameter Value dialog box.
9. Type **W**, press the **Enter** key, and then scroll to the right, if necessary, to display the City field values. The recordset displays the 19 records for patients in Windsor, West Hartford, and Waterbury.
10. Close the query.
11. If you are not continuing on to the next session, close the Clinic database and click the **Yes** button if necessary to empty the Clipboard.

The queries you created will make the Clinic database easier to use. In the next session, you'll create a top values query and use query wizards to create three additional queries.

REVIEW

Session 5.1 Quick Check

1. According to the naming conventions used in this session, you use the ____________ prefix tag to identify queries.
2. Which comparison operator selects records based on a specific pattern?
3. What is the purpose of the asterisk (*) in a pattern match query?
4. When do you use the In comparison operator?
5. How do you negate a selection criterion?
6. The ____________ function returns one of two values based on whether the condition being tested is true or false.
7. When do you use a parameter query?

Session 5.2 Visual Overview:

A **crosstab query** uses aggregate functions such as Sum and Count to perform arithmetic operations on selected records.

A simple query selects records from one of more tables that satisfy criteria.

A **find duplicates query** is a select query that finds duplicate records in a table or query.

A **find unmatched query** is a select query that finds all records in a table or query that have no related records in a second table or query.

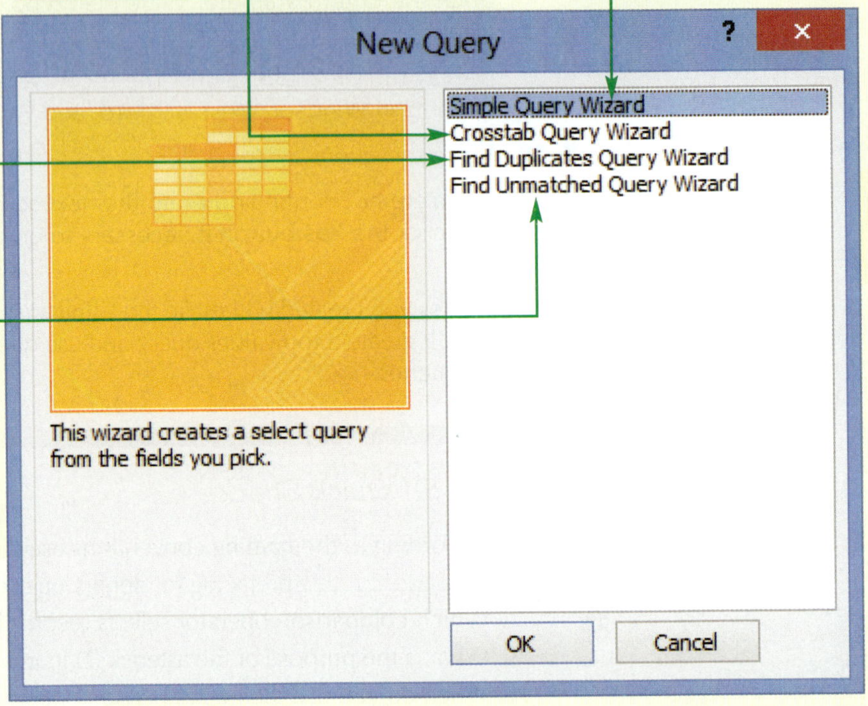

Each column and row intersection will display the sum of the InvoiceAmt values.

The selected field (InvoiceAmt) is used in the calculations for each column and row intersection.

This option determines whether to display an overall totals column in the crosstab query.

The crosstab query will display one column for the paid invoices and a second column for the unpaid invoices.

The crosstab query will display one row for each unique City field value.

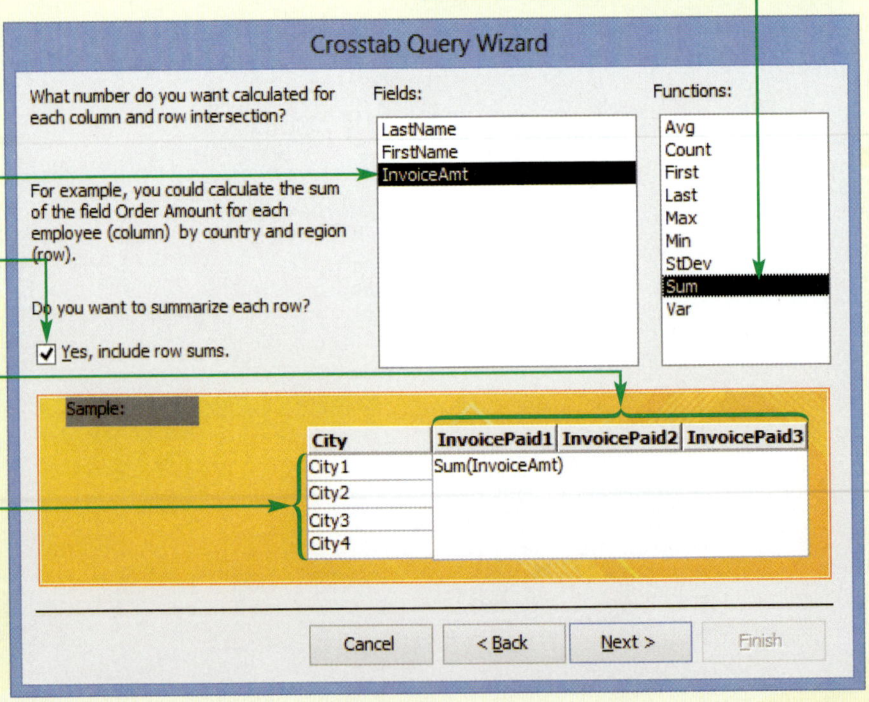

Advanced Query Wizards

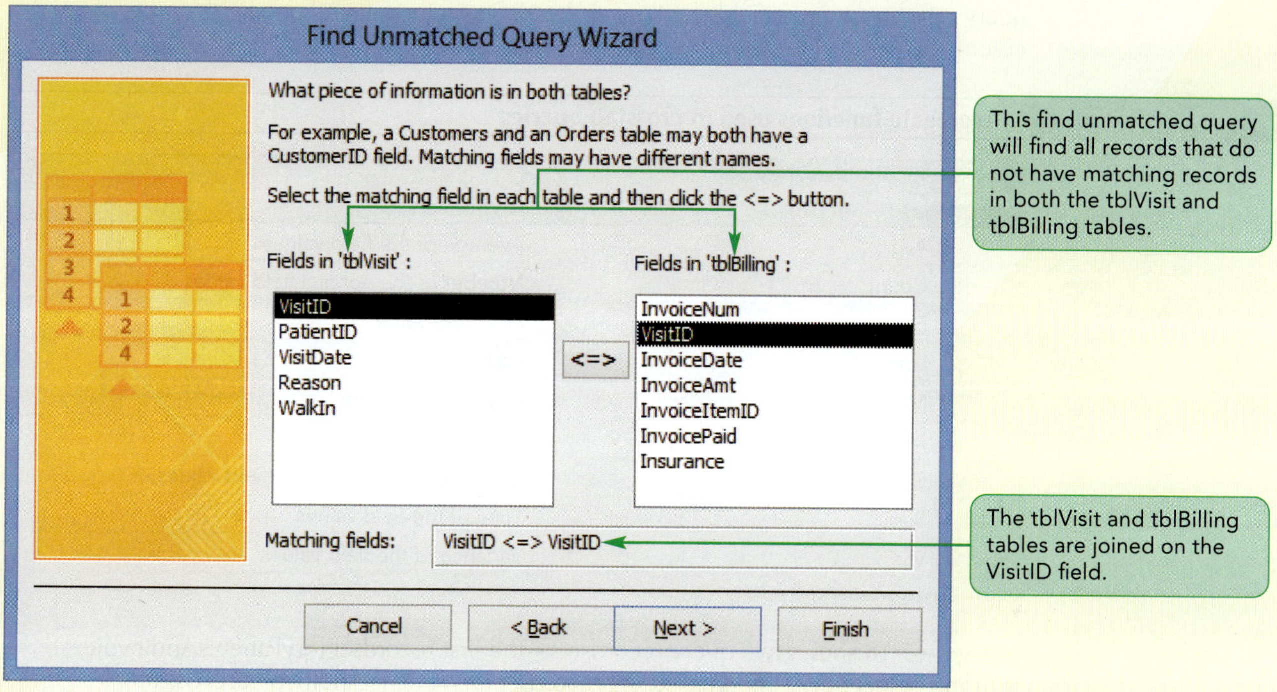

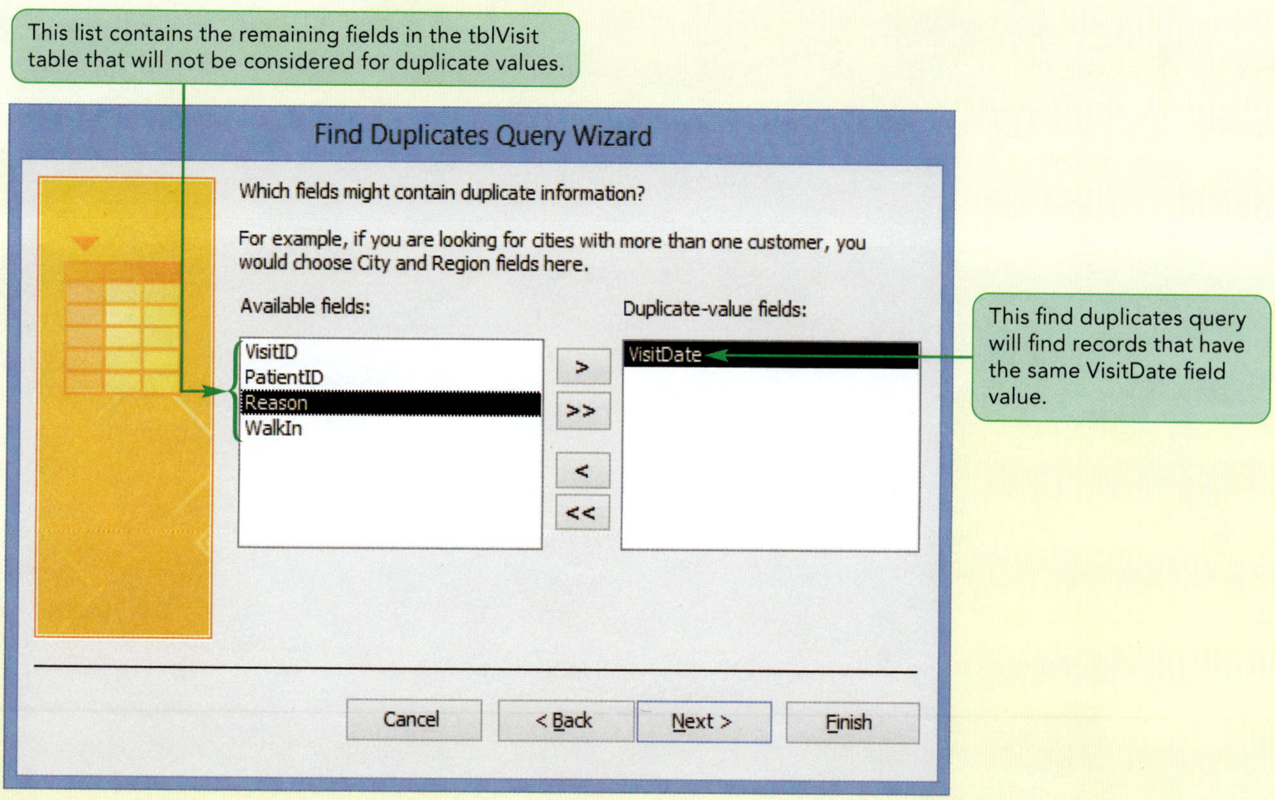

Creating a Crosstab Query

Cindi wants to analyze the Chatham Community Health Services invoices by city, so she can view the paid and unpaid invoice amounts for all patients located in each city. Crosstab queries use the aggregate functions shown in Figure 5-17 to perform arithmetic operations on selected records. A crosstab query can also display one additional aggregate function value that summarizes the set of values in each row. The crosstab query uses one or more fields for the row headings on the left and one field for the column headings at the top.

Figure 5-17 **Aggregate functions used in crosstab queries**

Aggregate Function	Definition
Avg	Average of the field values
Count	Number of the nonnull field values
First	First field value
Last	Last field value
Max	Highest field value
Min	Lowest field value
StDev	Standard deviation of the field values
Sum	Total of the field values
Var	Variance of the field values

Figure 5-18 shows two query recordsets—the first recordset (qryPatientsAndInvoices) is from a select query and the second recordset (qryPatientsAndInvoicesCrosstab) is from a crosstab query based on the select query.

Figure 5-18 Comparing a select query to a crosstab query

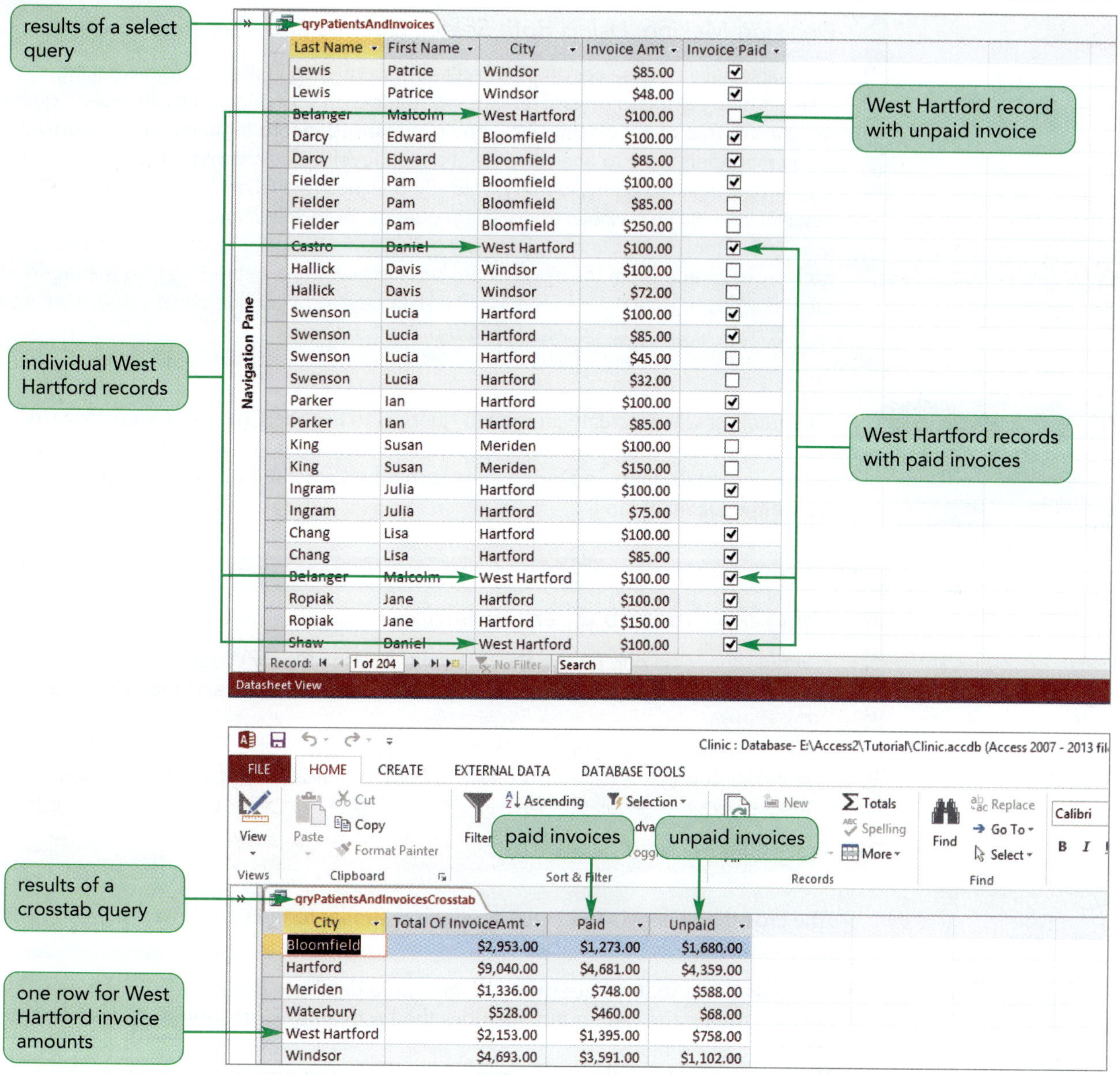

The qryPatientsAndInvoices query, a select query, joins the tblPatient, tblVisit, and tblBilling tables to display selected data from those tables for all invoices. The qryPatientsAndInvoicesCrosstab query, a crosstab query, uses the qryPatientsAndInvoices query as its source query and displays one row for each unique City field value. The City column in the crosstab query identifies each row. The crosstab query uses the Sum aggregate function on the InvoiceAmt field to produce the displayed values in the Paid and Unpaid columns for each City row. An entry in the Total Of InvoiceAmt column represents the sum of the Paid and Unpaid values for the City field value in that row.

PROSKILLS

Decision Making: Using Both Select Queries and Crosstab Queries

Companies use both select queries and crosstab queries in their decision making. A select query displays several records—one for each row selected by the select query—while a crosstab query displays only one summarized record for each unique field value. When managers want to analyze data at a high level to see the big picture, they might start with a crosstab query, identify which field values to analyze further, and then look in detail at specific field values using select queries. Both select and crosstab queries serve as valuable tools in tracking and analyzing a company's business, and companies use both types of queries in the appropriate situations. By understanding how managers and other employees use the information in a database to make decisions, you can create the correct type of query to provide the information they need.

TIP

Microsoft Access Help provides more information on creating a crosstab query without using a wizard.

The quickest way to create a crosstab query is to use the **Crosstab Query Wizard**, which guides you through the steps for creating one. You could also change a select query to a crosstab query in Design view using the Crosstab button in the Query Type group on the DESIGN tab.

REFERENCE

Using the Crosstab Query Wizard

- In the Queries group on the CREATE tab, click the Query Wizard button.
- In the New Query dialog box, click Crosstab Query Wizard, and then click the OK button.
- Complete the Wizard dialog boxes to select the table or query on which to base the crosstab query, select the row heading field (or fields), select the column heading field, select the calculation field and its aggregate function, and enter a name for the crosstab query.

The crosstab query you will create, which is similar to the one shown in Figure 5-18, has the following characteristics:

- The qryPatientsAndInvoices query in the Clinic database is the basis for the new crosstab query. The base query includes the LastName, FirstName, City, InvoiceAmt, and InvoicePaid fields.
- The City field is the leftmost column in the crosstab query and identifies each crosstab query row.
- The values from the InvoicePaid field, which is a Yes/No field, identify the rightmost columns of the crosstab query.
- The crosstab query applies the Sum aggregate function to the InvoiceAmt field values and displays the resulting total values in the Paid and Unpaid columns of the query results.
- The grand total of the InvoiceAmt field values appears for each row in a column with the heading Total Of InvoiceAmt.

Next you will create the crosstab query based on the qryPatientsAndInvoices query.

To start the Crosstab Query Wizard:

1. If you took a break after the previous session, make sure that the Clinic database is open and the Navigation Pane is closed.

   Trouble? If the security warning is displayed below the ribbon, click the Enable Content button next to the security warning.

2. Click the **CREATE** tab on the ribbon.
3. In the Queries group, click the **Query Wizard** button. The New Query dialog box opens.
4. Click **Crosstab Query Wizard**, and then click the **OK** button. The first Crosstab Query Wizard dialog box opens.

You'll now use the Crosstab Query Wizard to create the crosstab query for Cindi.

To finish the Crosstab Query Wizard:

1. Click the **Queries** option button in the View section to display the list of queries in the Clinic database, and then click **Query: qryPatientsAndInvoices**. See Figure 5-19.

Figure 5-19 Choosing the query for the crosstab query

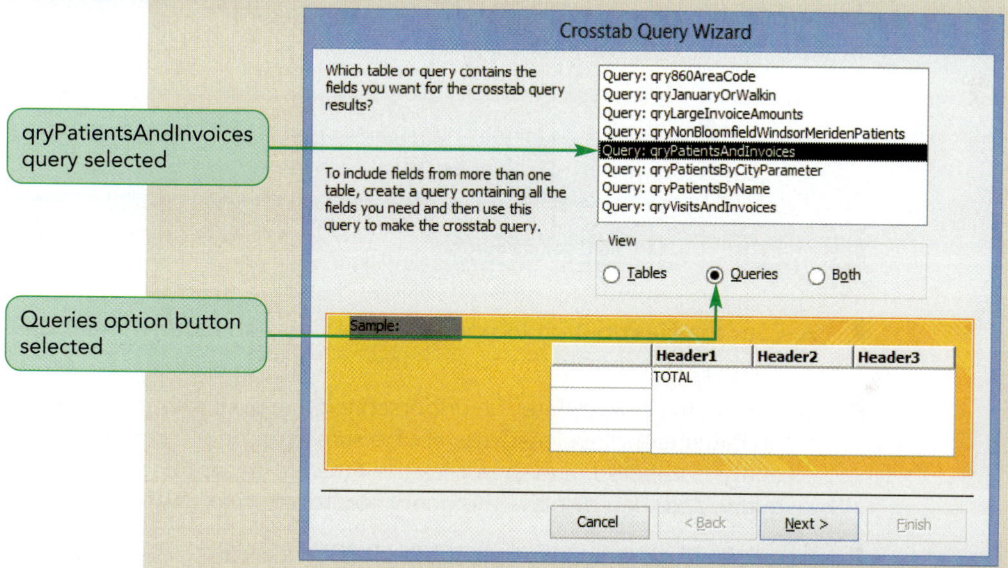

2. Click the **Next** button to open the next Crosstab Query Wizard dialog box. This is the dialog box where you choose the field (or fields) for the *row* headings. Because Cindi wants the crosstab query to display one row for each unique City field value, you will select that field for the row headings.
3. In the Available Fields box, click **City**, and then click the > button to move the City field to the Selected Fields box.
4. Click the **Next** button to open the next Crosstab Query Wizard dialog box, in which you select the field values that will serve as *column* headings. Cindi wants to see the paid and unpaid total invoice amounts, so you need to select the InvoicePaid field for the column headings.
5. Click **InvoicePaid** in the box, and then click the **Next** button.

   In the next Crosstab Query Wizard dialog box, you choose the field that will be calculated for each row and column intersection and the function to use for the calculation. The results of the calculation will appear in the row and column intersections in the query results. Cindi needs to calculate the sum of the InvoiceAmt field value for each row and column intersection.

TIP

When you select a field, Access changes the sample crosstab query in the dialog box to illustrate your choice.

6. Click **InvoiceAmt** in the Fields box, click **Sum** in the Functions box, and then make sure that the "Yes, include row sums" check box is checked. The "Yes, include row sums" option creates a column showing the overall totals for the values in each row of the query recordset. See Figure 5-20.

Figure 5-20 **Completed crosstab query design**

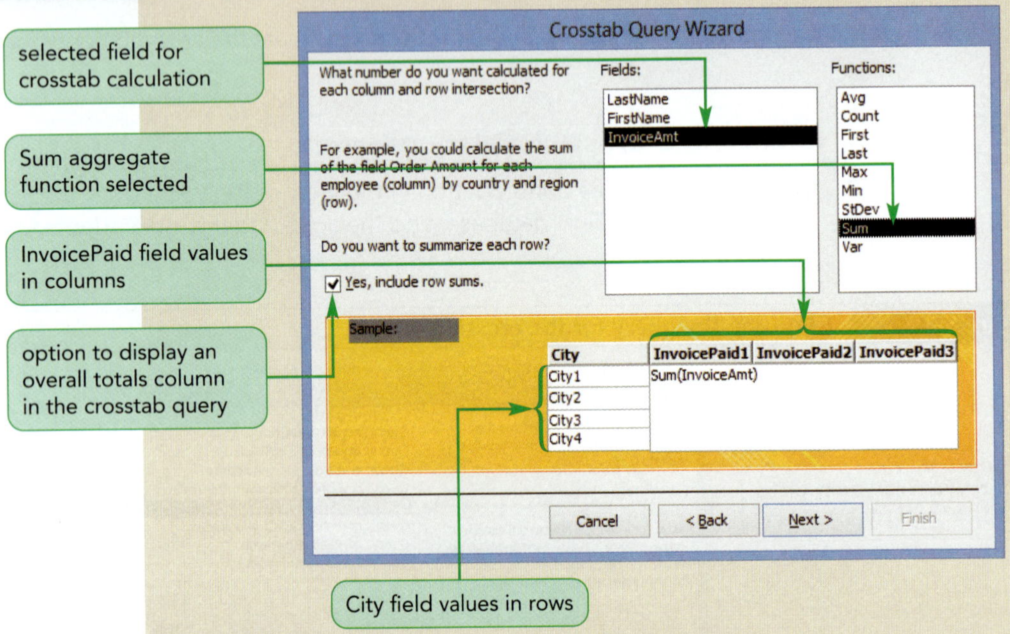

7. Click the **Next** button to open the final Crosstab Query Wizard dialog box, in which you choose the query name.

8. Click in the box, delete the underscore character so that the query name is qryPatientsAndInvoicesCrosstab, be sure the option button for viewing the query is selected, and then click the **Finish** button. Access saves the crosstab query, and then displays the query recordset.

9. Resize all the columns in the query recordset to their best fit, and then click the City field value in the first row (**Bloomfield**). See Figure 5-21.

Figure 5-21 **Crosstab query recordset**

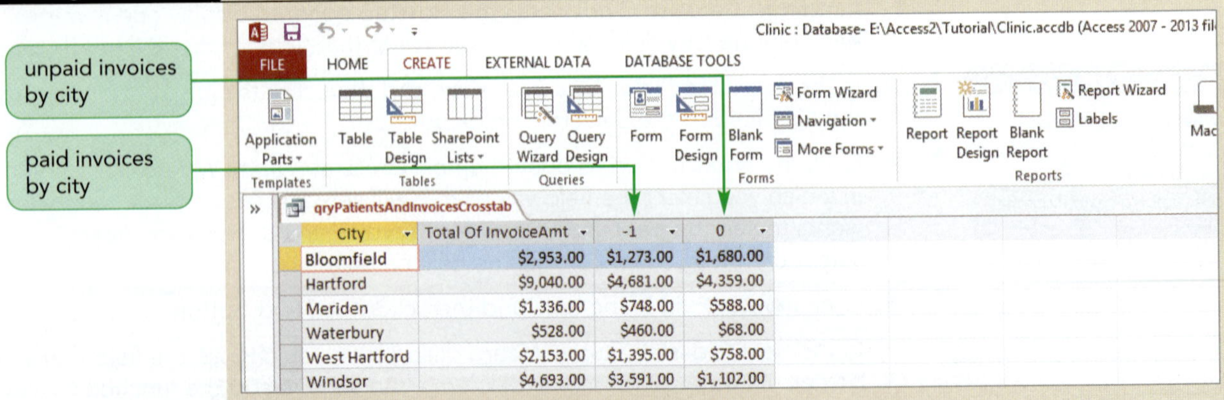

The query recordset contains only one row for each City field value. The Total Of InvoiceAmt column shows the total invoice amount for the patients in each city. The columns labeled -1 and 0 show the sum total paid (-1 column) and sum total unpaid (0 column) invoice amounts for patients in each city. Because the InvoicePaid field is a Yes/No field, by default, Access displays field values in datasheets, forms, and reports in a check box (either checked or unchecked), but stores a checked value in the database as a -1 and an unchecked value as a 0. Instead of displaying check boxes, the crosstab query displays the stored values as column headings.

Cindi wants you to change the column headings of -1 to Paid and 0 to Unpaid. You'll use the IIf function to change the column headings, using the expression *IIf (InvoicePaid,"Paid","Unpaid")*—if the InvoicePaid field value is true (because it's a Yes/No field or a True/False field), or is checked, use "Paid" as the column heading; otherwise, use "Unpaid" as the column heading. Because the InvoicePaid field is a Yes/No field, the condition *InvoicePaid* is the same as the condition *InvoicePaid = -1*, which uses a comparison operator and a value. For all data types except Yes/No fields, you must use a comparison operator in a condition.

To change the crosstab query column headings:

1. Click the **HOME** tab on the ribbon, and then switch to Design view. The design grid has four entries. See Figure 5-22.

Figure 5-22 Crosstab query in the design grid

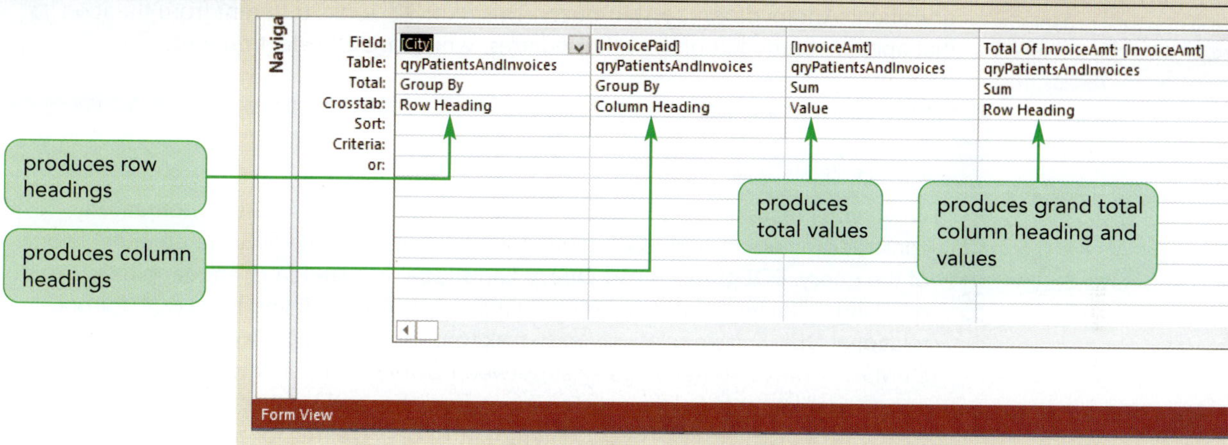

From left to right, the [City] entry produces the row headings, the [InvoicePaid] entry produces the column headings, the [InvoiceAmt] entry produces the totals in each row/column intersection, and the Total Of InvoiceAmt entry produces the row total column heading and total values. The field names are enclosed in brackets; the Total Of InvoiceAmt entry is the name of this calculated field, which displays the sum of the InvoiceAmt field values for each row.

You need to replace the Field box value in the second column with the IIf function expression to change the -1 and zero column headings to Paid and Unpaid. You can type the expression in the box, use Expression Builder to create the expression, or type the expression in the Zoom dialog box. You'll use the last method.

2. Right-click the **InvoicePaid Field** box, and then open the Zoom dialog box.
3. Delete the InvoicePaid expression, and then type **IIf (InvoicePaid,"Paid", "Unpaid")** in the Zoom dialog box. See Figure 5-23.

Figure 5-23 IIf function for the crosstab query column headings

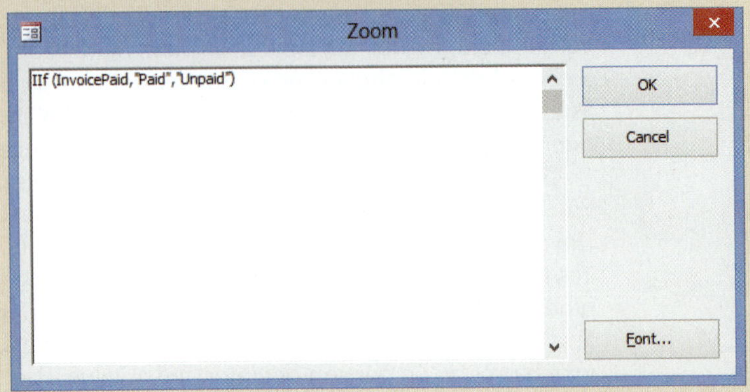

4. Click the **OK** button, and then save and run the query. Access displays the completed crosstab query with Paid and Unpaid as the last two column headings, in alphabetical order, as shown in Figure 5-18.
5. Close the query, and then open the Navigation Pane.

TIP

Point to an object in the Navigation Pane to display the full object name in a ScreenTip.

In the Navigation Pane, Access uses unique icons to represent different types of queries. The crosstab query icon appears in the Queries list to the left of the qryPatientsAndInvoicesCrosstab query. This icon looks different from the icon that appears to the left of the other queries, which are all select queries.

INSIGHT

Using Special Database Features Cautiously

When you create a query in Design view or with a wizard, Access automatically constructs an equivalent SQL statement and saves only the SQL statement version of the query. **SQL (Structured Query Language)** is a standard language used in querying, updating, and managing relational databases. If you learn SQL for one relational DBMS, it's a relatively easy task to begin using SQL for other relational DBMSs. However, differences exist between DBMSs in their versions of SQL—somewhat like having different dialects in English—and in what additions they make to SQL. The SQL-equivalent statement that Access creates for a crosstab query is one such SQL-language addition. If you need to convert an Access database to SQL Server, Oracle, or another DBMS, crosstab queries created in Access will not work in these other DBMSs. You'd have to construct a set of SQL statements in the other DBMS to replace the SQL statement automatically created by Access. Constructing this replacement set of statements is a highly technical process that only an experienced programmer can complete, so you should use special features of a DBMS judiciously.

Next, Cindi wants to identify any visit dates that have the same visit dates as other patients because these are the ones that might have potential scheduling difficulties. To find the information Cindi needs, you'll create a find duplicates query.

Creating a Find Duplicates Query

A find duplicates query is a select query that finds duplicate records in a table or query. You can create this type of query using the **Find Duplicates Query Wizard**. A find duplicates query searches for duplicate values based on the fields you select when answering the Wizard's questions. For example, you might want to display all employers that have the same name, all students who have the same phone number, or all products that have the same description. Using this type of query, you can locate duplicates to avert potential problems (for example, you might have inadvertently assigned two different numbers to the same product), or you can eliminate duplicates that cost money (for example, you could send just one advertising brochure to all patients having the same address).

REFERENCE

Using the Find Duplicates Query Wizard

- In the Queries group on the CREATE tab, click the Query Wizard button.
- In the New Query dialog box, click Find Duplicates Query Wizard, and then click the OK button.
- Complete the Wizard dialog boxes to select the table or query on which to base the query, select the field (or fields) to check for duplicate values, select the additional fields to include in the query results, enter a name for the query, and then click the Finish button.

You'll use the Find Duplicates Query Wizard to create and run a new query to display duplicate visit dates in the tblVisit table.

To create the query using the Find Duplicates Query Wizard:

1. Close the Navigation Pane, click the **CREATE** tab on the ribbon, and then, in the Queries group, click the **Query Wizard** button to open the New Query dialog box.
2. Click **Find Duplicates Query Wizard**, and then click the **OK** button. The first Find Duplicates Query Wizard dialog box opens. In this dialog box, you select the table or query on which to base the new query. You'll use the tblVisit table.
3. Click **Table: tblVisit** (if necessary), and then click the **Next** button. Access opens the next Find Duplicates Query Wizard dialog box, in which you choose the fields you want to check for duplicate values.
4. In the Available fields box, click **VisitDate**, click the > button to select the VisitDate field as the field to check for duplicate values, and then click the **Next** button. In the next Find Duplicates Query Wizard dialog box, you select the additional fields you want displayed in the query results.

   Cindi wants all remaining fields to be included in the query results.
5. Click the >> button to move all fields from the Available fields box to the Additional query fields box, and then click the **Next** button. Access opens the final Find Duplicates Query Wizard dialog box, in which you enter a name for the query. You'll use qryDuplicateVisitDates as the query name.
6. Type **qryDuplicateVisitDates** in the box, be sure the option button for viewing the results is selected, and then click the **Finish** button. Access saves the query, and then displays the 50 records for visits with duplicate visit dates. See Figure 5-24.

Figure 5-24 Query recordset for duplicate visit dates

qryDuplicateVisitDates

Date of Visit	Visit ID	Patient ID	Reason/Diagnosis	Walk-in?
11/9/2015	1528	22507	Diabetes mellitis Type 2 - initial diagnosis	☑
11/9/2015	1527	22522	Allergies - environmental	☑
11/17/2015	1536	22526	Gastroenteritis	☐
11/17/2015	1538	22500	Migraine	☑
11/24/2015	1541	22526	Gastroenteritis - follow up	☐
11/24/2015	1542	22537	Influenza	☑
11/30/2015	1548	22519	Hypertension	☐
11/30/2015	1549	22501	Influenza	☑
1/11/2016	1569	22558	COPD management visit	☐
1/11/2016	1570	22561	Nasopharyngitis	☑
1/13/2016	1573	22511	Cardiac monitoring	☐
1/13/2016	1575	22513	Broken leg	☑
1/13/2016	1572	22560	Acute sinusitis	☑
1/25/2016	1586	22523	Nasopharyngitis	☑
1/25/2016	1588	22535	Hypertension	☐
1/25/2016	1585	22555	Acute viral rhinopharyngitis	☑
1/26/2016	1590	22505	Annual wellness visit	☐
1/26/2016	1591	22544	Acute viral rhinopharyngitis	☑
2/1/2016	1597	22517	Annual wellness visit	☐
2/1/2016	1598	22530	Plantar faciitis	☑
2/8/2016	1605	22535	Hypertension monitoring	☐
2/8/2016	1606	22520	Gastric reflux	☑
2/9/2016	1610	22529	Sinusitis	☑
2/9/2016	1608	22527	UTI	☑
2/9/2016	1607	22507	Diabetes mellitis Type 2 - serum glucose che	☐
2/24/2016	1626	22513	Follow-up - cast removal	☐
2/24/2016	1625	22551	Elevated blood lipids-monitoring meds	☐

Record: 1 of 50 No Filter Search

Navigation Pane

Date of Visit

7. Close the query.

Cindi now asks you to find the records for patients with no visits. These are patients who have been referred to Chatham Community Health Services but have not had a first visit. Cindi wants to contact these patients to see if they would like to book initial appointments. To provide Cindi with this information, you need to create a find unmatched query.

Creating a Find Unmatched Query

A find unmatched query is a select query that finds all records in a table or query that have no related records in a second table or query. For example, you could display all patients who have had an appointment but have never been invoiced, or all students who are not currently enrolled in classes. Such a query provides information for a medical office to ensure all patients who have received services have also been billed for those services, and for a school administrator to contact the students to find out their future educational plans. You can use the **Find Unmatched Query Wizard** to create this type of query.

REFERENCE

Using the Find Unmatched Query Wizard

- In the Queries group on the CREATE tab, click the Query Wizard button.
- In the New Query dialog box, click Find Unmatched Query Wizard, and then click the OK button.
- Complete the Wizard dialog boxes to select the table or query on which to base the new query, select the table or query that contains the related records, specify the common field in each table or query, select the additional fields to include in the query results, enter a name for the query, and then click the Finish button.

Cindi wants to know which patients have no visits. She will contact these patients to determine if they will be visiting Chatham Community Health Services Clinic or whether they are receiving their medical services elsewhere. To create a list of patients who have not had a visit to the clinic, you'll use the Find Unmatched Query Wizard to display only those records from the tblPatient table with no matching PatientID field value in the related tblVisit table.

To create the query using the Find Unmatched Query Wizard:

1. On the CREATE tab, in the Queries group, click the **Query Wizard** button to open the New Query dialog box.
2. Click **Find Unmatched Query Wizard**, and then click the **OK** button. The first Find Unmatched Query Wizard dialog box opens. In this dialog box, you select the table or query on which to base the new query. You'll use the qryPatientsByName query.
3. In the View section, click the **Queries** option button to display the list of queries, click **Query: qryPatientsByName** in the box to select this query, and then click the **Next** button. The next Find Unmatched Query Wizard dialog box opens, in which you choose the table that contains the related records. You'll select the tblVisit table.
4. Click **Table: tblVisit** in the box (if necessary), and then click the **Next** button. The next dialog box opens, in which you choose the common field for both tables. See Figure 5-25.

Figure 5-25 Selecting the common field

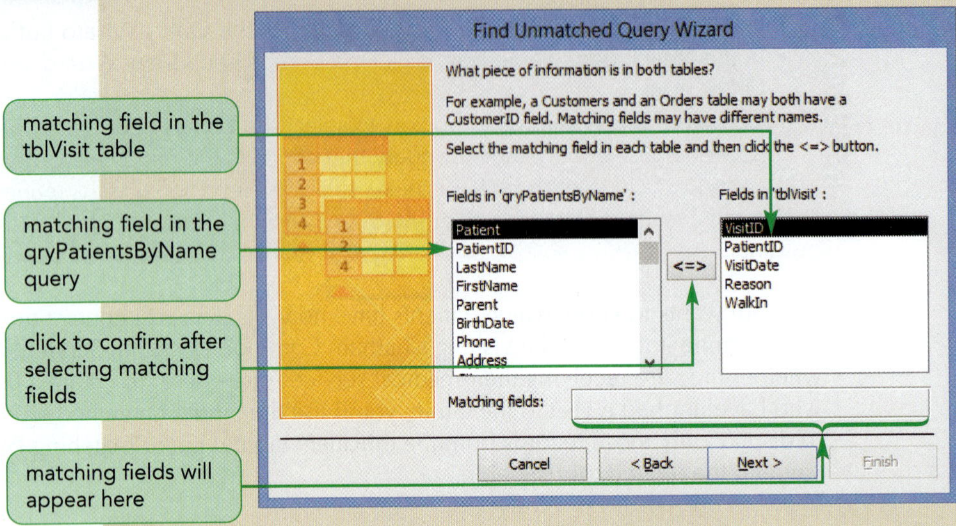

The common field between the query and the table is the PatientID field. You need to click the common field in each box, and then click the <=> button between the two boxes to join the two objects. The Matching fields box then will display PatientID <=> PatientID to indicate the joining of the two matching fields. If the two selected objects already have a one-to-many relationship defined in the Relationships window, the Matching fields box will join the correct fields automatically.

Be sure you click the Patient ID field in both boxes.

5. In the Fields in 'qryPatientsByName' box click **PatientID**, in the Fields in 'tblVisit' box click **PatientID**, click the <=> button to connect the two selected fields, and then click the **Next** button. The next Find Unmatched Query Wizard dialog box opens, in which you choose the fields you want to see in the query recordset. Cindi wants the query recordset to display all available fields.

6. Click the >> button to move all fields from the Available fields box to the Selected fields box, and then click the **Next** button. The final dialog box opens, in which you enter the query name.

7. Type **qryInactivePatients**, be sure the option button for viewing the results is selected, and then click the **Finish** button. Access saves the query and then displays four records in the query recordset. See Figure 5-26.

Figure 5-26 Query recordset displaying four patients without visits

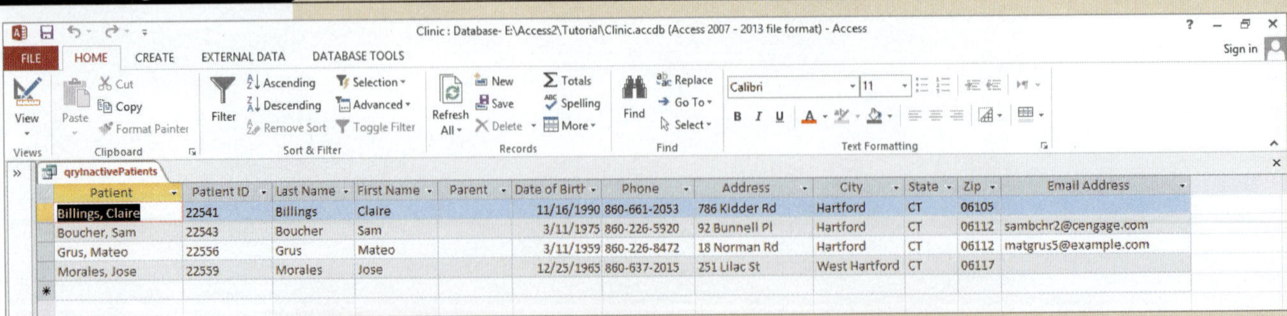

8. Close the query.

Next, Cindi wants to contact those patients who have the highest invoice amounts to make sure that Chatham Community Health Services is providing satisfactory service. To display the information Cindi needs, you will create a top values query.

Creating a Top Values Query

Whenever a query displays a large group of records, you might want to limit the number to a more manageable size by displaying, for example, just the first 10 records. The **Top Values property** for a query lets you limit the number of records in the query results. To find a limited number of records using the Top Values property, you can click one of the preset values from a list, or enter either an integer (such as 15, to display the first 15 records) or a percentage (such as 20%, to display the first fifth of the records).

For instance, suppose you have a select query that displays 45 records. If you want the query recordset to show only the first five records, you can change the query by entering a Top Values property value of either 5 or 10%. If the query contains a sort and the last record that Access can display is one of two or more records with the same value for the primary sort field, Access displays all records with that matching key value.

Cindi wants to view the same data that appears in the qryLargeInvoiceAmounts query for patients with the highest 25 percent contract amounts. Based on the number or percentage you enter, a top values query selects that number or percentage of records starting from the top of the recordset. Thus, you usually include a sort in a top values query to display the records with the highest or lowest values for the sorted field. You will modify the query and then use the Top Values property to produce this information for Cindi.

To set the Top Values property for the query:

1. Open the Navigation Pane, open the **qryLargeInvoiceAmounts** query in Datasheet view, and then close the Navigation Pane. Access displays 14 records, all with InvoiceAmt field values greater than $200, in descending order by InvoiceAmt.
2. Switch to Design view.
3. In the Query Setup group on the DESIGN tab, click the **Return** arrow (with the ScreenTip "Top Values"), and then click **25%**. See Figure 5-27.

Figure 5-27 Creating the top values query

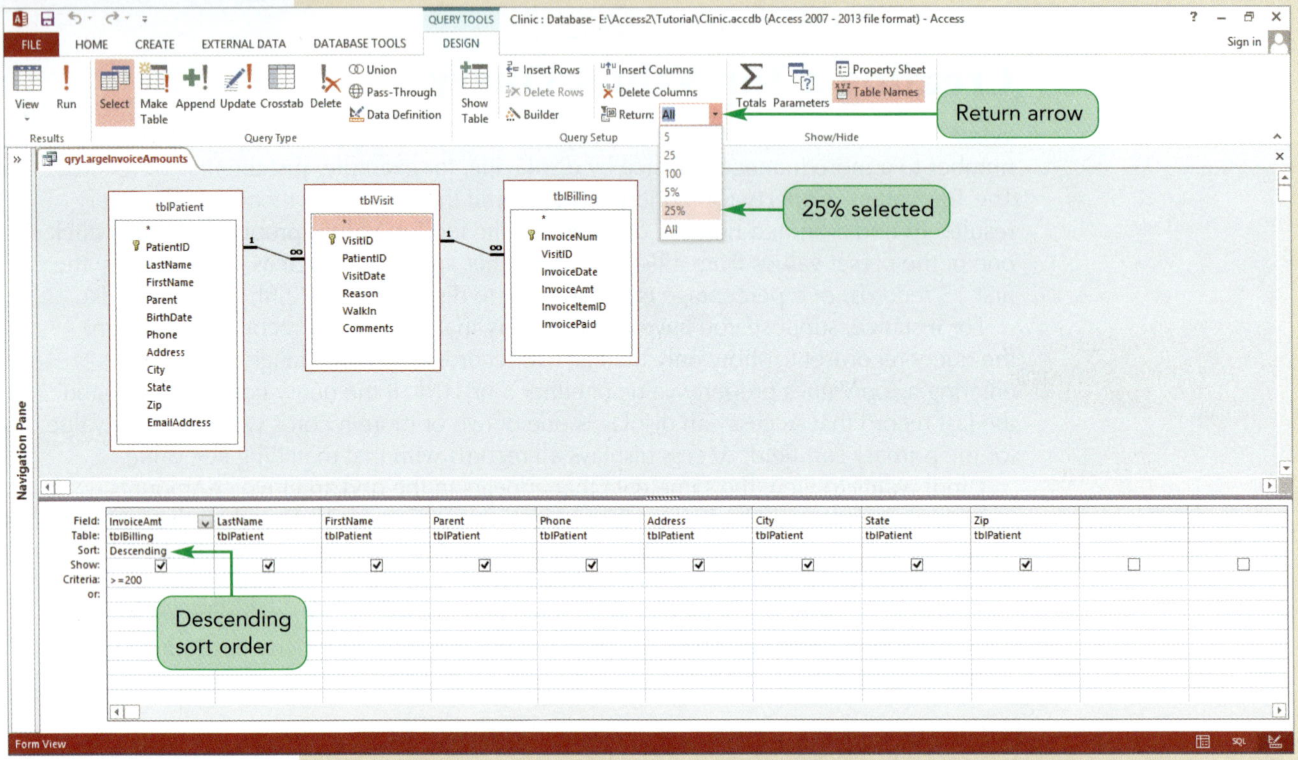

If the number or percentage of records you want to select, such as 15 or 20%, doesn't appear in the Top Values list, you can type the number or percentage in the Return box.

4. Run the query. Access displays four records in the query recordset; these records represent the patients with the highest 25 percent of the invoice amounts (25 percent of the original 14 records). See Figure 5-28.

Figure 5-28 **Top values query recordset**

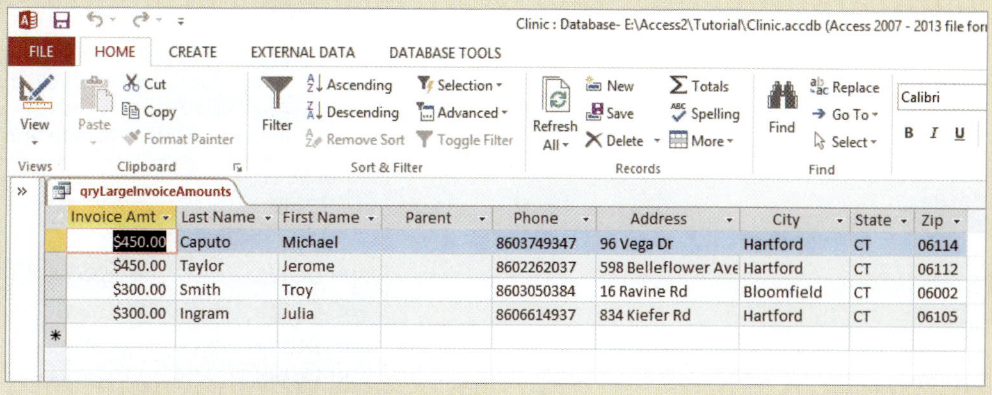

5. Save and close the query.
6. If you are not continuing on to the next session, close the Clinic database.

Cindi will use the information provided by the queries you created to analyze the Chatham Community Health Services business and to contact patients. In the next session, you will enhance the tblPatient and tblVisit tables.

REVIEW

Session 5.2 Quick Check

1. What is the purpose of a crosstab query?
2. What are the four query wizards you can use to create a new query?
3. What is a find duplicates query?
4. What does a find unmatched query do?
5. What happens when you set a query's Top Values property?
6. What happens if you set a query's Top Values property to 2 and the first five records have the same value for the primary sort field?

Session 5.3 Visual Overview:

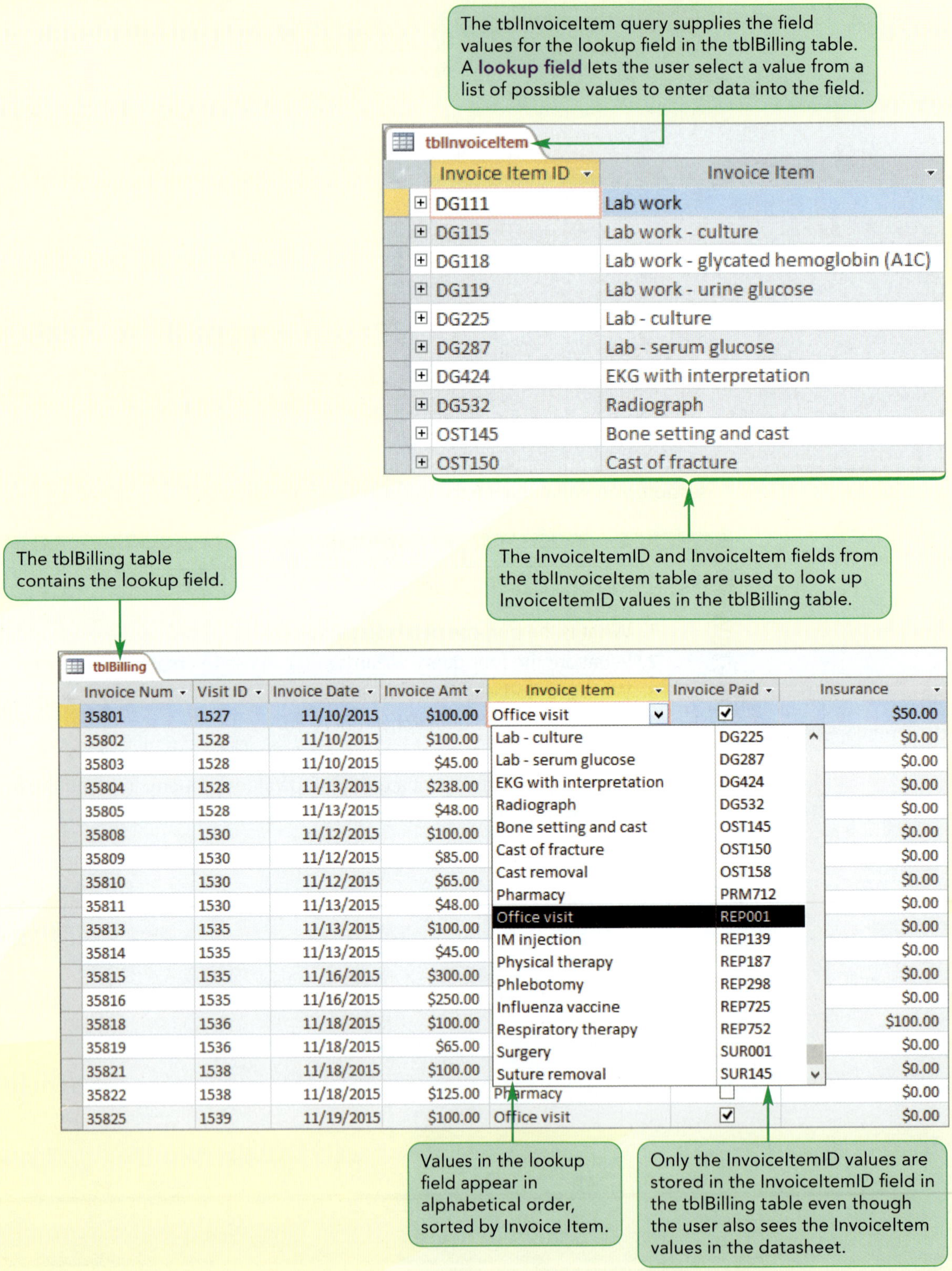

Lookup Fields and Input Masks

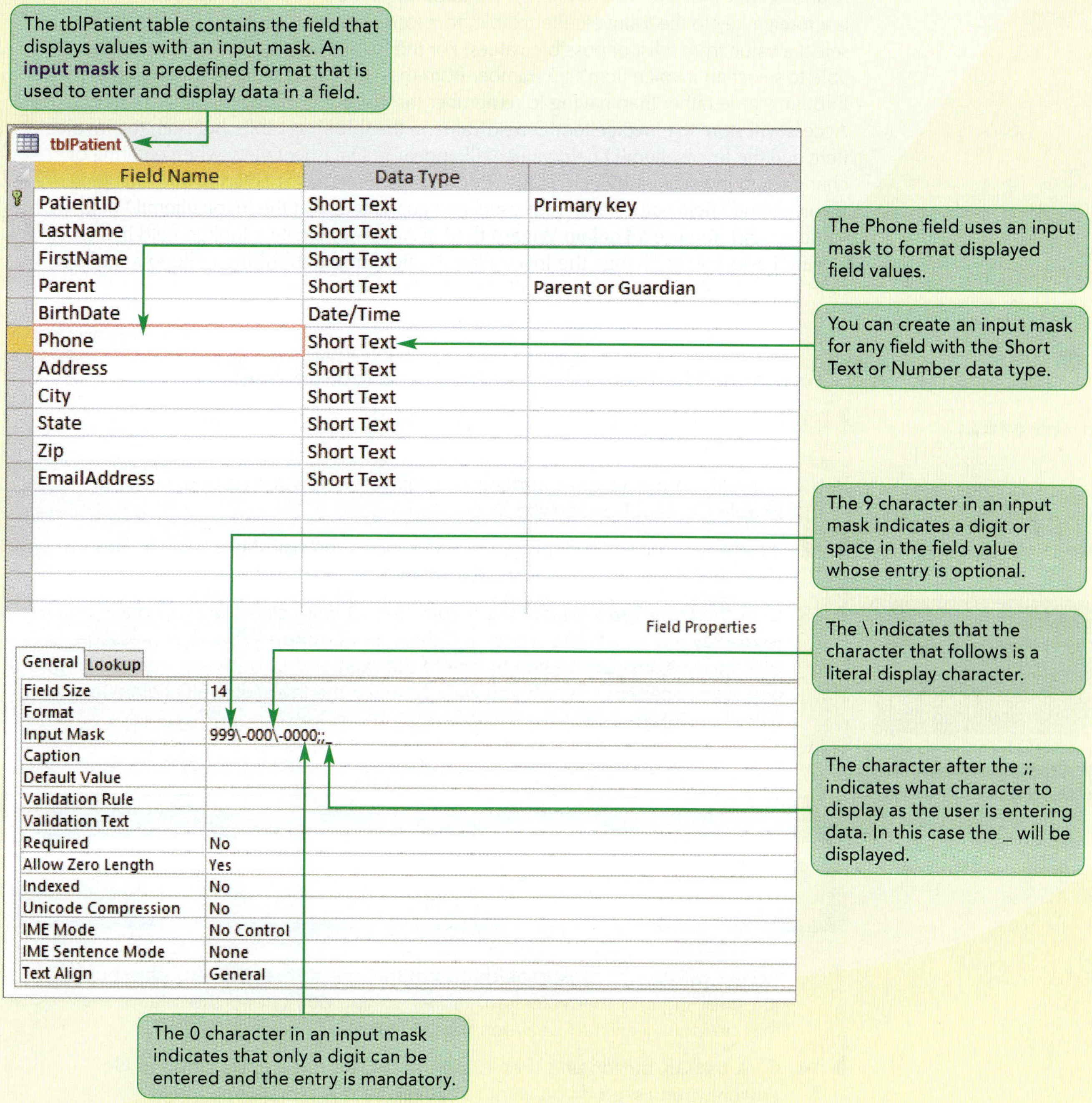

Creating a Lookup Field

The tblBilling table in the Clinic database contains information about patient invoices. Cindi wants to make entering data in the table easier for her staff. In particular, data entry is easier if they do not need to remember the correct InvoiceItemID field value for each treatment. Because the tblInvoiceItem and tblBIlling tables have a one-to-many relationship, Cindi asks you to change the tblBilling table's InvoiceItemID field, which is a foreign key to the tblInvoiceItem table, to a lookup field. A lookup field lets the user select a value from a list of possible values. For the InvoiceItemID field, a user will be able to select an invoice item's ID number from the list of invoice item names in the tblBilling table rather than having to remember the correct InvoiceItemID field value. Access will store the InvoiceItemID field value in the tblBilling table, but both the invoice item and the InvoiceItemID field value will appear in Datasheet view when entering or changing an InvoiceItemID field value. This arrangement makes entering and changing InvoiceItemID field values easier for users and guarantees that the InvoiceItemID field value is valid. You use a **Lookup Wizard field** in Access to create a lookup field in a table.

Cindi asks you to change the InvoiceItemID field in the tblBilling table to a lookup field. You'll begin by opening the tblBilling table in Design view.

To change the InvoiceItemID field to a lookup field:

1. If you took a break after the previous session, make sure that the Clinic database is open.

   Trouble? If the security warning is displayed below the ribbon, click the Enable Content button next to the warning.

2. If necessary, open the Navigation Pane, open the **tblBilling** table in Design view, and then close the Navigation Pane.

3. Click the **Data Type** box for the InvoiceItemID field, click the drop-down arrow to display the list of data types, and then click **Lookup Wizard**. A message box appears, instructing you to delete the relationship between the tblBilling and tblInvoiceItem tables if you want to make the InvoiceItemID field a lookup field. See Figure 5-29.

TIP

You can display the arrow and the menu simultaneously if you click the box near its right side.

Figure 5-29 Warning message for an existing table relationship

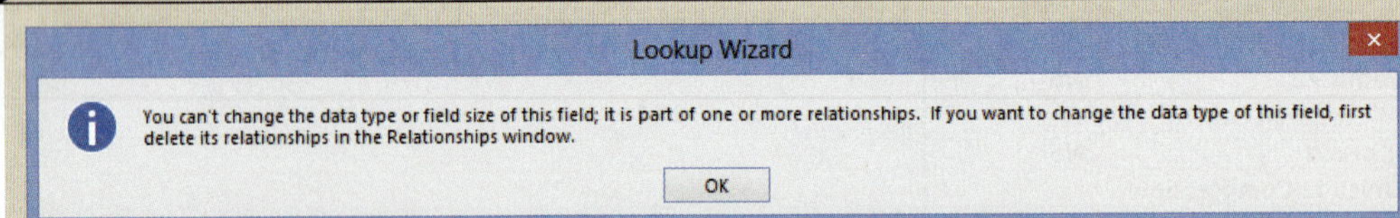

Access will use the lookup field to form the one-to-many relationship between the tblBilling and tblInvoiceItem tables, so you don't need the relationship that previously existed between the two tables.

4. Click the **OK** button and then close the tblBilling table, clicking the **No** button when asked if you want to save the table design changes.

5. Click the **DATABASE TOOLS** tab on the ribbon, and then in the Relationships group, click the **Relationships** button to open the Relationships window.

6. Right-click the join line between the tblBilling and tblInvoiceItem tables, click **Delete**, and then click the **Yes** button to confirm the deletion.

Trouble? If the Delete command does not appear on the shortcut menu, click a blank area in the Relationships window to close the shortcut menu, and then repeat Step 6, ensuring you right-click on the relationship line.

7. Close the Relationships window.

Now you can resume changing the InvoiceItemID field to a lookup field.

To finish changing the InvoiceItemID field to a lookup field:

1. Open the **tblBilling** table in Design view, and then close the Navigation Pane.
2. Click the right side of the **Data Type** box for the InvoiceItemID field, if necessary click the drop-down arrow, and then click **Lookup Wizard**. The first Lookup Wizard dialog box opens.

   This dialog box lets you specify a list of allowed values for the InvoiceItemID field in a record in the tblBilling table. You can specify a table or query from which users select the value, or you can enter a new list of values. You want the InvoiceItemID values to come from the tblInvoiceItem table.
3. Make sure the option for "I want the lookup field to get the values from another table or query" is selected, and then click the **Next** button to display the next Lookup Wizard dialog box.
4. Click the **Tables** option button in the View section to display the list of tables, if it is not already displayed, click **Table: tblInvoiceItem**, and then click the **Next** button to display the next Lookup Wizard dialog box. See Figure 5-30.

Figure 5-30 **Selecting the lookup fields**

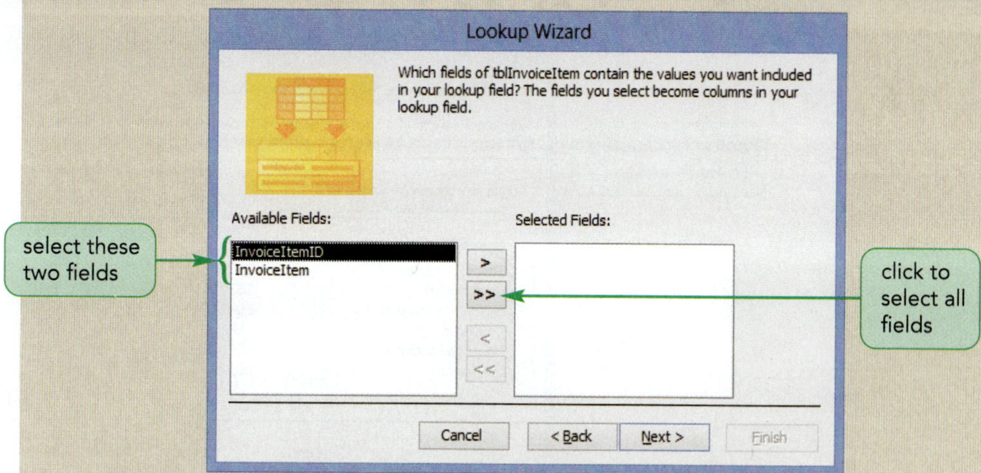

This dialog box lets you select the lookup fields from the tblInvoiceItem table. You need to select the InvoiceItemID field because it's the common field that links the tblInvoiceItem table and the tblBilling table. You also must select the InvoiceItem field because Cindi wants the user to be able to select from a list of invoice item names when entering a new contract record or changing an existing InvoiceItemID field value.

5. Click the >> button to move the InvoiceItemID and InvoiceItem fields to the Selected Fields box, and then click the **Next** button to display the next Lookup Wizard dialog box. This dialog box lets you choose a sort order for the box entries. Cindi wants the entries to appear in ascending Invoice Item order. Note that ascending is the default sort order.
6. Click the **arrow** for the first box, click **InvoiceItem**, and then click the **Next** button to open the next dialog box.

   In this dialog box, you can adjust the widths of the lookup columns. Note that when you resize a column to its best fit, Access resizes the column so that the widest column heading and the visible field values fit the column width. However, some field values that aren't visible in this dialog box might be wider than the column width, so you must scroll down the column to make sure you don't have to repeat the column resizing.
7. Click the Hide key column check box to remove the checkmark and display the InvoiceItemID field.
8. Click the InvoiceItemID column heading to select it. With the mouse pointer on the InvoiceItemID heading, drag it to the right of the InvoiceItem field to move the InvoiceItemID field to the right.
9. Place the pointer on the right edge of the InvoiceItem field column heading, and then when the pointer changes to ↔, double-click to resize the column to its best fit.
10. Scroll down the columns and repeat Step 9 as necessary until the InvoiceItem column accommodates all contents, and then press **Ctrl + Home** to scroll back to the top of the InvoiceItem column. See Figure 5-31.

Figure 5-31 **Adjusting the width of the lookup column**

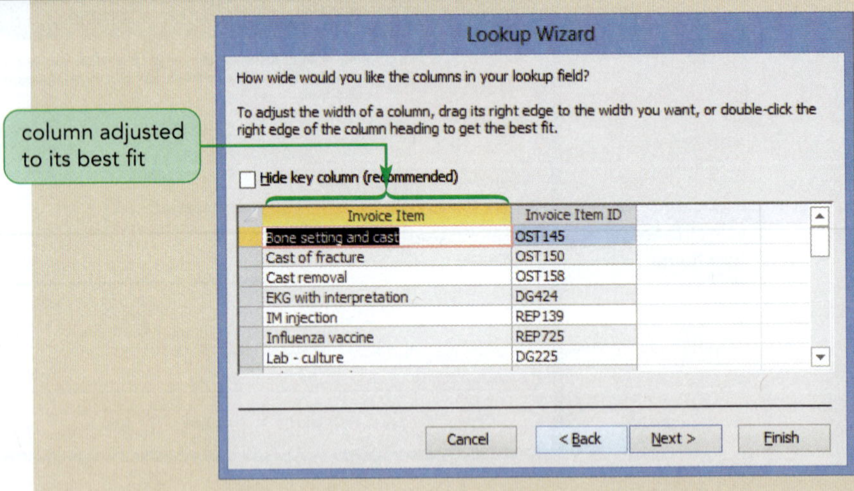

11. Click the **Next** button.

    In the next dialog box, you select the field you want to store in the table. You'll store the InvoiceItemID field in the tblBilling table because it's the foreign key to the tblInvoiceItem table.
12. Click **InvoiceItemID** in the Available Fields box if it's not already selected, and then click the **Next** button.

In the next dialog box, you specify the field name for the lookup field. Because you'll be storing the InvoiceItemID field in the table, you'll accept the default field name, InvoiceItemID.

13. Click the **Finish** button, and then click Yes to save the table.

The Data Type value for the InvoiceItemID field is still Short Text because this field contains text data. However, when you update the field, Access uses the InvoiceItemID field value to look up and display in the tblBilling table datasheet both the InvoiceItem and InvoiceItemID field values from the tblInvoiceItem table.

In reviewing patient visits recently, Cindi noticed that the InvoiceItemID field value stored in the tblBilling table for visit number 1552 is incorrect. She asks you to test the new lookup field to select the correct field value. To do so, you need to switch to Datasheet view.

To change the InvoiceItemID field value:

1. Switch to Datasheet view, and then resize the **Invoice Item** column to its best fit.

   Notice that the Invoice Item column displays InvoiceItem field values, even though the InvoiceItemID field values are stored in the table.

2. For Visit Num 1552, click **Office visit** in the Invoice Item column, and then click the **arrow** to display the list of InvoiceItem and InvoiceItemID field values from the tblInvoiceItems table. See Figure 5-32.

Figure 5-32 List of InvoiceItem and InvoiceItemID field values

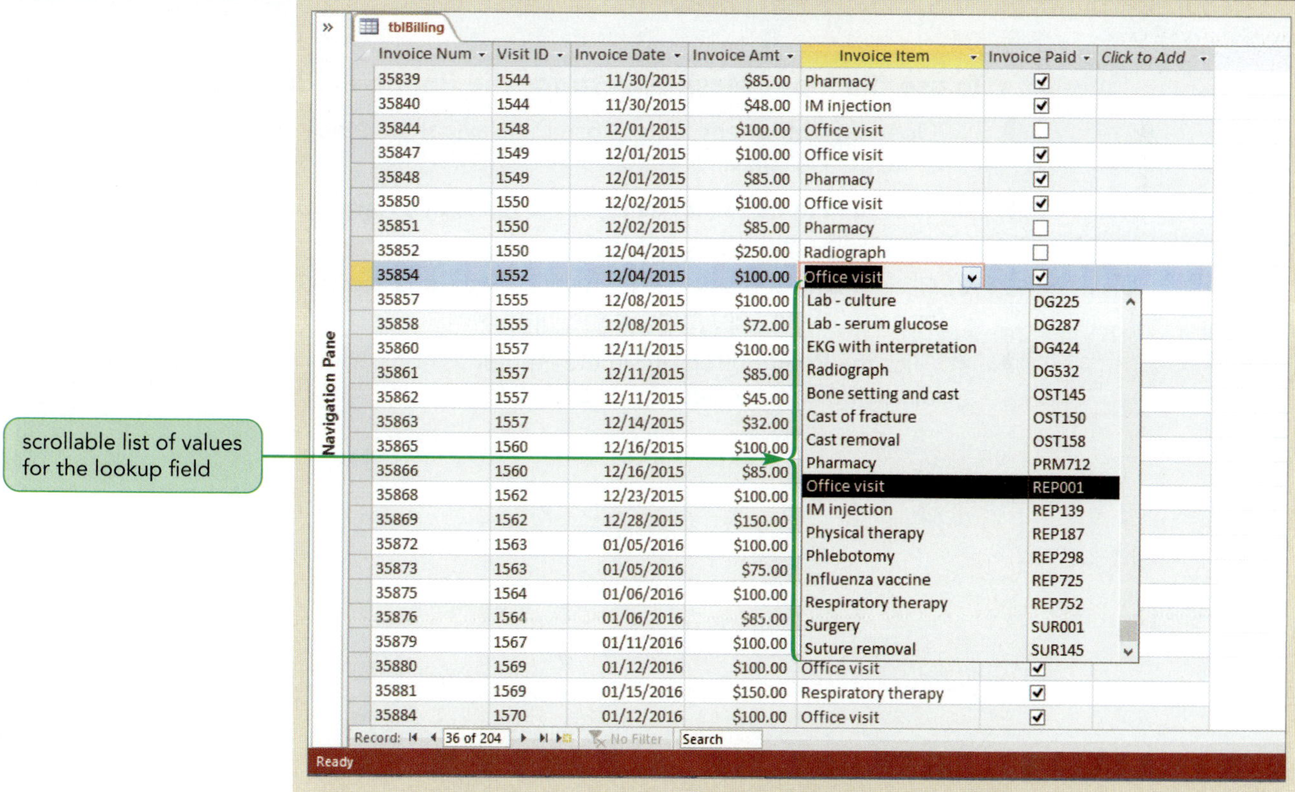

The invoice item for visit 1552 is Pharmacy, so you need to select this entry in the list to change the InvoiceItemID field value.

3. Scroll through the list if necessary, and then click **Pharmacy** to select that value to display in the datasheet and to store the InvoiceItemID field value of PRM712 in the table. The list closes and "Pharmacy" appears in the InvoiceItemID column.
4. Save and close the tblBilling table.

Next, Cindi asks you to change the appearance of the Phone field in the tblPatient table to a standard telephone number format.

Using the Input Mask Wizard

The Phone field in the tblPatient table is a 10-digit number that's difficult to read because it appears with none of the special formatting characters usually associated with a telephone number. For example, the Phone field value for Darcy Edward, which appears as 8603053985, would be more readable in any of the following formats: 860-305-3985, 860.305.3985, 860/305-3985, or (860) 305-3985. Cindi asks you to use the (860) 305-3985 style for the Phone field.

Cindi wants the parentheses and hyphens to appear as literal display characters whenever users enter Phone field values. A literal display character is a special character that automatically appears in specific positions of a field value; users don't need to type literal display characters. To include these characters, you need to create an input mask, which is a predefined format used to enter and display data in a field. An easy way to create an input mask is to use the **Input Mask Wizard**, an Access tool that guides you in creating a predefined format for a field. You must be in Design view to use the Input Mask Wizard.

To use the Input Mask Wizard for the Phone field:

1. Open the **tblPatient** table, close the Navigation Pane, and then, if necessary, switch to Design view.
2. Click the **Phone Field Name** box to make that row the current row and to display its Field Properties options.
3. Click the **Input Mask** box in the Field Properties pane. The Build button ... appears at the right edge of the Input Mask box.
4. Click the **Build** button ... in the Input Mask box. The first Input Mask Wizard dialog box opens. See Figure 5-33.

Figure 5-33 Input Mask Wizard dialog box

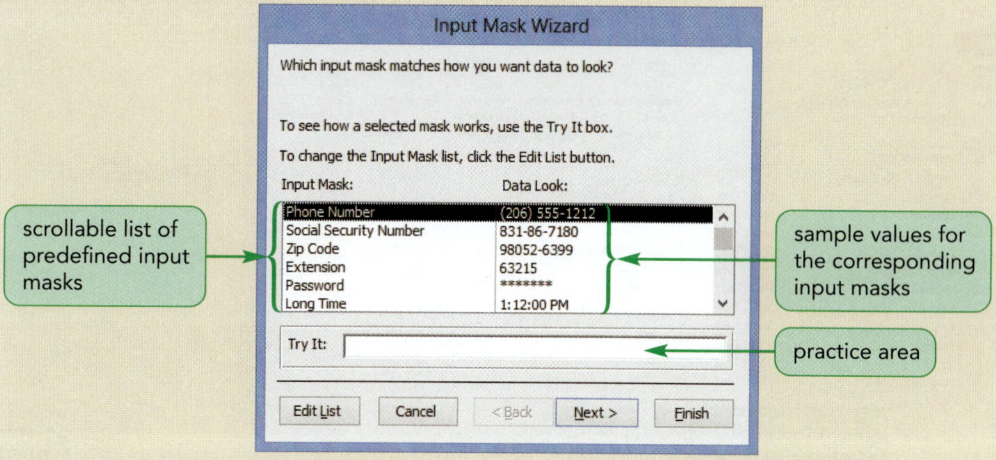

You can scroll the Input Mask box, select the input mask you want, and then enter representative values to practice using the input mask.

5. If necessary, click **Phone Number** in the Input Mask box to select it.
6. Click the far left side of the **Try It** box. (___) ___-____ appears in the Try It box. As you type a phone number, Access replaces the underscores, which are placeholder characters.

   Trouble? If your insertion point is not immediately to the right of the left parenthesis, press the ← key until it is.
7. Type **8603053985** to practice entering a sample phone number. The input mask formats the typed value as (860) 305-3985.
8. Click the **Next** button. The next Input Mask Wizard dialog box opens. In it, you can change the input mask and the placeholder character. Because you can change an input mask easily after the Input Mask Wizard finishes, you'll accept all wizard defaults.
9. Click the **Finish** button, and then click to the right of the value in the Input Mask box to deselect the characters. The Input Mask Wizard creates the phone number input mask, placing it in the Input Mask box for the Phone field. See Figure 5-34.

Figure 5-34 **Phone number input mask created by the Input Mask Wizard**

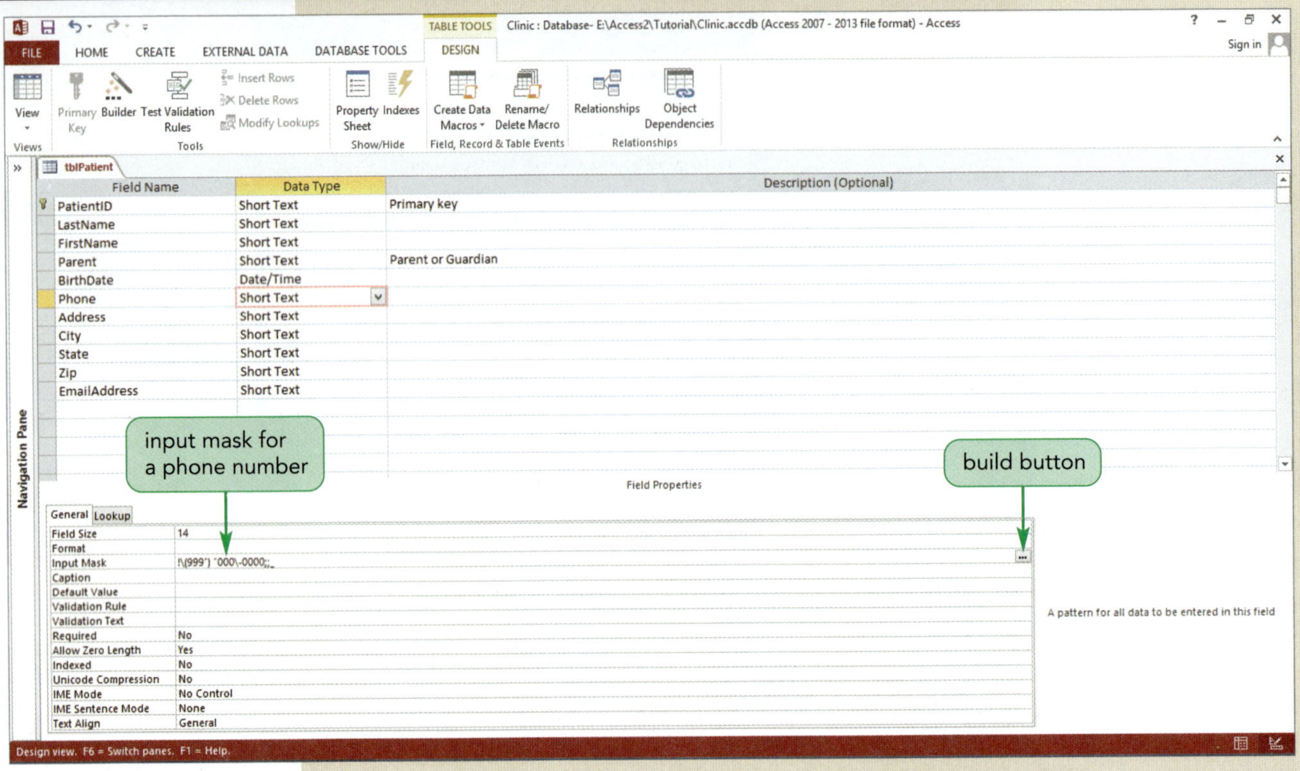

The characters used in a field's input mask restrict the data you can enter in the field, as shown in Figure 5-35. Other characters that appear in an input mask, such as the left and right parentheses in the phone number input mask, are literal display characters.

Figure 5-35 Input mask characters

Input Mask Character	Description
0	Digit only must be entered. Entry is required.
9	Digit or space can be entered. Entry is optional.
#	Digit, space, or a plus or minus sign can be entered. Entry is optional.
L	Letter only must be entered. Entry is required.
?	Letter only can be entered. Entry is optional.
A	Letter or digit must be entered. Entry is required.
a	Letter or digit can be entered. Entry is optional.
&	Any character or a space must be entered. Entry is required.
C	Any character or a space can be entered. Entry is optional.
>	All characters that follow are displayed in uppercase.
<	All characters that follow are displayed in lowercase.
"	Enclosed characters treated as literal display characters.
\	Following character treated as a literal display character. This is the same as enclosing a single character in quotation marks.
!	Input mask is displayed from right to left, rather than the default of left to right. Characters typed into the mask always fill in from left to right.
;;	The character between the first and second semicolons determines whether to store the literal display characters in the database. If the value is 1 or if no value is provided, the literal display characters are not stored. If the value is 0, the literal display characters are stored. The character following the second semicolon is the placeholder character that appears in the displayed input mask.

Cindi wants to view the Phone field with the default input mask.

To view and change the input mask for the Phone field:

1. Save the table, and then switch to Datasheet view. The Phone field values now have the format specified by the input mask.

   Cindi decides that she would prefer to omit the parentheses around the area codes and use only hyphens as separators in the displayed Phone field values, so you'll change the input mask in Design view.

2. Switch to Design view.

   The input mask is set to !\(999”) ”000\-0000;;_. The backslash character (\) causes the character that follows it to appear as a literal display character. Characters enclosed in quotation marks also appear as literal display characters. (See Figure 5-35.) The exclamation mark (!) forces the existing data to fill the input mask from right to left instead of left to right. This does not affect new data. This only applies to the situation when data already exists in the table and a new input mask is applied. For instance, if the existing data is 5551234 and the input mask fills from left to right, the data with the input mask would look like: (555) 123-4. If the input mask fills from right to left, the data with the input mask applied would look like: () 555-1234.

   If you omit the backslashes preceding the hyphens, Access will automatically insert them when you press the Tab key. However, Access doesn't add backslashes automatically for other literal display characters, such as periods and slashes, so it's best to always type the backslashes. Since all of the existing data includes the area code, it will not make a difference whether the input mask applied to the data fills the data from left to right or from right to left, so you'll omit the ! symbol.

3. In the Input Mask box for the Phone field, change the input mask to **999\-000\-0000;;_** and then press the **Tab** key.

   Because you've modified a field property, the Property Update Options button appears to the left of the Input Mask property.

4. Click the **Property Update Options** button. A menu opens below the button, as shown in Figure 5-36.

Figure 5-36 Property Update Options button menu

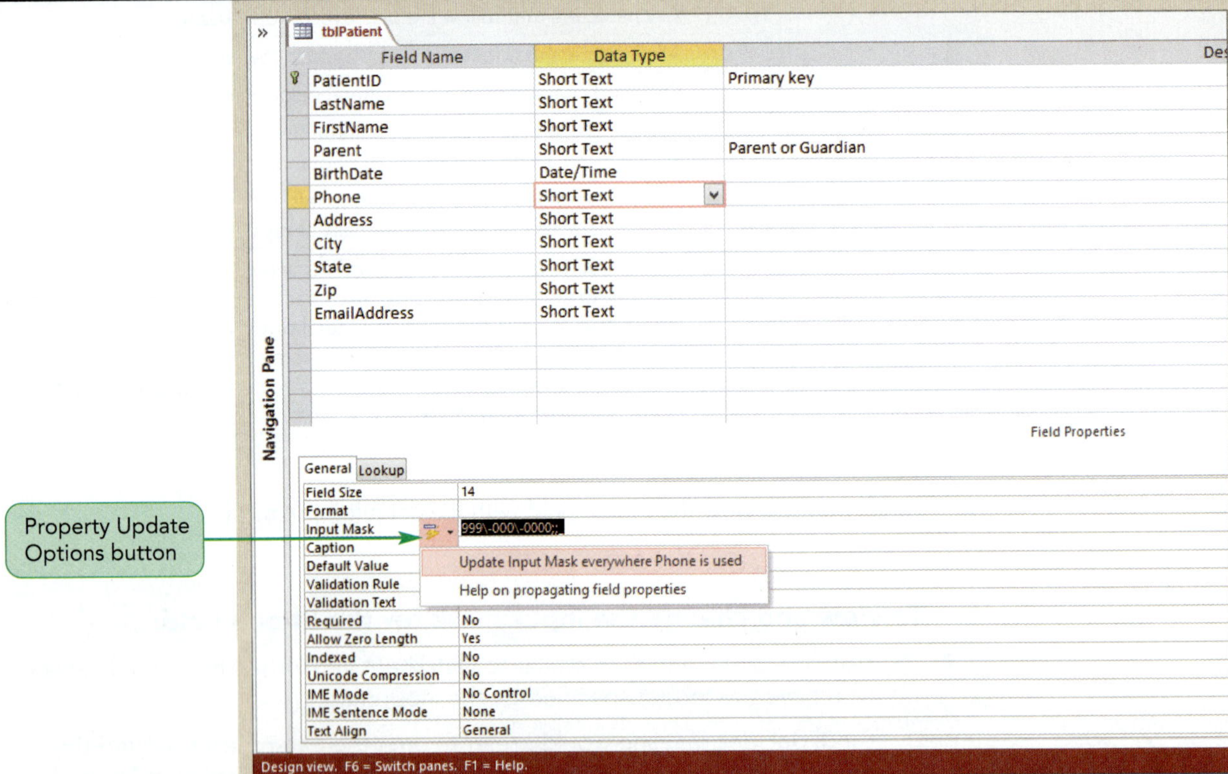

5. Click **Update Input Mask everywhere Phone is used**. The Update Properties dialog box opens. See Figure 5-37.

Figure 5-37 Update Properties dialog box

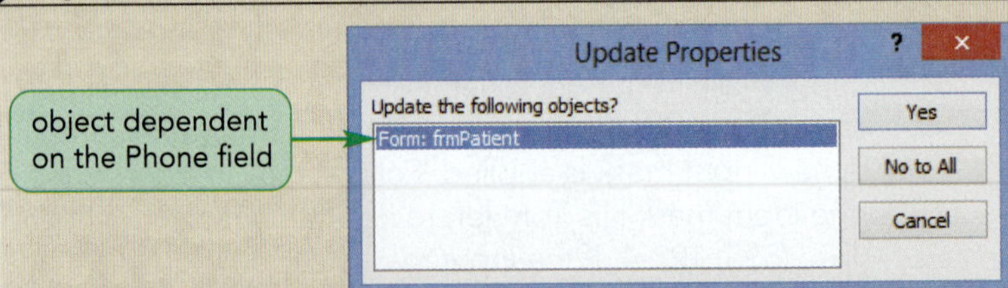

Because the frmPatient form displays the Phone field values from the tblPatient table, Access will automatically change the Phone field's Input Mask property in this object to your new input mask. If other form objects included the Phone field from the tblPatient table, they would be included in this dialog box as well. This capability to update field properties in objects automatically when you modify a table field property is called **property propagation**. Although the Update Properties dialog box displays no queries, property propagation also does occur with queries automatically. Property propagation is limited to field properties such as the Decimal Places, Description, Format, and Input Mask properties.

6. Click the **Yes** button, save the table, switch to Datasheet view, and then resize the Phone column to its best fit. The Phone field values now have the format Cindi requested. See Figure 5-38.

Figure 5-38 After changing the Phone field input mask

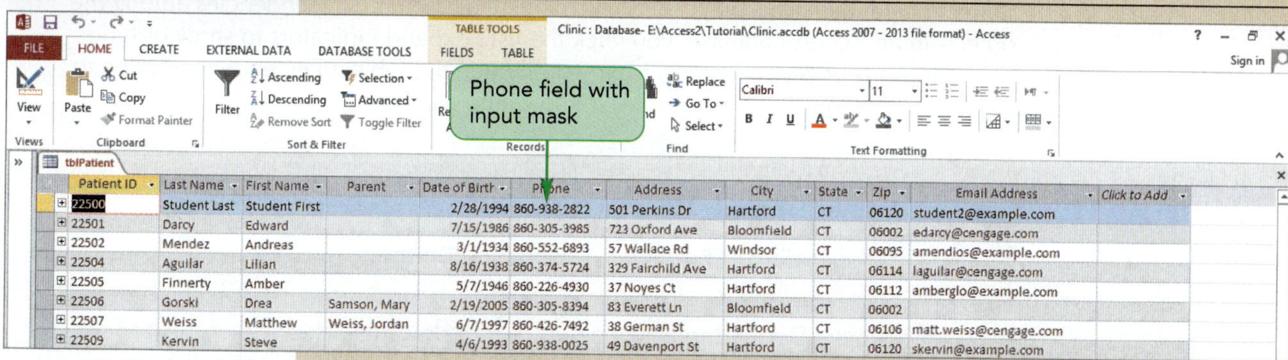

Because Cindi wants her staff to store only standard 10-digit U.S. phone numbers for patients, the input mask you've created will enforce the standard entry and display format that Cindi desires.

INSIGHT

Understanding When to Use Input Masks

An input mask is appropriate for a field only if all field values have a consistent format. For example, you can use an input mask with hyphens as literal display characters to store U.S. phone numbers in a consistent format of 987-654-3210. However, a multinational company would not be able to use an input mask to store phone numbers from all countries because international phone numbers do not have a consistent format. In the same way, U.S. zip codes have a consistent format, and you could use an input mask of 00000#9999 to enter and display U.S. zip codes such as 98765 and 98765-4321, but you could not use an input mask if you need to store and display foreign postal codes in the same field. If you need to store and display phone numbers, zip/postal codes, and other fields in a variety of formats, it's best to define them as Short Text fields without an input mask so users can enter the correct literal display characters.

After the change to the Phone field's input mask, Access gave you the option to update, selectively and automatically, the Phone field's Input Mask property in other objects in the database. Cindi is thinking about making significant changes to the way data is stored in the tblPatient table, and wants to understand which other elements those changes might impact. To determine the dependencies among objects in an Access database, you'll open the Object Dependencies pane.

Identifying Object Dependencies

An **object dependency** exists between two objects when a change to the properties of data in one object affects the properties of data in the other object. Dependencies between Access objects, such as tables, queries, and forms, can occur in various ways. For example, the tblVisit and tblBilling tables are dependent on each other because they have a one-to-many relationship. In the same way, the tblVisit table uses the qryPatientsByName query to obtain the Patient field to display along with the PatientID field, and this creates a dependency between these two objects. Any query, form, or other object that uses fields from a given table is dependent on that table. Any form or report that uses fields from a query is directly dependent on the query and is indirectly dependent on the tables that provide the data to the query. Large databases contain hundreds of objects, so it is useful to have a way to easily view the dependencies among objects before you attempt to delete or modify an object. The **Object Dependencies pane** displays a collapsible list of the dependencies among the objects in an Access database; you click the list's expand indicators to show or hide different levels of dependencies. Next, you'll open the Object Dependencies pane to show Cindi the object dependencies in the Clinic database.

To open and use the Object Dependencies pane:

1. Click the **DATABASE TOOLS** tab on the ribbon.
2. In the Relationships group, click the **Object Dependencies** button to open the Object Dependencies pane, and then drag the left edge of the pane to the left until the horizontal scroll bar at the bottom of the pane disappears. See Figure 5-39.

Figure 5-39 After opening the Object Dependencies pane

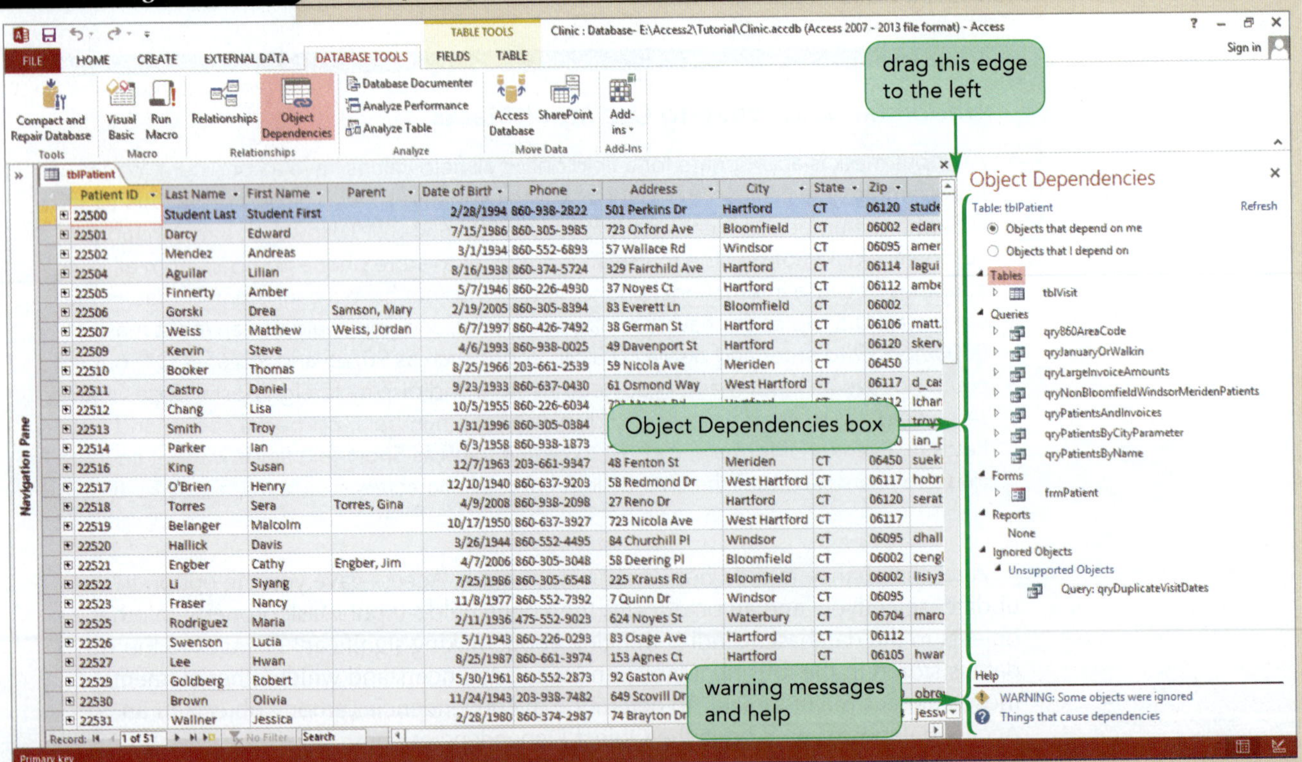

Trouble? If the "Objects that depend on me" option button is not selected, click the option button to select it.

The Object Dependencies pane displays the objects that depend on the tblPatient table, the object name that appears at the top of the pane. If you change the design of the tblPatient table, the change might affect objects in the pane. Changing a property for a field in the tblPatient table that's also used by a listed object affects that listed object. If a listed object does not use the field you are changing, that listed object is not affected.

Objects listed in the Ignored Objects section of the box might have an object dependency with the tblPatient table, and you'd have to review them individually to determine if a dependency exists. The Help section at the bottom of the pane displays links for further information about object dependencies.

3. Click the **frmPatient** link in the Object Dependencies pane. The frmPatient form opens in Design view. All the fields in the form are fields from the tblPatient table, which is why the form has an object dependency with the table.
4. Switch to Form view for the frmPatient form. Note that the Phone field value is displayed using the input mask you applied to the field in the tblPatient table. Access propagated this change from the table to the form.
5. Close the frmPatient form, open the Navigation Pane, open the **tblVisit** table in Datasheet view, and then click the **Refresh** link near the top of the Object Dependencies pane. The Object Dependencies box now displays the objects that depend on the tblVisit table.
6. Click the **Objects that I depend on** option button near the top of the pane to view the objects that affect the tblVisit table.
7. Click the **Objects that depend on me** option button and then click the **expand indicator** ▷ for the qryVisitsAndInvoices query in the Object Dependencies pane. The list expands to display the rptVisitsAndInvoices report, which is a report that the query depends upon.
8. Close the tblVisit table, close the Object Dependencies pane, and then save and close the tblPatient table.

Cindi now better understands object dependencies and how to identify them by using the Object Dependencies pane. She's decided to leave the tblPatient table the way it is for the moment to avoid making changes to forms and/or queries.

Defining Data Validation Rules

Cindi wants to minimize the amount of incorrect data in the database caused by typing errors. To do so, she wants to limit the entry of InvoiceAmt field values in the tblBilling table to values greater than $10 because Chatham Community Health Services does not invoice patients for balances of $10 or less. In addition, she wants to make sure that the Insurance field value entered in each tblBilling table record is either the same or less than the InvoiceAmt field value. The InvoiceAmt value represents the total price for the visit or procedure, and the Insurance value is the amount covered by the patient's insurance. The Insurance value may be equal to or less than the InvoiceAmt value, but it will never be more, so comparing these numbers is an additional test to ensure the data entered in a record makes sense. To provide these checks on entered data, you'll set field validation properties for the InvoiceAmt field in the tblBilling table and set table validation properties in the tblBilling table.

Defining Field Validation Rules

To prevent a user from entering an unacceptable value in the InvoiceAmt field, you can create a **field validation rule** that verifies a field value by comparing it to a constant or to a set of constants. You create a field validation rule by setting the Validation Rule and the Validation Text field properties. The **Validation Rule property** value specifies the valid values that users can enter in a field. The **Validation Text property** value will be displayed in a dialog box if a user enters an invalid value (in this case, an InvoiceAmt field value of $10 or less). After you set these two InvoiceAmt field properties in the tblBilling table, Access will prevent users from entering an invalid InvoiceAmt field value in the tblBilling table and in all current and future queries and future forms that include the InvoiceAmt field.

You'll now set the Validation Rule and Validation Text properties for the InvoiceAmt field in the tblBilling table.

To create and test a field validation rule for the InvoiceAmt field:

1. Open the **tblBilling** table in Design view, close the Navigation Pane, and then click the **InvoiceAmt Field Name** box to make that row the current row.

   To make sure that all values entered in the InvoiceAmt field are greater than 10, you'll use the > comparison operator in the Validation Rule box.

2. In the Field Properties pane, click the **Validation Rule** box, type **>10**, and then press the **Tab** key.

   You can set the Validation Text property to a value that appears in a dialog box that opens if a user enters a value not listed in the Validation Rule box.

3. In the Validation Text box, type **Invoice amounts must be greater than 10**. See Figure 5-40.

Figure 5-40 **Validation properties for the InvoiceAmt field**

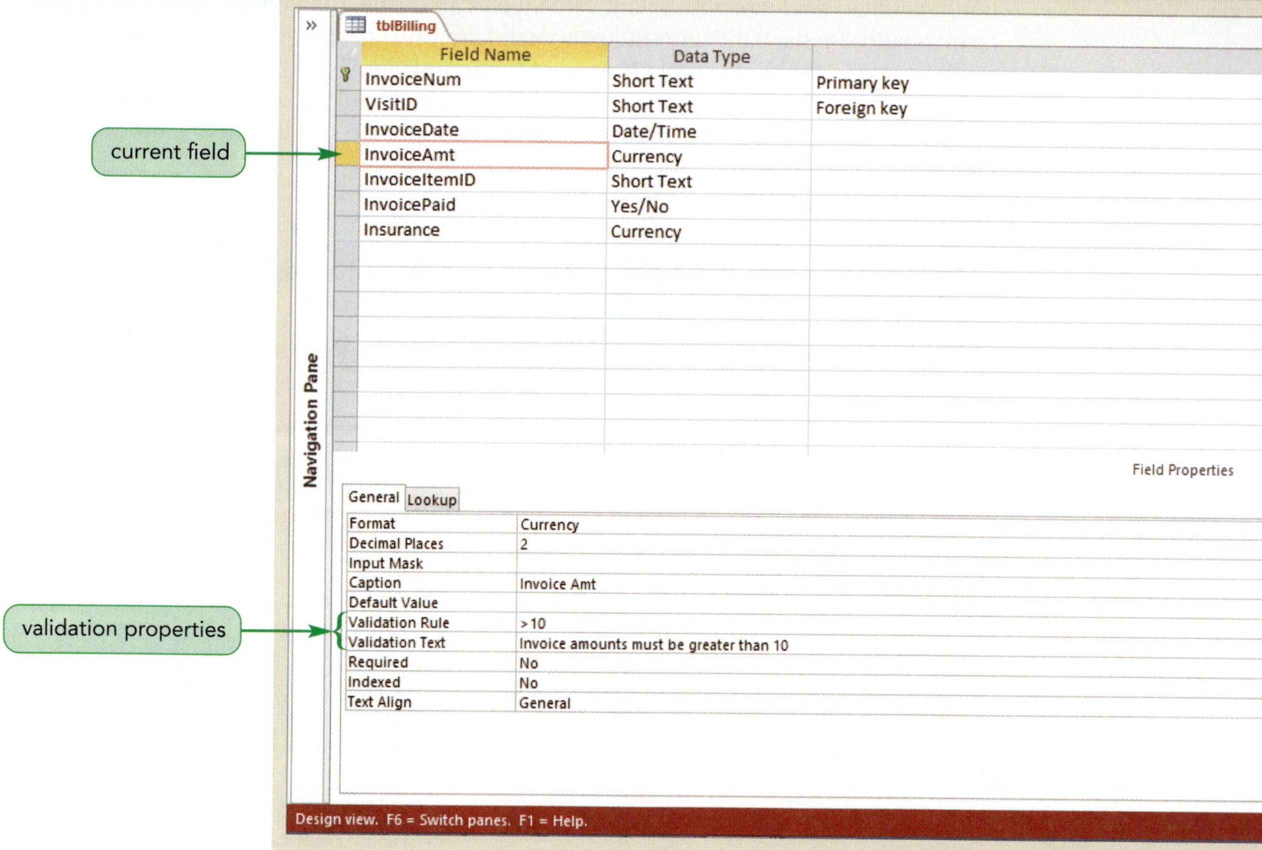

You can now save the table design changes and then test the validation properties.

4. Save the table, and then click the **Yes** button when asked if you want to test the existing InvoiceAmt field values in the tblBilling table against the new validation rule.

   Access tests the existing records in the tblBilling table against the validation rule. If any existing record violated the rule, you would be prompted to continue testing or to revert to the previous Validation Rule property setting. Next, you'll test the validation rule.

5. Switch to Datasheet view, select **$100.00** in the first row's InvoiceAmt field box, type **5**, and then press the **Tab** key. A dialog box opens containing the message "Invoice amounts must be greater than 10," which is the Validation Text property setting you created in Step 3.

6. Click the **OK** button, and then press the **Esc** key. The first row's InvoiceAmt field reverts to its original value, $100.00.

7. Close the tblBilling table.

Now that you've finished entering the field validation rule for the InvoiceAmt field in the tblBilling table, you'll enter the table validation rule for the date fields in the tblVisit table.

Defining Table Validation Rules

To make sure that the Insurance field value that a user enters in the tblBilling table is not larger than the InvoiceAmt field value, you can create a **table validation rule**. Once again, you'll use the Validation Rule and Validation Text properties, but this time you'll set these properties for the table instead of for an individual field. You'll use a table validation rule because this validation involves multiple fields. A field validation rule is used when the validation involves a restriction for only the selected field, and does not depend on other fields.

To create and test a table validation rule in the tblBilling table:

Be sure "Table Properties" is listed as the selection type in the property sheet.

1. Open the tblBilling table in Design view and then on the DESIGN tab, in the Show/Hide group, click the **Property Sheet** button to open the property sheet for the table.

   To make sure that each Insurance field value is less than or equal to the InvoiceAmt field value, you use the Validation Rule box for the table.

2. In the property sheet, click the **Validation Rule** box.
3. Type **Insur**, press the **Tab** key to select Insurance in the AutoComplete box, type **<= InvoiceAm**, and then press the **Tab** key.
4. In the Validation Text box, type **Insurance coverage cannot be larger than the invoice amount**, and then if necessary widen the Property Sheet so the Validation Rule text is visible. See Figure 5-41.

Figure 5-41 Setting table validation properties

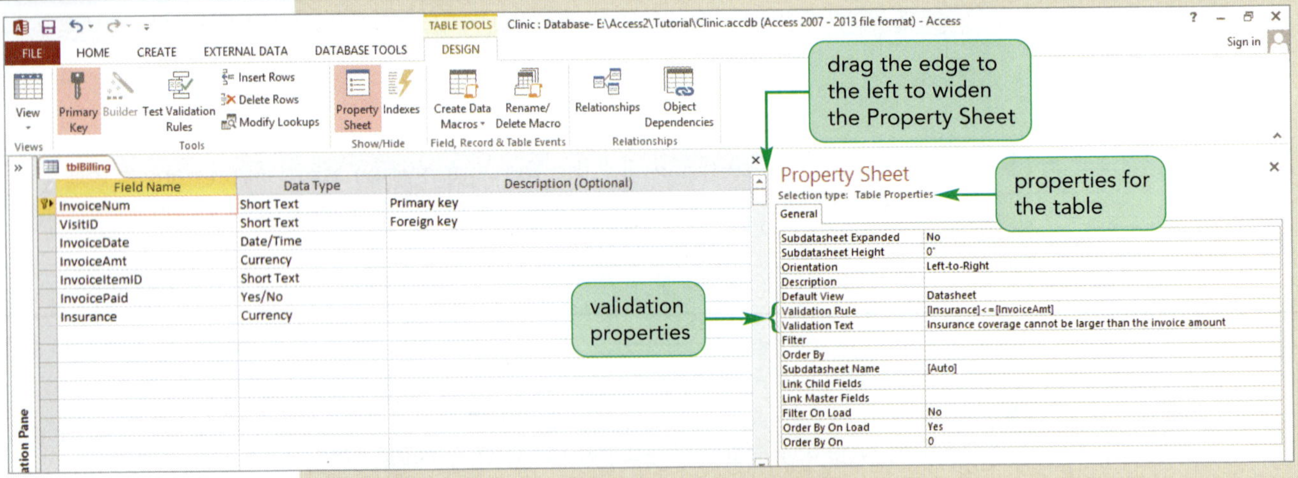

You can now test the validation properties.

5. Close the property sheet, save the table, and then click the **Yes** button when asked if you want to test the existing dates in the tblBilling table against the new validation rule.
6. Close the Navigation Pane, switch to Datasheet view, and then click the Insurance column value in the first record. Edit the Insurance value to change it to $150.00, and then press the **Tab** key to complete your changes to the record. A dialog box opens containing the message "**Insurance coverage cannot be larger than the invoice amount,**" which is the Validation Text property setting you entered in Step 4.

Unlike field validation rule violations, which Access detects immediately after you finish a field entry and advance to another field, Access detects table validation rule violations only when you finish all changes to the current record and advance to another record.

7. Click the **OK** button, and then press the **Esc** key to undo your change to the Insurance column value.
8. Close the tblBilling table.

PROSKILLS

Problem Solving: Perfecting Data Quality

It's important that you design useful queries, forms, and reports and that you test them thoroughly. But the key to any database is the accuracy of the data stored in its tables. It's critical that the data be as error-free as possible. Most companies employ people who spend many hours tracking down and correcting errors and discrepancies in their data, and you can greatly assist and minimize their problem solving by using as many database features as possible to ensure the data is correct from the start. Among these features for fields are selecting the proper data type, setting default values whenever possible, restricting the permitted values by using field and table validation rules, enforcing referential integrity, and forcing users to select values from lists instead of typing the values. Likewise, having an arsenal of queries—such as find duplicates and top values queries—available to users will expedite the work they do to find and correct data errors.

Based on a request from Cindi, Raj added a Long Text field to the tblVisit table, and now you'll review Raj's work.

Working with Long Text Fields

You use a Long Text field to store long comments and explanations. Short Text fields are limited to 255 characters, but Long Text fields can hold up to 65,535 characters. In addition, Short Text fields limit you to plain text with no special formatting, but you can define Long Text fields to store plain text similar to Short Text fields or to store rich text, which you can selectively format with options such as bold, italic, and different fonts and colors.

You'll review the Long Text field, named Comments, that Raj added to the tblVisit table.

To review the Long Text field in the tblVisit table:

1. Open the Navigation Pane, open the **tblVisit** table in Datasheet view, and then close the Navigation Pane.
2. Increase the width of the **Comments** field so most of the comments fit in the column.

   Although everything fits on the screen size and resolution shown in the figure, on some computer systems freezing panes is necessary to be able to view everything at once. On a smaller screen, if you scroll to the right to view the Comments field, you'll no longer be able to identify which patient applies to a row because the Patient ID column will be hidden. You'll also see this effect if you shrink the size of the Access window. You'll freeze the Visit ID, Patient ID, and Date of Visit columns so they remain visible in the datasheet as you scroll to the right.

3. Click the **Visit ID** column selector, press and hold down the **Shift** key, click the **Date of Visit** column selector, and then release the **Shift** key. The Visit ID, Patient ID, and Date of Visit columns should be selected.
4. On the HOME tab, in the Records group, click the **More** button, and then click **Freeze Fields**.
5. Scroll to the right until you see the Comments column. If all columns fit in the Access window, size the Access window smaller until the horizontal scroll bar is visible and not all columns are visible. Notice that the Visit ID, Patient ID, and Date of Visit columns, the three leftmost columns, remain visible. See Figure 5-42.

Figure 5-42 **Freezing three datasheet columns**

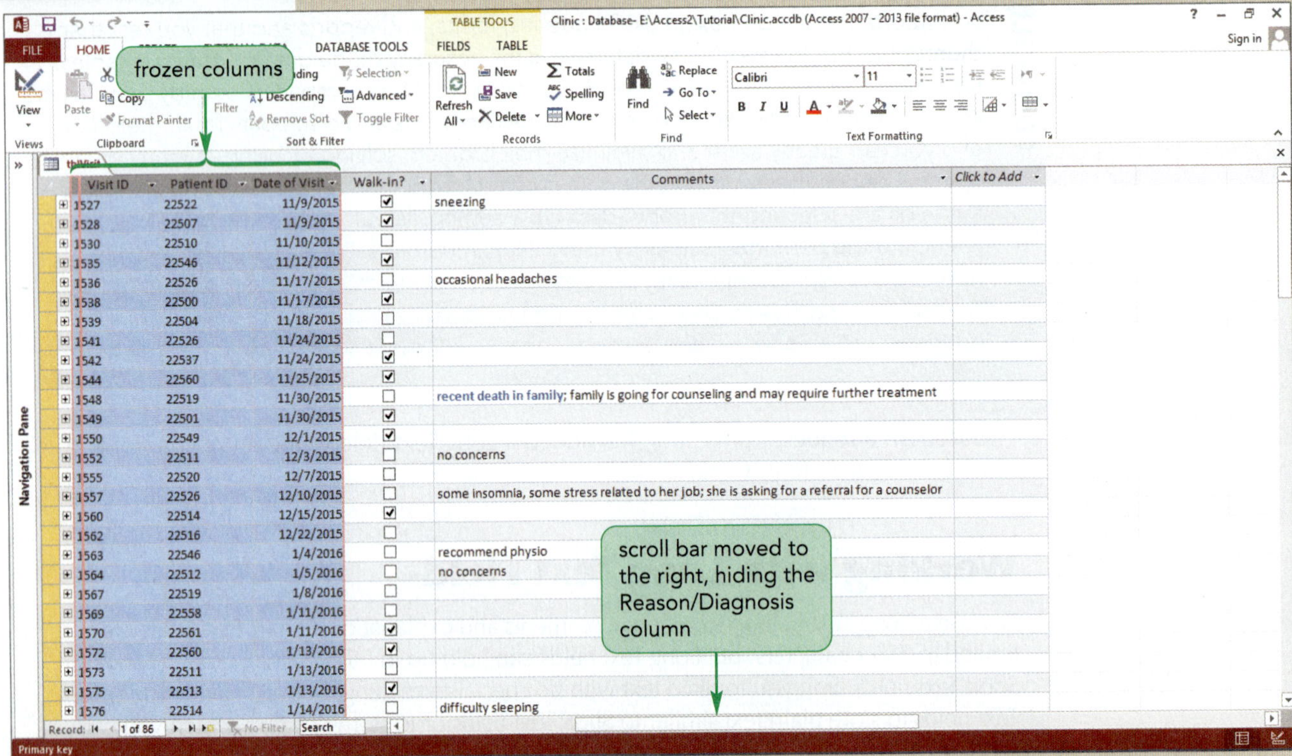

The Comments column is a Long Text field that Chatham Community Health Services clinicians use to store observations and other commentary about each patient. Note that the Comment for Visit ID 1548 displays rich text using a bold and blue font. Comments field values are partially hidden because the datasheet column is not wide enough. You'll view a record's Comments field value in the Zoom dialog box.

6. Click the **Comments** box for the record for Visit ID 1548, hold down the **Shift** key, press the **F2** key, and then release the **Shift** key. The Zoom dialog box displays the entire Comments field value.
7. Click the **OK** button to close the Zoom dialog box.

INSIGHT

Viewing Long Text Fields with Large Contents in Datasheet View

For a Long Text field that contains many characters, you can widen the field's column to view more of its contents by dragging the right edge of the field's column selector to the right or by using the Field Width command when you click the More button in the Records group on the HOME tab. However, increasing the column width reduces the number of other columns you can view at the same time. Further, for Long Text fields containing thousands of characters, you can't widen the column enough to be able to view the entire contents of the field at one time across the width of the screen. Therefore, increasing the column width of a Long Text field isn't necessarily the best strategy for viewing table contents.

Alternatively, you can increase the row height of a datasheet by dragging the bottom edge of a row selector down or by using the Row Height command when you click the More button in the Records group on the HOME tab. Increasing the row height causes the text in a Long Text field to wrap to the next line, so that you can view multiple lines at one time. Once again, however, for a Long Text field containing thousands of characters, you can't increase the row height enough to ensure that you can view the entire contents of the field at one time on screen. Additionally, you'd view fewer records at one time, and the row height setting for a table propagates to all queries that have an object dependency with the table. Thus, you generally shouldn't increase the row height of a table datasheet to accommodate a Long Text field.

What is the best way to view the contents of a Long Text field that contains a large number of characters? It is best to use the Zoom dialog box in a datasheet, or to use a large scrollable box on a form. It's really a matter of your own preference.

Now you'll review the property settings for the Comments field Raj added to the tblPatient table.

To review the property settings of the Long Text field:

1. Save the table, switch to Design view, click the **Comments Field Name** box to make that row the current row, and then, if necessary, scroll to the bottom of the list of properties in the Field Properties pane.
2. Click the **Text Format** box in the Field Properties pane, and then click its **arrow**. The list of available text formats appears in the box. See Figure 5-43.

Figure 5-43 Viewing the properties for a Long Text field

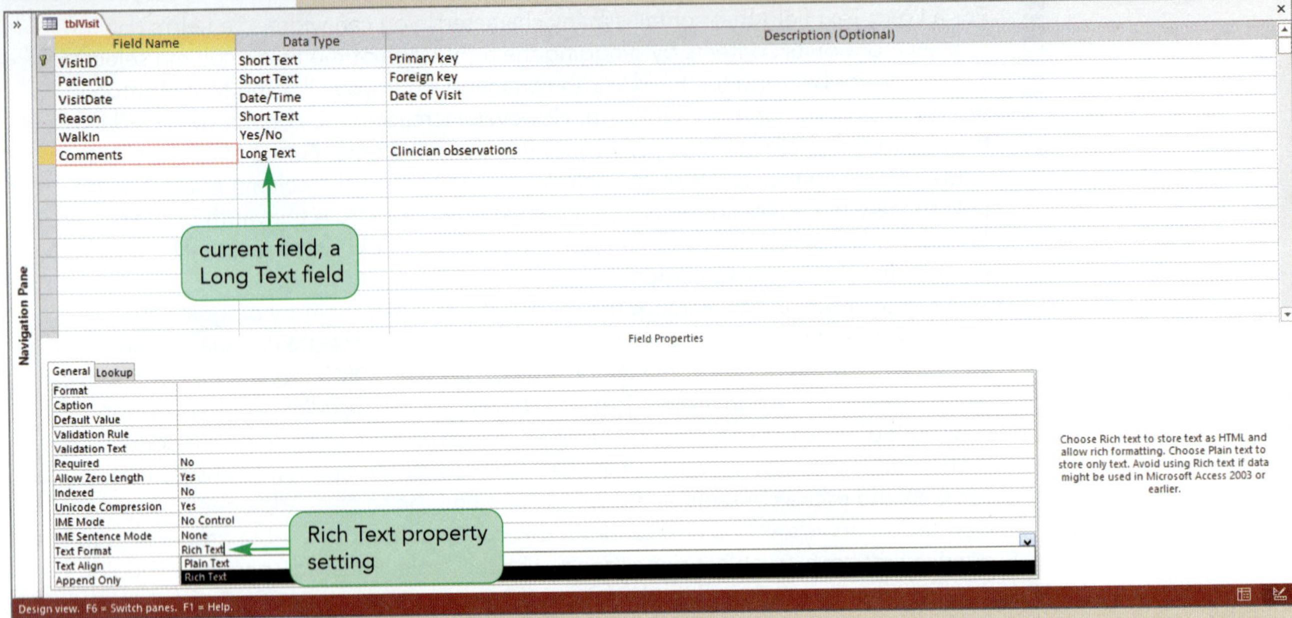

Raj set the **Text Format property** for the Comments field to Rich Text, which lets you format the field contents using the options in the Font group on the HOME tab. The default Text Format property setting for a Long Text field is Plain Text, which doesn't allow text formatting.

3. Click the **arrow** on the Text Format box to close the list, and then click the **Append Only** box.

   The **Append Only property,** which appears at the bottom of the list of properties, enables you to track the changes that you make to a Long Text field. Setting this property to Yes causes Access to keep a historical record of all versions of the Long Text field value. You can view each version of the field value, along with a date and time stamp of when each version change occurred.

   You've finished your review of the Long Text field, so you can close the table.

4. Close the tblVisit table.

When employees at Chatham Community Health Services open the Clinic database, a security warning might appear below the ribbon, and they must enable the content of the database before beginning their work. Cindi asks if you can eliminate this extra step when employees open the database.

Designating a Trusted Folder

A database is a file, and files can contain malicious instructions that can damage other files on your computer or files on other computers on your network. Unless you take special steps, Access treats every database as a potential threat to your computer. One special step that you can take is to designate a folder as a trusted folder. A **trusted folder** is a folder on a drive or network that you designate as trusted and where you place databases you know are safe. When you open a database located in a trusted folder, Access treats it as a safe file and no longer displays a security warning. You can also place files used with other Microsoft Office programs, such as Word documents and Excel workbooks, in a trusted folder to eliminate warnings when you open them.

Because the Clinic database is from a trusted source, you'll specify its location as a trusted folder to eliminate the security warning when a user opens the database.

To designate a trusted folder:

1. Click the **FILE** tab, and then click **Options** in the navigation bar. The Access Options dialog box opens.
2. In the left section of the dialog box, click **Trust Center**. The Trust Center options are displayed in the dialog box.
3. In the right section of the dialog box, click the **Trust Center Settings** button to open the Trust Center dialog box.
4. In the left section of the Trust Center dialog box, click **Trusted Locations**. The trusted locations for your installation of Access and other trust options are displayed on the right. See Figure 5-44.

Figure 5-44 Designating a trusted folder

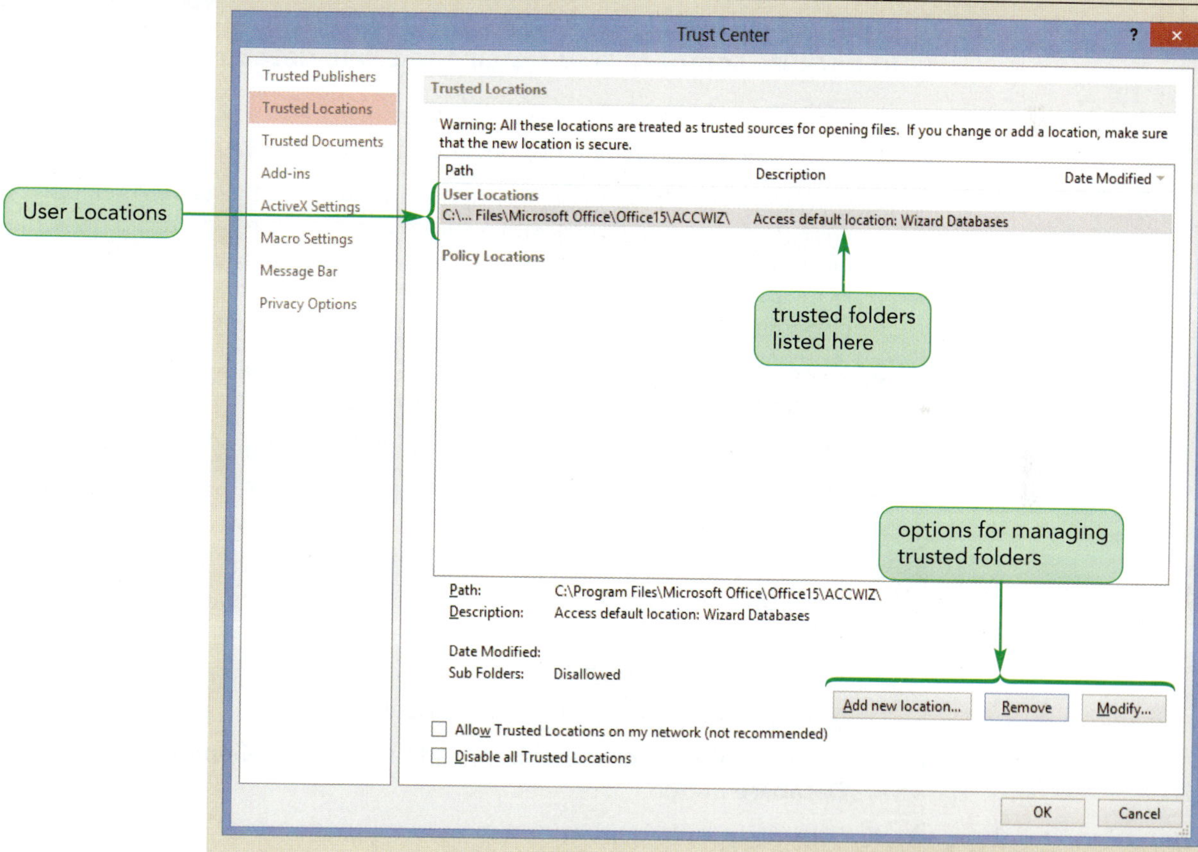

Existing trusted locations appear in the list at the top, and options to add, remove, and modify trusted locations appear at the bottom.

Trouble? Check with your instructor before adding a new trusted location. If your instructor tells you not to create a new trusted location, skip to Step 8.

5. Click the **Add new location** button to open the Microsoft Office Trusted Location dialog box.
6. In the Microsoft Office Trusted Location dialog box, click the **Browse** button, navigate to the Access2 ▸ Tutorial folder where your Data Files are stored, and then click the **OK** button.

You can also choose to designate subfolders of the selected location as trusted locations, but you won't select this option. By default, files in subfolders are not trusted.

7. Click the **OK** button. Access adds the Access2 ▸ Tutorial folder to the list of trusted locations.
8. Click the **OK** button to close the Trust Center dialog box, and then click the **OK** button to close the Access Options dialog box.

You've created several queries and completed several table design changes, so you should compact and repair the Clinic database. Raj doesn't use the Compact on Close option with the Clinic database because it's possible to lose the database if there's a computer malfunction when the Compact on Close operation runs. As a precaution, you'll make a backup copy of the database before you compact and repair it. Making frequent backup copies of your critical files safeguards your data from hardware and software malfunctions, which can occur at any time.

To backup, compact, and repair the Clinic database:

First, you'll make a backup of the Clinic database.

1. Click the **FILE** tab on the ribbon, and then click the **Save As** menu item.
2. Click the **Back Up Database** option, and then click the **Save As** button. The Save As dialog box opens with a suggested filename of Clinic_date in the File name box, where date is the current date in the format year-month-day. For instance, if you made a backup on February 15, 2016, the suggested filename would be Clinic_2016-02-15.
3. Navigate to the location of a USB drive or other external medium, if available, and then click the **Save** button to save the backup file.

   Next, you'll verify that the trusted location is working.
4. Click the **FILE** tab on the ribbon, and then click the **Close** command to close the Clinic database.
5. Click the **FILE** tab on the ribbon, click **Open** on the navigation bar, and then click **Clinic.accdb** in the Recent list. The database opens, and no security warning appears below the ribbon because the database is located in the trusted location you designated.

   Next, you'll compact and repair the database.
6. Click the **FILE** tab on the ribbon, and then click the **Compact & Repair Database** button.
7. Close the Clinic database.

You've completed the table design changes to the Clinic database, which will make working with it easier and more accurate.

REVIEW

Session 5.3 Quick Check

1. What is a lookup field?
2. A(n) ______________ is a predefined format you use to enter and display data in a field.
3. What is property propagation?
4. Define the Validation Rule property, and give an example of when you would use it.
5. Define the Validation Text property, and give an example of when you would use it.
6. Setting a Long Text field's Text Format property to ______________ lets you format its contents.
7. A(n) ______________ folder is a location where you can place databases that you know are safe.

ASSESS

SAM Projects

Put your skills into practice with SAM Projects! SAM Projects for this tutorial can be found online. If you have a SAM account, go to www.cengage.com/sam2013 to download the most recent Project Instructions and Start Files.

PRACTICE

Review Assignments

Data File needed for the Review Assignments: Supplier.accdb

Cindi asks you to create several new queries and enhance the table design for the Supplier database. This database contains information about the vendors that Chatham Community Health Services works with to obtain medical supplies and equipment for the clinic, as well as the vendors who service and maintain the equipment. Complete the following steps:

1. Open the **Supplier** database located in the Access2 ▸ Review folder provided with your Data Files.
2. Modify the first record in the **tblSupplier** table datasheet by changing the Contact First Name and Contact Last Name field values to your first and last names. Close the table.
3. Create a query to find all records in the tblSupplier table in which the City field value starts with the letter T. Display all fields in the query recordset, and sort in ascending order by CompanyName. Save the query as **qryTSelectedCities**, run the query, and then close it.
4. Make a copy of the qryTSelectedCities query using the new name **qryOtherSelectedCities**. Modify the new query to find all records in the tblSupplier table in which the City field values are not Dayton, Madison, or Edison. Save and run the query, and then close it.
5. Create a query to find all records from the tblSupplier table in which the State value is CT, NJ, or NY. Use a list-of-values match for the selection criteria. Display all fields in the query recordset, and sort in descending order by CompanyName. Save the query as **qrySelectedStates**, run the query, and then close it.
6. Create a query to display all records from the tblSupplier table, selecting the CompanyName, City, and ContactPhone fields, and sorting in ascending order by CompanyName. Add a calculated field named **ContactName** as the first column that concatenates the ContactFirstName, a space, and the ContactLastName. Set the Caption property for the ContactName field to **Contact Name**. Save the query as **qryCompanyContacts**, run the query, resize the Contact Name column to its best fit, and then save and close the query.
7. Create a parameter query to select the tblSupplier table records for a State field value that the user specifies. If the user doesn't enter a State field value, select all records from the table. Display the CompanyName, Category, City, State, ContactFirstName, ContactLastName, and ContactPhone fields in the query recordset, sorting in ascending order by City. Save the query as **qryStateParameter**. Run the query and enter no value as the State field value, and then run the query again and enter **CT** as the State field value. Close the query.
8. Create a find duplicates query based on the tblProduct table. Select ProductName as the field that might contain duplicates, and select the ProductID, SupplierID, Price, and Units fields as additional fields in the query recordset. Save the query as **qryDuplicateProductTypes**, run the query, and then close it. Because the tblProduct table does not have any duplicate ProductName values, running this query should show that no duplicate records are found.
9. Create a find unmatched query that finds all records in the tblSupplier table for which there is no matching record in the tblProduct table. Display the SupplierID, CompanyName, City, State, ContactPhone, ContactFirstName, and ContactLastName fields from the tblSupplier table in the query recordset. Save the query as **qrySuppliersWithoutMatchingProducts**, run the query, and then close it. Because the tblSupplier and tblProduct tables do not have unmatched records, running this query should show that no unmatched records are found.

10. Create a query to display all records from the tblProduct table, selecting the ProductID, SupplierID, ProductName, and Price fields, and sorting in descending order by Price. Use the Top Values property to select the top 25 percent of records. Save the query as **qryTop25Price** run the query, and then close it.
11. In the **tblProduct** table, change the SupplierID field to a lookup field. Select the CompanyName field and then the SupplierID field from the tblSupplier table. Sort in ascending order by the CompanyName field, do not hide the key column, make sure the Company Name column is the leftmost column, resize the lookup columns to their best fit, select SupplierID as the field to store in the table, and accept the default label for the lookup column. View the tblProduct table datasheet, resize the Supplier ID column to its best fit, test the lookup field without changing a value permanently, and then save and close the table.
12. Use the Input Mask Wizard to add an input mask to the ContactPhone field in the **tblSupplier** table. The ending input mask should use periods as separators, as in 987.654.3210 with only the last seven digits required; do not store the literal display characters, if you are asked to do so. Update the Input Mask property everywhere the ContactPhone field is used. Resize all columns in the datasheet to their best fit, and then test the input mask by typing over an existing Phone field value, being sure not to change the value by pressing the Esc key after you type the last digit in the Phone field.
13. Designate the Access2 ▸ Review folder as a trusted folder. (*Note:* Check with your instructor before adding a new trusted location.)
14. Make a backup copy of the database, compact and repair the database, and then close it.

APPLY

Case Problem 1

Data File needed for this Case Problem: Task.accdb

GoGopher! Amol Mehta, a recent college graduate living in Boulder, Colorado, spent months earning money by running errands and completing basic chores for family members and acquaintances, while looking for full-time employment. As his list of customers needing such services continued to grow, Amol decided to start his own business called GoGopher! The business, which Amol operates completely online from his home, offers customers a variety of services—from grocery shopping and household chores to yard work and pet care—on a subscription basis. Clients become members of GoGopher! by choosing the plan that best suits their needs. Each plan provides a certain number of tasks per month to members for a specified period of time. Amol created an Access database named Task to store data about members, plans, and contracts. He wants to create several new queries and make design changes to the tables. Complete the following steps:

1. Open the **Task** database located in the Access2 ▸ Case1 folder provided with your Data Files.
2. Modify the first record in the **tblMember** table datasheet by changing the First Name and Last Name column values to your first and last names. Close the table.
3. Create a query to find all records in the tblPlan table in which the PlanCost field is 600, 900, or 1500. Use a list-of-values match for the selection criterion, and include all fields from the table in the query recordset. Sort the query in descending order by the PlanID field. Save the query as **qryLowVolumePlans**, run the query, and then close it.
4. Make a copy of the qryLowVolumePlans query using the new name **qryHighVolumePlans**. Modify the new query to find all records in the tblPlan table in which the PlanCost field is not 600, 900, or 1500. Save and run the query, and then close it.
5. Create a query to display all records from the tblMember table, selecting the LastName, FirstName, Street, and Phone fields, and sorting in ascending order by LastName and then in ascending order by FirstName. Add a calculated field named **MemberName** as the first column that concatenates FirstName, a space, and LastName. Set the Caption property for the MemberName field to **Member Name**. Do not display the LastName and FirstName fields in the query recordset. Create a second calculated field named **CityLine**, inserting it between the

Street and Phone fields. The CityLine field concatenates City, a space, State, two spaces, and Zip. Set the Caption property for the CityLine field to **City Line**. Save the query as **qryMemberNames**, run the query, resize all columns to their best fit, and then save and close the query.

6. Create a query to display all matching records from the tblPlan and tblMember tables, selecting the LastName and FirstName fields from the tblMember table and the PlanDescription and PlanCost fields from the tblPlan table. Add a calculated field named **FeeStatus** as the last column that equals *Fee Waived* if the FeeWaived field is equal *to yes*, and that equals *Fee Not Waived* otherwise. Set the Caption property for the calculated field to **Fee Status**. Sort the list in ascending order on the LastName field. Save the query as **qryFeeStatus**, run the query, resize all columns to their best fit, and then save and close the query.
7. Create a query based on the tblPlan and tblMember tables, selecting the LastName, FirstName, and City fields from the tblMember table and the FeeWaived, PlanDescription, and PlanCost fields from the tblPlan table. The query should find the records in which the City field value is Boulder or Erie and the FeeWaived field value is *Yes*. Save the query as **qryBoulderAndErieFeeWaived**. Save and run the query, and then close the query.
8. Create a parameter query to select the tblMember table records for a City field value that the user specifies. If the user doesn't enter a City field value, select all records from the table. Display all fields from the tblMember table in the query recordset. Save the query as **qryMemberCityParameter**. Run the query and enter no value as the City field value, and then run the query again and enter **Boulder** as the City field value. Close the query.
9. Create a find duplicates query based on the tblMember table. Select Expiration as the field that might contain duplicates, and select all other fields in the table as additional fields in the query recordset. Save the query as **qryDuplicateMemberExpirationDates**, run the query, and then close it.
10. Create a find unmatched query that finds all records in the tblMember table for which there is no matching record in the tblPlan table. Select FirstName, LastName, and Phone fields from the tblMembers table. Save the query as **qryMembersWithoutPlans**, run the query, and then close it.
11. Create a new query based on the tblMember table. Display the FirstName, LastName, Phone, Expiration, and PlanID fields, in this order, in the query recordset. Sort in ascending order by the Expiration field, and then use the Top Values property to select the top 25 percent of records. Save the query as **qryUpcomingExpirations**, run the query, and then close it.
12. Use the Input Mask Wizard to add an input mask to the Phone field in the **tblMember** table. Create the input mask such that the phone number is displayed with a dot separating each part of the phone number. For instance, if the phone number is (303) 123-4567 it should be displayed as 303.123.4567 for new entries. Test the input mask by typing over an existing Phone column value, being certain not to change the value by pressing the Esc key after you type the last digit in the Phone column, and then save and close the table.
13. Define a field validation rule for the PlanCost field in the **tblPlan** table. Acceptable field values for the PlanCost field are values greater than 500. Enter the message **Value must be greater than 500** so it appears if a user enters an invalid PlanCost field value. Save your table changes, and then test the field validation rule for the PlanCost field; be certain the field values are the same as they were before your testing, and then close the table.
14. Define a table validation rule for the **tblMember** table to verify that DateJoined field values precede Expiration field values in time. Use an appropriate validation message. Save your table changes, and then test the table validation rule, making sure any tested field values are the same as they were before your testing.
15. Add a Long Text field named **MemberComments** as the last field in the tblMember table. Set the Caption property to **Member Comments** and the Text Format property to Rich Text. In the table datasheet, resize the new column to its best fit, and then add a comment in the Member Comments column in the first record about a job you would do for someone else, formatting the text with blue, italic font. Save your table changes, and then close the table.
16. Designate the Access2 ▸ Case1 folder as a trusted folder. (*Note:* Check with your instructor before adding a new trusted location.)
17. Make a backup copy of the database, compact and repair the database, and then close it.

APPLY

Case Problem 2

Data File needed for this Case Problem: Tutoring.accdb

O'Brien Educational Services After teaching English in a public high school for 15 years, Karen O'Brien decided to channel her experience in education in a new direction and founded O'Brien Educational Services, a small educational consulting company located in South Bend, Indiana. The company offers tutoring services to high school students to help prepare them for standardized tests, such as the SAT and the ACT. The company provides group, private, and semiprivate tutoring sessions to best meet the needs of its students. To make the database easier to use, Karen wants you to create several queries and modify its table design. Complete the following steps:

1. Open the **Tutoring** database located in the Access2 ▸ Case2 folder provided with your Data Files.
2. Change the record in the **tblTutor** table datasheet that contains Student First and Student Last so the First Name and Last Name field values contain your first and last names. Close the table.
3. Create a query to find all records in the tblStudent table in which the LastName field value begins with M. Display the FirstName, LastName, City, and HomePhone fields in the query recordset, and sort in ascending order by LastName. Save the query as **qryLastNameM**, run the query, and then close it.
4. Create a query that finds all records in the tblTutor table in which the Degree field value is either BA or MA. Use a list-of-values criterion and include the fields First Name, Last Name, and Degree in the recordset, sorted in ascending order on the LastName field. Save the query using the name **qrySelectedDegrees**. Run the query, and then close it.
5. Create a query to find all records in the tblStudent table in which the City field value is not equal to South Bend. Display the FirstName, LastName, City, and HomePhone fields in the query recordset, and sort in ascending order by City. Save the query as **qryNonSouthBend**, run the query, and then close it.
6. Create a query to display all records from the tblTutor table, selecting all fields, and sorting in ascending order by LastName and then in ascending order by FirstName. Add a calculated field named **TutorName** as the second column that concatenates FirstName, a space, and LastName for each teacher. Set the Caption property for the TutorName field to **Tutor Name**. Do not display the FirstName and LastName fields in the query recordset. Save the query as **qryTutorNames**, run the query, resize the Tutor Name column to its best fit, and then save and close the query.
7. Create a parameter query to select the tblContract table records for a SessionType field value that the user specifies. If the user doesn't enter a SessionType field value, select all records from the table. Include all fields from the tblContract table in the query recordset. Save the query as **qrySessionTypeParameter**. Run the query and enter no value as the SessionType field value, and then run the query again and enter **Private** as the SessionType field value. Close the query.
8. Create a crosstab query based on the tblContract table. Use the SessionType field values for the row headings, the Length field values for the column headings, and the count of the ContractID field values as the summarized value, and include row sums. Save the query as **qrySessionTypeCrosstab**. Change the column heading for the row sum column to **Total Number of Sessions.** Resize the columns in the query recordset to their best fit, and then save and close the query.
9. Create a find duplicates query based on the tblContract table. Select StudentID and SessionType as the fields that might contain duplicates, and select all other fields in the table as additional fields in the query recordset. Save the query as **qryMultipleSessionsForStudents**, run the query, and then close it.
10. Create a find unmatched query that finds all records in the tblStudent table for which there is no matching record in the tblContract table. Display all fields from the tblStudent table in the query recordset. Save the query as **qryStudentsWithoutContracts**, run the query, and then close it.

11. In the **tblContract** table, change the TutorID field data type to Lookup Wizard. Select the FirstName, LastName, and TutorID fields from the tblTutor table, sort in ascending order by LastName, resize the lookup columns to their best fit, select TutorID as the field to store in the table, and accept the default label for the lookup column. View the tblContract table datasheet, resize the Tutor ID column to its best fit, and then save and close the table.
12. Use the Input Mask Wizard to add an input mask to the HomePhone field in the **tblStudent** table. The ending input mask should use periods as separators, as in 987.654.3210, with only the last seven digits required; do not store the literal display characters, if you are asked to do so. Resize the Home Phone column to its best fit, and then test the input mask by typing over an existing Phone field value, being sure not to change the value permanently by pressing the Esc key after you type the last digit in the Phone field.
13. Define a field validation rule for the Gender field in the tblStudent table. Acceptable field values for the Gender field are F or M. Use the message "Gender value must be F or M" to notify a user who enters an invalid Gender field value. Save your table changes, test the field validation rule for the Gender field, making sure any tested field values are the same as they were before your testing, and then close the table.
14. Designate the Access2 ▸ Case2 folder as a trusted folder. (*Note:* Check with your instructor before adding a new trusted location.)
15. Make a backup copy of the database, compact and repair the database, and then close it.

CHALLENGE

Case Problem 3

Data File needed for this Case Problem: Rosemary.accdb

Rosemary Animal Shelter Ryan Lang is the director of the Rosemary Animal Shelter in Cobb County, Georgia. The main goals of the shelter, which has several locations in the county, are to rescue dogs and cats and to find people who will adopt them. The shelter was established by Rosemary Hanson, who dedicated her life to rescuing pets and finding good homes for them. Residents of Cobb County generously donate money, food, and equipment in support of the shelter. Some of these patrons also adopt animals from the shelter. Ryan has created an Access database to manage information about the animals, patrons, and donations. Ryan now wants to create several queries and to make changes to the table design of the database. You'll help Ryan by completing the following steps:

1. Open the **Rosemary** database located in the Access2 ▸ Case3 folder provided with your Data Files.
2. Modify the first record in the **tblPatron** table datasheet by changing the Title, FirstName, and LastName column values to your title and name. Close the table.
3. Create a query to find all records in the tblAnimal table for dogs that have been adopted. Display the AnimalName, AnimalGender, AnimalType, AdoptionDate, and Adopted fields in the query recordset. Sort by ascending order by AnimalName. Save the query as **qryDogsAdopted**, run the query, and then close it.
4. Create a query to find all records in the tblDonation table in which the DonationDesc field value is not equal to Cash Donation. Display the Title, FirstName, and LastName, from the tblPatron table, and DonationDesc from the tblDonation table. Sort in ascending order by LastName. Save the query as **qryNonCashDonations**, run the query, and then close it.
5. Create a query called **qryNetDonationsAprilOrLater** that will contain all fields from the tblDonation and tblPatron tables except for PatronID and DonationID, for all donations that are on or after April 1, 2016. Sort this query by DonationValue in descending order. Save and run the query, and then close it.
6. Create a query to display all records from the tblPatron table, selecting the Title and Phone fields. Add a calculated field named **PatronName** that concatenates FirstName, a space, and LastName. Position this column as the second column, and sort the recordset in ascending order by LastName. Set the Caption property for the PatronName field to **Patron Name**. Save the query as **qryPatronNames**, run the query, resize the new column to its best fit, and then save and close the query.

7. Create a parameter query to select the tblAnimal table records for an AnimalType field value that the user specifies. If the user doesn't enter an AnimalType field value, select all records from the table. Display all fields from the tblAnimal table in the query recordset, and sort in ascending order by AnimalName. Save the query as **qryAnimalTypeParameter**. Run the query and enter no value as the AnimalType field value, and then run the query again and enter **Cat** as the AnimalType field value. Close the query.
8. Create a crosstab query based on the qryNetDonationsAprilOrLater query. Use the DonationDate field values for the row headings, the DonationTypeID field values for the column headings, and the sum of the DonationValue field values as the summarized value, and include row sums. Save the query as **qryNetDonationsAprilOrLaterCrosstab**. Change the format of the displayed values (DonationValue and Total Of DonationValue columns in Design view) to Fixed. Resize the columns in the query recordset to their best fit, and then save and close the query.
9. Create a find duplicates query based on the qryNetDonationsAprilOrLater query. Select FirstName and LastName as the fields that might contain duplicates, and select the DonationTypeID and DonationValue fields in the query as additional fields in the query recordset. Save the query as **qryMultipleDonorDonations**, run the query, and then close it.
10. Create a find unmatched query that finds all records in the tblPatron table for which there is no matching record in the tblDonation table. Include all fields from the tblPatron table, except for PatronID, in the query recordset. Save the query as **qryPatronsWithoutDonations**, run the query, and then close it.
11. Make a copy of the qryNetDonationsAprilOrLater query using the new name **qryTopNetDonations**. Modify the new query by using the Top Values property to select the top 40 percent of the records. Save and run the query, and then close the query.
12. Use the Input Mask Wizard to add an input mask to the Phone field in the **tblPatron** table. The ending input mask should use hyphens as separators, as in 987-654-3210, with only the last seven digits required; do not store the literal display characters, if you are asked to do so. Update the Input Mask property everywhere the Phone field is used. Test the input mask by typing over an existing Phone field value, being sure not to change the value permanently by pressing the Esc key after you type the last digit in the Phone field. Close the table.
13. Designate the Access2 ▸ Case3 folder as a trusted folder. (*Note:* Check with your instructor before adding a new trusted location.)
14. Make a backup copy of the database, compact and repair the database, and then close it.

CHALLENGE

Case Problem 4

Data File needed for this Case Problem: Ecotour.accdb

Stanley EcoTours Janice and Bill Stanley live in Pocatello, Idaho, and are the proud owners and operators of Stanley EcoTours. Their passion is to encourage people to visit natural areas around the world in a responsible manner that does not harm the environment. Their advertising has drawn clients from Idaho, Wyoming, Montana, and Canada. As the interest in ecotourism grows, Janice and Bill's business is also expanding to include more tours in Africa and South America. Janice and Bill have created an Access database for their business and now want you to create several queries and modify the table design. To do so, you'll complete the following steps:

1. Open the **Ecotour** database located in the Access2 ▸ Case4 folder provided with your Data Files.
2. Modify the first record in the **tblGuest** table datasheet by changing the Guest First Name and Guest Last Name column values to your first and last names, and then close the table.
3. Create a query to find all records in the tblGuest table in which the GuestLast field value starts with the letter G, sorted in ascending order by GuestLast. Display all fields except the GuestID field in the query recordset. Save the query as **qryGuestLastNameG**, run the query, and then close it.
4. Create a query to find all records in the tblTour table where the country is not Brazil or Peru. Name this query **qryNonBrazilOrPeruTours**. Display all fields, sorting by Country and then by Location. Save and run the query, and then close it.

5. Create a query to find all records in the tblGuest table in which the StateProv field value is MT, WY, or ID and display all fields from the tblGuest table in the query recordset, sorted by GuestLast in ascending order. Save the query as **qrySelectedStates**, run the query, and then close it.
6. Create a query to select all records from the tblTour with tour rates of $5,000 or less, where the TourType is either Hiking or Jeep. Display all fields in the query recordset, sorted by Nights in descending order. Save the query as **qryHikingOrJeepSelectedTours**, run the query, and then close it.
7. Create a parameter query to select the tblTour table records for a Country field value that the user specifies. If the user doesn't enter a Country field value, select all records from the table. Display all fields from the tblTour table in the query recordset, and sort in ascending order by TourName. Save the query as **qryCountryParameter**. Run the query and enter no value as the Country field value, and then run the query again and enter **Peru** as the Country field value. Close the query.
8. Create a query that contains all records from the tblGuest table and all matching records from the tblReservation table. Display all fields from the tblGuest table and all fields except GuestID from the tblReservation table. Save the query as **qryGuestsAndReservations**, run the query, and then close it.
9. Create a crosstab query based on the qryGuestsAndReservations query. Use the TourID field values for the row headings, the Country field values for the column headings, and the sum of the People field as the summarized value, and include row sums. Save the query as **qryReservationsCrosstab**, resize the columns in the query recordset to their best fit, and then save and close the query.
10. Create a find duplicates query based on the **qryGuestsAndReservations** query. Select GuestID as the field that might contain duplicates, and select the fields GuestFirst, GuestLast, TourID, StartDate, and People in the table as additional fields in the query recordset. Save the query as **qryMultipleReservations**, run the query, and then close it.
11. Create a find unmatched query that finds all records in the tblGuest table for which there is no matching record in the tblReservation table. Display the GuestFirst, GuestLast, City, StateProv. and Phone fields from the tblGuest table in the query recordset. Save the query as **qryGuestsWithoutReservations**, run the query, and then close it.
12. Copy the **qryHikingOrJeepSelectedTours** and save it as **qryTopHikingOrJeepSelectedTours.** Use the Top Values property to select the top 30 percent of the records. Save and run the query, and then close it.
13. In the **tblReservation** table, change the TourID field data type to Lookup Wizard. Select the TourID, TourName, Location, and Country fields from the tblTour table, sort in ascending order by TourName, hide the key column, resize the lookup columns to their best fit, select TourID as the field to store in the table, and accept the default label for the look up column. View the tblReservation datasheet, resize the TourID column to its best fit, test the lookup field without changing a field value permanently, and then close the table.
14. Define a field validation rule for the People field in the **tblReservation** table. Acceptable field values for the People field are values less than or equal to 12. Display the message **Please book a custom tour for large groups.** when a user enters an invalid People field value. Save your table changes, and then test the field validation rule for the People field; be certain the field values are the same as they were before your testing.
15. Define a table validation rule for the **tblTour** table to verify that SingleSupplement field values are less than the PricePerPerson values. Use an appropriate validation message. Save your table changes, test the table validation rule, making sure any tested field values are the same as they were before your testing, and then close the table.
16. Designate the Access2 ▸ Case4 folder as a trusted folder. (*Note:* Check with your instructor before adding a new trusted location.)
17. Make a backup copy of the database, compact and repair the database, and then close it.

TUTORIAL 6

Using Form Tools and Creating Custom Forms

Creating Forms for Chatham Community Health Services

OBJECTIVES

Session 6.1

- Change a lookup field to a Short Text field
- View and print database documentation
- Create datasheet, multiple item, and split forms
- Modify a form and anchor form controls in Layout view

Session 6.2

- Plan, design, and create a custom form in Design view and in Layout view
- Select, move, align, resize, delete, and rename controls in a form
- Add a combo box to a form
- Add headers and footers to a form

Session 6.3

- Add a combo box to a form to find records
- Add a subform to a form
- Add calculated controls to a form and a subform
- Change the tab order in a form
- Improve the appearance of a form

Case | *Chatham Community Health Services*

Cindi Rodriguez hired Raj Gupta to enhance the Clinic database, and he initially concentrated on standardizing the table design and creating queries for Chatham Community Health Services. Cindi and her staff created a few forms before Raj came onboard, and Raj's next priority is to work with Cindi to create new forms that will be more functional and easier to use.

In this tutorial, you will create new forms for Chatham Community Health Services. In creating the forms, you will use many Access form customization features, such as adding controls and a subform to a form, using combo boxes and calculated controls, and adding color and special effects to a form. These features make it easier for database users like Cindi and her staff to interact with a database.

STARTING DATA FILES

Access2 → Tutorial, Review, Case1, Case2, Case3, Case4

Tutorial	Clinic.accdb (*cont.*)
Review	Supplier.accdb (*cont.*)
Case1	Task.accdb (*cont.*)
Case2	Tutoring.accdb (*cont.*)
Case3	Rosemary.accdb (*cont.*)
Case4	Ecotour.accdb (*cont.*)

Session 6.1 Visual Overview:

A **tabular layout** arranges text box controls in a datasheet format with a label above each column.

A **stacked layout** arranges text box controls vertically with a label control to the left of each text box control.

This form was created using the **Split Form Tool**, which creates a customizable form that simultaneously displays the data in both Form view and Datasheet view.

These controls are anchored to the top left.

These controls have been removed from the stacked layout.

This form is displayed in Layout view.

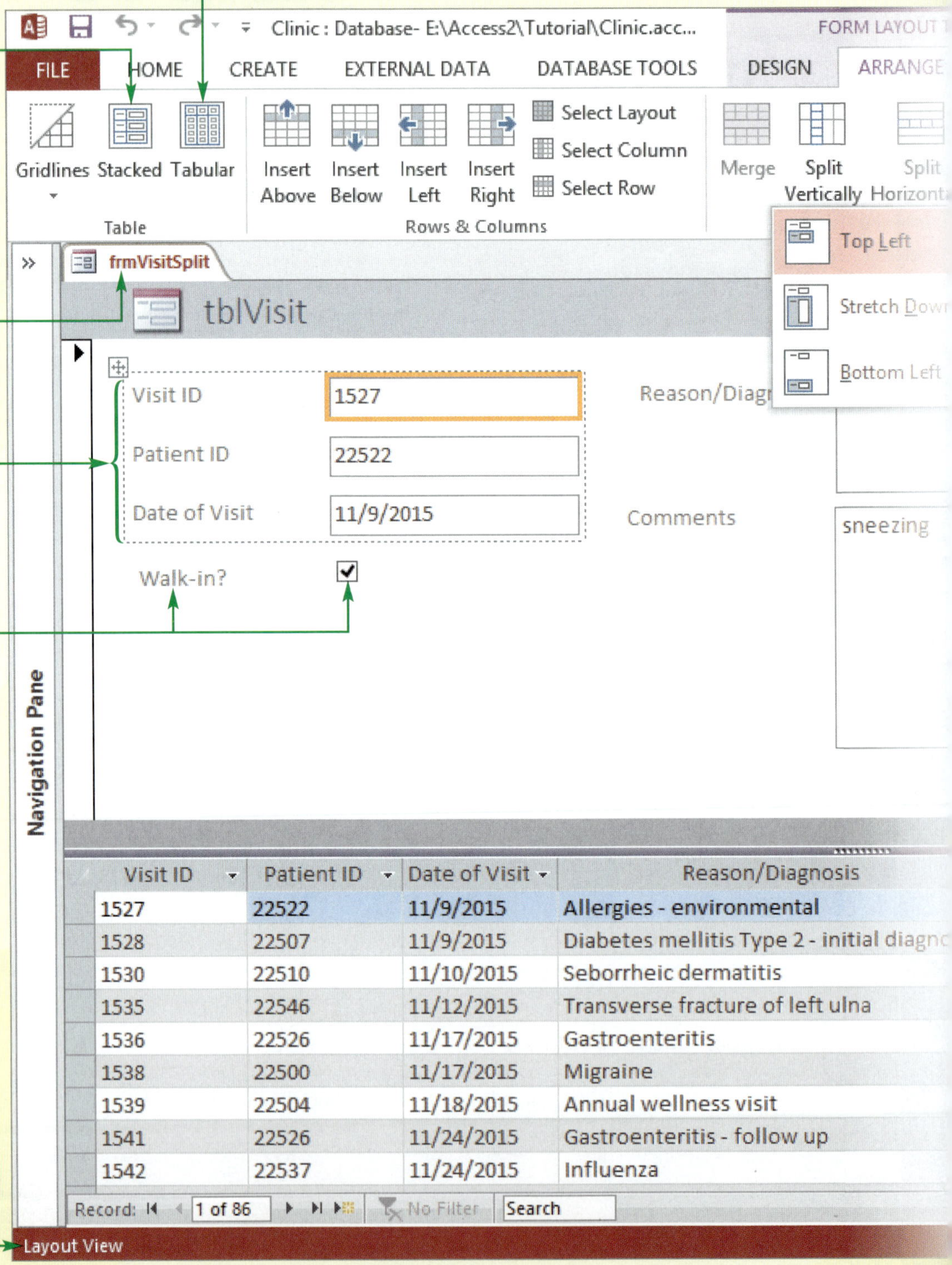

Anchoring Controls

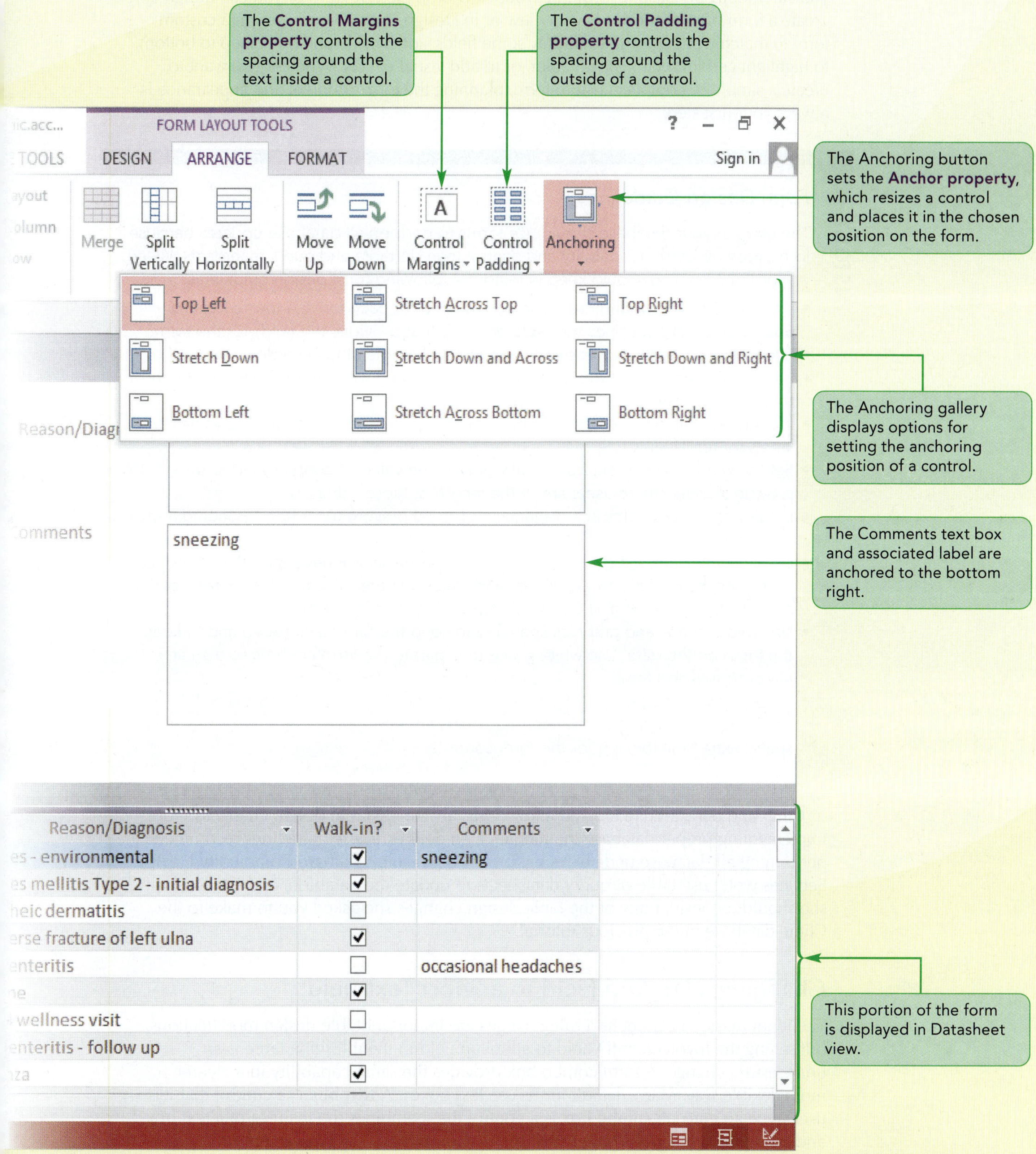

Designing Forms

You've used wizards to create forms, and you've modified a form by changing its design in Layout view, which is one method of creating a custom form. To create a **custom form**, you can modify an existing form in Layout view or in Design view, or you can design and create a form from scratch in Layout view or in Design view. You can design a custom form to match a paper form, to display some fields side by side and others top to bottom, to highlight certain sections with color, or to add visual effects. Whether you want to create a simple or complex custom form, planning the form's content and appearance is always your first step.

INSIGHT

Form Design Guidelines

The users of your database should use forms to perform all database updates because forms provide better readability and control than do table and query recordsets. When you plan a form, you should keep in mind the following form design guidelines:

- Determine the fields and record source needed for each form. A form's **Record Source property** specifies the table or query that provides the fields for the form.
- Group related fields and position them in a meaningful, logical order.
- If users will refer to a source document while working with the form, design the form to match the source document closely.
- Identify each field value with a label that names the field, and align field values and labels for readability.
- Set the width of each text box to fully display the values it contains and also to provide a visual cue to users about the length of those values.
- Display calculated fields in a distinctive way, and prevent users from changing and updating them.
- Use default values, list boxes, and other form controls whenever possible to reduce user errors by minimizing keystrokes and limiting entries. A control is an item, such as a text box or command button, that you place in a form or report.
- Use colors, fonts, and graphics sparingly to keep the form uncluttered and to keep the focus on the data. Use white space to separate the form controls so they are easier to find and read.
- Use a consistent style for all forms in a database. When forms are formatted differently, with form controls in different locations from one form to another, users must spend extra time looking for the form controls.

Cindi and her staff had created a few forms and made table design changes before implementing proper database maintenance guidelines. These guidelines recommend performing all database updates using forms. As a result, Chatham Community Health Services won't use table or query datasheets to update the database, and Cindi asks if she should reconsider any of the table design changes she asked you to make to the Clinic database in the previous tutorial.

Changing a Lookup Field to a Short Text field

The input mask and validation rule changes are important table design modifications, but setting the InvoiceItemID field to a lookup field in the tblBilling table is an unnecessary change. A form combo box provides the same capability in a clearer, more flexible way. Many default forms use text boxes. A **text box** is a control that lets users type an entry. A **combo box** is a control that combines the features of a text box and a list box; it lets users either choose a value from a list or type an entry. A text box should be used when users must enter data, while a combo box should be used when there is a finite number of choices. Before creating the new forms for Cindi, you'll change the data type of the InvoiceItemID field in the tblBilling table from a Lookup Wizard field to a Short Text field, so you can create the relationship with referential integrity between the tblBilling and tblInvoiceItems tables.

To change the data type of the InvoiceItemID field:

1. Start Access, and then open the **Clinic** database you worked with in Tutorial 5.

   Trouble? If the security warning is displayed below the Ribbon, either the Clinic database is not located in the Access2 ▸ Tutorial folder or you did not designate that folder as a trusted folder. Make sure you opened the database in the Access2 ▸ Tutorial folder, and make sure that it's designated as a trusted folder.

TIP

You can press the F11 key to open or close the Navigation Pane.

2. Open the Navigation Pane, open the **tblBilling** table in Design view, and then close the Navigation Pane.
3. Click the **InvoiceItemID** Field Name box, and then click the **Lookup** tab in the Field Properties pane. The Field Properties pane now displays the lookup properties for the InvoiceItemID field. See Figure 6-1.

Figure 6-1 Lookup properties for the InvoiceItemID field

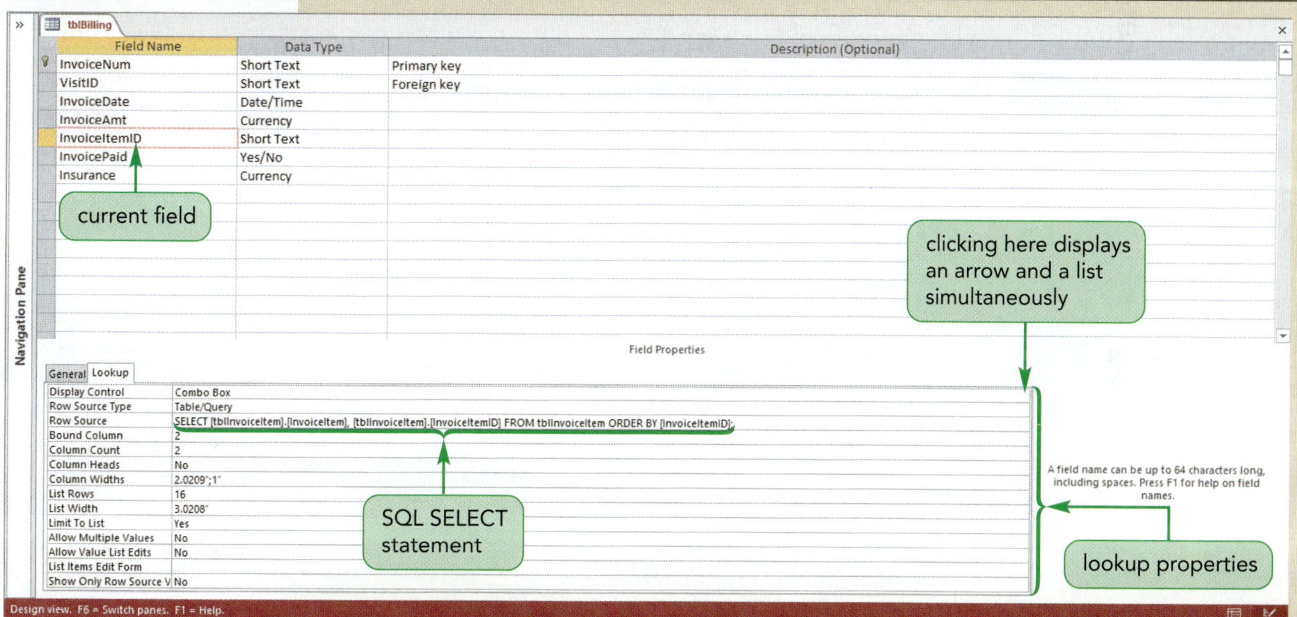

Notice the **Row Source property**, which specifies the data source for a control in a form or report or for a field in a table or query. The Row Source property is usually set to a table name, a query name, or an SQL statement. For the InvoiceItemID field, the Row Source property is set to an SQL SELECT statement. You'll learn more about SQL later in this text.

To remove the lookup feature for the InvoiceItemID field, you need to change the **Display Control property**, which specifies the default control used to display a field, from Combo Box to Text Box.

4. Click the right side of the **Display Control** box, and then click **Text Box**. All the lookup properties in the Field Properties pane disappear, and the InvoiceItemID field changes back to a standard Short Text field without lookup properties.

5. Click the **General** tab in the Field Properties pane and notice that the properties for a Short Text field still apply to the InvoiceItemID field.
6. Save the table, switch to Datasheet view, resize the Invoice Item column to its best fit, and then click one of the Invoice Item boxes. An arrow does not appear in the Invoice Item box because the InvoiceItemID field is no longer a lookup field.
7. Save the table, and then close the tblBilling table.

Before you could change the InvoiceItemID field in the tblBilling table to a lookup field in the previous tutorial, you had to delete the one-to-many relationship between the tblInvoiceItem and tblBilling tables. Now that you've changed the data type of the InvoiceItemID field back to a Short Text field, you'll view the table relationships to make sure that the tables in the Clinic database are related correctly.

To view the table relationships in the Relationships window:

1. On the Ribbon, click the **DATABASE TOOLS** tab, and then in the Relationships group, click the **Relationships** button to open the Relationships window. See Figure 6-2.

Figure 6-2 Clinic database tables in the Relationships window

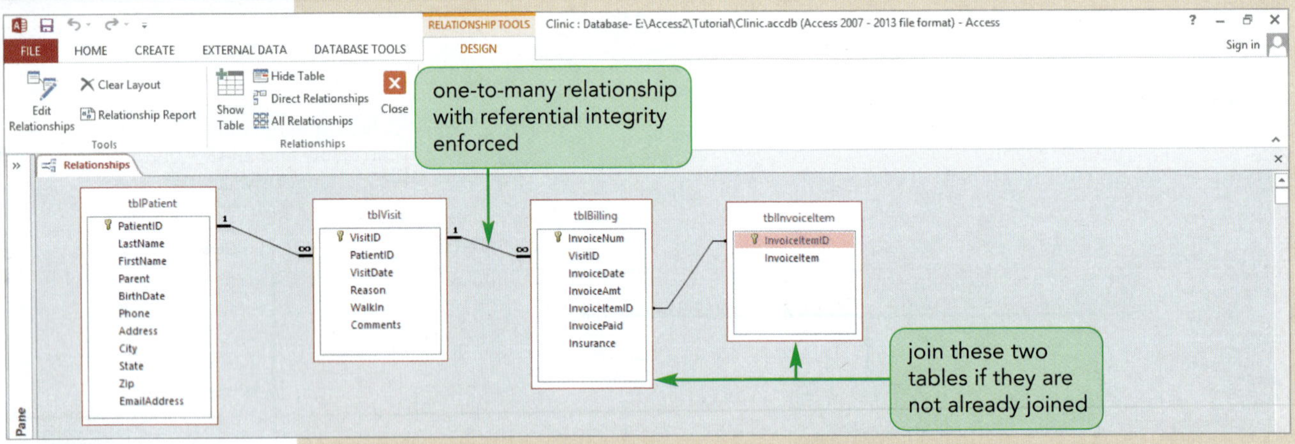

The tblVisit table and the related tblBilling table have a one-to-many relationship with referential integrity enforced. You need to establish a similar one-to-many relationship between the tblInvoiceItem and tblBilling tables.

2. Double-click the **relationship line** between the tblInvoiceItem and tblBilling tables to open the Edit Relationships dialog box.
3. Click the **Enforce Referential Integrity** check box, click the **Cascade Update Related Fields** check box, and then click the **OK** button to define the one-to-many relationship between the two tables and to close the dialog box. The join line connecting the tblInvoiceItem and tblBilling tables indicates the type of relationship (one-to-many) with referential integrity enforced.

Cindi asks you to print a copy of the database relationships to use as a reference, and she asks if other Access documentation is available.

Printing Database Relationships and Using the Documenter

You can print the Relationships window to document the fields, tables, and relationships in a database. You can also use the **Documenter**, another Access tool, to create detailed documentation of all, or selected, objects in a database. For each selected object, the Documenter lets you print documentation, such as the object's properties and relationships, and the names and properties of fields used by the object. You can use the documentation to help you understand an object and to help you plan changes to that object.

REFERENCE

Using the Documenter

- Start Access and open the database you want to document.
- In the Analyze group on the DATABASE TOOLS tab, click the Database Documenter button.
- Select the object(s) you want to document.
- If necessary, click the Options button to select specific documentation options for the selected object(s), and then click the OK button.
- Click the OK button, print the documentation, and then close the Object Definition window.

Next, you'll print the Relationships window and use the Documenter to create documentation for the tblVisit table.

PROSKILLS

Written Communication: Satisfying User Documentation Requirements

The Documenter produces object documentation that is useful to the technical designers, analysts, and programmers who develop and maintain Access databases and who need to understand the minutiae of a database's design. However, users who interact with databases generally have little interest in the documentation produced by the Documenter. Users need to know how to enter and maintain data using forms and how to obtain information using forms and reports, so they require special documentation that matches these needs; this documentation isn't produced by the Documenter, though. Many companies assign one or more users the task of creating the documentation needed by users based on the idea that users themselves are the most familiar with their company's procedures and understand most clearly the specific documentation that they and other users require. Databases with dozens of tables and with hundreds of other objects are complicated structures, so be sure you provide documentation that satisfies the needs of users separate from the documentation for database developers.

Cindi will show her staff the tblVisit table documentation as a sample of the information that the Documenter provides.

To view the Relationships report and use the Documenter:

1. On the DESIGN tab, in the Tools group, click the **Relationship Report** button to open the Relationships for Clinic report in Print Preview. See Figure 6-3.

Figure 6-3 Relationships for Clinic report

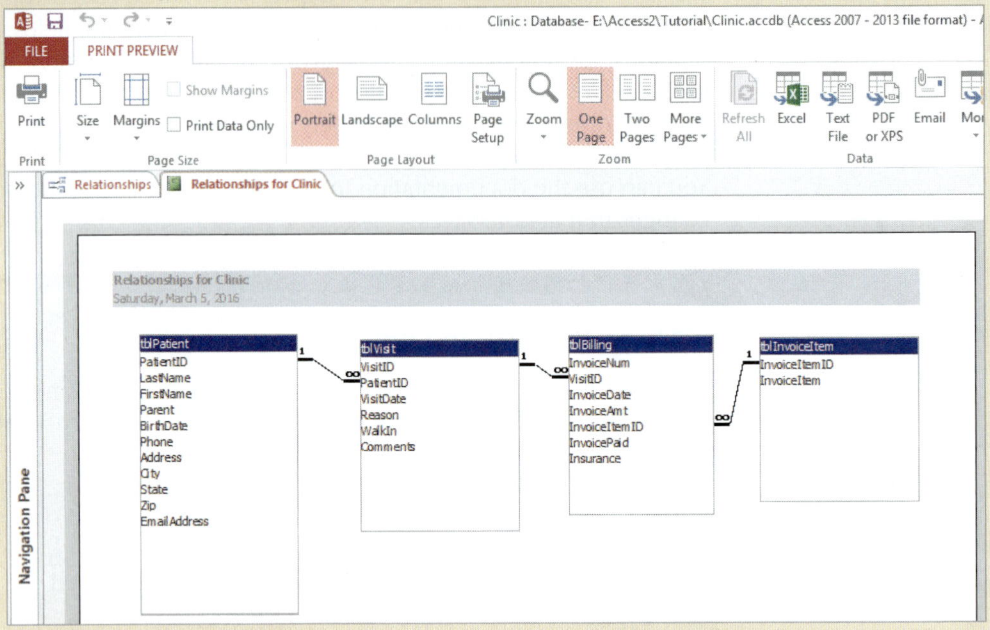

2. Right-click the **Relationships for Clinic** tab and click **Close** to close the tab. A dialog box opens and asks if you want to save the report.

3. Click the **Yes** button to save the report, click the OK button to save using the default name Relationships for Clinic, and then close the Relationships window.

   Now you'll use the Documenter to create detailed documentation for the tblVisit table as a sample to show Cindi.

4. On the Ribbon, click the **DATABASE TOOLS** tab. In the Analyze group, click the **Database Documenter** button, and then click the **Tables** tab (if necessary) in the Documenter dialog box. See Figure 6-4.

Figure 6-4 Documenter dialog box

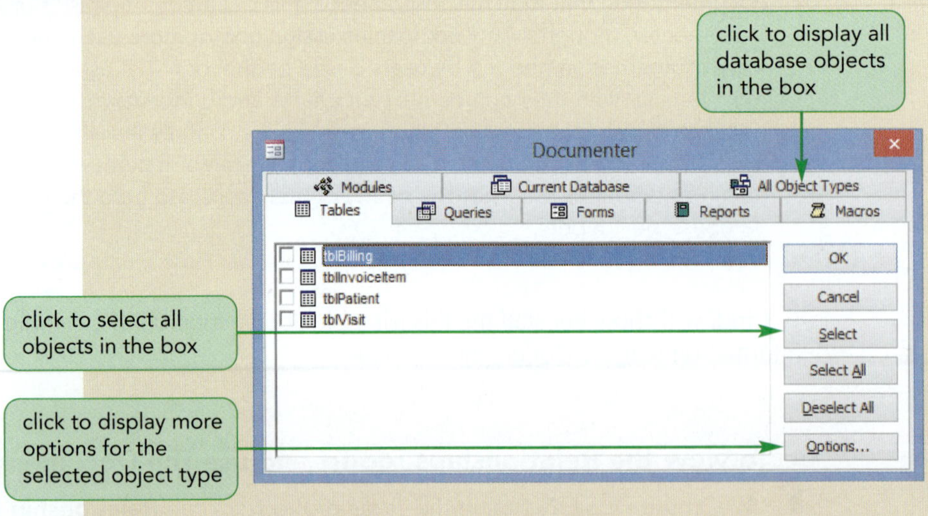

Form view and Layout view are not options in the list, which means that they are unavailable for this form type. Datasheet view allows you to view and update data, and Design view is the only other view option for this form.

You'll save this form to show Cindi as one of the options for the forms for patient visits.

5. Save the form as **frmVisitDatasheet** and close the form.

Cindi might not like the datasheet view since the Comments field is not fully displayed. She might like the form created using the Multiple Items tool better since it will provide larger text boxes for the data. Next, you'll create a form for Cindi using the Multiple Items tool.

Creating a Form Using the Multiple Items Tool

The **Multiple Items tool** creates a customizable form that displays multiple records from a source table or query in a datasheet format. You'll use the Multiple Items tool to create a form based on the tblVisit table.

To create the form using the Multiple Items tool:

1. Make sure that the tblVisit table is selected in the Navigation Pane, and then click the **CREATE** tab on the Ribbon.
2. In the Forms group, click the **More Forms** button and then click **Multiple Items**. The Multiple Items tool creates a form showing every field in the tblVisit table and opens the form in Layout view. See Figure 6-9.

Figure 6-9 Form created by the Multiple Items tool

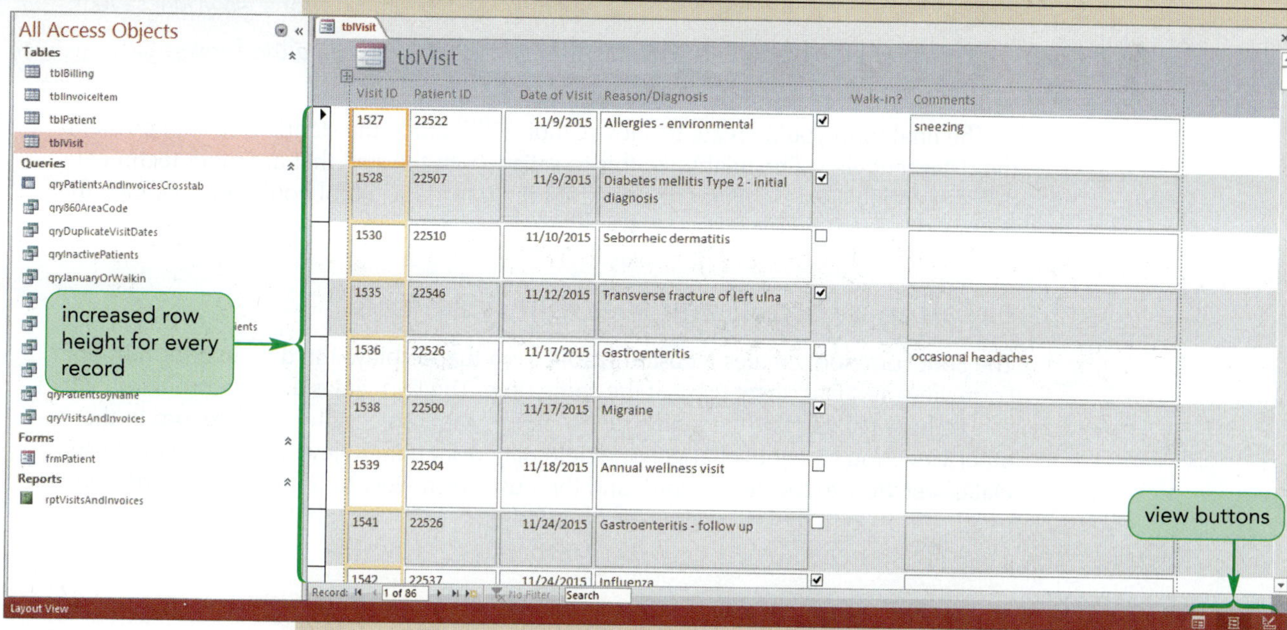

The new form displays all the records and fields from the tblVisit table in a format similar to a datasheet, but the row height for every record is increased compared to a standard datasheet. Unlike a form created by the Datasheet tool, which has only Datasheet view and Design view available, a Multiple Items form is a standard form that can be displayed in Form view, Layout view, and Design view, as indicated by the buttons on the right side of the status bar.

TIP

You can click one of the view buttons on the right side of the status bar to switch to another view.

For the form created with the Multiple Items tool, you'll check the available view options.

3. On the DESIGN tab, in the Views group, click the **View button arrow**. Form view, Layout view, and Design view are the available views for this form. See Figure 6-10.

Figure 6-10 View options for a form created by the Multiple Items tool

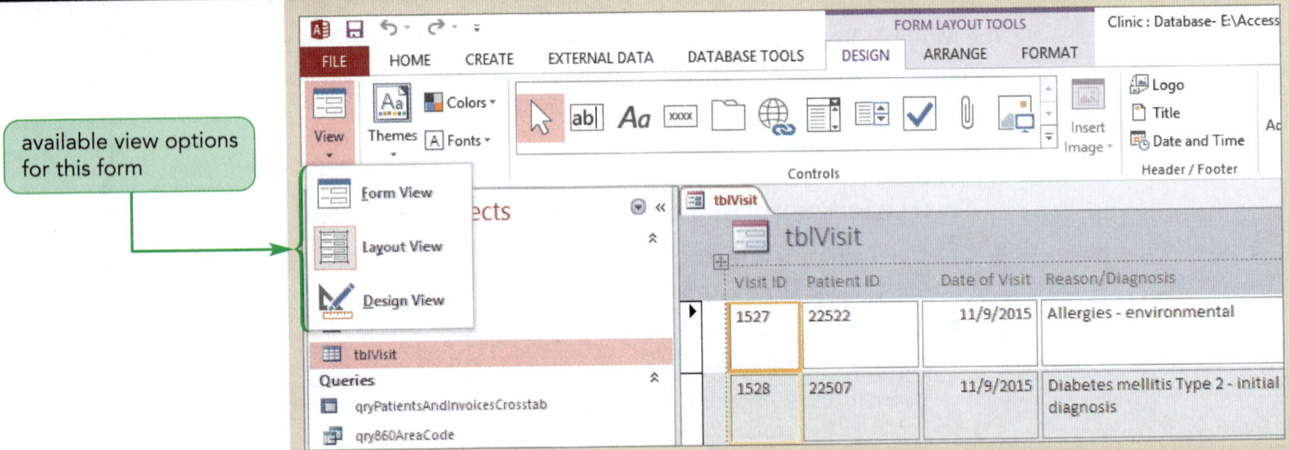

You'll want to show this form to Cindi as one of the options, so you'll save it.

4. Save the form as **frmVisitMultipleItems**, and then close the form.

The final form you'll create to show Cindi will include the standard form inputs and the datasheet view. She might like this to satisfy both the staff that are more technical and the staff that would like a more user-friendly form. The tool you'll use to create this is the Split Form tool.

Creating a Form Using the Split Form Tool

The Split Form tool creates a customizable form that displays the data in a form in both Form view and Datasheet view at the same time. The two views are synchronized with each other at all times. Selecting a record in one view selects the same record in the other view. You can add, change, or delete data from either view. Typically, you'd use Datasheet view to locate a record, and then use Form view to update the record. You'll use the Split Form tool to create a form based on the tblVisit table.

To create the form using the Split Form tool:

1. Make sure that the tblVisit table is selected in the Navigation Pane, and then click the **CREATE** tab on the Ribbon.

2. In the Forms group, click the **More Forms** button, click **Split Form** on the menu, and then close the Navigation Pane. The Split Form tool creates a split form that opens in Layout view and displays a form with the contents of the first record in the tblVisit table on the top and a datasheet of the first several records in the tblVisit table on the bottom. The position of the form in Layout view will be either a single column or two columns, depending on the height of the Access window when the form was created. If you have a two-column layout, that won't affect your ability to complete the steps that follow. Figure 6-11 shows the single column layout.

Figure 6-11 Form created by the Split Form tool

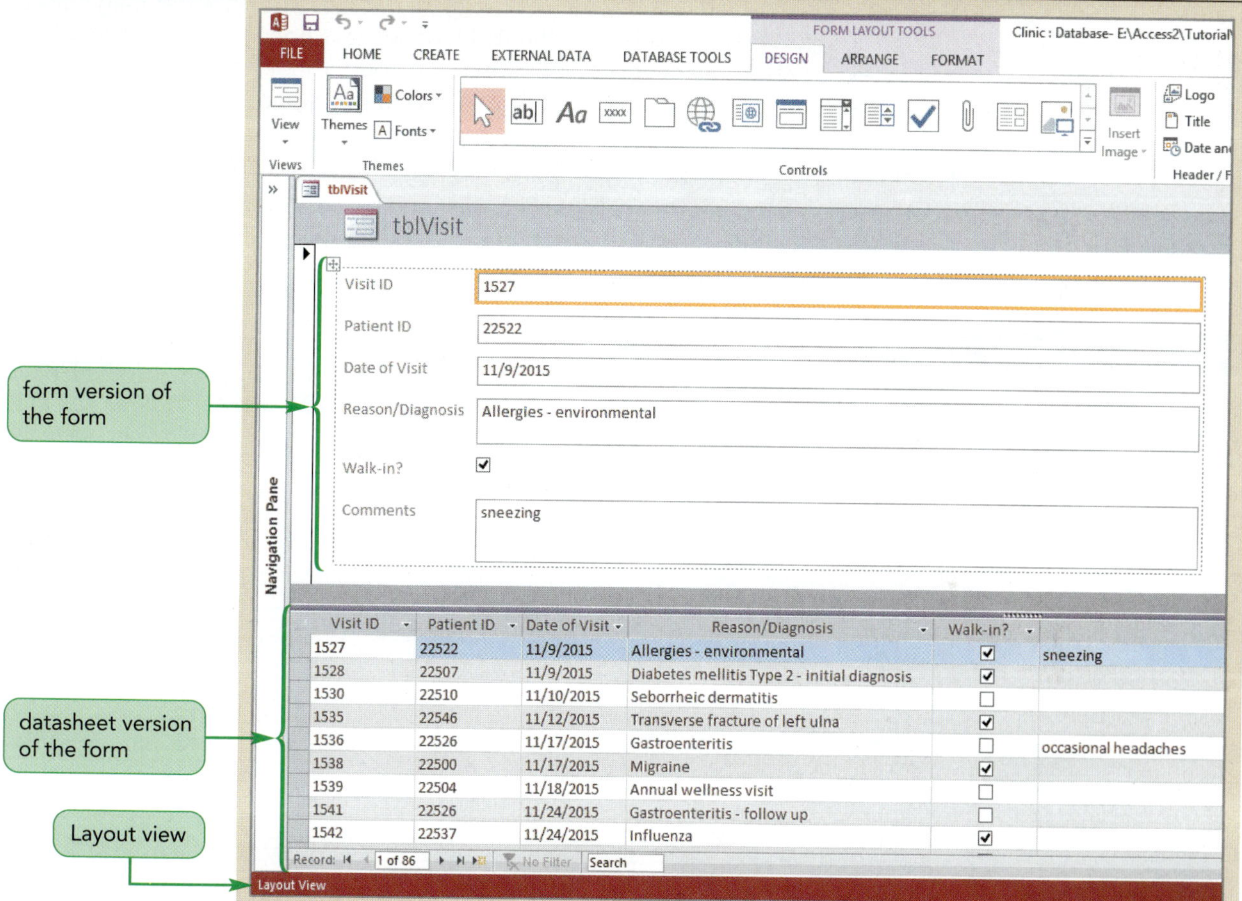

In Layout view, you can make layout and design changes to the form and layout changes to the datasheet. Cindi thinks the split form will be a useful addition to the Clinic database, and she wants you to show her the types of design modifications that are possible with a split form.

Modifying a Split Form in Layout View

You use the options on the DESIGN tab on the Ribbon to add controls and make other modifications to the form but not to the datasheet. In previous tutorials, you've modified forms using options on the FORMAT tab. Other powerful options are available on the ARRANGE tab. For a split form, options on the ARRANGE tab apply only to the form and do not apply to the datasheet.

To modify the form in Layout view:

1. Click the **ARRANGE** tab on the Ribbon.

   The form's label and field value box controls for the fields from the tblVisit table are grouped in a control layout. A **control layout** is a set of controls grouped together in a form or report, so that you can manipulate the set as a single control. For example, you can move and resize all the controls in a control layout as a group; moving or resizing one control in the control layout moves or resizes all controls in the control layout. You also can rearrange fields and their attached labels within the control layout.

   All the text boxes in the control layout are the same width. The first three text boxes, Visit ID, Patient ID and Date of Visit, are much wider than necessary. However, if you reduce the width of any text box in a control layout, all text boxes in the control layout are also resized. Cindi wants you to reduce the width of the first three text boxes and to move and resize the Reason/Diagnosis label and text box.

2. Click the **layout selector** ⊞ which is located at the top-left corner of the Visit ID label, to select all controls in the control layout. An orange outline, which identifies the controls that you've selected, appears around the labels and field value boxes in the form. See Figure 6-12.

Figure 6-12 Control layout selected in the form

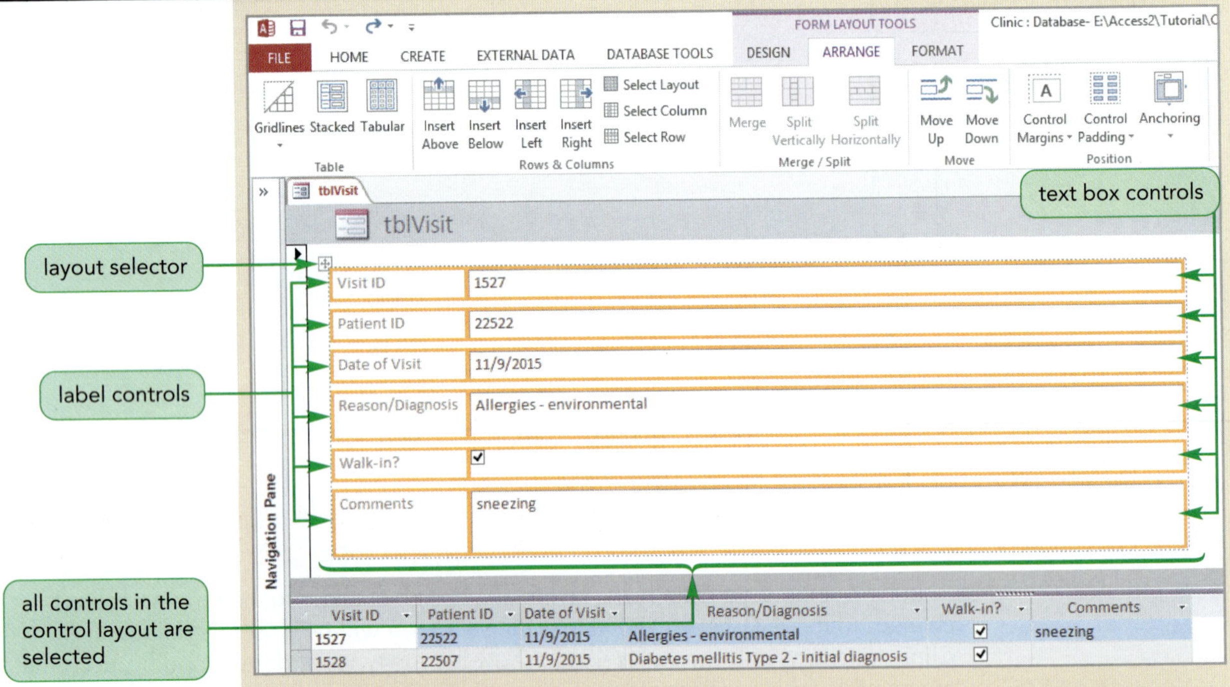

   Trouble? If the layout selector wasn't visible, or if only one large orange outline appears outside the controls but not around each individual control, click the VisitID text box, and then repeat Step 2.

   Next, you'll resize the text boxes in the control layout.

3. Click the **VisitDate** text box (the text box that contains the value 11/9/2015) to deselect the control layout and select the VisitDate text box.

4. Position the pointer on the right edge of the VisitDate text box until the pointer changes to a ↔ shape, click and drag to the left until the right edge is just to the right of the VisitDate field value, and then release the mouse button. If you have a one-column layout, you've resized all five text boxes. If you have a two-column layout, you've resized the three text boxes on the left. Figure 6-13 shows the single-column layout.

Figure 6-13 After resizing the text boxes in the control layout

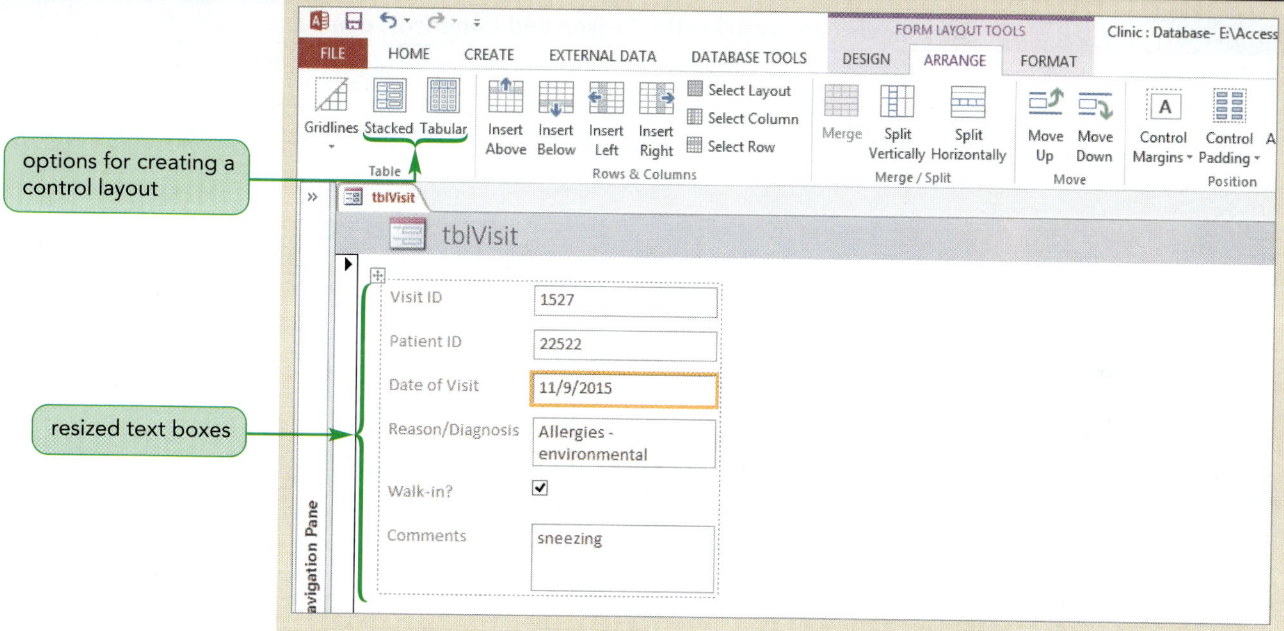

Trouble? If you resize the text boxes too far to the left, number signs appear inside the VisitDate and PatientID text boxes. Drag the right edge of the VisitDate text box slightly to the right and repeat the process until the date values are visible inside the text boxes.

The control layout for the form is a stacked layout, which arranges field value box controls vertically with a label control to the left of each field value box control in one or more vertical columns; you click the Stacked button in the Table group to place selected controls in a stacked layout. You can also choose a tabular layout, which arranges field value box controls in a datasheet format with labels above each column; you click the Tabular button in the Table group to place selected controls in a tabular layout.

You can now remove the Reason/Diagnosis text box, the Walk-in? check box, the Comments text box, and their labels from the stacked layout, move the four controls, and then resize the text boxes.

5. Click the **Reason** text box, hold down the **Ctrl** key, click the **Reason/ Diagnosis label**, the **Walk-in? label**, the **Walk-in? check box**, the **Comments text box,** and the **Comments label** to select all six controls, and then release the **Ctrl** key. Right-click the **Reason** text box to open the shortcut menu, point to **Layout**, and then click **Remove Layout**. You've removed the six selected controls from the stacked layout.

6. If your form has the single-column layout shown in Figure 6-13, make sure that the six controls are selected, and then drag them up and to the right until their tops are aligned with the top of the VisitID controls.

Trouble? If your form already has a two-column layout, you don't need to complete Step 6; proceed to Step 7.

7. Click the **Walk-in? label** to select it, hold down the **Ctrl** key, and click the **Walk-in? checkbox** to select it. Drag these back to the left, below the Date of Visit label and text box.

   See Figure 6-14. (Note: You will resize the Reason/Diagnosis and Comments text boxes in the next step.)

Figure 6-14 After moving and resizing the Reason and Comments controls

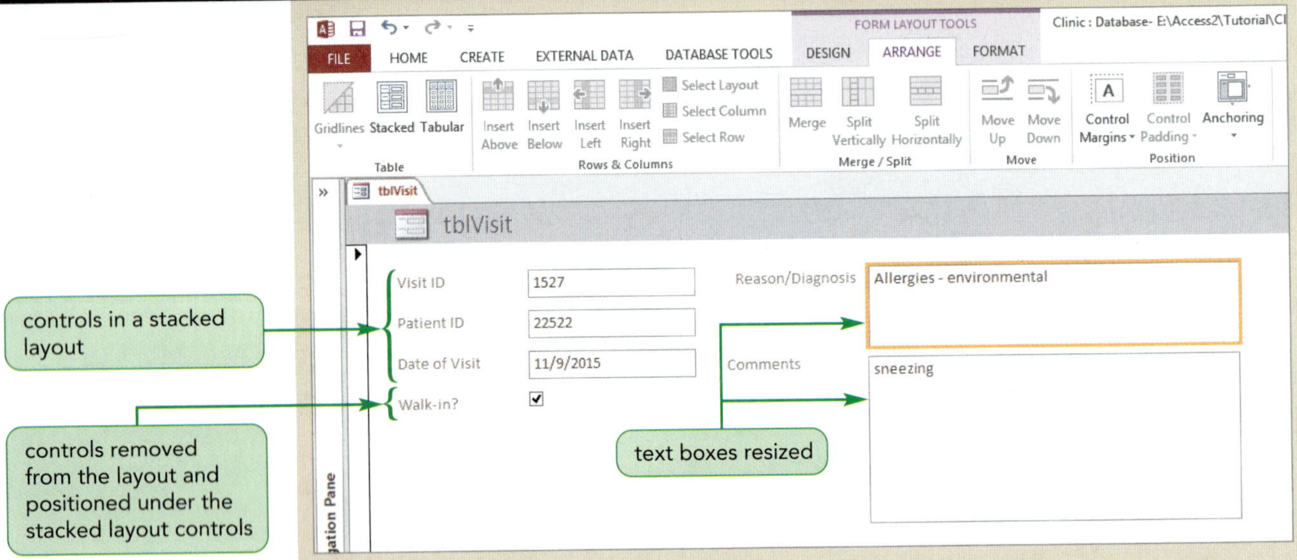

8. Click the **Comments** label, hold down the **Ctrl** key, click the **Comments** text box, and then drag both controls down. Click the **Comments** text box, and then drag the right edge of the control to the right and the bottom edge of the control down to the positions shown in Figure 6-14.

9. Click the **Reason** text box so that it's the only selected control, and then drag the right edge of the control to the right and the bottom edge of the control down to the positions shown in Figure 6-14.

   Trouble? It won't cause any problems if the controls on your screen are in slightly different positions than the ones shown in the figure.

   You do not usually need to change the default settings for the Control Margins property, which controls the spacing around the text inside a control, or the Control Padding property, which controls the spacing around the outside of a control. However, you'll explore the effects of changing these properties.

10. Click one of the controls in the stacked layout, and then click the **layout selector** to select all controls in the stacked layout.

11. Click the **ARRANGE** tab, in the Position group click the **Control Margins** button, and then click **Medium**. The text inside the stacked layout controls moves down slightly.

12. Click the **Control Margins** button, click **Wide** and observe the effect of this setting on the text inside the controls, click the **Control Margins** button, click **None** and observe the effect of this setting, click the **Control Margins** button, and then click **Narrow**. Narrow is the default setting for the Control Margins property.

    Narrow is also the default setting for the Control Padding property.

13. In the Position group, click the **Control Padding** button, click **Medium** and observe the change to the spacing around the controls, and then repeat for the other settings of this property, making sure you set the property to **Narrow** as your final step.

Next, you'll anchor the controls.

Anchoring Controls in a Form

You can design forms that use the screen dimensions effectively when all the users of a database have the same sized monitors and use the same screen resolution. How do you design forms when users have a variety of monitor sizes and screen resolutions? If you design a form to fit on large monitors using high screen resolutions, then only a portion of the controls in the form fit on smaller monitors with lower resolutions, forcing users to scroll the form. If you design a form to fit on smaller monitors with low screen resolutions, then the form displays on larger monitors in a small area in the upper-left corner of the screen, making the form look unattractively cramped. As a compromise, you can anchor the controls in the form. As shown in the Visual Overview for this session, as the screen size and resolution change, the Anchor property for a control automatically resizes the control and places it in the same relative position on the screen. Unfortunately, when you use the Anchor property, Access doesn't scale the control's font size to match the screen size and resolution. Sometimes the results of anchoring controls works well, but sometimes the controls are spaced across a large screen and the form may seem unorganized with controls moved to the corners of the screen.

Next, you'll anchor controls in a form. Because all monitors at Chatham Community Health Services are the same size and use the same resolution, first you'll save the split form, so that you can demonstrate anchoring and then discard the anchoring changes to the form.

To anchor controls in the form:

1. Save the form as **frmVisitSplit**.

    You can't anchor individual controls in a control layout; you can only anchor the entire control layout as a group. You've already removed the Reason/Diagnosis, Walk-in?, and Comments controls from the stacked layout, so you can anchor them separately from the stacked layout. You'll have four sets of controls to anchor—the stacked layout is one set, the Reason/Diagnosis controls are in the second set, the Comments controls are the third set, and the Walk-in? controls make up the fourth set.

    First, you'll select and anchor the Walk-in? controls.

2. Click the **Walk-in?** label, hold down the **Ctrl** key, and then click the **WalkIn** check box.

3. On the ARRANGE tab, in the Position group, click the **Anchoring** button to open the Anchoring gallery. See Figure 6-15.

Figure 6-15 **Displaying the Anchoring gallery**

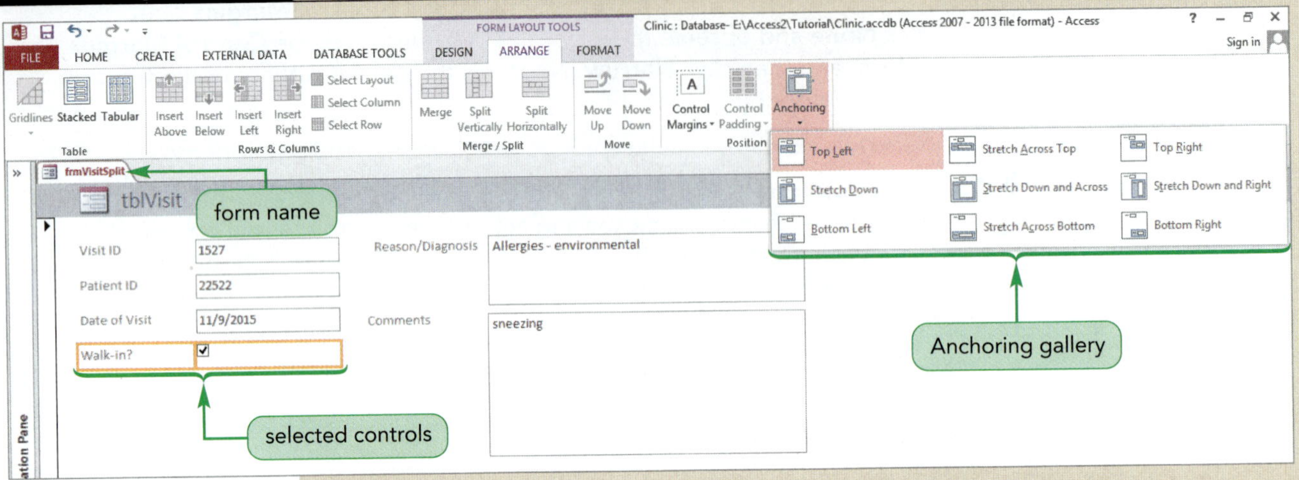

Four of the nine options in the Anchoring gallery fix the position of the selected controls in the top left (the default setting), bottom left, top right, or bottom right positions in the form. If other controls block the corner positions for controls you're anchoring for the first time, the new controls are positioned in relation to the blocking controls. The other five anchoring options resize (or stretch) and position the selected controls.

You'll anchor the Walk-in? controls in the bottom left, the Reason/Diagnosis controls in the top right, and the Comments controls in the bottom right.

4. Click **Bottom Left** in the Anchoring gallery, click the **Reason** text box, click the **Anchoring** button, and then click **Top Right**. Click the **Comments** text box, click the **Anchoring** button, then click **Bottom Right**. The Walk-in? controls are shifted down, the Reason controls are shifted up and to the right, and the Comments controls are shifted down and to the right.

   Next, you'll increase the height of the form to simulate the effect of a larger screen for the form.

5. Open the Navigation Pane. The four sets of controls on the left shift to the right because the horizontal dimensions of the form decreased from the left, and these four sets of controls are anchored to the left in the form. The Reason and Comments controls remain in the same position in the form.

6. Position the pointer on the border between the form and the datasheet until the pointer changes to a ↕ shape, and then drag down until you see only the column headings and the first row in the datasheet. The bottom sets of controls shift down, because they are anchored to the bottom, and the two sets of controls at the top remain in the same positions in the form. See Figure 6-16.

Figure 6-16 Anchored controls in a resized form

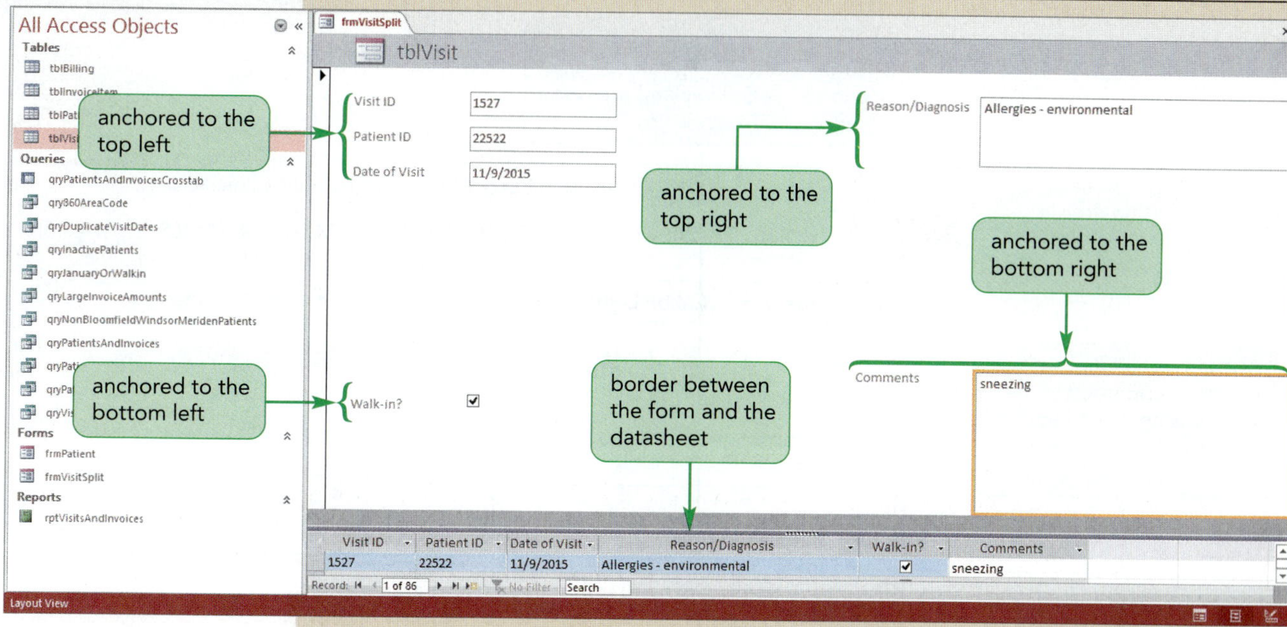

Finally, you'll use another anchoring option to resize the Comments text box as the form dimensions change.

7. Click the **Comments** text box (if necessary), click the **Anchoring** button, and then click **Stretch Down and Right**. Because the Comments text box is already anchored to the bottom right, it can't stretch any more to the right, but it does stretch up while leaving the label in place, to increase the height of the text box.
8. Position the pointer on the border between the form and the datasheet until the pointer changes to a ✛ shape, and then drag up until you can see several rows in the datasheet. The bottom set of controls shifts up, and the bottom edge of the Comments text box shifts up, reducing its height.

   You've finished adjusting the Layout view changes to the split form, so you can close the form without saving the anchoring changes.
9. Save the frmVisitSplit form, and then close the form.
10. If you are not continuing on to the next session, close the Clinic database.

    You've used form tools to create forms, and you've modified forms in Layout view. In the next session, you will continue your work with forms.

REVIEW

Session 6.1 Quick Check

1. Which object(s) should you use to perform all database updates?
2. The ______________ property specifies the data source for a control in a form or report or for a field in a table or query.
3. What is the Documenter?
4. What is the Multiple Items tool?
5. What is a split form?
6. As the screen's size and resolution change, the ______________ property for a control automatically resizes the control.

Session 6.2 Visual Overview:

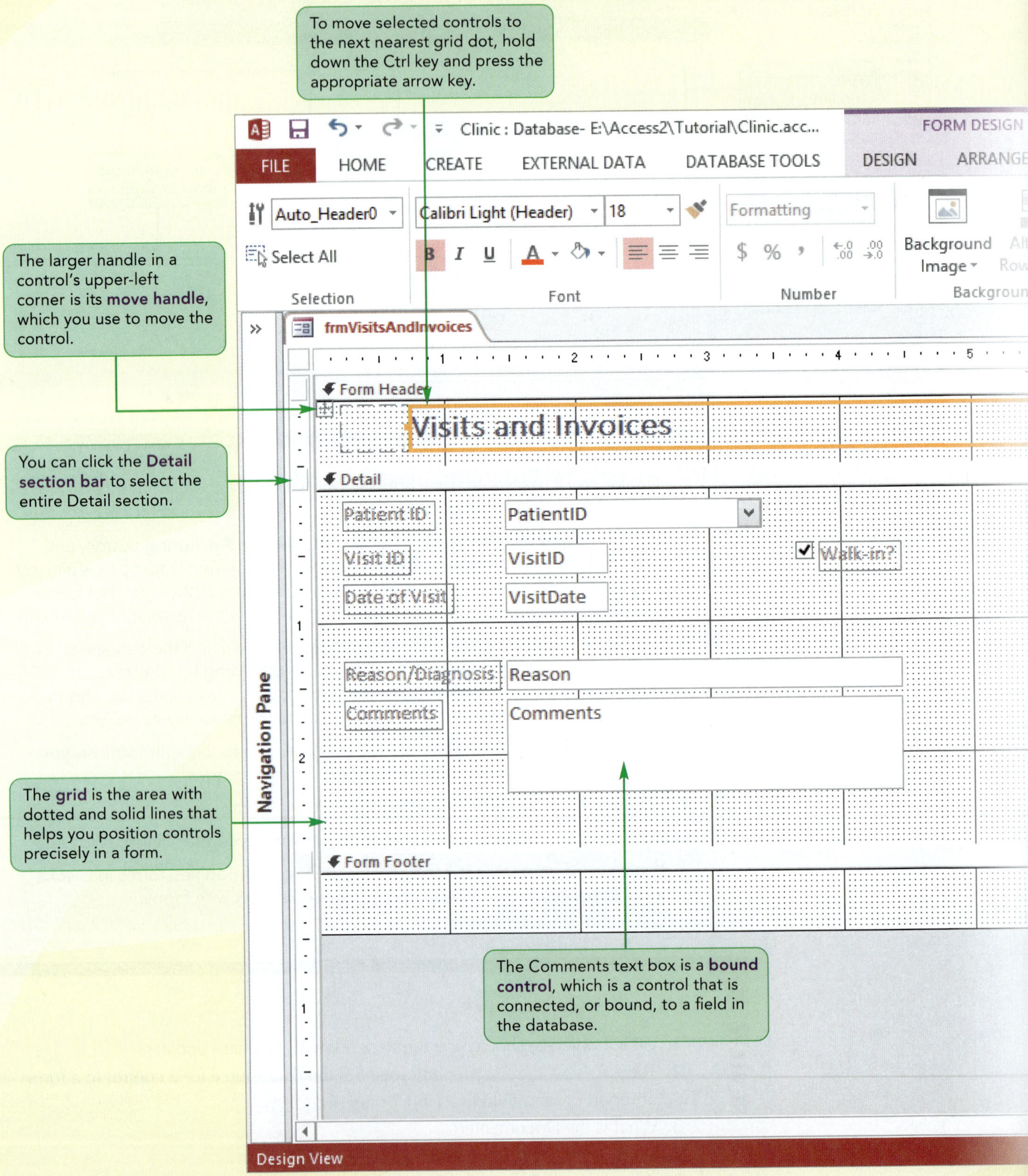

Form in Design View

The **sizing handles** located on the edges and corners are used to resize the control.

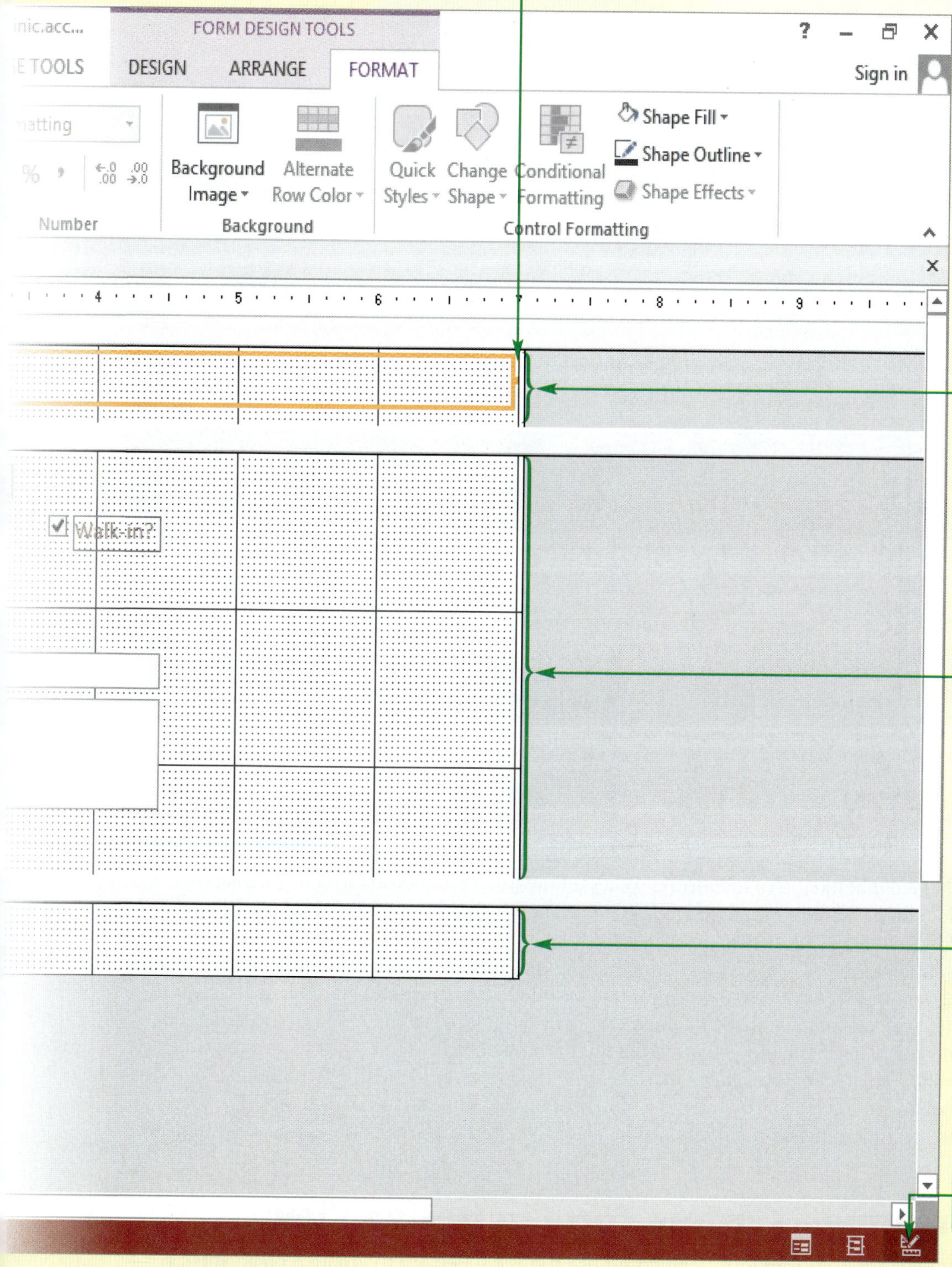

The Form Header section contains a title object and can contain other objects that will appear at the top of the form.

The **Detail section** is the main section of the form.

The Form Footer section contains objects that will appear at the bottom of the form.

The Design View button displays the form with the grid.

Planning and Designing a Custom Form

Cindi needs a form to enter and view information about Chatham Community Health Services visits and their related invoices. She wants the information in a single form, and she asks Raj to design a form for her review.

After several discussions with Cindi and her staff, Raj prepared a sketch for a custom form to display a patient visit and its related invoices. Raj then used his paper design to create the form shown in Figure 6-17.

Figure 6-17 Raj's design for the custom form

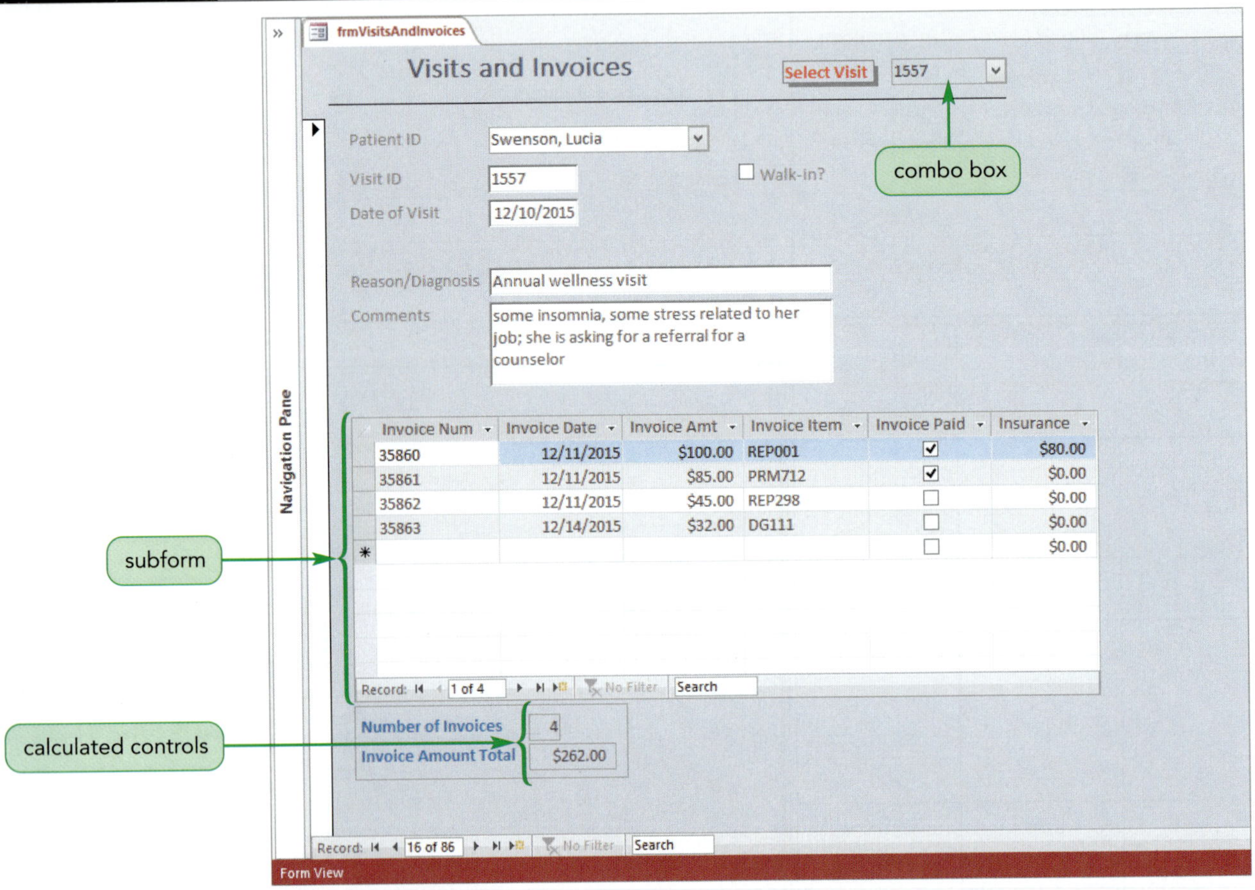

Notice that the top of the form displays a title and a combo box to select a visit record. Below these items are six field values with identifying labels from the tblVisit table; these fields are the PatientID, VisitID, WalkIn, VisitDate, Reason, and Comments fields. The PatientID field is displayed in a combo box, the WalkIn field is displayed as a check box, and the other field values are displayed in text boxes. The tblBilling table fields appear in a subform, a separate form contained within another form. Unlike the tblVisit table data, which displays identifying labels to the left of the field values in field value boxes, the tblBilling table data is displayed in datasheet format with identifying column headings above the field values. Finally, the Number of Invoices and Invoice Amount Total calculated controls in the main form display values based on the content of the subform.

Creating a Custom Form in Design View

To create Raj's custom form, you could use the Form Wizard to create a basic version of the form and then customize it in Layout and Design views. However, for the form that Raj designed, you would need to make many modifications to a basic form created by a wizard. You can instead build the form in a more straightforward manner by creating it directly in Design view. Creating forms in Design view allows you more control and precision, and provides more options than creating forms in Layout view. You'll also find that you'll create forms more productively if you switch between Design view and Layout view because some design modifications are easier to make in one of the two views than in the other view.

The Form Window in Design View

You can use the Form window in Design view to create and modify forms. To create the custom form based on Raj's design, you'll create a blank form, add the fields from the tblVisit and tblBilling tables, and then add other controls and make other form modifications.

REFERENCE

Creating a Form in Design View

- Click the CREATE tab on the Ribbon.
- In the Forms group, click the Blank Form button.
- Click the Design View button on the status bar.
- Make sure the Field List pane is open, and then add the required fields to the form.
- Add other required controls to the form.
- Modify the size, position, and other properties as necessary for the fields and other controls in the form.
- Save the form.

The form you'll create will be a bound form. A **bound form** is a form that has a table or query as its record source. You use bound forms for maintaining and displaying table data. **Unbound forms** are forms that do not have a record source and are usually forms that help users navigate among the objects in a database. Now you'll create a blank bound form based on the tblVisit table.

To create a blank form in Design view:

1. If you took a break after the previous session, make sure that the Clinic database is open and the Navigation Pane is open.
2. Click the **CREATE** tab on the Ribbon and then, in the Forms group, click the **Blank Form** button. Access opens the Form window in Layout view.
3. Click the **Design View** button on the status bar to switch to Design view, and then close the Navigation Pane. See Figure 6-18.

Figure 6-18 **Blank form in Design view**

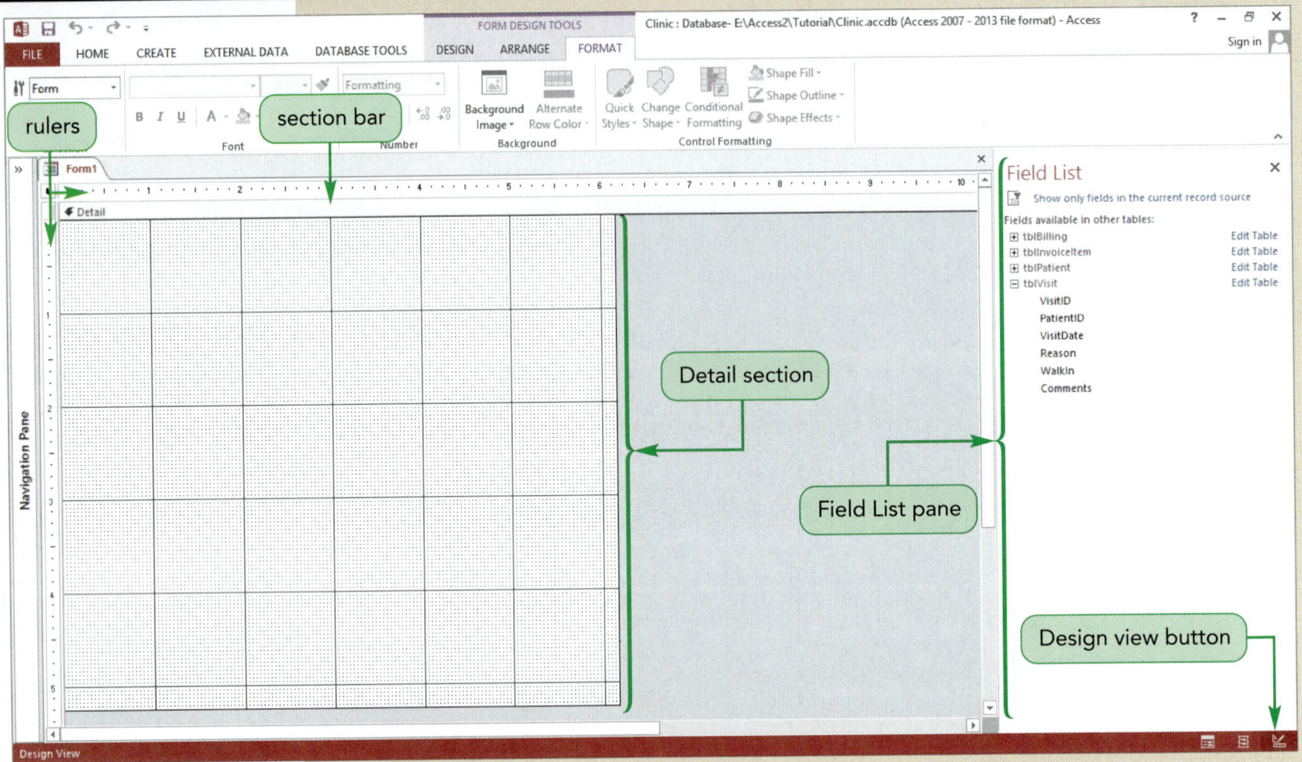

Trouble? If the Field List pane displays the "No fields available to be added to the current view" message, click the "Show all tables" link to display the tables in the Clinic database, and then click the plus sign next to tblVisit in the Field List pane to display the fields in the table.

Trouble? If the tblVisit table in the Field List pane is not expanded to show the fields in the table, click the plus sign next to tblVisit to display the fields.

Design view contains the tools necessary to create a custom form. You create the form by placing controls in the blank form. You can place three kinds of controls in a form:

- A bound control is connected, or bound, to a field in the database. The field could be selected from the fields in a table or query that are used as the record source. You use bound controls to display and maintain table field values.
- An **unbound control** is not connected to a field in the database. You use unbound controls to display text, such as a form title or instructions; to display lines, rectangles, and other objects; or to display graphics and pictures created using other software programs. An unbound control that displays text is called a **label**.
- A **calculated control** displays a value that is the result of an expression. The expression usually contains one or more fields, and the calculated control is recalculated each time any value in the expression changes.

To create a bound control, you add fields from the Field List pane to the Form window, and then position the bound controls where you want them to appear in the form. To place other controls in a form or a report, you use the tools in the Controls and Header/Footer groups on the DESIGN tab; a ScreenTip is available for each control in these groups. The tools in the Controls group let you add controls such as lines, rectangles, images, buttons, check boxes, and list boxes to a form.

Design view for a form contains a Detail section, which is a rectangular area consisting of a grid with a section bar above the grid. You click the section bar to select the section in preparation for setting properties for the entire section. Some forms use Header, Detail, and Footer sections, but a simple form might have only a Detail section. The grid consists of the area with dotted and solid lines that help you position controls precisely in a form. In the Detail section, you place bound controls, unbound controls, and calculated controls in your form. You can change the size of the Detail section by dragging its edges. Rulers at the top and left edges of the Detail section define the horizontal and vertical dimensions of the form and serve as guides for placing controls in a form.

Your first task is to add bound controls to the Detail section for the six fields from the tblVisit table.

Adding Fields to a Form

When you add a bound control to a form, Access adds a field value box and, to its left, an attached label. The field value box displays a field value from the record source. The attached label displays either the Caption property value for the field, if the Caption property value has been set, or the field name. To create a bound control, you first display the Field List pane by clicking the Add Existing Fields button in the Tools group on the DESIGN tab. Then you double-click a field in the Field List pane to add the bound control to the Detail section. You can also drag a field from the Field List pane to the Detail section.

Next, you'll add bound controls to the Detail section for the six fields in the Field List pane. The Field List pane displays the four tables in the Clinic database, and the six fields in the tblVisit table.

To add bound controls from the tblVisit table to the grid:

1. Double-click **VisitID** in the Field List pane. Access adds a bound control in the Detail section of the form, places the tblVisit table in the "Fields available for this view" section of the Field List pane, and places the tblBilling and tblPatient tables in the "Fields available in related tables" section.
2. Repeat Step 1 for the **VisitDate, PatientID, Reason, Comments,** and **WalkIn** fields, in this order, in the Field List pane. Six bound controls—one for each of the six fields in the Field List pane—are added in the Detail section of the form. See Figure 6-19.

Figure 6-19 **Adding field value boxes and attached labels as bound controls to a form**

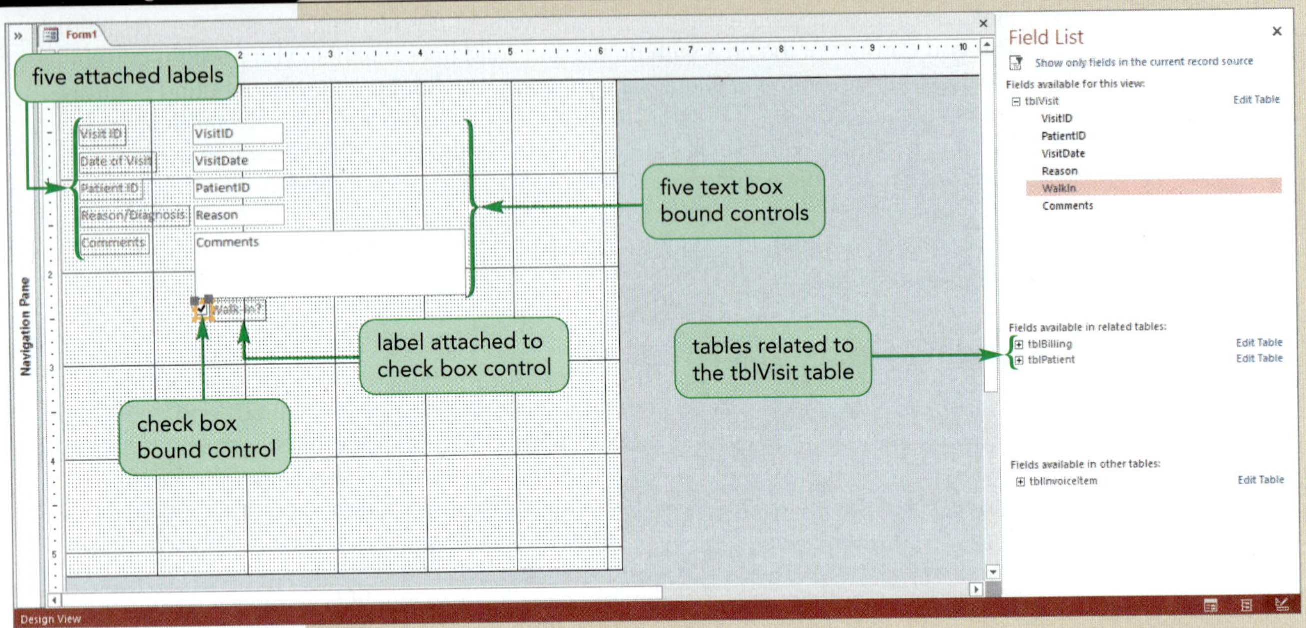

You should periodically save your work as you create a form, so you'll save the form now.

3. Click the **Save** button on the Quick Access Toolbar. The Save As dialog box opens.
4. With the default name Form1 (your name might be different) selected in the Form Name box, type **frmVisitsAndInvoices**, and then press the **Enter** key. The tab for the form now displays the form name, and the form design is saved in the Clinic database.

You've added the fields you need to the grid, so you can close the Field List pane.

5. Click the DESIGN tab and then, in the Tools group, click the **Add Existing Fields** button to close the Field List pane.

INSIGHT

Suggestions for Building Forms

To help prevent common problems and more easily recover from errors while building forms, you should keep in mind the following suggestions:

- You can click the Undo button one or more times immediately after you make one or more errors or make form adjustments you don't wish to keep.
- You should back up your database frequently, especially before you create new objects or customize existing objects. If you run into difficulty, you can revert to your most recent backup copy of the database.
- You should save your form after you've completed a portion of your work successfully and before you need to perform steps you've never done before. If you're not satisfied with subsequent steps, close the form without saving the changes you made since your last save, and then open the form and perform the steps again.
- You can always close the form, make a copy of the form in the Navigation Pane, and practice with the copy.
- Adding controls, setting properties, and performing other tasks correctly in Access should work all the time with consistent results, but in rare instances, you might find a feature doesn't work properly. If a feature you've previously used successfully suddenly doesn't work, you should save your work, close the database, make a backup copy of the database, open the database, and then compact and repair the database. Performing a compact and repair resolves most of these types of problems.

To make your form's Detail section match Raj's design (Figure 6-17), you need to move the WalkIn bound control up and to the right. To do so, you must start by selecting the bound control.

Selecting, Moving, and Aligning Controls

Six field value boxes now appear in the form's Detail section, one below the other. Each field value box is a bound control connected to a field in the underlying table, with an attached label to its left. Each field value box and each label is a control in the form; in addition, each pairing of a field value box and its associated label is itself a control. When you select a control, the control becomes outlined in orange, and eight squares, called handles, appear on its four corners and at the midpoints of its four edges. The larger handle in a control's upper-left corner is its move handle, which you use to move the control. You use the other seven handles, called sizing handles, to resize the control. When you work in Design view, controls you place in the form do not become part of a control layout, so you can individually select, move, resize, and otherwise manipulate one control without also changing the other controls. However, at any time you can select a group of controls and place them in a control layout—either a stacked layout or a tabular layout.

REFERENCE

Selecting and Moving Controls

- Click a control to select it. To select several controls at once, press and hold down the Shift key while clicking each control. Handles appear around all selected controls.
- To move a single selected control, drag the control's move handle, which is the handle in the upper-left corner, to its new position.
- To move a group of selected controls, point to any selected control until the pointer changes to a move pointer, and then drag the group of selected controls to its new position.
- To move selected controls in a small increment, press the appropriate arrow key.
- To move selected controls to the next nearest grid dot, hold down the Ctrl key and press the appropriate arrow key.

Based on Raj's design for the custom form, shown in Figure 6-17, you must select the WalkIn bound control and move it up and to the right in the Detail section. The WalkIn bound control consists of a check box and an attached label, displaying the text "Walk-in?" to its right.

To select the WalkIn bound control:

1. If necessary, click the **Walk-in?** label box to select it. Move handles, which are the larger handles, appear on the upper-left corners of the selected label box and its associated bound control. Sizing handles also appear, but only on the label box. See Figure 6-20.

Figure 6-20 Selecting the Walk-in? label control

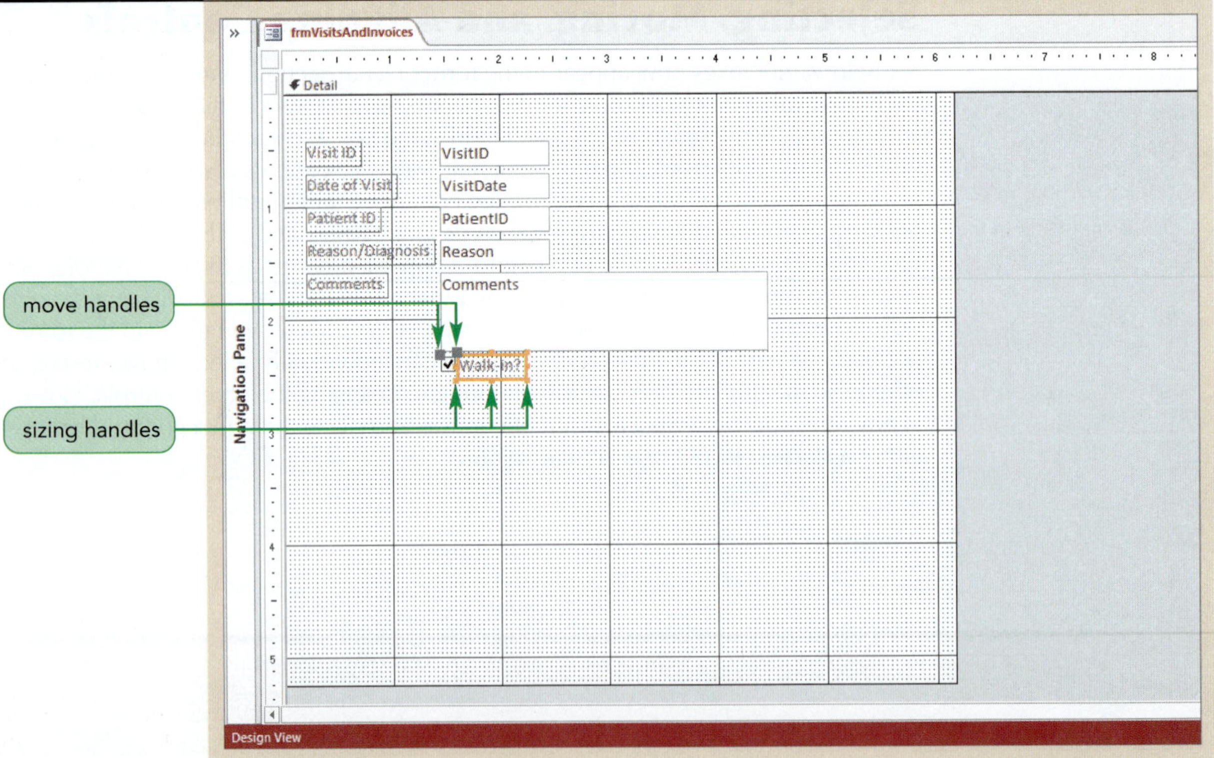

You can move a field value box and its attached label together. To move them, you place the pointer anywhere on the border of the field value box, but not on a move handle or a sizing handle. When the pointer changes to a shape, you can drag the field value box and its attached label to the new location. As you move a control, an outline of the control moves on the rulers to indicate the current position of the control as you drag it. To move a group of selected controls, point to any selected control until the pointer changes to a shape, and then drag the group of selected controls to its new position. You can move controls with more precision when you use the arrow keys instead of the mouse. To move selected controls in a small increment, press the appropriate arrow key on the keyboard. To move selected controls to the next nearest grid dot, hold down the Ctrl key and press the appropriate arrow key on the keyboard.

You can also move either a field value box or its label individually. If you want to move the field value box but not its label, for example, place the pointer on the field value box's move handle. When the pointer changes to a shape, drag the field value box to the new location. You use the label's move handle in a similar way to move only the label.

You'll now arrange the controls to match Raj's design.

To move the WalkIn bound control:

Be sure to position the pointer on one of the edges, but not on a move handle or a sizing handle.

1. Position the pointer on one of the edges of the Walk-in? label, but not on a move handle or a sizing handle. When the pointer changes to a shape, drag the control to the upper-right area and then release the mouse button. See Figure 6-21.

Figure 6-21 After moving the Walk-in? label and associated bound control

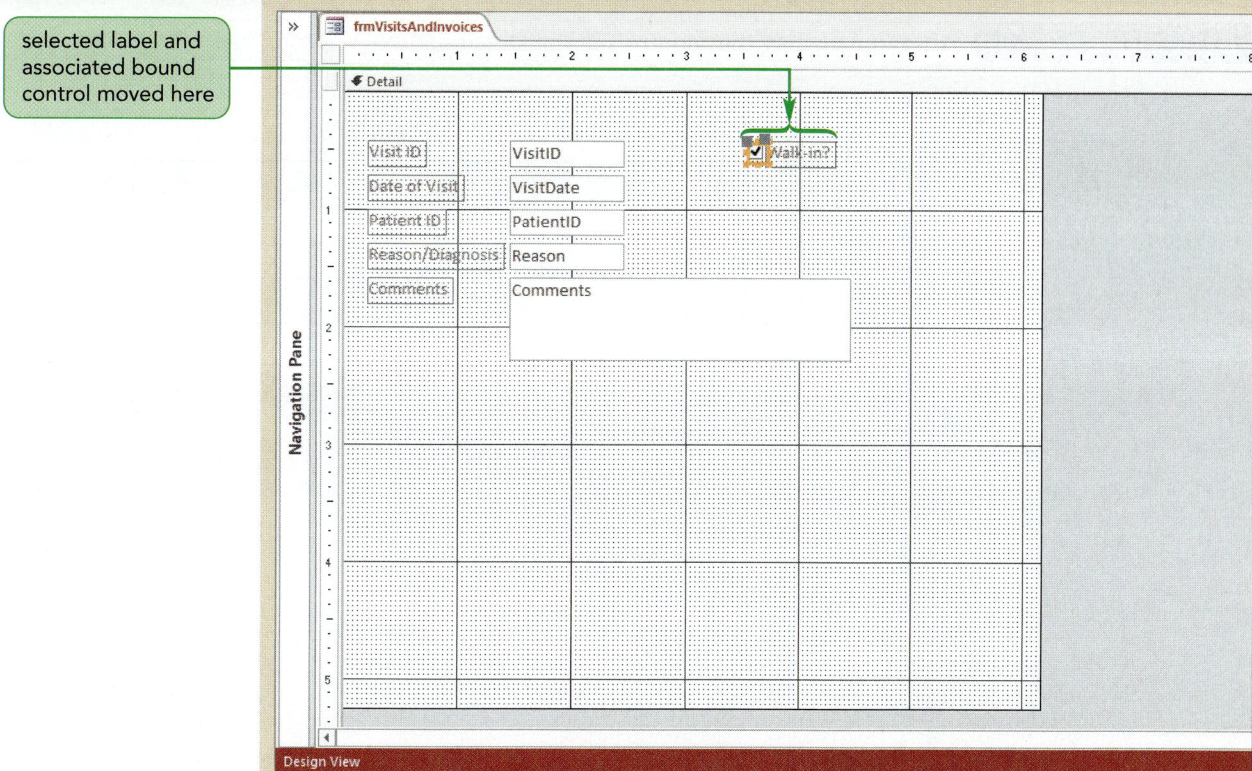

Trouble? If you need to make major adjustments to the placement of the WalkIn bound control, click the Undo button on the Quick Access Toolbar one or more times until the bound control is back to its starting position, and then repeat Step 1. If you need to make minor adjustments to the placement of the WalkIn bound control, use the arrow keys on the keyboard.

Now you need to align the WalkIn and VisitID bound controls on their top edges. When you select a column of controls, you can align the left edges or the right edges of the controls. When you select a row of controls, you can align the top edges or the bottom edges of the controls. A fifth alignment option, To Grid, aligns selected controls with the dots in the grid. You can find the five alignment options on the ARRANGE tab on the ribbon or on the shortcut menu for the selected controls.

You'll use the shortcut menu to align the two bound controls. Then you'll save the modified form and review your work in Form view.

To align the WalkIn and VisitID bound controls:

1. Make sure the Walk-in? label box is selected, hold down the **Shift** key, click the **WalkIn check box**, click the **VisitID** text box, click the **Visit ID** label, and then release the **Shift** key. This action selects the four controls; each selected control has an orange border.
2. Right-click one of the selected controls, point to **Align** on the shortcut menu, and then click **Top**. The four selected controls are aligned on their top edges. See Figure 6-22.

Figure 6-22 After top-aligning four controls in the Detail section

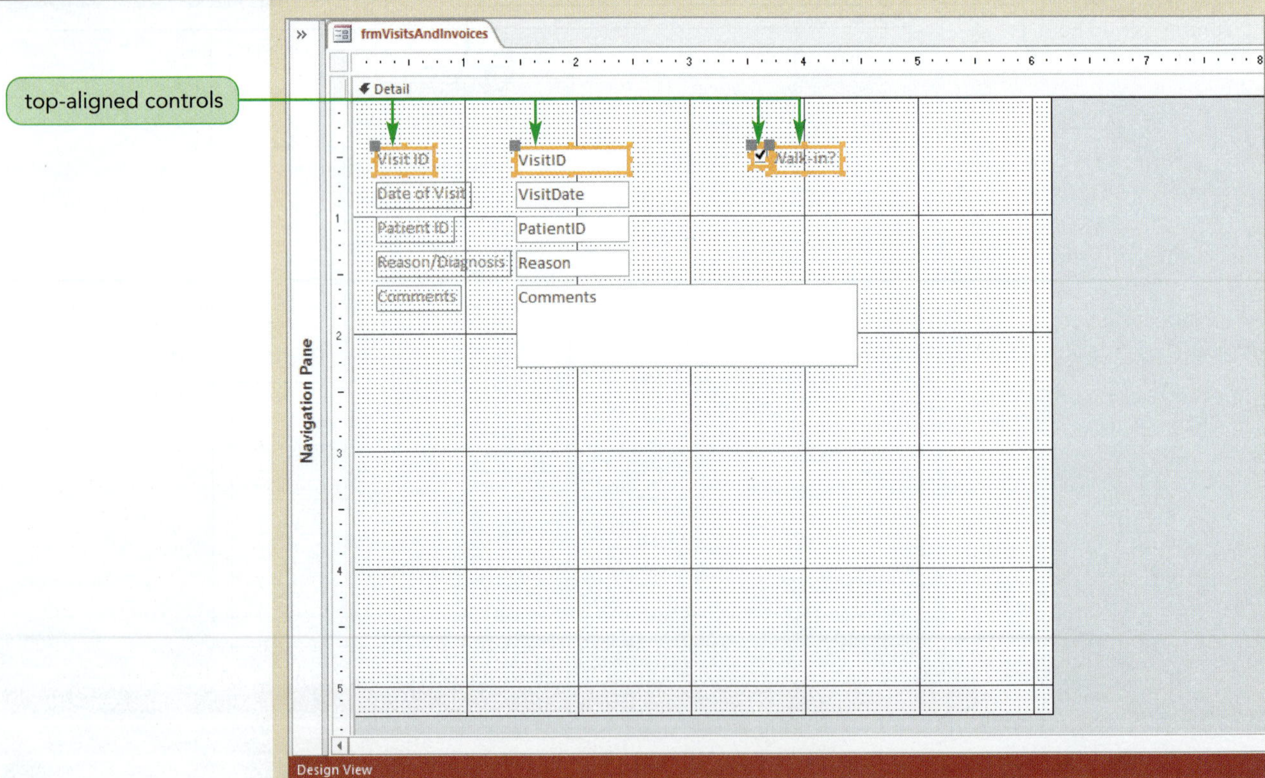

As you create a form, you should periodically save your modifications to the form and review your progress in Form view.

3. Save your form design changes, and then switch to Form view. See Figure 6-23.

Figure 6-23 Form displayed in Form view

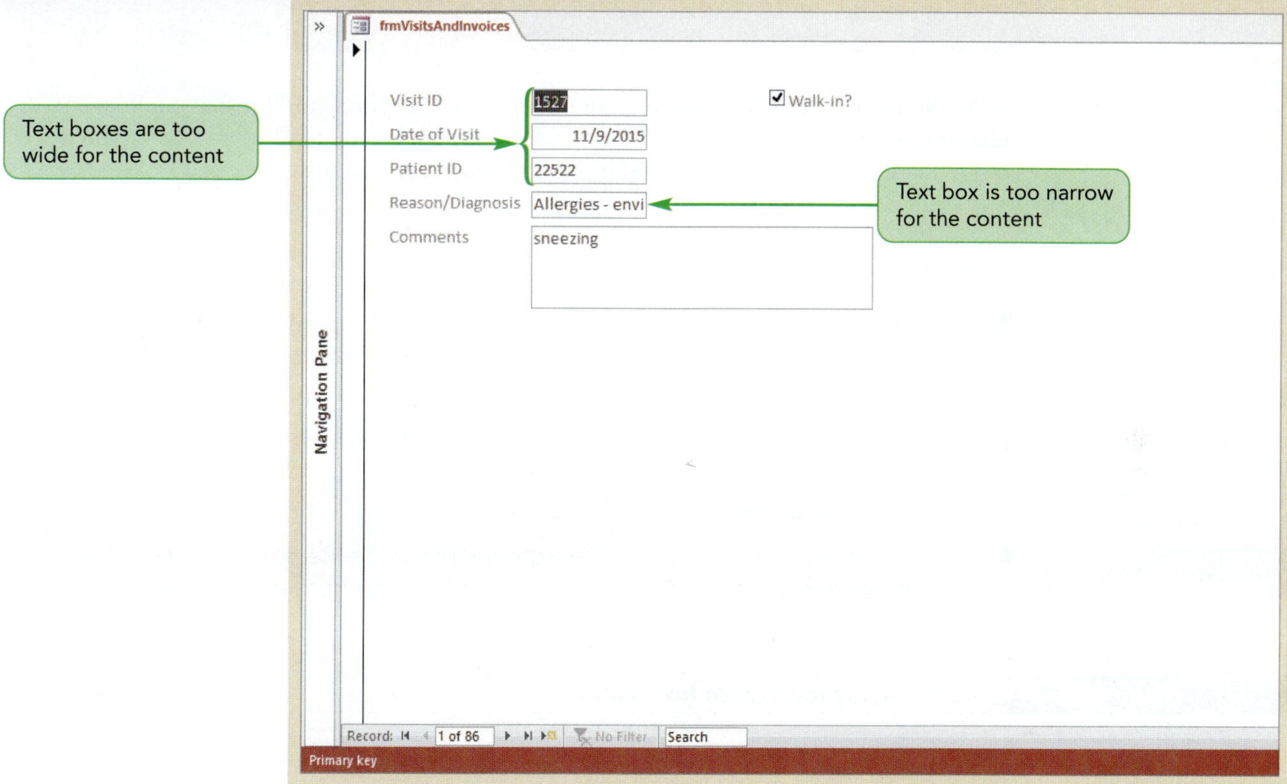

The value in the Reason text box is not fully displayed, so you need to increase the width of the text box. The widths of the VisitID and VisitDate text boxes are wider than necessary, so you'll reduce their widths. Also, the PatientID bound control consists of a label and a text box, but the plan for the form shows a combo box for the PatientID positioned below the WalkIn bound control. You'll delete the PatientID bound control in preparation for adding it to the form as a combo box.

Resizing and Deleting Controls

A selected control displays seven sizing handles: four at the midpoints on each edge of the control and one at each corner except the upper-left corner. Recall that the upper-left corner displays the move handle. Positioning the pointer over a sizing handle changes the pointer to a two-headed arrow; the directions in which the arrows point indicate in which direction you can resize the selected control. When you drag a sizing handle, you resize the control. As you resize the control, a thin line appears inside the sizing handle to guide you in completing the task accurately, along with outlines that appear on the horizontal and vertical rulers.

REFERENCE

Resizing a Control in Design View

- Click the control to select it and display the sizing handles.
- Place the pointer over the sizing handle you want to use, and then drag the edge of the control until it is the size you want.
- To resize selected controls in small increments, hold down the Shift key and press the appropriate arrow key on the keyboard. This technique applies the resizing to the right edge and the bottom edge of the control.

You'll begin by deleting the PatientID bound control. Then you'll resize the Reason text box, which is too narrow and too short to display Reason field values. Next you'll resize the VisitID and VisitDate text boxes to reduce their widths.

TIP

If you want to delete a label but not its associated field value box, right-click the label, and then click Delete on the shortcut menu.

To delete a bound control and resize the text boxes:

1. Switch to Design view, click an unused portion of the grid to deselect all controls, and then click the **PatientID** text box to select it.
2. Right-click the **PatientID** text box to open the shortcut menu, and then click **Delete**. The label and the text box for the PatientID bound control are deleted.
3. Click the **Reason** text box to select it.
4. Place the pointer on the middle-right handle of the Reason text box. When the pointer changes to a ↔ shape, drag the right border horizontally until it is approximately the same width as the Comments text box. See Figure 6-24.

Figure 6-24 After resizing the Reason text box

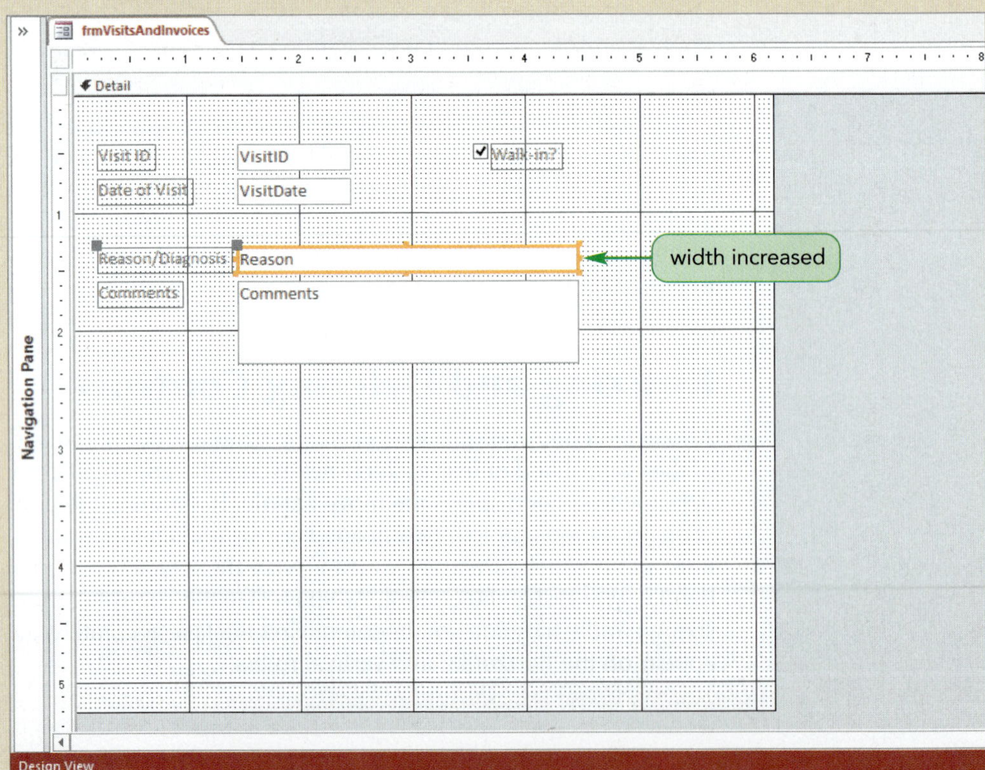

Resizing controls in Design view is a trial-and-error process, in which you resize a control in Design view, switch to Form view to observe the effect of the resizing, switch back to Design view to make further refinements to the control's size, and continue until the control is sized correctly. It's easier to resize controls in Layout view because you can see actual field values while you resize the controls. You'll resize the other two text boxes in Layout view. The sizes of the VisitID and VisitDate text boxes will look fine if you reduce them to have the same widths, so you'll select both text boxes and resize them as a group.

5. Switch to Layout view, and then click the **VisitID** text box (if necessary) to select it. Hold the **Shift** key down and click the **VisitDate** text box (next to the label "Date of Visit") to select it.
6. Position the pointer on the right edge of the **VistDate** text box. When the pointer changes to a ↔ shape, drag the right border horizontally to the left until the text box is slightly wider than the field value it contains, and the date in the VisitID field is also visible. See Figure 6-25.

Figure 6-25 After resizing field value boxes in Layout view

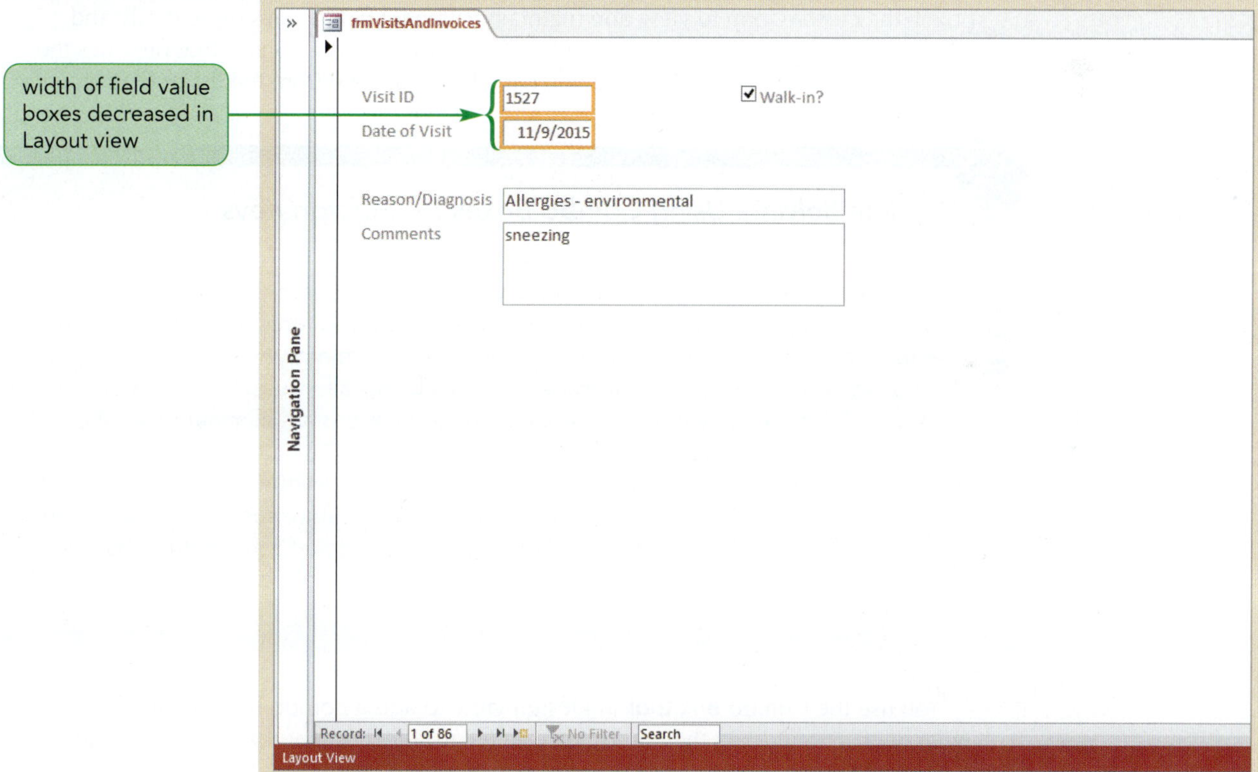

Trouble? If you resized the text boxes too far to the left, number signs will be displayed inside the VisitDate text box. Drag the right edge of the text boxes slightly to the right and repeat the process until the date value is visible inside the text box.

TIP

If you select a control by mistake, hold down the Shift key, and then click the selected control to deselect it.

7. Navigate through the first several records to make sure the three text boxes are sized properly and display the full field values. If any text box is too small, select the text box and increase its width the appropriate amount.
8. Save your form design changes, switch to Design view, and then deselect all controls by clicking in an unused portion of the grid.

INSIGHT

Making Form Design Modifications

When you design forms and other objects, you'll find it helpful to switch frequently between Design view and Layout view. Some form modifications are easier to make in Layout view, other form modifications are easier to make in Design view, and still other form modifications can be made only in Design view. You should check your progress frequently in either Layout view or Form view, and you should save your modifications after completing a set of changes successfully.

Recall that you removed the lookup feature from the PatientID field because a combo box provides the same lookup capability in a form. Next, you'll add a combo box for the PatientID field to the custom form.

Adding a Combo Box to a Form

The tblPatient and tblVisit tables are related in a one-to-many relationship. The PatientID field in the tblVisit table is a foreign key to the tblPatient table, and you can use a combo box in the custom form to view and maintain PatientID field values more easily and accurately than using a text box. Recall that a combo box is a control that provides the features of a text box and a list box; you can choose a value from the list or type an entry.

PROSKILLS

Problem Solving: Using Combo Boxes for Foreign Keys

When you design forms, combo boxes are a natural choice for foreign keys because foreign key values must match one of the primary key values in the related primary table. If you do not use a combo box for a foreign key, you force users to type values in the text box. When they make typing mistakes, Access rejects the values and displays frustrating nonmatching error messages. Combo boxes allow users to select only from a list of valid foreign key values, so nonmatching situations are eliminated. At the same time, combo boxes allow users who are skilled at data entry to more rapidly type the values, instead of using the more time-consuming technique of choosing a value from the combo box list. Whenever you use an Access feature such as combo boxes for foreign keys, it takes extra time during development to add the feature, but you save users time and improve their accuracy for the many months or years they use the database.

You use the **Combo Box tool** in Design view to add a combo box to a form. If you want help when adding the combo box, you can select one of the Control Wizards. A **Control Wizard** asks a series of questions and then uses your answers to create a control in a form or report. Access offers Control Wizards for the Combo Box, List Box, Option Group, Command Button, Subform/Subreport, and other control tools.

You will use the Combo Box Wizard to add a combo box to the form for the PatientID field.

To add a combo box to the form:

1. Click the DESIGN tab, and then in the Controls group, click the **More** button to open the Controls gallery. See Figure 6-26.

Figure 6-26 Controls gallery

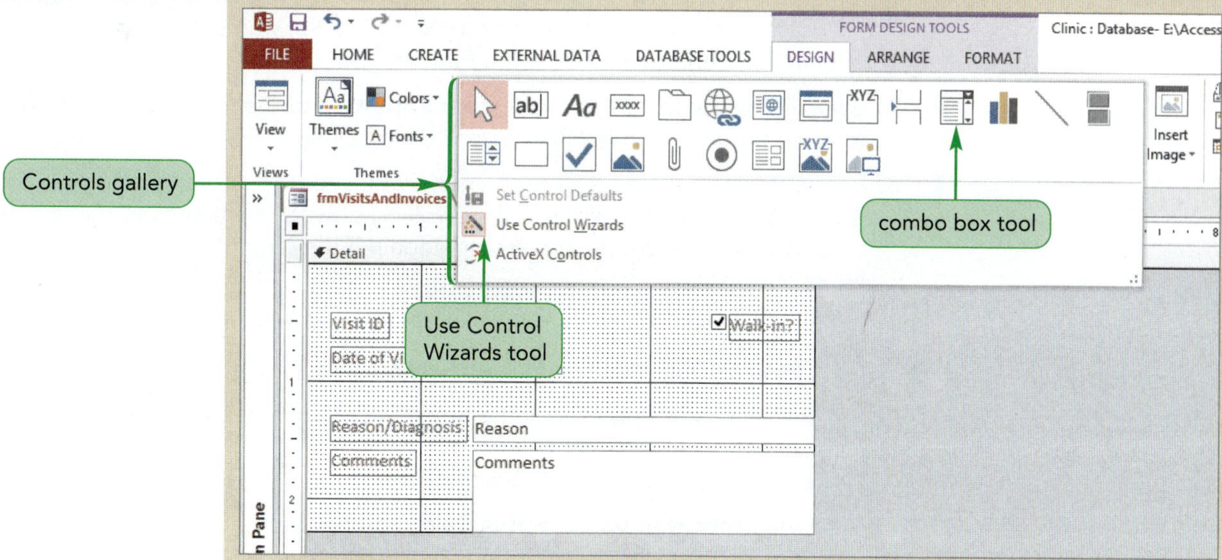

The Controls gallery contains tools that allow you to add controls (such as text boxes, lines, charts, and labels) to a form. You drag a control from the Controls gallery and place it in position in the grid.

2. In the gallery, make sure the Use Control Wizards tool is selected (with an orange background) in the Controls gallery. If the tool is not selected, click the **Use Control Wizards** tool to select it, and then click the **More** button to open the Controls gallery again.

3. In the Controls gallery, click the **Combo Box** tool. The Controls gallery closes. After you click the Combo Box tool or most other tools in the Controls gallery, nothing happens until you move the pointer over the form. When you move the pointer over the form, the pointer changes to a shape that is unique for the control with a plus symbol in its upper-left corner. You position the plus symbol in the location where you want to place the upper-left corner of the control.

   You'll place the combo box near the top of the form, below the WalkIn bound control, and then position it more precisely after you've finished the wizard.

4. Position the + portion of the pointer below the WalkIn bound control and at the 4-inch mark on the horizontal ruler, and then click the mouse button. Access places a combo box control in the form and opens the first Combo Box Wizard dialog box.

   You can use an existing table or query as the source for a new combo box or type the values for the combo box. In this case, you'll use the qryPatientsByName query as the basis for the new combo box. This query includes the Patient calculated field, whose value equals the concatenation of the LastName and FirstName field values.

5. Click the **I want the combo box to get the values from another table or query** option button (if necessary), click the **Next** button to open the next Combo Box Wizard dialog box, click the **Queries** option button in the View group, click **Query: qryPatientsByName**, and then click the **Next** button. Access opens the third Combo Box Wizard dialog box. This dialog box lets you select the fields from the query to appear as columns in the combo box. You'll select the first two fields.

6. Double-click **Patient** to move this field to the Selected Fields box, double-click **PatientID**, and then click the **Next** button. This dialog box lets you choose a sort order for the combo box entries. Raj wants the entries to appear in ascending order on the Patient field.

7. Click the **arrow** for the first box, click **Patient**, and then click the **Next** button to open the next Combo Box Wizard dialog box.

8. Resize the columns a bit wider than the widest data because the form font is a bit larger than the wizard font, scrolling down the columns to make sure all values are visible and resizing again if they're not, and then click the **Next** button.

   In this dialog box, you select the foreign key, which is the PatientID field.

9. Click **PatientID** and then click the **Next** button.

   In this dialog box, you specify the field in the tblVisit table where you will store the selected PatientID value from the combo box. You'll store the value in the PatientID field in the tblVisit table.

10. Click the **Store that value in this field** option button, click its **arrow**, click **PatientID**, and then click the **Next** button.

    Trouble? If PatientID doesn't appear in the list, click the Cancel button, press the Delete key to delete the combo box, click the Add Existing Fields button in the Tools group on the DESIGN tab, double-click PatientID in the Field List pane, press the Delete key to delete PatientID, close the Field List pane, and then repeat Steps 1–10.

    In this dialog box, you specify the name for the combo box control. You'll use the field name of PatientID.

11. Type **PatientID** and then click the **Finish** button. The completed PatientID combo box appears in the form.

You need to position and resize the combo box control, but first you'll change the text for the attached label from PatientID to Patient ID to match the format used for other label controls in the form. To change the text for a label control, you set the control's Caption property value.

REFERENCE

Changing a Label's Caption

- Right-click the label to select it and to display the shortcut menu, and then click Properties to display the Property Sheet.
- If necessary, click the All tab to display the All page in the Property Sheet.
- Edit the existing text in the Caption box; or click the Caption box, press the F2 key to select the current value, and then type a new caption.
- On the DESIGN tab, in the Tools group, click the Property Sheet button to close the Property Sheet.

Next, you'll change the text that displays in the combo box label.

TIP

After selecting a control, you can press the F4 key to open and close the Property Sheet for the control.

To set the Caption property value for the PatientID label:

1. Right-click the **PatientID** label, which is the control to the left of the PatientID text box, to select it and to display the shortcut menu, and then click **Properties** on the shortcut menu. The Property Sheet for the PatientID label opens.
2. If necessary, click the **All** tab to display all properties for the selected PatientID label.

   Trouble? If the Selection type entry below the Property Sheet title bar is not "Label," then you selected the wrong control in Step 1. Click the PatientID label to change to the Property Sheet for this control.
3. Click before the "ID" in the Caption box, press the **spacebar**, and then press the **Tab** key to move to the next property in the Property Sheet. The Caption property value should now be Patient ID and the label for the PatientID bound control should now display Patient ID. See Figure 6-27.

Figure 6-27 **PatientID combo box and updated label added to the form**

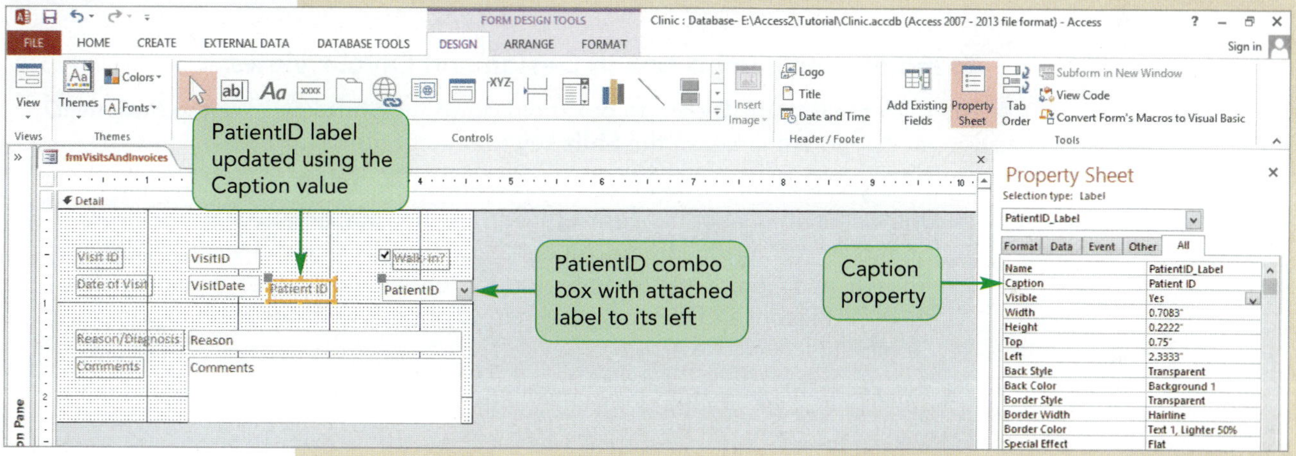

Trouble? Some property values in your Property Sheet, such as the Width and Top property values, might differ if your label's position slightly differs from the label position used as the basis for Figure 6-27. These differences cause no problems.

Trouble? You won't see the effects of the new property setting until you select another property, select another control, or close the Property Sheet.

The Selection type entry, which appears below the Property Sheet title bar, displays the control type (Label in this case) for the selected control. Below the Selection type entry in the Property Sheet is the Control box, which you can use to select another control in the form and then change its properties in the Property Sheet. Alternately, you can simply click a control in the form to change its properties in the Property Sheet. The first property in the Property Sheet, the **Name property**, specifies the name of a control, section, or object (PatientID_Label in this case). The Name property value is the same as the value displayed in the Control box, unless the Caption property has been set. For bound controls, the Name property value matches the field name. For unbound controls, Access adds an underscore and a suffix of the control type (for example, Label) to the Name property setting. For unbound controls, you can set the Name property to another, more meaningful value at any time.

4. Close the Property Sheet, and then save your design changes.

Now that you've added the combo box to the form, you can position the combo box and its attached label and resize the combo box. You'll need to view the form in Form view to determine any fine tuning necessary for the width of the combo box.

To modify the combo box in Design and Layout views:

1. Click the **PatientID** combo box, hold down the **Shift** key, click the **Patient ID** label, and then release the **Shift** key to select both controls.

   First, you'll move the selected controls above the VisitID controls. Then you'll align the PatientID, VisitID, VisitDate, Reason, and Comments labels on their left edges, align the PatientID combo box with the VisitID, VisitDate, Reason, and Comments text box controls on their left edges, and then align the WalkIn label and check box with the right edges of the Reason and Comments text boxes.

2. Drag the selected controls to a position above the VisitID controls. Do not try to align them.
3. Click in an unused area of the grid to deselect the selected controls, press and hold the **Shift** key while you click the **Patient ID** label, the **Visit ID** label, **Date of Visit** label, **Reason/Diagnosis** label, and the **Comments** label, and then release the **Shift** key.
4. Click the **ARRANGE** tab on the Ribbon, in the Sizing & Ordering group click the **Align** button, and then click **Left**. The selected controls are aligned on their left edges.
5. Repeat Steps 3 and 4 to align the **PatientID** combo box, **VisitID** text box, **VisitDate** text box, **Reason** text box, and the **Comments** text box on their left edges.
6. Select the **Walk-in?** label, **Walkin?** check box, **Reason** text box, and **Comments** text box, and in the Sizing & Ordering group on the ARRANGE tab, click the **Align** button, and then click **Right**. The selected controls are aligned on their right edges.
7. Switch to Form view, and then click the **PatientID** arrow to open the control's list box. Note that the column is not wide enough to show the full data values. See Figure 6-28.

Figure 6-28 PatientID combo box in Form view

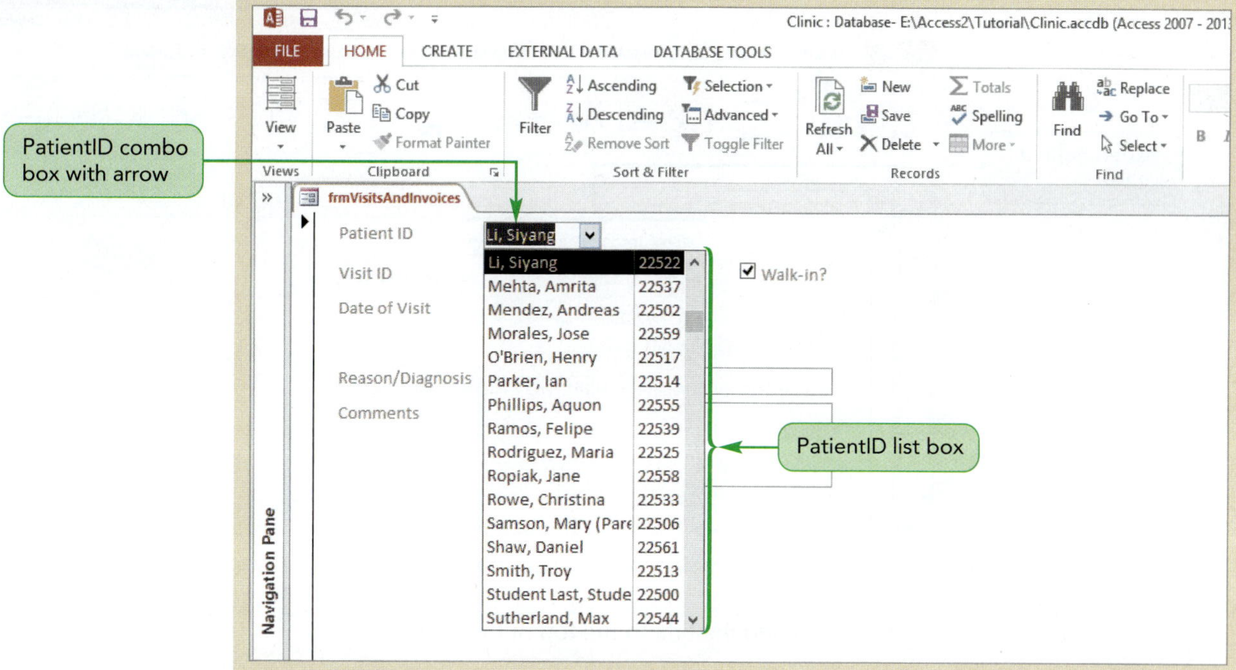

You need to widen the PatientID combo box, so that the widest customer value in the list is displayed in the combo box. You can widen the combo box in Layout view or in Design view. Because Form view and Layout view display actual data from the table rather than placeholder text in each bound control, these views let you immediately see the effects of your layout changes. You'll use Layout view instead of Design view to make this change because you can determine the proper width more accurately in Layout view.

8. Switch to Layout view, and then navigate to record 2. Weiss, Jordan (Parent), which is the patient value for this record, is one of the widest values that is displayed in the combo box. You want to widen the combo box so that the value in record 2 is completely visible, with a little bit more room.
9. Make sure that only the combo box is selected, and then pointing to the right edge, widen the combo box until the entire patient value is visible. See Figure 6-29.

Figure 6-29 After resizing the PatientID combo box in Layout view

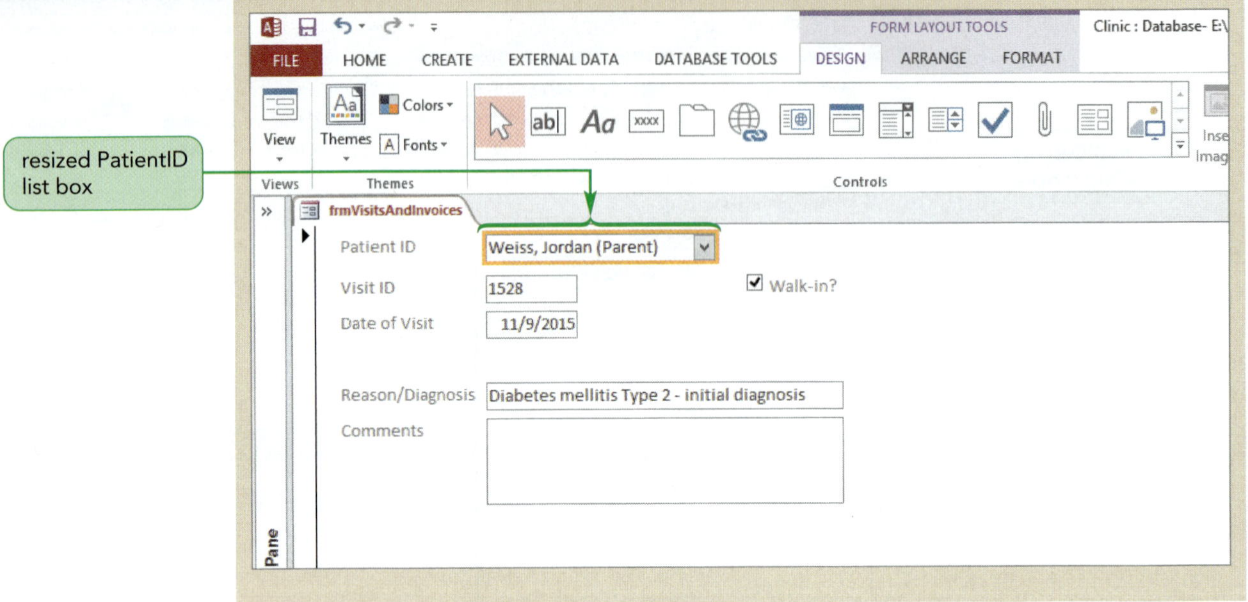

Now you'll add the title to the top of the form.

Using Form Headers and Form Footers

The **Form Header** and **Form Footer sections** let you add titles, instructions, command buttons, and other controls to the top and bottom of your form, respectively. Controls placed in the Form Header or Form Footer sections remain on the screen whenever the form is displayed in Form view or Layout view; they do not change when the contents of the Detail section change as you navigate from one record to another record.

To add either a form header or footer to your form, you must first add both the Form Header and Form Footer sections as a pair to the form. If your form needs one of these sections but not the other, you can remove a section by setting its height to zero, which is the same method you would use to remove any form section. You can also prevent a section from appearing in Form view or in Print Preview by setting its Visible property to No. The **Visible property** determines if Access displays a control or section. You set the Visible property to Yes to display the control or section, and set the Visible property to No to hide it.

If you've set the Form Footer section's height to zero or set its Visible property to No and a future form design change makes adding controls to the Form Footer section necessary, you can restore the section by using the pointer to drag its bottom edge back down or by setting its Visible property to Yes.

You can add the Form Header and Form Footer sections as a pair to a form either directly or indirectly. The direct way to add these sections is to right-click the Detail section selector, and then click Form Header/Footer. This direct method is available only in Design view. The indirect way to add the Form Header and Form Footer sections in Layout view or Design view is to use one of three buttons on the DESIGN tab in the Header/Footer group: the Logo button, the Title button, or the Date and Time button. Clicking any of these three buttons causes Access to add the Form Header and Form Footer sections to the form and to place an appropriate control in the Form Header section. If you use the indirect method in Layout view, Access sets the Form Footer section's height to zero. In Design view, the indirect method creates a Form Footer section with the Height property set to one-quarter inch.

REFERENCE

Adding and Removing Form Header and Form Footer Sections

- In Design view, right-click the Detail section selector, and then click Form Header/Footer on the shortcut menu; or in Layout view or Design view, click a button on the DESIGN tab in the Header/Footer group to add a logo, title, or date and time to the form.
- To remove a Form Header or Form Footer section, drag its bottom edge up until the section area disappears or set the section's Visible property to No.

Raj's design includes a title at the top of the form. Because the title will not change as you navigate through the form records, you will add the title to the Form Header section in the form.

Adding a Title to a Form

You'll add the title to Raj's form in Layout view. When you add a title to a form in Layout view, Access adds the Form Header section to the form and places the title in the Form Header section. At the same time, Access adds the Page Footer section to the form and sets its height to zero.

To add a title to the form:

1. On the DESIGN tab, in the Header/Footer group, click the **Title** button. Access adds the title to the form, displaying it in the upper-left of the form and using the form name as the title.

   You need to change the title. Because the title is already selected, you can type over or edit the selected title.

2. Type **Visits and Invoices** to replace the default title text. See Figure 6-30.

Figure 6-30 Title placed in the Form Header section

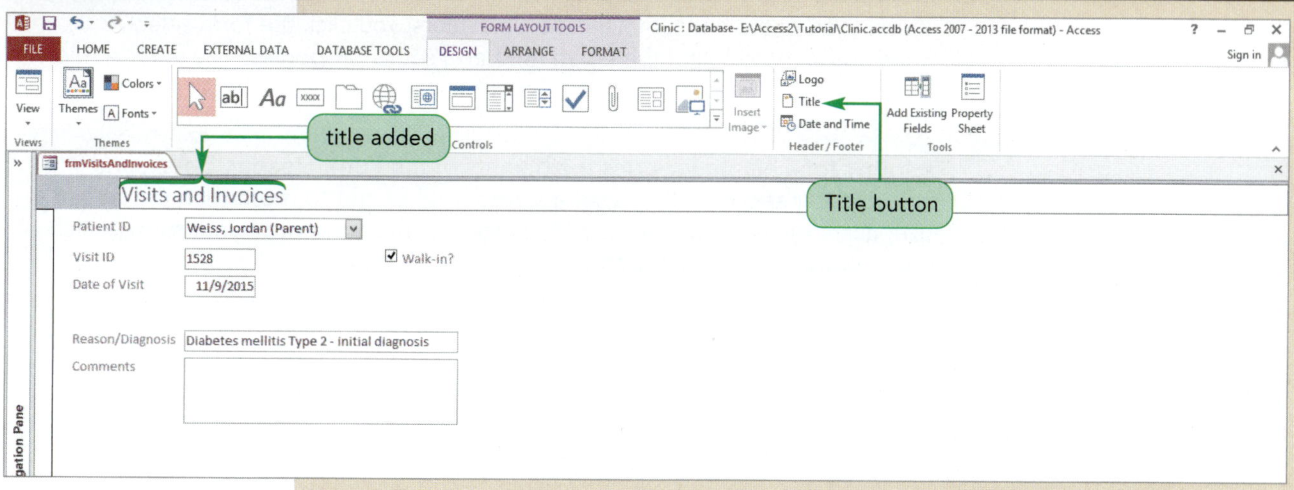

Raj wants the title to be prominent in the form. The title is already a larger font size than the font used for the form's labels and field value boxes, so you'll change the title's font weight to bold to increase its prominence.

3. Select the title control, click the **FORMAT** tab, and then in the Font group, click the **Bold** button **B**. The title is displayed in 18-point, bold text.

   It is not obvious in Layout view that the title is displayed in the Form Header section, so you'll view the form design in Design view.

4. Switch to Design view, click outside the grid to deselect all controls, and then save your design changes. The title is displayed in the Form Header section. See Figure 6-31.

Figure 6-31 Form Header and Form Footer sections in Design view

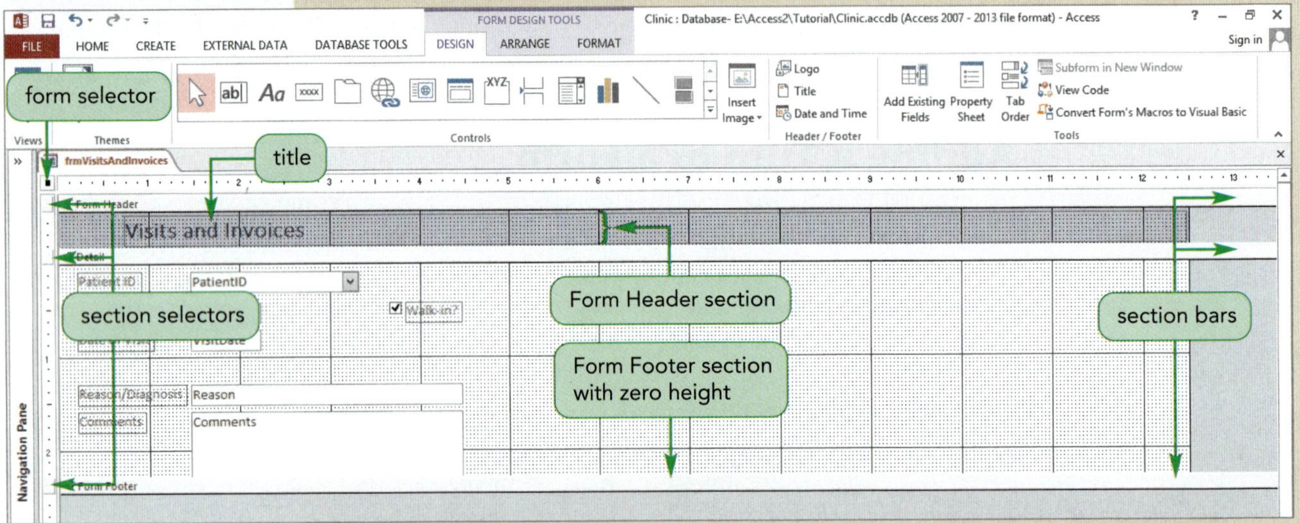

The form now contains a Form Header section that displays the title, a Detail section that displays the bound controls and labels, and a Form Footer section that is set to a height of zero. Each section consists of a **section selector** and a section bar, either of which you can click to select and set properties for the entire section, and a grid or background, which is where you place controls that you want to display in the form. The **form selector** is the selector at the intersection of the horizontal and vertical rulers; you click the form selector when you want to select the entire form and set its properties. The vertical ruler is segmented into sections for the Form Header section, the Detail section, and the Form Footer section.

A form's total height includes the heights of the Form Header, Detail, and Form Footer sections. If you set a form's total height to more than the screen size, users will need to use scroll bars to view the content of your form, which is less productive for users and isn't good form design.

So far, you've added controls to the form and modified the controls by selecting, moving, aligning, resizing, and deleting them. You've added and modified a combo box and added a title in the Form Header section. In the next session, you will continue your work with the custom form by adding a combo box to find records, adding a subform, adding calculated controls, changing form and section properties, and changing control properties.

REVIEW

Session 6.2 Quick Check

1. What is a bound form, and when do you use bound forms?
2. What is the difference between a bound control and an unbound control?
3. The ______________ consists of the dotted and solid lines that appear in the Header, Detail, and Footer sections to help you position controls precisely in a form.
4. The handle in a selected object's upper-left corner is the ______________ handle.
5. How do you move a selected field value box and its label at the same time?
6. How do you resize a control?
7. A(n) ______________ control provides the features of a text box and a list box.
8. How do you change a label's caption?
9. What is the Form Header section?

Session 6.3 Visual Overview:

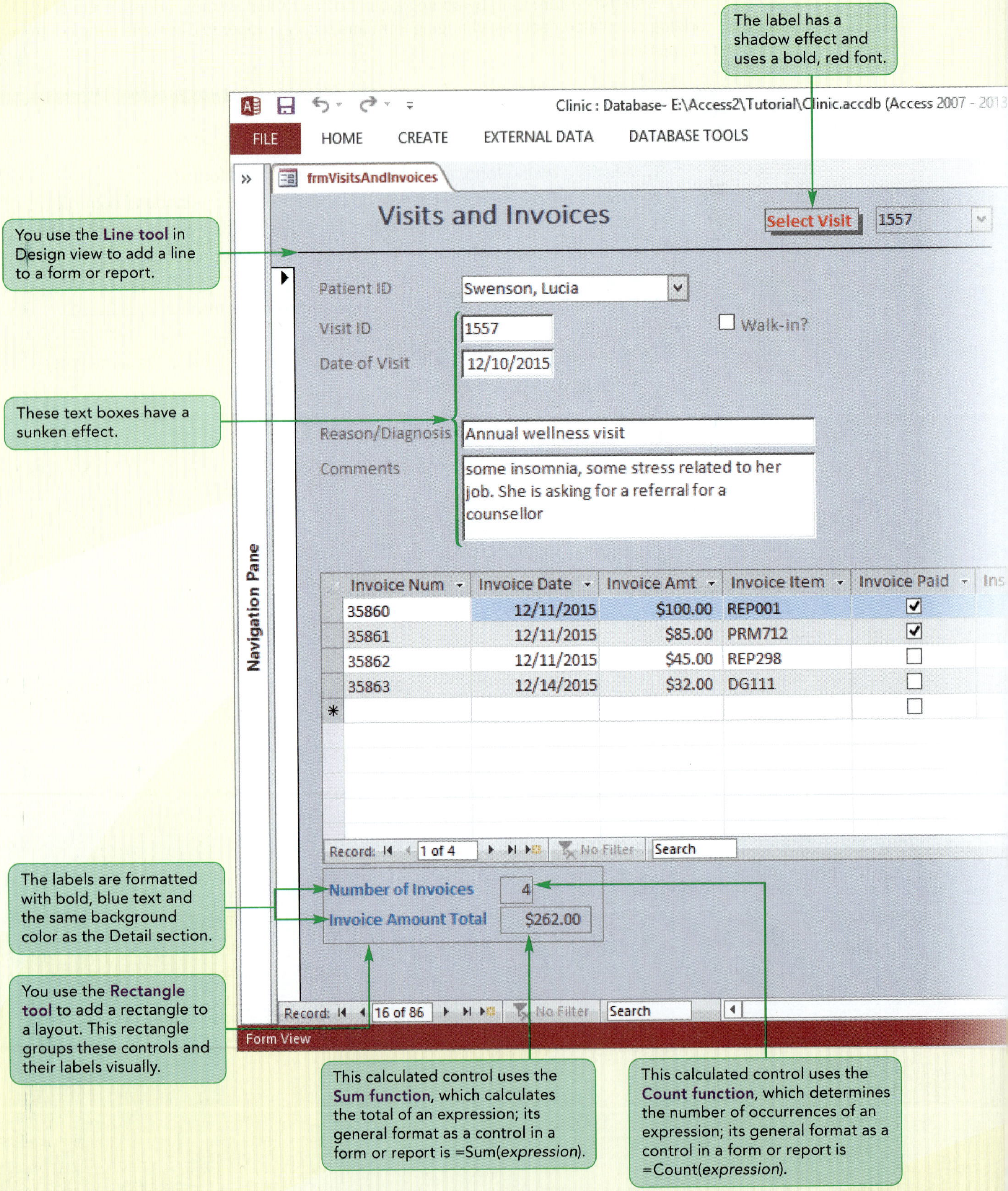

Custom Form in Form View

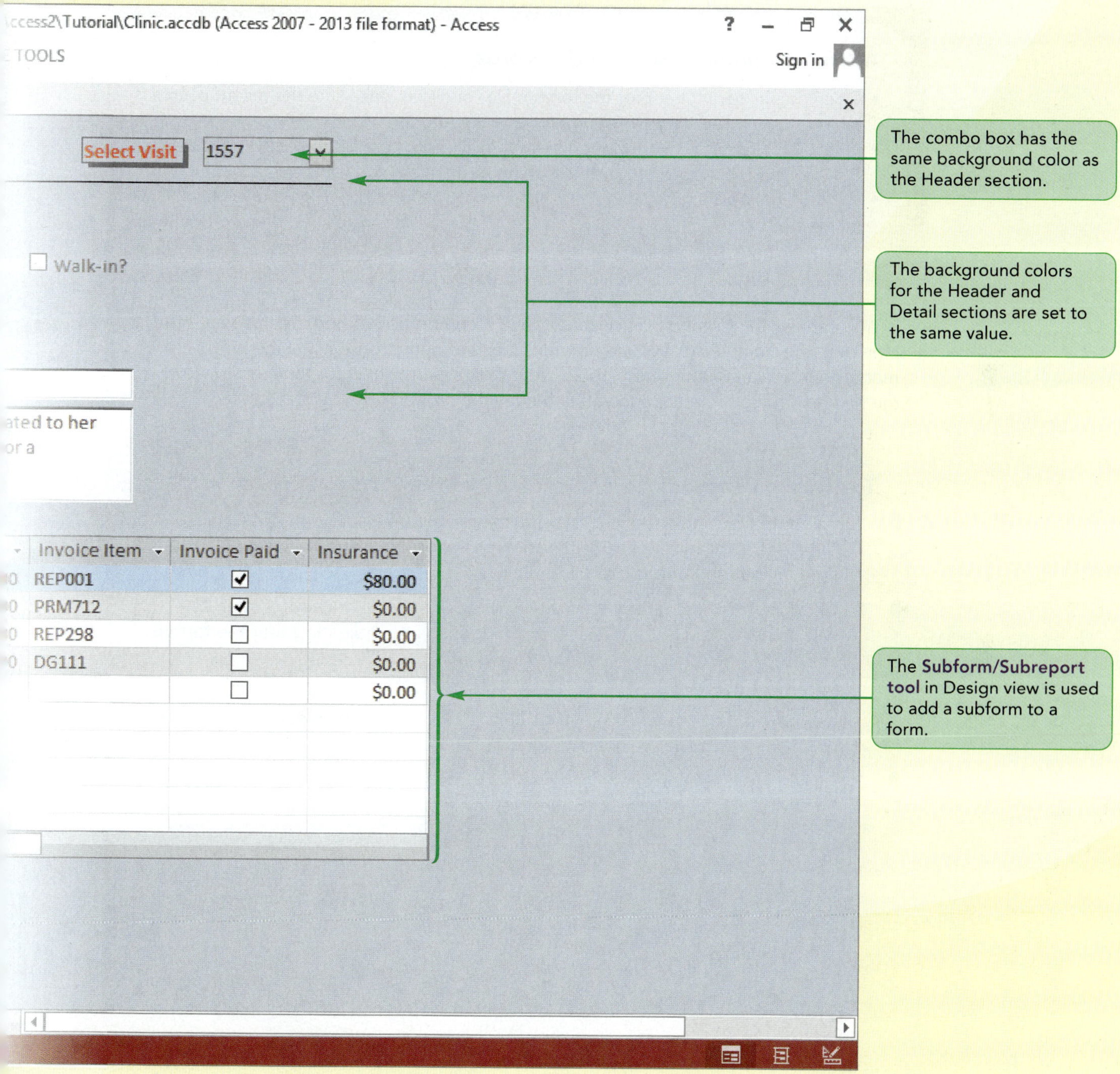

Adding a Combo Box to Find Records

Most combo boxes are used to display and update data. You can also use combo boxes to find records. To continue creating the form that Raj sketched, you will add a combo box to the Form Header section to find a specific record in the tblVisit table to display in the form.

REFERENCE

Adding a Combo Box to Find Records

- Open the Property Sheet for the form in Design view, make sure the record source is a table or query, and then close the Property Sheet.
- On the DESIGN tab, in the Controls group, click the More button, click the Combo Box tool, and then click the position in the form where you want to place the control.
- Click the third option button ("Find a record on my form based on the value I selected in my combo box") in the first Combo Box Wizard dialog box, and then complete the remaining Combo Box Wizard dialog boxes.

You can use the Combo Box Wizard to add a combo box to find records in a form. However, the Combo Box Wizard provides this find option only when the form's record source is a table or query. You'll view the Property Sheet for the form to view the Record Source property, and you'll change the property setting, if necessary.

To add a combo box to find records to the form:

1. If you took a break after the previous session, make sure that the Clinic database is open, the frmVisitsAndInvoices form is open in Design view, and the Navigation Pane is closed.
2. Click the **form selector** ☐ (located to the left of the horizontal ruler) to select the form. The form selector changes to ▣, indicating that the form is selected.

   Trouble? If the Form Header section head instead turns black, you might have clicked the header selector button. Click the form selector button, which is just above the header selector button.
3. Click the DESIGN tab, and then in the Tools group, click the Property Sheet button. The Property Sheet displays the properties for the form. See Figure 6-32.

Figure 6-32 **Property sheet for the form**

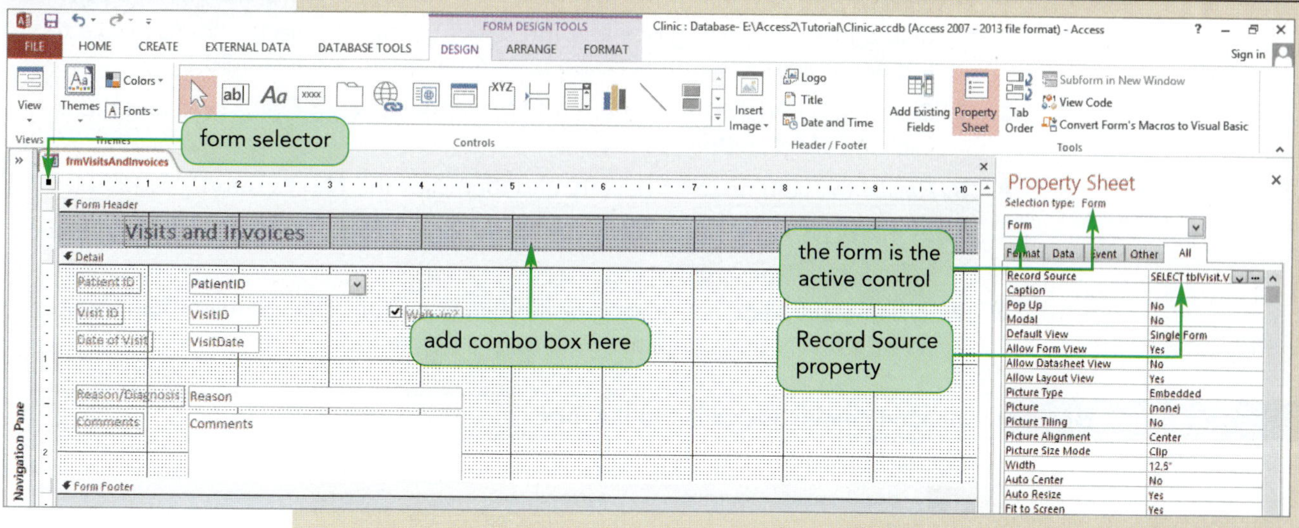

The Record Source property is set to an SQL SELECT statement, which is code that references a table. You need to change the Record Source property to a table or query, or the Combo Box Wizard will not present you with the option to find records in a form. You'll change the Record Source property to the tblVisit table because this table is the record source for all the bound controls you added to the Detail section.

4. Click the **All** tab if necessary, and click the **Record Source** box. Click the arrow, select **tblVisit**, and then close the Property Sheet.

You'll now use the Combo Box Wizard to add a combo box to the form's Form Header section, which will enable a user to find a record in the tblVisit table to display in the form.

5. On the DESIGN tab, in the Controls group, click the **More** button to open the Controls gallery, make sure the Use Control Wizards tool is selected in the Controls gallery, click the **Combo Box** tool, position the + portion of the pointer at the top of the Form Header section and at the 5-inch mark on the horizontal ruler (see Figure 6-32), and then click the mouse button. Access places a combo box control in the form and opens the first Combo Box Wizard dialog box.

Trouble? If the Combo Box Wizard dialog box does not open, delete the new controls and try again, ensuring the + pointer is very near the top of the Form Header grid.

The dialog box now displays a third option to "Find a record on my form based on the value I selected in my combo box," which you'll use for this combo box. You would choose the first option, which you used for the PatientID combo box, if you wanted to select a value from a list of foreign key values from an existing table or query. You would choose the second option if you wanted users to select a value from a short fixed list of values that don't change. For example, if Chatham Community Health Services wanted to include a field in the tblPatient table to identify the state in which the patient resides, you could use a combo box with this second option to display a list of states.

6. Click the **Find a record on my form based on the value I selected in my combo box** option button, and then click the **Next** button to open the next dialog box. This dialog box lets you select the fields from the tblVisit table to appear as columns in the combo box. You'll select the first field.
7. Double-click **VisitID** to move this field to the Selected Fields box, and then click the **Next** button.
8. Resize the column to its best fit, and then click the **Next** button.

   In this dialog box, you specify the name for the combo box's label. You'll use Select Visit as the label.
9. Type **Select Visit**, and then click the **Finish** button. The completed unbound combo box is displayed in the form. See Figure 6-33.

Figure 6-33 **Unbound combo box added to the form**

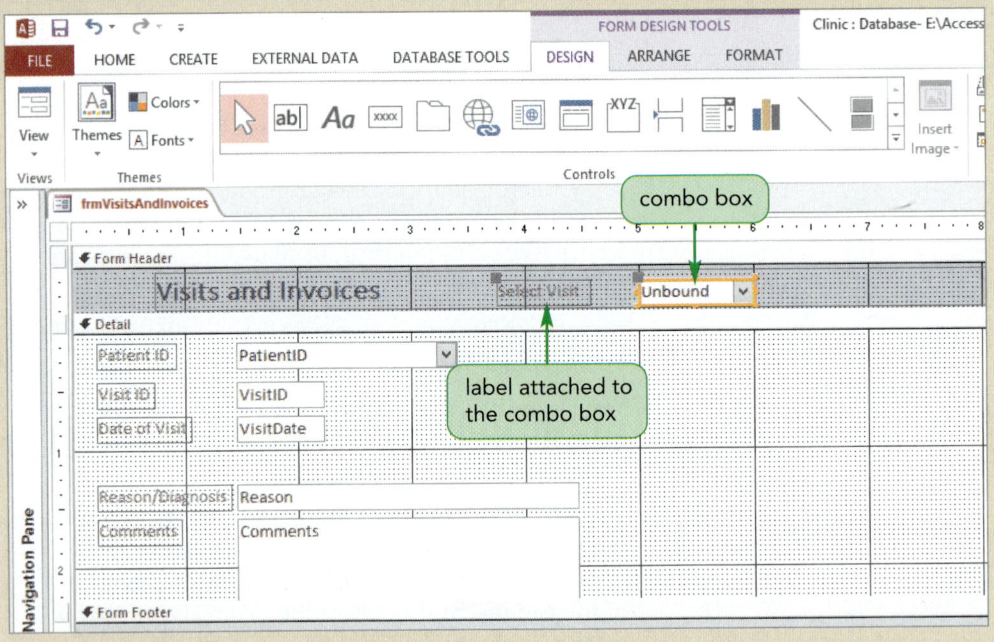

You'll move the attached label closer to the combo box, and then you'll align the bottoms of the combo box and its attached label with the bottom of the title in the Form Header section.

10. Click the **Select Visit** label, point to the label's move handle (upper left corner), and then drag the label to the right until its right edge is two grid dots to the left of the combo box.
11. Select the combo box in the Form Header section, the **Select Visit** label, and the title, right-click one of the selected controls, point to **Align**, and then click **Bottom**. The three selected controls are aligned on their bottom edges. See Figure 6-34.

Figure 6-34 After aligning the combo box control and the title

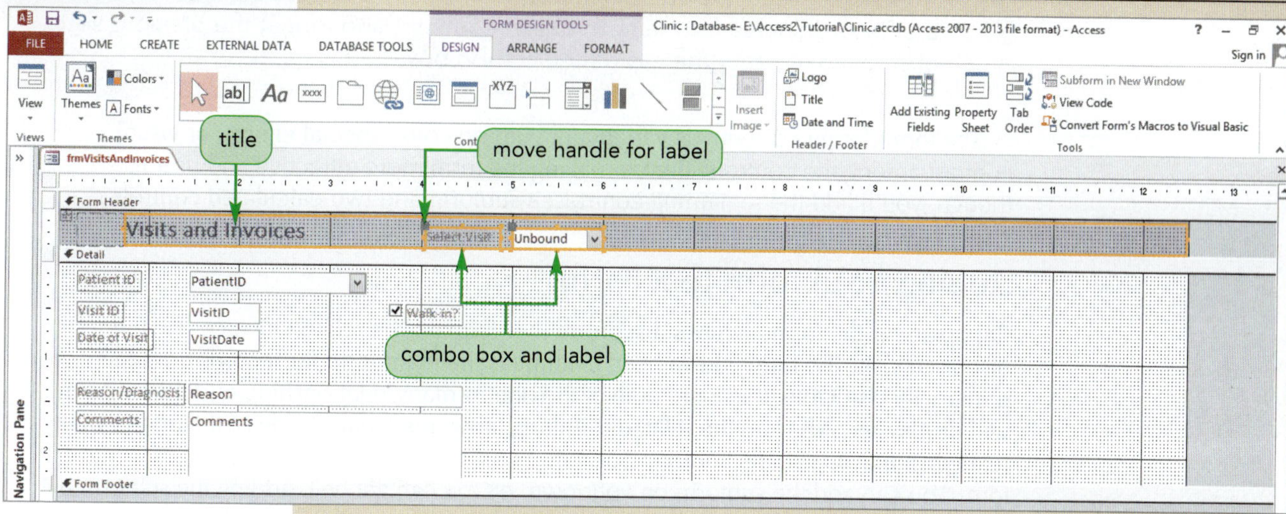

You'll save your form changes and view the new combo box in Form view.

To find contract records using the combo box:

1. Save the form design changes, and then switch to Form view.
2. Click the **Select Visit** combo box arrow to open the list box. See Figure 6-35.

Figure 6-35 Displaying the combo box's list of visit IDs

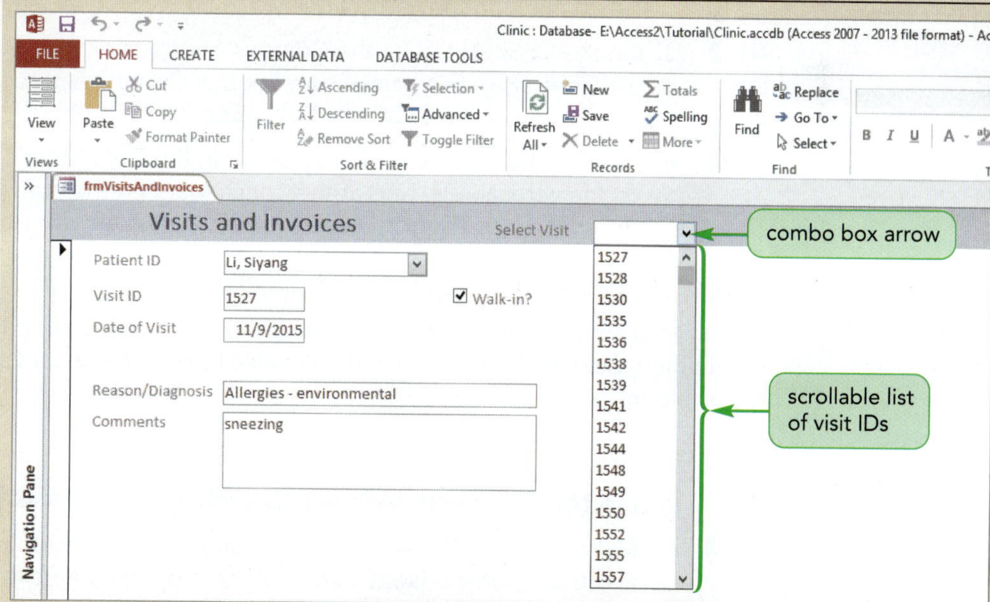

3. Scroll down the list, and then click **1557**. The current record changes from record 1 to record 16, which is the record for visit ID 1557.

Trouble? If you see the data for record 1, the navigation combo box is not working correctly. Delete the combo box, check to ensure that you have set the Record Source for the form object correctly, and repeat the previous set of steps to recreate the navigation combo box.

The form design currently is very plain, with no color, special effects, or visual contrast among the controls. Before making the form more attractive and useful, though, you'll add the remaining controls: a subform and two calculated controls.

Adding a Subform to a Form

Raj's plan for the form includes a subform that displays the related invoices for the displayed visit. The form you've been creating is the main form for records from the primary tblVisit table (the "one" side of the one-to-many relationship), and the subform will display records from the related tblBilling table (the "many" side of the one-to-many relationship). You use the Subform/Subreport tool in Design view to add a subform to a form. You can add the subform on your own, or you can get help adding the subform by using the SubForm Wizard.

You will use the SubForm Wizard to add the subform for the tblBilling table records to the bottom of the form. First, you'll increase the height of the Detail section to make room for the subform.

To add the subform to the form:

1. Switch to Design view.
2. Place the pointer on the bottom edge of the Detail section. When the pointer changes to a shape, drag the section's edge down until it is at the 5-inch mark on the vertical ruler.

TIP

Drag slightly beyond the desired ending position to expose the vertical ruler measurement, and then decrease the height back to the correct position.

3. On the DESIGN tab, in the Controls group, click the **More** button to open the Controls gallery, make sure the Use Control Wizards tool is selected, and then click the **Subform/Subreport** tool.
4. Position the + portion of the pointer in the Detail section at the 2.5-inch mark on the vertical ruler and at the 1-inch mark on the horizontal ruler, and then click the mouse button. Access places a subform control in the form's Detail section and opens the first SubForm Wizard dialog box.

You can use a table, a query, or an existing form as the record source for a subform. In this case, you'll use the related tblInvoice table as the record source for the new subform.

To use the SubForm Wizard to configure the subform:

1. Make sure the Use existing Tables and Queries option button is selected, and then click the **Next** button. Access opens the next SubForm Wizard dialog box, which lets you select a table or query as the record source for the subform and pick which fields to use from the selected table or query.
2. Click the **Tables/Queries arrow** to display the list of tables and queries in the Clinic database, scroll to the top of the list, and then click **Table: tblBilling**. The Available Fields box shows the fields in the tblBilling table.

Raj's form design includes all fields from the tblBilling table in the subform, except for the VisitID field, which you already placed in the Detail section of the form from the tblVisit table.

3. Click the >> button to move all available fields to the Selected Fields box, click **VisitID** in the Selected Fields box, click the < button, and then click the **Next** button to open the next SubForm Wizard dialog box. See Figure 6-36.

Figure 6-36 Selecting the linking field

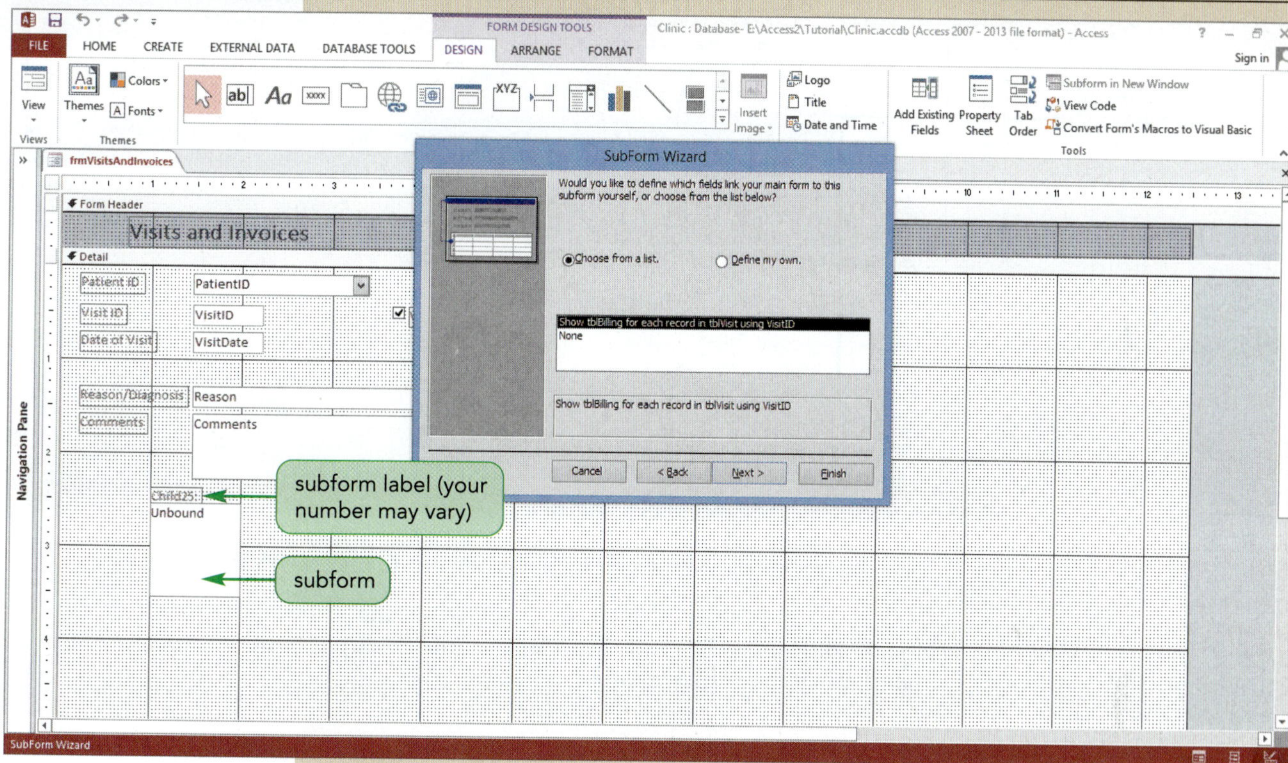

In this dialog box, you select the link between the primary tblVisit table and the related tblBilling table. The common field in the two tables, VisitID, links the tables. Access uses the VisitID field to display a record in the main form, which displays data from the primary tblVisit table, and to select and display the related records for that contract in the subform, which displays data from the related tblBilling table.

4. Make sure the "Choose from a list" option button is selected, make sure "Show tblBilling for each record in tblVisit using VisitID" is highlighted in the list, and then click the **Next** button. The next SubForm Wizard dialog box lets you specify a name for the subform.

5. Type **frmBillingSubform** and then click the **Finish** button. Access increases the height and width of the subform in the form. The subform will display the related tblBilling records; its label appears above the subform and displays the subform name.

6. Deselect all controls, save your form changes, switch to Form view, and then click the **VisitID** text box to deselect the value. If the record for VisitID 1557 is not selected, then click the drop-down arrow for the Select Visit combo box and scroll down the list to select VisitID 1557. See Figure 6-37.

Figure 6-37 Viewing the subform in Form view

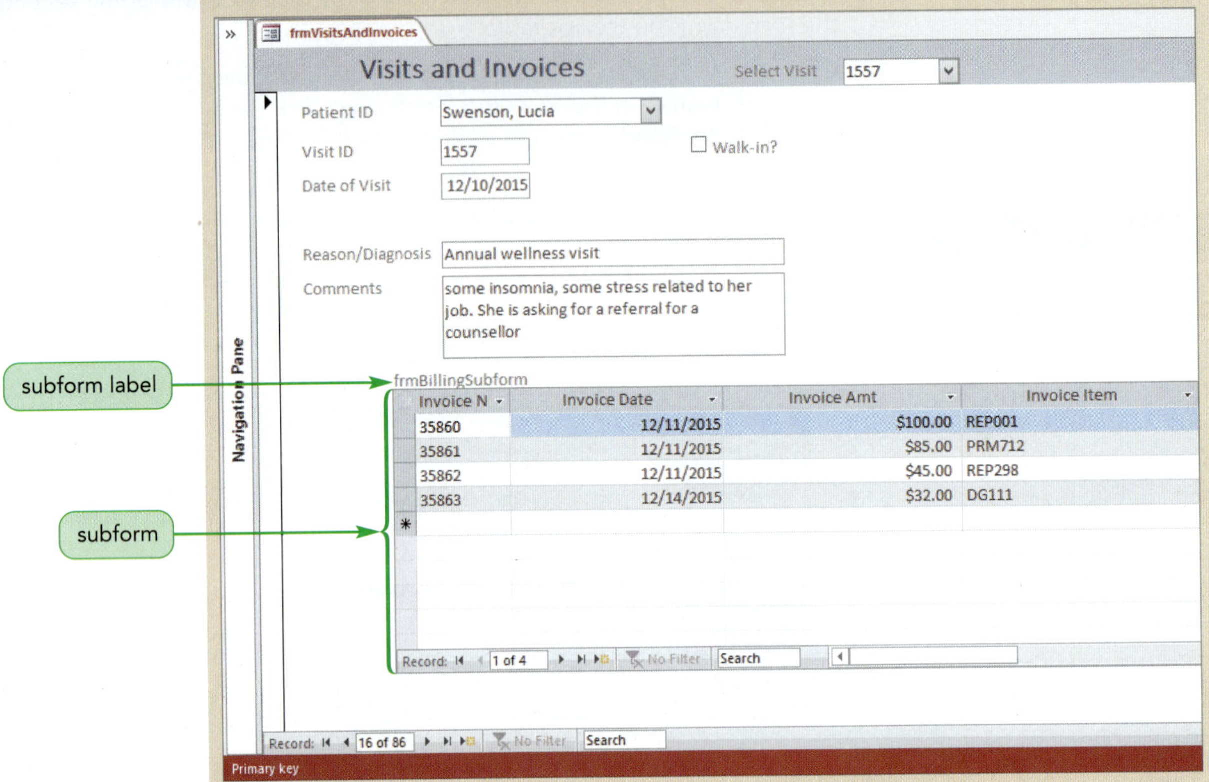

The subform displays the four invoices related to visit ID 1557.

Trouble? If the widths of the columns in your datasheet differ or the position of your subform is different, don't worry. You'll resize all columns to their best fit and move the subform later.

After viewing the form, Raj identifies some modifications he wants you to make. The subform is not properly sized and the columns in the subform are not sized to their best fit. He wants you to resize the subform and its columns, so that all columns in the subform are entirely visible. Also, he asks you to delete the subform label, because the label is unnecessary for identifying the subform contents. You'll use Design view and Layout view to make these changes.

To modify the subform's design:

1. Switch to Design view. Notice that in Design view, the subform data does not appear in a datasheet format as it does in Form view. That difference causes no problem; you can ignore it.

   First, you'll delete the subform label.

2. Deselect all controls (if necessary), right-click the **frmBillingSubform** subform label to open the shortcut menu (make sure no other controls have handles), and then click **Cut**.

   Next, you'll move the subform by aligning it with the Comments label.

3. Click the edge of the subform to select it (an orange border and handles appear on the subform's border when the subform is selected), hold down the **Shift** key, click the **Comments** label, and then release the **Shift** key. The subform and the Comments label are selected. Next you'll align the two controls on their left edges.
4. Right-click the **Comments** label, point to **Align** on the shortcut menu, and then click **Left**. The two controls are aligned on their left edges. You'll resize the subform in Layout view, so you can see your changes as you make them.
5. Switch to Layout view, click the edge of the subform to select it, and then drag the right edge of the subform to the right until all six datasheet columns are fully visible.

   Before resizing the columns in the subform, you'll display record 16 in the main form. The subform for this record contains the related records in the tblBilling table with one of the longest field values.
6. Use the record navigation bar for the main form (at the bottom left of the form window) to display record 16, for visit number 1557, and then resize each column in the subform to its best fit.

   Next, you'll resize the subform again so its width matches the width of the five resized columns.
7. Resize the subform's right edge, so it is aligned with the right edge of the Insurance column. See Figure 6-38.

Figure 6-38 After moving and resizing the subform

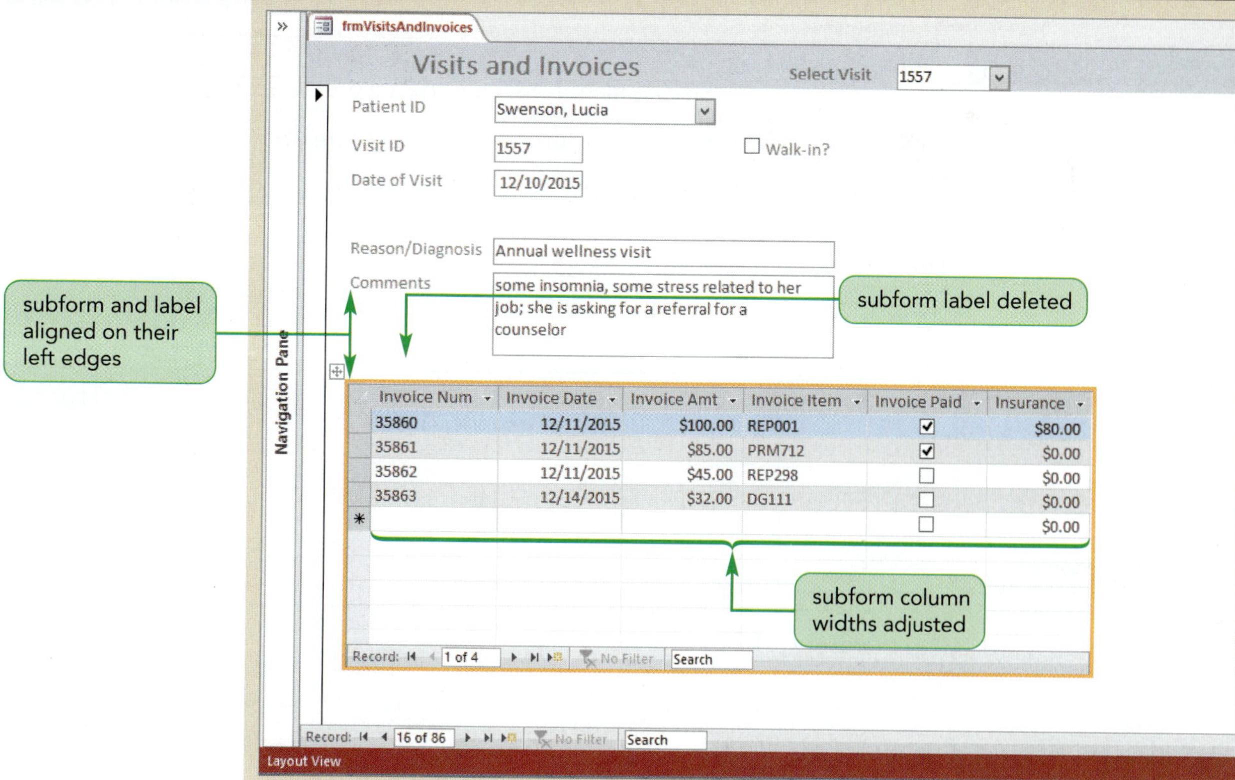

You've finished your work with the subform. Now you need to add two calculated controls to the main form.

Displaying a Subform's Calculated Controls in the Main Form

TIP

You precede expressions with an equal sign to distinguish them from field names, which do not have an equal sign.

Raj's form design includes the display of calculated controls in the main form that tally the number of invoices and the total of the invoice amounts for the related records displayed in the subform. To display these calculated controls in a form or report, you use the Count and Sum functions. The Count function determines the number of occurrences of an expression; its general format as a control in a form or report is =Count(*expression*). The Sum function calculates the total of an expression, and its general format as a control in a form or report is =Sum(*expression*). The number of invoices and total of invoice amounts are displayed in the subform's Detail section, so you'll need to place the calculated controls in the subform's Form Footer section.

Adding Calculated Controls to a Subform's Form Footer Section

First, you'll open the subform in Design view in another window and add the calculated controls to the subform's Form Footer section.

To add calculated controls to the subform's Form Footer section:

1. Save your form design changes, switch to Design view, click an unused area of the grid to deselect any selected controls, click the subform border to select the subform, right-click the border, and then click **Subform in New Window** on the shortcut menu. The subform opens in Design view. See Figure 6-39.

Figure 6-39 Subform in Design view

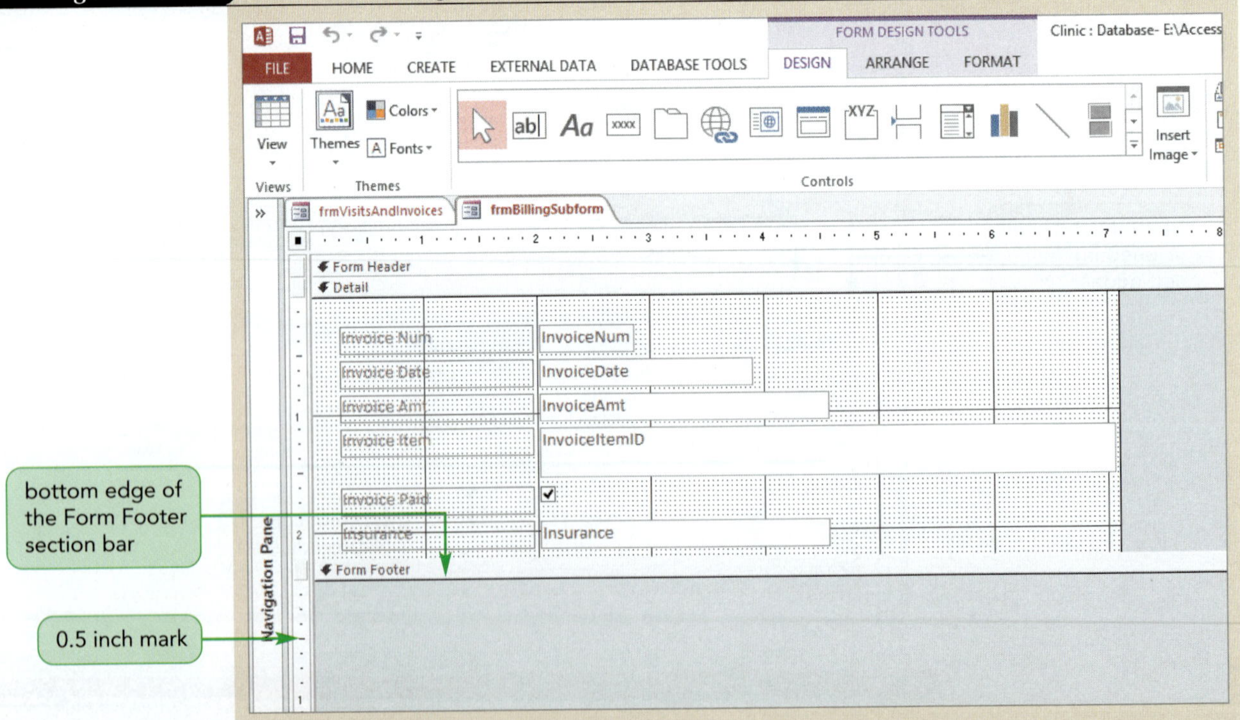

The subform's Detail section contains the tblBilling table fields. As a subform in the main form, the fields appear in a datasheet even though the fields do not appear that way in Design view. The heights of the subform's Form

Header and Form Footer sections are zero, meaning that these sections have been removed from the subform. You'll increase the height of the Form Footer section so that you can add the two calculated controls to the section.

2. Place the pointer at the bottom edge of the Form Footer section bar. When the pointer changes to a ↕ shape, drag the bottom edge of the section down to the 0.5-inch mark on the vertical ruler.

Now you'll add the first calculated control to the Form Footer section. To create the text box for the calculated control, you use the **Text Box tool** in the Controls group on the DESIGN tab. Because the Form Footer section is not displayed in a datasheet, you do not need to position the control precisely.

3. On the DESIGN tab, in the Controls group, click the **Text Box** tool ab|.

4. Position the + portion of the pointer near the top of the Form Footer section and at the 1-inch mark on the horizontal ruler, and then click the mouse button. Access places a text box control and an attached label control to its left in the Form Footer section.

Next, you'll set the Name and Control Source properties for the text box. Recall that the Name property specifies the name of an object or control. Later, when you add the calculated control in the main form, you'll reference the subform's calculated control value by using its Name property value. The **Control Source property** specifies the source of the data that appears in the control; the Control Source property setting can be either a field name or an expression.

TIP

Read the Naming Conventions section in the appendix titled "Relational Databases and Database Design" for more information about naming conventions.

5. Open the Property Sheet for the text box in the Form Footer section (the word "Unbound" is displayed inside the text box), click the **All** tab (if necessary), select the value in the Name box, type **txtInvoiceAmtSum** in the Name box, press the **Tab** key, type **=Sum(Inv** in the Control Source box, press the **Tab** key to accept the rest of the field name of InvoiceAmt suggested by Formula AutoComplete, type **)** (a right parenthesis), and then press the **Tab** key. InvoiceAmt is enclosed in brackets in the expression because it's a field name. See Figure 6-40.

Figure 6-40 **Setting properties for the subform calculated control**

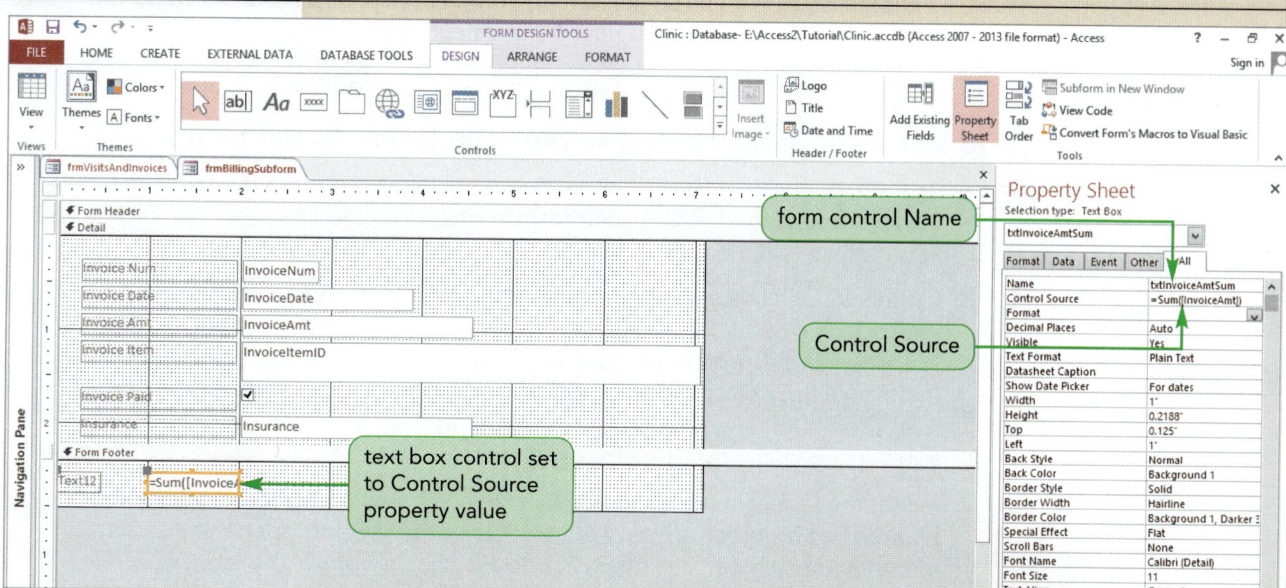

You've finished creating the first calculated control; now you'll create the other calculated control.

TIP

In txtInvoiceNum-Count, txt identifies the control type (a text box), InvoiceNum is the related field name, and Count identifies the control as a count control.

6. Repeat Steps 3 through 5, positioning the + portion of the pointer near the top of the Form Footer section and at the 4-inch mark on the horizontal ruler, setting the Name property value to **txtInvoiceNumCount**, and setting the Control Source property value to **=Count([InvoiceNum])**.

   When you use the Count function, you are counting the number of displayed records—in this case, the number of records displayed in the subform. Instead of using InvoiceNum as the expression for the Count function, you could use any of the other fields displayed in the subform.

   You've finished creating the subform's calculated controls, so you can close the Property Sheet, save your subform design changes, and return to the main form.

7. Close the Property Sheet, save your subform changes, and then close the subform. The active object is now the main form in Design view.

   Trouble? The subform in the frmContractsAndInvoices form might appear to be blank after you close the frmInvoiceSubform form. This is a temporary effect; the subform's controls do still exist. Switch to Form view and then back to Design view to display the subform's controls.

8. Switch to Form view. The calculated controls you added in the subform's Form Footer section are *not* displayed in the subform.

9. Switch to Design view.

Next, you'll add two calculated controls in the main form to display the two calculated controls from the subform.

Adding Calculated Controls to a Main Form

The subform's calculated controls now contain a count of the number of invoices and a total of the invoice amounts. Raj's design has the two calculated controls displayed in the main form, not in the subform. You need to add two calculated controls in the main form that reference the values in the subform's calculated controls. Because it's easy to make a typing mistake with these references, you'll use Expression Builder to set the Control Source property for the two main form calculated controls.

To add a calculated control to the main form's Detail section:

1. Adjust the length of the Detail section if necessary so there is approximately 0.5 inch below the frmBillingSubform control. The Detail section should be approximately 5.5 inches.
2. On the DESIGN tab, in the Controls group, click the **Text Box** tool ab|, and then add the text box and its attached label in the Detail section, clicking the + portion of the pointer at the 1-inch mark on the horizontal ruler and below the frmBillingSubform control, approximately the 5-inch mark on the vertical ruler. Don't be concerned about positioning the control precisely because you'll resize and move the label and text box later.
3. Select the label and open the Property Sheet, set its Caption property to **Number of Invoices**, right-click an edge of the label to open the shortcut menu, point to **Size**, and then click **To Fit**. Don't worry if the label now overlaps the text box.

You'll use Expression Builder to set Control Source property for the text box.

4. Click the text box (the word "Unbound" is displayed inside the text box) to select it, click the **Control Source** box in the Property Sheet, and then click the property's **Build** button [...] to open Expression Builder.

5. In the Expression Elements box, click the **expand indicator** [▷] next to frmVisitsAndInvoices, click **frmBillingSubform** in the Expression Elements box, scroll down the Expression Categories box, and then double-click **txtInvoiceNumCount** in the Expression Categories box. See Figure 6-41.

Figure 6-41 **Text box control's expression in the Expression Builder dialog box**

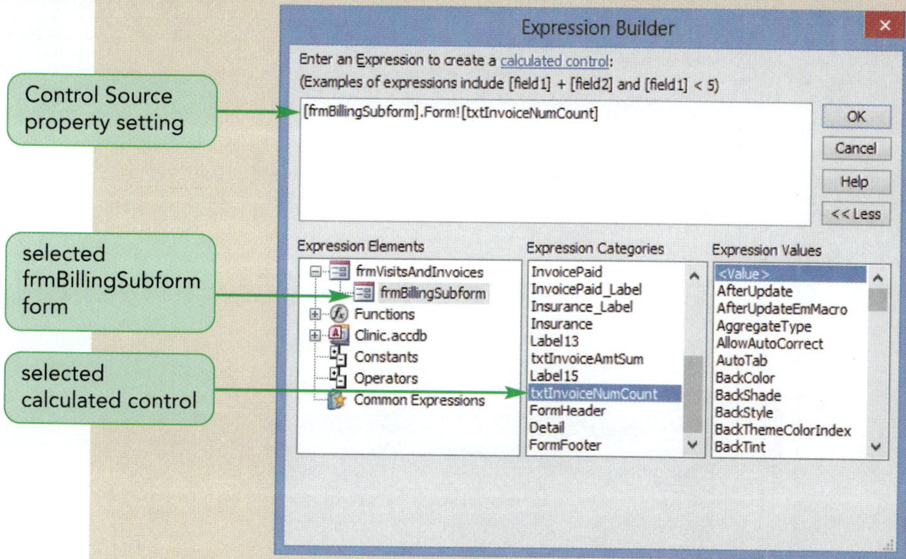

Instead of adding txtInvoiceNumCount to the expression box at the top, Access changed it to Form![frmBillingSubform]![txtInvoiceNumCount]. This expression asks Access to display the value of the txtInvoiceNumCount control that is located in the frmBillingSubform form, which is a form object.

You need to add an equal sign to the beginning of the expression.

6. Press the **Home** key, type = (an equal sign), and then click the **OK** button. Access closes the Expression Builder dialog box and sets the Control Source property.

Next, you'll add a second text box to the main form, set the Caption property for the label, and use Expression Builder to set the text box's Control Source property.

Be sure you resize the label to its best fit.

7. Repeat Steps 2 and 3 to add a text box to the main form, clicking the + portion of the pointer at the 4-inch mark on the horizontal ruler and approximately the 5-inch mark on the vertical ruler, and setting the label's Caption property to **Invoice Amount Total**.

8. Click the new text box (containing the word "Unbound") to select it, click the **Control Source** box in the Property Sheet, and then click the property's **Build** button [...] to open Expression Builder.

9. With the Expression Builder dialog box open for the new text box, type **=** (an equal sign), click the **expand indicator** next to frmVisitsAndInvoices in the Expression Elements box, click **frmBillingSubform** in the Expression Elements box, scroll down the Expression Categories box, and then

double-click **txtInvoiceAmtSum** in the Expression Categories box. Access changes the txtInvoiceAmtSum calculated field to the expression = [frmBillingSubform].Form![txtInvoiceAmtSum].

Next, you'll save your form changes and view the form in Layout view.

10. Click the **OK** button to accept the expression and close the Expression Builder dialog box, close the Property Sheet, save your form changes, and then switch to Form view. If the record for VisitID 1557 is not selected, then click the drop-down arrow for the Select Visit combo box and scroll down the list to select VisitID 1557. See Figure 6-42.

Figure 6-42 After adding two calculated controls

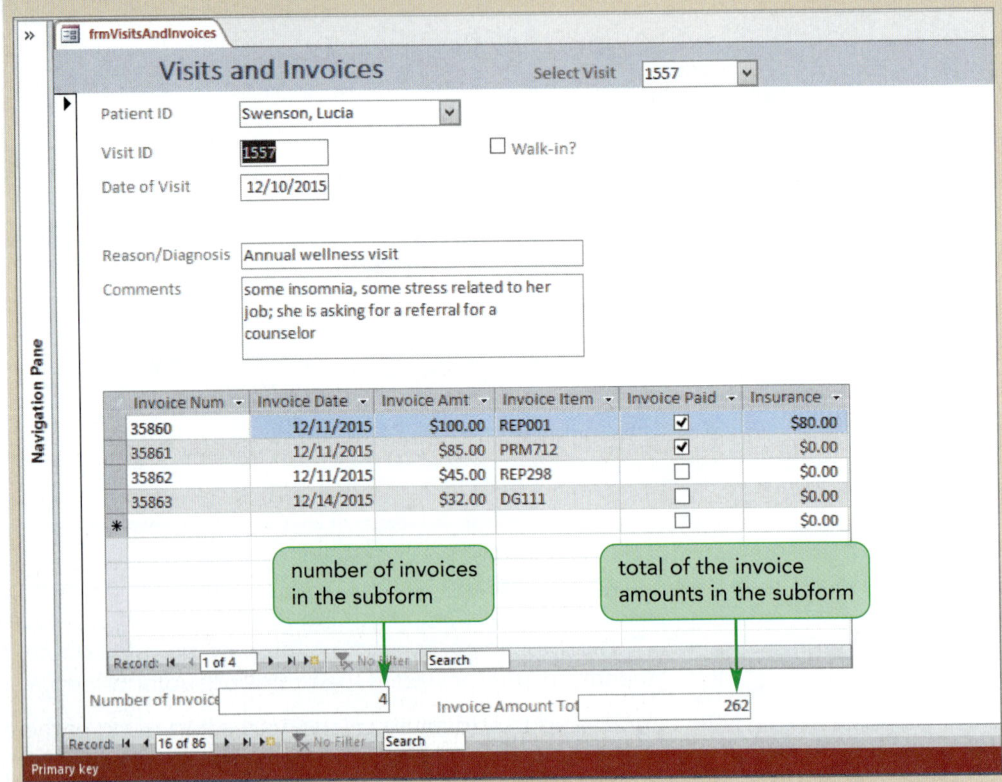

Next, you need to resize, move, and format the two calculated controls and their attached labels.

Resizing, Moving, and Formatting Calculated Controls

In addition to resizing and repositioning the two calculated controls and their attached labels, you need to change the format of the rightmost calculated control to Currency and to set the following properties for both calculated controls:

- Set the Tab Stop property to a value of No. The **Tab Stop property** specifies whether users can use the Tab key to move to a control on a form. If the Tab Stop property is set to No, users can't tab to the control.
- Set the ControlTip Text property to a value of "Calculated total number of invoices for this patient visit" for the calculated control on the left and "Calculated invoice total for this patient visit" for the calculated control on the right. The **ControlTip Text property** specifies the text that appears in a ScreenTip when users hold the mouse pointer over a control in a form.

INSIGHT

Setting Properties in the Property Sheet

You can set many properties in the Property Sheet by typing a value in the property's box, by clicking the arrow on the property and then selecting a value from the menu, or by double-clicking the property name. If you need to set a property by typing a long text entry, you can open the Zoom dialog box and type the entry in the dialog box. You can also use Expression Builder to help you enter expressions.

Now you'll resize, move, and format the calculated controls and their attached labels, and you'll set other properties for the calculated controls.

To modify the calculated controls and their attached labels:

1. Switch to Layout view, right-click the calculated control on the right, click **Properties** on the shortcut menu to open the Property Sheet, click the **All** tab in the Property Sheet (if necessary), set the Format property to **Currency**, and then close the Property Sheet. The value displayed in the calculated control changes from 262 to $262.00.

   Now you'll resize the calculated controls, adjust the positions of each paired label and field value box with respect to each other, and then move the controls into their final positions in the form.

2. Individually, reduce the widths of the two calculated controls by dragging the left or right border to shrink the text box width.
3. Click the **Number of Invoices** label, use the → key on the keyboard to move the text box and label into the position shown in Figure 6-43, repeat the process for the **Invoice Amount Total** label and its related calculated control, and then deselect all controls. See Figure 6-43.

Figure 6-43 After modifying the calculated controls and their labels

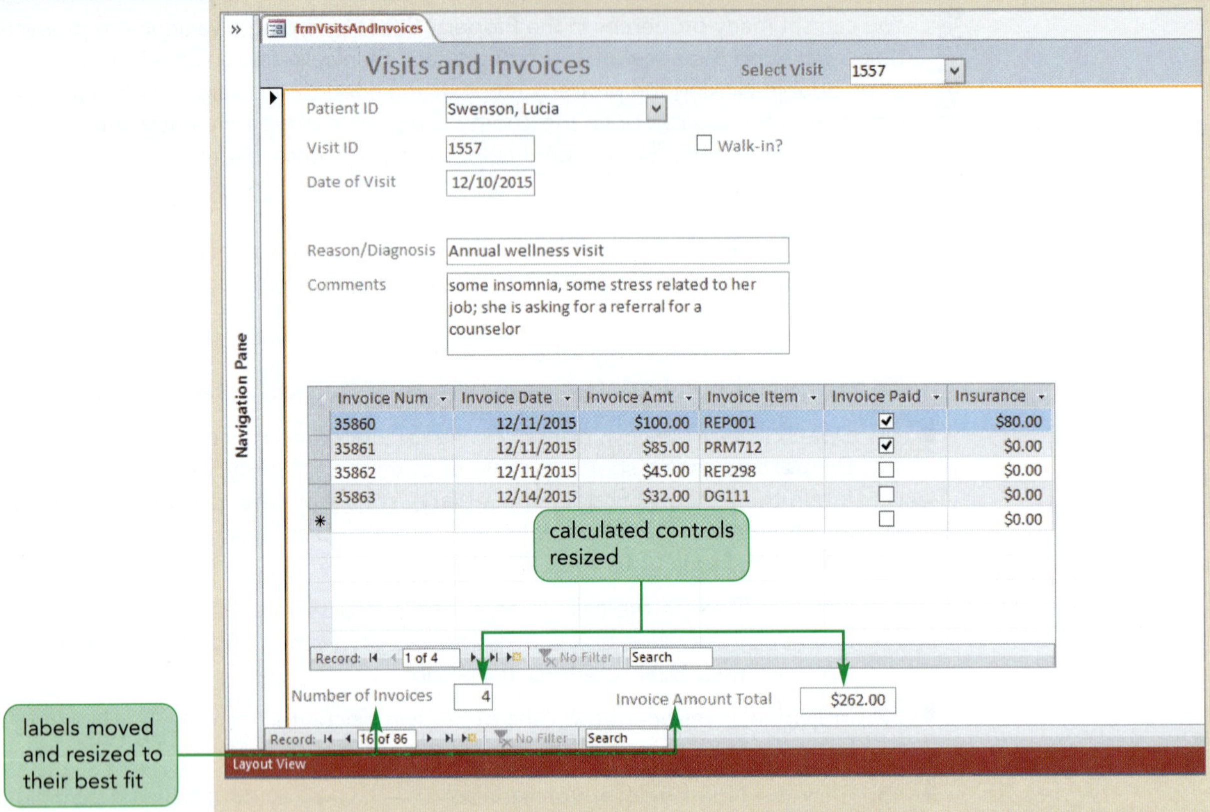

4. Switch to Design view and double-click the HOME tab to minimize the ribbon. Select the **Number of Invoices** label and its related calculated control, and use the right arrow key to move the label and its related text box to the right, aligning the left edges of the label with the left edge of the Comments label as much as possible, moving the controls two grid dots from the bottom of the subform control.

5. Lengthen the Detail section to approximately 6 inches. Deselect the selected controls, and then use the Shift key to select the **Invoice Amount Total** label and its related calculated control. Use the move handle on the calculated control text box to move it below the Number of Invoices label and its related text box.

TIP

In Design view you must use the move handle to move only a text box or its label, while in Layout view you can use either the move handle or the arrow keys.

6. Select the **Invoice Amount Total** label and its related calculated control and use the arrow keys to align the two calculated control text boxes on their left edges as shown in Figure 6-44, deselect all controls, and then switch to Form view and select record 1557. If the label controls are not fully visible, select the calculated controls, and use the right arrow key to move the controls to the right.

Figure 6-44 After moving and aligning the calculated controls and their labels

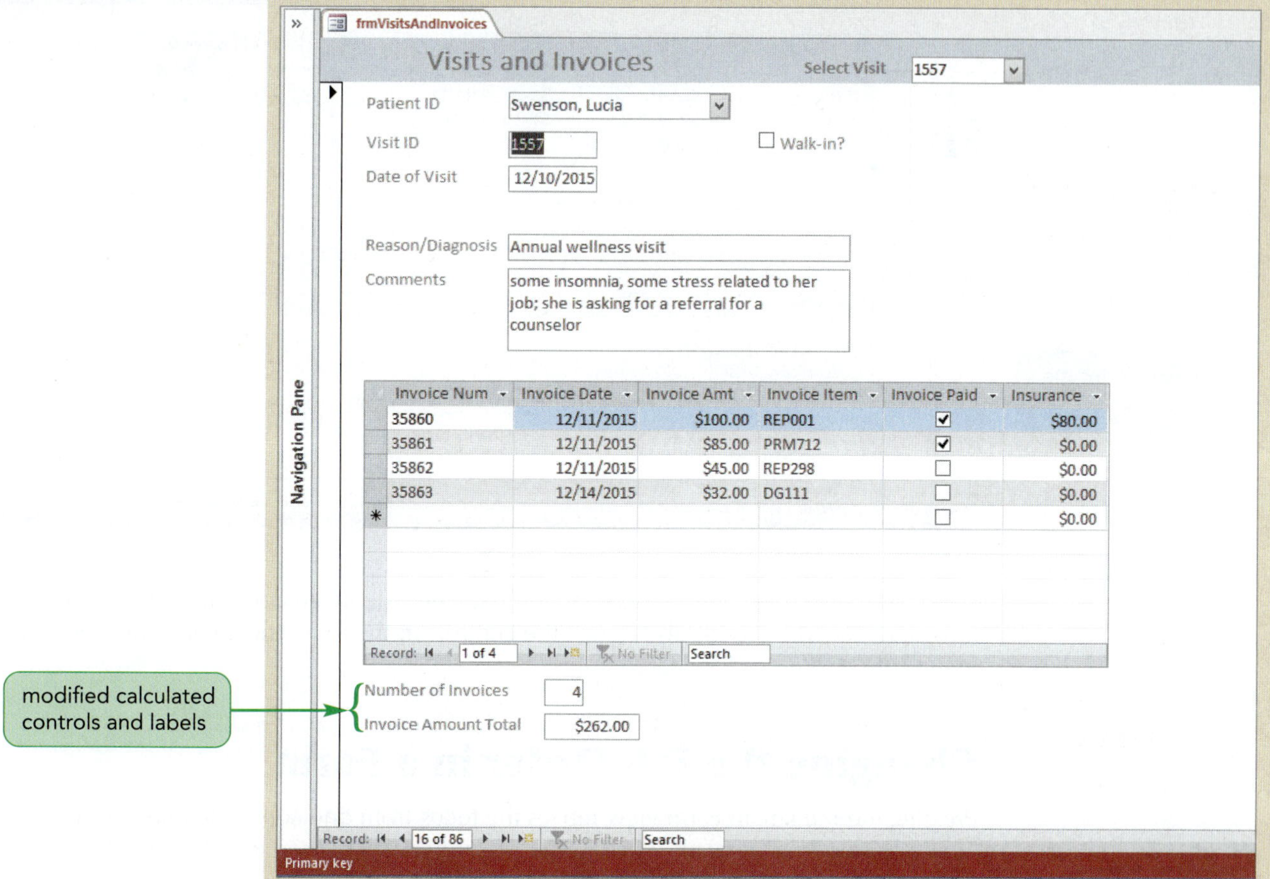

7. Switch to Layout view, select only the bottom calculated control, right-click, click **Properties** on the shortcut menu, and then click the **Other** tab in the Property Sheet.
8. Set the Tab Stop property to **No**, and then set the ControlTip Text property to **Calculated invoice total for this patient visit.**
9. Click the top calculated control, set the Tab Stop property to **No**, and then set the ControlTip Text property to **Calculated total number of invoices for this patient visit**.
10. Close the Property Sheet, save your form design changes, and then switch to Form view. Select visit 1557 from the Visit combo box if necessary.
11. Click the **Number of Invoices** text box, position the pointer on the Number of Invoices text box to display its ScreenTip, click the **Invoice Amount Total** text box, and then position the pointer on the Invoice Amount Total text box to display its ScreenTip. You may have to pause while you position the mouse pointer over the text box, until the ScreenTip appears. See Figure 6-45.

Figure 6-45 Displaying a control's ScreenTip

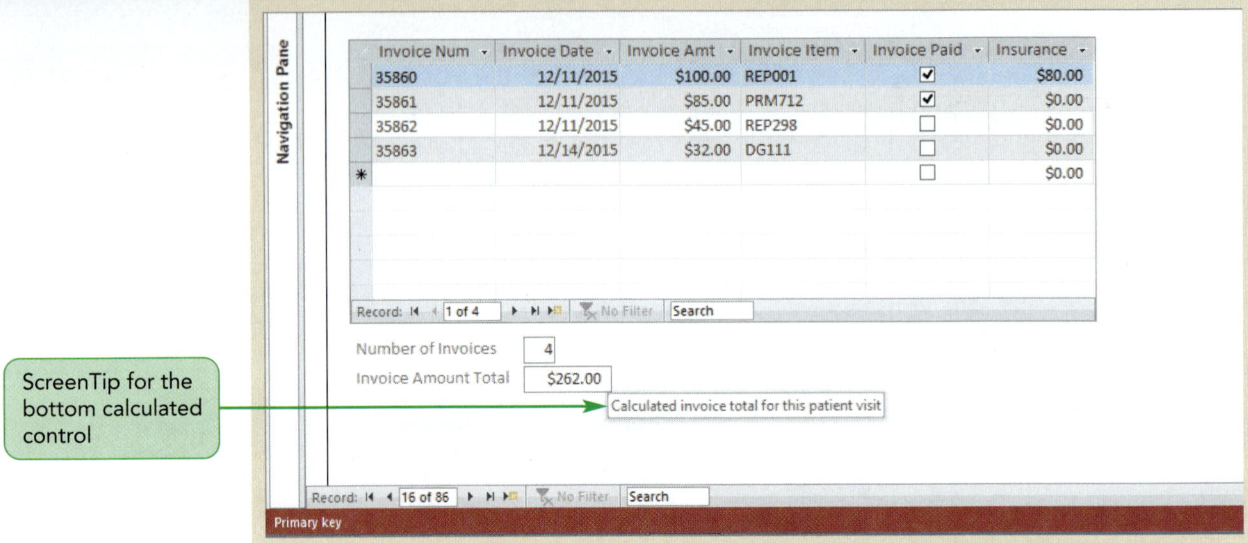

Raj asks you to verify that users can't update the calculated controls in the main form and that when users tab through the controls in the form, the controls are selected in the correct order.

Changing the Tab Order in a Form

Pressing the Tab key in Form view moves the focus from one control to another. A control is said to have **focus** when it is active and awaiting user action. The order in which the focus moves from control to control when a user presses the Tab key is called the **tab order**. Setting tab stops enables the user to keep his or her hands on the keyboard without reaching for the mouse and speeds up the process of data entry in a form. Raj wants to verify that the tab order in the main form is top-to-bottom, left-to-right. First, you'll verify that users can't update the calculated controls.

To test the calculated controls and modify the tab order:

1. Select the value in the Number of Invoices text box, and then type **8**. The Number of Invoices value remains unchanged, and a message is displayed on the status bar. See Figure 6-46.

Figure 6-46 After attempting to update a calculated control

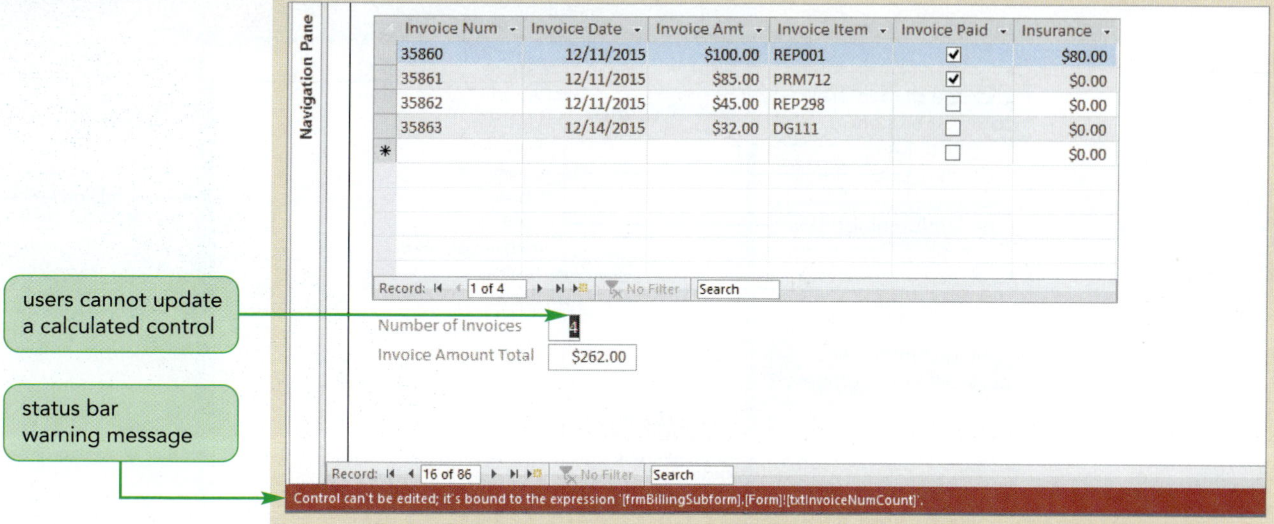

The status bar message warns you that you can't update, or edit, the calculated control because it's bound to an expression. The calculated control in the main form changes in value only when the value of the expression changes in the subform.

2. Click the **Invoice Amount Total** text box, and then type **8**. The value remains unchanged, and a message again displays on the status bar because you cannot edit a calculated control.

   Next, you'll determine the tab order of the fields in the main form. Raj wants the tab order to be down and then across.

3. Select the value in the Visit ID text box, press the **Tab** key to advance to the VisitDate text box, and then press the **Tab** key five more times to advance to the Reason text box, Comments text box, WalkIn check box, and PatientID combo box, in order, and then to the subform.

   Access sets the tab order in the same order in which you add controls to a form, so you should always check the form's tab order when you create a custom form in Layout or Design view. In this form your testing reveals that you tab through the field value boxes in the main form before tabbing through the fields in the subform. In the main form, tabbing bypasses the two calculated controls because you set their Tab Stop properties to No, and you bypass the Select Visit combo box because it's an unbound control. Also, you tab through only the field value boxes in a form, but not the labels.

   The tab order Raj wants for the field value boxes in the main form (top-to-bottom, left-to-right) should be the following: PatientID, VisitID, WalkIn, VisitDate, Reason, Comments, and then the subform. The default tab order doesn't match the order Raj wants, so you'll change the tab order. You can change the tab order only in Design view.

4. Double-click the HOME tab to maximize the ribbon, switch to Design view, and then on the DESIGN tab, in the Tools group, click the **Tab Order** button. The Tab Order dialog box opens. See Figure 6-47.

TIP

Setting the Name property for all your controls to meaningful names avoids having to guess which control a name references in this and similar situations.

Figure 6-47 **Changing the tab order for the Detail section in the main form**

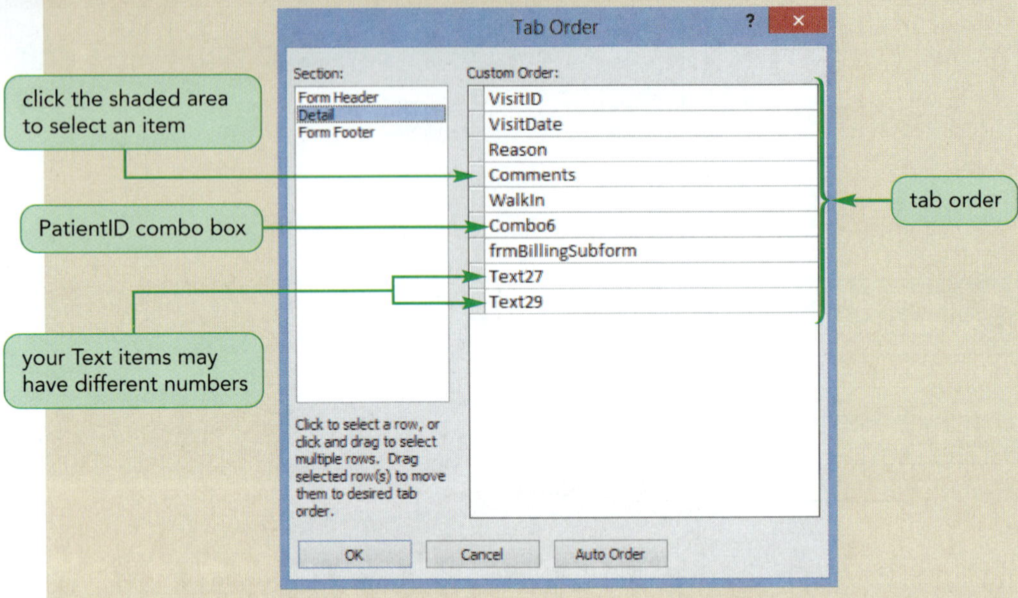

Because you did not set the Name property for the combo box control and the calculated controls, Access assigned their names: Combo6 (your name might be different) for the PatientID combo box, Text27 (your name might be different) for the Number of Invoices calculated control, and Text29 (your name might be different) for the Invoice Amount Total calculated control. The Auto Order button lets you create a left-to-right, top-to-bottom tab order automatically, which is not the order Raj wants. You need to move the Combo6 entry above the VisitID entry.

5. Click the **row selector** to the left of Combo6, drag the row selector above the VisitID entry, and then repeat to move WalkIn above VisitDate. The entries are now correct and in the correct order.

6. Click the **OK** button, save your form design changes, switch to Form view, and then tab through the controls in the main form to make sure the tab order is correct (Combo6, VisitID, WalkIn, VisitDate, Reason, Comments, frmBillingSubform, Text27, Text29).

Trouble? If the tab order is incorrect, switch to Design view, click the Tab Order button in the Tools group on the DESIGN tab, change your tab order in the Tab Order dialog box to match the order described in Step 6, and then repeat Step 6.

PROSKILLS

Written Communication: Enhancing Information Using Calculated Controls

For a small number of records in a subform, it's easy for users to quickly count the number of records and to calculate numeric total amounts when the form doesn't display calculated controls. For instance, when students have completed few courses or when people have made few tax payments, it's easy for users to count the courses and calculate the student's GPA or to count and total the tax payments. But for subforms with dozens or hundreds of records—for instance, students with many courses, or people with many tax payments—displaying summary calculated controls is mandatory. By adding a few simple calculated controls to forms and reports, you can increase the usefulness of the information presented and improve the ability of users to process the information, spot trends, and be more productive in their jobs.

You've finished adding controls to the form, but the form is plain looking and lacks visual clues for the different controls in the form. You'll complete the form by making it more attractive and easier for Cindi and her staff to use.

Improving a Form's Appearance

The frmVisitsAndInvoices form has four distinct areas: the Form Header section containing the title and the Select Visit combo box, the six bound controls in the Detail section, the subform in the Detail section, and the two calculated controls in the Detail section. To visually separate these four areas, you'll increase the height of the Form Header section, add a horizontal line at the bottom of the Form Header section, and draw a rectangle around the calculated controls.

Adding a Line to a Form

You can use lines in a form to improve the form's readability, to group related information, or to underline important values. You use the Line tool in Design view to add a line to a form or report.

REFERENCE

Adding a Line to a Form or Report

- Display the form or report in Design view.
- On the DESIGN tab, in the Controls group, click the More button, and then click the Line tool.
- Position the pointer where you want the line to begin.
- Drag the pointer to the position for the end of the line, and then release the mouse button. If you want to ensure that you draw a straight horizontal or vertical line, hold down the Shift key before and during the drag operation.
- To make small adjustments to the line length, select the line, hold down the Shift key, and then press an arrow key. To make small adjustments in the placement of a line, select the line, hold down the Ctrl key, and then press an arrow key.

You will add a horizontal line to the Form Header section to separate the controls in this section from the controls in the Detail section.

To add a line to the form:

1. Switch to Design view, and then drag down the bottom of the Form Header section to the 1-inch mark on the vertical ruler to make room to draw a horizontal line at the bottom of the Form Header section.
2. On the DESIGN tab, in the Controls group, click the **More** button to open the Controls gallery, and then click the **Line** tool.
3. Position the pointer's plus symbol (+) at the left edge of the Form Header section just below the title.
4. Hold down the **Shift** key, drag a horizontal line from left to right so the end of the line ends at the 6-inch mark on the vertical ruler, release the mouse button, and then release the **Shift** key. See Figure 6-48.

Figure 6-48 **Adding a line to the form**

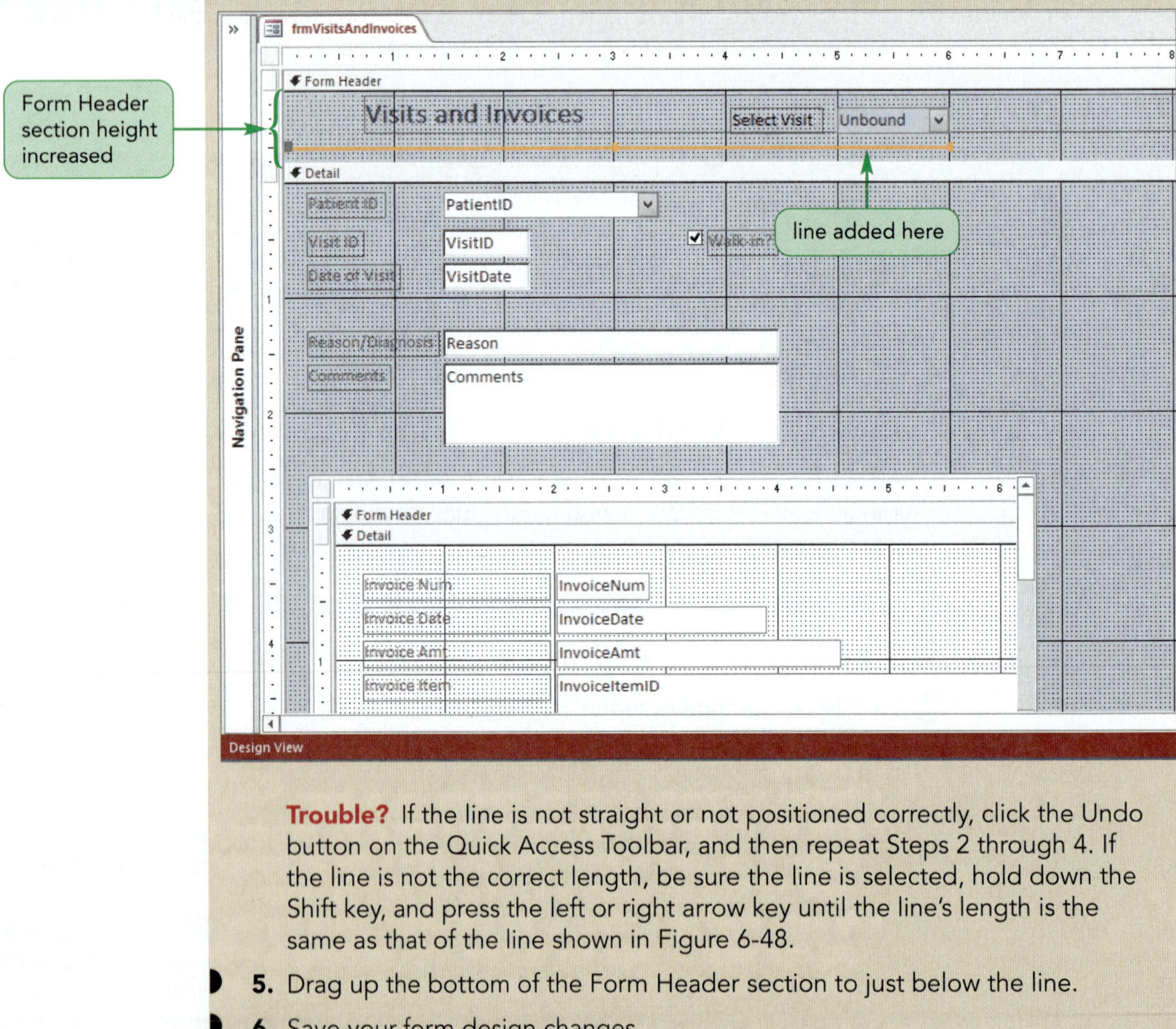

Trouble? If the line is not straight or not positioned correctly, click the Undo button on the Quick Access Toolbar, and then repeat Steps 2 through 4. If the line is not the correct length, be sure the line is selected, hold down the Shift key, and press the left or right arrow key until the line's length is the same as that of the line shown in Figure 6-48.

5. Drag up the bottom of the Form Header section to just below the line.
6. Save your form design changes.

Next, you'll add a rectangle around the calculated controls in the Detail section.

Adding a Rectangle to a Form

You can use a rectangle in a form to group related controls and to separate the group from other controls. You use the **Rectangle tool** in Design view to add a rectangle to a form or report.

REFERENCE

Adding a Rectangle to a Form or Report

- Display the form or report in Design view.
- On the DESIGN tab, in the Controls group, click the More button, and then click the Rectangle tool.
- Click in the form or report to create a default-sized rectangle, or drag a rectangle in the position and size you want.

You will add a rectangle around the calculated controls and their labels to separate them from the subform and from the other controls in the Detail section.

To add a rectangle to the form:

1. On the DESIGN tab, in the Controls group, click the **More** button to open the Controls gallery, and then click the **Rectangle** tool .
2. Position the pointer's plus symbol (+) approximately two grid dots above and two grid dots to the left of the Number of Invoices label.
3. Drag a rectangle down and to the right until all four sides are approximately two grid dots from the two calculated controls and their labels. See Figure 6-49.

Figure 6-49 **Adding a rectangle to the form**

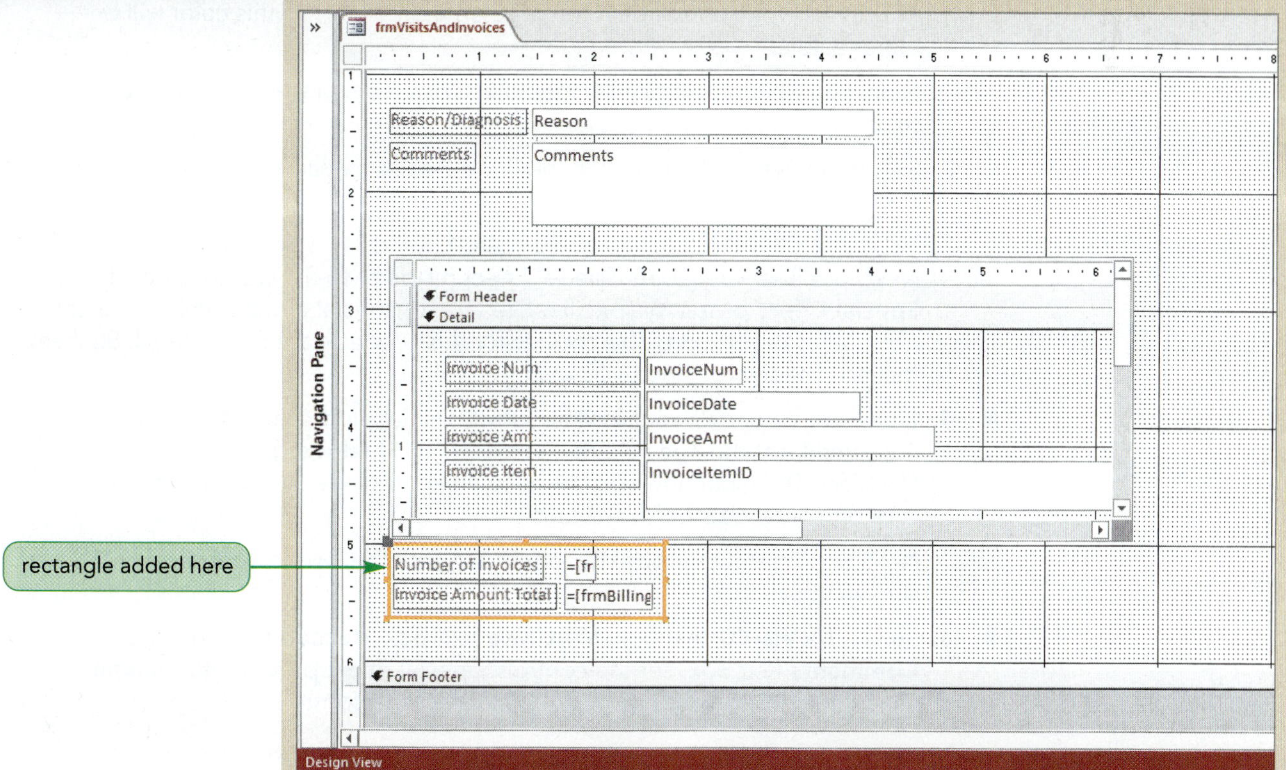

Trouble? If the rectangle is not sized or positioned correctly, use the sizing handles to adjust its size and the move handle to adjust its position.

Next, you'll set the thickness of the rectangle's lines.

4. Click the **FORMAT** tab.
5. In the Control Formatting group, click the **Shape Outline arrow**, point to **Line Thickness** at the bottom of the gallery, and then click the line with the ScreenTip **1 pt** in the list (2nd line from the top).
6. Deselect the control.

Next, you'll add color and visual effects to the form's controls.

Modifying the Visual Effects of the Controls in a Form

TIP

Using a theme can improve a form's appearance, but a theme doesn't provide the control you can achieve by setting properties in Design or Layout view.

Distinguishing one group of controls in a form from other groups is an important visual cue to the users of the form. For example, users should be able to distinguish the bound controls in the form from the calculated controls and from the Select Visit control in the Form Header section. You'll now modify the controls in the form to provide these visual cues. You'll start by setting font properties for the calculated control's labels.

To modify the controls in the form:

1. Select the **Number of Invoices** label and the **Invoice Amount Total** label, using the Shift key to select multiple controls.
2. On the FORMAT tab, in the Font group, click the **Font Color button arrow** A, click the **Blue** color (row 7, column 8 in the Standard Colors palette), and then on the FORMAT tab in the Font group, click the **Bold** button B. The labels' captions now use a bold, blue font. In the Form view, the controls will have a white background rather than a gray one, so this color will be more legible.

   Next, you'll set properties for the Select Visit label in the Form Header section.
3. Select the **Select Visit** label in the Form Header section, set the label's font color to **Red** (row 7, column 2 in the Standard Colors palette), and then set the font style to bold.

   Next, you'll set the label's Special Effect property to a shadowed effect. The **Special Effect property** specifies the type of special effect applied to a control in a form or report. The choices for this property are Flat, Raised, Sunken, Etched, Shadowed, and Chiseled.
4. Open the Property Sheet for the Select Visit label, click the **All** tab (if necessary), set the Special Effect property to **Shadowed**, and then deselect the label. The label now has a shadowed special effect, and the label's caption now uses a bold, red font.

   Next, you'll set the Special Effect property for the bound control labels to a sunken effect.
5. Select the **VisitID** text box, **VisitDate** text box, **Reason** text box, and **Comments** text box, set the controls' Special Effect property to **Sunken**, close the Property Sheet, and then deselect the controls.

Finally, you'll set the background color of the Form Header section, the Detail section, the combo box, and the two calculated controls. You can use the **Background Color button** in the Font group on the DESIGN tab to change the background color of a control, section, or object (form or report).

6. Click the Form Header section bar.
7. On the FORMAT tab, in the Font group, click the **Background Color button arrow**, and then click the **Light Blue 2** color (row 3, column 5 in the Standard Colors palette). The Form Header's background color changes to the Light Blue 2 color.
8. Click the Detail section bar, and then on the FORMAT tab, in the Font Group, click the **Background Color** button to change the Detail section's background color to the **Light Blue 2** color.
9. Select the **Select Visit** combo box, **Number of Invoices** text box, and the **Invoice Amount Total** text box, set the selected controls' background color to the **Light Blue 2** color, and then deselect all controls by clicking to the right of the Detail section's grid. See Figure 6-50.

Figure 6-50 Completed custom form in Design view

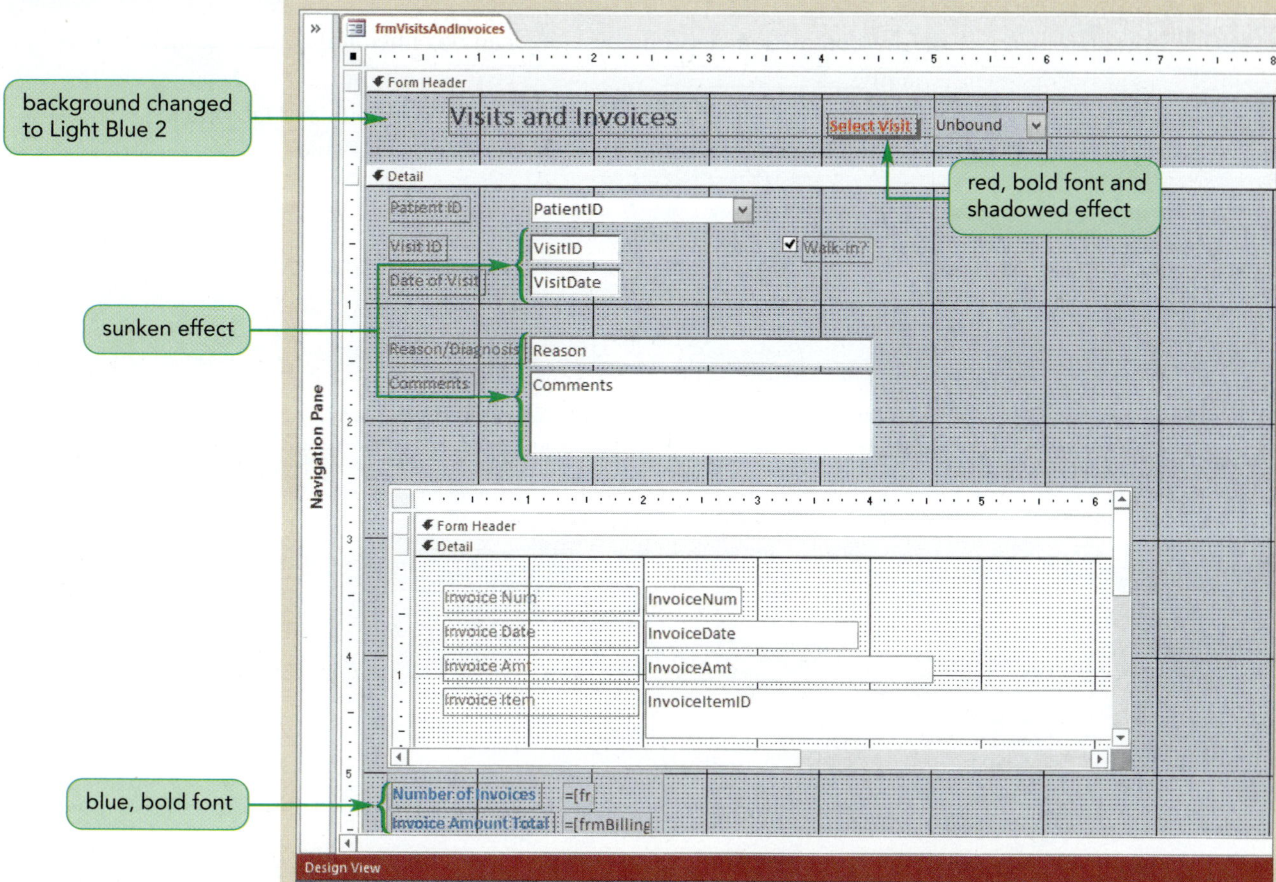

10. Switch to Form view, and then click the **VisitID** text box to select the first value in the list, 1527. The Session 6.3 Visual Overview shows the completed form.

11. Test the form by tabbing between fields, navigating between records, and using the Select Visit combo box to find records, making sure you don't change any field values and observing that the calculated controls display the correct values.
12. Save your form design changes, close the form, make a backup copy of the database, compact and repair the database, and then close the database.

Cindi looked at the datasheet form, the multiple items form, and the custom form. She is really pleased with the choices you provided for her and she'll discuss the choices with her staff.

REVIEW

Session 6.3 Quick Check

1. To create a combo box to find records in a form with the Combo Box Wizard, the form's record source must be a(n) ____________.
2. You use the ____________ tool to add a subform to a form.
3. To calculate subtotals and overall totals in a form or report, you use the ____________ function.
4. The Control Source property setting can be either a(n) ____________ or a(n) ____________.
5. Explain the difference between the Tab Stop property and tab order.
6. What is focus?
7. The ____________ property has settings such as Raised and Sunken.

ASSESS

SAM Projects

Put your skills into practice with SAM Projects! SAM Projects for this tutorial can be found online. If you have a SAM account, go to www.cengage.com/sam2013 to download the most recent Project Instructions and Start Files.

PRACTICE

Review Assignments

Data File needed for the Review Assignments: Supplier.accdb (*cont. from Tutorial 5*)

Cindi wants you to create several forms, including a custom form that displays and updates companies and the products they offer. Complete the following steps:

1. Open the **Supplier** database you worked with in Tutorial 5.
2. In the **tblProduct** table, remove the lookup feature from the SupplierID field, and then resize the Supplier ID column in the datasheet to its best fit. Save and close the table.
3. Edit the relationship between the primary tblSupplier and related tblProduct tables to enforce referential integrity and to cascade update related fields. Create the relationship report, save the report as **rptRelationshipsForProducts**, and then close it.
4. Use the Documenter to document the qryCompanyContacts query. Select all query options; use the Names, Data Types, and Sizes option for fields; and use the Names and Fields option for indexes. Print the report produced by the Documenter and then close it.
5. Use the Datasheet tool to create a form based on the tblProduct table, save the form as **frmProductDatasheet**, and then close it.
6. Use the Multiple Items tool to create a form based on the qryDuplicateProductTypes query, save the form as **frmProductTypeMultipleItems**, and then close it.
7. Use the Split Form tool to create a split form based on the tblProduct table, and then make the following changes to the form in Layout view:
   a. Remove the two Units controls from the stacked layout, reduce the width of the Units text box by about half, and then anchor the two Units controls to the bottom left. Depending on the size of your window, the two Units controls may be positioned at the bottom left of the right column.
   b. Remove the five control pairs in the right column from the stacked layout, and then anchor the group to the bottom right. You may see a dotted border outlining the location of the previously removed controls. This may be automatically selected as well.
   c. Remove the ProductName control pair from the stacked layout, move them to the top right, and then anchor them to the top right.
   d. Reduce the widths of the ProductID and SupplierID text boxes to a reasonable size.
   e. Change the title to **Product**, save the modified form as **frmProductSplitForm**, and then close it.
8. Use Figure 6-51 and the following steps to create a custom form named **frmSuppliersWithProducts** based on the tblSupplier and tblProduct tables.

Figure 6-51 Vendor database custom form design

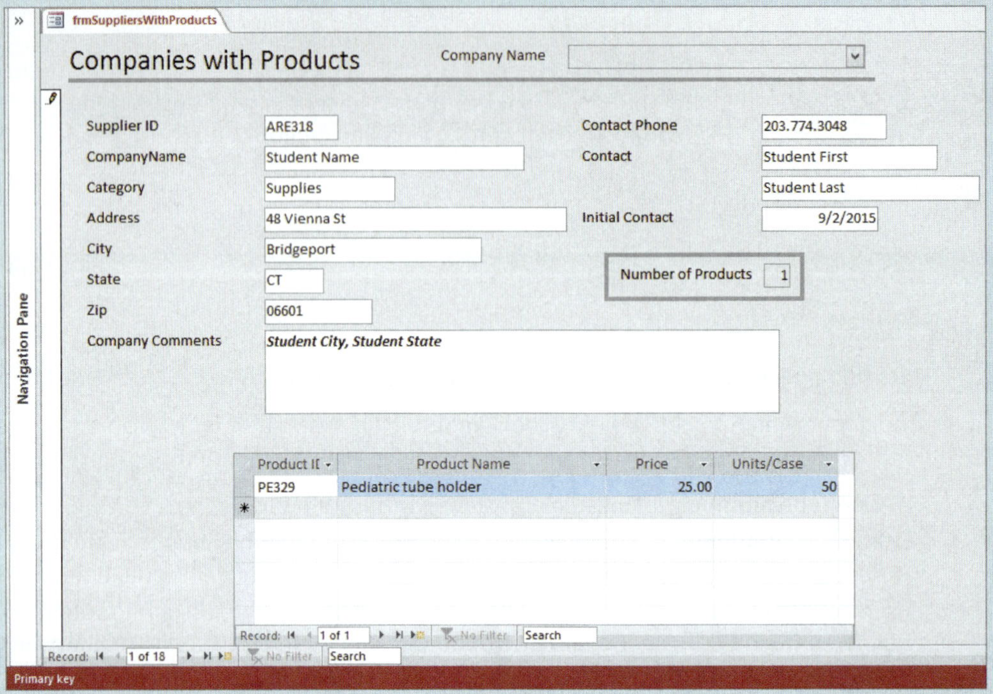

a. Place the fields from the tblSupplier table at the top of the Detail section. Delete the Contact Last Name label and change the caption for the Contact First Name label to Contact.

b. Move the fields into two columns in the Detail section, as shown in Figure 6-51, resizing and aligning controls, as necessary, and increasing the width of the form.

c. Add the title in the Form Header section.

d. Make sure the form's Record Source property is set to tblSupplier, and then add a combo box in the Form Header section to find CompanyName field values. In the wizard steps, select the CompanyName and SupplierID fields, and hide the key column. Resize and move the control. Ensure the label displays the text Company Name.

e. Add a subform based on the tblProduct table, include only the fields shown in Figure 6-51, link with SupplierID, name the subform **frmPartialProductSubform**, delete the subform label, resize the columns in the subform to their best fit, and resize and position the subform.

f. Add a calculated control that displays the number of products displayed in the subform. Set the calculated control's Tab Stop property to No, and the ControlTip Text property to **Calculated number of products**.

g. Add a line in the Form Header section, and add a rectangle around the calculated control and its label, setting the line thickness of both controls to the line style with the ScreenTip 3 pt. Set the rectangle's color the same as the line's color.

h. In the main form, use the Black, Text 1 font color (row 1, column 2 in the Theme Colors palette) for all text boxes and for the title text in the Header section, and use the White, Background 1, Darker 5% fill color (row 2, column 1 in the Theme Colors palette) for the sections, the calculated control, and the Company Name combo box.

i. Make sure the tab order is top-to-bottom, left-to-right for the main form text boxes.

9. Make a backup copy of the database, compact and repair the database, and then close the database.

APPLY

Case Problem 1

Data File needed for this Case Problem: Task.accdb (*cont. from Tutorial 5*)

GoGopher! Amol Mehta wants you to create several forms, including two custom forms that display and update data in the database. Complete the following steps:

1. Open the **Task** database you worked with in Tutorial 5.
2. Use the Documenter to document the qryMemberNames query. Select all query options; use the Names, Data Types, and Sizes option for fields; and use the Names and Fields option for indexes. Print the first page of the report produced by the Documenter.
3. Use the Datasheet tool to create a form based on the tblPlan table, and then save the form as **frmPlanDatasheet**.
4. Create a custom form based on the qryUpcomingExpirations query. Display all fields from the query in the form. Create your own design for the form. Add a label to the bottom of the Detail section that contains your first and last names. Change the label's font so that your name appears in bold, blue text. Change the ExpirationDate text box format so that the field value displays in bold, red text. Save the form as **frmUpcomingExpirations**.
5. Use Figure 6-52 and the following steps to create a custom form named **frmPlansWithMembers** based on the tblPlan and tblMember tables.

Figure 6-52 Plans custom form design

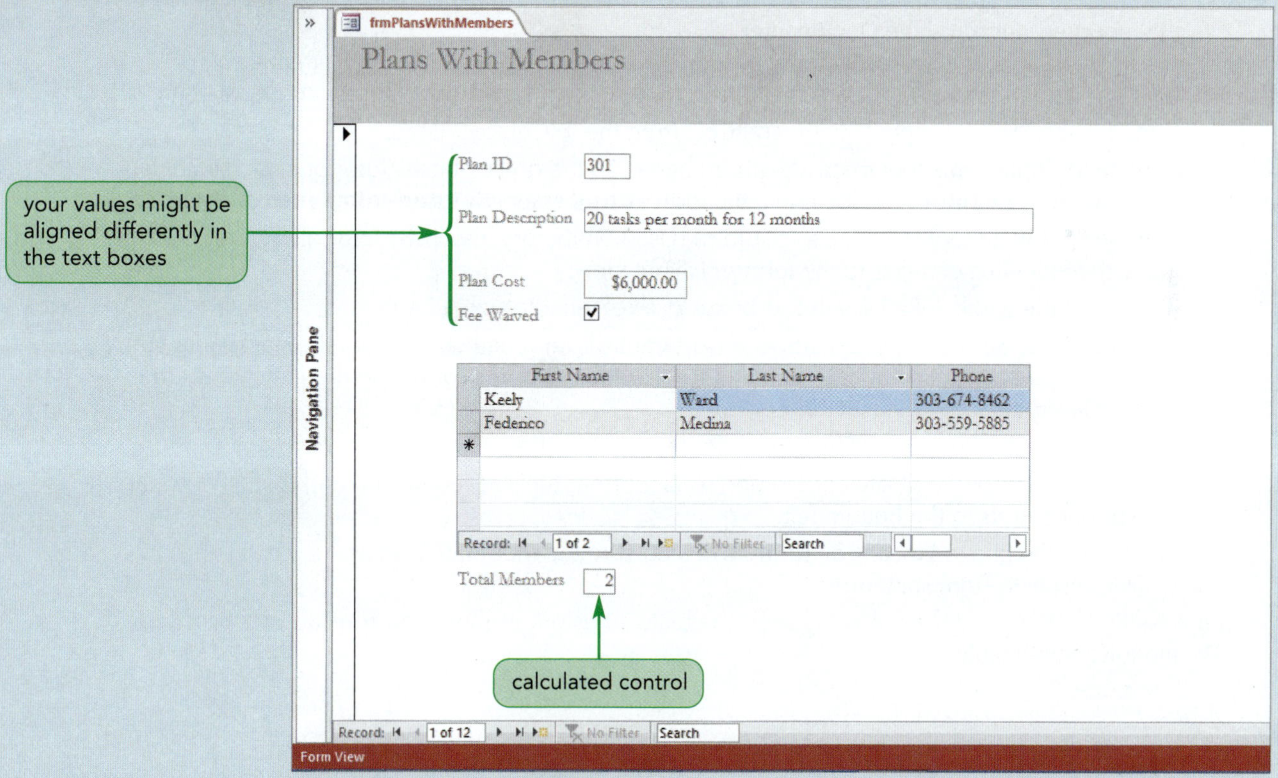

a. Place the fields from the tblPlan table at the top of the Detail section and edit the captions in the associated label controls as shown.

b. Selected fields from the tblMember table appear in a subform named **frmPlanMemberSubform**.

   c. The calculated control displays the total number of records that appear in the subform. Set the calculated control's ControlTip Text property to **Total number of members in this plan**. Set the calculated control's Tab Stop property to No.
   d. Apply the Organic theme to the form.
   e. Save and view the form, and then print the first record.
6. Make a backup copy of the database, compact and repair the database, and then close the database.

APPLY

Case Problem 2

Data File needed for this Case Problem: Tutoring.accdb (*cont. from Tutorial 5*)

O'Brien Educational Services Karen O'Brien wants you to create several forms, including a custom form that displays and updates the tutoring service's contracts with students. Complete the following steps:

1. Open the **Tutoring** database you worked with in Tutorial 5.
2. Remove the lookup feature from the TutorID field in the tblContract table, and then resize the Tutor ID column to its best fit. Save and close the table.
3. Define a one-to-many relationship between the primary tblTutor table and the related tblContract table. Select the referential integrity option and the cascade updates option for this relationship.
4. Use the Documenter to document the tblContract table. Select all table options; use the Names, Data Types, and Sizes option for fields; and use the Names and Fields option for indexes. Print the report produced by the Documenter.
5. Create a query called **qryLessonsByTutor** that uses the tblTutor and tblContract tables and includes the fields FirstName and LastName from the tblTutor table, and the fields StudentID, ContractDate, SessionType, Length, and Cost from the tblContract table.
6. Use the Multiple Items tool to create a form based on the qryLessonsByTutor query, change the title to **Lessons by Tutor**, and then save the form as **frmLessonsByTutorMultipleItems**.
7. Use the Split Form tool to create a split form based on the qryLessonsByTutor query, and then make the following changes to the form in Layout view.
   a. Reduce the widths of all seven text boxes to a reasonable size.
   b. Remove the SessionType, Length, and Cost controls and their labels from the stacked layout, move these six controls to the right and then to the top of the form, and then anchor them to the top right.
   c. Select the Cost control and its label, and then anchor them to the bottom right.
   d. Remove the Contract Date control and its label from the stacked layout, and then anchor the pair of controls to the bottom left.
   e. Change the title to **Lessons by Tutor**, and then save the modified form as **frmLessonsByTutorSplitForm**.
8. Use Figure 6-53 and the following steps to create a custom form named **frmContract** based on the tblContract table.

Figure 6-53 **Tutoring database custom form design**

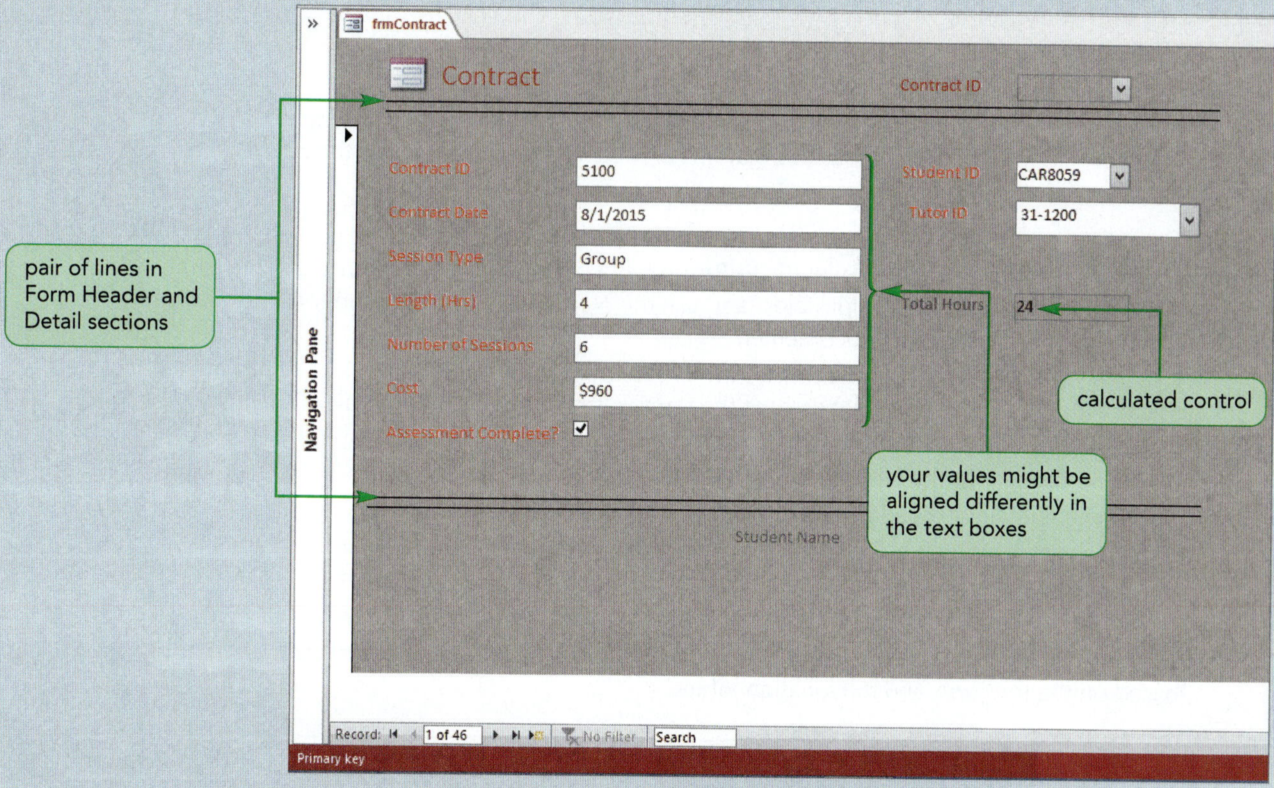

a. For the StudentID combo box, select the LastName, FirstName, and StudentID fields from the tblStudent table, in order, and sort in ascending order by the LastName field and then by the FirstName field.
b. For the TutorID combo box, select the LastName, FirstName, and TutorID fields from the tblTutor table, in order, and sort in ascending order by the LastName field and then by the FirstName field.
c. Make sure the form's Record Source property is set to tblContract, and then add a combo box in the Form Header section to find ContractID field values.
d. Add a calculated control that displays the total number of hours (length multiplied by sessions). *Hint*: Use the * symbol for multiplication. Set the calculated control's Tab Stop property to No and format the values with one decimal place.
e. Add a line in the Form Header section, add a second line below it, and then add a second pair of lines near the bottom of the Detail section. Set the line thickness of all lines to the line setting with the ScreenTip 1 pt.
f. Use the Label tool to add your name below the pair of lines at the bottom of the Detail section.
g. For the labels in the Detail section, except for the Total Hours label and the label displaying your name, use the Red font color (row 7, column 2 in the Standard Colors palette).
h. For the title and Contract ID label, use the Dark Red font color (row 7, column 1 in the Standard Colors palette).
i. For the calculated control and its label, bold the font.
j. For the background fill color of the sections, the calculated control, and the Contract ID combo box, use the Medium Gray color (row 1, column 3 in the Standard Colors palette).
k. Make sure the tab order is top-to-bottom, left-to-right for the main form field value boxes.

9. Make a backup copy of the database, compact and repair the database, and then close the database.

CREATE

Case Problem 3

Data File needed for this Case Problem: Rosemary.accdb (*cont. from Tutorial 5*)

Rosemary Animal Shelter Ryan Lang asks you to create several forms, including a custom form for the Rosemary Animal Shelter database so that he can better track donations for the animal shelter. Complete the following steps:

1. Open the **Rosemary** database you worked with in Tutorial 5.
2. Use the Documenter to document the tblPatron table. Select all table options; use the Names, Data Types, and Sizes option for fields; and use the Names and Fields option for indexes. Print the report produced by the Documenter.
3. Use the Multiple Items tool to create a form based on the qryPatronPhoneList query, change the title to **Patron Phone List**, and then save the form as **frmPatronPhoneListMultipleItems**.
4. Use the Split Form tool to create a split form based on the tblPatron table, and then make the following changes to the form in Layout view.
   a. Reduce the widths of all five text boxes to a reasonable size.
   b. Remove the FirstName, LastName, and Phone controls and their labels from the stacked layout, move them to the top right, and then anchor them to the top right.
   c. Change the title to **Patron**, and then save the modified form as **frmPatronSplitForm**.
5. Use Figure 6-54 and the following steps to create a custom form named **frmPatronDonations** based on the tblPatron and tblDonation tables.

Figure 6-54 Rosemary database custom form design

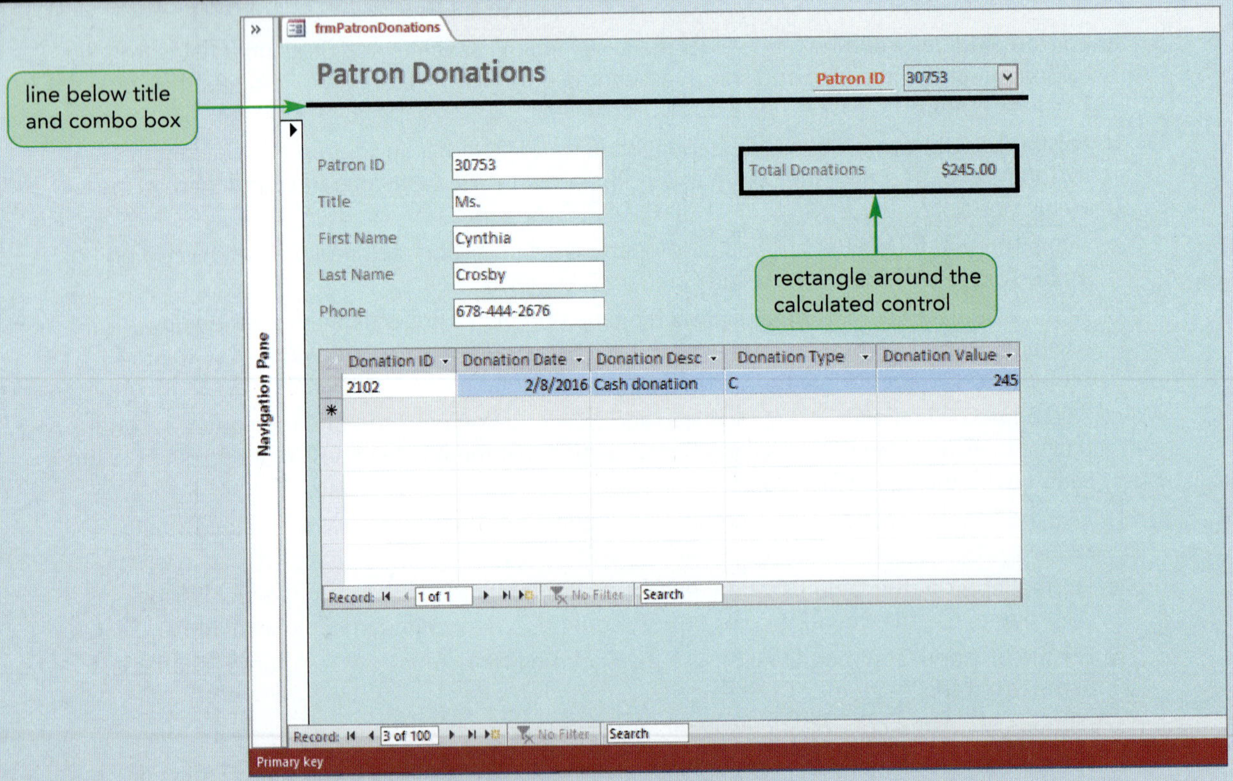

a. Add the title in the Form Header section.
b. Make sure the form's Record Source property is set to tblPatron, and then add a combo box in the Form Header section to find PatronID field values. In the wizard steps, select the PatronID field. Format the label using the Red font (row 7, column 2 in the Standard Colors palette), bold, and the Chiseled special effect.
c. Add a subform based on the tblDonation table, name the subform **frmPatronDonationSubform**, delete the subform label, and resize the columns in the subform to their best fit and resize and position the subform.
d. Add a calculated control that displays the total of the DonationValue field displayed in the subform with the Currency format. Set the calculated control's Tab Stop property to No, and the Border Style property to Transparent.
e. Add a line in the Form Header section, and add a rectangle around the calculated control and its label, setting the line thickness of both controls to the line style with the ScreenTip 3 pt. Set the rectangle color to Black (row 1, column 2 in the Standard Colors section) using the Shape Outline button in the Control Formatting group on the FORMAT tab.
f. Use the background color Aqua Blue 2 (row 3, column 9 in the Standard Colors palette) for the sections, the calculated control, and the Patron ID combo box.
g. Make sure the tab order is top-to-bottom for the main form text boxes.

6. Make a backup copy of the database, compact and repair the database, and then close the database.

CREATE

Case Problem 4

Data File needed for this Case Problem: Ecotour.accdb (*cont. from Tutorial 5*)

Stanley EcoTours Janice and Bill Stanley want you to create several forms, including a custom form that displays and updates guest and reservation data in the Stanley database. Complete the following steps:

1. Open the **Ecotour** database you worked with in Tutorial 5.
2. Remove the lookup feature from the TourID field in the **tblReservation** table. Size the TourID field and save and close the table.
3. Edit the relationship between the primary tblTour and related tblReservation tables to enforce referential integrity and to cascade update related fields. Create the relationship report, and then save the report as **rptRelationshipsForVacation.pdf**, without exporting steps.
4. Use the Documenter to document the qrySelectedStates query. Select all query options; use the Names, Data Types, and Sizes option for fields; and use the Nothing option for indexes. Print the report produced by the Documenter.
5. Use the Datasheet tool to create a form based on the qryGuestLastNameG query, and then save the form as **frmGuestLastNameG**.
6. Create a custom form based on the qryHikingOrJeepSelectedTours query. Display all fields in the form. Use your own design for the form, but use the title **Hiking Or Jeep Selected Tours** in the Form Header section, and use the Label tool to add your name to the Form Header section. Save the form as **frmHikingOrJeepSelectedTours**.
7. Use Figure 6-55 and the following steps to create a custom form named **frmGuestsWithReservations** based on the tblGuest and tblReservation tables.

Figure 6-55 **Ecotour database custom form design**

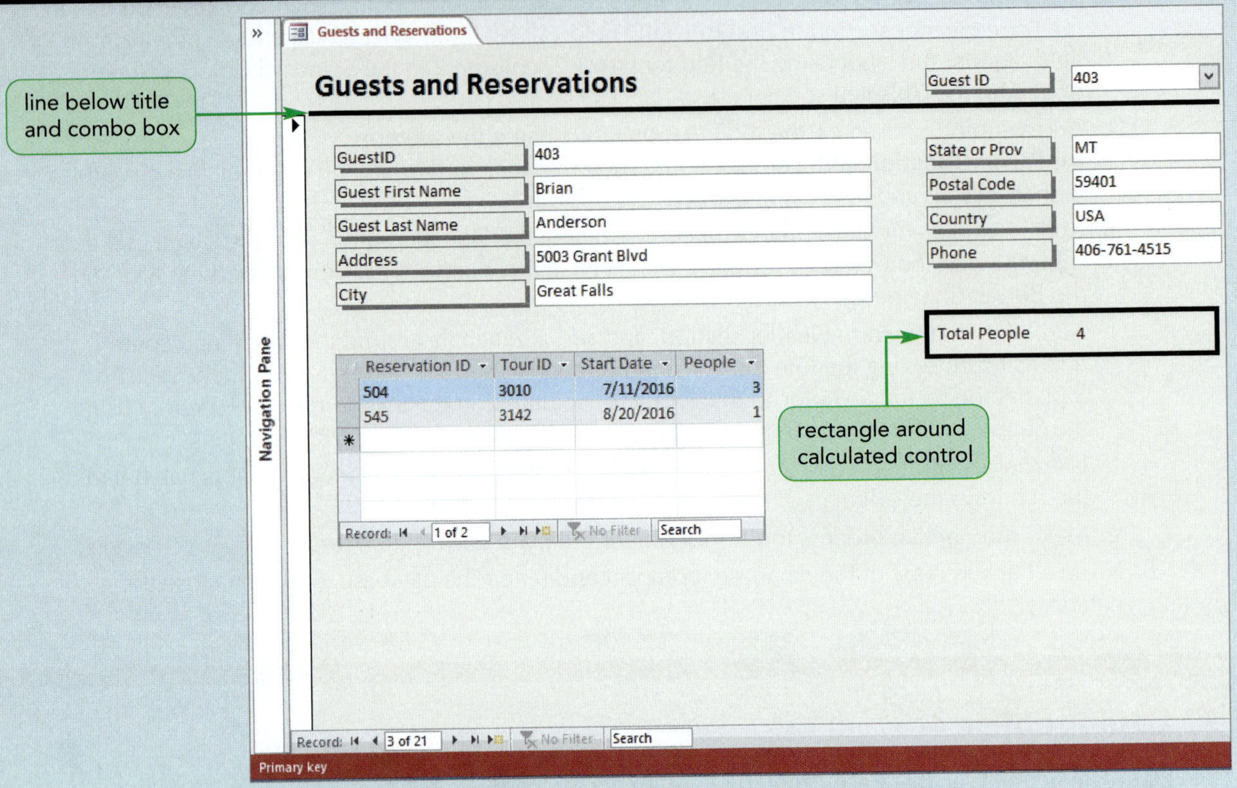

a. Add the title in the Form Header section and apply bold formatting.
b. Add the fields from the tblGuest table. Size the associated labels so they're all the same length. Size the text boxes in variable lengths to fit a reasonable amount of data, as shown in Figure 6-55.
c. Make sure the form's Record Source property is set to tblGuest, and then add a combo box in the Form Header section to find GuestID field values.
d. Add a subform based on the tblReservation table, name the subform **frmGuestsWithReservationsSubform**, delete the subform label, resize the columns in the subform to their best fit, and then resize and position the subform.
e. Add a calculated control that displays the total of the People field displayed in the subform. Set the calculated control's Tab Stop property to No, and set the calculated control's Border Style property to Transparent.
f. Add a line in the Form Header section, and add a rectangle around the calculated control and its label, setting the line thickness of both controls to the line style with the ScreenTip 3 pt. Set the rectangle color to Black (row 1, column 2 in the Standard Colors section) using the Shape Outline button in the Control Formatting group on the Format tab.
g. Use black font color for all controls, including the controls in the subform.
h. Use the "Green 1" fill color (row 2, column 7 in the Standard Colors palette) for the sections and the calculated control.
i. Use the Shadowed special effect for the labels in the Detail section, except for the calculated control label, and the Form Header section, except for the title.
j. Make sure the tab order is top-to-bottom and left-to-right for the main form text boxes.

8. Make a backup copy of the database, compact and repair the database, and then close the database.

TUTORIAL 7

Creating Custom Reports

ACCESS

OBJECTIVES

Session 7.1

- View, filter, and copy report information in Report view
- Modify a report in Layout view
- Modify a report in Design view

Session 7.2

- Design and create a custom report
- Sort and group data in a report
- Add, move, resize, and align controls in a report
- Add lines to a report
- Hide duplicate values in a report

Session 7.3

- Add the date, page numbers, and title to a report
- Create and modify mailing labels

Creating Custom Reports for Chatham Community Health Services

Case | *Chatham Community Health Services*

At a recent staff meeting, Kelly Schwarz, the office manager, indicated that she would like to make some changes to an existing report in the database. She also requested a new report that she can use to produce a printed list of all invoices for all visits.

In this tutorial, you will modify an existing report and create the new report for Kelly. In modifying and building these reports, you will use many Access report customization features, including grouping data, calculating totals, and adding lines to separate report sections. These features will enhance Kelly's reports and make them easier to read and use.

STARTING DATA FILES

Access2 → Tutorial: Clinic.accdb (*cont.*)

Review: Supplier.accdb (*cont.*)

Case1: Task.accdb (*cont.*)

Case2: Tutoring.accdb (*cont.*)

Case3: Rosemary.accdb (*cont.*)

Case4: Ecotour.accdb (*cont.*)

Session 7.1 Visual Overview:

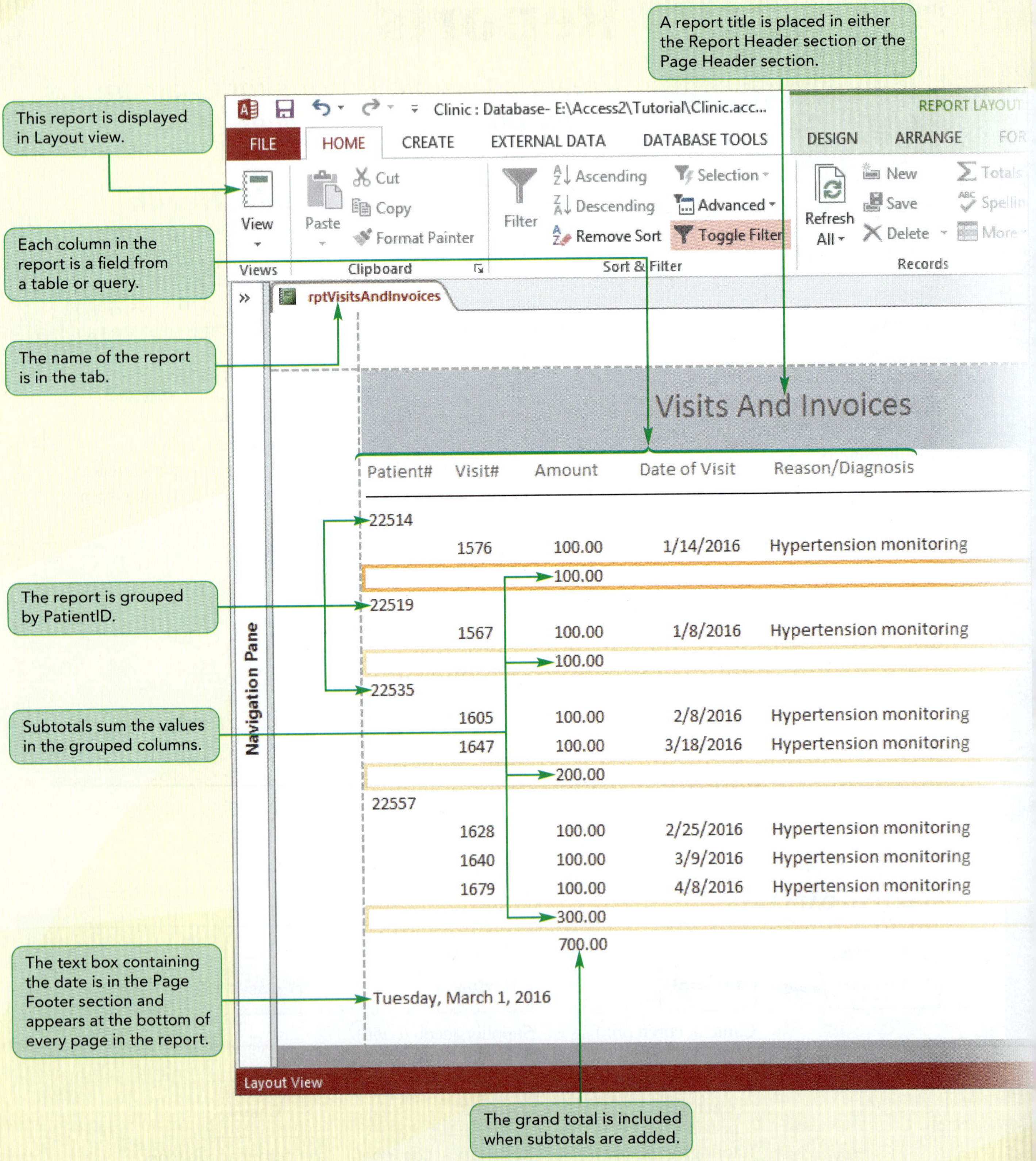

Report Sections

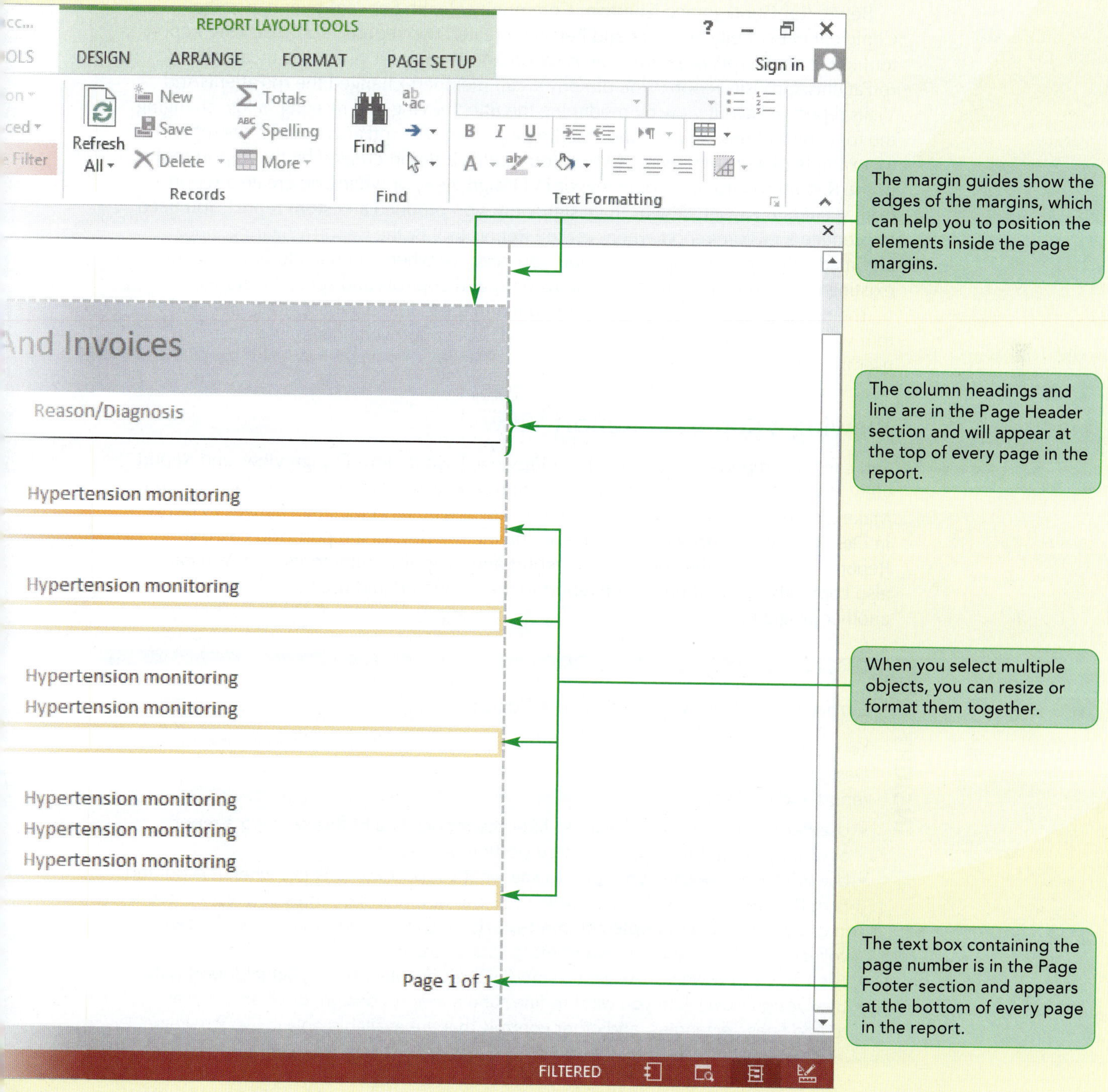

Customizing Existing Reports

A report is a formatted output (screen display or printout) of the contents of one or more tables in a database. Although you can format and print data using datasheets, queries, and forms, reports offer greater flexibility and provide a more professional, readable appearance. For example, a billing statement created using a datasheet would not look professional, but the staff at Chatham Community Health Services can easily create professional-looking billing statements from the database using reports.

Before Raj Gupta joined Chatham Community Health Services to enhance the Clinic database, Kelly Schwarz and her staff created two reports. Kelly used the Report tool to create the rptVisitsAndInvoices report and the Report Wizard to create the rptPatientsAndVisits report. One of Kelly's staff members changed the rptPatientsAndVisits report in Layout view by modifying the title, moving and resizing fields, changing the font color of field names, and inserting a picture. The rptPatientsAndVisits report is an example of a custom report. When you modify a report created by the Report tool or the Report Wizard in Layout view or in Design view, or when you create a report from scratch in Layout view or in Design view, you produce a **custom report**. You need to produce a custom report whenever the Report tool or the Report Wizard cannot automatically create the specific report you need, or when you need to fine-tune an existing report to fix formatting problems or to add controls and special features.

The rptVisitsAndInvoices report is included in the Clinic database. Kelly asks Raj to review the rptVisitsAndInvoices report and make improvements to it so it's more user friendly.

Viewing a Report in Report View

You can view reports on screen in Print Preview, Layout view, Design view, and Report view. You've already viewed and worked with reports in Print Preview and Layout view. Making modifications to reports in Design view is similar to making changes to forms in Design view. **Report view** provides an interactive view of a report. You can use Report view to view the contents of a report and to apply a filter to its data. You can also copy selected portions of the report to the Clipboard and use the selected data in another program.

INSIGHT

Choosing the View to Use for a Report

You can view a report on screen using Report view, Print Preview, Layout view, or Design view. Which view you choose depends on what you intend to do with the report and its data.

- Use Report view when you want to filter the report data before printing a report, or when you want to copy a selected portion of a report.
- Use Print Preview when you want to see what a report will look like when it is printed. Print Preview is the only view in which you can navigate the pages of a report, zoom in or out, or view a **multiple-column report**, which is a report that prints the same collection of field values in two or more sets across the page.
- Use Layout view when you want to modify a report while seeing actual report data.
- Use Design view when you want to fine-tune a report's design, or when you want to add lines, rectangles, and other controls that are available only in Design view.

You'll open the rptVisitsAndInvoices report in Report view and you'll interact with the report in this view.

To interact with the rptVisitsAndInvoices report in Report view:

1. Start Access, and then open the **Clinic** database you worked with in Tutorials 5 and 6.

   Trouble? If the Security Warning is displayed below the Ribbon, either the Clinic database is not located in the Access2 ▸ Tutorial folder or you did not designate that folder as a trusted folder. Make sure you opened the database in the Access2 ▸ Tutorial folder, and make sure that it's designated as a trusted folder.

2. Open the Navigation Pane, scroll down the Navigation Pane (if necessary), double-click **rptVisitsAndInvoices**, and then close the Navigation Pane. The rptVisitsAndInvoices report opens in Report view.

   In Report view, you can view the live version of the report prior to printing it, just as you can do in Print Preview. Unlike Print Preview, Report view lets you apply filters to the report before printing it. You'll apply a text filter to the rptVisitsAndInvoices report.

3. Scroll down to Patient ID 22514: Visit ID 1576, right-click **Hypertension monitoring** in the Reason column to open the shortcut menu, and then point to **Text Filters**. A submenu of filter options for the Text field opens. See Figure 7-1.

Figure 7-1 Filter options for a Text field in Report view

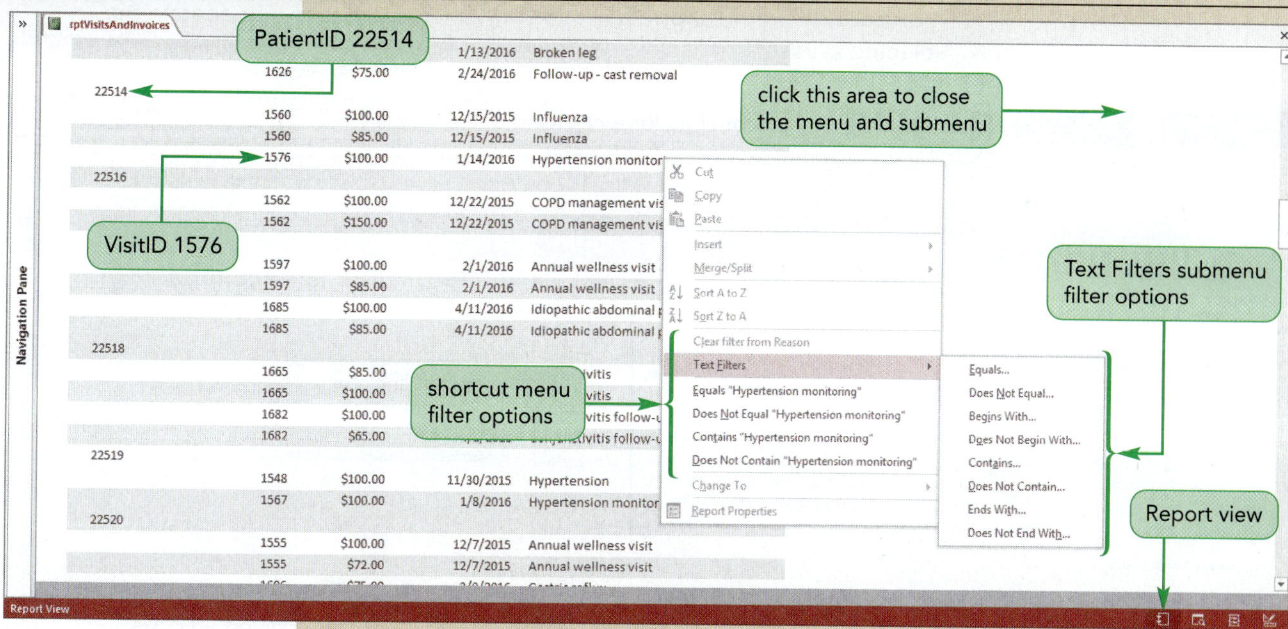

Trouble? Your Text Filters submenu may open to the left of the shortcut menu when you click the right side of the text in the Reason column. This will not cause a problem.

The filter options that appear on the shortcut menu depend on the selected field's data type and the selected value. Because you clicked the Reason field value without selecting a portion of the value, the shortcut menu displays filter options—various conditions using the value "Hypertension monitoring"—for the entire Reason field value. You'll close the menus and select a portion of the Reason column value to explore a different way of filtering the report.

4. Click a blank area in the report (see Figure 7-1) to close the menus. In the Patient ID 22514 for Visit ID 1576, double-click **monitoring** in the Reason column to select it and then right-click **monitoring**. The filter options now apply to the selected text.

   Notice that the filter options on the shortcut menu include the options such as "Ends With" and "Does Not End With" because the text you selected is at the end of the field value in the Reason column.

5. Click **Contains "monitoring"** on the shortcut menu. The report content changes to display only those visits that contain the word "monitoring" anywhere in the Reason column.

6. Double-click the word **Hypertension** in the Reason column for the report detail line for Visit ID 1576 to select it, right-click **Hypertension** to open the shortcut menu, and then point to **Text Filters**. The filter options now include the "Begins With" and "Does Not Begin With" options because the text you selected is at the beginning of the field value in the Reason column.

   Kelly wants to view only those visits that contain the phrase "Hypertension monitoring" in the Reason column.

7. Click a blank area in the report to close the menus, and then click a blank area again to deselect the selected text.

8. In the report detail line for Visit ID 1576, right-click **Hypertension monitoring** in the Reason column, and then click **Equals "Hypertension monitoring"** on the shortcut menu. Only the seven visits that contain the selected phrase are displayed in the report. See Figure 7-2.

Figure 7-2 **Filter applied to the report in Report View**

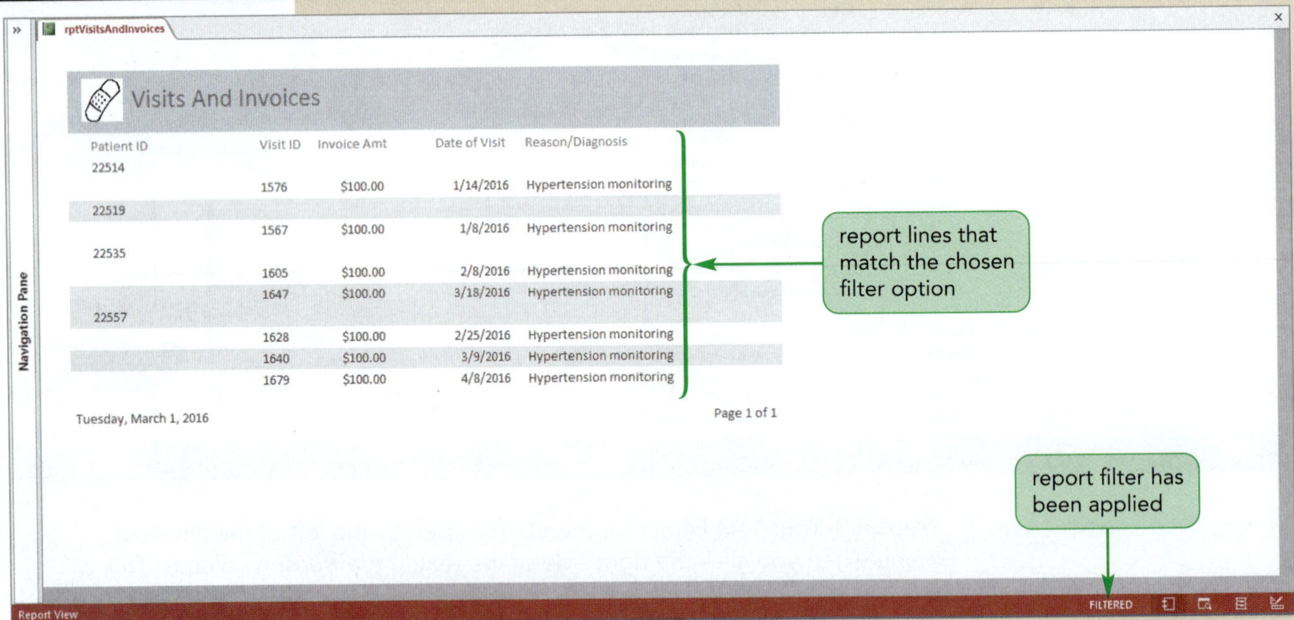

Clip art used with permission from Microsoft Corporation

You can print the filtered report, or you can select the entire filtered report or a portion of it. Then you can copy the selection to the Clipboard and paste it into another file, such as a Word document or an Excel spreadsheet. Next, you'll copy the entire filtered report to the Clipboard.

Kelly would like you to create a Word document that contains the records from the Hypertension Monitoring filter so she can provide this information to the nurse who will follow up with these patients.

TIP

To select a portion of the report, click to the left of the top of the selection and drag down to the bottom of the selection.

To create a Word document that contains filtered records:

1. Click to the left of the title graphic at the top of the report (but don't click in the Navigation Pane), drag down to the end of the last record in the report, release the mouse button to select the report title, field titles, and all of the records in the report, and then in the Clipboard group on the HOME tab, click the **Copy** button. Alternatively, you can use the Ctrl + A key combination only if you want to select all items in the report. In this case, you're selecting only the titles and records. See Figure 7-3.

   Trouble? If you selected nothing, you clicked above the title graphic. Make sure the mouse pointer is to the left of the title graphic, but not above it, and then repeat Step 1.

   Trouble? If you selected only a portion of the report, press the Esc key to deselect your selection, and then repeat Step 9.

Figure 7-3 After selecting the filtered report in Report view

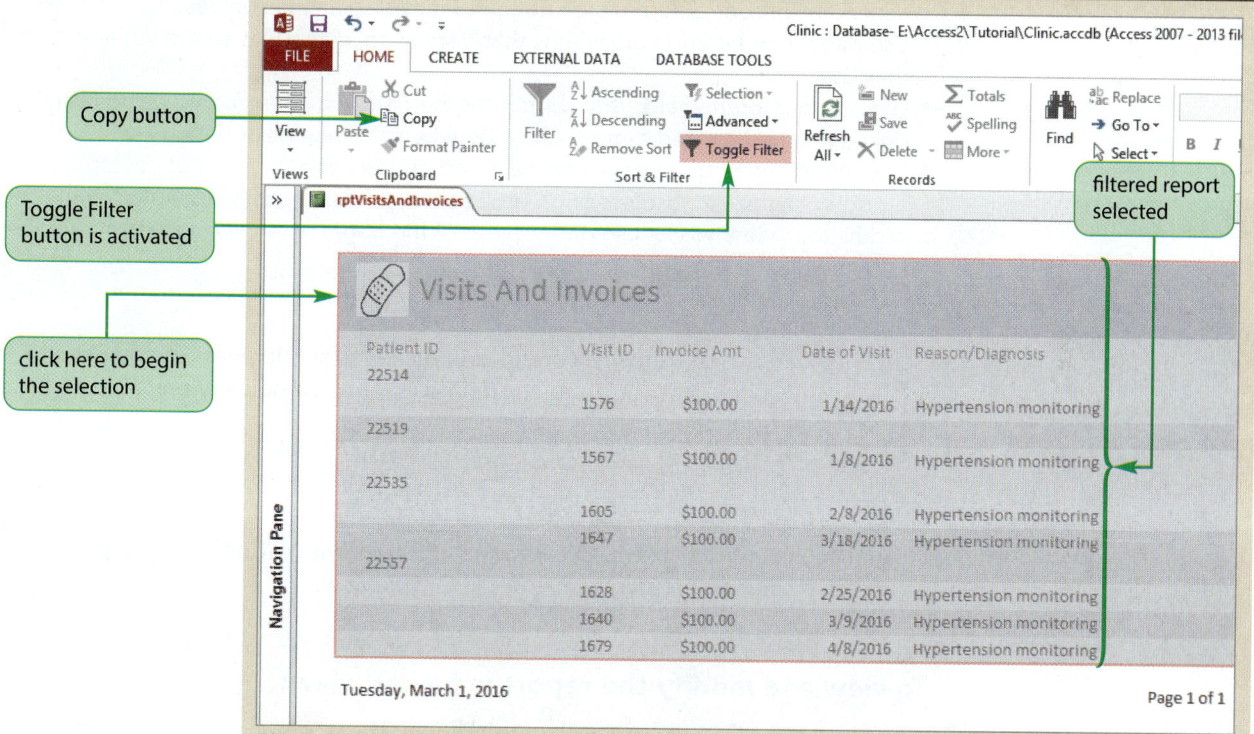

Clip art used with permission from Microsoft Corporation

   If you needed to copy the selection to the Clipboard, you would click the Copy button (see Figure 7-3). You'll copy this report data into a Word document.

2. Open Word, click **Blank document** (if necessary), and then on the HOME tab in the Clipboard group, click the **Paste** button to paste the report data.
3. Save the Word document with the filename **HypertensionMonitoring.docx** in the Access2 ▸ Tutorial folder, and then close Word.
4. In Access, on the HOME tab in the Sort & Filter group, click the **Toggle Filter** button. Access removes the filter.

Kelly wants you to modify the Reason column in the rptVisitsAndInvoices report so that all field values are fully displayed on one line, while decreasing the width of other columns and adjusting the page margins. She also wants you to rename some of the column headings, format the InvoiceAmt field values using the Standard format, resize the column headings, delete the picture from the Report Header section, remove the alternate row color from the detail and group header lines, and add a grand total of the InvoiceAmt field values. These changes will make the report more useful for Kelly.

PROSKILLS

Written Communication: Enhancing Reports Created by the Report Tool and the Report Wizard

Creating a report using the Report tool or the Report Wizard can save time, but you should review the report to determine if you need to make any of the following types of common enhancements and corrections:

- Change the report title from the report object name (with an rpt prefix and no spaces) to one that has meaning to the users.
- Reduce the widths of the date and page number controls, and move the controls so that they are not printed on a separate page.
- Review the report in Print Preview and, if the report displays excess pages, adjust the page margins and the placement of controls.
- Verify that all controls are large enough to fully display their values.
- Use page margins and field widths that display equal margins to the left and right of the data.
- Use a layout for the fields that distributes the data in a balanced way across the document, and use the same spacing between all columns of data.
- The report and page titles can be centered on the page, but do not center the report data. Instead, use spacing between the columns and reasonable column widths to make the best use of the width of the page, extending the data from the left margin to the right margin.

Some of the report adjustments you need to make are subtle ones, so you need to carefully review all report controls to ensure the report is completely readable and usable for those using the report.

Modifying a Report in Layout View

You can make the report changes Kelly wants in Layout view. Modifying a report in Layout view is similar to modifying a form in Layout view.

To view and modify the report in Layout view:

1. On the status bar, click the **Layout View** button, and then scroll to the top of the report (if necessary). See Figure 7-4.

Figure 7-4 Viewing the report in Layout view

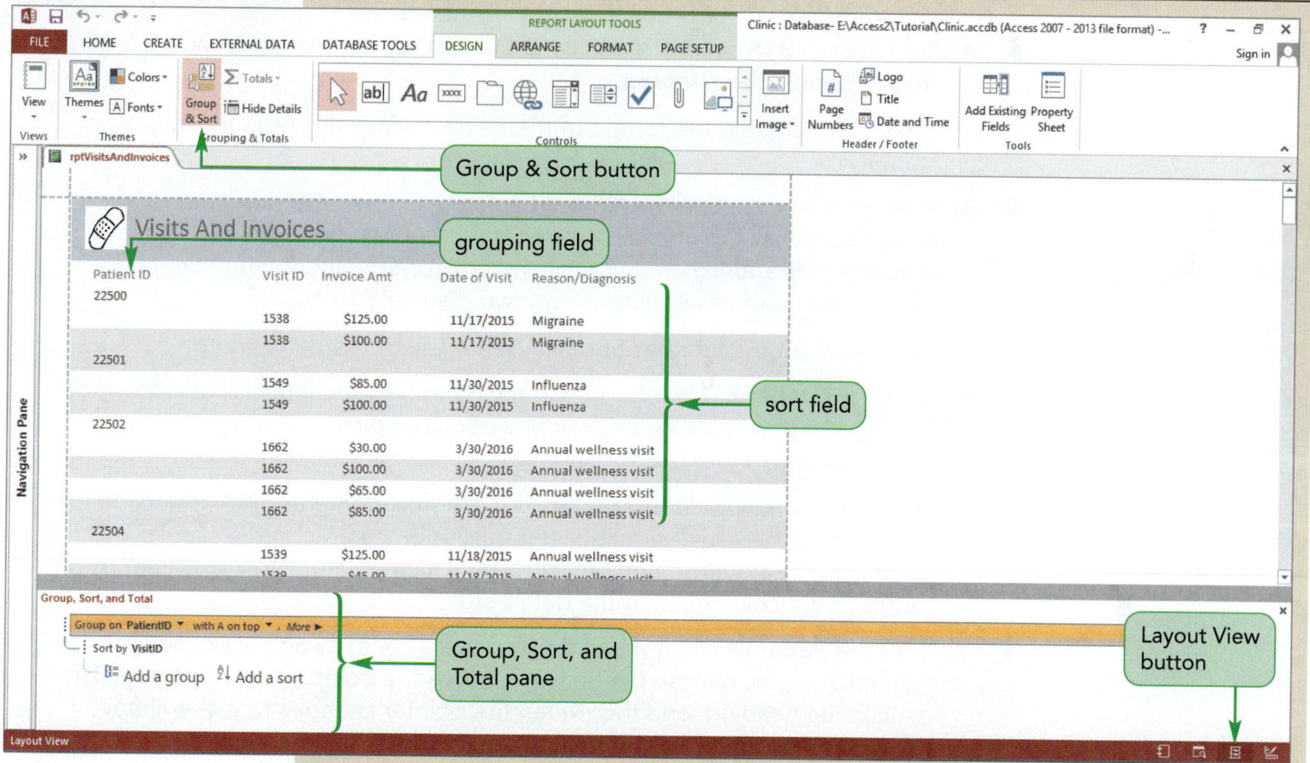

Clip art used with permission from Microsoft Corporation

Trouble? If the Group, Sort, and Total pane is not open at the bottom of the screen, on the DESIGN tab in the Grouping & Totals group, click the Group & Sort button.

TIP

You can click the Group & Sort button in the Grouping & Totals group to open and close the Group, Sort, and Total pane.

The rptVisitsAndInvoices report has a grouping field (the PatientID field) and a sort field (the VisitID field). At the bottom of the screen, the **Group, Sort, and Total pane** provides you with the options to modify the report's grouping fields and sort fields and the report calculations for the groups. A **grouping field** is a report sort field that includes a Group Header section before a group of records having the same sort field value and a Group Footer section after the group of records. A Group Header section usually displays the group name and the sort field value for the group. A Group Footer section usually displays subtotals or counts for the records in that group. The rptVisitsAndInvoices report's grouping field is the PatientID field, which is displayed in a Group Header section that precedes the set of visits for the Patient; the grouping field does not have a Group Footer section. The VisitID field is a secondary sort key, as shown in the Group, Sort, and Total pane.

Because you don't need to change the grouping or sort fields for the report, you'll close the pane and then make Sarah's modifications to the report.

2. On the DESIGN tab, in the Grouping & Totals group, click the **Group & Sort** button to close the Group, Sort, and Total pane.

First, you'll change the column headings for the first three columns to Patient#, Visit#, and Amount. Kelly prefers to see all the detail data on one line, even when it means abbreviating column headings for columns whose headings are wider than the data. After reducing the column headings, you'll reduce the column widths, freeing up space on the detail lines to widen the Reason column.

3. Double-click the **PatientID** column heading to change to editing mode, change it to **Patient#**, and then press the **Enter** key.
4. Repeat Step 3 to change the second column heading to **Visit#** and the third column heading to **Amount**.

   Next, you'll change the format of the field values in the Amount column to Standard.

5. Right-click any value in the **Amount** column to open the shortcut menu, if necessary click **Properties** to open the Property Sheet, set the Format property to **Standard**, and then close the Property Sheet. The Standard format adds comma separators and two decimal places.

   Now you'll set the margins to make better use of the page width.

6. Click the **PAGE SETUP** tab, then in the Page Size section, click the **Margins** button, and then click **Wide**. This sets page margins to 1" on the top and bottom and 0.75" on the left and right.

   Sometimes when margins are decreased, some elements appear outside the margins and this causes additional pages to be created in the report. This has occurred with the page number, and you'll fix that later. Now you'll adjust the widths of the columns to fit the data better.

7. Click the **Patient#** column heading, hold the Shift key and click any of the PatientID values, release the Shift key, move the pointer to the left edge of the column heading, and then when the pointer changes to a ↔ shape, drag the left edge to the left-margin guide (dotted line) then drag the right edge to the left to fit the column heading and the PatientID values.

   Now, you'll move the VisitID column to the left, closer to the PatientID column.

8. Click the **Visit#** column heading, hold the Shift key and click any of the VisitID values, release the Shift key, and then move the mouse pointer over the Visit# heading until it changes to a ✥ shape.
9. Drag the mouse pointer to the left, close to the Patient ID column, and then release the mouse button. The column does not appear to move until you release the mouse button.

   Trouble? Access may also scroll to the bottom of the report after you release the mouse button. If that happens, just scroll up to the top of the report and try again if necessary. It may take a couple of attempts to move the column to the right spot.

   Now you'll resize and move the Amount heading and InvoiceAmt values to the left, closer to the VisitID column, and then you'll move the Date of Visit and Reason/Diagnosis columns to the left, closer to the Amount column.

10. Click the **Amount** column heading, hold the Shift key and click any of the InvoiceAmt values, release the Shift key, and then drag the left edge of one of the items in the column to the right to reduce the width of the **Amount** column to fit the data better.
11. With the Amount column heading and the InvoiceAmt values still selected, drag the objects to the left, closer to the Visit# column.
12. Repeat steps 10 and 11 for the Date of Visit column, resizing it from the right edge and moving it to the left. See Figure 7-5.

Figure 7-5 **After resizing columns in Layout view**

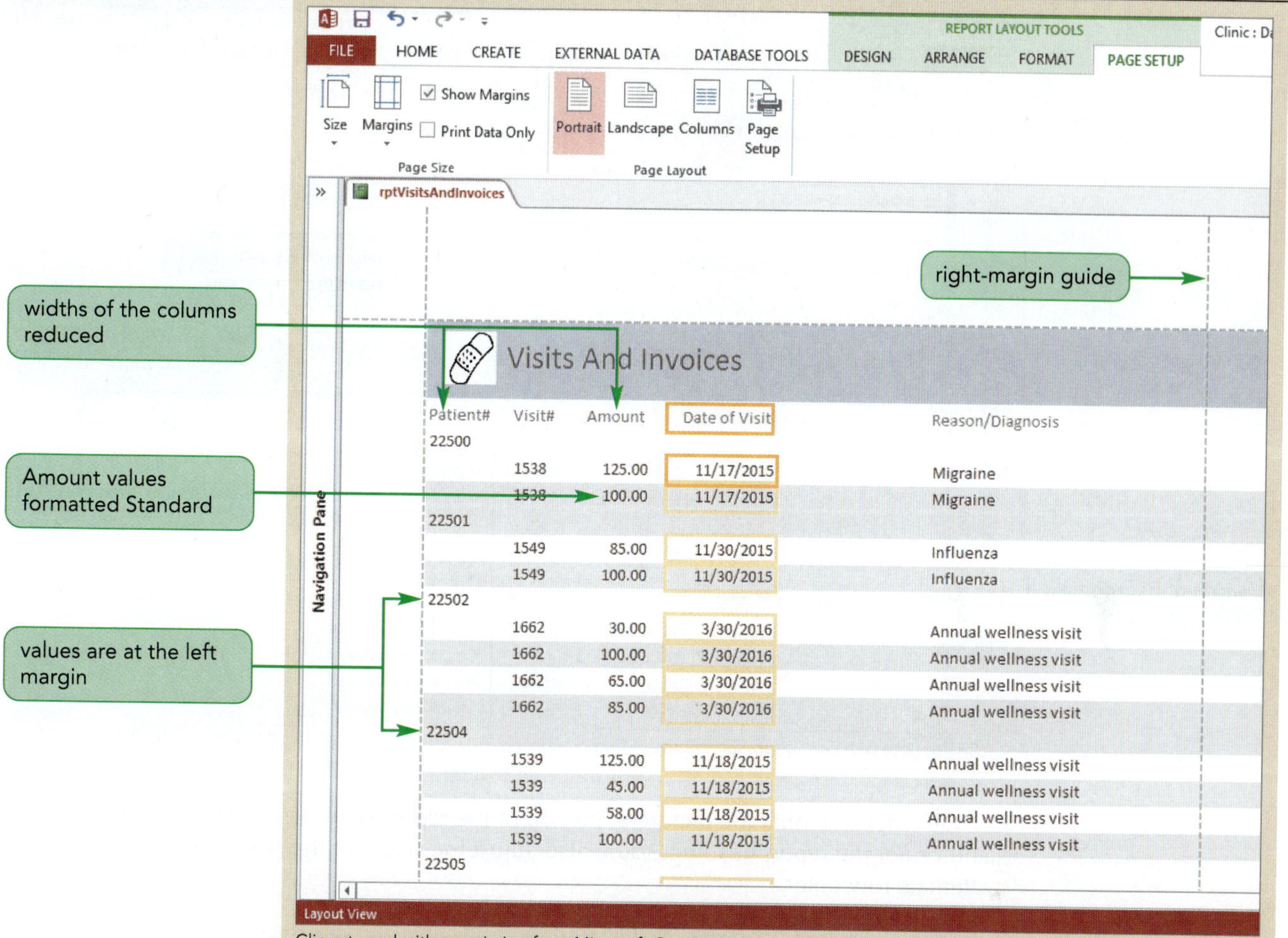

Clip art used with permission from Microsoft Corporation

Now, you'll move the Reason field to the left, and size it to fit the data better, aligning it with the page's right-margin.

13. Select the Reason column heading and values, and then move them to the left, closer to the Date of Visit column.

    Because the Reason field heading is wider than the Reason column data items, you'll size them separately.

14. Click a blank area of the report to deselect the selected objects, click the **Reason** field heading to select it, drag its right edge to the right-margin guide (dotted line), deselect the Reason field heading, click one of the **Reason field values** to select all of the Reason field values, and then drag one of the right edges to the right-margin guide. See Figure 7-6.

Figure 7-6 After resizing columns in Layout view

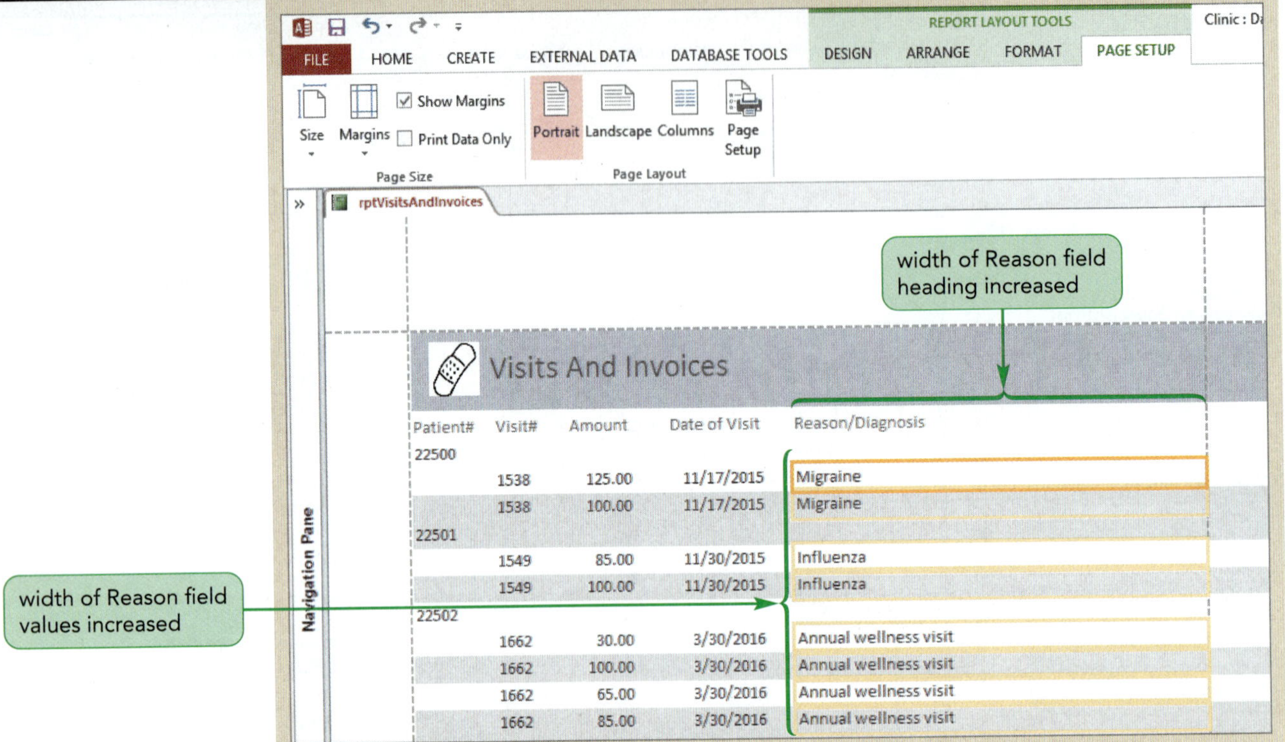

Clip art used with permission from Microsoft Corporation

Kelly doesn't think the picture at the top of the report is necessary, so you'll delete it and center the report heading. You'll also adjust the width of the page and remove the alternate row color.

To modify the appearance of the report:

1. Scroll to the top of the report, right-click the picture at the top of the report to open the shortcut menu, and then click **Delete** to remove the picture.
2. Click the **Visits And Invoices** title to select it, and then move it to the left-margin guide.
3. Drag the right edge of the title to the right-margin guide to increase the size of the title box to the full width of the page.
4. Click the **FORMAT** tab, and then in the Font group, click the **Center** button to center the title in the title box.

   Kelly finds the alternate row color setting in the group header and detail lines distracting, and asks you to remove this feature.
5. Click to the left of the left-margin guide to the left of the first PatientID value to select the group headers, in the Background group click the **Alternate Row Color** arrow to display the gallery of available colors, and then at the bottom of the gallery, click **No Color**. The alternate row color is removed from the PatientID rows.

You've removed the alternate row color from the PatientID values in the report, and next you'll remove the alternate row color from the detail lines. Because the Alternate Row Color button is now set to "No Color," you can just click the button to remove the color.

6. Click to the left of the left-margin guide next to the first VisitID in the first Patient record detail lines, and then in the Background group click the **Alternate Row Color** button to remove the alternate row color from the group header lines.

Kelly's last change to the report is to add a grand total of the Amount field values. First, you must select the Amount column or one of the values in the column.

To add a grand total to the report in Layout view:

1. In the detail line for VisitID 1538, click **125.00** in the Amount column, click the **DESIGN tab**, and then in the Grouping & Totals group, click the **Totals** button to display the Totals menu. See Figure 7-7.

Figure 7-7 Displaying options on the Totals menu

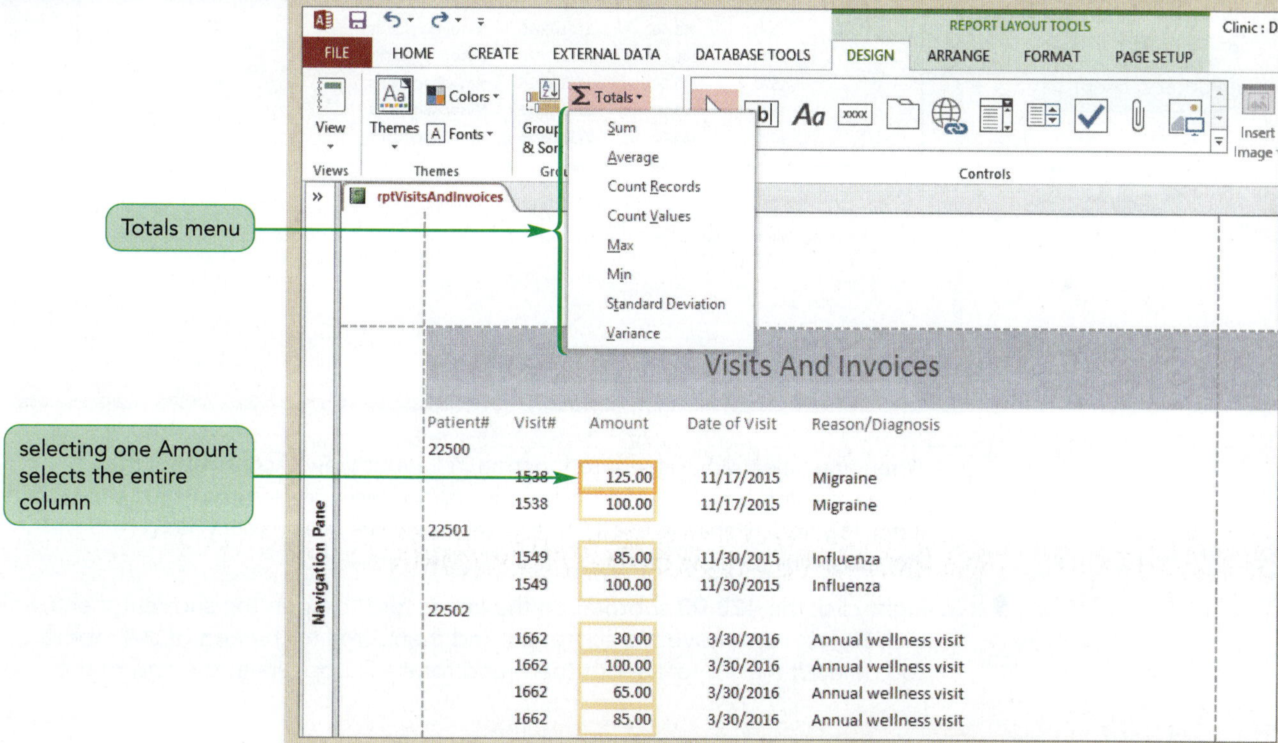

You select one of the eight aggregate functions on the Totals menu to summarize values in the selected column. To calculate and display the grand total visit amount, you'll select the Sum aggregate function.

TIP

A text box displays pound signs when the text box is too narrow to display the full field value.

2. Click **Sum** in the Totals menu, scroll to the bottom of the report, and then if the last text box contains ###### instead of numbers, click the text box to select it, then drag its left edge to the left to increase its width. In addition to the grand total of 20,703.00, subtotals for each group of visits are displayed for each PatientID field value (423.00 for the last patient). See Figure 7-8.

Trouble? If the text box still contains ###### after you resize it, increase the width again until the grand total value of 20,703.00 is visible.

Figure 7-8 After adding subtotals and a grand total of the Amount field values

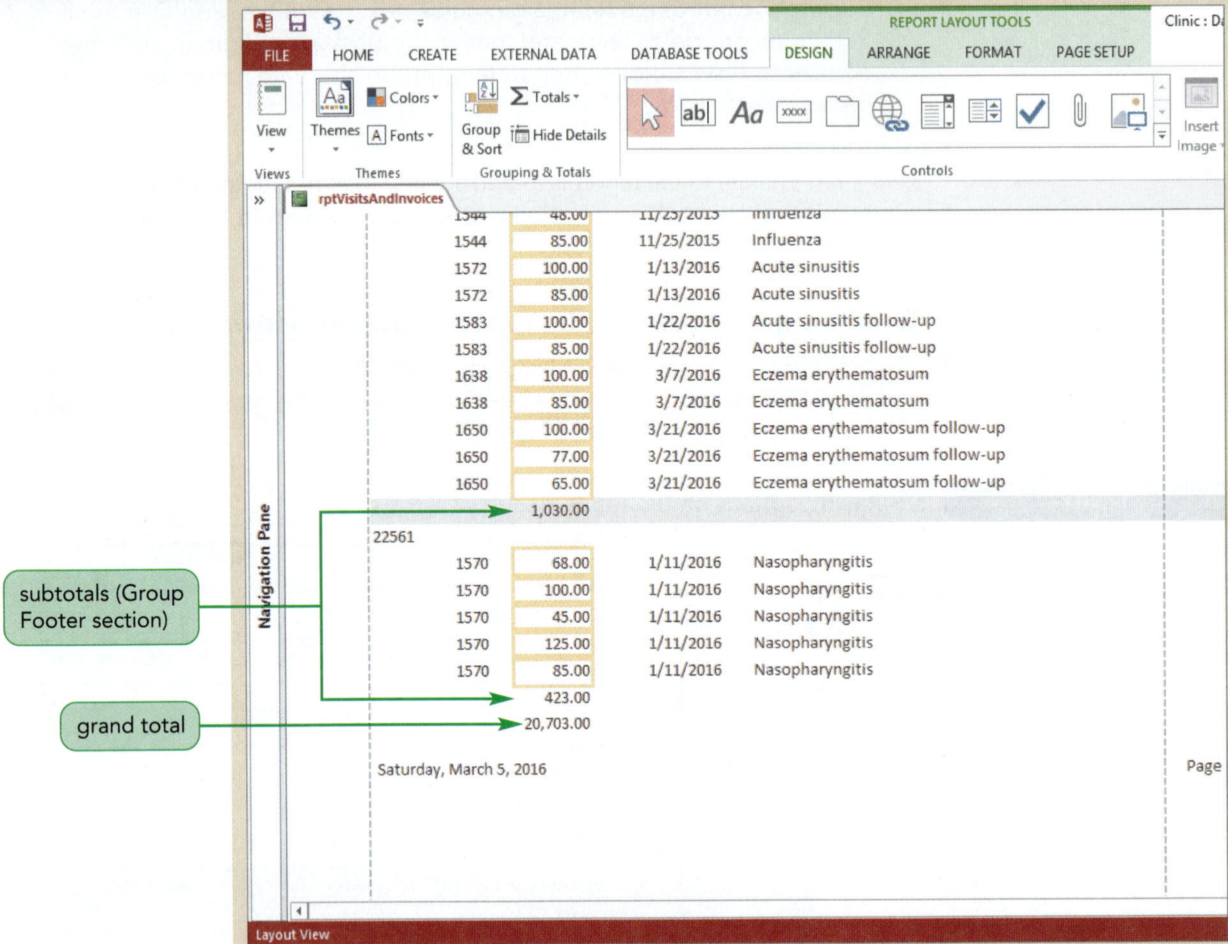

When you select an aggregate function in Layout view, Access adds the results of the function to the end of the report and adds subtotals for each grouping field. Because each Patient has few visits, Kelly asks you to remove the subtotals from the report.

3. Right-click the **423.00** subtotal on the last record to open the shortcut menu, click **Delete** to remove the subtotals, and then scroll to the end of the report. You deleted the subtotals, but the grand total still appears at the end of the report.

Kelly wants to review the rptVisitsAndInvoices report in Print Preview.

4. Save your report changes, switch to Print Preview, and then use the navigation buttons to page through the report, ending on the second-to-last page of the report.

You can use the Zoom control on the status bar to zoom in or out on the report view in 10% increments (using the Zoom In button or Zoom Out button) or in variable increments (by dragging the Zoom slider control).

5. Click the **Zoom In** button on the status bar to increase the zoom percentage to 110%. See Figure 7-9.

Figure 7-9 **Viewing the rptVisitsAndInvoices report in Print Preview**

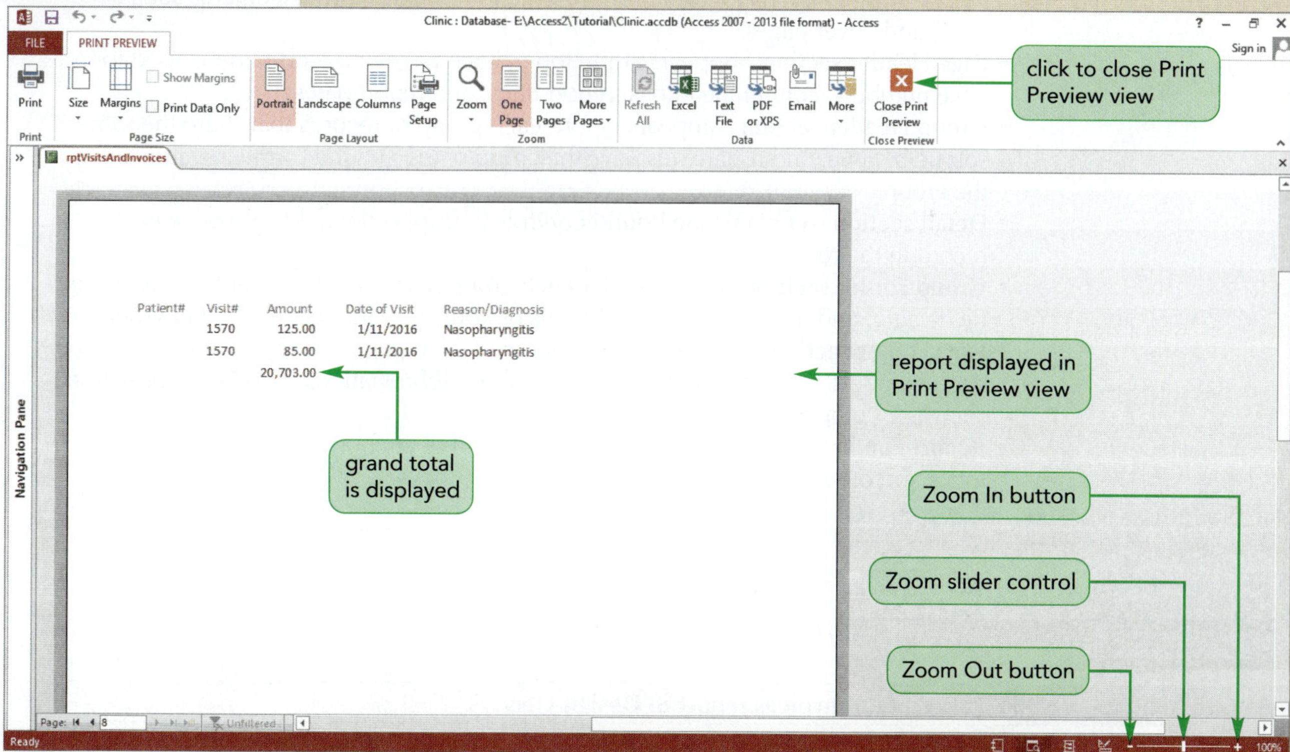

Trouble? Depending on the printer you are using, the last page of your report might differ. If so, don't worry. Different printers format reports in different ways, sometimes affecting the total number of pages and the number of records printed per page.

6. Click the **Zoom Out** button on the status bar to decrease the zoom percentage to 100%, and then click the **Close Print Preview** button to close the Print Preview view for the report.

Kelly identifies two additional modifications she wants you to make to the report. The page numbers are outside the right-margin and are causing extra pages in the report. She wants you to move the page number that appears at the bottom of each page. She wants you to move it to the left so that its right edge is aligned with the right edge of Reason text box in the Detail section and the extra pages are no longer created. She also wants you to add a line below the column heading labels.

Modifying a Report in Design View

To make Kelly's changes to the report, you need to move the page number control in the Page Footer section to the left, and then create a line control below the column headings in the Page Header. Although you can make Kelly's modifications in Layout view, you'll make them in Design view so you can more precisely position the line using the grid. Design view for reports is similar to Design view for forms, which you used in Tutorial 6 to customize forms.

A report in Design view is divided into seven sections:

- **Report Header section**—appears once at the beginning of a report and is used for report titles, company logos, report introductions, dates, visual elements such as lines, and cover pages.
- **Page Header section**—appears at the top of each page of a report and is used for page numbers, column headings, report titles, and report dates.
- **Group Header section**—appears before each group of records that share the same sort field value, and usually displays the group name and the sort field value for the group.
- **Detail section**—contains the bound controls to display the field values for each record in the record source.
- **Group Footer section**—appears after each group of records that share the same sort field value, and usually displays subtotals or counts for the records in that group.
- **Page Footer section**—appears at the bottom of each page of a report and is used for page numbers, brief explanations of symbols or abbreviations, or other information such as a company name.
- **Report Footer section**—appears once at the end of a report and is used for report totals and other summary information.

To view and modify the report in Design view:

1. Switch to Design view. See Figure 7-10.

Figure 7-10 rptVisitsAndInvoices report in Design view

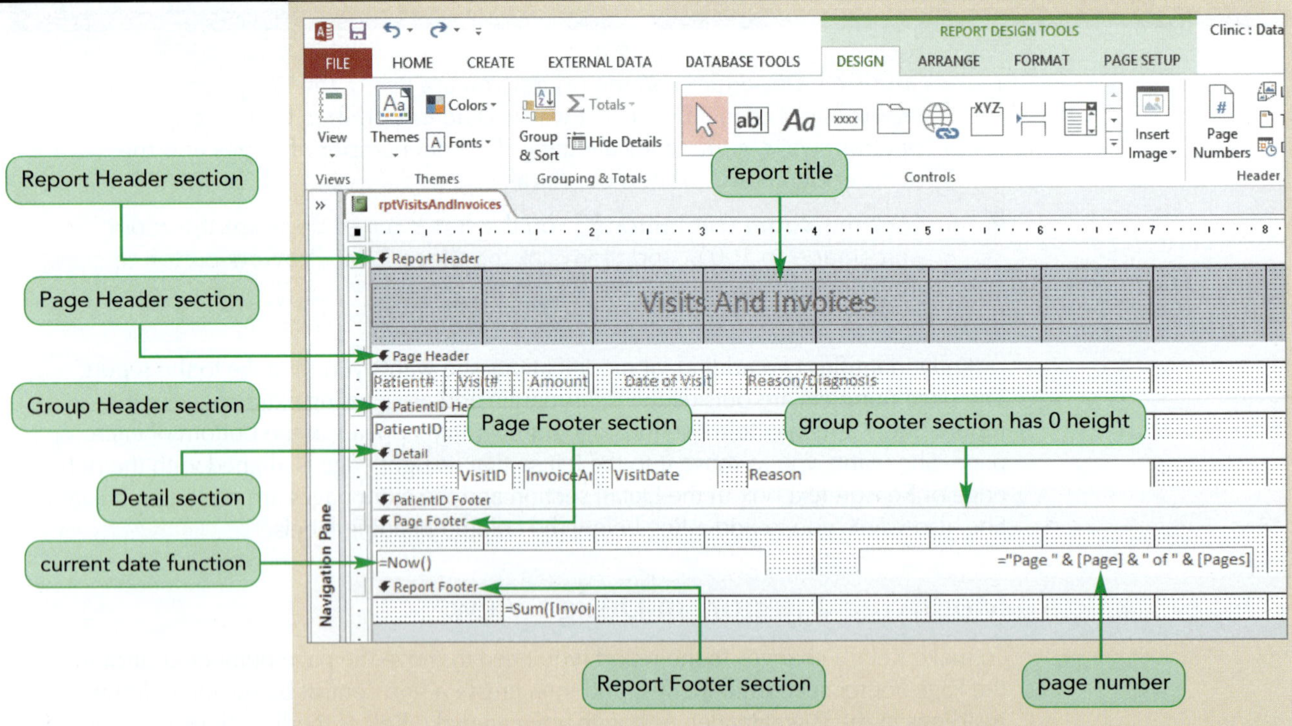

Notice that Design view for a report has most of the same components as Design view for a form. For example, Design view for forms and reports includes horizontal and vertical rulers, grids in each section, and similar buttons in the groups on the DESIGN tab.

Design view for the rptVisitsAndInvoices report displays seven sections: the Report Header section contains the report title; the Page Header section contains the column heading labels; the Group Header section (PatientID Header) contains the PatientID grouping field; the Detail section contains the bound controls to display the field values for each record in the record source (tblVisit); the Group Footer section (PatientID Footer) isn't displayed in the report; the Page Footer section contains the current date and the page number; and the Report Footer section contains the Sum function, which calculates the grand total of the InvoiceAmt field values.

You'll begin on Kelly's changes by moving the page number control in the Page Footer section.

2. Click the **Page Number** text box (the control on the right side of the Page Footer section), and then press the ← key to move the text box to the left until the right edge of the text box is roughly aligned with the right edge of the Reason text box in the Detail section.

   Trouble? If the page number text box overlaps the date text box, don't worry about it. The contents of both will still be displayed.

3. With the Page Number text box still selected, hold down the **Shift** key, click the **Reason** text box, and then release the **Shift** key. Both controls are now selected.

4. Right-click one of the selected controls, point to **Align** on the shortcut menu, and then click **Right**. Both controls are now aligned on their right edges.

   Finally, you'll create the line in the Page Header section.

5. Drag the lower edge of the Page Header section down to increase the height approximately half an inch more. You'll resize this again after the line is created.

   You'll hold the Shift key down while dragging the mouse pointer to create a horizontal line easily.

6. On the DESIGN tab, in the Controls group, click the **More** button and then click the **Line** button.

7. Under the headings in the Page Header section, position the mouse pointer approximately two grid dots below the page header text boxes, press and hold the **Shift** key, drag to the right to create a horizontal line that will stretch the width of the page and align with the right edge of the Reason text boxes, and then release the Shift key. Holding the Shift key while drawing or extending a line snaps the line to either horizontal or vertical—whichever is nearest to the angle at which the line is drawn.

8. Drag the lower edge of the Page header section up so it is approximately two grid dots below the line. See Figure 7-11.

Figure 7-11 **After modifying the rptVisitsAndInvoices report in Design view**

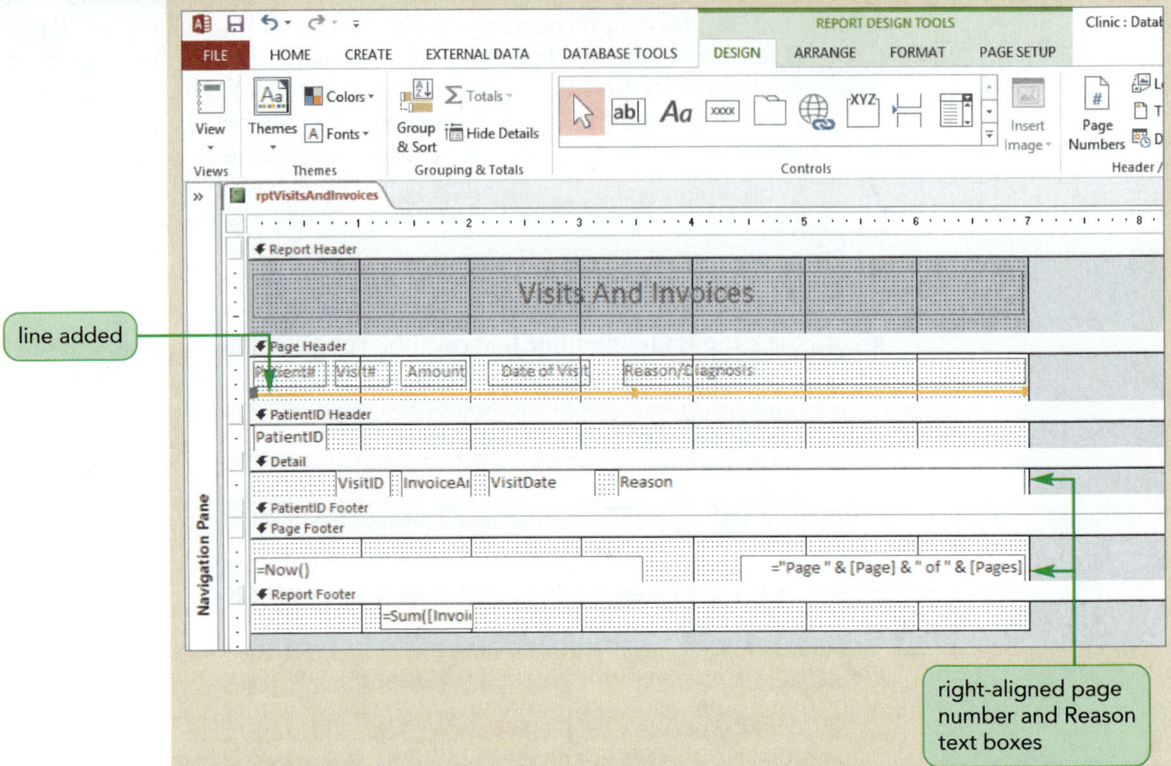

9. Save your report changes, switch to Print Preview, and then scroll and use the navigation buttons to page through the report, paying particular attention to the placement of the line in the Page Header section and the page number in the Page Footer section. The page number data is right-aligned in the text box, so the text appears flush with the right margin. The data in the Reason field value text boxes are left-aligned, so this data does not appear flush with the right margin.

   Trouble? If you resize a field to position it outside the current margin, the report may widen to accommodate it, triggering a dialog box about the section width being greater than the page width. If this dialog box opens, click OK, manually move form elements as necessary so that no elements extend past 7.5 inches, and then adjust the report width to 7.5 inches.

10. Save and close the report.
11. If you are not continuing on to the next session, close the Clinic database.

Kelly is happy with the changes you've made to the rptVisitsAndInvoices report. In the next session, you create a new custom report for her based on queries instead of tables.

REVIEW

Session 7.1 Quick Check

1. What is a custom report?
2. You can view a report in Report view. What other actions can you perform in Report view?
3. What is a grouping field?
4. List and describe the seven sections of an Access report.

Session 7.2 Visual Overview:

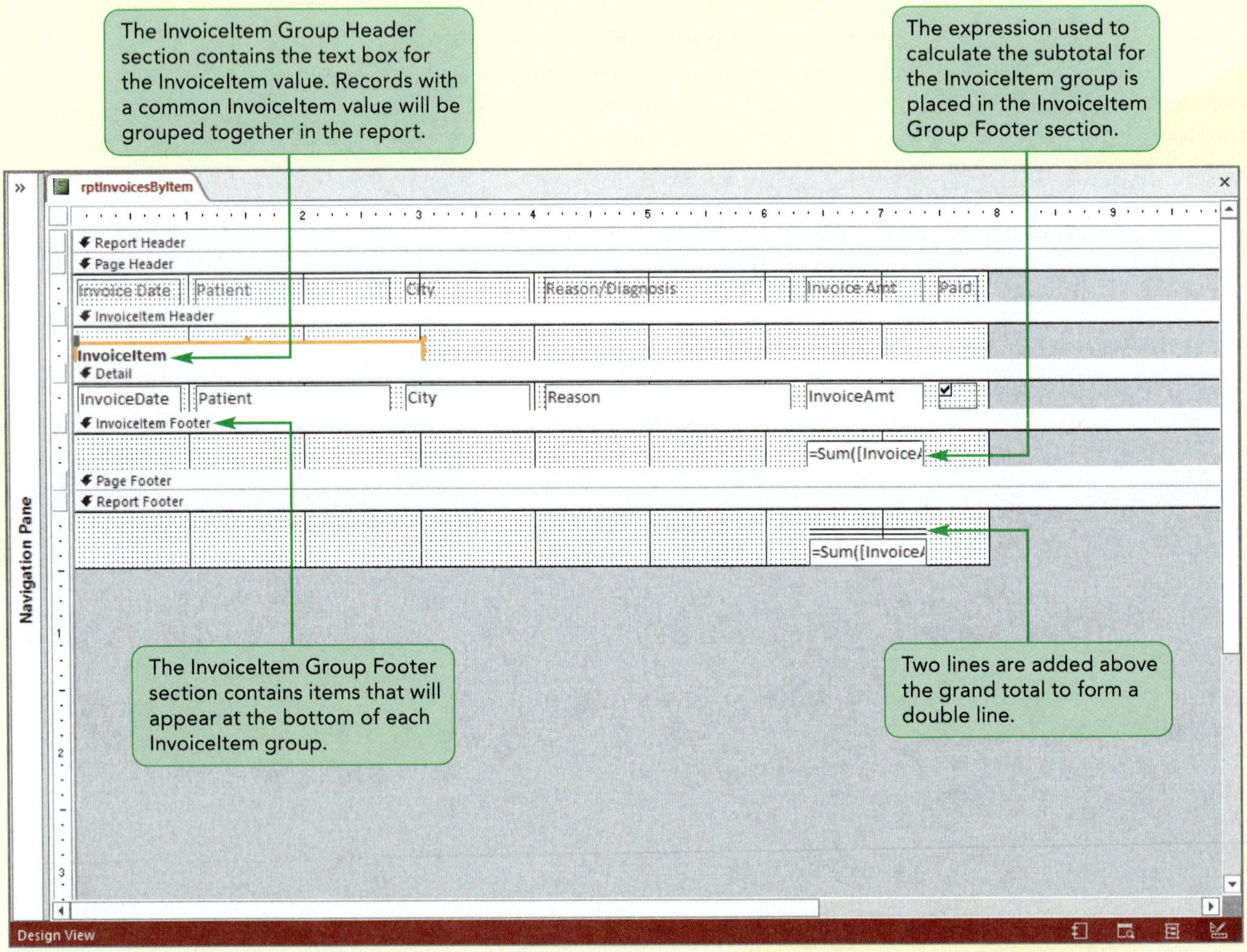

Report Design view and Print Preview

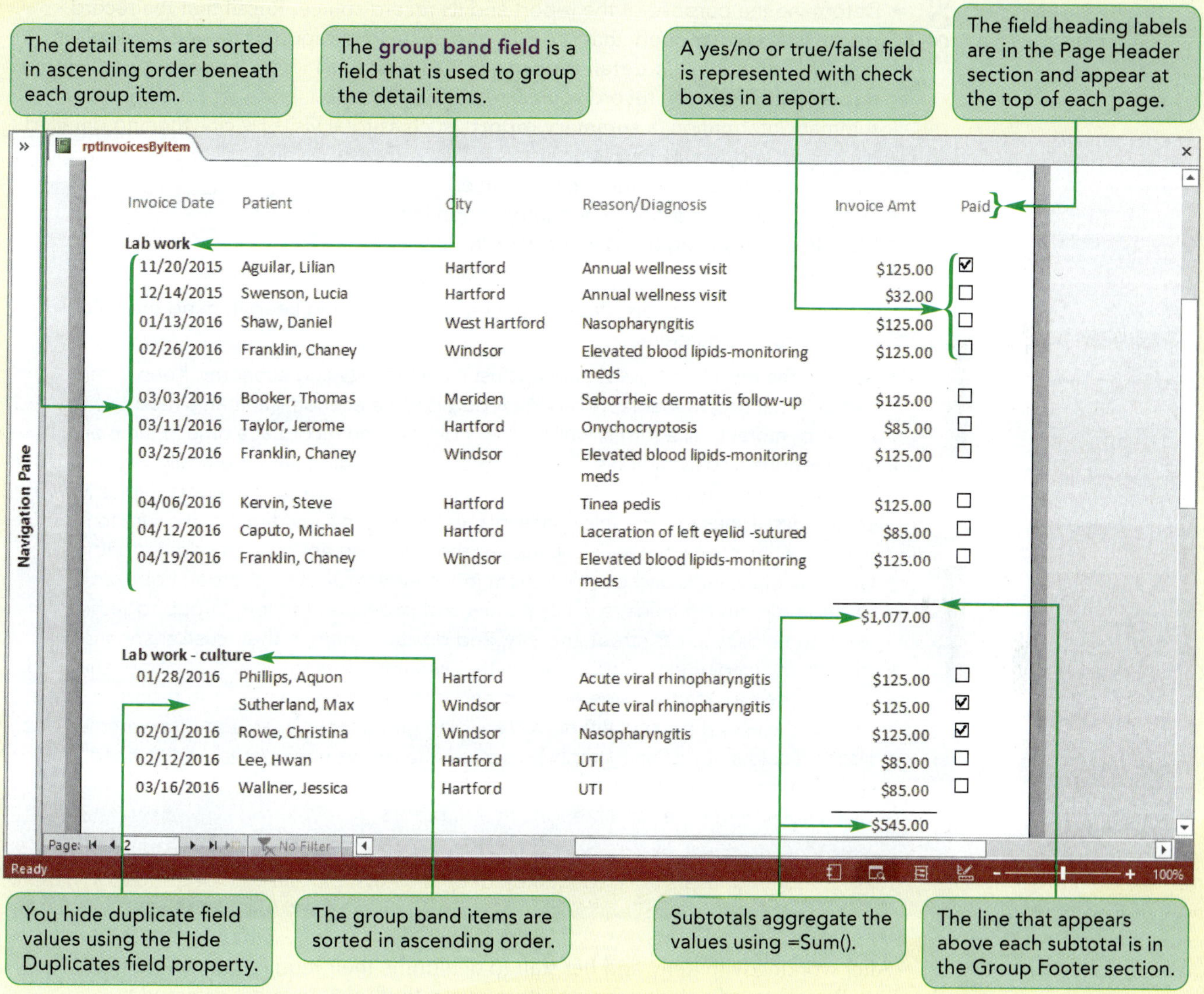

Designing a Custom Report

Before you create a custom report, you should first plan the report's contents and appearance.

PROSKILLS

Decision Making: Guidelines for Designing and Formatting a Report

When you plan a report, you should keep in mind the following report design guidelines:

- Determine the purpose of the report and its record source. Recall that the record source is a table or query that provides the fields for a report. If the report displays detailed information (a **detail report**), such as a list of all visits, then the report will display fields from the record source in the Detail section. If the report displays only summary information (a **summary report**), such as total visits by city, then no detailed information appears; only grand totals and possibly subtotals appear based on calculations using fields from the record source.
- Determine the sort order for the information in the report.
- Identify any grouping fields in the report.
- Consider creating a sketch of the report design using pen and paper.

At the same time you are designing a report, you should keep in mind the following report formatting guidelines:

- Balance the report's attractiveness against its readability and economy. Keep in mind that an attractive, readable, two-page report is more economical than a report of three pages or more. Unlike forms, which usually display one record at a time in the main form, reports display multiple records. Instead of arranging fields vertically as you do in a form, you usually position fields horizontally across the page in a report. Typically, you set the detail lines to be single space in a report. At the same time, make sure to include enough white space between columns so the values do not overlap or run together.
- Group related fields and position them in a meaningful, logical order. For example, position identifying fields, such as names and codes, on the left. Group together all location fields, such as street and city, and position them in their customary order.
- Identify each column of field values with a column heading label that names the field.
- Include the report title, page number, and date on every page of the report.
- Identify the end of a report either by displaying grand totals or an end-of-report message.
- Use few colors, fonts, and graphics to keep the report uncluttered and to keep the focus on the information.
- Use a consistent style for all reports in a database.

By following these report design and formatting guidelines, you'll create reports that make it easier for users to conduct their daily business and to make better decisions.

After working with Kelly and her staff to determine their requirements for a new report, Raj prepared a design for a custom report to display invoices grouped by invoice item. Refer to the Session 7.2 Visual Overview for Raj's report design.

The custom report will list the records for all invoices and will contain five sections:

- The Page Header section will contain the report title ("Invoices by Item") centered between the current date on the left and the page number on the right. A horizontal line will separate the column heading labels from the rest of the report page. From your work with the Report tool and the Report Wizard, you know that, by default, Access places the report title in the Report Header section and the date and page number in the Page Footer section. Sarah prefers that the date, report title, and page number appear at the top of each page, so you need to place this information in the custom report's Page Header section.

- The InvoiceItem field value from the tblBilling table will be displayed in a Group Header section.
- The Detail section will contain the InvoiceDate, InvoiceAmt, and InvoicePaid field values from the tblBilling table; the Reason field value from the tblVisit table; the City field value from the tblPatient table; and the Patient calculated field value from the qryPatientsByName query. The detail records will be sorted in ascending value by the InvoiceDate field.
- A subtotal of the InvoiceAmt field values will be displayed below a line in the Group Footer section.
- The grand total of the InvoiceAmt field values will be displayed below a double line in the Report Footer section.

Before you start creating the custom report, you need to create a query that will serve as the record source for the report.

Creating a Query for a Custom Report

TIP

Create queries to serve as the record source for forms and reports. As requirements change, you can easily add fields, including calculated fields, to the queries.

The data for a report can come from a single table, from a single query based on one or more tables, or from multiple tables and/or queries. Raj's report will contain data from the tblBilling, tblVisit, and tblPatient tables, and from the qryPatientsByName query. You'll use the Simple Query Wizard to create a query to retrieve all the data required for the custom report and to serve as the report's record source. A query filters data from one or more tables using criteria that can be quite complex. Creating a report based on a query allows you to display and distribute the results of the query in a readable, professional format, rather than only in a datasheet view.

To create the query to serve as the report's record source:

1. If you took a break after the previous session, make sure that the Clinic database is open and the Navigation Pane is closed.
2. Click the **CREATE tab**, in the Queries group click the **Query Wizard** button, make sure **Simple Query Wizard** is selected, and then click the **OK** button. The first Simple Query Wizard dialog box opens.

   You need to select fields from the tblBilling, tblVisit, and tblPatient tables, and from the qryPatientsByName query, in that order.
3. In the Tables/Queries box, select **Table:tblInvoiceItem**, and then move the **InvoiceItem** field to the Selected Fields box.
4. In the Tables/Queries box, select **Table: tblBilling**, and then move the **InvoiceItemID**, **InvoiceDate**, **InvoiceAmt**, and **InvoicePaid** fields, in that order, to the Selected Fields box.
5. In the Tables/Queries box, select **Table: tblVisit**, and then move the **Reason** field to the Selected Fields box.
6. In the Tables/Queries box, select **Table: tblPatient**, and then move the **City** field to the Selected Fields box.
7. In the Tables/Queries box, select **Query: qryPatientsByName**, move the **Patient** calculated field to the Selected Fields box, and then click the **Next** button.
8. Make sure the **Detail (shows every field of every record)** option button is selected, and then click the **Next** button to open the final Simple Query Wizard dialog box.

9. Change the query name to **qryInvoicesByItem**, click the **Modify the query design** option button, and then click the **Finish** button. The query is displayed in Design view.

   Next you need to set the sort fields for the query. The InvoiceItem field will be a grouping field, which means it's the primary sort field, and the InvoiceDate field is the secondary sort field.

10. In the design grid, set the value in the InvoiceItem Sort box to **Ascending** and then set the value in the InvoiceDate Sort box to **Ascending**.

11. Lengthen the field lists as necessary to view all fields and drag the tables if necessary to see the join lines between them, and then save your query changes. The completed query contains eight fields from four tables and one query and has two sort fields, the InvoiceItem primary sort field and the InvoiceDate secondary sort field. See Figure 7-12.

Figure 7-12 Finished qryInvoicesByItem query in Design view

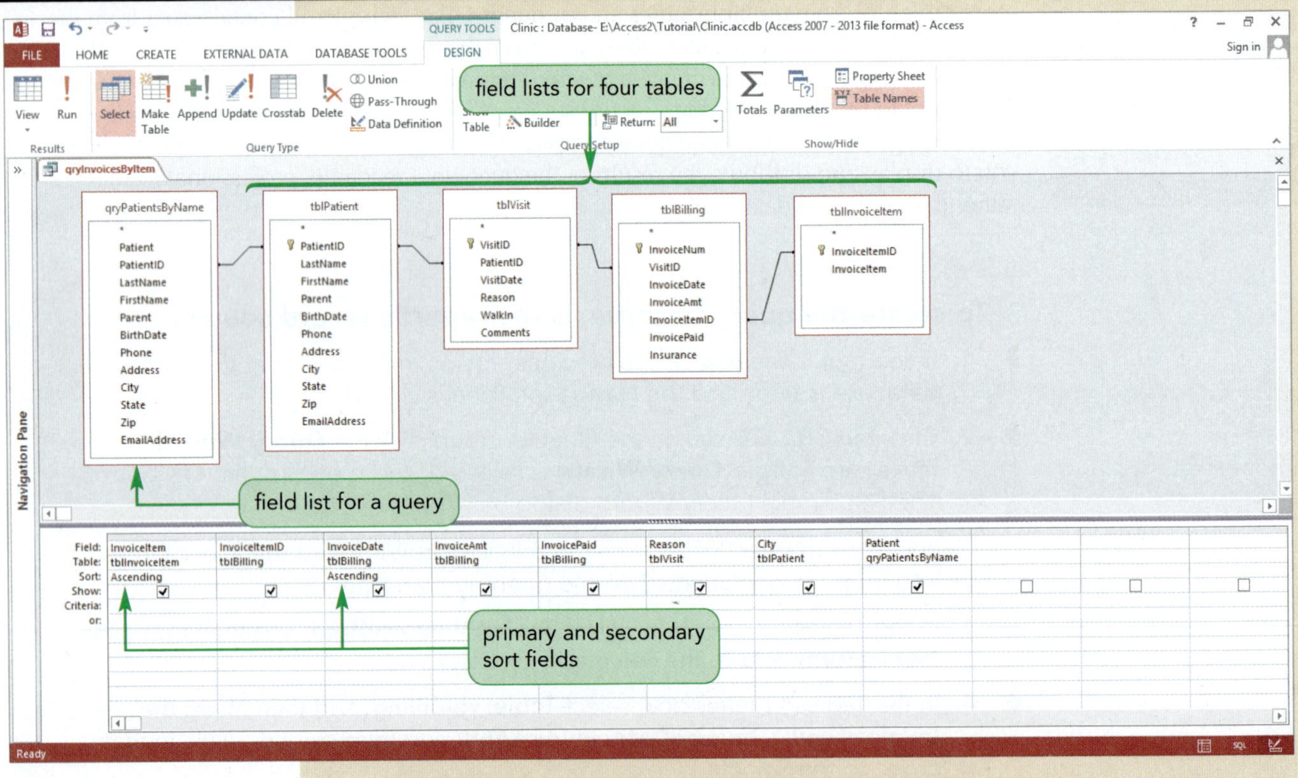

Trouble? After you've finished creating the query and close it, if you later open the query in Design view, you'll see the thicker join lines with referential integrity enforced, connecting the tblPatient and tblVisit table field lists and the tblVisit and tblBilling table field lists.

Before closing the query, you'll run it to view the query recordset.

12. Click the DESIGN tab if it is not already active, run the query, verify that it displays 204 records, and then save and close the query.

You'll use the qryInvoicesByItem query as the record source for Raj's custom report.

Creating a Custom Report

Now that you've created the record source for the custom report, you could use the Report Wizard to create the report and then modify it to match the report design. However, because you need to customize several components of the report, you will create a custom report in Layout view, and then switch between Layout and Design view to fine-tune the report. As the first step in creating the report, you need to create a blank report in Layout view.

INSIGHT

Making Report Design Modifications

You perform operations in Layout and Design views for reports in the same way that you perform operations in these views for forms. These operations become easier with practice. Remember to use the Undo button when necessary, back up your database frequently, save your report changes frequently, work from a copy of the report for complicated design changes, and compact and repair the database on a regular basis. You can also display the report in Print Preview at any time to view your progress on the report.

You'll create a blank report in Layout view, set the record source, and then add controls to the custom report.

To create a blank report and add bound controls in Layout view:

1. Click the **CREATE** tab on the Ribbon, and then in the Reports group, click the **Blank Report** button. A new report opens in Layout view, with the Field List pane open. See Figure 7-13.

Figure 7-13 **Blank report in Layout view**

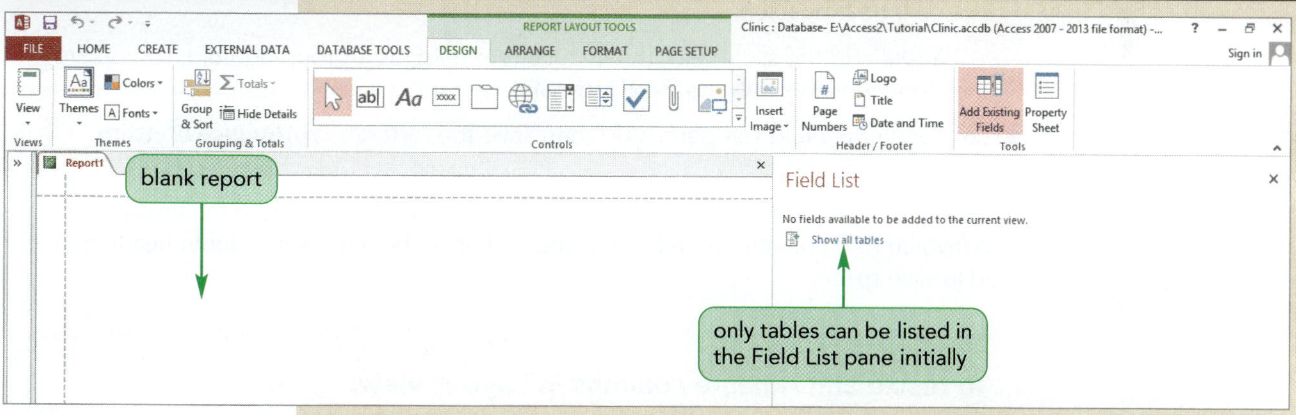

2. On the DESIGN tab, in the Tools group, click the **Property Sheet** button to open the Property Sheet for the report.
3. In the Property Sheet, click the **All** tab (if necessary), click the **Record Source** arrow, click **qryInvoicesByItem**, and then close the Property Sheet.
4. On the DESIGN tab, in the Tools group, click the **Add Existing Fields** button to open the Field List pane. The Field List pane displays the eight fields in the qryInvoicesByItem query, which is the record source for the report.

Referring to Raj's report design, you'll add six of the eight fields to the report in a tabular layout, which is the default control layout when you add fields to a report in Layout view.

5. Double-click **InvoiceDate** in the Field List pane, and then, in order, double-click **Patient**, **City**, **Reason**, **InvoiceAmt**, and **InvoicePaid** in the Field List pane. The six bound controls are displayed in a tabular layout in the report. See Figure 7-14.

Figure 7-14 After adding fields to the report in Layout view

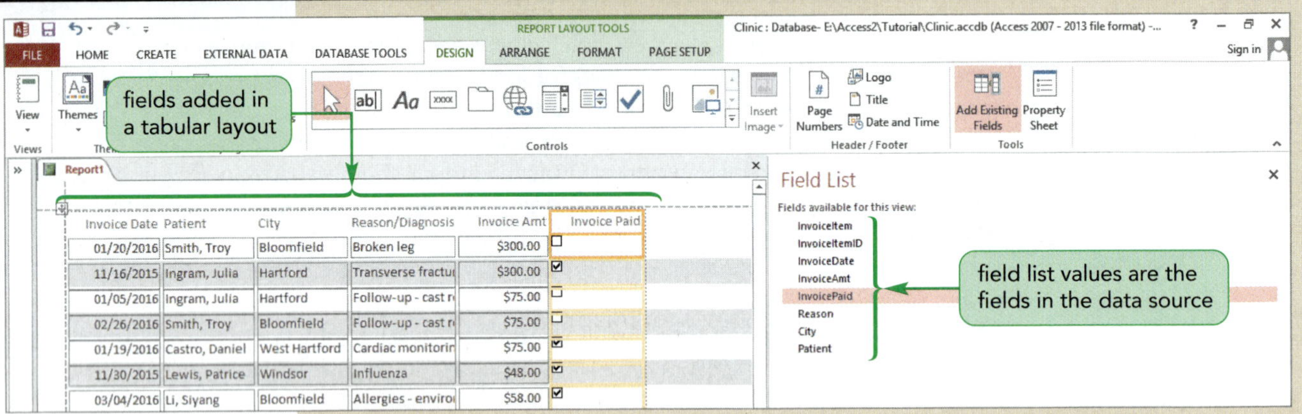

Trouble? If you add the wrong field to the report, click the field's column heading, press and hold the Shift key, click one of the field values in the column to select the column, release the Shift key, click the HOME tab on the Ribbon, and then in the Records group, click the Delete button to delete the field. If you add a field in the wrong order, click the column heading in the tabular layout, press and hold the Shift key, click one of the field values in the column, release the Shift key, and then drag the column to its correct columnar position.

You'll add the sixth field, the InvoiceItem field, as a grouping field, so you are done working with the Field List pane.

6. Close the Field List pane, and then save the report as **rptInvoicesByItem**.

Next, you'll adjust the column widths in Layout view. Also, because the Invoice Amt and Invoice Paid columns are adjacent, you'll change the rightmost column heading to Paid to save space.

To resize and rename columns in Layout view:

1. Double-click **Invoice Paid** in the rightmost column, delete **Invoice** and the following space, and then press the **Enter** key.
2. Drag the right edge of the **Paid** control to the left to decrease the column's width so it just fits the column heading.
3. Click **Patient** to select the column, and then drag the right edge of the control to the right to increase its width, until it accommodates the contents of all data in the column.
4. Repeat Step 3 to resize the **City** and **Reason** columns, as shown in Figure 7-15.

The full text will not be displayed in the Reason text boxes, which is okay for now. You'll fine-tune the adjustments and the spacing between columns later in Design view.

Figure 7-15 **After resizing and renaming columns in Layout view**

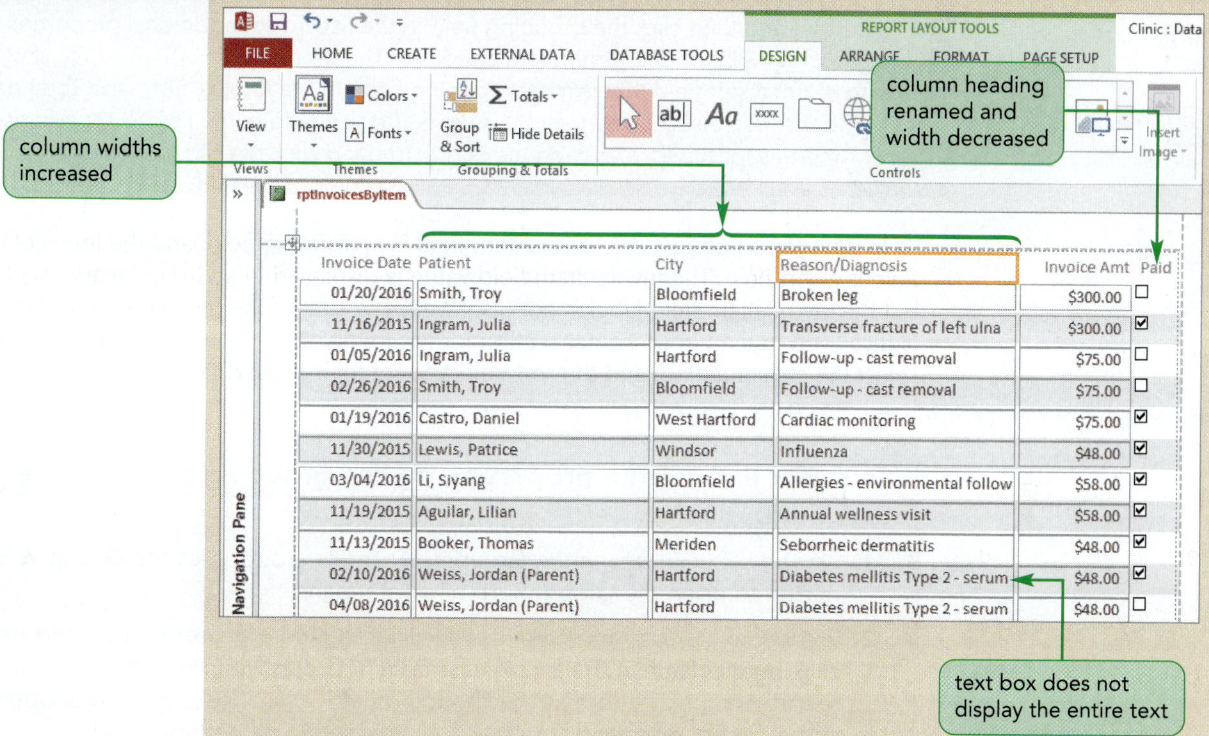

According to Raj's plan for the report (see the Session 7.2 Visual Overview), the InvoiceItem field is a grouping field that is displayed in a Group Header section. Subtotals for the InvoiceAmt field are displayed in a Group Footer section for each InvoiceItem field value. Next you need to add the sorting and grouping data to the report.

Sorting and Grouping Data in a Report

Access lets you organize records in a report by sorting them using one or more sort fields. Each sort field can also be a grouping field. If you specify a sort field as a grouping field, you can include a Group Header section and a Group Footer section for the group. A Group Header section typically includes the name of the group, and a Group Footer section typically includes a count or subtotal for records in that group. Some reports have a Group Header section but not a Group Footer section, some reports have a Group Footer section but not a Group Header section, and some reports have both sections or have neither section.

You use the Group, Sort, and Total pane to select sort fields and grouping fields for a report. Each report can have up to 10 sort fields, and any of its sort fields can also be grouping fields.

REFERENCE

Sorting and Grouping Data in a Report

- Display the report in Layout view or Design view.
- If necessary, on the DESIGN tab, in the Grouping & Totals group, click the Group & Sort button to display the Group, Sort, and Total pane.
- To select a grouping field, in the Group, Sort, and Total pane click the Add a group button, and then click the grouping field in the list. To set additional properties for the grouping field, on the group field band click the More button.
- To select a sort field that is not a grouping field, in the Group, Sort, and Total pane click the Add a sort button, and then click the sort field in the list. To set additional properties for the sort field, on the sort field band click the More button.

In Raj's report design, the InvoiceItem field is a grouping field, and the InvoiceDate field is a sort field. The InvoiceItem field value is displayed in a Group Header section, but the InvoiceItem field label is not displayed. The sum of the InvoiceAmt field values is displayed in the Group Footer section for the InvoiceItem grouping field. Next, you'll select the grouping field and the sort field and set their properties.

To select and set the properties for the grouping field and the sort field:

1. On the DESIGN tab, in the Grouping & Totals group, click the **Group & Sort** button to open the Group, Sort, and Total pane.
2. In the Group, Sort, and Total pane, click the **Add a group** button, and then click **InvoiceItem** in the list. Access adds a Group Header section to the report with InvoiceItem as the grouping field, and adds group band options in the Group, Sort, and Total pane for this section. See Figure 7-16.

Figure 7-16 After selecting InvoiceItem as a grouping field in Layout view

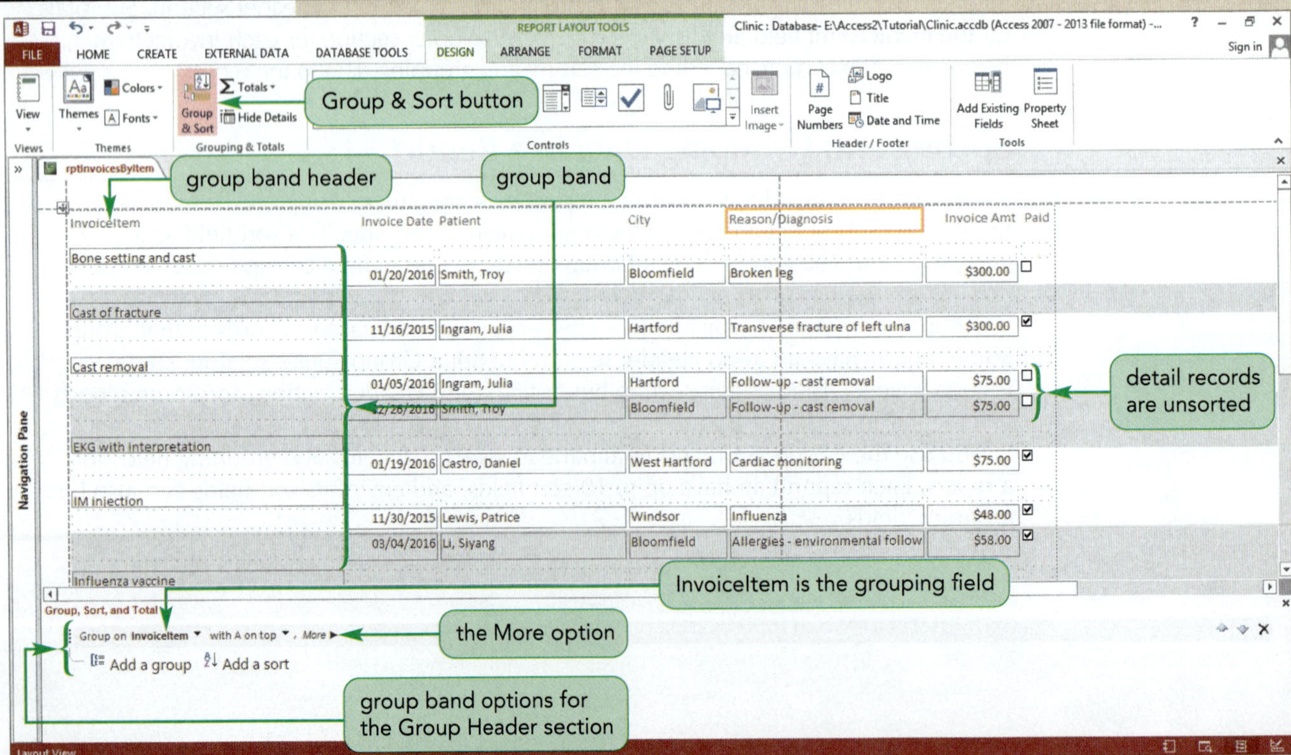

InvoiceItem is now a bound control in the report in a Group Header section that displays a field value text box. The group band options in the Group, Sort, and Total pane contains the name of the grouping field (InvoiceItem), the sort order ("with A on top" to indicate ascending), and the More option, which you click to display more options for the grouping field. You can click the "with A on top" arrow to change to descending sort order ("with Z on top").

Notice that the addition of the grouping field has moved the detail records to the right; you'll move them back to the left later in this tutorial. Also, notice that the detail records are unsorted, and Raj's design specifies an ascending sort on the InvoiceDate field. Next, you'll select this field as a secondary sort field; the InvoiceItem grouping field is the primary sort field.

3. In the Group, Sort, and Total pane, click the **Add a sort** button, and then click **InvoiceDate** in the list. Access displays the detail records in ascending order by InvoiceDate and adds a sort band for the InvoiceDate field in the Group, Sort, and Total pane.

   Next, you'll display all the options for the InvoiceItem group band field, and set group band options as shown in Raj's report design.

4. Click ⋮ to the left of the group band options to select them, and then click **More** to display all group band options. See Figure 7-17. Next, you need to delete the Invoice Item label.

Figure 7-17 After expanding the group band

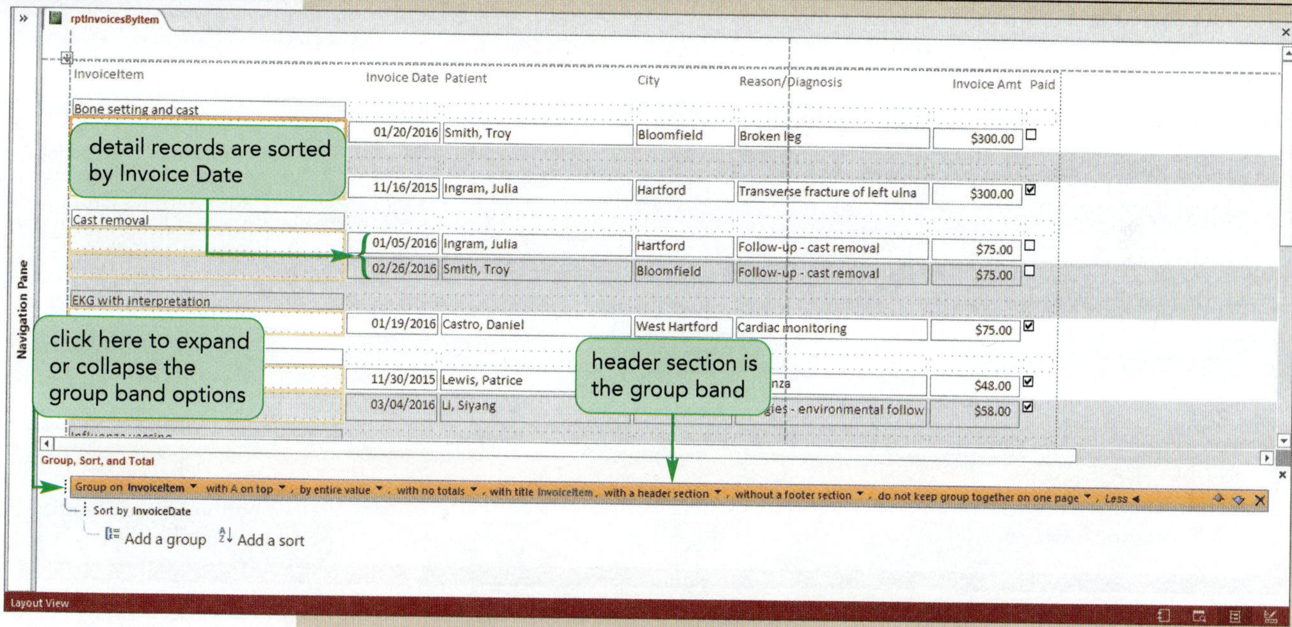

5. In the "with title Invoice Item" option, click the **Invoice Item** link to open the Zoom dialog box, press the **Delete** key to delete the expression, and then click the **OK** button. The Invoice Item label is deleted from the report, and the option in the group band options changes to "with title click to add."

   Next you'll set the Keep Together property. The **Keep Together property** prints a group header on a page only if there is enough room on the page to print the first detail record for the group; otherwise, the group header prints at the top of the next page.

6. In the group band options, click the **do not keep group together on one page** arrow, and then click **keep header and first record together on one page**.
7. In the group band options, click **More** to expand the options (if necessary), click the **without a footer section** arrow, and then click **with a footer section**. Access adds a Group Footer section for the InvoiceItem grouping band field, but the report doesn't display this new section until you add controls to it.
8. In the group band options, click **More** to expand the options (if necessary), click the **with no totals** arrow to open the Totals menu, click the **Total On** arrow, click **InvoiceAmt**, make sure **Sum** is selected in the Type box, and then click the **Show Grand Total** check box. The group band options collapse.
9. In the group band options, click **More** to expand the options (if necessary), click the **with InvoiceAmt totaled** arrow, click the **Total On** arrow, click **InvoiceAmt**, and then click the **Show subtotal in group footer** check box. This adds subtotals in the Amount column, at the bottom of each group.
10. In the group band options, click **More** to expand the options (if necessary). The group band options shows the InvoiceAmt subtotals and a grand total added to the report. See Figure 7-18.

Figure 7-18 After setting properties in the group band

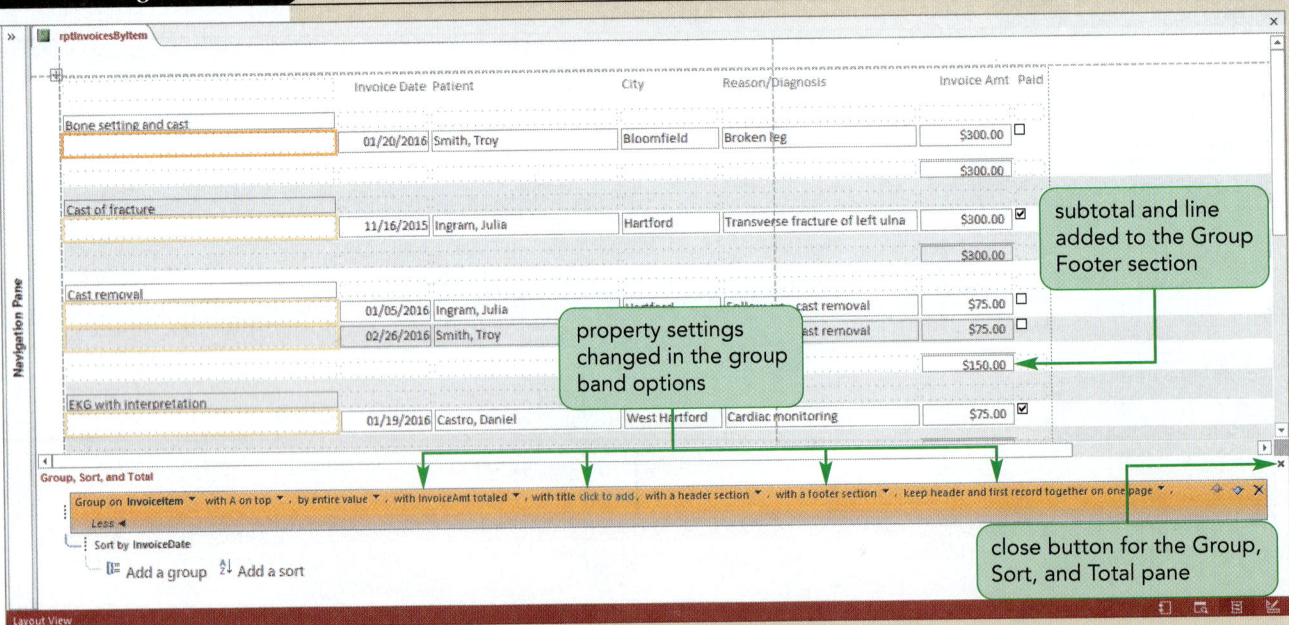

11. Save your report changes, switch to Print Preview, and then use the navigation buttons to review every page until you reach the end of the report—noticing in particular the details of the report format and the effects of the Keep Together property. Also, notice that because the grouping field forces the detail values to the right, the current report design prints the detail values across two pages.

Before you can move the detail values to the left onto one page, you need to remove all controls from the control layout.

To remove controls from a control layout in Layout view:

1. Switch to Layout view.
2. Click the **layout selector**, which is located at the top-left corner of the column heading line, to select the entire control layout. An orange outline, which identifies the controls that you've selected, appears around the labels and text boxes in the report, and a yellow outline appears around the other controls in the report.
3. Right-click one of the selected controls to open the shortcut menu, point to **Layout**, and then click **Remove Layout**. This removes the selected controls from the layout so they can be moved without affecting the other controls.

   Next you'll move all the controls to the left except for the InvoiceItem text box. You have to be careful when you move the remaining controls to the left. If you try to select all the column headings and the text boxes, you're likely to miss the subtotal and grand total controls. The safest technique is to select all controls in the report, and then remove the InvoiceItem text box from the selection. This latter step, removing individual controls from a selection, must be done in Design view because it doesn't work in Layout view.
4. Switch to Design view, click the **Format** tab, and then in the Selection group, click the **Select All** button. All controls in the report are now selected.
5. Hold down the **Shift** key, click the **InvoiceItem** text box in the InvoiceItem Header section to remove this control from the selection, and then release the **Shift** key.
6. Hold down the ← key to move the selected controls rapidly to the left edge of the report, and then release the ← key. See Figure 7-19.

Figure 7-19 After moving all controls to the left in the report

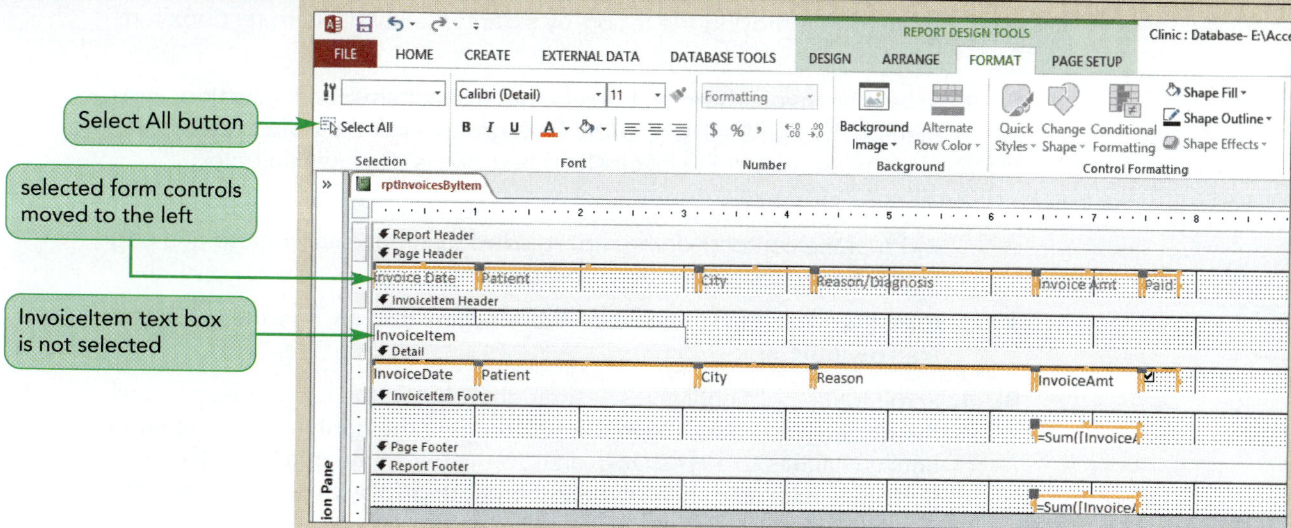

The grand total of the InvoiceAmt field values is displayed at the end of the report, and subtotals are displayed for each unique InvoiceItem field value in the Group Footer section. It's possible for subtotals to appear in an orphaned footer section. An **orphaned footer section** appears by itself at the top of a page, and the detail lines for the section appear on the previous page. When you set the Keep Together property for the grouping field, you set it to keep the group and the first detail record together on one page to prevent an **orphaned header section**, which is a section that appears by itself at the bottom of a page. To prevent both types of orphaned sections, you'll set the Keep Together property to keep the whole group together on one page.

In addition, you need to fine-tune the sizes of the text boxes in the Detail section, adjust the spacing between columns, and make other adjustments to the current content of the report design before adding a report title, the date, and page number to the Page Header section. You'll make most of these report design changes in Design view.

Working with Controls in Design View

Compared to Layout view, Design view gives you greater control over the placement and sizing of controls, and lets you add and manipulate many more controls; however, this power comes at the expense of not being able to see live data in the controls to guide you as you make changes.

The rptInvoicesByItem report has five sections that contain controls: the Page Header section contains the six column heading labels; the InvoiceItem Header section (a Group Header section) contains the InvoiceItem text box; the Detail section contains the six bound controls; the InvoiceItem Footer section (a Group Footer section) contains a line and the subtotal text box; and the Report Footer section contains a line and the grand total text box.

You'll move and resize controls in the report in Design view. The Group, Sort, and Total pane is still open, so first you'll change the Keep Together property setting.

To change the report size:

1. In the Group, Sort, and Total pane, click ⋮ to the left of the group band options to select it, click **More** to display all group options, click the **keep header and first record together on one page** arrow, click **keep whole group together on one page**, and then click the Close button ✕ in the top right corner of the Group, Sort, and Total pane to close it.

   You'll start improving the report by setting the InvoiceItem text box font to bold.

2. Select the **InvoiceItem** text box in the InvoiceItem Header section, and then on the FORMAT tab, in the Font group, click the **Bold** button. The placeholder text in the InvoiceItem text box is displayed in bold.

   The report's width is approximately 16 inches, which is much wider than the width of the contents of the report, so you'll reduce its width to fit a page that is 8.5 inches wide with narrow margins.

3. Click the PAGE SETUP tab, click the **Margins button**, and then click the **Narrow button**.

4. Scroll to the right until you see the right edge of the report (the point where the dotted grid ends), move the pointer over the right edge of the report until it changes to a ↔ shape, drag to the left to the 8-inch mark on the horizontal ruler, and then scroll to the left to display the entire report from the left (if necessary). See Figure 7-20.

Figure 7-20 After reducing the width of the report

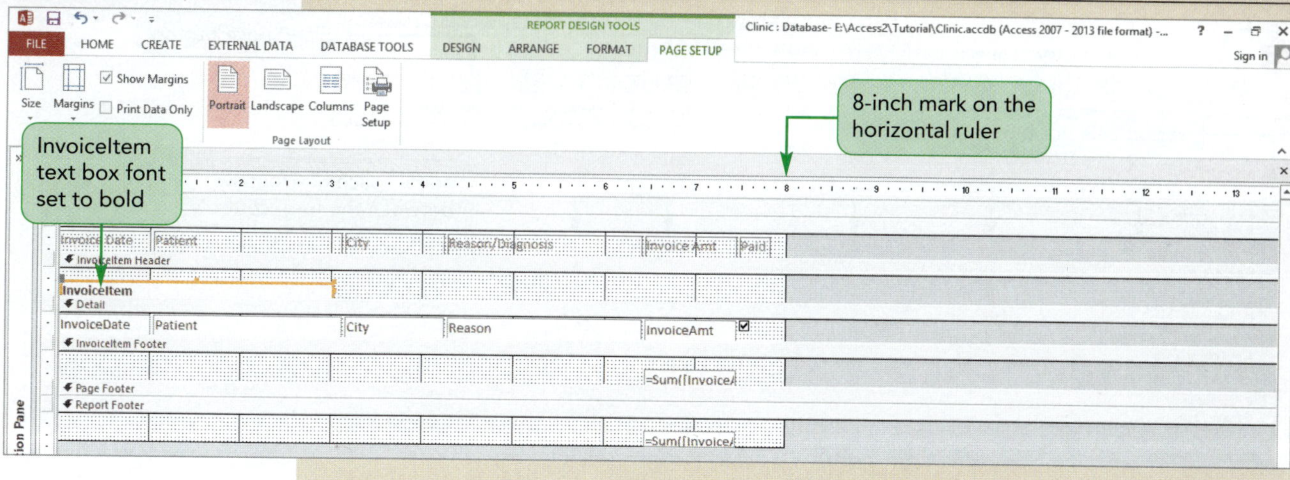

The text boxes in the Detail section are crowded together with little space between them, and the form controls are too wide for a page with normal margins. Your reports shouldn't have too much space between columns, but reports are easier to read when the columns are separated more than they are in the rptInvoicesByItem report. Sometimes the amount of spacing is dictated by the users of the report, but you also need to work with the minimum size of the form controls as well. To design this report to fit on a page with narrow margins, the report width will have to be 8.5 inches minus the left and right margins of 0.25 inches each, which results in a maximum report width of 8 inches (8.5"–0.25"–0.25"). This is the size you already used to reduce the report grid in Design view. Next, you'll add some space between the columns while ensuring they still fit in the 8-inch report width. First, you'll resize the Invoice Date and Patient form controls in Layout view, and then you'll arrange the columns in Design view. You'll size the corresponding heading and field value text boxes for each column to be the same width.

TIP

You can resize labels and controls added with the Label tool using Size, To Fit, but you can't resize text boxes using the To Fit method.

To move and resize controls in the report:

1. Switch to Layout view, click the **Invoice Date** heading, press and hold the **Shift** key, and then click on one of the Invoice Date field values to select all of the Invoice Date text boxes.
2. Drag the right side of the controls to the left to reduce the size of the text boxes to fit the data better.
3. Repeat Steps 1 and 2 for the Patient heading and field values to reduce their widths to fit the data better.

   Next you'll adjust the spacing between the controls to distribute them evenly across the page.

4. Switch to Design view, click the **FORMAT** tab, and then in the Selection group click the **Select All button** to select all controls.
5. Press and hold the **Shift** key and click the **Invoice Item** control to deselect it.
6. Click the **ARRANGE** tab, in the Size & Ordering group click the **Size/Space button**, and then click **Equal Horizontal**. The form controls are shifted horizontally so the spacing between them is equal. See Figure 7-21.

Figure 7-21 After resizing and spacing controls in Design view

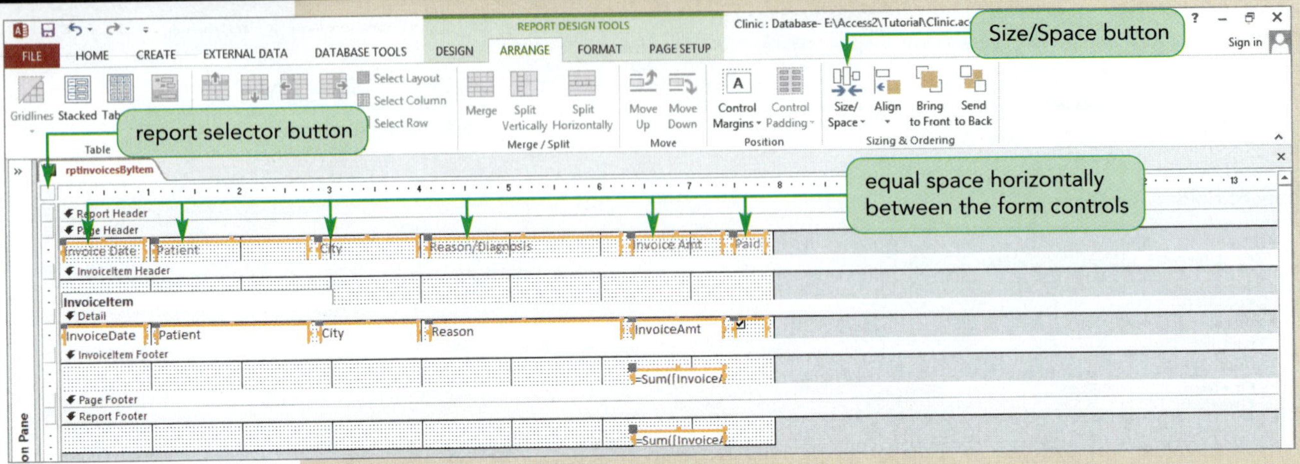

The Patient and Reason text boxes may not be wide enough to display the entire field value in all cases. For the Patient and Reason text boxes, you'll set their Can Grow property to Yes. The **Can Grow property**, when set to Yes, expands a text box vertically to fit the field value when the report is printed, previewed, or viewed in Layout and Report views.

TIP

You can select two or more controls, and then set common properties for the selected controls, instead of setting them one control at a time.

7. Click the **DESIGN** tab, click the **Report Selector** button to deselect all controls, select the **Patient** and **Reason** text boxes in the Detail section, right-click one of the selected controls, and then on the contextual menu click **Properties**.
8. On the Property Sheet, click the **Format** tab, scroll down the Property Sheet to the Can Grow property, and then if the Can Grow property is set to Yes, set it to **No**. The default setting for this feature may not work properly, so to ensure the setting is applied correctly, you must make sure it is first set to No.

   Trouble? If you don't see the CanGrow property on the Format tab, double-check to ensure you've selected the Patient and Reason controls in the Detail section, not in the Page Header section.
9. Change the Can Grow property value to **Yes**, close the Property Sheet, and then save your report changes.
10. Switch to Print Preview, and then review every page of the report, ending on the last page. See Figure 7-22.

Figure 7-22 Reviewing the report changes in Print Preview

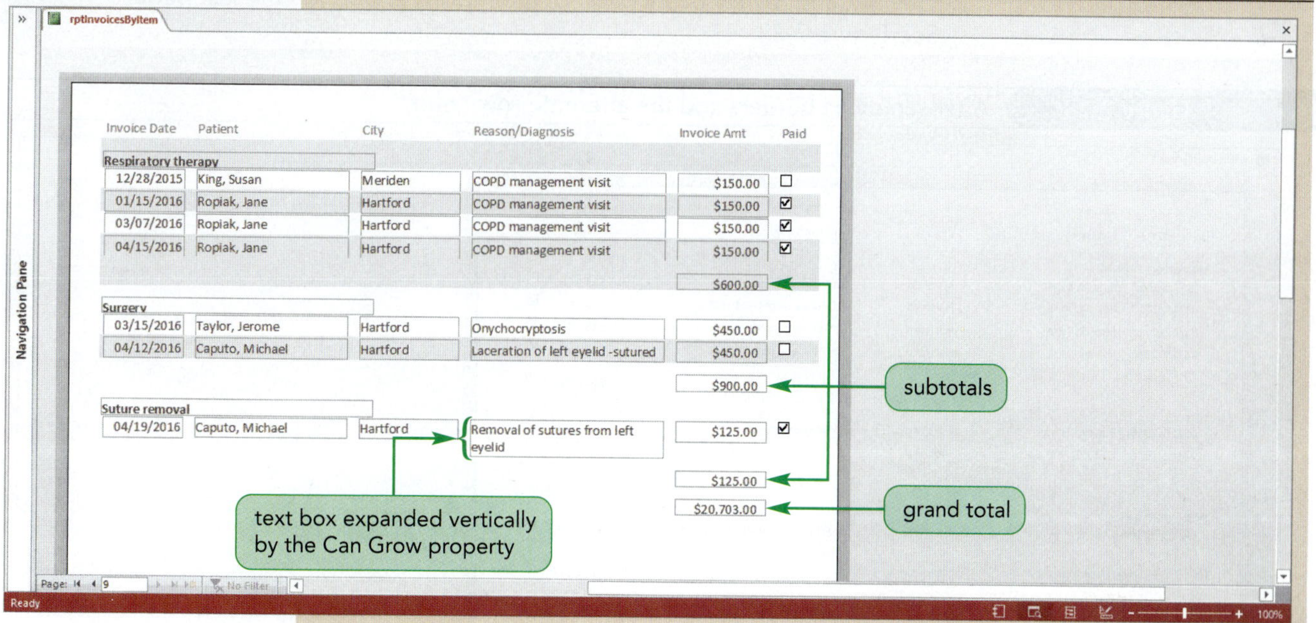

The groups stay together on one page, except for the groups that have too many detail lines to fit on one page. The Can Grow property correctly expands the height of the Patient and Reason text boxes.

Also, the lines that were displayed above the subtotals and grand total are no longer displayed, and the commas in the values are not fully visible. You'll add those lines back in the report and resize the text boxes. First, Raj thinks the borders around the text boxes and the alternate row color are too distracting, so you'll remove them from the report.

To remove the borders and alternate row color:

1. Close the Print Preview and switch to Design view.
2. Click the **FORMAT** tab, and then in the Selection group, click the **Select All** button.
3. Right-click one of the selected controls, and then click **Properties** on the shortcut menu to open the Property Sheet.
4. Click the **Format** tab (if necessary) in the Property Sheet, click the right side of the **Border Style** box, and then click **Transparent**. The transparent setting will remove the boxes from the report by making them transparent.
5. Click the **InvoiceItem Header** section bar, click the right side of the **Alternate Back Color** box in the Property Sheet, and then click **No Color** at the bottom of the gallery. This setting removes the alternate row color from the InvoiceItem Header section.
6. Click the **Detail** section bar, and then on the **FORMAT** tab, in the Background group, click the **Alternate Row Color** button, and then click **No Color** at the bottom of the gallery. The Alternate Back Color property setting in the Property Sheet is now set to No Color.
7. Repeat Step 6 for the **InvoiceItem Footer** section.

TIP

You can also control the Alternate Back Color property using the Alternate Row Color button because the two options set the same property.

8. Close the Property Sheet, save your report changes, switch to Print Preview, and review every page of the report, ending on the last page. See Figure 7-23.

Figure 7-23 After removing borders and the alternate row color

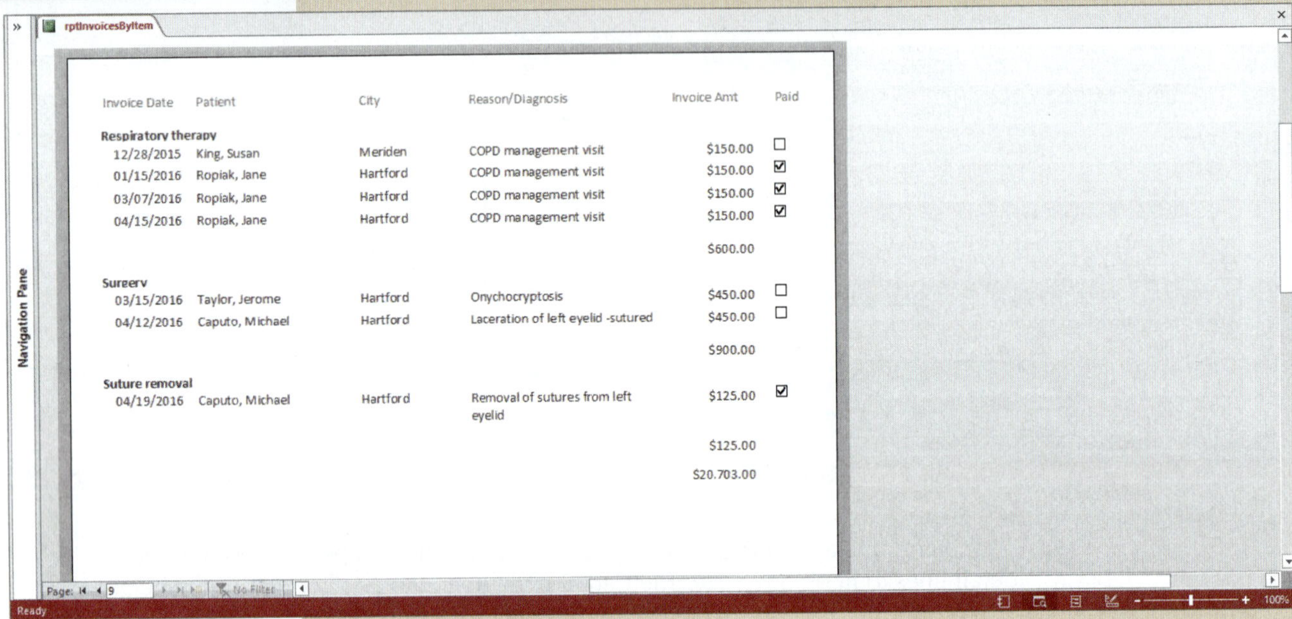

Next, you'll add lines to the report.

Adding Lines to a Report

You've used the Line tool to add lines to a form. You can also use the Line tool to add lines to a report. Previously, you added a line to separate the header content from the rest of the report. Now you'll add lines to separate the values from the subtotals and grand total. You'll switch to Design view and use the Line tool to add a single line above the subtotal control and a double line above the grand total control. First, you'll resize the subtotal and grand total text boxes.

To add lines to the report:

1. Close the Print Preview and switch to Design view.
2. In the InvoiceItem Footer section, click the text box control to select it, and then resize the control from the top so its height increases by one row of grid dots.
3. Repeat Step 2 to resize the text box control in the Report Footer section.
4. On the DESIGN tab, in the Controls group, click the **More** button to open the Controls gallery.
5. Click the **Line** tool, position the pointer's plus symbol (+) in the InvoiceItem Footer section at the upper-left corner of the text box, hold down the **Shift** key, drag a horizontal line from left to right so the end of the line aligns with the upper-right corner of the text box, release the mouse button, and then release the **Shift** key.

6. In the Report Footer section, click the text box, press the ↓ key four times to move the control down slightly in the section, and then deselect all controls.
7. On the DESIGN tab, in the Controls group, click the **More** button, click the **Line** tool, position the pointer's plus symbol (+) in the Report Footer section at the grid dot just above the upper-left corner of the text box, hold down the **Shift** key, drag a horizontal line from left to right so the end of the line aligns with the right edge of the text box, release the mouse button, and then release the **Shift** key.

   Next, you'll copy and paste the line in the Report Footer section, and then align the copied line into position.
8. Right-click the selected line in the Report Footer section, and then click **Copy** on the shortcut menu.
9. Right-click the **Report Footer** section bar, and then click **Paste** on the shortcut menu. A copy of the line is pasted in the upper-left corner of the Report Footer section.
10. Press the ↓ key four times to move the copied line down in the section, hold down the **Shift** key, click the original line in the Report Footer section to select both lines, release the **Shift** key, right-click the copied line to open the shortcut menu, point to **Align**, and then click **Right**. A double line is now positioned above the grand total text box.
11. Save your report changes, switch to Print Preview, and then navigate to the last page of the report. See Figure 7-24.

Figure 7-24 After adding lines to the report

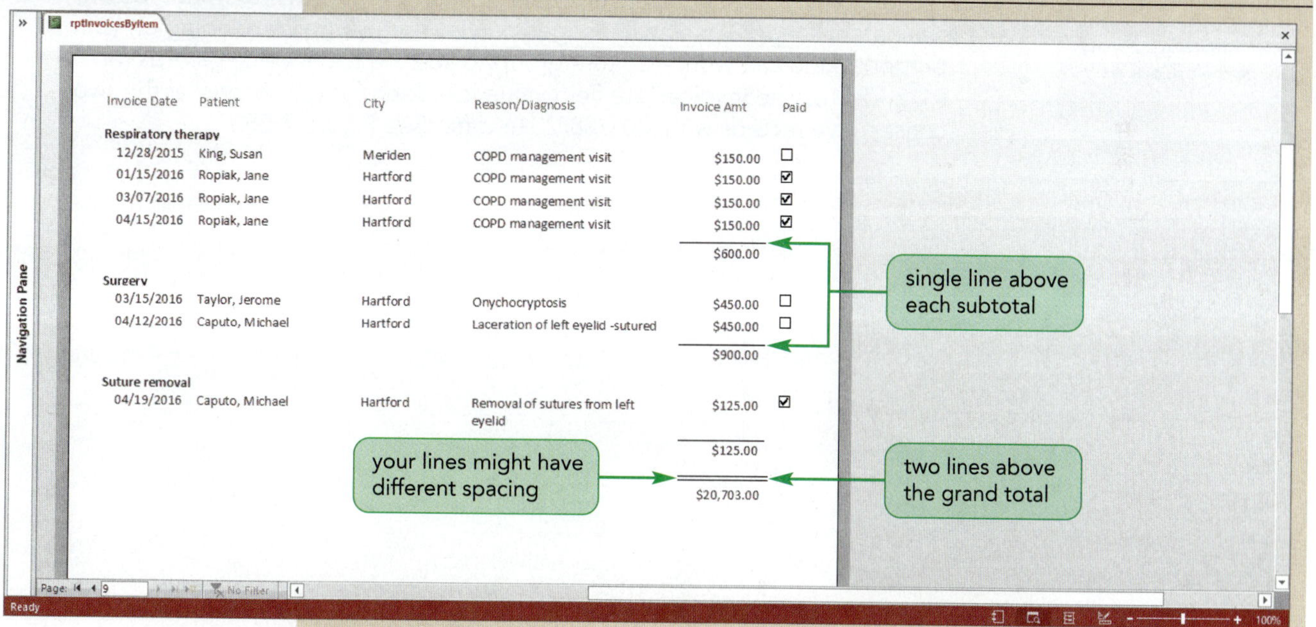

For the rptInvoicesByItem report, the InvoiceDate field is a sort field. Two or more consecutive detail report lines can have the same InvoiceDate field value. In these cases, Raj wants the InvoiceDate field value printed for the first detail line but not for subsequent detail lines because he believes it makes the printed information easier to read.

Hiding Duplicate Values in a Report

You use the **Hide Duplicates property** to hide a control in a report when the control's value is the same as that of the preceding record in the group.

REFERENCE

Hiding Duplicate Values in a Report

- Display the report in Layout or Design view.
- Open the Property Sheet for the field whose duplicate values you want to hide.
- Set the Hide Duplicates property to Yes, and then close the Property Sheet.

TIP

Use Hide Duplicates only on fields that are sorted. Otherwise it may look as if data is missing.

Your next design change to the report is to hide duplicate InvoiceDate field values in the Detail section. This change will make the report easier to read.

To hide the duplicate InvoiceDate field values:

1. Close Print Preview, switch to Design view, and then click below the grid to deselect all controls.
2. Open the Property Sheet for the **InvoiceDate** text box in the Detail section.
3. Click the **Format** tab (if necessary), scroll down the Property Sheet (if necessary), click the right side of the **Hide Duplicates** box, and then click **Yes**.
4. Close the Property Sheet, save your report changes, switch to Print Preview, navigate to page 2 (the actual page you view might vary depending on your printer) to the Lab work - Culture group to see the two invoice records for 01/28/2016. The InvoiceDate field value is hidden for the second of the two consecutive records with a 01/28/2016 date. See Figure 7-25.

TIP

For properties offering a list of choices, you can double-click the property name repeatedly to cycle through the options in the list.

Figure 7-25 **Report in Print Preview with hidden duplicate values**

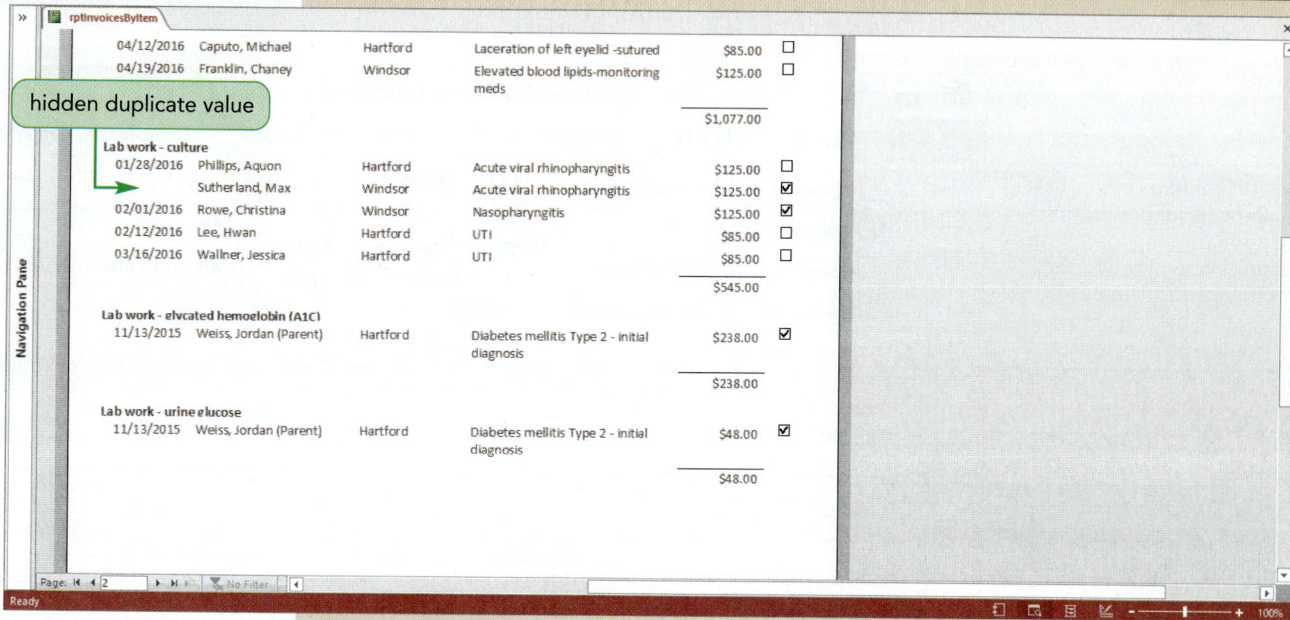

5. If you are not continuing on to the next session, close the Clinic database.

You have completed the Detail section, the Group Header section, and the Group Footer section of the custom report. In the next session, you will complete the custom report according to Raj's design by adding controls to the Page Header section.

REVIEW

Session 7.2 Quick Check

1. What is a detail report? A summary report?
2. The ______________ property prints a group header on a page only if there is enough room on the page to print the first detail record for the group; otherwise, the group header prints at the top of the next page.
3. A(n) ______________ section appears by itself at the top of a page, and the detail lines for the section appear on the previous page.
4. The ______________ property, when set to Yes, expands a text box vertically to fit the field value when a report is printed, previewed, or viewed in Layout and Report views.
5. Why might you want to hide duplicate values in a report?

Session 7.3 Visual Overview:

The contents in the Report Header section appear at the top of the first page of the report. This Report Header section has a height of 0 and no contents.

The **Date function** will display the current date.

The Group Footer section contents appear at the bottom of each group.

The Page Footer section contents appear at the bottom of every page. This Page Footer section has 0 height and no contents.

The Report Footer section contents appear at the bottom of the last page of the report.

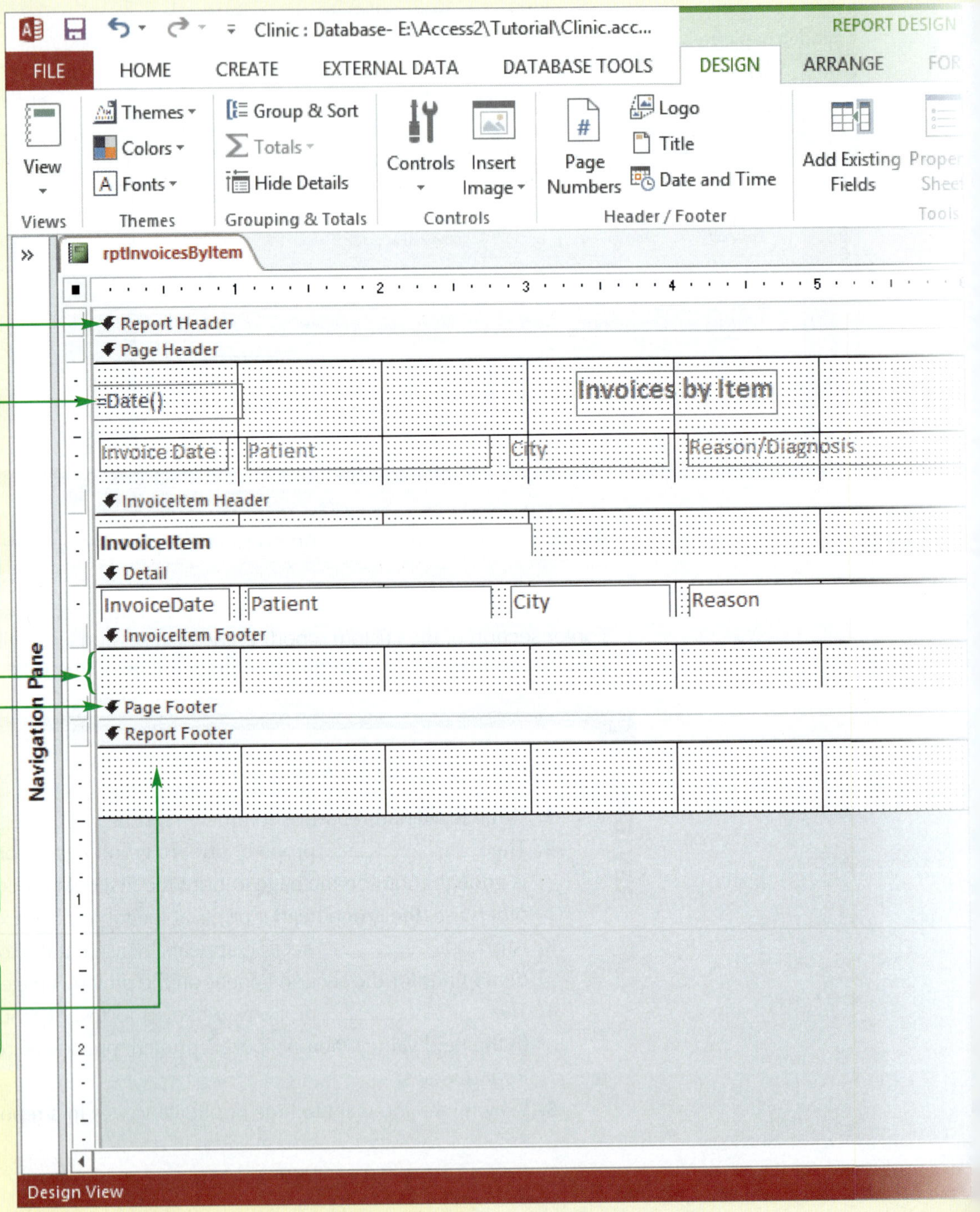

Custom report in Design view

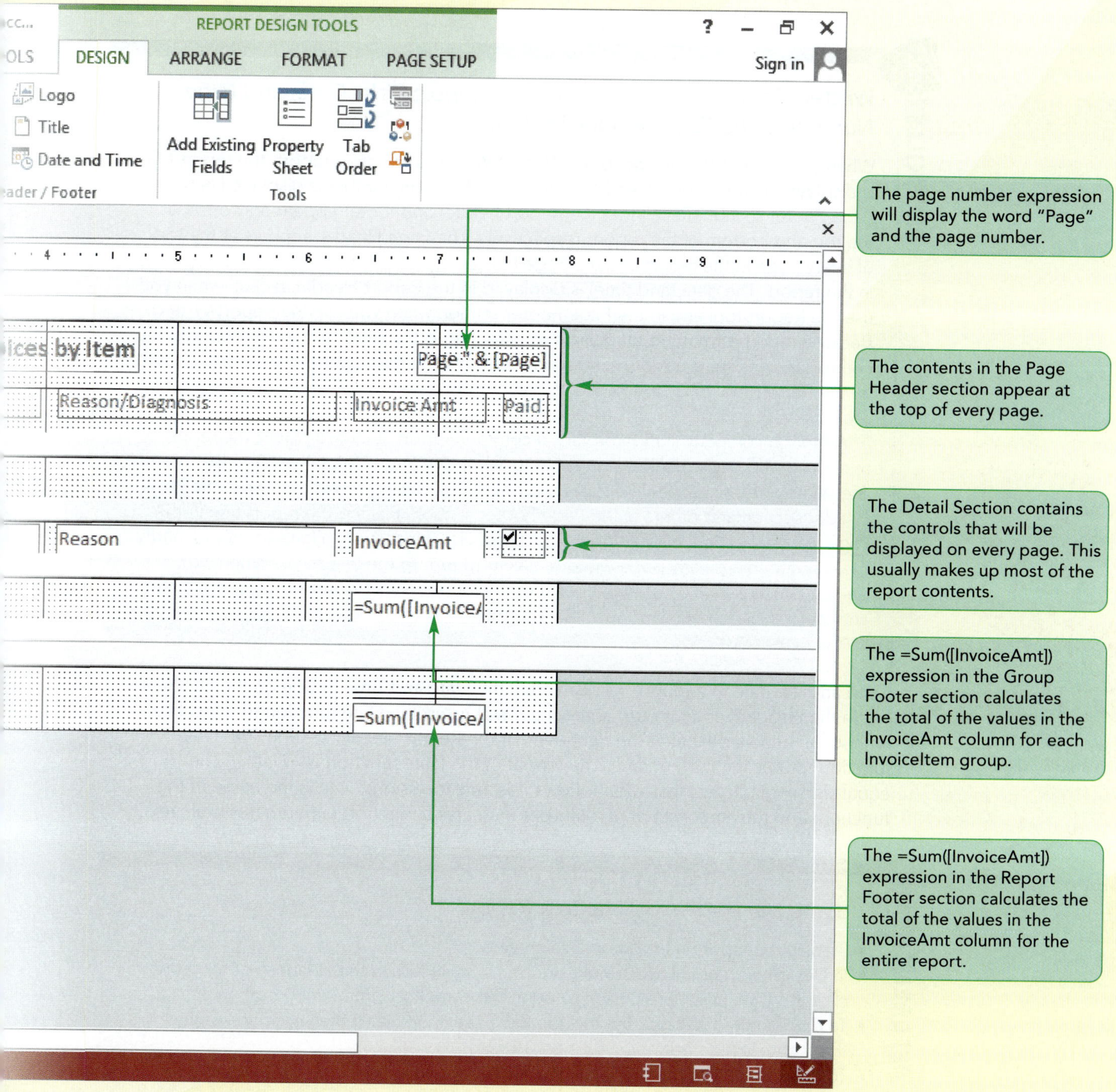

Adding the Date to a Report

According to Raj's design, the rptInvoicesByItem report includes the date in the Page Header section, along with the report title, the page number, the column heading labels, and a line below the labels.

PROSKILLS

Written Communication: Placing the Report Title, Date, and Page Number in the Page Header Section

When you use the Report tool or the Report Wizard to create a report, the report title is displayed in the Report Header section and the page number is displayed in the Page Footer section. Recall that the Report header and footer appear only once, at the top and bottom of the report, respectively. The Page Header appears at the top of every page in the report and the Page Footer appears at the bottom of every page in the report. The date (and time) is displayed in the Report Header section when you use the Report tool and in the Page Footer section when you use the Report Wizard. Because report formatting guidelines require that all the reports in a database display controls in consistent positions, you have to move the date control for reports created by the Report tool or by the Report Wizard so the date is displayed in the same section for all reports.

Although company standards vary, a common report standard places the report title, date, and page number on the same line in the Page Header section. Using one line saves vertical space in the report compared to placing some controls in the Page Header section and others in the Page Footer section. Placing the report title in the Page Header section, instead of in the Report Header section, allows users to identify the report name on any page without having to turn to the first page. When you develop reports with a consistent format, the report users become more productive and more confident working with the information in the reports.

To add the date to a report, you can click the Date and Time button on the DESIGN tab in the Header/Footer group, and Access will insert the Date function in a text box without an attached label at the right edge of the Report Header section. The Date function returns the current date. The format of the Date function is *=Date()*. The equal sign (=) indicates that what follows it is an expression; *Date* is the name of the function; and the empty set of parentheses indicates a function rather than simple text.

REFERENCE

Adding the Date and Time to a Report

- Display the report in Layout or Design view.
- In Design view or in Layout view, on the DESIGN tab, in the Header/Footer group, click the Date and Time button to open the Date and Time dialog box.
- To display the date, click the Include Date check box, and then click one of the three date option buttons.
- To display the time, click the Include Time check box, and then click one of the three time option buttons.
- Click the OK button.

In Raj's design for the report, the date appears at the left edge of the Page Header section. You'll add the date to the report, and then cut the date from its default location in the Report Header section and paste it into the Page Header section.

To add the date to the Page Header section:

1. If you took a break after the previous session, make sure that the Clinic database is open, that the rptInvoicesByItem report is open, and that the Navigation Pane is closed.

   You can add the current date in Layout view or Design view. However, because you can't cut and paste controls between sections in Layout view, you'll add the date in Design view. First, you'll move the column heading labels down in the Page Header section to make room for the controls you'll be adding above them.

2. Switch to Design view, increase the height of the Page Header section by dragging down the bottom of the Page Header border until the 1-inch mark on the vertical ruler appears, select all six labels in the Page Header section, and then move the labels down until the tops of the labels are at the 0.5-inch mark on the vertical ruler. You may find it easier to use the arrow keys to position the labels, rather than the mouse.

   Raj's report design has a horizontal line below the labels. You'll add this line next.

3. On the DESIGN tab, in the Controls group, click the **More** button, click the **Line** tool, position the pointer's plus symbol (+) one grid dot below the lower-left corner of the Invoice Date label in the Page Header section, hold down the **Shift** key, drag a horizontal line from left to right so the end of the line aligns with the right edge of the Paid label, release the mouse button, and then release the **Shift** key.

4. Reduce the height of the Page Header section by dragging the bottom of the section up until it touches the bottom of the line you just added.

5. On the DESIGN tab, in the Header/Footer group, click the **Date and Time** button to open the Date and Time dialog box, make sure the **Include Date** check box is checked and the **Include Time** check box is unchecked, and then click the third date option button. See Figure 7-26.

Figure 7-26 Completed Date and Time dialog box

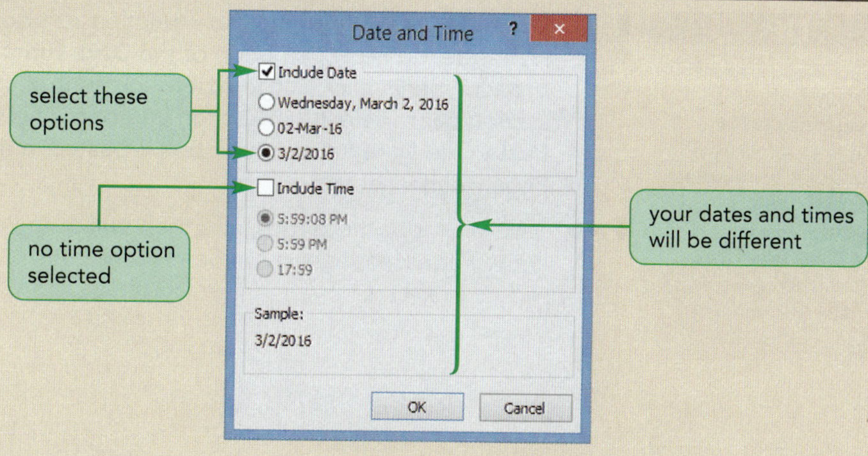

6. Click the **OK** button. The Date function is added to the Report Header section.

7. Click the **Date function** text box, and then click the **layout selector** ⊞ in the upper-left corner of the Report Header section. The Date function text box is part of a control layout with three additional boxes, which are empty cells. See Figure 7-27.

Figure 7-27 **Date function added to the Report Header section**

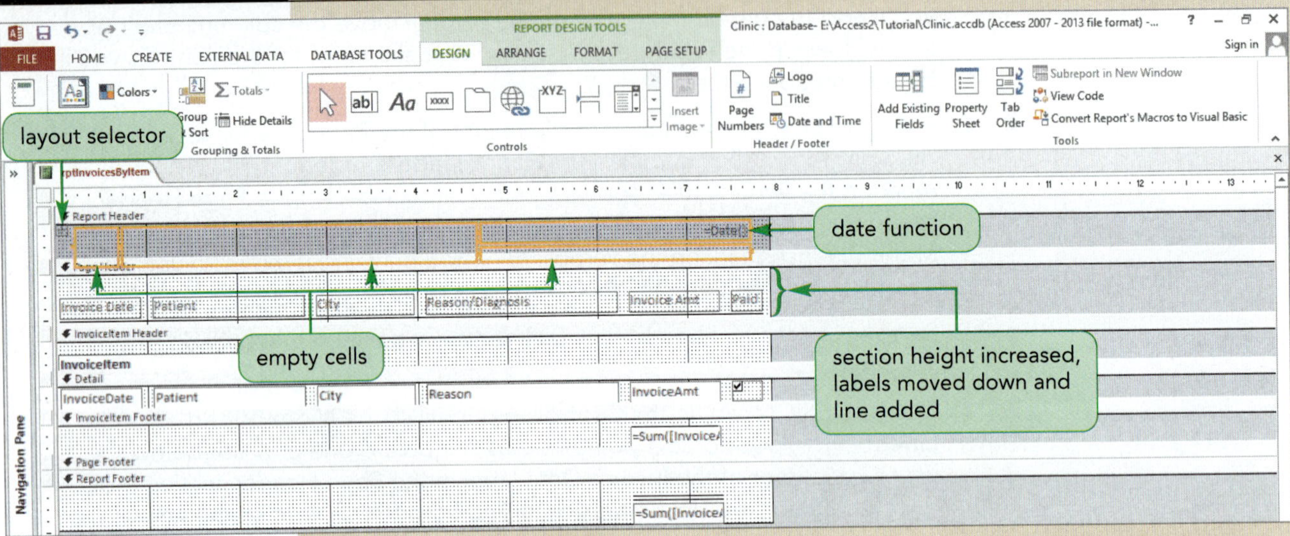

You need to remove these controls from the control layout before you work further with the Date function text box.

8. Right-click one of the selected controls, point to **Layout** on the shortcut menu, and then click **Remove Layout**. The three empty cells are deleted, and the Date function text box remains selected.

   The default size for the Date function text box accommodates long dates and long times, so the text box is much wider than needed for the date that will appear in the custom report. You'll decrease its width and move it to the Page Header section.

TIP

If a report includes a control with the Date function, the current date will be displayed each time the report is run. If you instead want a specific date to appear each time the report is run, use a label control that contains the date, rather than the Date function.

9. Decrease the width of the Date function text box from the left until it is one inch wide, right-click an edge of the **Date function** text box to open the shortcut menu, click **Cut** to delete the control, right-click the **Page Header** section bar to select that section and open the shortcut menu, and then click **Paste**. The Date function text box is pasted in the upper-left corner of the Page Header section.

10. Save your report changes, and then switch to Print Preview to view the date in the Page Header section. See Figure 7-28.

Figure 7-28 **Viewing the date in Print Preview**

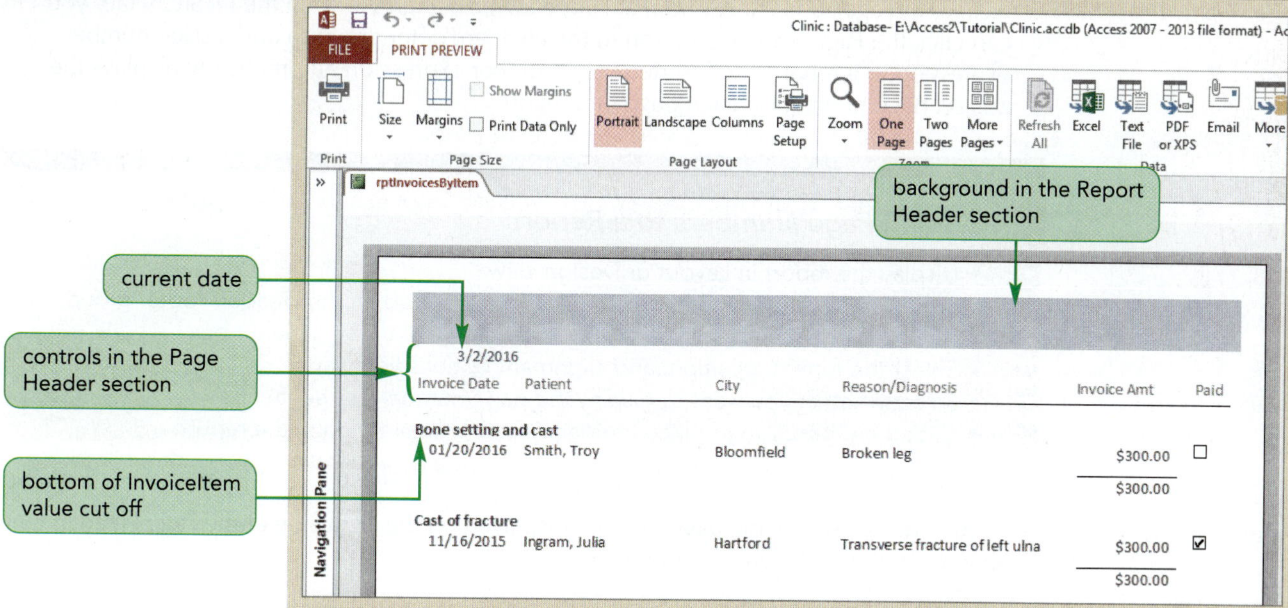

Trouble? Your year might appear with two digits instead of four digits as shown in Figure 7-28. Your date format might also differ, depending on your computer's date settings. These differences do not cause any problems.

Next you'll left-align the date in the text box in Design view.

11. Switch to Design view, make sure the Date function text box is selected, click the **FORMAT** tab, and then in the Font group, click the **Align Left** button.

Finally, notice that when you bolded the font in the InvoiceItem text box, you increased the size of the characters. You need to increase the height of the text boxes to fully display all characters in the text box.

12. Click the **InvoiceItem** text box, and then increase the height of the text box from the top by one row of grid dots.

INSIGHT

Choosing a Theme for a Database

Access has nine themes that you can use to set the font type and size and the color and other effects for the objects in a database. The default theme is the Office theme, which uses Calibri 11 font. You should either use the default theme or choose a theme immediately after creating the first table in the database. If you wait to choose a theme until after you've created a large number of objects in the database, the theme you choose will probably have a font different from Calibri 11, and you'll have to go back and resize the table and query datasheets and the form and report text boxes and labels.

You are now ready to add page numbers to the Page Header section. You'll also delete the empty Report Header section by decreasing its height to zero.

Adding Page Numbers to a Report

You can display page numbers in a report by including an expression in the Page Header or Page Footer section. In Layout view or Design view, on the DESIGN tab, you can click the Page Numbers button in the Header/Footer group to add a page number expression to a report. The inserted page number expression automatically displays the correct page number on each page of a report.

REFERENCE

Adding Page Numbers to a Report

- Display the report in Layout or Design view.
- In Design view or in Layout view, on the DESIGN tab, in the Header/Footer group, click the Page Numbers button to open the Page Numbers dialog box.
- Select the format, position, and alignment options you want.
- Select whether you want to display the page number on the first page.
- Click the OK button to place the page number expression in the report.

Raj's design shows the page number displayed on the right side of the Page Header section, bottom-aligned with the date.

To add page numbers to the Page Header section:

1. In the Report Header section, drag the bottom border up to the top of the section so the section's height is reduced to zero.
2. Click the **DESIGN tab**, and then in the Header/Footer group, click the **Page Numbers** button. The Page Numbers dialog box opens.

   You use the Format options to specify the format of the page number. Raj wants page numbers to appear as Page 1, Page 2, and so on. This is the "Page N" format option. You use the Position options to place the page numbers at the top of the page in the Page Header section or at the bottom of the page in the Page Footer section. Raj's design shows page numbers at the top of the page.
3. In the Format section, make sure that the **Page N** option button is selected, and then in the Position section, make sure that the **Top of Page [Header]** option button is selected.

   The report design shows page numbers at the right side of the page. You can specify this placement in the Alignment box.
4. Click the **Alignment** arrow, and then click **Right**.
5. Make sure the **Show Number on First Page** check box is checked, so the page number prints on the first page and all other pages as well. See Figure 7-29.

Figure 7-29 Completed Page Numbers dialog box

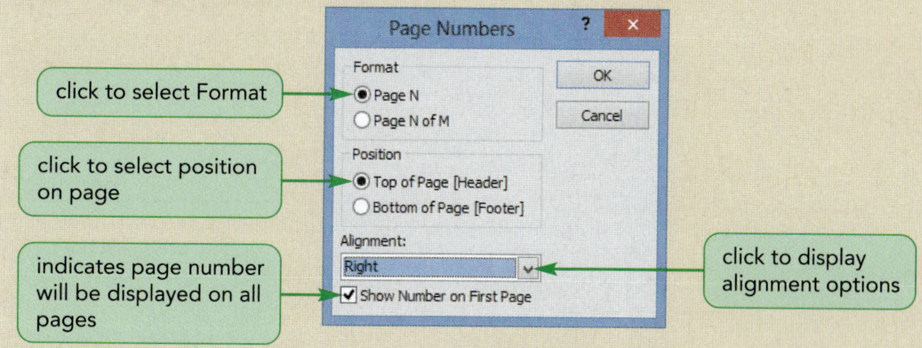

6. Click the **OK** button. A text box containing the expression *="Page " & [Page]* appears in the upper-right corner of the Page Header section. See Figure 7-30. The expression *="Page " & [Page]* in the text box means that the printed report will show the word "Page" followed by a space and the page number.

Figure 7-30 Page number expression added to the Page Header section

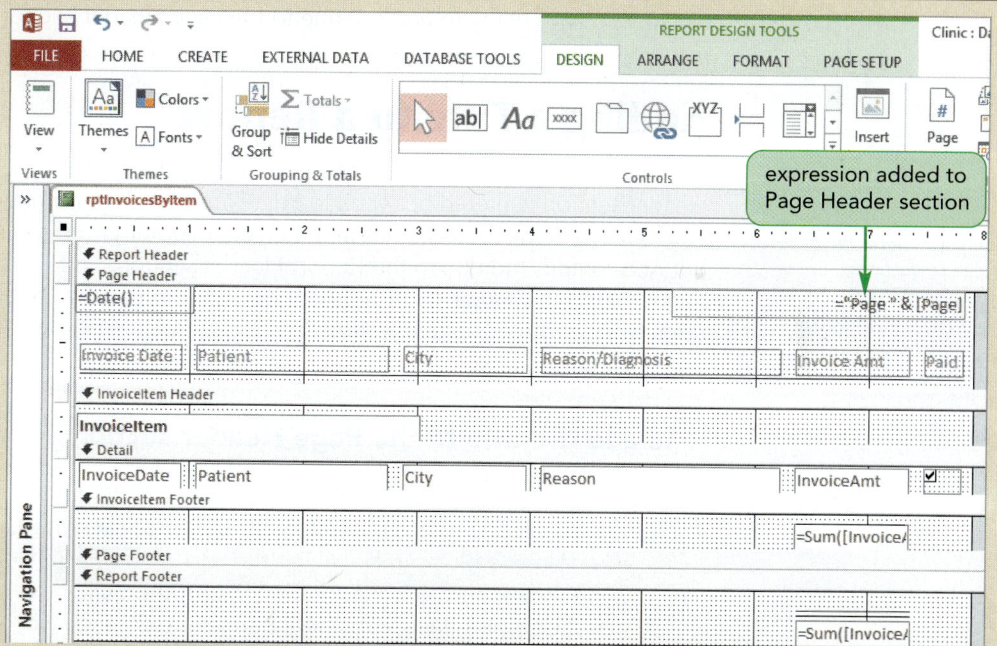

The page number text box is much wider than needed for the page number expression that will appear in the custom report. You'll decrease its width.

7. Click the **Page Number** text box, decrease its width from the left until it is one inch wide, and then move it to the left so its right edge aligns with the right edge of the Paid text box.
8. Save your report changes, and then switch to Print Preview. See Figure 7-31.

Figure 7-31 Date and page number in the Page Header section

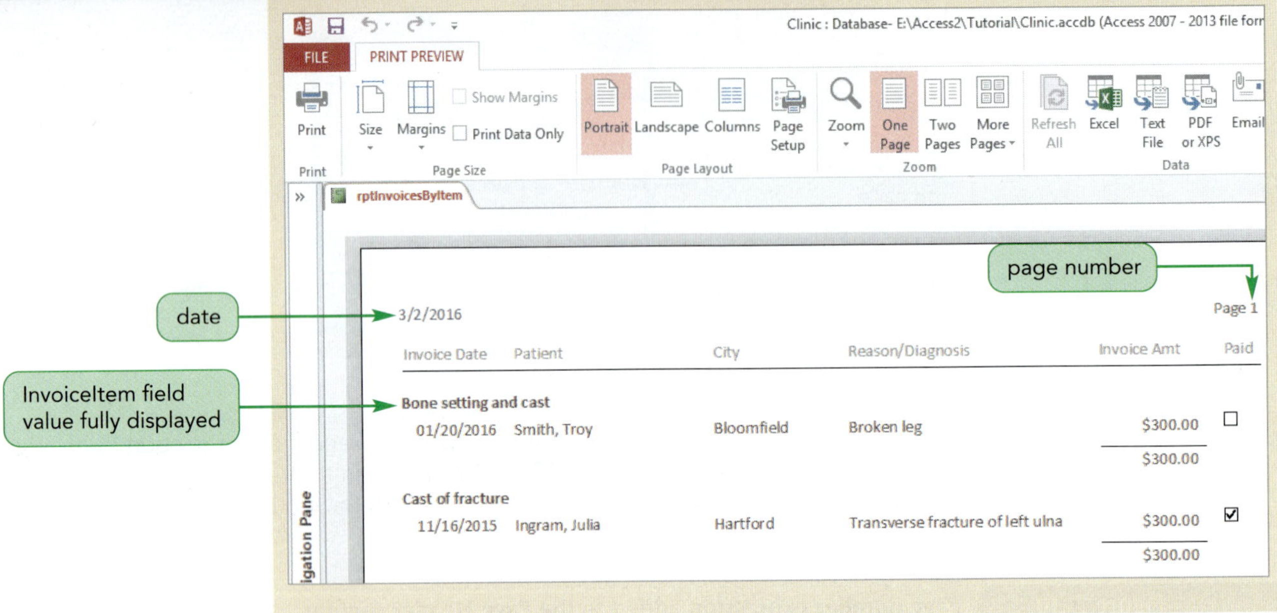

Now you are ready to add the title to the Page Header section.

Adding a Title to a Report

> **TIP**
>
> All reports should contain a title, either in the Report Header section to display only on the first page, or in the Page Header section to display on all pages.

Raj's report design includes the title "Invoices by Item," which you'll add to the Page Header section centered between the date and the page number. You could use the Title button on the DESIGN tab in the Header/Footer group to add the report title, but Access adds the title to the Report Header section, and Raj's design positions the title in the Page Header section. It will be easier to use the Label tool to add the title directly in the Page Header section.

To add the title to the Page Header section:

1. Close Print Preview and switch to Design view.
2. On the DESIGN tab, in the Controls group, click the **Label** tool Aa, position the pointer's plus symbol (+) at the top of the Page Header section at the 3-inch mark on the horizontal ruler, and then click the mouse button. The insertion point flashes inside a narrow box, which will expand as you type the report title.

   To match Raj's design, you need to type the title as "Invoices by Item," and then change its font size to 14 points and its style to bold.
3. Type **Invoices by Item**, and then press the **Enter** key.

4. Click the **FORMAT** tab, in the Font group click the **Font Size** arrow, click **14**, and then click the **Bold** button **B**. Increase the width of the label to fit the title, increase the height by two grid dots and move the label to the right so it is centered at the 4-inch mark. See Figure 7-32.

Figure 7-32 **Report title in the Page Header section**

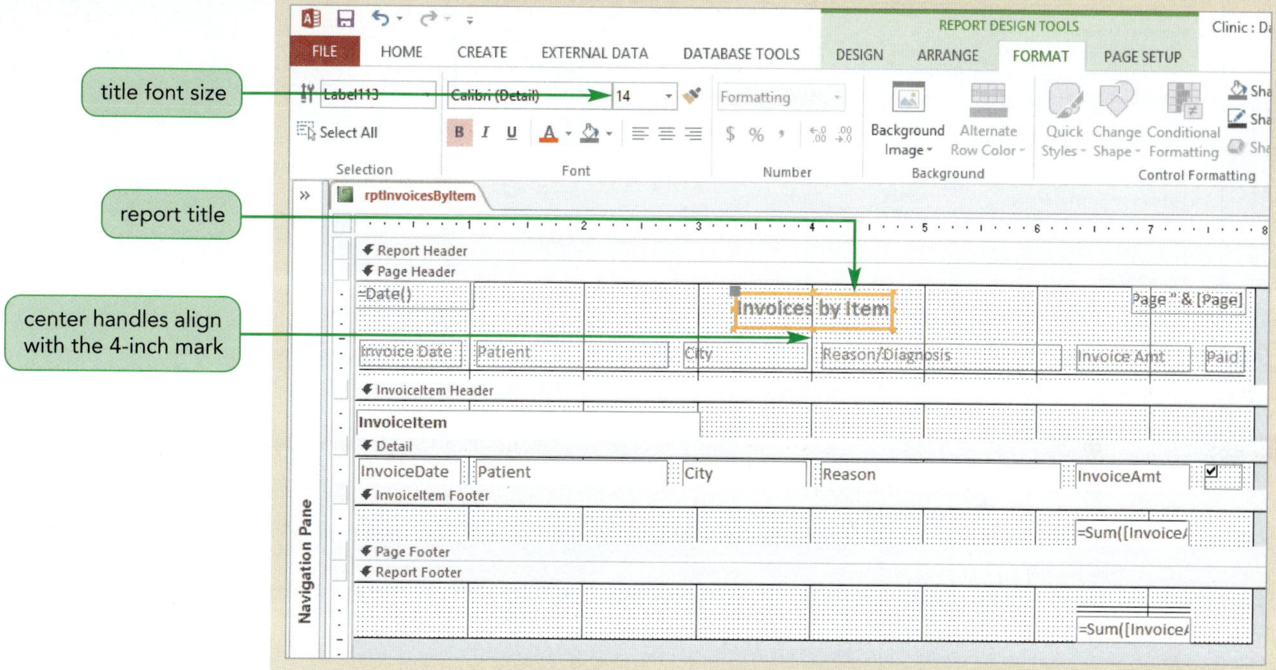

Finally, you'll align the date, report title, and page number controls on their bottom edges. Yours may be aligned already, but if not, this step will align the controls.

5. Select the date, report title, and page number controls in the Page Header section, right-click one of the selected controls, point to **Align**, and then click **Bottom**.
6. Save your report changes. You have completed the design of the custom report as shown in the Session 7.3 Visual Overview.
7. Switch to Print Preview to review the completed report, and then navigate to the top of the last page of the report to view your changes. See Figure 7-33.

Figure 7-33 **Completed rptInvoicesByItem report in Print Preview**

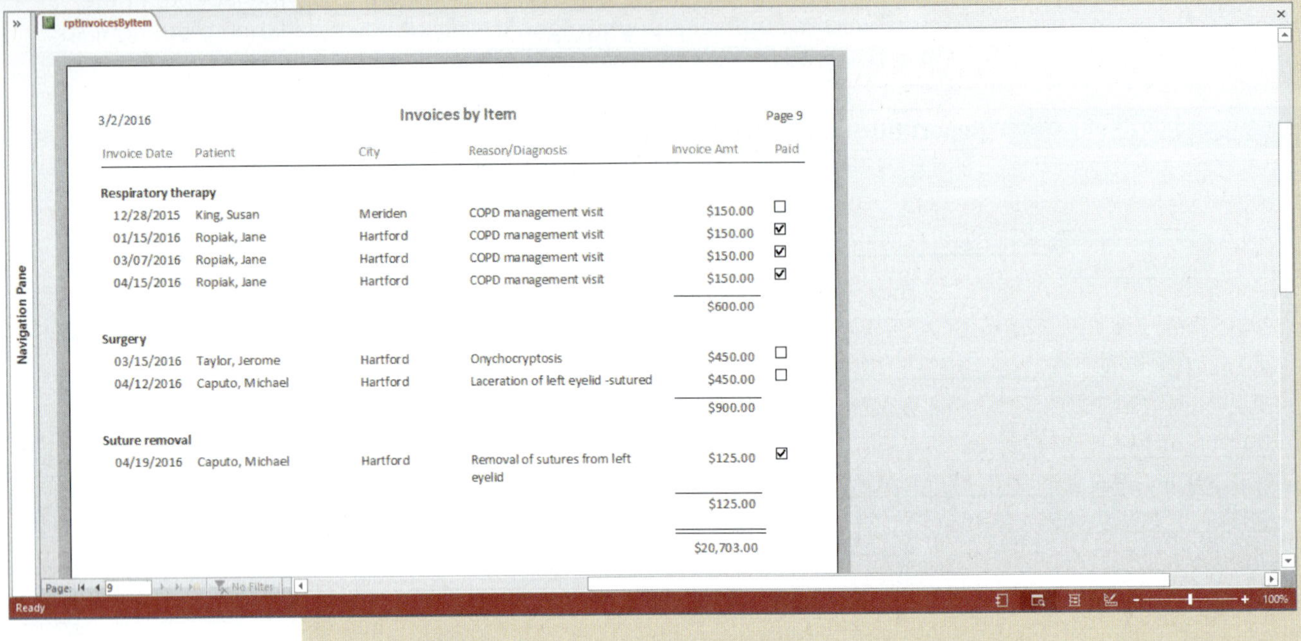

8. Close the report.

Next, Sarah wants you to create mailing labels that she can use to address materials to Chatham Community Health Services patients.

Creating Mailing Labels

Sarah needs a set of mailing labels printed for all Patients so she can mail a marketing brochure and other materials to them. The tblPatient table contains the name and address information that will serve as the record source for the labels. Each mailing label will have the same format: first name and last name on the first line; address on the second line; and city, state, and zip code on the third line.

You could create a custom report to produce the mailing labels, but using the Label Wizard is an easier and faster way to produce them. The **Label Wizard** provides templates for hundreds of standard label formats, each of which is uniquely identified by a label manufacturer's name and number. These templates specify the dimensions and arrangement of labels on each page. Standard label formats can have between one and five labels across a page; the number of labels printed on a single page also varies. Sarah's mailing labels are manufactured by Avery and their product number is C2163. Each sheet contains twelve labels; each label is 1.5 inches by 3.9 inches, and the labels are arranged in two columns and six rows on the page.

REFERENCE

Creating Mailing Labels and Other Labels

- In the Navigation Pane, click the table or query that will serve as the record source for the labels.
- In the Reports group on the CREATE tab, click the Labels button to start the Label Wizard and open its first dialog box.
- Select the label manufacturer and product number, and then click the Next button.
- Select the label font, color, and style, and then click the Next button.
- Construct the label content by selecting the fields from the record source and specifying their placement and spacing on the label, and then click the Next button.
- Select one or more optional sort fields, click the Next button, specify the report name, and then click the Finish button.

You'll use the Label Wizard to create a report to produce mailing labels for all patients.

To use the Label Wizard to create the mailing label report:

1. Open the Navigation Pane, click **tblPatient** to make it the current object that will serve as the record source for the labels, close the Navigation Pane, and then click the **CREATE tab**.
2. In the Reports group, click the **Labels** button. The first Label Wizard dialog box opens and asks you to select the standard or custom label you'll use.
3. In the Unit of Measure section make sure that the **English** option button is selected, in the Label Type section make sure that the **Sheet feed** option button is selected, in the Filter by manufacturer box make sure that **Avery** is selected, and then in the Product number box click **C2163**. See Figure 7-34.

Figure 7-34 **Selecting a standard label**

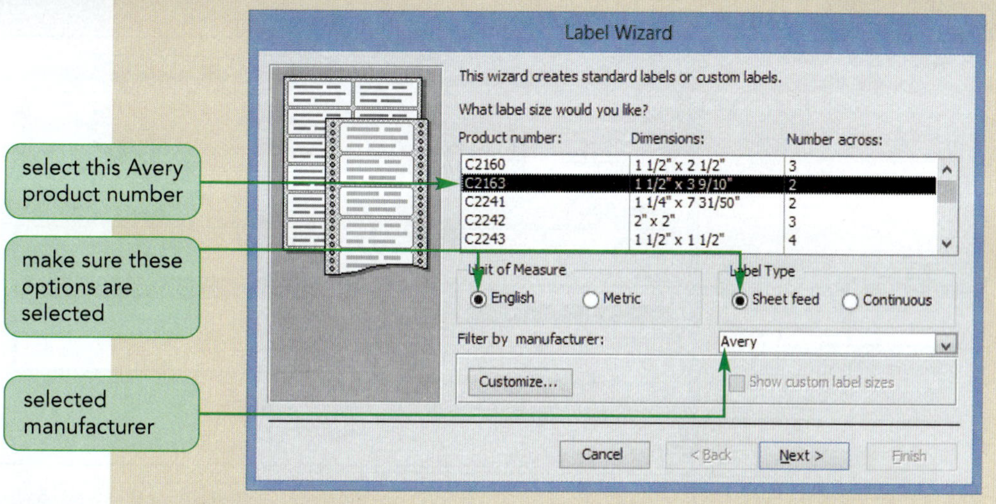

TIP

If your label manufacturer or its labels do not appear in the box, you can create your own custom format for them.

Because the labels are already filtered for products manufactured by Avery, the top box shows the Avery product number, dimensions, and number of labels across the page for each of its standard label formats. You can display the dimensions in the list in either inches or millimeters by choosing the appropriate option in the Unit of Measure section. You can also specify in the Label Type section whether the labels are on individual sheets or are continuous forms.

4. Click the **Next** button to open the second Label Wizard dialog box, in which you choose font specifications for the labels.

   Kelly wants the labels to use 10-point Arial with a medium font weight and without italics or underlines. The font weight determines how light or dark the characters will print; you can choose from nine values ranging from thin to heavy.

5. If necessary, select **Arial** for the font name, **10** for the font size, and **Medium** for the font weight, make sure the Italic and the Underline check boxes are not checked and that black is the text color, and then click the **Next** button. The third Label Wizard dialog box opens, from which you select the data to appear on the labels.

   Kelly wants the mailing labels to print the FirstName and LastName fields on the first line, the Address field on the second line, and the City, State, and Zip fields on the third line. A single space will separate the FirstName and LastName fields, the City and State fields, and the State and Zip fields.

TIP

As you select fields from the Available fields box or type text for the label, the Prototype label box shows the format for the label.

6. In the Available fields box click **FirstName**, click the > button to move the field to the Prototype label box, press the **spacebar**, in the Available fields box click **LastName** (if necessary), and then click the > button. The braces around the field names in the Prototype label box indicate that the name represents a field rather than text that you entered.

   Trouble? If you select the wrong field or type the wrong text, click the incorrect item in the Prototype label box, press the Delete key to remove the item, and then select the correct field or type the correct text.

7. Press the **Enter** key to move to the next line in the Prototype label box, and then use Figure 7-35 to complete the entries in the Prototype label box. Make sure you press the spacebar after selecting the City field and the State field.

Figure 7-35 Completed label prototype

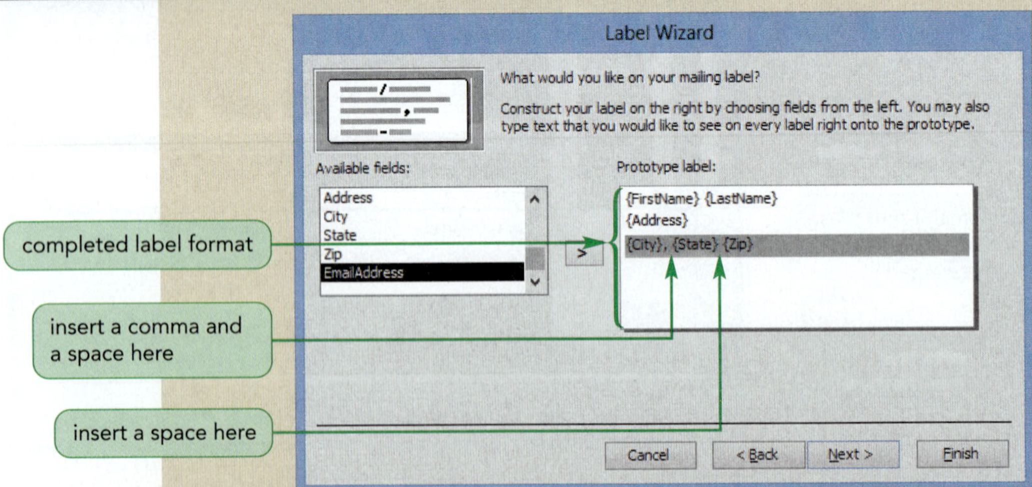

8. Click the **Next** button to open the fourth Label Wizard dialog box, in which you choose the sort fields for the labels.

   Kelly wants Zip to be the primary sort field and LastName to be the secondary sort field.

9. Scroll down the list and click the **Zip** field, click the [>] button to select Zip as the primary sort field, click the **LastName** field, click the [>] button to select LastName as the secondary sort field, and then click the **Next** button to open the last Label Wizard dialog box, in which you enter a name for the report.

10. Change the report name to **rptPatientMailingLabels**, and then click the **Finish** button. Access saves the report as rptPatientMailingLabels and then opens the first page of the report in Print Preview. Note that two columns of labels appear across the page. See Figure 7-36.

Figure 7-36 Previewing the label content and sequence

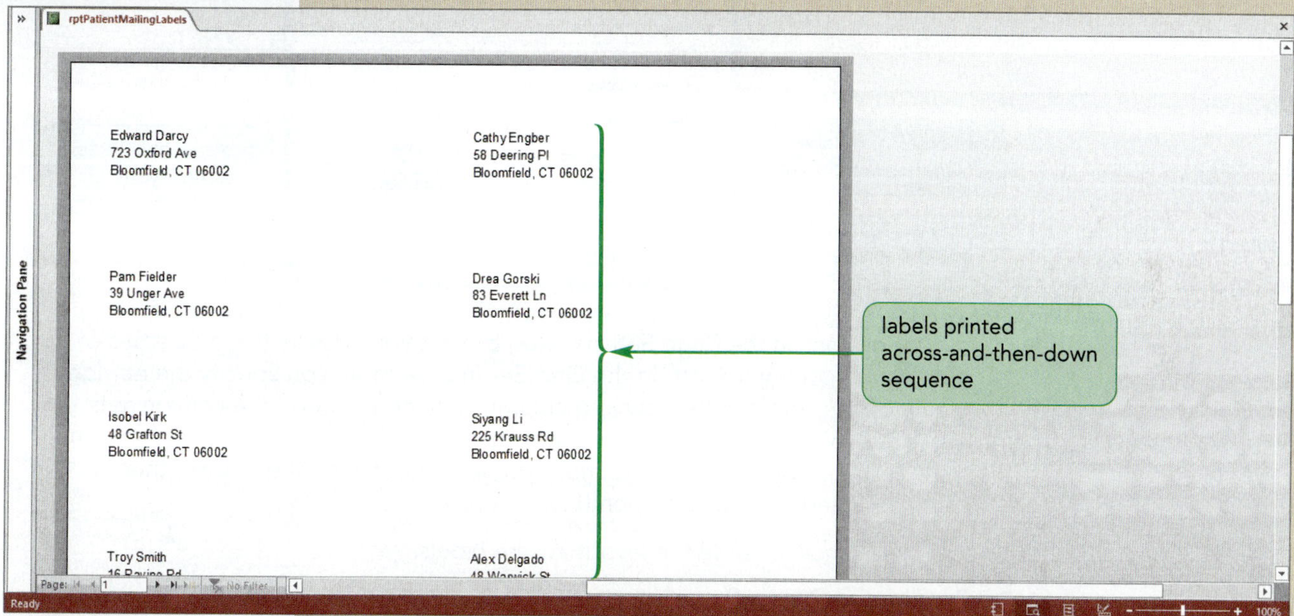

The rptPatientMailingLabels report is a multiple-column report. The labels will be printed in ascending order by zip code and, within each zip code, in ascending order by last name. The first label will be printed in the upper-left corner on the first page, the second label will be printed to its right, the third label will be printed below the first label, and so on. This style of multiple-column report is the "across, then down" layout. Instead, Kelly wants the labels to print with the "down, then across" layout because she prefers to pull the labels from the sheet in this manner. In this layout, the first label is printed, the second label is printed below the first, and so on. After the bottom label in the first column is printed, the next label is printed at the top of the second column. The "down, then across" layout is also called **newspaper-style columns**, or **snaking columns**.

To change the layout of the mailing label report:

1. Close Print Preview and switch to Design view. The Detail section, the only section in the report, is sized for a single label.

   First, you'll change the layout to snaking columns.

2. Click the **PAGE SETUP** tab, in the Page Layout group click the **Page Setup** button, and then click the **Columns** tab. The Page Setup dialog box displays the column options for the report. See Figure 7-37.

Figure 7-37 Column options in the Page Setup dialog box

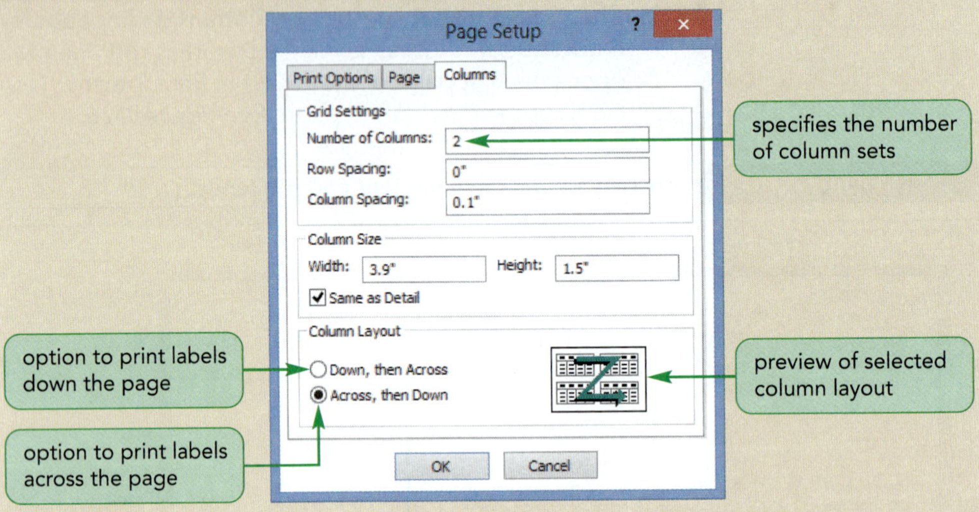

> **TIP**
> When you select a label using a manufacturer's name and product code, the options in the dialog box are set automatically.

The options in the Page Setup dialog box let you change the properties of a multiple-column report. In the Grid Settings section, you specify the number of column sets and the row and column spacing between the column sets. In the Column Size section, you specify the width and height of each column set. In the Column Layout section, you select between the "down, then across" and the "across, then down" layouts.

You can now change the layout for the labels.

3. Click the **Down, then Across** option button, and then click the **OK** button.

   You've finished the report changes, so you can now save and preview the report.

4. Save your report design changes, and then switch to Print Preview. The labels appear in the snaking columns layout.

   You've finished all work on Kelly's reports.

5. Close the report, make a backup copy of the database, compact and repair the database, and then close it.

Kelly is very pleased with the modified report and the two new reports, which will provide her with improved information and help expedite her written communications with patients.

REVIEW

Session 7.3 Quick Check

1. What is the function and syntax to print the current date in a report?
2. How do you insert a page number in the Page Header section?
3. Clicking the Title button in the Header/Footer group on the DESIGN tab adds a report title to the ______________ section.
4. What is a multiple-column report?

ASSESS

SAM Projects

Put your skills into practice with SAM Projects! SAM Projects for this tutorial can be found online. If you have a SAM account, go to www.cengage.com/sam2013 to download the most recent Project Instructions and Start Files.

PRACTICE

Review Assignments

Data File needed for the Review Assignments: Supplier.accdb (*cont. from Tutorial 6*)

Kelly wants you to create a custom report for the Supplier database that prints all companies and the products they offer. She also wants you to customize an existing report. Complete the following steps:

1. Open the **Supplier** database you worked with in Tutorials 5 and 6.
2. Modify the **rptSupplierDetails** report by completing the following steps:
   a. Change the report title to **Chatham Suppliers**.
   b. Remove the alternate row color from the detail lines in the report.
   c. Change the fourth column heading to First Name and the fifth column heading to Last Name.
   d. In the Report Footer section, add a grand total count of the number of suppliers that appear in the report, make sure the text box control has a transparent border, and left-align the count with the left edge of the CompanyName text box. Left-align the count value in the text box.
   e. Add a label that contains the text **Suppliers:** to the left of the count of the total number of suppliers, aligned to the left margin, and aligned with the bottom of the count text box.
   f. Set the Margins to Normal, and adjust the width of the grid to 7.8 inches. Extend the width of the controls in the Report Header to one grid point to the left of the width of the right margin. Increase the width of the Company header label and CompanyName detail text box to approximately double, until the Contact Last Name controls are one grid dot to the left of the right margin.
   g. Move the page number text box control to the right until it is one grid dot to the left of the right margin. Right-align the page number value in the text box control.
3. After you've completed and saved your modifications to the rptSupplierDetails report, filter the report in Report view, selecting all records that contain the word "surgical" in the Company field. Copy the entire filtered report and paste it into a new Word document. Save the document as **surgical** in the Access2 ▸ Review folder. Close Word, save your changes to the Access report, and then close it.
4. Create a query that displays the CompanyName and Category fields from the tblSupplier table, and the ProductName, Price, and Units fields from the tblProduct table. Sort in ascending order by the first three fields in the query, and then save the query as **qrySupplierProducts**.
5. Create a custom report based on the qrySupplierProducts query. Figure 7-38 shows a sample of the completed report. Refer to the figure as you create the report. Distribute the fields horizontally to produce a visually balanced report.

Figure 7-38 Products database custom report

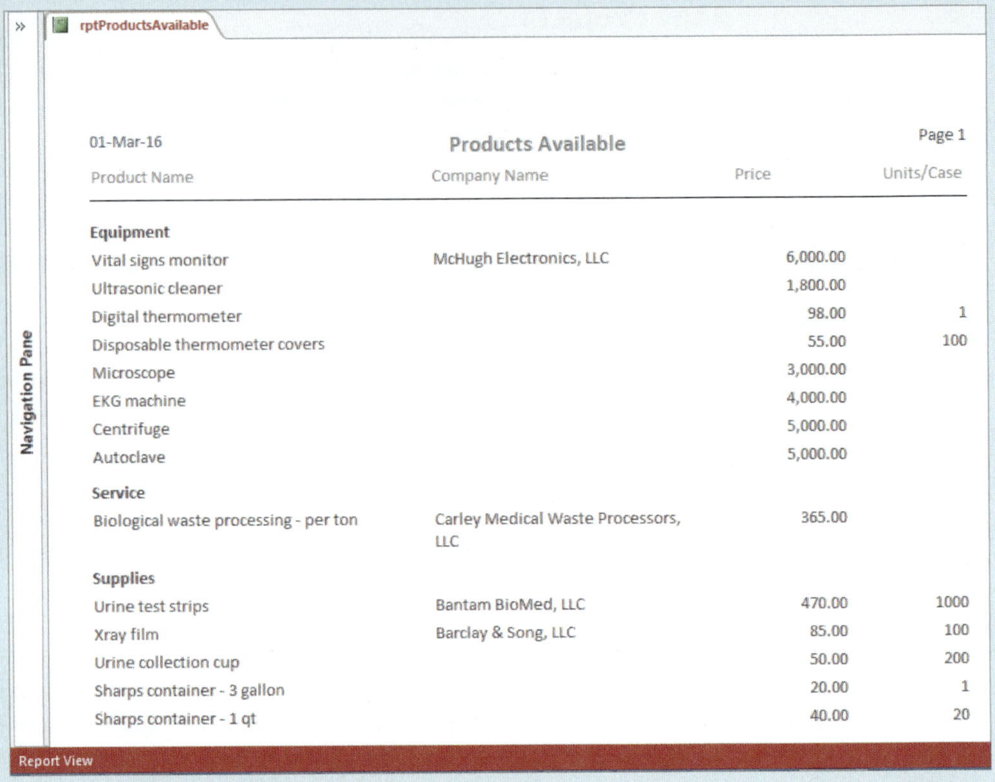

01-Mar-16 **Products Available** Page 1

Product Name	Company Name	Price	Units/Case
Equipment			
Vital signs monitor	McHugh Electronics, LLC	6,000.00	
Ultrasonic cleaner		1,800.00	
Digital thermometer		98.00	1
Disposable thermometer covers		55.00	100
Microscope		3,000.00	
EKG machine		4,000.00	
Centrifuge		5,000.00	
Autoclave		5,000.00	
Service			
Biological waste processing - per ton	Carley Medical Waste Processors, LLC	365.00	
Supplies			
Urine test strips	Bantam BioMed, LLC	470.00	1000
Xray film	Barclay & Song, LLC	85.00	100
Urine collection cup		50.00	200
Sharps container - 3 gallon		20.00	1
Sharps container - 1 qt		40.00	20

a. Save the report as **rptProductsAvailable**.

b. Use the Category field (from the tblSupplier table) as a grouping field, and use the CompanyName field (from the tblSupplier table) as a sort field.

c. Hide duplicate values for the CompanyName field.

d. Keep the whole group together on one page.

e. Remove the text box borders.

f. Remove the alternate row color from the group header and detail line.

g. Add a Page title **Products Available** using 14-point font, centered horizontally.

h. Apply a text filter for companies that contain "LLC" in the Company Name.

6. Create a mailing label report according to the following instructions:
   a. Use the tblSupplier table as the record source.
   b. Use Avery C2160 labels, and use the default font, size, weight, and color.
   c. For the prototype label, add the ContactFirstName, a space, and ContactLastName on the first line; the CompanyName on the second line; the Address on the third line; and the City, a comma and a space, State, a space, and Zip on the fourth line.
   d. Sort by Zip and then by CompanyName, and then enter the report name **rptCompanyMailingLabels**.
7. Make a backup copy of the database, compact and repair, and then close the Supplier database.

APPLY

Case Problem 1

Data File needed for this Case Problem: Task.accdb (*cont. from Tutorial 6*)

GoGopher! Amol Mehta wants you to create a custom report and mailing labels for the Gopher database. The custom report will be based on the results of a query you will create. Complete the following steps:

1. Open the **Task** database you worked with in Tutorials 5 and 6.
2. Create a query that displays the PlanID, FeeWaived, PlanDescription, and PlanCost fields from the tblPlan table, and the FirstName, and LastName fields from the tblMember table. Sort in ascending order by the PlanID, FeeWaived, and LastName fields, and then save the query as **qryPlanMembership**.
3. Create a custom report based on the qryPlanMembership query. Figure 7-39 shows a sample of the first page of the completed report. Refer to the figure as you create the report.

Figure 7-39 **Task database custom report**

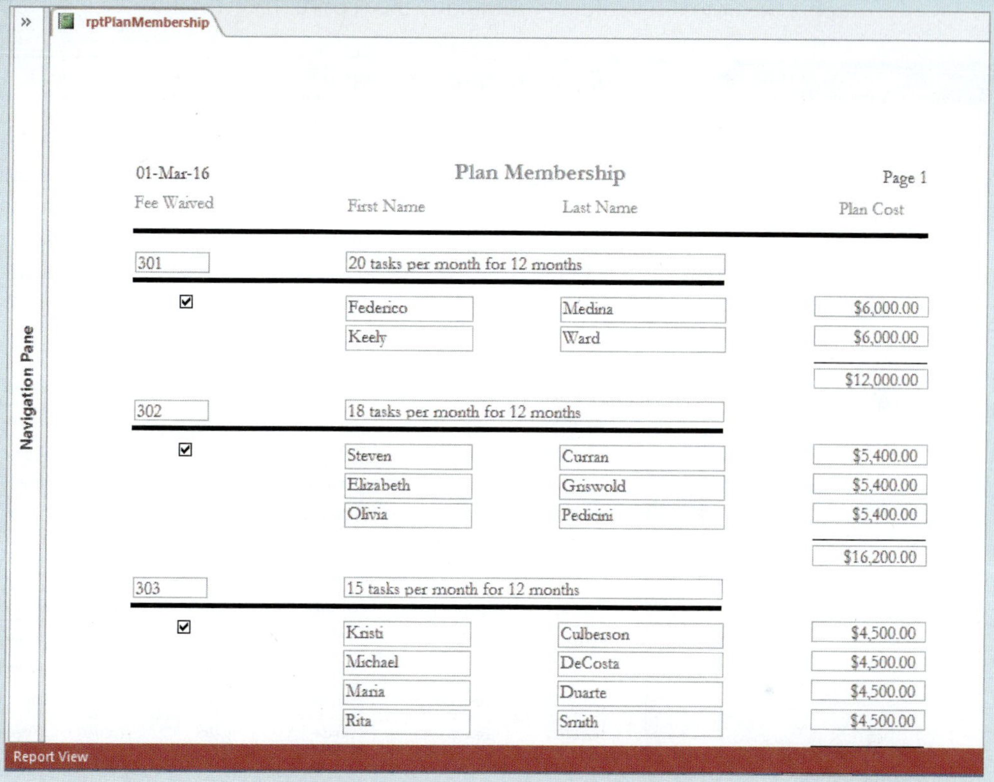

   a. Save the report as **rptPlanMembership**.
   b. Use the PlanID field as a grouping field.
   c. Select the FeeWaived field as a sort field, and the LastName field as a secondary sort field.
   d. Hide duplicate values for the FeeWaived field.
   e. Add the PlanDescription field to the Group Header section, and then delete its attached label.
   f. Keep the whole group together on one page.
   g. Use Wide margins and spacing to distribute the columns evenly across the page.
   h. Remove the alternate row color for all sections.
   i. Use black font for all the controls, and set the lines' thickness to 3 pt.
4. Use the following instructions to create the mailing labels:
   a. Use the tblMember table as the record source for the mailing labels.
   b. Use Avery C2160 labels, and use the default font, size, weight, and color.
   c. For the prototype label, place FirstName, a space, and LastName on the first line; Street on the second line; and City, a comma and space, State, a space, and Zip on the third line.
   d. Sort by Zip and then by LastName, and then type the report name **rptMemberLabels**.
5. Make a backup copy of the database, compact and repair it, and then close the Task database.

APPLY

Case Problem 2

Data File needed for this Case Problem: Tutoring.accdb *(cont. from Tutorial 6)*

O'Brien Educational Services Karen O'Brien wants you to modify an existing report and to create a custom report and mailing labels for the Tutoring database. Complete the following steps:

1. Open the **Tutoring** database you worked with in Tutorials 5 and 6.
2. Modify the **rptTutorList** report. Figure 7-40 shows a sample of the last page of the completed report. Refer to the figure as you modify the report.

Figure 7-40 Tutoring database enhanced report

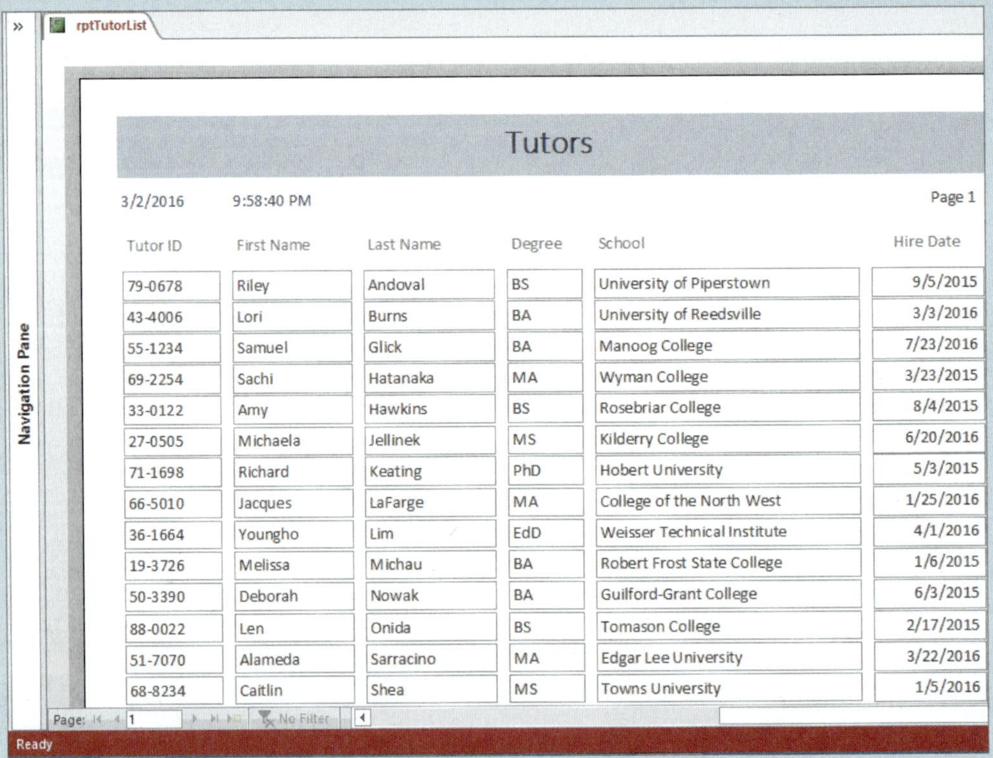

Tutor ID	First Name	Last Name	Degree	School	Hire Date
79-0678	Riley	Andoval	BS	University of Piperstown	9/5/2015
43-4006	Lori	Burns	BA	University of Reedsville	3/3/2016
55-1234	Samuel	Glick	BA	Manoog College	7/23/2016
69-2254	Sachi	Hatanaka	MA	Wyman College	3/23/2015
33-0122	Amy	Hawkins	BS	Rosebriar College	8/4/2015
27-0505	Michaela	Jellinek	MS	Kilderry College	6/20/2016
71-1698	Richard	Keating	PhD	Hobert University	5/3/2015
66-5010	Jacques	LaFarge	MA	College of the North West	1/25/2016
36-1664	Youngho	Lim	EdD	Weisser Technical Institute	4/1/2016
19-3726	Melissa	Michau	BA	Robert Frost State College	1/6/2015
50-3390	Deborah	Nowak	BA	Guilford-Grant College	6/3/2015
88-0022	Len	Onida	BS	Tomason College	2/17/2015
51-7070	Alameda	Sarracino	MA	Edgar Lee University	3/22/2016
68-8234	Caitlin	Shea	MS	Towns University	1/5/2016

a. Delete the picture at the top of the report.
b. Set Normal margins, and a grid width of 7.8 inches.
c. Center the report title and ensure the text is "Tutors", bold and 22 pt.
d. Move the Hire Date column to the right margin, and center the Hire Date label value. Use horizontal spacing to evenly distribute the columns.
e. Remove the alternate row color from the detail lines in the report.
f. Change the page number format from "Page n of m" to "Page n" and align the text to the right.
g. Move the date, time, and page number to the Page Header section.
h. Change the date format to short date and align the text to the left.
i. Add a grand total control that calculates the total number of tutors and add a label with the text "Total Tutors".
j. Sort the tutors by Last Name.

3. Create a query that displays, in order, the LastName and FirstName fields from the tblTutor table, the SessionType field from the tblContract table, the FirstName and LastName fields from the tblStudent table, and the NumSessions and Cost fields from the tblContract table. Sort in ascending order by the first three fields in the query, and then save the query as **qryTutorSessions**.

4. Create a custom report based on the qryTutorSessions query. Figure 7-41 shows a sample of the first page of the completed report. Refer to the figure as you create the report.

Figure 7-41 **Contract database custom report**

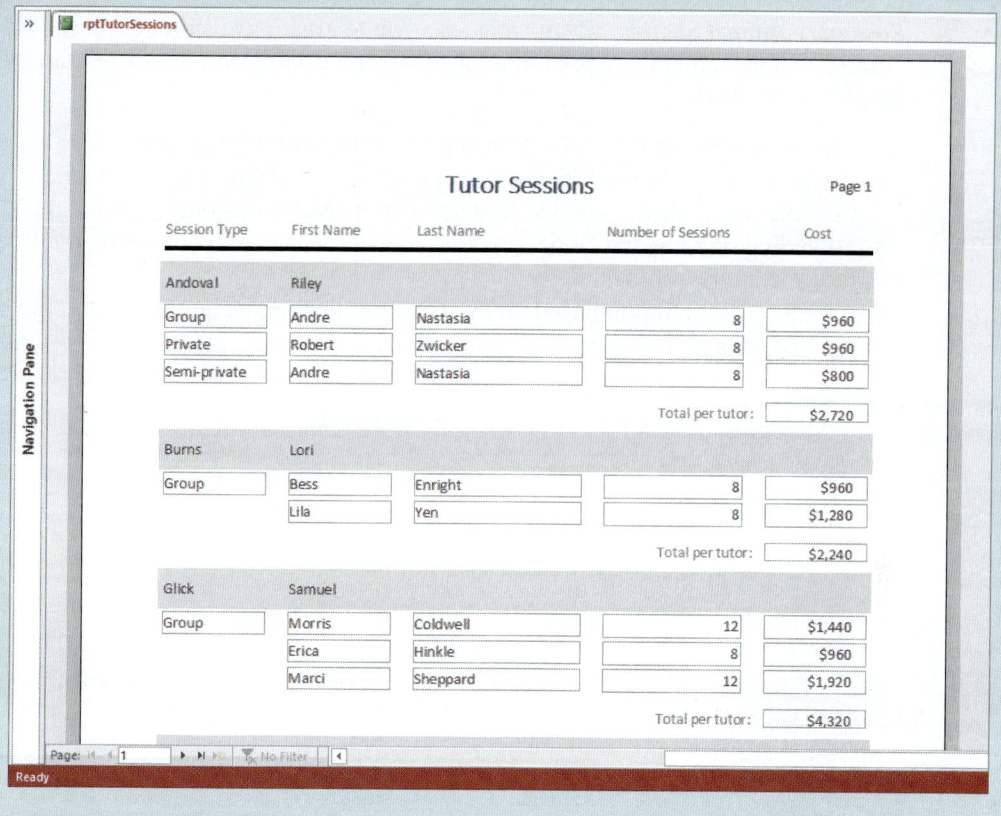

a. Save the report as **rptTutorSessions**.
b. The LastName field (from the tblTutor table) is a grouping field, and the FirstName field also appears in the Group Header section.
c. The SessionType field is a sort field, and the LastName field (from the tblStudent table) is a sort field.
d. Hide duplicate values for the SessionType field.
e. Use Wide margins and set the grid width to 7 inches. Size fields as shown and distribute horizontally using spacing to create a balanced look.
f. Set the background color for the grouped header and its controls to Background 2 in the Theme colors.
g. Use black font for all the controls, setting the lines' thickness to 3 pt.

5. Create a mailing label report according to the following instructions:
   a. Use the tblStudent table as the record source.
   b. Use Avery C2160 labels, use a 12-point font size and use the other default font and color options.
   c. For the prototype label, place FirstName, a space, and LastName on the first line; Address on the second line; and City, a comma and a space, State, a space, and Zip on the third line.
   d. Sort by Zip and then by LastName, and then enter the report name **rptStudentMailingLabels**.
   e. Change the mailing label layout to snaking columns.
6. Make a backup copy of the database, compact and repair it, and then close the Tutoring database.

Case Problem 3

CREATE

Data File needed for this Case Problem: Rosemary.accdb (*cont. from Tutorial 6*)

Rosemary Animal Shelter Ryan Lang asks you to create a custom report for the Rosemary database so that he can better track donations made by donors and to create mailing labels. Complete the following steps:

1. Open the **Rosemary** database you worked with in Tutorials 5 and 6.
2. Create a query that displays the DonationDesc, DonationDate, and DonationValue fields from the tblDonation table, and the FirstName and LastName fields from the tblPatron table. Sort in ascending order by the DonationDesc, DonationDate, and LastName fields, and then save the query as **qryPatronDonations**.
3. Create a custom report based on the qryPatronDonations query. Figure 7-42 shows a sample of the first page of the completed report. Refer to the figure as you create the report.

Figure 7-42 Rosemary database custom report

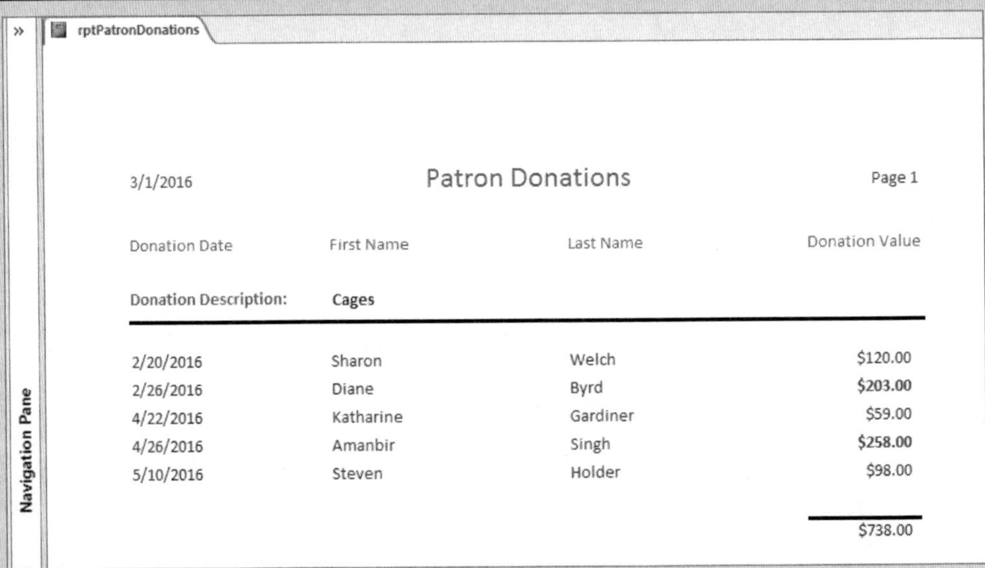

   a. Save the report as **rptPatronDonations**.
   b. Ryan would like you to use the DonationDesc field as a grouping field; however, it is currently a Long Text field, and you can't group on a Long Text field. Ryan realized that the donation description will always be a short description. In the tblDonation table, change the data type of the DonationDesc field to Short Text.
   c. Use the DonationDesc field as a grouping field.
   d. Select the DonationDate field as a sort field, and the LastName field as a secondary sort field.
   e. Hide duplicate values for the DonationDate field.
   f. Use black font for all the controls, and set the lines' thickness to 2 pt.
   g. Keep the whole group together on one page.
   h. Use Wide margins and set the grid width to 7 inches. Size fields as shown and distribute horizontally, using spacing to create a balanced look.
   i. Create a conditional formatting rule for the DonationValue field to display the value in blue, bold font when the amount is more than $200.
   j. Make any additional changes to the layout and formatting of the report that are necessary for it to match Figure 7-42.

4. After you've created and saved the rptPatronDonations report, filter the report in Report view, selecting all records that contain the name "Lew" in the LastName field. Copy the entire filtered report and paste it into a new Word document. Save the document as **PatronLew** in the Access2 ▸ Case3 folder. Close Word, and then save and close the Access report.
5. The Rosemary Animal Shelter is having a fundraiser dinner and Ryan would like name tags for the patrons. Use the following instructions to create mailing labels that will be used as name tags:
   a. Use the tblPatron table as the record source for the mailing labels.
   b. Use Avery C2160 labels, and use a font size of 16, with Normal weight, and black color.
   c. For the prototype label, place FirstName, a space, and LastName on the first line.
   d. Sort by LastName, and then type the report name **rptPatronNameTags**.
   e. Change the mailing label layout to snaking columns.
6. Make a backup copy of the database, compact and repair it, and then close it.

CREATE

Case Problem 4

Data File needed for this Case Problem: Ecotour.accdb (*cont. from Tutorial 6*)

Stanley EcoTours Janice and Bill Stanley want you to create a custom report and mailing labels for the Ecotour database. Complete the following steps:

1. Open the **Ecotour** database you worked with in Tutorials 5 and 6.
2. Create a query that displays the TourName and Country fields from the tblTour table; the GuestFirst, GuestLast, and StateProv field from the tblGuest table; and the StartDate and People fields from the tblReservation table. Sort in ascending order by the TourName, StateProv, and StartDate fields, and then save the query as **qryTourReservations**.
3. Create a custom report based on the qryTourReservations query. Figure 7-43 shows a sample of the last page of the completed report. Refer to the figure as you create the report.

Figure 7-43 Ecotour database custom report

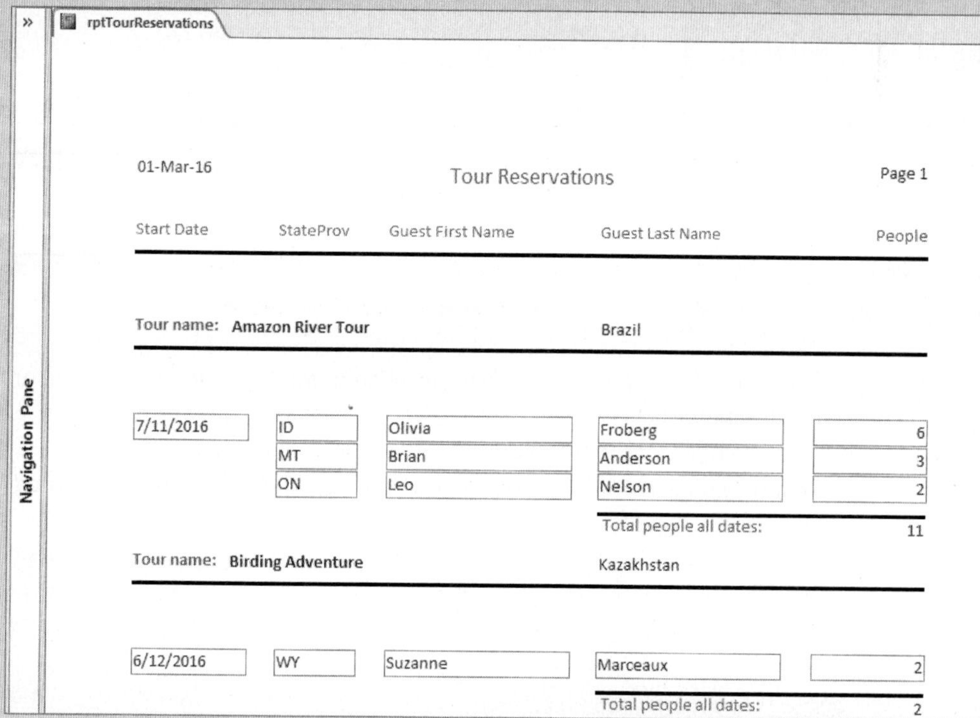

   a. Save the report as **rptTourReservations**.
   b. Use the TourName field as a grouping field.
   c. Select the StartDate field as a sort field, and the StateProv field as a secondary sort field.
   d. Hide duplicate values for the StartDate field.
   e. Use black font for all the controls, and set the lines' thickness to 2 pt.
   f. Keep the whole group together on one page.
   g. Add the Country field to the Group Header section.
   h. Use Wide margins and set the grid width to 7 inches. Size fields as shown and distribute horizontally, using spacing to create a balanced look.
   i. Remove the color for alternate rows, and then make any other layout and formatting changes necessary to match the report shown in Figure 7-43.

4. Use the following instructions to create the mailing labels:
   a. Use the tblGuest table as the record source for the mailing labels.
   b. Use Avery C2163 labels, with 12 point font size, Medium weight, and black color settings.
   c. For the prototype label, place GuestFirst, a space, and GuestLast on the first line; Address on the second line; City, a comma and a space, StateProv, a space, and PostalCode on the third line; and Country on the fourth line.
   d. Sort by PostalCode, then by GuestLastName, and then enter the report name **rptGuestLabels**.
   e. Change the mailing label layout to snaking columns.
5. Make a copy of the rptTourReservations report using the name **rptTourReservationsSummary**, and then customize it according to the following instructions. Figure 7-44 shows a sample of the first page of the completed report.

Figure 7-44 Ecotour database custom summary report

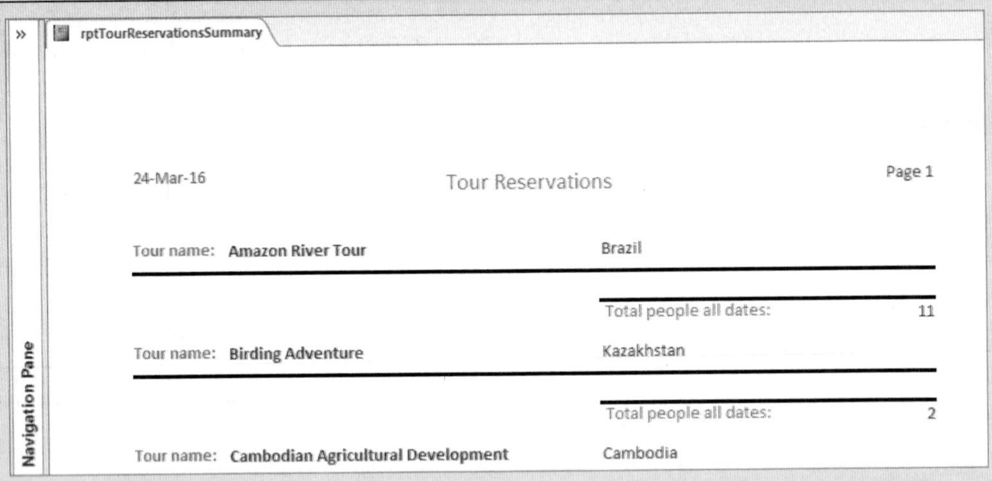

   a. Delete the column heading labels and line in the Page Header section, and then reduce the height of the section.
   b. Add subtotals for the number of reservations and number of people.
6. Make a backup copy of the database, compact and repair it, and then close the Ecotour database.

TUTORIAL **8**

Sharing, Integrating, and Analyzing Data

Importing, Exporting, Linking, and Analyzing Data in the Clinic Database

OBJECTIVES

Session 8.1
- Export an Access query to an HTML document and view the document
- Import a CSV file as an Access table
- Use the Table Analyzer
- Import a table from another Access database
- Import and export XML files
- Save and run import and export specifications

Session 8.2
- Create a tabbed form using a tab control
- Understand the difference between importing, embedding, and linking external objects
- Embed a chart in a form
- Create and use an application part
- Export a PDF file
- Link data from an Excel workbook

Case | *Chatham Community Health Services*

Cindi Rodriguez, Kelly Schwarz, and Ethan Ward are pleased with the design and contents of the Clinic database. Cindi feels that other employees would benefit from gaining access to the Clinic database and from sharing data among the different programs employees use. Cindi and Kelly would also like to be able to analyze the data in the database.

In this tutorial, you will import, export, link, and embed data, and you will create application parts. You will also explore the charting features of Access.

STARTING DATA FILES

Access2 →

Tutorial
Clinic.accdb (*cont.*)
NewPatientReferrals.accdb
peoplecalled.csv
Referral.xml
Volunteer.xlsx

Review
Ads.xlsx
Partners.accdb
Payables.csv
Payments.xml
Vendor.accdb (*cont.*)

Case1
CreditCard.xml
Schedule.xlsx
Task.accdb (*cont.*)

Case2
AddSubject.xml
NewStudentReferrals.accdb
Room.xlsx
Subject.csv
Tutoring.accdb (*cont.*)

Case3
Facility.csv
Rosemary.accdb (*cont.*)
Volunteer.accdb

Case4
Ecotour.accdb (*cont.*)
Personnel.xlsx
PotentialTours1.xml
PotentialTours2.xml

Session 8.1 Visual Overview:

Each piece of data is encapsulated in paired tags.

Access includes tools for exporting data on the EXTERNAL DATA tab.

Extensible Markup Language (XML) is a programming language that uses customizable tags to describe the data it contains and how that data should be structured.

```
<tblReferral>
<PatientID>36229</PatientID>
<FirstName>Larissa</FirstName>
<LastName>Waller</LastName>
<Phone>860-661-3098</Phone>
<Address>7297 Dolor St</Address>
<City>Hartford</City>
<State>CT</State>
<Zip>06105</Zip>
<Email>lwaller@example.com</Email>
</tblReferral>
<tblReferral>
<PatientID>36232</PatientID>
<FirstName>Maria</FirstName>
<LastName>Marquez</LastName>
<Phone>860-938-1123</Phone>
<Address>27 Frankfurt St</Address>
<City>Hartford</City>
<State>CT</State>
<Zip>06120</Zip>
<Email>mmarq@example.com</Email>
</tblReferral>
<tblReferral>
<PatientID>36239</PatientID>
<FirstName>Betty</FirstName>
<LastName>Gallagher</LastName>
<Phone>860-552-2987</Phone>
<Address>127 Rain Ct</Address>
<City>Windsor</City>
<State>CT</State>
<Zip>06095</Zip>
<Email>bettyg@example.com</Email>
</tblReferral>
<tblReferral>
<PatientID>36241</PatientID>
<FirstName>Jonathan</FirstName>
<LastName>Holloway</LastName>
<Phone>860-552-2341</Phone>
<Address>128 Charning Ave</Address>
```

The field names from the table are used as XML tags to identify data.

Each record begins with the tag <tblReferral> and ends with the tag </tblReferral>.

Access table exported as an XML file

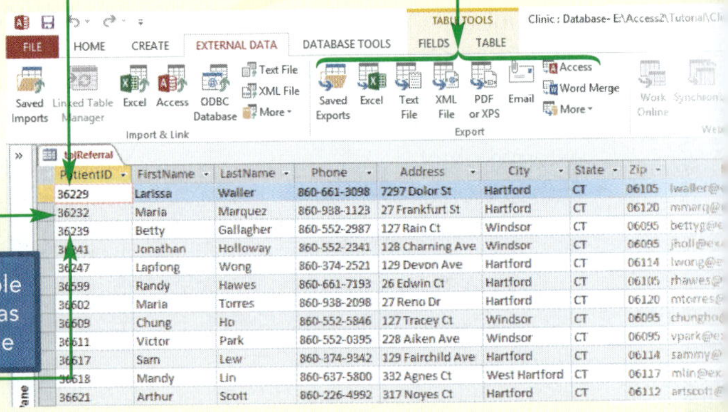

Exporting data to XML and HTML

The table field names are used as column headings in the table on the web page.

The Export to HTML tool generates an HTML document, embedding the Access content in the document. An **HTML document** contains tags and other instructions that a web browser processes and displays as a web page.

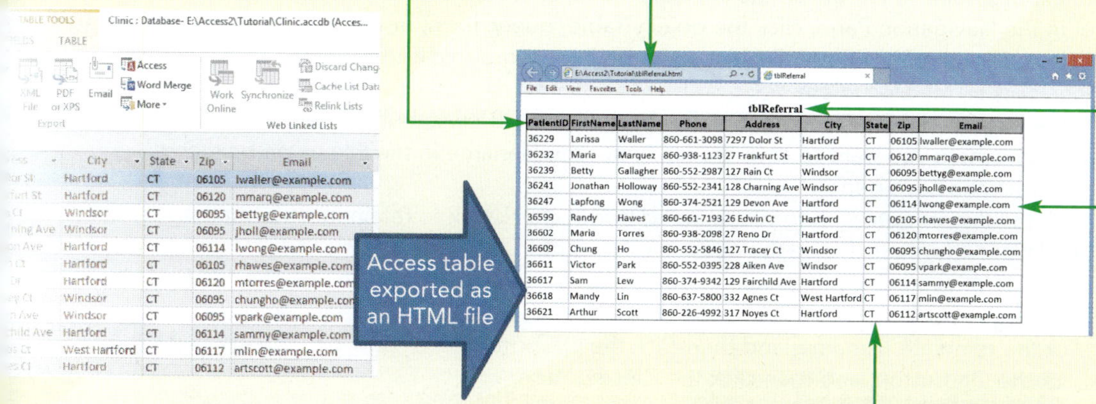

The name of the table is used as a heading on the web page.

The values are formatted using the formatting property for each field.

The Export to HTML tool creates a **static web page**, which reflects the state of the query at the time you created it. If the data in the query changed, you would need to export the query as an HTML document again.

Exporting an Access Query to an HTML Document

Cindi wants to display the summary data in the qryPatientsAndInvoicesCrosstab query on the company's intranet so that all employees working in the office are able to view it. To store the data on the company's intranet, you'll create a web page version of the qryPatientsAndInvoicesCrosstab query.

An HTML document contains tags and other instructions that a Web browser, such as Microsoft Internet Explorer, Apple Safari, or Google Chrome, processes and displays as a Web page. Creating the necessary HTML document to provide Cindi with the information she wants is not as difficult as it might appear at first. You can use Access to export the query and convert it to an HTML document automatically.

REFERENCE

Exporting an Access Object to an HTML Document

- In the Navigation Pane, right-click the object (table, query, form, or report) you want to export, point to Export on the shortcut menu, and then click HTML Document; or in the Navigation Pane, click the object (table, query, form, or report) you want to export, click the EXTERNAL DATA tab, in the Export group click the More button, and then click HTML Document.
- In the Export – HTML Document dialog box, click the Browse button, select the location where you want to save the file, enter the filename in the File name box, and then click the Save button.
- Click the Export data with formatting and layout check box to retain most formatting and layout information, and then click the OK button.
- In the HTML Output Options dialog box, if using a template click the Select a HTML Template check box, click the Browse button, select the location for the template, click the template filename, and then click the OK button.
- Click the OK button, and then click the Close button.

You'll export the qryPatientsAndInvoicesCrosstab query as an HTML document. The qryPatientsAndInvoicesCrosstab query is a select query that joins the tblPatient, tblVisit, and tblBilling tables to display selected data from those tables for all invoices. The query displays one row for each unique City field value.

To export the qryPatientsAndInvoicesCrosstab query as an HTML document:

1. Start Access, and then open the **Clinic** database you worked with in Tutorials 5–7.
2. Open the Navigation Pane (if necessary), right-click **qryPatientsAndInvoicesCrosstab** to display the shortcut menu, point to **Export**, and then click **HTML Document**. The Export - HTML Document dialog box opens.
3. Click the **Browse** button to open the File Save dialog box, navigate to the **Access2 ▸ Tutorial** folder in the location where your data files are stored, select the text in the File name box, type **Crosstab.html**, and then click the **Save** button. The File Save dialog box closes, and you return to the Export – HTML Document dialog box.

TIP

Always select the "Export data with formatting and layout" option, or the HTML document you create will be poorly formatted and difficult to read.

Figure 8-1 **Export - HTML Document dialog box**

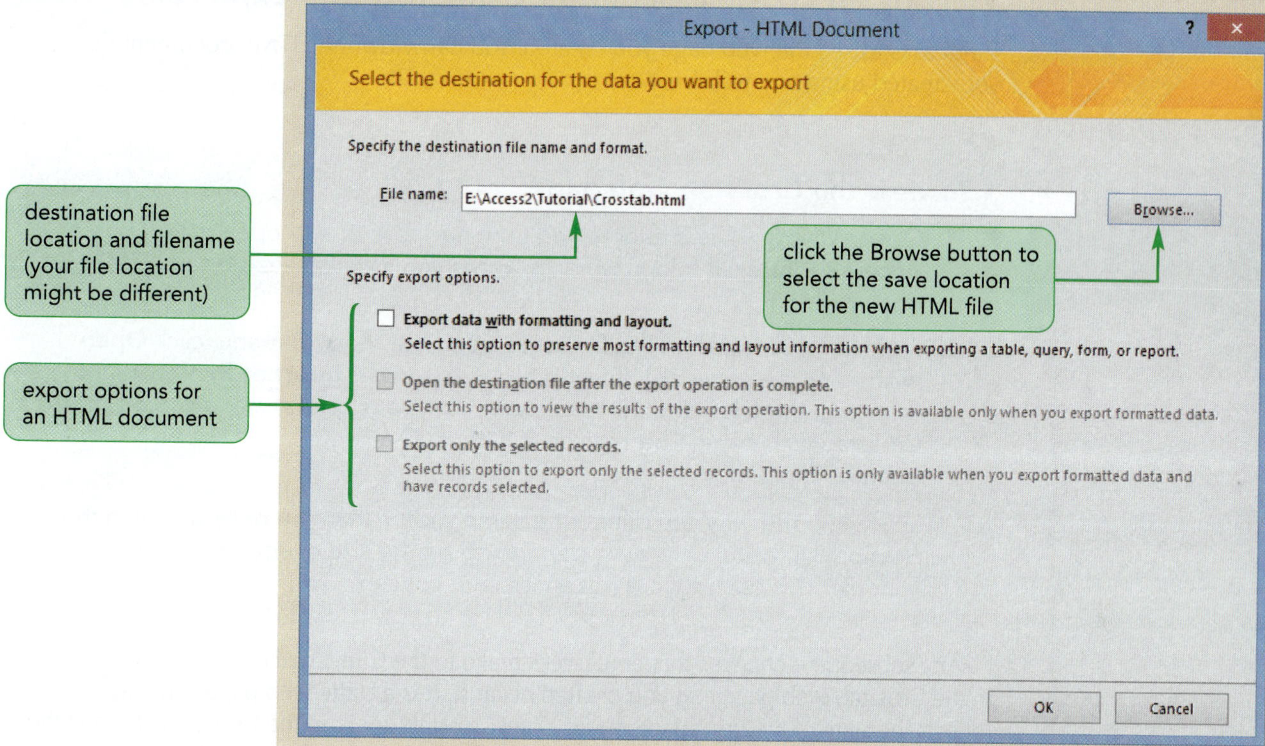

The dialog box provides options for exporting the data with formatting and layout, opening the exported file after the export operation is complete, and exporting selected records from the source object (available only when you select records in an object instead of selecting an object in the Navigation Pane). You need to select the option for exporting the data with formatting and layout.

4. Click the **Export data with formatting and layout** check box to select it, and then click the **OK** button. The Export - HTML Document dialog box closes and the HTML Output Options dialog box opens. See Figure 8-2.

Figure 8-2 **HTML Output Options dialog box**

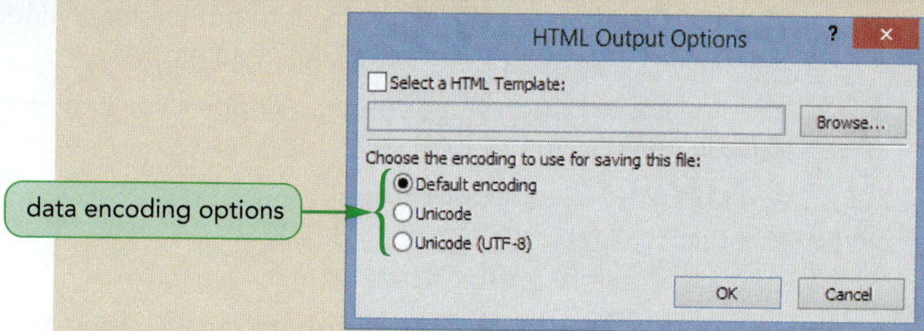

5. Click the **OK** button. The HTML Output Options dialog box closes, the HTML document named Crosstab is saved in the Access2 ▸ Tutorial folder, and the Export - HTML Document dialog box is displayed with an option to save the export steps. You won't save these export steps.
6. Click the **Close** button in the dialog box to close it without saving the steps and to close the Navigation Pane.

Now you can view the web page.

Viewing an HTML Document Using Internet Explorer

Cindi asks to see the web page you created. You can view the HTML document that you created using any web browser.

To view the Crosstab web page:

1. Open Windows File Explorer, and then navigate to and open the **Access2 ▸ Tutorial** folder, which is where you saved the exported HTML document.
2. Right-click **Crosstab** in the file list to open the shortcut menu, click **Open with**, click the name of your web browser, such as **Internet Explorer**, and then click the **OK** button (if necessary). Internet Explorer starts and opens the Crosstab web page. The Session 8.1 Visual Overview shows the web page in Internet Explorer.

   Trouble? You may see different column widths than the ones shown in the Session 8.1 Visual Overview, depending on the size of your web browser window. This difference is not an issue of concern.

Any subsequent changes that employees make to the Clinic database will not appear in the Crosstab web page that you created because it is a static web page—that is, it reflects the state of the qryPatientsAndInvoicesCrosstab query in the Clinic database at the time you created it. If data in the qryPatientsAndInvoicesCrosstab query changes, you will need to export the query as an HTML document again.

Because this static web page is not linked to the qryPatientsAndInvoicesCrosstab query on which it is based, you cannot use your browser to make changes to its data. Before closing the Crosstab web page, you'll verify this by trying to change one of its field values.

To attempt to change a field value in the web page:

1. Double-click **Hartford** in the City column for the second record, type **D**, and then notice that no change occurs. The value of Hartford remains highlighted and unchanged because the Crosstab web page is a static page.
2. Click the **Close** button on the Internet Explorer window title bar to close it and to return to Windows File Explorer.
3. Click the **Close** button on the Windows File Explorer window title bar to close it and to return to Access.

   Trouble? If the Access window is not active on your screen, click the Microsoft Access program button on the taskbar.

Now that you've completed your work creating the web page, Kelly has a file containing information for potential new patients that she needs to add to the Clinic database. Instead of typing the information into new records, she asks you to import the data into the Clinic database.

Importing a CSV File as an Access Table

Kelly has been maintaining an Excel workbook containing contact information for people who have called the Chatham Community Health Services clinic to inquire about the services, but have not yet booked appointments. She has exported the Excel data to a CSV file. A **CSV (comma-separated values) file** is a text file in which commas separate values, and each line is a record containing the same number of values in the same positions. This is a common format for representing data in a table and is used by spreadsheet applications such as Excel as well as database applications. Many people use Excel to manage a simple table, such as a table of contact information or product information. They may not want to provide the entire Excel file if it also contains formulas or other data that they do not want to distribute. Instead, they may choose to save one worksheet of the Excel workbook as a CSV file so you can import it into Access.

REFERENCE

Importing a CSV File as an Access Table

- On the EXTERNAL DATA tab, in the Import & Link group, click the Text File button to open the Get External Data - Text File dialog box.
- Click the Browse button in the dialog box, navigate to the location where the file to import is stored, click the filename, and then click the Open button.
- Click the "Import the source data into a new table in the current database" option button, and then click the OK button.
- In the Import Text Wizard dialog box, click the Delimited option button, and then click the Next button.
- Make sure the Comma option button is selected. If appropriate, click the First Row Contains Field Names check box to select it, and then click the Next button.
- For each field, if necessary, select the column, type its field name and select its data type, and then click the Next button.
- Choose the appropriate option button to let Access create a primary key, to choose your own primary key, or to avoid setting a primary key, click the Next button, type the table name in the Import to Table box, and then click the Finish button.

Access can import data from a CSV file directly into a database table. Kelly's CSV file is named peoplecalled.csv, and you'll import the data as a new table in the Clinic database.

To view and import the CSV file as an Access table:

1. Open Windows File Explorer, navigate to the **Access2 ▸ Tutorial** folder included with your Data Files, right-click **peoplecalled.csv** in the file list to open the shortcut menu, click **Open with**, and then click **Notepad**.

   Trouble? If Notepad isn't an option when you click Open with, click More options, and then click Notepad in the expanded list that is displayed.

2. Examine the contents of the peoplecalled.csv file. The file contains rows of data, with commas separating pieces of data.
3. Close the Notepad window.

   Trouble? If a dialog box appears prompting you to save the file, click **Don't Save**. You may have accidentally added or deleted a character, and you don't want to save this change to the file.

4. In Access, click the **EXTERNAL DATA** tab, and then in the Import & Link group, click the **Text File** button (with the ScreenTip "Import text file") to open the Get External Data - Text File dialog box.

   Trouble? If the Export - Text File dialog box opens, you clicked the Text File button in the Export group. Click the Cancel button and then repeat Step 4, being sure to select the Text File button from the Import & Link group.

5. Click the **Browse** button, navigate to the **Access2 ▸ Tutorial** folder, click **peoplecalled.csv**, click the **Open** button, and then click the **Import the source data into a new table in the current database** option button (if necessary). The selected path and filename appear in the File name box. See Figure 8-3.

Figure 8-3 Get External Data - Text File dialog box

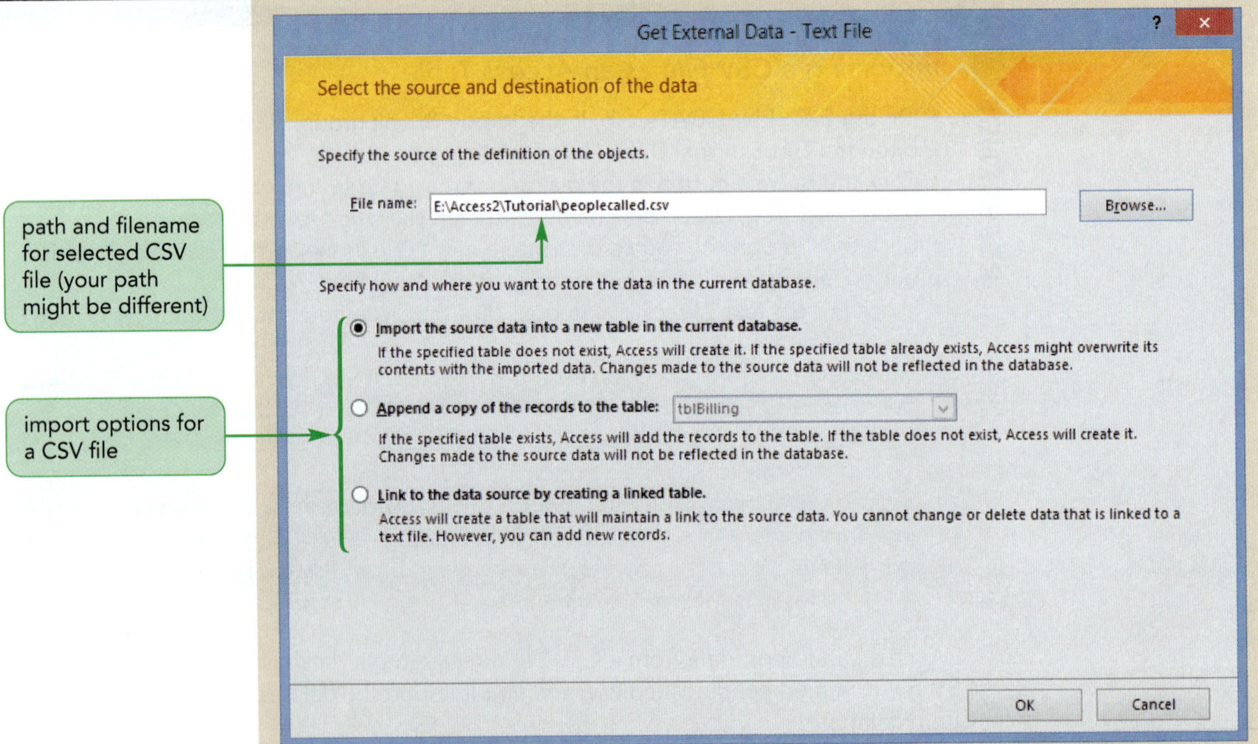

The dialog box provides options for importing the data into a new table in the database, appending a copy of the data to an existing table in the database, and linking to the source data. In the future, Kelly wants to maintain the potential new patient data in the Clinic database, instead of using her Excel workbook, so you'll import the data into a new table.

6. Click the **OK** button to open the first Import Text Wizard dialog box, in which you designate how to identify the separation between field values in each line in the source data. The choices are the use of commas, tabs, or another character to separate, or delimit, the values, or the use of fixed-width columns with spaces between each column. The wizard has correctly identified that values are delimited by commas.

7. Click the **Next** button to open the second Import Text Wizard dialog box, in which you verify the delimiter for values in each line. See Figure 8-4.

Figure 8-4 Verifying the delimiter for values in the CSV file

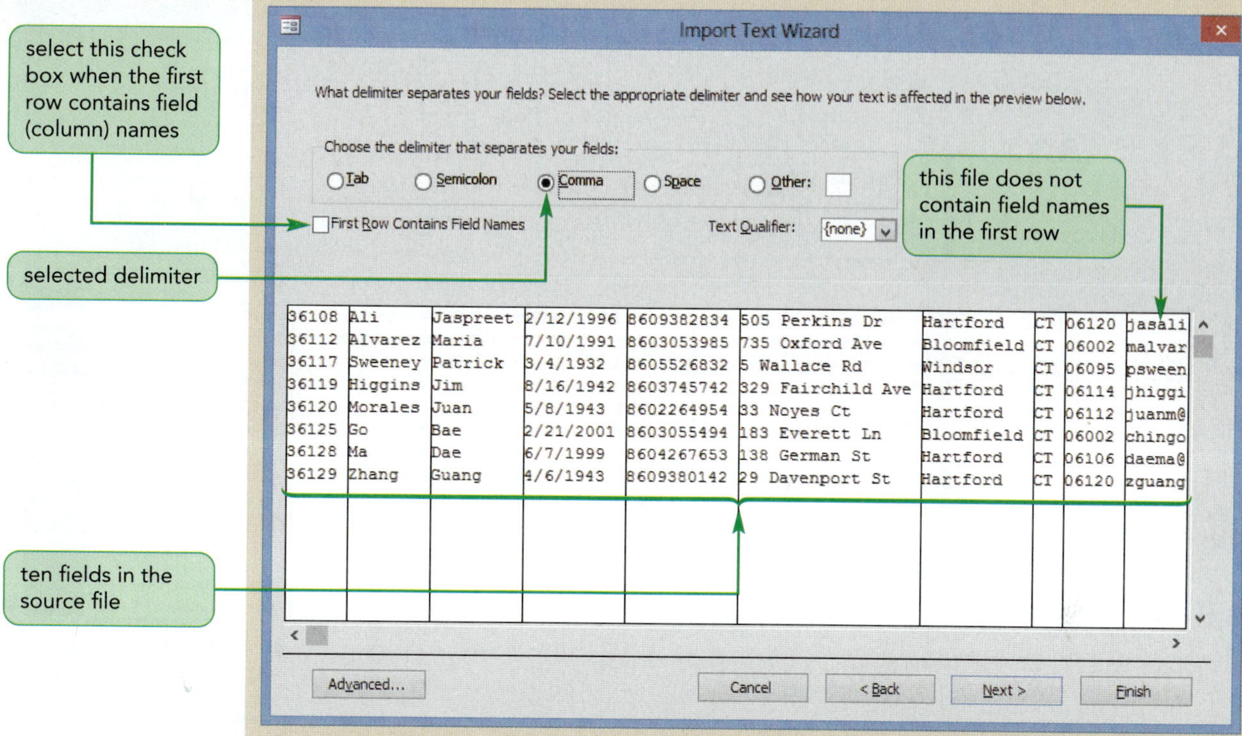

The CSV source file contains eight records with ten fields in each record. A comma serves as the delimiter for values in each line, so the Comma option button is selected. The first row in the source file contains the first record, not field names, so the "First Row Contains Field Names" check box is not checked. If the source file used either single or double quotation marks to enclose values, you would click the Text Qualifier arrow to choose the appropriate option.

8. Click the **Next** button to open the third Import Text Wizard dialog box, in which you enter the field name and set other properties for the imported fields. You will import all fields from the source file and use the default data type and indexed settings for each field, except for the first field's data type.

9. Type **PatientID** in the Field Name box, click the **Data Type** arrow, click **Short Text** in the list, and then click **Field2** in the table list. The heading for the first column changes to PatientID (partially hidden) in the table list, and the second column is selected.

Be sure the data type for DOB is Date With Time, and the data type for Phone and Zip is Short Text.

10. Repeat Step 9 for the remaining nine columns, making sure Short Text is the data type for all fields, except for DOB, which should be Date With Time, typing **LastName**, **FirstName**, **DOB**, **Phone**, **Address**, **City**, **State**, **Zip**, and **Email** in the Field Name box. See Figure 8-5.

Figure 8-5 After setting field names for the ten fields in the source file

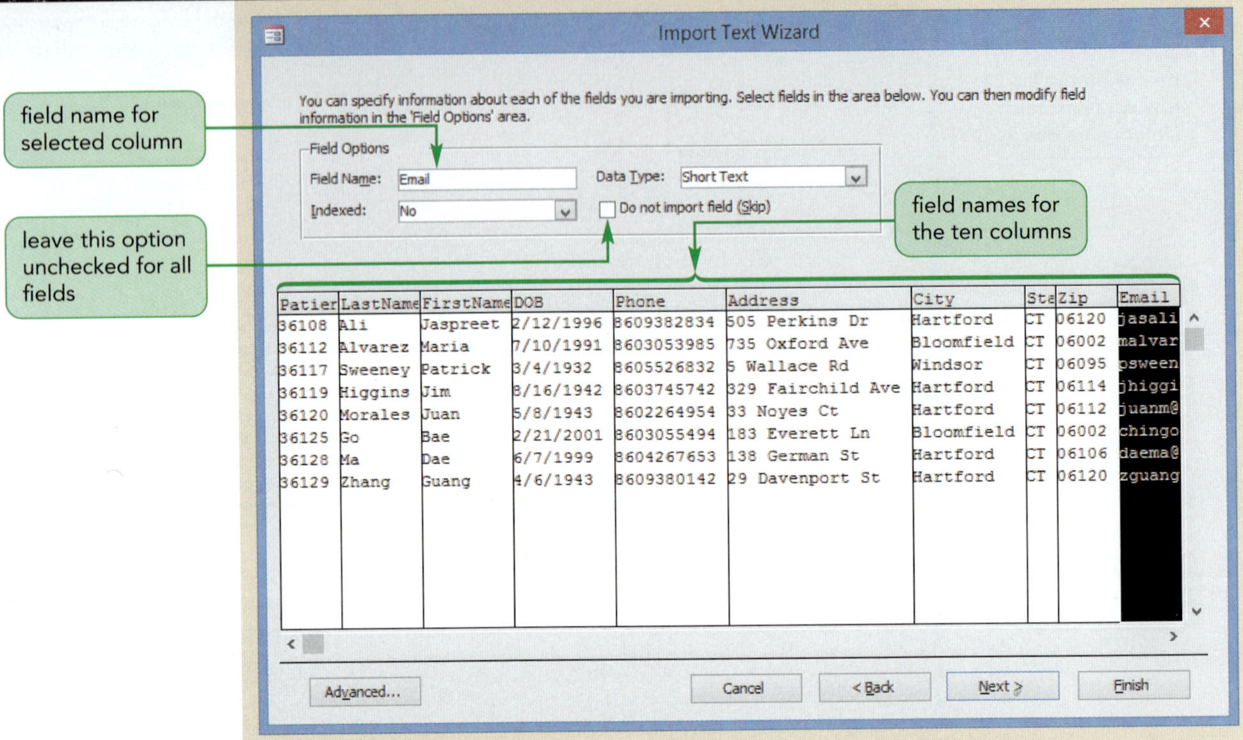

11. Click the **Next** button to open the fourth Import Text Wizard dialog box, in which you select the primary key for the imported table. PatientID, the first column, will be the primary key. When you select this column as the table's primary key, Access will delete the ID column it created.
12. Click the **Choose my own primary key** option button, make sure **PatientID** appears in the box for the option, click the **Next** button, type **tblPeopleCalled** as the table name in the Import to Table box, click the **I would like a wizard to analyze my table after importing the data** check box to select it, and then click the **Finish** button. An Import Text Wizard dialog box opens asking if you want to analyze the table; you'll continue working with this dialog box in the next set of steps.

After importing data and creating a new table, you can use the Import Text Wizard to analyze the imported table. When you choose this option, you start the Table Analyzer.

Analyzing a Table with the Table Analyzer

TIP

Read the Normalization section in the appendix titled "Relational Databases and Database Design" for more information about normalization and third normal form.

The **Table Analyzer** analyzes a single table and, if necessary, splits it into two or more tables that are in third normal form. The Table Analyzer looks for redundant data in the table. When the Table Analyzer encounters redundant data, it removes redundant fields from the table and then places them in new tables. The analyzer results must always be reviewed carefully by the database designer to determine if the suggestions are appropriate.

TIP

You can start the Table Analyzer directly by clicking the DATABASE TOOLS tab, and then in the Analyze group clicking the Analyze Table button.

To use the Table Analyzer to analyze the imported table:

1. Click the **Yes** button to close the dialog box and to open the first Table Analyzer Wizard dialog box. The wizard identifies duplicate data in your table and displays a diagram and explanation in the dialog box describing the potential problem.
2. Click the first **Show me an example** button [»], read the explanation, close the example box, click the second **Show me an example** button [»], read the explanation, close the example box, and then click the Next button to open the second Table Analyzer Wizard dialog box. The diagram and explanation in this dialog box describe how the Table Analyzer solves the duplicate data problem.
3. Again, click the first **Show me an example** button [»], read the explanation, close the example box, click the second **Show me an example** button [»], read the explanation, close the example box, and then click the **Next** button to open the third Table Analyzer Wizard dialog box. In this dialog box, you choose whether to let the wizard decide the appropriate table placement for the fields, if the table is not already normalized. Normalizing is the process of identifying and eliminating anomalies from a collection of tables. You'll let the wizard decide.
4. Make sure the **Yes, let the wizard decide** option button is selected, and then click the **Next** button. The wizard indicates that the City and State fields should be split into a separate table. Although this data is redundant, it is an industry practice to keep the city, state, and zip information with the address information in a table, so you'll cancel the wizard rather than split the table.
5. Click the **Cancel** button to close the message box and exit the wizard. Access returns you to the Get External Data - Text File dialog box, in which you are asked if you want to save the import steps. You don't need to save these steps because you're importing the data only this one time.
6. Click the **Close** button to close the dialog box.

The tblPeopleCalled table is now listed in the Tables section in the Navigation Pane. You'll open the table to verify the import results.

To open the imported tblPeopleCalled table:

1. Open the Navigation Pane and double-click **tblPeopleCalled** to open the table datasheet, resize all columns to their best fit, and then click **36108** in the first row in the PatientID column to deselect all values. Close the Navigation Pane. See Figure 8-6.

Figure 8-6 **Imported tblPeopleCalled table datasheet**

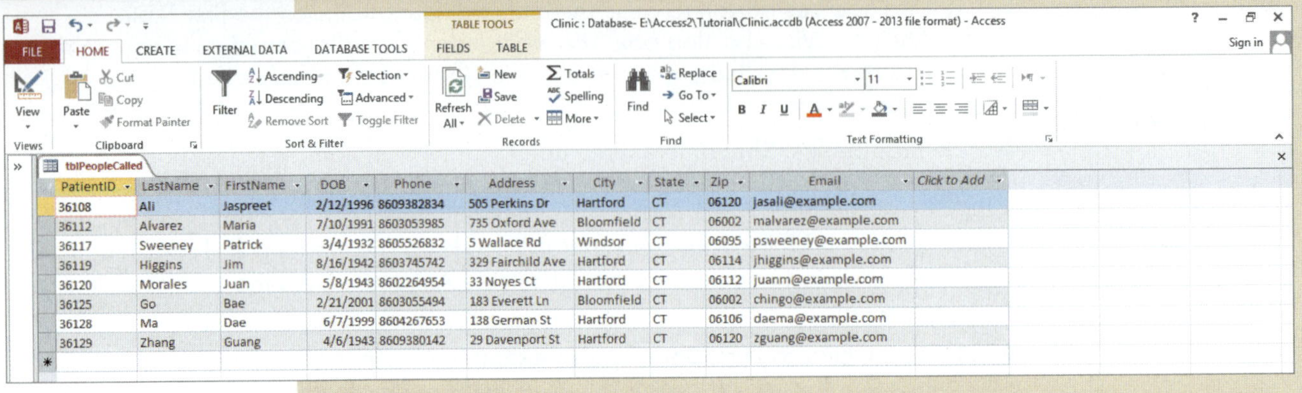

PatientID	LastName	FirstName	DOB	Phone	Address	City	State	Zip	Email
36108	Ali	Jaspreet	2/12/1996	8609382834	505 Perkins Dr	Hartford	CT	06120	jasali@example.com
36112	Alvarez	Maria	7/10/1991	8603053985	735 Oxford Ave	Bloomfield	CT	06002	malvarez@example.com
36117	Sweeney	Patrick	3/4/1932	8605526832	5 Wallace Rd	Windsor	CT	06095	psweeney@example.com
36119	Higgins	Jim	8/16/1942	8603745742	329 Fairchild Ave	Hartford	CT	06114	jhiggins@example.com
36120	Morales	Juan	5/8/1943	8602264954	33 Noyes Ct	Hartford	CT	06112	juanm@example.com
36125	Go	Bae	2/21/2001	8603055494	183 Everett Ln	Bloomfield	CT	06002	chingo@example.com
36128	Ma	Dae	6/7/1999	8604267653	138 German St	Hartford	CT	06106	daema@example.com
36129	Zhang	Guang	4/6/1943	8609380142	29 Davenport St	Hartford	CT	06120	zguang@example.com

2. Save and close the table.

Kelly has received a file from another clinic that contains a table of referral patients in an Access database. She'd like you to import this table into the Clinic database, creating a new table called tblReferral.

Importing a table from an Access Database

You can import tables, queries, reports, and other Access database objects. While you can import only a table's structure to create a blank new table, Kelly wants the data in the referral file imported into the Clinic database as well. You'll import the structure and data of the table into the Clinic database as a new table.

To import an Access table:

1. Click the **EXTERNAL DATA** tab (if necessary), and then in the Import & Link group, click the **Access** button. The Get External Data-Access Database dialog box opens.

   Trouble? If the Export - Access File dialog box opens, you clicked the Access File button in the Export group. Click the Cancel button and then repeat Step 1, being sure to select the Access File button from the Import & Link group.

2. Click the **Browse** button. The File Open dialog box opens. The Access database file from which you need to import the table structure is named NewPatientReferrals and is located in the Access2 ▸ Tutorial folder provided with your Data Files.
3. Navigate to the **Access2 ▸ Tutorial** folder where your starting Data Files are stored, click the **NewPatientReferrals** database file to select it, and then click the **Open** button.
4. Make sure the **Import tables, queries, forms, reports, macros, and modules into the current database** option button is selected, and then click the **OK** button. The Import Objects dialog box opens.
5. Click the **Options** button in the dialog box to see all the options for importing tables.

There is only one table in the NewPatientReferrals database. You'll import the tblReferral table and all of its data.

6. On the Tables tab, click **tblReferral** to select this table. See Figure 8-7.

Figure 8-7 **Import Objects dialog box showing tblReferral**

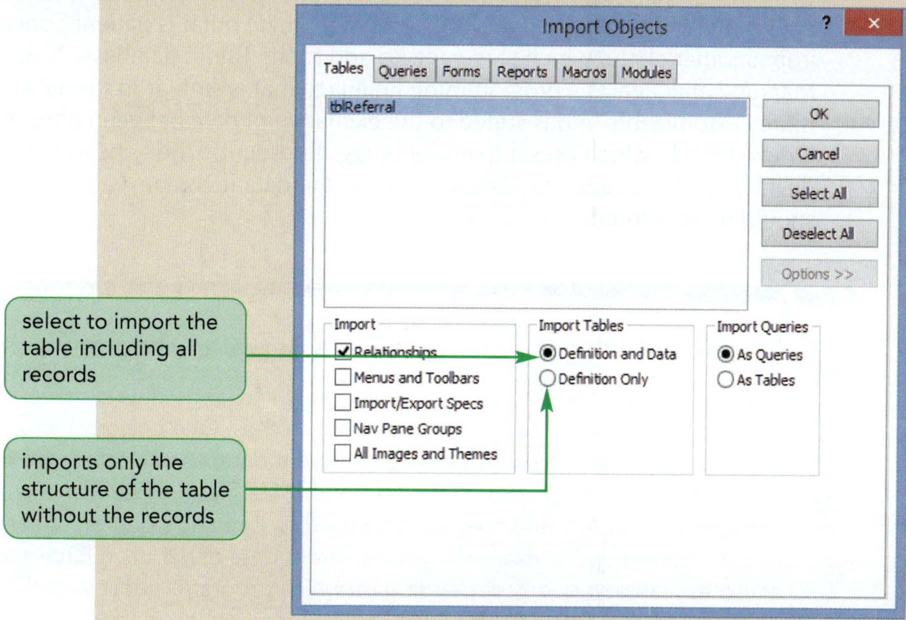

7. In the Import Tables section of the dialog box, click the **Definition and Data** option button if necessary, and then click the **OK** button. Access creates the tblReferral table in the Clinic database using the structure and contents of the tblReferral table in the NewPatientReferrals database, and opens a dialog box asking if you want to save the import steps.
8. Click the **Close** button to close the dialog box without saving the import steps.
9. Open the Navigation Pane (if necessary) and note that the tblReferral table is listed in the Tables section.
10. Double-click **tblReferral** to open the table. The tblReferral table opens in Datasheet view. See Figure 8-8.

Figure 8-8 **Imported tblReferral table datasheet**

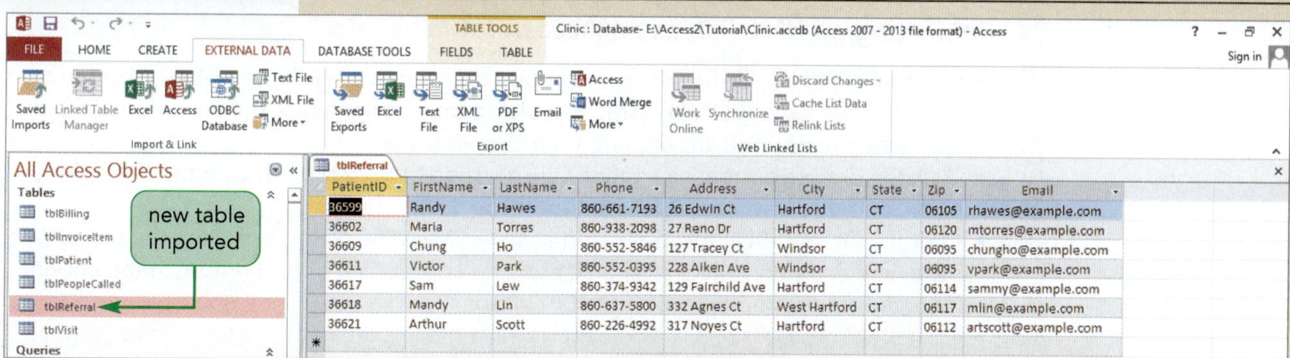

11. Close the tblReferral table.

Next, Kelly would like you to import data from another file containing new patient referrals from another clinic. However, this data is not in an Access table; instead, it's stored in XML format.

Using XML

Chatham Community Health Services occasionally receives patient referrals from other clinics. Kelly was provided an XML document that contains patient contact information from another clinic, which she wants to add to the Clinic database. XML (Extensible Markup Language) is a programming language that is similar in format to HTML, but is more customizable and is suited to the exchange of data between different programs. Unlike HTML, which uses a fixed set of tags to describe the appearance of a web page, developers can customize XML to describe the data it contains and how that data should be structured.

PROSKILLS

Decision Making: Exchanging Data Between Programs

If all companies used Access, you could easily exchange data between any two databases. However, not all companies use Access. One universal and widely used method for transferring data between different database systems is to export data to XML files and import data from XML files. XML files are used to exchange data between companies, and they are also used to exchange data between programs within a company. For example, you can store data either in an Excel workbook or in an Access table or query, depending on which program is best suited to the personnel working with the data and the business requirements of the company. Because the XML file format is a common format for both Excel and Access—as well as many other programs—whenever the data is needed in another program, you can export the data from one program as an XML file and then import the file into the other program. You should consider the needs of the users and the characteristics of the programs they use when deciding the best means for exchanging data between programs.

Importing Data from an XML File

Access can import data from an XML file directly into a database table. Kelly's XML file is named Referral.xml, and you'll import it into the tblReferral table in the Clinic database, adding the XML records to the end of the table.

REFERENCE

Importing an XML File as an Access Table

- On the EXTERNAL DATA tab, in the Import & Link group, click the XML File button to open the Get External Data - XML File dialog box; or right-click the table name in the Navigation pane, click Import, and then click XML File.
- Click the Browse button, navigate to the location of the XML file, click the XML filename, and then click the Open button.
- Click the OK button in the Get External Data - XML File dialog box, click the table name in the Import XML dialog box, click the appropriate option button in the Import Options section, and then click the OK button.
- Click the Close button; or if you need to save the import steps, click the Save import steps check box, enter a name for the saved steps in the Save as box, and then click the Save Import button.

Now you will import the Referral XML document as an Access database table.

To import the contents of the XML document:

1. In the Navigation Pane, right-click the **tblReferral** table name in the Tables objects listing, point to **Import**, then click **XML File**. The Get External Data - XML File dialog box opens.
2. Click the **Browse** button, navigate to the **Access2 ▸ Tutorial** folder, click **Referral**, and then click the **Open** button. The selected path and filename now appear in the File name box.
3. Click the **OK** button. The Import XML dialog box opens. See Figure 8-9.

Figure 8-9 **Import XML dialog box**

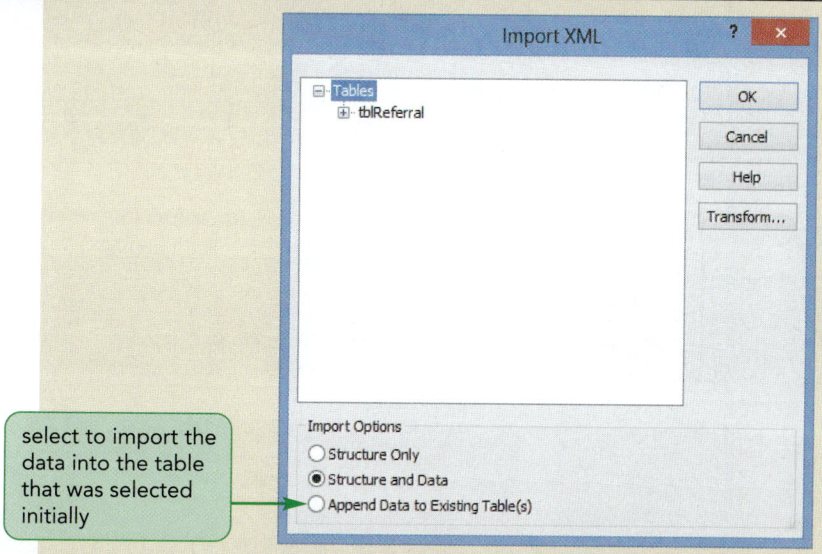

From the XML file, you can import only the table structure to a new table, import the table structure and data to a new table, or append the data in the XML file to an existing table. You'll import the data to the tblReferral table, which you selected to begin this import process.

TIP

To add records from an XML file to an existing table, in the Import XML dialog box click the Append Data to Existing Table(s) option button.

4. Make sure the **Append Data to Existing Table(s)** option button is selected, click **tblReferral** in the box, and then click the **OK** button. The Import XML dialog box closes, and the last Get External Data - XML File dialog box is displayed. You'll continue to work with this dialog box in the next set of steps.

Saving and Running Import Specifications

If you need to repeat the same import procedure many times, you can save the steps for the procedure and expedite future imports by running the saved import steps without using a wizard. Because the other clinic will send Kelly additional lists of patient referrals in the future, you'll save the import steps for Kelly so she can reuse them whenever she receives a new list.

To save the XML file import steps:

1. In the Get External Data – XML File dialog box, click the **Save import steps** check box to select it. The dialog box displays additional options for the save operation. See Figure 8-10.

Figure 8-10 Saving the import steps

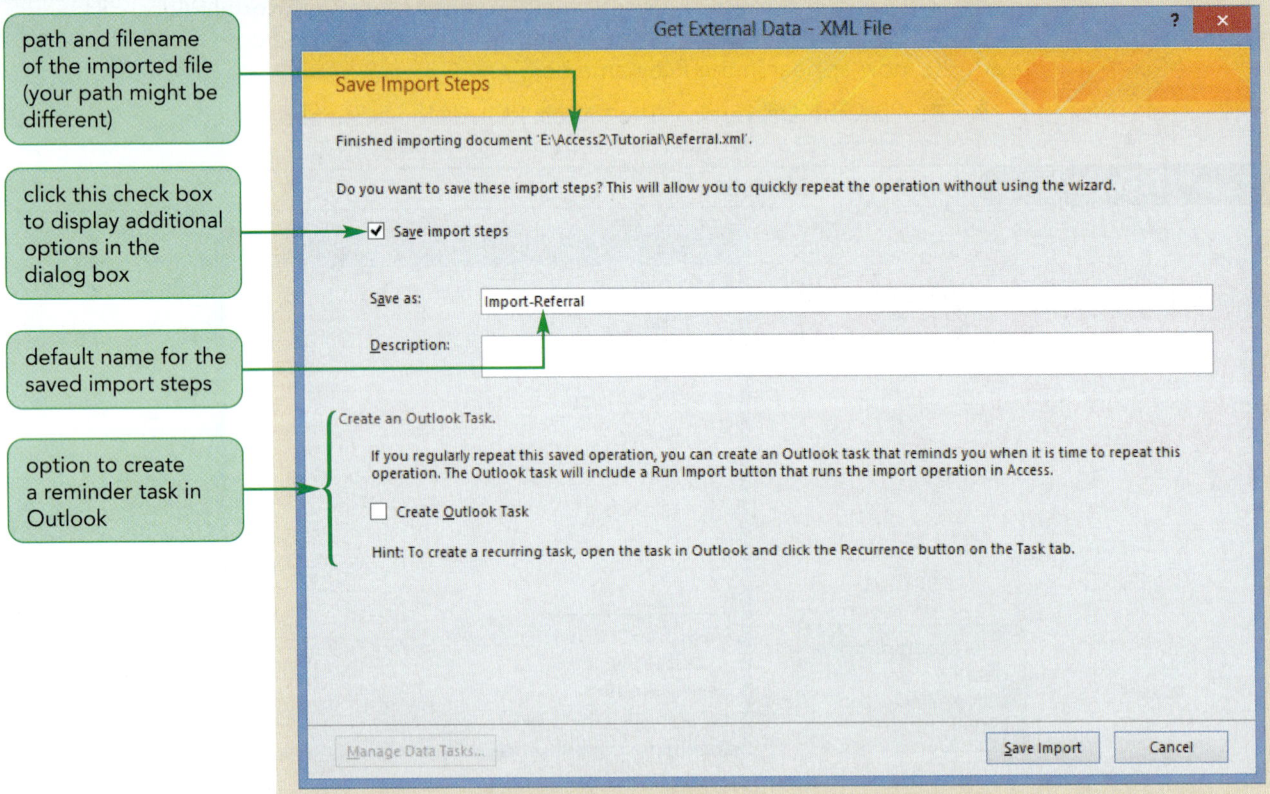

You can accept the default name for the saved import steps or specify a different name, and you can enter an optional description. If the import will occur on a set schedule, you can also create a reminder task in Microsoft Outlook. You'll accept the default name for the saved steps, and you won't enter a description or schedule an Outlook task.

2. Click the **Save Import** button. The import steps are saved as Import-Referral, the Get External Data - XML File dialog box closes, and the tblReferral records from the Referral.xml file have been imported into the tblReferral table in the Clinic database. Before reviewing the imported table, you'll add a description to the saved import steps.
3. On the EXTERNAL DATA tab, in the Import & Link group, click the **Saved Imports** button. The Manage Data Tasks dialog box opens. See Figure 8-11.

Figure 8-11 Manage Data Tasks dialog box

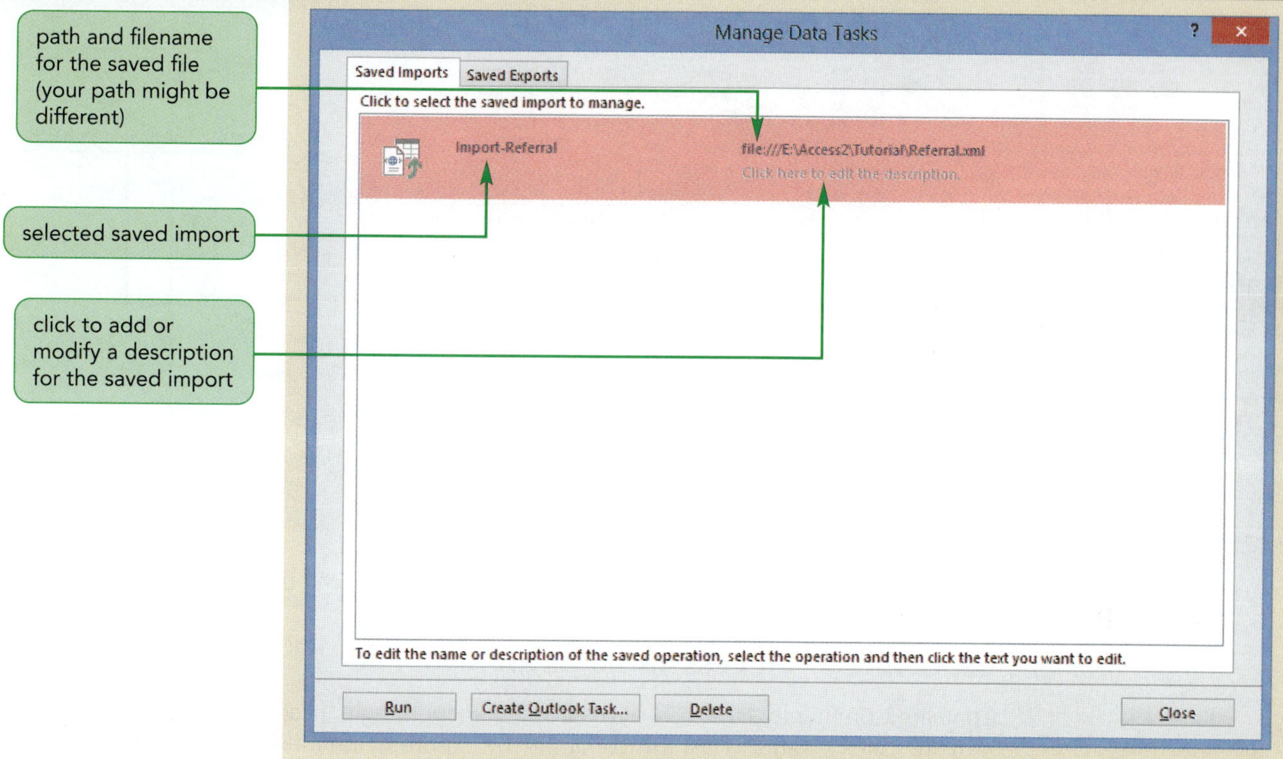

In this dialog box, you can change the name of a saved import, add or change its description, create an Outlook task for it, run it, or delete it. You can also manage any saved export by clicking the Saved Exports tab. You'll add a description for the saved procedure.

4. Click the **Click here to edit the description** text to open a box that contains an insertion point, type **XML file containing patient referrals from other clinics**, click an unused portion of the highlighted selection band to close the box and accept the typed description, and then click the **Saved Exports** tab. You have not saved any export steps, so no saved exports are displayed.
5. Click the **Close** button to close the Manage Data Tasks dialog box.
6. Double-click the **tblReferral** table in the Navigation Pane to open the table datasheet, close the Navigation Pane, resize all columns to their best fit, and then click **36229** in the first row in the PatientID column to deselect all values. See Figure 8-12.

Figure 8-12 Imported XML records added to the tblReferral table

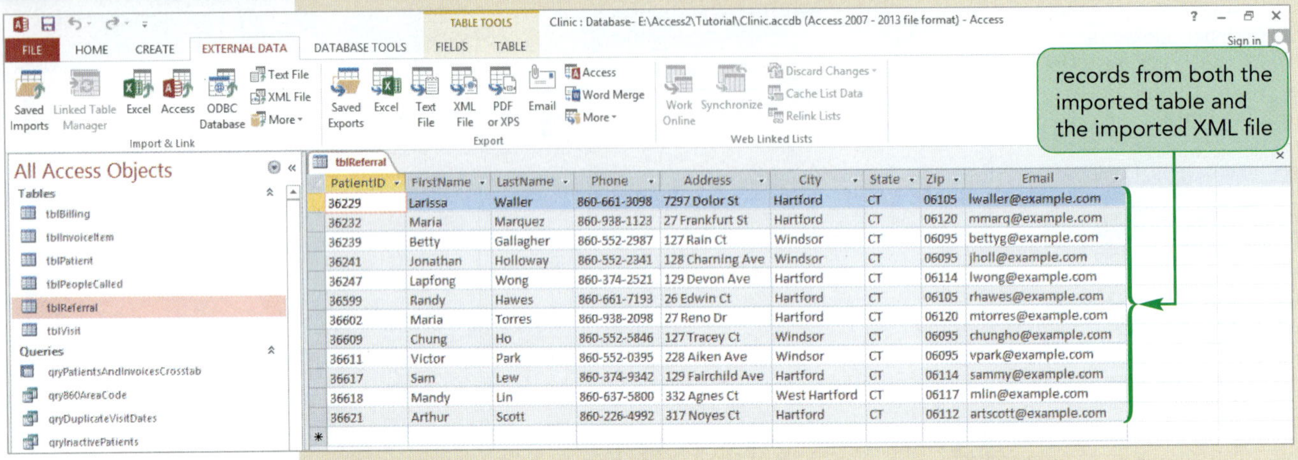

7. Save and close the table.

Next, Kelly asks you to export the tblBilling table as an XML file.

Exporting an Access Table as an XML File

Chatham Community Health Services uses an accounting package that accepts data in XML files. Kelly wants to test this capability by exporting the tblBilling table as an XML file and giving the XML file to the company's accounting manager for testing with the accounting package.

REFERENCE

Exporting an Access Object as an XML File

- Right-click the object (table, query, form, or report) in the Navigation Pane, point to Export, and then click XML File; or click the object (table, query, form, or report) in the Navigation Pane, and then on the EXTERNAL DATA tab, in the Export group, click XML File button.
- Click the Browse button in the Export - XML File dialog box, navigate to the location where you will save the XML file, and then click the Save button.
- Click the OK button in the dialog box, select the options in the Export XML dialog box or click the More Options button and select the options in the expanded Export XML dialog box, and then click the OK button.
- Click the Close button; or if you need to save the export steps, click the Save export steps check box, enter a name for the saved steps in the Save as box, and then click the Save Export button.

You'll export the tblBilling table as an XML file now.

To export the tblBilling table as an XML file:

1. Open the Navigation Pane (if necessary), right-click **tblBilling**, point to **Export** on the shortcut menu, and then click **XML File**. The Export - XML File dialog box opens.

2. Click the **Browse** button, navigate to the **Access2 ▸ Tutorial** folder included with your data files, change the name in the File name box to **Billing.xml**, and then click the **Save** button. The selected path and filename now appear in the File name box in the Export-XML File dialog box.
3. Click the **OK** button. The Export XML dialog box opens.

   Clicking the More Options button in the Export XML dialog box expands the dialog box and lets you view and change detailed options for exporting a database object to an XML file.
4. Click the **More Options** button to reveal detailed export options in the Export XML dialog box. See Figure 8-13.

Figure 8-13 **Data tab in the Export XML dialog box**

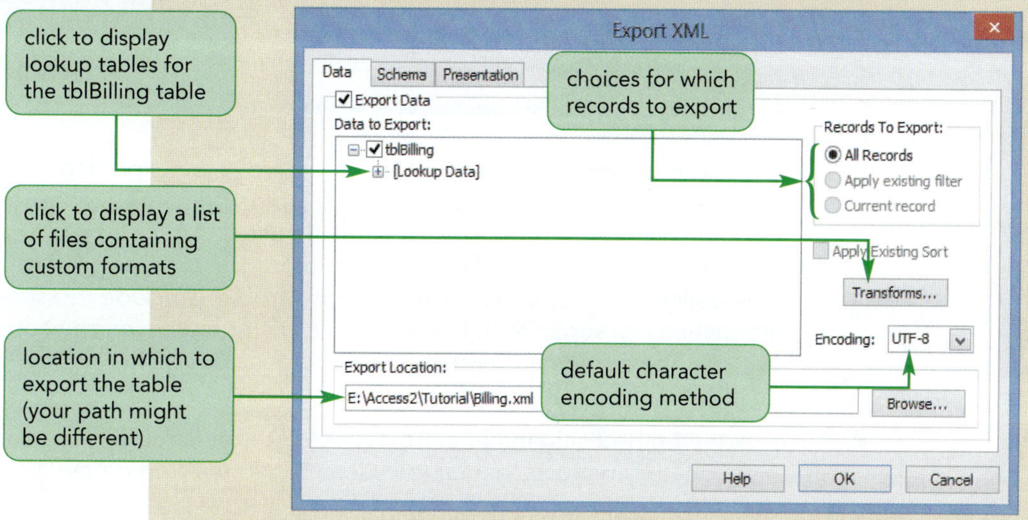

The "Export Data" check box, the "Export Location" box, and the "Records To Export" option group display the selections you made in the previous steps. You're exporting all records from the tblBilling table, including the data in the records and the structure of the table, to the Billing.xml file in the Access2 ▸ Tutorial folder. The encoding option determines how characters will be represented in the exported XML file. The encoding choices are UTF-8, which uses 8 bits to represent each character, and UTF-16, which uses 16 bits to represent each character. You can also click the Transforms button if you have a special file that contains instructions for changing the exported data.

The accounting package doesn't have a transform file and requires the default encoding, but Kelly wants to review the tables that contain lookup data.

5. In the Data to Export box, click the plus box to the left of [Lookup Data], and then verify that the tblVisit check box is not checked. The tblVisit table contains lookup data because it's the primary table in the one-to-many relationship with the related tblBilling table. The accounting package requirements don't include any lookup data from the tblVisit table, so you don't want the tblVisit check box to be checked.

   The Data tab settings are correct, so next you'll verify the Schema tab settings.
6. Click the **Schema** tab. See Figure 8-14.

Figure 8-14 Schema tab in the Export XML dialog box

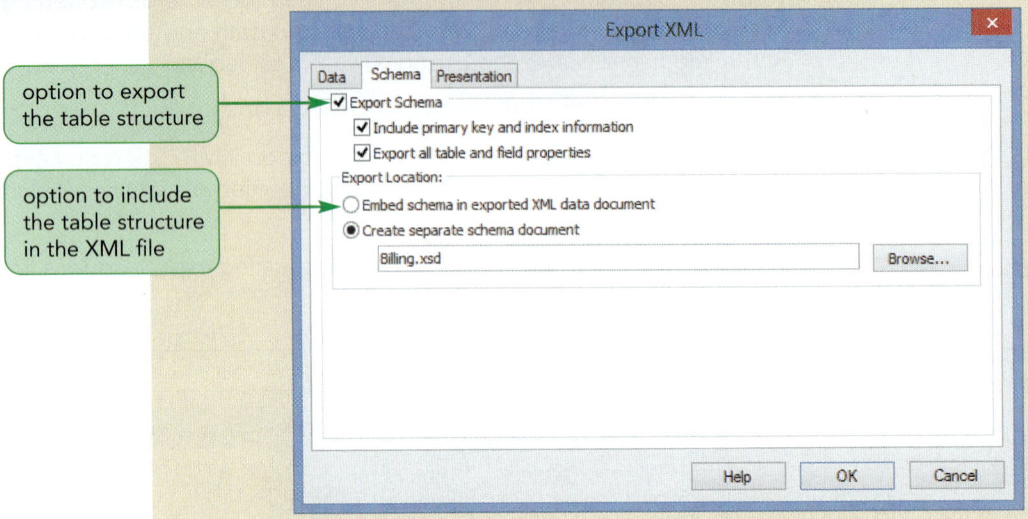

Along with the data from the tblBilling table, you'll be exporting its table structure, including information about the table's primary key, indexes, and table and field properties. An **XSD (XML Structure Definition) file** is a file that defines the structure of the XML file, much like the Design view of a table defines the fields and their data types. You can include this structure information in a separate XSD file or you can embed the information in the XML file. The accounting package expects a single XML file, so you'll embed the structure information in the XML file.

7. Click the **Embed schema in exported XML data document** option button. The "Create separate schema document" option button is now grayed out.
8. Click the **Presentation** tab. See Figure 8-15.

Figure 8-15 Presentation tab in the Export XML dialog box

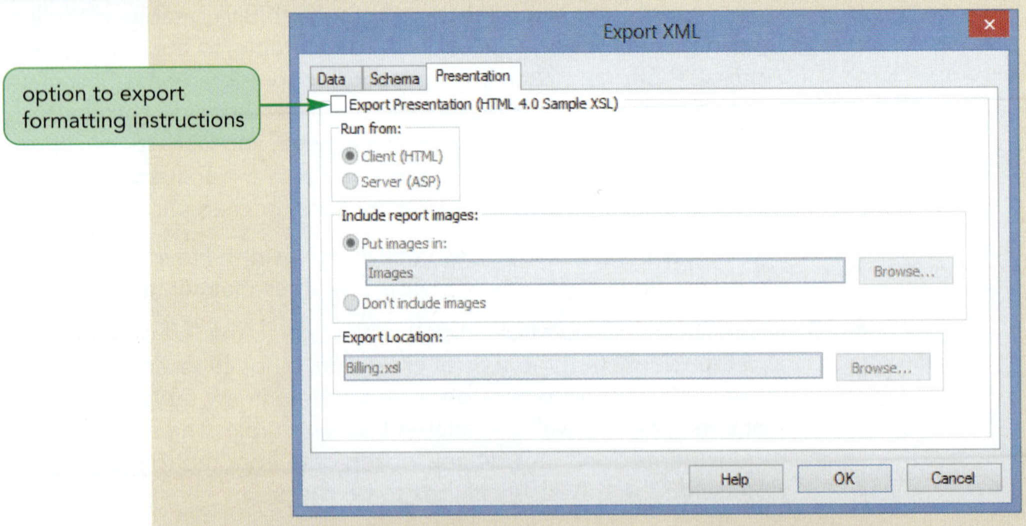

The Presentation tab options let you export a separate **XSL (Extensible Stylesheet Language) file** containing the format specifications for the tblBilling table data. The accounting package contains its own formatting instructions for any imported data, so you will not export an XSL file.

9. Make sure that the **Export Presentation (HTML 4.0 Sample XSL)** check box is not checked, and then click the **OK** button. Access closes the Export XML dialog box, exports the data in the tblBilling table as an XML file to the Access2 ▸ Tutorial folder, and returns you to the final Export - XML File dialog box. You'll see the results of creating this file in the next set of steps.

Kelly plans to make further tests exporting the tblBilling table as an XML file, so you'll save the export steps.

INSIGHT

Importing and Exporting Data

Access supports importing data from common file formats such as an Excel workbook, a text file, and an XML file. Additional Access options include importing an object from another Access database, importing data from other databases (such as Microsoft SQL Server, mySQL, and others), and importing an HTML document, an Outlook folder, or a SharePoint list.

In addition to exporting an Access object as an XML file or an HTML document, Access includes options for exporting data to another Access database, other databases (Microsoft SQL Server, mySQL), an Excel workbook, a text file, a Word document, a SharePoint list, or a PDF or XPS file. You can also export table or query data directly to Word's mail merge feature, or export an object to an e-mail message.

The steps you follow for other import and export options work similarly to the import and export steps you've already used.

Saving and Running Export Specifications

Saving the steps to export the tblBilling table as an XML file will save time and eliminate errors when Kelly repeats the export procedure. You'll save the export steps and then run the saved steps.

To save and run the XML file export steps:

1. Click the **Save export steps** check box. The dialog box displays additional options for the save operation.

   The dialog box has the same options you saw earlier when you saved the XML import steps. You'll enter a description, and you won't create an Outlook task because Kelly will be running the saved export steps on an as-needed basis.

2. In the Description box, type **XML file accounting entries from the tblBilling table**. See Figure 8-16.

Figure 8-16 Saving the export steps

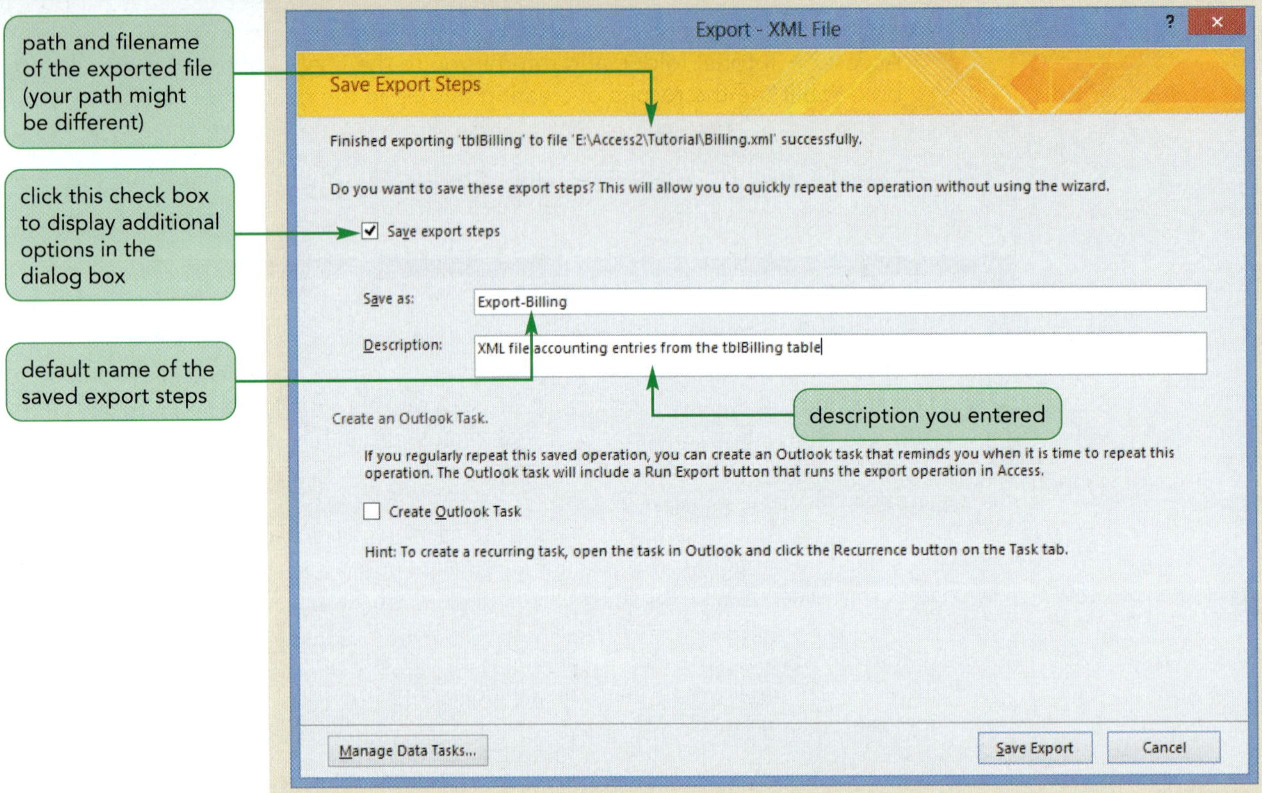

3. Click the **Save Export** button. The export steps are saved as Export-Billing and the Export - XML File dialog box closes.

   Now you'll run the saved steps.

4. Click the **EXTERNAL DATA** tab (if necessary), and then in the Export group, click the **Saved Exports** button. The Manage Data Tasks dialog box opens with the Saved Exports tab selected. See Figure 8-17.

   Trouble? If the Saved Imports tab is visible, then you selected the Saved Imports button instead of the Saved Exports button. Click the Close button and repeat Step 4.

Figure 8-17 Manage Data Tasks dialog box

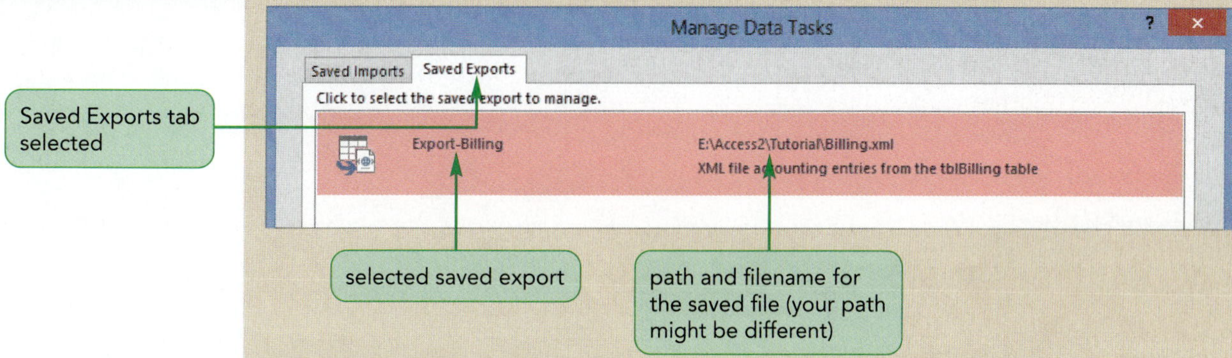

5. Verify that the Export-Billing procedure you created in Step 3 is selected, and then click the **Run** button. The saved procedure runs and a message box opens, asking if you want to replace the existing XML file you created earlier.
6. Click the **Yes** button to replace the existing XML file. A message box informs you that the export was completed successfully.
7. Click the **OK** button to close the message box, and then click the **Close** button to close the Manage Data Tasks dialog box.
8. Open Windows File Explorer, navigate to the **Access2 ▸ Tutorial** folder, right-click **Billing.xml** in the file list to open the shortcut menu, click **Open with**, and then click **Notepad**.

   The Billing.xml file contains the data itself, along with code that describes the data, as shown in Visual Overview 8.1.
9. Close the Notepad window.
10. If you are not continuing on to the next session, close the Clinic database.

You've imported and exported data, analyzed a table's design, and saved and run import and export specifications. In the next session, you will analyze data by working with a chart, create and use an application part, link external data, and add a tab control to a form.

REVIEW

Session 8.1 Quick Check

1. What is HTML?
2. What is an HTML template?
3. What is a static web page?
4. What is a CSV file?
5. What is the Table Analyzer?
6. ____________ is a programming language that describes data and its structure.

Session 8.2 Visual Overview:

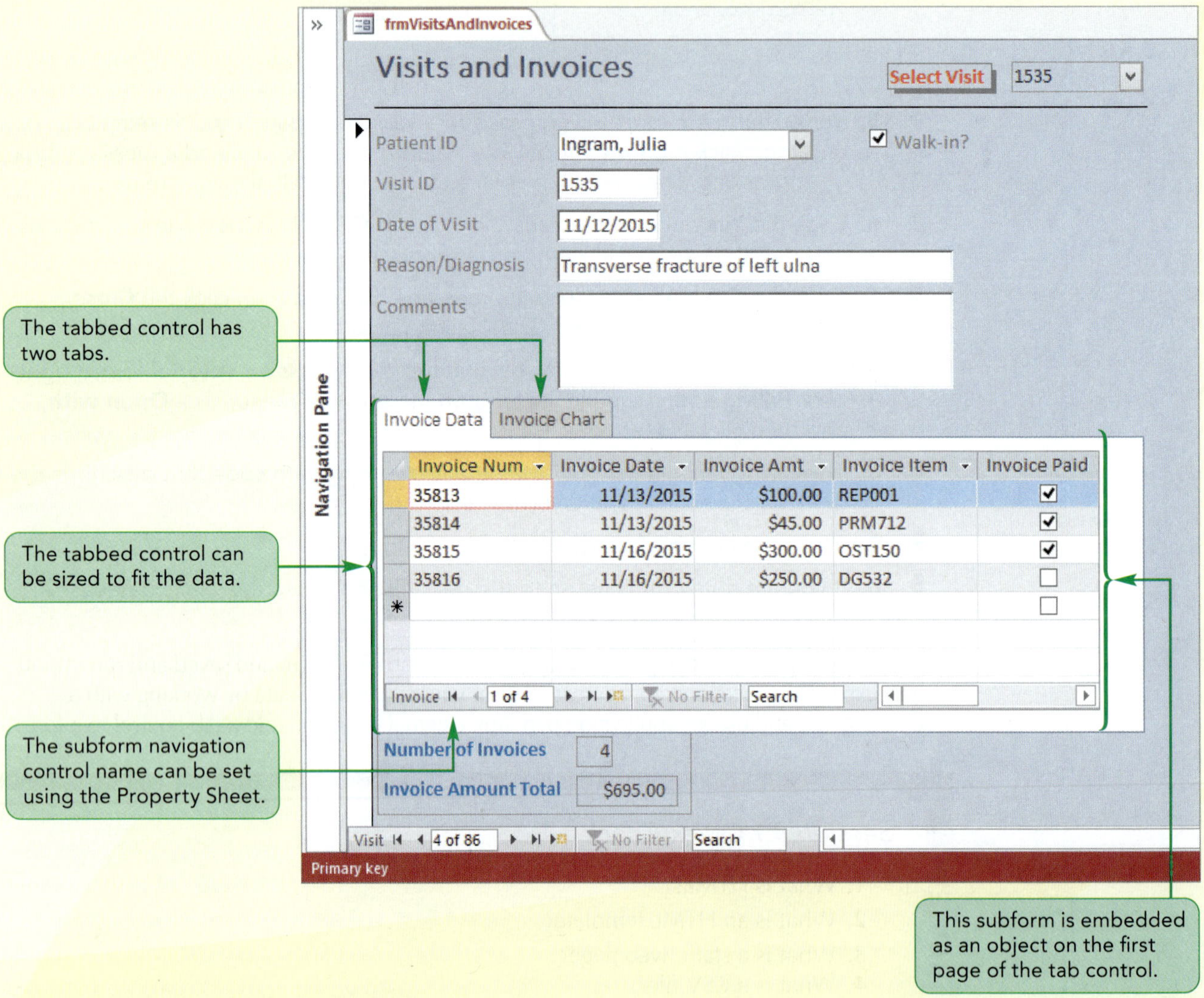

Tabbed Control with a Chart

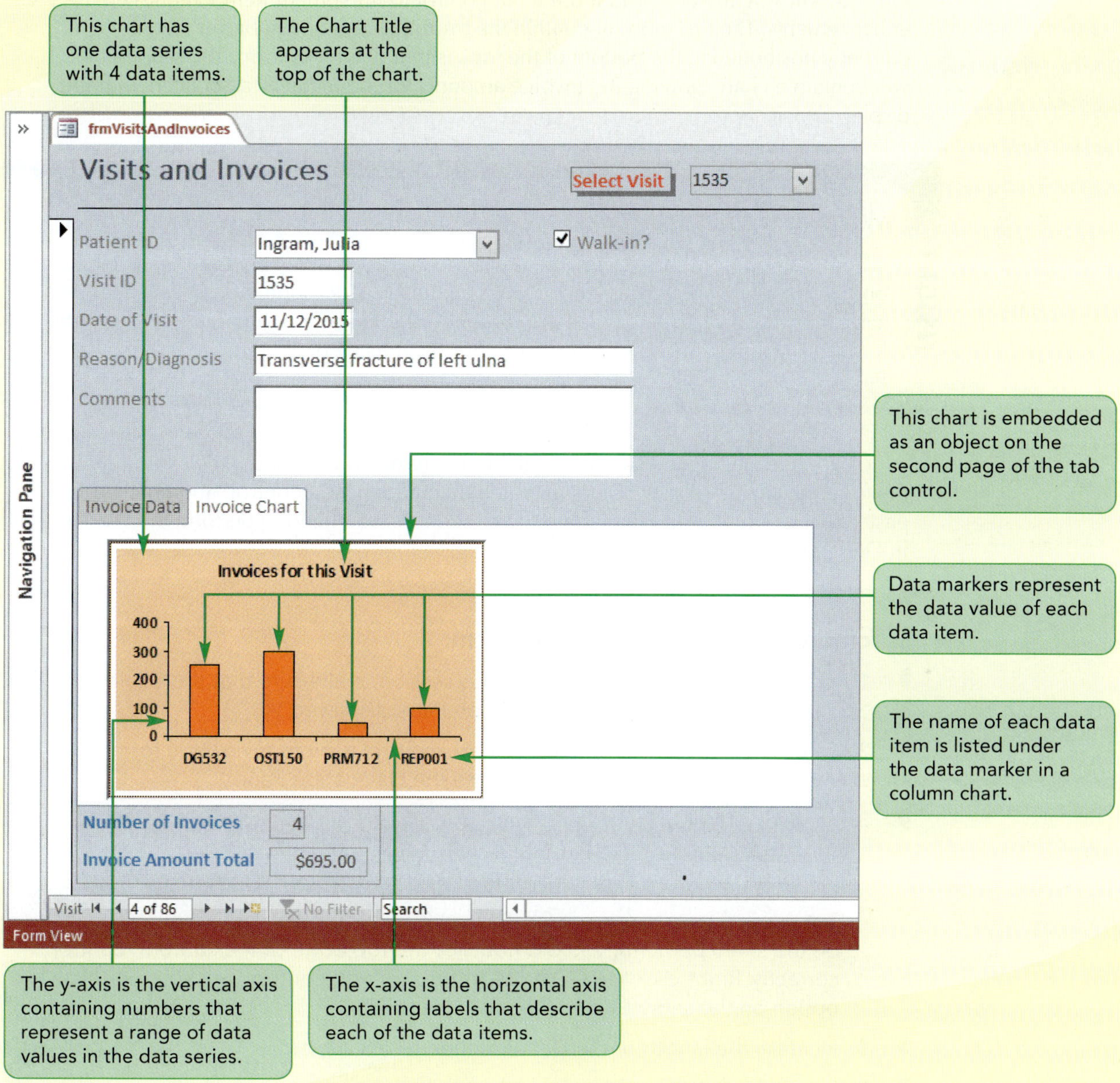

Creating a Tabbed Form Using a Tab Control

Kelly wants you to enhance the frmVisitsAndInvoices form to enable users to switch between different content. Specifically, she wants users to be able to choose between viewing the frmBillingSubform subform or viewing a chart showing the invoices associated with the displayed visit.

You can use the **Tab Control tool** to insert a tab control, which is a control that appears with tabs at the top, with one tab for each form. Users can switch between forms by clicking the tabs. You'll use a tab control to implement Kelly's requested enhancements. The first tab will contain the frmBillingSubform subform that is currently positioned at the bottom of the frmVisitsAndInvoices form. The second tab will contain a chart showing the invoice amounts for the invoices associated with the displayed visit.

INSIGHT

Working with Large Forms

When you want to work with a form that is too large to display in the Access window, one way to help you navigate the form is to manually add page breaks, where it makes sense to do so. You can use the **Page Break tool** to insert a page break control in the form, which lets users move between the form pages by pressing the Page Up and Page Down keys.

To expedite placing the subform in the tab control, you'll first cut the subform from the form, placing it on the Clipboard. You'll then add the tab control, and finally you'll paste the subform into the left tab on the tab control. You need to perform these steps in Design view.

To add the tab control to the form:

1. If you took a break after the previous session, make sure that the Clinic database is open with the Navigation Pane displayed.
2. Open the **frmVisitsAndInvoices** form in Form view to review the form, switch to Design view, and then close the Navigation Pane.
3. Scroll down to the subform (if necessary), right-click the top edge of the subform control to open the shortcut menu, and then click **Cut** to delete the subform control and place it on the Clipboard.

   Trouble? If you do not see Subform in New Window as one of the options on the shortcut menu, you did not click the top edge of the subform control correctly. Right-click the top edge of the subform control until you see this option on the shortcut menu, and then click Cut.
4. Increase the length of the Detail section to 6.5 inches.
5. Select the Number of Invoices label and control, the Invoice Amount Total label and control, and the rectangle shape surrounding them, and then move them below the 6-inch horizontal line in the grid.
6. On the DESIGN tab, in the Controls group, click the **Tab Control** tool .
7. Position the + portion of the pointer in the Detail section at the 2.75-inch mark on the vertical ruler and three grid dots from the left edge of the grid, and then click the mouse button. Access places a tab control with two pages in the form.

8. Right-click in the middle of the tab control, and then when an orange outline appears inside the tab control, click **Paste** on the shortcut menu. The subform is pasted in the tab control. See Figure 8-18.

Figure 8-18 **Subform on the tab control in the Detail section**

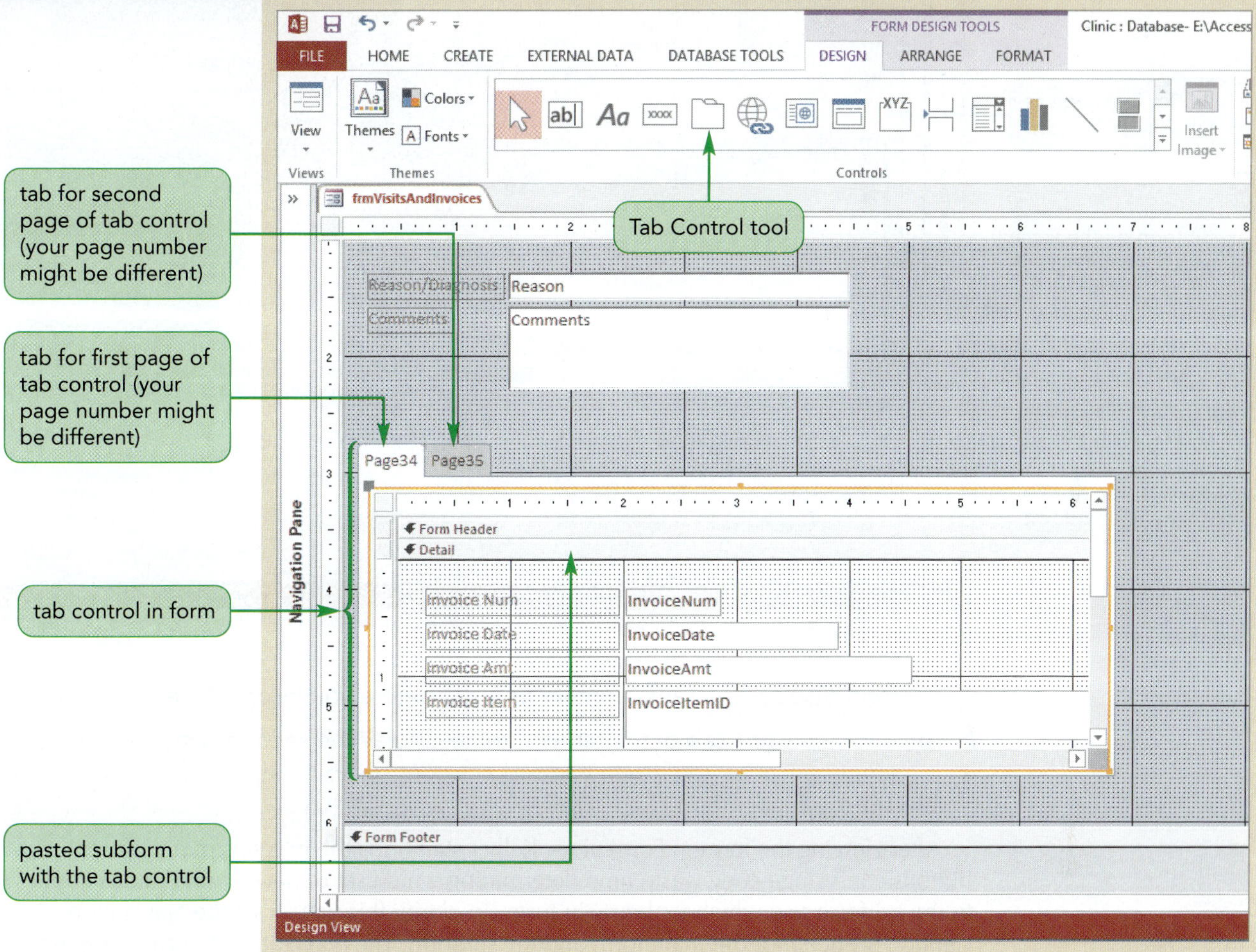

9. Switch to Form view, and then click **1527** in the VisitID text box to deselect all controls. The left tab, which represents the first page in the tab control, is the active tab. See Figure 8-19.

Figure 8-19 Subform on the tab control in Form view

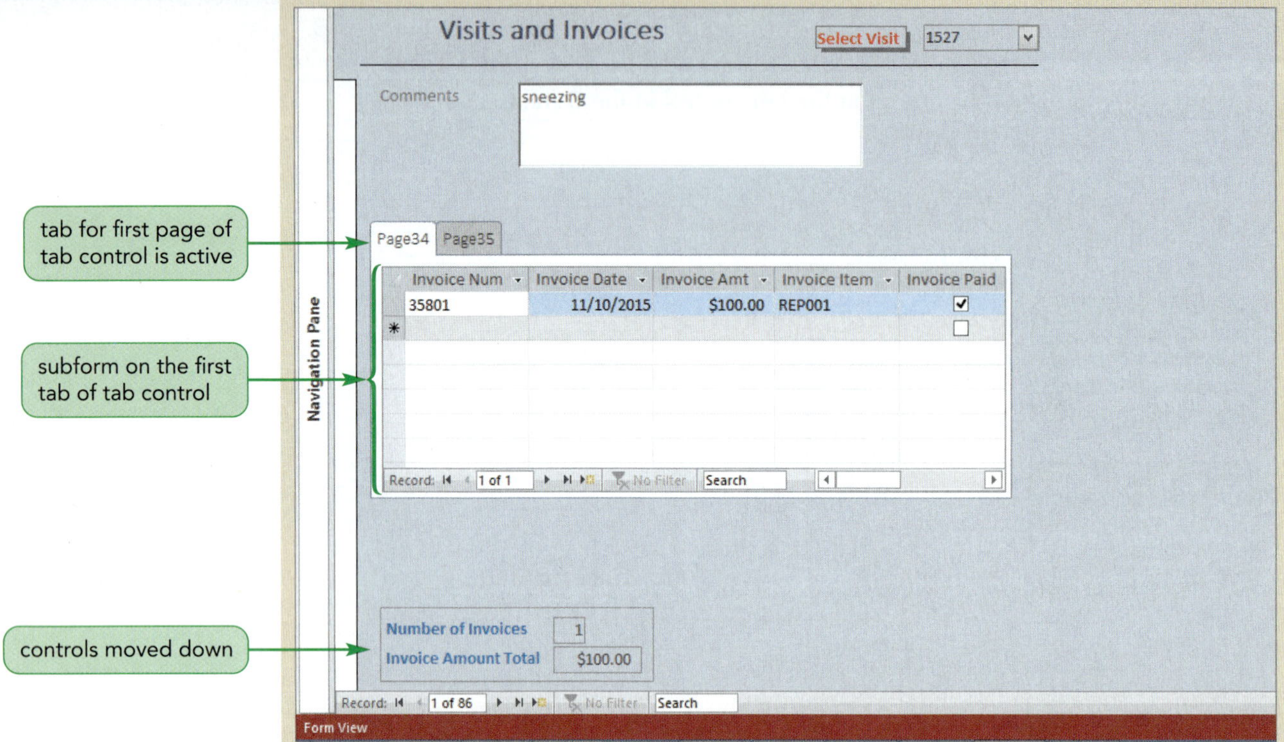

The subform is now displayed on the first page of the tab control, and the form displays the same content as it did before you inserted the tab control.

10. Click the **right tab** of the tab control to display the second page. The page is empty because you haven't added any controls to it yet.

After viewing the form in Form view, Kelly's staff finds the two sets of navigation buttons confusing—they waste time determining which set of navigation buttons applies to the subform and which to the main form. To clarify this, you'll set the Navigation Caption property for the main form and the subform. The **Navigation Caption property** lets you change the navigation label from the word "Record" to another value. Because the main form displays data about visits and the subform displays data about invoices, you'll change the Navigation Caption property for the main form to "Visit" and for the subform to "Invoice."

You'll also edit the labels for the tabs in the tab control, so they indicate the contents of each page.

To change the captions for the navigation buttons and the tabs:

1. Switch to Design view.
2. Click the **form selector** for the main form to select the form control in the main form, open the property sheet to display the properties for the selected form control, click the **All** tab (if necessary), click the **Navigation Caption** box, and then type **Visit**. See Figure 8-20.

Figure 8-20 Setting the Navigation Caption property for the main form

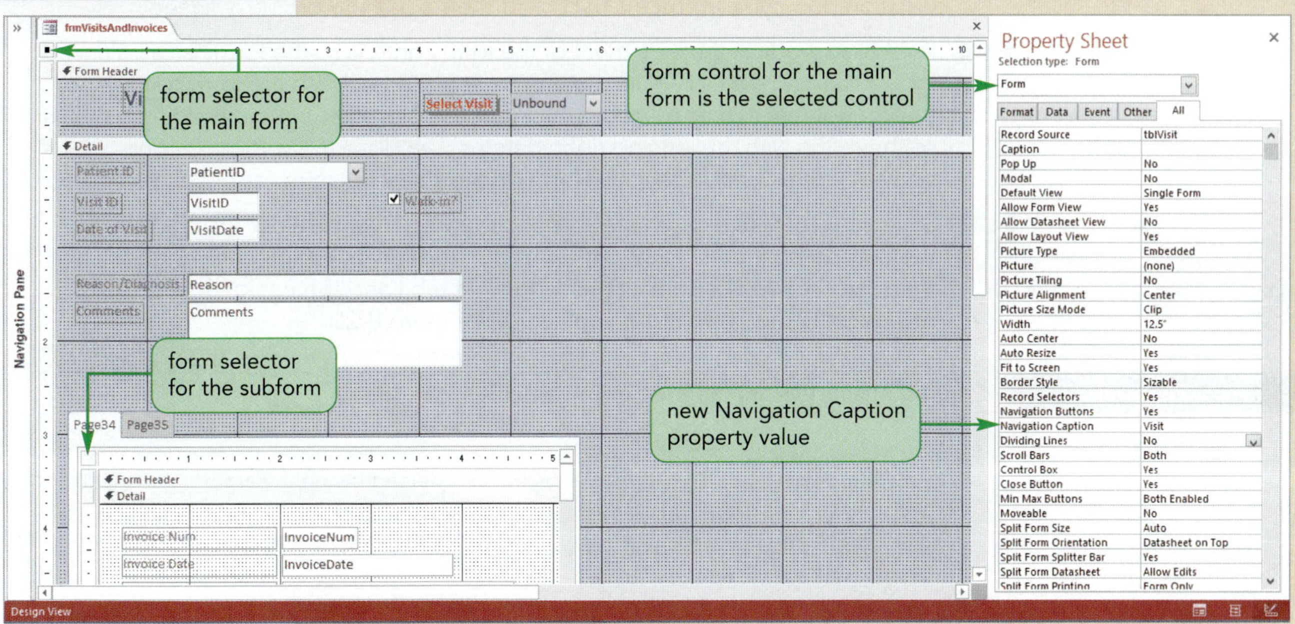

3. Click the **form selector** for the subform to select the subform, click the **form selector** for the subform again to select the form control in the subform and to display the properties for the selected form control, on the Property Sheet click the **Navigation Caption** box, and then type **Invoice**. Navigation buttons don't appear in Design view, so you won't see the effects of the Navigation Caption property settings until you switch to Form view.
4. Click the **left tab** in the subform, click the **left tab** in the subform again to select it, on the Property Sheet in the Caption box type **Invoice Data**, and then press the **Tab** key. The Caption property value now appears in the left tab. See Figure 8-21.

Figure 8-21 Setting the Caption property for the left tab

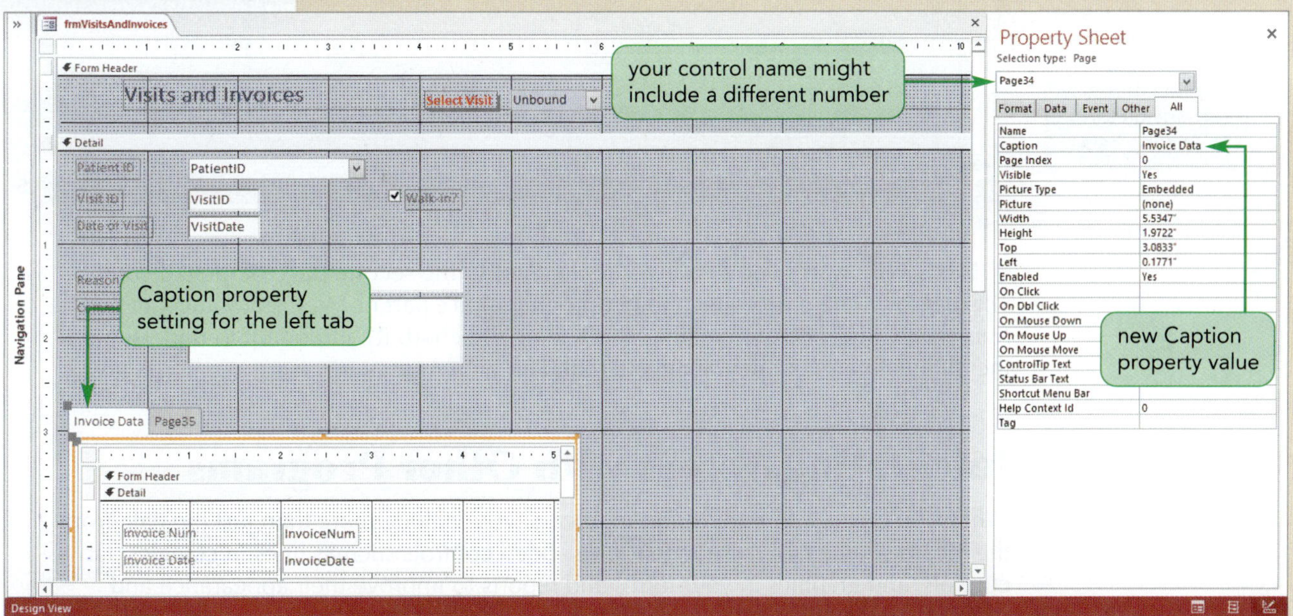

5. Click the **right tab** in the subform to select it, on the Property Sheet in the Caption box, type **Invoice Chart**, and then close the property sheet.
6. If necessary, adjust the alignment of the form controls so the form has a balanced look. You may need to adjust the vertical spacing between the form controls so the controls are evenly spaced, and adjust the placement of the heading controls so they align with the left and right margins. Decrease the vertical spacing between form controls to fit the form on the screen as much as possible.
7. Save your form design changes, switch to Form view, select VisitID 1527 in the combo box, click **1527** in the VisitID text box to deselect all controls, and then scroll to the bottom of the form. The tabs and the navigation buttons now display the new caption values. See Figure 8-22.

Figure 8-22 **Caption properties and aligned form controls**

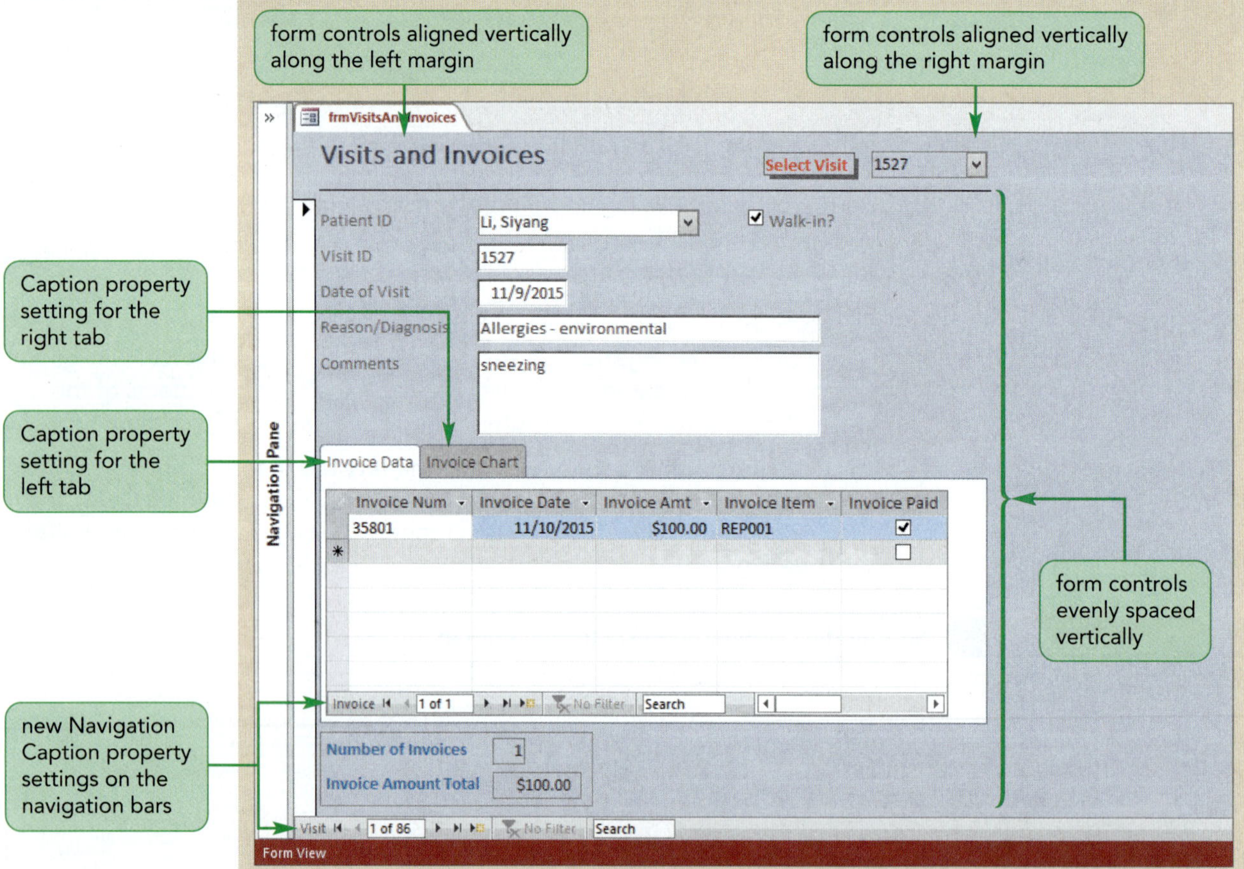

Next, Kelly wants you to add a simple chart to the second page of the tab control. This chart will be created by another program that's part of Microsoft Office, called Microsoft Graph. Before creating and adding the chart, it's important to understand the different ways of integrating external data with Access.

Integrating Access with Other Programs

When you create a form or report in Access, you include more than just the data from the record source table or query. You've added controls such as lines, rectangles, tab controls, and graphics in your forms and reports to improve their appearance and usability. You can also add charts, drawings, and other objects to your forms and reports, but Access doesn't have the capability to create them. Instead, you create these objects using other programs and then place them in a form or report using the appropriate integration method.

When you integrate information between programs, the program containing the original information, or object, is called the **source program**, and the program in which you place the information created by the source program is called the **destination program**. Access offers three ways for you to integrate objects created by other programs.

- **Importing**. When you import an object, you include the contents of a file in a new table or append it to an existing table, or you include the contents of the file in a form, report, or field. For example, when you add a picture to a form, you import it into the form; likewise, in this tutorial you imported CSV and XML files as new tables in the Clinic database. An imported picture is a file with a .bmp extension that was created by a graphics program, and the CSV and XML files you imported were also created by other programs. After importing an object, it no longer has a connection to the program that created it. Any subsequent changes you make to the object using the source program are not reflected in the imported object.
- **Embedding**. When you embed an object in a form, report, or field, you preserve its connection to the source program, which enables you to edit the object, if necessary, using the features of the source program. However, any changes you make to the object are reflected only in the form, report, or field in which it is embedded; the changes do not affect the original object in the file from which it was embedded. Likewise, if you start the source program outside Access and make any changes to the original object, these changes are not reflected in the embedded object. The features of the source program determine which features are available for the embedded object.
- **Linking**. When you link an object to a form, report, or field, you include a connection in the destination program to the original file maintained by the source program; you do not store data from the file in the destination program. Any changes you make to the original file using the source program are reflected in the linked file version in the destination program.

PROSKILLS

Decision Making: Importing, Embedding, and Linking Data

How do you decide which method to use when you need to include in an Access database data that is stored in another file or format? When you intend to use Access to maintain the data and no longer need an updated version of the data in the source program, you can import a file as a new table or append the records in the file to an existing table. You link to the data when the source program will continue to maintain the data in the file, and you need to use an updated version of the file at all times in the destination program. When linking to the data, you can also maintain the data using the destination program, and the source program will always use the updated version of the file.

- For objects in forms or reports, you import an object (such as a picture) when you want a copy of the object in your form or report and you don't intend to make any changes to the object. You embed or link an object when you want a copy of the object in your form or report and you intend to edit the object using the source program in the future. You embed the object when you do not want your edits to the object in the destination program to affect any other copies of the object used by other programs. You link the object when you want your edits to the object in the destination program to affect the object used by other programs.
- The decision to import, embed, or link to data depends on how you will use the data in your database, and what connection is required to the original data. You should carefully consider the effect of changes to the original data and to the copied data before choosing which method to use.

To add the chart that Kelly wants on the second page of the tab control, you'll embed data from another program.

Embedding a Chart in a Form

The Chart Wizard in Access helps you to embed a chart in a form or report. The chart is actually created by another program, Microsoft Graph, but the Chart Wizard does the work of embedding the chart. After embedding the chart in a form or report, you can edit it using the Microsoft Graph program.

REFERENCE

Embedding a Chart in a Form or Report

- In Design view, on the DESIGN tab, in the Controls group, click the More button, and then click the Chart tool.
- Position the + portion of the pointer where you want to position the upper-left corner of the chart, and then click the mouse button to start the Chart Wizard.
- Select the record source, fields, and chart type.
- Edit the chart contents, and select the fields that link the object and chart, if necessary.
- Enter a chart title, select whether to include a legend, and then click the Finish button.

The tblBilling table contains the information needed for the chart Kelly wants you to include in the form's right tab in the tab control.

To add a chart in the tab control and start the Chart Wizard:

1. Switch to Design view, then on the Invoice Chart tab on the tab control click the **subform**, and then click the **subform** again to ensure the tab content is selected.
2. On the DESIGN tab, in the Controls group, click the **Chart** tool, and then move the pointer to the tab control. When the pointer is inside the tab control, the rectangular portion of the tab control you can use to place controls is filled in black.
3. Position the + portion of the pointer in the upper-left corner of the black portion of the tab control, and then click the mouse button. Access places a chart control in the form and opens the first Chart Wizard dialog box, in which you select the source record for the chart.

Kelly wants the chart to provide her staff with a simple visual display of the relative proportions of the invoice amounts for the invoice items for the currently displayed patient visit. You'll use the tblBilling table as the record source for the chart and select the InvoiceAmt and InvoiceItem fields as the fields to use in the chart.

The order of the items is important. Be sure to add InvoiceItemID first, then InvoiceAmt. If you make a mistake, move both back to the Available Fields and start again.

To create the chart with the Chart Wizard:

1. Click **Table: tblBilling** in the box, and then click the **Next** button to display the second Chart Wizard dialog box.
2. Add the InvoiceItemID and InvoiceAmt fields to the Fields for Chart box, in that order, and then click the **Next** button to display the third Chart Wizard dialog box, in which you choose the chart type.

3. Click the **Pie Chart** button (row 4, column 1) to select the pie chart as the chart type to use for Kelly's chart. The box on the right displays a brief description of the selected chart type. See Figure 8-23.

Figure 8-23 Selecting the chart type

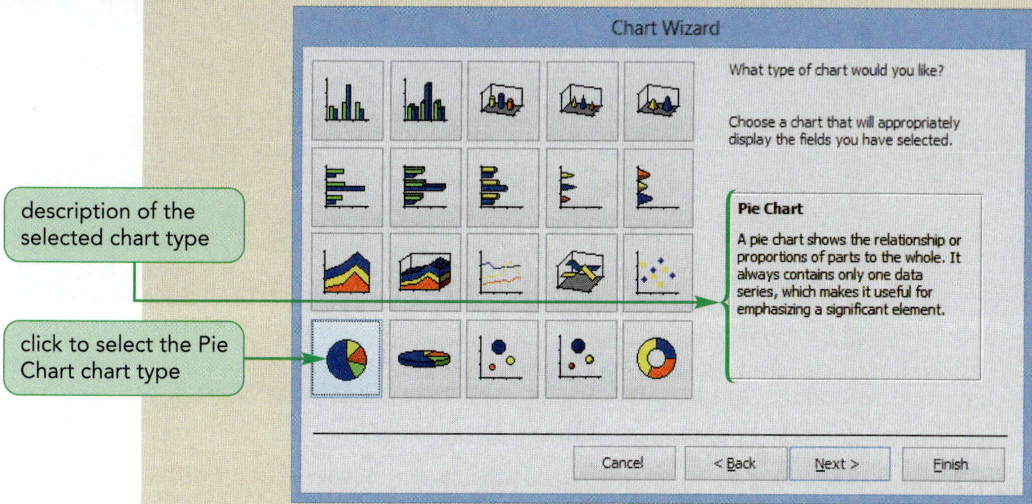

4. Click the **Next** button to display the next Chart Wizard dialog box, which displays a preview of the chart and options to modify the data and its placement in the chart. You'll use the default layout based on the two selected fields. You can easily modify the chart after you create it.

5. Click the **Next** button to display the next Chart Wizard dialog box, which lets you choose the fields that link records in the main form (which uses the tblVisit table as its record source) to records in the chart (which uses the tblBilling table as its record source). You don't need to make any changes in this dialog box, as the wizard has already identified VisitID as the common field linking these two tables. You can use the VisitID field as the linking field even though you didn't select it as a field for the chart.

6. Click the **Next** button to display the final dialog box, which allows you to enter the title that will appear at the top of the chart and choose whether to include a legend in the chart.

7. Type **Invoices for this Visit**, make sure the **Yes, display a legend** option button is selected, and then click the **Finish** button. The completed chart appears in the tab control.

   You'll view the form in Form view, where it's easier to assess the chart's appearance.

8. Save your form design changes, switch to Form view, in the combo box select Visit ID **1535**, click the **Invoice Chart** tab to display the chart, and then scroll down to the bottom of the form (if necessary). See Figure 8-24.

Figure 8-24 Embedded chart in Form view

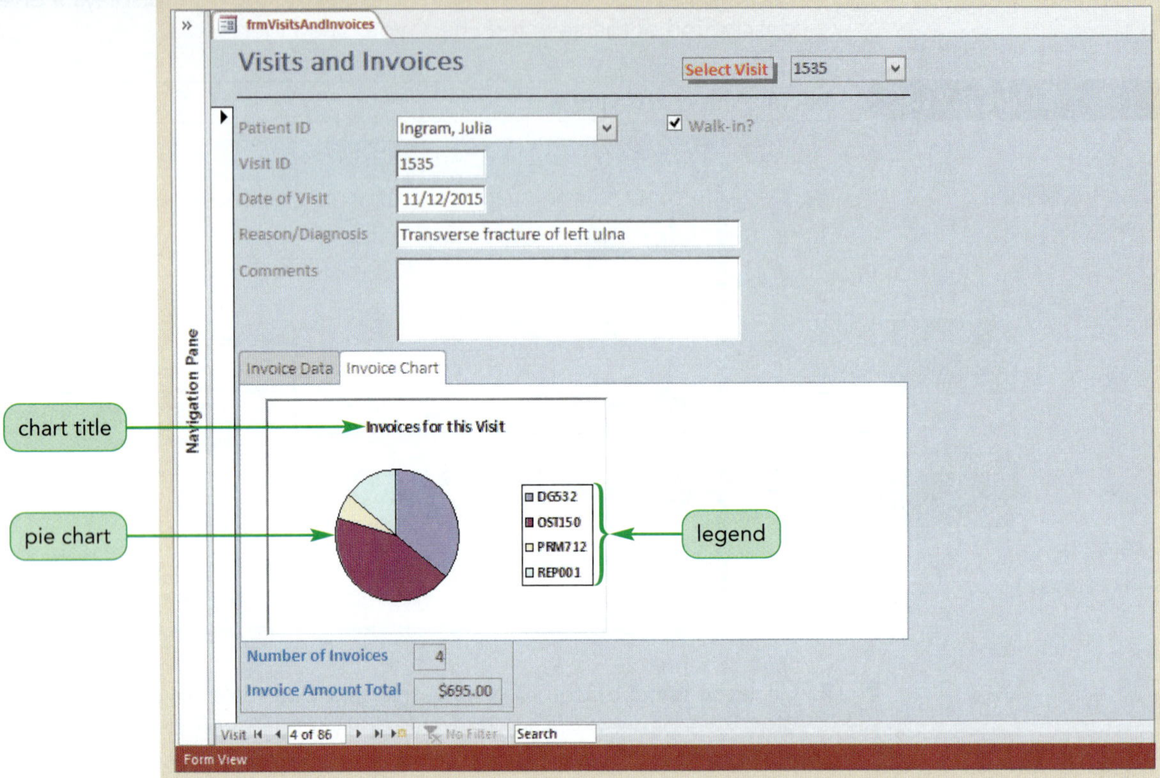

INSIGHT

Linking Record Sources

The record source for a primary main form must have a one-to-many relationship to the record source for a related subform or chart. The subform or chart object has its Link Master Fields property set to the primary key in the record source for the main form and its Link Child Fields property set to the foreign key in the record source for the subform or chart.

After viewing the chart, Kelly decides it needs some modifications. She wants you to change the chart type from a pie chart to a bar chart, remove the legend, and modify the chart's background color. To make these changes, you'll switch to Design view and then you'll start Microsoft Graph.

To edit the chart using Microsoft Graph:

1. Switch to Design view, right-click an edge of the chart object to open the shortcut menu, point to **Chart Object**, and then click **Open**. Microsoft Graph starts and displays the chart. See Figure 8-25.

   Trouble? If Chart Object doesn't appear on the shortcut menu, right-click the edge until it does.

Figure 8-25 Editing the chart with Microsoft Graph

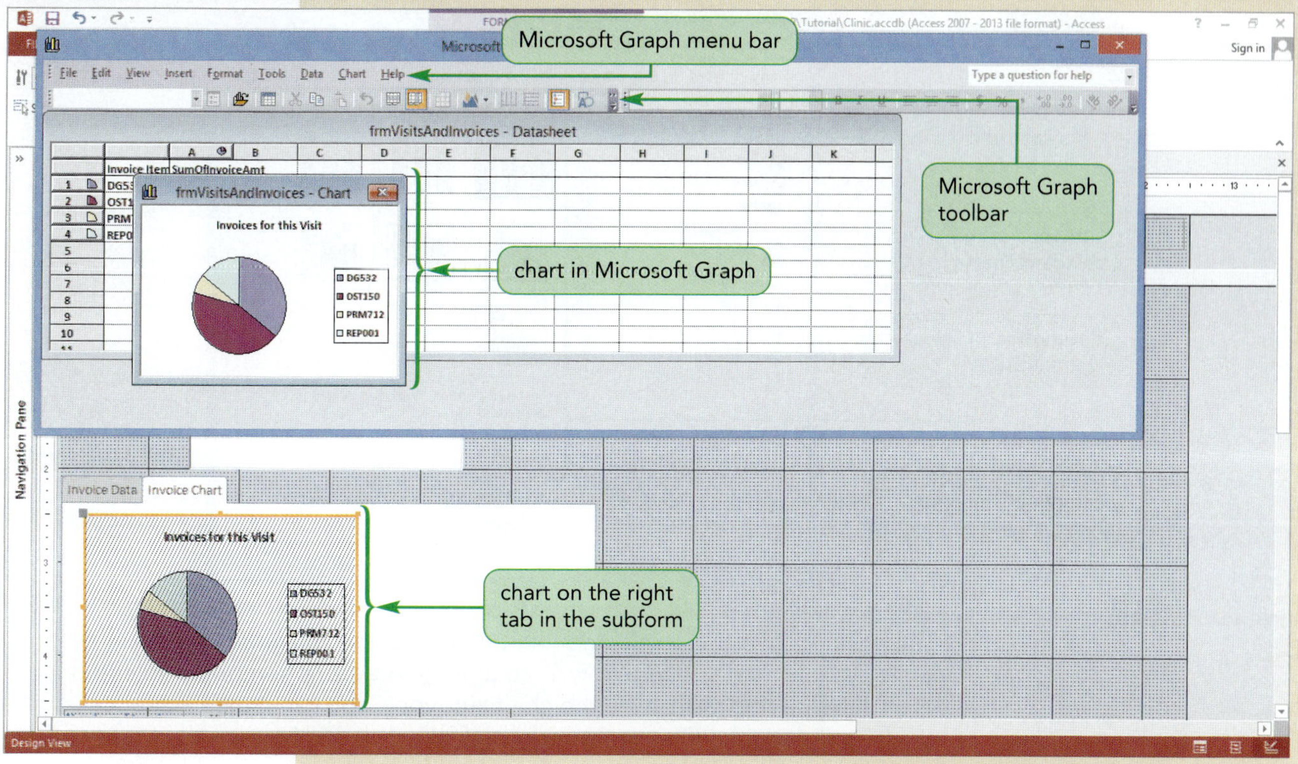

Microsoft Graph is the source program that the Chart Wizard used to create the chart. Because the chart was embedded in the form, editing the chart object starts Graph and allows you to edit the chart using the Graph menu bar and toolbar. In addition to displaying the selected chart, the Graph window displays a datasheet containing the data on which the chart is based. You'll now make Kelly's chart changes using Graph.

2. On the Graph menu bar, click **Chart**, click **Chart Type** to open the Chart Type dialog box, and then click **Column** in the Chart type box to display the types of column charts. See Figure 8-26.

Figure 8-26 **Chart Type dialog box**

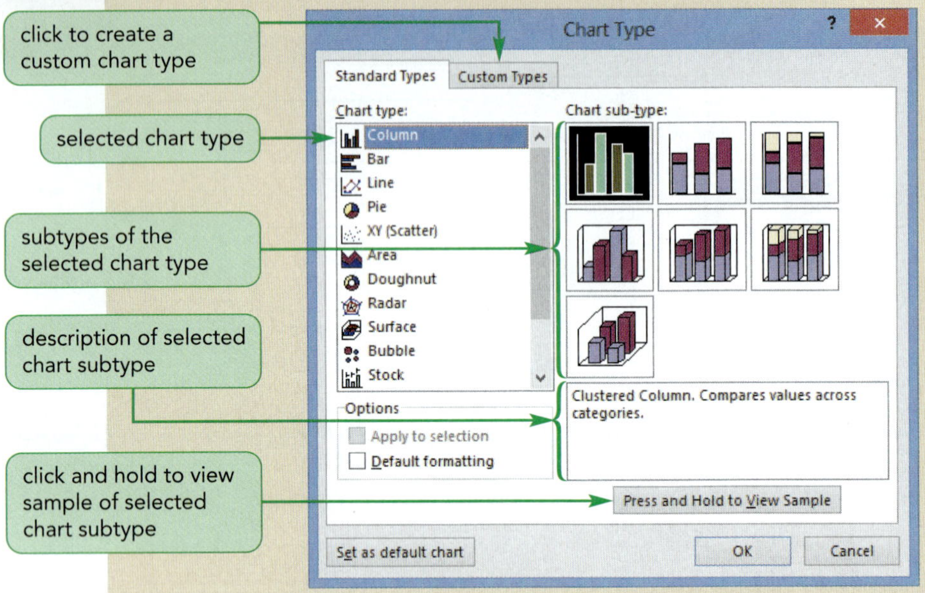

The column chart is the selected chart type, and the clustered column chart is the default chart subtype (row 1, column 1). A description of the selected chart subtype appears below the chart subtypes. You can create a custom chart by clicking the Custom Types tab. If you click and hold on the Press and Hold to View Sample button, you'll see a sample of the selected subtype.

3. Click the **Press and Hold to View Sample** button to view a sample of the chart, release the mouse button, and then click the **OK** button to close the dialog box and change the chart to a column chart in the Graph window and in the form.
4. On the Graph menu bar, click **Chart**, click **Chart Options** to open the Chart Options dialog box, click the **Legend** tab to display the chart's legend options, click the **Show legend** check box to clear it, and then click the **OK** button. The legend is removed from the chart object in the Graph window and in the form.

   To change the color or other properties of a chart control—the chart background (or chart area), axes, labels to the left of the y-axis, labels below the x-axis, or data markers (columnar bars for a column chart)—you need to double-click the control.

TIP

A data marker is a bar, dot, segment, or other symbol that represents a single data value.

5. In the Chart window, double-click one of the blue data markers inside the chart to open the Format Data Series dialog box, and then in the Area section, in the color palette, click the orange box (row 2, column 2). The sample color in the dialog box changes to orange to match the selected color in the color palette. See Figure 8-27.

   Trouble? If you click off the chart in MS Graph, and the chart disappears, just click View on the menu bar, and then click Datasheet to bring the chart back.

Figure 8-27 Format Data Series dialog box

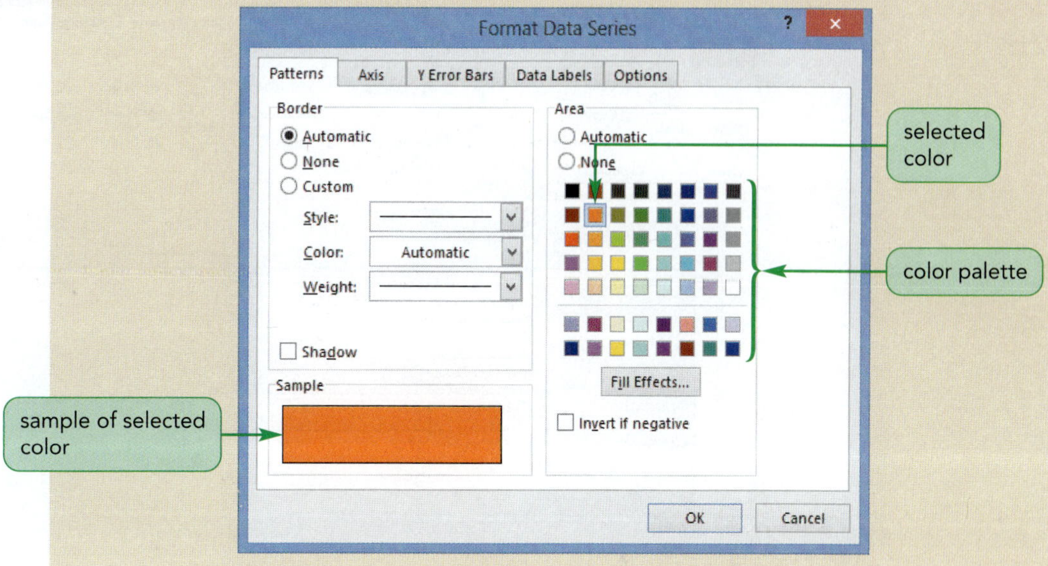

6. Click the **OK** button to close the dialog box. The color of the data markers in the chart in the Graph window and in the form changes to orange.

   Trouble? If only one of the bars changed color, you selected one bar instead of the entire series. Click Edit, click Undo, and then repeat Steps 5 and 6.

7. In the Chart window, double-click the white chart background to the left of the title to open the Format Chart Area dialog box, in the Area section in the color palette click the light orange box (row 5, column 2), and then click the **OK** button. The chart's background color changes from white to light orange in the chart in the Graph window and in the form.

8. Click **File** on the Graph menu bar, and then click **Exit & Return to frmVisitsAndInvoices** to exit Graph and return to the form.

9. Save your form design changes, switch to Form view, in the combo box select Visit ID **1535** and then click the **Invoice Chart** tab to display the chart. See Figure 8-28.

Figure 8-28 **Completed chart in Form view**

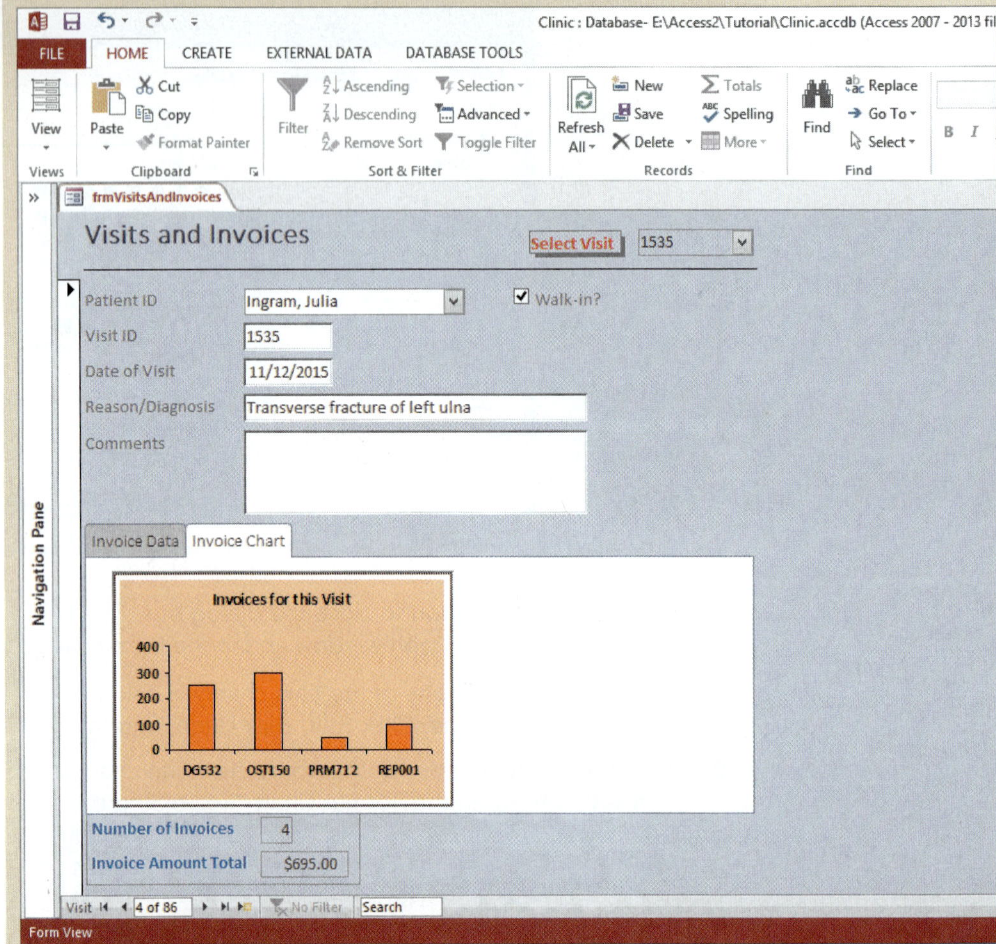

10. Close the form.

Kelly has found the tblReferral table so useful that she'd like to be able to use the same table structure in other databases. One option would be to import the table structure from the NewPatientReferrals.accdb database file into each database. Another option is to create an application part from the NewPatientReferrals database, which could then easily be included in any Access database file on Kelly's computer.

Using Templates and Application Parts

A template is a predefined database that can include tables, relationships, queries, forms, reports, and other database objects. When you create a new database using Backstage view, Access displays a list of predefined templates. You can also create your own template from an existing database file. In addition to creating a standard template, you can also create an **application part**, which is a specialized template that can be imported into an existing database. A standard template would be used to create a new database file. An application part is used when you already have a database file that you're working with, and would like to include the content from an application part in your existing database. Like a template, an application part can contain tables, relationships, queries, forms, reports, and other database objects.

Kelly would like to reuse the tblReferral table structure to store a table of referrals from local pharmacists. You'll use the NewPatientReferrals.accdb database file to create an Application Part for the tblReferral table structure, then you'll import the new application part into the Clinic database to use for referrals from local pharmacists.

To create an application part from a database file:

1. Click the **CREATE tab**, and then in the Templates group, click the **Application Parts** button to open the gallery of predefined application parts. See Figure 8-29.

Figure 8-29 Predefined Application Parts

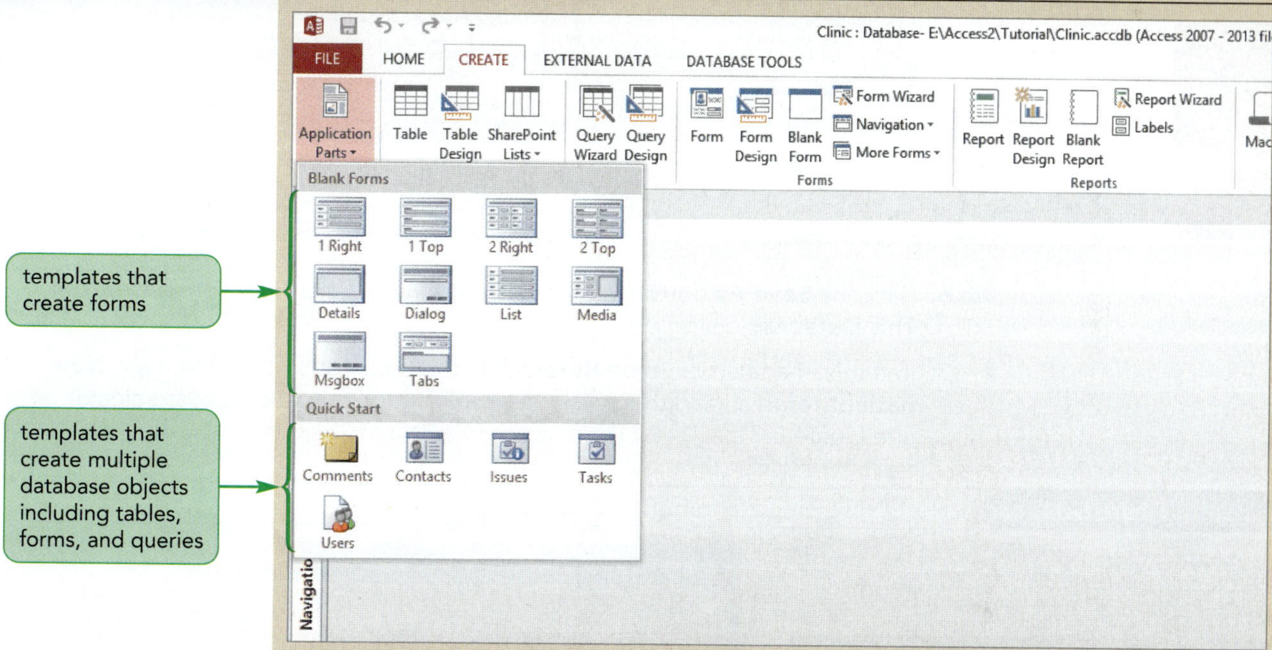

Note that there are Blank Forms and Quick Start Application Parts, but there are no user-defined application parts.

Trouble? If you see user-application parts listed in the Application Parts gallery it could be that these application parts were created by other users. Access will store Application Parts created from any Access database file and they will be available in all Access database files on the computer. You can disregard any user-defined application parts that you may see on your local computer.

2. Close the Clinic database file.
3. Open the NewPatientReferrals database file from the Access2 ▸ Tutorial folder included with your Data Files.

   When you save this file as a template, all database objects that are in the file will be included in the template file. This file contains only the tblReferral table.
4. Click the **FILE** tab to display Backstage view, and then click **Save As**.
5. Click **Save Database As** (if necessary) and then in the Save Database As box in the Database File Types list click **Template**. See Figure 8-30.

Figure 8-30 Saving a database as a template

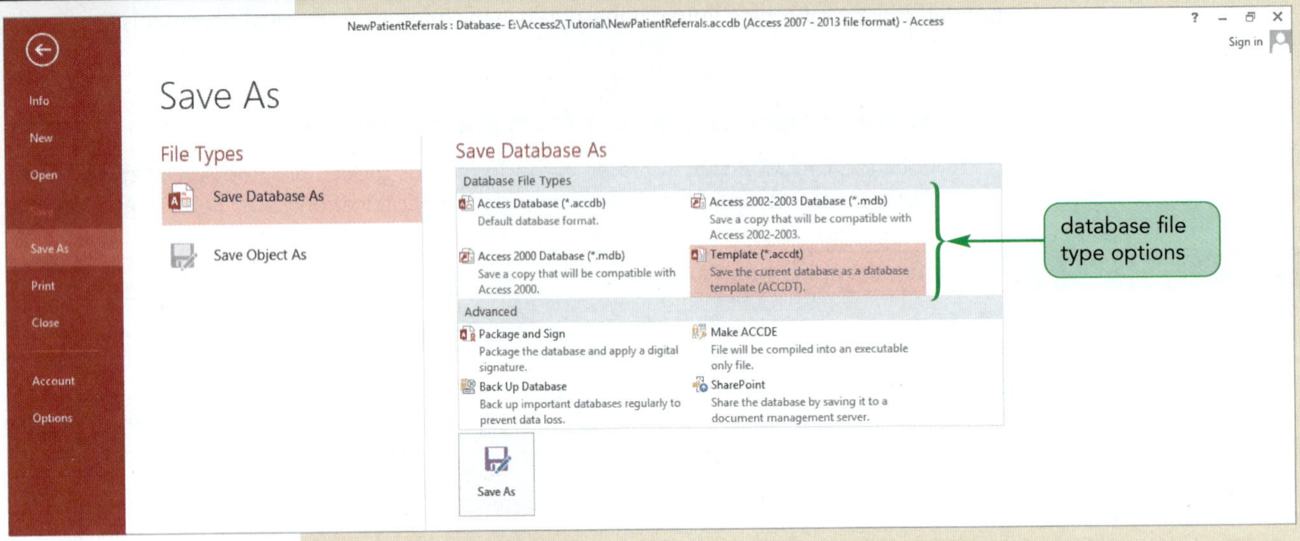

6. Click the **Save As** button. Access displays the **Create New Template from This Database** dialog box .
7. In the Name text box, type **Referral**. In the Description text box, type **New patient referral**, and then click the Application Part check box to select it. See Figure 8-31.

Figure 8-31 Create New Template from This Database dialog box

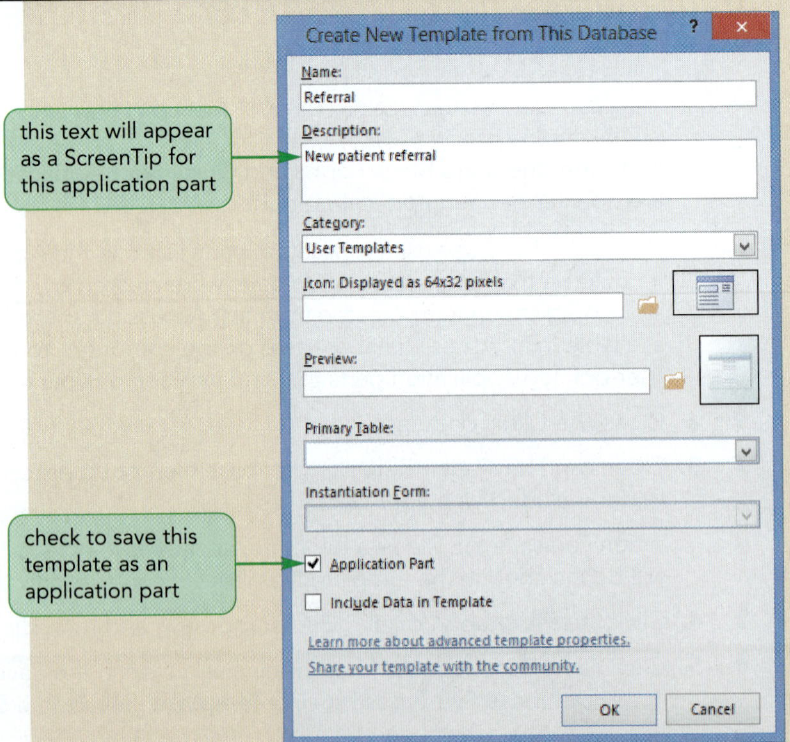

8. Click the **OK** button to close the dialog box. An alert box opens indicating that the template has been saved.
9. Click the **OK** button to close the message box, and then close the NewPatientReferrals database.

Now that you've created the application part, you'll use it in the Clinic database to create the referral table for patients who have been referred to the clinic by a pharmacist.

To use the application part to create the referral table:

1. Open the **Clinic** database, click the **CREATE** tab, and then click the **Application Parts** button. The Referral template is displayed in the User Templates section in the Application Parts list. See Figure 8-32.

Figure 8-32 Application Parts showing Referral template

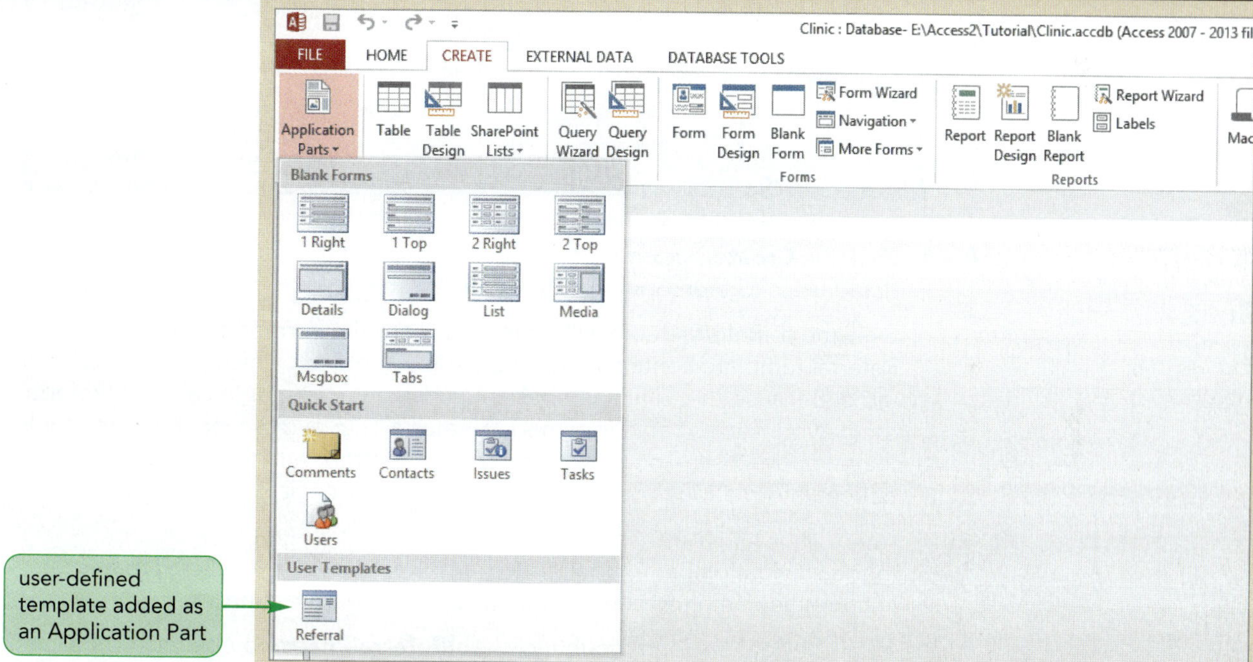

2. Click **Referral**. The Create Relationship dialog box opens because the application part includes a table.
3. Click the **There is no relationship** option button. This indicates that the new table is not related to other tables in the current database. See figure 8-33.

Figure 8-33 Create Relationship dialog box

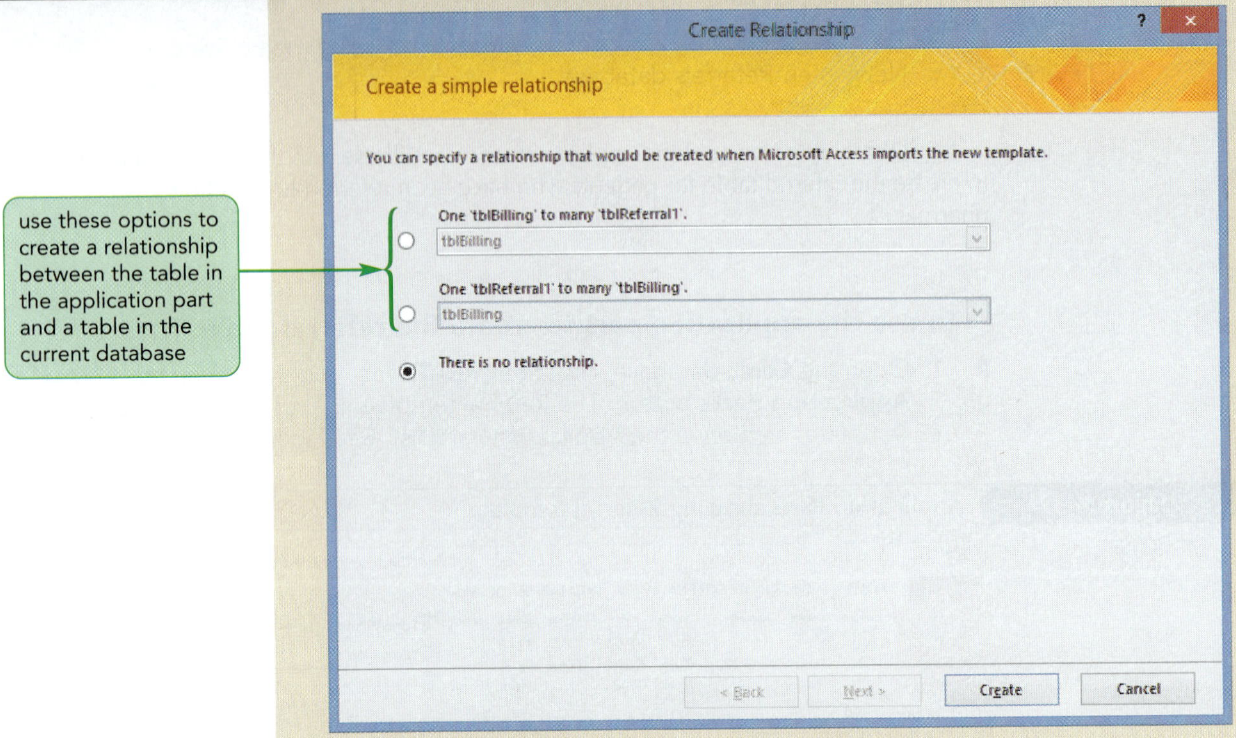

4. Click the **Create** button to insert the Referral database object into the current database, and then open the Navigation Pane.

   Only the tblReferral table will be inserted into the current database since the Referral template contains only one database object, which is the tblReferral table. Because the Clinic database already contains a table called tblReferral, the newly inserted table is named tblReferral1, to avoid overwriting the table that already exists. The newly inserted tblReferral1 will be used to store the patient information for patients referred by pharmacists. You'll rename this table as tblReferralPharm.

5. In the Navigation Pane, right-click the **tblReferral1** table, click **Rename**, change the name to **tblReferralPharm**, and then press **Enter**.
6. In the Navigation Pane, double-click **tblReferralPharm** to open it in Datasheet view.

   Note that the tblReferralPharm table contains the same fields as the tblReferral table but does not contain any records.

7. Close the tblReferralPharm table.

Kelly would like to be able to send an electronic copy of the rptVisitDetails report that other people can read on their computers, rather than distributing printed reports. You can export tables, queries, reports, and other database objects as files that can be opened in other programs such as Excel and PDF readers. Kelly would like to distribute rptVisitDetails as a PDF and asks you to export the report in this format.

Exporting a Report to a PDF File

PDF (portable document format) is a file format that preserves the original formatting and pagination of its contents no matter where it's viewed. Current versions of all major operating systems for desktop computers and handheld devices include software that opens PDF files. Most web browsers allow you to view PDF files as well. You'll create a PDF document from the rptVisitDetails report so Kelly can send this report to colleagues.

To export the rptVisitDetails report to a PDF file:

1. In the Navigation Pane, right-click **rptVisitDetails**, point to **Export** on the shortcut menu, and then click **PDF or XPS**. The Publish as PDF or XPS dialog box opens.
2. Navigate to the **Access2 ▸ Tutorial** folder included with your Data Files, and then change the name in the File name box to **Visit Details Report.pdf**. See Figure 8-34.

Figure 8-34 Publish as PDF or XPS file dialog box

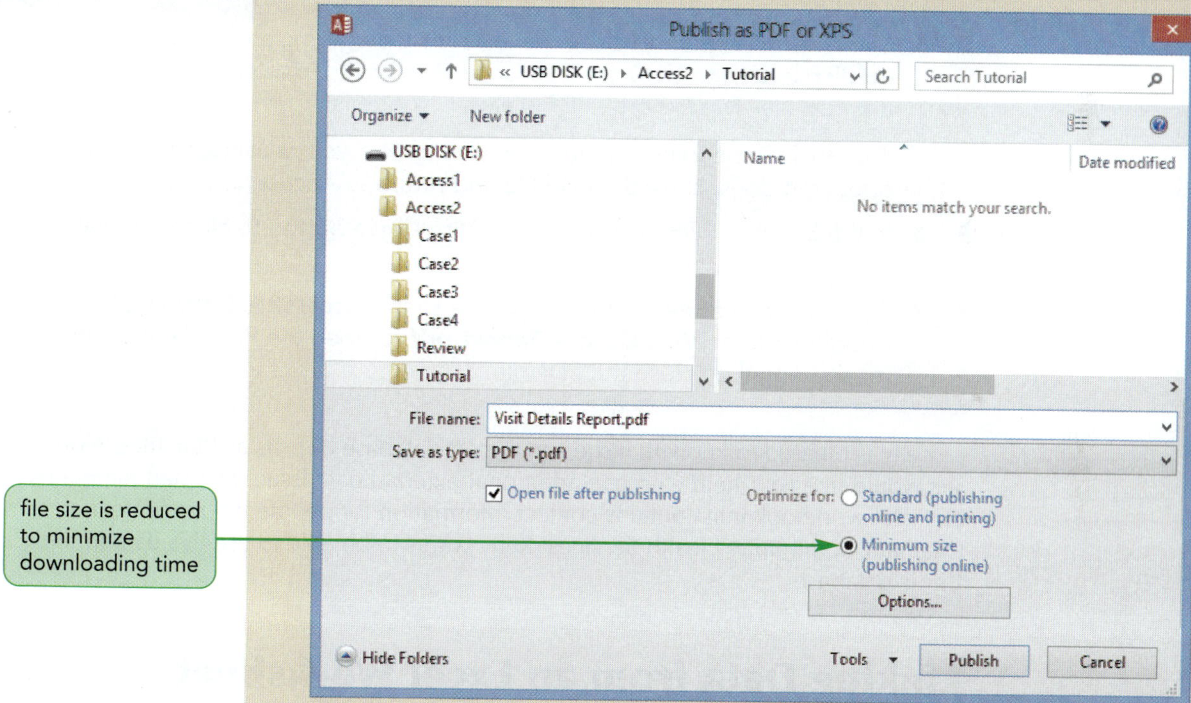

Kelly would like people who are visually impaired to be able to use the PDF document with their screen readers. When a PDF file is saved using the minimum size option, there is no additional functionality for screen readers. You can include document structure tags that allow people using screen readers to navigate the document easily. Screen reader software voices the structure tags, such as a tag that provides a description of an image. Structure tags also reflow text so that screen readers understand the flow of information and can read it in a logical order. For instance, a page with a sidebar shouldn't be read as two columns; the main column needs to be read as a continuation of the previous page.

In order to add this functionality, you'll specify that document structure tags should be included.

3. Click the **Options** button. The Options dialog box opens.
4. Click the **Document structure tags for accessibility** check box to select it. See Figure 8-35.

Figure 8-35 Options dialog box for PDF file export

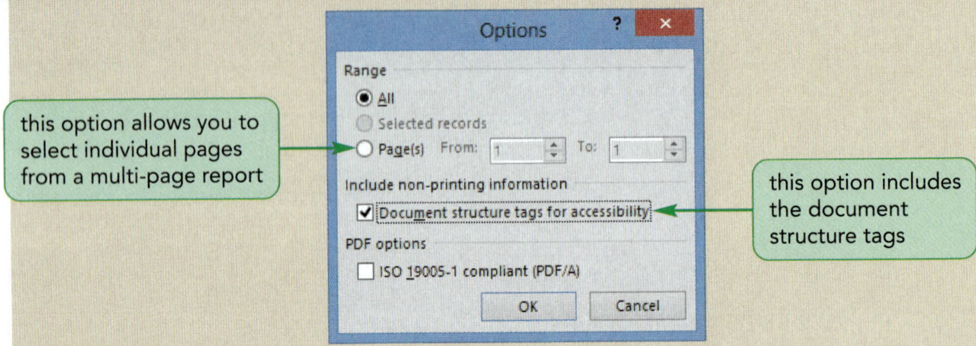

5. Click the **OK** button to close the Options dialog box, and then click the **Publish** button to close the Publish as PDF or XPS dialog box and to create the PDF file. The Export – PDF dialog box opens.

   Trouble? Depending on the operating system you're using, the PDF file may open. If it does, close the PDF file and return to Access.
6. In the Export – PDF dialog box, click the **Close** button to close the dialog box without saving the export steps.
7. Open Windows File Explorer, navigate to the **Access2 ▸ Tutorial** folder, double-click the **Visit Details Report.pdf** to open the PDF file, examine the results, and then close the PDF file.

Kelly is pleased to know that she can export database objects as PDF files. Now she would like your help with one additional external data issue. Her staff maintains an Excel workbook that contains contact information for people who volunteer at Chatham Community Health Services. Kelly wants to be able to use this data in the Clinic database.

Linking Data from an Excel Worksheet

Kelly's staff has extensive experience working with Excel, and one of her staff members prefers to maintain the data for people who volunteer in the Volunteer workbook using Excel. However, Kelly needs to reference the volunteer data in the Clinic database on occasion, and the data she's referencing must always be the current version of the worksheet data. Importing the Excel workbook data as an Access table would provide Kelly with data that's quickly out of date unless she repeats the import steps each time the data in the Excel workbook changes. Because Kelly doesn't personally need to update the volunteer data in the Clinic database, you'll link to the workbook from the database. When the staff changes the Volunteer workbook, the changes will be reflected automatically in the linked version of the database table. At the same time, Kelly won't be able to update the volunteer data from the Clinic database, which ensures that only the staff members responsible for maintaining the volunteer workbook can update the data.

To link to the data in the Excel workbook:

1. Click the **EXTERNAL DATA** tab, and then in the Import & Link group, click the **Excel** button (with the ScreenTip "Import Excel spreadsheet"). The Get External Data - Excel Spreadsheet dialog box opens.

   Trouble? If the Export - Excel File dialog box opens, you clicked the Excel File button in the Export group. Click the Cancel button and then repeat Step 1, being sure to select the Excel File button from the Import & Link group.

2. Click the **Browse** button, navigate to the **Access2 ▸ Tutorial** folder included with your Data Files, click **Volunteer**, click the **Open** button, and then click the **Link to the data source by creating a linked table** option button. This option links to the data instead of importing or appending it. The selected path and filename are displayed in the File name box. See Figure 8-36.

Figure 8-36 **Linking to data in an Excel workbook**

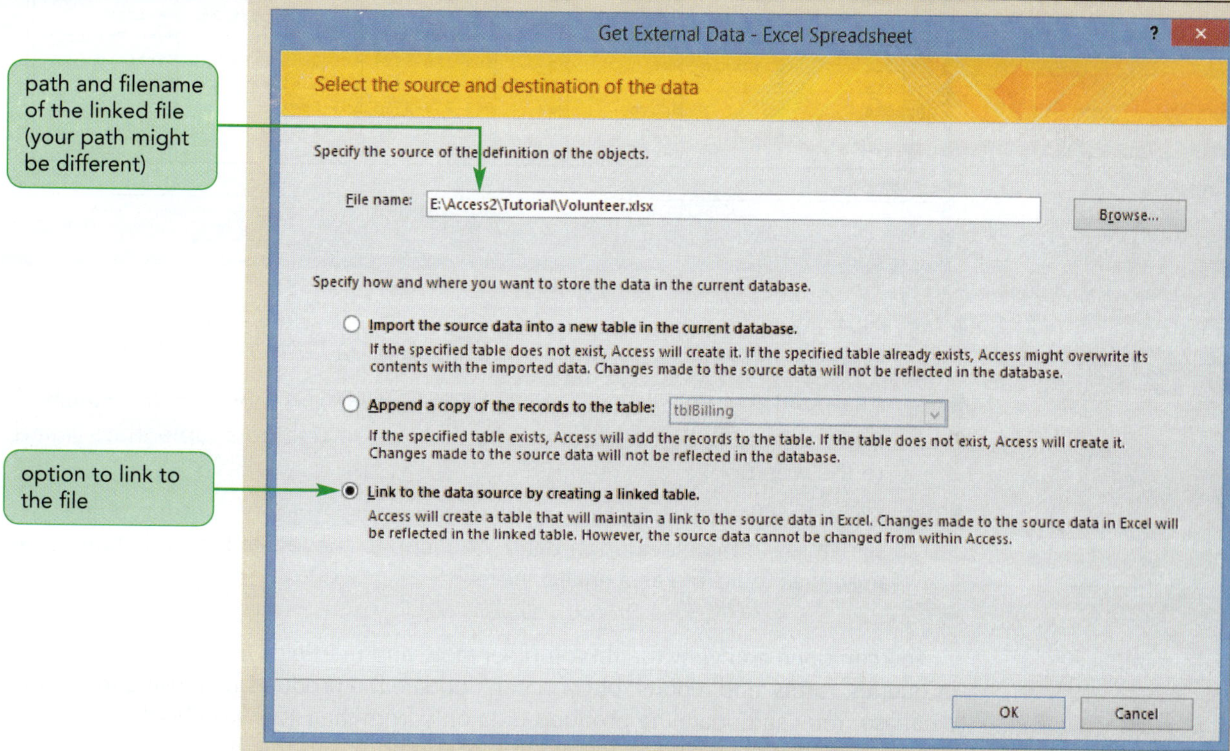

3. Click the **OK** button. The first Link Spreadsheet Wizard dialog box opens.

   The first row in the worksheet contains column heading names, and each row in the worksheet represents the data about a single product.

4. Click the **First Row Contains Column Headings** check box to select it. See Figure 8-37.

Figure 8-37 Link Spreadsheet Wizard dialog box

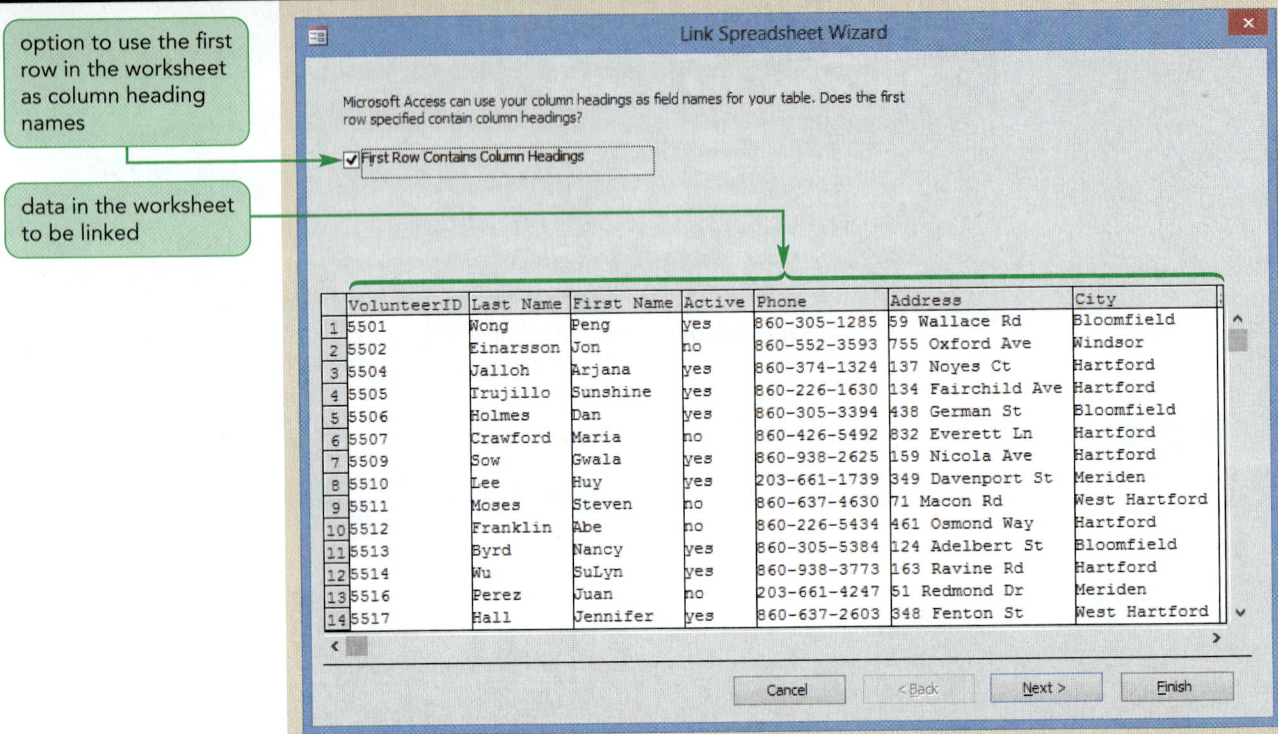

	VolunteerID	Last Name	First Name	Active	Phone	Address	City
1	5501	Wong	Peng	yes	860-305-1285	59 Wallace Rd	Bloomfield
2	5502	Einarsson	Jon	no	860-552-3593	755 Oxford Ave	Windsor
3	5504	Jalloh	Arjana	yes	860-374-1324	137 Noyes Ct	Hartford
4	5505	Trujillo	Sunshine	yes	860-226-1630	134 Fairchild Ave	Hartford
5	5506	Holmes	Dan	yes	860-305-3394	438 German St	Bloomfield
6	5507	Crawford	Maria	no	860-426-5492	832 Everett Ln	Hartford
7	5509	Sow	Gwala	yes	860-938-2625	159 Nicola Ave	Hartford
8	5510	Lee	Huy	yes	203-661-1739	349 Davenport St	Meriden
9	5511	Moses	Steven	no	860-637-4630	71 Macon Rd	West Hartford
10	5512	Franklin	Abe	no	860-226-5434	461 Osmond Way	Hartford
11	5513	Byrd	Nancy	yes	860-305-5384	124 Adelbert St	Bloomfield
12	5514	Wu	SuLyn	yes	860-938-3773	163 Ravine Rd	Hartford
13	5516	Perez	Juan	no	203-661-4247	51 Redmond Dr	Meriden
14	5517	Hall	Jennifer	yes	860-637-2603	348 Fenton St	West Hartford

5. Click the **Next** button to open the final Link Spreadsheet Wizard dialog box, in which you choose a name for the linked table.
6. Change the default table name to **tblVolunteer** and then click the **Finish** button. A message box informs you that you've created a table that's linked to the workbook.
7. Click the **OK** button to close the message box. The tblVolunteer table is displayed in the Navigation Pane. The icon to the left of the table name identifies the table as a linked table.

You can open and view the tblVolunteer table and use fields from the linked table in queries, forms, and reports, but you can't update the products data using the Clinic database. You can update the products data only from the Excel workbook.

Next, you'll make a change to data in the workbook and see the update in the linked table. Kelly tells you that the volunteer Crawford had not been able to volunteer for a while, so her Active status was **no**. She's now able to volunteer, and Kelly would like to change her Active status to **yes**.

To update the Excel workbook and view the data in the linked table:

1. Open Windows File Explorer, navigate to the **Access2 ▸ Tutorial** folder, right-click **Volunteer.xlsx**, and then open the file using **Microsoft Excel**. The Volunteer workbook opens and displays the Volunteer worksheet.

   Trouble? If you attempt to open the table in Access before you open the workbook in Excel, you'll get an error message and won't be able to open the workbook. Make sure you always open the workbook or other source file before you open a linked table.

2. Switch to the Clinic database, and then open the **tblVolunteer** datasheet. The fields and records in the tblVolunteer table display the same data as the Volunteer worksheet.
3. Switch to the Volunteer workbook, select the value **no** in the Active column for Maria Crawford (row 7), type **yes** to replace the value, and then press the **Enter** key.
4. Switch to the Clinic database. Maria Crawford's Active status is now **yes**.

   You've completed your work for Kelly and her staff.
5. Close the tblVolunteer table in Access.
6. Switch to the Volunteer workbook, save your worksheet change, and then exit Excel.
7. Make a backup copy of the database, compact and repair the database, and then close it.

Knowing how to create tabbed form controls and Application Parts, export data to PDF documents, and link to data maintained by other programs will make it easier for Kelly and her staff to work efficiently and manage their data.

REVIEW

Session 8.2 Quick Check

1. The ______________ property lets you change the default navigation label from the word "Record" to another value.
2. What is the Microsoft Graph program?
3. What is a PDF file?
4. What is an application part?
5. What is the difference between an application part and a template?
6. How can you edit data in a table that has been linked to an Excel file?

ASSESS

SAM Projects

Put your skills into practice with SAM Projects! SAM Projects for this tutorial can be found online. If you have a SAM account, go to www.cengage.com/sam2013 to download the most recent Project Instructions and Start Files.

PRACTICE

Review Assignments

Data Files needed for the Review Assignments: Ads.xlsx, Partners.accdb, Payables.csv, Payments.xml, and Supplier.accdb ***(cont. from Tutorial 7)***

Kelly wants you to integrate the data in the Supplier database with other programs, and she wants to be able to analyze the data in the database. Complete the following steps:

1. Open the **Supplier** database you worked with in Tutorials 5–7.
2. Export the qrySupplierProducts query as an HTML document to the Access2 ▸ Review folder provided with your Data Files, saving the file as **qrySupplierProducts.html**. Do not save the export steps.
3. Import the CSV file named Payables, which is located in the Access2 ▸ Review folder, as a new table in the database. Use the names in the first row as field names, use Currency as the data type for the numeric fields, choose your own primary key, name the table **tblPayable**, run the Table Analyzer, record the Table Analyzer's recommendation, and then cancel out of the Table Analyzer Wizard without making the recommended changes. Do not save the import steps.
4. Import the data and structure from the XML file named Payments, which is located in the Access2 ▸ Review folder, as a new table named **tblPayments** in the database. Save the import steps, and then rename the table **tblPayment**.
5. Export the tblSupplier table as an XML file named **Supplier.xml** to the Access2 ▸ Review folder; do not create a separate XSD file. Save the export steps.
6. The Chatham Community Health Services clinic also pays for advertisements. Link to the Ads.xlsx workbook, which is located in the Access2 ▸ Review folder, using **tblAd** as the table name. Change the cost of the flyer for Ad Num 5 to $300 and save the workbook.
7. Modify the **frmSuppliersWithProducts** form in the following ways:
   a. Size the text box controls for SupplierID, Company Name, Category, City, State, and Zip so that they are all the same width as the Address text box.
   b. Size the text box controls for ContactPhone, ContactFirstName, and ContactLastName so that they are all the same width as the InitialContact text box.
   c. Move the Number of Products label, text box, and rectangle so the right edge of the rectangle is aligned with the right edge of the InitialContact text box.
   d. Add a tab control to the bottom of the Detail section, so the left edge is aligned with the left edge of the Company Comments label, and then place the existing subform on the first page of the tab control.
   e. Change the caption for the left tab to **Product Data** and for the right tab to **Product Chart**.
   f. Change the caption for the main form's navigation buttons to **Supplier**.
   g. Add a chart to the second page of the tab control. Use the tblProduct table as the record source, select the ProductName and Price, use the 3-D Column Chart type (row 1, column 2), do not include a legend, and use **Products Offered** as the chart title.
   h. Change the chart to a 3-D Bar chart, and change the blue colored data markers to pink.
8. Export the **tblPayment** table as a PDF file called Payments.pdf, using document structure tags for accessibility. Do not save the export steps.

9. Open the **Partners** database from the Access2 ▸ Review folder, and then create and implement an application part as follows:
   a. Create an application part called **vendor** with the description **New vendor**, and do not include the data.
   b. Close the **Partners** database.
   c. Open the **Supplier** database and import the **vendor** application part, which has no relationship to any of the other tables. Open the tblNewVendor table to verify the data has been imported.
10. Make a backup copy of the database, compact and repair the database, and then close it.

APPLY

Case Problem 1

Data Files needed for this Case Problem: CreditCard.xml, Task.accdb (*cont. from Tutorial 7*), and Schedule.xlsx.

GoGopher! Amol Mehta wants you to integrate the data in the Task database with other programs, and he wants to be able to analyze the data in the database. Complete the following steps:

1. Open the **Task** database you worked with in Tutorials 5–7.
2. Export the qryMemberNames query as an HTML document to the Access2 ▸ Case1 folder using a filename of **MemberNames.html**. Save the export steps.
3. Export the rptPlanMembership report as a PDF document with a filename of **Plan.pdf** to the Access2 ▸ Case1 folder. Include the document structure tags for accessibility, and do not save the export steps.
4. Import the data and structure from the XML file named CreditCard, which is located in the Access2 ▸ Case1 folder, as a new table. Save the import steps. Rename the table as **tblCreditCard**.
5. Export the tblPlan table as an XML file named **Plan** to the Access2 ▸ Case1 folder; do not create a separate XSD file. Save the export steps.
6. Link to the Schedule workbook, which is located in the Access2 ▸ Case1 folder, using **tblSchedule** as the table name. For TaskID 301, change the Day value to **F**.
7. Modify the **frmPlansWithMembers** form in the following ways:
   a. Add a tab control to the bottom of the Detail section, and place the existing subform on the first page of the tab control.
   b. Change the caption for the left tab to **Member Data** and for the right tab to **Member Chart**.
   c. Change the caption for the main form's navigation buttons to **Plan** and for the subform's navigation buttons to **Member**.
   d. Add a chart to the second page of the tab control. Use the tblPlan table as the record source, select the PlanID and PlanCost fields, use the Column Chart chart type, do not include a legend, and use **Plan Cost** as the chart title.
   e. Change the color of the data marker to red (row 3, column 1).
8. Make a backup copy of the database, compact and repair the database, and then close it.

CHALLENGE

Case Problem 2

Data Files needed for this Case Problem: AddSubject.xml, NewStudentReferrals.accdb, Tutoring.accdb *(cont. from Tutorial 7)*, Room.xlsx and Subject.csv.

O'Brien Educational Services Karen O'Brien wants you to integrate the data in the Tutoring database with other programs, and she wants to be able to analyze the data in the database. Complete the following steps:

1. Open the **Tutoring** database you worked with in Tutorials 5–7.
2. Export the rptTutorSessions report as a PDF document with a filename of **TutorSessions.pdf** to the Access2 ▸ Case2 folder. Include the document structure tags for accessibility, and do not save the export steps.
3. Import the CSV file named Subject.csv, which is located in the Access2 ▸ Case2 folder, as a new table in the database. Use the names in the first row as field names, set the third column's data type to Currency and the other fields' data types to Short Text, choose your own primary key, name the table **tblSubject**, run the Table Analyzer, and record the Table Analyzer's recommendation, but do not accept the recommendation. Do not save the import steps.
4. Export the tblTutor table as an XML file named **Tutor** to the Access2 ▸ Case2 folder; do not create a separate XSD file. Save the export steps.
5. Link to the Room workbook, which is located in the Access2 ▸ Case2 folder, using **tblRoom** as the table name. Add the following new record to the Room workbook: Room Num 5, Rental Cost **$25**, and Type **Private**.

Explore 6. Import the **AddSubject.xml** file, which is located in the Access2 ▸ Case2 folder, appending the records to the tblSubject table. Do not save the import steps. Open the tblSubject table in Datasheet view and then verify that the record with SubjectID 50 and Subject Math4 has been appended, along with other records. Close the tblSubject table and then close the Tutoring database.

Explore 7. Open the **NewStudentReferrals** database from the Access2 ▸ Case2 folder, and then create and work with an application part as follows:
   a. Create an application part called **NewStudentContact** with the description **New student referrals** and include the data.
   b. Close the **NewStudentReferrals** database.
   c. Open the **Tutoring** database and import the **NewStudentContact** Application Part, which has no relationship to any of the other tables. Open the tblContact table to verify the data has been imported.
   d. Karen would like to import an empty tblContact table in the future. Delete the **NewStudentContact** Application Part by clicking on the Application Parts button, right-clicking on the **NewStudentContact** template, selecting **Delete Template Part from Gallery**, and then clicking **Yes** in the dialog box that opens.
   e. Save and close the Tutoring database.
   f. Open the **NewStudentReferrals** database, then create an Application Part called **Contact** with the description **Contact information** and do not include the data.
   g. Close the NewStudentReferrals database.
   h. Open the Tutoring database and then add the Contact Application Part. Open the tblContact1 table to verify that it does not contain records.

8. Make a backup copy of the database, compact and repair the database, and then close it.

CHALLENGE

Case Problem 3

Data Files needed for this Case Problem: Facility.csv, Rosemary.accdb (*cont. from Tutorial 7*), and Volunteer.accdb.

Rosemary Animal Shelter Ryan Lang wants you to integrate the data in the Rosemary database with other programs, and he wants to be able to analyze the data in the database. Complete the following steps:

1. Open the **Rosemary** database you worked with in Tutorials 5–7.
2. Export the qryNetDonationsAprilOrLaterCrosstab query as an HTML document named **Crosstab** to the Access2 ▸ Case3 folder. Save the export steps.

3. Export the rptPatronDonations report as a PDF document with a filename of **PatronDonations.pdf** to the Access2 ▸ Case3 folder. Include the document structure tags for accessibility, and do not save the export steps.
4. **Explore** Import the CSV file named Facility, which is located in the Access2 ▸ Case3 folder, as a new table in the database. Use the Short Text data type for all fields, choose your own primary key, name the table **tblTemporary**, and run the Table Analyzer. Accept the Table Analyzer's recommendations, which will be to create two tables. Rename the tables as **tblStorage** and **tblFacility**. (*Hint*: Use the Rename Table button to the right of "What name do you want for each table?") Make sure each table has the correct primary key. (*Hint*: Use the Set Unique Identifier button to set a primary key if necessary.) Let the Table Analzyer create a query. Do not save the import steps. Review the tblTemporary query, review the tblTemporary table (it might be named tblTemporary_OLD), and then review the tblStorage and tblFacility tables. Close all tables.
5. Export the tblDonation table as an XML file named **Donation.xml** to the Access2 ▸ Case3 folder; do not create a separate XSD file. Save the export steps.
6. Modify the **frmPatronDonations** form in the following ways:
   a. Add a tab control to the bottom of the Detail section, and place the existing subform on the first page of the tab control.
   b. Change the caption for the left tab to **Donation Data** and for the right tab to **Donation Chart**.
   c. Change the caption for the main form's navigation buttons to **Donor** and for the subform's navigation buttons to **Donation**.
   d. Add a chart to the second page of the tab control. Use the tblDonation table as the record source, select the PatronID, DonationValue, and DonationDate fields, use the 3-D Column Chart type, include a legend, and use **Donations by Patron** as the chart title.
   e. Change the chart to a Clustered Bar chart.
7. Close the Rosemary database.
8. Open the **Volunteer** database, which is located in the Access2 ▸ Case3 folder. Create an application part called **Volunteer** with the description **Volunteer information**, and do not include the data. Close the Volunteer database.
9. Open the **Rosemary** database. Create a table called **tblPotentialVolunteer** from the Volunteer application part.
10. Make a backup copy of the database, compact and repair the database, and then close it.

CHALLENGE

Case Problem 4

Data Files needed for this Case Problem: Personnel.xlsx, PotentialTours1.xml, PotentialTours2.xml, and Ecotour.accdb (*cont. from Tutorial 7*)

Stanley EcoTours Janice and Bill Stanley want you to integrate the data in the Stanley database with other programs, and they want to be able to analyze the data in the database. Complete the following steps:

1. Open the **Ecotour** database you worked with in Tutorials 5–7.
2. Export the qryGuestsWithoutReservations query as an HTML document named **GuestsWithoutReservations.html** to the Access2 ▸ Case4 folder. Do not save the export steps.
3. Import the data and structure from the XML file named **PotentialTours1.xml**, which is located in the Access2 ▸ Case4 folder, as a new table in the database. Do not save the import steps. Open the PotentialTours table to verify the records were imported. Close the PotentialTours table.
4. **Explore** Import the data from the XML file named **PotentialTours2.xml**, which is located in the Access2 ▸ Case4 folder, appending the data to the **PotentialTours** table. Rename the table as **tblPotentialTours**. Open the tblPotentialTours table to verify the records were appended. Close the tblPotentialTours table.

5. Export the qryTourReservations query as an XML file named **TourReservations** to the Access2 ▸ Case4 folder; do not create a separate XSD file. Do not save the export steps.
6. Link to the Personnel Excel workbook, which is located in the Access2 ▸ Case4 folder, using **tblPersonnel** as the table name. Change the Job Title in the last record from Staff Manager to **HR Staff Manager**.
7. Modify the **frmGuestsWithReservations** form in the following ways:
   a. Add a tab control to the bottom of the Detail section, and place the existing subform on the first page of the tab control.
   b. Change the caption for the left tab to **Reservation Data** and for the right tab to **Reservation Chart**.
   c. Change the caption for the main form's navigation buttons to **Guest** and for the subform's navigation buttons to **Reservation**.
   d. Add a chart to the second page of the tab control. Use the tblReservation table as the record source, select the StartDate, TourID, and People fields, use the Column Chart chart type, do not include a legend, and use **Reservations** as the chart title.
8. Export the rptTourReservations report as a PDF document with a filename of **TourReservations.pdf** to the Access2 ▸ Case4 folder. Include the document structure tags for accessibility, and do not save the export steps.
9. Make a backup copy of the database, compact and repair the database, and then close it.

ProSkills

Decision Making

Deciding When to Create a Personal Database

Decision making is a process of choosing between alternative courses of action. When you make decisions, you normally follow these steps:

1. Gather information relevant to the decision
2. Consider viable alternatives
3. Select the best alternative
4. Prepare an implementation action plan
5. Take action and monitor results
6. Verify the accuracy of the decision

For some decisions, you might combine some steps, and you might even skip steps for the simplest decisions.

Gathering Information, Considering Alternatives, and Selecting the Best Alternative

Suppose you were charged with tracking volunteers and their jobs for a service organization or other entity that requires coordination of a large group of people. The first step in decision making—gathering relevant information—starts with the choice of how to organize the people and their jobs. For example, if your information shows that each person completes only one job, few people are involved in the process, and volunteers all report to the same coordinator, then you could use a Word document or an Excel workbook to manage the volunteers and their jobs.

However, what if your information shows a very large number of volunteers, and many volunteers work in multiple jobs and report to more than one coordinator? When the relevant information changes so that one volunteer is no longer completing only one job and no longer reporting to a single coordinator, managing the data in a Word document or Excel workbook becomes problematic.

When making the decision to use a database to manage your data, at first you might find that some data exists in another format, such as in an Excel workbook. After considering the data that you have already collected (such as in a workbook) or data that you will collect in the future, consider the types of decisions you need to make. These decisions might include determining whether a database will effectively and efficiently manage your data, deciding which DBMS you will use, and evaluating the ability of users to manage and use the database to get the information they need.

Preparing an Implementation Action Plan

Once you have made the choice to use a DBMS, determine the steps needed to design and create the database. The first step is to analyze the data you have collected or will collect and start compiling it into tables. Then, you can begin identifying the primary and foreign keys in the tables to create the relationships between those tables. Finally, you can determine the field properties in anticipation of making data entry easier and reducing the likelihood of errors. For example, you might use the Default Value property to enter a city or state field value if all of your volunteers reside in the same area.

Taking Action and Monitoring Results

The next step in decision making involves implementation, which includes creating the database, defining the tables, and entering the data. After designing and installing the database, you need to make decisions about the types of queries, forms, and reports to create to produce the data in the format that users need. After implementation, you should make decisions about how the database will be updated so it remains current and ready for any future decisions you need to make.

Verifying the Accuracy of the Decision

At the end of your decision-making process, review your steps and evaluate how well they worked. Did you discover data you wish you had originally collected and stored in the database, but didn't have available? How did that limitation affect your ability to make a good decision? What changes do you need to make to your database so that it will provide better information for future decisions?

PROSKILLS

Create a Personal Database

Most businesses use databases for decision making, and you can also use databases to track data in your personal life. Examples of personal database use include tracking personal collections, such as music or books; hobby data, such as crafts or antiques; or items related to sports teams, theater clubs, or other organizations to which you might belong. In this exercise, you'll use Access to create a database that will contain information of your choice, using the Access skills and features you've learned in these tutorials.

Note: Please be sure *not* to include any personal information of a sensitive nature in the database you create to be submitted to your instructor for this exercise. Later on, you can update the data in your database with such information for your own personal use.

1. Consider your personal interests and activities, school-related functions, and work-related duties, and select from them one set of requirements that includes data that is best tracked using a DBMS. (If you completed Tutorials 1–4 of this book and the ProSkills Exercise at the end of Tutorial 4, you can use and enhance the database you've already created, and you can skip this step and the next step.) Make sure the data is sufficiently complex that a Word document or Excel workbook would not be viable alternatives to store and manage the data.
2. Create a new Access database to contain the data you want to track. The database must include two or more tables that you can join through one-to-many relationships. Define the properties for each field in each table. Make sure you include a mix of data types for the fields (for example, do not include only Text fields in each table). Specify a primary key for each table, define the table relationships with referential integrity enforced, and enter records in each table.
3. Create queries that include at least one of each of the following: pattern query match, list-of-values match, parameter, crosstab, find duplicates, find unmatched, and the use of a conditional value in a calculated field.
4. For one or more fields, apply an input mask and specify field validation rules.
5. Create a split form and modify the form.
6. Create a custom form that uses at least one of each of the following: combo box for a lookup, combo box to find records, subform, lines and rectangles, and tab control. Add one or more calculated controls to the main form based on the subform's calculated control(s), and add a chart, if appropriate. Check the main form's tab order, and improve the form's appearance.
7. Create a custom report that uses at least one of each of the following: grouping field, sort field(s), lines, and rectangles. Hide duplicates, and add the date, page numbers, and a report title.
8. Export two or more objects in different formats, and save the step specifications.
9. Designate a trusted folder, make a backup copy of the database, and compact and repair it.
10. Submit your completed database to your instructor as requested. Include printouts of any database objects, if required. Also, prepare a document that addresses the specific data you selected to store and track and why a DBMS was the best choice.

TUTORIAL 9

Using Action Queries and Advanced Table Relationships

Enhancing User Interaction with the Health Database

OBJECTIVES

Session 9.1
- Create an action query to create a table
- Create action queries to append, delete, and update data

Session 9.2
- Define many-to-many and one-to-one relationships between tables
- Learn about joining tables
- Join a table using a self-join
- View and create indexes for tables

Case | *Chatham Community Health Services*

Chatham Community Health Services is a nonprofit health clinic located in Hartford, Connecticut. It provides a range of medical services to patients of all ages. The clinic specializes in the areas of pulmonology, cardiac care, and chronic disease management. Cindi Rodriguez, the office manager for Chatham Community Health Services, oversees a small staff and is responsible for maintaining the medical records of the clinic's patients. The Chatham staff developed the Health database of patient, visit, billing, employee, and treatment data, and the employees use Microsoft Access 2013 (or simply Access) to manage it. Raj Gupta, the company's database expert and developer, has been enhancing the Health database containing tables, queries, forms, and reports that Kelly Schwarz, office manager, and Ethan Ward, marketing manager, use to track patients and their visits. Cindi, Kelly, and Ethan have asked you to continue enhancing the database by creating some advanced queries and integrating more tables into the database.

STARTING DATA FILES

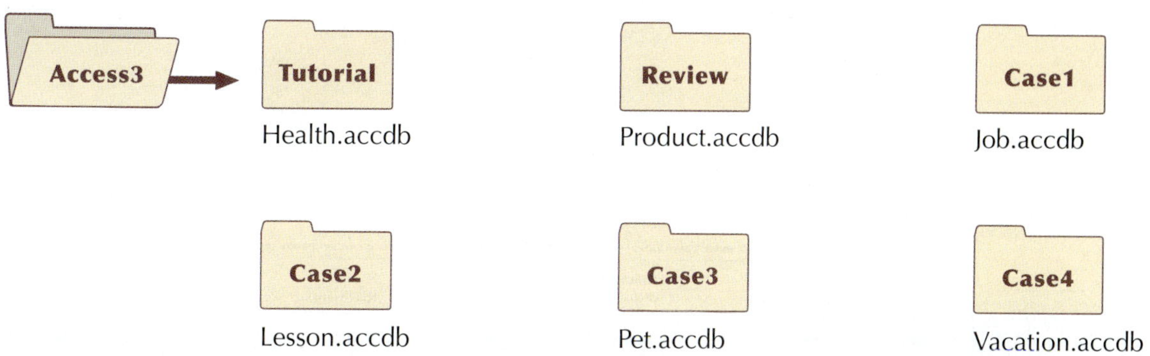

Session 9.1 Visual Overview:

The selected Make Table button indicates this query is a **make-table query**, which is an action query that creates a new table by copying records from one or more existing tables.

The design grid for a make-table query contains the same elements as the design grid for a select query.

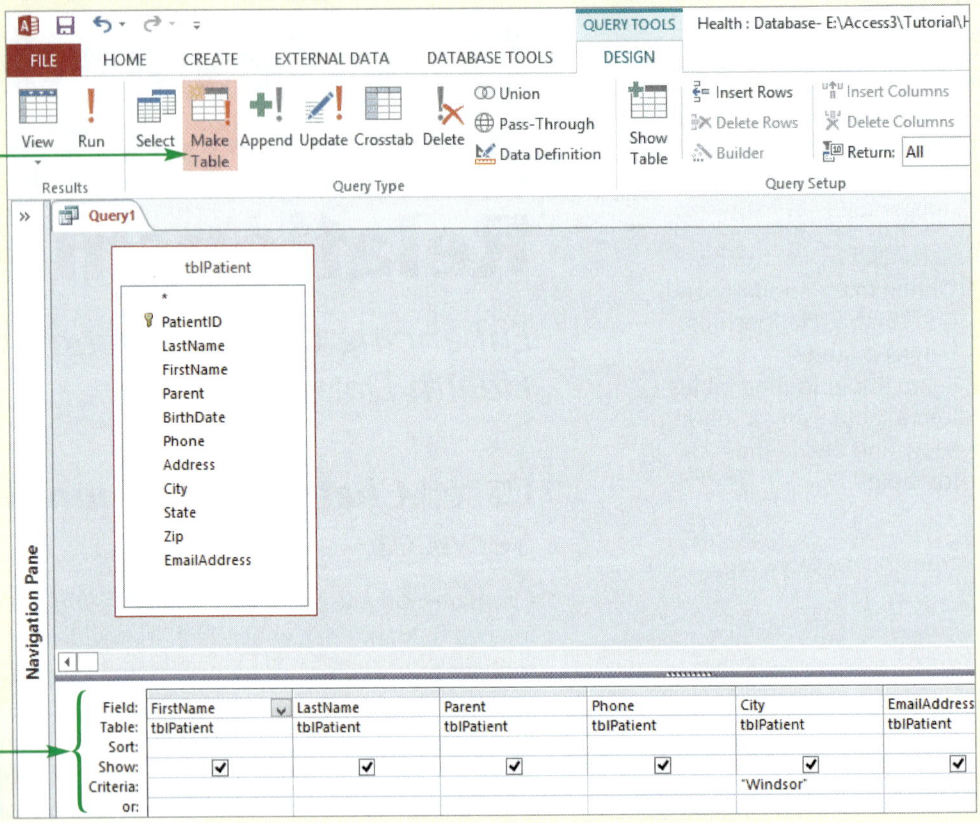

The selected Append button indicates this query is an **append query**, which is an action query that adds records from existing tables or queries to the end of another table.

For an append query, the Append To row replaces the Show row.

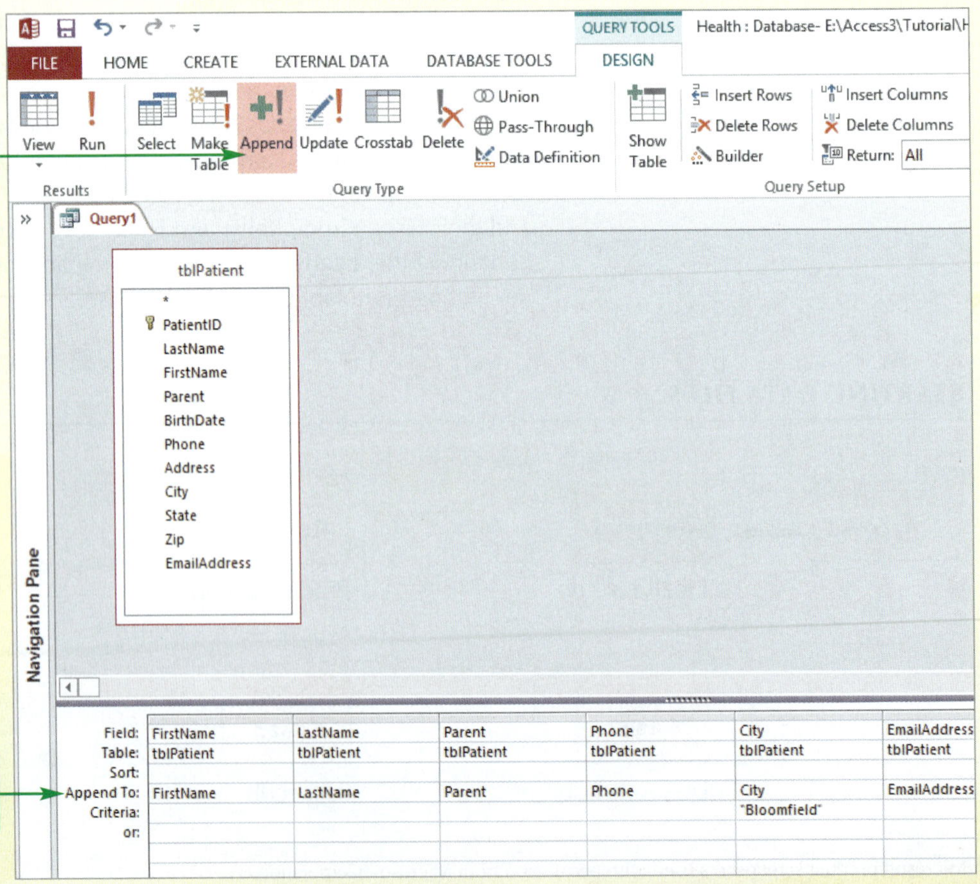

Action Queries

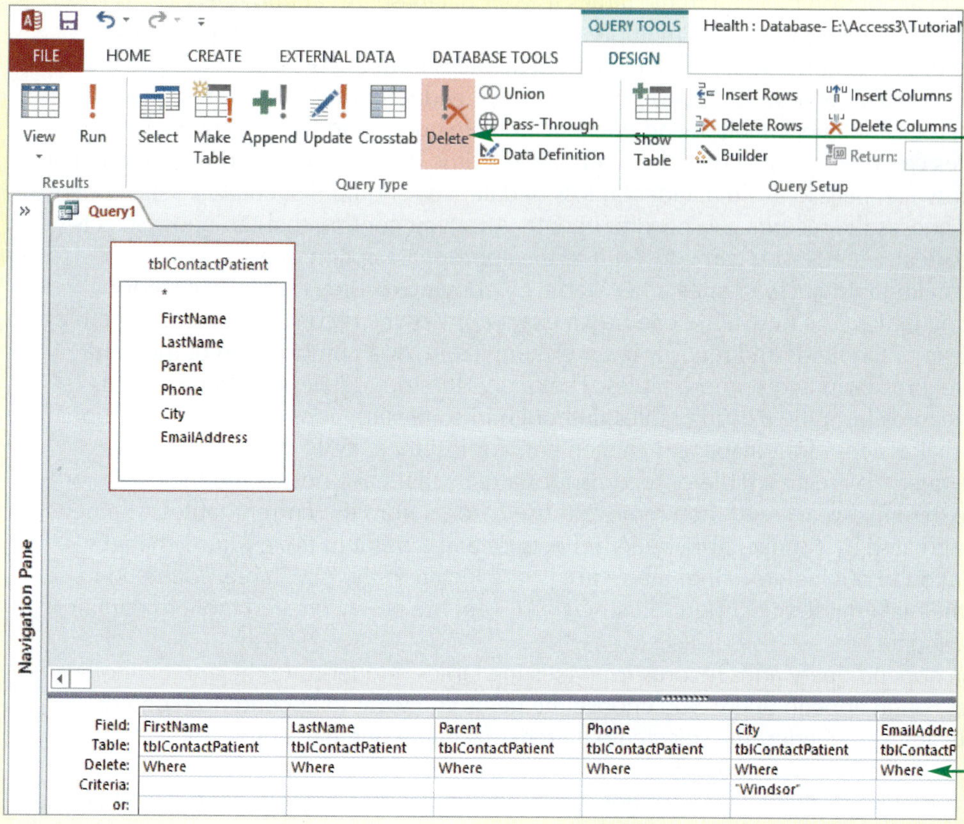

The selected Delete button indicates this query is a **delete query**, which is an action query that deletes a group of records matching the criteria you specify from one or more tables.

For a delete query, the Delete row replaces the Sort and Show rows.

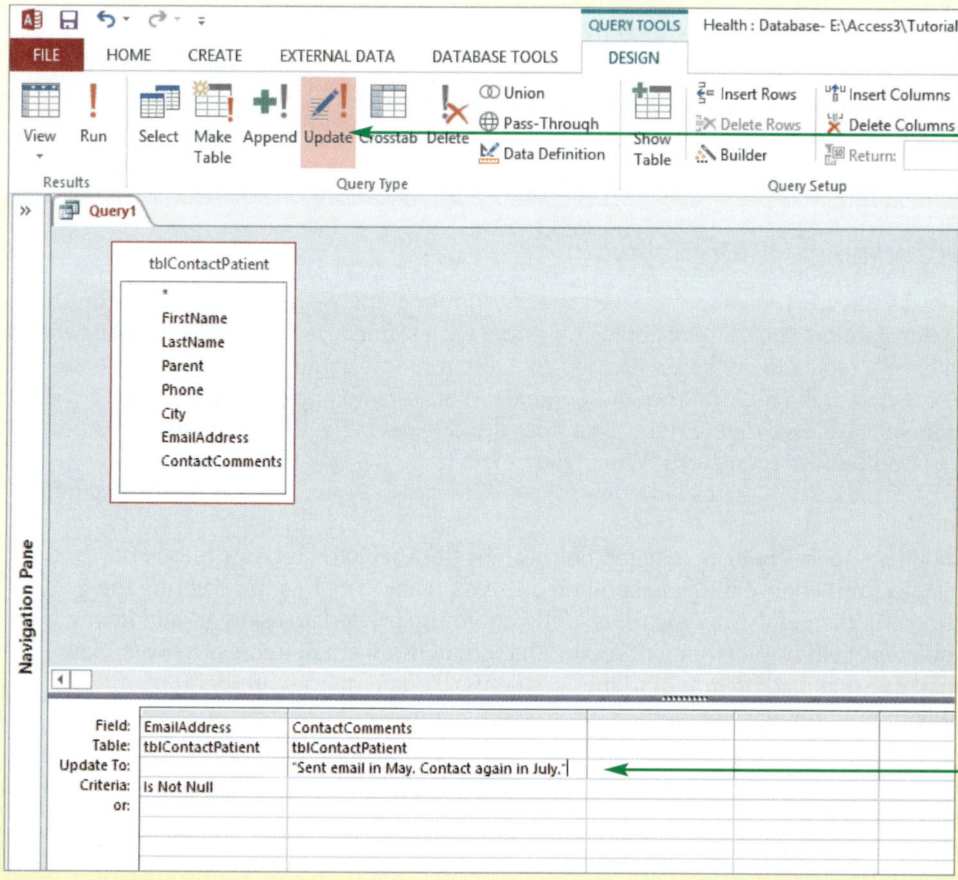

The selected Update button indicates this query is an **update query**, which is an action query that changes selected field values from selected records in one or more tables.

For an update query, the Update To row replaces the Sort and Show rows.

Action Queries

Queries can do more than display answers to the questions you ask; they can also perform actions on the data in the tables in your database. An **action query** is a query that adds, changes, or deletes multiple table records at a time. For example, Kelly could use an action query to delete all paid invoices from the previous year. As shown in the Visual Overview for Session 9.1, Access provides four types of action queries: the make-table query, the append query, the delete query, and the update query. Action queries can modify many records in a table at a time. Even though enforcing referential integrity can help to avoid accidental loss of data, you should first create a select query that chooses the records you need to update. After you confirm that the query selects the correct records, you can convert it to the appropriate action query.

A make-table query creates a new table by copying records from one or more existing tables. The new table can be an exact copy of the records in an existing table, a subset of the fields and records in an existing table, or a combination of the fields and records from two or more tables. The query does not delete the selected fields and records from the existing tables, although in some situations taking this additional step makes sense for database management. For instance, Kelly could use a make-table query to create a table of records for patients that have not visited the clinic for more than five years, and then remove those records from the current tables. The new table created by a make-table query reflects data at a point in time; future changes made to the original (existing) tables are not reflected in the new table. You need to run the make-table query periodically if you want the newly created table to contain current data.

An append query adds records from existing tables or queries to the end of another table. For an append query, you choose the fields you want to append from one or more tables or queries; the selected data remains in the original tables. Append queries are most often used to append records to history tables. A **history table** contains data that is no longer needed for current processing but that you might need to reference in the future.

A delete query deletes a group of records matching the criteria you specify from one or more tables. You choose which records you want to delete by entering selection criteria. Deleting records removes them permanently from the database after the database is compacted.

INSIGHT

Appending to History Tables

Tables containing data about cleared checks, former employees, inactive customers, and obsolete products are examples of history tables. Because the records you append to a history table are no longer needed for current processing in the original table, you can delete the records from the original table after you append the records to the history table. Before deleting the data from the original table, be sure to verify that you appended the correct records. When you delete data, the deletion is permanent.

An update query changes selected field values from selected records in one or more tables. You choose the fields and records you want to change by entering the selection criteria and the update rules. Kelly could use an update query to add text in the comment field of every patient record that contains an email address to note that an email message had been sent to these patients. Update queries are particularly valuable in performing multiple updates to large tables.

Creating a Make-Table Query

Ethan wants to call all patients who live in Windsor to inform them about the importance of annual flu vaccinations. He asks you to create a new temporary table containing the FirstName, LastName, Parent, Phone, City, and EmailAddress fields from the tblPatient table for all patients whose City field value is Windsor. He only wants to keep this table for this phone call campaign, after which he would not need the table anymore. He wants to create a temporary table so he can modify it by adding notes that he will take when he calls the patients who live in Windsor. By creating a new temporary table, Ethan won't need to worry about disrupting or changing the data in any existing tables or in any objects on which those existing tables are based. After Ethan is satisfied that all patients have been called and he's gathered their feedback, he could delete the table.

INSIGHT

Making Temporary Tables

Duplicating data in a database is frowned upon. When there are multiple copies of data in a database, and a change is made, it is possible that there will be errors in the data if some instances of the data are changed and others are not changed. However, sometimes it is useful to create a temporary table for a specific purpose. When the table is no longer needed it is deleted. For instance, the manager of a small appliance retail store might wish to notify all customers who purchased a toaster more than two years ago that a new model is now available. The manager could create a temporary table that contains the First Name, Last Name, and Phone Number for each of these customers, and add a field that contains Comments so the staff can indicate when the customer was called and if a message was left or the staff spoke to the customer directly. It would not make sense to track this information in the database because this does not directly relate to the patients' visits. Once the telephone campaign is finished, the table could be deleted.

You can create the new temporary table for Ethan by using a make-table query that uses fields from the tblPatient table in the Health database. When you run a make-table query, you create a new table. The records in the new table are based on the records in the query's underlying tables. The fields in the new table will have the data type and field size of the fields in the query's underlying tables. The new table will not preserve the primary key designation or field properties such as the format or lookup properties.

REFERENCE

Creating a Make-Table Query

- Create a select query with the necessary fields and selection criteria.
- On the DESIGN tab, in the Results group, click the Run button to preview the results.
- Switch to Design view to make any necessary changes to the query. When the query is correct, on the DESIGN tab in the Query Type group click the Make Table button.
- In the Make Table dialog box, type the new table name in the Table Name box. Make sure the Current Database option button is selected to include the new table in the current database; or, click the Another Database option button and enter the database name in the File Name box. Then click the OK button.
- Click the Run button, and then click the Yes button to confirm the creation of the new table.

You'll create the new temporary table now using a make-table query. You'll base the make-table query on the tblPatient table.

To create and run the select query based on the tblPatient table:

1. Make sure you have the Access Data Files on your computer.

   Trouble? If you don't have the starting Data Files, you need to get them before you can proceed. Your instructor will either give you the Data Files or ask you to obtain them from a specified location (such as a network drive). If you have any questions about the Data Files, see your instructor or technical support person for assistance.

2. Start Access, open the **Health** database in the Access3\Tutorial folder provided with your Data Files, and then click the **Enable Content** button next to the Security Warning.

   Next you'll eliminate the Security Warning by designating the Access3\Tutorial folder as a trusted folder.

3. Click the **FILE** tab to display Backstage view, and then click **Options** in the navigation bar to open the Access Options dialog box.

4. In the left section of the dialog box, click **Trust Center**, in the window on the right, click the **Trust Center Settings** button to open the Trust Center dialog box, and then in the left section, click **Trusted Locations**. The trusted locations for your installation of Access and other trust options are displayed on the right.

   Trouble? Check with your instructor before adding a new trusted location. If your instructor tells you not to create a new trusted location, click the Cancel button, click the Cancel button again, and then skip to Step 6.

5. Click the **Add new location** button to open the Microsoft Office Trusted Location dialog box, click the **Browse** button, navigate to the **Access3\Tutorial** folder where your Data Files are stored, click the **OK** button, click the **OK** button to add the Access3\Tutorial folder to the list of trusted locations, click the **OK** button to close the Trust Center dialog box, and then click the **OK** button to close the Access Options dialog box.

6. Make sure the Navigation Pane is closed, click the **CREATE tab** and then, in the Queries group, click the **Query Design** button. The Show Table dialog box opens on top of the Query window in Design view.

7. Click **tblPatient** in the Tables list, click the **Add** button, and then click the **Close** button. The tblPatient table field list is displayed in the Query window and the Show Table dialog box closes.

8. Drag down the bottom of the tblPatient field list to display all its fields, double-click **FirstName**, double-click **LastName**, double-click **Parent**, double-click **Phone**, double-click **City**, and then double-click **EmailAddress** to add these six fields to the design grid.

   Next, you'll enter the City field's selection criterion of Windsor.

9. Click the **City Criteria** box, type **Windsor**, and then press the **Tab** key. The condition changes to "Windsor". See Figure 9-1.

Figure 9-1 Select query on which make-table query will be based

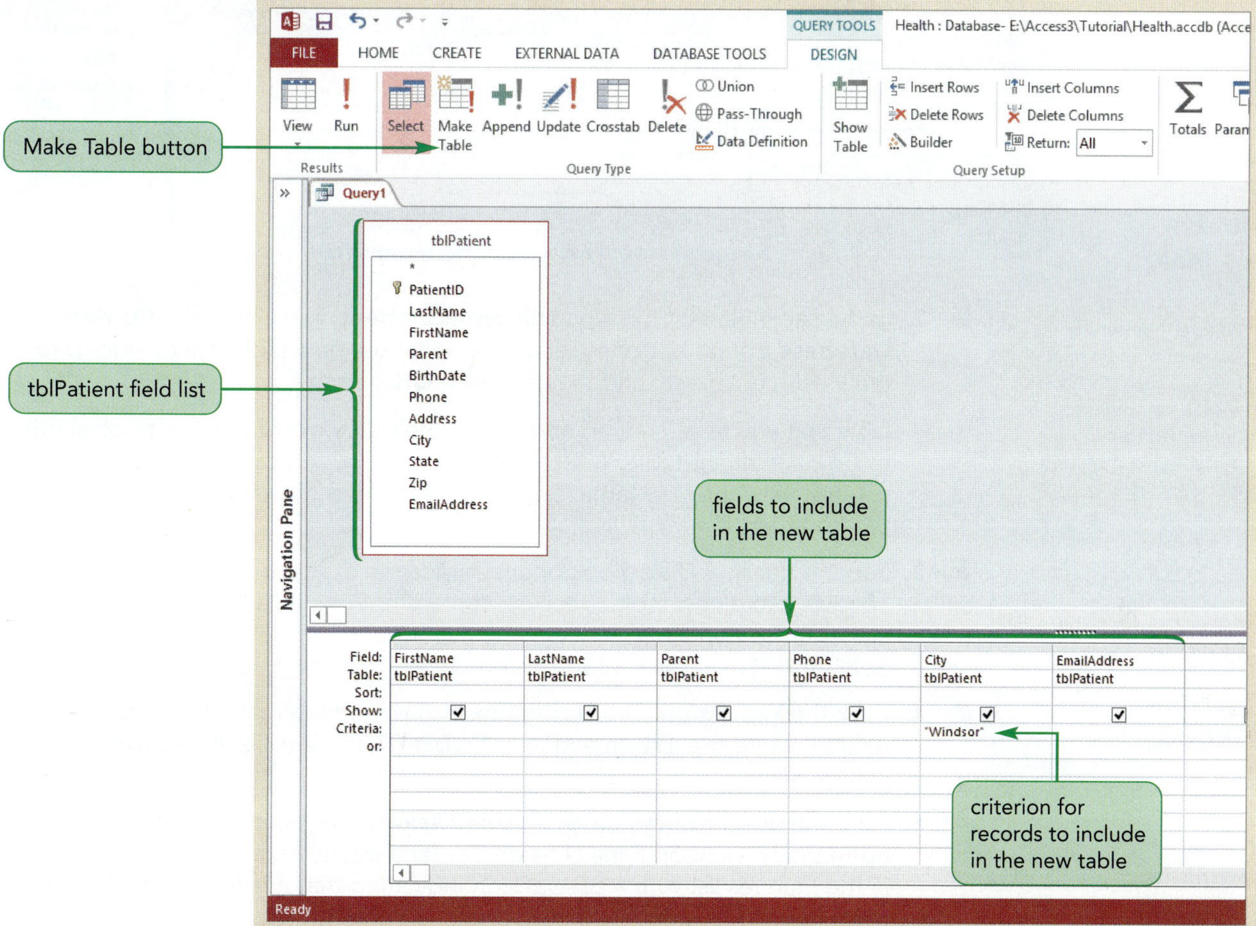

You've completed the select query, so now you can run it to make sure the recordset contains the data Ethan needs.

10. Run the query. The query recordset shows the 10 records for Windsor patients.

Now that you have verified that the records selected contain the city Windsor, you can be confident these are the same records that will be selected for the make-table query. Next you'll change the query to a make-table query.

To change the query type, and then run and save the make-table query:

1. Switch to Design view, and then on the DESIGN tab, in the Query Type group, click the **Make Table** button. The Make Table dialog box opens. You use the dialog box to enter the name of the new table and designate the database to be used to store the table. See Figure 9-2.

Figure 9-2 Make Table dialog box

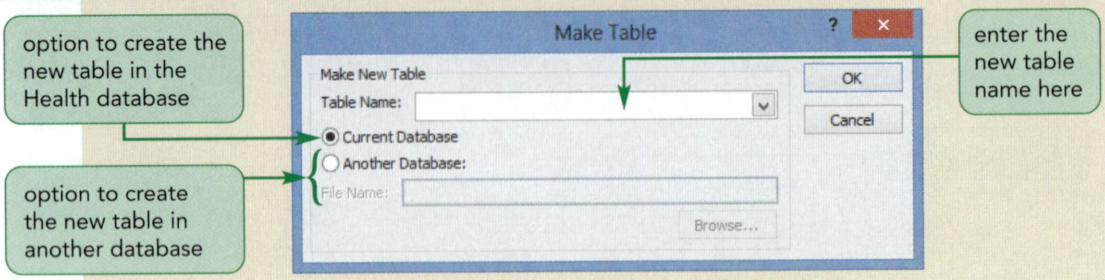

Be sure to select the Current Database option button; otherwise Access will require you to specify the name of another database file in which to place the table.

2. In the Table Name box, type **tblContactPatient**, make sure the **Current Database** option button is selected so that the new table will be added to the Health database, and then click the **OK** button.

   Now that you have created and tested the query, you can run it to create the tblContactPatient table. After you run the query, you can save it, and then you can view the new table. Because the query is not saved, the name on the tab is Query1.

3. Run the query. A dialog box opens, indicating that you are about to paste 10 rows into a new table. Because you are running an action query that alters the contents of the database, you have the opportunity to cancel the operation, if necessary, or to confirm it.

4. Click the **Yes** button. The dialog box closes, and the make-table query runs to create the tblContactPatient table. The query is still displayed in Design view.

5. Save the query as **qryContactPatientMakeTable**, close the query, and then open the Navigation Pane. The qryContactPatientMakeTable query appears in the Queries list with a special icon indicating that it is a make-table query. See Figure 9-3.

Figure 9-3 Query type icons in the Navigation Pane

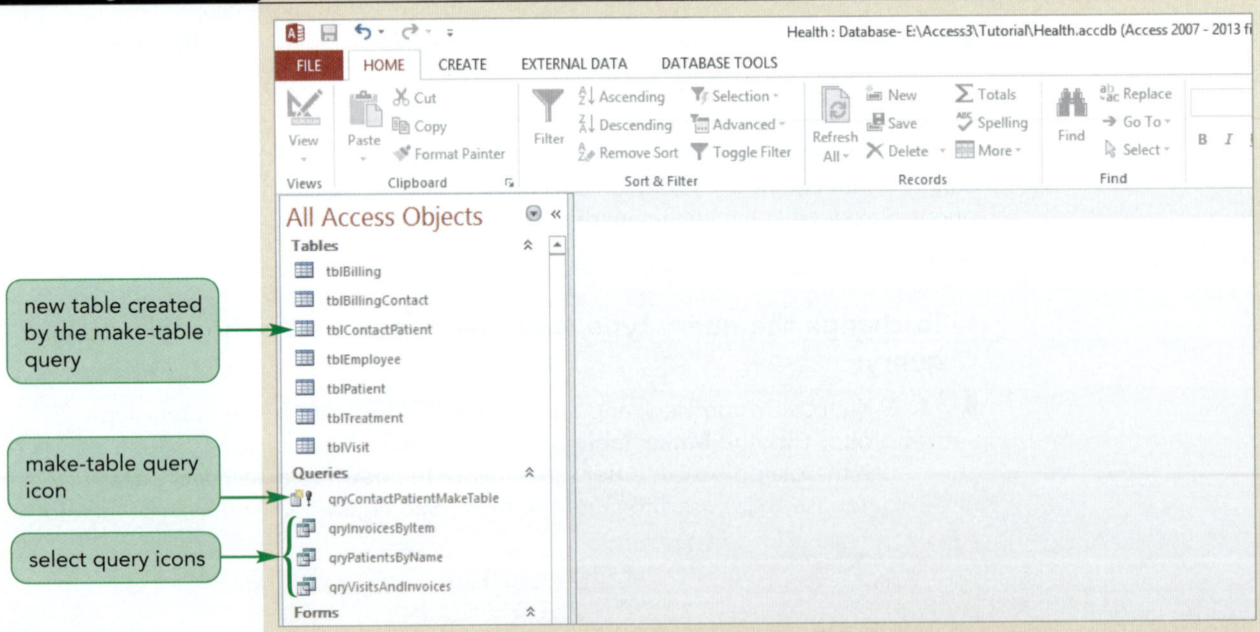

You can now open the tblContactPatient table to view the results of the make-table query.

6. Open the **tblContactPatient** table in Datasheet view, resize all datasheet columns to their best fit, and then click the first row's **FirstName** field value to deselect all values. See Figure 9-4.

Figure 9-4 **tblContactPatient table datasheet**

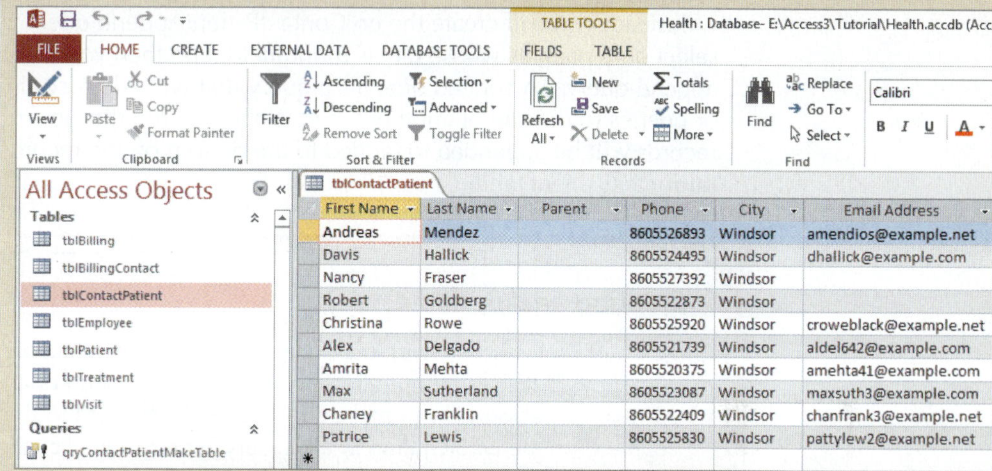

The tblContactPatient table includes the FirstName, LastName, Parent, Phone, City, and EmailAddress fields for patients who live in Windsor. Make-table queries do not transfer Caption property settings to the created tables. The tblContactPatient table also does not include formatting for the phone number. Other field properties that do not transfer include Decimal Places, Default Value, Format, Input Mask, Validation Rule, and Validation Text.

7. Save your datasheet changes, and then close the table.

Ethan can now make any necessary changes to the tblContactPatient table records when he contacts customers without affecting the tblPatient table in the Health database.

INSIGHT

Deleting database objects

A database evolves to meet the needs of its users, and eventually some database objects are no longer needed. A table, query, or report created for a special event, for instance, would no longer be useful after that event is over. Likewise, a database might contain a form created to enter data that is no longer relevant. As time goes by, you may want to delete such tables, queries, forms, and reports. To delete any database object, you can right-click the name of the object in the Navigation Pane and click the Delete option.

Creating an Append Query

Ethan has decided to expand the list of patients that he will call to include the patients who live in Bloomfield. He asks you to add these new records to the tblContactPatient table. You could make this change by modifying the selection criterion in the qryContactPatientMakeTable query to select patients with City field values of Bloomfield. If you ran this modified query, however, you would overwrite the existing tblContactPatient table with a new table. If Ethan had made any changes to the existing tblContactPatient table records, creating a new table would overwrite these changes as well.

Instead, you will create the qryContactPatientAppend query as a select query to select only patients whose city is Bloomfield, and then you'll change the query to an append query. An append query is a query that will add records from existing tables or queries to the end of another table. When you run this new query, the selected records will be appended to (added to the bottom of) the records in the existing tblContactPatient table.

REFERENCE

Creating an Append Query

- Create a select query with the necessary fields and selection criteria.
- On the DESIGN tab, in the Results group, click the Run button to preview the results.
- Switch to Design view to make any necessary changes to the query. When the query is correct, on the DESIGN tab in the Query Type group click the Append button.
- In the Append dialog box, select the table name in the Table Name box. Make sure the Current Database option button is selected to include the new table in the current database; or click the Another Database option button, enter the database name in the File Name box, and then click the OK button. The Append To row replaces the Show row in the design grid.
- Click the Run button, and then click the Yes button to confirm appending the records to the table.

You can now create the qryContactPatientAppend query to create the append query you'll use to include the additional customer data Ethan wants in the tblContactPatient table.

To create the append query:

1. Make sure the Navigation Pane is closed, click the **CREATE tab**, and then, in the Queries group, click the **Query Design** button. The Show Table dialog box opens on top of the Query window in Design view.
2. Click **tblPatient** in the Tables list, click the **Add** button, and then click the **Close** button. The tblPatient table field list is displayed in the Query window and the Show Table dialog box closes.
3. Drag down the bottom of the tblPatient field list to display all its fields, double-click **FirstName**, double-click **LastName**, double-click **Parent**, double-click **Phone**, double-click **City**, and then double-click **EmailAddress** to add these six fields to the design grid. The selected fields match the fields in the table to which the records will be appended.

   Next, you'll enter the selection criterion of Bloomfield for the City field.
4. Click the **City Criteria** box, type **Bloomfield**, and then press the **Tab** key. See Figure 9-5.

Figure 9-5 Changing the selection criterion

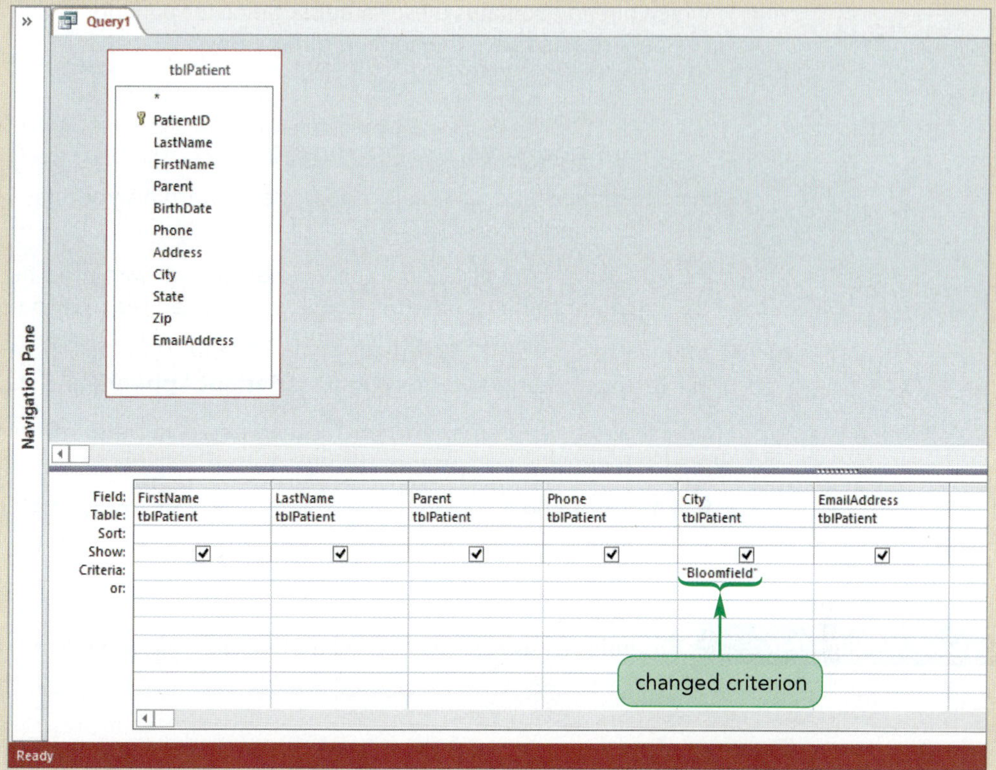

Before you can run the query to append the records to the tblContactPatient table, you have to change the query type to an append query. It is always a good idea to test an action query before you run it, so you will first run this select query to make sure the correct records are selected. Then you will change the query type to an append query and run it to append the new records to the tblContactPatient table.

5. On the DESIGN tab, in the Query Type group, click the **Select** button to select it (if necessary).

6. Run the query. The query recordset shows the seven records for patients who live in Bloomfield.

   These seven records are the additional records you will append to the tblContactPatient table. Now that you've verified that the results shown in the query are correct, you can change the query type to an append query.

7. Switch to Design view, and then on the DESIGN tab, in the Query Type group, click the **Append** button. The Append dialog box opens. You use this dialog box to select the name of the table to which you want to append the data, and to designate the database to be used to store the table.

8. In the Table Name box, click the arrow, click **tblContactPatient**, ensure that the **Current Database** option button is selected, and then click the **OK** button. The Append To row replaces the Show row in the design grid. See the Session 9.1 Visual Overview.

The Append To row in the design grid identifies the fields that the query will append to the designated table. The FirstName, LastName, Parent, Phone, City, and EmailAddress fields are selected and will be appended to the tblContactPatient table, which already contains these same six fields for patients.

You'll run and save the append query now.

To run and save the append query:

1. Run the query. A dialog box opens, warning you that you are about to append seven rows.
2. Click the **Yes** button to acknowledge the warning. The dialog box closes and the append query runs, adding the seven records to the tblContactPatient table. The Query window is still displayed in Design view.
3. Save the query as **qryContactPatientAppend**, and then close the query.

   Next, you'll open the tblContactPatient table to make sure that the seven records were appended to the table.
4. Open the Navigation Pane, open the **tblContactPatient** table datasheet, size the fields to display all the data, and then click the first row's **FirstName** field value to deselect all values. See Figure 9-6.

Figure 9-6 tblContactPatient table datasheet after appending records

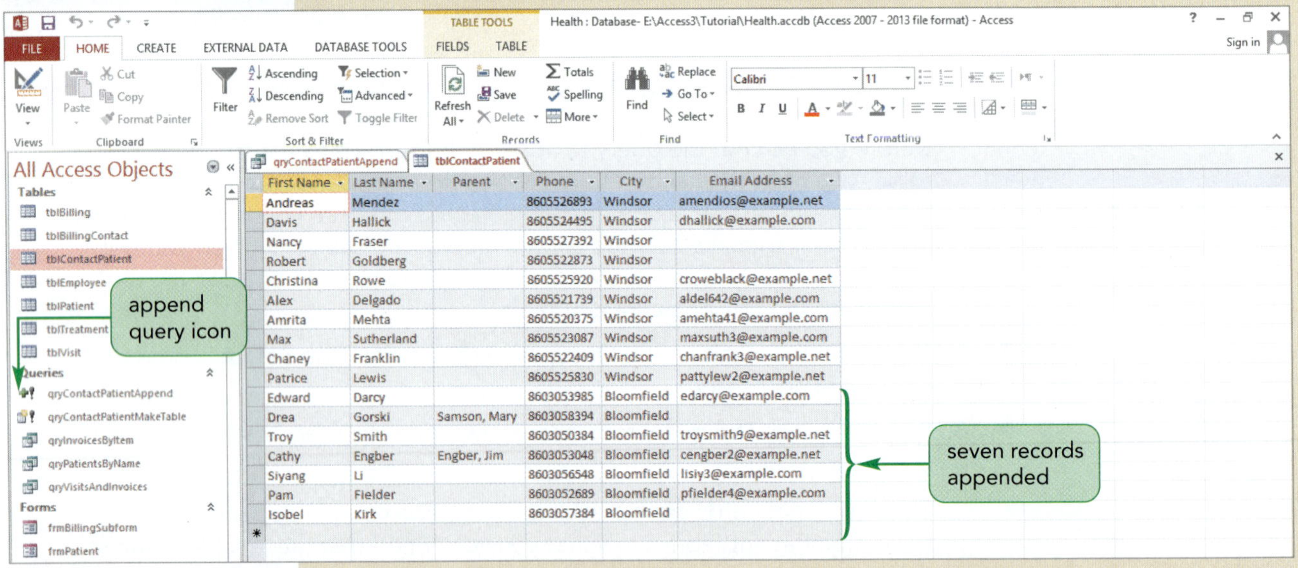

TIP

You can arrange the records in a different order by sorting the records using the Ascending button or the Descending button and then saving the table.

The new records have been added to the tblContactPatient table. Because the tblContactPatient table does not have a primary key, the new records appear at the end of the table.

5. Save your changes to the table, close the table, and then close the Navigation Pane.

Creating a Delete Query

Ethan has contacted all the patients in the tblContactPatient table that are located in the city of Windsor. He asks you to delete these records from the tblContactPatient table so that the table contains only those records for patients he has not yet contacted. You can either delete the table records individually or create a delete query to remove them all at once.

REFERENCE

Creating a Delete Query

- Create a select query with the necessary fields and selection criteria.
- On the DESIGN tab, in the Results group, click the Run button to preview the results.
- Switch to Design view to make any necessary changes to the query. When the query is correct, on the DESIGN tab in the Query Type group click the Delete button. The Delete row replaces the Show and Sort rows in the design grid.
- Click the Run button, and then click the Yes button to confirm deleting the records.

You'll create a delete query to delete the patient records in the tblContactPatient table whose city is Windsor. First, you'll create a select query to choose the correct records and run the query to verify you're selecting the correct records. Then you'll change the query to a delete query and run it.

To create the delete query:

1. Click the **CREATE tab** and then, in the Queries group, click the **Query Design** button.
2. Add the **tblContactPatient** table field list to the Query window, close the Show Table dialog box, and then drag down the bottom of the tblContactPatient field list to display all its fields.
3. Double-click the title bar of the tblContactPatient field list to select all the fields in the table, drag the highlighted area of the field list to the design grid's first column Field box, and then release the mouse button. All the fields are added to the design grid.
4. Click the **City Criteria** box, type **Windsor**, and then press the **Tab** key. The criterion changes to "Windsor". Only the records with a City field value of Windsor will be selected when you run the query.
5. Run the query. The query recordset shows the ten records with City field values of Windsor. The select query is correct. See Figure 9-7.

Figure 9-7 Ten records to be deleted

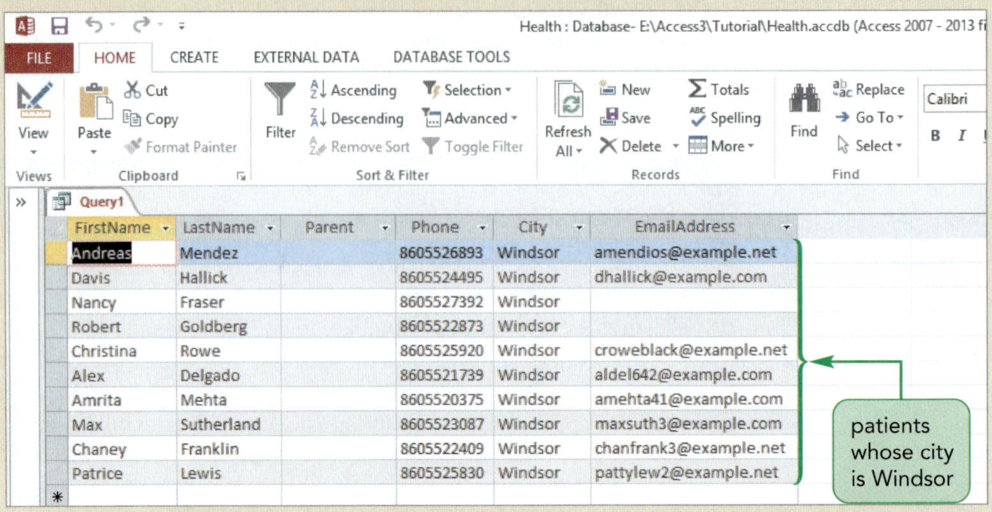

Trouble? If your query did not select the correct ten records, switch to Design view, correct the selection criterion, and then run the query again.

Now that you have verified that the correct records are selected, you can change the query to a delete query.

6. Switch to Design view, and then on the DESIGN tab in the Query Type group, click the **Delete** button. In the design grid, the Delete row replaces the Sort and Show rows. See the Session 9.1 Visual Overview.
7. Run the query. A dialog box opens, warning that you are about to delete ten rows.
8. Click the **Yes** button to close the dialog box and run the delete query. The ten records in the tblContactPatient table are deleted. The Query window is still displayed in Design view. Once records have been deleted from a table using a delete query, they cannot be restored using the Undo command.
9. Save the query as **qryContactPatientDelete**, and then close the query.

Next you'll open the tblContactPatient table to verify that the records have been deleted.

10. Open the Navigation Pane, and then open the **tblContactPatient** table in Datasheet view. The table contains seven records, and the Windsor records were correctly deleted. See Figure 9-8.

Figure 9-8 tblContactPatient table after deleting ten records

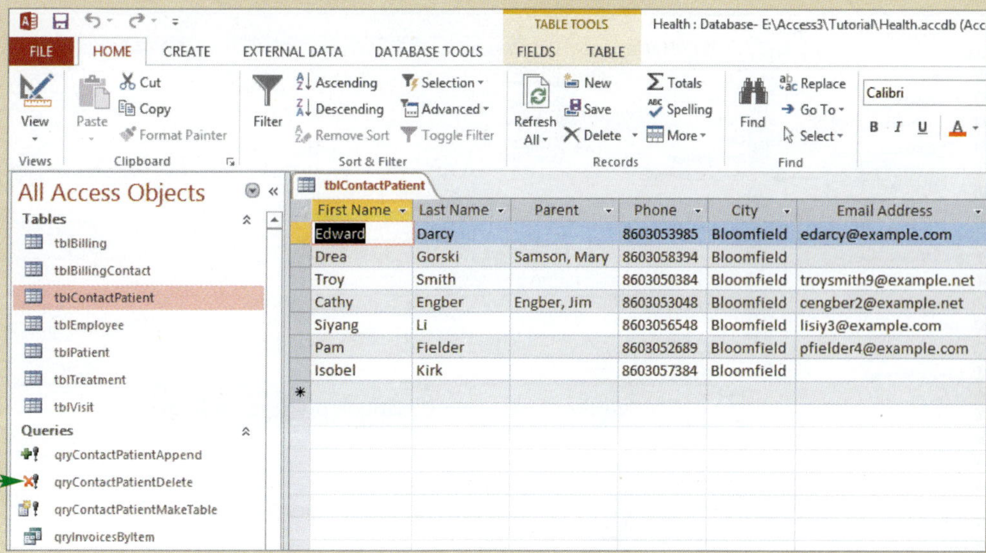

Ethan wants you to add a field named ContactComments to the tblContactPatient table in which he can keep notes about the calls he makes. You can add the field to the tblContactPatient table without affecting the other objects in the Health database, including the tblPatient table, because the tblContactPatient table was created as a temporary table only to meet Ethan's specific need to contact patients for specific reasons.

To add the new ContactComments field to the tblContactPatient table:

1. Switch to Design view.

   You'll set the data type for the new field to Long Text, so that Ethan is not limited to 255 characters of data in the field, which would be the case with the Short Text data type.

2. Click the **Field Name** box below the EmailAddress field, type **ContactComments**, press the **Tab** key, type the letter **l**, and then press the **Tab** key to select the Long Text data type.

3. Press the **F6** key to position the insertion point in the Format property in the Field Properties pane, press the **Tab** key, and then type **Contact Comments** in the Caption box. You've completed adding the ContactComments field to the table. See Figure 9-9.

Figure 9-9 ContactComments field added to the tblContactPatient table

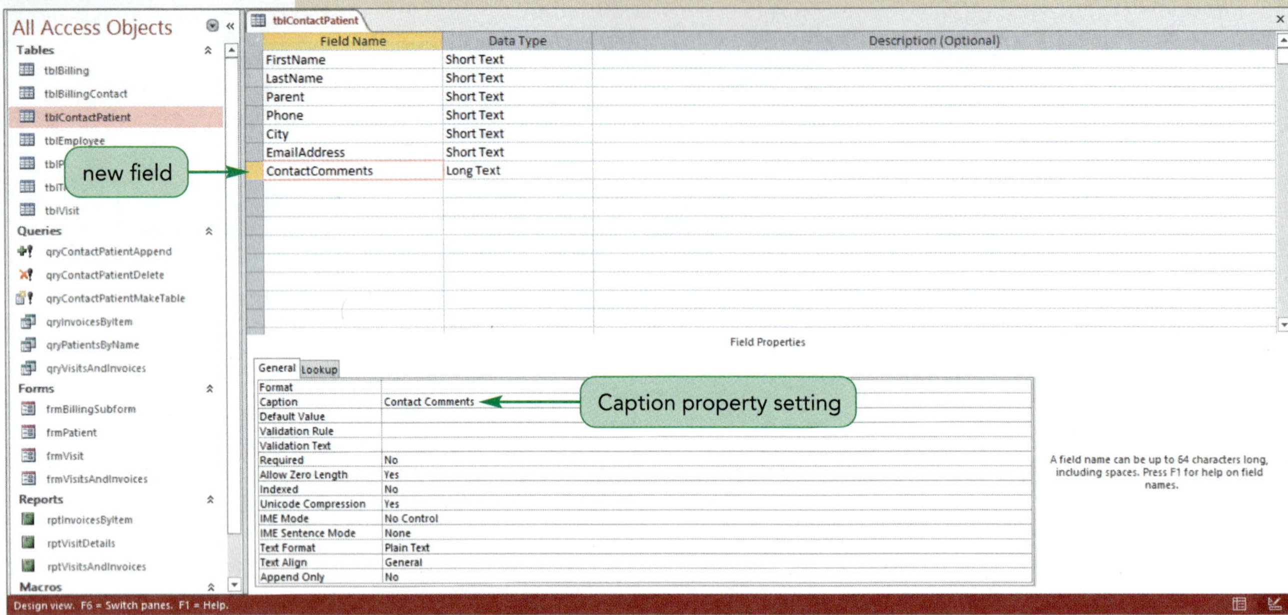

4. Add the caption **First Name** to the FirstName field, add the caption **Last Name** to the LastName field, and then add the caption **Email Address** to the EmailAddress field.
5. Save your changes to the table structure, and then switch to Datasheet view. Notice that the captions and new field are displayed.
6. Close the table, and then close the Navigation Pane.

Ethan has sent an email message to each patient that has an email address in the EmailAddress field, and he wants to update the ContactComments field in the tblContactPatient table with the same comments for all records with an email address in the EmailAddress field. He could type the comments in the ContactComments field for one of the records, and then copy and paste the comments to the other records. However, performing these steps takes time and could result in updating an incorrect record or miss one of the records. Instead, you'll create an update query.

Creating an Update Query

Recall that an update query changes selected field values and records in one or more tables.

REFERENCE

Creating an Update Query

- Create a select query with the necessary fields and selection criteria.
- On the DESIGN tab, in the Results group, click the Run button to preview the results.
- Switch to Design view to make any necessary changes to the query. When the query is correct, on the DESIGN tab in the Query Type group, click the Update button. The Update To row replaces the Show and Sort rows in the design grid.
- Type the updated values in the Update To boxes for the fields you want to update.
- Click the Run button, and then click the Yes button to confirm changing the records.

Now you can create an update query to update the ContactComments field in the tblContactPatient table for records that contain an email address in the EmailAddress field.

To create the update query:

1. Click the **CREATE tab**, in the Queries group, click the **Query Design** button, add the **tblContactPatient** table field list to the Query window, close the Show Table dialog box, and then drag down the bottom of the tblContactPatient field list to display all its fields.

   You will select the EmailAddress and ContactComments fields for the query results. The EmailAddress field lets you select records for patients that have an email address listed in this field. The ContactComments field is the field Ethan needs to update.
2. In the tblContactPatient field list, double-click **EmailAddress** and **ContactComments** to add these fields to the design grid.
3. Click the **EmailAddress Criteria** box, type **Is Not Null**, and then press the **Tab** key. The query will select a record only if there is a value in the EmailAddress field—in other words, if the field is not null.
4. Run the query. The query recordset displays five records, each of which contains an EmailAddress value. The selected query is correct.

   Now that you have verified that the correct records are selected, you can change the query to an update query.
5. Switch to Design view, and then on the DESIGN tab in the Query Type group, click the **Update** button. In the design grid, The Update To row replaces the Sort and Show rows.

   You specify how you want to change a field value for the selected records by entering an expression in the field's Update To box. An expression is a calculation resulting in a single value. You can type a simple expression directly into the Update To box.
6. Click the **ContactComments Update To** box, type **"Sent email in May. Contact again in July."** (be sure to type the quotation marks), and then drag the right edge of the ContactComments column to the right to display the entire expression value. See the Session 9.1 Visual Overview.
7. Run the query. A dialog box opens, warning that you are about to update five rows in the tblContactPatient table.
8. Click the **Yes** button to close the dialog box and run the update query. The query updates the ContactComments field values for patients who have an email address in the EmailAddress field. The Query window is still displayed in Design view.

   You are finished updating the tblContactPatient table, so you'll save and close the query.
9. Save the query as **qryContactPatientUpdate**, and then close the query.

TIP

For text expressions that contain quotation marks, you need to type the quotation marks twice. For example, to enter the expression A *"text" expression*, type "A ""text"" expression".

Now you can view the tblContactPatient table to see the results of the update operation.

To view the updated tblContactPatient table:

1. Open the Navigation Pane, open the **tblContactPatient** table in Datasheet view, and then resize the **Contact Comments** column to its best fit. The ContactComments field values for patients who have email addresses have been updated correctly. See Figure 9-10.

Figure 9-10 tblContactPatient table with updated ContactComments field values

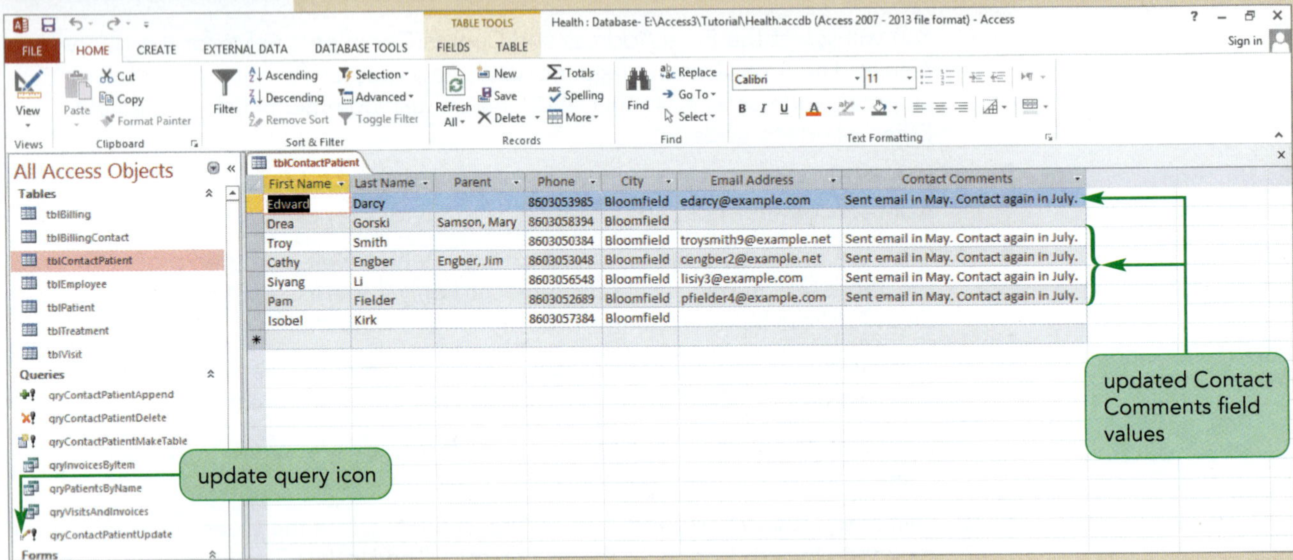

2. Save your table datasheet changes, and close the table.
3. If you are not continuing on to the next session, close the Health database.

PROSKILLS

Decision Making: Deleting Action Queries

You usually create an action query and run it for a special purpose, and in most cases you need to run the query only once. If you create and run an action query, and then save it, you might accidentally run it again. Doing so would result in the update of tables in unintended ways. Therefore, after you've run an action query, you shouldn't save it in your database; this will prevent users from running it by mistake.

Ethan can now use action queries in his future work with the Health database. In the next session, you'll learn about the different types of relationships you can create between tables, and you'll view and create indexes to increase a database's efficiency.

REVIEW

Session 9.1 Quick Check

1. What is an action query?
2. What precautions should you take before running an action query?
3. What is the difference between a make-table query and an append query?
4. What does a delete query do?
5. What does an update query do?
6. How does the design grid change when you create an update query?

Session 9.2 Visual Overview:

The tblBilling and tblEmployee tables have a many-to-many relationship. A **many-to-many relationship** (abbreviated **M:N**) exists between two tables when each record in the first table matches many records in the second table, and each record in the second table matches many records in the first table.

A primary table has a one-to-many relationship with a relationship table.

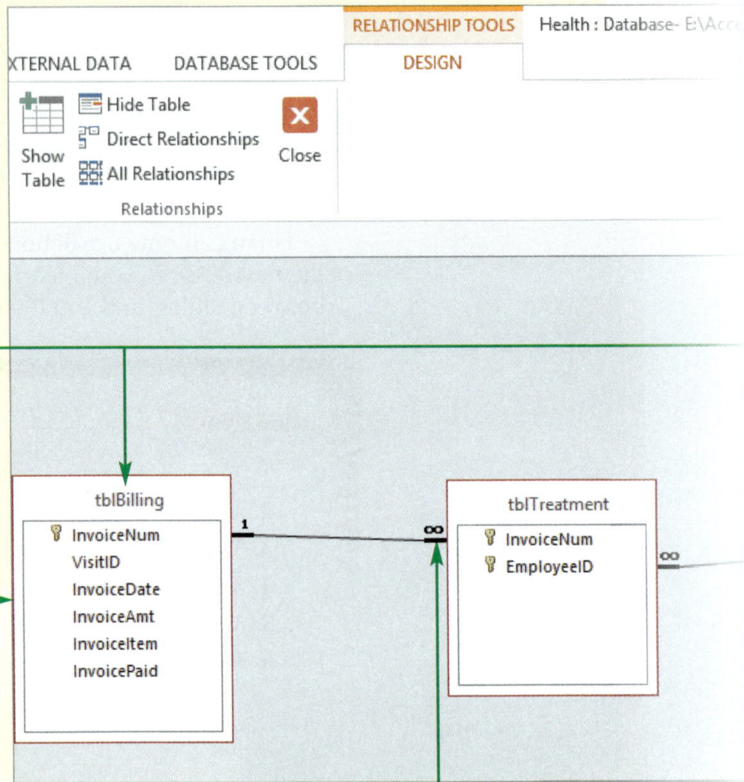

The ∞ symbol indicates there can be many records that contain the same InvoiceNum in the tblTreatment table.

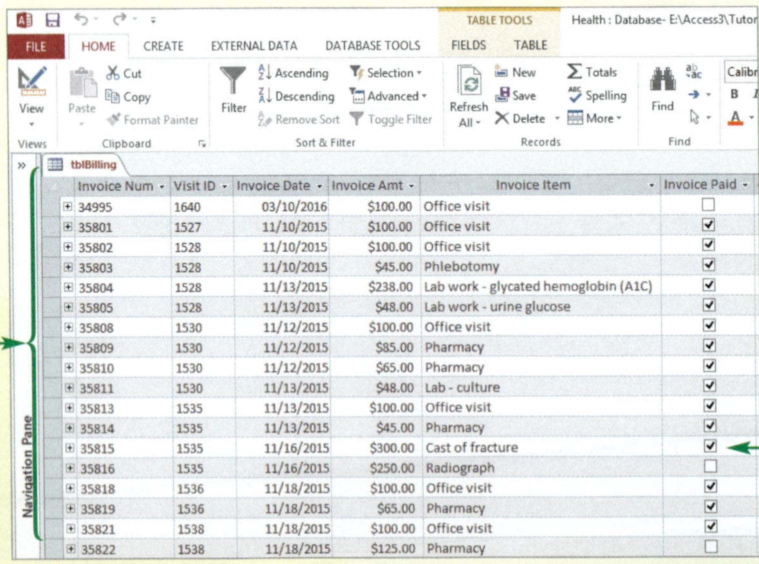

The tblBilling table contains one record for each invoice, and is one of the two primary tables in the many-to-many relationship.

InvoiceNum 35815 occurs just once in the tblBilling table but twice in the tblTreatment table.

Many-to-Many Relationship

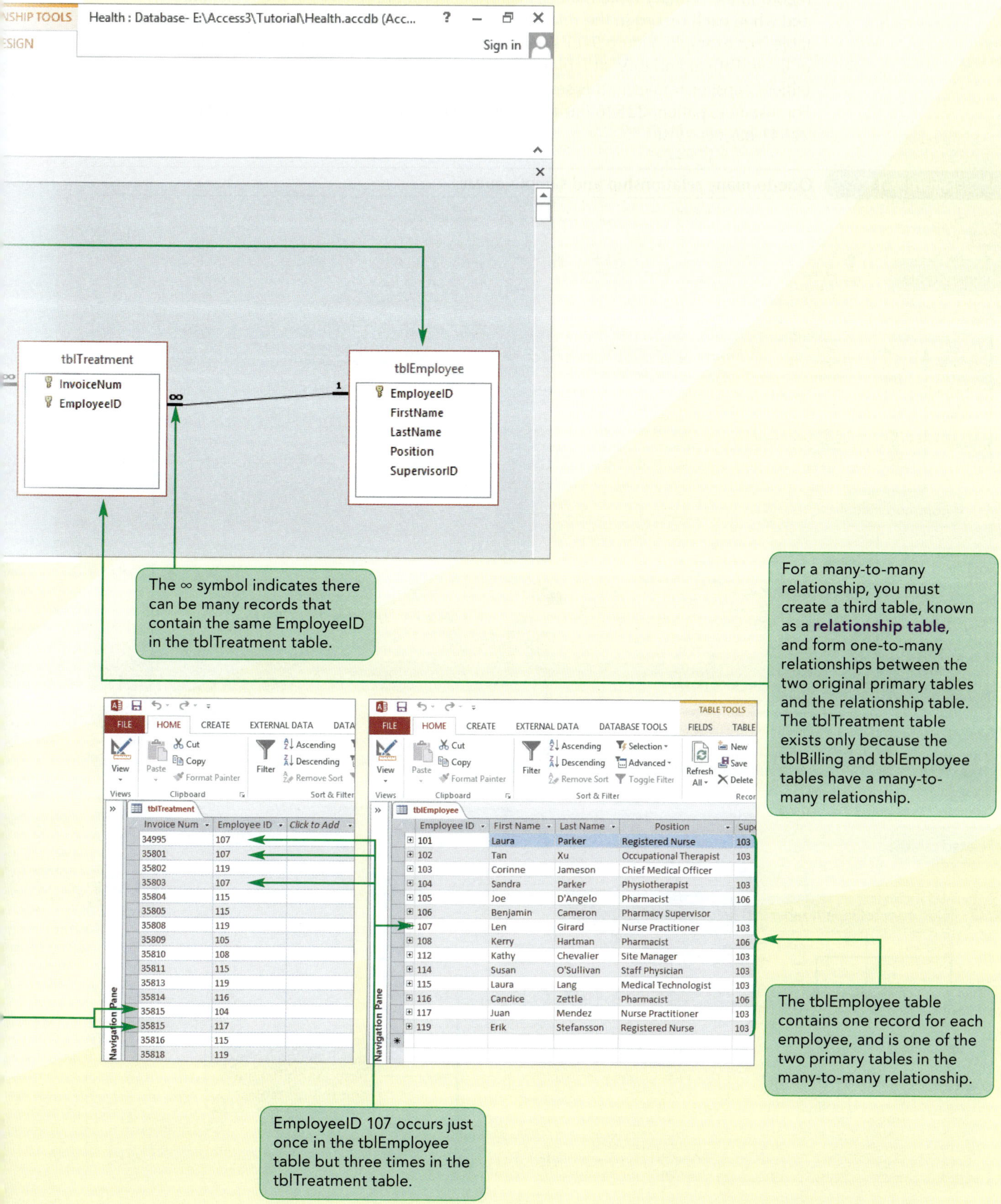

Relationships Between Database Tables

A one-to-many relationship (abbreviated as 1:M) exists between two tables when each record in the primary table matches zero, one, or more records in the related table, and when each record in the related table matches at most one record in the primary table. For example, Figure 9-11 shows a one-to-many relationship between portions of the tblPatient and tblVisit tables and also shows a sample query based on the two tables. (Most examples in this session use portions of tables for illustrative purposes.) For instance, patient 22526 has three visits, patient 22527 has one visit, and patient 22541 has zero visits.

Figure 9-11 One-to-many relationship and sample query

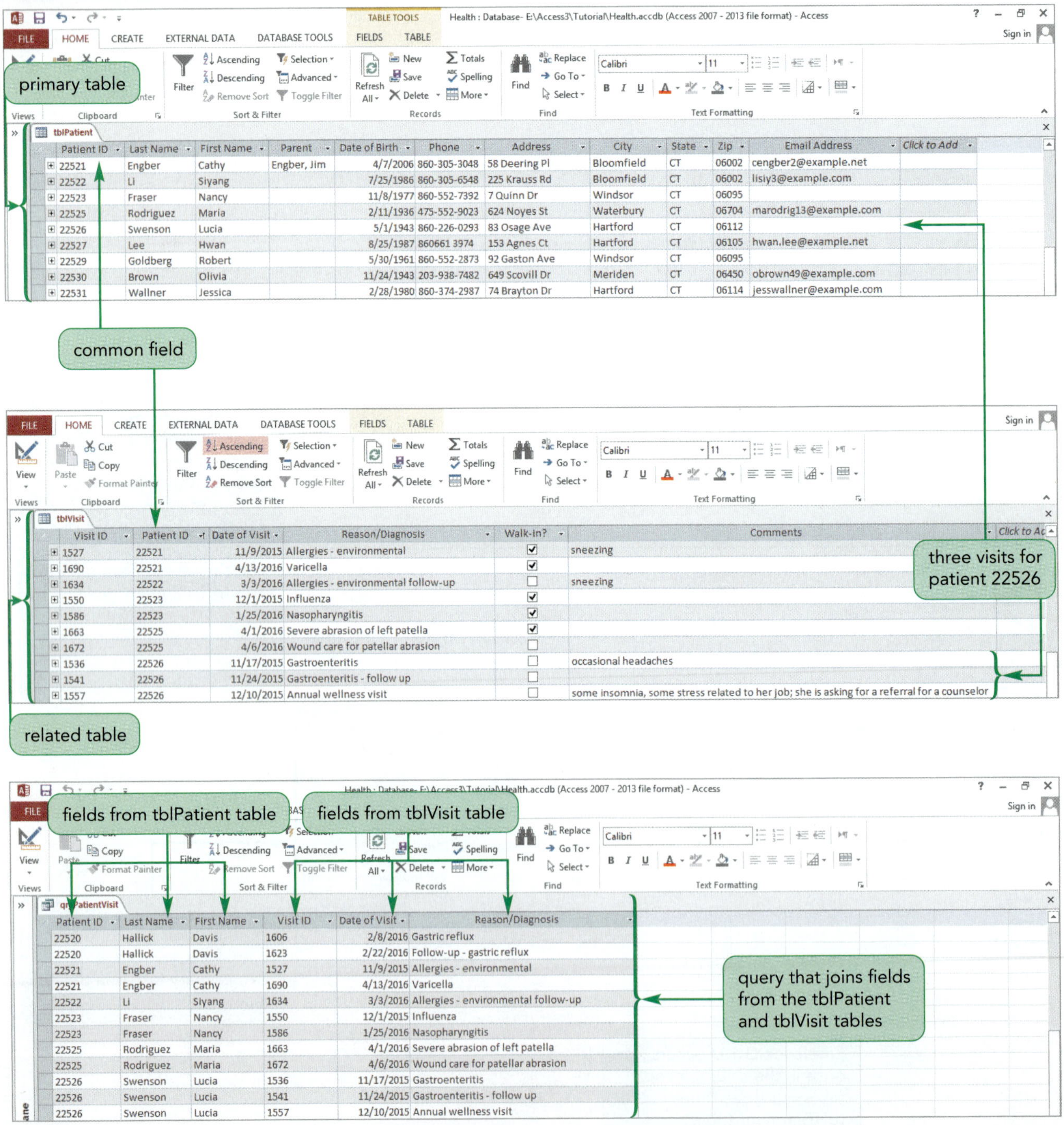

You use the common field—the PatientID field—to form the one-to-many relationship between the tblPatient and tblVisit tables. When you join the two tables based on PatientID field values, you can extract data from them as if they are one larger table. For example, you can join the tblPatient and tblVisit tables to create the qryPatientVisit query shown in Figure 9-11. In the qryPatientVisit query, the PatientID, Last Name, and First Name columns are from the tblPatient table, and the VisitID, Date of Visit and Reason/Diagnosis columns are from the tblVisit table.

In addition to one-to-many relationships between tables, you can also relate tables through many-to-many and one-to-one relationships.

Many-to-Many Relationships

In the Health database, an invoice can represent treatment performed by many employees, and each employee can provide treatment on many invoiced treatments, so the tblBilling and tblEmployee tables have a many-to-many relationship, as shown in the Session 9.2 Visual Overview.

When you have a many-to-many relationship (abbreviated as M:N) between two tables, you must create a third table, known as a relationship table, and form one-to-many relationships between the two original primary tables and the relationship table. For instance, the tblTreatment table, shown in the Session 9.2 Visual Overview, exists only because the tblBilling and tblEmployee tables have a many-to-many relationship. Each record in the tblTreatment table contains two foreign keys: the EmployeeID field is a foreign key that allows you to join the tblEmployee table to the tblTreatment table; and the InvoiceNum field is a foreign key that allows you to join the tblBilling table to the tblTreatment table. The primary key of the tblTreatment table is a composite key, consisting of the combination of the EmployeeID and InvoiceNum fields. Each pair of values in this primary key is unique.

You can see the one-to-many relationship between each primary table and the relationship table by examining the records. For example, the first record in the tblTreatment table represents an Office Visit for InvoiceNum 34995 that was performed by Louis Gerard, who has EmployeeID 107. EmployeeID 107 appears in many records in the tblTreatment table that represent treatment Louis Gerard provided for many other invoices including 35801, 35803, and more. Also, InvoiceNum 35815 appears in two tblTreatment table records, each for a different employee: Linda Park and Louis Gerard.

PROSKILLS

Decision Making: Identifying Many-to-Many Relationships

Although one-to-many relationships are the most common type of table relationship, many-to-many relationships occur frequently, and most databases have one or more many-to-many relationships, as in the following examples:

- In a college database, a student takes more than one class, and each class has more than one student enrolled; a course has many prerequisites and can be the prerequisite to many courses.
- In a pharmacy database, a medication is prescribed to many customers, and a customer can take many medications.
- In an airline database, a flight has many passengers, and a passenger can take many flights.
- In a publisher database, an author can write many books, and a book can have multiple authors.
- In a manufacturing database, a manufactured product consists of many parts, and a part can be a component in many manufactured products.
- In a film database, a movie has many actors, and each actor appears in many movies.

Common one-to-many relationships can turn into many-to-many relationships when circumstances change. For example, a department in an organization has many employees, and an employee usually works in a single department. However, an instructor can have a joint appointment to two departments, and some companies hire employees and split their time between two departments. You must carefully analyze each situation and design your table relationships to handle the specific requirements for today and for the future.

When you join tables that have a many-to-many relationship, you can extract data from them as if they were one larger table. For example, you can join the tblBilling and tblEmployee tables to create the qryTreatment query shown in the Session 9.2 Visual Overview. In the tblTreatment table, the EmployeeID field joins the tblEmployee and tblTreatment tables, and the InvoiceNum field joins the tblBilling and tblTreatment tables.

One-to-One Relationships

A **one-to-one relationship** (abbreviated as **1:1**) exists between two tables when each record in the first table matches at most one record in the second table, and each record in the second table matches at most one record in the first table. Most relationships between tables are either one-to-many or many-to-many; the primary use for one-to-one relationships is as entity subtypes. An **entity subtype** is a table whose primary key is a foreign key to a second table and whose fields are additional fields for the second table.

For most patients, the Address, City, State, and Zip fields in the tblPatient table identify both the patient's location and billing address, which is where Chatham Community Health Services sends the patient's invoices. In a few cases, however, a friend or relative will be paying the medical bills, so the billing name and address is different from the patient's name and address. There are two ways to handle these two sets of names and addresses. One way is to add the BillingCompany, BillingAddress, BillingCity, BillingState, and BillingZip fields to the tblPatient table. For each patient with an additional billing name and address, you store the appropriate values in these billing fields. For those patients who do not have additional billing information, you leave these billing fields null.

Another way to handle the two sets of addresses is to create an entity subtype, which in this case is named tblBillingContact. In the tblBillingContact table, the PatientID field, which is the primary key, is also a foreign key to the tblPatient table. A record appears in the tblBillingContact table only for those patients who have different billing names and addresses. All billing data appears only in the tblBillingContact table. The tblPatient table and the tblBillingContact table, which is an entity subtype, have a one-to-one relationship, as shown in Figure 9-12. Appendix A provides further explanation on designing databases and why this type of relationship is a good choice.

Figure 9-12 **tblPatient and tblBillingContact tables with a 1:1 relationship**

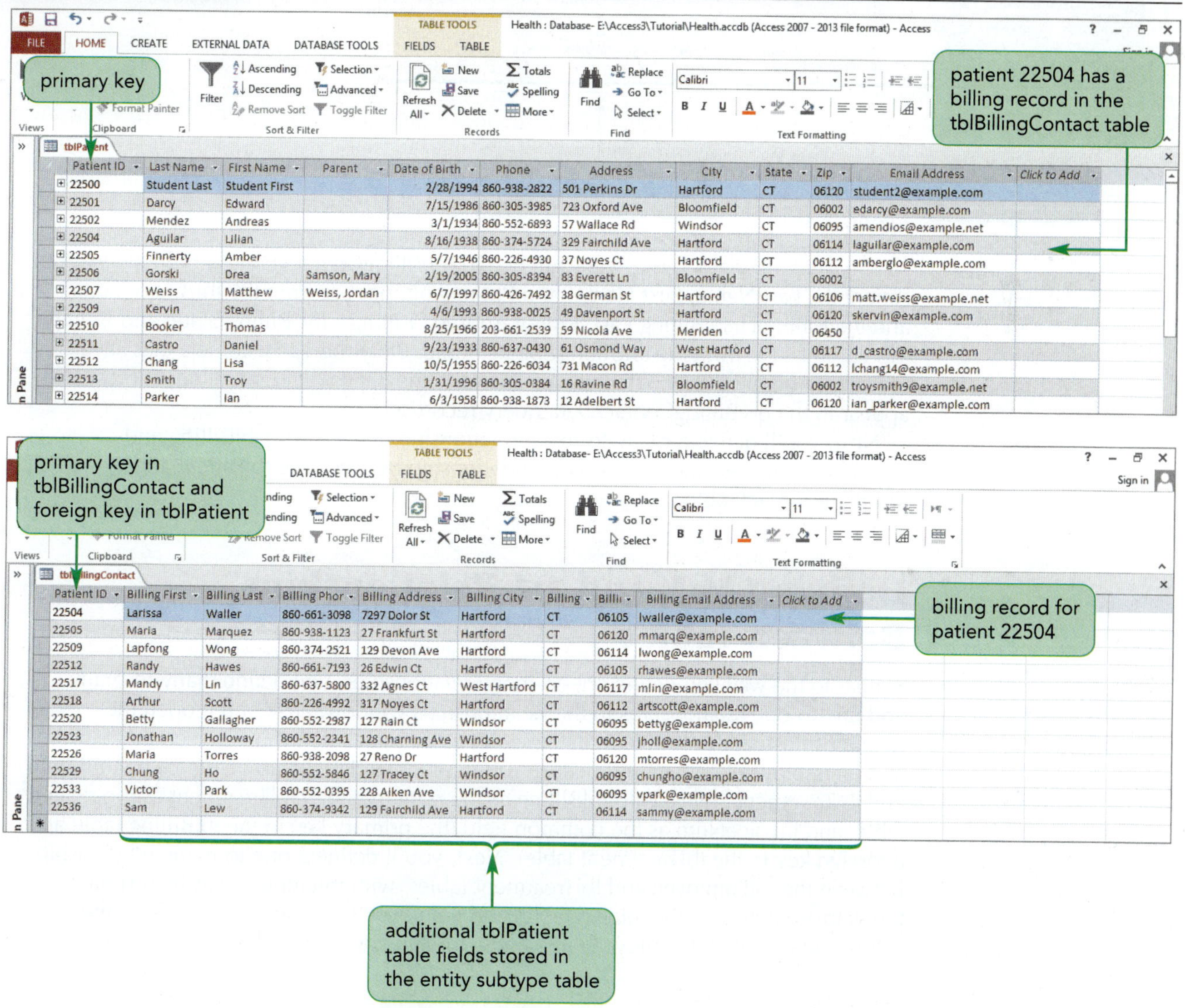

When you join tables that have a one-to-one relationship, you can extract data from them as if they were one larger table. For example, you can join the tblPatient and tblBillingContact tables to create the qryBillingContactData query shown in Figure 9-13.

Figure 9-13 **Query results produced by joining tables having a 1:1 relationship**

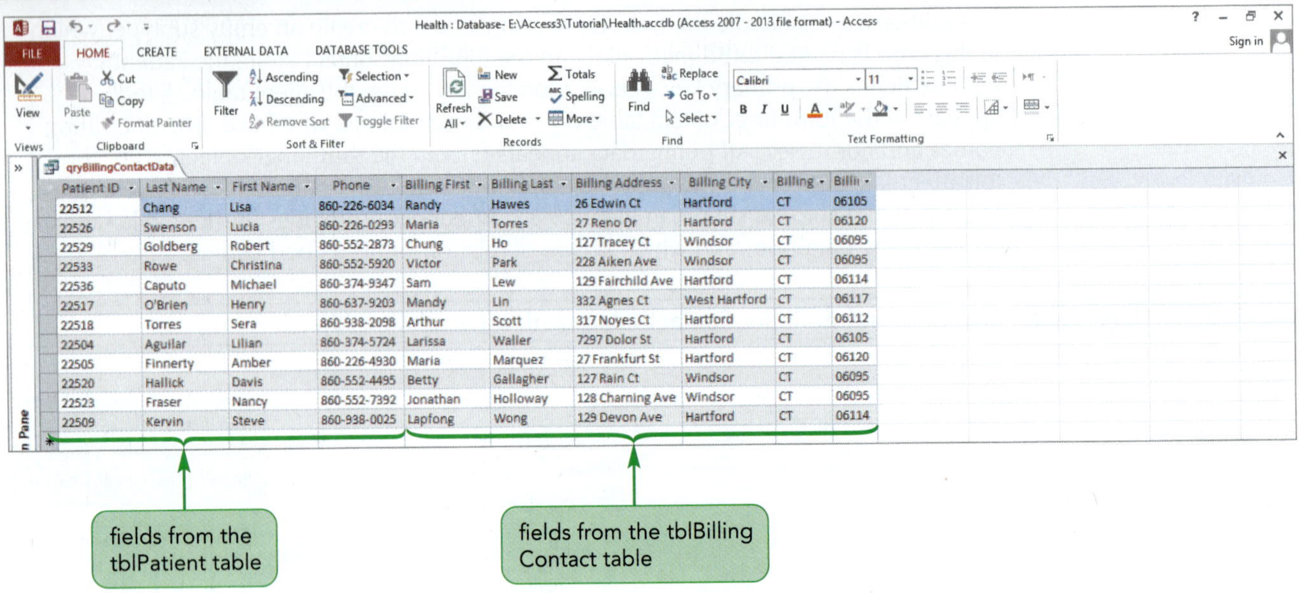

Patient ID	Last Name	First Name	Phone	Billing First	Billing Last	Billing Address	Billing City	Billing	Billi
22512	Chang	Lisa	860-226-6034	Randy	Hawes	26 Edwin Ct	Hartford	CT	06105
22526	Swenson	Lucia	860-226-0293	Maria	Torres	27 Reno Dr	Hartford	CT	06120
22529	Goldberg	Robert	860-552-2873	Chung	Ho	127 Tracey Ct	Windsor	CT	06095
22533	Rowe	Christina	860-552-5920	Victor	Park	228 Aiken Ave	Windsor	CT	06095
22536	Caputo	Michael	860-374-9347	Sam	Lew	129 Fairchild Ave	Hartford	CT	06114
22517	O'Brien	Henry	860-637-9203	Mandy	Lin	332 Agnes Ct	West Hartford	CT	06117
22518	Torres	Sera	860-938-2098	Arthur	Scott	317 Noyes Ct	Hartford	CT	06112
22504	Aguilar	Lilian	860-374-5724	Larissa	Waller	7297 Dolor St	Hartford	CT	06105
22505	Finnerty	Amber	860-226-4930	Maria	Marquez	27 Frankfurt St	Hartford	CT	06120
22520	Hallick	Davis	860-552-4495	Betty	Gallagher	127 Rain Ct	Windsor	CT	06095
22523	Fraser	Nancy	860-552-7392	Jonathan	Holloway	128 Charning Ave	Windsor	CT	06095
22509	Kervin	Steve	860-938-0025	Lapfong	Wong	129 Devon Ave	Hartford	CT	06114

The PatientID field joins the tblPatient and tblBillingContact tables. In the query, the Patient ID, Last Name, First Name, and Phone columns are from the tblPatient table; and the Billing First, Billing Last, Billing Address, Billing City, Billing State, and Billing Zip columns are from the tblBillingContact table. Only the 12 customers that have records in the tblBillingContact table—because they have different billing addresses—appear in the qryBillingContactData query recordset.

Next, you'll define a many-to-many relationship between the tblBilling and tblEmployee tables, and a one-to-one relationship between the tblPatient and tblBillingContact tables.

Defining M:N and 1:1 Relationships Between Tables

Similar to the way you define one-to-many relationships, you define many-to-many and one-to-one relationships in the Relationships window. First, you'll open the Relationships window and define the many-to-many relationship between the tblBilling and tblEmployee tables. You'll define a one-to-many relationship between the tblBilling and tblTreatment tables, with tblBilling as the primary table, tblTreatment as the related table, and InvoiceNum as the common field (the primary key in the tblBilling table and a foreign key in the tblTreatment table). Next, you'll define a one-to-many relationship between the tblEmployee and tblTreatment tables, with tblEmployee as the primary table, tblTreatment as the related table, and EmployeeID as the common field (the primary key in the tblEmployee table and a foreign key in the tblTreatment table).

To define a many-to-many relationship between the tblBilling and tblEmployee tables:

1. If you took a break after the previous session, make sure that the Health database is open.
2. Close the Navigation Pane (if necessary), click the **DATABASE TOOLS** tab, and then in the Relationships group, click the **Relationships** button to open the Relationships window.

3. On the DESIGN tab, in the Relationships group, click the **Show Table** button to open the Show Table dialog box, double-click **tblTreatment** to add the tblTreatment field list to the Relationships window, double-click **tblBillingContact** to add the tblBillingContact field list to the Relationships window, double-click **tblEmployee** to add the tblEmployee field list to the Relationships window, and then close the Show Table dialog box.
4. Drag the bottom of the tblBillingContact field list down until all field names are visible, and then drag the field list title bars of the field lists for the tblBillingContact, tblBilling, tblEmployee, and tblTreatment tables to arrange them as shown in Figure 9-14.

Figure 9-14 **After adding three table field lists to the Relationships window**

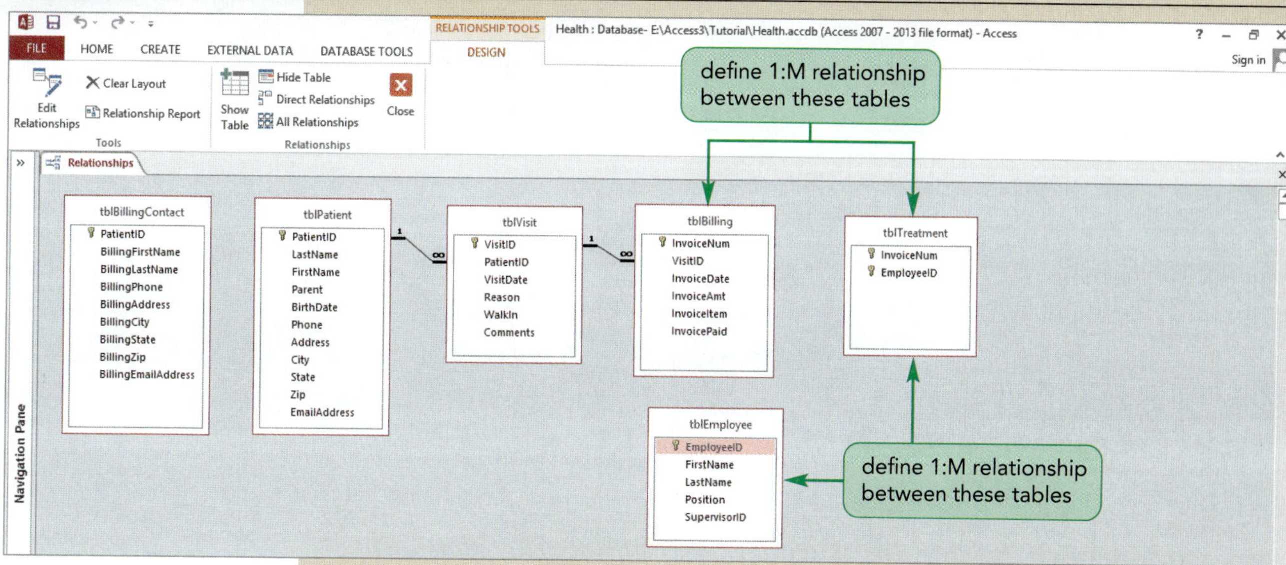

First, you'll define the one-to-many relationship between the tblBilling and tblTreatment tables.

5. In the tblBilling field list, click **InvoiceNum** and then drag it to **InvoiceNum** in the tblTreatment field list. When you release the mouse button, the Edit Relationships dialog box opens.

   The primary table, related table, and common field appear at the top of the dialog box. The type of relationship, One-To-Many, appears at the bottom of the dialog box. When you click the Enforce Referential Integrity check box, the two cascade options become available. If you select the Cascade Update Related Fields option, Access will change the appropriate foreign key values in the related table when you change a primary key value in the primary table. If you select the Cascade Delete Related Records check box, when you delete a record in the primary table, Access will delete all records in the related table that have a matching foreign key value. You'll enforce referential integrity and cascade updates to related fields, but you won't cascade deletions to related records because you want to preserve the Billing contact information in case it will be used again later.

6. Click the **Enforce Referential Integrity** check box, and then click the **Cascade Update Related Fields** check box. You have now selected all the necessary relationship options.

7. Click the **Create** button to close the dialog box and define the one-to-many relationship between the two tables. The completed relationship appears in the Relationships window.

   The thick join line indicates that you've chosen to enforce referential integrity in the relationship.

8. Repeat Steps 5 through 7 to define the one-to-many relationship between the primary tblEmployee table and the related tblTreatment table, using EmployeeID as the common field. See Figure 9-15.

Figure 9-15 M:N relationship defined between the tblBilling and tblEmployee tables

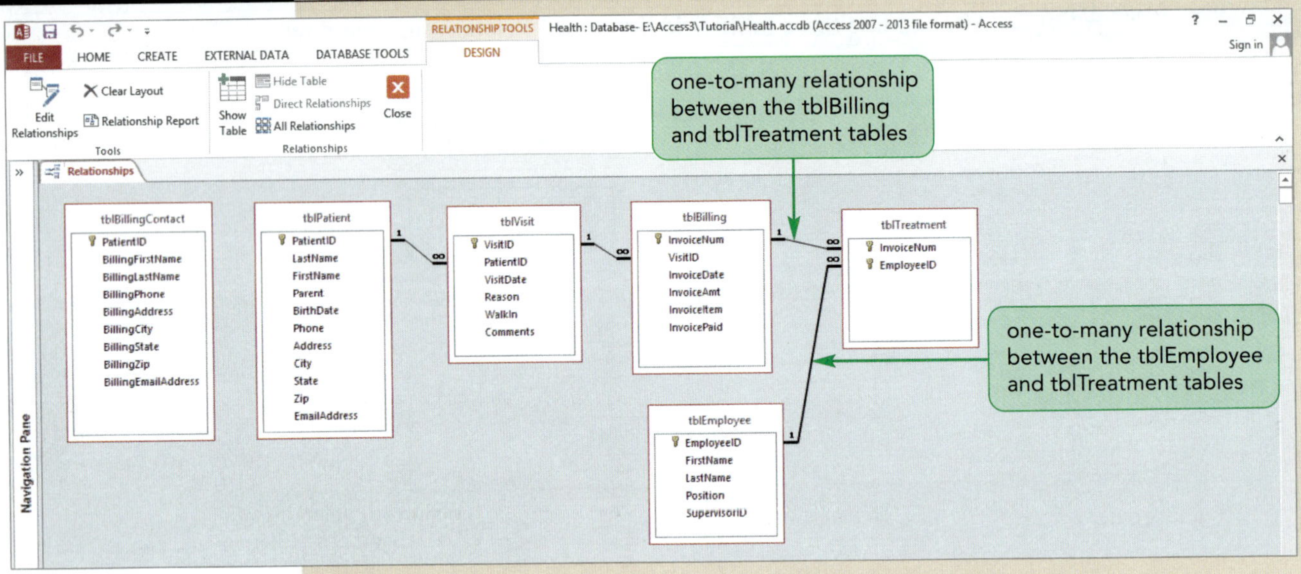

Now you'll define a one-to-one relationship between the tblPatient and tblBillingContact tables. Not all patients have billing contact information, so it will be important to create the relationship by dragging from the tblPatient table to the tblBillingContact table to preserve referential integrity.

To define a one-to-one relationship between the tblPatient and tblBillingContact tables:

Be sure to drag from the tblPatient to the tblBilling-Contact table, and not the reverse.

1. In the tblPatient field list, click **PatientID**, and then drag it to **PatientID** in the tblBillingContact field list. When you release the mouse button, the Edit Relationships dialog box opens.

   The primary table, related table, and common field appear at the top of the dialog box. The type of relationship, One-To-One, appears at the bottom of the dialog box.

   Trouble? If you mistakenly drag from the tblBillingContact table to the tblPatient table, you'll see an error message that indicates a violation of referential integrity. Just click the Cancel button and try again, dragging from the tblPatient table to the tblBillingContact table.

2. Click the **Enforce Referential Integrity** check box, click the **Cascade Update Related Fields** check box, and then click the **Create** button to define the one-to-one relationship between the two tables and close the dialog box. The completed relationship appears in the Relationships window. See Figure 9-16.

Figure 9-16 1:1 relationship defined between the tblPatient and tblBillingContact tables

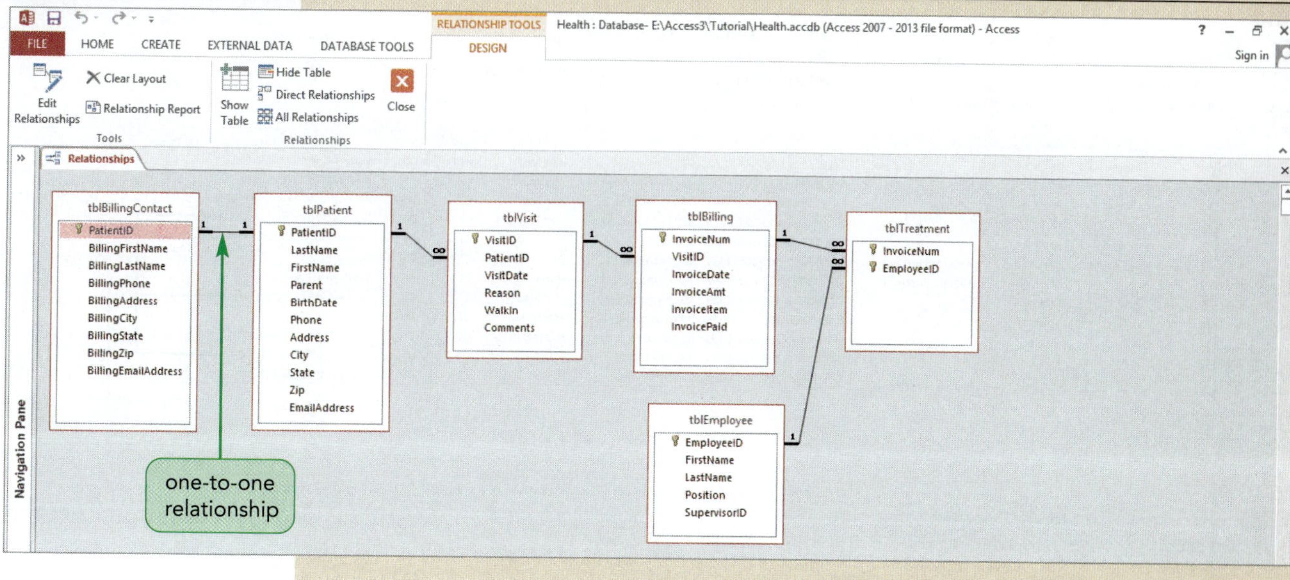

Each side of the relationship has the digit 1 at its end of the join line to indicate a one-to-one relationship between the two tables.

3. Save your relationship changes.

The tblEmployee table contains data about the employees at Chatham Community Health Services who are health care workers. Kelly asks you to create a select query to display the employees in the tblEmployee table and their supervisors. The select query you'll create will require a special join using the tblEmployee table.

Joining Tables

The design of the Health database includes a one-to-many relationship between the tblPatient and tblVisit tables using PatientID as the common field, which allows you to join the two tables to create a query based on data from both tables. The type of join you have used so far is an inner join. Two other types of joins are the outer join and the self-join.

Inner and Outer Joins

An **inner join** is a join in which the DBMS selects records from two tables only when the records have the same value in the common field that links the tables. For example, in a database containing a table of student information and a table of class information, an inner join would show all student records that have a matching class record and all class records that have a matching student record. In the Health database, PatientID is the common field for the tblPatient and tblBillingContact tables. As shown in Figure 9-17, the results of a query based on an inner join of these two tables include only those records that have a matching PatientID value. The record in the tblPatient table with a Patient ID column value of 22500 is not included in the query recordset because it fails to match a record with the same Patient ID column value in the tblBillingContact table. (That patient does not have a different billing address.) Because primary key values can't be null, records with null foreign key values do not appear in a query recordset based on an inner join. You usually use an inner join whenever you perform a query based on more than one table; it is the default join you have used to this point. When you create a join, you can specify the type of join in the dialog box.

Figure 9-17 Example of an inner join

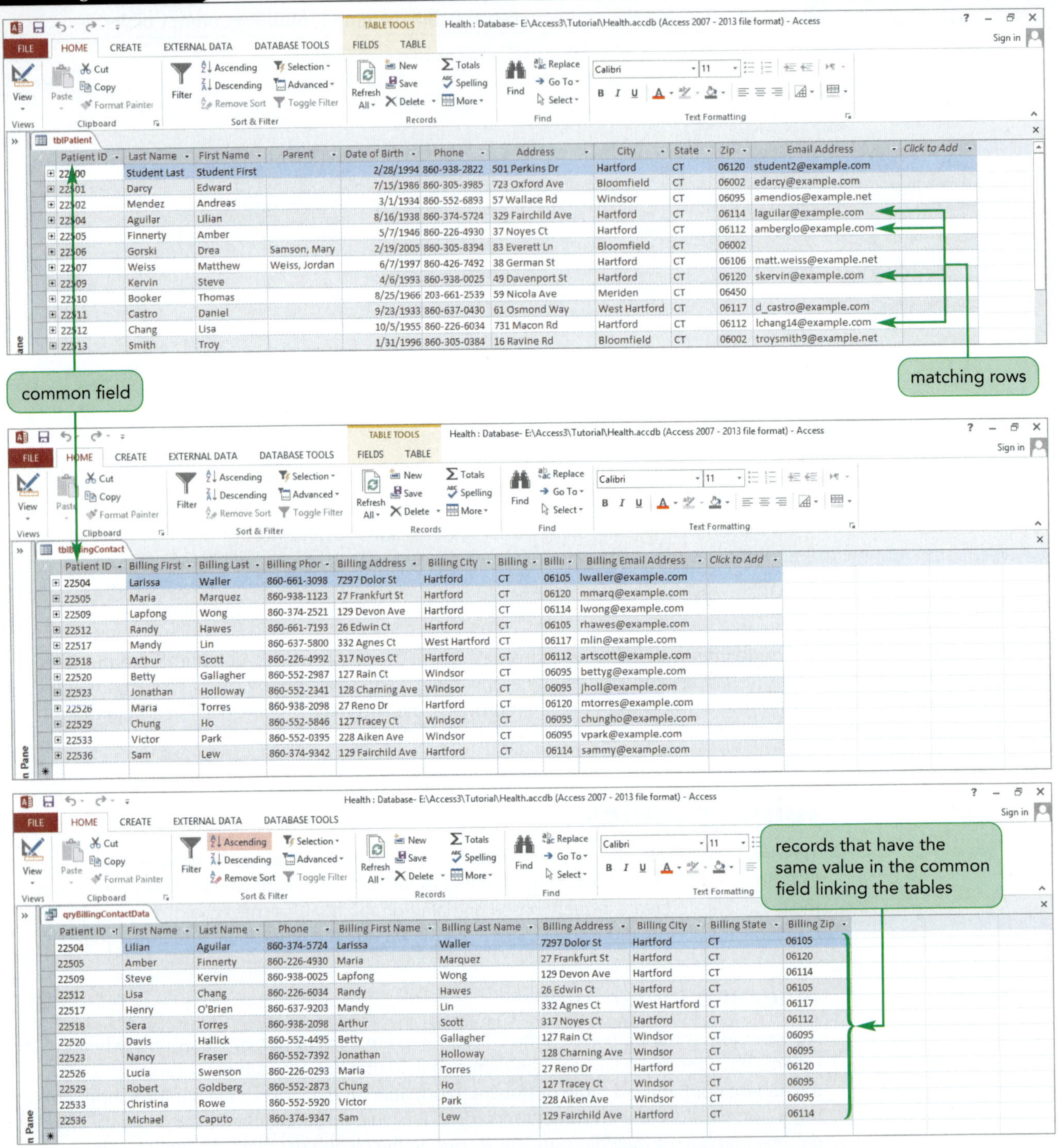

An **outer join** is a join in which the DBMS selects *all* records from one table and only those records from a second table that have matching common field values. For example, in a database containing a student table and a class table, an outer join would show all students whether or not the students are enrolled in classes, and another outer join would show all classes whether or not any students are enrolled in them. In the Health database, you would use this kind of join if you wanted to see, for example, all records from the tblPatient table and also any and all matching records from the tblBillingContact table. Figure 9-18 shows an outer join for the tblPatient and tblBillingContact tables. All records from the tblPatient table appear in the query recordset, along with only matching records from the tblBillingContact table. Notice that the record from the tblPatient table for Patient ID 22519 appears in the query recordset even though it does not match a record in the tblBillingContact table.

Figure 9-18 Example of an outer join

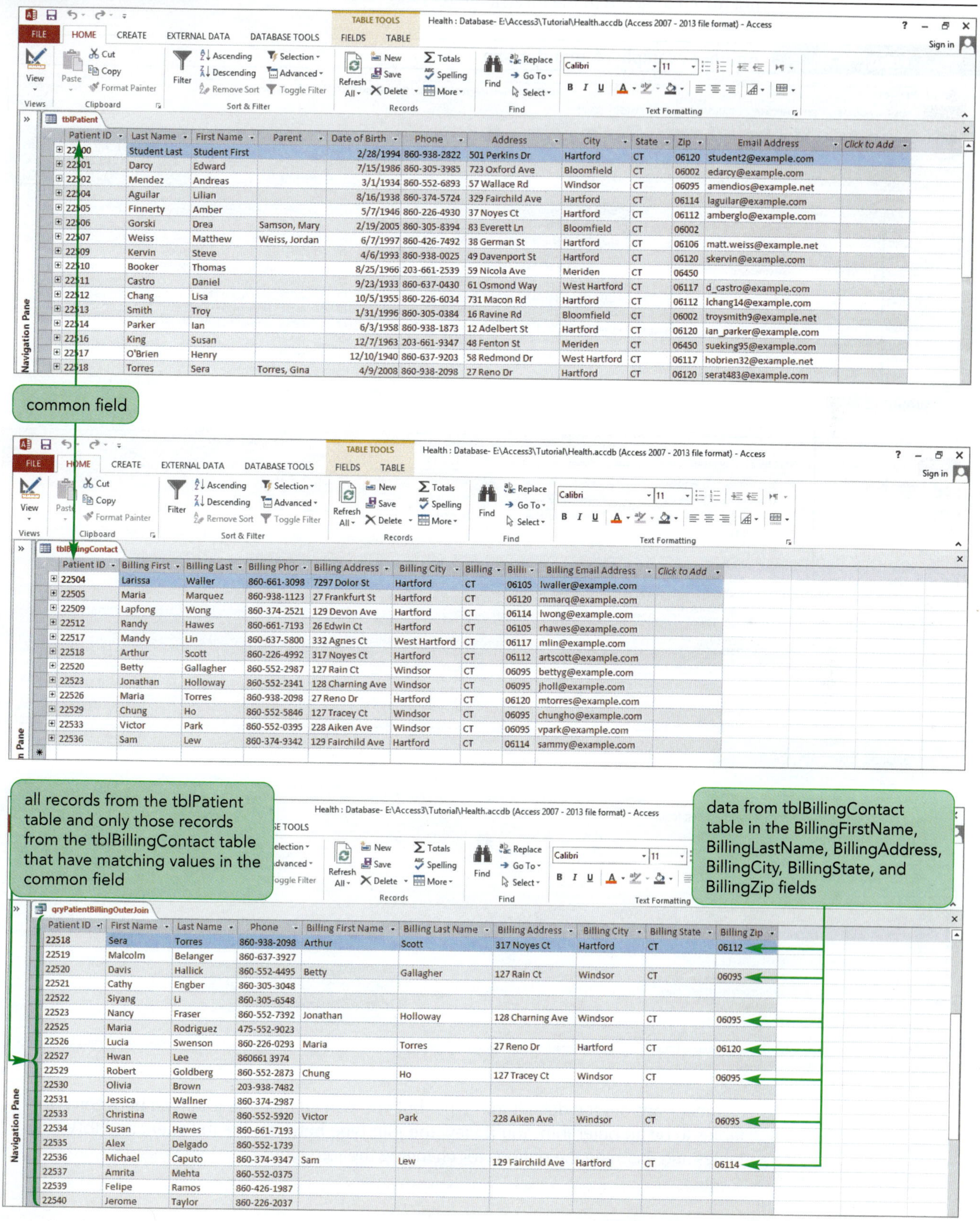

Another example of an outer join using the tblPatient and tblVisit tables is shown in Figure 9-19. All records from the tblVisit table appear in the query recordset. If any tblVisit records had a Patient ID that did not match a Patient ID in the tblPatient table, these records would still be in the query recordset. The Patient ID 22541 record from the tblPatient table does not appear in the query recordset, however, because it does not match a record in the tblVisit table.

Figure 9-19 Another example of an outer join

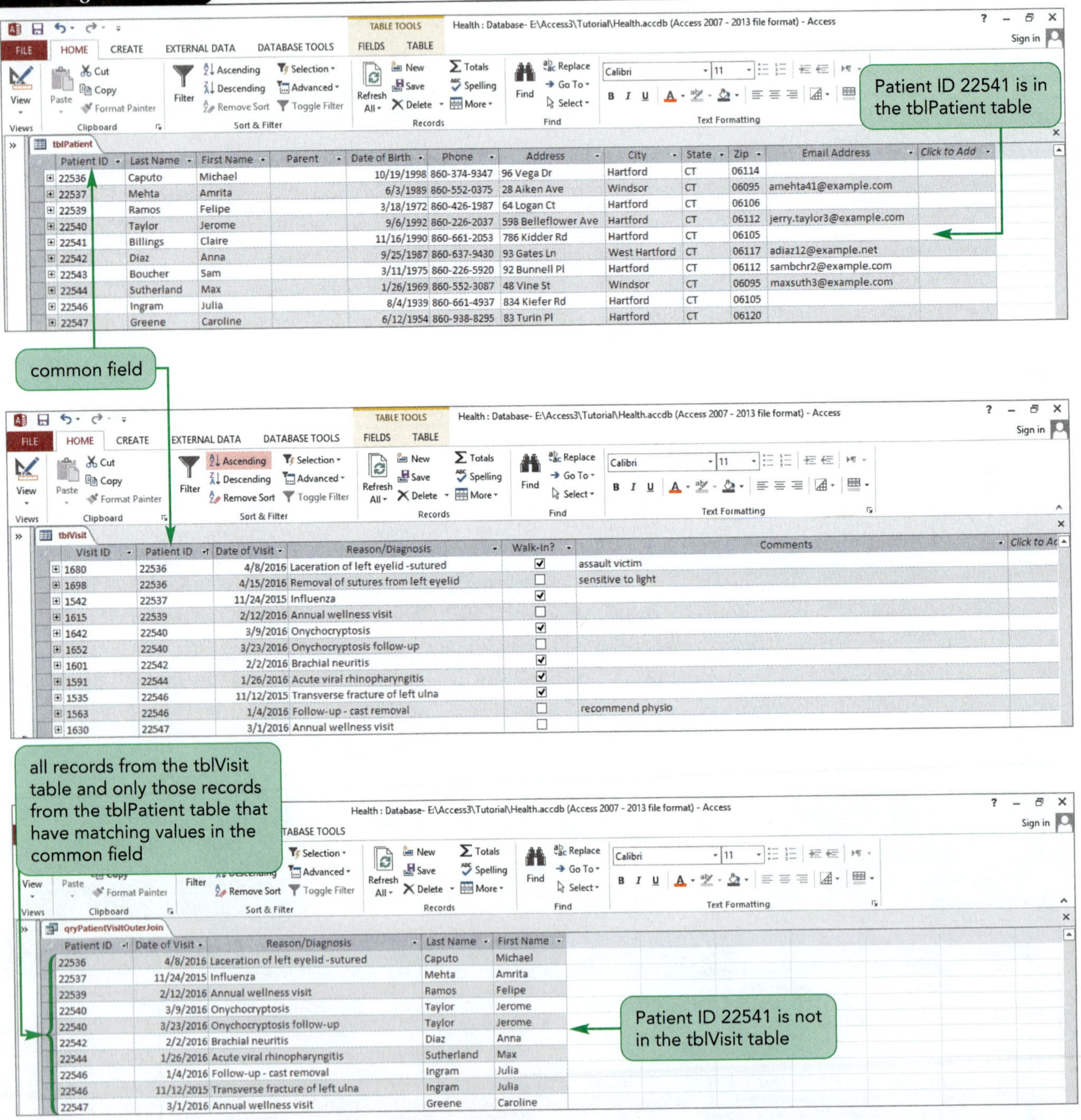

Inner joins are the default join type, but you can change the join type between two tables to be an outer join. You'll view the join type between the tblPatient and tblVisit tables and examine the options for changing the join type.

To view the join type between the tblPatient and tblVisit tables:

1. Right-click the join line between the tblPatient and tblVisit tables, and then click **Edit Relationship** on the shortcut menu to open the Edit Relationships dialog box.

   Trouble? If right-clicking the join line does not work, click the join line, and then on the DESIGN tab, in the Tools group, click the Edit Relationships button.

2. Click the **Join Type** button in the dialog box to open the Join Properties dialog box. See Figure 9-20.

Figure 9-20 Join Properties dialog box

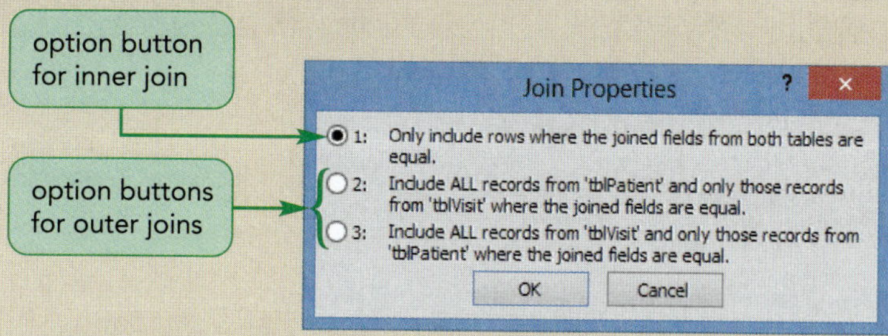

In the Join Properties dialog box, the first option button is selected, indicating that the join type between the tblPatient and tblVisit tables is an inner join. You would click the second or third option button to establish an outer join between the two tables. You'd select the second option if you wanted to select all records from the tblPatient table and any matching records from the tblVisit table based on the PatientID common field. You'd select the third option if you wanted to select all records from the tblVisit table and any matching records from the tblPatient table based on the PatientID common field.

When you change the join type between two tables in the Relationships window, every new query based on the two tables uses the join type you selected in the Join Properties dialog box. Existing queries, reports, or forms based on the two tables continue to use the join type that was in effect at the time you created the queries.

Kelly wants to continue to use an inner join for all queries based on the tblPatient and tblVisit tables.

3. Click the **Cancel** button to close the Join Properties dialog box without making any changes, click the **Cancel** button to close the Edit Relationships dialog box without making any changes, close the Relationships window, and then if you are prompted to save changes, click **No** to ensure that you don't change the relationship type.

Self-Joins

A table can also be joined with itself; this join is called a **self-join**. A self-join can be either an inner or outer join. For example, the tblEmployee table lists all employees, and for each employee that has a supervisor, the SupervisorID is included. The SupervisorID is the EmployeeID of the supervisor. It doesn't make sense to have separate SupervisorID and Employee ID fields. Imagine a situation where there are multiple supervisors, and each of the supervisors also has a supervisor. Separate tables for supervisors would be very confusing. The supervisors are also employees, and thus the EmployeeID for a supervisor is entered in the SupervisorID field. This is a case where a self-join would be used. The tblEmployee table would be joined to itself so the SupervisorID field could be related to the EmployeeID field in order to display the name of the supervisor for each employee. You would use a self-join to relate the SupervisorID field to the EmployeeID field to determine the name of the supervisor if you wanted to see records from the tblEmployee table together with information about each employee's supervisor. Figure 9-21 shows a self-join for the tblEmployee table. In this case, the self-join is an inner join because records appear in the query results only if the SupervisorID field value matches an EmployeeID field value. To create this self-join, you would add two copies of the tblEmployee table to the Query window in Design view, and then join the SupervisorID field of one tblEmployee table to the EmployeeID field of the other tblEmployee table.

Figure 9-21 Example of a self-join

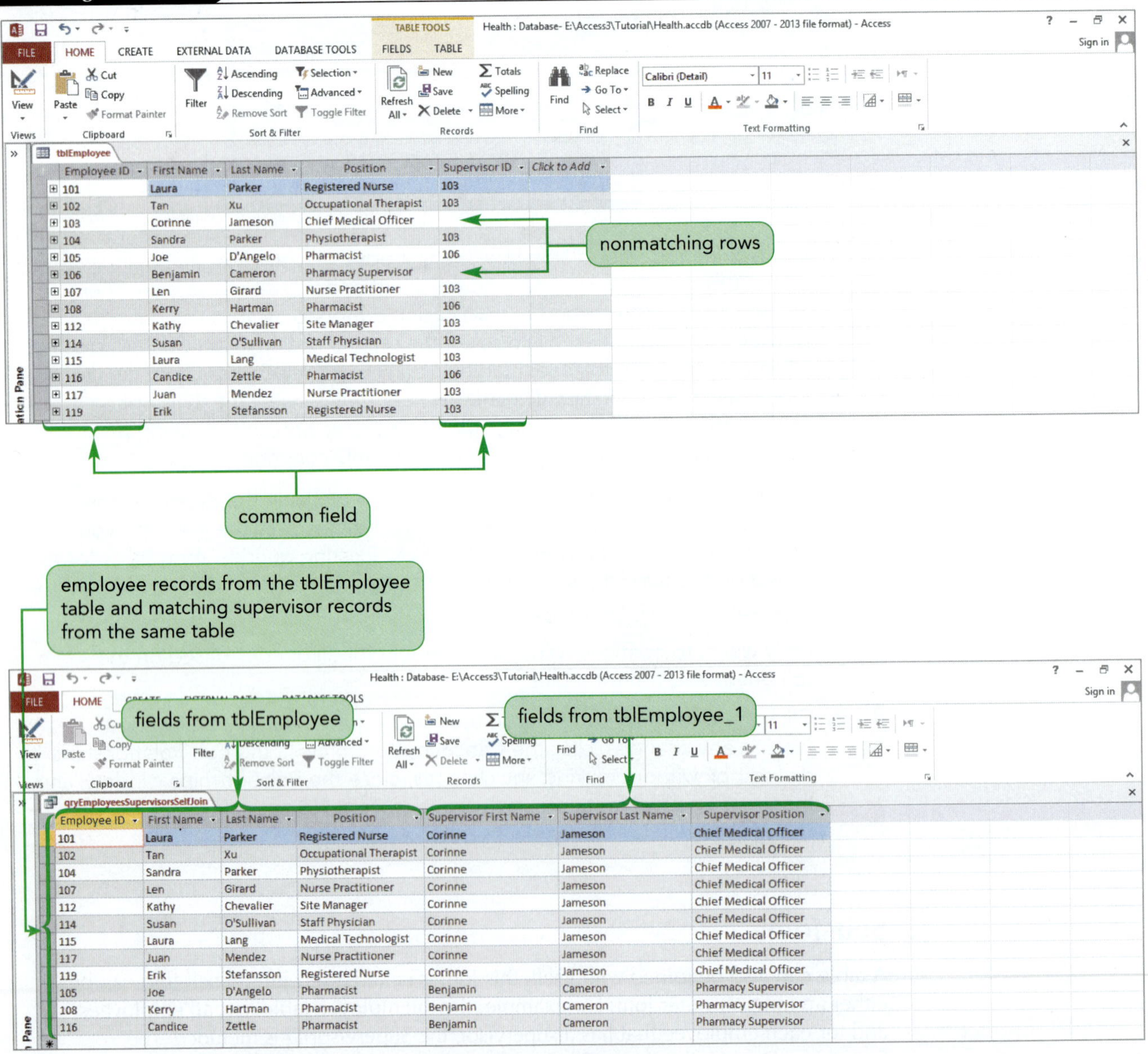

tblEmployee

Employee ID	First Name	Last Name	Position	Supervisor ID
101	Laura	Parker	Registered Nurse	103
102	Tan	Xu	Occupational Therapist	103
103	Corinne	Jameson	Chief Medical Officer	
104	Sandra	Parker	Physiotherapist	103
105	Joe	D'Angelo	Pharmacist	106
106	Benjamin	Cameron	Pharmacy Supervisor	
107	Len	Girard	Nurse Practitioner	103
108	Kerry	Hartman	Pharmacist	106
112	Kathy	Chevalier	Site Manager	103
114	Susan	O'Sullivan	Staff Physician	103
115	Laura	Lang	Medical Technologist	103
116	Candice	Zettle	Pharmacist	106
117	Juan	Mendez	Nurse Practitioner	103
119	Erik	Stefansson	Registered Nurse	103

qryEmployeesSupervisorsSelfJoin

Employee ID	First Name	Last Name	Position	Supervisor First Name	Supervisor Last Name	Supervisor Position
101	Laura	Parker	Registered Nurse	Corinne	Jameson	Chief Medical Officer
102	Tan	Xu	Occupational Therapist	Corinne	Jameson	Chief Medical Officer
104	Sandra	Parker	Physiotherapist	Corinne	Jameson	Chief Medical Officer
107	Len	Girard	Nurse Practitioner	Corinne	Jameson	Chief Medical Officer
112	Kathy	Chevalier	Site Manager	Corinne	Jameson	Chief Medical Officer
114	Susan	O'Sullivan	Staff Physician	Corinne	Jameson	Chief Medical Officer
115	Laura	Lang	Medical Technologist	Corinne	Jameson	Chief Medical Officer
117	Juan	Mendez	Nurse Practitioner	Corinne	Jameson	Chief Medical Officer
119	Erik	Stefansson	Registered Nurse	Corinne	Jameson	Chief Medical Officer
105	Joe	D'Angelo	Pharmacist	Benjamin	Cameron	Pharmacy Supervisor
108	Kerry	Hartman	Pharmacist	Benjamin	Cameron	Pharmacy Supervisor
116	Candice	Zettle	Pharmacist	Benjamin	Cameron	Pharmacy Supervisor

In Figure 9-21, the query results show the record for each employee in the tblEmployee table with a value in the SupervisorID field, and the detail for each record includes information about the supervisor for that employee. The supervisor information also comes from the tblEmployee table through the SupervisorID field. The join for the query is an inner join, so only employees with nonnull SupervisorID field values appear in the query recordset.

To create a select query to display the employees in the tblEmployee table and their supervisors, you need to create a self-join.

Creating a Self-Join

You need to create a query to display the employees and their supervisors in the tblEmployee table. This query requires a self-join. To create the self-join, you need to add two copies of the tblEmployee field list to the Query window in Design view, and then add a join line from the EmployeeID field in one field list to the SupervisorID field in the other. The SupervisorID field is a foreign key that matches the primary key field EmployeeID. You can then create a query to display employee information from one copy of the table and supervisor information from the other copy of the table.

REFERENCE

Creating a Self-Join

- Click the CREATE tab on the Ribbon.
- In the Queries group, click the Query Design button.
- In the Show Table dialog box, double-click the table for the self-join, double-click the table a second time, and then click the Close button.
- Click and drag the primary key field from one field list to the foreign key field in the other field list.
- Right-click the join line between the two tables, and then click Join Properties to open the Join Properties dialog box.
- Click the first option button to select an inner join, or click the second option button or the third option button to select an outer join, and then click the OK button.
- Select the fields, specify the selection criteria, select the sort options, and set other properties as appropriate for the query.

Now you'll create the self-join query to display supervisor information with the relevant employee records.

To create the self-join query:

1. Click the **CREATE tab**, and then in the Queries group, click the **Query Design** button to open the Show Table dialog box on top of the Query window in Design view.
2. Double-click **tblEmployee** to add the tblEmployee field list to the Query window.
3. Double-click **tblEmployee** again to add a second copy of the tblEmployee field list to the Query window, and then click the **Close** button. Access identifies the left field list as tblEmployee and the right field list as tblEmployee_1 to distinguish the two copies of the table.

   You will now create a join between the two copies of the tblEmployee table by linking the EmployeeID field in the tblEmployee field list to the SupervisorID field in the tblEmployee_1 field list. The SupervisorID field is a foreign key that matches the primary key field EmployeeID.
4. In the tblEmployee field list, click the **EmployeeID** field and then drag it to the **SupervisorID** field in the tblEmployee_1 field list. Access adds a join line between the two fields. You can verify that this is an inner join query by opening the Join Properties dialog box.

TIP

To remove a table from the Query window, right-click the field list and then click Remove Table on the shortcut menu.

5. Right-click the join line between the two tables, and then click **Join Properties** on the shortcut menu to open the Join Properties dialog box. See Figure 9-22.

Figure 9-22 Join Properties dialog box

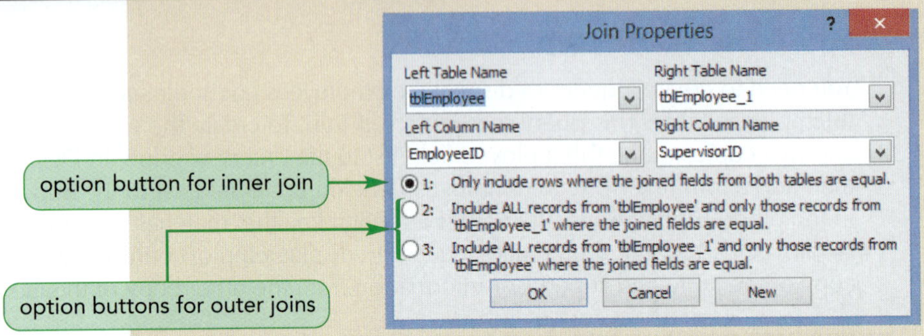

The first option button is selected, indicating that this is an inner join. Because the inner join is correct, you can close the dialog box and then add the necessary fields in the design grid.

6. Click the **Cancel** button, and then double-click the following fields (in order) from the tblEmployee_1 field list: **EmployeeID**, **FirstName**, **LastName**, and **Position**.

7. Double-click the following fields (in order) from the tblEmployee field list: **FirstName** and **LastName**.

8. Run the query. Access displays the query recordset with six fields and 12 records. See Figure 9-23.

Figure 9-23 Initial self-join on the tblEmployee table

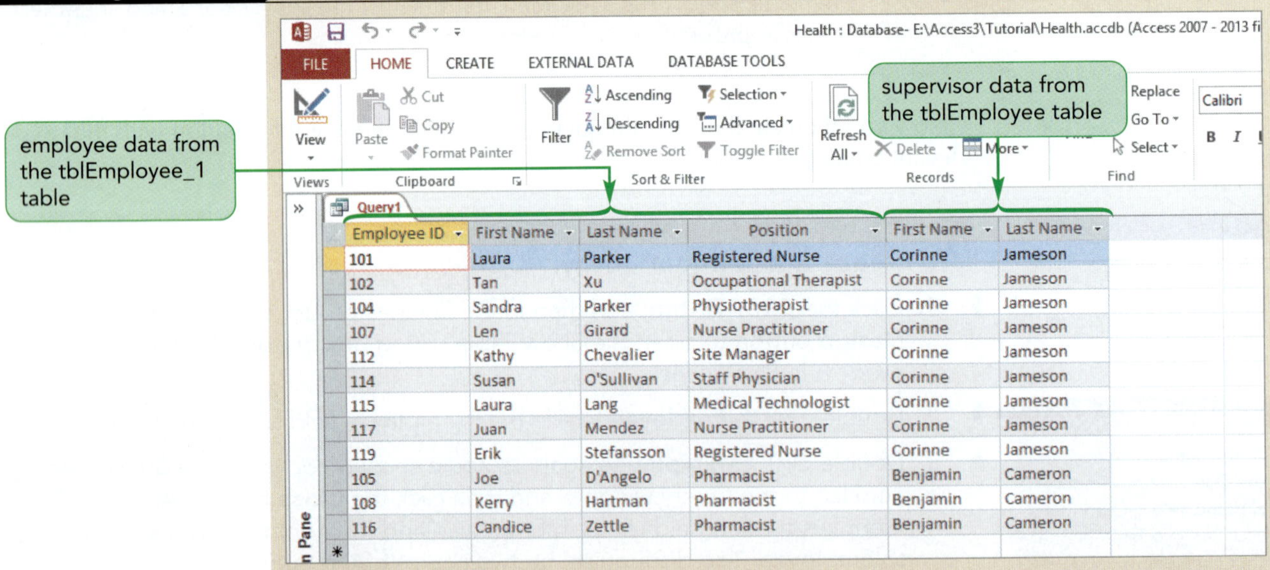

The query recordset displays all employees and their supervisors with the exception of the records for Corinne Jameson and Benjamin Cameron because their records contain null SupervisorID field values. (They are supervisors of the other employees and do not have assigned supervisors.) Remember that an inner join doesn't display records from the second table unless it contains a matching value in the common field. In the tblEmployee_1 table, the SupervisorID field values for Corinne Jameson and Benjamin Cameron are null, so the inner join doesn't select their records in the tblEmployee table.

Trouble? If your query results do not match Figure 9-23, switch to Design view and review the preceding steps to make any necessary corrections to your query design. Then run the query again.

Two columns in the query recordset are titled "First Name," and two columns are titled "Last Name." Kelly asks you to rename the two rightmost columns so that the query recordset will be easier to read. After you set the Caption property for the two rightmost fields, the column names in the query recordset will be, from left to right, Employee ID, First Name, Last Name, Position, Supervisor First Name, and Supervisor Last Name. You'll also sort the query in increasing EmployeeID order.

To set the Caption property for two query fields and sort the query:

1. Switch to Design view.
2. Click the **Field** box for the sixth column.
3. On the DESIGN tab, in the Show/Hide group, click the **Property Sheet** button, and then set the Caption property to **Supervisor Last Name**.
4. Click the **Field** box for the fifth column, and then set the Caption property to **Supervisor First Name**.
5. Close the property sheet, click the right side of the **EmployeeID Sort** box to display the sort order options, and then click **Ascending**.
6. Save the query as **qryEmployeesSupervisors**, run the query, resize all columns to their best fit, and then click the first row's **Employee ID** field value to deselect all values. The query recordset displays the new names for the fifth and sixth columns. See Figure 9-24.

Figure 9-24 Final self-join on the tblEmployee table

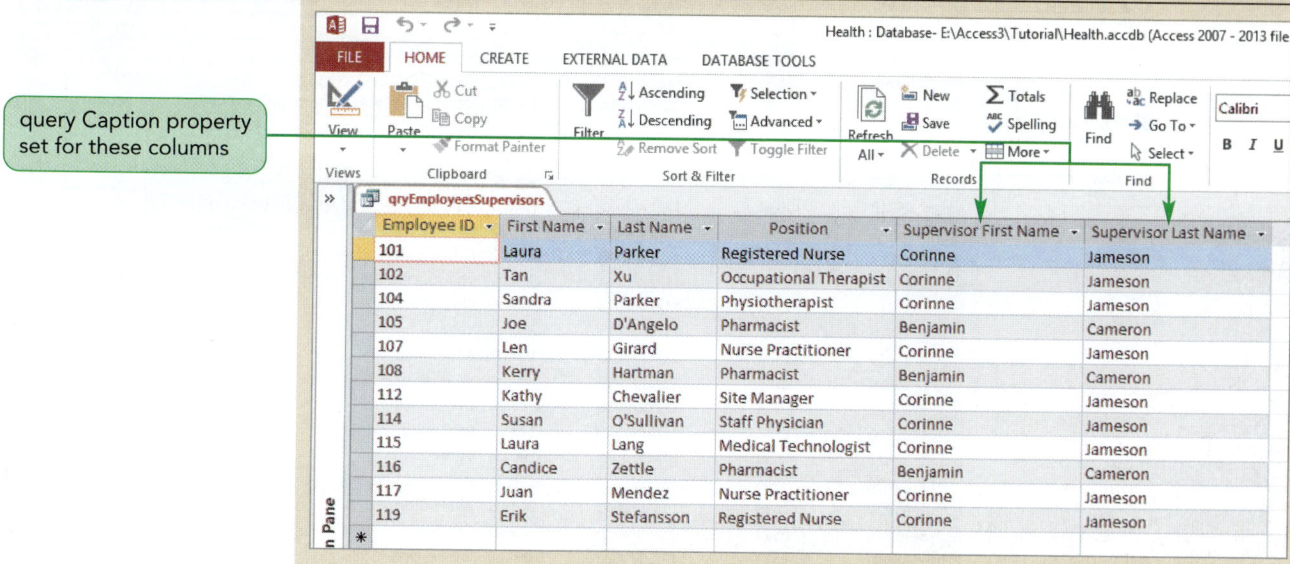

7. Save and close the query.

Kelly asks you if her staff's work will take longer as the Health database grows in size with the addition of more table records. Specifically, she wants to know if queries will take longer to run. Using indexes will help make her queries run faster.

Using Indexes for Table Fields

Suppose you need to find all the pages in a book that discuss a specific topic. The fastest, most accurate way to perform your search is to look up the topic in the book's index. In a similar fashion, you can create indexes for fields in a table, so that Access can quickly locate all the records in a table that contain specific values for one or more fields. An **index** is a list that relates field values to the records that contain those field values.

Access automatically creates and maintains an index for a table's primary key. When you view a table in datasheet view, the records are always in Primary key order, even though they may not have been entered in that order. This is because Access has created an index for the primary key. For example, the tblBilling table in the Health database includes an index for the InvoiceNum field, which is the table's primary key. Conceptually, as shown in Figure 9-25, Access identifies each record in the tblBilling table by its record number, and the InvoiceNum index has two columns. The first column contains an InvoiceNum value, and the second column contains the record number in the tblBilling table for that InvoiceNum value. For instance, InvoiceNum 35802 in the index has a record number value of 3; and record number 3 in the tblBilling table contains the data for InvoiceNum 35802.

Figure 9-25 tblBilling table with index for the InvoiceNum field

Index Value (Record Number)	Invoice Num
1	34995
2	35801
3	35802
4	35803

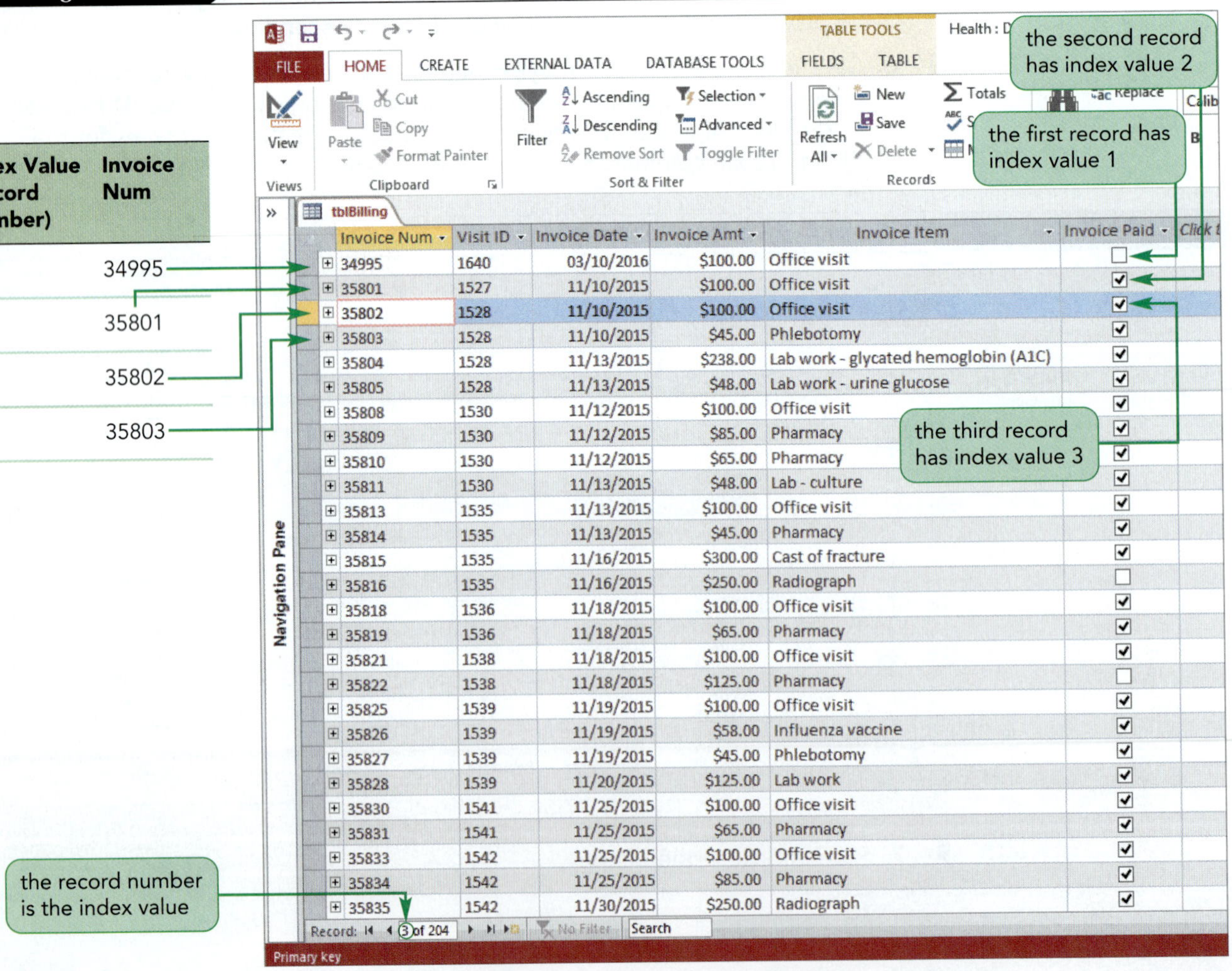

Because InvoiceNum values in the tblBilling table are unique, each row in the InvoiceNum index has a single record number. An index for a non-primary-key field, however, may contain multiple record numbers in a row. Figure 9-26 illustrates a VisitID index for the tblBilling table. Because VisitID is a foreign key in the tblBilling table (a visit can have many invoices), each VisitID entry in the index can be associated with many record numbers in the tblBilling table. For instance, VisitID 1528 in the index has record number values of 3, 4, 5, and 6, and record numbers 3, 4, 5, and 6 in the tblBilling table contain the invoice data for ContractNum 1528.

Figure 9-26 **tblBilling table with index for the VisitID field**

Index Value (Record Number)	Visit ID
1	1640
2	1527
3, 4, 5, 6	1528
7, 8, 9, 10	1530

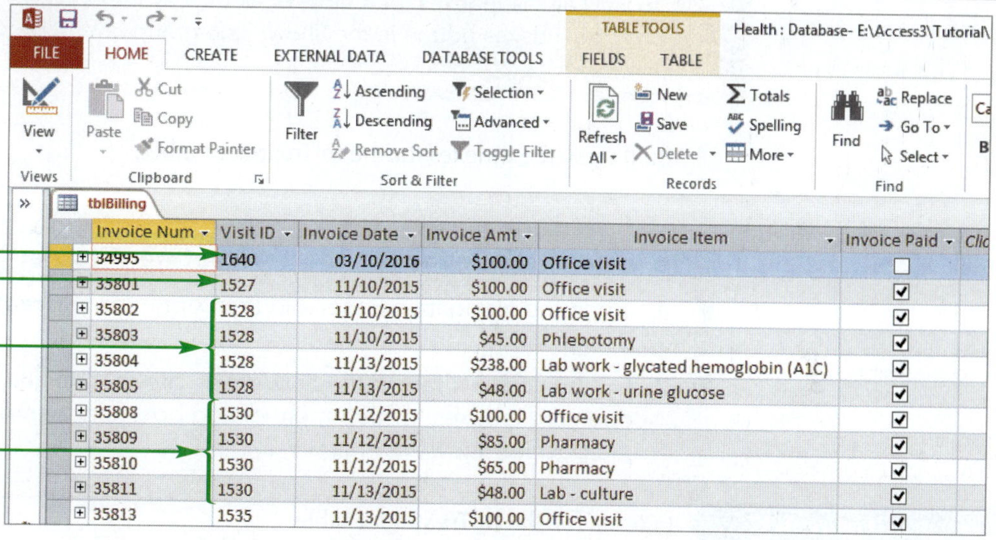

If an index exists for the VisitID field in the tblBilling table, queries that use VisitID as a sort field or as a selection criterion will run faster.

INSIGHT

Tradeoffs of Using Indexes

With small tables, the increased speed associated with indexes is not readily apparent. In practice, tables with hundreds of thousands or millions of records are common. In such cases, the increase in speed is dramatic. In fact, without indexes, many database operations in large tables would not be practical because they would take too long to complete. Why the speed difference in these cases? To sort or select records from a large table without an index, Access must make numerous accesses to disk storage to retrieve table records because the entire table can't fit in computer memory. In contrast, indexes are usually small enough to fit completely in computer memory, and Access sorts and selects records based on indexes with minimal need to access disk storage. Because accessing disk storage is very slow and performing operations in computer memory is very fast, using indexes in large tables is faster.

The speed advantage of using an index must be weighed against two disadvantages: the index adds disk storage requirements to the database, and it takes time to update the index as you add and delete records. Except for primary key indexes, you can add and delete indexes at any time. Thus, you can add an index if you think searching and querying would be faster as the number of records in the database increases. You can also delete an existing index if you later deem it to be unnecessary.

Viewing Existing Indexes

You can view the existing indexes for a table by opening the table in Design view.

REFERENCE

View a Table's Existing Indexes

- Open the table in Design view.
- To view an index for a single field, click the field, and then view the Indexed property in the Field Properties pane.
- To view all the indexes for a table or to view an index consisting of multiple fields, click the Indexes button in the Show/Hide group on the DESIGN tab.

You'll view the indexes for the tblTreatment table.

To view the indexes for the tblTreatment table:

1. Open the Navigation Pane, and then open the **tblTreatment** table in Design view.
2. On the DESIGN tab, in the Show/Hide group, click the **Indexes** button to open the Indexes: tblTreatment dialog box, and then drag the dialog box to the position shown in Figure 9-27.

Figure 9-27 Indexes for the tblTreatment table

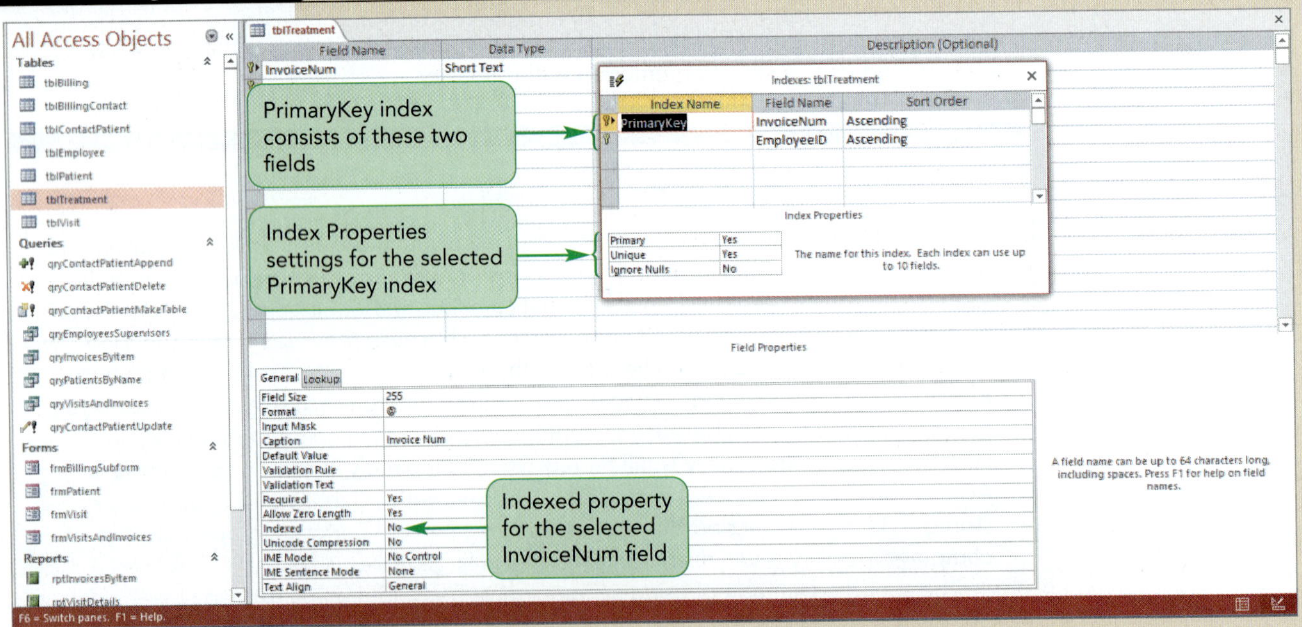

3. Close the Indexes: tblTreatment dialog box, and then close the table.

Because the InvoiceNum field was selected when you opened the Indexes: tblTreatment dialog box, the properties in the Field Properties pane pertained to this field. In particular, the Indexed property value of No for the InvoiceNum field specifies there's no index for this field.

In the Indexes: tblTreatment dialog box, the properties in the Index Properties section apply to the selected PrimaryKey index, which consists of the table's composite key of the InvoiceNum and EmployeeID fields. Because EmployeeID in the second row of the dialog box does not have an Index Name property value, both InvoiceNum and EmployeeID make up the PrimaryKey index. Access automatically created the PrimaryKey index when the table was created and the InvoiceNum and EmployeeID fields were designated as the table's composite key. The properties for the PrimaryKey index indicate that this index is the primary key index (Primary property setting of Yes), and that values in this index must be unique (Unique property setting of Yes)—that is, each InvoiceNum and EmployeeID pair of field values must be unique. The Ignore Nulls property setting of No means that records with null values for the InvoiceNum field or EmployeeID field are included in the index, but this setting is ignored because the Yes setting for the Primary property doesn't allow either field to have a null value.

INSIGHT

Default Automatic Indexes

Access automatically creates an index for the primary key field in a table. In addition, Access automatically creates an index for any field name that contains the following letter sequences: "code", "ID", "key", or "num". You can add, change, and delete from this list of letter sequences to manage the automatic indexes created in a database. To do so, click the FILE tab, click Options in the navigation bar, and then click Object Designers. In the Table design view section, the AutoIndex on Import/Create box displays, by default, ID;key;code;num. Modify the entries in the AutoIndex on Import/Create box if you want a different list of letter sequences that Access will use to automatically create indexes for the fields in your tables.

Over the past few weeks, Kelly's staff has been monitoring the performance of the Health database by timing how long it takes to run queries. She wants her staff to let her know if the performance changes over the next several days as a result of creating an index for the City field in the tblPatient table. Many queries use the City field as a sort field or selection criterion, and adding an index might speed up those queries.

Creating an Index

You can create an index for a single field in the Indexes dialog box or by setting the Indexed property for the field in Design view. However, for a multiple-field index, you must create the index in the Indexes dialog box.

REFERENCE

Creating an Index

- Open the table in Design view.
- To create an index for a single field, click the field, and then set the Indexed property in the Field Properties pane.
- To create an index consisting of multiple fields, on the DESIGN tab in the Show/Hide group, click the Indexes button, enter a name for the index in the first Index Name box, and select the first field in the Field Name box. In the next Index Name Box, leave the name blank, and select the second field in the Field Name box. Set additional field names in each row as needed, leaving the Index Name Box blank for each row except the first one. Set other properties as necessary for the index.

Next, you'll create an index for the City field in the tblPatient table by setting the field's Indexed property.

To create an index for the City field in the tblPatient table:

1. Open the **tblPatient** table in Design view, close the Navigation Pane, and then on the DESIGN tab in the Show/Hide group, click the **Indexes** button to open the Indexes: tblPatient dialog box.
2. Make sure the dialog box is positioned as shown in Figure 9-28, click the **tblPatient** tab to make the Table window the active window, and then click **City** in the Field Name column to make it the current field. See Figure 9-28.

Figure 9-28 Indexes for the tblPatient table

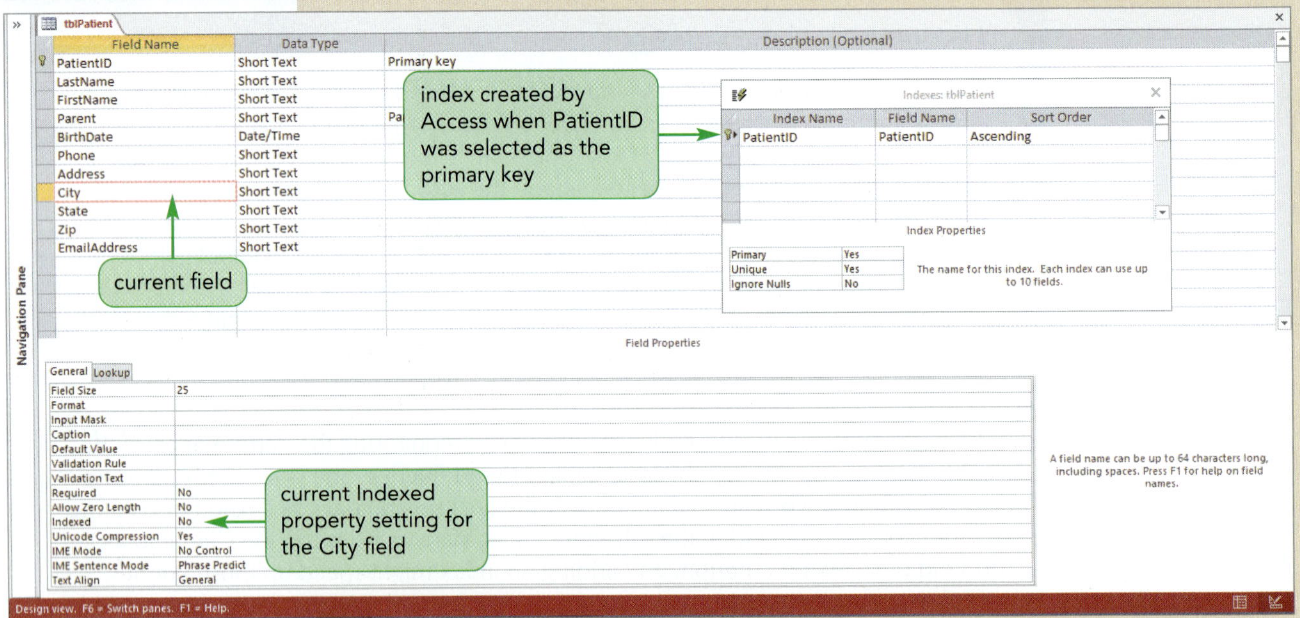

Access created an index for the PatientID field because it is the primary key. The PatientID index would have been created even if the field wasn't the primary key because the field name has an ID suffix. No other indexes exist for the tblPatient table. You'll create an index for the City field allowing duplicates because the same City field value can appear in many records in the tblPatient table.

3. Click the right side of the **Indexed** box in the Field Properties pane, and then click **Yes (Duplicates OK)**. An index for the City field is created with duplicate values allowed. Setting the Indexed property automatically created the City index in the Indexes: tblPatient dialog box. See Figure 9-29.

Figure 9-29 **After creating the City index**

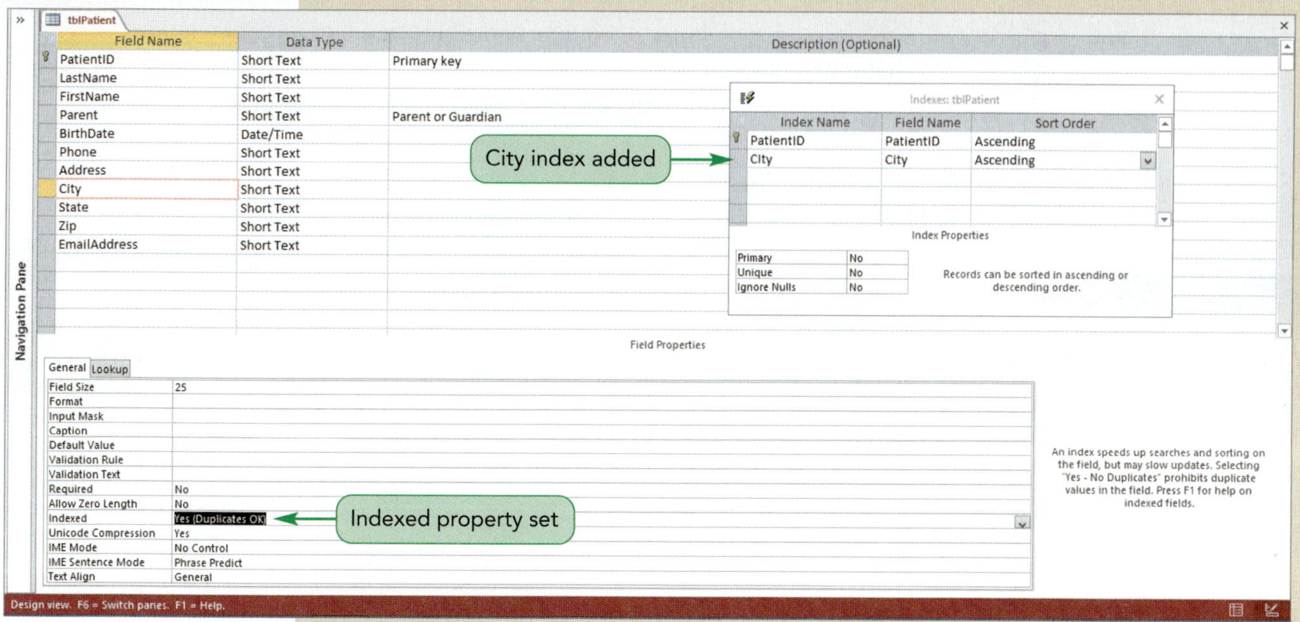

4. Close the dialog box, save your table design changes, and then switch to Datasheet view.
5. Change the first record in the table so the Last Name and First Name columns contain your last and first names, respectively.
6. Close the table, make a backup copy of the Health database, compact and repair the database, and then close it.

The work you completed with table relationships, table and query joins, and indexes will make it much easier for Kelly and her staff to enter, retrieve, and view information in the Health database.

REVIEW

Session 9.2 Quick Check

1. What are the three types of relationships you can define between tables?
2. What is an entity subtype?
3. What is the difference between an inner join and an outer join?
4. What is a self-join?
5. What is an index?
6. Figure 9-30 lists the field names from two tables: tblDepartment and tblEmployee.

Figure 9-30 **Fields for the tblDepartment and tblEmployee tables**

tblDepartment	tblEmployee
DepartmentID	EmployeeSSN
DepartmentName	EmployeeName
PhoneNumber	DepartmentID
	Salary
	SupervisorSSN

a. What is the primary key for each table?
b. What type of relationship exists between the two tables?
c. Is an inner join possible between the two tables? If so, give one example of an inner join.
d. Is an outer join possible between the two tables? If so, give one example of an outer join.

ASSESS

SAM Projects

Put your skills into practice with SAM Projects! SAM Projects for this tutorial can be found online. If you have a SAM account, go to www.cengage.com/sam2013 to download the most recent Project Instructions and Start Files.

PRACTICE

Review Assignments

Data File needed for the Review Assignments: Product.accdb

The Product database contains data about Chatham Community Health Services suppliers and their products, as well as data about the invoices from the suppliers and the payments made by Chatham Community Health Services to the suppliers. The database also contains queries, forms, and reports. Kelly wants you to define relationships between the tables and to create some new queries for her. To meet these requests, complete the following steps:

1. Open the **Product** database located in the Access3\Review folder provided with your Data Files.
2. Designate the Access3\Review folder as a trusted folder. (*Note:* Check with your instructor before adding a new trusted location.)
3. Modify the first record in the **tblSupplier** table datasheet so the Contact First Name and Contact Last Name columns contain your first and last names, and the Company Comments field contains your city and state or country. Close the table.
4. Define a many-to-many relationship between the tblInvoice and tblPayment tables, using the tblInvoicePayment table as the related table. Define a one-to-one relationship between the primary tblSupplier table and the related tblSupplierCreditLine table. Select the referential integrity option and the cascade updates option for the relationships.
5. Create a make-table query based on the tblProduct table, selecting the ProductID, SupplierID, ProductName, Price, TempControlled, and Sterile fields, and selecting only those records for products that require a temperature-controlled environment. Use **tblProductSpecialEnviron** as the new table name, store the table in the current database, and then run the query. Save this query as **qryMakeSpecialEnviron**. Open the tblProductSpecialEnviron table and format the TempControlled and Sterile fields to yes/no. (*Hint*: In Design View, select the fieldname, then select the Format property for yes/no.) Save and close the tblProductSpecialEnviron table.
6. Create an append query based on the tblProduct table, selecting the ProductID, SupplierID, ProductName, Price, TempControlled, and Sterile fields, and selecting only those records that are sterile and do not require a temperature controlled environment. Append the records to the tblProductSpecialEnviron table, run the query, and save it as **qryAppendSterile**.
7. Suppliers are offering a 10 percent discount off the regular price for all products in the tblProductSpecialEnviron table. Create an update query to select all records in the tblProductSpecialEnviron table, decrease the Price field values by 10 percent, run the query, save it as **qrySpecialDiscount** then close the query. (*Hint*: Use the expression **0.9*[Price]**.)
8. Create a delete query that deletes all records in the tblProductSpecialEnviron table in which the Price is less than $200.00. Run the query, and save it as **qryDeletePriceLess200**. Open the tblProductSpecialEnviron table, resize all columns to their best fit, and then save and close the table.
9. Open the **tblProductSpecialEnviron** table in Design view, specify the primary key, add an index that allows duplicates for the SupplierID field, and then save and close the table.
10. Make a backup copy of the database, compact and repair the database, and then close it.

APPLY

Case Problem 1

Data File needed for this Case Problem: Job.accdb

GoGopher! Amol Mehta owns and operates a business that offers customers a variety of services—from grocery shopping and household chores to yard work and pet care—on a subscription basis. Clients become members of GoGopher! by choosing the plan that best suits their needs. Each plan provides a certain number of tasks per month to members, for a specified period of time. Amol created an Access database named Job to store information for the members, payments, plans, and task schedules. The tblTask table contains data about members and the scheduled tasks, the tblCreditCard table contains data about members' credit cards, the tblMember table contains data about members, the tblPlan table contains data about task plans offered to members, and the tblSchedule table contains data about each scheduled task. The database also contains several other objects, including queries, forms, and reports. Amol wants you to define a many-to-many relationship between the tblMember and tblSchedule tables, create a one-to-one relationship between the tblMember and tblCreditCard tables, and create several new queries. To do so, complete the following steps:

1. Open the **Job** database located in the Access3\Case2 folder provided with your Data Files.
2. Designate the Access3\Case1 folder as a trusted folder. (*Note:* Check with your instructor before adding a new trusted location.)
3. Modify the first record in the **tblMember** table datasheet so the First Name and Last Name columns contain your first and last names. Close the table.
4. Define a many-to-many relationship between the tblMember and tblSchedule tables, using the tblTask table as the related table. Define a one-to-one relationship between the primary tblMember table and the related tblCreditCard table. Select the referential integrity option and the cascade updates option for the relationships.
5. Create a make-table query based on the tblMember table, selecting all fields from the table except the Street, City, State, and Zip fields, and only those records where the MemberStatus field value is **on hold**. Use **tblSpecialMember** as the new table name, store the table in the current database, and then run the query. Save the query as **qryMakeOnHold** and close the query.
6. Create an append query based on the tblMember table (selecting all fields from the table except the Street, City, State, and Zip fields) that selects only those records where the MemberStatus field value is **inactive**. Append the records to the tblSpecialMember table and run the query. Save the query as **qryAppendInactive** and then close the query.
7. Create an update query to select all records in the tblSpecialMember table in which the MemberStatus field value is **inactive**, changing the MemberComments field value to **Contact member** and run the query. Save the query as **qryUpdateSpecialPlan** and close the query.
8. Create a delete query that deletes all records in the tblSpecialMember table where the PlanID field value equals **312**. Run the query, save it as **qryDelete312**, and close the query. Open the **tblSpecialMember** table, resize all columns to their best fit, and then save and close the table.
9. Create a select query with an outer join between the tblMember and tblCreditCard tables, selecting all records from the tblMember table and any matching records from the tblCreditCard table. Display all fields from the tblMember table, and the CardNum and ExpDate fields from the tblCreditCard table. Save the query as **qryMemberCreditCardOuterJoin**, and then run and close the query.
10. In the tblMember table, add an index that allows duplicates using the **DateJoined** field, change the PlanID index to **No**, and then save and close the table.
11. Make a backup copy of the database, compact and repair the database, and then close it.

CHALLENGE

Case Problem 2

Data File needed for this Case Problem: Lesson.accdb

O'Brien Educational Services Karen O'Brien decided to channel her experience in education in a new direction and founded O'Brien Educational Services, a small educational consulting company located in South Bend, Indiana. The company offers tutoring services to high school students to help prepare them for standardized tests, such as the SAT and the ACT. The company provides group, private, and semi-private tutoring sessions to best meet the needs of its students, and also rents equipment such as calculators and laptop and tablet computers to the students. Karen created an Access database named Lesson, which includes seven tables. The tblStudent table contains data about the students taking lessons, the tblTutor table contains data about the lesson instructors, the tblCreditCard table contains data about the credit cards used to pay the monthly fees for lessons, the tblContract table contains data about the student contracts, the tblEquipment table contains data about the equipment students can rent, and the tblEquipmentContract table contains data about the equipment rental agreements. Karen asks you to define table relationships and create some new queries for her. To do so, complete the following steps:

1. Open the **Lesson** database located in the Access3\Case2 folder provided with your Data Files.
2. Designate the Access3\Case2 folder as a trusted folder. (*Note*: Check with your instructor before adding a new trusted location.)
3. Change the first record in the **tblStudent** table datasheet so the First Name and Last Name columns contain your first and last names. Close the table.
4. Define a many-to-many relationship between the tblContract and tblEquipment tables, using the tblEquipmentContract table as the related table. Define a one-to-one relationship between the primary tblStudent table and the related tblCreditCard table. Select the referential integrity option and the cascade updates option for the relationships.
5. Create a make-table query based on the qryLessonsByTutor query, selecting all fields from the query and only those records where the SessionType field value is **Group**. Use **tblSpecialSession** as the new table name, store the table in the current database, and then run the query. Save the query as **qryMakeSpecialSession** and close the query. Open the tblSpecialSession table and verify the SessionType value is Group for all records. Close the tblSpecialSession table.
6. Create an append query based on the qryLessonsByTutor query that selects all fields for only those records where the SessionType field value is **Semi-private**. Append the records to the tblSpecialSession table and run the query. Save the query as **qryAppendSemiPrivate**, and then close the query. Open the tblSpecialSession table and verify that the SessionType column includes values of both Group and Semi-private. Close the tblSpecialSession table.
7. Create an update query to select all records in the tblSpecialSession table where the value in the Length field value is **4**, changing the field value to **5**. Run the query, save it as **qryUpdateLength4To5**, and then close the query. Open the tblSpecialSession table and verify there are no records whose Length field is 4. Close the tblSpecialSession table.
8. Create a delete query that deletes all records in the tblSpecialSession table in which the ContractDate field value is less than **1/1/2016**. Run the query, save it as **qryDeleteLess2016**, and then close the query. Open the **tblSpecialSession** table, resize all columns to their best fit, and then verify there are no records whose ContractDate is earlier than 1/1/2016. Save your layout changes and then close the tblSpecialSession table.
9. Create a select query with an outer join between the tblStudent and tblCreditCard tables, selecting all records from the tblStudent table and any matching records from the tblCreditCard table. Display the FirstName and LastName fields from the tblStudent table, and the FirstName, LastName, and CreditRelationship fields from the tblCreditCard table. Change the caption for the FirstName and LastName fields from the tblCreditCard table to **Credit First Name** and **Credit Last Name**. Save the query as **qryStudentCreditCardOuterJoin**, run the query, resize all columns to their best fit, and then save and close the query.

Explore 10. Create a self-join query based on the tblTutor table with the TutorID field as the primary key and Coordinator as the foreign key. Select the TutorID, FirstName, LastName, and HireDate fields from the related table (the table that has the Coordinator field connected to the join line), and the FirstName and LastName fields from the primary table. The column names in the query recordset should be **Tutor ID**, **First Name**, **Last Name**, **Hire Date**, **Coordinator First Name**, and **Coordinator Last Name**, respectively. Use an outer join on the related table so the query lists all tutors from the related table, and coordinators from the primary table for all tutors who aren't coordinators. Run the query and resize all columns to their best fit. The query should list all tutors, and coordinators should not have a Coordinator First Name and Coordinator Last Name in their records. Save the query as **qryTutorSelfJoin** and then close the query.

11. Open the **tblSpecialSession** table in Design view, add an index that allows duplicates for the StudentID field, and then save and close the table.
12. Make a backup copy of the database, compact and repair the database, and then close it.

APPLY

Case Problem 3

Data File needed for this Case Problem: Pet.accdb

Rosemary Animal Shelter Ryan Lang is the director of the Rosemary Animal Shelter in Cobb County, Georgia. The main goals of the shelter, which has several locations in the county, are to rescue dogs and cats and to find people who will adopt them. The shelter was established by Rosemary Hanson, who dedicated her life to rescuing pets and finding good homes for them. Residents of Cobb County generously donate money, food, and equipment in support of the shelter. Some of these patrons also adopt animals from the shelter. Ryan created an Access database named Pet to track information for the shelter. In the Pet database, the tblPatron table contains data about people who donate cash or goods, the tblFacility table contains data about the building locations, the tblDonation table contains data about the donations people make, the tblAnimal table contains data about the animals residing in the shelter, the tblStorage table contains data about the storage locations in the facilities for the animals, and the tblAnimalLocation table contains data about the location of the animals. The database also contains other objects, including queries, forms, and reports. Tom wants you to define table relationships and create several new queries. To do so, you'll complete the following steps:

1. Open the **Pet** database located in the Access3\Case3 folder provided with your Data Files.
2. Designate the Access3\Case3 folder as a trusted folder. (*Note:* Check with your instructor before adding a new trusted location.)
3. Modify the first record in the **tblPatron** table datasheet so the Title, First Name, and Last Name columns contain your title and name. Close the table.
4. Define a one-to-many relationship between the primary tblFacility table and the related tblStorage table. Define a many-to-many relationship between the tblAnimal and tblStorage tables, using the tblAnimalLocation table as the related table. Select the referential integrity option and the cascade updates option for the relationships.
5. Create a make-table query based on the tblDonation table, selecting all fields from the table and only those records where the DonationDesc field value is **Cash donation**. Use **tblSpecialDonation** as the new table name, store the table in the current database, and then run the query. Save this query as **qryMakeSpecialDonation** and close the query. Open the tblSpecialDonation table and verify all records have a DonationDesc field value of Cash donation. Close the tblSpecialDonation table.
6. Create an append query based on the tblDonation table, selecting all fields from the table and only those records where the DonationDesc field value is **Cages**. Append the records to the **tblSpecialDonation** table and run the query. Save the query as **qryAppendCages**, and then close the query. Open the tblSpecialDonation table and verify all records have a DonationDesc field value of either Cash donation or Cages. Close the tblSpecialDonation table.

7. Create an update query to select all records in the tblSpecialDonation table in which the DonationDesc field value equals **Cash donation**, changing the DonationDesc field value to **Money**. Run the query, save it as **qryUpdateMoney**, and then close the query. Open the tblSpecialDonation table and verify all records have a DonationDesc field value of either Money or Cages. Close the tblSpecialDonation table.
8. Create a delete query that deletes all records in the **tblSpecialDonation** table in which the DonationValue field value is less than **$100**. Run the query, save it as **qryDeleteLess100**, and then close the query. Open the **tblSpecialDonation** table, resize all columns to their best fit, save the table, and then verify that all records have a DonationValue field value of 100 or more. Close the tblSpecialDonation table.
9. Create a select query with an outer join between the tblPatron and tblDonation tables, selecting all records from the tblPatron table and any matching records from the tblDonation table. Display the PatronID, FirstName, and LastName fields from the tblPatron table, and the DonationID, DonationDate, DonationDesc, and DonationValue fields from the tblDonation table. Save the query as **qryPatronDonationOuterJoin**, and then run and close the query.
10. Add an index that allows duplicate AnimalType values in the **tblAnimal** table, and then save and close the table.
11. Make a backup copy of the database, compact and repair the database, and then close it.

CHALLENGE

Case Problem 4

Data File needed for this Case Problem: Vacation.accdb

Stanley EcoTours Janice and Bill Stanley live in Pocatello, Idaho, and are the proud owners and operators of Stanley EcoTours. Their passion is to encourage people to visit natural areas around the world in a responsible manner that does not harm the environment. Their advertising has drawn clients from Idaho, Wyoming, Montana, and Canada. As the interest in ecotourism grows, Janice and Bill's business is also expanding to include more tours in Africa and South America. The Stanleys created an Access database called Vacation to track information for their business. In the Vacation database, the tblReservation table contains data about scheduled tours by their client guests, the tblGuest table contains data about guests, the tblTour table contains data about the ecotours, the tblPersonnel table contains data about the people who are tour guides and tour managers, and the tblTourGuideReservation table contains data about the tour guide assigned to each tour. The database also contains several other objects, including queries, forms, and reports. Janice and Bill want you to define a many-to-many relationship between the tblReservation and tblPersonnel tables, and to create several new queries. To do so, complete the following steps:

1. Open the **Vacation** database located in the Access3\Case4 folder provided with your Data Files.
2. Designate the Access3\Case4 folder as a trusted folder. (*Note:* Check with your instructor before adding a new trusted location.)
3. Modify the first record in the **tblGuest** table so the Guest First Name and Guest Last Name columns contain your first and last names.
4. Define a many-to-many relationship between the tblReservation and tblPersonnel tables, using the tblTourGuideReservation table as the related table. Select the referential integrity option and the cascade updates option for the relationships.
5. Create a make-table query based on the tblGuest and tblReservation tables, selecting the GuestFirst, GuestLast, and City fields from the tblGuest table and the StartDate and TourID fields from the tblReservation table. Select those records with a City field value of **Butte**. Save the table as **tblSelectedReservation** in the current database and then run the query. Save the query as **qryMakeSelectedReservation** and close the query. Open the tblSelectedReservation table and verify that all records have a City field value of Butte. Close the tblSelectedReservation table.

6. Create an append query based on the tblGuest and tblReservation tables, selecting the GuestFirst, GuestLast, and City fields from the tblGuest table and the StartDate and TourID fields from the tblReservation table. Select those records with a city field value of **Great Falls** or **Cheyenne** and append the selected records to the tblSelectedReservation table. Run the query, save it as **qryAppendCityReservation**, and then close the query. Open the tblSelectedReservation table and verify that all records have a City field value of Butte, Great Falls, or Cheyenne. Close the tblSelectedReservation table.
7. Create a delete query that deletes all records from the tblSelectedReservation table in which the StartDate field value is less than **6/1/2016**. Run the query, save it as **qryDeleteBeforeJune**, and then close the query. Open the **tblSelectedReservation** table, resize all columns to their best fit, verify that all records have StartDate value on or after 6/1/2016, and then close the tblSelectedReservation table.
8. Create a select query with an outer join between the tblGuest and tblReservation tables, selecting all records from the tblGuest table and any matching records from the tblReservation table. Display the GuestFirst, GuestLast, and City fields from the tblGuest table, and the StartDate and TourID fields from the tblReservation table. Save the query as **qryGuestReservationOuterJoin**, and then run and close the query.

Explore 9. Create a select query with a self-join based on the tblPersonnel table with the PersonID field as the primary key and Manager as the foreign key. Select the PersonID, FirstName, and LastName fields from the related table (the table that has the Manager field connected to the join line), and the PersonID, FirstName, and LastName fields from the primary table. The column names in the query recordset should be **Person ID**, **First Name**, **Last Name**, **Manager ID**, **Manager First Name**, and **Manager Last Name**, respectively. Use a join that will display the First Name and Last Name for all employees, and for the employees with managers, also display the Manager ID, Manager First Name, and Manager Last Name for those employees. Run the query, resize all columns to their best fit, save the query as **qryPersonnelSelfJoin**, and then close the query.

Explore 10. Add an index named **Location** to the **tblGuest** table that consists of the StateProv and City fields and uses the default property settings, delete the PostalCode index, and then save and close the table. (*Hint*: Create an index named Location using the first field name, and then in the next row, leave the index name blank but specify the second field name.)

11. Make a backup copy of the database, compact and repair the Vacation database, and then close the database.

TUTORIAL **10**

Automating Tasks with Macros

Creating a User Interface for the Health Database

OBJECTIVES

Session 10.1
- Run and add actions to macros
- Single step a macro
- Create a submacro
- Add a command button to a form
- Attach a macro to a command button

Session 10.2
- Create an unbound form
- Add a list box to a form
- Use a SQL statement to fill a list box with object names
- Create multiple macros for a form
- Create a navigation form

Case | *Chatham Community Health Services*

At a recent office automation conference, Raj Gupta, the database developer for Chatham Community Health Services, saw several database applications developed by database designers. The designers' applications used several advanced Access features to automate and control how a user interacts with Access. One of these features allowed the designers to create a custom user interface for a database. This interface made it much easier for inexperienced users to access the database, and it minimized the chance that an unauthorized user could change the design of any database object.

Raj would like to implement a similar user interface for the Health database. For less experienced users, he would like the interface to display specific forms and reports, and all the queries in the database, so that users can select objects they want to work with from the interface. This interface will make it much easier for employees to use the Health database, and it will reduce the chance that they will make undesirable changes to the design of these database objects. For more advanced users, Raj would like a form that has some buttons that users can click to perform common tasks.

STARTING DATA FILES

Access3 → Tutorial: Health.accdb (cont)
Review: Product.accdb (cont)
Case1: Job.accdb (cont)
Case2: Lesson.accdb (cont)
Case3: Pet.accdb (cont)
Case4: Vacation.accdb (cont)

Session 10.1 Visual Overview:

Click the Single Step button to **single step**, which executes one macro action at a time, pausing between actions.

The **Action Catalog button** is a toggle to open and close the Action Catalog pane, which lists all actions by category and all macros in the database.

Click the Run button to run the macro.

The mcr prefix tag identifies the object as a macro.

The **OpenForm action** opens a specified form in a specified view.

The arguments required to execute the action are displayed in detail lines.

A **comment** is a text description, and has no effect on the macro.

An **action** is an instruction to perform an operation such as sounding a beep or displaying a query

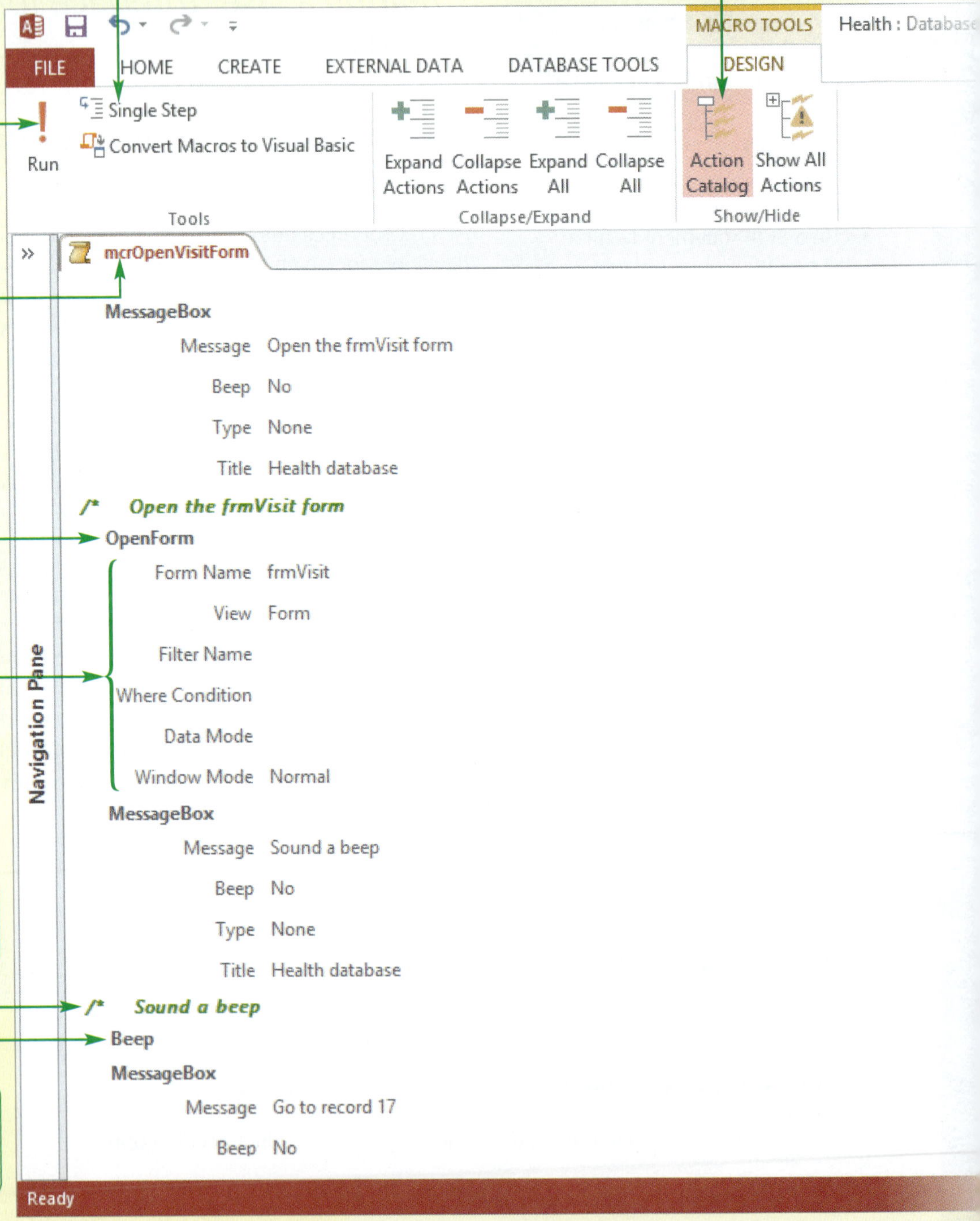

The Macro Designer

The **search box** allows you to enter a filter term to filter the list of objects displayed in the Action Catalog pane.

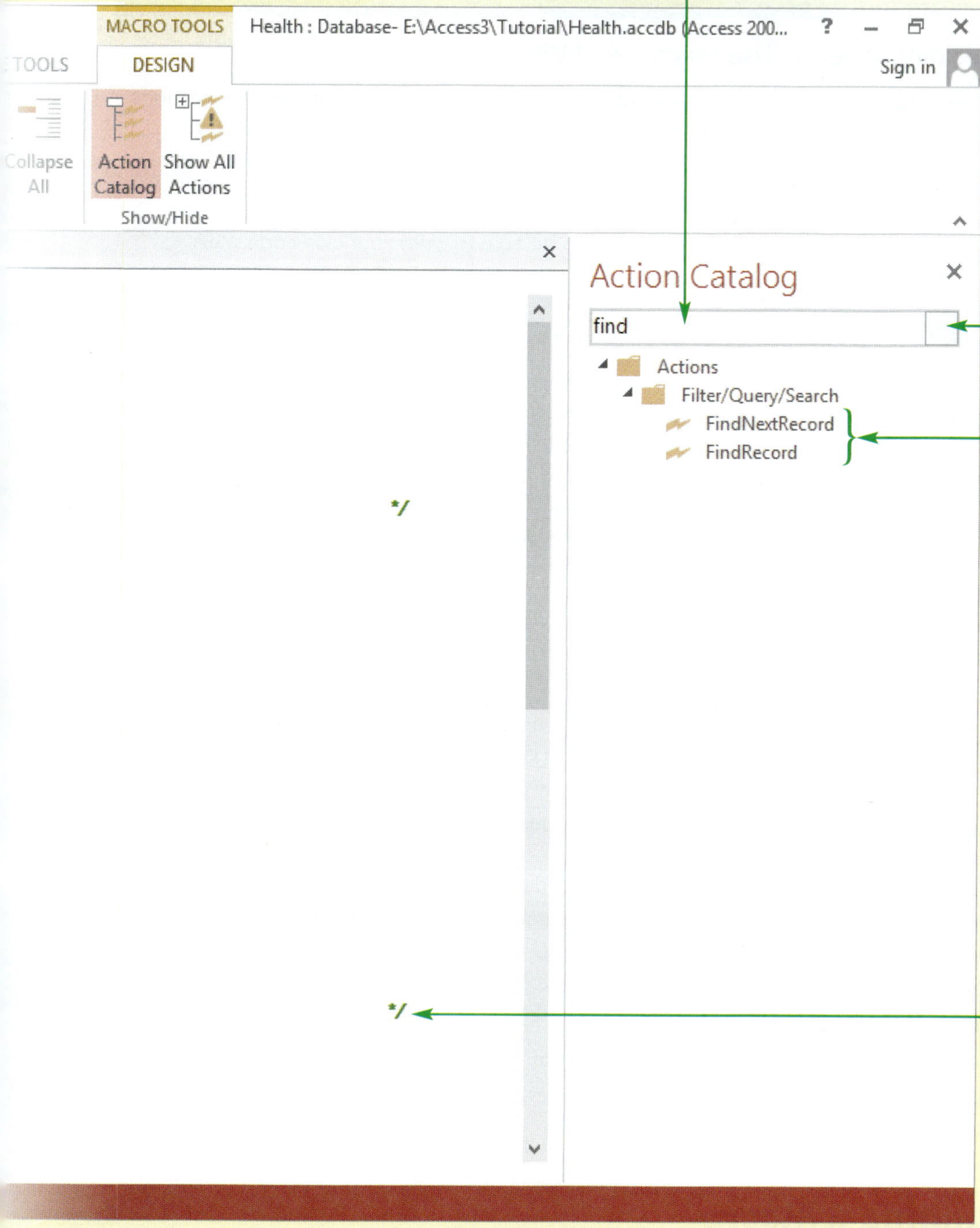

The **clear filter button** clears the search box and displays all actions and objects in the Action Catalog pane.

This list of Actions is filtered by the term entered in the search box.

A comment starts with /* and ends with */ and contains a description of one or more tasks.

Introduction to Macros

TIP

You'll learn about and use VBA in Tutorial 11.

Raj plans to automate some of the processing in the Health database, initially by using macros and then later by using Visual Basic for Applications code. A **macro** is a recorded action, or a set of actions, that Access can perform automatically for you. Macros automate repetitive tasks, such as opening forms, tables, and reports; printing selected form records; and running queries.

INSIGHT

Deciding When to Use Macros and VBA

Access lets you automate most tasks using either macros or Visual Basic for Applications (VBA), the programming language for Microsoft Office programs. As a beginner, you will likely find it easier to create macros than to build programs using VBA. To create a macro that performs a series of actions, you simply select the actions from a list in the order you want the macro to perform them.To use VBA, you need to understand the VBA command language well enough to be able to write your own code. VBA does provide advantages over using macros, such as better error-handling capabilities and making your applications easier to change. Macros, however, are useful for small applications and for simple tasks, such as opening and closing objects. Additionally, you cannot use VBA to assign actions to a specific key or key combination or to open an application in a special way, such as displaying a user interface. For these types of actions, you must use macros.

You can use macros to perform over 80 common actions in Access. Each of these actions has a designated name you use to reference it in a macro. Figure 10-1 lists the names for several frequently used Access actions and describes the actions they reference.

Figure 10-1 **Frequently used Access actions**

Action	Description
ApplyFilter	Applies a filter to a table, form, or report to restrict or sort the records in the recordset
Beep	Produces a beep tone through the computer's speakers
CloseWindow	Closes the specified window, or the active window if none is specified
FindRecord	Finds the first record (or the next record, if the action is used again) that meets the specified criteria
GoToControl	Moves the focus to a specified field or control on the active datasheet or form
MessageBox	Displays a message box containing a warning or informational message
OpenForm	Opens a form in the specified view
QuitAccess	Exits Microsoft Access
RunMacro	Runs a macro
SelectObject	Selects a specified object so you can run an action that applies to the object
SendKeys	Sends keystrokes to Microsoft Access or another active program

Running a Macro

TIP

A standard naming convention is to use *mcr* as the prefix for a macro.

Raj created a macro with multiple actions as a practice exercise after he returned from the conference. Before you begin creating the final macros Raj wants, you'll run Raj's first macro, named mcrOpenVisitForm, which performs multiple actions using the frmVisit form. You can reference and run a macro from within a form or report, or you can run an existing macro directly.

You can create, view, and edit a macro using the Macro Designer. The **Macro Designer** is a development environment built into Access that allows you create, view, and modify macros. See the Session 10.1 Visual Overview for descriptions and explanations of the Macro Designer components.

REFERENCE

Running an Existing Macro Directly

With the Macro Designer open, on the DESIGN tab, in the Tools group, click the Run button.

or

On the DATABASE TOOLS tab, in the Macro group, click the Run Macro button; in the Run Macro dialog box select the macro name in the Macro Name list, and then click the OK button.

or

In the Navigation Pane, in the Macros group, right-click the macro name, and then on the shortcut menu, click Run.

You'll use the shortcut menu to run the mcrOpenVisitForm macro.

To run the mcrOpenVisitForm macro and open the Macro Designer:

1. Start Access, and then open the **Health** database you worked with in Tutorial 9.

   Trouble? If the security warning is displayed below the ribbon, click the Enable Content button.

2. Make sure the Navigation Pane is open, scroll down the Navigation Pane (if necessary) to view the Macros section, right-click **mcrOpenVisitForm** in the Macros group, and then click **Run** on the shortcut menu. A message box opens. See Figure 10-2.

Figure 10-2 Using a macro action to open a message box

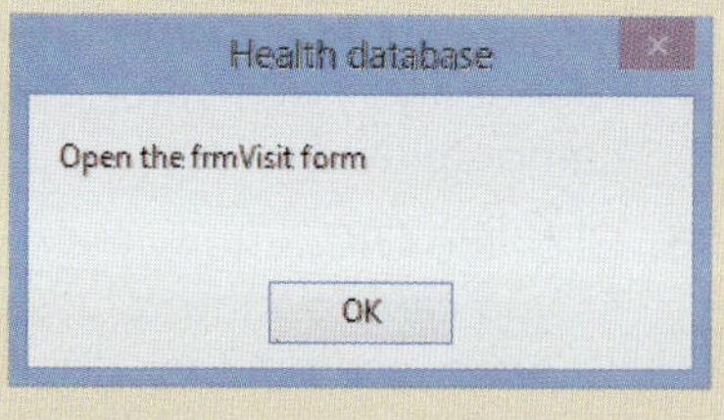

Opening the message box is the first action Raj added to the mcrOpenVisit-Form macro. A **message box** is a special dialog box that contains a message and a command button, but no options. A **command button** is a button that performs an action when a user clicks it. In this case, the command button, labelled OK, closes the message box. The message box that Raj created specifies that the next macro action will open the frmVisit form. When you click the OK button, the message box closes, and the macro resumes with the next action. Raj added this message box and other message boxes to the macro so that he could more easily observe the macro's actions as he experimented with the macro. With macros you create for working databases, you don't include message boxes between steps as Raj did in his macro.

3. Click the **OK** button. The next two actions in the mcrOpenVisitForm macro are performed: the frmVisit form opens, and the second message box opens. See Figure 10-3.

Figure 10-3 Second and third actions in the mcrOpenVisitForm macro

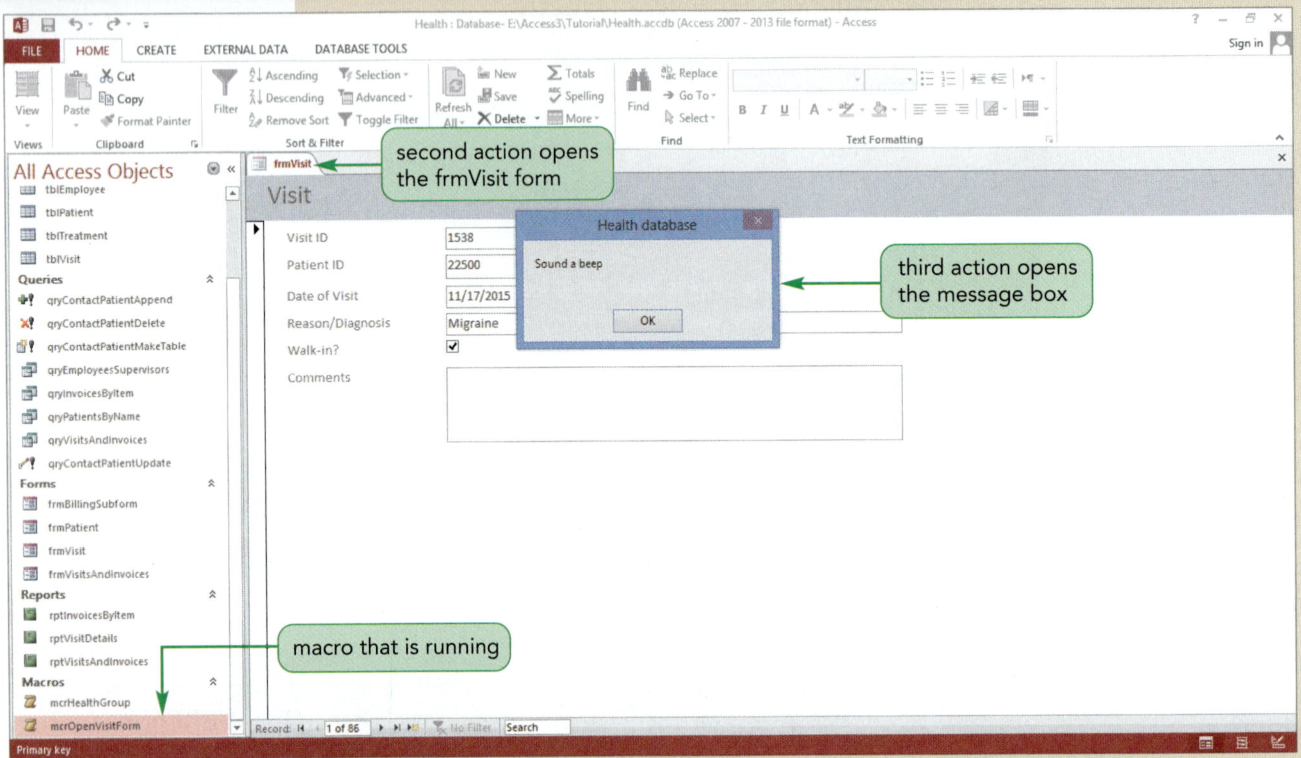

TIP

The macro uses the default alert sound for your system, which might not sound like a beep at all.

4. Click the **OK** button. A beep sounds, and the third message box opens. These are the fourth and fifth actions in the mcrOpenVisitForm macro.

   Trouble? If your computer doesn't have speakers, you won't hear the beep sound. If you do hear the beep, its sound may vary depending on your computer and its settings.

5. Click the **OK** button, and then drag the message box title bar to the right so you can view the values in the form's text boxes. The frmVisit form now displays record 17 for VisitID 1564. The sixth action in the mcrOpenVisitForm is displaying record 17, and the seventh action is displaying the message box with the message *Close the form.*

6. Click the **OK** button. The frmVisit form closes, and the mcrOpenVisitForm macro ends.

   Raj suggests that you add some actions to the mcrOpenVisitForm macro to learn about the Macro Designer and how to modify an existing macro. To open the Macro Designer, you'll open the macro in Design view.

7. Right-click **mcrOpenVisitForm** in the Navigation Pane, click **Design View** on the shortcut menu, and then close the Navigation Pane. The Macro Designer displays the mcrOpenVisitForm macro. See Figure 10-4.

Figure 10-4 Macro Designer displaying actions collapsed

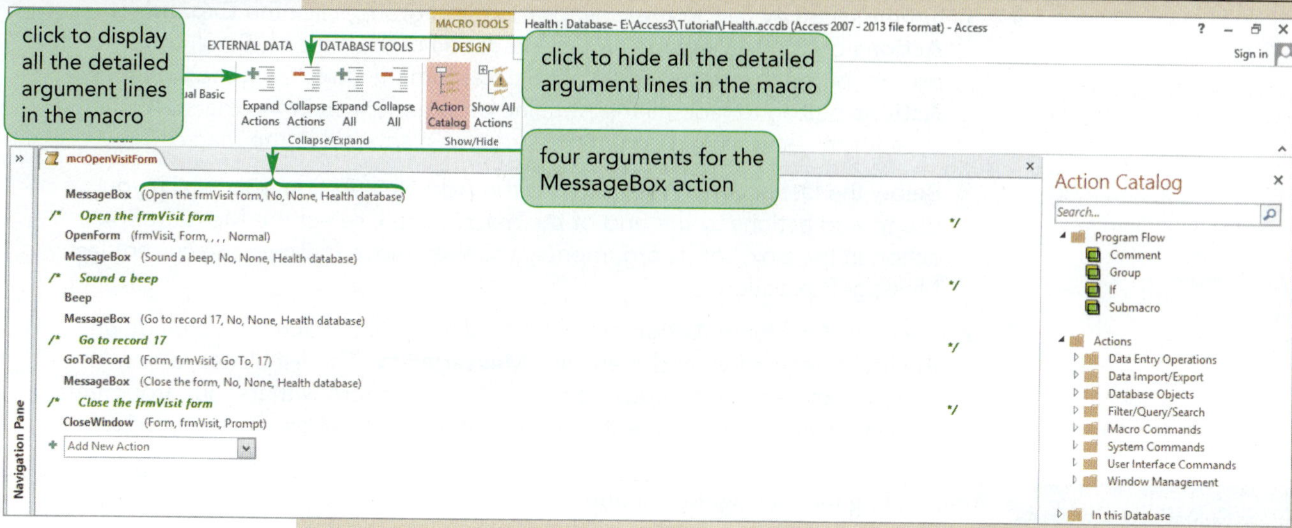

Adding Actions to a Macro

Some actions require information. For instance, if an action is going to open a form, the action needs to know the name of the form to open. A piece of data that is required by an action is known as an **argument**. An action can have more than one argument; multiple arguments are separated by commas.

> **TIP**
>
> When a macro contains a MessageBox action, the macro doesn't proceed to the next action until users click the OK button, so they have as much time as they need to read and react to the message box.

The mcrOpenVisitForm macro contains a MessageBox action as the first action. The name of the MessageBox action is followed by the four arguments needed by the action—Message, Beep, Type, and Title:

- The Message argument contains the text that will appear in the message box when it is displayed.
- The Beep argument is either Yes or No, to specify whether a beep will sound when the message box opens.
- The Type argument determines which icon, if any, appears in the message box to signify the critical level of the message. The icon choices are None (no icon), Critical (❌), Warning? (❓), Warning! (⚠), and Information (ℹ).
- The Title argument contains the word(s) that will appear in the message box title bar.

You'll add two actions, the MessageBox and FindRecord actions, to the mcrOpenVisitForm macro between the GoToRecord and the last MessageBox actions. For the FindRecord action, you'll find the record for VisitID 1665. You use the **FindRecord action** to find the first record, or the next record if the action is used again, that meets the criteria specified by the FindRecord arguments.

To add two actions to the mcrOpenVisitForm macro:

1. On the DESIGN tab, in the Collapse/Expand group, click the **Expand Actions** button to view the arguments for all of the actions. Scroll to the bottom of the macro to see all detailed argument lines. Click the **Collapse Actions** button to hide all the detailed argument lines in the macro. Only the lines for the actions and comments are now displayed in the macro.

   Below the last action in the macro is the Add New Action box, which you use to add actions to the end of the macro. You'll select the MessageBox action in the box, set its arguments, and then move it above the current last MessageBox action.

2. Click the **Add New Action** arrow to display the list of actions, scroll down the list (if necessary), and then click **MessageBox**. The list closes, a new MessageBox action is added to the end of the macro with its four arguments displayed, and two arguments are set with default values. See Figure 10-5.

Figure 10-5 After adding the MessageBox action

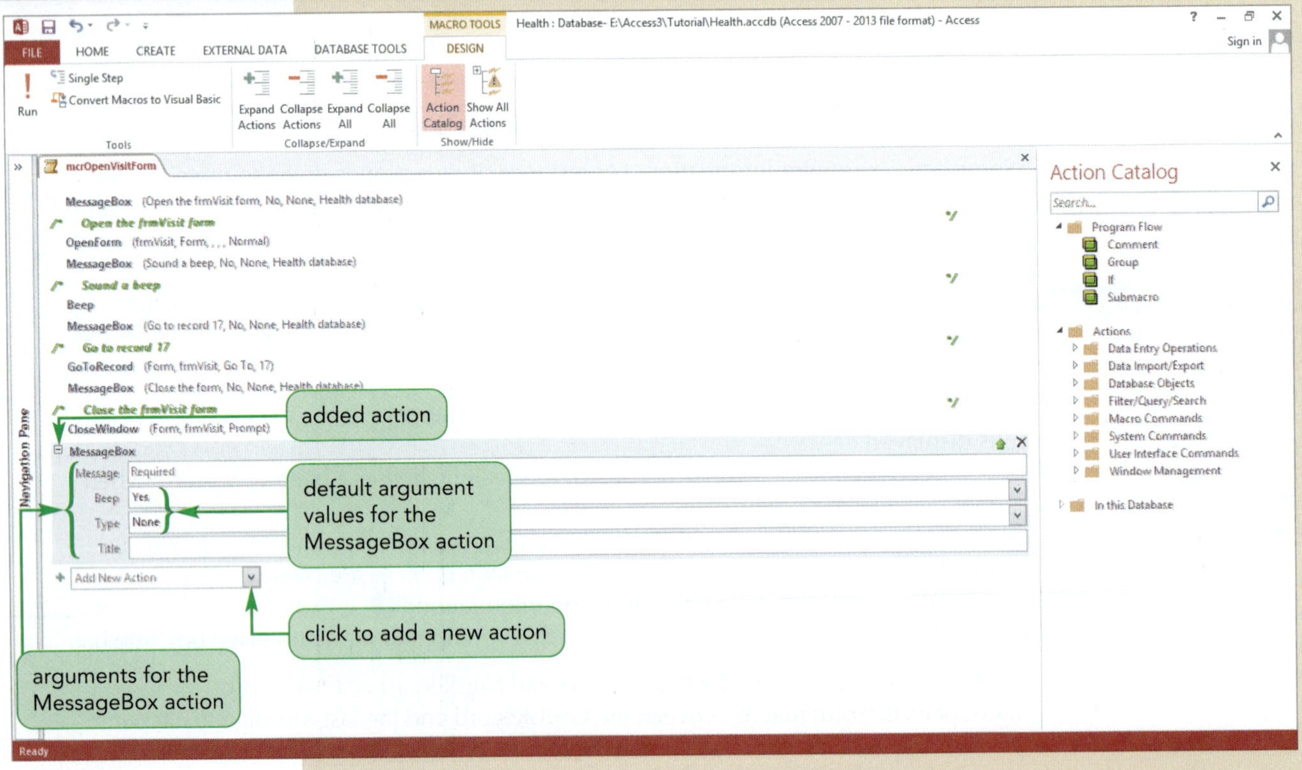

If you hover the mouse pointer on the MessageBox line or on any argument line, a ScreenTip displays a brief explanation of the action or argument. You can also use Help to learn about specific actions and their arguments, and about macros in general. You'll enter values for the Message and Title arguments, change the Beep argument value from Yes to No, and retain the default Type argument value of None.

3. Click the **Message** box (if necessary), type **Find visit 1665**, press the **Tab** key, click the **Beep** arrow, click **No**, press the **Tab** key twice, and then type **Health database** in the Title box. See Figure 10-6.

Figure 10-6 **Completed MessageBox action**

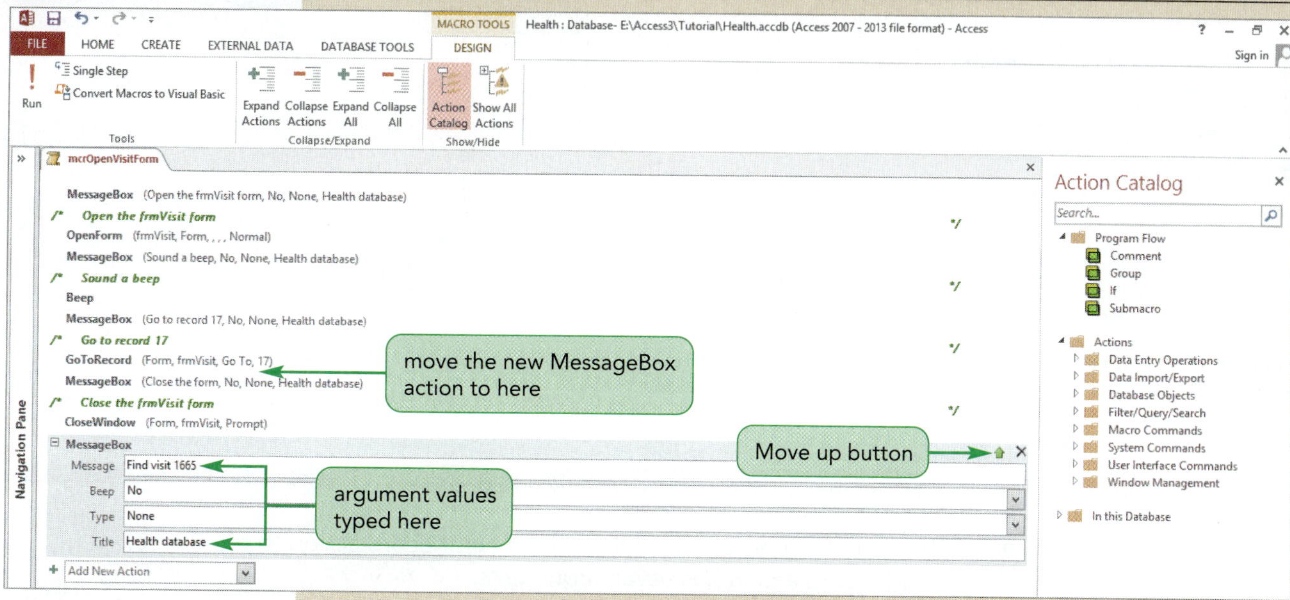

You now need to move the new MessageBox action three positions up in the macro because it needs to be above the two actions and one comment that precede it.

> **TIP**
> Use the Move down button to move actions down in a macro.

4. On the MessageBox line, click the **Move up** button three times to move the action to its correct position. Nine lines of actions and comments are now above the new MessageBox action, and two actions and one comment are now below the action.

You'll now add the FindRecord action to the macro. You could add the FindRecord action to the bottom of the macro and move it up three positions as you did for the MessageBox action. Instead, you'll search for the action in the Action Catalog pane, and then drag it to its correct position in the macro. First, you'll collapse the MessageBox action.

5. On the DESIGN tab, in the Collapse/Expand group, click the **Collapse Actions** button to hide all the argument lines in the MessageBox action.
6. In the Action Catalog pane, click the **search** box, and then type **find**. Access displays a filtered list of actions containing the search term *find*.
7. In the Action Catalog pane, drag **FindRecord** to the macro immediately below the newly added MessageBox action until a colored line appears just below the MessageBox action. See Figure 10-7.

Figure 10-7 Dragging the FindRecord action to the macro

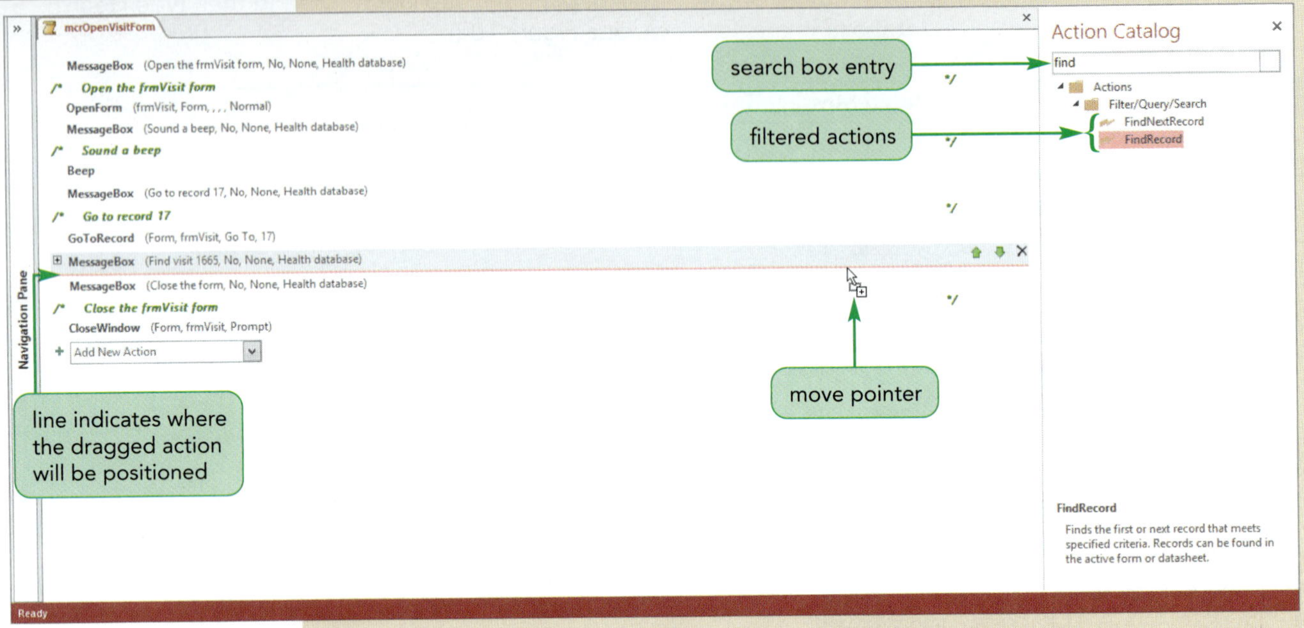

8. Release the mouse button to add the FindRecord action to the macro. The FindRecord action has seven arguments.

   Trouble? If you drag the wrong action or drag the action to the wrong location, delete the action by clicking the Delete button to the right of the Move up and Move down buttons, and then repeat Steps 7 and 8.

   You need to set the Find What argument to a value of 1665. You'll accept the defaults for the other action arguments.

9. Click the **Find What** box (if necessary), type **1665**, and then click the minus box ⊟ to the left of FindRecord to hide all the argument lines for the action.

   Finally, you'll add a comment above the FindRecord action to document the FindRecord action.

10. In the Action Catalog pane, click the **clear filter** button ☐ to remove the filter and display the entries in the box, drag **Comment** to the macro immediately above the MessageBox action, type **Find visit 1665** in the Comment box, and then click an empty area at the bottom of the Macro Designer to close the Comment box and complete your macro changes. See Figure 10-8.

Figure 10-8 After adding actions and a comment to the macro

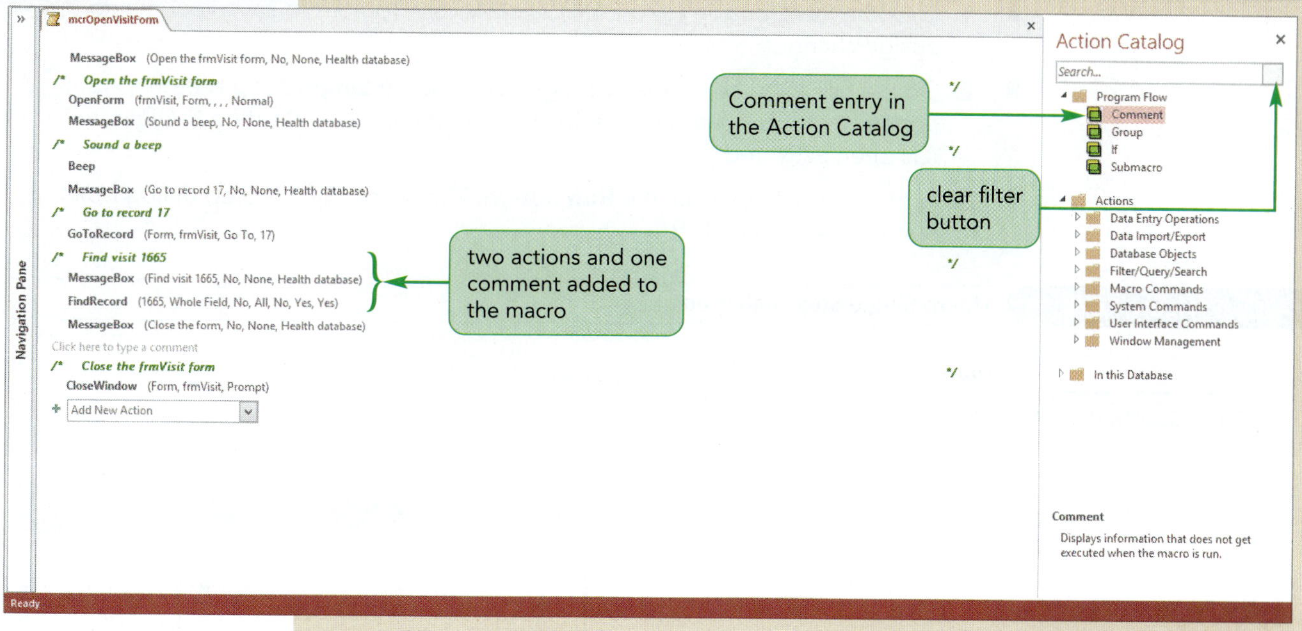

Single Stepping a Macro

When you create a complicated macro with many actions, you'll often find it useful to run through the macro one step at a time. In Access, you can do this using single step mode. In **single step mode**, Access executes a macro one action at a time, pausing between actions. Using single step mode is also referred to as single stepping. You single step a macro to make sure you have placed actions in the right order and with the correct arguments. If you have problems with a macro, you can use single step mode to find the causes of the problems and to determine their proper corrections. The Single Step button in the Tools group on the DESIGN tab is a toggle you use to turn single step mode on and off. Once you turn on single step mode, it stays on for all macros until you turn it off.

REFERENCE

Single Stepping a Macro

- In the Macro Designer, on the DESIGN tab, in the Tools group, click the Single Step button.
- In the Tools group, click the Run button.
- In the Macro Single Step dialog box, click the Step button to execute the next action, click the Stop All Macros button to stop the macro, or click the Continue button to execute all remaining actions in the macro and turn off single step mode.

To get a clearer understanding of the effects of the actions in the mcrOpenVisitForm macro, you can single step through it. First, you need to save your macro changes.

To save the macro changes and then single step through the macro:

1. Click the **Save** button on the Quick Access Toolbar to save your macro design changes.
2. On the DESIGN tab, in the Tools group, click the **Single Step** button to turn on the single step feature. The button is highlighted, indicating the feature has been activated.
3. In the Tools group, click the **Run** button. The Macro Single Step dialog box opens. See Figure 10-9.

Figure 10-9 Macro Single Step dialog box

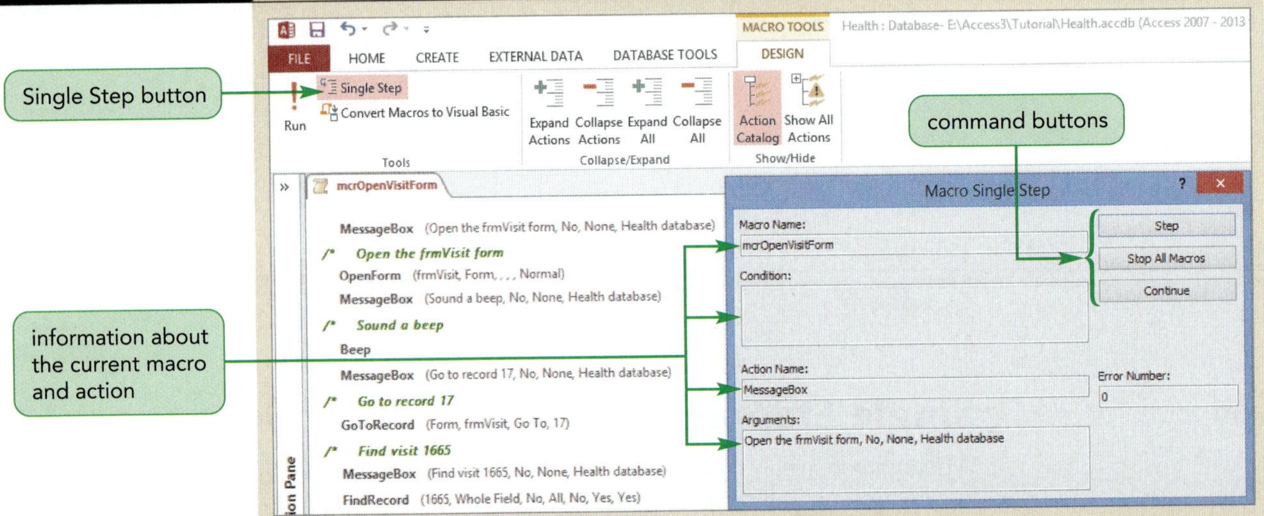

Trouble? If the first message box opens instead of the Macro Single Step dialog box, then you turned off single stepping in Step 2 when you clicked the Single Step button. Click the OK button to run through the end of the macro, and then repeat Steps 2 and 3.

When you single step through a macro, Access opens the Macro Single Step dialog box before performing each action. This dialog box shows the macro's name and the action's condition, name, and arguments. The action will be executed or not executed, depending on whether the condition is true or false. The three command buttons let you step through the macro one action at a time, stop the macro and return to the Macro Designer, or continue by executing all remaining actions without pausing. If you click the Continue button, you also turn off single step mode.

4. Click the **Step** button. Access runs the first action (MessageBox). Because the MessageBox action pauses the macro, the Macro Single Step dialog box remains hidden until you click the OK button in the message box.
5. Click the **OK** button to close the message box. The Macro Single Step dialog box shows the macro's second action (OpenForm).
6. Click the **Step** button. Access runs the second action by opening the frmVisit form and shows the macro's third action (MessageBox) in the Macro Single Step dialog box.

7. Continue clicking the **Step** button and the **OK** button until you see the "Find visit 1665" message box, making sure you read the Macro Single Step dialog box carefully and observe the actions that occur. At this point, record 17 is the current record in the frmVisit form.
8. Click the **OK** button, and then click the **Step** button. The FindRecord action runs, record 25 for VisitID 1665 is now the current record in the frmVisit form, and the Macro Single Step dialog box shows the macro's last MessageBox action.
9. Click the **Step** button, click the **OK** button, and then click the **Step** button. The Macro Single Step dialog box closes automatically after the last macro action is completed; the last macro action closes the frmVisit form.

   You've finished your work with Raj's macro, and can turn off the single step feature.
10. Click the **DESIGN tab**, in the Tools group click the **Single Step** button to turn off single step feature, and then click the **Close 'mcrOpenVisitForm'** button [X] to close the macro.

Raj suggests you next review a macro he created for the frmContract form.

Using a Command Button with an Attached Macro

Raj created a macro that he associated with a command button on the frmVisit form that you just opened using the mcrOpenVisitForm macro. A command button is a control that runs a macro or VB program when you click it. To add a command button to a form, you open the form in Design view and use the Button tool in the Controls group on the DESIGN tab. After adding the command button to the form and while still in Design view, you attach a macro to the command button. Then, when a user clicks the command button, the macro's actions are executed.

Raj asks you to use the Open Patient Table command button on the frmVisit form to see how the macro attaches to the command button, and then to view the macro.

To use the Open Patient Table command button:

1. Open the Navigation Pane, open the **frmVisit** form in Form view to display the first visit with VisitID 1538 and PatientID 22500, click **1538** in the Visit ID text box to deselect all values, and then close the Navigation Pane. See Figure 10-10.

Figure 10-10 Open Patient Table command button on the frmVisit form

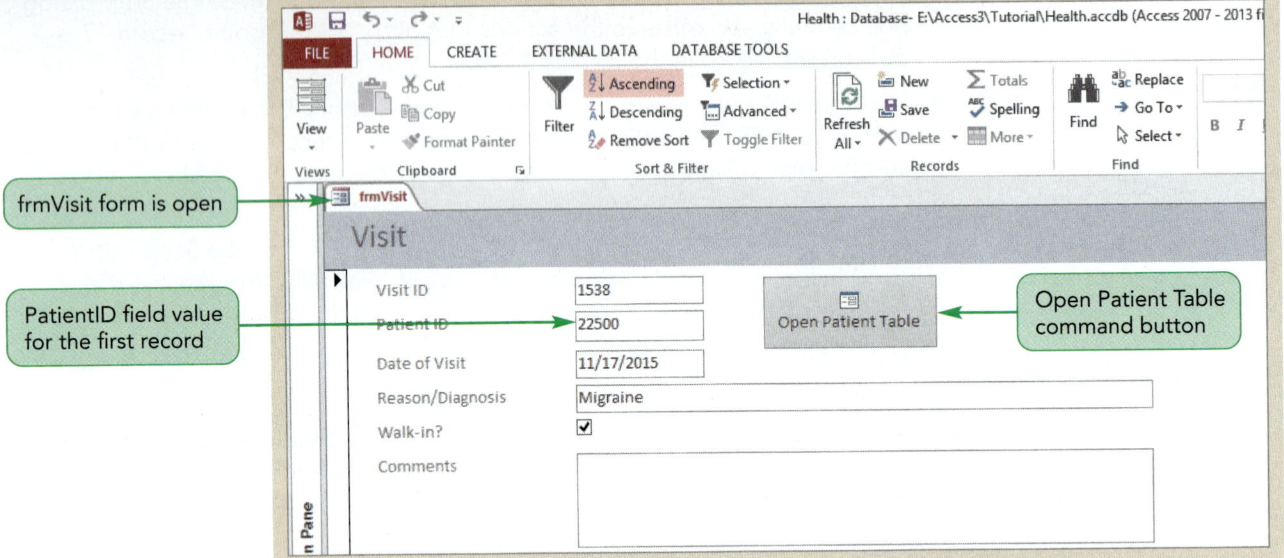

2. Click the **Open Patient Table** command button. The frmVisit form remains open, and the tblPatient table opens. The tblPatient table is the active object. See Figure 10-11.

Figure 10-11 After opening the tblPatient table with the Open Patient Table command button

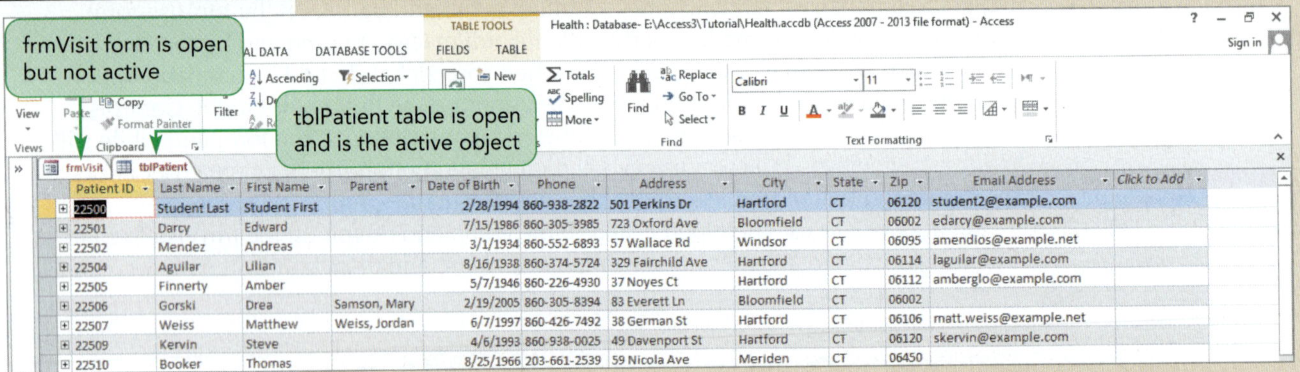

Clicking the Open Patient Table command button triggered an attached macro that opened the tblPatient table. The tblPatient table will remain open until it is closed manually or by another macro.

3. Close the tblPatient table. The frmVisit form is now the active object.

Events

> **TIP**
> When viewing a report, you can find specific data by clicking the Find button in the Find group on the HOME tab and selecting or typing entries in the Find dialog box.

Clicking the Open Patient Table command button is an event, and the opening of the tblPatient table is controlled by setting an event property. An **event** is a state, condition, or occurrence detectable by Access. For example, an event occurs when you click a command button on a form, when you use the mouse to position the pointer on a form, or when you press a key to choose an option. In your work with Access, you've initiated hundreds of events on forms, controls, records, and reports without any special effort. For example, events you've triggered in forms include Open, which occurs when you open a form; Activate, which occurs when the form becomes the active window; and Close, which occurs when you close a form and the form is removed from the screen. Each event has an associated event property. An **event property** specifies how an object responds when an event occurs. For example, each form has OnOpen, OnActivate, and OnClose event properties associated with the Open, Activate, and Close events, respectively.

Event properties appear in the property sheet when you create forms and reports. Unlike most properties you've used previously in property sheets, event properties do not have an initial value. If an event property contains no value, it means the event property has not been set. In this case, Access takes no special action when the associated event occurs. For example, if a form's OnOpen event property is not set and you open the form, then the Open event occurs (the form opens), and no special action occurs beyond the opening of the form. You can set an event property value to a macro name, and Access will run the macro when the event occurs. For example, you could write a macro that automatically selects a particular field in a form when you open it. You can also create a group of statements using VBA code and set the event property value to the name of that group of statements. Access will then execute the group of statements, or **procedure**, when the event occurs. Such a procedure is called an **event procedure**.

When you clicked the Open Patient Table command button on the frmVisit form, the Click event occurred and triggered an attached macro. The Open Patient Table command button contains an OnClick event property setting, which you will examine next.

TIP

Event properties do not contain a space, but the Event tab in the property sheet shows them with spaces. However, the OnClick event property and the On Click property in the property sheet are the same.

To view the OnClick event property setting for the Open Patient Table command button:

1. Switch to Design view, right-click the **Open Patient Table** command button, click **Properties** on the shortcut menu to open the property sheet if necessary, and then click the **Event** tab (if necessary) in the property sheet.
2. Right-click the **On Click** box, click **Zoom** on the shortcut menu to open the Zoom dialog box, and then click to the right of the selected text to deselect it. See Figure 10-12.

Figure 10-12 Macro attached to the OnClick event property

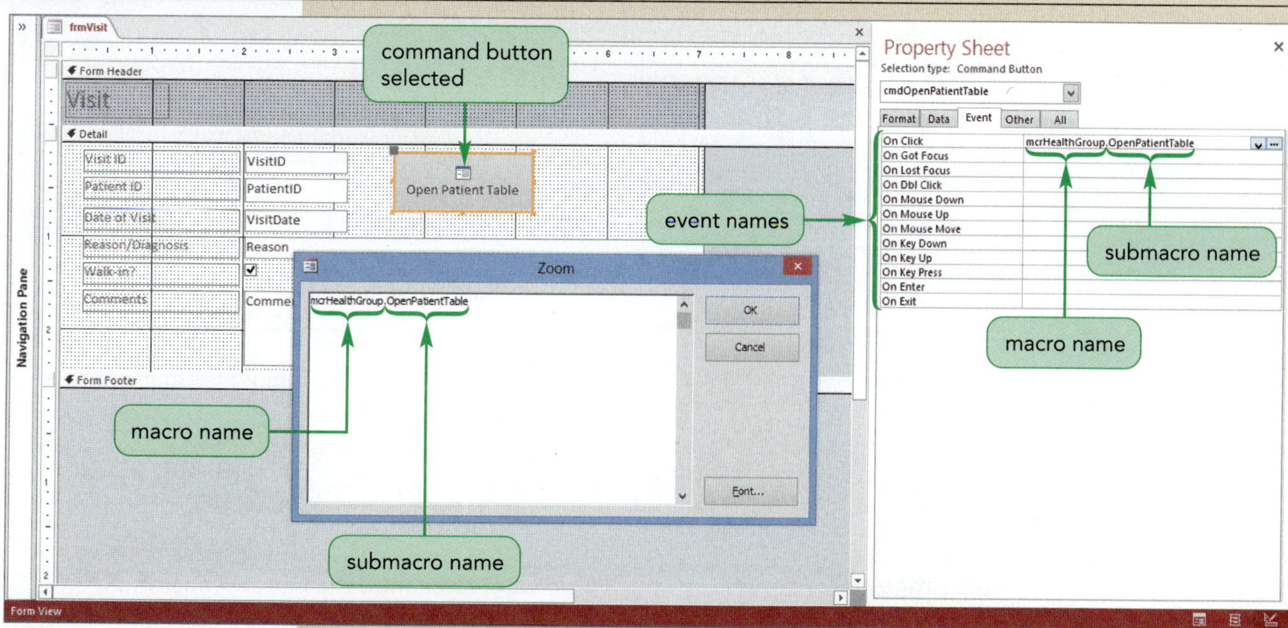

The OnClick event property value shown in the Zoom dialog box is *mcrHealthGroup.OpenPatientTable*. This is an example of a reference to a submacro in a macro.

Submacros

If you need to create several related macros, you can create them as submacros in a single macro instead of creating them as separate macros. A **submacro** is a complete macro with a Submacro header within a macro. Using submacros allows you to consolidate related macros and to manage large numbers of macros. For example, if a form's design uses command buttons to open a form with a related record and to print the related record displayed in the form, you can create one macro for the form that contains two submacros—one submacro to open the form, and a second submacro to print the related record. Because you created the macro specifically for the form object, you can store all the submacros you need in a single macro. When a macro contains a submacro, a period separates the macro name from the submacro name. For the OnClick event property value shown in Figure 10-12, for example, mcrHealthGroup is the macro name, and OpenPatientTable is the submacro name. When you click the Open Patient Table command button on the frmVisit form, Access processes the actions contained in the OpenPatientTable submacro, which is located in the mcrHealthGroup macro.

You'll now close the Zoom dialog box, and then open the Macro Designer from the property sheet.

To open the mcrHealthGroup macro in the Macro Designer:

1. Click the **Cancel** button in the Zoom dialog box to close it. In the property sheet for the selected Open Patient Table command button, the On Click box contains an arrow and a Build button to its right. The button is named cmdOpenPatientTable; *cmd* is a prefix tag to identify a command button control. See Figure 10-13.

Figure 10-13 OnClick event property value for the Open Patient Table command button

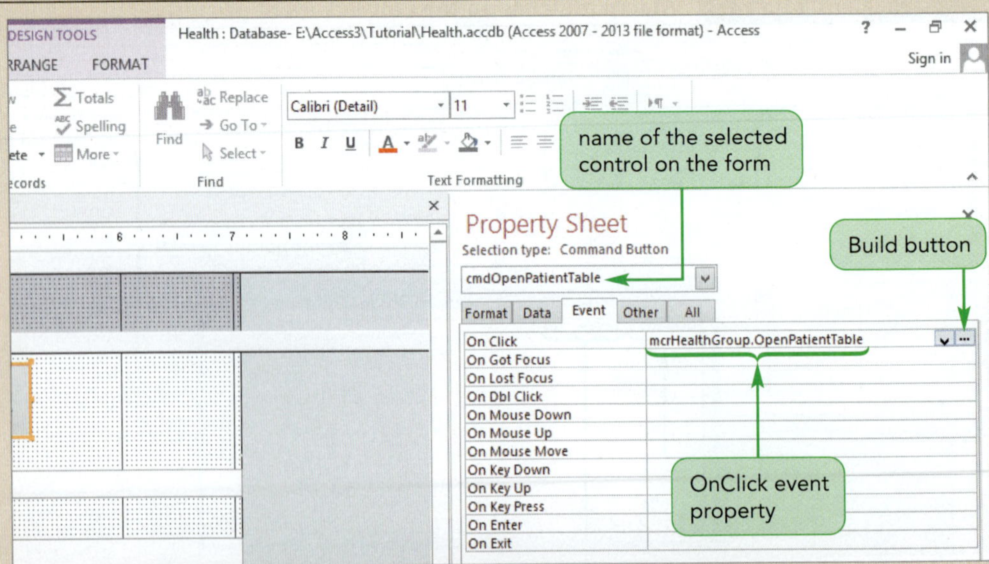

You click the On Click arrow if you want to change the current macro to a different macro, and you click the Build button if you want to use the Macro Designer to view or change the existing macro. The Build button is also called the **Macro Builder** when you use it to work with macros.

2. Click the **Build** button [...] on the right side of the On Click box. The Macro Designer opens and displays the mcrHealthGroup macro and the OpenPatientTable submacro. See Figure 10-14.

Figure 10-14 **Macro Designer displaying the mcrHealthGroup macro and its submacro**

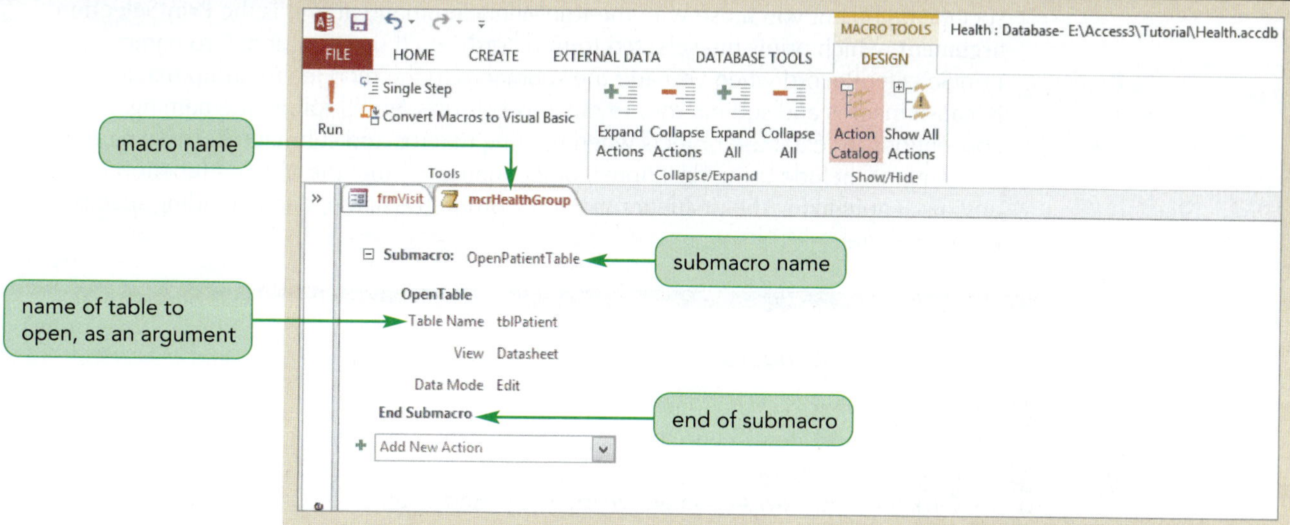

The mcrHealthGroup macro consists of one submacro that starts with the Submacro statement and ends with the End Submacro statement. These statements are not actions; they are control statements to identify the beginning and end of a submacro. If a macro contains several submacros, each submacro starts with a Submacro statement and ends with an End Submacro statement.

The OpenPatientTable submacro consists of a single action, OpenTable, which opens the tblPatient table. The OpenTable action arguments are as follows:

- The **Table Name argument** specifies the name of a table that will be opened when the macro is run.
- The **View argument** specifies the view in which the object opens. For tables, you can specify Datasheet, Design, Print Preview, PivotTable, or PivotChart.
- The **Data Mode argument** specifies the table's data-entry options. Allowable settings for this argument are Add (users can add new records but can't change or delete existing records), Edit (users can change and delete existing records and can add new records), and Read Only (users can only view records). If you don't select an argument value, Edit is the default setting.

Now that you've seen a macro that's attached to a command button, Raj asks you to add a command button to the frmVisit form, and then to attach a new macro to the command button. Users want to be able to print the current record in the frmVisit form by clicking a command button on the form. Raj created the mcrHealthGroup macro to group together all the submacros in the Health database. Because the Macro Designer is already open for the mcrHealthGroup macro, you'll add a submacro to it to print the current record.

Adding a Submacro

To print the contents of a form's current record, normally you have to click the FILE tab to display Backstage view, click Print on the navigation bar, click Print in the list of options, click Selected Record(s), and then click the OK button—a process that takes five steps and several seconds. Instead of following this process, you can create a command button on the form, create a macro that prints the contents of a form's current record, and then attach the macro to the command button on the form. To print the form's current record, you'd simply click the command button.

First, you'll add a submacro to the mcrHealthGroup macro. You'll use the SelectObject and RunMenuCommand actions for the new submacro. The **SelectObject action** selects a specified object so that you can run an action that applies to the object. The **RunMenuCommand action** selects and runs a command on the ribbon. The specific argument you'll use with the RunMenuCommand action is the **PrintSelection argument**, which prints the selected form record. You'll use the submacro name PrintSelectedRecord when you add the submacro to the mcrHealthGroup macro. Because macros and submacros are database objects, you'll follow the naming conventions for database objects when naming macros and submacros. These naming conventions include using descriptive object names so that the object's function is obvious, capitalizing the first letter of each word in the name, and excluding spaces from the name.

REFERENCE

Adding a Submacro

- Open the macro in the Macro Designer.
- Click the Add New Action arrow, click Submacro, and then type the submacro name in the Submacro box.
- Click the Add New Action arrow above the End Submacro statement, click the action you want to use, and then set the action's arguments.
- If the submacro consists of more than one action, repeat the previous step for each action.
- Add comments as needed to the submacro to document the submacro's function or provide other information.
- Save the macro.

You'll now add the PrintSelectedRecord submacro to the mcrHealthGroup macro.

To add the PrintSelectedRecord submacro to the mcrHealthGroup macro:

1. Click the minus box [−] to the left of Submacro OpenPatientTable to collapse the actions and arguments for the submacro.
2. Click the **Add New Action** arrow to display the list of actions and control statements, click **Submacro**, and then type **PrintSelectedRecord** in the Submacro box. The Submacro and End Submacro statements are added to the macro, and another Add New Action box is displayed between these two statements. See Figure 10-15.

Figure 10-15 Adding a new submacro

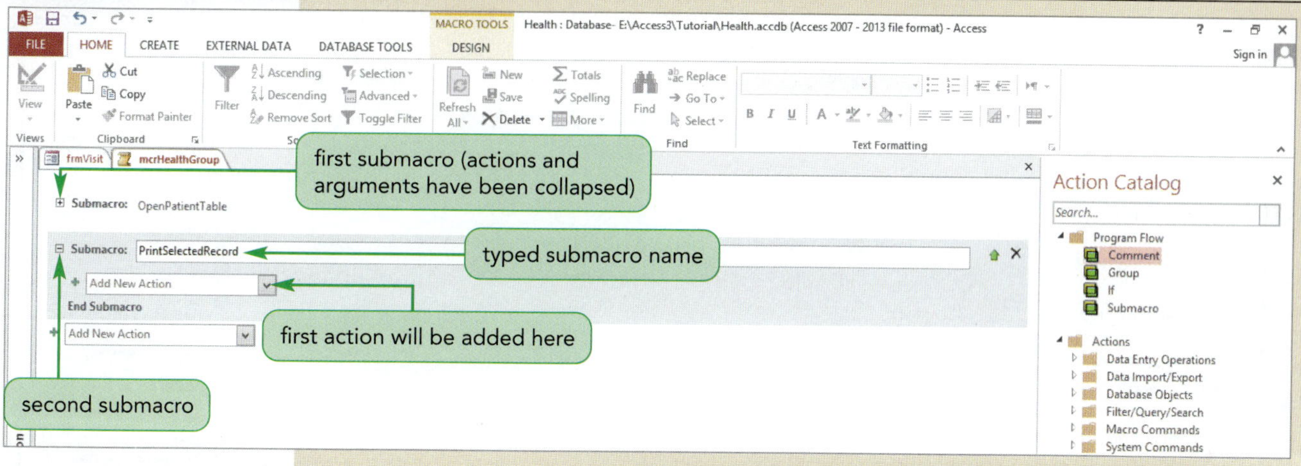

TIP

You can also type the first few letters of the action until the full action name appears, and then press the Tab key to select the action.

You need to select the SelectObject action and set its arguments.

3. Between the Submacro and End Submacro statements, click the **Add New Action** arrow, scroll down the list, and then click **SelectObject**. The SelectObject action is added to the PrintSelectedRecord submacro. This action has three arguments. The first argument, Object Type, specifies the type of database object to select. The second argument, Object Name, specifies the name of the object to open. The third argument, In Database Window, specifies whether to open the object in the database window (yes) or not (no). You would open a table, form, or report in the database window if it is not already open. If the table, form, or report is already open in the database window, you would select No as the value for the Database Window argument.

   You need to open a form named frmVisit, so you'll set these arguments first.

4. Click the **Object Type** arrow, click **Form**, click the **Object Name** arrow, and then click **frmVisit**. Because the form will be open when you run the macro, you'll leave the In Database Window argument set to No.

   You'll next select the RunMenuCommand action and set its arguments. The RunMenuCommand action lets you add a command available on the Ribbon to a submacro. The Command argument in this submacro lets you select the command. In this case, the Command argument is named PrintSelection.

5. Below the SelectObject action, click the **Add New Action** arrow, scroll down the list, click **RunMenuCommand**, click the **Command** arrow, scroll down the list, and then click **PrintSelection**.

   You've completed the second action. You'll add another SelectObject action to the submacro to return control back to the frmVisit form after printing the selected record to make the form the active object.

6. Below the RunMenuCommand action, click the **Add New Action** arrow, scroll down the list, click **SelectObject**, set the Object Type argument to **Form**, and then set the Object Name argument to **frmVisit**. You've finished adding the three actions to the PrintSelectedRecord submacro. See Figure 10-16.

Figure 10-16 After adding three actions to the PrintSelectedRecord submacro

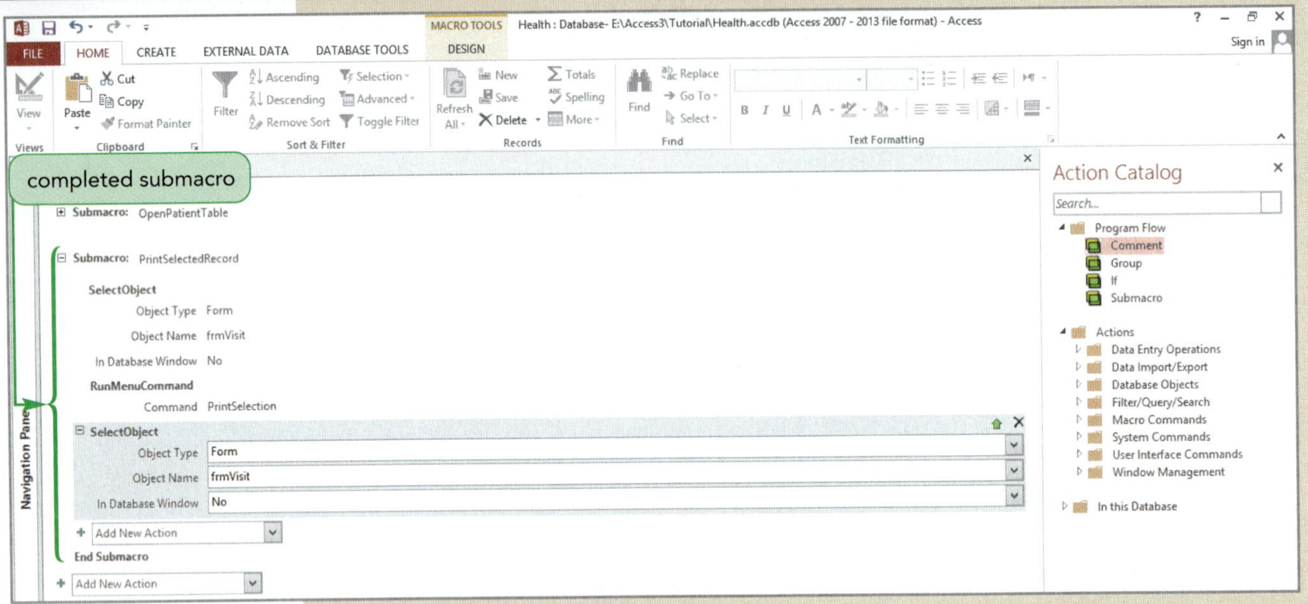

7. Save your macro design changes, and then close the Macro Designer. The frmVisit form is the active object.

Next, you'll add a command button to the frmVisit form. After you attach the PrintSelectedRecord macro to the command button, you'll be able to click the command button to print the current frmVisit form record.

INSIGHT

Using submacros, subforms, subqueries and subreports

You can create a small macro and embed it in another macro as a submacro. Likewise, you can create a small form and embed it in another form as a subform, create a small query and embed it in another query as a subquery, and create a small report and embed it in another report as a subreport. The techniques for each of these object types are quite different.

- To embed a macro as a submacro, you use the Macro Designer and add a submacro as a new action.
- To embed a subform, you view the main form in Design view and add the subform using the wizard, or you drag the subform to the main form.
- To embed a query as a subquery, you use SQL view to copy the SQL for the subquery, and then you paste it in the SQL statement for the main query.
- To embed a report as a subreport, you use the Subreport Wizard, or you drag the report to the main report in Design view.

Although the techniques are different, the underlying logic is the same. An embedded object works with the data that is used by the main object. That is, a subform uses the related data from the main form, a subreport uses the related data from the main report, a subquery uses the related data from the main query, and a submacro is executed as an action of the main macro.

Adding a Command Button to a Form

In Design view for a form, you use the Button tool in the Controls group on the DESIGN tab to add a command button to a form. If the Use Control Wizards tool is selected when you click the Button tool, the Command Button Wizard guides you through the process of adding the command button. You'll explore adding the command button directly to the frmVisit form without using the wizard, and then you'll set the command button's properties using its property sheet.

To add a command button to the frmVisit form:

1. Close the property sheet.
2. Click the **DESIGN tab**, in the Controls group click the **More** button, and then make sure the **Use Control Wizards** tool is not selected.

   Trouble? If the Use Control Wizards tool has an orange background, click it to disable the control wizards, and then continue with Step 3.
3. In the Controls group, click the **Button** tool.
4. Move the pointer over the Detail section, and then when the pointer's plus symbol (+) is positioned in the Detail section to the right of the Open Patient Table button, click the mouse button. Access adds a command button to the form. See Figure 10-17.

Figure 10-17 After adding a command button to the frmVisit form

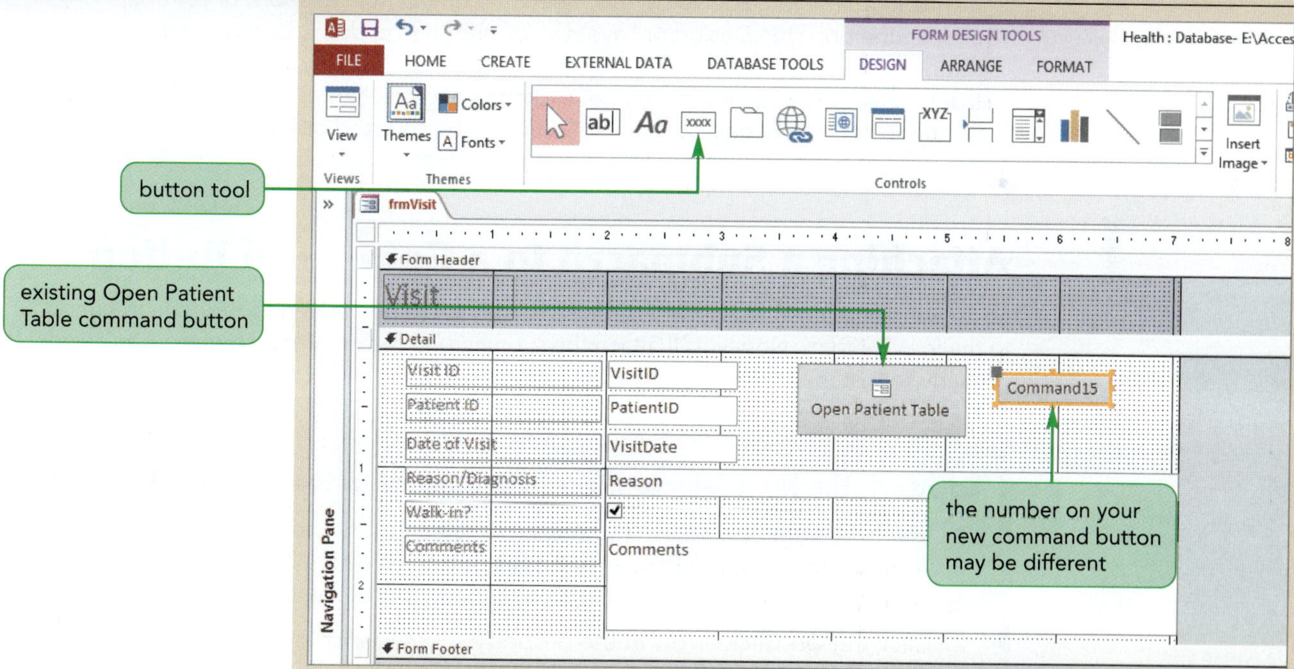

Trouble? If the Command Button Wizard dialog box opens, click the Cancel button to close it, on the DESIGN tab in the Controls group, click the More button, click the Use Control Wizards tool to deselect it, and then repeat Steps 3 and 4.

Trouble? The command button on your screen might show a different number in its label, depending on how you completed the previous steps. This difference will not affect the command button or macro.

You can now attach the PrintSelectedRecord submacro to the command button.

INSIGHT

Techniques for Formatting Controls in Forms and Reports

Access supports four especially useful methods for formatting controls and forms—the Format Painter tool, the Quick Styles gallery, conditional formatting, and setting a background image.

You can use the Format Painter tool to copy the formatting from one control to another. To do this, select a control on a form or report in Design view, click the Format Painter tool on the FORMAT tab, and then click on another control to apply the formatting.

You can use the Quick Styles gallery to apply a built-in style to a control on a form or report. To do this, select the control in Layout or Design view, and then on the FORMAT tab, click the Quick Styles button in the Control Formatting group to display the Quick Styles gallery. Click a style in the gallery to apply it to the control. You can also change the shape of a control on a form or report by clicking the Change Shape button in the Control Formatting group to display the Change Shape gallery, then click a shape to apply it to the selected control.

You can use conditional formatting to format a text box or field on a form or report to apply formatting when the condition defined in a rule has been met. To do this, select a text box or field on a form or report in Layout view, click the Conditional Formatting button on the Control Formatting group in the FORMAT tab, click the New Rule button, and then fill in the entries in the New Formatting Rule dialog box.

Finally, you can set an image as a background for a form, report, or control, rather than setting a solid color. To do this, select the object (form, report, or control), click on the object in Design or Layout view, and then click the Background Image button in the Background group on the FORMAT tab. Next, browse to the folder that contains the background image, click the image filename, and then click the OK button to set the image as the background for the selected object

Attaching a Submacro to a Command Button

So far you've created the PrintSelectedRecord submacro and added the command button to the frmVisit form. Now you'll attach the submacro to the command button's OnClick property so that the submacro is executed when the command button is clicked.

To attach the PrintSelectedRecord submacro to the command button:

1. Make sure the new command button is selected, on the DESIGN tab, in the Tools group, click the **Property Sheet** button to open the property sheet, and then, if necessary, click the **Event** tab in the property sheet.
2. Click the **On Click** arrow in the property sheet to display the macros list, and then click **mcrHealthGroup.PrintSelectedRecord**.

   You can change the text that appears on the command button (also known as the command button's label or caption). By changing its Caption property, you can replace the text with a picture by setting its Picture property, or you can include both text and a picture. Raj wants you to place a picture of a printer on the command button and to display text on the command button.

3. In the property sheet, click the **Format** tab, click the **Picture** box, and then click the **Build** button ... that appears on the right side of the Picture box. The Picture Builder dialog box opens. See Figure 10-18.

Be sure to select mcrHealthGroup. PrintSelectedRecord and not one of the other macros. If you can't see the entire macro and submacro name, drag the left edge of the property sheet to the left to widen it, and then repeat Step 2.

Figure 10-18 Picture Builder dialog box

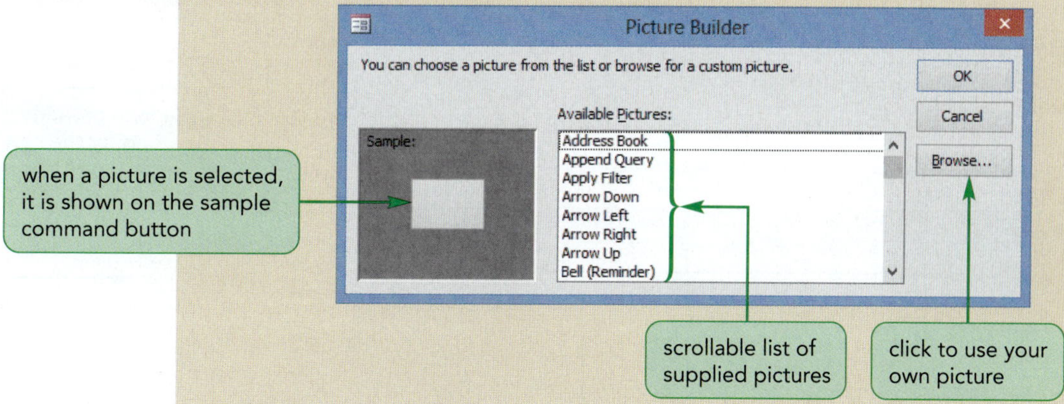

The Picture Builder dialog box contains an alphabetical list of pictures supplied with Access. You can scroll the list and select one of the pictures, or you can click the Browse button to select your own picture. When you select a picture, a sample of the picture is displayed on the command button in the Sample box on the left.

4. Scroll down the Available Pictures box, and then click **Printer**. A printer picture is displayed on the command button in the Sample box.
5. Click the **OK** button. The Picture Builder dialog box closes, and the printer picture is displayed on the command button in the form.
6. Click the **Caption** box in the property sheet, press the **F2** key to select the Caption property value, type **Print selected record**, and then press the **Tab** key.

   The **Picture Caption Arrangement property** specifies how a command button's Caption property value is arranged in relation to the picture placed on the command button. The choices are No Picture Caption, General, Top, Bottom, Left, and Right.

7. Click the **Picture Caption Arrangement** arrow, and then click **Bottom**.

   The command button is not tall enough or wide enough to display the picture and caption, so you'll resize it.

8. Use the middle-bottom sizing handle and the middle-right sizing handle to increase the width and height of the command button so it is approximately the same size as the Open Patient Table button and looks like the one shown in Figure 10-19.

Figure 10-19 **Command button with picture and caption**

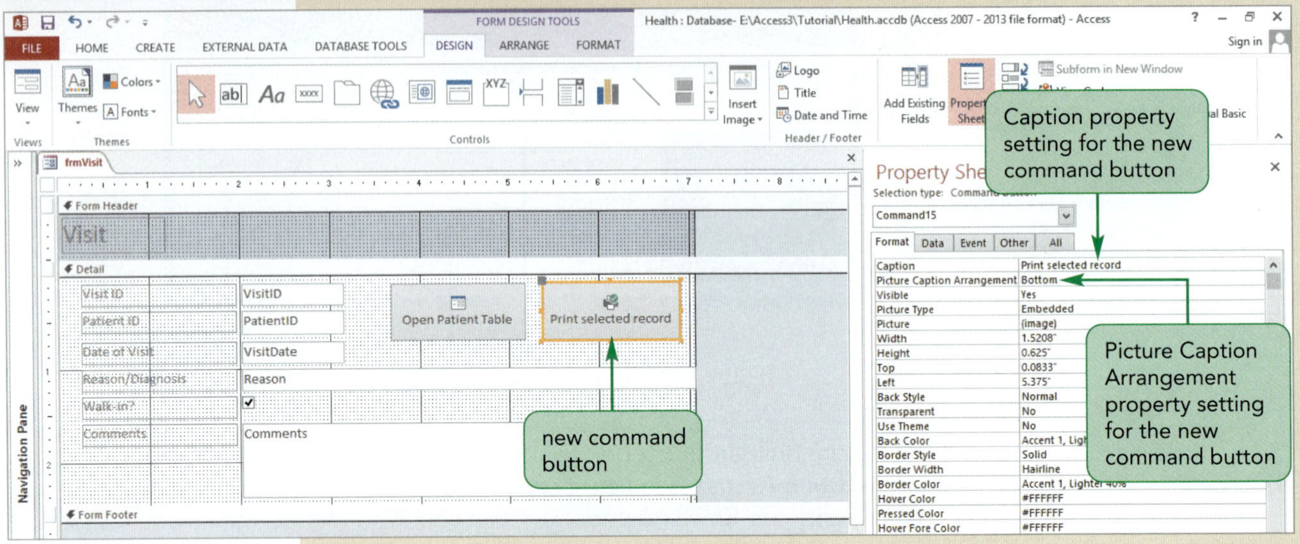

Next, you'll save the frmVisit form and test the command button.

To save the form and test the command button:

1. Close the property sheet, save your form design changes, and then switch to Form view.
2. On the Visit navigation bar, click the **Last record** navigation button to move to the last visit record for VisitID 1570.
3. Click the **Print selected record** command button on the form to open the Print dialog box. Notice that the submacro correctly set the print range to print the selected record.
4. Click the **OK** button to print the last visit record. The submacro returns control to the frmVisit form after the record was printed.
5. Close the form.
6. If you are not continuing on to the next session, close the Health database.

TIP

If the Print dialog box contains a Print To File checkbox, you can print to a file instead of printing on paper.

You've incorporated macros into a form to automate some tasks. Creating one or more forms such as this is suitable for providing some automation for a user who is fairly comfortable using Access. This method is not suitable for beginner users, though, because they could choose any database object and accidentally delete or corrupt data and objects.

In the next session, you'll create a navigation system for users with less experience that will prevent them from accessing the database objects. You'll create a form that contains a list box to display specific form, reports, and the queries in the Health database, use a SQL statement to select the values for the list box, and then add command buttons to the form.

REVIEW

Session 10.1 Quick Check

1. What is a macro?
2. What is the Macro Designer?
3. What does the MessageBox action do?
4. What are you trying to accomplish when you single step through a macro?
5. What is an event property?
6. What is the purpose of the Where Condition argument for the OpenForm action?
7. How do you change the picture on a command button?

Session 10.2 Visual Overview:

A **navigation form** is a form with tabs that allows you to display database objects in an organized way to users.

The Queries tab is the active upper tab.

The frmQueries tab is the active lower tab.

Clicking the Add New tab will add a new lower tab.

A **list box** displays a scrollable list of values. When the list of items is too long for the list box, a scroll bar will appear.

The frmNavigation form is the active form.

A button control can be used to execute a macro.

The active button control's properties are displayed in the Property Sheet.

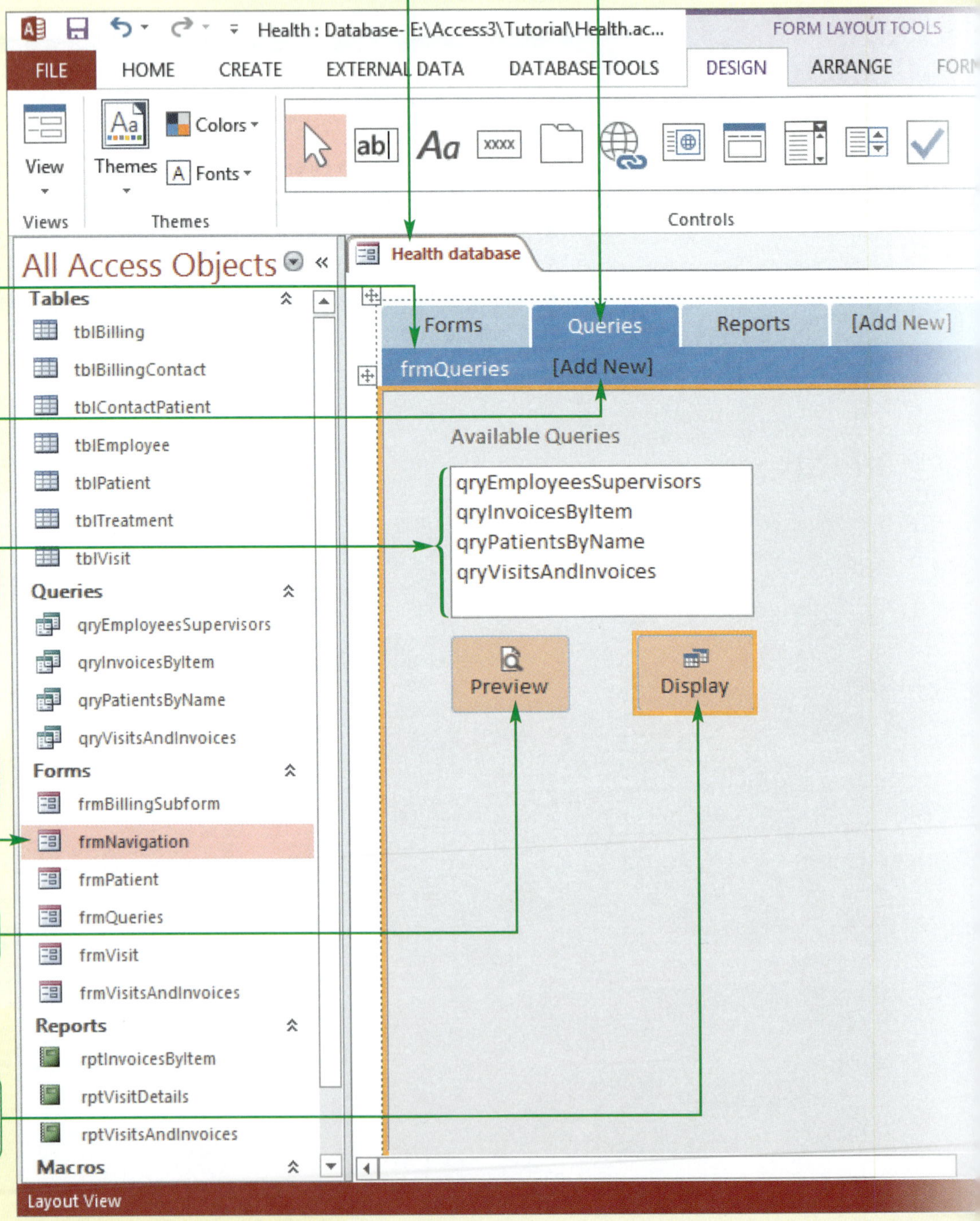

A Navigation Form

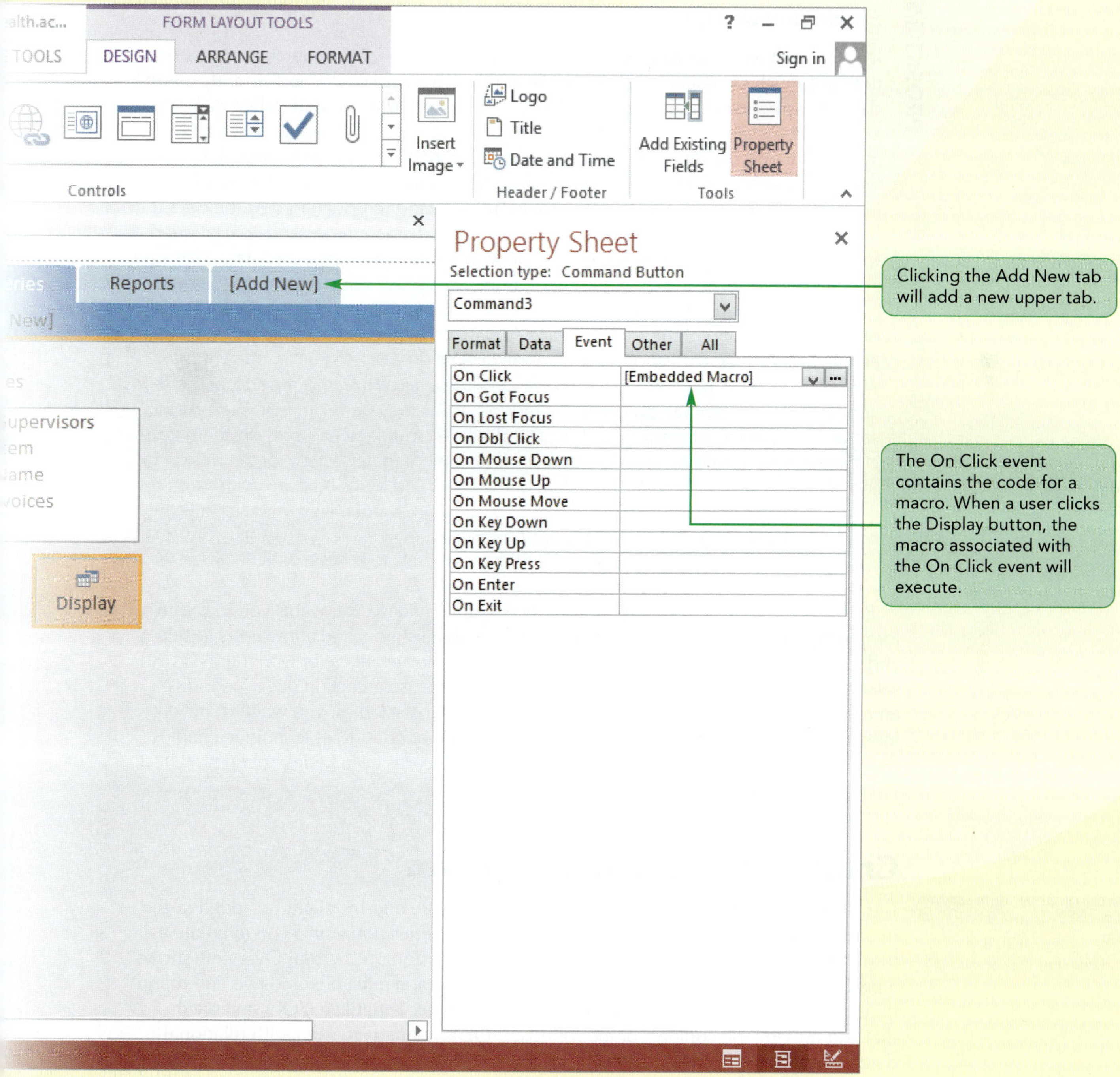

Designing a User Interface

A **user interface** is what you see and use when you communicate with a computer program. Raj wants to provide a simple user interface for the Health database.

PROSKILLS

Problem Solving: Restricting Access to Database Objects and Prohibiting Design Changes

It's important to ensure that data is as accurate as possible. Many database users do not have much experience with database applications, and could inadvertently corrupt data. However, database users need to be able to add, change, and delete data. If they make updates using forms and special queries, such as action queries, users can manipulate only the data on forms and queries, without accessing the rest of the data in the tables upon which the forms and queries are built. To minimize the risk of users inadvertently corrupting data, users should be restricted to updating only the data they need. For this reason, a database administrator might create forms and special queries for the purpose of restricting the users' ability to access only authorized data. Users also need to review and print information from a database using reports, forms, and queries. Similarly, users should not be allowed to change the design of any database object or the design of the user interface. You can create a user interface that meets all these needs and restrictions. When users open a database, you can present them with a form that allows them to choose among the available forms, reports, and queries and to navigate from one object to another object as they perform their work. At the same time, you can limit users to this controlled user interface and prevent them from circumventing it, so that you prevent them from changing any aspect of the design of the database. By considering the needs of the users and by using the features and tools provided by the DBMS, you can ensure users can work productively with a database and ensure the integrity of the data stored in the database.

Before he creates the user interface for the Health database, Raj wants you to create a form to display a list of the queries in the database in a list box, and allow users to select and run a query from the list box. This technique has the advantage of working well with select queries but not working with action queries. Because an action query performs an action (make table, append, delete, update) on database tables, you want to prevent inexperienced users from selecting and running action queries. Raj's technique enables users to choose and run select queries, which select records from tables but do not affect the records in a table.

Creating the frmQueries Form

TIP

The acronym SQL is often pronounced "see-kwel."

The Health database contains several queries, and more queries might be added in the future. To allow users to choose from the available queries, Raj wants you to create a form that will display the queries in a list box. The Session 10.2 Visual Overview shows a preview of the frmQueries form you'll create. You'll add a list box and two command buttons to the form, and you'll enter a Structured Query Language (SQL) statement that will provide the contents of the list box. (SQL is a language used with relational databases.)

If you completed the exercises in Tutorial 9, there will be some action queries in the Health database. First, you'll delete any action queries that are in the Health database, then you'll create the frmQueries form.

To delete the action queries in the Health database:

1. If you took a break after the previous session, make sure that the Health database is open and the Navigation Pane is displayed.
2. Delete the following queries from the database: qryContactPatientAppend, qryContactPatientDelete, qryContactPatientMakeTable, qryContactPatientUpdate.

   Trouble? If you want to keep the action queries, first make a copy of the Health database, and then delete the action queries.

   The remaining queries should be select queries.
3. Close the Navigation Pane.

Next, you'll create the frmQueries form. To create the frmQueries form, you'll begin by creating a blank form. Because a SQL statement will supply the list box with its values, none of the form controls needs data from a table or query, so you'll create an unbound form, which does not use a table or query as its source.

To create and save the frmQueries form:

1. Click the **CREATE tab**, and then in the Forms group, click the **Blank Form** button. Access creates a blank form, opens it in the Form window in Layout view, and opens the Field List pane.
2. Close the Field List pane, and then click the **Design View** button on the status bar to switch to Design view.
3. Click the **Save** button on the Quick Access Toolbar, type **frmQueries** in the Form Name box, and then press the **Enter** key.

All the objects you've created and used so far are standard objects in which users need to navigate from record to record, or from page to page in the case of reports, and to perform other operations such as copying data and closing the object. For unbound forms, users do not need to perform any of these operations, so you should remove these features from the form. Access includes a number of form properties that are especially helpful in designing a user interface; for Raj's form, you'll use properties that let you disable the display of the Close button, the navigation buttons, the record selector, and the right-click shortcut menu.

TIP

Some developers prefer to set form properties after they've created all the form controls.

In addition, to match Raj's design, you need to set the Caption property to "Queries," which is the value that will appear on the form's tab when you open the form.

Figure 10-20 shows the form property settings you will use to create the frmQueries form for Raj.

Figure 10-20 frmQueries form properties

Property	Setting	Function
Caption	Queries	Value that appears on the form's object tab when the form is open
Close Button	No	Disables the display of the Close button on the form's object tab
Navigation Buttons	No	Disables the display of navigation buttons at the bottom of the form
Record Selectors	No	Disables the display of a record selector on the left side of the form
Shortcut Menu	No	Disables the display of the shortcut menu when a user right-clicks the form

Next you'll use the property sheet to set the form properties shown in Figure 10-20.

To set the properties for the unbound form:

TIP

You can also double-click the form selector to open the property sheet.

1. Right-click the **form selector** ■, which is the box immediately to the left of the horizontal ruler, if it is not already selected, and then click **Properties** on the shortcut menu to open the form's property sheet.
2. If necessary, click the **Format** tab in the property sheet to display the Format page of the property sheet.

   You can now set the Caption property for the form. The Caption property value will appear on the tab when the form is displayed.
3. Click the **Caption** box, and then type **Queries**.

   Next, you'll set the Record Selectors property so that a record selector will not be displayed on the left side of the form. Because the form does not display any records, there's no need to include a record selector.
4. In the Record Selectors box, double-click **Yes** to change the property setting from Yes to No.

   You'll now set the remaining form properties.
5. Scrolling as necessary, set the Navigation Buttons property to **No**, and set the Close Button property to **No**.
6. Click the **Other** tab in the property sheet to display the Other page of the property sheet, and then set the Shortcut Menu property to **No**.
7. Close the property sheet, and then save your form design changes.

Now that you have set the form's properties, you can add a list box to it. The label associated with the list box will identify the list box for the user, and the list box will display the list of queries in the Health database. You will not use the Control Wizards tool for the list box because you'll be using a SQL statement to provide the query names for the list box.

Adding a List Box to a Form

The list box in the frmQueries form will display the list of queries that users can preview or view. A user will be able to click the name of a query to select it, and then click one of the command buttons to preview or view the query. Double-clicking a query name in the list box also will open the query datasheet.

REFERENCE

Adding a List Box to a Form

- Switch to Design view, if necessary.
- If necessary, on the DESIGN tab, in the Controls group, click the More button, and then click the Use Control Wizards tool to select or deselect it, depending on whether you want to use the wizard.
- On the DESIGN tab, in the Controls group, click the More button, and then click the List Box tool.
- Position the pointer's plus symbol (+) where you want to place the upper-left corner of the list box, and then click the mouse button.
- If you use the List Box Wizard, complete the dialog boxes to choose the source of the list, select the fields to appear in the list box, select a sort order, size the columns, and select the label; or if you do not use the List Box Wizard, set the Row Source property and size the list box.

Now you'll add the list box to the form.

To add the list box to the form and move the attached label:

1. Click the **DESIGN tab**, in the Controls group, click the **More** button, and then make sure the **Use Control Wizards** tool in the Controls group is not selected.

   Trouble? If the Use Control Wizards tool has an orange background, click it to disable the control wizards, and then continue with Step 2.

2. If the Controls gallery is not open, in the Controls group, click the **More** button to open it, and then in the Controls gallery, click the **List Box** tool.

3. Move the pointer over the Detail section, position the pointer's plus symbol (+) approximately ½ inch from the top and ½ inch from the left edge, and then click the mouse button. Access adds a list box and attached label to the form. See Figure 10-21.

Figure 10-21 Form's design after adding the label and list box

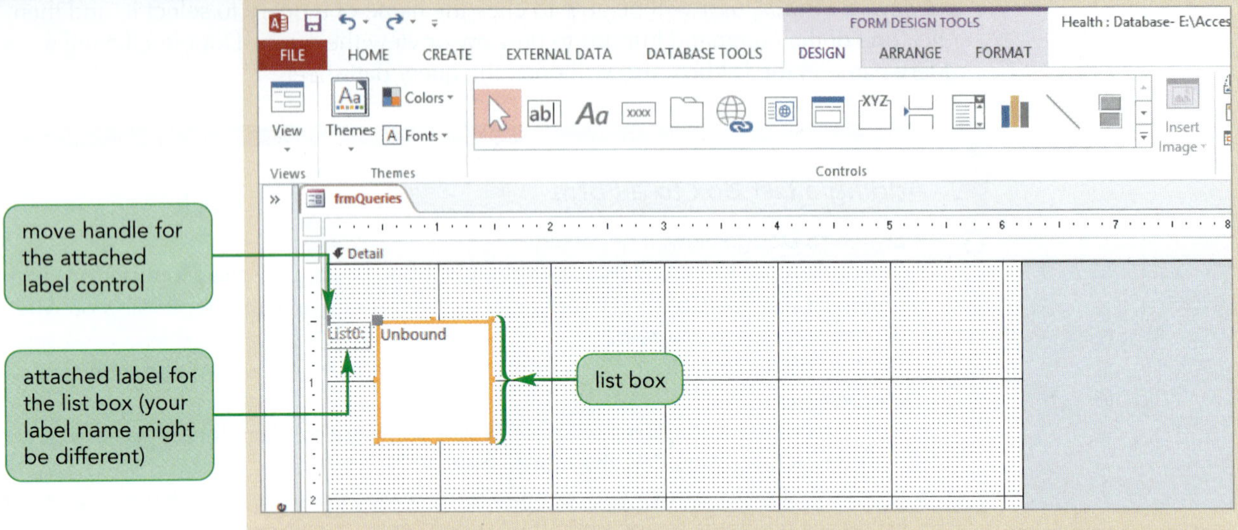

Trouble? If your list box is sized or positioned differently, resize it or move it until it matches the list box shown in Figure 10-21.

You'll move the attached label above the list box.

5. Click the label control to select it, position the mouse pointer on the move handle in the upper left corner of the label control, and then drag it to position the label 2 grid dots above the list box and the left edge of the label aligns with the left edge of the list box.

   You can now set the Caption property for the label control.

6. Display the property sheet (if necessary), and then click the **Format** tab in the property sheet to display the Format page of the property sheet.
7. Click the **Caption** box, press the **F2** key to select the Caption property value, type **Available Queries**, and then press the **Tab** key.
8. Drag the right edge of the label control to the right until it is wide enough to display all of the caption text.
9. Close the Property Sheet.

   Now you'll save the form and check your progress by switching to Form view.

10. Save your form design changes, and then switch to Form view. See Figure 10-22.

Figure 10-22 frmQueries form displayed in Form view

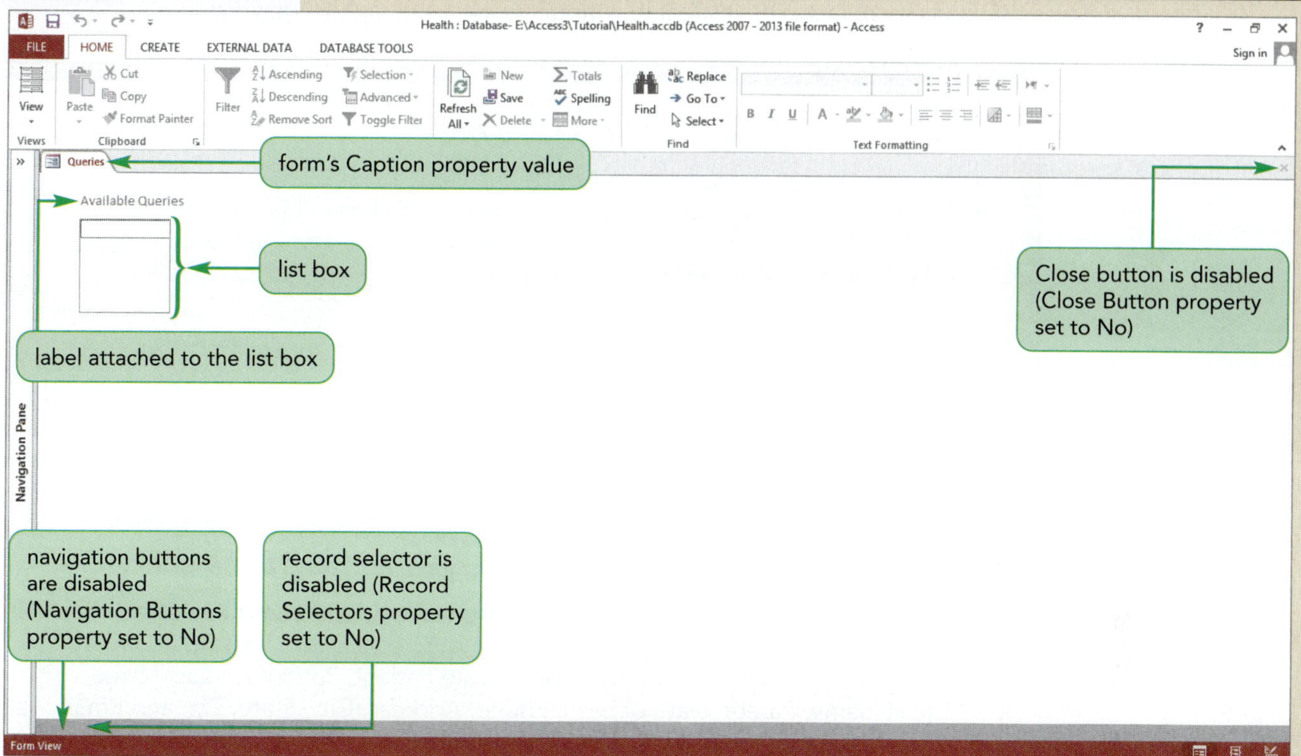

Now you're ready to enter the SQL statement that will provide the query names for the list box.

Using SQL

SQL (**Structured Query Language**) is a standard language used in querying, updating, and managing relational databases. Instead of using a drag-and-drop environment like Access, a database administrator in a large organization uses a relational DBMS such as mySQL or Oracle, and uses SQL statements to query, update, delete, and make tables. Every full-featured relational DBMS has its own version of the current standard SQL. If you learn SQL for one relational DBMS, it's a relatively easy task to begin using SQL for other relational DBMSs. When you work with two or more relational DBMSs, which is the case in most companies, you'll learn that few differences exist among the various SQL versions.

Much of what Access accomplishes behind the scenes is done with SQL. Whenever you create a query, for example, Access automatically constructs an equivalent SQL statement. When you save a query, Access saves the SQL statement version of the query.

When you start to view the SQL statements, you'll recognize the query statement names. This is not a coincidence! There are really only five SQL statement types: select, update, delete, insert, and create. These correspond with the Access queries Select, Update, Delete, Append, and Make Table. For example, the following simple SQL statement selects records in the tblPatient table, selecting the fields PatientID, LastName, FirstName and City where the city is Windsor:

```
SELECT tblPatient.PatientID, tblPatient.LastName, tblPatient.FirstName, tblPatient.City
FROM tblPatient
WHERE (((tblPatient.City)="Windsor"));
```

Viewing a SQL Statement for a Query

When you are working in Design view or viewing a query recordset, you can see the SQL statement that is equivalent to your query by switching to SQL view.

REFERENCE

Viewing a SQL Statement for a Query

- Open the query in Datasheet view or Design view.
- Click the SQL View button on the status bar, right-click the object tab and click SQL View on the shortcut menu, or click the View button arrow in the Views group (in Datasheet view) or in the Results group (in Design view) and click SQL View.

You'll start learning about SQL by examining the SQL statements that are equivalent to two existing queries: qryPatientsByName and qryVisitsAndInvoices.

To view the SQL statement for the qryPatientsByName query:

1. Open the Navigation Pane, open the **qryPatientsByName** query datasheet, and then close the Navigation Pane. The query displays 51 records from the tblPatient table. The columns displayed are Patient, Patient ID, Last Name, First Name, Parent, Date of Birth, Phone, Address, City, State, Zip, and Email Address.
2. Right-click the **qryPatientsByName** object tab to open the shortcut menu, click **SQL View** to display the query in SQL view, and then click an unused portion of the window to deselect the SQL statement. See Figure 10-23.

Figure 10-23 **SQL view for the qryPatientsByName query**

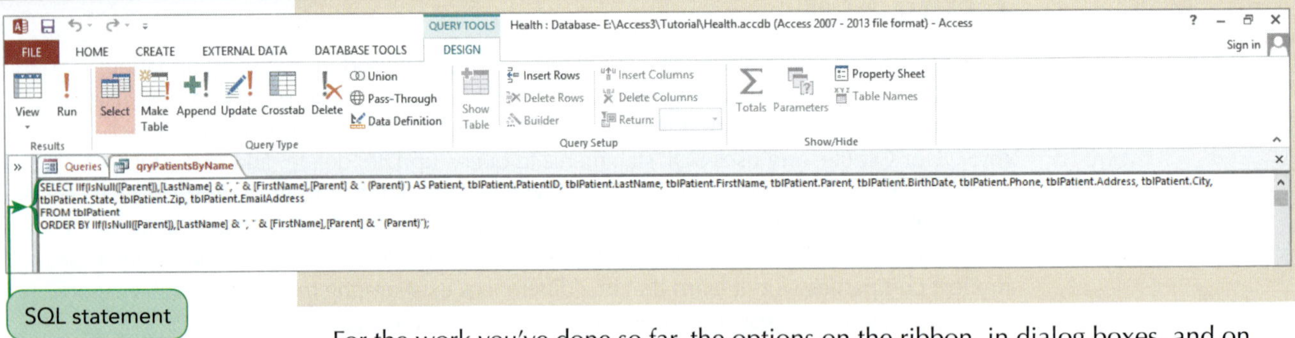

For the work you've done so far, the options on the ribbon, in dialog boxes, and on the property sheet have sufficed. If you learn SQL to the point where you can use it efficiently, you will be able to enter your own SQL statements in SQL view. If you work with more complicated databases, you might find that you need the extra power of the SQL language to implement your database strategies fully.

TIP

The first clause of a SQL statement begins with SELECT, CREATE, UPDATE, DELETE, or INSERT.

SQL uses the **SELECT statement** to define what data it retrieves from a database and how it presents the data. A SELECT statement like the one shown in Figure 10-23 must follow these rules:

- The basic form of a SQL SELECT statement includes four sections, known as clauses. Each clause starts with a different keyword: SELECT, FROM, WHERE, and ORDER BY. After the SELECT keyword, you list the fields you want to display. After FROM, you list the tables used in the query. After WHERE, you list the selection criteria. After ORDER BY, you list the sort fields.

- If a field name includes a space or a special symbol, you enclose the field name in brackets. Because the Health database does not use field names with spaces or special symbols, you don't have to enclose its field names in brackets. However, if your database had a field name such as *Contract Type*, then you would use [Contract Type] in a SQL statement. Some database administrators prefer to enclose every fieldname in square brackets to make it easier to identify field names in SQL statements.
- You precede a field name with the name of its table by connecting the table name to the field name with a period. For example, you would enter the PatientID field in the tblVisit table as *tblVisit.PatientID*.
- You use commas to separate values in a list of field names or a list of table names, and you end the SELECT statement with a semicolon.

The SQL statement shown in Figure 10-23 selects the Patient, PatientID, LastName, FirstName, Parent, BirthDate, Phone, Address, City, State, Zip, and EmailAddress fields from the tblPatient table; the records are sorted in ascending order by the Patient LastName field. The SQL statement does not contain a WHERE clause, so the recordset includes all records from the tblPatient table when the query is run.

You can enter or change SQL statements directly in SQL view. If you enter a SQL statement and then switch to Design view, you will see its equivalent in the design grid.

Next, you'll examine the SQL statement for the qryPatientsAndInvoices query.

To view the SQL statement for the qryVisitsAndInvoices query:

1. Close the qryPatientsByName query, open the Navigation Pane, open the **qryVisitsAndInvoices** query in Design view, and then close the Navigation Pane. The query selects data from the tblVisit and tblBilling tables and does not sort the records. The fields included in the query design are PatientID, VisitID, InvoiceAmt, VisitDate, and Reason.
2. On the DESIGN tab, in the Results group, click the **View** button arrow, click **SQL View** to change to SQL view, and then click an unused portion of the window to deselect the SQL statement. See Figure 10-24.

Figure 10-24 SQL view for the qryVisitsAndInvoices query

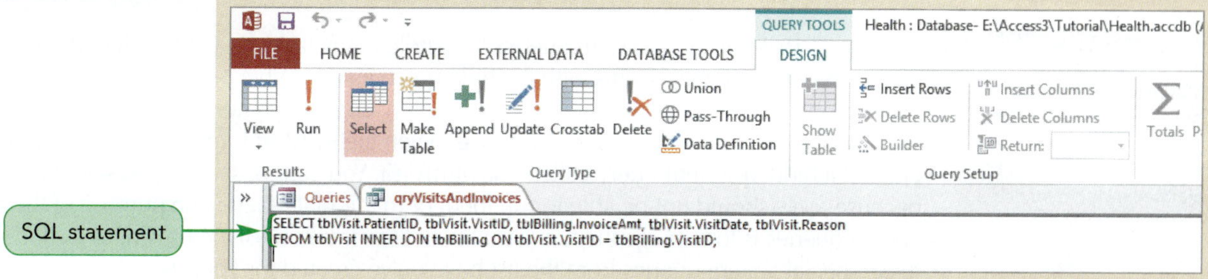

The SELECT statement for this query is similar to the one shown in Figure 10-23, except that it does not include an ORDER BY clause and it includes an INNER JOIN clause. The INNER JOIN clause selects records from the two tables only when the records have the same value in the common field that links the tables. The general syntax for a SQL statement with an inner join is the following:

SELECT *field list* FROM *Table1* INNER JOIN *Table2* ON *Table1.Field1* = *Table2.Field2*;

Access uses the ON clause here instead of the standard SQL WHERE clause.

3. Close the query. The frmQueries form in Design view is now the active object.

The SQL SELECT statements mirror the query options you viewed in Design view. In effect, every choice you make in Design view is reflected as part of the SQL SELECT statement. Viewing the SQL statements generated from queries that you design is an effective way to begin learning SQL.

You now can enter the SQL statement that will provide the query names for the list box.

Using a SQL Statement for a List Box

You'll use a SQL SELECT statement to retrieve the list of query names from one of the Access system tables. **System tables** are special tables maintained by Access that store information about the characteristics of a database and about the structure of the objects in the database. Although system tables do not appear in the Navigation Pane, you can retrieve information from system tables using SELECT statements. One of the system tables, the **MSysObjects table**, keeps track of the names, types, and other characteristics of every object in a database. The Name and Type fields are the two MSysObjects table fields you'll use in the SELECT statement. The type field value contains a numeric value that corresponds to an object type. Figure 10-25 shows the numbers that correspond to some commonly used objects. For instance, a table is a type 1 object and a query is a type 5 object. If the Type value of an MSObject is 5, then we know that the MSObject referred to must be a query. The values may seem cryptic, but think of them as values that Microsoft developers have assigned to these objects so they can use a number instead of a name.

Figure 10-25 **MSysObjects table Type field values**

Object Type	Type Field Value in MSysObjects Table
Table	1
Query	5
Form	-32768
Report	-32764
Macro	-32766
Module	-32761

TIP

SQL is case insensitive, but typing SQL keywords in uppercase is an industry convention and makes the statements more readable.

Access creates its own system queries to handle many tasks for you; each of these queries has a name that begins with the tilde (~) character. When a form contains a list box, combo box, or subform, Access automatically creates a system query to manage the functionality of these elements. For instance, when the frmVisit form was created, Access created a hidden system query called ~sq_ffrmVisit. You cannot see these system queries because users should not be able to run them or manipulate them. The purpose of these system queries is to manage the functionality of the form controls. You want to exclude these special system queries from the list box you've created for your user interface. Because every system query name begins with the ~ character, you'll use the Left function in your SELECT statement to identify the query names that begin with ~ and exclude those from the list of queries in the list box. The **Left function** provides the first character(s) in a text string. The format of the Left function is *Left*(text string, number of characters). You'll test the first character of the name of each query to determine if it is the ~ character. If the first character is not the ~ character, you'll include the query name in the list box. You'll use *Left([Name],1)* to retrieve the first character of the Name field, and you'll use the not equal operator (<>). To include only those queries whose names do not begin with the ~ character, you'll use the expression *Left([Name],1)<>"~"*. Access interprets this expression as "the first character of the Name field does not equal the ~ character." The complete SELECT statement that you will use to select the list of query names is as follows:

SELECT [Name] FROM MSysObjects WHERE [Type]=5 And Left([Name],1)<>"~" ORDER BY [Name];

The **Row Source property** for a list box specifies the data source, such as a table, a query, or a SQL statement. You'll enter the SELECT statement as the value for the Row Source property of the list box you created.

To set the Row Source property for the list box:

1. Switch to Design view, right-click the **list box** to open the shortcut menu, click **Properties** to open the property sheet, and then click the **Data** tab (if necessary).
2. Right-click the **Row Source** box to open the shortcut menu, and then click **Zoom**. The Zoom dialog box opens.
3. In the Zoom dialog box, type **SELECT [Name] FROM MSysObjects WHERE [Type]=5 And Left([Name],1)<>"~" ORDER BY [Name];**

   See Figure 10-26.

Be sure to type the semicolon at the end of the SELECT statement.

Figure 10-26 SELECT statement for the list box

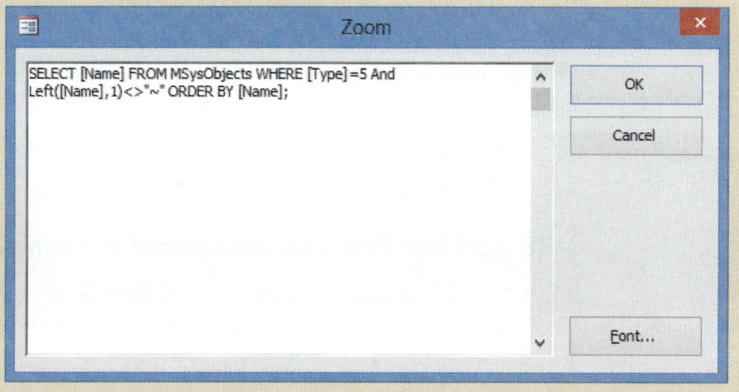

4. Click the **OK** button to close the Zoom dialog box.
5. Close the property sheet, save your form design changes, and then switch to Form view. The queries in the database (excluding system queries) now appear in alphabetical order in the list box. See Figure 10-27.

Figure 10-27 Completed list box

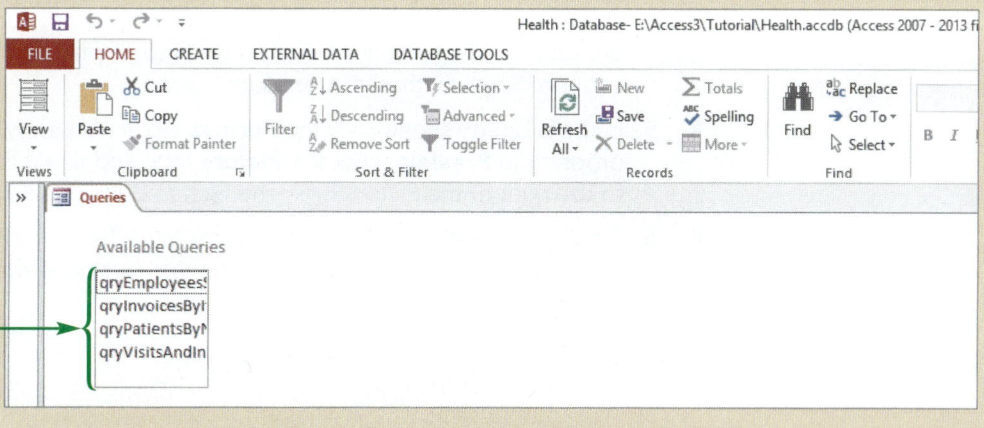

query names retrieved by a SQL statement from the MSysObjects table

Trouble? If a syntax-error message appears, click the OK button, switch to Design view, right-click the list box, click Properties, right-click the Row Source box, and then click Zoom. Correct the SELECT statement so it's the same as the statement shown in Step 3, click the OK button, and then repeat Step 5.

6. Switch to layout view, and then drag the right edge of the list box to the right until you can see the full names of all of the queries.

You can now add command buttons to the form.

Adding Command Buttons to a Form

You can add a command button to a form by placing the button directly on the form or by using the Use Control Wizards tool. If you use the Use Control Wizards tool, you can attach a standard Access action (such as opening a specific query or closing a window) or a macro to the button. Raj's design includes two command buttons: Preview and Display. The Preview command button will allow a user to view the query in Print Preview, and the Display command button will allow the user to view the query as a datasheet. When the user clicks either of the command buttons, the query that will be opened is the query the user has selected in the list box. For the Print Preview button, you'll attach a macro to the command button's On Click property that will display the selected query in Print Preview. Similarly, you'll attach a macro to the Display command button that will display the selected query as a datasheet. You'll add both command buttons and appropriate macros to the form. First, you'll add the Preview command button to the form.

To add the Preview command button to the form:

1. Switch to Design view, click the DESIGN tab, and then increase the width of the form to 4" and the length of the form to 4" (if necessary).
2. In the Controls group, click the **More** button, make sure the **Use Control Wizards** tool is deselected, and then in the Controls group, click the Button tool.
3. Move the pointer to the Detail section, position the pointer's plus symbol (+) below and aligned with the left edge of the list box, and then click the mouse button. Access adds a command button to the form.
4. If necessary, open the property sheet for the command button.

   You can now change the default text that appears on the command button to the word "Preview" and add the Print Preview picture. When you add the picture, the button will be too small to display both the picture and the caption. You'll fix that in subsequent steps.
5. In the property sheet, click the **Format** tab (if necessary), set the Caption property to **Preview**, click the **Picture** box, and then click the **Build** button to the right of the Picture box. The Picture Builder dialog box opens.
6. Scroll down the Available Pictures box, and then click **Preview**. A Print Preview picture appears on the command button in the Sample box.

7. Click the **OK** button to close the Picture Builder dialog box and to place the Print Preview picture on the command button.
8. Click the **Picture Caption Arrangement** box, click its **arrow**, and then click **Bottom**.

Raj wants you to change the background color of the command button. You'll change the color, then resize the button to display the caption as well.

9. On the Property Sheet, click the **Back Color** box, click its **Build** button [...], in the Theme Colors section click the **Orange Accent 2, lighter 60%** (row 3, column 6), and then close the property sheet.
10. Use the bottom-right sizing handle to change the size of the command button to match the size shown in Figure 10-28. The width of the button should be less than half the width of the list box because you'll be adding another button of the same size to the right. See Figure 10-28.

Figure 10-28 **After adding the Preview command button to the form**

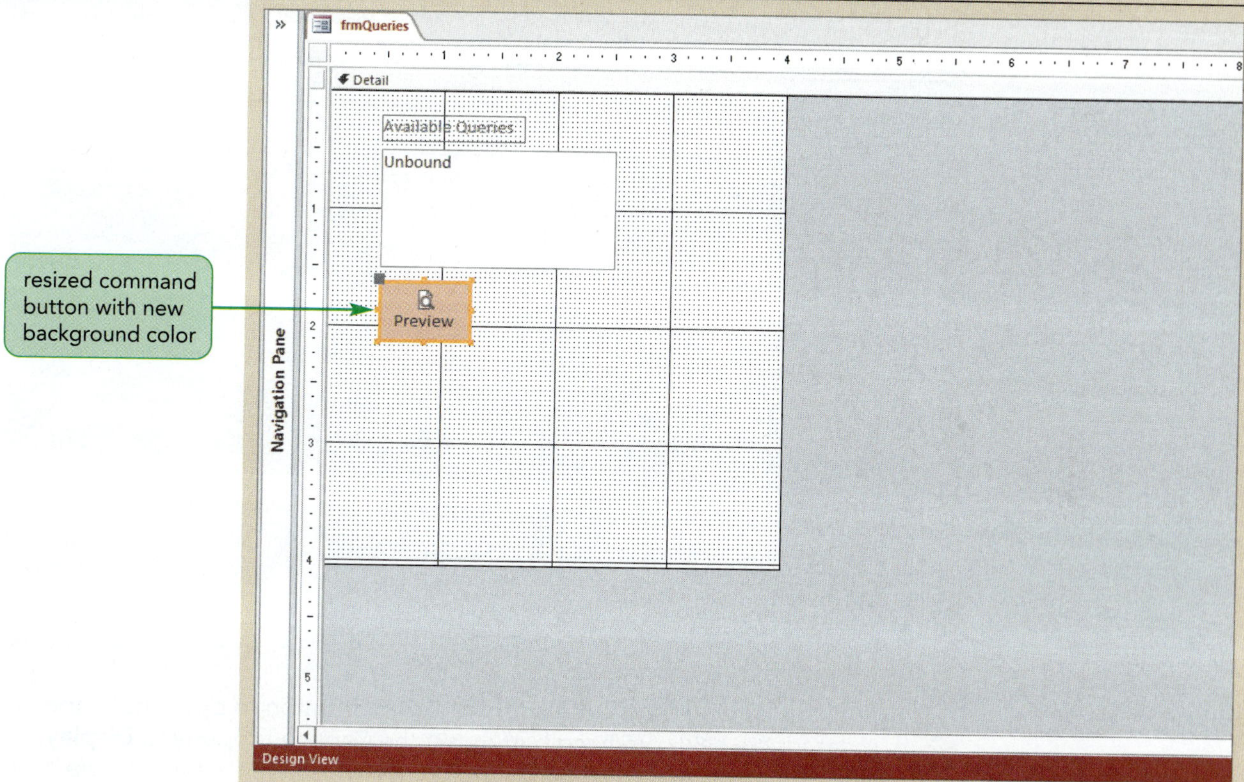

Instead of repeating the steps to add the command button for viewing a query recordset, you'll copy the first command button and paste it in the Detail section. This will also ensure the buttons are the same dimensions and save time adjusting the size of the new button. After moving the copied button into position, you can change the text and picture on it.

To add the Display command button to the form:

1. Right-click the **Preview** command button, and then click **Copy** on the shortcut menu.
2. Right-click the grid in an empty area of the form, and then click **Paste** on the shortcut menu. Access adds a copy of the command button in the upper-left corner of the Detail section.
3. Move the new command button into position to the right of the original command button, aligning the bottom edges of the two buttons and aligning the right edge of the new button with the right edge of the list box. See Figure 10-29.

Figure 10-29 After pasting and repositioning a copy of the command button

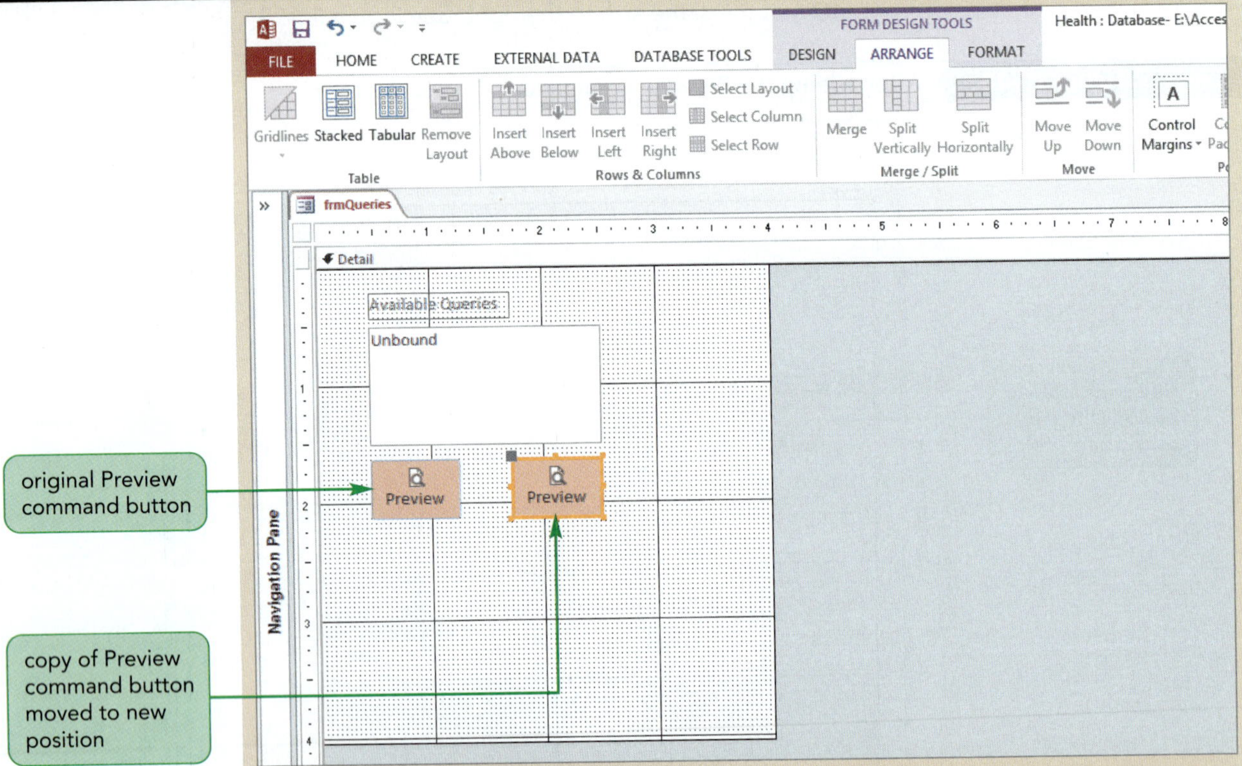

4. On the DESIGN tab, click the **Property Sheet** button to open the property sheet for the new command button, set the Caption property to **Display**, click the **Build button** on the Picture property, and then set the Picture property to **MS Access Query**.
5. Save your form design changes.

INSIGHT

Positioning Controls in Forms and Reports

When you need to create forms or reports that contain many fields and controls, it's best to try to fit the fields and controls as closely together as possible, while still creating a form or report that can be read easily. Here are some techniques that may help you to position controls on forms and reports.

- Position controls on a form or report by aligning them more precisely. Align controls on a form or report to the nearest dots in the design grid by right-clicking the selected controls, pointing to Align on the shortcut menu, and then clicking To Grid.
- Increase or decrease padding and margins for controls on a form or report to adjust space between controls. Modify the padding and margins for controls on a form or report in Design view by clicking the Control Padding button then clicking the Control Margins button in the position group on the ARRANGE tab.
- Insert a control on a form or report using the options in the ARRANGE tab in Layout view. You can select a control and click the Insert Above button to insert a new control above the selected control.
- Merge two text box controls on a form or report using the options in the ARRANGE tab in Layout view. You can select two text box controls and click the Merge button in the Merge/Split group. Similarly, select a merged control and split it using the Split Horizontally (or Split Vertically) button in the Merge/Split group to split the text box horizontally (or vertically) into two equal sized text boxes.
- Move a control up or down on a form or report using the options in the ARRANGE tab in Layout view. You can select the control and click the Move Up or Move Down button in the Move group to move the control.
- Add a page break to a report to ensure the automatic page breaks don't fragment the report data. In Design view, you can click the Page Break button in the Controls group on the DESIGN tab, then click in the location on the report or form where you'd like the page break to appear. A short line appears on the form or report at the page break location.

Before creating the macros for the form and for the command buttons to open the query selected by the user, you'll set the Name property for the list box. The naming convention for a list box is to use the three-letter prefix LST in lower case (lst). You'll enter the name lstQueryList for the list box control. You'll also set the background color of the Detail section and the list box.

Be sure to type the first character as a lower case L, not as a number 1.

To set the Name property for the list box and to set background colors:

1. Click the **list box** to make it the active control.
2. In the property sheet, click the **All tab**, select the value in the Name box, and then type **lstQueryList** in the Name box.
3. Click the **Back Color** box, click its **Build** button ..., and then in the Theme Colors section click the **White, Background 1** color (row 1, column 1).
4. Click the **Detail** section bar, and then set the section's Back Color property to **White, Background 1, Darker 5%** (row 2, column 1 in the Theme Colors section).
5. Save your form design changes, and then switch to Form view to display the completed frmQueries form. See Figure 10-30.

Figure 10-30 Completed list box

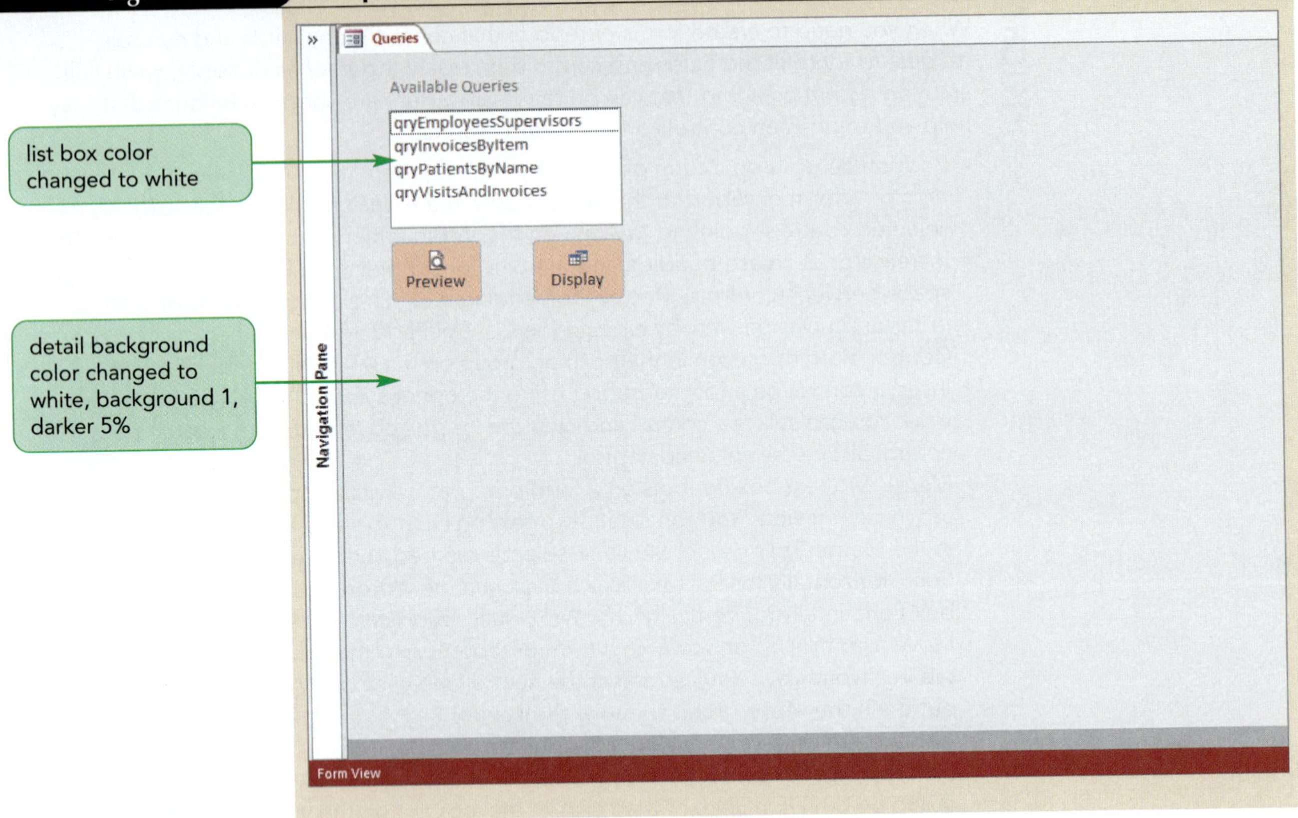

You now can create the macros for the frmQueries form.

Creating the Macros for the frmQueries Form

Raj wants Access to highlight the first query name in the list box when the frmQueries form first opens, by placing the focus on it. When an item has the focus, it may be highlighted, or a flashing insertion point is visible in the control. In general, it is a good practice to ensure a form element has the focus when the form opens. If no form controls have the focus, the user could press the Enter key, and an error message may be displayed. To avoid this situation, you'll place the focus on the first query name in the lstQueryList list box when the form opens.

When a user double-clicks a query name in the list box or selects a query name and then clicks the Display command button, the selected query should open in Datasheet view. When a user selects a query name in the list box and then clicks the Preview command button, the selected query should open in Print Preview. You'll create and attach four different macros to the objects on your form to enable these behaviors. You'll start by creating and attaching a macro to the On Load property for the form to place the focus on the first query name in the list box and highlight it when the form opens.

The **Load event** occurs when Access opens a form or report. When you attach a macro to the Load event through the form's On Load property, Access will process the actions in the macro each time the form is opened. You'll create a macro containing two actions. First, you'll use the GoToControl action to move the focus to the list box. This action does not set the focus to any specific query name in the list box, so you'll use the SendKeys action to send the down arrow keystroke to the list box. Access will respond to the SendKeys action by highlighting the first query name in the list box. The end result of these two actions will be that when a user opens the frmQueries form, the first query name will be highlighted and will have the focus.

To create the macro for the On Load property:

1. Switch to Design view, in the property sheet click the **Event** tab, click the **On Load** box, and then click its **Build** button [...]. The Choose Builder dialog box opens. See Figure 10-31.

Figure 10-31 Choose Builder dialog box

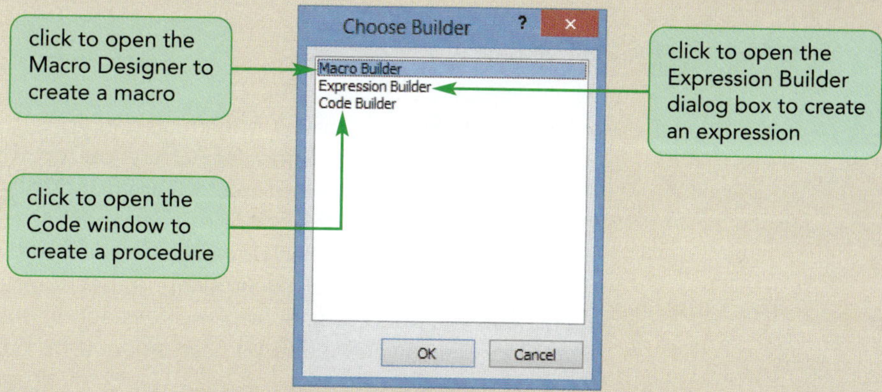

The Choose Builder dialog box presents three choices for setting the property value. You can attach a macro to the event property (Macro Builder), set the property to an expression (Expression Builder), or attach a VBA procedure to the event property (Code Builder).

You'll attach a macro to the event property.

2. Make sure **Macro Builder** is selected, and then click the **OK** button to open the Macro Designer.
3. Click the **Add New Action** arrow to display the list of actions, and then click **GoToControl**. The list closes, and GoToControl becomes the new action with one argument.
4. Type **lst** and then press the **Tab** key to select the AutoComplete box's value of lstQueryList, which is the Name property setting for the list box.

   Trouble? If you do not see the AutoComplete value, delete the characters you have typed and retype the first character as a lower case L, not as a number 1.

   The second and final action you need to add is the SendKeys action.The SendKeys action doesn't appear in the Add New Action list. You'll verify this, and then use the Show All Actions button to display the SendKeys action.

5. Click the **Add New Action** arrow, scroll down the list, notice that the SendKeys action doesn't appear in the list, click the **Add New Action** arrow to close the list, and then on the DESIGN tab, in the Show/Hide group, hover the mouse pointer over the **Show All Actions** button to display the button's ScreenTip. See Figure 10-32.

Figure 10-32 **Creating the macro for the form's On Load property**

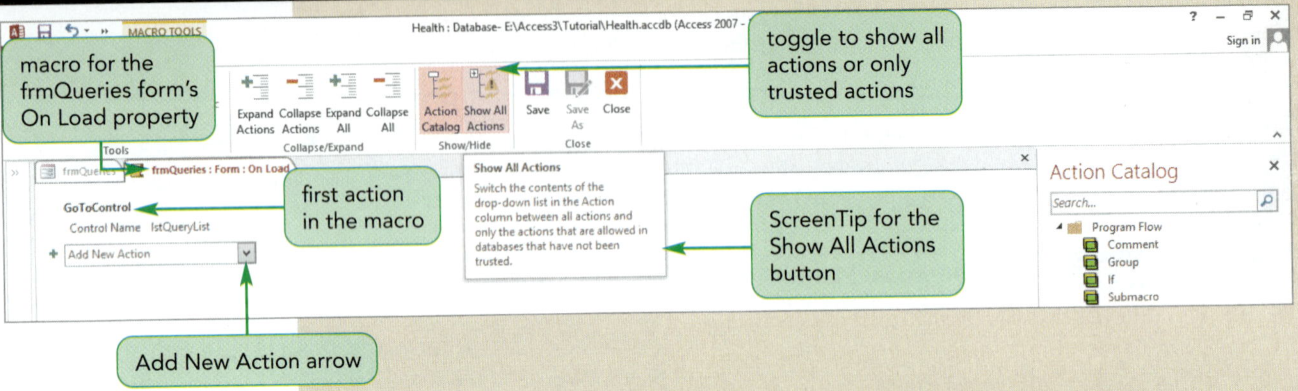

By default, Access displays only trusted actions, but you can display all actions by clicking the Show All Actions button. The actions that are categorized as unsafe actions (not trusted) are not displayed in the action list by default; this includes the SendKeys action. This action is considered unsafe because an inexperienced developer could use the SendKeys action to send keystrokes to the database application that could delete data, for instance. Because you need to use the SendKeys action and you understand the risks, you'll display all actions so you can select it from the menu.

6. On the DESIGN tab, in the Show/Hide group, click the **Show All Actions** button to toggle it on, click the **Add New Action** arrow, scroll down the list, and then click **SendKeys**. The list closes, and SendKeys becomes the new action with two arguments. You'll use the Keystrokes value of *{Down}*, which represents the down arrow keystroke, and a Wait value of *No*, which prevents the macro from pausing when it runs. (If the macro pauses, the down arrow keystroke might not be received right away and the first query in the list box may not receive the focus.)

   Trouble? If SendKeys isn't in the list, check the Show All Actions button; if it has a white background, it is toggled off. Click it again and then click the Add New Action arrow to select the SendKeys action.

7. Type **{Down}** in the Keystrokes box to complete the macro. See Figure 10-33.

Figure 10-33 **Completed macro for the form's On Load property**

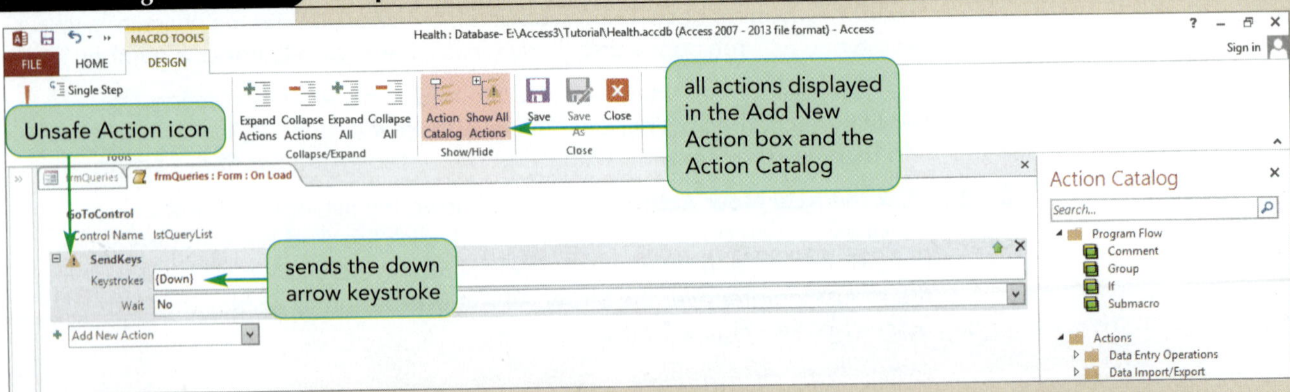

8. Hover the mouse pointer over the icon to the left of the SendKeys action. The icon's ScreenTip of "Unsafe Action" identifies that the action isn't a trusted action.

9. Save the macro, and then close the Macro Designer tab to return to the frmQueries form in Design view.

Now you'll create the macros for the Preview and Display command buttons and the list box.

To create the macros for the command buttons and the list box:

1. Click the **Preview** command button, click the **On Click** box (if necessary), click its **Build** button to open the Choose Builder dialog box, and then click the **OK** button to open the Macro Designer.

   When users click the Preview command button, the query selected in the list box should open in Print Preview.

2. Click the **Add New Action** arrow, scroll down the list, and then click **OpenQuery**. The list closes, and OpenQuery becomes the new action with three arguments.

   You'll enter the expression =[lstQueryList] in the Query Name box to indicate the query to be opened is equal to the name of the query that is selected in the lstQueryList list box.

3. In the Query Name box, type an **equal sign** (**=**). The Query Name arrow to the right of the Query Name box changes to the Expression Builder button.

4. Click the **Expression Builder** button to open the Expression Builder dialog box, double-click **lstQueryList** in the Expression Categories column, and then click the **OK** button to close the dialog box. The expression *= [lstQueryList]* is now displayed in the Query Name box.

5. Click the **View** arrow, and then click **Print Preview** to complete the macro. See Figure 10-34.

Figure 10-34 Completed macro for the Preview command button

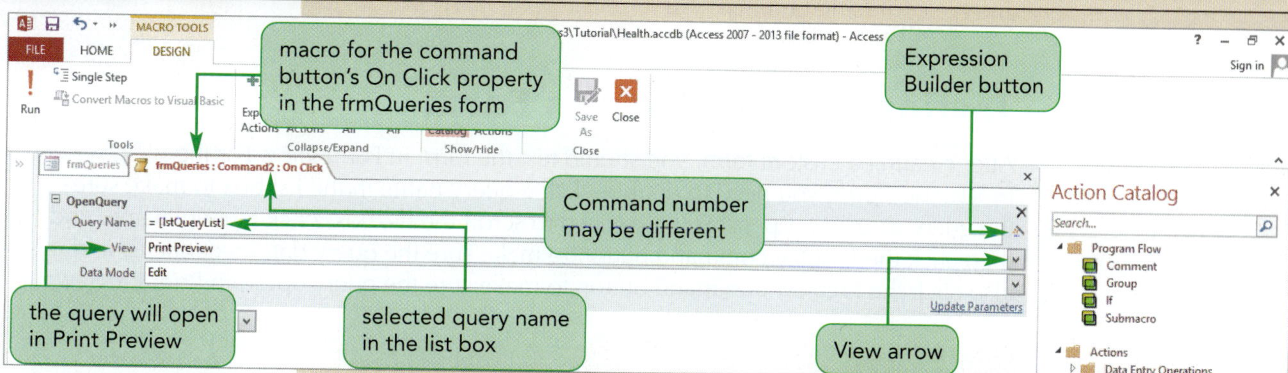

Because you did not set the Name property for the command buttons, the tab displays the default name of Command2 (your name might be different).

6. Save the macro, and then close the Macro Designer.

   Next you'll create the macro for the Display command button.

7. Repeat Steps 1 to 4 for the Display command button.

8. Set the View property for the OpenQuery action to **Datasheet** (if necessary). See Figure 10-35.

Figure 10-35 Completed macro for the Display command button

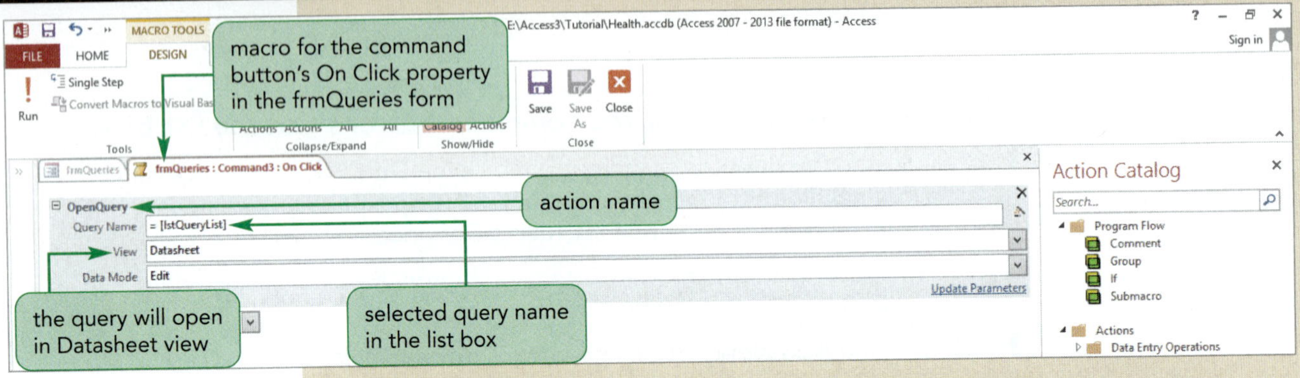

9. Save the macro, and then close the Macro Designer tab.

   Next you'll add a macro that will open a query in datasheet view if the user double-clicks on a query name in the list box.

10. Click the **list box**, click the **On Dbl Click** box, click its **Build** button ... to open the Choose Builder dialog box, and then click the **OK** button to open the Macro Designer.
11. Repeat Steps 2 to 4, and then set the View property for the OpenQuery action to **Datasheet** (if necessary).
12. Save the macro, and then close the Macro Designer tab.
13. Close the property sheet, save your form changes, and then switch to Form view.

You have finished creating the macros for the form. Next, you will test the list box and the command buttons.

Testing the frmQueries Form

After creating a custom form, you should test the form in Form view. For the frmQueries form, you need to double-click a query name in the list box to make sure the query datasheet opens. You also need to scroll the list box, click a query name, and then click the Display command button to make sure the query datasheet opens, and also click the Preview command button to make sure the query opens in Print Preview.

To test the form's design:

1. Double-click the first query name in the list box to verify that the correct query datasheet opens, and then close the query to make the frmQueries form the active object.
2. Repeat Step 1 for each of the other query names in the list box.
3. Click a query name in the list box, click the **Preview** command button to verify that the correct query opens in Print Preview, and then close the Print Preview window to make the frmQueries form the active object.

4. Repeat Step 3 for the other query names in the list box.
5. Click a query name in the list box, click the **Display** command button to verify that the correct query datasheet opens, and then close the query to make the frmQueries form the active object.
6. Repeat Step 5 for the other query names in the list box.

   Because the frmQueries form's Close button is disabled, you need to switch to Design view, which still has an enabled Close button, to close the form, or you can close the form by using the shortcut menu for the form object's tab.
7. Right-click the **Queries** tab, and then click **Close** on the shortcut menu.

You've completed the custom frmQueries form. The frmQueries form is a good example of a form that is designed to allow a user to easily choose a select query and view the records, without having to know how to run a query from the Navigation Pane. Next, Raj wants you to create the navigation form for the Health database. You'll incorporate the frmQueries form into this overall navigation system.

Creating a Navigation Form

The frmVisit form is a great example of navigation using a single form. You can set properties in Access to display only a single form if that's sufficient to provide the functionality users need and to restrict them from being able to accidentally use other database objects or to corrupt data. If users need access to several queries, forms, reports, or other database objects, though, another option is to build a separate navigation form. A navigation form is a form with tabs that allows you to display database objects in an organized way to users.

A database generally uses either one or more single, independent forms, or a navigation form. The choice to use one or the other generally depends on the designer's assessment of the abilities of the users of the database. If the users have little experience with databases, a navigation form approach might be better. If the users have more experience, a few well designed forms that the users could select themselves might be a better approach.

TIP

Navigation forms replace switchboards, which were available with all previous versions of Access.

Raj wants to restrict the access users have to the Health database to the queries that will be displayed in the frmQueries form, and to selected forms and reports. To control how users interact with the database, he wants you to create a navigation form that provides users access to only those database objects. Access has six predefined layouts for a navigation form with the layouts differing in the placement of tabs and subtabs. There are several navigation form styles available and Raj wants you to use the Horizontal Tabs, 2 Levels layout for the navigation form.

To create the navigation form:

1. Click the **CREATE tab**.
2. In the Forms group, click the **Navigation** button. The Navigation gallery opens. See Figure 10-36.

Figure 10-36 **Displaying the Navigation gallery**

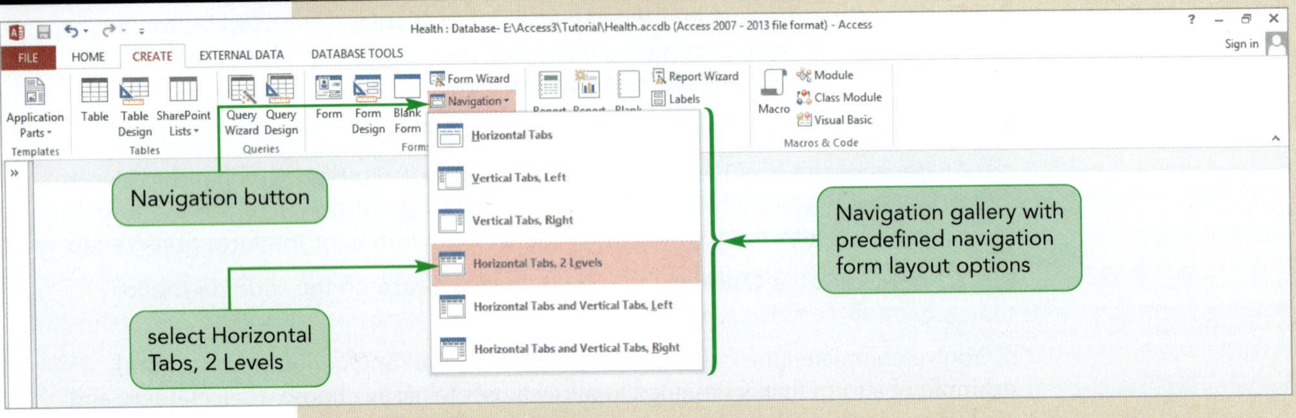

3. Click **Horizontal Tabs, 2 Levels** in the gallery, and then close the Field List pane. The navigation form with the default title of Navigation Form opens in Layout view. See Figure 10-37.

Figure 10-37 **Initial navigation form**

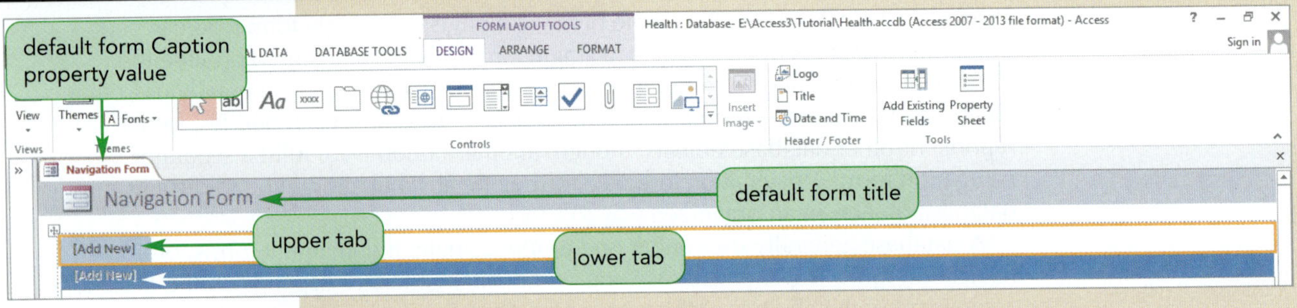

INSIGHT

Using Controls that Allow Users to Make Selections

The following controls are useful for allowing users to make selections, and you can add them to forms and reports.

- Use a tab control to switch between multiple pages on a form or report. Change the tab order for the controls in a form or report by clicking the Tab Order button in the Tools group on the DESIGN tab in Design view, and then rearrange the controls in the correct order in the Tab Order dialog box.
- Use the Auto Order option to quickly reset the tab order for all form controls so that the controls are selected top to bottom and left to right. When a form is active and a user presses the Tab key repeatedly, the focus should change from one control to another in an order that makes sense. If controls have been added or rearranged, the tab order can be affected. On the DESIGN tab, in the Tools group, click Tab Order, and then under Selection, choose Auto Order.
- Use a combo box to provide a drop-down list of options. In Design view, click the Combo Box tool in the Controls gallery on the DESIGN tab, and then select or enter options in the Combo Box Wizard dialog boxes.
- Use a hyperlink to link to an existing file, web page, database object, or email address. In Design view, click the Hyperlink button in the Controls gallery on the DESIGN tab. The Insert Hyperlink dialog box will appear, and you can select the source of the hyperlink in the Link to pane.

TIP

You can use the Chart Wizard to embed a chart in a form or report to show data visually instead of in datasheets.

Because the navigation form won't display data from the database, it will be an unbound form. You'll enter the labels *Forms*, *Reports*, and *Queries* for the upper tabs. You'll then drag the forms and reports that Raj wants to include in the navigation form from the Navigation Pane to the lower tabs. The Session 10.2 Visual Overview shows a preview of the completed upper tabs as well as a lower tab. You won't add the frmVisit form to the navigation form because the frmVisit form was created as a manual navigation form for a more advanced user. The macros for previewing and displaying the records would not function in the navigation form because they become submacros of the frmVisit subform of the frmNavigation form. The macros would have to be rewritten to work in a navigation form. If you wanted to have this functionality in a navigation form, you would create a new version of the frmVisit form that is designed to work as a subform of a navigation form. The frmVisit form you created is designed to work as a stand-alone form, not as a subform. However, the simple select queries, simple forms, and reports all work well as subforms in a navigation form.

To add names and objects to the navigation form:

1. Click the upper **[Add New]** tab, type **Forms**, and then press the **Enter** key. Forms is the name on the first tab, and a second tab appears to its right.

   Trouble? If you type the first letter and it does not appear in the tab, click the tab again to switch to editing mode.

   Trouble? If you need to correct or change a tab name, click the name, edit the name, and then press the Enter key.

2. Click the upper **[Add New]** tab to the right of the Forms tab, type **Queries**, and then press the **Enter** key.

3. Click the upper **[Add New]** tab to the right of the Queries tab, type **Reports**, and then press the **Enter** key.

   You'll next drag form and report objects from the Navigation Pane to the lower tabs. As you drag the objects, their names are added to the tabs.

TIP

You can drag only forms and reports, not queries, to tabs in a navigation form.

4. Open the Navigation Pane, click the **Forms** tab in the navigation form, and then drag the **frmVisitsAndInvoices** form from the Navigation Pane to the lower [Add New] tab. The frmVisitsAndInvoices form opens in the first tab below the Forms tab, and the tab displays the form's name.

   Trouble? If you drag the wrong object to a tab, right-click the tab, click Delete on the shortcut menu, and then drag the correct object to the tab.

   Trouble? You can rearrange the order of objects on the lower tabs by dragging the name of an object from its current tab to its new tab.

5. Drag the **frmPatient** form from the Navigation Pane to the next [Add New] tab to the right. You've added the two forms Raj wants users to work with in the Health database. See Figure 10-38.

Figure 10-38 After dragging two forms to the navigation form

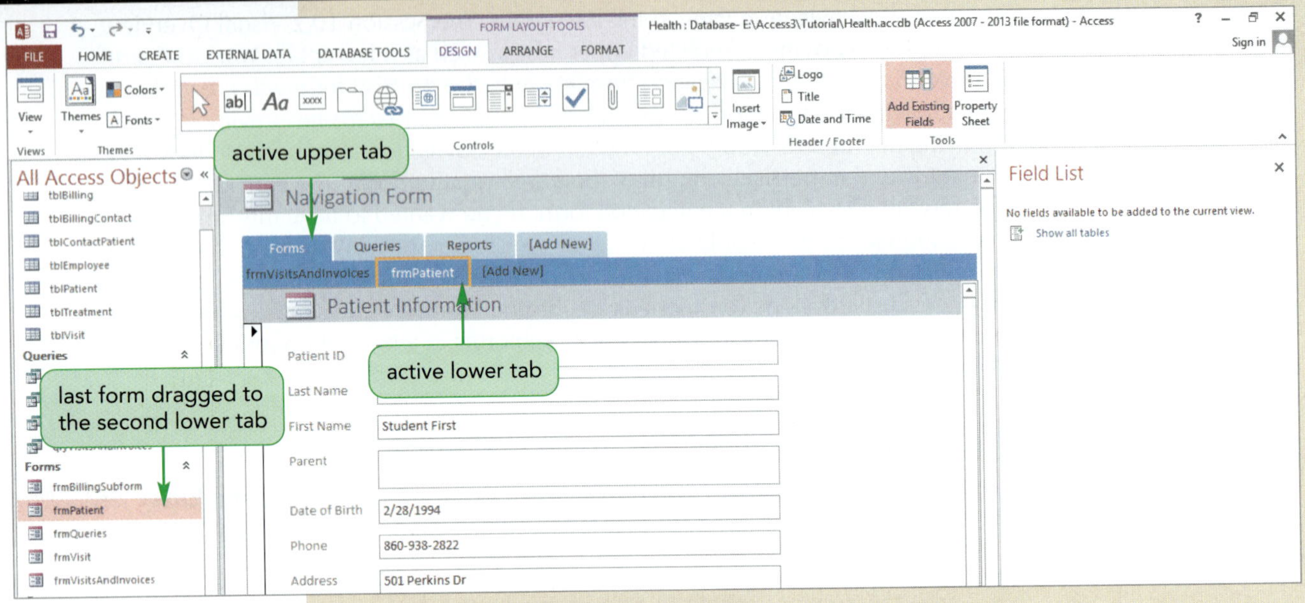

Next, you'll drag objects from the Navigation Pane to the lower tabs below the Queries and Reports tabs.

6. Click the **Queries** tab at the top of the navigation form, and then drag the **frmQueries** form from the Navigation Pane to the [Add New] tab below the Queries tab. Although you can't drag queries to a navigation form, in this case you're instead dragging a form that lists queries.
7. Click the **Reports** tab at the top of the navigation form, and then drag from the Navigation Pane to the lower tabs, in order, the **rptVisitDetails** report, the **rptVisitsAndInvoices** report, and the **rptInvoicesByItem** report. Notice that each report opens as you drag it to the form.
8. Close the Navigation Pane. You've finished adding objects to the navigation form. See Figure 10-39.

Figure 10-39 After dragging all required objects to the navigation form

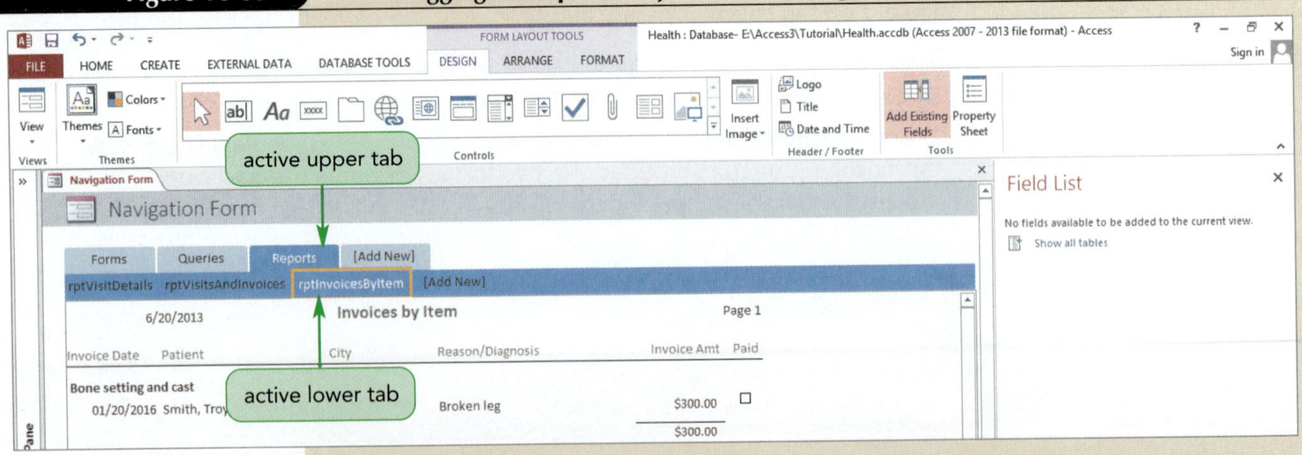

Raj asks you to delete the picture at the top of the navigation form, delete the form title, set the form's Caption property to "Health database," and then save the form.

9. Right-click the **picture** at the top of the form, click **Delete** on the shortcut menu, right-click the **form title**, and then click **Delete** on the shortcut menu.

10. Save the form as **frmNavigation**, switch to Design view, open the property sheet for the form, click the **Format** tab (if necessary), and then set the Caption property to **Health database**.

11. Switch to Form view. See Figure 10-40.

Figure 10-40 Completed navigation form

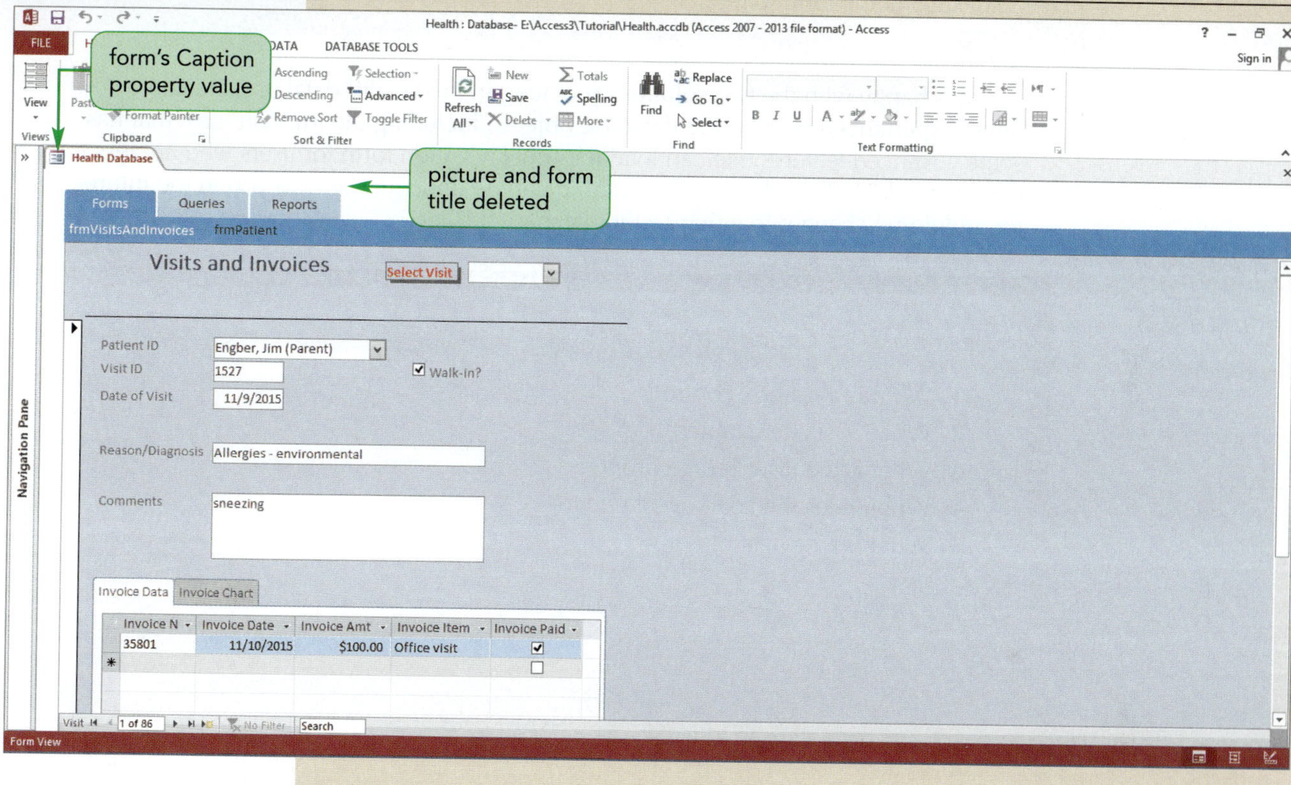

12. Navigate through the navigation form by clicking each upper tab and all of the lower tabs for each upper tab.

Trouble? When you open the navigation form, it also opens every object on the lower tabs. When you click a tab below the Forms tab, you need to click a blank area of the form to place the focus in the first field in the record.

When you click the Queries tab you may notice that the first query is not selected. This is because the frmQueries form is a subform of the frmNavigation form, and the Load event occurs on the frmNavigation form, but does not occur on its subforms. When you load the frmQueries form itself, the Load event occurs on the frmQueries form. You'll need to click a query in the Available Queries list box before you click one of the command buttons on the form.

13. Save and close the form, make a backup copy of the database, compact and repair the database, and then close it.

INSIGHT

Formatting the Print Layout for a Form

On occasion it may be important to print a form populated with data from the database. Multiple copies of the form could be printed, each containing data for a record in the database. By default, a form prints in portrait mode. However, you can change this and other aspects of print formatting using the Print Preview feature. To do so, display the form, click the FILE tab, click Print, and then click Print Preview to display the Print Preview options on the ribbon. These options allow you to set margins, set the print orientation (landscape or portrait), and specify the number of columns of the form to print.

Raj is happy with the two solutions provided in the Health database. He can direct experienced users to the database objects, including the frmVisit form that has some advanced features. He can load the frmNavigation form for users who are less experienced. He'll work with the Health database and will come to you in the future for additional changes to enhance the database further.

REVIEW

Session 10.2 Quick Check

1. What is a list box control?
2. What are system tables?
3. What is the Row Source property?
4. When does the Load event occur?
5. What is a navigation form?

ASSESS

SAM Projects

Put your skills into practice with SAM Projects! SAM Projects for this tutorial can be found online. If you have a SAM account, go to www.cengage.com/sam2013 to download the most recent Project Instructions and Start Files.

PRACTICE

Review Assignments

Data File needed for the Review Assignments: Product.accdb (*cont. from Tutorial 9*)

Raj wants you to create a user interface for the Product database. To help with this request, complete the following steps:

1. Open the **Product** database you worked with in Tutorial 9. Delete the action queries, qryAppendSterile, qryDeletePriceLess200, qryMakeSpecialEnviron, and qrySpecialDiscount. If you want to keep the action queries, first save a copy of the Product database as Product_T9, and then delete the action queries.
2. Design and create a form named **frmQueries** that has the following components and characteristics:
   a. Use the text **Health Queries** on the form's tab.
   b. In the attached label, change the caption to **Queries Available**, formatted with a 12-point, bold font, move the label above the list box, and increase the width of the label to fit the text.
   c. Add a list box with a Name property value of **lstQueryList** that displays all the query names contained in the Product database, excluding those that start with a "~" character. To place the query names in the list box, use a SQL SELECT statement to retrieve the query names from the MSysObjects table, and display the queries in alphabetical order. (*Hint*: Use the same SQL select query that you used in the tutorial.) Widen the list box to approximately 2.5 inches.
   d. Add two command buttons below the list box. The left command button displays the Preview icon above the word **Preview**, and the right command button displays the MS Access Query icon above the word **Display**.
   e. Create macros for the form (when the form loads, move the focus to the first query name in the list box), the list box (when a user double-clicks a query name), and both command buttons (when a user clicks a command button). Double-clicking a query name has the same effect as selecting a query name in the list box and clicking the right command button. Both events cause Access to display the query datasheet for the selected query. Clicking the left command button opens the selected query in Print Preview.
   f. Set the background color of the Detail section to Maroon 2 in the Standard Colors section and the background color of the list box to Maroon 1, and then disable the form's shortcut menu, record selectors, and navigation buttons.
   g. Test the form.
3. Create a navigation form named **frmNavigation**, using the Horizontal Tabs, 2 Levels layout that includes the following tab names and objects:
   a. Use **Forms** as the name for the left tab, and place the following forms below it, in order: frmSupplier, frmProduct, and frmSuppliersWithProducts.
   b. Use **Queries** as the name for the second tab, and place the frmQueries form below it.
   c. Use **Reports** as the name for the third tab, and place the following reports below it, in order: rptSupplier, rptSupplierProducts, and rptProductsAvailable.
   d. Delete the navigation form's picture and title, and change the tab name to **Vendor database**.
   e. Test the navigation form.
4. Make a backup copy of the database, compact and repair the database, and then close it.

APPLY

Case Problem 1

Data Files needed for this Case Problem: Job.accdb (*cont. from Tutorial 9*)

GoGopher! To make the Job database easier to use, Amol Mehta wants you to create a user interface for it. To help Amol with his request, complete the following steps:

1. Open the **Job** database you worked with in Tutorial 9. Delete the action queries qryAppendInactive, qryDelete312, qryMakeOnHold, and qryUpdateSpecialPlan. If you want to keep the action queries, first save a copy of the Job database as Job_T9, and then delete the action queries.
2. Design and create a form named **frmQueries** that has the following components and characteristics:
   a. Use the text **Task Queries** on the form's tab.
   b. In the attached label, change the caption to **Select a Query**, formatted with Century Gothic 12-point, bold font, position the label above the list box, and increase the width of the label to fit the text.
   c. Add a list box with a Name property value of **lstQueryList** that displays all the query names contained in the Job database, excluding those queries that start with a "~" character. To place the query names in the list box, use a SQL SELECT statement to retrieve the query names from the MSysObjects table, and display the queries in alphabetical order. (*Hint*: Use the same SQL select query that you used in the tutorial.) Widen the list box to approximately 2.75 inches.
   d. Add two command buttons below the list box. The left command button displays the Preview icon above the word **Preview**, and the right command button displays the MS Access Query icon above the word **Display**.
   e. Create macros for the form (when the form loads, move the focus to the first query name in the list box), the list box (when a user double-clicks a query name), and both command buttons (when a user clicks a command button). Double-clicking a query name has the same effect as selecting a query name in the list box and clicking the right command button. Both events cause Access to display the query datasheet for the selected query. Clicking the left command button opens the selected query in Print Preview.
   f. Set the background color of the Detail section to Aqua Blue 2 in the Standard Colors section and the background color of the list box to Aqua Blue 1, and then disable the shortcut menu, record selectors, and navigation buttons.
   g. Test the form.
3. Create a navigation form named **frmNavigation**, using the Horizontal Tabs, 2 Levels layout that includes the following tab names and objects:
   a. Use **Forms** as the name for the left tab, and place the following forms below it, in order: frmPlanInfo and frmPlansWithMembers.
   b. Use **Queries** as the name for the second tab, and place the frmQueries form below it.
   c. Use **Reports** as the name for the third tab, and place the following reports below it, in order: rptPlanList, rptPlanMembership, and rptMemberLabels.
   d. Delete the navigation form's picture and title, and change the tab name to **Task database**.
   e. Test the navigation form.
4. Make a backup copy of the database, compact and repair the database, and then close it.

TROUBLESHOOT

Case Problem 2

Data File needed for this Case Problem: Lesson.accdb (*cont. from Tutorial 9*)

O'Brien Educational Services Karen O'Brien wants the Lesson database to include an easy-to-use interface. To help Karen with her request, complete the following steps:

1. Open the **Lesson** database you worked with in Tutorial 9.

Troubleshoot 2. Open the **frmQueries** form. Troubleshoot and fix the following problems with this form:

   a. The following action queries appear in the lstQueryList list box but should not be displayed in the list box and should not be in the database: qryAppendSemiPrivate, qryDeleteLess216, qryMakeSpecialSession, and qryUpdateLength4to5.

   b. When you click the Preview button, the query is not displayed in Print Preview.

   c. When you click the Display button, nothing happens. When the user clicks the Display button, the datasheet for the selected query should be displayed.

Troubleshoot 3. Open the navigation form named **frmNavigation.** Troubleshoot and fix the following problems with this form:

   a. The **Forms** tab should have the following forms below it: frmStudent and frmTutorInfo.

   b. The **Queries** form should have the following form below it: frmQueries.

   c. The **Reports** tab should have the following reports below it: rptTutorList, rptTutorSessions, and rptStudentMailingLabels.

   d. There should be only three tabs; Forms, Queries, Reports.

   e. The text on the tab for the navigation form should be **O'Brien database**.

4. Make a backup copy of the database, compact and repair the database, and then close it.

APPLY

Case Problem 3

Data File needed for this Case Problem: Pet.accdb (*cont. from Tutorial 9*)

Rosemary Animal Shelter Ryan Lang wants the Pet database to include an easy-to-use user interface. To help him with his request, complete the following steps:

1. Open the **Pet** database you worked with in Tutorial 9. Delete the action queries qryAppendCages, qryDeleteLess100, qryMakeSpecialDonation, and qryUpdateMoney. If you want to keep the action queries, first save a copy of the Pet database as Pet_T9, and then delete the action queries.
2. Design and create a form named **frmQueries** that has the following components and characteristics:

   a. Use the text **Animal Shelter Queries** on the form's tab.

   b. In the attached label, change the caption to **Choose a query**, formatted with a 14-point, bold font, move the label above the list box, and increase the width of the label to fit the text.

   c. Add a list box with a Name property value of **lstQueryList** that displays all the query names contained in the Pet database, excluding those queries that start with a "~" character. To place the query names in the list box, use a SQL SELECT statement to retrieve the query names from the MSysObjects table, and display the queries in alphabetical order. (*Hint*: Use the same SQL select query that you used in the tutorial.) Widen the list box to approximately 2.5 inches.

   d. Add two command buttons below the list box. The left command button displays the Preview icon above the word **Preview**, and the right command button displays the MS Access Query icon above the word **Display**.

   e. Create macros for the form (when the form loads, move the focus to the first query name in the list box), the list box (when a user double-clicks a query name), and both command buttons (when a user clicks a command button). Double-clicking a query name has the same effect as selecting a query name in the list box and clicking the right command button. Both events cause Access to display the query datasheet for the selected query. Clicking the left command button opens the selected query in Print Preview.

f. Set the background color of the Detail section to Light Gray 2 in the Standard Colors section and the background color of the list box to Light Gray 1, and then disable the form's shortcut menu, record selectors, and navigation buttons.

g. Test the form.

3. Create a navigation form named **frmNavigation**, using the Horizontal Tabs, 2 Levels layout that includes the following tab names and objects:
   a. Use **Forms** as the name for the left tab, and place the following forms below it, in order: frmPatronDonations and frmPatronInfo.
   b. Use **Queries** as the name for the second tab, and place the frmQueries form below it.
   c. Use **Reports** as the name for the third tab, and place the following reports below it, in order: rptDogsAdopted, rptPatronList, and rptPatronDonations.
   d. Delete the navigation form's picture and title, and change the tab name to **Animal Shelter database**.
   e. Test the navigation form.
4. Make a backup copy of the database, compact and repair the database, and then close it.

CREATE

Case Problem 4

Data File needed for this Case Problem: Vacation.accdb *(cont. from Tutorial 9)*

Stanley EcoTours Janice and Bill Stanley want you to create a user-friendly interface for the Vacation database. To help them with their request, complete the following steps:

1. Open the **Vacation** database you worked with in Tutorial 9. Delete the action queries. If you want to keep the action queries, first save a copy of the Vacation database as Vacation_T9, and then delete the action queries.
2. Design and create a form named **frmQueries** that has the following components and characteristics:
   a. Appropriate text on the form's tab.
   b. A list box that will contain all of the queries except for the system queries. Recall that system query names begin with the ~ character. The list box should have an appropriate label above the list box, and should be wide enough to display the longest query name.
   c. Add two command buttons below the list box. Choose appropriate functionality for the command buttons that will display the results of the selected query, or display the query in Design view. Create macros that will perform the appropriate functions for each command button.
   d. Set appropriate formatting including font, font size, and color for the list box and Detail section. Disable the form's shortcut menu, record selectors, and navigation buttons.
   e. Test the form.
3. Create a navigation form named **frmNavigation**, using an appropriate layout that will display the following database objects: frmGuestInfo, frmGuestsWithReservations, frmQueries, rptTourReservations, and rptGuestLabels.
   a. Delete the navigation form's picture and title, and change the tab name to **Stanley database**.
   b. Apply an appropriate design theme.
   c. Test the navigation form.
4. Make a backup copy of the database, compact and repair the database, and then close it.

TUTORIAL **11**

Using and Writing Visual Basic for Applications Code

Creating VBA Code for the Health Database

OBJECTIVES

Session 11.1

- Learn about user-defined functions, Sub procedures, and modules
- Review and modify an existing Sub procedure in an event procedure
- Create a function in a standard module
- Test a procedure in the Immediate window

Session 11.2

- Create event procedures
- Compile and test functions, Sub procedures, and event procedures
- Create a field validation procedure

Case | ***Chatham Community Health Services***

Raj Gupta and Kelly Schwarz are pleased with your progress in developing the user interface for the Health database. They realize that many different people will be entering information in the Health database. Whenever there is manual entry of data, there is always the potential for typographical errors. Raj and Kelly want you to modify the frmVisit, frmPatient, and frmVisitsAndInvoices forms to make data entry easier and to highlight important information on them. To make these modifications, you will write Visual Basic for Applications code to perform the necessary operations.

STARTING DATA FILES

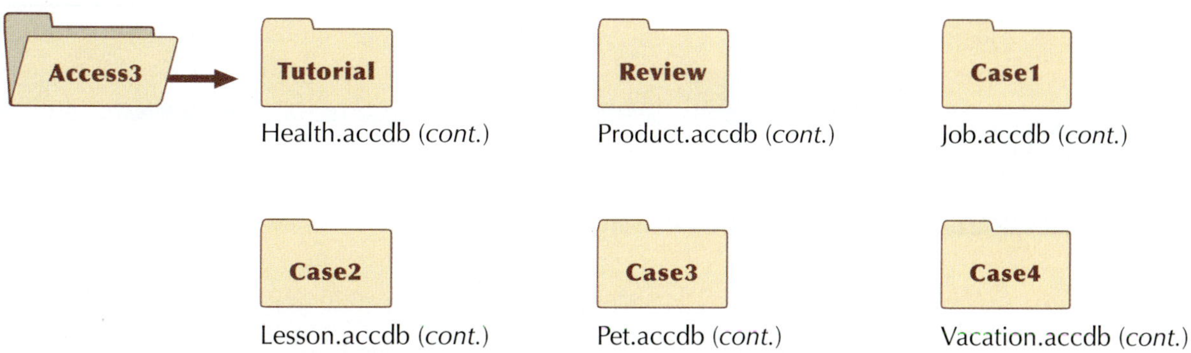

Session 11.1 Visual Overview:

Each Sub procedure begins with a **Sub statement**, which marks the start of a new Sub procedure.

Each **Case statement** designates the start of an alternative set of actions.

An **assignment statement** assigns the value of an expression to a field, control, or property.

The **End Sub statement** designates the end of a Sub procedure.

The **End Select statement** designates the end of a Case control structure.

Access displays a control when its Visible property is True, and hides the control when its Visible property is False.

You can use the **Immediate window** to test VBA procedures without changing any data in the database.

Access executes the function in the Immediate window and displays the value returned by the function.

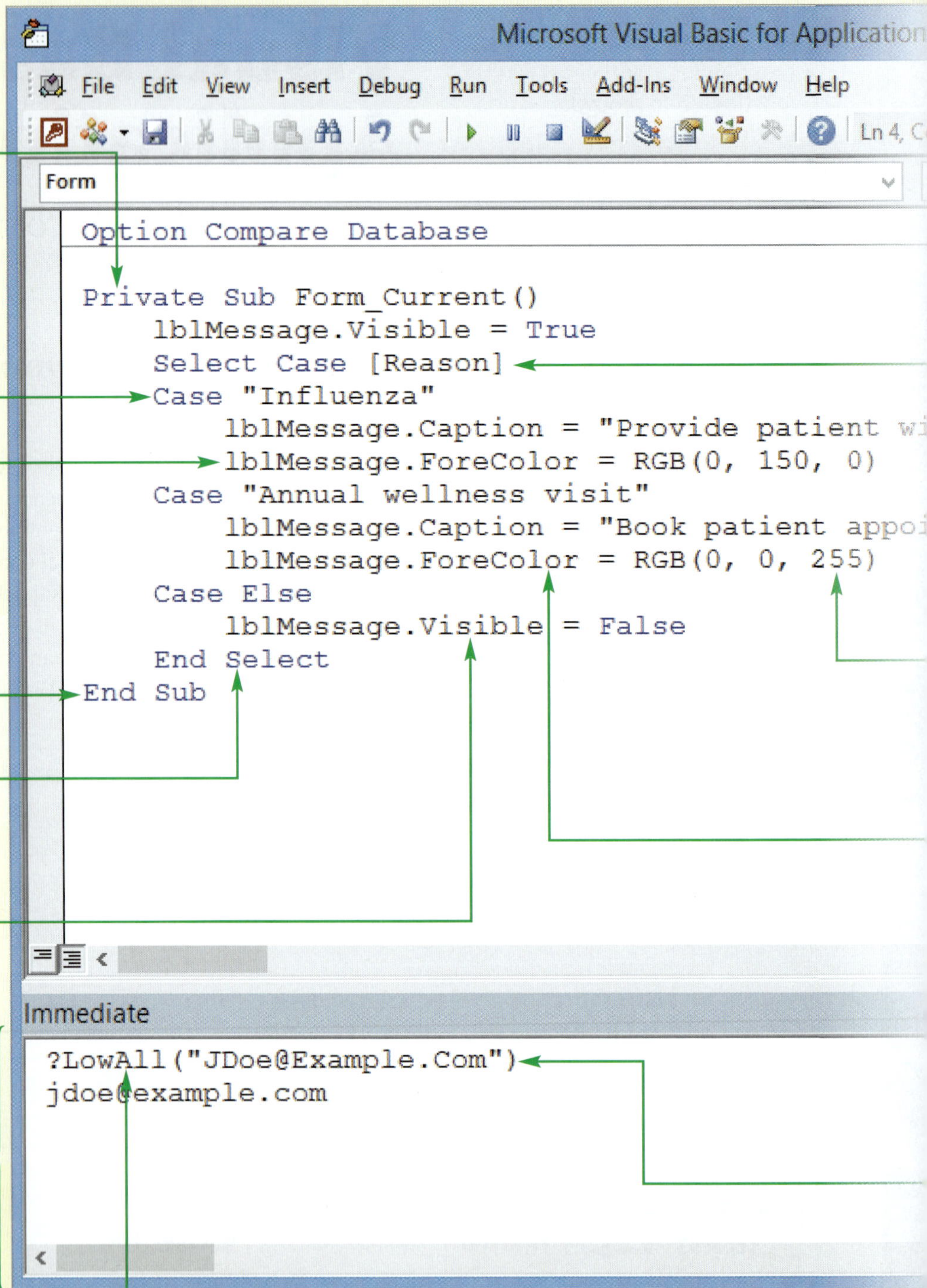

VBA Code Window

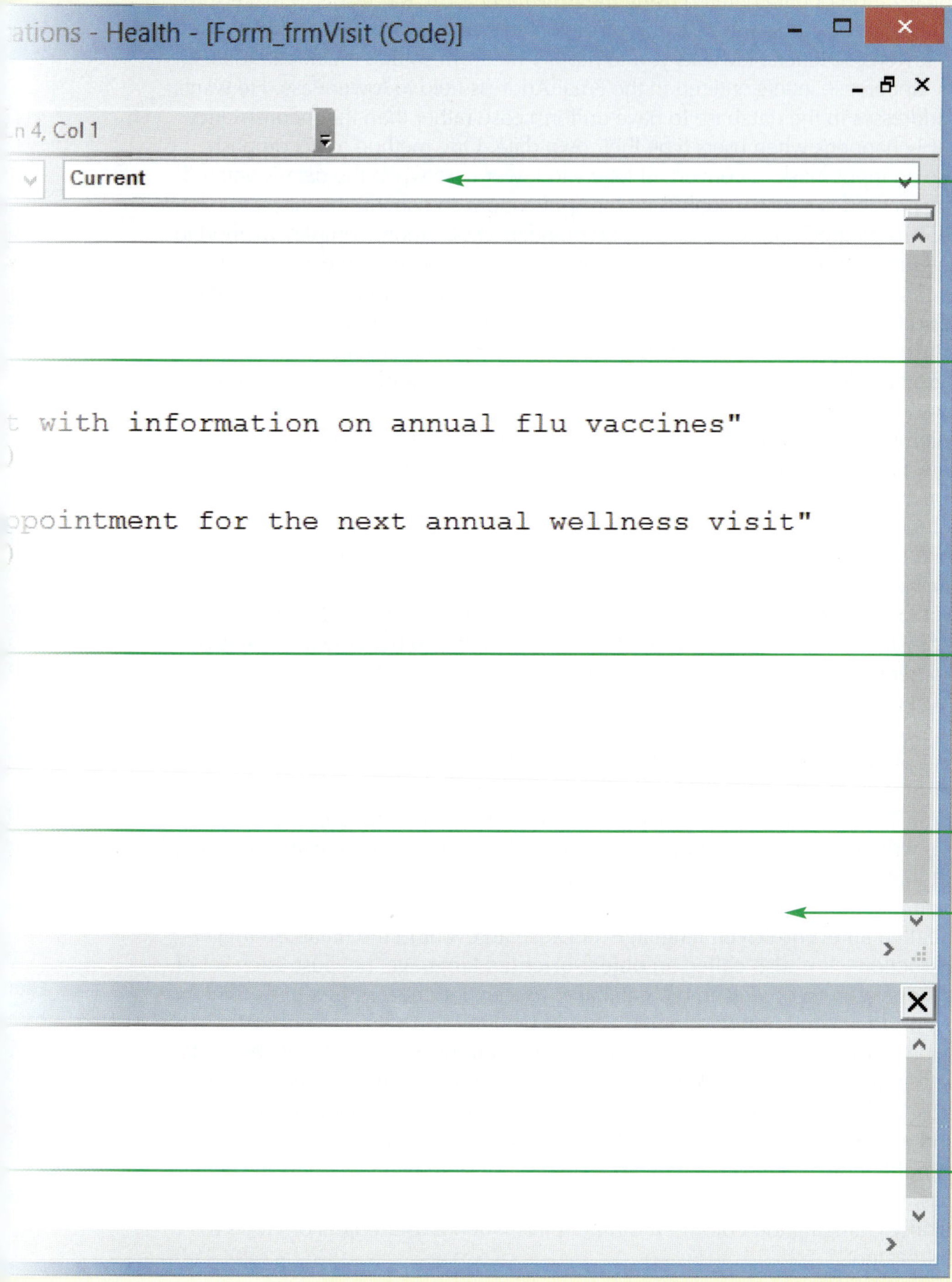

The **Procedure box** displays the event name for the current event procedure.

The **Case control structure** evaluates an expression and performs one of several alternative actions based on the resulting value of the evaluated expression.

The **RGB function** returns an RGB (red, green, blue) color value, indicating the relative intensity of red (first value), green (second value), and blue (third value) in the color of a property for a control.

A control's **ForeColor property** determines the control's foreground, or font, color.

The **Code window** is the window in which you create, modify, and display specific VBA procedures.

To test a procedure, in the Immediate window, type the *Print* keyword or a question mark (?), followed by the procedure name, and then the value you want to test in parentheses.

Introduction to Visual Basic for Applications

Your next task in the development of the Health database is to add a procedure to ensure proper capitalization of data entered using the frmPatient form. Raj wants to make sure that all values entered in this form's EmailAddress field will be stored in the tblPatient table using lowercase letters. He asks you to modify the form so that it will automatically convert any uppercase letters entered in the EmailAddress field to lower case. He wants the email addresses in the database to have uniform case rather than the inconsistency that inevitably happens when users type their own data. One method to accomplish this is to use an input mask to convert all letters to lower case when the data is entered. An alternate method is to use Visual Basic for Applications to convert the letters to lower case. This method could be used as the foundation of a more complex method to validate an email address. An input mask can restrict characters during data entry, but Visual Basic for Applications could also check to see if the email address contains the @ symbol, and a valid suffix such as .com, which an input mask cannot do.

Visual Basic for Applications (VBA) is the programming language provided with Access and other Office programs. VBA has a common syntax and a set of common features for all Microsoft Office programs, but it also has features that are unique for each Microsoft Office program due to each program's distinct structure and components. For example, because Access has fields, tables, queries, forms, other objects, tab controls, subforms, and other controls that are unique to Access, VBA for Access includes features that support these particular components. In contrast, because Microsoft Excel does not have these same Access components, VBA for Excel does not support them, but does support cells, ranges, and worksheets—three of the basic structures of Excel. The fundamental VBA skills you learn for one of the Microsoft Office programs transfer to any other Microsoft Office program, but to become proficient with VBA in another program, you first need to master its unique aspects.

When you use a programming language, such as VBA, you write a set of instructions to direct the computer to perform specific operations in a specific order, similar to writing a set of instructions for a recipe or an instruction manual. The Visual Overview for Session 11.1 shows the VBA Code window with instructions for Access to use in the frmVisit form. The process of writing instructions in a programming language is called **coding**. You write the VBA instructions, each of which is called a **statement**, to respond to an event that occurs with an object or a form control in a database. An event could be a click on a button, or activating a textbox control. A language such as VBA is, therefore, called an **event-driven language**, because an event in the database triggers a set of instructions. It is also called an **object-oriented language**, because each set of instructions operates on objects in the database. Your experience with macros, which are also event-driven and object-oriented, should facilitate your learning of VBA. Although you must use macros if you need to assign actions to a specific keyboard key or key combination, you can use VBA for everything else you normally accomplish with macros. VBA provides advantages over using macros, such as better error-handling features and easier updating capabilities. You can also use VBA in situations that macros do not handle, such as creating your own set of statements to perform special calculations, verifying a field value based on the value of another field or set of fields, or dynamically changing the color of a form control when a user enters or views a specific field value.

Events

Recall from Tutorial 10 that an event is a state, condition, or action that Access recognizes. For example, an event occurs when you click a field or command button on a form, open an object, change a field value in a form, or press a key. Each event has an associated event property that specifies how an object responds when an event occurs. For example, each report has an OnOpen event property that specifies what happens when a user opens the report and triggers the Open event, and each form control has an OnClick event property that specifies what happens when a user clicks the control and triggers the Click event. Event properties appear in the property sheet for forms, reports, and controls. By default, an event property is not set to an initial value, which means that no special action takes place when the event occurs.

In Tutorial 10, you set event property values to macro names and Access executed the macros when those events occurred. You can also create a group of statements using VBA code and set an event property value to the name of that group of statements. Access then executes the group of statements, or procedure, when the event occurs. Such a procedure is called an event procedure. Access has over 60 events and associated event properties. Figure 11-1 describes some frequently used Access events. Each event (such as the AfterUpdate event) has an associated event property (AfterUpdate) and event procedure (ContractNum_AfterUpdate for the AfterUpdate event procedure for the ContractNum control).

Figure 11-1 **Frequently used Access events**

Event	Description
AfterUpdate	Occurs after changed data in a control or a record is updated
BeforeUpdate	Occurs before changed data in a control or a record is updated
Click	Occurs when a user presses and then releases a mouse button over a control in a form
Current	Occurs when the focus moves to a record, making it the current record, or when a form is refreshed or requeried
DblClick	Occurs when a user presses and releases the left mouse button twice over a control in a form within the double-click time limit
Delete	Occurs when a user performs some action, such as pressing the Delete key, to delete a record, but before the record is actually deleted
GotFocus	Occurs when a form or a form control receives the focus
Load	Occurs when a form is opened and its records are displayed
MouseDown	Occurs when a user presses a mouse button
NoData	Occurs after Access formats a report for printing that has no data (the report is bound to an empty recordset), but before the report is printed; you use this event to cancel the printing of a blank report
Open	Occurs when a form is opened, but before the first record is displayed; for reports, the event occurs before a report is previewed or printed

Procedures

When you work with VBA, you code a group of statements to perform a set of operations or calculate a value, and then you attach the group of statements to the event property of an object. Access then executes these statements every time the event occurs for that object or control. Each group of statements is called a procedure. The two types of procedures are Function procedures and Sub procedures.

A **user-defined function**, or **function**, performs operations, returns a value, accepts input values, and can be used in expressions (recall that an expression is a calculation resulting in a single value). For example, some of the Health database queries use built-in Access functions, such as Sum, Count, and Avg, to calculate a sum, a record count, or an average. To meet Raj's request, you will create a function named LowAll by entering the appropriate VBA statements. The LowAll function will accept the value entered in a field text box—in this case, the EmailAddress field—as an input value, convert all characters of the field value to lower case, and then return the changed field value to be stored in the database and displayed in the field text box.

A **Sub procedure** executes instructions and accepts input values, but does not return a value and cannot be used in expressions. Most Access procedures are Sub procedures because you need the procedures to perform a series of actions or operations in response to an event. Later in this tutorial, you will create a Sub procedure that displays a message in the frmVisitsAndInvoices form only when the visit date is earlier than a specified date.

Modules

You store a group of related procedures together in an object called a **module**. Figure 11-2 shows the structure of a typical module.

Figure 11-2 **Structure of a VBA module and its procedures**

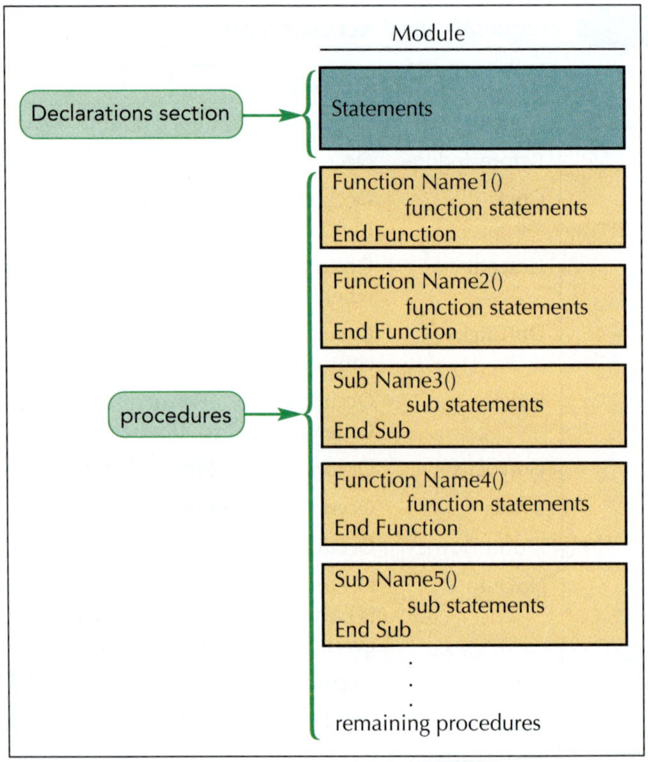

Each module starts with a **Declarations section**, which contains statements that apply to all procedures in the module. One or more procedures, which follow the Declarations section and which can be a mixture of functions and Sub procedures, constitute the rest of the module. The two basic types of modules are standard modules and class modules.

A **standard module** is a database object that is stored in memory with other database objects (queries, forms, and so on) when you open the database. You can use the procedures in a database's standard modules from anywhere in the database—even from procedures in other modules. A procedure that more than one object can use is called a **public procedure**. For example, the LowAll procedure that you will create converts all letters in the value passed to it to lower case. Although you are creating this procedure specifically to work with Email Address field values, you will place it in a standard module and make it public. You could then use the LowAll procedure for any object in the database. All standard modules are listed under the Modules bar in the Navigation Pane.

A **class module** is usually associated with a particular form or report. When you create the first event procedure for a form or report, Access automatically creates an associated form or report class module. When you add additional event procedures to the form or report, Access adds them to the class module for that form or report. Each event procedure in a class module is a **local procedure**, or a **private procedure**, which means that only the form or report for which the class module was created can use the event procedure.

Using an Existing Procedure

Before creating the LowAll procedure for Raj, you'll use an existing procedure that Raj created in the class module for the frmVisit form. The Chatham Community Health Services team would like to provide information about annual flu vaccines for patients who come to the clinic for influenza. They would also like to book the next annual wellness visit for all patients who come to the clinic for an annual wellness visit.
To remind the staff to provide information and book the next annual wellness visit, Raj created a class module that displays the message about annual flu vaccines in red text in a text box to the right of the walk-in check box, and displays the message reminding the user to book the next annual wellness visit in blue text.

For patients with any other reason for visiting the clinic, the class module makes the text box invisible.

You'll navigate through the records using the frmVisit form to observe the effects of the procedure.

To navigate a form that uses a VBA procedure:

1. Start Access, and then open the **Health** database you worked with in Tutorials 9 and 10.
2. Open the Navigation Pane (if necessary), open the **frmVisit** form in Form view, and then close the Navigation Pane. For the first record for VisitID 1538, no value is displayed to the right of the Walk-in check box because the Reason field value is neither "Influenza" nor "Annual wellness visit."
3. Click the Visit **Next record** navigation button ▶. The frmVisit form displays record 2 for VisitID 1549. Because this patient visit Reason is Influenza, "Provide patient with information on annual flu vaccines" appears in a red font to the right of the Walk-in check box. See Figure 11-3.

Figure 11-3 **Using an existing VBA procedure**

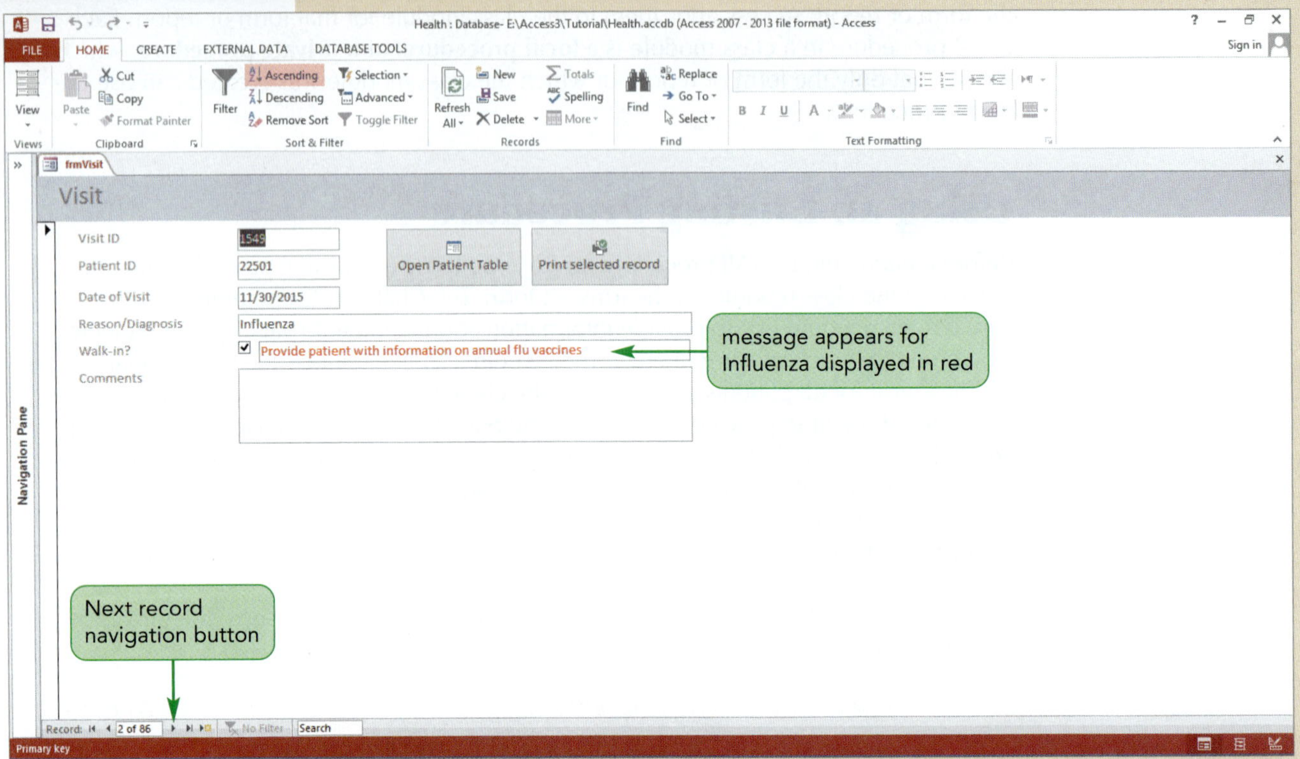

4. Click the **Next record** navigation button to display record 3 for VisitID 1662. Because the Reason/Diagnosis value for this visit is "Annual wellness visit," the text "Book patient appointment for the next annual wellness visit" is displayed in a blue font to the right of the Walk-in? check box.

Kelly asks you to change the red color for the display of "Provide patient with information on annual flu vaccines" to green so that it doesn't appear to be an urgent warning.

Displaying an Event Procedure

TIP

The control that is currently active and awaiting user interaction is said to have focus; the object and record that are currently active have focus as well.

The VBA procedure that controls the display of the message and its color for each record is in the class module for the frmVisit form. Access processes the statements in the procedure when you open the frmVisit form and also when the focus leaves one record and moves to another. The event called the **Current event** occurs when the focus shifts to the next record loaded in a form, making it the current record. This also happens when the form loads and when the form is refreshed. The **OnCurrent property** contains a reference to a macro, VBA code, or some other expression that runs when the Current event occurs.

To change the color of the display of the text "Provide patient with information on annual flu vaccines" from red to green, you'll modify the event procedure for the form's OnCurrent property. First, you'll switch to Design view, and then you'll display the event procedure.

To display the event procedure for the form's OnCurrent property:

1. Switch to Design view.
2. Right-click the **form selector** to display the shortcut menu, and then (if necessary) click **Properties** to open the property sheet for the form.
3. Click the **Event** tab (if necessary) to display the Event page of the property sheet, click the **On Current** box, and then (if necessary) drag the left edge of the property sheet to the left until the On Current property value is visible. See Figure 11-4.

Figure 11-4 **Event properties for the frmVisit form**

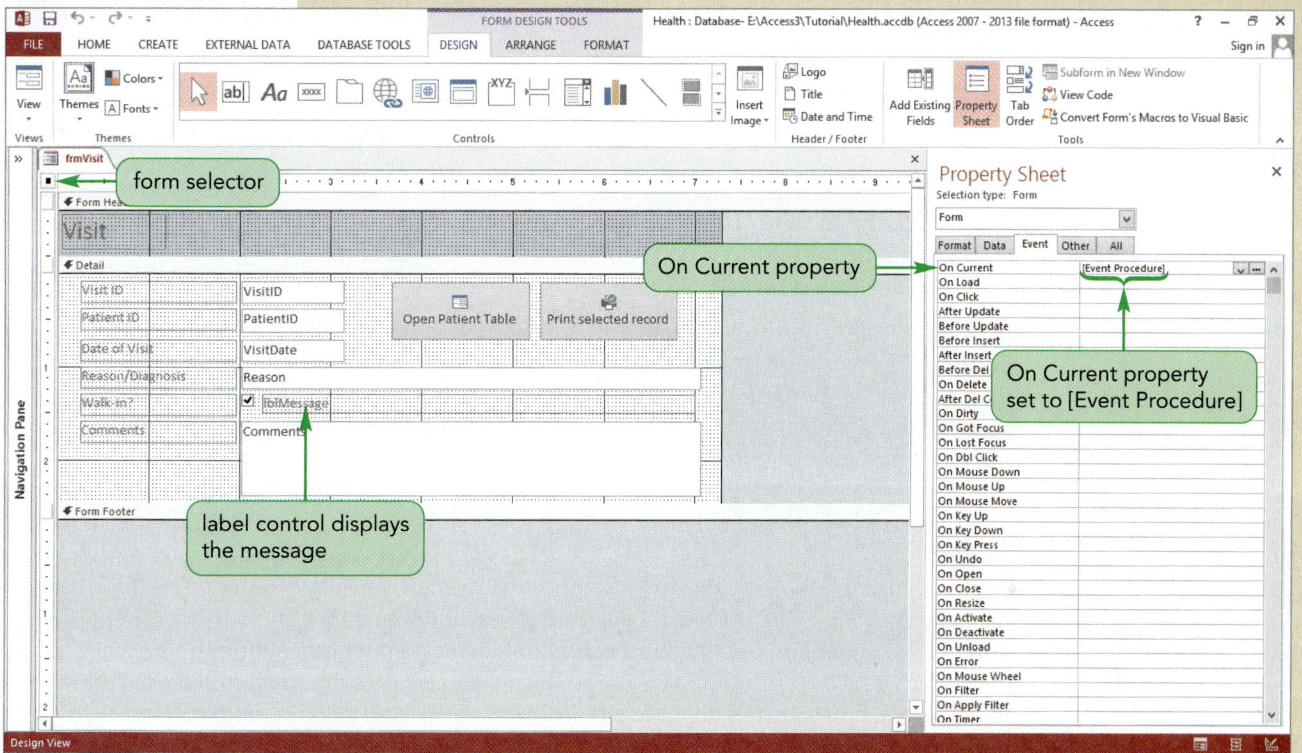

The On Current property is set to [Event Procedure], indicating that Access calls a VBA procedure when the Current event occurs. You'll click the Build button to display the procedure.

4. Click the **Build** button [...] to the right of the On Current box. The Code window opens in the Visual Basic window. See Figure 11-5.

Figure 11-5 **Code window in the Visual Basic window**

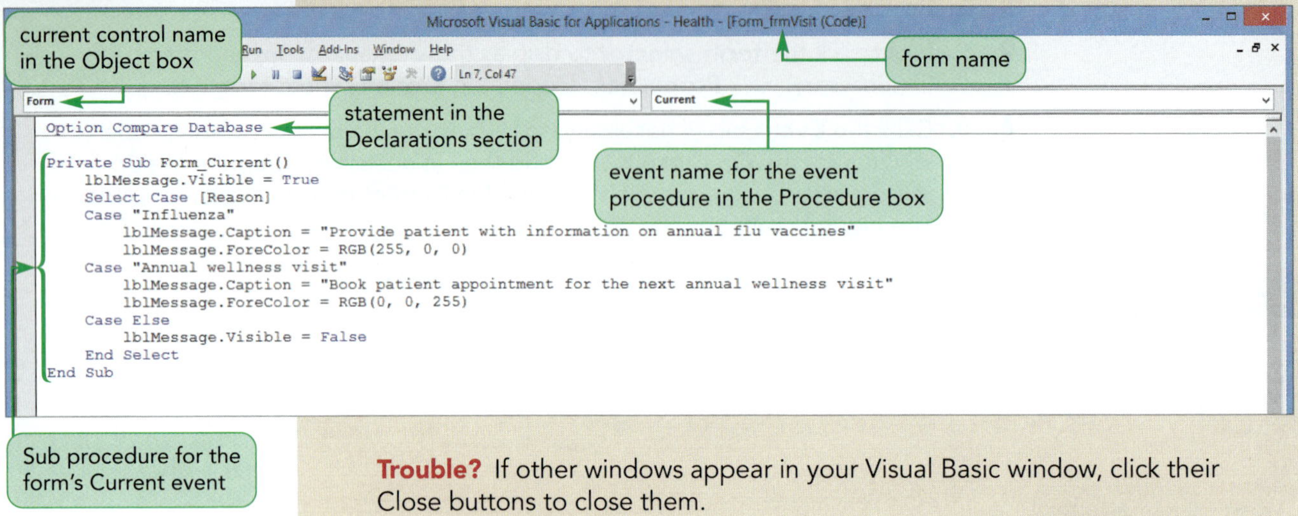


```
Option Compare Database

Private Sub Form_Current()
    lblMessage.Visible = True
    Select Case [Reason]
    Case "Influenza"
        lblMessage.Caption = "Provide patient with information on annual flu vaccines"
        lblMessage.ForeColor = RGB(255, 0, 0)
    Case "Annual wellness visit"
        lblMessage.Caption = "Book patient appointment for the next annual wellness visit"
        lblMessage.ForeColor = RGB(0, 0, 255)
    Case Else
        lblMessage.Visible = False
    End Select
End Sub
```

Trouble? If other windows appear in your Visual Basic window, click their Close buttons to close them.

Trouble? If the code window isn't maximized within the VBA window, click the maximize button.

The program you use to create and modify VBA code is called the **Visual Basic Editor** (**VBE**, or **editor** for short), and the **Visual Basic window** is the program window that opens when you use VBE. The Code window is the window in which you create, modify, and display specific VBA procedures. You can have as many Code windows open as you have modules in the database. In the Code window, the Object box (the upper-left box) indicates the current control (Form), and the Procedure box (the upper-right box) indicates the event name (Current) for the event procedure you are viewing.

All event procedures are Sub procedures. A horizontal line visually separates each procedure in the Code window. Each Sub procedure begins with a Sub statement and ends with an End Sub statement. The Sub statement includes the scope of the procedure (private or public), the name of the procedure (for example, Form_Current, which means the Current event for the form control), and opening and closing parentheses. The **scope** of a procedure indicates where the procedure is available. If its scope is public, the procedure is available in all objects in the database. If its scope is private, the procedure is available only in the object in which it is created. Event procedures are private, by default. For instance, the event procedure in the OnCurrent property in the frmVisit form is private, and other forms do not have access to this procedure code.

Notice the Option Compare statement in the Declarations section above the horizontal line. The Option Compare statement designates the technique Access uses to compare and sort text data. The default method "Database," as shown in Figure 11-5, means that Access compares and sorts letters in normal alphabetical order, using the language settings specified for Access on your computer.

The remaining statements in the Form_Current procedure shown in Figure 11-5 use only two controls in the form: the Reason field from the tblVisit table; and lblMessage, which is a label control that displays "Book patient appointment for the next annual wellness visit" or "Provide patient with information on annual flu vaccines" when it's visible. Based on the Reason field value, the statements in the procedure do the following:

- When the Reason field value is "Influenza," set Caption property for the lblMessage control to "Provide patient with information on annual flu vaccines" and set its font color to red.
- When the Reason field value is "Annual wellness visit," set the Caption property for the lblMessage control to "Book patient appointment for the next annual wellness visit" and set its font color to blue.
- When the Reason field has any other value, hide the lblMessage control.

The statements from the *Select Case [Reason]* statement to the *End Select* statement are an example of a control structure. A **control structure** is a set of VBA statements that work together as a unit. The Case control structure is a conditional control structure. A **conditional control structure** evaluates an expression—the value of the Reason field, in this case—and then performs one of several alternative actions based on the resulting value (or condition) of the evaluated expression. Each Case statement, such as *Case "Influenza"* and *Case Else*, designates the start of an alternative set of actions.

Statements such as *lblMessage.Caption = "Book patient appointment for the next annual wellness visit"* are assignment statements. An assignment statement assigns the value of an expression—"Book patient appointment for the next annual wellness visit", in this case—to a field, control, or property—the Caption property of the lblMessage control, in this case.

TIP

The RGB color model is commonly used by graphic designers and enables you to specify over 16 million different colors.

Because a property is associated with a control, you use the general form of *ControlName.PropertyName* to specify a property for a control. An assignment statement such as *lblMessage.ForeColor = RGB(255, 0, 0)*, for example, assigns a value to the ForeColor property of the lblMessage control. A control's ForeColor property determines the control's foreground, or font, color. The expression in this assignment statement uses a built-in VBA function named RGB. The RGB function returns an RGB (red, green, blue) color value, indicating the relative intensity of red (first value), green (second value), and blue (third value) in the color of a property for a control. Figure 11-6 displays a list of some common colors and the red, green, and blue values for the RGB function that produces those colors. Each color component value must be in the range 0 through 255. Instead of using the RGB function for the eight colors shown in Figure 11-6, you can use one of the VBA constants (vbBlack, vbBlue, vbCyan, vbGreen, vbMagenta, vbRed, vbWhite, or vbYellow). A **VBA constant** is a predefined memory location that is initialized to a value that doesn't change. For example, *lblMessage.ForeColor = vbRed* and *lblMessage.ForeColor = RGB(255, 0, 0)* would set the color of the lblMessage control to red. You must use the RGB function when you want colors that differ from the eight colors shown in Figure 11-6.

Figure 11-6 **RGB function values for some common colors**

Color	Red Value	Green Value	Blue Value	VBA Constant
Black	0	0	0	vbBlack
Blue	0	0	255	vbBlue
Cyan	0	255	255	vbCyan
Green	0	255	0	vbGreen
Magenta	255	0	255	vbMagenta
Red	255	0	0	vbRed
White	255	255	255	vbWhite
Yellow	255	255	0	vbYellow

INSIGHT

Assigning a Color Value

A color value can be assigned to a control property using a variety of methods. A color value could be one of the following:

- A built-in VB constant such as vbRed, vbWhite, or vbBlack.
- A set of red, green, and blue values, each ranging from 0 to 255, specified in the RGB function. For instance, RGB(0,255,0) represents the color green.
- A hexadecimal value that represents color intensities of red, green, and blue. For instance, 00FF00 represents the color green. The first two characters represent red, the second two characters represent green, and the last two characters represent blue. Similar to the RGB function, these triplets represent the intensity of each color, mixed to form the resulting color.
- A ColorIndex property value, which uses a color code specific to VBA. For instance, the color green has a ColorIndex value of 4.
- A Microsoft Access color code, which is a code specific to Microsoft Access. For instance, the color green has the Microsoft Access color code 32768.

With all those choices, which one should you use? The most common are the built-in VB constants, RGB function, and hexadecimal values. The RGB function and hexadecimal values are also used in web design and VB.NET programming, so you may find these techniques especially useful if you modify web page code as well.

The Visible property determines whether or not Access displays a control. Access displays a control when its Visible property is True, and hides the control when its Visible property is False. The *lblMessage.Visible = True* statement, which Access processes before the *Select Case [Reason]* statement, displays the lblMessage control. Because Kelly doesn't want the lblMessage control to appear for reasons other than Influenza and Annual wellness visit, the *lblMessage.Visible = False* statement hides the lblMessage control when the Reason field value doesn't equal one of the two reasons.

Modifying an Event Procedure

Kelly wants you to change the red color for the display of "Provide patient with information on annual flu vaccines". This requires changing the red RGB function value of (255, 0, 0) to the green value (0, 150, 0). To make this change, you'll modify the first set of RGB function values in the event procedure. Then you'll close the Visual Basic window and save and test your modifications.

To modify, save, and test the event procedure:

1. In the first RGB function, double-click **255** to select it, and then type **0** to replace the selected value. The RGB function is now RGB(0, 0, 0).
2. In the first RGB function, double-click the second **0**, and then type **150**. The RGB function is now RGB(0, 150, 0), which is a value that will produce a medium shade of green. See Figure 11-7.

Figure 11-7 Changing the RGB values

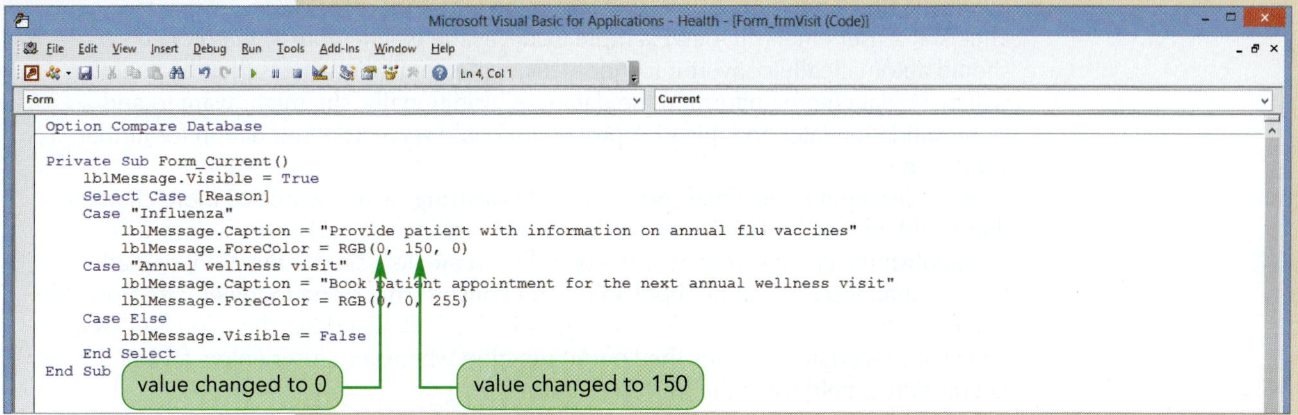

3. Click the **Save** button on the Standard toolbar to save your changes, and then click the **Close** button on the Visual Basic window title bar to close it and return to the Form window in Design view.
4. Close the property sheet, save your form design changes, and then switch to Form view.
5. Navigate to record 2 for the VisitID 1549. The text "Provide patient with information on annual flu vaccines" displays in green to the right of the Walk-in check box. Your modification to the event procedure was completed successfully. See Figure 11-8.

Figure 11-8 Viewing the forecolor change

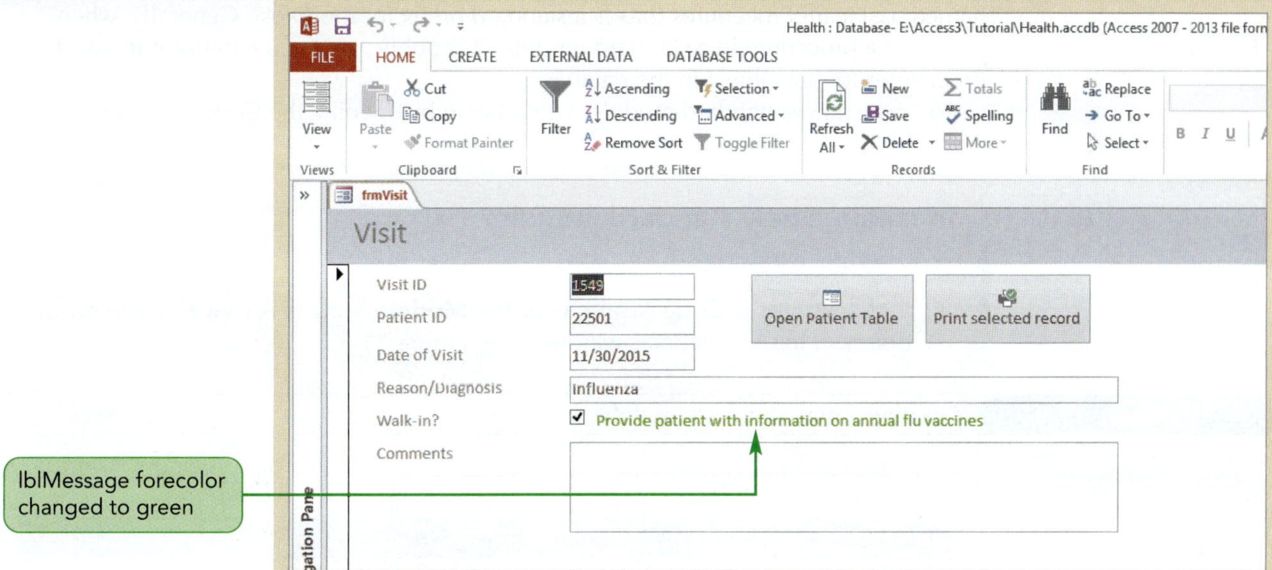

6. Close the frmVisit form.

You've completed your modifications to the event procedure. Next, you'll create the LowAll function.

Creating Functions in a Standard Module

Kelly wants you to create a VBA procedure for the frmPatient form that will automatically convert the values entered in the EmailAddress field to lower case. That is, if a user enters "JDoe@Example.Com" as the email address, the procedure should automatically convert it to "jdoe@example.com". Kelly feels that this function will make data more uniform in the database. Additionally, she might want to add some validation later and this VBA procedure could serve as a foundation for further validation code.

Any user input in the Email Address field is a **string**, which is one or more characters that could include alphabetic characters, numbers, spaces, and punctuation. To accomplish the change Kelly wants, you will first create a simple function, named LowAll, that accepts a string input value and converts that string to lower case. You will create the function by typing the statements in the Code window. Then you will create an event procedure that calls the LowAll function whenever a user enters a value in the EmailAddress field using the frmPatient form.

Whenever a user enters or changes a field value in a control or in a form and then changes the focus to another control or record, Access automatically triggers the **AfterUpdate event**, which, by default, simply accepts the new or changed entry. However, you can set the AfterUpdate event property of a control to a specific event procedure in order to have something else happen when a user enters or changes the field value. In this case, you need to set the Email Address field's AfterUpdate event property to [Event Procedure], and then code an event procedure to call the LowAll function. Calling the LowAll function will cause the entry in the Email Address field to be converted to lowercase letters before storing it in the database.

You will use the LowAll function with the frmPatient form, so you could add it to the class module for that form. Adding the function to the class module for the frmPatient form would make it a private function; that is, you could not use it in other forms or database objects. Because you might use the LowAll function in other forms in the Health database, you'll instead place the LowAll function in a new standard module named basHealthProcedures (*bas* is a standard prefix for modules). Generally, when you enter a procedure in a standard module, it is public, and you can use it in event procedures for any object in the database.

To create a new standard module, you'll begin by opening the Code window.

To create a new standard module:

1. Click the **CREATE tab**.
2. In the Macros & Code group, click the **Module** button. A new Code window opens in the Visual Basic window. See Figure 11-9.

Figure 11-9 Creating a new standard module

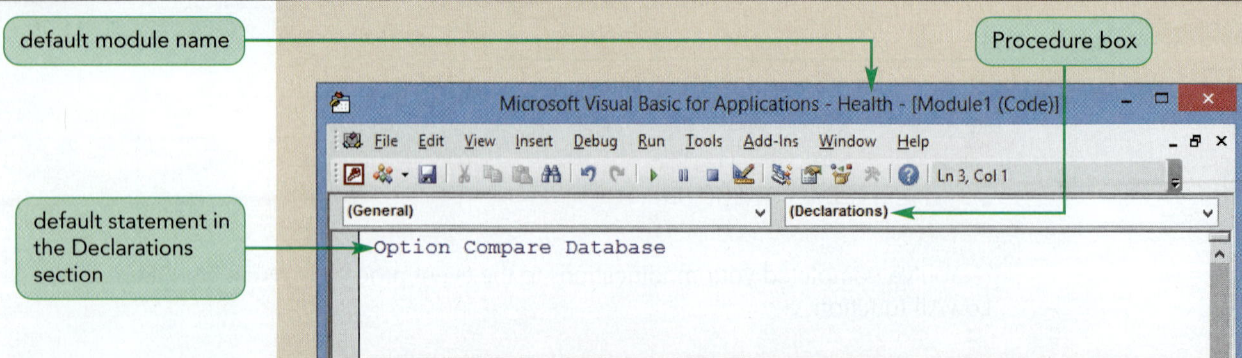

Trouble? If other windows appear in your Visual Basic window, click their Close buttons to close them.

In the Code window for the new standard module, the Procedure box displays the Declarations section as the current procedure in the module. Access automatically includes the Option Compare statement in the Declarations section of a new module. The LowAll function is a simple function that does not require additional statements in the Declarations section.

Creating a Function

Each function begins with a **Function statement** and ends with an **End Function statement**. Access visually separates each procedure in the Code window with a horizontal line. You can view a procedure's statements by selecting the procedure name from the Procedure box.

You'll start the LowAll function with the statement *Function LowAll(FValue)*. LowAll is the function name and FValue is used as a placeholder for the input value in the function definition. When a user enters a value for the Email Address field in the frmPatient form, that value will be passed to the LowAll function and substituted for FValue in the function definition. A placeholder like FValue is called a **parameter**. The value passed to the function and used in place of the parameter when the function is executed is called an **argument**. In other words, the value passed to the function is the argument, which is assigned to the parameter named FValue.

INSIGHT

VBA Naming Rules

Each VBA function name, Sub procedure name, argument name, and any other name you create must conform to the following rules:

- It must begin with a letter.
- It cannot exceed 255 characters.
- It can include letters, numbers, and the underscore character (_). You cannot use a space or any punctuation characters.
- It cannot contain keywords—such as Function, Sub, Case, and Option—that VBA uses as part of its language.
- It must be unique; that is, you can't declare the same name twice within the same procedure.

You'll enter the LowAll function in the Code window and then you'll test it. Finally, you'll attach it to an event procedure for the frmPatient form. You now can start entering the LowAll function.

To start a new function:

1. If necessary, position the insertion point two lines below the Option Compare statement.
2. Type **Function LowAll(FValue)** and then press the **Enter** key. The editor displays a horizontal line that visually separates the new function from the Declarations section and adds the End Function statement. See Figure 11-10.

Figure 11-10 **Starting a new function**

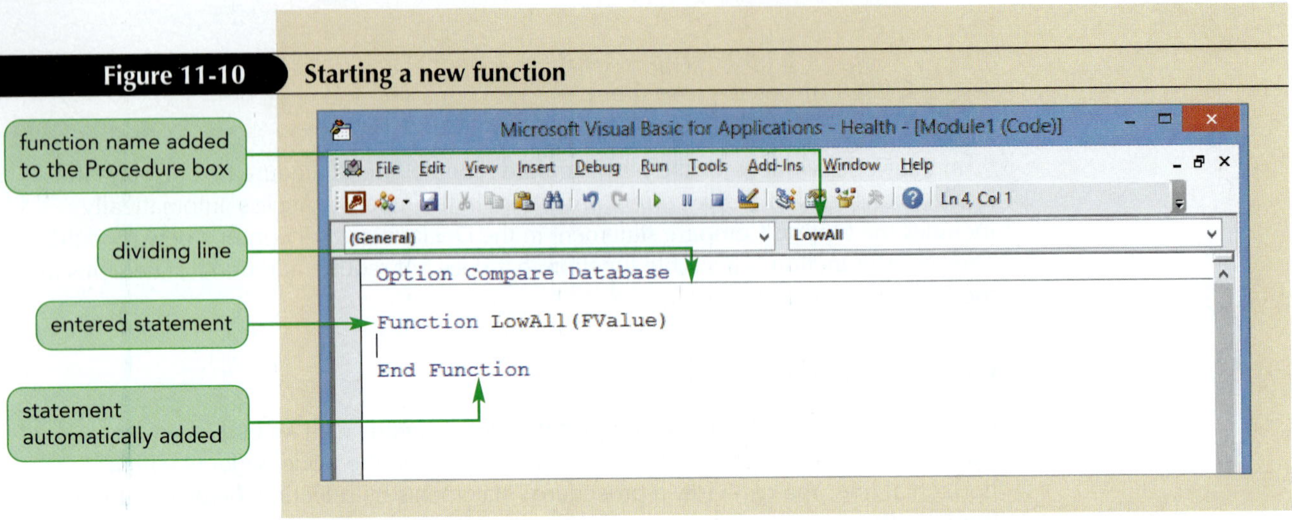

The function name LowAll now appears in the Procedure box. The editor automatically added the End Function statement and moved the insertion point to the beginning of the blank line between the Function and End Function statements, where you will enter the procedure statements. The editor displays the reserved words Function and End Function in blue. The function name and the parameter name appear in black.

The LowAll function will consist of a single executable assignment statement that you will place between the Function and End Function statements. The assignment statement you'll enter is *LowAll = LCase(FValue)*. The value of the expression, which is LCase(FValue), will be assigned to the function, which is LowAll.

The expression in the assignment statement uses a built-in Access function named LCase. The **LCase function** accepts a single string argument as input, converts the value of the argument to lowercase letters, and then returns the converted value. The assignment statement assigns the converted value to the LowAll function. Figure 11-11 illustrates this process.

Figure 11-11 **Evaluation of the assignment statement**

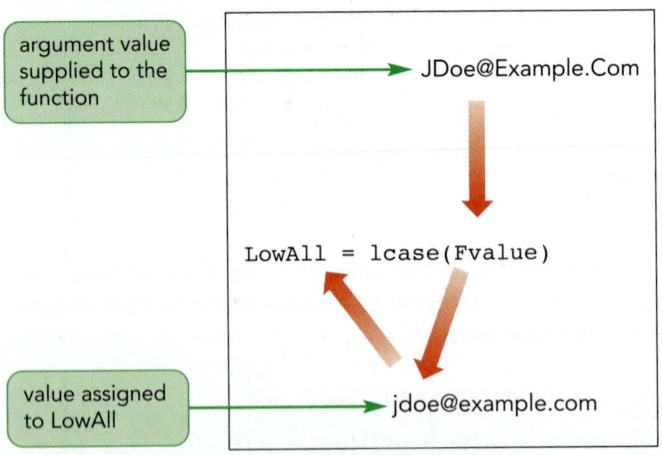

TIP

Because VBA ignores the contents of comments, you can include spaces, special characters, and mixed-case strings in your comments.

Before entering the assignment statement, you will add a comment line to explain the procedure's purpose. You can include comments anywhere in a VBA procedure to describe what the procedure does or what a statement does. Comments make it easier for you and other programmers to identify the purpose of statements in your code. You begin a comment with the word Rem (for "Remark") or with a single quotation mark ('). VBA ignores anything following the word Rem or the single quotation mark on a single line.

PROSKILLS

Written Communication: Commenting, Indenting, and Proper Case for VBA Code

Different people can use multiple approaches to solving a problem, so you should use comments in a VBA procedure to explain the purpose of the procedure and to clarify any complicated programming logic used. Most companies have documentation standards that specify the types of comments that should be included in each procedure. These standards typically require comments that identify the name of the original creator of a procedure, the purpose of the procedure, and a history of changes made to the procedure, including who made each change and for what purpose.

VBA does not require statements to be indented in procedures. However, experienced programmers indent statements to make procedures easier to read and maintain. Pressing the Tab key once indents a line four spaces to the right, which is a sufficient amount of indentation, and pressing the Shift+Tab key combination or the Backspace key once moves the insertion point four spaces to the left. As an example of indenting statements, you left-align Select Case and End Select statements to clearly show the start and end of the Case control structure, and you indent the statements between them four spaces. Commenting and indenting your procedures will help you recall the logic of the procedures you created months or years ago, and will help others understand your work.

Just as there are industry conventions for commenting and indentation, experienced programmers also use proper case for VB statements. That is, the first character of each keyword is capitalized, as in the statement End If.

To add a comment and statement to the function:

1. Click on the line between the Function and End Function statements (if necessary), and then press the **Tab** key.

   Next, you'll add the comment. The single quotation mark is a comment marker and it indicates that the text that follows is a comment and will not be executed.

Be sure to type the single quotation mark at the beginning of the comment.

2. Type **'Convert all letters of a field value to lower case** and then press the **Enter** key.

   Notice that the editor displays the comment in green and indents the new line. After entering the comment line, you can enter the assignment statement, which is the executable statement in the function that performs the actual conversion of the argument to upper case.

TIP

The editor displays a similar Quick Info banner after you type LowAll and press the spacebar; you should ignore this banner because its reminder is incorrect.

3. Type **LowAll = LCase(**

   The editor provides assistance as you enter the statement. After you type LCase and the opening parenthesis, the editor displays a Quick Info banner with a reminder that LCase accepts a single string argument. See Figure 11-12.

Figure 11-12 Entering the LowAll function in the Code window

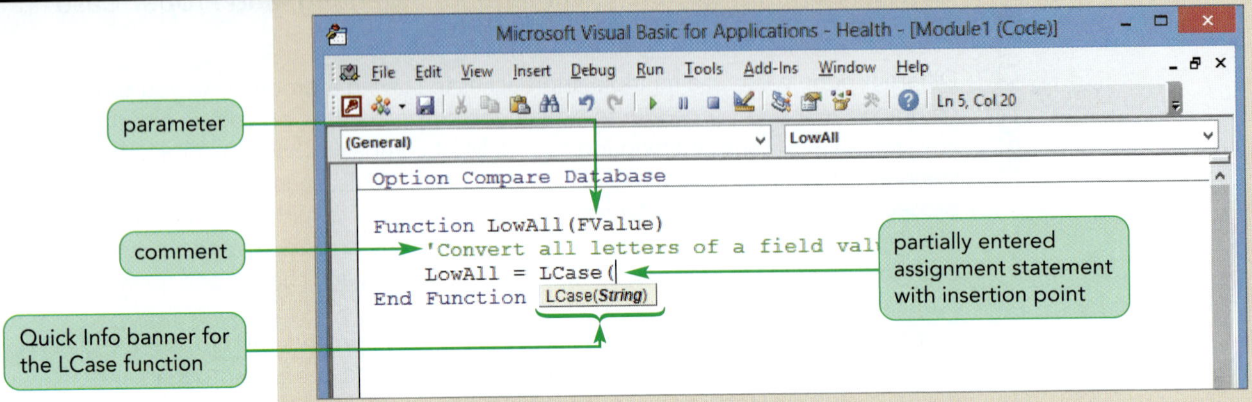

Trouble? If the Quick Info banner does not open, click Tools on the menu bar, click Options, click the Editor tab (if necessary), click the Auto Quick Info check box to select it, and then click the OK button.

You'll now finish typing the assignment statement.

4. Type **FValue)** to finish the assignment statement.

   The editor scans each statement for errors when you press the Enter key or change the focus to another statement. Because the function is complete and you want the editor to scan the line you just entered for errors, you must move the insertion point to another line.

5. Press the ↓ key to move the insertion point to the next line. Because Access finds no errors, the insertion point continues to blink on the last line. See Figure 11-13.

Figure 11-13 Complete LowAll function in the Code window

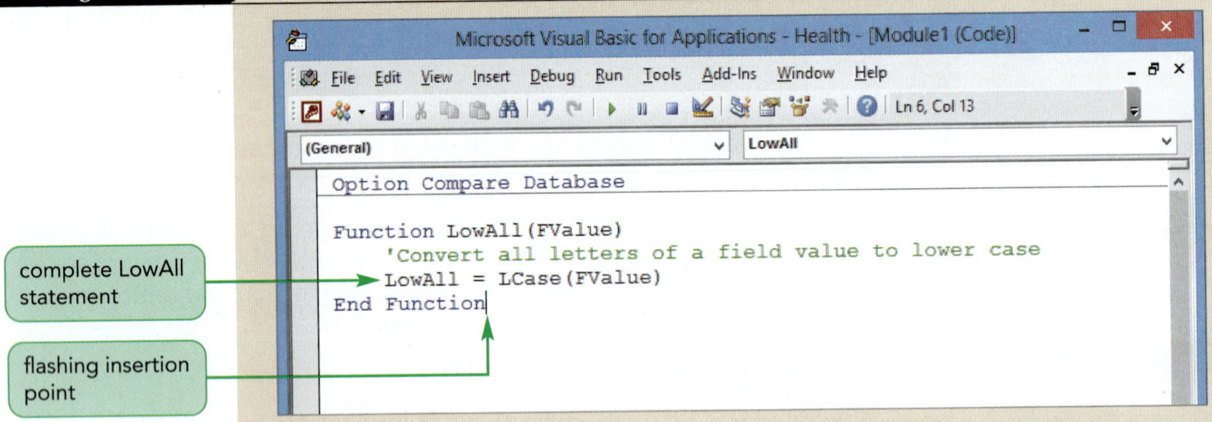

You have finished entering the function, so you'll save it before continuing with your work.

Saving a Function

When you click the Save button in the Visual Basic window, the editor saves the module and its procedures. If you are entering a long procedure, it's a good idea to save your work periodically.

To save the module:

1. Click the **Save** button on the Standard toolbar.
2. Type **basHealthProcedures** in the Module Name box, and then press the **Enter** key. The editor saves the module and places the new module name in the title bar.

Before making the changes to the frmPatient form so that the LowAll function automatically acts on every entry in the EmailAddress field, you'll test the function using the Immediate window.

Testing a Procedure in the Immediate Window

TIP

VBA functions that you create won't run if the database is not trusted. One way to designate the database as trusted is by opening it from a trusted folder.

When you finish entering a VBA statement, the editor checks the statement to make sure its syntax is correct. Even though you may have entered all procedure statements with the correct syntax, however, the procedure may still contain logic errors. A **logic error** occurs when a procedure produces incorrect results. For example, the LowAll function would have a logic error if you typed JDoe@Example.Com and the function changed it to JDOE@EXAMPLE.COM or anything other than the correct result of jdoe@example.com. Even the simplest procedure can contain errors. Be sure to test each procedure thoroughly to ensure that it does exactly what you expect it to do in all situations.

When working in the Code window, you can use the **Immediate window** to test VBA procedures without changing any data in the database. In the Immediate window, you can enter different values to test the procedure you just entered. To test a procedure, you type the *Print* keyword or a question mark (?), followed by the procedure name, and then the value you want to test in parentheses. For example, to test the LowAll function in the Immediate window using the test word JDoe@Example.Com, you type *?LowAll("JDoe@Example.Com")* and then press the Enter key. Access executes the function and displays the value returned by the function (you expect it to return jdoe@example.com). Note that you must enclose a string of characters within quotation marks in the test statement.

REFERENCE

Testing a Procedure in the Immediate Window

- In the Code window, click View on the menu bar, and then click Immediate Window to open the Immediate window.
- Type a question mark (?), the procedure name, and the procedure's arguments in parentheses. If an argument contains a string of characters, enclose the argument in quotation marks.
- Press the Enter key and verify that the result displayed is the expected output.

Now you'll use the Immediate window to test the LowAll function.

To test the LowAll function in the Immediate window:

1. Click **View** on the menu bar, and then click **Immediate Window**. The editor opens the Immediate window across the bottom of the screen and places the insertion point inside the window.

The Immediate window allows you to run individual lines of VBA code for **debugging**, or testing. You will use the Immediate window to test the LowAll function.

2. Type **?LowAll("JDoe@Example.Com")** and then press the **Enter** key. The editor executes the function and prints the function result, jdoe@example.com, on the next line. See Figure 11-14.

Figure 11-14 LowAll function executed in the Immediate window

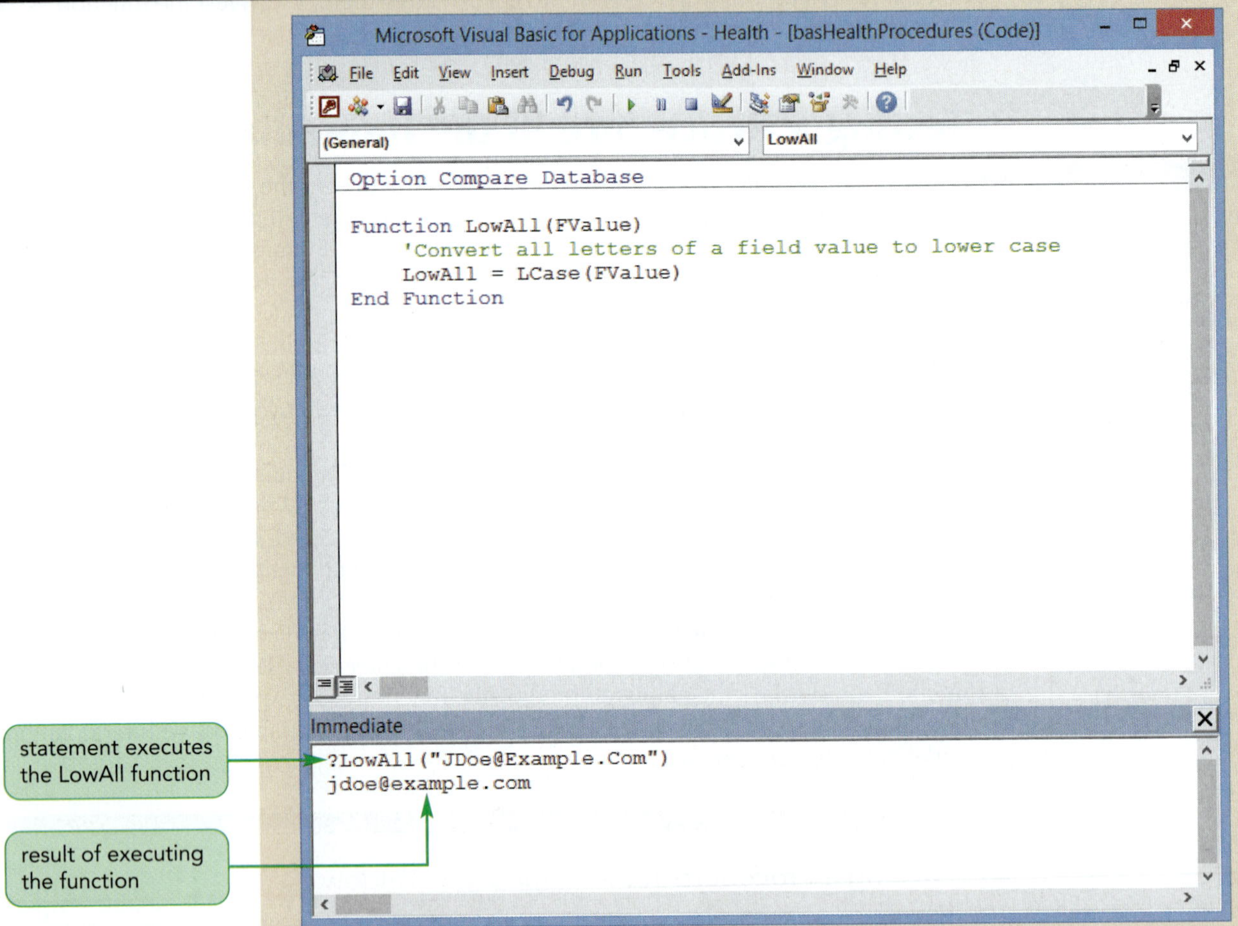

Trouble? If Access displays a dialog box with an error message, click the OK button in the dialog box, correct the error in the Immediate window, and then press the Enter key. If the function does not produce the correct output (jdoe@example.com), compare your code to Figure 11-13, correct the LowAll function statements in the Code window as necessary, save your changes, click a blank line in the Immediate window, and then repeat Step 2.

To test the LowAll function further, you could enter several other test values, retyping the entire statement each time. Instead, you'll select the current test value, type another value, and then press the Enter key.

3. Delete the email address **JDoe@Example.Com** in the first line of the Immediate window.

4. Type **JDOE@EXAMPLE.COM** and then press the **Enter** key. The editor executes the function and prints the function result, jdoe@example.com, on a new line.

5. Repeat Steps 3 and 4 two more times, using **Jdoe@example.com** and then **JDOE@example.COM** as the test values. The editor prints the correct values, jdoe@example.com.
6. Click the **Close** button on the Immediate window title bar to close it, and then click the **Close** button on the Visual Basic window title bar to return to the Access window.
7. If you are not continuing on to the next session, close the Health database.

Your initial test of the LowAll function is successful. In the next session, you'll modify the frmPatient form to execute the LowAll function for the Email Address field.

INSIGHT

Converting a Macro to Visual Basic

Creating a macro can be a bit more user-friendly than learning VBA code. Some people may find it easier to create a macro, and then convert it to VBA. They may find that they have a database with several macros, but have learned some VBA and would like to convert the macros to VBA so they can copy them and use them in other databases, or keep as much code as possible in a standard module.

To convert a macro to VBA, you open the macro you'd like to convert, then use the Convert Macros to Visual Basic button in the Tools group on the DESIGN tab.

REVIEW

Session 11.1 Quick Check

1. Why is Visual Basic for Applications called an event-driven, object-oriented language?
2. What is an event procedure?
3. What are the differences between a user-defined function and a Sub procedure?
4. Describe the two different types of modules.
5. The ______________ of a procedure is either private or public.
6. What can you accomplish in the Immediate window?

Session 11.2 Visual Overview:

Click the Save button to save the Macros.

The Object box displays the current control name.

This AfterUpdate Sub procedure will execute after the Address is updated.

This Sub procedure executes every time the EmailAddress field value changes.

The BeforeUpdate event occurs before changed data in a control or a record is updated.

The not equals operator is <> (less than symbol, greater than symbol).

The *DoCmd.CancelEvent* statement executes the CancelEvent action, which cancels the event that caused the procedure or macro containing the action to execute.

The fieldname is encapsulated in square brackets.

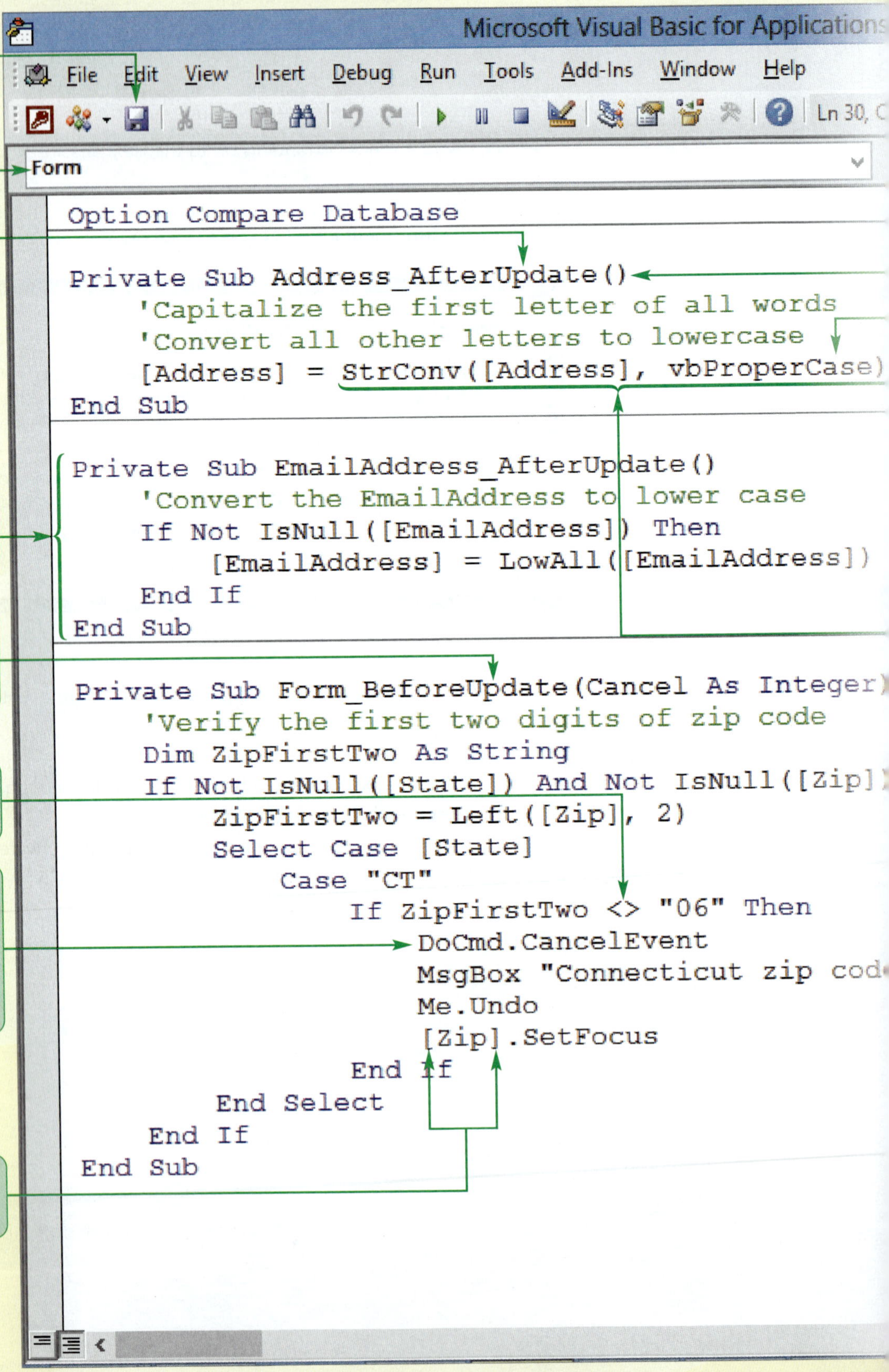

Event Procedures

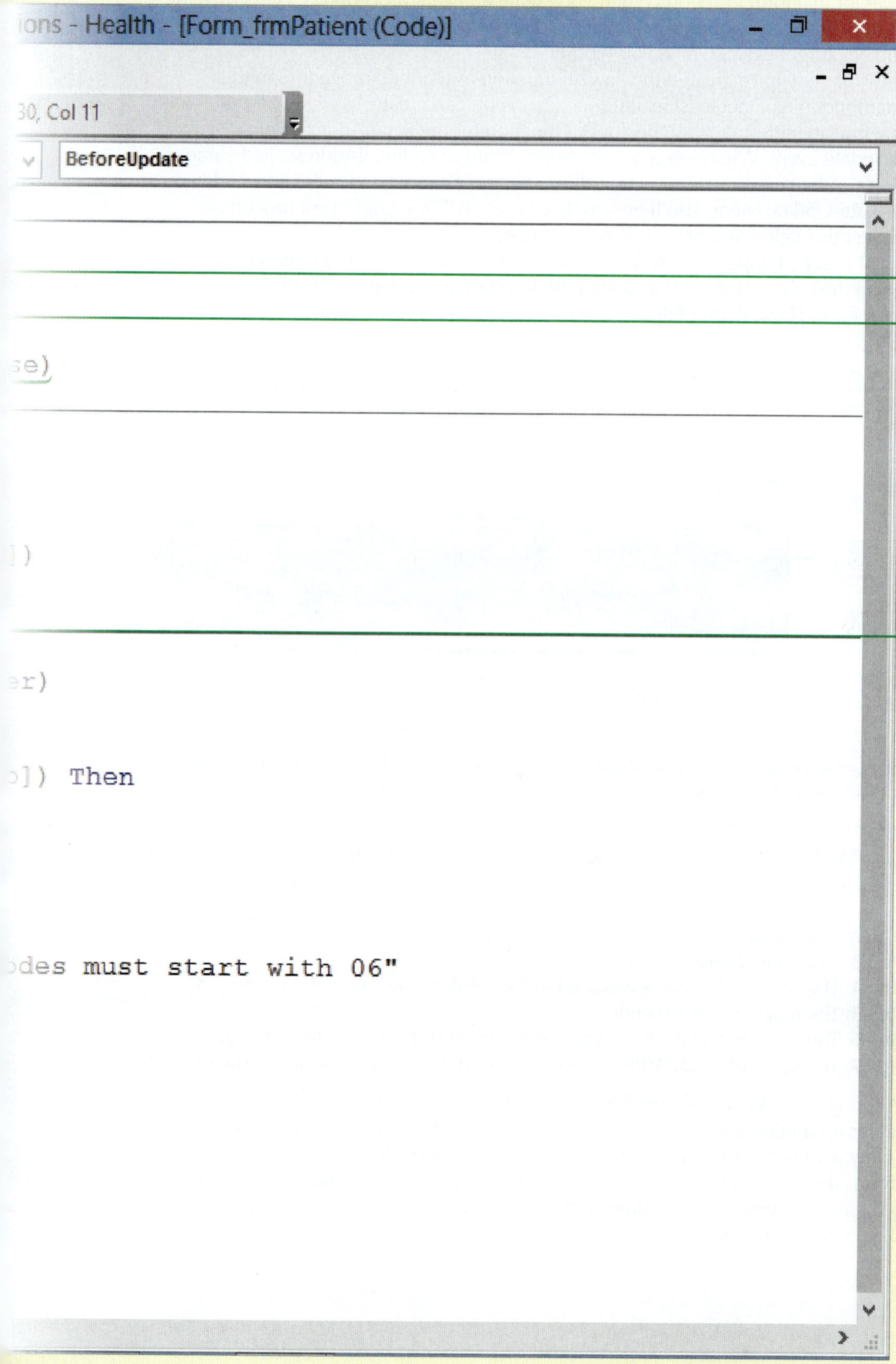

Whenever a user enters or changes a field value in a control or in a form and changes the focus to another control or record, Access automatically triggers the **AfterUpdate event**.

The **vbProperCase constant** is a VBA constant that specifies the conversion of the first letter in every word in a string to uppercase letters and the conversion of all other letters to lowercase letters.

The **StrConv function** converts the letters in a string to a form indicated in the second argument in the function.

Creating an Event Procedure

When you add a procedure to a form or report, Access automatically creates a class module for that form or report. When you create an event procedure, Access runs the procedure when a specific event occurs. The frmVisit form contains an event procedure for the onCurrent event, which you modified.

Now that you have created the LowAll function as a public procedure in the standard module named basHealthProcedures, you can create an event procedure for the frmPatient form to call the LowAll function for the EmailAddress field's AfterUpdate event. Whenever a user enters or changes an EmailAddress field value, the AfterUpdate event occurs, so by calling the LowAll function for the EmailAddress field's AfterUpdate event, you'll ensure that Access will run your event procedure whenever this field has a new or changed value.

What exactly happens when Access calls a procedure? There is an interaction between the calling statement and the function statements. Figure 11-15 shows the process for the LowAll procedure.

Figure 11-15 Process of executing a function

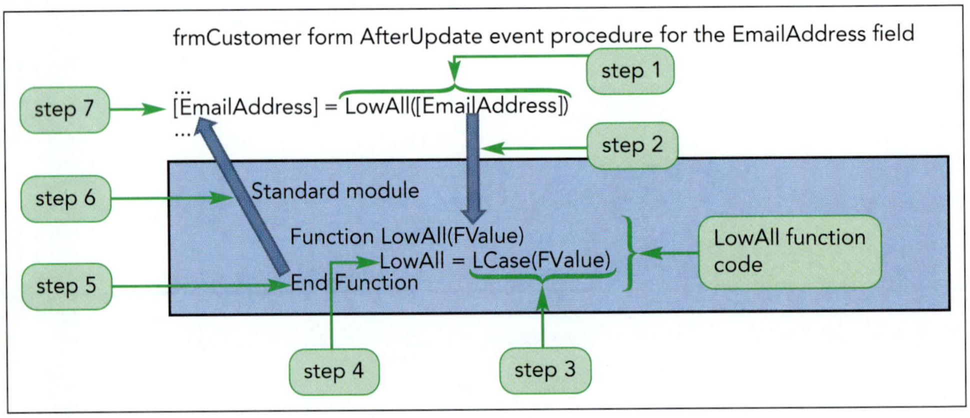

The steps in Figure 11-15 are numbered in the order in which they occur as Access processes the statement and the function. Access goes through the following steps:

- **Step 1**: The call to the function LowAll passes the value of the argument [EmailAddress]. This is the value of the EmailAddress field that is entered or changed by the user.
- **Step 2**: The function LowAll begins, and the parameter FValue receives the value of [EmailAddress].
- **Step 3**: FValue is changed to lower case.
- **Step 4**: The value of LowAll is assigned to the result of the calculation in Step 3.
- **Step 5**: The function LowAll ends.
- **Step 6**: The value of LowAll is returned to the point of the call to the function.
- **Step 7**: The value of [EmailAddress] is set equal to the returned value of LowAll.

Although it looks complicated, the general function process is simple. The statement contains a **function call**, which is a statement that contains the name of the function plus any parameters required by the function. When the statement is executed, Access performs the function call, executes the function, returns a single value to the original statement, and completes that statement's execution. Study the steps in Figure 11-15 and trace their sequence until you understand the complete process.

Designing an Event Procedure

Whenever a user enters a new value or modifies an existing value in the EmailAddress field in the frmPatient form, Kelly wants Access to execute the LowAll function to ensure that all EmailAddress field values are displayed in lowercase letters. After a user changes an EmailAddress field value, the AfterUpdate event occurs. You can set the AfterUpdate event property to run a macro, call a built-in Access function, or execute an event procedure. Because you want to call your user-defined function from within the event procedure, you'll set the AfterUpdate event property to [Event Procedure], and then add the VBA statements needed to use the LowAll function.

All event procedures are Sub procedures. Access automatically adds the Sub and End Sub statements to an event procedure. All you need to do is place the statements between the Sub and End Sub statements. Figure 11-16 shows the completed event procedure. The following text describes the parts of the procedure.

Figure 11-16 AfterUpdate event procedure for the EmailAddress field

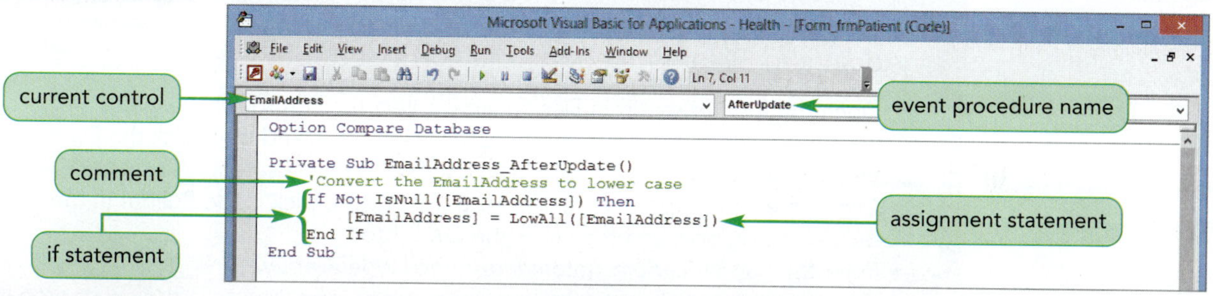

TIP

If the name of a control contains spaces or special characters, Access substitutes underscores for them in the event procedure name.

Access names each event procedure in a standard way, using the name of the control, an underscore (_), and the event name. No parameters are passed to an event procedure, so Access places nothing in the parentheses following the name of the Sub procedure.

A user might delete an existing EmailAddress field value, so that it contains no value, or becomes null. In this case, calling the function accomplishes nothing. The procedure is designed to call the LowAll function only when a user changes the EmailAddress field to a value that is not null. The If statement screens out the null values. In its simplest form, an **If statement** executes one of two groups of statements based on a condition, similar to common English usage. For example, consider the English statements, "If the door is unlocked, I'll open it and walk through it. Otherwise, I'll knock on the door and wait until someone unlocks it." In these sentences, the two groups of statements come before and after the "otherwise," depending on the condition, "if the door is unlocked." The first group of statements consists of the clause "I'll open it and walk through it." This clause is called the **true-statement group** because it's what happens if the condition ("the door is unlocked") is true. The second group of statements contains "I'll knock on the door and wait until someone unlocks it." This clause is called the **false-statement group** because it is what happens if the condition is false. VBA uses the keyword *If* to precede the condition. The keyword *Then* precedes the true-statement group and the keyword Else precedes the false-statement group. The general syntax of a VBA If statement is:

```
If condition Then
   true-statement group
[Else
   false-statement group]
End If
```

Access executes the true-statement group when the condition is true and the false-statement group when the condition is false. In this statement's syntax, the bracketed portions are optional. Therefore, you must omit the *Else* and its related false-statement group when you want Access to execute a group of statements only when the condition is true.

TIP

Notice that the EmailAddress field name is enclosed in brackets, even though brackets are optional for field names and control names that do not contain spaces and special characters.

In Figure 11-16, the If statement uses the VBA **IsNull function**, which returns a value of True when the EmailAddress field value is null and False when it is not null. The *Not* in the If statement is the same logical operator you've used previously to negate an expression. So, Access executes the statement *[EmailAddress] = LowAll([EmailAddress])* only when the EmailAddress field value is not null.

Adding an Event Procedure

To add an event procedure to the State field's AfterUpdate event property, you need to open the frmPatient form in Design view.

REFERENCE

Adding an Event Procedure to a Form or Report

- Open the form or report in Design view, select the control whose event property you want to set, open the property sheet for the control, and then click the Event tab in the property sheet.
- Click the event property box, click its Build button, click Code Builder in the Choose Builder dialog box, and then click the OK button.
- Enter the Sub procedure statements in the Code window.
- Compile the procedure, fix any statement errors, and then save the event procedure.

Next you'll add the event procedure to the frmPatient form.

To add the event procedure to the frmPatient form:

1. If you took a break after the previous session, make sure that the Health database is open.
2. Open the Navigation Pane, and then open the **frmPatient** form in Design view.
3. Right-click the **EmailAddress** text box to select it and to display the shortcut menu, click **Properties** to open the property sheet, and then, if necessary, click the **Event** tab in the property sheet. Access displays only the event properties in the property sheet. You need to set the AfterUpdate property for the EmailAddress text box.

   Trouble? If you do not see any events in the Event tab, you might have clicked on the Email Address label control instead of the text box. Right-click the EmailAddress text box.
4. Click the **After Update** box, click the **Build** button ... to the right of the After Update box to open the Choose Builder dialog box, click **Code Builder**, and then click the **OK** button. The Code window opens in the Visual Basic window. See Figure 11-17.

Figure 11-17 Starting a new event procedure in the Code window

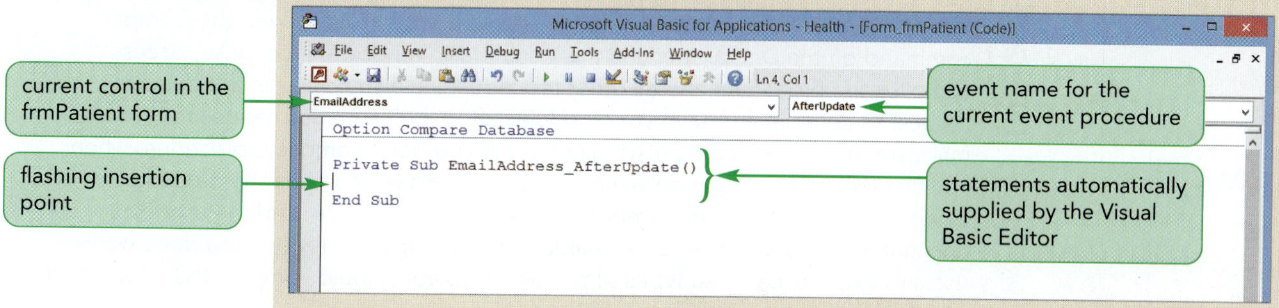

Trouble? If the Object box does not display the EmailAddress control, close the Visual Basic window, delete "[Event Procedure]" from the After Update box in the property sheet, click the EmailAddress text box control on the form, and then repeat Step 4.

5. Enter the statements shown in Figure 11-18. Use the Tab key to indent the lines as shown in the figure (if necessary), press the Enter key at the end of each line, and press the Backspace key to move one tab stop to the left. Compare your screen with Figure 11-18, and make any necessary corrections.

Figure 11-18 Completed event procedure

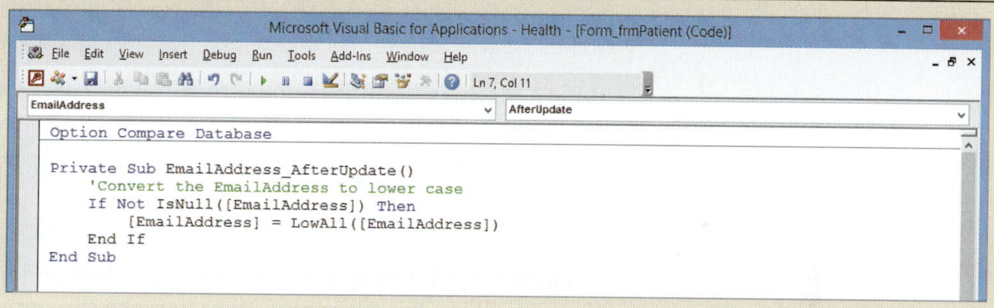

Trouble? If your event procedure contains errors, correct them by highlighting the errors and typing the corrections. Use the Backspace or Delete keys to delete characters.

Before saving the event procedure, you'll compile it.

Compiling Modules

The VBA programming language is not the computer's native language. Although you can learn VBA and become fluent in it, computers cannot understand or learn VBA. For a computer to understand the statements in your VBA modules, Access must translate the statements into a form that the computer processor can use. The process of translating modules from VBA to a form your computer processor understands is called **compilation**; you say that you **compile** the module when you translate it.

When you run a procedure for the first time, Access compiles it for you automatically and opens a dialog box only when it finds syntax errors in the procedure. If it finds an error, Access does not translate the procedure statements. If no errors are detected, Access translates the procedure and does not display a confirmation.

INSIGHT

Compiling Procedures

You can compile a procedure at any time as you enter it by clicking the Compile command on the Debug menu in the Visual Basic window. In response, Access compiles the procedure and all other procedures in all modules in the database. It's best to compile and save your modules after you've made changes to them, to make sure they don't contain syntax errors. If you don't compile a procedure when you first create it or after you've changed it, Access will compile the procedure when a first user opens the form or report that uses the procedure, and the user could encounter a syntax error and be unable to use the form or report. You don't want users to experience these types of problems, so you should compile and fully test all procedures as you create them.

You'll now compile the procedures in the Health database and save the class module for the frmPatient form.

To compile the procedures in the Health database and save the class module:

1. Click **Debug** on the menu bar, and then click **Compile Health**. Access compiles all the modules in the Health database. Because you have no syntax errors, Access translates the VBA statements and returns control to the Visual Basic window. It may seem as if nothing has happened.

   Trouble? If Access identifies any errors in your code, correct the errors and repeat Step 1.

2. Save your module changes, close the Visual Basic window, and then close the property sheet.

You have created the function and the event procedure and have set the event property. Next, you'll test the event procedure to make sure it works correctly.

Testing an Event Procedure

You need to display the frmPatient form in Form view and test the EmailAddress field's event procedure by entering a few different test EmailAddress field values in the first record of the form. Moving the focus to another control on the form or to another record triggers the AfterUpdate event for the EmailAddress field and executes your attached event procedure. Because the LowAll function is attached only to the frmPatient form, the automatic conversion to lower case of EmailAddress field values is not in effect when you enter them in the tblPatient table or in any other object in the Health database.

To test the event procedure:

1. Switch to Form view.
2. Click the frmPatient Next record navigation button ▶ to advance to record 2.
3. Select the **EmailAddress** field value (edarcy@example.com), type **EDARCY@EXAMPLE.COM** in the EmailAddress text box, and then click the Zip text box control to enter the data. Access executes the AfterUpdate event procedure for the EmailAddress field and changes the EmailAddress field value to "edarcy@example.com." See Figure 11-19.

Figure 11-19 **frmPatient form after executing the event procedure**

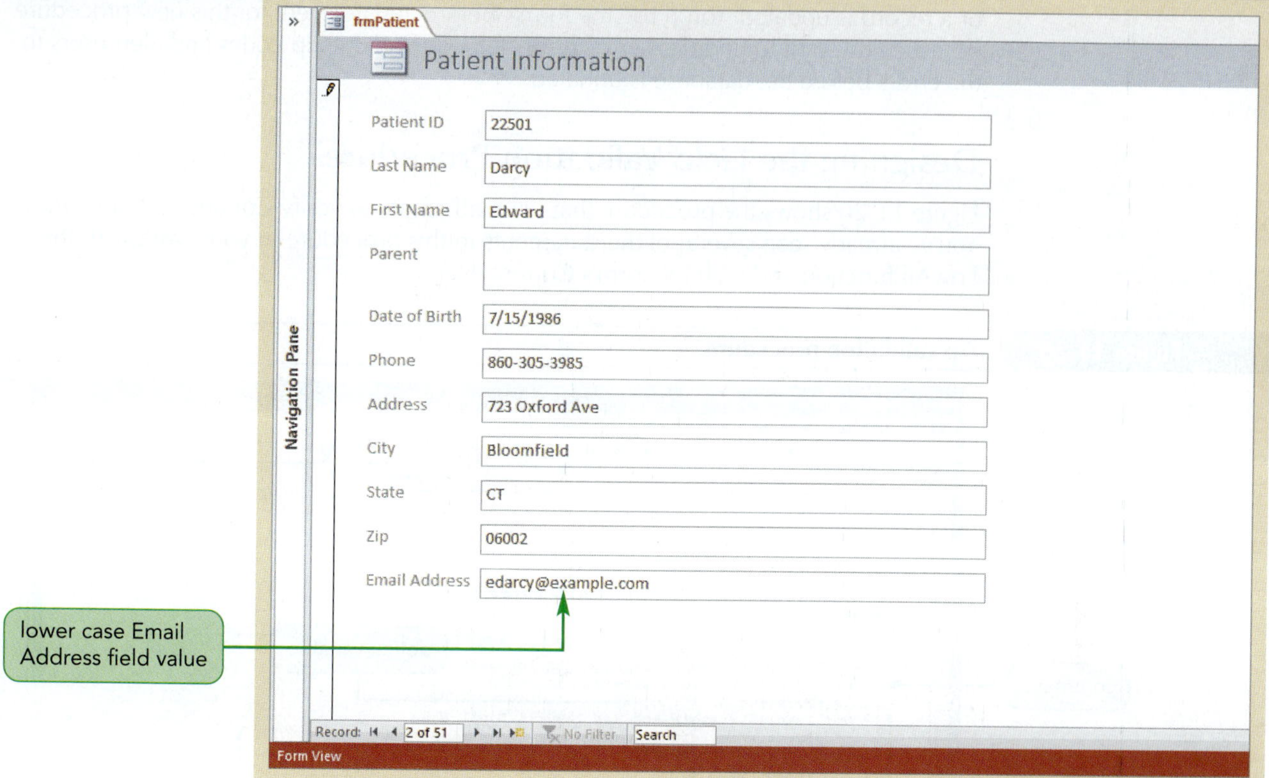

Trouble? If you see the data for record 3, you pressed the Enter key instead of clicking on the Zip text box. Click the **Previous record** navigation button to return to record 2.

4. Repeat Step 3 three more times, entering **EDarcy@Example.com**, then **eDarCY@EXAMPLE.com**, and finally **EDARcy@Example.COM** in the EmailAddress text box. Access displays the correct value of "edarcy@example.com" each time.

Kelly is happy with the functionality you've added to the EmailAddress text box. Next she wants you to create a more complex function for the Zip field in the frmPatient form.

Adding a Second Procedure to a Class Module

Kelly has found that her staff makes frequent errors when entering Connecticut zip codes, whose first two digits are always 06. She asks you to create a procedure that will verify that Connecticut zip codes are in the correct range (beginning with 06) when her staff updates the Zip field in the frmPatient form. One option is to use a form validation rule, but Kelly would like to be able to add complexity later, to validate other Zip codes as patients from other states may use the clinic. Also, Kelly would like to be able to use this VBA code in other databases. If the validation property is used in the tblPatient table instead of using VBA, then this validation rule would have to be re-created in another database. Instead, Kelly will be able to copy the VBA code, and paste it into another VBA window in another database.

You'll build a simple procedure that could later be used to add more complexity. For this procedure, you will use an event procedure attached to the BeforeUpdate event for the frmPatient form. The BeforeUpdate event occurs before changed data in a control or a record is updated. You'll use the form's BeforeUpdate event for this new procedure because you want to find data-entry errors for Connecticut zip codes and alert users to the errors before the database is updated.

Designing the Field Validation Procedure

Figure 11-20 shows the procedure that you will create to verify Connecticut zip codes. You've already seen several of the statements in this procedure in your work with the LowAll function and with the form's Current event.

Figure 11-20 Zip validation procedure

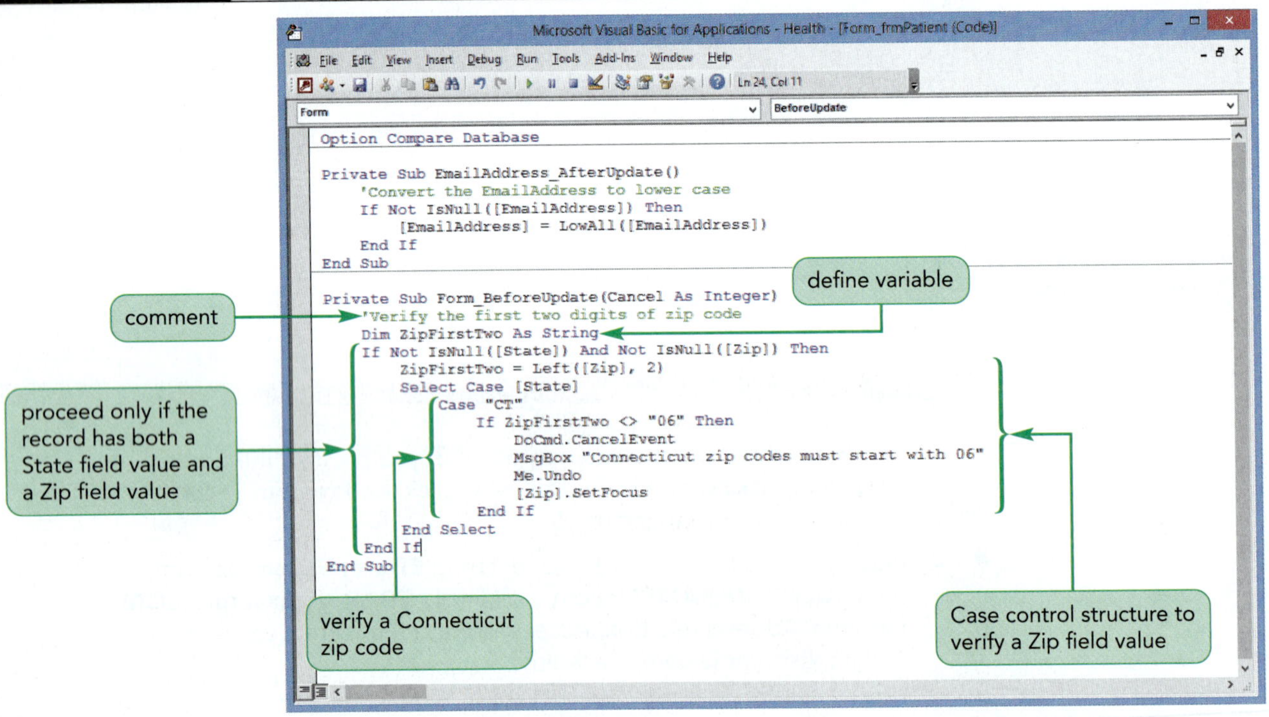

The Sub and End Sub statements begin and end the Sub procedure. As specified in the Sub statement, the Sub procedure executes when the form's BeforeUpdate event occurs. Within parentheses in the Sub statement, *Cancel As Integer* defines Cancel as a parameter with the Integer data type. VBA has data types that are different from the Access data types you've used to define table fields, but each Access data type is equivalent to one of the VBA data types. For example, the Access Number data type with an Integer field size is the same as the VBA Integer data type, and the Access Short Text data type is the same as the VBA String data type. Figure 11-21 shows the primary VBA data types.

Figure 11-21 **Primary VBA data types**

Data Type	Stores
Boolean	True/False values
Byte	Integer values from 0 to 255
Currency	Currency values from –922,337,203,685,477.5808 to 922,337,203,685,477.5807
Date	Date and time values from 1 January 100 to 31 December 9999
Decimal	Non-integer values with 0 to 28 decimal places
Double	Non-integer values from $-1.79769313486231*10^{308}$ to $-4.94065645841247*11^{-324}$ for negative values, from $4.94065645841247*11^{-324}$ to $1.79769313486232*10^{308}$ for positive values, and 0
Integer	Integer values from –32,768 to 32,767
Long	Integer values from –2,147,483,648 to 2,147,483,647
Object	Any object reference
Single	Non-integer values from $-3.402823*10^{38}$ to $-1.401298*11^{-45}$ for negative values, from $1.401298*11^{-45}$ to $3.402823*10^{38}$ for positive values, and 0
String	Text values up to 2 billion characters in length
Variant	Any numeric or string data type

When an event occurs, Access performs the default behavior for the event. For some events, such as the BeforeUpdate event, Access executes the event procedure or macro before performing the default behavior. Thus, if something is wrong and the default behavior should not occur, you can cancel the default behavior in the event procedure or macro. For this reason, Access automatically includes the Cancel parameter for the BeforeUpdate event.

The second procedure statement, which starts with a single quotation mark, is a comment. The third statement, *Dim ZipFirstTwo As String*, declares the String variable named ZipFirstTwo that the Sub procedure uses. A **variable** is a named location in computer memory that can contain a value. If you use a variable in a module, you must explicitly declare it in the Declarations section or in the procedure where the variable is used. You use the **Dim statement** to declare variables and their associated data types in a procedure. The Sub procedure will assign the first two digits of a zip code (the Zip field) to the ZipFirstTwo variable, and then use the variable when verifying that a Connecticut zip code begins in the correct range. Because the zip code could contain a value that begins with zero (0), the ZipFirstTwo variable uses the String data type instead of a numeric data type. The first two characters of any zip code for Connecticut are represented as the string value "06".

The procedure should not attempt to verify records that contain null field values for the State field and the Zip field. To screen out these conditions, the procedure uses the fourth procedure statement, *If Not IsNull([State]) And Not IsNull([Zip]) Then*, which pairs with the last *End If* statement. The *If* statement determines whether both the State and Zip fields are nonnull. If both conditions are true (both fields contain values), then Access executes the next statement in the procedure. If either condition is false, then Access executes the paired End If statement, and the following End Sub statement ends the procedure without the execution of any other statement.

The fifth procedure statement, *ZipFirstTwo = Left([Zip], 2)*, uses a built-in VBA function, the Left function, to assign the first two characters of the Zip field value to the ZipFirstTwo variable. The Left function returns a string containing a specified number of characters from the left side of a specified string. In this case, the Left function returns the leftmost two characters of the Zip field value.

You encountered the Case control structure previously in the frmVisit form's Current event procedure. For the BeforeUpdate event procedure, the *Select Case [State]* statement evaluates the State field value. For a State field value equal to CT (indicating the record should have a Connecticut zip code), the next If statement is executed. For all other State field values, nothing further in the procedure is executed; Access performs the default behavior, and control returns back to the form for further processing. The procedure uses the Case control structure because although Kelly wants the procedure to verify the first two characters of only Connecticut zip codes for now, she might want to expand the procedure in the future to verify the first two digits of zip codes for other states as Chatham Community Health Services expands its business.

Because valid Connecticut zip codes begin with "06", invalid values for the Zip field will not be equal to "06". The not equals operator in VBA is <> (less than symbol followed by the greater than symbol). The next VBA statement, *If ZipFirstTwo <> "06" Then*, is true only for invalid Connecticut zip codes. When the If statement is true, the next four statements are executed. When the If statement is false, nothing further in the procedure is executed, Access performs the default behavior, and control returns back to the form for further processing.

The first of the four VBA statements that executes for invalid Connecticut zip codes is the DoCmd statement. The DoCmd statement executes an action in a procedure. The *DoCmd.CancelEvent* statement executes the CancelEvent action. The CancelEvent action cancels the event that caused the procedure or macro containing the action to execute. In this case, Access cancels the BeforeUpdate event and does not update the database with the changes to the current record. In addition, Access cancels subsequent events that would have occurred if the BeforeUpdate event had not been canceled. For example, in addition to the form's BeforeUpdate event being triggered when you move to a different record, the following events are also triggered when you move to a different record, in the order listed: BeforeUpdate event for the form, AfterUpdate event for the form, Exit event for the control with the focus, LostFocus event for the control with the focus, RecordExit event for the form, and Current event for the form. When the CancelEvent action is executed, all these events are canceled and the focus remains with the record being edited.

TIP

The macro MessageBox action is the same as the VBA MsgBox statement.

The second of the four VBA statements that are executed for invalid Connecticut zip codes is the MsgBox statement. The *MsgBox "Connecticut zip codes must start with 06"* statement displays its message in a message box that remains on the screen until the user clicks the OK button. The message box appears on top of the frmPatient form so the user can view the changed field values in the current record.

For invalid Connecticut zip codes, after the user clicks the OK button in the message box, the *Me.Undo* statement is executed. The Me keyword refers to the current object—in this case, the frmPatient form. Undo is a method that clears all changes made to the current record in the frmPatient form, so that the field values in the record return to the way they were before the user made the current changes. A **method** is an action that operates on specific objects or controls.

Finally, for invalid Connecticut zip codes, the *[Zip].SetFocus* statement is executed. SetFocus is a method that moves the focus to the specified object or control. In this case, Access moves the focus to the Zip field in the current record in the frmPatient form.

Adding a Second Event Procedure

You can now add an event procedure for the frmPatient form's BeforeUpdate event property. Access will execute the event procedure whenever field values in a record are entered or updated.

To add the event procedure for the frmPatient form's BeforeUpdate event:

1. Switch to Design view.
2. Right-click the **form selector** to display the shortcut menu, and then click **Properties** to open the property sheet for the form.
3. If necessary, click the **Event** tab in the property sheet.
4. Click the **Before Update** box, click the **Before Update** arrow, click **[Event Procedure]**, and then click the **Build** button [...] to the right of the Before Update box. The Code window, which contains new Private Sub and End Sub statements, opens in the Visual Basic window. Horizontal lines separate the Option Compare statement from the new procedure and from the AfterUpdate event procedure you entered earlier.

When entering "06" be sure to enter the number zero, not the letter O.

5. Press the **Tab** key, and then type the Sub procedure statements exactly as shown in Figure 11-22. Press the Enter key after you enter each statement, press the Tab key to indent lines as necessary, and press the Backspace key to move the insertion point one tab stop to the left. When you are finished, your screen should look like Figure 11-22.

   Remember that capitalization is important in all statements so that your code is readable and maintainable.

Figure 11-22 Event procedure for the frmPatient form's BeforeUpdate event

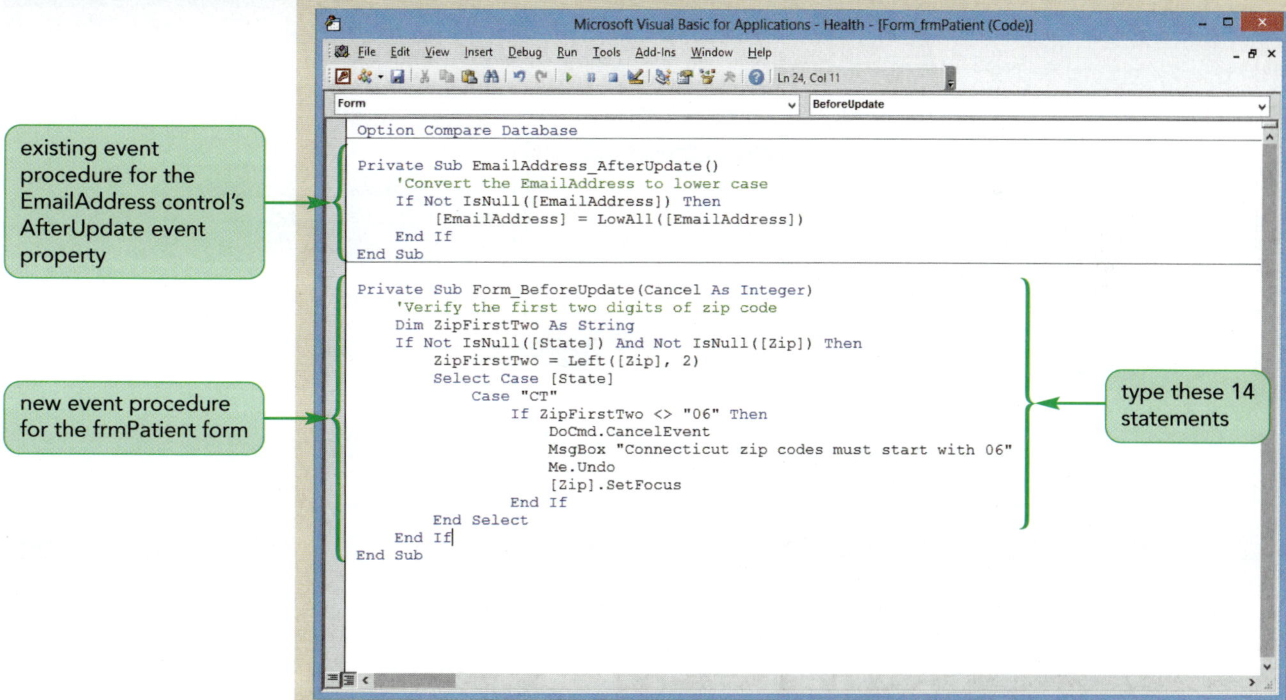

6. Click **Debug** on the menu bar, and then click **Compile Health**. Access compiles all the modules in the Health database.

   Trouble? If the editor finds an error, it highlights the error and opens a dialog box with a message describing the nature of the error. Click the OK button and then change the highlighted error by comparing your entries with those shown in Figure 11-22. Then repeat Step 6 to scan the statements for errors again and to compile the module.

7. Save your class module changes.
8. Close the Visual Basic window to return to the Form window, close the property sheet, and then close the Navigation Pane.

You can now test the event procedure. To do so, you'll switch to Form view for the frmPatient form and test the form's BeforeUpdate event procedure by entering valid and invalid Zip field values.

To test the form's BeforeUpdate event procedure:

1. Switch to Form view. Access displays record 1. The first two digits of the Zip field value, 06, represent a valid Connecticut zip code.

TIP

You must navigate to another record, not just to another field, to trigger a form's BeforeUpdate event procedure.

2. Select **06120** in the Zip text box, type **98765**, press the **Tab** key to move to the Email Address text box, and then click the **Next record** navigation button ▶ to move to the next record. Access executes the BeforeUpdate event procedure for the frmPatient form, determines that the Connecticut zip code's first two digits are incorrect, and displays the message box you included in the procedure. See Figure 11-23.

Figure 11-23 **After the frmPatient form's BeforeUpdate event procedure detects an error**

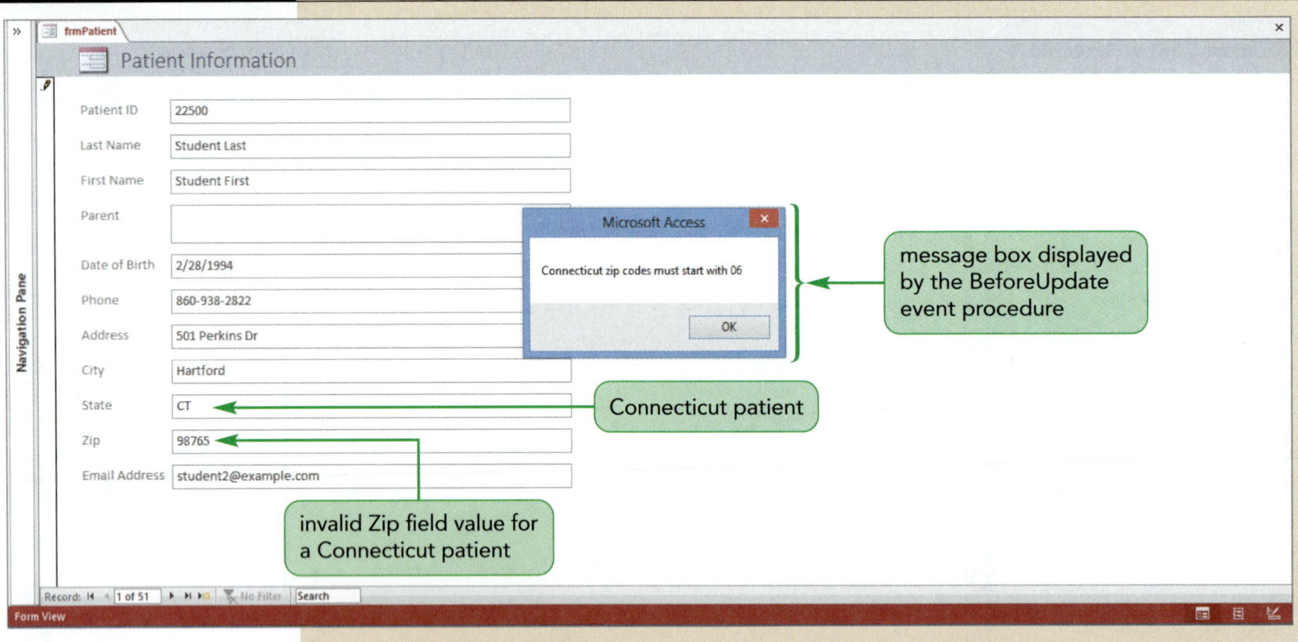

While the message box is open, the updated Zip field value of 98765 remains on screen for you to review.

3. Click the **OK** button. The message box closes, the Undo method changes the Zip field value to 06120 (its original value), and the SetFocus method moves the focus to the Zip text box.

Next, you'll change the Zip field value to 06095, which is a valid Connecticut zip code.

4. Change the Zip field value to **06095**, and then click the **Next record** navigation button [▶] to move to the next record. The form's BeforeUpdate event procedure verifies that the zip code is a valid value for a Connecticut customer, and the focus moves to the Zip text box in the next record.
5. Click the **Previous record** navigation button [◀] to move to the first record, change the State field value to **TX**, change the Zip field value to **98765**, and then click the **Next record** navigation button [▶] to move to the next record. The form's BeforeUpdate event procedure checks zip codes only when the State field value is "CT" (Connecticut), so even though the zip code 98765 is not valid for Texas (abbreviated TX), the focus moves to the Zip text box in the next record anyway.

   Next, you'll change the first record's State field value to CT and the Zip field value to 06120, which are the original values for the record.
6. Click the **Previous record** navigation button [◀] to move to the first record, change the State field value to **CT**, and then change the Zip field value to **06120**.

Kelly is impressed with the zip code validation you've added to the frmPatient form. She has one additional procedure she wants you to create for the form.

Changing the Case of a Field Value

Kelly wants to make it easier for users to enter an address when using the frmPatient form, so she asks you to create a procedure that will automatically convert the case of letters entered in the address field. This procedure will capitalize the first letter of each word in the field and change all other letters to lower case. You'll use an event procedure attached to the AfterUpdate event for the address field to perform this automatic conversion. For example, if a user enters "12 mAin sT" as the address field value, the event procedure will correct the field value to "12 Main St".

You'll use the StrConv function in the event procedure to perform the conversion. The **StrConv function** converts the letters in a string to all uppercase letters or to all lowercase letters, or converts the first letter of every word in the string to uppercase letters and all other letters to lowercase letters, which is a pattern known as proper case. The StrConv function ignores numbers. The statement you'll use in the event procedure is *[Address] = StrConv([Address], vbProperCase)*. The StrConv function's second argument, the **vbProperCase constant**, is a VBA constant that specifies the conversion of the first letter in every word in a string to uppercase letters and the conversion of all other letters to lowercase letters. Recall that the LowAll function you created earlier in this tutorial used the statement *LowAll = LCase(FValue)* to convert every character in a string to lower case. Instead, you could have used the statement *LowAll = StrConv(FValue, vbLowerCase)* to accomplish the same result. Other VBA constants you can use with the StrConv function are the **vbUpperCase constant**, which specifies the conversion of the string to all uppercase letters, and the **vbLowerCase constant**, which specifies the conversion of the string to all lowercase letters.

Next, you'll create the AfterUpdate event procedure for the Address field in the frmPatient form to perform the automatic conversion of entered and updated Address field values.

To add the event procedure for the Address field's AfterUpdate event:

1. Switch to Design view.
2. Right-click the **Address** text box to display the shortcut menu, and then click **Properties** to open the property sheet for the control.
3. If necessary, click the **Event** tab in the property sheet.
4. Click the **After Update** box, click the **After Update** arrow, click **[Event Procedure]**, and then click the **Build** button ... to the right of the After Update box. The Code window, which contains new Private Sub and End Sub statements, opens in the Visual Basic window. The Code window also contains two other event procedures defined in the form's class module: one event procedure for the form's BeforeUpdate event, and another event procedure for the EmailAddress field's AfterUpdate event.
5. Press the **Tab** key, and then type the Sub procedure statements exactly as shown in Figure 11-24.

Figure 11-24 Event procedure for the Address control's AfterUpdate event

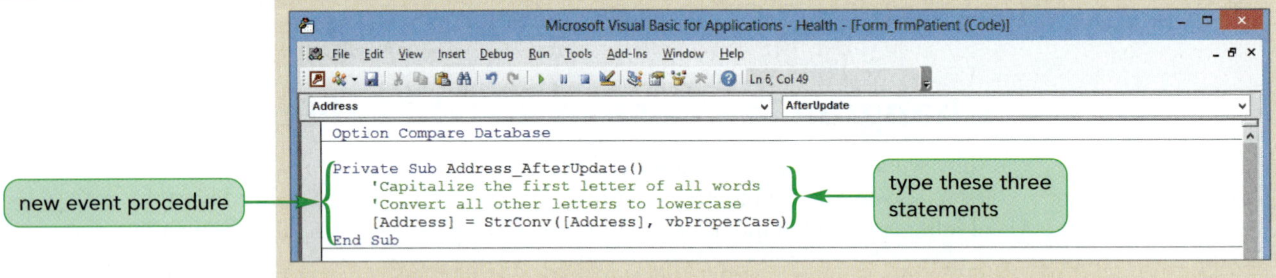

6. Click **Debug** on the menu bar, click **Compile Health**, save your class module changes, close the Visual Basic window, and then close the property sheet.

You can now test the event procedure. To do so, you'll view the frmPatient form in Form view and test the Address field's event procedure by entering different Address field values.

To test the new event procedure:

1. Switch to Form view, and then press the **Tab** key as many times as necessary to move to the Address text box for the first record.

   You'll test the new event procedure by entering Address field values in record 1.

2. Type **501 perKins dR** and then press the **Enter** key. Access executes the AfterUpdate event procedure for the Address field and changes the Address field value to "501 Perkins Dr".
3. Press the ↑ key to select the Address field value.
4. Repeat Steps 2 and 3 two more times, entering **501 pERKINS dR** (correctly changed to "501 Perkins Dr"), and then entering **501 perkins dr** (correctly changed to "501 Perkins Dr").
5. Close the form.

Hiding a Control and Changing a Control's Color

Kelly wants you to add a message to the frmVisitsAndInvoices form that will remind her staff when a visit record should be considered for archiving from the tblVisit table. Specifically, when the visit date is prior to the year 2016, Kelly wants the VisitDate field value displayed in red; all other VisitDate field values should be displayed in black. She also wants to display a message to the right of the VisitDate text box in red only when the visit is a candidate for archiving. The red font will help to draw attention to these visit records. Figure 11-25 shows a preview of the formatting she's requesting.

Figure 11-25 **Archive message and red VisitDate field value in frmVisitsAndInvoices form**

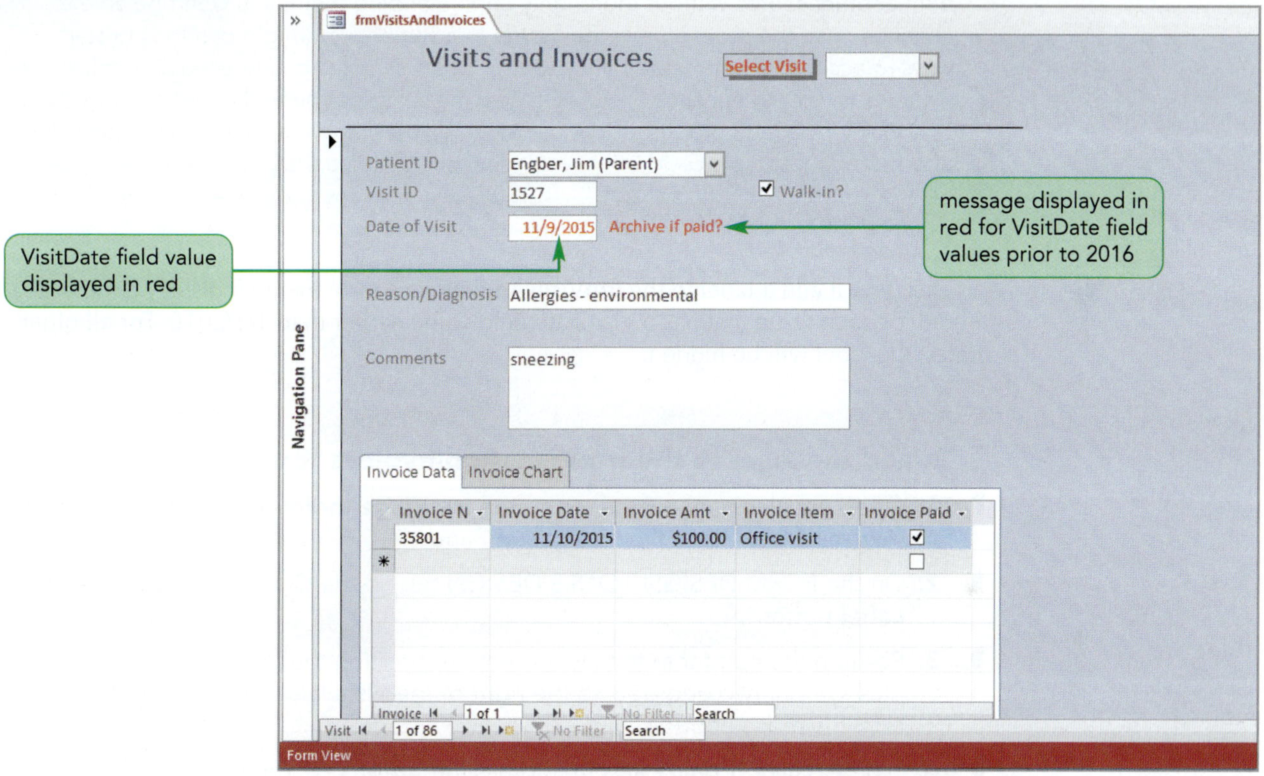

In the frmVisitsAndInvoices form, you will add a label to the right of the VisitDate text box that will display the text "Archive if paid?" in red. Because Kelly wants the text to appear only when the VisitDate field has a value earlier than 1/1/2016, you will change the label's Visible property during execution. You will also change the foreground color of the value in the VisitDate text box to red when the VisitDate field value is earlier than 1/1/2016, and to black for all other dates.

Because the change to the Visible property takes place during execution, you will add code to the Current event procedure in the frmVisitsAndInvoices form. To set a property in a VBA statement, you enter the object name followed by a period and the property name. For example, if the label name for the message is lblArchiveMsg, then the statement *lblArchiveMsg.Visible = False* hides the label on the form.

PROSKILLS

Problem Solving: Reusing Code from Other Sources

Creating your first few VBA procedures from scratch can be a daunting task. To get started, you should take advantage of the available resources that discuss various ways of designing and programming commonly encountered situations. These resources include the sample databases available from Microsoft, Access VBA books, periodicals, web sites that provide sample code, and Access Help. These resources contain sample procedures and code segments, often with commentary about what the procedures and statements accomplish and why. However, when you create a procedure, you are responsible for knowing what it does, how it does it, when to use it, how to enhance it in the future, and how to fix it when problems occur. If you simply copy statements from another source without thoroughly understanding them, you won't be able to enhance or fix the procedure in the future. In addition, you might overlook better ways to accomplish the same thing—better because the procedure would run faster or would be easier to enhance. In some cases, the samples you find might be flawed, so that they won't work properly for you. The time you spend researching and completely understanding sample code will pay dividends in your learning experience to create VBA procedures.

First, you'll add a label to the frmVisitsAndInvoices form that will display a message in red for each value that has a VisitDate field value earlier than 1/1/2016. For all other dates, the label will be hidden.

To add the label to the frmVisitsAndInvoices form:

1. Open the Navigation Pane, open the **frmVisitsAndInvoices** form in Design view, and then close the Navigation Pane.
2. On the FORM DESIGN TOOLS DESIGN tab, in the Controls group, click the **Label** button Aa.
3. Position the pointer in the Detail section, position the center of the pointer's plus symbol two grid dots to the right of the VisitDate text box, and then click the mouse button.
4. Type **Archive if paid?** and then press the **Enter** key. The new label box appears in the form and displays the Error Checking Options button. See Figure 11-26.

Figure 11-26 Label control added to the form

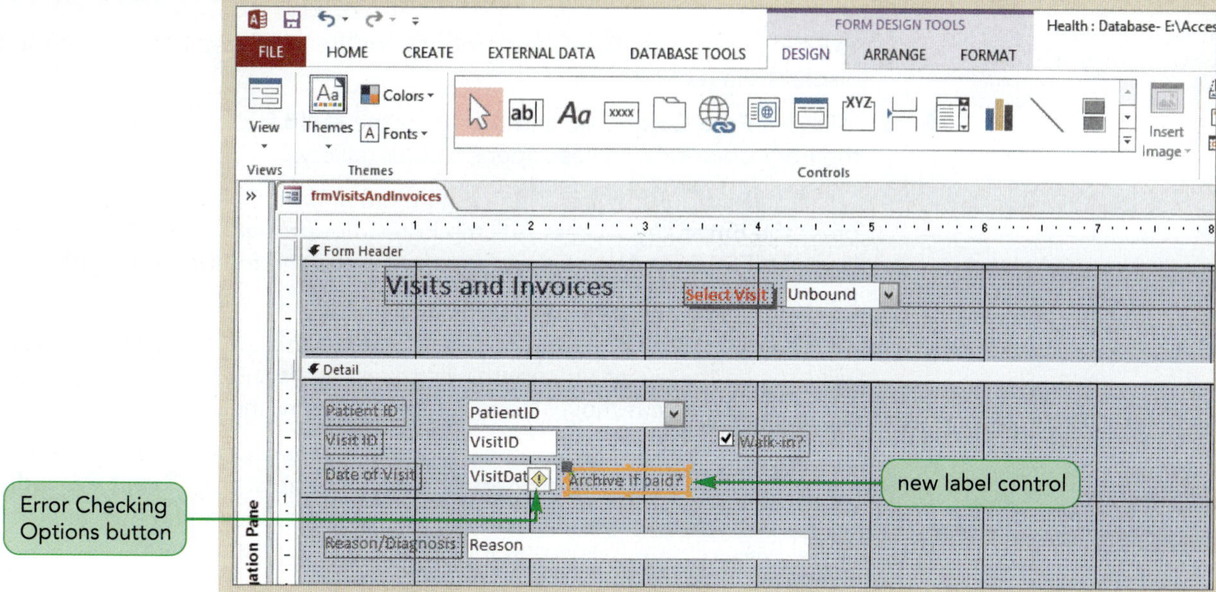

Trouble? If you do not see the Error Checking Options button, error checking is disabled in Access. Click the FILE tab, click Options in the navigation bar, click Object Designers, scroll down the page, click the Enable error checking check box to add a check mark to it, click the OK button, click a blank area in the form, and then click the "Archive if paid?" label box. Continue with Step 5.

5. Position the pointer on the **Error Checking Options** button. The message, "This is a new label and is not associated with a control," appears. Because the new label should not be associated with a control, you'll choose to ignore this error.
6. Click the **Error Checking Options arrow**, and then click **Ignore Error**. The Error Checking Options button disappears.
7. Hold down the **Shift** key, click the **VisitDate** text box to select this control and the label control, release the **Shift** key, right-click one of the selected controls, point to **Align**, and then click **Top** to align both controls on their top edges.

Trouble? If the Error Checking Options button appears, click the Error Checking Options button arrow, and then click Dismiss Error.

You'll now set the label's Name and ForeColor properties, and you'll add the Current event procedure to the frmVisitsAndInvoices form.

To set the label's properties and add the Current event procedure to the form:

1. Deselect all controls, right-click the **Archive if paid?** label to display the shortcut menu, and then click **Properties** to open the property sheet (if necessary).

TIP

The *lbl* (the consonants in the word "label") prefix tag identifies a label control.

2. Click the **All** tab (if necessary), select the value in the **Name** box (if necessary), and then type **lblArchiveMsg**.

   You can now set the ForeColor property for the label so that the message is displayed in red.

3. Click the **Fore Color** box, and then click the **Build** button [...] to the right of the Fore Color box. Access opens a color gallery.

4. Click the **Red** box (row 7, column 2 in the Standard Colors palette), and then press the **Enter** key. Access sets the ForeColor property value to the code for red (#ED1C24). Notice that Access changed the foreground (font) color of the "Archive if paid?" label to red.

   You'll now enter the event procedure for the form's Current event. Access will execute this event procedure whenever the frmVisitsAndInvoices form is opened or the focus moves from one record to another.

5. Click the **form selector**, scroll down the property sheet to the On Current box, click the **On Current** box, click the **On Current** arrow, click [**Event Procedure**], and then click the **Build** button [...]. Access opens the Code window in the Visual Basic window, displaying the Sub and End Sub statements.

6. Press the **Tab** key, and then type the Sub procedure statements exactly as shown in Figure 11-27.

Figure 11-27 **Current event procedure for the frmVisitsAndInvoices form**

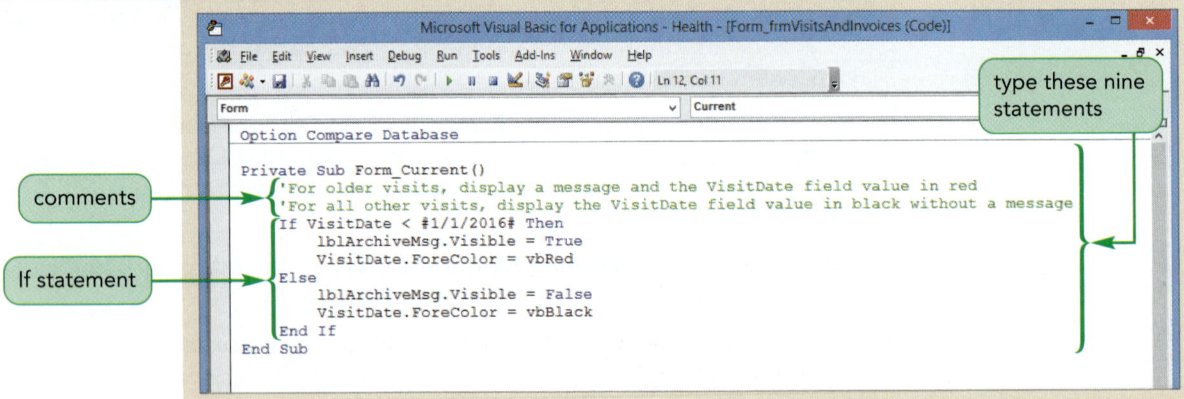

The form's Current procedure uses an If statement to determine whether the current value of the VisitDate field is less than 1/1/2016. If the current value of the VisitDate field is less than 1/1/2016, the procedure sets the lblArchiveMsg control's Visible property to True (which means the "Archive if paid?" message will appear in the frmVisitsAndInvoices form), and it sets the VisitDate control's ForeColor property to vbRed (red). If the current value of the VisitDate field is greater than 1/1/2016, the procedure sets the lblArchiveMsg control's Visible property to False, hiding the message in the form, and sets the VisitDate control's ForeColor property to vbBlack.

7. Click **Debug** on the menu bar, and then click **Compile Health**. Access compiles all the modules in the Health database.

8. Save your class module changes, close the Visual Basic window, and then close the property sheet.

You'll now test the frmVisitsAndInvoices form's Current event procedure.

To test the Current event procedure for the frmVisitsAndInvoices form:

1. Switch to Form view. Access displays the first record for ContractNum 1527, for which the start date is prior to 1/1/2016. The "Archive if paid?" message appears in red, as does the VisitDate field value of 11/9/2015.

   Trouble? If Access displays a dialog box indicating a run-time error, Access could not execute the event procedure. Click the Debug button in the dialog box. Access displays the event procedure in the Code window and highlights the line containing the error. Check the statements carefully against those shown in Figure 11-27. Make the necessary changes so they match the figure exactly, compile the module, save the module, and then close the Code window. Then repeat Step 1.

2. Click the Visit **Last record** navigation button ▶| to display record 86 for Visit ID 1700, for which the visit date is 4/18/2016. The "Archive if paid?" message is not displayed, and the VisitDate field value is displayed in black.
3. Close the form, make a backup copy of the database, compact and repair the database, and then close it.

Raj and Kelly are pleased with the VBA modifications you've made to the forms. They'll come to you for any additional enhancements to the database and the user interface that they need.

REVIEW

Session 11.2 Quick Check

1. The VBA ______________ statement executes one of two groups of statements based on a condition.
2. What happens when you compile a module?
3. What is the purpose of the Dim statement?
4. The ______________ function returns a value of true if the field value is empty and false if the field value is not empty.
5. What is the purpose of the DoCmd statement?
6. What is a method?
7. What is a VBA constant?
8. You can use the UCase function or the ______________ function to convert a string to all uppercase letters.
9. What does the Visible property determine?
10. What does the ForeColor property determine?

ASSESS

SAM Projects

Put your skills into practice with SAM Projects! SAM Projects for this tutorial can be found online. If you have a SAM account, go to www.cengage.com/sam2013 to download the most recent Project Instructions and Start Files.

PRACTICE

Review Assignments

Data File needed for the Review Assignments: Product.accdb (*cont. from Tutorial 10*)

Raj asks you to continue your work on the Product database by enhancing the appearance of the frmSuppliersWithProducts form. To help with this request, complete the following steps:

1. Open the **Product** database you worked with in Tutorials 9 and 10.
2. Create an event procedure for the **frmSuppliersWithProducts** form to convert SupplierName field values to proper case—capitalize the first letter of each word, and convert all other letters to lower case, on the **AfterUpdate** event. Test the procedure, and then close the form.
3. Create an event procedure on the OnCurrent event for the **frmProduct** form to do the following:
   a. Display the Price field value in red when the value is greater than $100 and in black for other values.
   b. Display the message **high price** to the right of the Price text box in bold, red text. Display the message only when the Price field value is greater than $100.
   c. Test the procedure, and then save and close the form.
4. Create a user-defined function called **CapAll** that will accept one argument called **FValue**, convert it to upper case, and return the uppercase value back to the instruction that called it. (*Hint*: Use the UCase function to convert characters to upper case.) Store this user-defined function in a standard module called **basProductProcedures**.
5. In the frmSupplier form, create an event procedure on the AfterUpdate event for the State field that will convert the characters to upper case only if the text box is not empty. Call the CapAll function to perform the character conversion.
6. Make a backup copy of the database, compact and repair the Product database, and then close the database.

APPLY

Case Problem 1

Data File needed for this Case Problem: Job.accdb (*cont. from Tutorial 10*)

GoGopher! Amol Mehta asks you to continue your work on the Job database by enhancing the frmMemberInfo form. To help Amol with his request, complete the following steps:

1. Open the **Job** database you worked with in Tutorials 9 and 10.
2. Create an event procedure for the FirstName field's AfterUpdate event in the frmMemberInfo form to convert the FirstName field values to proper case—capitalize the first letter of each word, and convert all other letters to lower case. Test the procedure.

3. Create an event procedure for the form's OnCurrent event in the frmMemberInfo form to do the following:
   a. If the Expiration date value is earlier than January 1, 2017, display the words "Time to renew" in a label control to the right of the Expiration text box in bold, and red, and display the text in the Expiration control in red.
   b. No special action is required for other Expiration field values.
   c. Test the procedure, and then save your form changes.
4. Create an event procedure for the form's BeforeUpdate event for the frmMemberInfo form to do the following:
   a. The MemberStatus value must be either "active", "inactive", or "on hold". If the MemberStatus field value is invalid, display an appropriate message, cancel the event, undo the change, and move the focus to the MemberStatus field.
   b. Test the procedure, and then save your form changes.
5. Make a backup copy of the database, compact and repair the database, and then close it.

CHALLENGE

Case Problem 2

Data File needed for this Case Problem: Lesson.accdb (*cont. from Tutorial 10*)

O'Brien Educational Services Karen O'Brien wants you to continue your work on the Lesson database by enhancing the frmTutorInfo, frmStudent, and frmContract forms. To help Karen with her request, complete the following steps:

1. Open the **Lesson** database you worked with in Tutorials 9 and 10.
2. Create an event procedure for the AfterUpdate event for the frmTutorInfo form on the School field to convert School field values to proper case—capitalize the first letter of each word, and convert all other letters to lower case. Test the procedure, and then close the form.

Explore 3. Create an event procedure for the form's BeforeUpdate event to verify the Zip field values in the frmStudent form by doing the following:
   a. For a State field value of IN, the first two digits of the Zip field value must equal 46 or 47. If the Zip field value is invalid, display an appropriate message, cancel the event, undo the change, and move the focus to the Zip field. (*Hint*: The condition in the If statement will indicate a Zip field is invalid if the first two digits are not equal to "46" and the first two digits are not equal to "47".)
   b. No special action is required for other Zip field values.
   c. Test the procedure, and then save your form changes.

Explore 4. Create an event procedure for the form's OnCurrent event for the frmContract form to do the following:
   a. Display the SessionType field value in a bold, blue text when the value is "Private" and in normal, black text for all other values. (*Hint*: Use the FontBold property set with the value True for bold or False for not bold, and use the color vbBlue for blue.)
   b. Display the message "Small study room" to the right of the SessionType text box in a label control, in bold, blue text only when the SessionType field value is "Private".
   c. Test the procedure, and then save your form changes.

5. Make a backup copy of the database, compact and repair the database, and then close it.

CHALLENGE

Case Problem 3

Data File needed for this Case Problem: Pet.accdb (*cont. from Tutorial 10*)

Rosemary Animal Shelter Ryan Lang wants you to continue working on the Pet database by creating and enhancing the appearance of the frmDonation form. To help him with his request, complete the following steps:

1. Open the **Pet** database you worked with in Tutorials 9 and 10.
2. Create a form called **frmDonation** form that contains all of the fields from the tblDonation table in tabular layout.
3. Create an event procedure for the AfterUpdate event for the frmDonation form's DonationTypeID field to convert the values to upper case. Although each value in the DonationTypeID field should be a single character, if more than one character is entered, they should all be upper case. Test the procedure.

Explore 4. Create an event procedure for the form's OnCurrent event for the frmDonation form to do the following:

   a. Display the calculated field value (the donation total) in bold, red text when the value is greater than $200 and in regular, black text otherwise. (*Hint*: Use the FontBold property with the value True for bold or False for not bold.)

   b. Display the message "Large donation" to the right of the calculated field text box in a label control, in bold, red text only when the calculated field value is greater than $200.

   c. Test the procedure, and then save your form design changes.

5. Make a backup copy of the database, compact and repair the database, and then close it.

TROUBLESHOOT

Case Problem 4

Data File needed for this Case Problem: Vacation.accdb (*cont. from Tutorial 10*)

Stanley EcoTours Janice and Bill Stanley ask you to continue your work on the Vacation database by enhancing the frmGuestInfo form's accuracy and appearance. To help them with their request, complete the following steps:

1. Open the **Vacation** database you worked with in Tutorials 9 and 10.
2. Open the **frmGuestInfo** form in Design view and ensure the form contains the fields GuestID, GuestFirst, GuestLast, Address, City, StateProv, PostalCode, Country, and Phone.

Troubleshoot 3. The event procedure for the frmGuestInfo form to convert new Country field values to all uppercase letters is not working correctly. Test the procedure and fix the event procedure code to convert the Country field values to uppercase letters.

4. Create an event procedure for the form's OnCurrent event that adds the message "Remind guests about U.S. customs requirements" in a label control on the frmGuestInfo form. Display the message in 14-point, bold, orange text and position it to the right of the GuestID text box. Display the message only when the Country field equals "USA". Save your form changes, and then test the procedure.
5. Make a backup copy of the database, compact and repair the database, and then close it.

TUTORIAL 12

Managing and Securing a Database

Administering the Health Database

ACCESS

OBJECTIVES

Session 12.1
- Filter data in a table and a form
- Save a filter as a query and apply the saved query as a filter
- Create a subquery
- Create a multivalued field

Session 12.2
- Create an Attachment field
- Use an AutoNumber field
- Save a database as a previous version
- Analyze a database's performance
- Link a database to a table in another database
- Use the Linked Table Manager
- Split a database
- Encrypt a database with a password
- Set database properties and startup options

Case | *Chatham Community Health Services*

Raj Gupta and Kelly Schwarz have planned training sessions for staff members to learn how to use the Health database. These training sessions are scheduled to begin right after you finalize the Health database. Your remaining work will address advanced Access features, such as multivalued fields and Attachment fields, and Kelly's concerns about database management, database security, and the database's overall performance. You'll also set database properties and startup options to complete the development of the Health database.

STARTING DATA FILES

Access3 →

Tutorial
- Health.accdb (*cont.*)
- Referral.accdb
- Sandra Parker Associate Degree.docx
- Sandra Parker Bachelor Degree.pdf
- Sandra Parker Expenses.xlsx

Review
- Ads.accdb
- Autoclave_Specification_Sheet.pdf
- Autoclave.xlsx
- Product.accdb (*cont.*)

Case1
- Job.accdb (*cont.*)
- NewTasks.accdb

Case2
- Amy_Hawkins_Associate_Degree.docx
- Amy_Hawkins_Bachelor_Degree.pdf
- Lesson.accdb (*cont.*)
- Room.accdb

Case3
- Pet.accdb (*cont.*)
- Receipt2100.xlsx
- Receipt2101.xlsx
- Rescuers.accdb

Case4
- Leary_1.txt
- Leary_2.txt
- Vacation.accdb (*cont.*)

Session 12.1 Visual Overview:

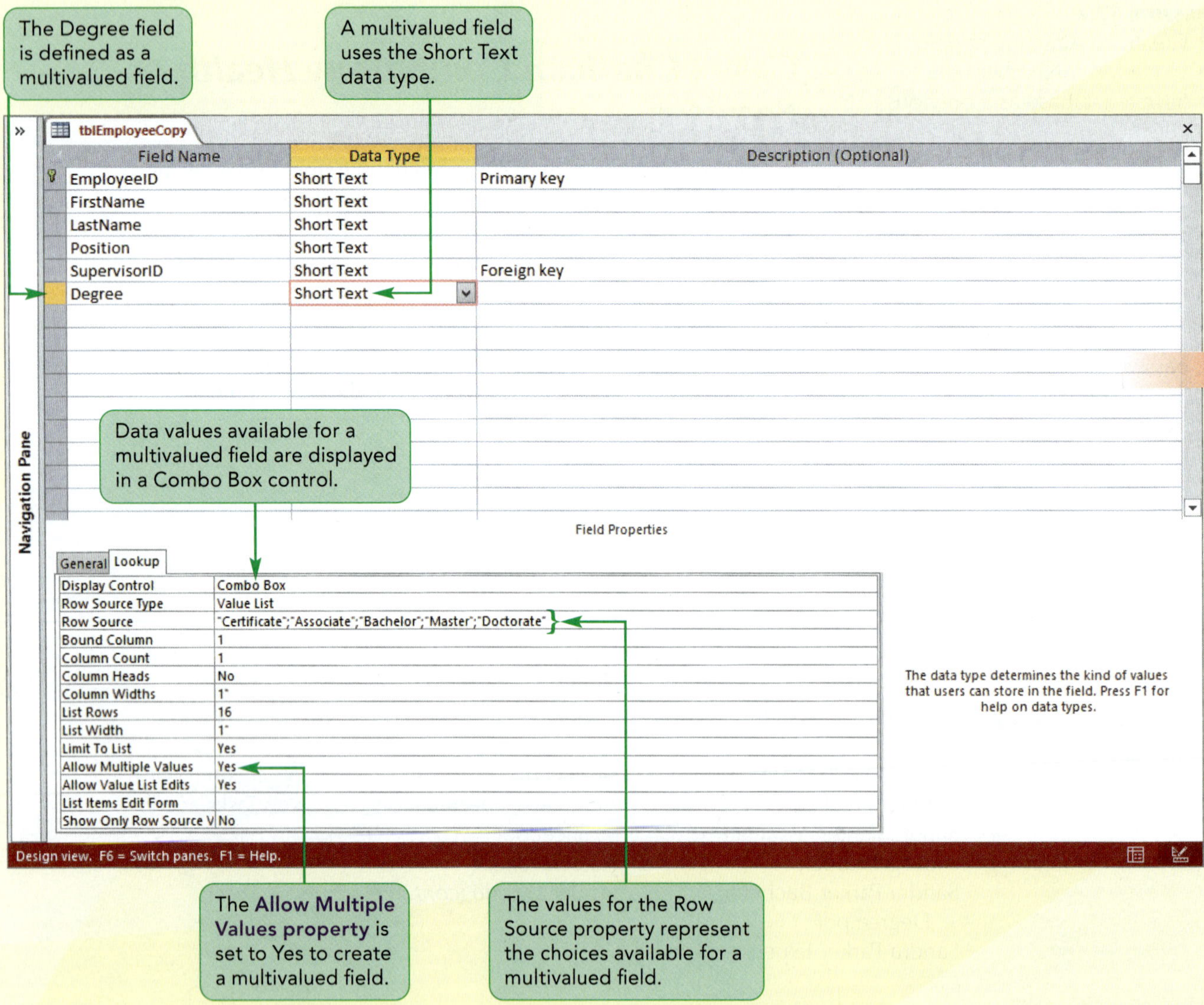

Multivalued Fields and Subqueries

The Degree field is a **multivalued field**, which is a lookup field that allows you to store more than one value in a field in each record.

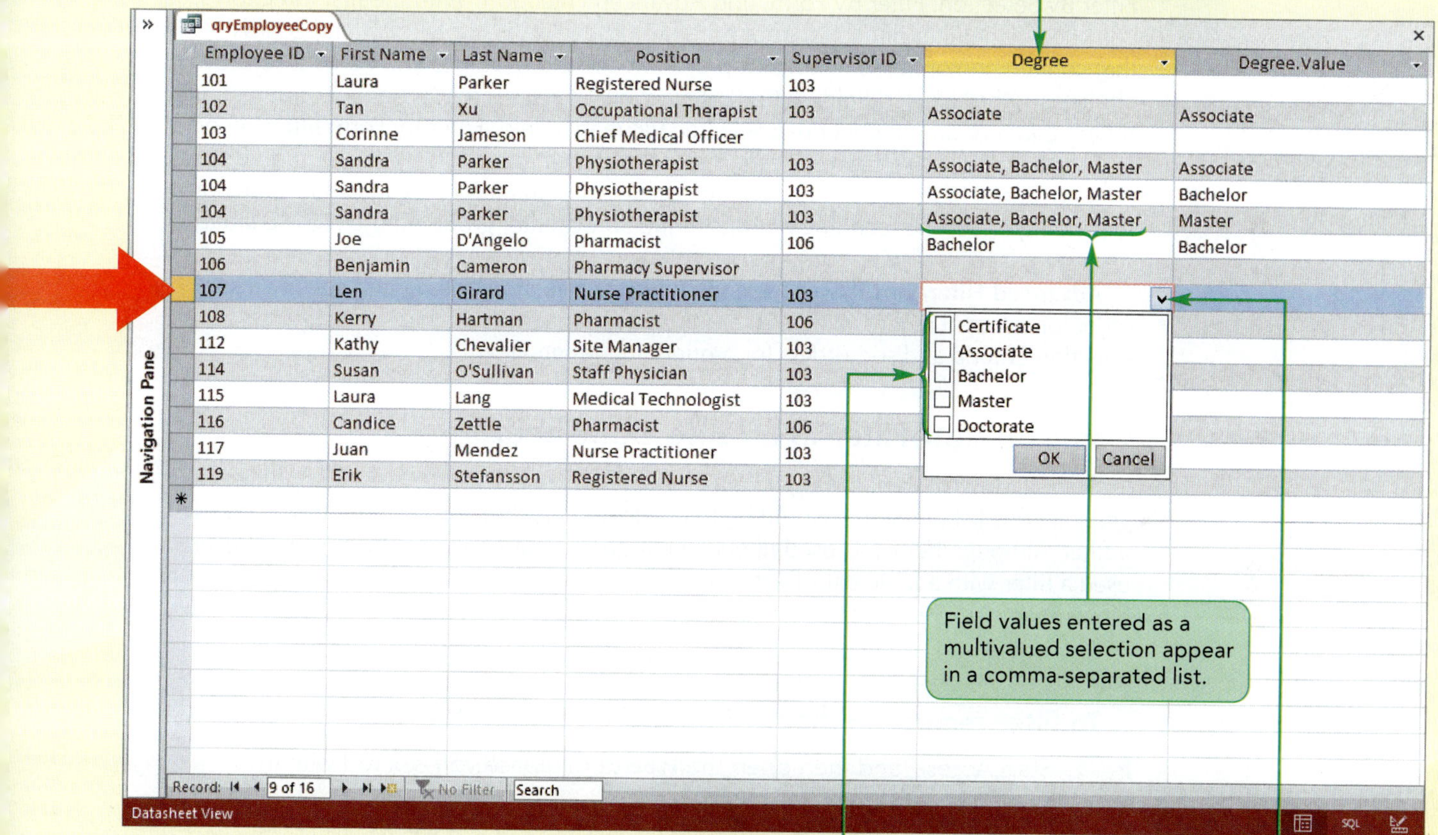

Field values entered as a multivalued selection appear in a comma-separated list.

The values for the multivalued field contain checkboxes to allow you to select more than one value.

When a multivalued field is selected, a drop-down arrow appears.

Filtering Data

Kelly needs answers to a couple questions from the Health database. She needs to know who visited the clinic in November 2015, as well as which patients in Hartford and Windsor have Private health insurance. She'd like a quick method to access this information, without creating a query. You can use a filter to display records from a table or form.

A filter is a set of criteria you place on the records in an open form or datasheet to isolate a subset of the records temporarily. A filter is similar to a query, but it applies only to the open form or datasheet. If you want to use a filter at another time, you can save the filter as a query. A filter can be used only on one datasheet or form, and only with simple criteria. For this reason, it's ideal when you need a quick method to perform a simple query, but it is limited in that you cannot use multiple tables and forms.

Four filter tools let you specify and apply filters in a form or datasheet: AutoFilter, Filter By Selection, Filter By Form, and Advanced Filter/Sort. With the first three tools, you specify the filter directly in the form or datasheet. An AutoFilter filters records that contain one of the selections displayed in a menu of values and context-sensitive choices for the selected field. Filter By Selection filters records that equal or contain (or do not equal or do not contain) a selected value in a field. Filter By Form filters records that match multiple selection criteria using the same Access logical and comparison operators used in queries. After applying one of these filter tools, you can use the Sort Ascending or Sort Descending buttons in the Sort & Filter group on the HOME tab to rearrange the records, if necessary.

Advanced Filter/Sort lets you specify multiple selection criteria and specify a sort order for selected records in the Filter window, in the same way you specify record selection criteria and sort orders for a query in Design view.

Using an AutoFilter in a Table Datasheet

Kelly would like to look through the list of visits in November 2015. One option to generate this list of records would be to create a query, but a quicker method is to use a filter. Although Kelly has used filters with a query datasheet and a form, she's never used a filter with a table datasheet. You'll use a filter to display all clinic visits with November 2015 visit dates in the tblVisit table datasheet.

To filter records in the tblVisit table datasheet:

1. Start Access, and then open the **Health** database you worked with in Tutorials 9–11.
2. Open the Navigation Pane (if necessary), open the **tblVisit** table in Datasheet view, and then close the Navigation Pane.
3. Click the **arrow** on the Date of Visit column heading to open the AutoFilter menu, point to **Date Filters** to open a submenu of context-sensitive options, and then point to **All Dates In Period** to open an additional submenu. See Figure 12-1.

Figure 12-1 **AutoFilter menu and submenus for a date field**

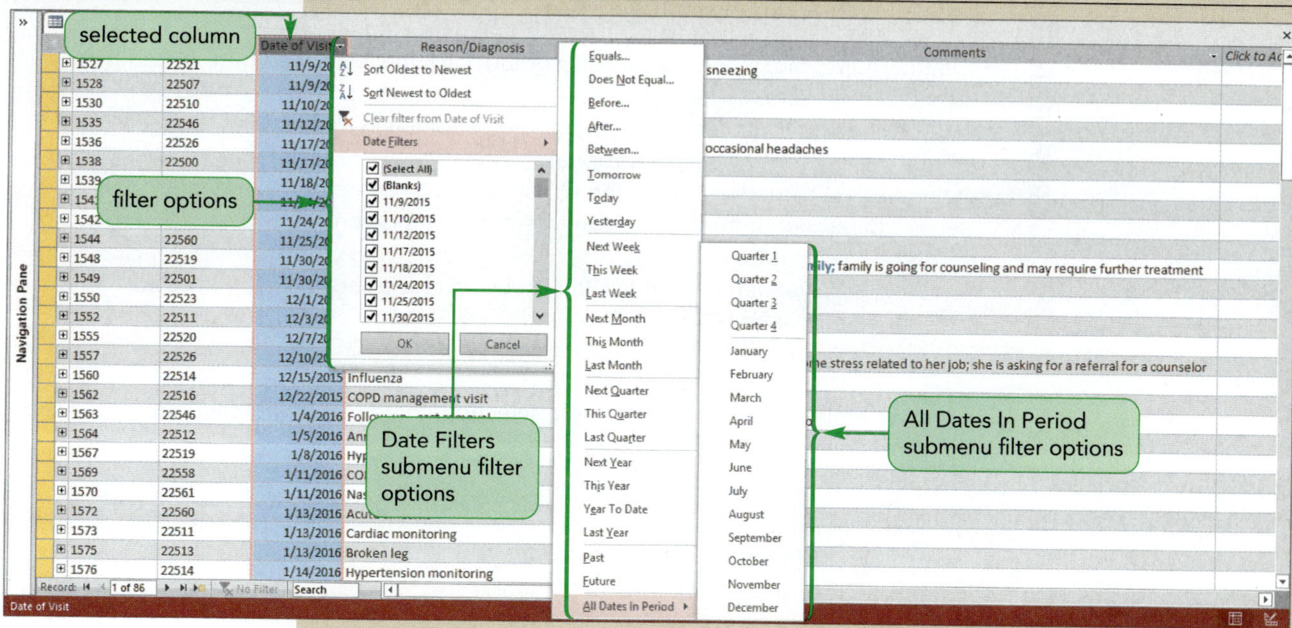

The Date of Visit menu displays all the values that appear in the Date of Visit column; you use the Date of Visit menu when you want to select specific values for the filter. The Date Filters submenu displays filter options that apply to a Date field, and the All Dates In Period submenu displays additional filter options for a Date field.

4. In the All Dates In Period submenu, click **November**. Only the 12 records with November visit dates are displayed in the recordset.

   If you save a table with an applied filter, the filter is saved, and you can reapply the filter anytime you open the table datasheet.

5. Save and close the table.

6. Open the Navigation Pane, open the **tblVisit** table datasheet to display all 86 records, and then on the HOME tab, in the Sort & Filter group, click the **Toggle Filter** button (with the ScreenTip "Apply Filter"). Access applies the VisitDate filter, displaying the 12 records with November visit dates.

7. Close the table.

Next, you'll use Filter By Form to produce the other results Kelly wants—the list of patients from Hartford or Windsor with Private health insurance.

Filter By Form

You can use Filter By Form to display only those records for customers in Hartford or Windsor who have private insurance.

REFERENCE

Selecting Records Using Filter By Form

- Open the table or query datasheet, or the form in Form view.
- On the HOME tab, in the Sort & Filter group, click the Advanced button, and then click Filter By Form.
- Enter a simple selection criterion or an And condition in the first datasheet or form, using the text boxes for the appropriate fields.
- If there is an Or condition, click the Or tab and then enter the Or condition in the second datasheet or form. Continue to enter Or conditions on separate datasheets or forms by using the Or tab.
- On the HOME tab, in the Sort & Filter group, click the Toggle Filter button (with the ScreenTip "Apply Filter").

To answer Kelly's question, the multiple selection criteria you will enter are: Hartford *and* Private *or* Windsor *and* Private.

To select the records using Filter By Form:

1. Open the **tblPatient** datasheet to display the 51 records in the recordset, and then close the Navigation Pane.
2. On the HOME tab, in the Sort & Filter group, click the **Advanced** button, click **Filter By Form** to display a blank datasheet, and then if the City and Insurance Type fields are not visible, press the **Tab** key until both the City and Insurance Type columns are visible. See Figure 12-2.

Figure 12-2 Blank form for Filter By Form option

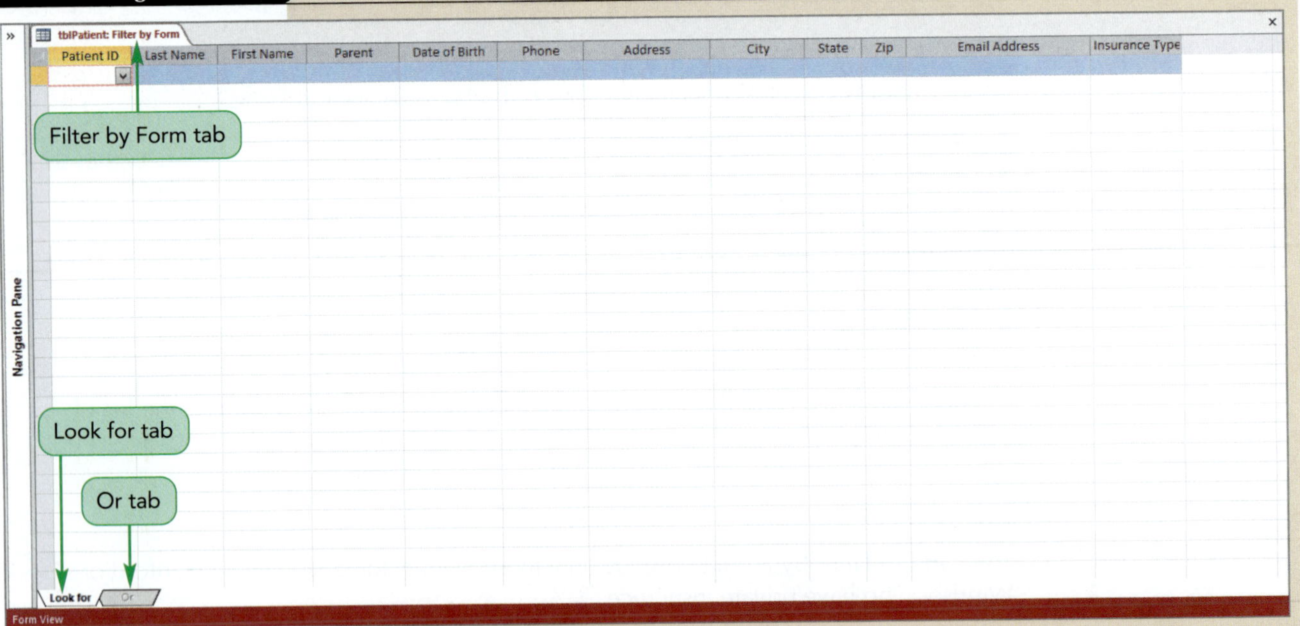

On the blank datasheet, you specify multiple selection criteria by entering conditions in the text boxes for the fields. If you enter criteria in more than one field, you create the equivalent of an And condition—Access selects any record that matches all criteria. To create an Or condition, you enter the criteria for the first part of the condition in the field on the first ("Look for") blank datasheet, and then click the Or tab to display a new blank datasheet.

You enter the criteria for the second part of the condition on the second ("Or") blank datasheet. Access selects any record that matches all criteria on the Look for datasheet or all criteria on the Or datasheet.

For a criterion, you can select a value from the list of values in a text box, or you can use a comparison operator (such as <, >=, <>, and Like) and a value, similar to conditions you enter in the query design grid.

3. Click the **City** box, click the **City** arrow, and then click **Hartford**. Access adds the criterion "Hartford" to the City box.
4. Click the **Insurance Type** box, click the **Insurance Type** arrow, and then click **Private**. Access adds the criterion "Private" to the Insurance Type box.

   Before you add additional options to the filter, you'll verify that the filter is working.

5. In the Sort & Filter group, click the **Toggle Filter** button (with the ScreenTip "Apply Filter").

   The records that contain Hartford for the city and Private for the Insurance Type are displayed. Now you'll return to the Filter by Form window to continue creating the filter.

6. On the HOME tab, in the Sort & Filter group, click the **Advanced** button, and then click **Filter By Form** to return to the filter.

   You've specified the logical operator (And) for the condition "Hartford" And "Private". To add the rest of the criteria, you need to display the Or blank datasheet.

TIP

Notice that a third tab, also labeled "Or," is now available in case you need to specify another Or condition.

7. Click the **Or** tab to display a second blank datasheet. The insertion point is in the Insurance Type box.
8. Click the **Insurance Type** arrow, and then click **Private**.
9. Click the right side of the **City** box to display the list, and then click **Windsor**. The filter now contains the second And condition: "Windsor" And "Private". See Figure 12-3.

Figure 12-3 Completed filter using Filter By Form option

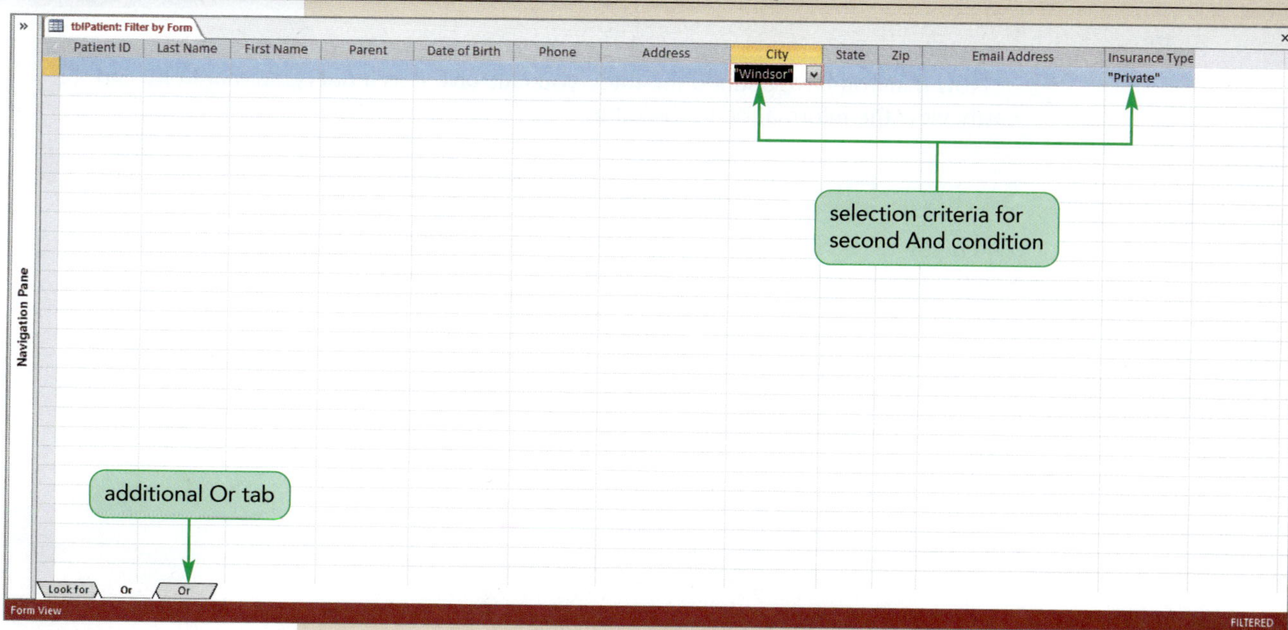

Combined with the Look for conditions, you now have the Or conditions and the complete Filter By Form conditions. Much like building queries, all data that is on the same line in the criteria must be satisfied in order for the record to satisfy the criteria.

10. In the Sort & Filter group, click the **Toggle Filter** button (with the ScreenTip "Apply Filter"), and then scroll to the right until both the City and Insurance Type columns are visible (if necessary). Access applies the filter, displays the four records that match the selection criteria, and displays "Filtered" in the navigation bar. See Figure 12-4.

Figure 12-4 Records that match the Filter By Form criteria

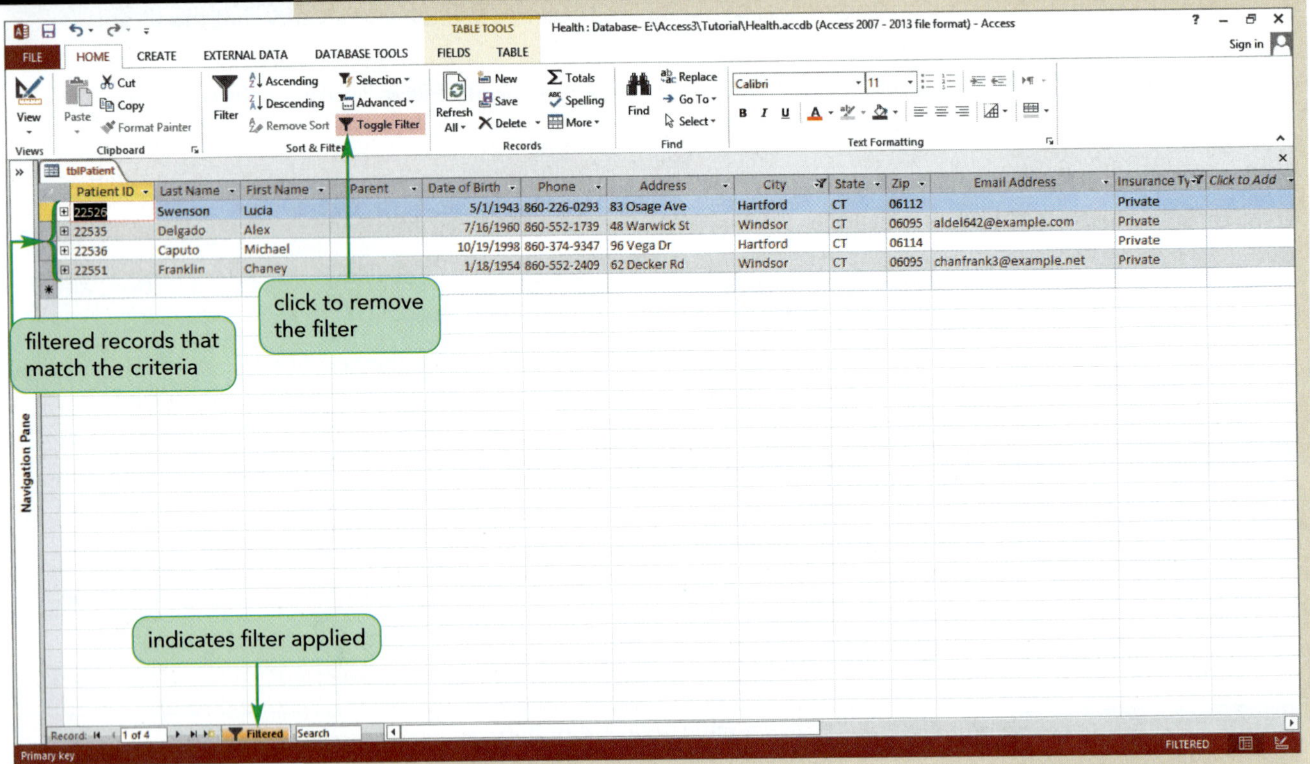

Now that you have defined the filter, you can save it as a query, so that Kelly can easily view the information in the future.

Saving a Filter as a Query

When you save a filter as a query, you can reuse the filter in the future by opening the saved query.

REFERENCE

Saving a Filter as a Query

- Create a filter using Filter By Selection, Filter By Form, or Advanced Filter/Sort.
- If you applied the filter using Filter By Form, click the Advanced button, and then click Filter By Form.
- On the HOME tab, in the Sort & Filter group, click the Advanced button, and then click Save As Query.
- Type the name for the query, and then press the Enter key.

Next, you'll save the filter as a query named qryHartfordWindsorPrivateFilter.

To save the filter as a query:

1. On the HOME tab, in the Sort & Filter group, click the **Advanced** button, and then click **Filter By Form**. Access displays the datasheet with the selection criteria.
2. In the Sort & Filter group, click the **Advanced** button, and then click **Save As Query**. The Save As Query dialog box opens.
3. Type **qryHartfordWindsorPrivateFilter** in the Query Name box, and then click the **OK** button. Access saves the filter as a query in the Health database and closes the dialog box.

   Now you can clear the selection criteria, close the Filter by Form window, and return to Datasheet view.
4. In the Sort & Filter group, click the **Advanced** button, and then click **Clear Grid**. Access removes the selection criteria from the filter datasheet.
5. Close the Filter by Form tab to return to Datasheet view for the tblPatient table. The four filtered records are still displayed in the datasheet and the filter is still applied.
6. In the Sort & Filter group, click the **Toggle Filter** button (with the ScreenTip "Remove Filter"), click the **Advanced** button, and then click **Clear All Filters**. The recordset displays 51 records and the recordset has no filters.

   Next, you'll leave the datasheet open while you open the qryHartfordWindsorPrivateFilter query in Design view.
7. Open the Navigation Pane, open the **qryHartfordWindsorPrivateFilter** query in Design view, and then close the Navigation Pane. In the design grid, the first And condition ("Hartford" And "Private") appears in the Criteria row, the second And condition ("Windsor" And "Private") appears in the or row, and the Or condition combines the first And condition with the second And condition. The Insurance Type condition "Private" appears in each or row. You can interpret this criteria as "the records that contain Hartford and Private, or contain Windsor and Private". See Figure 12-5.

Figure 12-5 Filter saved as a query in Design view

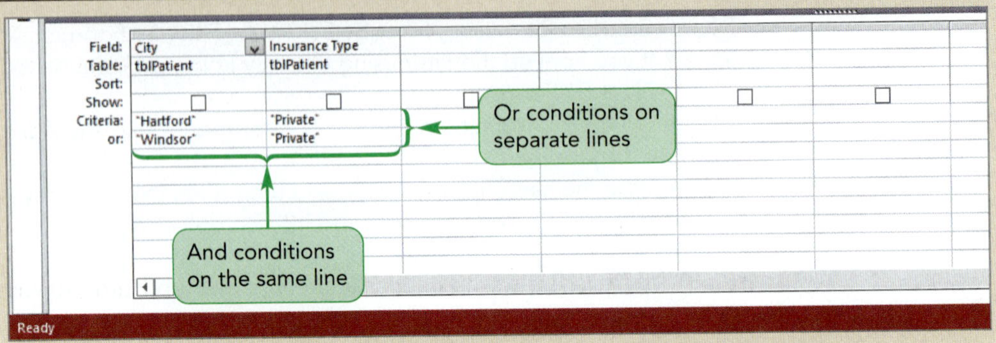

8. Run the query to display the four records that satisfy the selection criteria, close the query, close the table, and then click the **No** button if asked if you want to save the table design changes. You don't want to save the filter with the table because you've already saved the filter as a separate query.

The next time Kelly wants to view the records selected by the filter, she can run the qryHartfordWindsorPrivateFilter query.

Applying a Filter Saved as a Query

To see how to apply a query as a filter to a table, you will open the tblPatient table and apply the qryHartfordWindsorPrivateFilter query as a filter.

REFERENCE

Applying a Filter Saved as a Query

- Open the table to which you want to apply the filter in Datasheet view.
- On the HOME tab, in the Sort & Filter group, click the Advanced button, and then click Filter By Form.
- In the Sort & Filter group, click the Advanced button, and then click Load from Query.
- In the Applicable Filter dialog box, click the query you want to apply as a filter, and then click the OK button.
- On the HOME tab, in the Sort & Filter group, click the Toggle Filter button (with the ScreenTip "Apply Filter") to apply the filter.

To apply the qryHartfordWindsorPrivateFilter query as a filter, you'll first need to open the tblPatient table.

To apply the filter saved as a query:

1. Open the Navigation Pane, open the **tblPatient** table datasheet, and then close the Navigation Pane.
2. In the Sort & Filter group, click the **Advanced** button, and then click **Filter By Form**. Access displays a blank datasheet.
3. In the Sort & Filter group, click the **Advanced** button, and then click **Load from Query**. Access opens the Applicable Filter dialog box. See Figure 12-6.

Figure 12-6 **Applicable Filter dialog box**

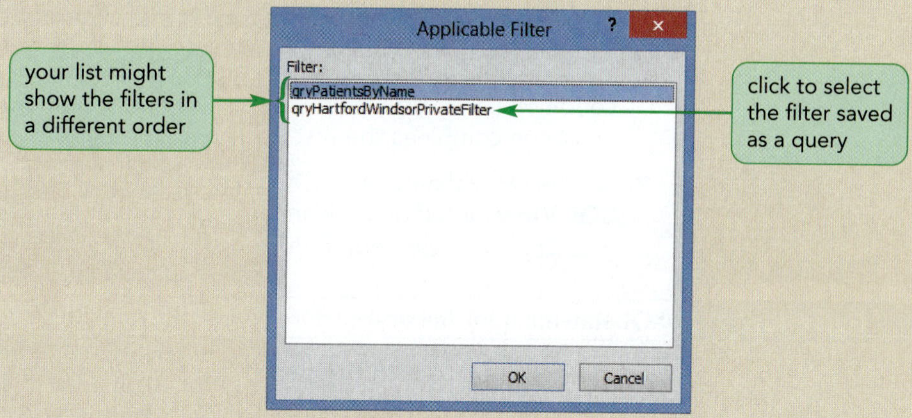

4. Click **qryHartfordWindsorPrivateFilter** in the Filter box if it is not already selected, and then click the **OK** button. Access loads the saved query into the Filter by Form window.
5. In the Sort & Filter group, click the **Toggle Filter** button. Access applies the filter and displays the four filtered records in the datasheet.
6. Click the **Advanced** button, click **Clear All Filters**, and then close the table without saving your design changes.

Kelly finds the qryHartfordWindsorPrivateFilter useful, but she'd also like a list of the patients who visited the clinic, and their visit information, for patients who live in either Hartford or Windsor, and who have private health insurance coverage. To generate this list, you can use the qryHartfordWindsorPrivateFilter as a subquery within a query that searches for these patient visit records in the tblVisit table. You'll modify the qryHartfordWindsorPrivateFilter query to use a subquery.

Creating a Subquery

When you create a query using a SQL SELECT statement, you can place a second SELECT statement inside it; this second query is called a **subquery**. Access runs the subquery first, and then Access uses the results of the subquery to run the outer query. A subquery is also known as an **inner query**. It runs inside another query, referred to as a **parent query**, which is simply a query that contains a subquery. A parent query can also be referred to as an **outer query**.

The records that result from the parent query are the only records that will be used as the dataset for the subquery. You can think of this arrangement as a query within a query. For instance, you might have a query that finds all patients from Hartford, then use a subquery to find all patients within those records who visited the clinic in November. The subquery would be patients who visited in November, and the parent query would be patients whose city is Hartford. This is a simple example and you could certainly create one query that contains both the tblVisit and tblPatient tables, with criteria that sets the city and visit date appropriately. However, in other situations you may be dealing with much more complex parent queries and subqueries. In these cases, rather than dealing with troubleshooting one very complex query, you could build two simpler queries and combine them in this manner. This can be a time-saving technique because you can create a very complex query by combining queries that are easier to understand.

To view the qryHartfordWindsorPrivateFilter query in SQL view:

1. Open the **qryHartfordWindsorPrivateFilter** query in Design view, and then close the Navigation Pane. In the design grid, the first And condition ("Hartford" And "Private") appears in the Criteria row, the second And condition ("Windsor" And "Private") appears in the or row, and the Or condition combines the first And condition with the second And condition.
2. On the DESIGN tab, in the Results group, click the **View button arrow**, click **SQL View**, and then click an unused portion of the window to deselect the SQL SELECT statement. See Figure 12-7.

Figure 12-7 SQL statement for the qryHartfordWindsorPrivateFilter query

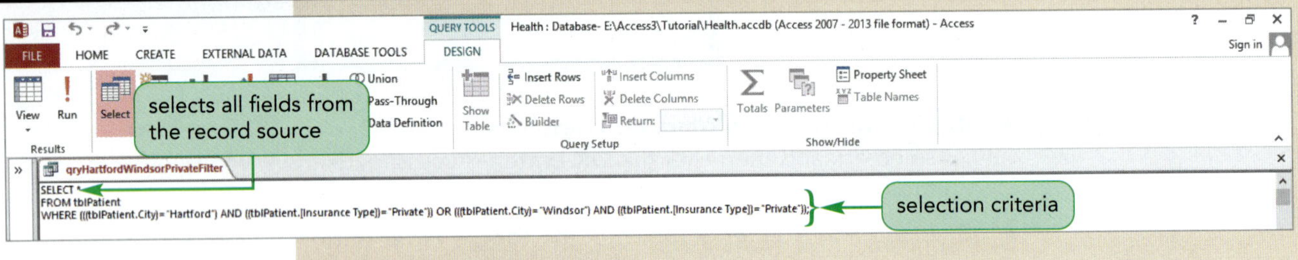

*SELECT * FROM tblPatient* selects all fields from the tblPatient table in the order in which they appear in the table. The WHERE clause specifies the selection criteria: records with a City field value of Hartford and an InsuranceType field value of Private, or records with a City field value of Windsor and an InsuranceType field value of Private.

In the next set of steps, you'll add the following outer query to modify the query to use it as a subquery:

SELECT * FROM tblVisit WHERE PatientID IN (

This will perform a SELECT query to find all fields (*) in the tblVisit table. The IN function will contain the SQL code for the qryHartfordWindsorPrivateFilter query, which becomes the subquery. You'll need to add a right parenthesis) before the final semi-colon to end the subquery. The finished SQL statement is shown in Figure 12-8.

Figure 12-8 SQL SELECT statement using a subquery

outer query SQL code

subquery with additional (at the beginning and) before the ;

```
SELECT *
FROM tblVisit
WHERE PatientID IN
(SELECT PatientID
FROM tblPatient
WHERE (((tblPatient.City)="Hartford") AND ((tblPatient.[Insurance Type])="Private")) OR
(((tblPatient.City)="Windsor") AND ((tblPatient.[Insurance Type])="Private")));
```


Now you'll change the query to use a subquery. Rather than writing the SQL code for the subquery, you'll copy the qryHartfordWindsorPrivateFilter query and then add to this SQL code to form the query that uses this as a subquery.

To create the query that uses a subquery:

1. Close the qryHartfordWindsorPrivateFilter tab, and then open the Navigation Pane.
2. Copy the qryHartfordWindsorPrivateFilter query, and then save it as **qryHartfordWindsorPrivateFilterVisit**.
3. Open the **qryHartfordWindsorPrivateFilterVisit** query in Design view, and then close the Navigation pane.
4. On the DESIGN tab, in the Results group, click the **View button arrow**, click **SQL View**, and then click an unused portion of the window to deselect the SQL SELECT statement.
5. Click to the left of the SELECT statement, press the Enter key three times, and then type the following on the blank lines you inserted:

   SELECT *

   FROM tblVisit

   WHERE PatientID IN

6. Edit the next line to add **(** (a left parenthesis) to the left of SELECT, and then delete the asterisk (*) and replace it with PatientID so the statement is:

   (SELECT PatientID

7. Click to the left of the semicolon at the end of the SQL statement and type **)** (a right parenthesis). See Figure 12-9.

The complete SQL statement should have the same number of left and right parentheses. Be sure to add the left parenthesis before the second SELECT statement, and add a right parenthesis to the left of the semicolon at the end of the SQL statement.

Figure 12-9 SQL statement using a subquery

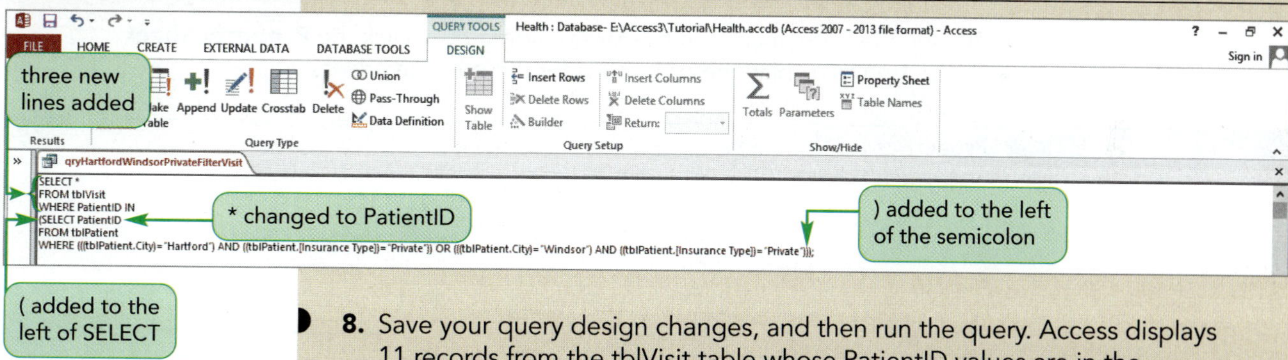

8. Save your query design changes, and then run the query. Access displays 11 records from the tblVisit table whose PatientID values are in the qryHartfordWindsorPrivateFilter.
9. Switch to Design view, and then click the first column's **Field** box to deselect all values. The value in the PatientID Criteria box is a subquery that selects Hartford and Windsor patients who have Private health insurance. See Figure 12-10.

Figure 12-10 **Query using a subquery in the Design window**

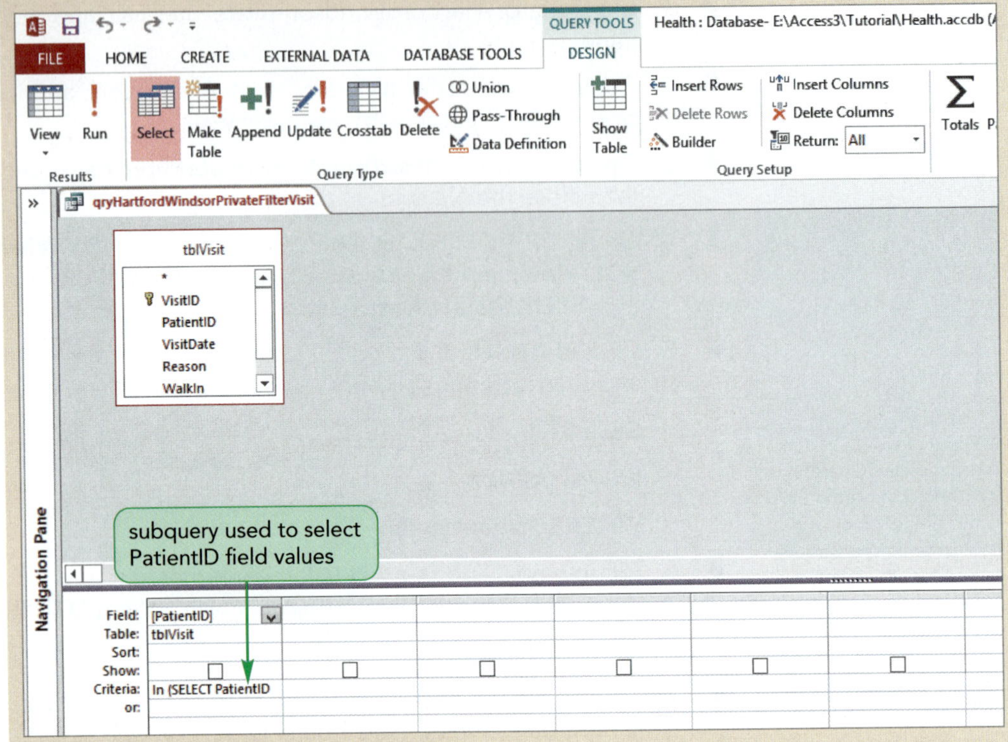

It's unclear from looking at the column in the design grid that all fields are displayed from the tblVisit table.

10. On the DESIGN tab, in the Show/Hide group, click the **Property Sheet** button to display the properties for the query (if necessary). See Figure 12-11.

Figure 12-11 **Properties for the query**

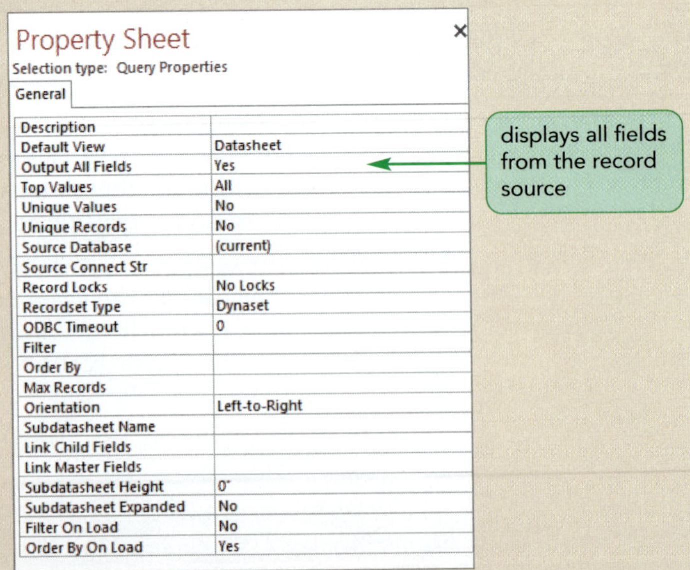

The Output All Fields property setting of Yes specifies that Access displays all fields from the record source, the tblVisit table, without these fields being added to the design grid.

11. Close the property sheet, close the query, and then click the **Yes** button if you're asked to save changes to the query design.

Kelly wants to keep track of the degrees—such as associate's degree, bachelor's degree, and master's degree—earned by employees. Because each employee can earn more than one degree, and each degree can be earned by more than one employee, there's a many-to-many relationship between employees and degrees. To implement this many-to-many relationship, you could use the existing tblEmployee table, create a separate tblDegree table to store the Degree field values, and then create a third table to tie together the other two tables. Instead, you can use a multivalued field.

Using Multivalued Fields

A multivalued field is a lookup field that allows you to store more than one value. Using a multivalued field, you can add a Degree field to the tblEmployee table and use the Lookup Wizard to enter the Degree field values and specify that you want to store multiple values in the Degree field. Kelly and her staff can then select one or more Degree field values from the list of degrees.

INSIGHT

Using Multivalued Fields

When you define a multivalued field in a table, Access does not actually store values in the field in that table. Instead, Access stores the values in hidden, system tables in a many-to-many relationship with the table. Access manages, manipulates, and displays the data to make it appear as if the data was stored in the multivalued field in the table.

Users with limited Access and database experience are the intended audience for multivalued fields because understanding the concepts of many-to-many relationships and creating them are difficult for beginning or casual database users. Experienced database users generally avoid multivalued fields and instead implement many-to-many relationships because that method provides total control over the data, rather than limiting options as working with multivalued fields does. One of the limitations of multivalued fields is that except in special circumstances, you can't sort records based on the values stored in a multivalued field in queries, forms, and reports. Also, multivalued fields do not convert properly to a database managed by a DBMS such as SQL Server or Oracle. If you need to convert an Access database using a multivalued field to another DBMS in the future, you'd have to change the multivalued field to many-to-many relationships, which is a change that's much more difficult at that point than if you had avoided using a multivalued field from the beginning. As a precaution, you should save a copy of the database file before you create a multivalued field.

You'll use the multivalued field feature without modifying the existing tables and relationships, so Raj can decide whether you should keep the multivalued field, or use a traditional many-to-many implementation. You'll make a copy of the tblEmployee table and you will add the multivalued field to the copied version of the table. This way, you can delete the copy of the tblEmployee table if Raj decides not to use a multivalued field. If Raj decides to keep it, you could instead delete the tblEmployee table and rename this new table as the tblEmployee table.

To create a copy of the tblEmployee table:

1. Open the Navigation Pane, right-click **tblEmployee**, and then on the shortcut menu, click **Copy**.
2. In the Clipboard group on the HOME tab, click the **Paste** button to open the Paste Table As dialog box, and then click the **Table Name** box to deselect all values. See Figure 12-12.

Figure 12-12 Paste Table As dialog box

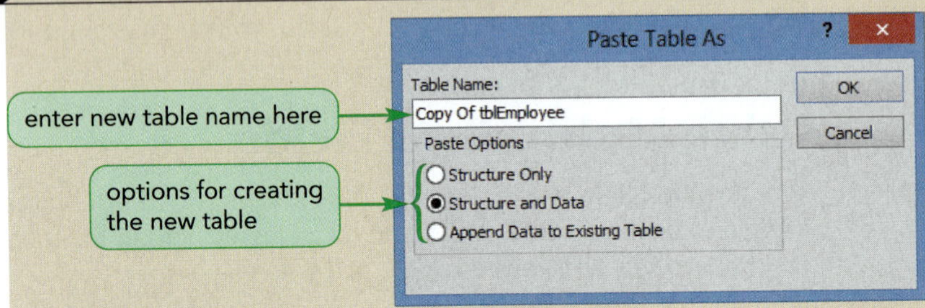

When you copy a table to create a new table, you can use the design of the table without copying its data (Structure Only), use the design and copy the data from the table (Structure and Data), or add the data to an existing table (Append Data to Existing Table).

You'll create the new table using the design and data from the tblEmployee table.

3. Change the name in the Table Name box to **tblEmployeeCopy**, make sure the **Structure and Data** option button is selected, and then click the **OK** button. Access creates a new table named tblEmployeeCopy that contains the same structure and data as the tblEmployee table.

Now you can add the multivalued field to the tblEmployeeCopy table.

To add the multivalued field to the tblEmployeeCopy table:

1. Open the **tblEmployeeCopy** table in Design view, and then close the Navigation Pane.
2. In the blank row below the SupervisorID field, click the **Field Name** box, type **Degree**, press the **Tab** key, click the **Data Type** arrow, and then click **Lookup Wizard**. The first Lookup Wizard dialog box opens.

   You'll type the Degree field values instead of obtaining them from a table or query.

3. Click the **I will type in the values that I want** option button, and then click the **Next** button to open the second Lookup Wizard dialog box, in which you'll type the Degree field values.
4. Click the **Col1** box in the first row, type **Certificate**, press the **Tab** key, type **Associate**, press the **Tab** key, type **Bachelor**, press the **Tab** key, type **Master**, press the **Tab** key, and then type **Doctorate**. These are the five values that users can choose among for the Degree multivalued field. See Figure 12-13.

Figure 12-13 Values for the Degree multivalued field

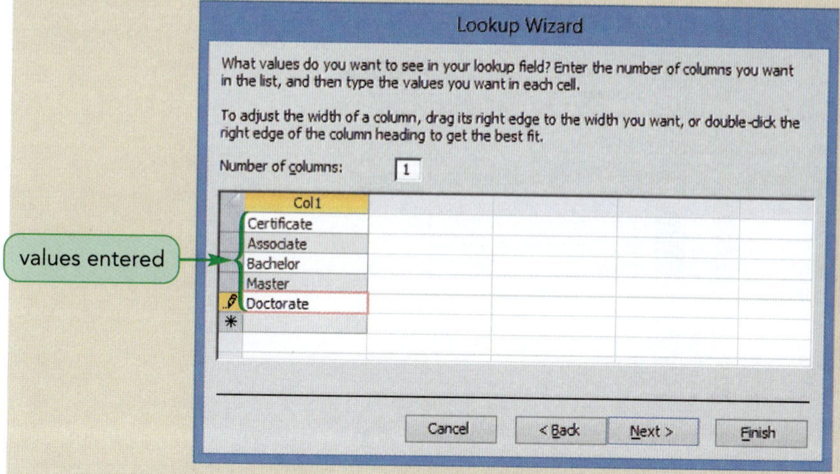

5. Click the **Next** button to open the last Lookup Wizard dialog box, and then click the **Allow Multiple Values** check box to add a check mark to it. See Figure 12-14.

Figure 12-14 Specifying a multivalued field

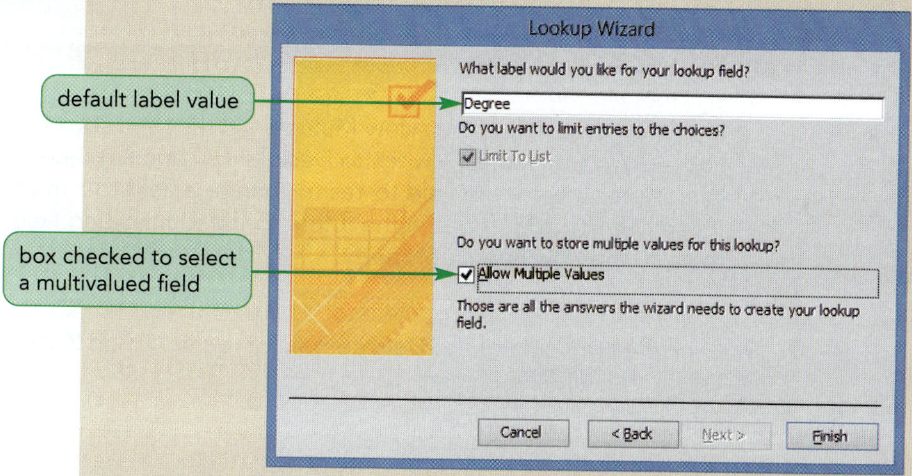

You'll accept the default label name of Degree for the field. When you click the Allow Multiple Values check box to place a check mark in it, you are specifying that you want the Degree field to be a multivalued field.

6. Click the **Finish** button to complete the definition of the Degree field as a lookup field that allows multiple values, or a multivalued field.
7. In the Field Properties pane, click the **Lookup** tab. The Degree field has its Row Source property set to the five values you typed in one of the Lookup Wizard dialog boxes, and the Allow Multiple Values property is set to Yes. See Figure 12-15.

Figure 12-15 After defining the Degree field as a multivalued field

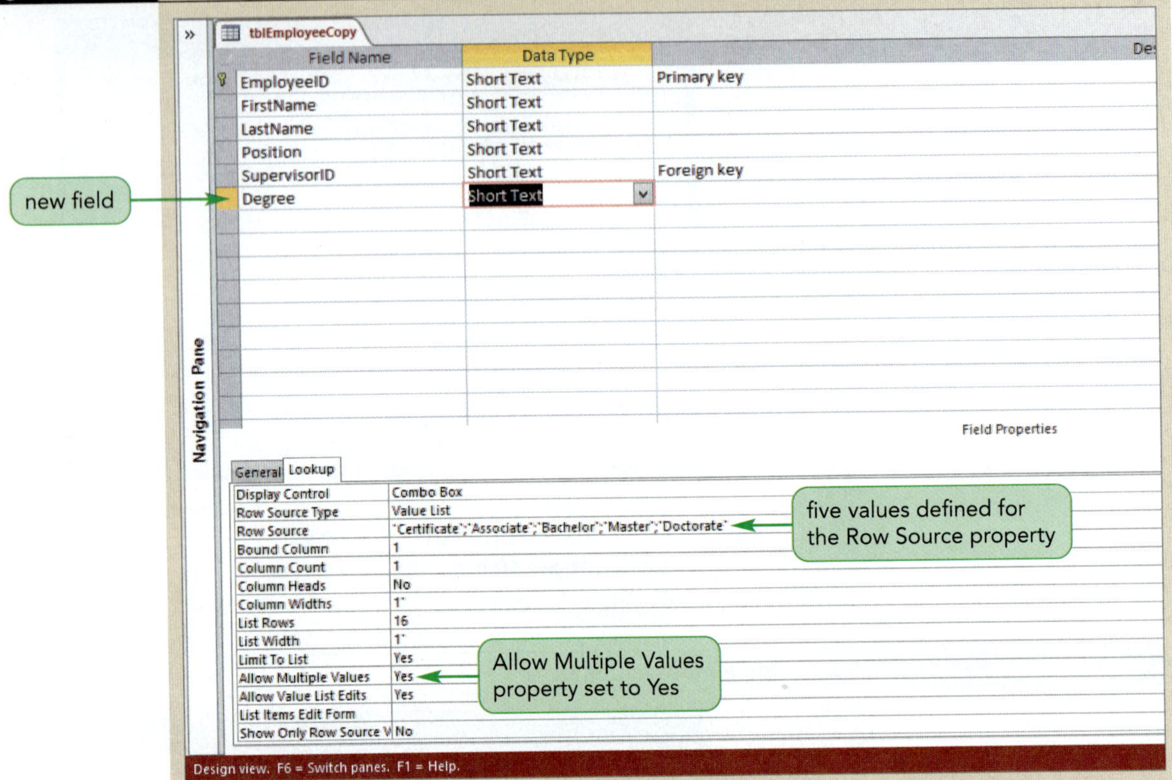

If you forget to select the Allow Multiple Values check box when you use the Lookup Wizard, you can switch to Design view and set the Allow Multiple Values property for the field to Yes to change a field to a multivalued field. If you need to add values in the future to the multivalued field, you can add them to the Row Source property.

8. Save your table design changes, and then switch to Datasheet view.
9. Click the right side of the **Degree** box for record 2 (Tan Xu) to open the value list for the field. See Figure 12-16.

Figure 12-16 Value list for the Degree multivalued field

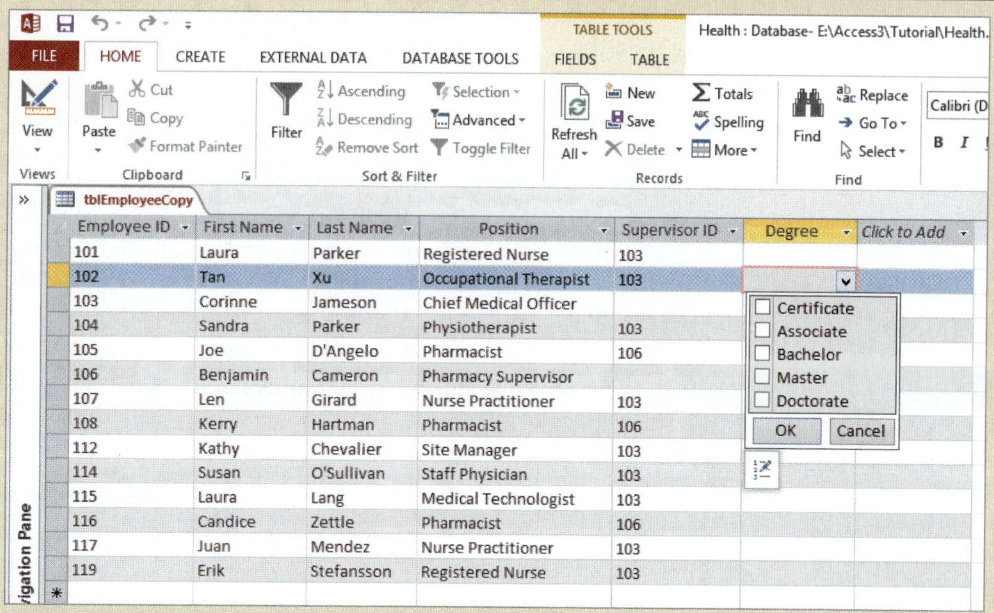

> **TIP**
> In the Sort & Filter group, the Ascending and Descending buttons are dimmed because you can't sort records based on multivalued fields.

10. Click the **Associate** check box, and then click the **OK** button.
11. Repeat Steps 9 and 10 for record 4 (Sandra Parker), selecting **Associate**, **Bachelor**, and **Master**, and for record 5 (Joe D'Angelo), selecting **Bachelor**, and then resize the Degree column to its best fit. Records 2 (Tan Xu) and 5 (Joe D'Angelo) each have one value in the Degree field, and record 4 (Sandra Parker) has three values selected for the Degree field. See Figure 12-17.

Figure 12-17 After selecting values for the multivalued field

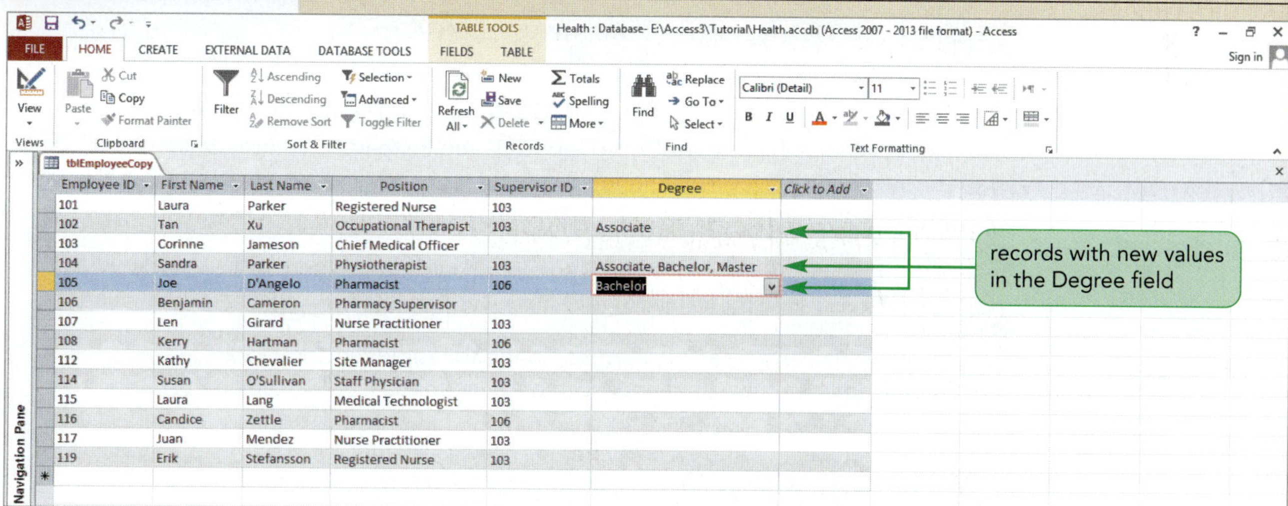

Next, you'll create queries to display all field values from the tblEmployeeCopy table to display the multivalued field values.

To create queries to display the Degree multivalued field:

1. Save and close the tblEmployeeCopy table, click the **CREATE tab**, and then in the Queries group, click the **Query Wizard** button to open the New Query dialog box.
2. Make sure the **Simple Query Wizard** option is selected, click the **OK** button to open the Simple Query Wizard dialog box, from the tblEmployeeCopy table select all fields, click the **Next** button, change the query title to **qryEmployeeCopy**, click the **Finish** button, and then click the first row's Employee ID column value to deselect all values (if necessary). Size the Degree.Value column to fit the data. Access displays 16 records in the query recordset. See Figure 12-18.

Figure 12-18 **Query that displays the Degree multivalued field**

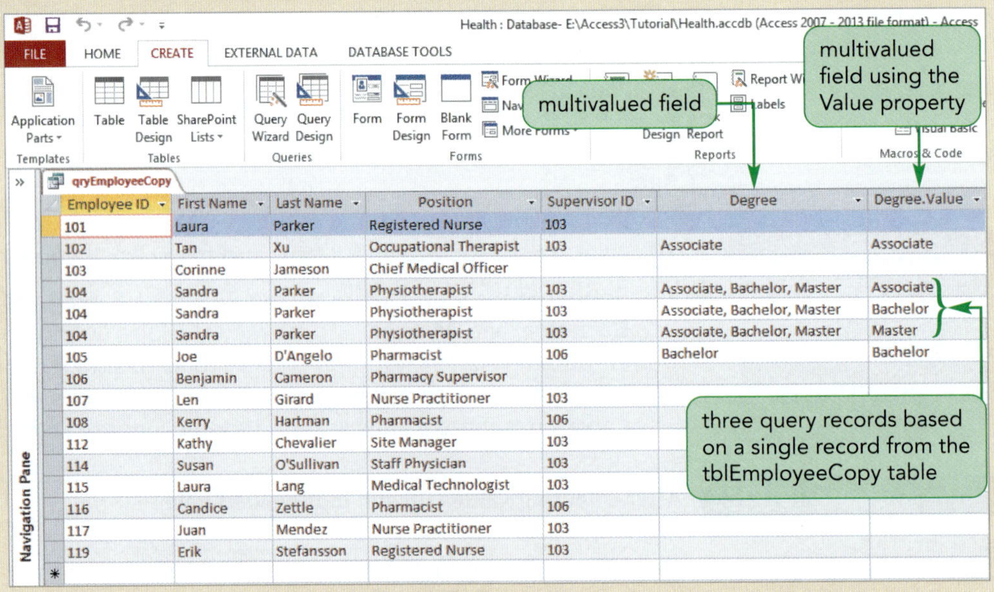

Employee ID	First Name	Last Name	Position	Supervisor ID	Degree	Degree.Value
101	Laura	Parker	Registered Nurse	103		
102	Tan	Xu	Occupational Therapist	103	Associate	Associate
103	Corinne	Jameson	Chief Medical Officer			
104	Sandra	Parker	Physiotherapist	103	Associate, Bachelor, Master	Associate
104	Sandra	Parker	Physiotherapist	103	Associate, Bachelor, Master	Bachelor
104	Sandra	Parker	Physiotherapist	103	Associate, Bachelor, Master	Master
105	Joe	D'Angelo	Pharmacist	106	Bachelor	Bachelor
106	Benjamin	Cameron	Pharmacy Supervisor			
107	Len	Girard	Nurse Practitioner	103		
108	Kerry	Hartman	Pharmacist	106		
112	Kathy	Chevalier	Site Manager	103		
114	Susan	O'Sullivan	Staff Physician	103		
115	Laura	Lang	Medical Technologist	103		
116	Candice	Zettle	Pharmacist	106		
117	Juan	Mendez	Nurse Practitioner	103		
119	Erik	Stefansson	Registered Nurse	103		

Trouble? The rightmost column heading on your screen might be the equivalent tblEmployeeCopy.Degree.Value instead of Degree.Value, indicating the Degree field in the tblEmployeeCopy table. This difference does not affect the contents of the column.

The six fields from the tblEmployeeCopy table are displayed in seven columns in the query recordset because the Degree field is displayed in two columns: the Degree column and the Degree.Value column. The Degree column displays field values exactly as they appear in the tblEmployeeCopy table; all values for the Degree multivalued field, such as those for Sandra Parker, are displayed in one row in the query. The Degree.Value column displays the Degree multivalued field in expanded form so that each value appears in a separate row in the query. *Degree.Value* identifies the Degree field and the Value property for the Degree field.

In queries that contain a multivalued field, you should display the field in a single column, not in two columns, with values appearing as they are in the table or in expanded form. You can eliminate the extra column by deleting it, by clearing its Show check box in Design view, or by selecting just one of the two fields in the Simple Query Wizard when you select the fields for the query.

3. Click the **HOME tab**, notice that the Ascending and Descending buttons in the Sort & Filter group are active, click the first row's **Degree** box, notice that the Ascending and Descending buttons are dimmed, and then click the first row's **Degree.Value** box. The Ascending and Descending buttons are active and you can sort records in the query based on the values in the Degree.Value column.

   Next, you'll review the query design.

4. Switch to Design view, and then drag down the bottom of the tblEmployeeCopy field list to show all values in the list. See Figure 12-19.

Figure 12-19 **Design of the query containing the Degree multivalued field**

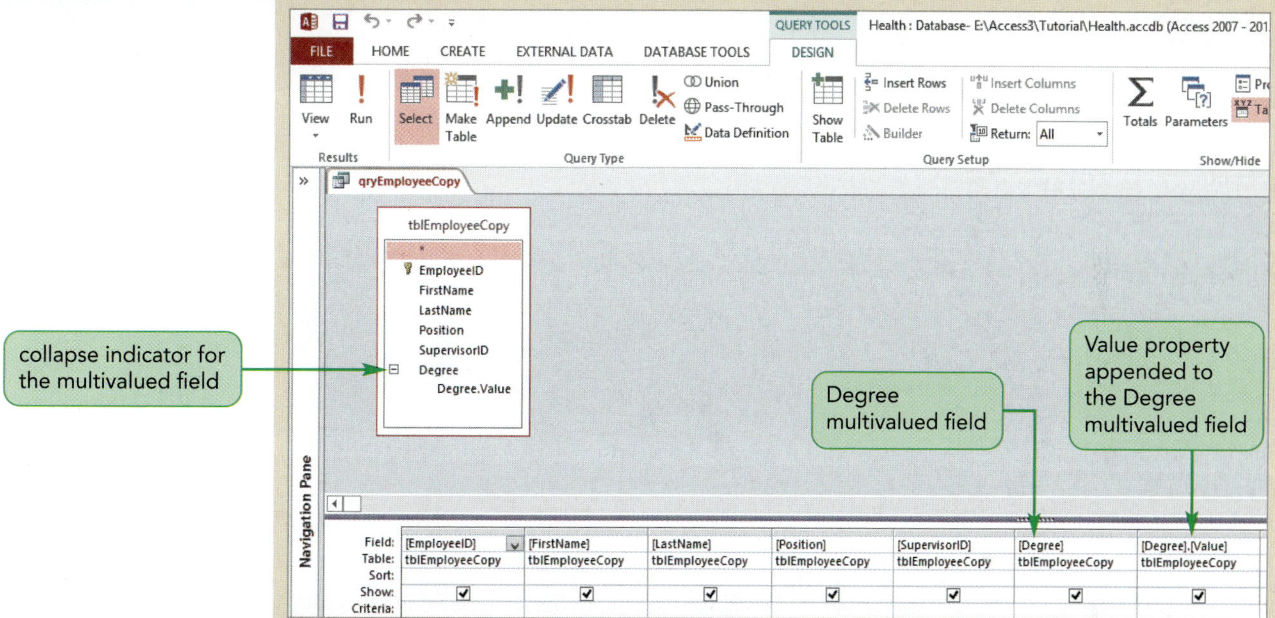

The Degree field in the tblEmployeeCopy field list has a collapse indicator to its left that you can click to hide the Degree.Value entry below it. The right-most column in the design grid, [Degree].[Value], uses the Value property for the Degree field. Using the **Value property** with a multivalued field displays the multivalued field in expanded form so that each value is displayed in a separate row.

You'll delete the [Degree] column from the query design, retaining the [Degree].[Value] column and setting its Caption property, and then you'll save the query with a new name.

5. Right-click the **column selector bar** for the [Degree] column to highlight the column and open the shortcut menu, and then click **Cut**.

6. Click the **column selector bar** for the [Degree].[Value] column to select it, open the property sheet for the [Degree].[Value] column, set the Caption property to **Degree**, and then close the property sheet.

7. Click the **File** tab, click **Save As**, then **Save Object As**, then click the **Save As button** to open the Save As dialog box, change the query name to **qryEmployeeCopyValue**, click the **OK** button, click the **HOME** tab, and then switch to Datasheet view. Access displays 16 records in the query recordset.

8. Close the query, open the Navigation Pane, open the **qryEmployeeCopy** query in Design view, and then close the Navigation Pane.
9. Delete the **Degree.Value** column, save the query, and then run the query. Access displays the 14 records from the tblEmployeeCopy table and displays the Degree multivalued field values in one row.
10. Close the query, and then if you are not continuing on to the next session, close the Health database.

Kelly and Raj are pleased with your work, and Raj will review it as he decides whether to use the multivalued Degree field or a many-to-many relationship. In the next session, you'll add Attachment fields using the tblEmployeeCopy table.

REVIEW

Session 12.1 Quick Check

1. Filter By ____________ filters records that match multiple selection criteria using the same Access comparison operators used in queries.
2. You can save a filter as a(n) ____________ and reuse the filter by opening the saved object.
3. What is a subquery?
4. What is a multivalued field?
5. You use the ____________ property to display a multivalued field in expanded form so that each value is displayed in a separate row in a query.

Session 12.2 Visual Overview:

The Current Database option displays options that apply only to the currently open database.

The **Application Title property** value appears in the Access window title bar.

The **Display Form property** specifies the form that opens automatically when you open the database.

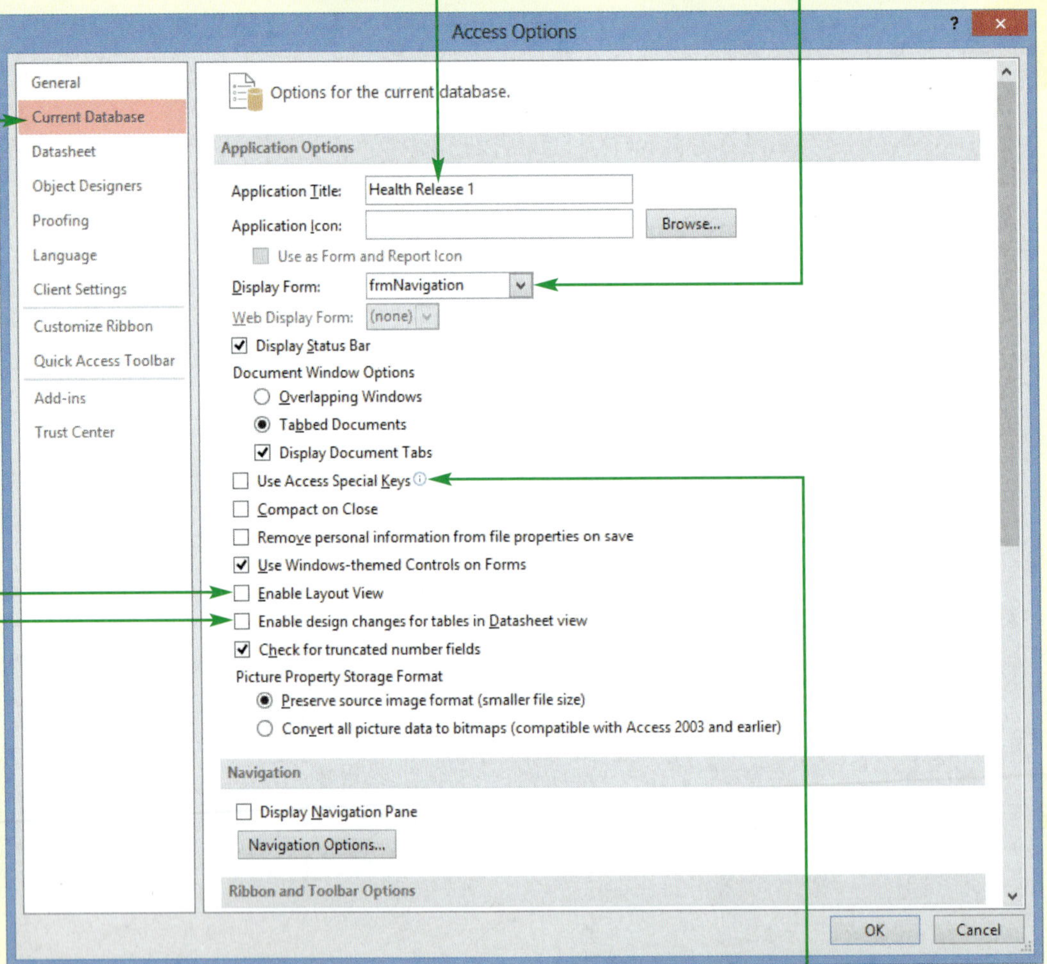

The **Enable Layout View property** shows/hides the Layout View button on the Access status bar and on shortcut menus.

The **Enable design changes for tables in Datasheet view property** allows you to change a table's design in Datasheet view.

The **Use Access Special Keys property** enables or disables the F11 key (show/hide the Navigation Pane), Ctrl+G (show/hide the Immediate window in VB editor), and Alt+F1 (start VB Editor).

Database Properties

The **Display Navigation pane property** controls whether the Navigation Pane is available in the Access window.

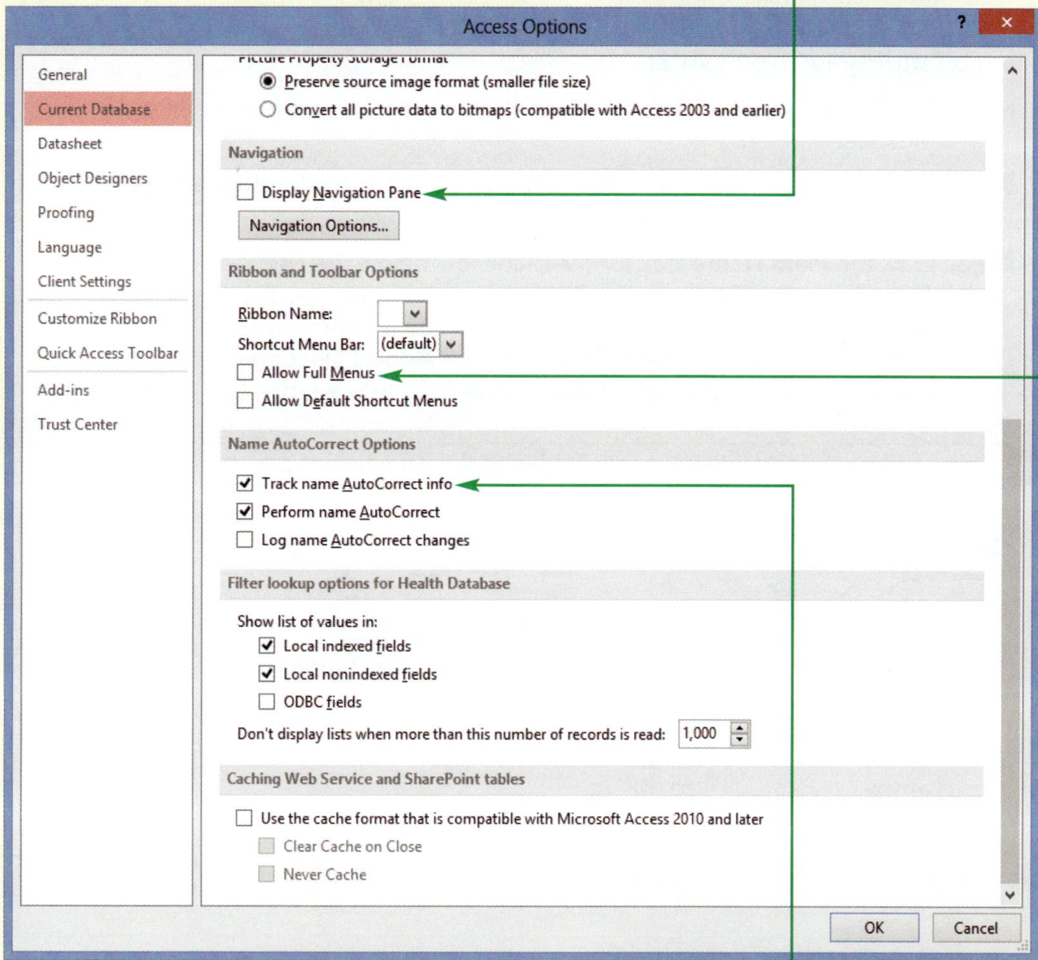

The **Allow Full Menus property** shows/hides all options on the ribbon. Uncheck to display only the FILE and HOME tabs.

The **Track name AutoCorrect info property** stores information about changes to the names of fields, controls, and objects.

Creating an Attachment Field

In addition to storing data such as text, numbers, and dates in a database, you can attach external files such as Excel workbooks, Word documents, and images, similar to how you attach external files to email messages. You use the **Attachment data type** to attach one or more files to a table record. Access stores attachments as part of the database. An attachment data field can contain one or more file attachments in a table record.

TIP

After you change a field type to Attachment, you can't change the field type again. Instead, you have to delete the field and re-create it with a new field type.

Raj wants to be able to attach documents to the tblEmployeeCopy table that contains information about Sandra Parker's degrees and expenses. You'll add a field with the Attachment data type and use it to attach the documents to the table.

To add a new field with the Attachment data type to the tblEmployeeCopy table:

1. If you took a break after the previous session, make sure that the Health database is open.
2. Open the Navigation Pane (if necessary), open the **tblEmployeeCopy** table in Design view, and then close the Navigation Pane.
3. Click the **Field Name** box for the blank row below the Degree field, type **AddedDocuments**, press the **Tab** key, type **at**, press the **Tab** key to select Attachment as the data type, press the **F6** key to switch to the Caption box in the Field Properties pane, and then type **Added Documents**. You've completed adding the AddedDocuments field to the table. See Figure 12-20.

Figure 12-20 After adding the AddedDocuments field with the Attachment data type

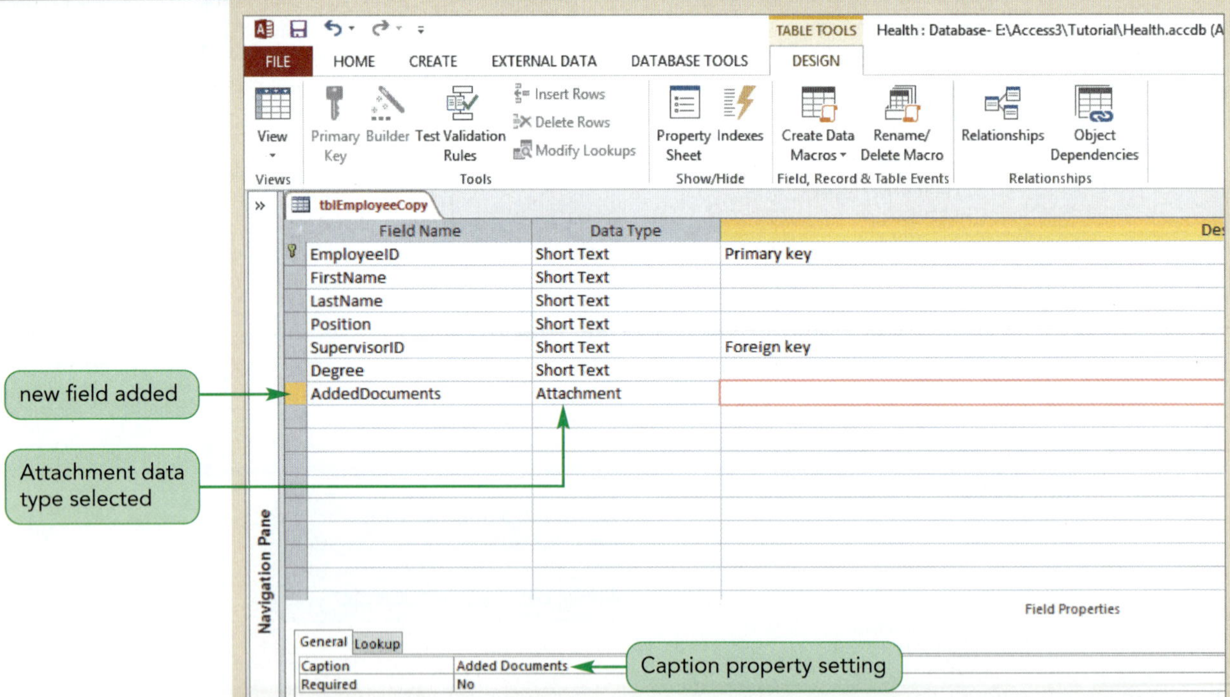

4. Save your table design changes, switch to Datasheet view, resize the Added Documents column to its best fit, click the first row's **Employee ID** box to deselect all values, and then save your datasheet format changes. See Figure 12-21.

Figure 12-21 Attachment field displayed in the table datasheet

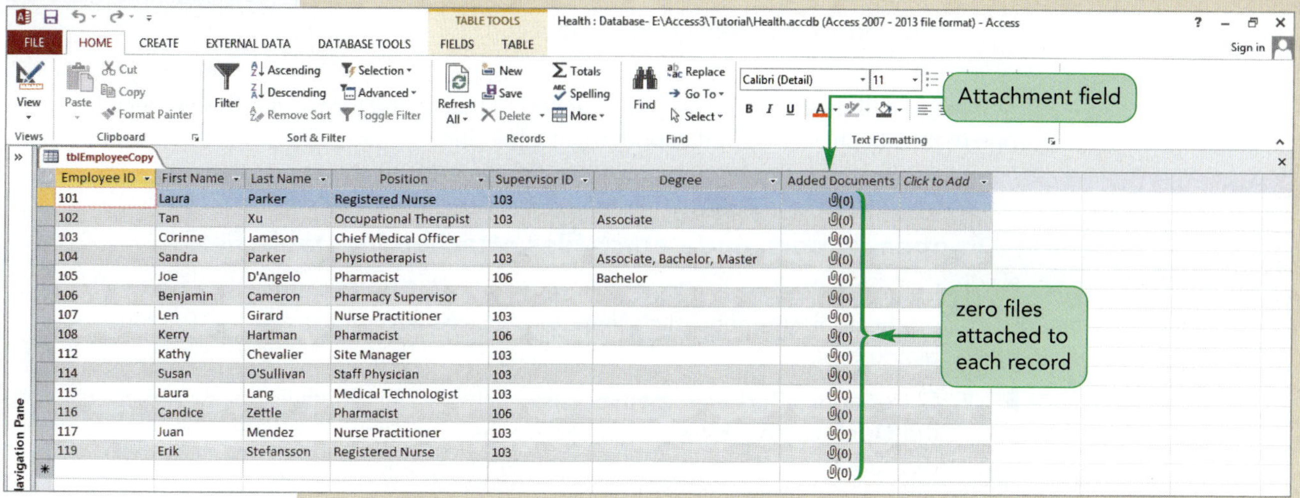

Each AddedDocuments field value displays an attachment icon in the shape of a paper clip followed by a number in parentheses that indicates the number of files attached in that field for the record. You haven't attached any files, so each record displays zero file attachments.

Raj has some files from Sandra Parker that he would like you to attach to her record in the Added Documents column.

5. In the row for Sandra Parker, right-click the **Added Documents** box to open the shortcut menu, and then click **Manage Attachments** to open the Attachments dialog box.

   You'll add all three of Sandra's files (Sandra Parker Associate Degree.docx, Sandra Parker Bachelor Degree.pdf, and Sandra Parker Expenses.xlsx) as attachments to the AddedDocuments field for Sandra Parker.

6. Click the **Add** button to open the Choose File dialog box, navigate to the Access3 ▸ Tutorial folder, click **Sandra Parker Associate Degree**, and then click the **Open** button to add the Sandra Parker Associate Degree.docx file to the Attachments dialog box.

7. Click the **Add** button to open the Choose File dialog box, click **Sandra Parker Bachelor Degree**, hold down the **Ctrl** key, click **Sandra Parker Expenses**, release the **Ctrl** key, and then click the **Open** button. The three files you've added now appear in the Attachments dialog box. See Figure 12-22.

Figure 12-22 Attachments dialog box

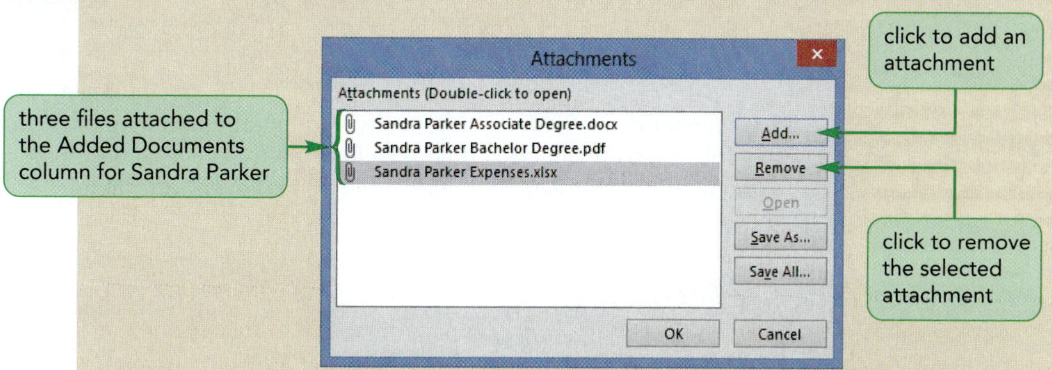

8. Click the **OK** button to close the dialog box. The table datasheet now indicates that three files (as noted by the 3 in parentheses) are attached to the AddedDocuments field in the record for Sandra Parker.

Next, you'll open one of the files attached in the record for Sandra Parker, detach one of the attached files, and export an attached file.

To open, export, and detach files attached in a table field:

1. In the row for Sandra Parker, right-click the **AddedDocuments** box, and then on the shortcut menu click **Manage Attachments** to open the Attachments dialog box.
2. Click **Sandra Parker Expenses.xlsx** in the Attachments list, and then click the **Open** button. Excel starts and opens the Sandra Parker Expenses workbook.
3. Exit Excel.
4. Click **Sandra Parker Associate Degree.docx** in the Attachments list, and then click the **Remove** button. Access removes the Sandra Parker Associate Degree document from the Attachments list and detaches the Sandra Parker Associate Degree document from her row's AddedDocuments field.

> **TIP**
> The Sandra Parker Associate Degree.xlsx document remains in the Access3 ▸ Tutorial folder because detaching a file doesn't delete it.

5. Click **Sandra Parker Bachelor Degree.pdf** in the Attachments list, click the **Save As** button to open the Save Attachment dialog box, type **Sandra Parker Bachelor Degree Export.pdf** in the File name box, make sure the Access3 ▸ Tutorial folder is the current destination folder, and then click the **Save** button. Access exports the Sandra Parker Bachelor Degree.pdf file with the name Sandra Parker Bachelor Degree Export.pdf and saves it in the Access3 ▸ Tutorial folder.
6. Click the **OK** button to close the Attachments dialog box. Because you removed the Sandra Parker Associate Degree.docx file as an attachment, the Added Documents column for the Sandra Parker record now shows that there are two attachments.

Raj is considering adding an employee number for each employee that could be automatically generated when a new employee record is added. You can do this by adding an AutoNumber field to the tblEmployeeCopy table.

Using an AutoNumber Field

> **TIP**
> Read the Natural, Artificial, and Surrogate Keys section in the appendix titled "Relational Databases and Database Design" for more information about AutoNumber fields and primary keys.

When you create a table in Datasheet view, Access assigns the AutoNumber data type to the default ID primary key field because the AutoNumber data type automatically inserts a unique number in this field for every record in the table. Therefore, it can serve as the primary key for any table you create. When defining a field with the AutoNumber data type, you can specify sequential numbering or random numbering, either of which guarantees a unique field value for every record in the table.

You'll add an AutoNumber field to the tblEmployeeCopy table.

To add an AutoNumber field to the tblEmployeeCopy table:

1. Switch to Design view, right-click the **row selector** for the EmployeeID field to open the shortcut menu, and then click **Insert Rows**. Access adds a blank row above the EmployeeID row. Next, you'll add the AutoNumber field to this new first row in the table design.
2. Click the first row's **Field Name** box, type **EmployeeNum**, press the **Tab** key, type **a**, press the **Tab** key to accept AutoNumber as the data type, press the **F6** key to switch to the Field Properties pane, press the **Tab** key three times to navigate to the Caption box, and then type **Employee Num** in the Caption box and press the **Tab** key to finish the entry. You've finished adding the EmployeeNum field to the table. See Figure 12-23.

Figure 12-23 After adding the EmployeeNum field with the AutoNumber data type

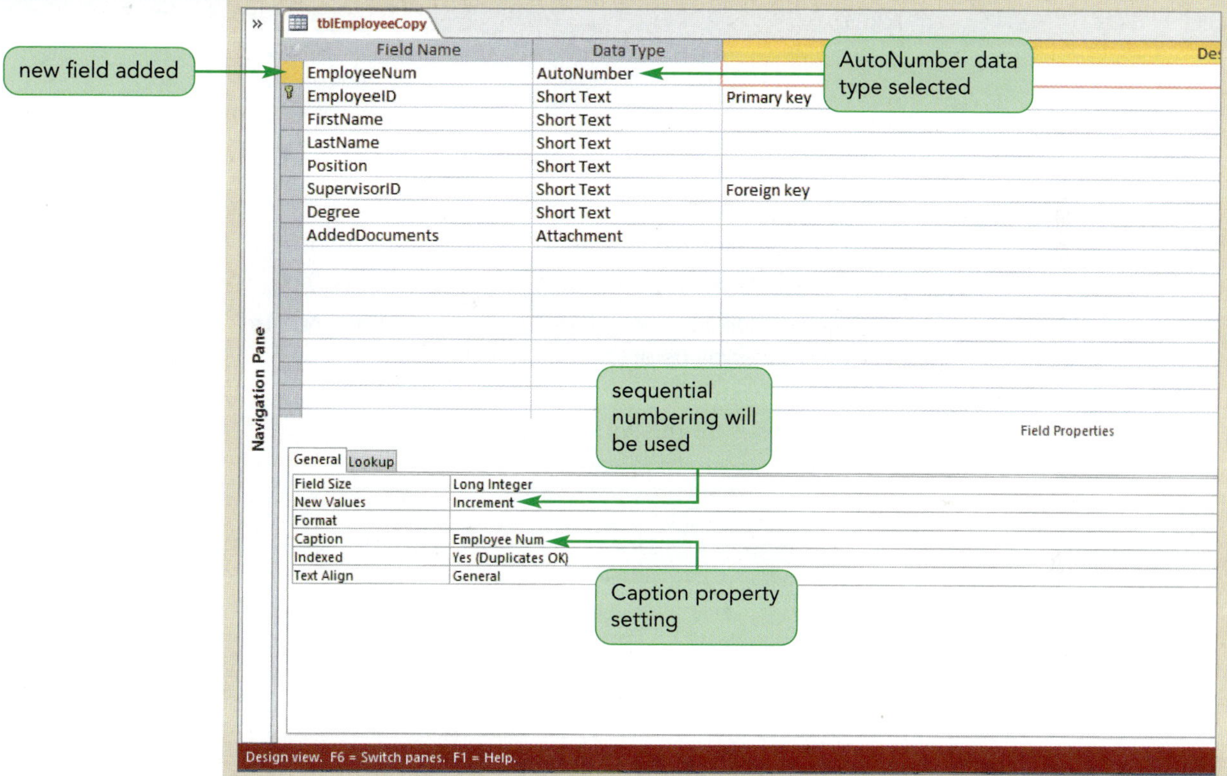

The default New Values property setting of Increment specifies that sequential numbering will be used for the AutoNumber field. The other New Values property value you can select is Random.

3. Save your table design changes, switch to Datasheet view, resize the first column to its best fit, and then click the first row's **Employee Num** box to deselect all values. The new EmployeeNum field is displayed as the first column in the table, and Access has automatically assigned unique sequential numbers to the EmployeeNum field for the 14 records in the table. See Figure 12-24.

Figure 12-24 AutoNumber field displayed in the table datasheet

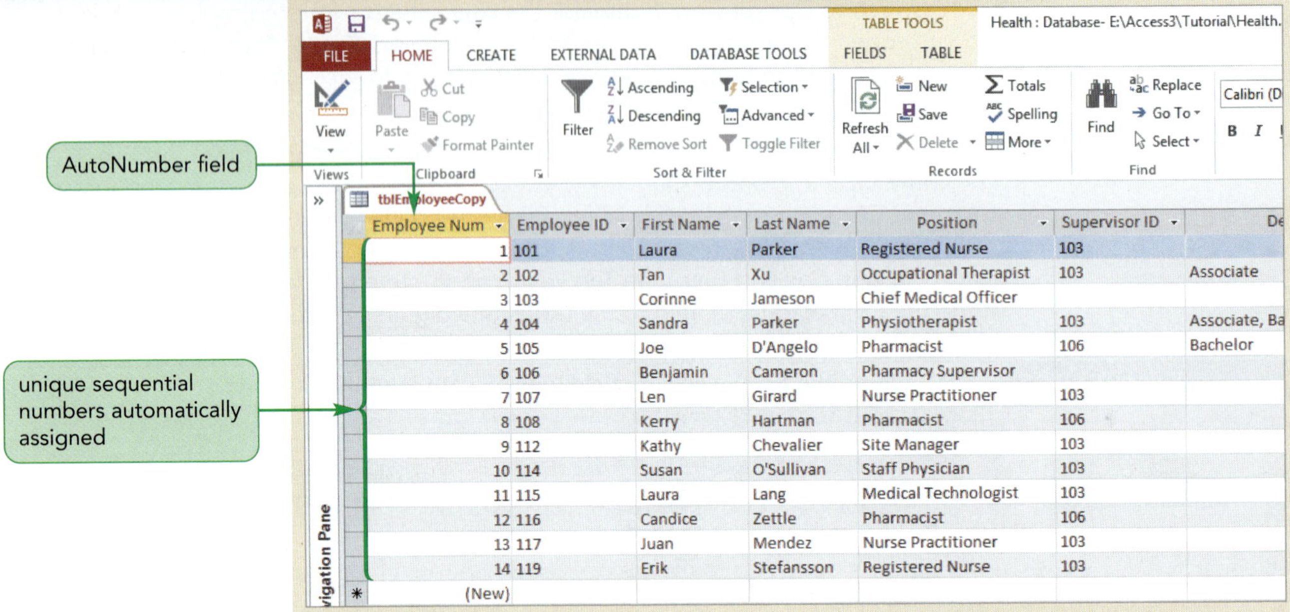

Next, you'll review the property settings for the Position field in the tblEmployeeCopy table to verify they are correct.

4. Switch to Design view, and then click the **Field Name** box for the **Position field** to display its properties. See Figure 12-25.

Figure 12-25 Property settings for the Position field

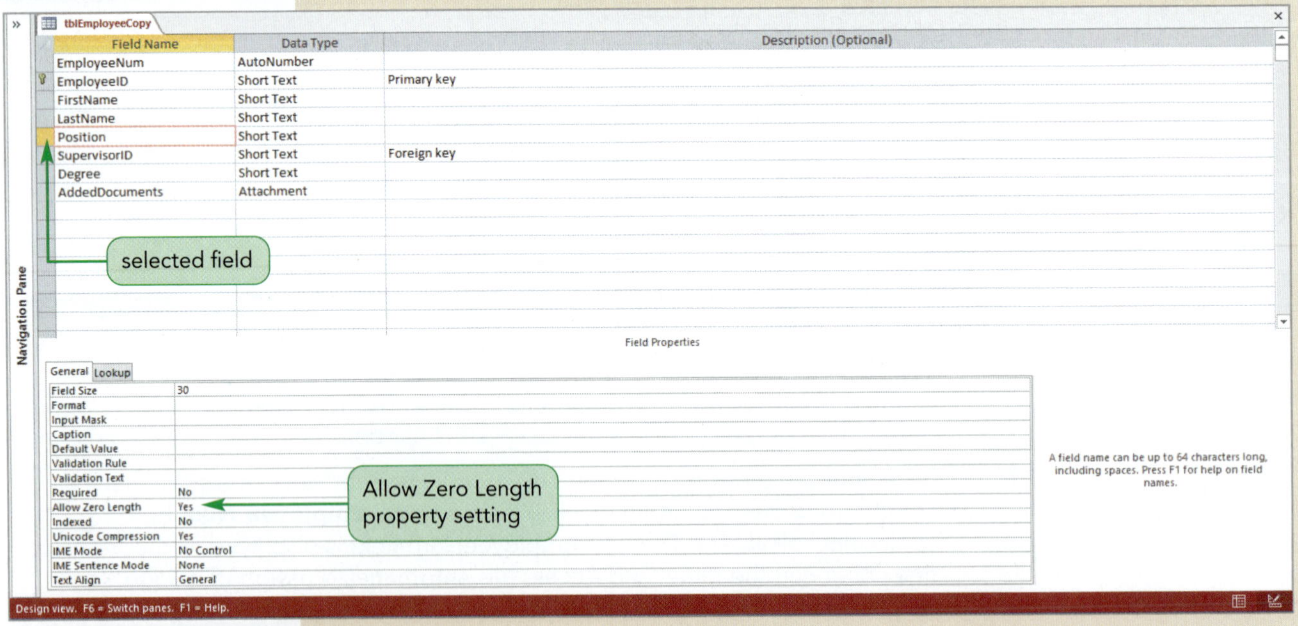

The Position field's Required property is set to No, which means field value entries are optional. The Allow Zero Length property is set to Yes, which is the default setting for Text fields and Memo fields. When its **Allow Zero Length property** is set to Yes, a field can store a zero length string value.

INSIGHT

Setting the Allow Zero Length Property to No

For a Text or Memo field, there is a difference between how you specify a null field value and a zero length value and how Access interprets the two values. Recall that null means that the field does not contain any value at all and describes a text field or a numeric field that is empty. A numeric field that contains the number zero is not empty. Similarly, a text field that contains a zero length value is not empty. You specify a zero length value in a Text or a Memo field by typing two consecutive double quotation marks (""), and you specify a null value by entering no value. When you view a value for a Text or Memo field that has its Allow Zero Length property set to Yes, you can't determine if the field value has been set to null or has a zero length value because both field values look the same—the absence of a visible value.

However, Access treats the two values differently. If you run a query to display all records in the table that have a null value in the field using the IsNull function, only the records with null field values appear in the query recordset; the records with zero length values in the field do not appear. And if you change the query to display all records that have a nonnull value, the records with zero length values in the field appear in the query recordset, which often raises questions by users about why those records are displayed. A typical user doesn't understand the distinction between a null value and a zero length value and doesn't need to make this distinction, so you should set the Allow Zero Length property to No for Text and Memo fields.

Kelly has a previous version of Access on her home computer and wonders if she can open the Health database on that computer.

Saving an Access Database as a Previous Version

The default file format for databases you create in Access 2013 uses the .accdb filename extension, and is referred to as the Access 2007 file format because it was introduced with Access 2007. None of the versions of Access prior to Access 2007 can open a database that has the .accdb filename extension. However, you can save an .accdb database to a format that is compatible with previous versions of Access—specifically, to a format that is compatible with Access 2000 or to a format that is compatible with Access 2002-2003; both have the .mdb filename extension. For people who don't have Access 2013, Access 2010, or Access 2007 but do have one of the previous versions of Access, saving the database to a previous version allows them to use the database. Unfortunately, when an Access 2007 file format database uses features such as multivalued and Attachment fields, you cannot save the database in a previous version.

To save an Access 2007 file format database as a previous version, you would complete the following steps (note that you will not actually save the database now):

1. Make sure that the database you want to save is open and all database objects are closed, and that the database does not contain any multivalued fields, Attachment fields, or any other features that are included only in Access 2007 file-formatted databases.
2. Click the FILE tab to display Backstage view, click Save As in the navigation bar, click Save Database As, and then click Access 2002-2003 Database or click Access 2000 Database, depending on which file format you want to use.
3. Click the Save As button. In the Save As dialog box, navigate to the folder where you want to save the file, enter a name for the database in the File name box, and then click the Save button.

Kelly is happy to know it's possible for her to open the database on her home computer. Because the Health database currently uses multivalued and Attachment fields, she'll continue to work on the database only at the office, so you don't need to save it as a previous version now.

Next, Raj asks you to analyze the performance of the Health database.

Analyzing Database Performance with the Performance Analyzer

Raj wants the Health database to respond as quickly as possible to user requests, such as running queries and opening reports. You'll use the Performance Analyzer to check the performance of the Health database. The **Performance Analyzer** is an Access tool that you can use to optimize the performance of an Access database. You select the database objects you want to analyze for performance and then run the Performance Analyzer. You can select tables, queries, forms, reports, and macros either as a group or individually. The Performance Analyzer lists three types of analysis results: recommendation, suggestion, and idea. Access can complete the recommendation and suggestion optimizations for you, but you must implement the idea optimizations. Analysis results include changes such as those related to the storage of fields and the creation of indexes and relationships.

REFERENCE

Using the Performance Analyzer

- Start Access and open the database you want to analyze.
- On the DATABASE TOOLS tab, in the Analyze group, click the Analyze Performance button.
- Select the object(s) you want to analyze, and then click the OK button.
- Select the analysis result(s) you want the Performance Analyzer to complete for you, and then click the Optimize button.
- Note the idea optimizations and perform those optimizations, as appropriate.
- Click the Close button.

You'll use the Performance Analyzer to optimize the performance of the Health database.

To use the Performance Analyzer to optimize the performance of the Health database:

1. Save and close the tblEmployeeCopy table.
2. Click the **DATABASE TOOLS** tab, and then in the Analyze group, click the **Analyze Performance** button. The Performance Analyzer dialog box opens. See Figure 12-26.

Figure 12-26 Performance Analyzer dialog box

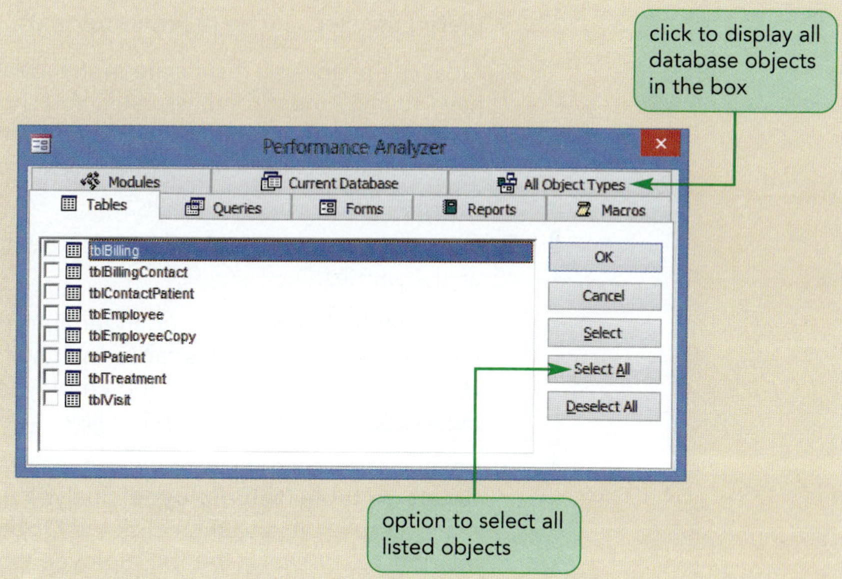

You'll analyze every object in the Health database.

3. Click the **All Object Types** tab, and then click the **Select All** button. All objects in the Health database appear in the box, and all of them are now selected.

4. Click the **OK** button. The Performance Analyzer analyzes all the objects in the Health database and, after a few moments, displays its analysis results. See Figure 12-27.

Figure 12-27 Performance Analyzer analysis results

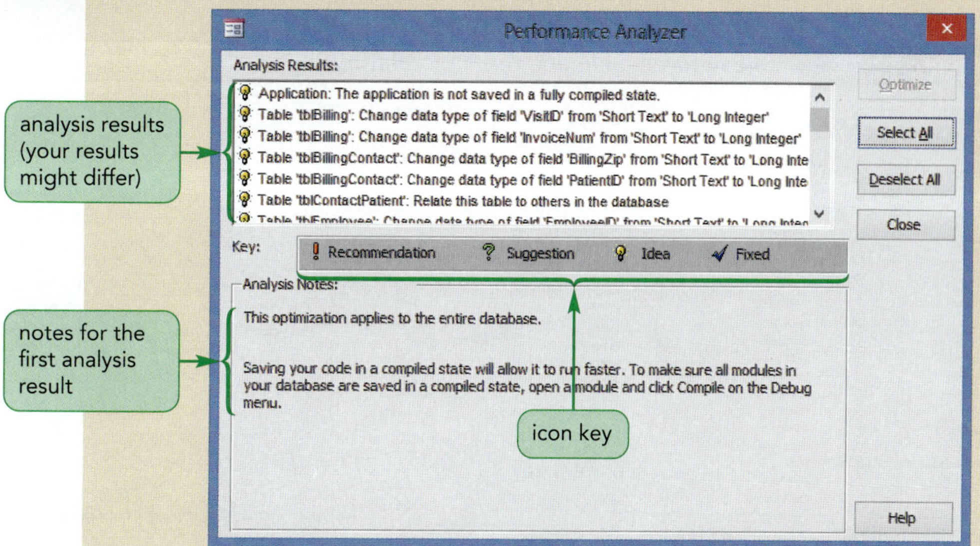

Trouble? If the Visual Basic window opens containing the code for the frmVisitsAndInvoices form, close the Visual Basic window.

Trouble? The contents of the Analysis Results box on your screen might be different from those shown in Figure 12-27, depending on how you've completed the steps in the previous tutorials.

Most of the analysis results are in the idea category, which means that you have to implement them yourself. You should consider all idea analysis results, but more important now are the recommendation and suggestion analysis results, which the Performance Analyzer can complete for you automatically.

5. Click several entries in the Analysis Results box, and read each entry and its analysis notes.

   You'll let the Performance Analyzer automatically create a relationship between the tblEmployee table and itself because the table has a one-to-many relationship based on the EmployeeID field as the primary key and the SupervisorID field as the foreign key.

6. Scroll the Analysis Results box as necessary, click the **Table 'tblEmployee': Relate to table 'tblEmployee'** analysis result (its icon is a green question mark) to select it, and then click the **Optimize** button. Access creates a relationship between the tblEmployee table and itself, and the icon for the selected analysis result changes to a check mark to indicate a "Fixed" status.

7. Click the **Close** button to close the dialog box.

Next, you'll open the Relationships window to view the new relationship created by the Performance Analyzer.

To view the relationship created by the Performance Analyzer:

1. Click the **DATABASE TOOLS** tab, and then in the Relationships group, click the **Relationships** button to open the Relationships window. See Figure 12-28.

Figure 12-28 tblEmployee table one-to-many relationship

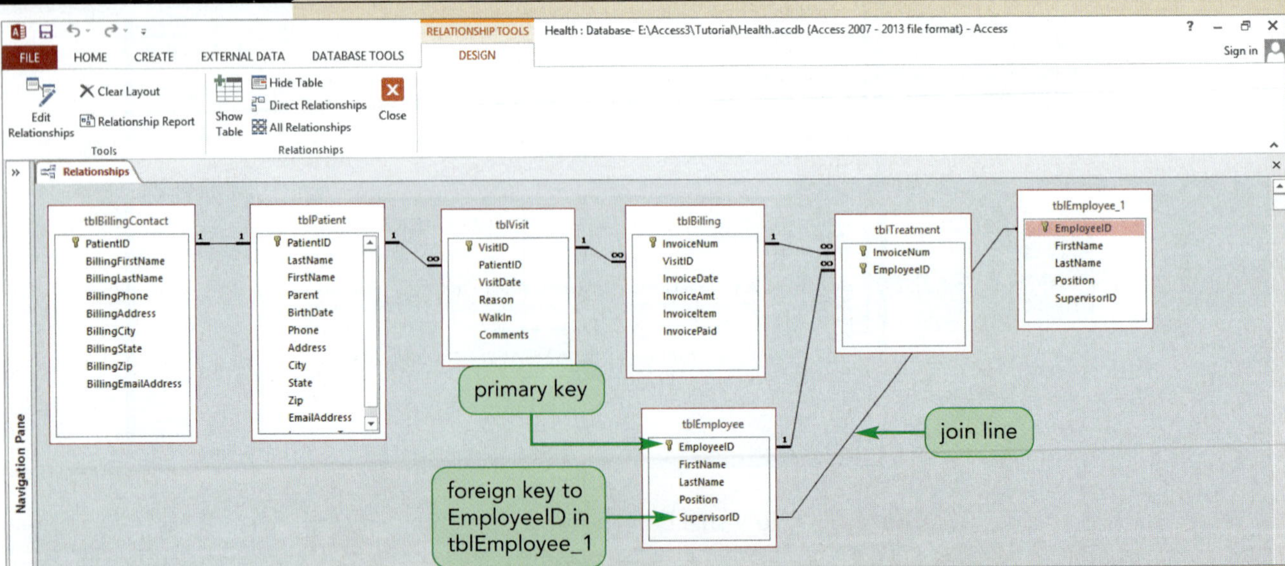

Trouble? The field lists in the Relationships window might be in different positions from what is shown in Figure 12-28. This difference causes no problems.

The Performance Analyzer added a second copy of the tblEmployee table (named tblEmployee_1) and a join line between the tblEmployee and tblEmployee_1 tables to the Relationships window. The join line connects the primary table (tblEmployee_1) to the related table (tblEmployee) using the EmployeeID field as the primary key and the SupervisorID field as the foreign key. You'll use the Edit Relationships dialog box to view the join properties for the relationship.

2. Right-click the join line between the tblEmployee_1 and tblEmployee tables, and then click **Edit Relationship** on the shortcut menu to open the Edit Relationships dialog box. See Figure 12-29.

Figure 12-29 **Edit Relationships dialog box for the new relationship**

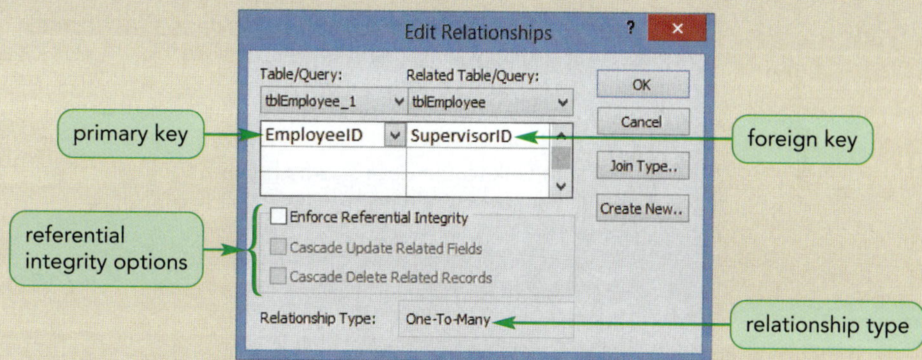

The referential integrity options are not selected, so you'll select them now for the new one-to-many relationship to show this as a one-to-many relationship in the relationship window.

3. Click the **Enforce Referential Integrity** check box, click the **Cascade Update Related Fields** check box, and then click the **OK** button to close the dialog box.
4. Close the Relationships window, and then click the **Yes** button, if necessary, to save your changes.

Ethan Ward, marketing manager, has the responsibility at Chatham Community Health Services for maintaining a separate database named Referral in which he stores information about patients who have been referred by other physicians but who have not yet contacted the Chatham Community Health Services clinic. Kelly wants to be able to retrieve the data in the tblReferral table in the Referral database from within the Health database. To provide Kelly with access to this table, you'll create a link to the tblReferral table in the Health database.

Linking Tables and Using the Linked Table Manager

You'll provide Kelly and other users of the Health database with access to the tblReferral table by using a linked table in the Health database. A **linked table** is a table that is stored in a file outside the open database and that can be updated from the open database. You can retrieve and update (add, change, and delete) records in a linked table, but you can't change its structure. From the Health database, you'll be able to update the tblReferral table as a linked table, but you won't be able to change its structure. However, from the Referral database, Ethan will be able to update the tblReferral table ***and*** change its structure. You can link a database to data stored in Excel worksheets, HTML documents, text files, other Access databases, and databases created by other DBMSs, such as Microsoft SQL Server and mySQL. Although Access works faster with its own tables than it does with linked tables, you must use linked tables when you need to edit data maintained in another Access database or in other programs.

REFERENCE

Linking to a Table in Another Access Database

- Click the EXTERNAL DATA tab.
- In the Import & Link group, click the Access button (with the ScreenTip "Import Access database").
- Click the Link to the data source by creating a linked table option button.
- Click the Browse button, select the folder and file containing the linked data, and then click the Open button.
- Click the OK button, select the table(s) in the Link Tables dialog box, and then click the OK button.

You'll link to the tblReferral table in the Referral database from the Health database.

To link to the tblReferral table in the Referral database:

1. Click the **EXTERNAL DATA tab**, and then in the Import & Link group, click the **Access** button (with the ScreenTip "Import Access database") to open the Get External Data - Access Database dialog box.
2. Click the **Link to the data source by creating a linked table** option button, and then click the **Browse** button to open the File Open dialog box.
3. Navigate to the Access3 ▸ Tutorial folder, click **Referral.accdb**, and then click the **Open** button to close the File Open dialog box and return to the Get External Data - Access Database dialog box. The path and file you selected now appear in the File name box.
4. Click the **OK** button. Access opens the Link Tables dialog box. See Figure 12-30.

Figure 12-30 Link Tables dialog box

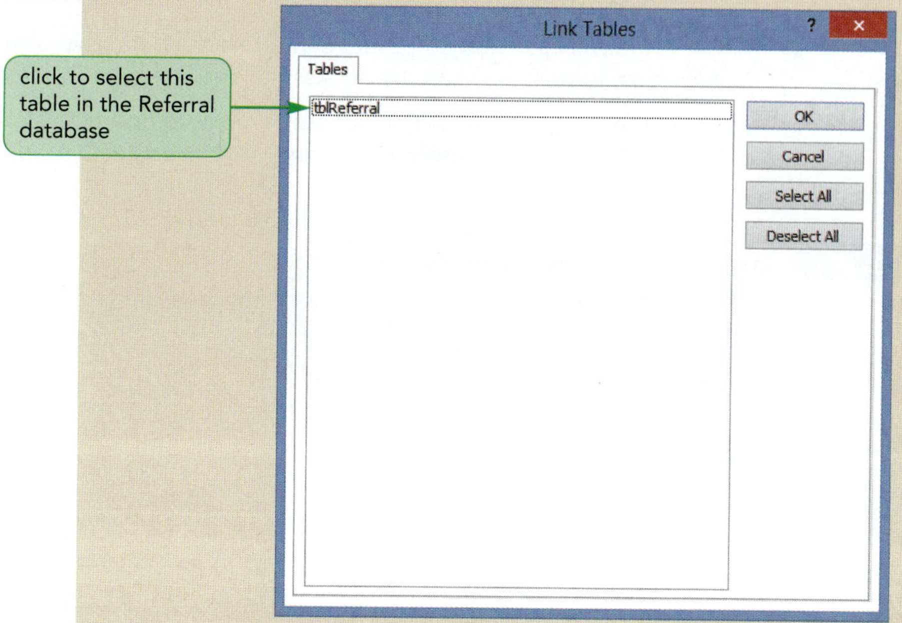

5. Click **tblReferral** in the Tables box, and then click the **OK** button. The Link Tables dialog box closes, and you return to the Access window. A small blue arrow appears to the left of the tblReferral table icon in the Navigation Pane to identify the tblReferral table as a linked table.

Kelly will be reorganizing the company network folders soon and might move the Referral database to a different folder. She asks if moving the Referral database would cause a problem for the linked tblReferral table. You'll use the Linked Table Manager to handle this situation. The **Linked Table Manager** is an Access tool you use to change the filename or drive location for linked tables in an Access database. When you use Access to link to data in another file, Access stores the file's location (drive, folder, and filename) in the database and uses the stored location to connect to the linked data. If you change the file's location, you can use the Linked Table Manager to change the stored file location, or **refresh the link**, in the Access database.

REFERENCE

Using the Linked Table Manager

- In the Navigation Pane, right-click the linked table name, and then click Linked Table Manager on the shortcut menu; or on the EXTERNAL DATA tab, in the Import & Link group, click the Linked Table Manager button.
- Click the check box(es) for the linked table(s) you want to refresh, and then click the OK button.
- Navigate to the linked table location, click the filename, and then click the Open button.
- Click the OK button, and then close the Linked Table Manager dialog box.

Next, you'll move the Referral database to a different folder, and then you'll use the Linked Table Manager to refresh the link to the tblReferral table in the Health database.

To move the Referral database and refresh the link to the tblReferral table:

1. Use Windows File Explorer to move the **Referral** database from the Access3 ▸ Tutorial folder to the Access3 folder, and then switch back to Access.
2. In the Navigation Pane, right-click **tblReferral** to open the shortcut menu, and then click **Linked Table Manager**. The Linked Table Manager dialog box opens. See Figure 12-31.

Figure 12-31 Linked Table Manager dialog box

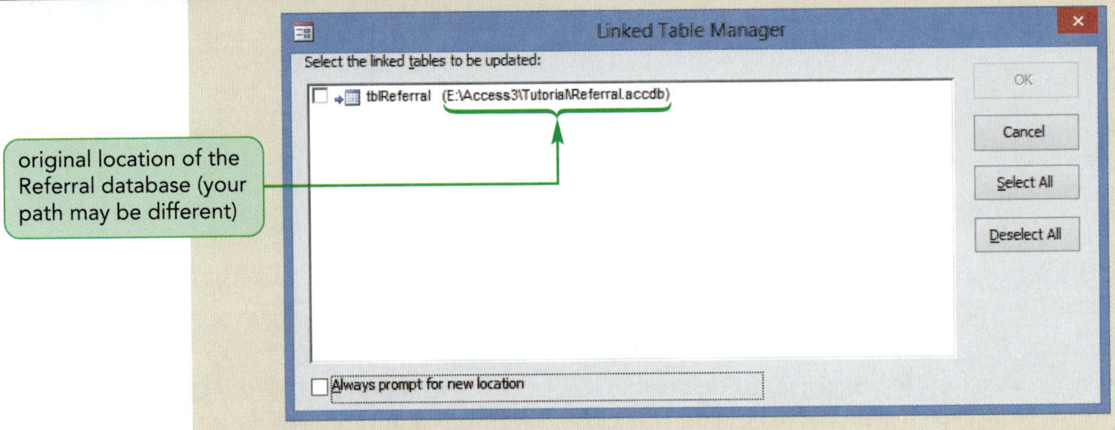

The tblReferral table is the only linked table, so it's the only table listed. The Access3 ▸ Tutorial folder provided with your Data Files, which is the original location of the Referral database, is listed as the current location for the tblReferral table.

3. Click the **Select All** button, and then click the **OK** button. The Select New Location of tblReferral dialog box opens.
4. Navigate to the **Access3** folder, click **Referral** in the file list, and then click the **Open** button. A dialog box informs you that all selected linked tables were successfully refreshed.
5. Click the **OK** button to close the dialog box. The Linked Table Manager dialog box now displays the Access3 folder as the current location of the linked tblReferral table.
6. Close the Linked Table Manager dialog box.

Next, you'll open the tblReferral table to update it as a linked table from the new location.

To update the tblReferral table and view its design in the Health database:

1. Open the **tblReferral** table in Datasheet view, and then close the Navigation Pane. The tblReferral table datasheet displays four records.

   First, you'll add a new record to the tblReferral table.

2. Click the **New (blank) record** navigation button, type **12005** in the Patient ID column, press the **Tab** key, type **Gail** in the First Name column, press the **Tab** key, type **Browning** in the Last Name column, press the **Tab**

key, type **203-661-9353** in the Phone column, press the **Tab** key, type **248 Fenton St** in the Address column, press the **Tab** key, type **Meriden** in the City column, press the **Tab** key, type **CT** in the State column, press the **Tab** key, type **06450** in the Zip column, press the **Tab** key, type **gbrowning@example.org** in the Email Address column, and then press the **Tab** key.

Next, you'll switch to Design view to verify that you can't change the design of the tblReferral table from the Health database.

3. Switch to Design view. The PatientID field is the current field, and the Help message in the Field Properties section indicates that you can't change the Field Name property value for linked tables. See Figure 12-32.

Figure 12-32 **Linked table in Design view**

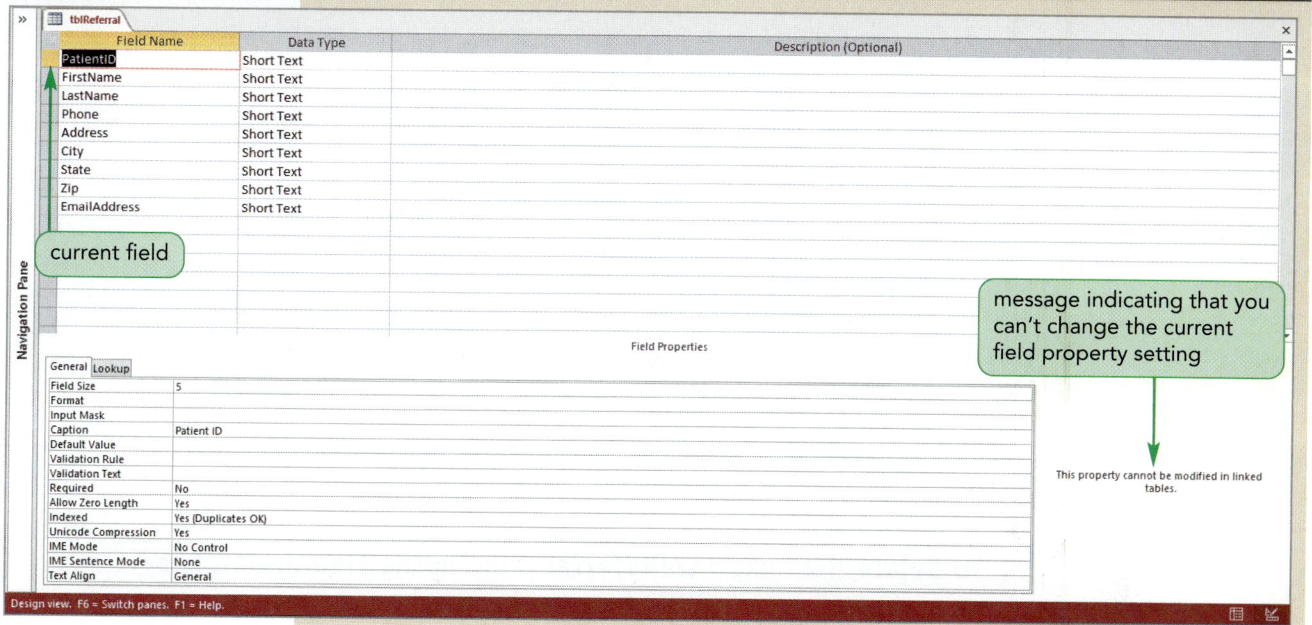

4. Press the **F6** key to highlight the Field Size property in the Field Properties pane. The Help message indicates that you can't change the Field Size property.
5. Press the **Tab** key to position the insertion point in the Format box. The normal Help message for the Format property appears, so you can change this field property.
6. Close the table.

Now you'll open the Referral database to see the new record in the tblReferral table that you added from the Health database. Then you'll delete that record and view the table in Design view.

To update the tblReferral table and view its design in the Referral database:

1. Start another instance of Access, keeping the Health database open as well, and then open the **Referral** database located in the Access3 folder on the drive where you are storing your Data Files.

   Trouble? If the security warning is displayed below the Ribbon, click the Enable Content button next to the security warning.

2. Open the Navigation Pane (if necessary), open the **tblReferral** table datasheet, and then click the **row selector** for record 5. The record for Gail Browning, which you added to the tblReferral linked table in the Health database, appears as record 5 in the tblReferral table in the Referral database.
3. On the HOME tab, in the Records group, click the **Delete** button, and then click the **Yes** button to delete record 5.
4. Switch to Design view. Because the tblReferral table is not a linked table in the Referral database (its own database), the Help message in the Field Properties pane does not warn you that you can't change the Field Name property. You can make any design changes you want to the tblReferral table in the Referral database.
5. Close the tblReferral table, and then close the Referral database.

Kelly decides that she'd like to maintain the Referral database separately and asks you to delete the linked tblReferral table in the Health database. If you delete the linked tblReferral table in the Health database, Access will delete the link to the tblReferral table but will not delete the tblReferral table in the Referral database.

To delete the linked tblReferral table in the Health database:

1. In the Health database, open the Navigation Pane, right-click **tblReferral** in the Navigation Pane to open the shortcut menu, and then click **Delete**. A dialog box asks if you want to remove the link to the tblReferral table. See Figure 12-33.

Figure 12-33 Dialog box that opens when attempting to delete a linked table

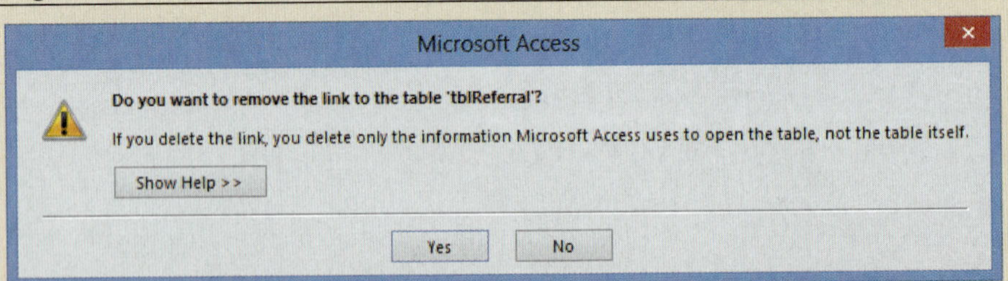

   The dialog box confirms that you'll delete only the link to the tblReferral table, but not the tblReferral table itself in the Referral database.

2. Click the **Yes** button. Access deletes the link to the tblReferral table, and the tblReferral table no longer appears in the Navigation Pane for the Health database.

Kelly now understands how to link to Ethan's tblReferral table and to other data if she needs to do so in the future.

Next, Kelly wants to create several queries for the Health database, but she doesn't want the user interface for other users to be cluttered with queries they won't need to use. She asks if there's a way for her to have a special user interface to access the data in the Health database. You can accomplish this by splitting the database.

Using the Database Splitter

TIP

In addition to making regular backups of databases, be sure to make a backup before making a significant change, such as splitting a database.

Users might want to customize the user interface to create their own custom versions of the interface, while accessing the same central table data. The **Database Splitter** is an Access tool that splits an Access database into two files: one file contains the tables, and the other file contains the queries, forms, reports, and other database objects. Although a single master copy of the file containing the tables is stored and accessed, users can have their own copies of the other file and add their own queries, reports, and other objects to handle their processing needs. Each file created by the Database Splitter is an Access database. The database that contains the tables is called the **back-end database**; and the database that contains the other objects, including the user interface, is called the **front-end database**.

REFERENCE

Using the Database Splitter

- Make a backup copy of the database that you want to split.
- Start Access and open the database you want to split.
- Click the DATABASE TOOLS tab, and then in the Move Data group, click the Access Database button.
- Click the Split Database button, select the drive and folder for the back-end database, type a name for the database in the File name box, and then click the Split button.
- Click the OK button.

After you split a database, when users open a front-end database, the objects they open use data in the tables in the back-end database. Because the tables in the front-end database are linked tables that are stored in the back-end database, the front-end database contains the physical drive locations of the tables in the back-end database. You can move the front-end database to a different drive location without affecting the physical connections to the back-end database. However, if you move the back-end database to a different drive location, you'll need to use the Linked Table Manager to change the physical drive locations of the back-end database's tables in the front-end database.

PROSKILLS

Decision Making: Splitting a Database

People who develop databases and sell them to multiple companies usually split their databases. When a developer delivers a split database, the initial back-end database does not include the company's data, and the initial front-end database is complete as created by the developer. Companies use the front-end database to update their data in the back-end database, but they do not modify the front-end database in any way. Periodically, the database developer improves the front-end database by modifying and adding queries, reports, and other objects without changing the structure of the tables. In other words, the developer changes the front-end database, but does not change the back-end database. The developer gives its client companies replacement front-end databases, which continue to work with the back-end database that contains the company's data.

Splitting a database also lets you place the files on different computers. You can place a copy of the front-end database on each user's computer, and the back-end database on a network server that users access through their front-end databases; this arrangement distributes the workload across the network. Finally, as a company grows, it might need a more powerful DBMS such as Oracle, SQL Server, DB2, or MySQL. You could retain the original Access front-end database and replace the Access back-end database with a new non-Access back-end database, which is an easier task than replacing all database objects.

Because splitting an Access database causes minimal disruption to a company's database processing as you periodically enhance the user interface, and because splitting provides greater flexibility for future growth, you should always develop your databases with splitting in mind. The entire process of splitting a database is illustrated in Figure 12-34, which follows this ProSkills box.

Figure 12-34 **Split Access database**

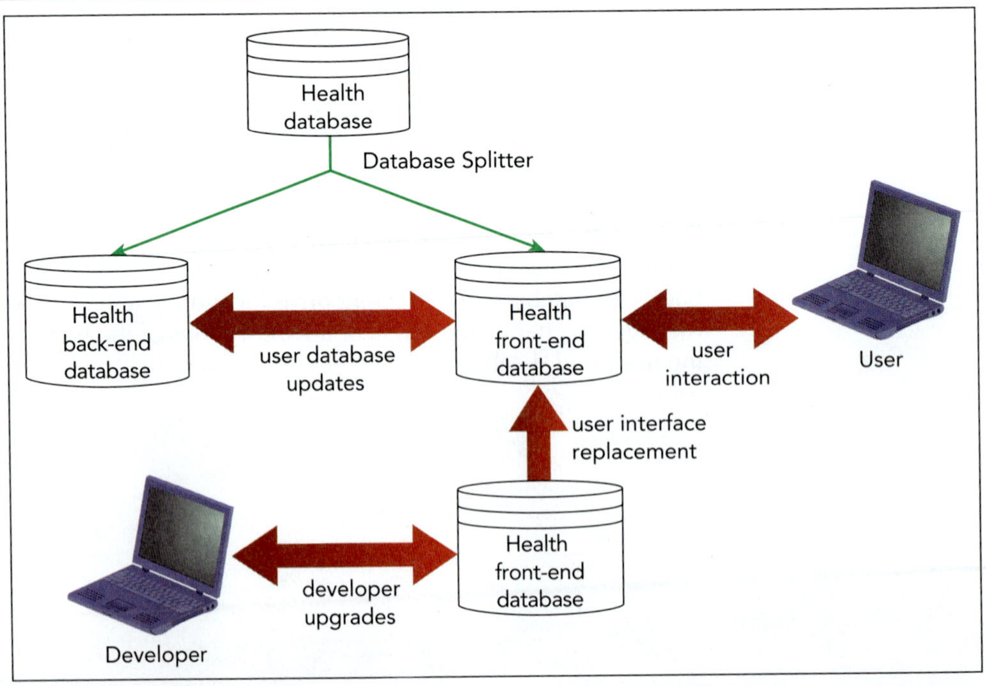

You'll use the Database Splitter to split the Health database into two files. As a precaution, you'll make a backup copy of the database before you split the database.

To use the Database Splitter:

1. Make a backup copy of the Health database.
2. Click the **DATABASE TOOLS** tab, and then in the Move Data group, click the **Access Database** button. The Database Splitter dialog box opens. See Figure 12-35.

Figure 12-35 Database Splitter dialog box

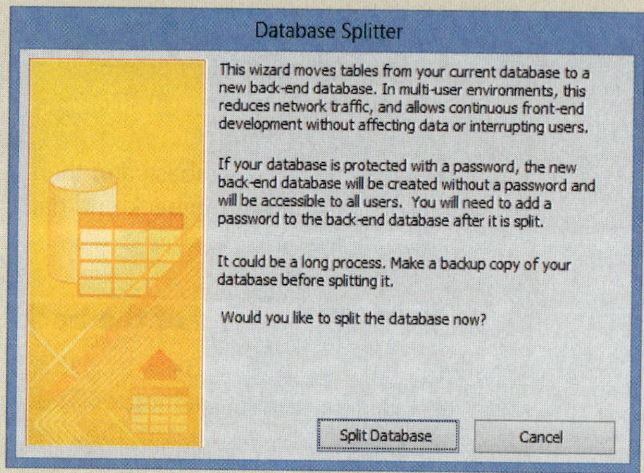

3. Click the **Split Database** button. The Create Back-end Database dialog box opens. The back-end database will contain the tables from the Health database. You'll use the default filename (Health_be with the .accdb extension) for the back-end database.
4. Navigate to the **Access3 ▸ Tutorial** folder (if necessary), and then click the **Split** button. After a few moments, a dialog box informs you that the database was successfully split.
5. Click the **OK** button to close the dialog boxes, and then scroll up to the top of the Navigation Pane, if necessary. See Figure 12-36.

Figure 12-36 Linked tables in the Health database

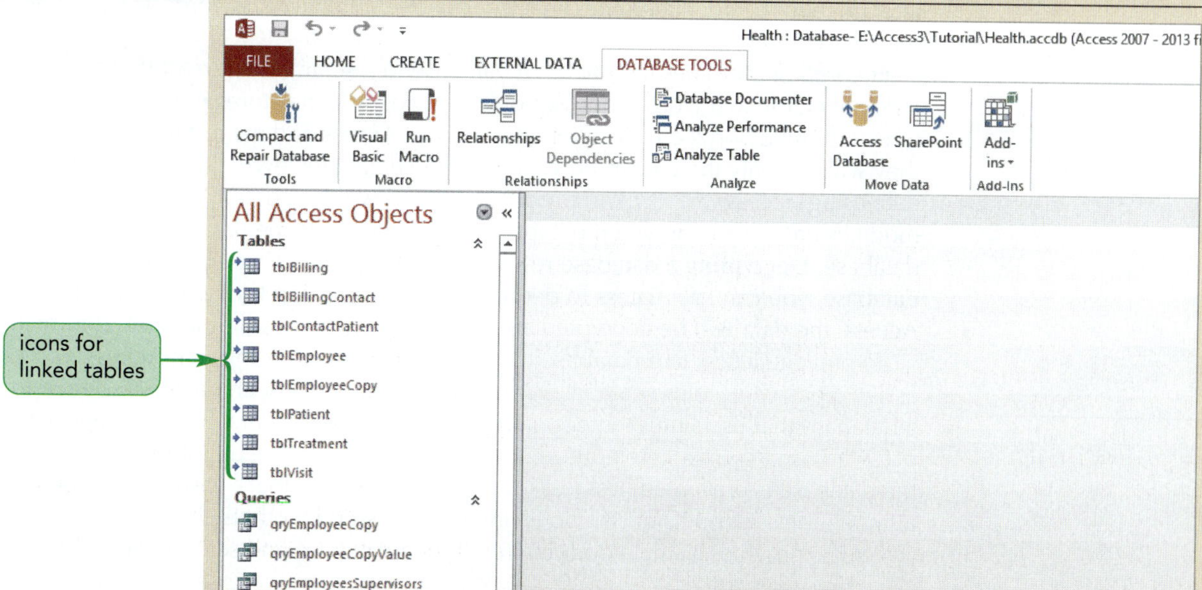

Each table in the Health database has an icon next to its name indicating that there's a link to that table in another file. The tables are no longer stored in the Health database; they are stored in the Health_be database file you just created with the Database Splitter.

You can use the linked tables as if they were stored in the Health database, except that you cannot change a table's design from the Health database. You have to close the Health database and open the Health_be database to change a table's design.

6. Scroll down the Navigation Pane. The queries, forms, reports, macros, and modules you've created appear in the Navigation Pane and are still stored in the Health database.

You'll close the Health database and then open the Health_be database to verify which objects are stored in the back-end database.

To verify the contents of the back-end database:

1. Close the Health database, and then open the **Health_be** database located in the Access3 ▸ Tutorial folder. The tables from the Health database appear in the Navigation Pane with their usual icons, indicating the tables are now stored in the Health_be database. No other objects exist in the Health_be database.
2. Open the **tblBilling** table in Design view. You can modify the design of the tables in the Health_be database because they are stored in that database; they are not linked from another database as they are in the Health database.
3. Close the table, close the Health_be database, and then open the **Health** database.

Securing an Access Database

Security refers to the protection of a database against unauthorized access, either intentional or accidental. Access provides encryption and passwords as two of its security features.

Encryption translates the data in a database to a scrambled format that's indecipherable to a word processor or other program and stores it in an encrypted format. If unauthorized users attempt to bypass Access and get to the data directly, they will see only the encrypted version of the data. However, users accessing the data using Access will have no problem working with the data. When a user stores or modifies data in an encrypted database, Access encrypts the data before updating the database. **Decrypting** a database reverses the encryption. Once you've encrypted a database, you can use Access to decrypt it. Before a user retrieves encrypted data using Access, the data will be decrypted and presented to the user in the normal format.

To prevent access to a database by an unauthorized user through Access, you can assign a password to the database. A **password** is a string of characters assigned to a database that users must enter before they can open the database. As long as the password is known only to authorized users of the database, unauthorized access to the database is prevented. It's best if you use a password that's easily remembered by authorized users, but is not obvious or easily guessed by others.

Access provides a single option to encrypt a database and set a password at the same time.

PROSKILLS

Decision Making: Determining When to Encrypt Data Using a Password

You might be familiar with setting a password and using it to unlock a cell phone, or to sign into your email or another device or software application. In these cases, the password acts as an authorization for you to use the device or software. Some software applications use a password for more than simply opening the file. Microsoft Access uses the password to actually encrypt the data. The password itself isn't stored anywhere. Instead, the password is used as part of a mathematical formula to encrypt the data. When a user tries to open an encrypted file, Microsoft Access prompts the user for the password, and attempts to open the file. If the entered password is correct, Microsoft Access is able to use it to decrypt the data and open the file. If the password is incorrect, the data is not readable when Microsoft Access uses the entered password to decrypt the file, and Microsoft Access does not open the file.

Because the password itself isn't stored anywhere and the data is actually encrypted, the contents of the database cannot be recovered if a user forgets a password. This is a security feature, and also a potential problem if there are concerns about losing the password. Unlike your cell phone, which can be reset and still used if the password is lost, an encrypted Microsoft Access file cannot be used if the password is lost.

If the data isn't sensitive, it's not as important to encrypt the data with a password. An encrypted Microsoft Access database provides security for data and should be considered when the data it contains is sensitive, such as credit card information or private health record information. If the database is accessible only from a desktop computer in a secured, locked office, that may be enough security and it may not be necessary to add encryption.

If you've decided to set a password, keep in mind that passwords are more secure when they consist of a mixture of numbers, symbols, and both lowercase and uppercase letters.

Access has some built-in security so that users cannot accidentally change data. The way you usually open an Access database allows **shared access** of the database with others; that is, two or more users can open and use the same database at the same time. When you set a password, you need to open the database with exclusive access. When you open an Access database with **exclusive access**, you prevent other users from opening and using the database at the same time. You must open the database with exclusive access in order to set a password, so that you can guarantee that only one copy of the database is open when you set the password.

If you want someone to be able to view the data without changing it, you can open a database as a read-only file. Clicking the Open option in the list opens the selected database with shared access for both reading and updating, whereas clicking the Open Read-Only option opens the selected database with shared access for reading only. **Reading** includes any database action that does not involve updating the database, such as running queries (but not action queries) and viewing table records. Actions that are prohibited when you open a database as read-only (because they involve updating the database) include changing the database design and updating table records. The other two open options in the Open list open the selected database with exclusive access for reading and updating (Open Exclusive) or for reading only (Open Exclusive Read-Only).

When multiple users update the database at the same time, Access uses row-level locking so that one user can't change the row content while another user is viewing it. **Locking** denies access by other users to data while Access processes one user's updates to the database. **Row-level locking** denies access by other users to the table rows one user is in the process of updating; other users can update the database simultaneously as long as the rows they need to update are not being updated, and therefore not being locked, by other users at the same time.

INSIGHT

Setting and Unsetting a Password

In order to set a password, you first open an Access database file with exclusive access to ensure there are no other users who are viewing or manipulating the data when you add or remove the password. After you open the file with exclusive access, you go to Backstage view, where the Encrypt with Password button is displayed. If you decide to apply encryption, Access prompts you to type the password twice. This is a security feature to ensure that you did not make a mistake the first time you typed the password. Both password entries must be identical in order to set the password encryption. In order to remove password encryption, you go to Backstage view and click the Decrypt Database button. Unsetting a password cancels the password protection for the database and also decrypts the database.

Kelly is pleased with the changes you have made. As a final enhancement to the user interface, she asks you to set Access to open the navigation form you created in Tutorial 10 automatically when a user opens the Health database.

Setting the Database Properties and Startup Options

TIP

To bypass the startup options that you set, press and hold down the Shift key when you open the database, or after entering the password in an encrypted database.

Access lets you specify certain actions, called **startup options**, that take place when a database opens. For example, you can specify the name that appears in the Access window title bar, prevent users from using the Navigation Pane, or specify a form that is automatically opened when you open a database.

Kelly wants users to be able to open the Health database and have the navigation form you created in Tutorial 10 open automatically. In this way, users won't need to use the Navigation Pane to access the navigation form.

REFERENCE

Setting the Database Properties and Startup Options

- Open the database, click the FILE tab, and then click Options in the navigation bar.
- In the Access Options dialog box, click Current Database in the left section.
- Set the database properties and startup options, and then click the OK button. Most options will take effect the next time the database is opened.

See the Session 12.2 Visual Overview for a description of the database properties and startup options you'll set for the Health database. In addition, you'll disable the **Enable error checking property**, which checks for design errors in forms and reports and alerts you to errors by displaying the Error Checking Options button. Disabling the Enable error checking property will suppress the display of the triangle-shaped error indicators that appear in the upper-right or upper-left corner of a control when a potential error occurs. Disabling this property will affect only the current database. Unlike all the other properties, which appear on the Current Database page in the Access Options dialog box, the Enable error checking property appears on the Object Designers page in the Access Options dialog box.

INSIGHT

Setting Database Properties and Startup Options

After you've developed and split a database and turned it over to its users, you've completed the design and creation of all fields and objects. Users don't need to change the design, so you should disable any Access property or feature that allows them to change the design. For this reason, you should disable the following properties: Use Access Special Keys, Enable Layout View, Enable design changes for tables in Datasheet view, Allow Full Menus, Allow Default Shortcut Menus, Track name AutoCorrect info, and Enable error checking.

When your database design includes a navigation form, you should display the navigation form when the database opens (set the Display Form property); therefore, users do not need the Navigation Pane (disable the Display Navigation Pane property).

You'll finish developing the Health database by setting the database properties and startup options.

To set the database properties and startup options in the Health database:

1. Click the FILE tab, and then click **Options** on the left side to open the Access Options dialog box.
2. In the left section of the dialog box, click **Current Database** to display the list of options for the current database.
3. In the Application Title box, type **Health Release 1**, click the **Display Form** arrow, and then click **frmNavigation**. This sets the title in the Access title bar, and sets the frmNavigation form as the initial form loaded in the application when Access opens the Health file.
4. Scrolling as necessary, click the following check boxes to disable (uncheck) the properties:

   Use Access Special Keys

   Enable Layout View

   Enable design changes for tables in Datasheet view

   Display Navigation Pane

   Allow Full Menus

   Allow Default Shortcut Menus

   Track name AutoCorrect info.

   See the Session 12.2 Visual Overview.
5. In the left section of the dialog box, click **Object Designers** to display the list of options for creating and modifying database objects, and then scroll to the bottom of the dialog box.
6. If necessary, click the **Enable error checking** check box to clear it and disable all error checking options. See Figure 12-37.

   Trouble? If the Error checking check box does not contain a check mark, continue on to the next step.

TIP

Unlike the other database properties, which apply only to the current database, the Enable error checking property applies to all databases.

Figure 12-37 Error checking options in the Access Options dialog box

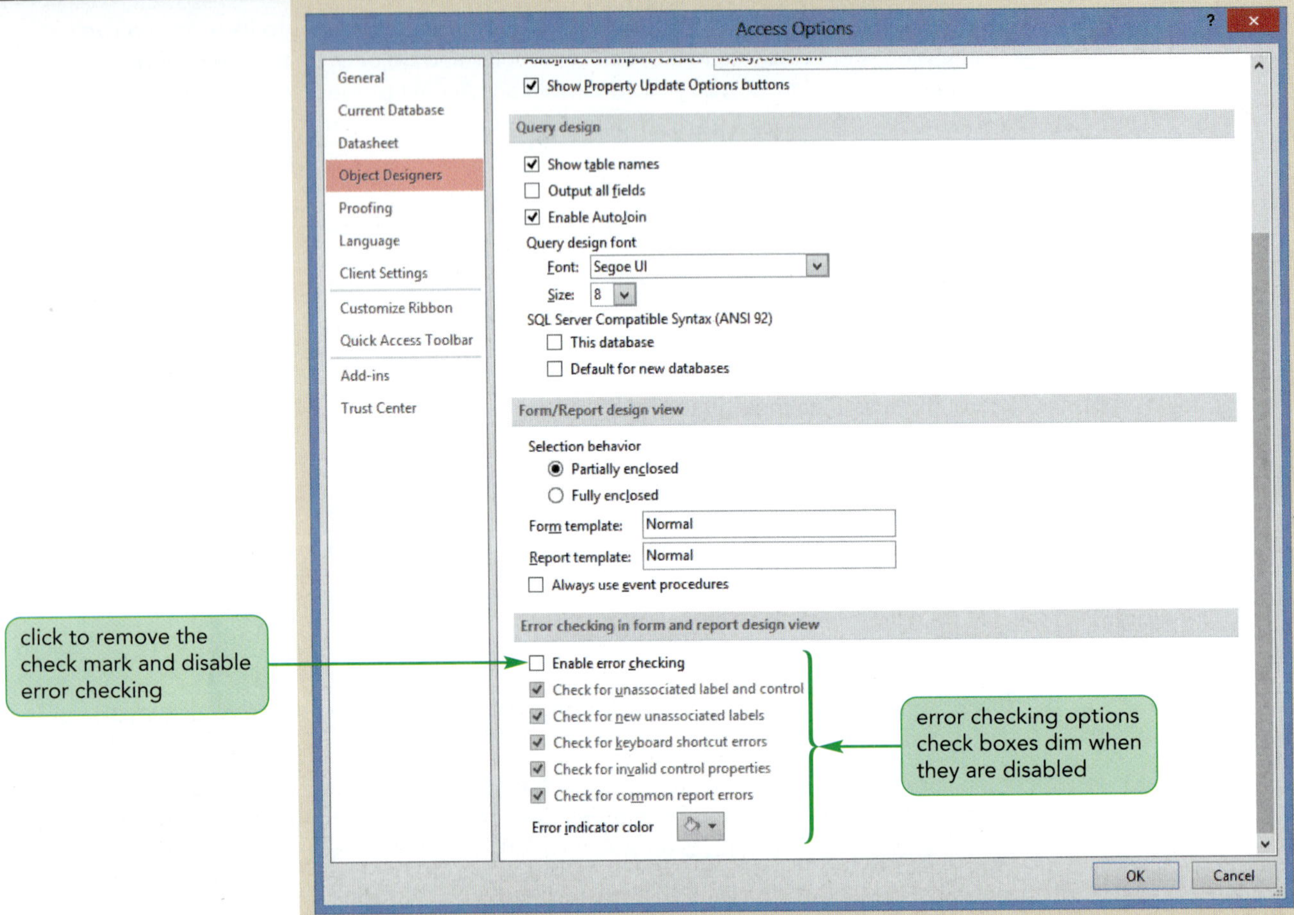

7. Click the **OK** button to close the Access Options dialog box. A dialog box informs you that you must close and reopen the Health database for the options you selected to take effect.
8. Click the **OK** button to close the dialog box.

To test the database properties and startup options, you need to close and reopen the Health database.

To test the database properties and startup options:

1. Click the **FILE tab**, and then click **Close** to close the Health database without exiting Access.
2. Click the **FILE** tab, click **Open**, and then in the Recent list, click **Health.accdb** to open the Health database. See Figure 12-38.

Figure 12-38 Health database user interface

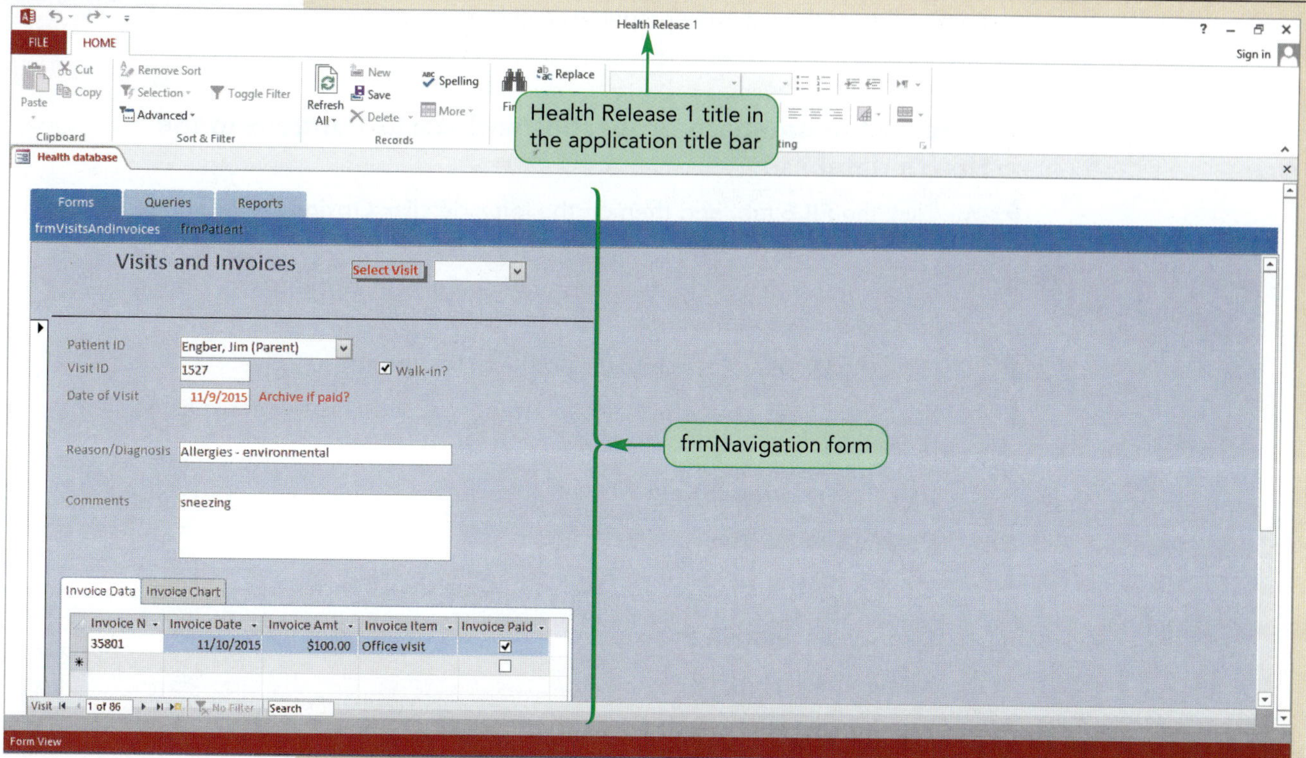

Access opens the Health database, opens the frmNavigation form, disables the Navigation Pane, displays a restricted Ribbon with only the FILE and HOME tabs, and displays "Health Release 1" in the Access window title bar.

Now you can make one final test of the Health database user interface.

3. Click each of the tabs on the navigation form to verify that all features work properly on the Health database user interface.

Kelly likes the navigation startup setting but realizes that some of her staff will need access to the Ribbon and database objects. One method her staff could use is to press and hold down the Shift key when they open the database. You'll open the database using this method to bypass the startup options now.

To bypass the startup options when opening the database:

1. Close the Health database.
2. Open Windows File Explorer if necessary, navigate to the Access3 ▸ Tutorial folder, and then press and hold the **Shift** key while you double-click the **Health** file to open the file.

   The Health database opens without the startup options you set. For instance, you can now use the shortcut keys to close a table, which had been disabled previously in the startup options when Allow Default Shortcut Menus was disabled.
3. Open the tblEmployee table, and then right-click the tab to display the shortcut menu.
4. Close the tblEmployee table.

Using the Shift key to open the file bypasses the startup options, but Kelly thinks this method also defeats the purpose of having startup options. Instead, she would like you to change the database options to display the Ribbon and enable the database objects again. You'll reset the database properties and startup options.

To reset the database properties and startup options in the Health database:

1. Click the **FILE** tab, and then on the left side click **Options** to open the Access Options dialog box.
2. In the left section of the dialog box, click **Current Database** to display the list of options for the current database.
3. Click the **Display Form** arrow, and then click **(none)**.
4. Scrolling as necessary, click the following check boxes to enable (check) the properties:

   Use Access Special Keys

   Enable Layout View

   Enable design changes for tables in Datasheet view

   Display Navigation Pane

   Allow Full Menus

   Allow Default Shortcut Menus

   Track name AutoCorrect info
5. A dialog box opens that indicates the Track name AutoCorrect info option generates name maps for the database objects and may take several minutes. Click **OK** to accept and close the dialog box.
6. In the left section of the dialog box, click **Object Designers** to display the list of options for creating and modifying database objects, and then scroll to the bottom of the dialog box.
7. Click the **Enable error checking** check box to add the check mark and enable all error checking options.
8. Click the **OK** button to close the Access Options dialog box. A dialog box may inform you that the Health database must close all objects and update dependency Information.
9. Click the **Yes** button to close the dialog box (if necessary).

   A dialog box informs you that you must close and reopen the Health database for the changes to take effect.
10. Click the **OK** button to close the dialog box, and then close Access.
11. Open the **Health** database again to verify the ribbon and database objects are displayed.
12. Close the Health database and exit Access.

INSIGHT

Saving a Database as an ACCDE File

If a database contains VBA code, you can save an ACCDE file version of the database to prevent people from viewing or changing the VBA code. Saving an Access database as an **ACCDE file**, which has the .accde extension instead of the .accdb extension for a normal Access database, compiles all VBA modules, removes all editable VBA source code, and compacts the resulting database. The database and its VBA code continue to run as normal, but users cannot view or edit the VBA code. Also, users can't view, modify, or create forms, reports, or modules in Design view, nor can they import or export forms, reports, or modules. Because an ACCDE file limits database design changes to tables and queries, saving a database as an ACCDE file is best suited to a front-end database. You should keep a backup copy of the complete front-end database in case you need to modify the database design. To save a database as an ACCDE file, follow these steps:

1. Open the database you want to save as an ACCDE file.
2. Click the FILE tab, click Save As in the navigation bar, and then click Make ACCDE.
3. Click the Save As button. In the Save As dialog box, type the name for the file in the File name box, navigate to the location where you want to store the file, and then click the Save button.

Your work with the Health database is now complete. Raj and Kelly are happy with your work and agree that the database will fully satisfy the clinic's requirements.

REVIEW

Session 12.2 Quick Check

1. Access stores attachments in ____________ form to minimize file size and maximize disk space usage.
2. You can specify sequential numbering or random numbering for a(n) ____________ field.
3. What is the Performance Analyzer?
4. When do you use the Linked Table Manager?
5. What is the Database Splitter?
6. ____________ refers to the protection of a database against unauthorized access, either intentional or accidental.
7. What is a startup option?

ASSESS

SAM Projects

Put your skills into practice with SAM Projects! SAM Projects for this tutorial can be found online. If you have a SAM account, go to www.cengage.com/sam2013 to download the most recent Project Instructions and Start Files.

PRACTICE

Review Assignments

Data Files needed for the Review Assignments: Ads.accdb, Autoclave_Specification_Sheet.pdf, Autoclave.xlsx, and Product.accdb (*cont. from Tutorial 11*)

Raj asks you to complete your work with the user interface for the Product database. To meet this request, complete the following steps:

1. Open the **Product** database you worked with in Tutorials 9–11.
2. Open the **tblProduct** table datasheet, use an AutoFilter to filter records using the TempControlled field for values of Yes and Sterile field for values of Yes, and then save and close the table.
3. Use Filter By Form with the **tblSupplier** table to select all records in which the city is Madison or Tarrytown and the category is Supplies. Apply the filter, save the filter as a query named **qryCitySuppliesFilter**, clear all filters, and then close the table.
4. Create a query named **qryProductSubquery** that selects the SupplierID field from the tblProduct table for all products that weigh more than 50 pounds (*Hint*: Do not show the weight field.) Switch to SQL view, copy the SQL code, and save the qryProductSubquery query.
5. Create a new query in SQL view. Paste the SQL code that you copied in the previous step from qryProductSubquery, add code that uses the existing code as a subquery and selects all fields from the tblInvoice table where the SupplierID is in the tblInvoice table. Run the query, save the query as **qryProductSubqueryInvoice**, and then close the query.
6. Add a multivalued field to the end of the **tblInvoice** table, defining permitted values of **Courier**, **Email**, **Fax**, and **USPS**, and naming the field **Transmitted**. Save the table, and then add the following values to the field in the table datasheet: for record 11—Email and USPS, for record 16—Courier, and for record 17—Fax and USPS. Close the table.
7. Use the Simple Query Wizard to create a query named **qryInvoiceValue** that displays all fields from the tblInvoice table; for the Transmitted field, display only the version of the field that uses the Value property and change its Caption property setting to **Transmitted**. Save and close the query.
8. Add an Attachment field named **ProductFiles** to the end of the **tblProduct** table, using a Caption property setting of **Product Files**. Attach the files **Autoclave_Specification_Sheet.pdf** and **Autoclave.xlsx** to the ProductFiles field for record 4 in the tblProduct table, and then close the table.
9. Add an AutoNumber field named **ProductNum** to the beginning of the **tblProductSpecialEnviron** table, using a Caption property setting of **Product Num** and a New Values property setting of Random. View the table in Datasheet view to see the random numbers. Save and close the table.
10. Use the Performance Analyzer to analyze the entire Product database, but do not implement any of the analysis results. How many analysis results of the recommendation type did the Performance Analyzer find? Of the suggestion type? Of the idea type? Record the answers in a Word document and submit it to your instructor. Close the Performance Analyzer dialog box.
11. Use Windows File Explorer to move the Ads database from the Access3 ▸ Review folder to the Access3 folder. Link to the tblAd table, and then move the Ads database to the Access3 ▸ Review folder. Use the Linked Table Manager to refresh the link to the tblAd table. Open the **tblAd** table in Datasheet view, and then add a new record to the table: Ad Num 7, Ad Date **9/13/2016**, Ad Cost **$227.60**, and Placed **Web ad**.

12. Close the Product database without exiting Access, create a copy of the Product database in the Access3 ▸ Review folder, and then rename the copy as **Sellers**. Open the **Product** database in the Access3 ▸ Review folder, and then use the Database Splitter to split the Product database. Use the default name for the back-end database and store it in the Access3 ▸ Review folder.
13. Set the same database properties and startup options for the Product database that you set in Tutorial 12 for the Health database, using a value of **Vendor for Chatham Community Health Services** for the Application Title property.
14. Compact and repair the database, exit Access, open the **Product** database, test all the navigation options, and then exit Access.

APPLY

Case Problem 1

Data Files needed for this Case Problem: Job.accdb (*cont. from Tutorial 11*), and NewTasks.accdb

GoGopher! Amol Mehta asks you to complete your work with the user interface for the Gopher database. To meet his request, complete the following steps:

1. Open the **Job** database you worked with in Tutorials 9–11.
2. Open the **tblMember** table datasheet, use an AutoFilter to filter records using the MemberStatus field for values of Inactive and On Hold, and then save and close the table.
3. Use Filter By Form with the **frmMemberInfo** form to select all records in which the Last Name is Grant or Ward and the membership status is Active. Apply the filter, save the filter as a query named **qryNameStatusFilter**, and then close the form.
4. Create a query named **qryTaskTHSubquery** that selects the TaskID field from the tblSchedule table for all tasks that are on TaskDay TH. (*Hint*: Do not show the TaskDay field.) Switch to SQL view, copy the SQL code, and then save and close the qryTaskTHSubquery query.
5. Create a new query in SQL view. Paste the SQL code you copied in the previous step from qryTaskTHSubquery, add code that uses the current code as a subquery and selects all fields from the tblTask table where the TaskID is in the tblTask table, and then run the query. Save the query as **qryTaskTHSubqueryMemberID**, and then save and close the query.
6. Add an Attachment field named **MemberAttachment** to the end of the **tblMember** table, using a Caption property setting of **Member Attachment**. Create two Notepad documents named **davidson_1.txt** and **davidson_2.txt**, each containing a thank-you note written by Denis Davidson, thanking the Gopher team for helping with tasks, and store them in the Access3 ▸ Case1 folder. Attach both documents to the MemberAttachment field for record 2 in the tblMember table, resize the Member Attachment column to its best fit, and then save and close the table.
7. Add an AutoNumber field named **MemberNum** to the beginning of the **tblSpecialMember** table, using a Caption property setting of **Member Num** and a New Values property setting of Random. Specify the MemberNum field as the primary key. Resize the Member Num column to its best fit in the datasheet, and then save and close the table.
8. Use the Performance Analyzer to analyze the entire Job database, but do not implement any of the analysis results. How many analysis results of the recommendation type did the Performance Analyzer find? Of the suggestion type? Of the idea type? Record the answers in a Word document and submit it to your instructor. Close the Performance Analyzer dialog box.
9. Use Windows File Explorer to move the NewTasks database from the Access3 ▸ Case1 folder to the Access3 folder. Link to the **tblNewTask** table in the **NewTasks** database located in the Access3 folder. Use Windows File Explorer to move the NewTasks database to the Access3 ▸ Case1 folder, and then use the Linked Table Manager to refresh the link to the **tblNewTask** table. Open the tblNewTask table in Datasheet view, and then add a new record to the table: Task ID **130**, and Task Desc **Mow Lawn**. Save and close the tblNewTask table.

10. Close the Job database without exiting Access, create a copy of the Job database in the Access3 ▸ Case1 folder, and then rename the copy as **InProgress**. Open the **Job** database in the Access3 ▸ Case1 folder, and then use the Database Splitter to split the Job database. Use the default name for the back-end database and store it in the Access3 ▸ Case1 folder.
11. Set the same database properties and startup options for the Job database that you set in Tutorial 12 for the Health database, using a value of **Final Exercise** for the Application Title property.
12. Compact and repair the database, exit Access, open the **Job** database, test all the navigation options, and then exit Access.

CHALLENGE

Case Problem 2

Data Files needed for this Case Problem: Amy_Hawkins_Associate_Degree.docx, Amy_Hawkins_Bachelor_Degree.pdf, Lesson.accdb (*cont. from Tutorial 11*), and Room.accdb

O'Brien Educational Services Karen O'Brien wants you to complete your work with the user interface for the Lesson database. To meet her request, complete the following steps:

1. Open the **Lesson** database you worked with in Tutorials 9–11.
2. Open the **tblEquipment** table datasheet, use an AutoFilter to filter records using the Equipment field for values of Desktop computer, Laptop computer, and Tablet computer, and then save and close the table.
3. Use Filter By Form with the **frmStudent** form to select all records in which the city is South Bend or Oscela and the gender is F. Apply the filter, save the filter as a query named **qryCityGenderFilter**, and then close the form.
4. **Explore** Create a query named **qryStudentGenderSubquery** that selects all students from the tblStudent table who are male. Create a query named **qryStudentGenderContracts** that contains all fields from the tblContract table for records whose StudentID is in the subquery qryStudentGenderSubquery. Use SQL view to create the qryStudentGenderContracts query. The results should be sorted in ascending order by StudentID. Save and close the query. (*Hint*: Create the qryStudentGenderSubquery first, copy the SQL code from the subquery to create the new query qryStudentGenderContracts, then open the new qryStudentGenderContracts in design view to apply the sort order.)
5. Add a multivalued field to the end of the **tblTutor** table, defining permitted values of **Math**, **Biology**, **Chemistry**, and **History**, and naming the field **Subject**. Allow the user to choose more than one subject. Save the table, and then add the following values to the field in the table datasheet: for record 1—Biology and Chemistry; for record 2—Math; for record 3—History; for record 4—Math, Biology and Chemistry; and for record 5—Math. Resize the Subject column to its best fit, and then save and close the table.
6. Use the Simple Query Wizard to create a query named **qryTutorMultivalued** that displays the TutorID, FirstName, LastName, and Subject from the tblTutor table; for the Subject field, display only the version of the field that displays multiple values in a text box. Resize the Subject column to its best fit, and then save and close the query.
7. Add an Attachment field named **Documents** to the end of the **tblTutor** table, using a Caption property setting of **Diplomas and References**. Attach two files named **Amy_Hawkins_Associate_Degree.docx** and **Amy_Hawkins_Bachelor_Degree.pdf**, to the Documents field for record 4 in the tblTutor table, resize the Documents column to its best fit, and then save and close the table.
8. Add an AutoNumber field named **SpecialNum** to the top of the **tblSpecialSession** table, using a Caption property setting of **Special Num** and a New Values property setting of Increment. Specify the SpecialNum field as the primary key. Resize the Special Num column to its best fit in the datasheet, and then save and close the table.

9. Use the Performance Analyzer to analyze the entire Lesson database. How many analysis results of the recommendation type did the Performance Analyzer find? Of the suggestion type? Of the idea type? Record the answers in a Word document and submit it to your instructor. Use the Performance Analyzer to implement any suggestion task, and perform any subsequent task(s) required due to implementing the suggestion(s). Close the Performance Analyzer dialog box.
10. Use Windows File Explorer to move the Room database from the Access3 ▸ Case2 folder to the Access3 folder. Link to the tblRoom table in the Room database located in the Access3 folder. Use Windows File Explorer to move the Room database to the Access3 ▸ Case2 folder, and then use the Linked Table Manager to refresh the link to the **tblRoom** table. Open the tblRoom table in Datasheet view, and then add a new record to the table: Room Num **2**, Rental Cost **$75**, and Room Type **Group**. Close the table.
11. Close the Lesson database without exiting Access, create a copy of the Lesson database in the Access3 ▸ Case2 folder, and then rename the copy as **Sessions**. Open the **Lesson** database in the Access3 ▸ Case2 folder, and then use the Database Splitter to split the Lesson database. Use the default name for the back-end database and store it in the Access3 ▸ Case2 folder.
12. Set the same database properties and startup options for the Lesson database that you set in Tutorial 12 for the Health database, using a value of **O'Brien Final** for the Application Title property.
13. Compact and repair the database, exit Access, open the **Lesson** database, test all the navigation options, and then exit Access.

APPLY

Case Problem 3

Data Files needed for this Case Problem: Pet.accdb (*cont. from Tutorial 11*), Receipt2100.xlsx, Receipt2101.xlsx, and Rescuers.accdb

Rosemary Animal Shelter Ryan Lang wants you to complete your work with the user interface for the Shelter database. To meet his request, complete the following steps:

1. Open the **Pet** database you worked with in Tutorials 9–11.
2. Open the **tblDonation** table datasheet, use an AutoFilter to filter records using the DonationDesc field for values of Dog Food and Cat Food, and then save and close the table.
3. Use Filter By Form with the **frmDonation** form to select all records in which the Patron ID is 34642 or 36020 and the DonationTypeID is E. Apply the filter, save the filter as a query named **qryPatronDescFilter**, and then close the form.
4. Create a query named **qryPatronOver100Subquery** that selects all PatronIDs from the tblDonation table where the DonationValue Is greater than 100. Use SQL view to create a query named **qryPatronNameOver100** that contains all fields from the tblPatron table for records whose PatronID is in the subquery qryPatronOver100Subquery. Save and close the query.
5. Add a multivalued field to the end of the **tblPatron** table, defining donation values of **Adopt**, **Donor**, and **Volunteer**, and naming the field **DonorType** with a Caption property value of **Donor Type**. Save the table, and then add the following values to the field in the table datasheet: for record 1—Donor and Volunteer; for record 2—Donor and Adopt; for record 3—Donor, Adopt, and Volunteer; and for record 4—Volunteer. Resize the Donor Type column to its best fit, and then save and close the table.
6. Create a query named **qryDonorValue** that displays all fields from the tblPatron table; for the DonorType field, display only the version of the field that uses the Value property and change its Caption property setting to **Donor Type**. Resize the Donor Type column to its best fit in the datasheet, and then save and close the query.
7. Add an Attachment field named **ReceiptFiles** to the end of the **tblDonation** table, using a Caption property setting of **Receipt Files**. Attach the document named **Receipt2100.xlsx** to record 1 and **Receipt2101.xlsx** to record 2, to the ReceiptFiles field in the tblDonation table, and then close the table.

8. Add an AutoNumber field named **DonationNum** to the top of the **tblSpecialDonation** table, using a Caption property setting of **Donation Num** and a New Values property setting of Increment. Specify the DonationNum field as the primary key. Resize the Donation Num column to its best fit in the datasheet, and then save and close the table.
9. Use the Performance Analyzer to analyze the entire Pet database, but do not implement any of the analysis results. How many analysis results of the recommendation type did the Performance Analyzer find? Of the suggestion type? Of the idea type? Record the answers in a Word document and submit it to your instructor. Close the Performance Analyzer dialog box.
10. Use Windows File Explorer to move the Room database from the Access3 ▸ Case3 folder to the Access3 folder. Link to the tblRescuer table in the Rescuers database located in the Access3 folder. Use Windows File Explorer to move the Rescuers database to the Access3 ▸ Case3 folder, and then use the Linked Table Manager to refresh the link to the tblRescuer table.
11. Close the Pet database without exiting Access, create a copy of the Pet database in the Access3 ▸ Case3 folder, and then rename the copy as **Animals**. Open the **Pet** database in the Access3 ▸ Case3 folder, and then use the Database Splitter to split the Pet database. Use the default name for the back-end database and store it in the Access3 ▸ Case3 folder.
12. Set the same database properties and startup options for the Pet database that you set in Tutorial 12 for the Health database, using a value of **Shelter Donations** for the Application Title property.
13. Compact and repair the database, exit Access, open the **Pet** database, test all the navigation options, and then exit Access.

CHALLENGE

Case Problem 4

Data File needed for this Case Problem: Leary_1.txt, Leary_2.txt, and Vacation.accdb (*cont. from Tutorial 11*)

Stanley EcoTours Janice and Bill Stanley ask you to complete your work with the user interface for the Vacation database. To meet their request, complete the following steps:

1. Open the **Vacation** database you worked with in Tutorials 9–11.
2. Open the **tblTour** table datasheet, use an AutoFilter to filter records using the Country field for values of Brazil, Ecuador, and Peru, and then save and close the table.
3. **Explore** Use Filter By Form with the **tblGuest** table to select all records in which the city is Boise or Pocatello and the state is ID. Apply the filter, save the filter as a query named **qryStateCityFilter**, and then save and close the table.
4. **Explore** Create a query named **qryTour3003Subquery** that selects all GuestIDs from the tblReservation table where the TourID is 3003. Use SQL view to create a query named **qryTour3003Guest** that contains all fields from the tblGuest table for records whose GuestID is in the subquery qryTour3003Subquery. Save and close the query.
5. Add an Attachment field named **Documents** to the end of the **tblPersonnel** table, using a Caption property setting of **Medical Documents**. Attach the documents **Leary_1.txt** and **Leary_2.txt** in the Access3 ▸ Case4 folder to the Documents field for record 4 in the tblPersonnel table, and then close the table.
6. Add an AutoNumber field named **GuestNum** to the beginning of the **tblSelectedReservation** table, using a Caption property setting of **Guest Num** and a New Values property setting of Increment. Specify the GuestNum field as the primary key. Save and close the table.
7. Use the Performance Analyzer to analyze the entire Vacation database, but do not implement any of the analysis results. How many analysis results of the recommendation type did the Performance Analyzer find? Of the suggestion type? Of the idea type? Record the answers in a Word document and submit it to your instructor. Use the Performance Analyzer to implement any suggestion task, and perform any subsequent task(s) required due to implementing the suggestion(s). Close the Performance Analyzer dialog box.

8. Close the Vacation database without exiting Access, create a copy of the Vacation database in the Access3 ▸ Case4 folder, and then rename the copy as **Tours**. Open the **Vacation** database in the Access3 ▸ Case4 folder, and then use the Database Splitter to split the Vacation database. Use the default name for the back-end database and store it in the Access3 ▸ Case4 folder.
9. Set the same database properties and startup options for the Vacation database that you set in Tutorial 12 for the Health database, using a value of **Stanley Tours** for the Application Title property.
10. Compact and repair the Vacation database, close the Vacation database without exiting Access, open the **Vacation** database, test all the navigation options, and then exit Access.

ProSkills

Written Communication

Writing Clear and Effective Database Documentation

The steps in developing a database include gathering all the data and processing requirements, analyzing the requirements, organizing the requirements, designing the database, documenting the database, and then creating the database. Notice that you prepare the documentation before you create the database because the documentation serves both as a blueprint for the database you will create and as a reference for users after the database is completed. In other words, database documentation must effectively convey to the database developers the technical details developers need to create the database, and convey to the users the data and processing requirements users need to perform their jobs using the database.

Having identified the dual audience for the database documentation; having gathered, analyzed, and organized the requirements; and having designed the database, you are ready to write the database documentation. Unlike writing business documents, essays, and other narrative documents in which you usually need to persuade or to present a point of view, you should write database documentation in a factual manner that accurately presents the data, processing, and technical requirements. It's helpful to prepare a draft of the database documentation and to schedule multiple review cycles. During the review cycles, you select database developers and users to read the documentation, provide feedback by pointing out errors, omissions, and other problems with the documentation, and then you revise the documentation and release it again for further review.

PROSKILLS

Document a Personal Database

Throughout this book, you have learned how to use Access to develop and manage a database. The appendix at the end of this book, titled "Relational Databases and Database Design," includes additional content about designing tables, examining the keys used in those tables, creating entity-relationship diagrams to describe the tables and their relationships, and setting integrity constraints. In this ProSkills exercise, you'll use a word processor or Access to design a database that will manage the data of your choice. You can choose any situation that interests you. For example, you might design a database based on your work experience, your involvement with a club or program at your school, your participation or interest in sports or a hobby, or something that you need to organize in your personal life. Be sure to choose a situation that contains enough variation so that you can design at least five to eight tables that are related to each other with at least one many-to-many and at least one one-to-one relationship.

Note: Please be sure *not* to include any personal information of a sensitive nature in the database you create to be submitted to your instructor for this exercise. Later on, you can update the data in your database with such information for your own personal use.

1. Read the appendix titled "Relational Databases and Database Design," which appears at the end of this book.
2. Identify each entity (table) in the database that you are designing. Your database should have at least five to eight tables. For each table, list the fields and their attributes, such as data types, field sizes, and validation rules. Place the set of tables in third normal form and identify all primary, alternate, and foreign keys. You can document these tables using a word processor or by using Access. If you use a word processor for your design, make sure that your work clearly indicates each table and the fields it contains, the attributes for each field, and the keys. If you use Access for your design, create the tables by defining each table's fields and field attributes, specify the primary key for each table, and establish the table relationships in the Relationships window.
3. Draw an entity-relationship diagram showing the entities and the relationships between the entities. Your database should have at least one many-to-many relationship and at least one one-to-one relationship.
4. For each table in the database, represent the functional dependencies and determinants in a bubble diagram or by using the shorthand representation shown in the appendix (that lists the determinant, followed by an arrow and the dependent fields).
5. Submit your completed database design to your instructor as requested.

ADDITIONAL CASE 1

Enhancing a Charity Database

ACCESS

OBJECTIVES

- Change field properties
- Add fields to a table
- Enter data in a table
- Create table relationships
- Create select, parameter, and crosstab queries
- Create a form using the Form Wizard
- Create calculated controls in a form
- Create a custom report
- Create an unbound form
- Create macros
- Create a navigation form
- Set database properties and startup options

In this case you will use skills you learned in the following tutorials:

- Tutorials 1–10 and 12 (startup options only)

Case | *The Hamilton Good Deed Club*

Doreen and Kyle Hamilton and some friends recently formed a club to support acts of kindness. The Hamilton Good Deed Club accepts cash donations that are used to finance the acts of kindness proposed by club members. Most of the club members have committed to contribute regular monthly donations.

The Hamilton Good Deed Club is a registered charitable organization, and accepts cash donations only. It does not accept donations of equipment or services. Examples of acts of kindness performed and financed by the Hamilton Good Deed Club include purchasing tickets to a baseball game for a family that has given extraordinary time and effort to help the community, purchasing a wheelchair for a teenager to play wheelchair basketball, and decorating a bedroom for a child who is ill.

The club members have committed to contribute regular monthly donations, and the club established contribution levels of a minimum of $200 monthly for level 1 donors and a minimum of $400 monthly for level 2 donors. Donors can donate more than their minimum monthly commitment if they wish. These donors are sometimes recognized by local businesses with coupons for dinner at local restaurants or free merchandise.

Donations are tracked using a small database, managed by Ron Khan, the club's treasurer. Ron's database consists of two tables, tblMember and tblDonation. Figure 1 shows the structure of the tblMember table, which stores data about each club member. Each tblMember table record contains a member ID number and each member's first name, last name, address, city, state or province, postal code, phone number, email address, join date, and donation level.

STARTING DATA FILES

AddCases

Hamilton.accdb

Figure 1 **Structure of the tblMember table**

Field Name	Data Type	Properties
MemberID	AutoNumber	Description: Primary key Caption: Member ID
FirstName	Short Text	Field Size: 15 Caption: First Name
LastName	Short Text	Field Size: 15 Caption: Last Name
Address	Short Text	Field Size: 32
Phone	Short Text	Field Size: 14
Email	Short Text	Field Size: 50 Caption: Email Address
JoinDate	Date/Time	Format: mm/dd/yyyy Caption: Join Date
Level	Number	Description: Donation level (1 = $200 per month, 2 = $400 per month) Field Size: Byte Decimal Places: 0

Figure 2 shows the structure of the tblDonation table, which contains one record for each monthly donation received. DonationID is the table's primary key. MemberID is a foreign key in the tblDonation table, and the tblMember table will have a one-to-many relationship with the tblDonation table. The other fields in the tblDonation table are DonationDate and DonationAmt.

Figure 2 **Structure of the tblDonation table**

Field Name	Data Type	Properties
DonationID	Number	Description: Primary key Caption: Donation ID Field Size: Long Integer Decimal Places: 0
MemberID	Number	Description: Foreign key Caption: Member ID Field Size: Long Integer Decimal Places: 0
DonationDate	Date/Time	Format: mm/dd/yyyy Caption: Donation Date
DonationAmt	Currency	Decimal Places: 2 Caption: Donation Amt

Ron wants to create special queries, forms, and reports in the database to help him mange club accounting. To help Ron finish his work with the database, complete the following steps:

1. Start Access, and then open the **Hamilton** database from the AddCases folder in the location where your Data Files are stored.
2. Review the **tblMember** and the **tblDonation** tables to become familiar with their structures and data. If you are unfamiliar with any property setting, use the Access Help system for an explanation of that property.
3. For the tblDonation table, specify the DonationID as the primary key and resize all datasheet columns to their best fit. For the tblMember table, add a validation rule for the Level field to store only values equal to 1 or 2, add an appropriate validation text message, and then add the following new text fields between the Address and Phone fields: **City** (Field Size **24**), **StateProv** (Field Size **2** and caption of **State/Prov**), and **PostalCode** (Field Size **10** and caption of **Postal Code**).
4. Modify the first record in the tblMember table datasheet by entering your name, city, state or province, postal code, and phone number; enter phone numbers in 987-654-3210 format. Select another city, state or province, postal code, and phone area code and enter this information for the last four records, along with a different phone number for each record. Select a second city, state or province, postal code, and phone area code, and then enter these values in records 2–6, using five different phone numbers. Finally, select another city, state or province, postal code, and phone area code and then enter these values in records 7–11, using five different phone numbers. Resize all datasheet columns to their best fit. An example of data is shown in Figure 3.

Figure 3 **Sample data for the tblMember table**

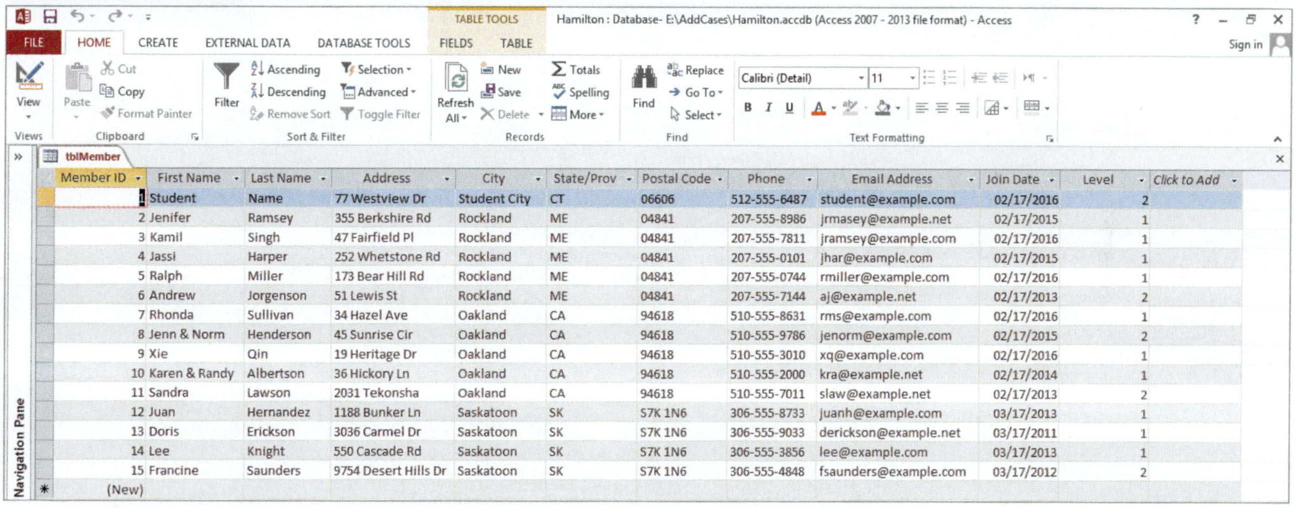

Member ID	First Name	Last Name	Address	City	State/Prov	Postal Code	Phone	Email Address	Join Date	Level	Click to Add
1	Student	Name	77 Westview Dr	Student City	CT	06606	512-555-6487	student@example.com	02/17/2016	2	
2	Jenifer	Ramsey	355 Berkshire Rd	Rockland	ME	04841	207-555-8986	jrmasey@example.net	02/17/2015	1	
3	Kamil	Singh	47 Fairfield Pl	Rockland	ME	04841	207-555-7811	jramsey@example.com	02/17/2016	1	
4	Jassi	Harper	252 Whetstone Rd	Rockland	ME	04841	207-555-0101	jhar@example.com	02/17/2015	1	
5	Ralph	Miller	173 Bear Hill Rd	Rockland	ME	04841	207-555-0744	rmiller@example.com	02/17/2016	1	
6	Andrew	Jorgenson	51 Lewis St	Rockland	ME	04841	207-555-7144	aj@example.net	02/17/2013	2	
7	Rhonda	Sullivan	34 Hazel Ave	Oakland	CA	94618	510-555-8631	rms@example.com	02/17/2016	1	
8	Jenn & Norm	Henderson	45 Sunrise Cir	Oakland	CA	94618	510-555-9786	jenorm@example.com	02/17/2015	2	
9	Xie	Qin	19 Heritage Dr	Oakland	CA	94618	510-555-3010	xq@example.com	02/17/2016	1	
10	Karen & Randy	Albertson	36 Hickory Ln	Oakland	CA	94618	510-555-2000	kra@example.net	02/17/2014	1	
11	Sandra	Lawson	2031 Tekonsha	Oakland	CA	94618	510-555-7011	slaw@example.net	02/17/2013	2	
12	Juan	Hernandez	1188 Bunker Ln	Saskatoon	SK	S7K 1N6	306-555-8733	juanh@example.com	03/17/2013	1	
13	Doris	Erickson	3036 Carmel Dr	Saskatoon	SK	S7K 1N6	306-555-9033	derickson@example.net	03/17/2011	1	
14	Lee	Knight	550 Cascade Rd	Saskatoon	SK	S7K 1N6	306-555-3856	lee@example.com	03/17/2013	1	
15	Francine	Saunders	9754 Desert Hills Dr	Saskatoon	SK	S7K 1N6	306-555-4848	fsaunders@example.com	03/17/2012	2	
(New)											

5. Define a one-to-many relationship between the primary tblMember table and the related tblDonation table, using MemberID as the common field, enforcing referential integrity, and selecting the Cascade Update Related Fields option. Resize the tblMember field list so that all fields are visible, and then create and print the Relationships for Hamilton report but do not save it.
6. Export the tblMember table as an XML file named **HamiltonMember** to the AddCases folder; do not create a separate XSD file. Save the export steps.
7. Create and save a query named **qryDistantMembers** that displays the FirstName, LastName, Address, City, StateProv, PostalCode, and Phone fields for all members not living in the same city where you live in ascending order by LastName. Print the query recordset in landscape orientation after testing and saving the query.
8. Create and save a query named **qryMarch17Donations** that displays the FirstName, LastName, Phone, and DonationAmt fields for all donations made on 3/17/2016 in ascending order by LastName. Print the query recordset after testing and saving the query.
9. Create and save a query named **qryDonationTotalsByMember** that displays each member's first name, last name, and total donation amount. For the total field, use the name **TotalDonated** and a Caption value of **Total Donated**. Sort in descending order by total donation amount, and resize all columns to best fit. Print the query recordset after testing and saving the query. Modify the query by deleting the FirstName and LastName fields, adding the DonationDate field as the first field in the query, sorting in ascending order by DonationDate (and not by the donation total), and then saving the query as **qryDonationTotalsByDate**. Resize all columns to best fit, and then print the query recordset.

10. Create and save a parameter query named **qryLevelParameter** that displays the FirstName, LastName, Phone, Email, JoinDate, and Level fields in ascending order by LastName for a Level field value that the user enters. If the user doesn't enter a field value, select and display all records. After creating and saving the query, run the query and enter **2** as the Level field value. Print the query results.

Explore 11. Create a crosstab query that uses DonationDate field values for the row headings, Level field values for the column headings, and the sum of the DonationAmt field as the summarized value. (*Hint*: Create a query named **qryDonationAmounts** that contains the three fields you need for the crosstab query.) Save the query as **qryDonationAmountsCrosstab**, resize the columns in the query recordset to their best fit, and then save and print the query recordset.

Explore 12. Create a form called **frmDonationsByMember** containing a main form and a subform called **frmDonationSubform**. Select all the fields from the tblMember table for the main form, and select all fields except MemberID from the tblDonation table for the subform. Use the Tabular layout for the subform. Change the form's title to **Contributions by Member**. Remove the subform's label and resize the columns to best fit. Add a calculated control to the frmDonationSubform footer that displays the sum of the DonationAmt field. Name this control **txtSumDonationAmt**. Change the text alignment of all the controls in the Detail section to Left.

Explore 13. Create a copy of the frmDonationsByMember form, and use **frmDonationsByMemberModified** as the new form's name. Modify the new form by adding a calculated control, as shown in Figure 4, which displays the sum of the DonationAmt field values that appear in the subform. (*Hint:* Set the Visible property for the Form Footer section in the subform to No.) Set the calculated control's Format property to Currency, set its ControlTip Text property to **Calculated total donation amount**, and set its Tab Stop property to No. If necessary, resize and reposition the controls in the form to match Figure 4. Print only the first main form record and its subform records.

Figure 4 **Modified Donations by Member form**

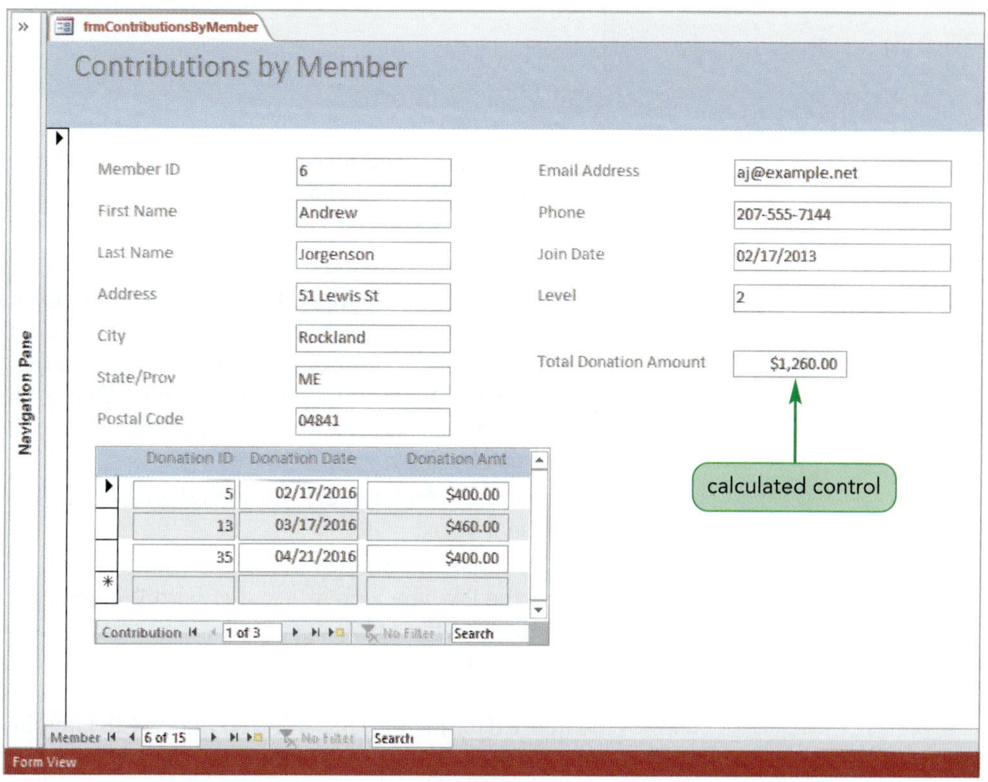

14. Create the custom Donations by Date report shown in Figure 5. The report contains Page Header, Detail, DonationDate Footer, and Report Footer sections. Sort the detail records in ascending order by the DonationDate field, and then in ascending order by the LastName field. Hide duplicate values for the DonationDate field. Calculate and print totals of the DonationAmt field for each DonationDate field value and a grand total. The color used in the lines and titles is Light Blue in the first row of the Standard Colors section, and the line thickness is 3 pt. Save the report as **rptDonationsByDate**. Print the report.

Figure 5 **Donations by Date report**

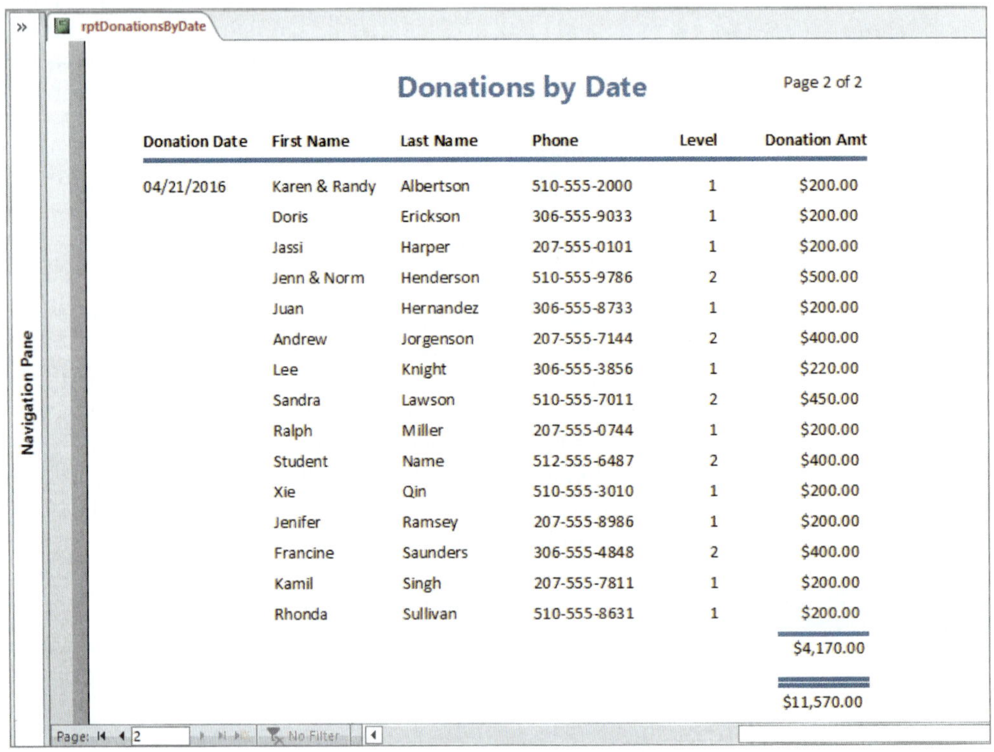

Donations by Date

Page 2 of 2

Donation Date	First Name	Last Name	Phone	Level	Donation Amt
04/21/2016	Karen & Randy	Albertson	510-555-2000	1	$200.00
	Doris	Erickson	306-555-9033	1	$200.00
	Jassi	Harper	207-555-0101	1	$200.00
	Jenn & Norm	Henderson	510-555-9786	2	$500.00
	Juan	Hernandez	306-555-8733	1	$200.00
	Andrew	Jorgenson	207-555-7144	2	$400.00
	Lee	Knight	306-555-3856	1	$220.00
	Sandra	Lawson	510-555-7011	2	$450.00
	Ralph	Miller	207-555-0744	1	$200.00
	Student	Name	512-555-6487	2	$400.00
	Xie	Qin	510-555-3010	1	$200.00
	Jenifer	Ramsey	207-555-8986	1	$200.00
	Francine	Saunders	306-555-4848	2	$400.00
	Kamil	Singh	207-555-7811	1	$200.00
	Rhonda	Sullivan	510-555-8631	1	$200.00
					$4,170.00
					$11,570.00

15. Create a form named **frmQueries** that will display the queries, and that has the following components and characteristics:
    a. Use the text **Hamilton Queries** on the form's tab.
    b. Add a list box with a Name property value of **lstQueryList** that displays all the query names contained in the Hamilton database, excluding those queries that start with a "~" character. To place the query names in the list box, use a SQL SELECT statement to retrieve the query names from the MSysObjects table, and display the queries in alphabetical order. Delete the label attached to the list box, widen the list box to approximately 2.5 inches, and set its height to approximately 1 inch.
    c. Add the label **Select a query**, formatted with Calibri 12-point, black, bold font, above the list box.
    d. Add two command buttons below the list box. The left command button displays the Preview icon above the word **Preview**, and the right command button displays the MS Access Query icon above the word **Display**. Double-clicking a query name has the same effect as selecting a query name in the list box and clicking the right command button. Both events cause Access to display the query datasheet for the selected query. Clicking the left command button opens the selected query in Print Preview.

e. Create macros for the form (when the form loads, move the focus to the first query name in the list box), the list box (when a user double-clicks a query name), and both command buttons (when a user clicks a command button).

f. Set the background color of the Detail section to the Maroon 1 color in the Standard Colors section and the background color of the list box to the Purple 1 color in the Standard Colors section, and then disable the form's shortcut menu, record selectors, and navigation buttons. Set the width of the Detail section to 5 inches, and set its height to 3 inches.

g. Test the form.

16. Create a navigation form named **frmNavigation**, using the Horizontal Tabs, 2 Levels layout, that includes the following tab names and objects:

a. Use **Forms** as the name for the left tab, and place the frmDonationsByMemberModified form below it.

b. Use **Queries** as the name for the second tab, and place the frmQueries form below it.

c. Use **Reports** as the name for the third tab, and place the rptDonationsByDate report below it.

d. Delete the navigation form's picture and title, and change the tab name to **Hamilton database**.

e. Test the navigation form.

17. Make a backup copy of the database, and then compact and repair the database.

18. Set the database properties for the Hamilton database so the frmNavigation form opens when the database is opened, set startup options to disable features as appropriate for a database that uses a navigation form, and change the database name in the title bar to **Hamilton Donation Club**.

19. Close the Hamilton database to activate the database startup options, open the database, test the navigation form options, and then exit Access.

ADDITIONAL CASE 2

Tracking Animal Licenses and Citations

ACCESS

OBJECTIVES

- Change field properties
- Create a new table
- Enter data in a table
- Create table relationships
- Create select, query wizard, parameter, and crosstab queries
- Create forms using wizards and customize forms
- Create calculated controls in a form
- Create a custom report
- Create an unbound form
- Create macros
- Create a navigation form
- Set database properties and startup options

In this case you will use skills you learned in the following tutorials:

- Tutorials 1–11 and 12 (startup options only)

Case | *North River Residences*

Leslie Fong is the office manager in the Animal Control department at North River Residences, a residence for seniors on 100 acres of land with accommodation for 6,000 residents. Residents must purchase licenses for their pets, and North River Residences issues citations for animal infractions on its property. Among her responsibilities, Leslie coordinates issuing licenses for the residents' pets and processing citations for on-site infractions. Budget reductions have forced her department to reduce the number of part-time workers. As a result, the department is experiencing an increase in the backlog for processing citations and pet licensing requests.

Pet licenses for dogs and cats are issued to residents. A license must be visible on the pet's collar, and must be renewed annually. Each license request form must include the license number, animal type, and the resident's name. With each license, the resident receives a brochure that describes the North River Residences animal regulations and the fines for violations of these regulations.

The animal control department is within the security department. The security department employs guards who maintain a secure facility and issue citations for violations including those related to the pet regulations. Each animal citation includes the citation number, the date and time of the violation, and a description of the violation. For animals with licenses, the citation includes the license number and the type of animal. For animals without licenses, the citation includes the animal type but not the license number. Leslie's staff also tracks payments for the fines levied with the citations.

Leslie needs to create a database that will allow her to track and update the animal licenses and citations. Leslie's initial database contains three tables: tblLicense, tblCitation, and tblPayment.

STARTING DATA FILES

AddCases

AnimalLicense.accdb

Figure 6 shows the structure of the tblLicense table, which stores data about each animal license issued to a resident. Each tblLicense table record contains a license number, the animal type, and the resident's name.

Figure 6 Structure of the tblLicense table

Field Name	Data Type	Properties
LicenseNum	Short Text	Description: Primary key; unique number issued to animal Field Size: 5 Caption: License Num
AnimalType	Short Text	Description: Type of animal (dog or cat) Field Size: 8 Caption: Animal Type
OwnerFirst	Short Text	Description: Animal owner's first name Field Size: 15 Caption: Owner First
OwnerLast	Short Text	Description: Animal owner's last name Field Size: 15 Caption: Owner Last

Figure 7 shows the structure of the tblCitation table, which contains one record for each issued citation. Each tblCitation record contains the citation number, date, and time; the license number, if a license is visible on the animal; the animal type; and the violation code.

Figure 7 Structure of the tblCitation table

Field Name	Data Type	Properties
CitationNum	Short Text	Description: Primary key; unique number assigned to a citation for an animal violation Field Size: 6 Caption: Citation Num
CitationDate	Date/Time	Description: Issue date for the citation Format: mm/dd/yyyy Caption: Citation Date
CitationTime	Date/Time	Description: Issue time for the citation Format: Medium Time Caption: Citation Time
LicenseNum	Short Text	Description: Null if the animal has no visible permit Field Size: 5 Caption: License Num
AnimalType	Short Text	Description: Type of animal (dog or cat) Field Size: 8 Caption: Animal Type
ViolationCode	Short Text	Description: Violation code for the infraction Field Size: 2 Caption: Violation Code

Figure 8 shows the structure of the tblPayment table, which contains one record for each animal violation payment. Each tblPayment record contains a unique payment ID, the payment amount and date, and the number of the citation to which the payment applies.

Figure 8 Structure of the tblPayment table

Field Name	Data Type	Properties
PaymentID	AutoNumber	Description: Primary key; unique number assigned to an animal violation payment Caption: Payment ID
PaymentAmt	Currency	Description: Amount paid Format: Currency Decimal Places: 2 Caption: Payment Amt
PaymentDate	Date/Time	Description: Payment date Format: mm/dd/yyyy Caption: Payment Date
CitationNum	Short Text	Description: Citation to which the payment applies Field Size: 6 Caption: Citation Num

Leslie wants some special queries, forms, and reports in the database to help her manage animal licenses and citations. To improve Leslie's database, complete the following steps:

1. Start Access, and then open the **AnimalLicense** database from the AddCases folder in the location where your Data Files are stored.
2. Review the **tblLicense**, **tblCitation**, and **tblPayment** tables to become familiar with their structures and data, and then resize all columns to best fit the data they contain. If you are unfamiliar with any property setting, use the Access Help system for an explanation of that property.
3. The tblCitation table contains a two-character ViolationCode field. Design and create a new table to store the violation codes, descriptions, and fine amounts, using the field names **ViolationCode**, **ViolationDesc**, and **FineAmt**, making ViolationCode the primary key, and setting the Caption property and other field properties to appropriate values. Save the table as **tblViolation**, add the eight records shown in Figure 9 to the table, resize all datasheet columns to their best fit, and then print the tblViolation table recordset.

Figure 9 tblViolation table records

ViolationCode	ViolationDesc	FineAmt
AU	Animal unsupervised	$20
DP	Animal damaged property	$15
EL	Expired license	$15
EN	Excessive noise	$20
NL	No license visible	$75
RA	No rabies vaccination	$50
VE	Animal left inside vehicle	$17
WL	Walking without a leash	$22

4. Modify the first record in the tblLicense table datasheet by entering your name in the Owner First and Owner Last columns.
5. Add all four tables to the Relationships window, make sure all fields are visible in the field lists, and then define the three one-to-many relationships. Enforce referential integrity, and select the Cascade Update Related Fields option for each relationship. Rearrange the field lists as appropriate so that join lines don't cross field lists, save your design, and then create and print the Relationships for AnimalLicense report but do not save it.
6. Create and save a query named **qryResidentCitations** that displays, in order, all fields from the tblCitation table, and the OwnerFirst and OwnerLast fields from the tblLicense table. Sort in ascending order by OwnerLast as the first sort field, OwnerFirst as the second sort field, CitationDate as the third sort field, and CitationTime as the fourth sort field. Print the query recordset in landscape orientation after testing and saving the query, but don't close the query.
7. Save the qryResidentCitations query as **qryAllCitations**, and then modify the new query to use an outer join to include all records from the tblCitation table and the matching records from the tblLicense table. Print the query recordset in landscape orientation after testing and saving the query, and then close the query.
8. Export the data with formatting and layout in the qryAllCitations query to an Excel workbook named **Citations** in the AddCases folder. Save the export steps.
9. Create and save a query named **qryTotalPaymentsByDate** that displays the PaymentDate field and the sum of the PaymentAmt field from the tblPayment table. For the total field, use a Caption value of **Total Payments**. Sort the query in ascending order by PaymentDate. Resize all datasheet columns to their best fit, and then print the query recordset after testing and saving the query.
10. Create a find duplicates query based on the tblCitation table. Select LicenseNum as the field that might contain duplicates, and select all the other fields in the table as additional fields in the query recordset. Save the query as **qryAnimalsWithMultipleCitations**, and then view and print the query recordset.
11. Make a copy of the qryAllCitations query, save the copy as **qryAllCitationsParameter**, and then modify the new query to display records for a ViolationCode field value that the user enters. If the user doesn't enter a field value, select and display all records. After modifying and saving the query, run the query and enter **AU** as the ViolationCode field value. Print the query recordset in landscape orientation.
12. **Explore** Make a copy of the qryAllCitations query, save the copy as **qryAllCitationsWithoutPermits**, and then modify the new query to display only those records that have a null LicenseNum field value. After modifying and saving the query, run the query and print the query results in landscape orientation.
13. Create a crosstab query that uses the tblCitation table. Select the CitationDate field values for the row headings, ViolationCode field values for the column headings, and the count of the CitationNum field as the summarized value. Save the query as **qryCitationCrosstab**, use a Caption value of **Total Citations** for the Count Row Heading column, resize the columns in the query recordset to their best fit, print the query results, and then save and close the query.
14. Create and save a query named **qryCitationsAndPayments** that displays, in order, all fields from the tblCitation table, and the PaymentID, PaymentAmt, and PaymentDate fields from the tblPayment table. Include all records from the tblCitation table and only the matching records from the tblPayment table. Sort in ascending order by CitationNum. Use the Totals row in the query datasheet to add a count of the number of citations in the Citation Num column, a count of the number of payments in the Payment ID column, and a total of the payment amounts in the Payment Amt column. Print the query recordset in landscape orientation after testing and saving the query.

15. Use the Form Wizard to create a form containing the main form and subform shown in Figure 10. Select all the fields from the tblLicense table for the main form, and select the appropriate fields from the qryCitationsAndPayments query for the subform. Use the Tabular layout. Save the main form as **frmLicensesAndCitations** and the subform as **frmCitationsAndPaymentsSubform**. Change the text in the main form's title control to **Licenses and Citations**. Delete the subform label, resize the widths of the columns in the subform, and adjust the width and height of the subform as necessary. Change the caption on the record navigation bar for the main form to **License** and for the subform to **Citation**. Make sure the tab order in the main form is top-to-bottom and the tab order in the subform is left-to-right. Modify the form by adding the Total Payments calculated control that displays the total PaymentAmt field values from the subform. (*Hint:* Set the Visible property for the Form Footer section in the subform to No.) Print only main form record 29 and its subform records.

Figure 10 **Licenses and Citations form**

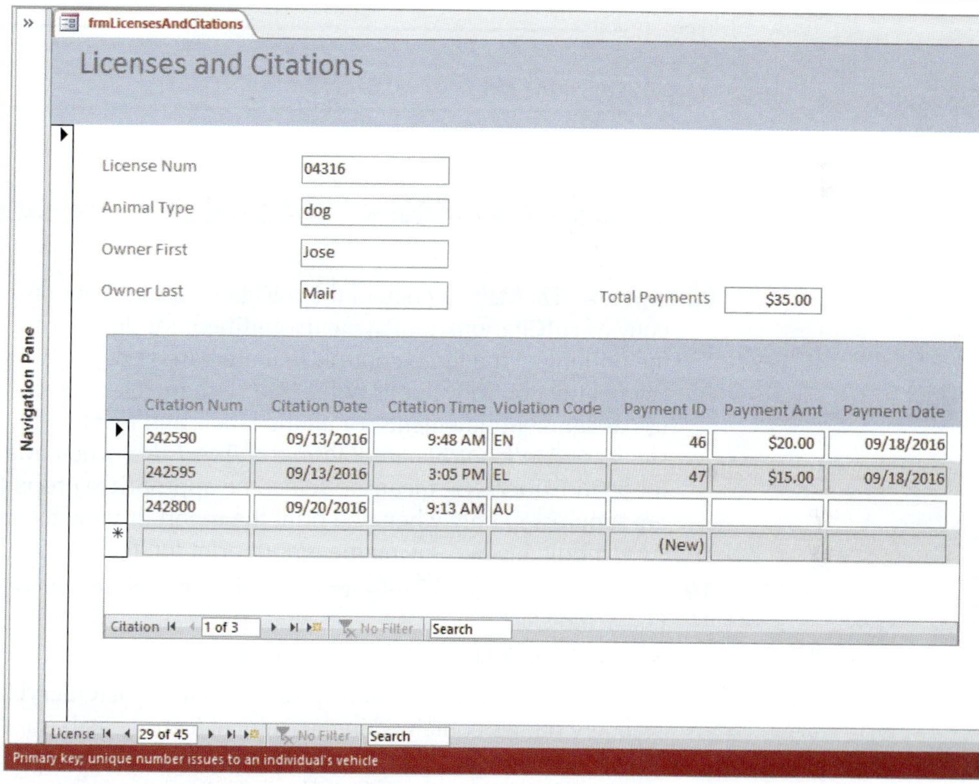

16. Create a blank form and add all fields from the tblCitation table to it, except for the ViolationCode field, in a Stacked layout. Add the ViolationCode field to the form as a combo box control that displays values from the tblViolation table. Display all three fields from the tblViolation table, sort the records in ascending order by ViolationCode, do not hide the key column, resize all columns to the widest control, store values in the ViolationCode field, and use the label **Violation Code**. Resize the text boxes and the combo box as appropriate for the displayed values, and so the text box and combo box controls do not overlap the label controls. Save the form as **frmCitation**, and then print only the last form record.

17. Create the report shown in Figure 11, which is based on the qryCitationsAndPayments query, and save it as **rptCitationsAndPayments**. Use landscape orientation, and increase the report width to at least 9.5 inches. Add the title, date, and time to the Report Header section. Print the first page of the report.

Figure 11 **Citations and Payments report**

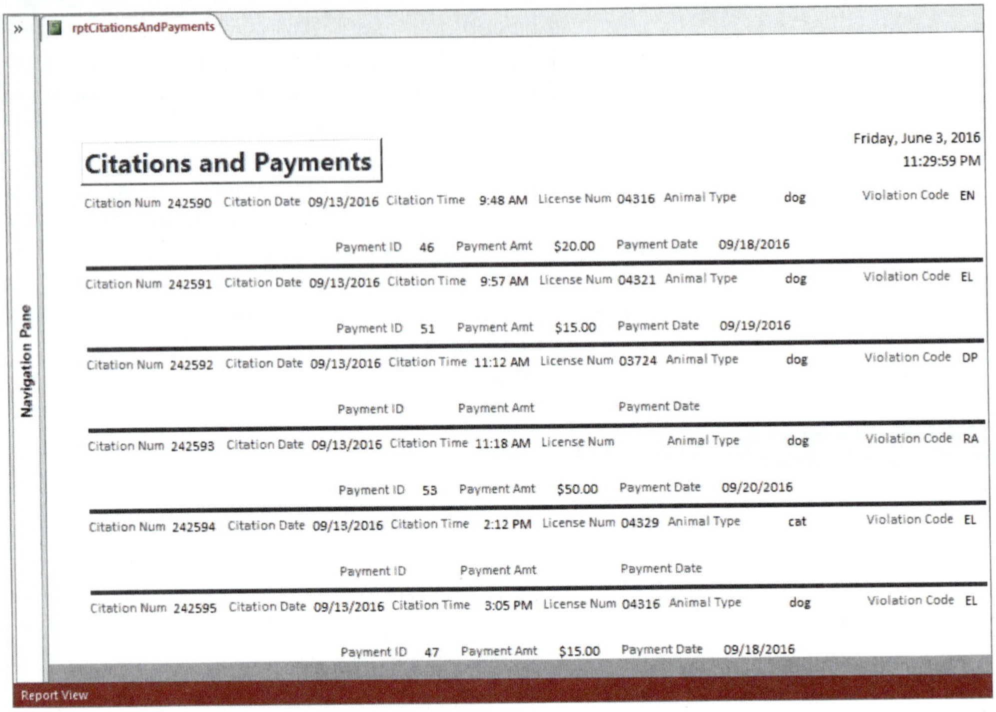

Explore **18.** Make a copy of the rptCitationsAndPayments report, and save the copy as **rptCitationsAndPaymentsModified**. Modify the new report to suppress the printing of the three controls that are based on the tblPayment table when the PaymentID control value is null. (*Hint:* Use the Detail section's Format event, and use assignment statements for all the labels and text boxes in the Detail section similar to *Me![control name].Visible = True/False*, where *Me* refers to the open form, and *True/False* means to select the appropriate property setting. The controls are suppressed only when you print the report or view the report in Print Preview.) After modifying and saving the report, print the first page of the report.

19. Create a form named **frmQueries** that has the following components and characteristics:

a. Use the text **North River Residences Queries** on the form's tab.

b. Add a list box with a Name property value of **lstQueryList** that displays all the query names contained in the AnimalLicense database, excluding those queries that start with a "~" character. To place the query names in the list box, use a SQL SELECT statement to retrieve the query names from the MSysObjects table, and display the queries in alphabetical order. Delete the label attached to the list box, widen the list box to approximately 2.5 inches, and set its height to approximately 1 inch.

c. Add the label **Available Queries**, formatted with Calibri 12-point, black, bold font, above the list box.

d. Add two command buttons below the list box. The left command button should display the Preview icon above the word **Preview**, and the right command button should display the MS Access Query icon above the word **Display**. Double-clicking a query name should have the same effect as selecting a query name in the list box and clicking the right command button. Both events should cause Access to display the query datasheet for the selected query. Clicking the left command button should open the selected query in Print Preview.

e. Create macros for the form (when the form loads, move the focus to the first query name in the list box), the list box (when a user double-clicks a query name), and both command buttons (when a user clicks a command button).

f. Disable the form's shortcut menu, record selectors, and navigation buttons. Set the width of the Detail section to 3.5 inches, and set its height to 3 inches.

g. Test the form.

20. Create a navigation form named **frmNavigation**, using the Horizontal Tabs, 2 Levels layout that includes the following tab names and objects:

a. Use **Forms** as the name for the left tab, and place the following forms below it, in order: frmCitation and frmLicensesAndCitations.

b. Use **Queries** as the name for the second tab, and place the frmQueries form below it.

c. Use **Reports** as the name for the third tab, and place the rptCitationsAndPaymentsModified report below it.

d. Delete the navigation form's picture and title, and change the tab name to **North River Residences database**.

e. Test the navigation form.

21. Make a backup copy of the database, and then compact and repair the database.

22. Set the database properties for the AnimalLicense database so the frmNavigation form opens when the database is opened, set startup options to disable features as appropriate for a database that uses a navigation form, and change the database name in the title bar to **North River Residences**.

23. Close the AnimalLicense database to activate the database startup options, open the database, test the navigation form options, and then exit Access.

ADDITIONAL CASE 3

ACCESS

Student Volunteer Activities for Southern Ridge College

OBJECTIVES

- Design a database and draw its entity-relationship diagram
- Create the tables and relationships for the database
- Create forms to maintain the database
- Design and enter test data for the database
- Create queries and reports from the database
- Create a navigation form
- Set database properties and startup options

In this case you will use skills you learned in the following tutorials:

- Tutorials 1–7, 9–11, 12 (startup options only), and the "Relational Databases and Database Design" appendix

Case | *Southern Ridge College*

Southern Ridge College provides students in New Mexico with opportunities to volunteer in the community, and these activities are recorded in their co-curricular transcripts. A co-curricular transcript is a record of volunteer activities that a student participates in while enrolled at the college. Volunteer activity is coordinated by the Student Life Office, which maintains the co-curricular transcript information. Volunteer activities include campus events such as Orientation and Open House, and work with nonprofit community agencies such as the local food bank and literacy outreach, which helps adults to learn how to read.

The college recently hired Jennifer Crowley as its new volunteer coordinator. She is eager to make information about the volunteer agencies, volunteer opportunities, and student volunteers more readily available to her office and to the students and agencies. Jennifer's most ambitious project is to develop a database for the volunteer program to help meet these goals. The database will allow potential volunteers to view the volunteer opportunities that meet criteria they specify. Jennifer would like you to design and develop the database.

The first steps in the volunteer program process are the following:

- Identify and document the available volunteers
- Arrange for student volunteer placements
- Assign and track student volunteers

As the first step in the volunteer program process, Jennifer receives a letter or phone call from a nonprofit agency. After some discussions, the agency proposes a volunteer opportunity and completes the Agency/Volunteer Position Information form shown in Figure 12.

STARTING DATA FILES

AddCases

(none)

Figure 12 Agency/Volunteer Request form

AGENCY INFORMATION

NAME OF AGENCY ______________________

ADDRESS ______________________
Street
____
City State Zip

CONTACT ______________ PHONE ______________

VOLUNTEER POSITION INFORMATION

TITLE ______________________

DESCRIPTION OF DUTIES ______________________

ORIENTATION & TRAINING ______________________

ACADEMIC BACKGROUND REQUIRED ______________________

REQUIRES CAR (Y/N) ______ REQUIRES POLICE CHECK (Y/N) ______

SUPERVISOR NAME ______________ PHONE ______________
EMAIL ______________

START DATE ______ (mm/dd/yyyy)

Office Use

Agency ID ______
Volunteer Position ID ______
Category ______

Many agencies offer more than one type of volunteer opportunity. For each possible volunteer position, the agency completes a separate form and assigns one person as the contact for all volunteer opportunity questions and problems. In addition, each volunteer opportunity lists a supervisor who will work with the student volunteer. The volunteer opportunity remains active until the agency notifies the Student Life Office that the volunteer opportunity is filled or no longer available.

Jennifer assigns a four-digit Agency ID to each new agency and a three-digit Volunteer Position ID to each new volunteer position using sequential numbers. She also classifies each volunteer position into a category that helps students identify volunteer positions that are related to their academic majors or interests. For example, a student might be interested in accounting, advertising, finance, health care, law, software engineering, social service, or marketing.

A copy of each Agency/Volunteer Position Information form is placed in reference books in the Student Life Office. Students browse through these books to find volunteer positions that interest them. If a volunteer position interests a student, the student copies the information about the volunteer position and contacts the agency directly to request an interview.

Students who are interested in volunteering fill out the Student Volunteer form, shown in Figure 13, to provide basic personal information for the office files.

Figure 13 Student Volunteer form

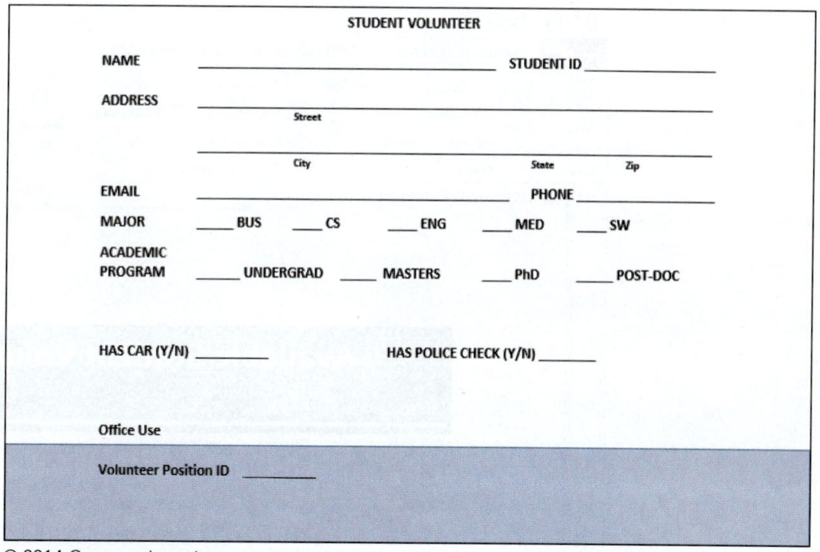
STUDENT VOLUNTEER

NAME ______________________ STUDENT ID __________

ADDRESS ______________________
Street

____
City State Zip

EMAIL ______________________ PHONE __________

MAJOR ____ BUS ____ CS ____ ENG ____ MED ____ SW

ACADEMIC PROGRAM ____ UNDERGRAD ____ MASTERS ____ PhD ____ POST-DOC

HAS CAR (Y/N) ______ HAS POLICE CHECK (Y/N) ______

Office Use

Volunteer Position ID ______

When a student has made arrangements with an agency to volunteer, Jennifer enters the Volunteer Position ID on the Student Volunteer form. Next, a clerk enters information from the form into a word processor to prepare lists of current volunteers and volunteer positions, and then prints and places the form in a binder.

Jennifer believes that getting these two forms into an Access database is the first priority; after that is accomplished, she would like several new reports. The first report, shown in Figure 14, lists all student volunteers who have volunteer positions with any agency, ordered alphabetically by last name. In order to identify the student volunteers who should be included in the report, the system prompts the user for the Major code and the Academic Code.

Figure 14 Student Volunteers report

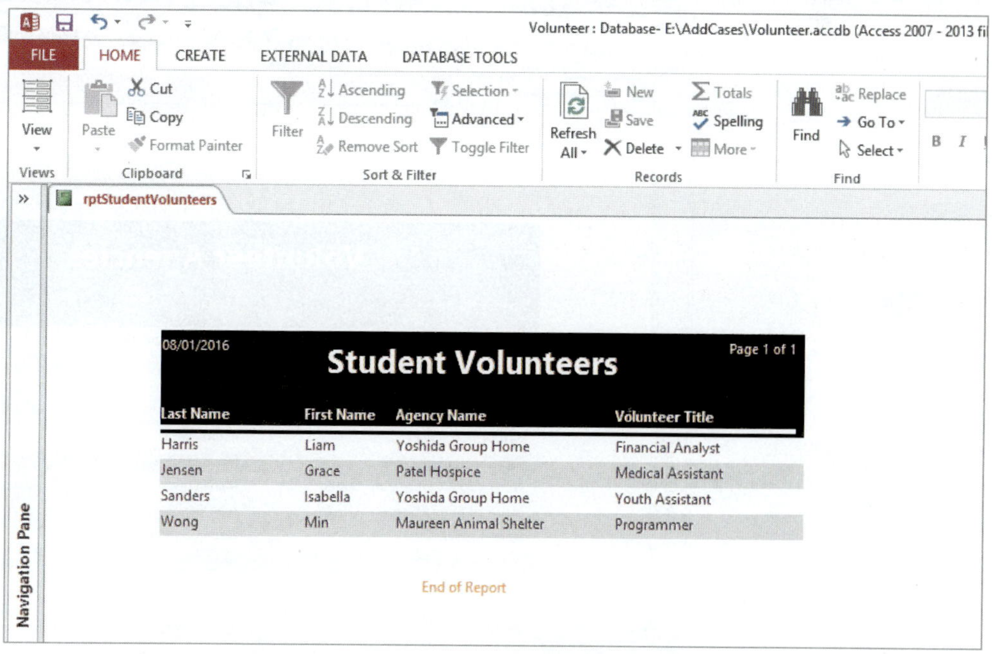

A second new report lists all students who do not currently have a volunteer job. This report is sorted by major, and within major, sorted by last name, shown in Figure 15.

Figure 15 Available Student Volunteers report

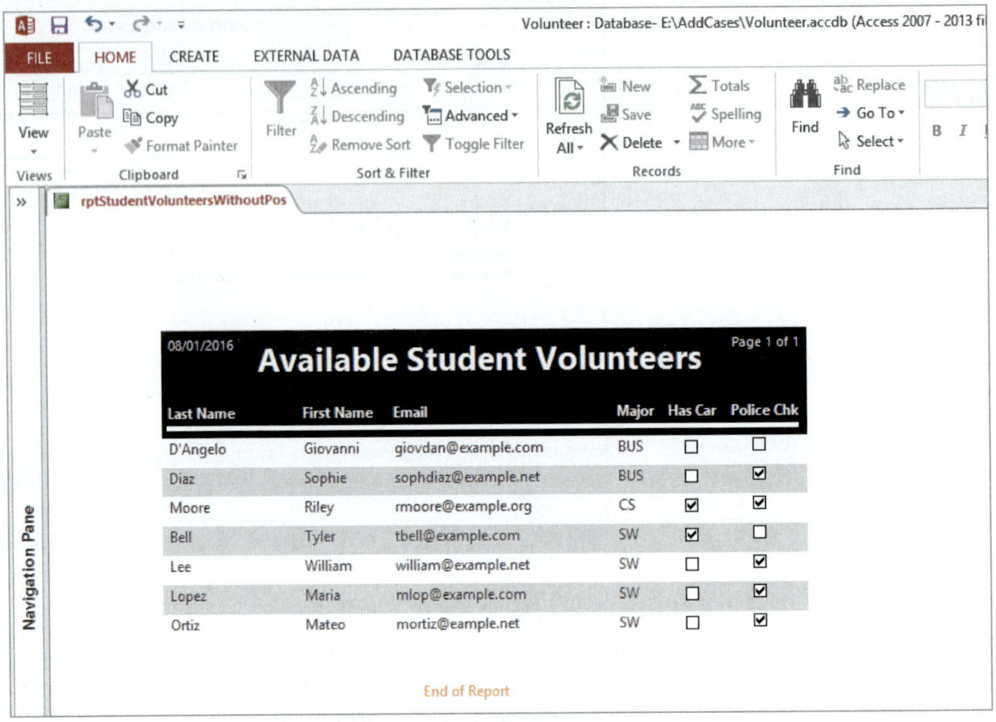

08/01/2016 **Available Student Volunteers** Page 1 of 1

Last Name	First Name	Email	Major	Has Car	Police Chk
D'Angelo	Giovanni	giovdan@example.com	BUS	☐	☐
Diaz	Sophie	sophdiaz@example.net	BUS	☐	☑
Moore	Riley	rmoore@example.org	CS	☑	☑
Bell	Tyler	tbell@example.com	SW	☑	☐
Lee	William	william@example.net	SW	☐	☑
Lopez	Maria	mlop@example.com	SW	☐	☑
Ortiz	Mateo	mortiz@eample.net	SW	☐	☑

End of Report

Another report lists all agencies in the database alphabetically by agency name. Figure 16 shows this report.

Figure 16 Volunteer Agencies report

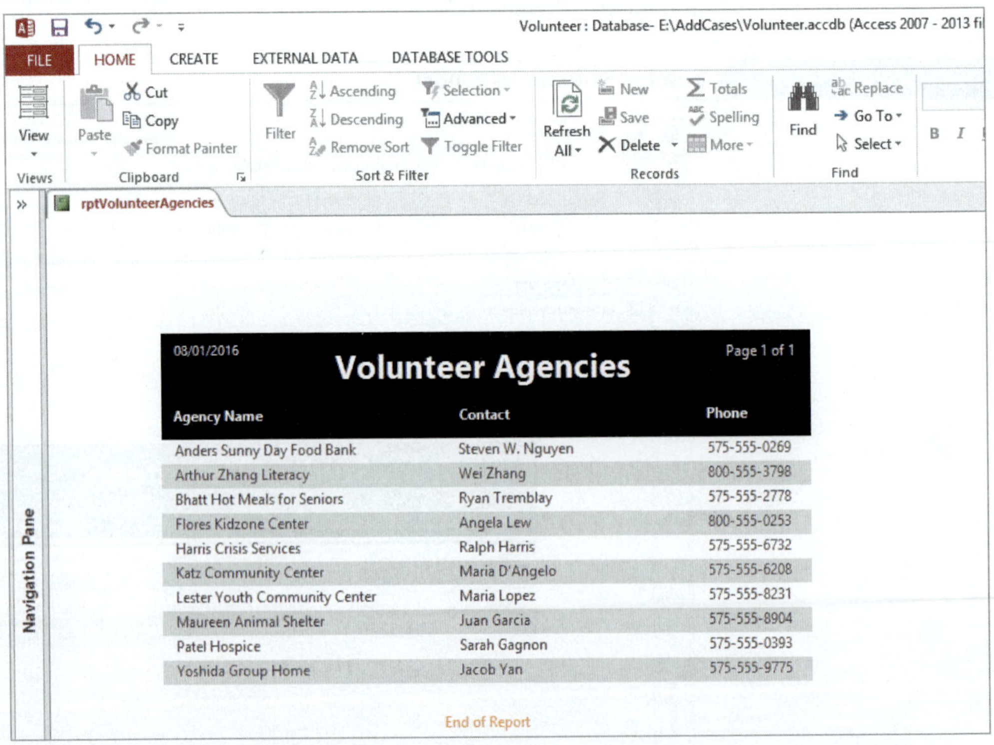

08/01/2016 **Volunteer Agencies** Page 1 of 1

Agency Name	Contact	Phone
Anders Sunny Day Food Bank	Steven W. Nguyen	575-555-0269
Arthur Zhang Literacy	Wei Zhang	800-555-3798
Bhatt Hot Meals for Seniors	Ryan Tremblay	575-555-2778
Flores Kidzone Center	Angela Lew	800-555-0253
Harris Crisis Services	Ralph Harris	575-555-6732
Katz Community Center	Maria D'Angelo	575-555-6208
Lester Youth Community Center	Maria Lopez	575-555-8231
Maureen Animal Shelter	Juan Garcia	575-555-8904
Patel Hospice	Sarah Gagnon	575-555-0393
Yoshida Group Home	Jacob Yan	575-555-9775

End of Report

The Volunteer Positions by Category report, shown in Figure 17, lists volunteer positions grouped by category. The staff will use this report when talking with students about the volunteer positions.

Figure 17 **Volunteer Positions by Category report**

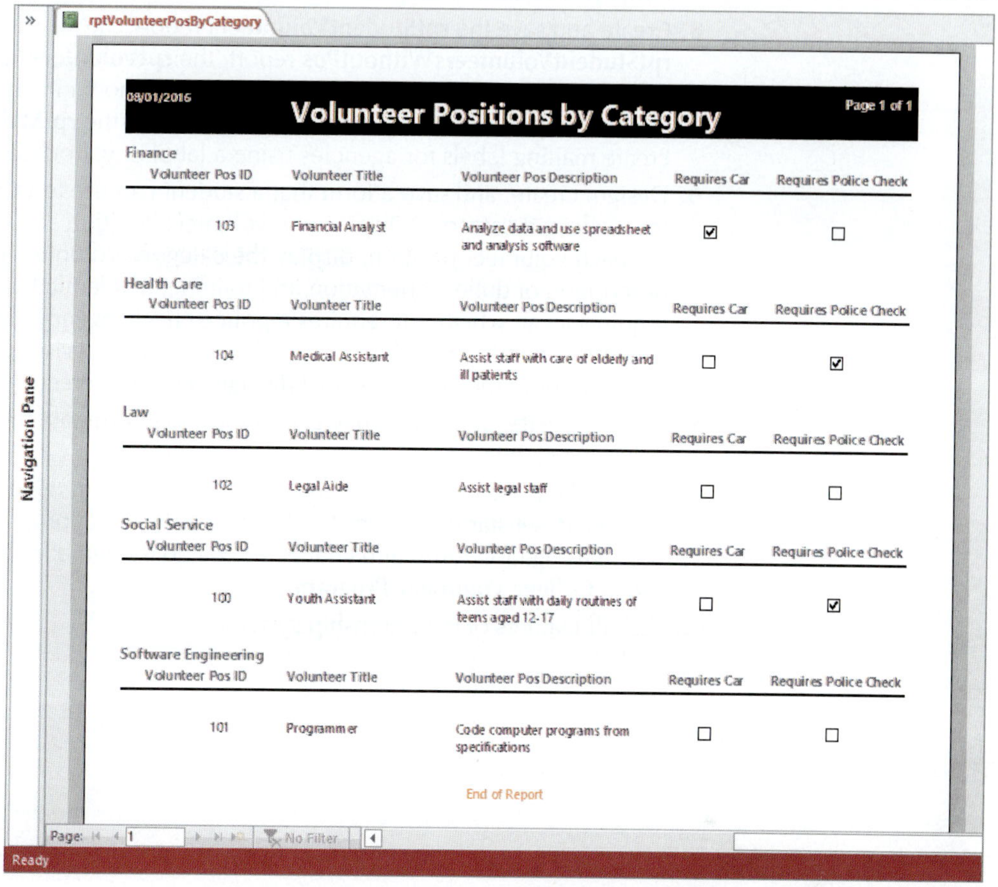

At the end of a volunteer commitment, the volunteer's supervisor evaluates the volunteer's work experience, using an evaluation form mailed from the Student Life office. Jennifer needs mailing labels addressed to the supervisor of each volunteer for the current term and year. The mailing labels should contain the supervisor's name on the first line; the agency name on the second line; the agency's street address on the third line; and the agency's city, state, and zip code on the fourth line. Jennifer wants the labels sorted by agency name.

To create the database, complete the following steps:

1. Read the appendix titled "Relational Databases and Database Design," which appears at the end of this book.

Explore 2. Identify each entity (table) in the database for the volunteer system.

Explore 3. Draw an entity-relationship diagram using Crow's Foot notation, showing the entities and the relationships between the entities.

Explore 4. Design the database for the volunteer system. For each table, list the fields and their attributes, such as data types, field sizes, and validation rules. Place the set of tables in third normal form and identify all primary, alternate, and foreign keys.

5. Use Access to create the **Volunteer** database in the AddCases folder with your Data Files. Be sure to define relationships between appropriate tables.

Explore 6. Create and save forms to maintain data on agencies, volunteer positions, student volunteers, and any other tables in your database structure. The forms should be used to view, add, edit, and delete records in the database.

7. Create test data for each table in the database and add the test data, using the forms you created in Step 6.
8. Create and save the **rptStudentVolunteers** report, the **rptStudentVolunteersWithoutPos** report, the **rptVolunteerAgencies** report, and the **rptVolunteerPosByCategory** report. The reports shown in Figures 14 through 17 are guides—improve them as you see fit. Then create the **rptMailingLabels** report to create mailing labels for agencies using a label of your choice.
9. Design, create, and save a form that a student can use to view volunteer positions for a selected category. Display one volunteer position at a time on the screen. For each volunteer position, display the category, volunteer position ID, title, description of duties, orientation and training, academic background, whether it requires a car, whether it requires a police check, agency name, agency address, supervisor name, supervisor email address, and supervisor phone. Provide an option to print the current record displayed on the screen.
10. Design, create, and save a navigation form to coordinate the running of the volunteer system.
11. Set the database properties so the frmNavigation form opens when the database is opened, set startup options to disable features as appropriate for a database that uses a navigation form, and change the database name in the title bar to **Southern Ridge College Volunteer Program**.
12. Test all features of the internship system.

APPENDIX A

Relational Databases and Database Design

OBJECTIVES

- Learn the characteristics of a table
- Learn about primary, candidate, alternate, composite, and foreign keys
- Study one-to-one, one-to-many, and many-to-many relationships
- Learn to describe tables and relationships with entity-relationship diagrams and with a shorthand method
- Study database integrity constraints for primary keys, referential integrity, and domains
- Learn about determinants, functional dependencies, anomalies, and normalization
- Understand the differences among natural, artificial, and surrogate keys
- Learn about naming conventions

This appendix introduces you to the basics of database design. Before trying to master this material, be sure you understand the following concepts: data, information, field, field value, record, table, relational database, common field, database management system (DBMS), and relational database management system (RDBMS).

STARTING DATA FILES

There are no starting Data Files needed for this appendix.

Tables

A relational database stores its data in tables. A **table** is a two-dimensional structure made up of rows and columns. The terms table, **record** (row), and **field** (column) are the popular names for the more formal terms **relation** (table), **tuple** (row), and **attribute** (column), as shown in Figure A-1.

Figure A-1 A table (relation) consisting of records and fields

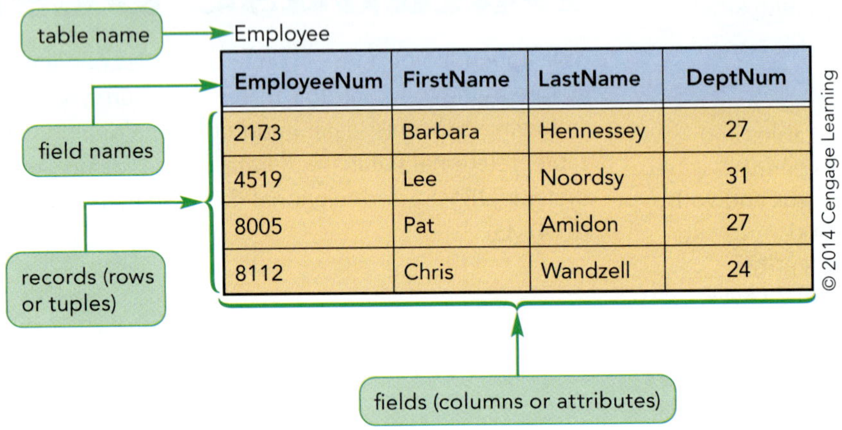

EmployeeNum	FirstName	LastName	DeptNum
2173	Barbara	Hennessey	27
4519	Lee	Noordsy	31
8005	Pat	Amidon	27
8112	Chris	Wandzell	24

The Employee table shown in Figure A-1 is an example of a relational database table, a two-dimensional structure with the following characteristics:

- Each row is unique. Because no two rows are the same, you can easily locate and update specific data. For example, you can locate the row for EmployeeNum 8005 and change the FirstName value, Pat, the LastName value, Amidon, or the DeptNum value, 27.
- The order of the rows is unimportant. You can add or view rows in any order. For example, you can view the rows in LastName order instead of EmployeeNum order.
- Each table entry contains a single value. At the intersection of each row and column, you cannot have more than one value. For example, each row in Figure A-1 contains one EmployeeNum value, one FirstName value, one LastName value, and one DeptNum value.
- The order of the columns is unimportant. You can add or view columns in any order.
- Each column has a unique name called the **field name**. The field name allows you to access a specific column without needing to know its position within the table.
- Each row in a table describes, or shows the characteristics of, an entity. An **entity** is a person, place, object, event, or idea for which you want to store and process data. For example, EmployeeNum, FirstName, LastName, and DeptNum are characteristics of the employees of a company. The Employee table represents all the employee entities and their characteristics. That is, each row of the Employee table describes a different employee of the company using the characteristics of EmployeeNum, FirstName, LastName, and DeptNum. The Employee table includes only characteristics of employees. Other tables would exist for the company's other entities. For example, a Department table would describe the company's departments and a Position table would describe the company's job positions.

Knowing the characteristics of a table leads directly to a definition of a relational database. A **relational database** is a collection of tables (relations).

Note that this book uses singular table names, such as Employee and Department, but some people use plural table names, such as Employees and Departments. You can use either singular table names or plural table names, as long as you consistently use the style you choose.

Keys

Primary keys ensure that each row in a table is unique. A **primary key** is a column, or a collection of columns, whose values uniquely identify each row in a table. In addition to being *unique*, a primary key must be *minimal* (that is, contain no unnecessary extra columns) and must not change in value. For example, in Figure A-2 the State table contains one record per state and uses the StateAbbrev column as its primary key.

Figure A-2 A table and its keys

alternate keys (StateName, EnteredUnionOrder)

primary key (StateAbbrev)

State

StateAbbrev	StateName	EnteredUnionOrder	StateBird	StatePopulation
CT	Connecticut	5	American robin	3,590,347
MI	Michigan	26	robin	9,883,360
SD	South Dakota	40	pheasant	833,354
TN	Tennessee	16	mockingbird	6,456,243
TX	Texas	28	mockingbird	26,059,203

Could any other column, or collection of columns, be the primary key of the State table?

- Could the StateBird column serve as the primary key? No, because the StateBird column does not have unique values (for example, the mockingbird is the state bird of more than one state).
- Could the StatePopulation column serve as the primary key? No, because the StatePopulation column values change periodically and are not guaranteed to be unique.
- Could the StateAbbrev and StateName columns together serve as the primary key? No, because the combination of these two columns is not minimal. Something less, such as the StateAbbrev column by itself, can serve as the primary key.
- Could the StateName column serve as the primary key? Yes, because the StateName column has unique values. In a similar way, you could select the EnteredUnionOrder column as the primary key for the State table. One column, or a collection of columns, that can serve as a primary key is called a **candidate key**. The candidate keys for the State table are the StateAbbrev column, the StateName column, and the EnteredUnionOrder column. You choose one of the candidate keys to be the primary key, and each remaining candidate key is called an **alternate key**. The StateAbbrev column is the State table's primary key in Figure A-2, so the StateName and EnteredUnionOrder columns become alternate keys in the table.

Figure A-3 shows a City table containing the fields StateAbbrev, CityName, and CityPopulation.

Figure A-3 A table with a composite key

composite primary key

City

StateAbbrev	CityName	CityPopulation
CT	Hartford	124,062
CT	Madison	18,803
CT	Portland	9,551
MI	Lansing	119,128
SD	Madison	6,482
SD	Pierre	13,899
TN	Nashville	569,462
TX	Austin	757,688
TX	Portland	16,490

What is the primary key for the City table? The values for the CityPopulation column periodically change and are not guaranteed to be unique, so the CityPopulation column cannot be the primary key. Because the values for each of the other two columns are not unique, the StateAbbrev column alone cannot be the primary key and neither can the CityName column (for example, there are two cities named Madison and two cities named Portland). The primary key is the combination of the StateAbbrev and CityName columns. Both columns together are needed to identify—uniquely and minimally—each row in the City table. A multiple-column key is called a **composite key** or a **concatenated key**. A multiple-column primary key is called a **composite primary key**.

The StateAbbrev column in the City table is also a foreign key. A **foreign key** is a column, or a collection of columns, in one table in which each column value must match the value of the primary key of some table or must be null. A **null** is the absence of a value in a particular table entry. A null value is not blank, nor zero, nor any other value. You give a null value to a column value when you do not know its value or when a value does not apply. As shown in Figure A-4, the values in the City table's StateAbbrev column match the values in the State table's StateAbbrev column. Thus, the StateAbbrev column, the primary key of the State table, is a foreign key in the City table. Although the field name StateAbbrev is the same in both tables, the names could be different. As a rule, experts use the same name for a field stored in two or more tables to broadcast clearly that they store similar values; however, some exceptions exist.

Figure A-4 StateAbbrev as a primary key (State table) and a foreign key (City table)

primary key (State table)

State

StateAbbrev	StateName	EnteredUnionOrder	StateBird	StatePopulation
CT	Connecticut	5	American robin	3,518,288
MI	Michigan	26	robin	9,969,727
SD	South Dakota	40	pheasant	812,383
TN	Tennessee	16	mockingbird	6,296,254
TX	Texas	28	mockingbird	24,782,302

composite primary key (City table)

foreign key

City

StateAbbrev	CityName	CityPopulation
CT	Hartford	124,062
CT	Madison	18,803
CT	Portland	9,551
MI	Lansing	119,128
SD	Madison	6,482
SD	Pierre	13,899
TN	Nashville	596,462
TX	Austin	757,688
TX	Portland	16,490

A **nonkey field** is a field that is not part of the primary key. In the two tables shown in Figure A-4, all fields are nonkey fields except the StateAbbrev field in the State and City tables and the CityName field in the City table. "Key" is an ambiguous word because it can refer to a primary, candidate, alternate, or foreign key. When the word key appears alone, however, it means primary key and the definition for a nonkey field consequently makes sense.

Relationships

In a database, a table can be associated with another table in one of three ways: a one-to-many relationship, a many-to-many relationship, or a one-to-one relationship.

One-to-Many Relationship

The Department and Employee tables, shown in Figure A-5, have a one-to-many relationship. A **one-to-many relationship** (abbreviated **1:M** or **1:N**) exists between two tables when each row in the first table (sometimes called the **primary table**) matches many rows in the second table and each row in the second table (sometimes called the **related table**) matches at most one row in the first table. "Many" can mean zero rows, one row, or two or more rows. As Figure A-5 shows, the DeptNum field, which is a foreign key in the Employee table and the primary key in the Department table, is the common field that ties together the rows of the two tables. Each department has many employees; and each employee works in exactly one department or hasn't been assigned to a department, if the DeptNum field value for that employee is null.

Figure A-5 **A one-to-many relationship**

primary key for the one-to-many relationship → DeptNum

Department

DeptNum	DeptName	DeptHead
24	Finance	8112
27	Marketing	2173
31	Technology	4519

foreign key for the one-to-many relationship → DeptNum

primary key → EmployeeNum

Employee

EmployeeNum	FirstName	LastName	DeptNum
2173	Barbara	Hennessey	27
4519	Lee	Noordsy	31
8005	Pat	Amidon	27
8112	Chris	Wandzell	24

Many-to-Many Relationship

In Figure A-6, the Employee table (with the EmployeeNum field as its primary key) and the Position table (with the PositionID field as its primary key) have a many-to-many relationship. A **many-to-many relationship** (abbreviated as **M:N**) exists between two tables when each row in the first table matches many rows in the second table and each row in the second table matches many rows in the first table. In a relational database, you must use a third table (often called an **intersection table**, **junction table**, or **link table**) to serve as a bridge between the two many-to-many tables; the third table has the primary keys of the two many-to-many tables as its primary key. The original tables now each have a one-to-many relationship with the new table. The EmployeeNum and PositionID fields represent the primary key of the Employment table that is shown in Figure A-6. The EmployeeNum field, which is a foreign key in the Employment table and the primary key in the Employee table, is the common field that ties together the rows of the Employee and Employment tables. Likewise, the PositionID field is the common field for the Position and Employment tables. Each employee may serve in many different positions within the company over time, and each position in the company will be filled by different employees over time.

Figure A-6 A many-to-many relationship

primary key (Employee table)

primary key (Position table)

Employee

EmployeeNum	FirstName	LastName	DeptNum
2173	Barbara	Hennessey	27
4519	Lee	Noordsy	31
8005	Pat	Amidon	27
8112	Chris	Wandzell	24

Position

PositionID	PositionDesc	PayGrade
1	Director	45
2	Manager	40
3	Analyst	30
4	Clerk	20

composite primary key of the intersection table

foreign keys related to the Employee and Position tables

Employment

EmployeeNum	PositionID	StartDate	EndDate
2173	2	12/14/2011	
4519	1	04/23/2013	
4519	3	11/11/2007	04/22/2013
8005	3	06/05/2012	08/25/2013
8005	4	07/02/2010	06/04/2012
8112	1	12/15/2012	
8112	2	10/04/2011	12/14/2012

One-to-One Relationship

In Figure A-5, recall that there's a one-to-many relationship between the Department table (the primary table) and the Employee table (the related table). Each department has many employees, and each employee works in one department. The DeptNum field in the Employee table serves as a foreign key to connect records in that table to records with matching DeptNum field values in the Department table.

Furthermore, each department has a single employee who serves as the head of the department, and each employee either serves as the head of a department or simply works in a department without being the department head. Therefore, the Department and Employee tables not only have a one-to-many relationship, but these two tables also have a second relationship, a one-to-one relationship. A **one-to-one relationship** (abbreviated **1:1**) exists between two tables when each row in each table has at most one matching row in the other table. As shown in Figure A-7, each DeptHead field value in the Department table represents the employee number in the Employee table of the employee who heads the department. In other words, each DeptHead field value in the Department table matches exactly one EmployeeNum field value in the Employee table. At the same time, each EmployeeNum field value in the Employee table matches at most one DeptHead field value in the Department table—matching one DeptHead field value if the employee is a department head, or matching zero DeptHead field values if the employee is not a department head. For this one-to-one relationship, the EmployeeNum field in the Employee table and the DeptHead field in the Department table are the fields that link the two tables, with the DeptHead field serving as a foreign key in the Department table and the EmployeeNum field serving as a primary key in the Employee table.

Some database designers might use EmployeeNum instead of DeptHead as the field name for the foreign key in the Department table because they both represent the employee number for the employees of the company. However, DeptHead better identifies the purpose of the field and would more commonly be used as the field name.

Figure A-7 **A one-to-one relationship**

Department

DeptNum	DeptName	DeptHead
24	Finance	8112
27	Marketing	2173
31	Technology	4519

Employee

EmployeeNum	FirstName	LastName	DeptNum
2173	Barbara	Hennessey	27
4519	Lee	Noordsy	31
8005	Pat	Amidon	27
8112	Chris	Wandzell	24

Entity Subtype

Suppose the company awards annual bonuses to a small number of employees who fill director positions in selected departments. As shown in Figure A-8, you could store the Bonus field in the Employee table because a bonus is an attribute associated with employees. The Bonus field would contain either the amount of the employee's bonus (record 4 in the Employee table) or a null value for employees without bonuses (records 1 through 3 in the Employee table).

Figure A-8 **Bonus field added to the Employee table**

Employee

EmployeeNum	FirstName	LastName	DeptNum	Bonus
2173	Barbara	Hennessey	27	
4519	Lee	Noordsy	31	
8005	Pat	Amidon	27	
8112	Chris	Wandzell	24	$20,000

Figure A-9 shows an alternative approach, in which the Bonus field is placed in a separate table, the EmployeeBonus table. The EmployeeBonus table's primary key is the EmployeeNum field, and the table contains one row for each employee earning a bonus. Because some employees do not earn a bonus, the EmployeeBonus table has fewer rows than the Employee table. However, each row in the EmployeeBonus table has a matching row in the Employee table, with the EmployeeNum field serving as the common field; the EmployeeNum field is the primary key in the Employee table and is a foreign key in the EmployeeBonus table.

Figure A-9 **Storing Bonus values in a separate table, an entity subtype**

Employee

EmployeeNum	FirstName	LastName	DeptNum
2173	Barbara	Hennessey	27
4519	Lee	Noordsy	31
8005	Pat	Amidon	27
8112	Chris	Wandzell	24

EmployeeBonus

EmployeeNum	Bonus
8112	$20,000

primary key (Employee table)
primary key (EmployeeBonus table)
foreign key
entity subtype

The EmployeeBonus table, in this situation, is called an **entity subtype**, a table whose primary key is a foreign key to a second table and whose fields are additional fields for the second table. Database designers create an entity subtype in two situations. In the first situation, some users might need access to all employee fields, including employee bonuses, while other employees might need access to all employee fields except bonuses. Because most DBMSs allow you to control which tables a user can access, you can specify that some users can access both tables and that other users can access the Employee table but not the EmployeeBonus table, keeping the employee bonus information hidden from the latter group. In the second situation, you can create an entity subtype when a table has fields that could have nulls, as was the case for the Bonus field stored in the Employee table in Figure A-8. You should be aware that database experts are currently debating the validity of the use of nulls in relational databases, and many experts insist that you should never use nulls. This warning against nulls is partly based on the inconsistent way different RDBMSs treat nulls and partly due to the lack of a firm theoretical foundation for how to use nulls. In any case, entity subtypes are an alternative to the use of nulls.

Entity-Relationship Diagrams

A common shorthand method for describing tables is to write the table name followed by its fields in parentheses, underlining the fields that represent the primary key and identifying the foreign keys for a table immediately after the table. Using this method, the tables that appear in Figures A-5 through A-7 and Figure A-9 are described in the following way:

Department (<u>DeptNum</u>, DeptName, DeptHead)
    Foreign key: DeptHead to Employee table
Employee (<u>EmployeeNum</u>, FirstName, LastName, DeptNum)
    Foreign key: DeptNum to Department table
Position (<u>PositionID</u>, PositionDesc, PayGrade)
Employment (<u>EmployeeNum</u>, <u>PositionID</u>, StartDate, EndDate)
    Foreign key: EmployeeNum to Employee table
    Foreign key: PositionID to Position table
EmployeeBonus (<u>EmployeeNum</u>, Bonus)
    Foreign key: EmployeeNum to Employee table

Another popular way to describe tables *and their relationships* is with entity-relationship diagrams. An **entity-relationship diagram (ERD)** shows a database's entities and the relationships among the entities in a symbolic, visual way. In an ERD, an entity and a table are equivalent. Figure A-10 shows an entity-relationship diagram for the tables that appear in Figures A-5 through A-7 and Figure A-9.

Figure A-10 An entity-relationship diagram (ERD)

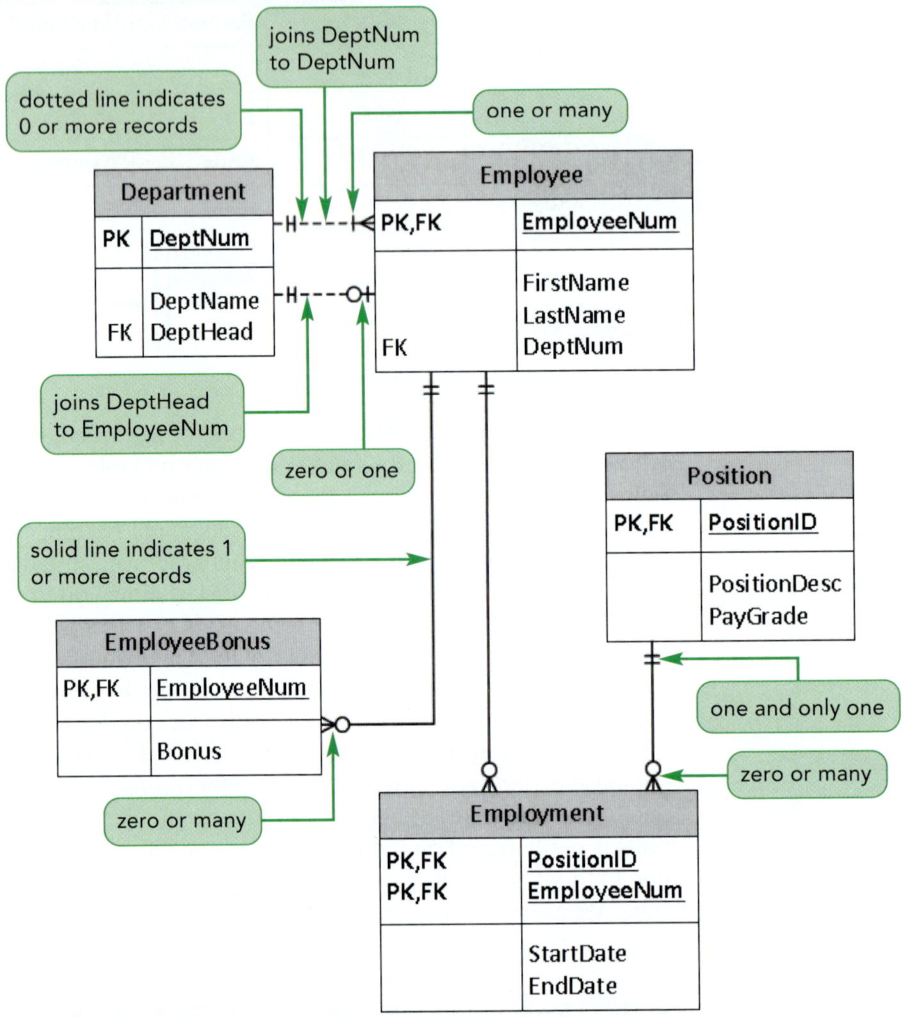

ERDs have the following characteristics:

- A table is represented by a rectangle that contains the table name and lists the field names. Within each rectangle, the primary key is identified with the abbreviation PK, and any foreign keys are designated with FK. Required fields are formatted in bold.
- Relationships are identified by lines joining the tables. A solid relationship line between two tables indicates there could be 1 or more related records. A dotted relationship line between two tables indicates there could be 0 or more related records.

- At the ends of each relationship line, symbols identify the minimum and maximum possible number of related records from each entity in the relationship. A single perpendicular line represents 1 record, a circle represents 0 records, and a group of three branching lines—known as a crow's foot—represents many records. A one-to-many relationship is represented by a 1 at one end of the relationship line and a crow's foot at the opposite end of the relationship line. For example, the Department and Employee tables have a one-to-many relationship from the DeptNum field in the Department table to the DeptNum field in the Employee table. In a similar manner, a one-to-many relationship exists between the Employee and EmployeeBonus tables and a one-to-one relationship exists between the Department and Employee tables from the DeptHead field in the Department table to the EmployeeNum field in the Employee table. The relationships in Figure A-10 illustrate all the possible designations for the ends of lines.

Integrity Constraints

A database has **integrity** if its data follows certain rules; each rule is called an **integrity constraint**. The ideal is to have the DBMS enforce all integrity constraints. If a DBMS can enforce some integrity constraints but not others, the other integrity constraints must be enforced by other programs or by the people who use the DBMS. Integrity constraints can be divided into three groups: primary key constraints, foreign key constraints, and domain integrity constraints.

- One primary key constraint is inherent in the definition of a primary key, which says that the primary key must be unique. The **entity integrity constraint** says that the primary key cannot be null. For a composite key, none of the individual fields can be null. The uniqueness and nonnull properties of a primary key ensure that you can reference any data value in a database by supplying its table name, field name, and primary key value.
- Foreign keys provide the mechanism for forming a relationship between two tables, and referential integrity ensures that only valid relationships exist. **Referential integrity** is the constraint specifying that each nonnull foreign key value must match a primary key value in the primary table. Specifically, referential integrity means that you cannot add a row containing an unmatched foreign key value. Referential integrity also means that you cannot change or delete the related primary key value and leave the foreign key orphaned. In some RDBMSs, when you create a relationship, you can specify one of these options: restricted, cascades, or nullifies. If you specify **restricted** and then change or delete a primary key, the DBMS updates or deletes the value only if there are no matching foreign key values. If you choose **cascades** and then change a primary key value, the DBMS changes the matching foreign key values to the new primary key value, or, if you delete a primary key value, the DBMS also deletes the matching foreign key rows. If you choose **nullifies** and then change or delete a primary key value, the DBMS sets all matching foreign key values to null.
- A **domain** is a set of values from which one or more fields draw their actual values. A **domain integrity constraint** is a rule you specify for a field. By choosing a data type for a field, you impose a constraint on the set of values allowed for the field. You can create specific validation rules for a field to limit its domain further. As you make a field's domain definition more precise, you exclude more and more unacceptable values for the field. For example, in the State table, shown in Figures A-2 and A-4, you could define the domain for the EnteredUnionOrder field to be a unique integer between 1 and 50 and the domain for the StateBird field to be any text string containing 25 or fewer characters.

Dependencies and Determinants

Just as tables are related to other tables, fields are also related to other fields. Consider the modified Employee table shown in Figure A-11. Its description is:

Employee (EmployeeNum, PositionID, LastName, PositionDesc, StartDate, HealthPlan, PlanDesc)

Figure A-11 **A table combining fields from three tables**

composite primary key

Employee

EmployeeNum	PositionID	LastName	PositionDesc	StartDate	HealthPlan	PlanDesc
2173	2	Hennessey	Manager	12/14/2011	B	Managed HMO
4519	1	Noordsy	Director	04/23/2013	A	Managed PPO
4519	3	Noordsy	Analyst	11/11/2007	A	Managed PPO
8005	3	Amidon	Analyst	06/05/2012	C	Health Savings
8005	4	Amidon	Clerk	07/02/2010	C	Health Savings
8112	1	Wandzell	Director	12/15/2012	A	Managed PPO
8112	2	Wandzell	Manager	10/04/2011	A	Managed PPO

The modified Employee table combines several fields from the Employee, Position, and Employment tables that appeared in Figure A-6. The EmployeeNum and LastName fields are from the Employee table. The PositionID and PositionDesc fields are from the Position table. The EmployeeNum, PositionID, and StartDate fields are from the Employment table. The HealthPlan and PlanDesc fields are new fields for the Employee table, whose primary key is now the combination of the EmployeeNum and PositionID fields.

In the Employee table, each field is related to other fields. To determine field relationships, you ask "Does a value for a particular field give me a single value for another field?" If the answer is Yes, then the two fields are **functionally** related. For example, a value for the EmployeeNum field determines a single value for the LastName field, and a value for the LastName field depends on the value of the EmployeeNum field. In other words, EmployeeNum functionally determines LastName, and LastName is functionally dependent on EmployeeNum. In this case, EmployeeNum is called a determinant. A **determinant** is a field, or a collection of fields, whose values determine the values of another field. A field is functionally dependent on another field (or a collection of fields) if that other field is a determinant for it.

You can graphically show a table's functional dependencies and determinants in a **bubble diagram**; a bubble diagram is also called a **data model diagram** or a **functional dependency diagram**. Figure A-12 shows the bubble diagram for the Employee table shown in Figure A-11.

Figure A-12 **A bubble diagram for the modified Employee table**

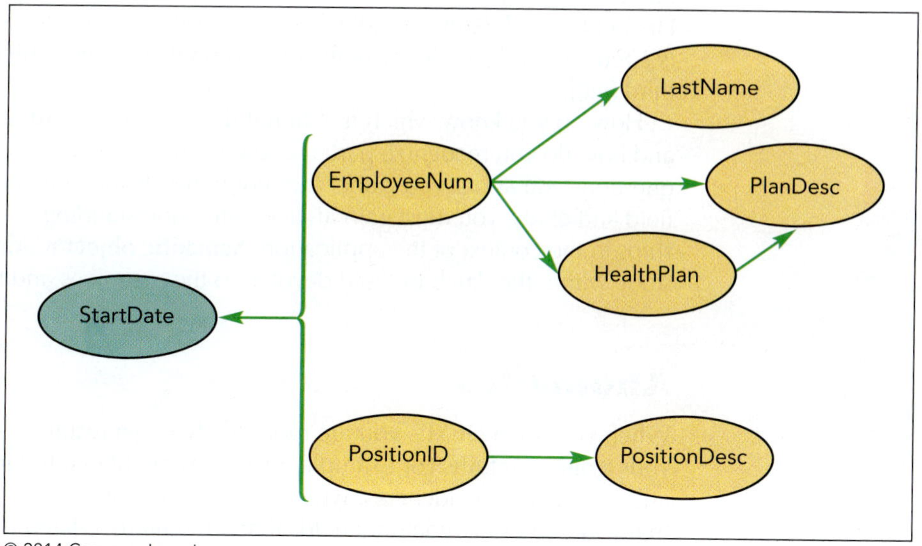

You can read the bubble diagram in Figure A-12 as follows:

- The EmployeeNum field is a determinant for the LastName, HealthPlan, and PlanDesc fields.
- The PositionID field is a determinant for the PositionDesc field.
- The StartDate field is functionally dependent on the EmployeeNum and PositionID fields together.
- The HealthPlan field is a determinant for the PlanDesc field.

Note that EmployeeNum and PositionID together serve as a determinant for the StartDate field and for all fields that depend on the EmployeeNum field alone and the PositionID field alone. Some experts include these additional fields and some don't. The previous list of determinants does not include these additional fields.

An alternative way to show determinants is to list the determinant, a right arrow, and then the dependent fields, separated by commas. Using this alternative, the determinants shown in Figure A-12 are:

EmployeeNum → LastName, HealthPlan, PlanDesc
PositionID → PositionDesc
EmployeeNum, PositionID → StartDate
HealthPlan → PlanDesc

Only the StartDate field is functionally dependent on the table's full primary key, the EmployeeNum and PositionID fields. The LastName, HealthPlan, and PlanDesc fields have partial dependencies because they are functionally dependent on the EmployeeNum field, which is part of the primary key. A **partial dependency** is a functional dependency on part of the primary key, instead of the entire primary key. Does another partial dependency exist in the Employee table? Yes, the PositionDesc field has a partial dependency on the PositionID field.

Because the EmployeeNum field is a determinant of both the HealthPlan and PlanDesc fields, and the HealthPlan field is a determinant of the PlanDesc field, the HealthPlan and PlanDesc fields have a transitive dependency. A **transitive dependency** is a functional dependency between two nonkey fields, which are both dependent on a third field.

How do you know which functional dependencies exist among a collection of fields, and how do you recognize partial and transitive dependencies? The answers lie with the questions you ask as you gather the requirements for a database application. For each field and entity, you must gain an accurate understanding of its meaning and relationships in the context of the application. **Semantic object modeling** is an entire area of study within the database field devoted to the meanings and relationships of data.

Anomalies

When you use a DBMS, you are more likely to get results you can trust if you create your tables carefully. For example, problems might occur with tables that have partial and transitive dependencies, whereas you won't have as much trouble if you ensure that your tables include only fields that are directly related to each other. Also, when you remove data redundancy from a table, you improve that table. **Data redundancy** occurs when you store the same data in more than one place.

The problems caused by data redundancy and by partial and transitive dependencies are called **anomalies** because they are undesirable irregularities of tables. Anomalies are of three types: insertion, deletion, and update.

To examine the effects of these anomalies, consider the modified Employee table that is shown again in Figure A-13.

Figure A-13 A table with insertion, deletion, and update anomalies

composite primary key

Employee

EmployeeNum	PositionID	LastName	PositionDesc	StartDate	HealthPlan	PlanDesc
2173	2	Hennessey	Manager	12/14/2011	B	Managed HMO
4519	1	Noordsy	Director	04/23/2013	A	Managed PPO
4519	3	Noordsy	Analyst	11/11/2007	A	Managed PPO
8005	3	Amidon	Analyst	06/05/2012	C	Health Savings
8005	4	Amidon	Clerk	07/02/2010	C	Health Savings
8112	1	Wandzell	Director	12/15/2012	A	Managed PPO
8112	2	Wandzell	Manager	10/04/2011	A	Managed PPO

- An **insertion anomaly** occurs when you cannot add a record to a table because you do not know the entire primary key value. For example, you cannot add the new employee Cathy Corbett with an EmployeeNum of 3322 to the Employee table if you do not know her position in the company. Entity integrity prevents you from leaving any part of a primary key null. Because the PositionID field is part of the primary key, you cannot leave it null. To add the new employee, your only option is to make up a PositionID field value, until you determine the correct position. This solution misrepresents the facts and is unacceptable, if a better approach is available.

- A **deletion anomaly** occurs when you delete data from a table and unintentionally lose other critical data. For example, if you delete EmployeeNum 2173 because Hennessey is no longer an employee, you also lose the only instance of HealthPlan B in the database. Thus, you no longer know that HealthPlan B is the "Managed HMO" plan.
- An **update anomaly** occurs when a change to one field value requires the DBMS to make more than one change to the database, and a failure by the database to make all the changes results in inconsistent data. For example, if you change a LastName, HealthPlan, or PlanDesc field value for EmployeeNum 8005, the DBMS must change multiple rows of the Employee table. If the DBMS fails to change all the rows, the LastName, HealthPlan, or PlanDesc field now has different values in the database and is inconsistent.

Normalization

Database design is the process of determining the content and structure of data in a database in order to support some activity on behalf of a user or group of users. After you have determined the collection of fields users need to support an activity, you need to determine the precise tables needed for the collection of fields and then place those fields into the correct tables. Understanding the functional dependencies of all fields; recognizing the anomalies caused by data redundancy, partial dependencies, and transitive dependencies when they exist; and knowing how to eliminate the anomalies are all crucial to good database design. Failure to eliminate anomalies leads to data redundancy and can cause data integrity and other problems as your database grows in size.

The process of identifying and eliminating anomalies is called **normalization**. Using normalization, you start with a collection of tables, apply sets of rules to eliminate anomalies, and produce a new collection of problem-free tables. The sets of rules are called **normal forms**. Of special interest for our purposes are the first three normal forms: first normal form, second normal form, and third normal form. First normal form improves the design of your tables, second normal form improves the first normal form design, and third normal form applies even more stringent rules to produce an even better design. Note that normal forms beyond third normal form exist; these higher normal forms can improve a database design in some situations but won't be covered in this section.

First Normal Form

Consider the Employee table shown in Figure A-14. For each employee, the table contains EmployeeNum, which is the primary key; the employee's first name, last name, health plan code and description; and the ID, description, pay grade, and start date of each position held by the employee. For example, Barbara Hennessey has held one position, while the other three employees have held two positions. Because each entry in a table must contain a single value, the structure shown in Figure A-14 does not meet the requirements for a table, or relation; therefore, it is called an **unnormalized relation**. The set of fields that includes the PositionID, PositionDesc, PayGrade, and StartDate fields, which can have more than one value, is called a **repeating group**.

Figure A-14 **Repeating groups of data in an unnormalized Employee table**

repeating group

Employee

EmployeeNum	PositionID	FirstName	LastName	PositionDesc	PayGrade	StartDate	HealthPlan	PlanDesc
2173	2	Barbara	Hennessey	Manager	40	12/14/2011	B	Managed HMO
4519	1 3	Lee	Noordsy	Director Analyst	45 30	04/23/2013 11/11/2007	A	Managed PPO
8005	3 4	Pat	Amidon	Analyst Clerk	30 20	06/05/2012 07/02/2010	C	Health Savings
8112	1 2	Chris	Wandzell	Director Manager	45 40	12/15/2012 10/04/2011	A	Managed PPO

First normal form addresses this repeating-group situation. A table is in **first normal form (1NF)** if it does not contain repeating groups. To remove a repeating group and convert to first normal form, you expand the primary key to include the primary key of the repeating group, forming a composite key. Performing the conversion step produces the 1NF table shown in Figure A-15.

Figure A-15 **After conversion to 1NF**

composite primary key

Employee

EmployeeNum	PositionID	FirstName	LastName	PositionDesc	PayGrade	StartDate	HealthPlan	PlanDesc
2173	2	Barbara	Hennessey	Manager	40	12/14/2011	B	Managed HMO
4519	1	Lee	Noordsy	Director	45	04/23/2013	A	Managed PPO
4519	3	Lee	Noordsy	Analyst	30	11/11/2007	A	Managed PPO
8005	3	Pat	Amidon	Analyst	30	06/05/2012	C	Health Savings
8005	4	Pat	Amidon	Clerk	20	07/02/2010	C	Health Savings
8112	1	Chris	Wandzell	Director	45	12/15/2012	A	Managed PPO
8112	2	Chris	Wandzell	Manager	40	10/04/2011	A	Managed PPO

The alternative way to describe the 1NF table is:

Employee (EmployeeNum, PositionID, FirstName, LastName, PositionDesc, PayGrade, StartDate, HealthPlan, PlanDesc)

The Employee table is now a true table and has a composite key. The table, however, suffers from insertion, deletion, and update anomalies. (As an exercise, find examples of the three anomalies in the table.) The EmployeeNum field is a determinant for the FirstName, LastName, HealthPlan, and PlanDesc fields, so partial dependencies exist in the Employee table. It is these partial dependencies that cause the anomalies in the Employee table, and second normal form addresses the partial-dependency problem.

Second Normal Form

A table in 1NF is in **second normal form (2NF)** if it does not contain any partial dependencies. To remove partial dependencies from a table and convert it to second normal form, you perform two steps. First, identify the functional dependencies for every field in the table. Second, if necessary, create new tables and place each field in a table such that the field is functionally dependent on the entire primary key, not part of the primary key. If you need to create new tables, restrict them to tables with a primary key that is a subset of the original composite key. Note that partial dependencies occur only when you have a composite key; a table in first normal form with a single-field primary key is automatically in second normal form.

First, identifying the functional dependencies leads to the following determinants for the Employee table:

EmployeeNum → FirstName, LastName, HealthPlan, PlanDesc
PositionID → PositionDesc, PayGrade
EmployeeNum, PositionID → StartDate
HealthPlan → PlanDesc

The EmployeeNum field is a determinant for the FirstName, LastName, HealthPlan, and PlanDesc fields. The PositionID field is a determinant for the PositionDesc and PayGrade fields. The composite key EmployeeNum and PositionID is a determinant for the StartDate field. The HealthPlan field is a determinant for the PlanDesc field. Performing the second step in the conversion from first normal form to second form produces the three 2NF tables shown in Figure A-16.

Figure A-16 After conversion to 2NF

Employee

primary key → EmployeeNum

EmployeeNum	FirstName	LastName	HealthPlan	PlanDesc
2173	Barbara	Hennessey	B	Managed HMO
4519	Lee	Noordsy	A	Managed PPO
8005	Pat	Amidon	C	Health Savings
8112	Chris	Wandzell	A	Managed PPO

Position

primary key → PositionID

PositionID	PositionDesc	PayGrade
1	Director	45
2	Manager	40
3	Analyst	30
4	Clerk	20

Employment

composite primary key → EmployeeNum, PositionID

EmployeeNum	PositionID	StartDate
2173	2	12/14/2011
4519	1	04/23/2013
4519	3	11/11/2007
8005	3	06/05/2012
8005	4	07/02/2010
8112	1	12/15/2012
8112	2	10/04/2011

The alternative way to describe the 2NF tables is:

Employee (EmployeeNum, FirstName, LastName, HealthPlan, PlanDesc)
Position (PositionID, PositionDesc, PayGrade)
Employment (EmployeeNum, PositionID, StartDate)
    Foreign key: EmployeeNum to Employee table
    Foreign key: PositionID to Position table

All three tables are in second normal form. Do anomalies still exist? The Position and Employment tables show no anomalies, but the Employee table suffers from anomalies caused by the transitive dependency between the HealthPlan and PlanDesc fields. (As an exercise, find examples of the three anomalies caused by the transitive dependency.) That is, the HealthPlan field is a determinant for the PlanDesc field, and the EmployeeNum field is a determinant for the HealthPlan and PlanDesc fields. Third normal form addresses the transitive-dependency problem.

Third Normal Form

A table in 2NF is in **third normal form (3NF)** if every determinant is a candidate key. This definition for 3NF is referred to as **Boyce-Codd normal form (BCNF)** and is an improvement over the original version of 3NF. What are the determinants in the Employee table? The EmployeeNum and HealthPlan fields are the determinants; however, the EmployeeNum field is a candidate key because it's the table's primary key, and the HealthPlan field is not a candidate key. Therefore, the Employee table is in second normal form, but it is not in third normal form.

To convert a table to third normal form, remove the fields that depend on the non-candidate-key determinant and place them into a new table with the determinant as the primary key. For the Employee table, the PlanDesc field depends on the HealthPlan field, which is a non-candidate-key determinant. Thus, you remove the PlanDesc field from the table, create a new HealthBenefits table, place the PlanDesc field in the HealthBenefits table, and then make the HealthPlan field the primary key of the HealthBenefits table. Note that only the PlanDesc field is removed from the Employee table; the HealthPlan field remains as a foreign key in the Employee table. Figure A-17 shows the database design for the four 3NF tables.

Figure A-17 After conversion to 3NF

Employee

primary key → EmployeeNum

EmployeeNum	FirstName	LastName	HealthPlan
2173	Barbara	Hennessey	B
4519	Lee	Noordsy	A
8005	Pat	Amidon	C
8112	Chris	Wandzell	A

HealthBenefits

primary key → HealthPlan

HealthPlan	PlanDesc
A	Managed PPO
B	Managed HMO
C	Health Savings

Position

primary key → PositionID

PositionID	PositionDesc	PayGrade
1	Director	45
2	Manager	40
3	Analyst	30
4	Clerk	20

Employment

composite primary key → EmployeeNum, PositionID

EmployeeNum	PositionID	StartDate
2173	2	12/14/2011
4519	1	04/23/2013
4519	3	11/11/2007
8005	3	06/05/2012
8005	4	07/02/2010
8112	1	12/15/2012
8112	2	10/04/2011

The alternative way to describe the 3NF relations is:

Employee (EmployeeNum, FirstName, LastName, HealthPlan)
    Foreign key: HealthPlan to HealthBenefits table
HealthBenefits (HealthPlan, PlanDesc)
Position (PositionID, PositionDesc, PayGrade)
Employment (EmployeeNum, PositionID, StartDate)
    Foreign key: EmployeeNum to Employee table
    Foreign key: PositionID to Position table

The four tables have no anomalies because you have eliminated all the data redundancy, partial dependencies, and transitive dependencies. Normalization provides the framework for eliminating anomalies and delivering an optimal database design, which you should always strive to achieve. You should be aware, however, that experts sometimes denormalize tables to improve database performance—specifically, to decrease the time it takes the database to respond to a user's commands and requests. Typically, when you denormalize tables, you combine separate tables into one table to reduce the need for the DBMS to join the separate tables to process queries and other informational requests. When you denormalize a table, you reintroduce redundancy to the table. At the same time, you reintroduce anomalies. Thus, improving performance exposes a database to potential integrity problems. Only database experts should denormalize tables, but even experts first complete the normalization of their tables.

Natural, Artificial, and Surrogate Keys

When you complete the design of a database, your tables should be in third normal form, free of anomalies and redundancy. Some tables, such as the State table (see Figure A-2), have obvious third normal form designs with obvious primary keys. The State table's description is:

State (<u>StateAbbrev</u>, StateName, EnteredUnionOrder, StateBird, StatePopulation)

Recall that the candidate keys for the State table are StateAbbrev, StateName, and EnteredUnionOrder. Choosing the StateAbbrev field as the State table's primary key makes the StateName and EnteredUnionOrder fields alternate keys. Primary keys such as the StateAbbrev field are sometimes called natural keys. A **natural key** (also called a **logical key** or an **intelligent key**) is a primary key that consists of a field, or a collection of fields, that is an inherent characteristic of the entity described by the table and that is visible to users. Other examples of natural keys are the ISBN (International Standard Book Number) for a book, the SSN (Social Security number) for a U.S. individual, the UPC (Universal Product Code) for a product, and the VIN (vehicle identification number) for a vehicle.

Is the PositionID field, which is the primary key for the Position table (see Figure A-17), a natural key? No, the PositionID field is not an inherent characteristic of a position. Instead, the PositionID field has been added to the Position table only as a way to identify each position uniquely. The PositionID field is an **artificial key**, which is a field that you add to a table to serve solely as the primary key and that is visible to users.

Another reason for using an artificial key arises in tables that allow duplicate records. Although relational database theory and most experts do not allow duplicate records in a table, consider a database that tracks donors and their donations. Figure A-18 shows a Donor table with an artificial key of DonorID and with the DonorFirstName and DonorLastName fields. Some cash donations are anonymous, which accounts for the fourth record in the Donor table. Figure A-18 also shows the Donation table with the DonorID field, a foreign key to the Donor table, and the DonationDate and DonationAmt fields.

Figure A-18 Donor and Donation tables

Donor

DonorID	DonorFirstName	DonorLastName
1	Christina	Chang
2	Franco	Diaz
3	Angie	Diaz
4		Anonymous
5	Tracy	Burns

primary key → DonorID

Donation

DonorID	DonationDate	DonationAmt
1	10/12/2013	$50.00
1	09/30/2014	$50.00
2	10/03/2014	$75.00
4	10/10/2014	$50.00
4	10/10/2014	$50.00
4	10/11/2014	$25.00
5	10/13/2014	$50.00

duplicate records → the two 10/10/2014 rows for DonorID 4

What is the primary key of the Donation table? No single field is unique, and neither is any combination of fields. For example, on 10/10/2014, two anonymous donors (DonorID value of 4) donated $50 each. You need to add an artificial key, DonationID for example, to the Donation table. The addition of the artificial key makes every record in the Donation table unique, as shown in Figure A-19.

Figure A-19 **Donation table after adding DonationID, an artificial key**

Donation

artificial key → DonationID

DonationID	DonorID	DonationDate	DonationAmt
1	1	10/12/2013	$50.00
2	1	09/30/2014	$50.00
3	2	10/03/2014	$75.00
4	4	10/10/2014	$50.00
5	4	10/10/2014	$50.00
6	4	10/11/2014	$25.00
7	5	10/13/2014	$50.00

The descriptions of the Donor and Donation tables now are:

Donor (DonorID, DonorFirstName, DonorLastName)
Donation (DonationID, DonorID, DonationDate, DonationAmt)
    Foreign key: DonorID to Donor table

For another common situation, consider the 3NF tables you reviewed in the previous section (see Figure A-17) that have the following descriptions:

Employee (EmployeeNum, FirstName, LastName, HealthPlan)
    Foreign key: HealthPlan to HealthBenefits table
HealthBenefits (HealthPlan, PlanDesc)
Position (PositionID, PositionDesc, PayGrade)
Employment (EmployeeNum, PositionID, StartDate)
    Foreign key: EmployeeNum to Employee table
    Foreign key: PositionID to Position table

Recall that a primary key must be unique, must be minimal, and must not change in value. In theory, primary keys don't change in value. However, in practice, you might have to change EmployeeNum field values that you incorrectly entered in the Employment table. Further, if you need to change an EmployeeNum field value in the Employee table, the change must cascade to the EmployeeNum field values in the Employment table. Also, changes to a PositionID field value in the Position table must cascade to the Employment table. For these and other reasons, many experts add surrogate keys to their tables. A **surrogate key** (also called a **synthetic key**) is a system-generated primary key that is hidden from users. Usually you can use an automatic numbering data type, such as the Access AutoNumber data type, for a surrogate key. Figure A-20 shows the four tables with surrogate keys added to each table.

Figure A-20 **Using surrogate keys**

Employee (EmployeeSK: surrogate key; HealthSK: foreign key)

EmployeeSK	EmployeeNum	FirstName	LastName	HealthSK
1	2173	Barbara	Hennessey	2
2	4519	Lee	Noordsy	1
3	8005	Pat	Amidon	3
4	8112	Chris	Wandzell	1

HealthBenefits (HealthSK: surrogate key)

HealthSK	HealthPlan	PlanDesc
1	A	Managed PPO
2	B	Managed HMO
3	C	Health Savings

Position (PositionID: artificial key)

PositionID	PositionDesc	PayGrade
1	Director	45
2	Manager	40
3	Analyst	30
4	Clerk	20

Employment (EmploymentSK: surrogate key; EmployeeSK: foreign key; PositionID: foreign key)

EmploymentSK	EmployeeSK	PositionID	StartDate
1	1	2	12/14/2011
2	2	1	04/23/2013
3	2	3	11/11/2007
4	3	3	06/05/2012
5	3	4	07/02/2010
6	4	1	12/15/2012
7	4	2	10/04/2011

The HealthSK field replaces the HealthPlan field as a foreign key in the Employee table, and the EmployeeSK field replaces the EmployeeNum field in the Employment table. Now when you change an incorrectly entered EmployeeNum field value in the Employee table, you don't need to cascade the change to the Employment table. Likewise, when you change an incorrectly entered HealthPlan field value in the HealthBenefits table, you don't need to cascade the change to the Employee table.

As you design a database, you should *not* consider the use of surrogate keys, and you should use an artificial key only for the rare table that has duplicate records. At the point when you implement a database, you might choose to use artificial and surrogate keys, but be aware that database experts debate their use and effectiveness. You need to consider the following tradeoffs between natural and surrogate keys:

- You use surrogate keys to avoid cascading updates to foreign key values. Surrogate keys can also replace lengthier foreign keys when those foreign keys reference composite fields.
- You don't need a surrogate key for a table whose primary key is not used as a foreign key in another table because cascading updates is not an issue.
- Tables with surrogate keys require more joins than do tables with natural keys. For example, if you need to know all employees with a HealthPlan field value of A, the surrogate key in Figure A-20 requires that you join the Employee and HealthBenefits tables to answer the question. Using natural keys as shown in Figure A-17, the HealthPlan field appears in the Employee table, so no join is necessary.
- Although surrogate keys are meant to be hidden from users, they cannot be hidden from users who create SQL statements and use other ad hoc tools.
- Because you need a unique index for the natural key and a unique index for the surrogate key, your database size is larger and index maintenance takes more time when you use a surrogate key. On the other hand, a foreign key using a surrogate key is usually smaller than a foreign key using a natural key, especially when the natural key is a composite key, so those indexes are smaller and faster to access for lookups and joins.

Microsoft Access Naming Conventions

In the early 1980s, Microsoft's Charles Simonyi introduced an identifier naming convention that became known as Hungarian notation. Microsoft and other companies use this naming convention for variable, control, and other object naming in Basic, Visual Basic, and other programming languages. When Access was introduced in the early 1990s, Stan Leszynski and Greg Reddick adapted Hungarian notation for Microsoft Access databases; their guidelines became known as the Leszynski/Reddick naming conventions. In recent years, the Leszynski naming conventions, the Reddick naming conventions, and other naming conventions have been published. Individuals and companies have created their own Access naming conventions, but many are based on the Leszynski/Reddick naming conventions, as are the naming conventions covered in this section.

An Access database can contain thousands of objects, fields, controls, and other items, and keeping track of their names and what they represent is a difficult task. Consequently, you should use naming conventions that identify the type and purpose of each item in an Access database. You can use naming conventions that identify items generally or very specifically.

For an object, include a prefix tag to identify the type of object, as shown in Figure A-21. In each example in Figure A-21, the final object name consists of a three-character tag prefixed to the base object name. For example, the form name of frmEmployeesAndPositions consists of the frm tag and the EmployeesAndPositions base form name.

Figure A-21 **Object naming tags**

Object type	Tag	Example
Form	frm	frmEmployeesAndPositions
Macro	mcr	mcrSwitchboard
Module	bas	basCalculations
Query	qry	qryEmployee
Report	rpt	rptEmployeesAndPositions
Table	tbl	tblEmployee

The tags in Figure A-21 identify each object type in general. If you want to identify object types more specifically, you could expand Figure A-21 to include tags such as fsub for a subform, qxtb for a crosstab query, tlkp for a lookup table, rsub for a subreport, and so on.

For controls in forms and reports, a general naming convention uses lbl as a prefix tag for labels and ctl as a prefix tag for other types of controls. For more specific naming conventions for controls, you'd use a specific prefix tag for each type of control. Figure A-22 shows the prefix tags for some common controls in forms and reports.

Figure A-22 **Control naming tags**

Control type	Tag
Check box	chk
Combo box	cbo
Command button	cmd
Image	img
Label	lbl
Line	lin
List box	lst
Option button	opt
Rectangle	shp
Subform/Subreport	sub
Text box	txt

Some database developers use a prefix tag for each field name to identify the field's data type (for example, dtm for Date/Time, num for Number, and chr for Text or Character), others use a prefix tag for each field name to identify in which table the field is located (for example, emp for the Employee table and pos for the Position table), and still others don't use a prefix tag for field names.

You might use suffix tags for controls that might otherwise have identical names. For example, if you have two text boxes in a form for calculated controls that display the average and the sum of the OrderAmt field, both could legitimately be named txtOrderAmt unless you used suffix tags to name them txtOrderAmtAvg and txtOrderAmtSum.

You should ensure that any name you use does not duplicate a property name or any keyword Access reserves for special purposes. In general, you can avoid property and keyword name conflicts by using two-word field, control, and object names. For example, use StudentName instead of Name, and use OrderDate instead of Date to avoid name conflicts.

All database developers avoid spaces in names, mainly because spaces are not allowed in server DBMSs, such as SQL Server, Oracle, and DB2. If you are prototyping a Microsoft Access database that you'll migrate to one of these server DBMSs, or if future requirements might force a migration, you should restrict your Access identifier names so that they conform to the rules common to them all. Figure A-23 shows the identifier naming rules for Access, SQL Server, Oracle, and DB2.

Figure A-23 **Identifier naming rules for common database management systems**

Identifier naming rule	Access	SQL Server	Oracle	DB2
Maximum character length	64	30	30	30
Allowable characters	Letters, digits, space, and special characters, except for period (.), exclamation point (!), grave accent (`), and square brackets ([ ])	Letters, digits, dollar sign ($), underscore (_), number symbol (#), and at symbol (@)	Letters, digits, dollar sign ($), underscore (_), and number symbol (#)	Letters, digits, at symbol (@), dollar sign ($), underscore (_), and number symbol (#)
Special rules		No spaces; first character must be a letter or at symbol (@)	No spaces; first character must be a letter; stored in the database in uppercase	No spaces; first character must be a letter, at symbol (@), dollar sign ($), or number symbol (#); stored in the database in uppercase

PRACTICE

Review Assignments

1. What are the formal names for a table, for a row, and for a column? What are the popular names for a row and for a column?
2. What is a domain?
3. What is an entity?
4. What is the relationship between a primary key and a candidate key?
5. What is a composite key?
6. What is a foreign key?
7. Look for an example of a one-to-one relationship, an example of a one-to-many relationship, and an example of a many-to-many relationship in a newspaper, magazine, book, or everyday situation you encounter.
8. When do you use an entity subtype?
9. What is the entity integrity constraint?
10. What is referential integrity?
11. What does the cascades option, which is used with referential integrity, accomplish?
12. What are partial and transitive dependencies?
13. What three types of anomalies can be exhibited by a table, and what problems do they cause?
14. Figure A-24 shows the Employee, Position, and Employment tables with primary keys EmployeeNum, PositionID, and both EmployeeNum and PositionID, respectively. Which two integrity constraints do these tables violate and why?

Figure A-24 Integrity constraint violations

Employee

EmployeeNum	FirstName	LastName	HealthPlan
2173	Barbara	Hennessey	B
4519	Lee	Noordsy	A
8005	Pat	Amidon	C
8112	Chris	Wandzell	A

Position

PositionID	PositionDesc	PayGrade
1	Director	45
2	Manager	40
3	Analyst	30
4	Clerk	20

Employment

EmployeeNum	PositionID	StartDate
2173	2	12/14/2011
4519	1	04/23/2013
4519		11/11/2007
8005	3	06/05/2012
8005	4	07/02/2010
8112	1	12/15/2012
9876	2	10/04/2011

15. The State and City tables, shown in Figure A-4, are described as follows:
    State (StateAbbrev, StateName, EnteredUnionOrder, StateBird, StatePopulation)
    City (StateAbbrev, CityName, CityPopulation)
    Foreign key: StateAbbrev to State table
    Add the field named CountyName for the county or counties in a state containing the city to this database, justify where you placed it (that is, in an existing table or in a new one), and draw the entity-relationship diagram for all the entities. Counties for some of the cities shown in Figure A-4 are Travis and Williamson counties for Austin TX; Hartford county for Hartford CT; Clinton, Eaton, and Ingham counties for Lansing MI; Davidson county for Nashville TN; Hughes county for Pierre SD; and Nueces and San Patricio counties for Portland TX.
16. Suppose you have a table for a dance studio. The fields are dancer's identification number, dancer's name, dancer's address, dancer's telephone number, class identification number, day that the class meets, time that the class meets, instructor name, and instructor identification number. Assume that each dancer takes one class, each class meets only once a week and has

one instructor, and each instructor can teach more than one class. In what normal form is the table currently, given the following alternative description?

Dancer (DancerID, DancerName, DancerAddr, DancerPhone, ClassID, ClassDay, ClassTime, InstrName, InstrID)

Convert this relation to 3NF and represent the design using the alternative description method.

17. Store the following fields for a library database: AuthorCode, AuthorName, BookTitle, BorrowerAddress, BorrowerName, BorrowerCardNumber, CopiesOfBook, ISBN (International Standard Book Number), LoanDate, PublisherCode, PublisherName, and PublisherAddress. A one-to-many relationship exists between publishers and books. Many-to-many relationships exist between authors and books and between borrowers and books.
    a. Name the entities for the library database.
    b. Create the tables for the library database and describe them using the alternative method. Be sure the tables are in third normal form.
    c. Draw an entity-relationship diagram for the library database.
18. In the database shown in Figure A-25, which consists of the Department and Employee tables, add one record to the end of the Employee table that violates both the entity integrity constraint and the referential integrity constraint.

Figure A-25 Creating integrity constraint violations

Department

DeptID	DeptName	Location
M	Marketing	New York
R	Research	Houston
S	Sales	Chicago

Employee

EmployeeID	EmployeeName	DeptID
1111	Sue	R
2222	Pam	M
3333	Bob	S
4444	Chris	S
5555	Pat	R
6666	Meg	R

19. Consider the following table:

    Patient (PatientID, PatientName, BalanceOwed, DoctorID, DoctorName, ServiceCode, ServiceDesc, ServiceFee, ServiceDate)

    This is a table concerning data about patients of doctors at a clinic and the services the doctors perform for their patients. The following dependencies exist in the Patient table:

    PatientID → PatientName, BalanceOwed

    DoctorID → DoctorName

    ServiceCode → ServiceDesc, ServiceFee

PatientID, DoctorID, ServiceCode → PatientName, BalanceOwed, DoctorName, ServiceDesc, ServiceFee, ServiceDate

a. Based on the dependencies, convert the Patient table to first normal form.

b. Next, convert the Patient table to third normal form.

20. Suppose you need to track data for mountain climbing expeditions. Each member of an expedition is called a climber, and one of the climbers is named to lead an expedition. Climbers can be members of many expeditions over time. The climbers in each expedition attempt to ascend one or more peaks by scaling one of the many faces of the peaks. The data you need to track includes the name of the expedition, the leader of the expedition, and comments about the expedition; the first name, last name, nationality, birth date, death date, and comments about each climber; the name, location, height, and comments about each peak; the name and comments about each face of a peak; comments about each climber for each expedition; and the highest height reached and the date for each ascent attempt by a climber on a face with commentary.

    a. Create the tables for the expedition database and describe them using the alternative method. Be sure the tables are in third normal form.

    b. Draw an entity-relationship diagram for the expedition database.

21. What is the difference among natural, artificial, and surrogate keys?

22. Why should you use naming conventions for the identifiers in a database?

GLOSSARY/INDEX

SPECIAL CHARACTERS

\ (backslash), AC 279, FM 11
< (left angle bracket), AC 142, AC 279
> (right angle bracket), AC 142, AC 279
! (exclamation point), AC 195, AC 279
" (double quotation mark), AC 279
(number symbol), AC 195, AC 237, AC 279
& (ampersand), AC 245, AC 279
* (asterisk), AC 195, AC 196, AC 237
+ (plus sign), AC 123–124
- (minus sign), AC 123, AC 195
= (equal sign), AC 142
? (question mark), AC 195, AC 237, AC 279
[] (square brackets), AC 195
. (dot), FM 16
; (semicolon), AC 279

A

.accdb file extension, AC 9

ACCDE file A special version of an Access database that runs as a normal database, but in which the VBA code can't be viewed or edited. In addition, users can't view, modify, or create forms, reports, or modules in Design view, and can't import or export forms, reports, or modules. The ACCDE file has an .accde extension instead of the usual .accdb extension. AC 697

Access. *See* Microsoft Access 2013

access
  to database objects, restricting, AC 574
  exclusive, to a database, AC 691

Access Help Information on Access commands and features as well as instructions for using them. AC 25, AC 40–41

Access Options dialog box, AC 693–694

Access window The program window that appears when you start the Access program to create a new database or open an existing database. AC 3

accuracy, data, AC 287

action An instruction to Access to perform an operation. AC 548
  adding to macros, AC 553–557

Action Catalog button A toggle to open and close the Action Catalog pane, which lists all actions by category and all macros in a database. AC 548

action query A query that adds, changes, or deletes multiple table records at a time. AC 498–515
  append, AC 498, AC 506–508
  delete, AC 499, AC 509–512
  deleting, AC 515
  make-table, AC 498, AC 501–505
  update, AC 499, AC 512–515

Add & Delete group A group on the FIELDS tab in Table Datasheet view that contains options for adding different types of fields to a table. AC 2

Address Quick Start selection The Quick Start Selection that adds a collection of fields related to an address to the table at one time. AC 86

Advanced Filter/Sort A form and datasheet tool that lets you specify multiple selection criteria and specify a sort order for selected records in the Filter window, in the same way you specify record selection criteria and sort orders for a query in Design view. AC 650

AfterUpdate event An event that occurs after changed data in a control or a record is updated. AC 607, AC 616, AC 625

aggregate function A function that performs an arithmetic operation on selected records in a database. AC 161–167
  creating queries using, AC 163–166
  record group calculations, AC 166–167
  Total row, AC 162–163
  used in crosstab queries, AC 256

alignment
  aligning controls, AC 332–333
  field values, changing, AC 213–214

All Access Objects The default category in the Navigation Pane; it lists all the objects in the database grouped by type (tables, queries, forms, reports, and so on). AC 40, AC 167–170

Allow Full Menus property A database property that specifies whether all options are available on the Ribbon. AC 671

Allow Multiple Values property The property that controls whether a field can store more than one value. AC 648

Allow Zero Length property A property that controls whether a field can store a zero length string value in a field. AC 676–677
  setting to No, AC 677

alternate key A candidate key that was not chosen to be the primary key. AC A3

ampersand (&), input mask character, AC 279

ampersand (&) operator A concatenation operator that joins text expressions. AC 245

Anchor property A form and report property that resizes a control and places it in the chosen position on a form. AC 303

Anchoring gallery, AC 319–320

And logical operator The logical operator you use in a query when you want a record selected only if two or more conditions are met. AC 149, AC 150–151
  Or logical operator vs. AC 153

anomaly Undesirable irregularity of a table caused by data redundancy and by partial and transitive dependencies. Anomalies are of three types: insertion, deletion, and update. AC A14–A15

Append Only property A field property for a Long Text field that lets you edit the field value and, when set to Yes, causes Access to keep a historical record of all versions of the field value. You can view each version of the field value, along with a date and time stamp of when each version change occurred. AC 290

append query An action query that adds records from existing tables or queries to the end of another table. AC 498, AC 506–508

application part A specialized template that can be imported into an existing database. You use an application part when you already have a database file that you're working with, and would like to include the content from an application part in your existing database. AC 480–484

Application Title property A database property that specifies the name for a database that appears in the Access window title bar. AC 670

ApplyFilter action, AC 550

archive A special type of folder containing compressed files. FM 26

argument A piece of data that is required by an action. AC 553

argument (for VBA) A value passed to a VBA function and used in place of a parameter when the function is executed. AC 617
  naming, AC 617

arrow button, FM 2, FM 3, FM 11

artificial key A field that you add to a table to serve solely as the primary key and that is visible to users. AC A21–A23

assignment statement A VBA statement that assigns the value of an expression to a field, control, or property. AC 604

asterisk (*), wildcard character, AC 195, AC 196, AC 237

Attachment data type A data type used to attach one or more files to a table record. AC 672–674

Attachments dialog box, AC 673–674

attribute The formal term for a column in a relation (table). AC A2

AutoFilter An Access feature, available by clicking the arrow to the right of a field name in Datasheet view for a table or query, that enables you to quickly sort and display the field's values in various ways. AC 132, AC 242–244

G

K

L

M

P

Q

R

S

TASK REFERENCE

TASK	PAGE #	RECOMMENDED METHOD
Access, start	AC 7	Click the Access 2013 tile on the Windows Start screen
Action, add to a macro	AC 554	In the Macro Designer, click the Add New Action arrow, click the action
Action, add to a macro by dragging	AC 556	In the Macro Designer, find the action in the Action Catalog, click and drag the action to the desired location in the macro
Action, find in Action Catalog	AC 556	Click the search box, type the action to find
Aggregate functions, use in a datasheet	AC 162	Open the table or query in Datasheet view, in Records group on HOME tab click Totals button, click Total field row, click function
Aggregate functions, use in a query	AC 163	Display the query in Design view, click the Totals button in the Show/Hide group on the DESIGN tab
Alternate row color, set and remove in a report	AC 415	In Design view, select the Detail section, click the FORMAT tab, in the Background group, click Alternate Row Color
Append query, create	AC 506	*See* Reference box: Creating an Append Query
Application Part, create	AC 481	Click the FILE tab, click Save Database As, click Template, click Save As, click enter a name and description, click Application Part, click OK
Autofilter, use in a table datasheet	AC 650	Click the arrow on the column heading, click Auto Filter, click appropriate filter type
AutoFilter, use in a table or query datasheet	AC 242	Click the arrow on the column heading, click one or more filter options, click OK
Borders, add or remove from a control in a form or report	AC 415	In Design view, select the control, click the FORMAT tab, open the Property Sheet, select a Border Style value
Built-in functions, use in a query	AC 246	Display the query in Design view, right-click a blank field, click Build, double-click Functions, click Built-In Functions, select a category, double-click a function, replace any placeholders, click OK
Calculated field, add to a query	AC 157	*See* Reference box: Using Expression Builder
Caption, change for a form's navigation bar	AC 470	Click the form selector, open the Property Sheet, type the value in the Navigation Caption box, press Enter
Caption, change for a label	AC 338	*See* Reference box: Changing a Label's Caption
Caption, set for a form	AC 576	Right-click the form selector, click the Format tab, click the Caption box, type the caption name
Chart Wizard, start	AC 474	In Design view, on the DESIGN tab, in the Controls group, click the More button, click the Chart tool
Chart, edit with Microsoft Graph	AC 476	In Design view, right-click the chart's edge, point to Chart Object, click Open, make desired changes, click File, click Exit & Return
Chart, embed in a form or report	AC 474	*See* Reference box: Embedding a Chart in a Form or Report
Color, change an object's background	AC 371	Click the object, click the arrow, click the desired color
Column, resize width in a datasheet	AC 18	Double-click on the right border of the column heading
Combo box, add to a form	AC 348	*See* Reference box: Adding a Combo Box to Find Records
Command button, add to a form	AC 566	Click the DESIGN tab, click the More button, make sure is not selected, in the Controls group click, position the pointer in the form, click the mouse button

TASK	PAGE #	RECOMMENDED METHOD
Control layout, remove control from a form	AC 317	In Layout view, right-click the control, point to Layout, click Remove Layout
Control tip property, set for a form control	AC 361	In Layout view, right-click the control, click Properties, click Other tab, type the tip in the ControlTip Text property box, press Enter
Control, anchor in a form	AC 318	In Layout view, select the control to anchor, click the ARRANGE tab, in the Position group, click the Anchoring button, click an option in the Anchoring gallery
Control, apply a special effect to	AC 370	Select the control, open the Property Sheet, set the Special Effect property
Control, delete	AC 334	Right-click the control, click Delete
Control, move in a form	AC 330	*See* Reference box: Selecting and Moving Controls
Control, resize in a form	AC 334	*See* Reference box: Resizing a Control in Design View
Control, select	AC 330	*See* Reference box: Selecting and Moving Controls
Controls, align selected	AC 332	Right-click one of the selected controls, point to Align, click desired alignment
Controls, move and resize in a form or report	AC 413	Select controls, click the ARRANGE tab in the Size & Ordering group, click Size/Space, click desired setting
Crosstab query, create	AC 258	*See* Reference box: Using the Crosstab Query Wizard
Crosstab query, edit column headings	AC 261	In Design view, right-click the Field box, click Zoom, edit the value or expression, click OK
CSV file, import as an Access table	AC 449	*See* Reference box: Importing a CSV File as an Access Table
Data, find	AC 194	*See* Reference box: Finding Data in a Form or Datasheet
Data, group in a report	AC 408	*See* Reference box: Sorting and Grouping Data in a Report
Data, sort in a report	AC 408	*See* Reference box: Sorting and Grouping Data in a Report
Database, back up	AC 292	Click the FILE tab, click Save As, click Back Up Database, click Save As, navigate to desired location, click Save
Database, compact and repair	AC 42	*See* Reference box: Compacting and Repairing a Database
Database, create a blank	AC 7	Start Access, click Blank desktop database, type the database name, select the drive and folder, click OK, click Create
Database, decrypt	AC 692	*See* Reference box: Setting and Unsetting a Password
Database, encrypt	AC 691	*See* Proskills box: Determining When to Encrypt Data Using a Password
Database, open	AC 26	*See* Reference box: Opening a Database
Database, save as an ACCDE file	AC 697	Open the database, click the FILE tab, click Save & Publish, click Make ACCDE, click Save As, type database name, select the destination folder, click Save
Database, save as a previous version	AC 677	Open the database to save and close all open objects, click the FILE tab, click Save & Publish, click Save Database As, click the desired Access format, click Save As, choose the destination folder and enter the database name, click Save
Database, split	AC 687	*See* Reference box: Using the Database Splitter
Database documentation, set	AC 693	*See* Reference box: Setting Database Documentation Properties
Database properties, set	AC 693	*See* Reference box: Setting the Database Properties and Startup Options
Datasheet view for tables, switch to	AC 75	In the Views group on the DESIGN tab, click the View button

TASK	PAGE #	RECOMMENDED METHOD
Data Type gallery, add fields to a table with	AC 86	Click the FIELDS tab, click More Fields in the Add & Delete group, click the field or Quick Start selection to add
Date and time, add to a report	AC 422	*See* Reference box: Adding the Date and Time to a Report
Delete query, create	AC 509	*See* Reference box: Creating a Delete Query
Design view, switch to	AC 73	In the Views group on the FIELDS tab, click the View button
Documenter, use	AC 307	*See* Reference box: Using the Documenter
Duplicate values, hide	AC 418	*See* Reference box: Hiding Duplicate Values in a Report
Event procedure, add to a form or report	AC 628	*See* Reference box: Adding an Event Procedure to a Form or Report
Event procedure, display an existing	AC 611	Open the property sheet for the control or object, click the Event tab, click the event property box, click ...
Excel worksheet, import data from	AC 81	Click the EXTERNAL DATA tab, click Excel in the Import & Link group, complete the import dialog boxes
Excel worksheet, link data from	AC 487	Click the EXTERNAL DATA tab, in the Import & Link group, click the Excel button, click Browse, select the workbook, click Open, click Link to the data source by creating a linked table, click OK, follow the steps in the Link Spreadsheet Wizard
Export steps, save	AC 463	In the Export dialog box, click the Save export steps check box, enter a description, click Save Export
Field, add to a form or report	AC 327	In Design view, on the DESIGN tab, in the Tools group, click Add Existing Fields, click the record source, double-click the field
Field, add to a table	AC 69	*See* Reference box: Adding a Field Between Two Existing Fields
Field, define in a table	AC 59	*See* Reference box: Defining a Field in Design View
Field, delete from a table	AC 87	*See* Reference box: Deleting a Field from a Table Structure
Field, move to a new location in a table	AC 69	Display the table in Design view, click the field's row selector, drag the field with the pointer
Field property change, update	AC 91	Click , select the option for updating the field property
File, attach to a record using an Attachment field	AC 672	Right-click the record's Attachment field, click Manage Attachments, click Add, select the file to attach, click Open, click OK
File, detach from a record's Attachment field	AC 674	Right-click the record's Attachment field, click Manage Attachments, select the file to detach, click Remove, click OK
File, export from a record's Attachment field	AC 674	Right-click the record's Attachment field, click Manage Attachments, select the file to export, click Save As, type the filename and choose the destination folder, click Save, click OK
File, open from a record's Attachment field	AC 674	Right-click the record's Attachment field, click Manage Attachments, select the file to open, click Open
Filter, apply to a form from a saved query	AC 656	*See* Reference box: Applying a Filter Saved as a Query
Filter, save as a query	AC 655	See Reference box: Saving a Filter as a Query
Filter By Form, use to select records	AC 652	*See* Reference box: Selecting Records Using Filter By Form
Filter By Selection, activate	AC 136	*See* Reference box: Using Filter By Selection
Find duplicates query, create	AC 263	*See* Reference box: Using the Find Duplicates Query Wizard
Find unmatched query, create	AC 265	*See* Reference box: Using the Find Unmatched Query Wizard
Form, create a custom	AC 325	*See* Reference box: Creating a Form in Design View

TASK	PAGE #	RECOMMENDED METHOD
Form, create in Design view	AC 325	*See* Reference box: Creating a Form in Design View
Form, create using the Datasheet tool	AC 311	Select the record source in the Navigation Pane, click the CREATE tab, in the Forms group, click More Forms, click Datasheet
Form, create using the Multiple Items tool	AC 313	Select the record source in the Navigation Pane, click the CREATE tab, in the Forms group, click More Forms, click Multiple Items
Form, create using the Split Form tool	AC 314	Select the record source in the Navigation Pane, click the CREATE tab, in the Forms group click More Forms, click Split Form
Form, select in Design view	AC 348	Click the form selector
Form Footer, add	AC 343	*See* Reference box: Adding and Removing Form Header and Form Footer Sections
Form Footer, remove	AC 343	*See* Reference box: Adding and Removing Form Header and Form Footer Sections
Form Header, add	AC 343	*See* Reference box: Adding and Removing Form Header and Form Footer Sections
Form Header, remove	AC 343	*See* Reference box: Adding and Removing Form Header and Form Footer Sections
Form Wizard, activate	AC 182	Click the CREATE tab, click Form Wizard in the Forms group, choose the table or query for the form, select fields, click Next
Function, create	AC 617	Enter function statements in the Code window
HTML document, export an Access object as	AC 446	*See* Reference box: Exporting an Access Object to an HTML Document
HTML Template, use	AC 446	*See* Reference box: Exporting an Access Object to an HTML Document
Import steps, save	AC 458	In the Get External Data dialog box, click the Save import steps check box, enter a description, click Save Import
Index, create	AC 537	*See* Reference box: Creating an Index
Indexes, view a table's existing	AC 536	*See* Reference box: Viewing a Table's Existing Indexes
Input Mask Wizard, start	AC 276	Click the field's Input Mask box, click ..., specify your choices in the Input Mask Wizard dialog boxes
Label Wizard, start	AC 431	Click the CREATE tab, in the Report group, click Labels
Line, add to a form or report	AC 367	*See* Reference box: Adding a Line to a Form or Report
Linked Table Manager, use	AC 683	*See* Reference box: Using the Linked Table Manager
List box, add to a form	AC 577	*See* Reference box: Adding a List Box to a Form
List-of-Values match, using in a query	AC 240	In Design view, in a field's Criteria box, type In, type an opening parenthesis, enter the first criterion in quotes, type a comma, type any additional criteria in quotes, separated by commas, type a closing parenthesis
Long Text field, change properties of	AC 289	Display the table in Design view, select the Long Text field, change the value in the Text Format box or in the Append Only box
Lookup field, change to a Text field	AC 305	Display the table in Design view, select the field, click the Lookup tab, set the Display Control property to Text Box
Lookup field, create	AC 272	Click the Data Type arrow, click Lookup Wizard, specify your choices in the Lookup Wizard dialog boxes
Macro, run an existing	AC 551	*See* Reference box: Directly Running an Existing Macro
Macro, single step	AC 557	*See* Reference box: Single Stepping a Macro

TASK	PAGE #	RECOMMENDED METHOD
Mailing labels, create	AC 431	*See* Reference box: Creating Mailing Labels and Other Labels
Make-table query, create	AC 501	*See* Reference box: Creating a Make-Table Query
Microsoft Access Help, search	AC 41	Click ? on the title bar, enter the search text in the search box, press Enter
Module, compile	AC 641	Click Debug, click Compile *database name*
Module, create	AC 616	On the CREATE tab, in the Macros & Code group, click the Module button
Module, save	AC 621	Click [Save], type module name, press Enter
Multivalued field, create in a table	AC 662	In Design view, enter the field name, choose the Lookup Wizard data type, select the method for looking up field values and choose the appropriate Lookup Wizard options, select the Allow Multiple Values check box, finish the Lookup Wizard
Navigation form, create	AC 593	On the CREATE tab, in the Forms group, click the Navigation button, choose the desired navigation form in gallery
Navigation form, drag form or report to	AC 595	Open the Navigation Pane, open the navigation form in Layout view, drag the object from Navigation Pane to desired tab on navigation form
Not logical operator, use in a query	AC 241	In Design view, click the Criteria box for a field, open the Zoom dialog box, type Not, press the spacebar, type the criteria
Object, open	AC 22	Double-click the object in the Navigation Pane
Object, save	AC 20	Click [Save], type the object name, click OK
Object dependencies, identify	AC 282	Click the DATABASE TOOLS tab, in the Relationships group, click the Object Dependencies button, click the object, click ▷
Padding, change in a form control	AC 316	In Layout view, click the control, click the ARRANGE tab, in the Position group, click Control Padding, click the desired setting
Page margins, setting in a report	AC 412	Click the PAGE SETUP tab, click Margins, click an option
Page numbers, add to a report	AC 426	*See* Reference box: Adding Page Numbers to a Report
Parameter query, create	AC 250	*See* Reference box: Creating a Parameter Query
Password, set a database	AC 692	*See* Reference box: Setting and Unsetting a Password
Password, unset a database	AC 692	*See* Reference box: Setting and Unsetting a Password
Pattern match, use in a query	AC 239	In Design view, in the Criteria box for a field, type Like, press the spacebar, type the text to match enclosed in quotes
PDF, create from report	AC 485	Right-click the name of the report in the Navigation pane, click Export, click PDF or XPS, navigate to the appropriate location, enter a name in the File name box, click Publish
Performance Analyzer, use	AC 678	*See* Reference box: Using the Performance Analyzer
Picture, add to or change on a command button	AC 568	Open the property sheet for the command button, click the Picture box, click ..., select the picture, click OK
Picture, insert in a form	AC 189	In Layout view, click the DESIGN tab, click the Logo button in the Header/Footer group, select the picture file, click OK
Picture caption, add to a command button	AC 568	Open the property sheet for the command button, click the Caption box, press F2, type the desired caption
Picture caption, change location of on a command button	AC 568	Open the property sheet for the command button, click the Picture Caption Arrangement arrow, click the desired setting
Primary key, specify	AC 67	*See* Reference box: Specifying a Primary Key in Design View

TASK	PAGE #	RECOMMENDED METHOD
Procedure, test in the Immediate Window	AC 621	*See* Reference box: Testing a Procedure in the Immediate Window
Property sheet, open	AC 159	Make the object current in Design view, click the Property Sheet button in the Show/Hide group on the DESIGN tab
Property sheet, open or close for a field or control	AC 248	Select the field or control, click the DESIGN tab, in the Show/Hide group click the Property Sheet button
Query, define	AC 125	Click the CREATE tab, click the Query Design button in the Queries group
Query, run	AC 127	Double-click the query in the Navigation Pane or, in the Results group on the DESIGN tab, click the Run button
Query results, sort	AC 133	*See* Reference box: Sorting a Query Datasheet
Quick Start selection, add	AC 86	Click the FIELDS tab, click More Fields in the Add & Delete group, click the Quick Start selection
Record, add new	AC 20	In the Records group on the HOME tab, click the New button
Record, delete	AC 122	*See* Reference box: Deleting a Record
Record, move to first	AC 30	Click 
Record, move to last	AC 30	Click 
Record, move to next	AC 30	Click 
Record, move to previous	AC 30	Click 
Records, print selected in a form	AC 199	Click the FILE tab, click Print in the navigation bar, click Print, click Selected Record(s), click OK
Records, redisplay all after filter	AC 138	In Sort & Filter group on HOME tab, click the Toggle Filter button
Rectangle, add to a form or report	AC 369	*See* Reference box: Adding a Rectangle to a Form or Report
Report, create a custom	AC 405	Click the CREATE tab, click Blank Report
Report, filter in Report view	AC 385	Right-click the value to filter, point to Text Filters, click a filter option
Report, print	AC 39	*See* Reference box: Printing a Report
Report, print specific pages of	AC 219	In the Print group on the PRINT PREVIEW tab, click Print, click Pages, enter number of pages to print in From and To boxes, click OK
Report, select and copy data in Report view	AC 387	Click the top of the selection, drag to the end of the selection, click the HOME tab, in the Clipboard group, click 
Report Wizard, activate	AC 208	Click the CREATE tab, click Report Wizard button in Reports group, choose the table or query for the report, select fields, click Next
Saved export, run	AC 464	Click the EXTERNAL DATA tab, in the Export group, click Saved Exports, click the saved export, click Run
Saved import, run	AC 458	Click the EXTERNAL DATA tab, in the Import & Link group, click Saved Imports, click the saved import, click Run
Self-join, create	AC 531	*See* Reference box: Creating a Self-Join
Sort, specify ascending in datasheet	AC 132	Click a column heading arrow, click Sort A to Z
Sort, specify descending in datasheet	AC 132	Click a column heading arrow, click Sort Z to A
Spacing, change in a form control	AC 316	In Layout view, click the control, click the ARRANGE tab, in the Position group, click Control Margins, click the desired setting
SQL statement, use for a list box	AC 583	Open the property sheet for the list box, click the Data tab, right-click the Row Source box, click Zoom, enter the SQL statement, click OK
SQL statement, view	AC 580	*See* Reference box: Viewing an SQL Statement for a Query

TASK	PAGE #	RECOMMENDED METHOD
Startup options, bypass	AC 695	In File Explorer, hold the Shift key while you double-click the filename
Startup options, set for a database	AC 693	*See* Reference box: Setting the Database Properties and Startup Options
Subform calculated controls, display in the main form	AC 358	Add calculated controls to the subform's footer section, in the main form, add a text box, select the text box, open the Property Sheet, click the Control Source box, click , navigate to the subform, select the text box In the subform that contains the calculation, insert = at the beginning of the expression, click OK
Subform, open in a new window	AC 356	Right-click the subform border, click Subform in New Window
Subform/Subreport Wizard, start	AC 352	Click the DESIGN tab, in the Controls group, click More, make sure is selected, click , click in the grid where the upper-left corner of the subform/subreport should be placed
Submacro, add to a macro	AC 564	*See* Reference box: Adding a Submacro
Submacro, attach to a command button	AC 567	Open the property sheet for the command button, click the Event tab, click the arrow for the event property box, click submacro name
Tab Control, add to a form	AC 468	Click the DESIGN tab, in the Controls group, click , click in the grid at the location of the upper-left corner for the tab control
Tab order, change in a form	AC 364	In Design view, click the DESIGN tab, in the Tools group, click Tab Order, drag the rows into the desired order, click OK
Tab Stop property, change for a form control	AC 361	In Layout view, right-click the control, click Properties, click the Other tab, set the Tab Stop property
Table, analyze	AC 453	Select the table, click DATABASE TOOLS tab, in the Analyze group, click Analyze Table
Table, create from Application Part	AC 483	Click the CREATE tab, click the Application Parts button, click the application part template, click the appropriate relationship option button, click Create
Table, create in Datasheet view	AC 11	*See* Reference box: Creating a Table in Datasheet View
Table, export as an XML file	AC 460	*See* Reference box: Exporting an Access Object as an XML File
Table, import into the open Access database	AC 454	Click the EXTERNAL DATA tab, in the Import & Link group, click Access, browse to the database location, click Open, select Import tables, queries, forms, reports, macros, and modules into the current database, click OK, click Options, click the Tables tab, click the table to import, click OK, click Close
Table, link to in another Access database	AC 682	*See* Reference box: Linking to a Table in Another Access Database
Table, open in a database	AC 22	Double-click the table in the Navigation Pane
Table, save in a database	AC 19	*See* Reference box: Saving a Table
Table relationships, view	AC 306	Click the DATABASE TOOLS tab, click Relationships
Template, create an Access database	AC 481	Open or create an Access database, click the FILE tab, click Save As, in the File Types column, click Save Database As (if necessary), click Template, click Save As, enter a name and description, click the Application Park check box, click OK, click OK again
Text file, import data from	AC 96	Click the EXTERNAL DATA tab, click Text File in the Import & Link group, complete the import dialog boxes

TASK	PAGE #	RECOMMENDED METHOD
Theme, apply to a form	AC 185	*See* Reference box: Applying a Theme to a Form
Title, add to a form or report	AC 343	On the DESIGN tab, in the Header/Footer group, click Title, type the title, press Enter
Top values query, create	AC 267	On the DESIGN tab, in the Query Setup group, in the Return (Top Values) box, enter the number of or percentage of records to select
Total, calculate in a report	AC 393	In Layout view, click any value in the column to calculate, click the DESIGN tab, in the Grouping & Totals group, click Totals, click the desired function
Trusted folder, create	AC 291	Click the FILE tab, click Options, click Trust Center, click Trust Center Settings, click Trusted Locations, click Add new location, click Browse, navigate to the desired folder, click OK four times
Update query, create	AC 512	*See* Reference box: Creating an Update Query
Validation Rule field or table property, set	AC 284	Display the table in Design view, select the field or table, enter the rule in the Validation Rule box
Validation Text property, set	AC 284	Display the table in Design view, select the field, enter the text in the Validation Text box
XML file, export an Access object as	AC 460	*See* Reference box: Exporting an Access Object as an XML File
XML file, import as an Access table	AC 456	*See* Reference box: Importing an XML File as an Access Table